2) Online Study Guide

Interactive Study Guide modules form the core of the student learning experience in the Companion Website. These modules are categorized according to their functionality:

- True-False
- Multiple Choice
- Essay questions

The True-False and Multiple Choice modules provide students with the ability to send answers to our grader and receive instant feedback on their progress through our Results Reporter. Coaching comments and references back to the textbook ensure that students take advantage of all resources available to enhance their learning experience.

3) Reference Material

Reference material broadens text coverage with up-to-date resources for learning. **Web Destinations** provides a directory of Web sites relevant to the subject matter in each chapter. **NetNews (Internet Newsgroups)** are a fundamental source of information about a discipline, containing a wealth of brief, opinionated postings. **NetSearch** simplifies key term search using Internet search engines.

4) Communication

Companion Websites contain the communication tools necessary to deliver courses in a **Distance Learning** environment. **Message Board** allows users to post messages and check back periodically for responses. **Live Chat** allows users to discuss course topics in real time, and enables professors to host on-line classes.

Communication facilities of Companion Websites provide a key element for distributed learning environments. There are two types of communication facilities currently in use in Companion Websites:

- **Message Board** – this module takes advantage of browser technology providing the users of each Companion Website with a national newsgroup to post and reply to relevant course topics.

- **Live Chat** – enables instructor-led group activities in real time. Using our chat client, instructors can display Website content while students participate in

---

Companion Websites are currently available for:

- Starke: Contemporary Management in Canada
- Kotler: Principles of Marketing
- Evans: Marketing Essentials
- Horngren: Cost Accounting
- Horngren: Introduction to Financial Accounting

Note: CW '99 content will vary slightly from site to site depending on discipline requirements.

The Companion Websites can be found at:

www.prenticehall.ca/griffin

PRENTICE HALL CANADA

1870 Birchmount Road
Scarborough, Ontario M1P 2J7

To order:
Call: 1-800-567-3800
Fax: 1-800-263-7733

For samples:
Call: 1-800-850-5813
Fax: (416) 299-2539
E-mail: phcinfo_pubcanada@prenhall.com

Third Canadian Edition

BUSINESS

Ricky W. Griffin
Texas A&M University

Ronald J. Ebert
University of Missouri-Columbia

Frederick A. Starke
University of Manitoba

Prentice Hall Canada Inc., Scarborough, Ontario

Canadian Cataloguing in Publication Data

Griffin, Ricky W.
     Business

3rd Canadian edition
Includes index.
ISBN 0-13-790437-1

1. Industrial management. 2. Business enterprises. 3. Industrial management–Canada.
4. Business enterprises–Canada. I. Ebert, Ronald J. II. Starke, Frederick A., 1942–   .
III. Title.

HD31.G75 1999 658 C98-930165-6

© 1999, 1996, 1993 Prentice-Hall Canada Inc., Scarborough, Ontario
A Division of Simon & Schuster/A Viacom Company

Prentice-Hall, Inc., Upper Saddle River, New Jersey
Prentice-Hall International (UK) Limited, London
Prentice-Hall of Australia, Pty. Limited, Sydney
Prentice-Hall Hispanoamericana, S.A., Mexico City
Prentice-Hall of India Private Limited, New Delhi
Prentice-Hall of Japan, Inc., Tokyo
Simon & Schuster Southeast Asia Private Limited, Singapore
Editora Prentice-Hall do Brasil, Ltda., Rio de Janeiro

ISBN 0-13-790437-1

Publisher: Patrick Ferrier
Acquisitions Editor: Mike Ryan
Senior Marketing Manager: Ann Byford
Senior Developmental Editor: Lesley Mann
Production Editor: Kelly Dickson
Copy Editor: Susan Broadhurst
Production Coordinator: Deborah Starks
Permissions/Photo Research: Susan Wallace-Cox
Cover and Interior Design: Alex Li
Cover Image (Background): Greg Pease/Tony Stone Images;
   Insert Images: 1, 4: Digital Vision Ltd.; 2, 3: P. Crowther and S. Carter/Tony Stone Images
Page Layout: Debbie Fleming/Joan M. Wilson

Original English Language edition published by Prentice-Hall Inc.,
Upper Saddle River, New Jersey, 07458
Copyright © 1996, 1993, 1991

1 2 3 4 5 CC 03 02 01 00 99

Printed and bound in the USA.

Visit the Prentice Hall Canada Web site! Send us your comments, browse our catalogues, and more at **www.ph-canada.com**. Or reach us through e-mail at **phcinfo_phcanada@prenhall.com**.

Every reasonable effort has been made to obtain permissions for all articles and data used in this edition. If errors or omissions have occurred, they will be corrected in future editions provided written notification has been received by the publisher.

Statistics Canada information is used with the permission of the Minister of Industry, as Minister responsible for Statistics Canada. Information on the availability of the wide range of data from Statistics Canada can be obtained from Statistics Canada's Regional Offices, its World Wide Web site at **http://www.statcan.ca**, and its toll-free access number 1-800-263-1136.

OVERVIEW

CONTENTS

4 Understanding International Business 91

5 Business Ethics, Social Responsibility, and Business Law 124

Part Two
The Business of Managing 163

6　Managing the Business Enterprise　164

7　Organizing the Business Enterprise　193

8　Understanding Entrepreneurship and Small Business　216

Part Three
Understanding People in Organizations   249

9   Managing Human Resources   250

10   Motivating and Leading Employees   277

14   Increasing Quality and Productivity   391

Part Five
Managing Marketing   423

15   Understanding Marketing Processes and Consumer Behaviour   424

16 Developing and Promoting Goods and Services   456

17 Pricing and Distributing Goods and Services   498

Part Six
*Managing
Information 543*

18 Managing Information Systems and Communication Technology   544

19 Understanding Accounting Issues   577

Part Seven
Managing
Financial Issues   613

20 Understanding Money and Banking   614

21 Understanding Securities and Investments   644

Video Resources

CBC Video Cases   CBC

Lands' End Video Cases

PREFACE

This is the third Canadian edition of *Business*. Our intent in this edition is to excite and inform students about today's business world, and to support instructors with an interesting and attractive book that explains the basic ideas that beginning business students must learn.

This new edition maintains the strengths that made the first two editions so successful. The text is well-organized, with a logical flow from one concept to another. It contains hundreds of examples of business practice, which help students bridge the gap from theory to practice. The text is globally focused, with examples from business firms around the world. The book retains its full-colour design, which attracts and holds students' attention.

Objectives

This third Canadian edition of *Business* was developed and guided by the following fundamental objectives:

- We wanted it to be *comprehensive*, providing a thorough survey of all the important facets of business.

- We wanted it to be *accurate*, with all statements of fact based on scientific research and/or actual managerial practice.

- We wanted it to be *current*, with illustrative examples and cases from business situations in Canada and elsewhere that are still unfolding.

- We wanted it to be *readable*, so that students will enjoy the experience of reading this edition as much as they tell us they have liked earlier editions.

We believe that we have met all these objectives, as the third Canadian edition of *Business* continues to offer significant coverage of both traditional topics and newer ideas.

The Theme of Change

The main theme of this edition is *change as a fact of life and a source of enrichment in the world of business*. This theme is evident in all aspects of this book—the opening chapter cases, the boxed inserts, the examples of business practice, the end-of-chapter cases, and the video cases. Change presents an exciting array of challenges, both externally and internally, including threats and opportunities that affect the ways in which contemporary companies are forced to develop and manage their activities. Today, more than ever, volatile environments demand day-to-day reactions along with longer-term adjustments for planned change. Our goal has been to communicate the theme of change by describing how real-world business firms cope with organizational change and conflict in the modern business world.

Other Themes

In support of our overall theme of change, the organization and content of this edition reflect six of today's major business subthemes—issues that will continue to gain in importance as the 20th century draws to a close and the 21st century dawns.

The growth of international business. Many analysts and businesspeople see the globalization of the economy as the dominant challenge to business firms at the close of the 20th century. To keep students aware of this challenge, we've based many of the examples and cases in this book on the experiences of global companies (and the global experiences of Canadian companies). We've also included material throughout the book that focuses student attention on important issues in international business. For example, Chapter 16 contains a new section on Product Development for International Markets; Chapter 19 contains a section on International Accounting; and Chapter 20 contains a section on International Banking and Finance. There is also an entire chapter devoted to Understanding International Business.

The role of ethics and social responsibility. Business ethics and social responsibility, while not new topics, continue to generate a great deal of discussion and debate. We reflect the attention that these topics deserve by devoting an entire chapter to them (Chapter 5, Business Ethics, Social Responsibility, and Business Law). Because ethical and social issues are so pervasive in the business world, we present them early in order to provide a continuing frame of ethical reference throughout the book.

The significance of small business. Because we recognize that many students will not go to work for major corporations, we have provided balanced coverage of both large and small companies throughout the text. In various chapters, the implications of the ideas for small business are discussed, and one full chapter is devoted to an analysis of small business in Canada (Chapter 8, Understanding Entrepreneurship and Small Business).

The need to manage information and communication technology. In our information-based society, the people and organizations that learn how to obtain and use information will be the ones that succeed. The explosive growth in these systems stems from the emergence of communication technologies such as multimedia communication systems. We cover this important topic in Chapter 18. Equally important, we make information available to both students and instructors through an unmatched set of resources: the text itself, an instructor's resource manual, a test bank, video cases at the end of each major part in the text, electronic transparencies, colour acetates, a Companion Website, and more.

The growth of the service sector. The 1990s have witnessed the continued growth of the service sector across the globe. We stress the importance of this sector by devoting a full chapter (Chapter 13) to the production of services, and by discussing the service sector in several other chapters as well.

The quality imperative. Quality and productivity became the key to competitive recovery for many companies in the global marketplace during the 1990s. These topics continue to be of special interest as we approach the 21st century. Chapter 14, Increasing Productivity and Quality, was born during intense debate at a reviewers' conference over the best means of presenting these important issues. The issues of quality and productivity are also discussed in various chapters throughout the text.

Changes to the Third Edition

The third edition of *Business* incorporates changes suggested by professors and students who used the first two editions. It also includes changes suggested by reviewers. Most chapters contain new or updated opening cases that describe real Canadian companies and the challenges and opportunities they face. Many new boxed inserts, end-of-chapter cases, video cases, and examples are contained in this edition. The boxed inserts, which describe Canadian and foreign business firms in action, are arranged on two themes: The Canadian Business Scene and International Report.

Chapters Containing Significant Revisions

Several chapters have been significantly revised to take into account new developments in the modern business world or to present to students interesting examples of business practice. These include:

Chapter 1: A new opening case detailing the nickel discovery at Voisey's Bay shows how the basic ideas of risk-taking, business activity, and profit are related. There are also two new end-of-chapter cases in this chapter.

Chapter 2: Two new end-of-chapter cases are included in this chapter.

Chapter 3: New material on the important trend of downsizing is included in this chapter. The chapter also includes in-depth treatment of the topic of business-government relations. Two new end-of-chapter cases are also included in this chapter.

Chapter 4: Several new boxed inserts focusing on international business are presented in this chapter. In addition, the section on free trade agreements has been revised and updated.

Chapter 6: Major revisions have been made to this chapter, which now focuses on planning and goal setting, the management process, and corporate culture. Two new end-of-chapter cases are included in this chapter.

Chapter 7: This chapter has also been significantly revised. It now focuses on organizing the business enterprise.

Chapter 13: Several new boxed inserts and a new opening case are presented in this chapter.

Chapter 14: The productivity paradox facing the industrialized nations is described in this chapter.

Chapter 15: A new section focusing on the external environment of marketing is introduced in this chapter.

Chapter 16: A new section on international promotion strategies is presented in this chapter. It describes the growth of worldwide advertising and the emergence of a global perspective in marketing.

Chapter 17: This chapter contains considerable new material, including an opening case describing Eaton's bankruptcy, a new section on distribution as a marketing strategy (including a discussion of the various types of distribution "hubs" that companies use), and two new end-of-chapter cases.

Chapter 18: This chapter contains new information on two issues that have recently received a great deal of publicity: the year 2000 problem and computer security.

Chapter 20: Major changes have been made to this chapter. The opening case presents an interesting description of how fluctuations in the value of a currency affect the people of a country. A new section on international banking and the international payments process is also presented in this chapter. This information is important, given the rapid rate of globalization of business activities that is taking place. Information on the latest technological developments in banking (such as smart cards and e-cash) is also included. The major changes that are taking place in banking and what Canadian banks are doing to cope with these changes are also discussed.

Chapter 21: A new opening case discusses the Bre-X scandal. New information is provided in this chapter on technological developments that are influencing securities markets. Cyberspace brokerage (buying stocks over the Internet) is one such important development. The chapter also includes information on mutual funds and their importance in securities markets in the 1990s.

Chapter 22: This chapter contains two new boxed inserts describing how insurance works in the field of entertainment, as well as a new Canadian box on insurance investigators.

Organization of the Text

The text is organized into seven parts as follows:

Part I: Introducing the Contemporary Business World

This section introduces students to the basic ideas underlying business activity. Chapter 1 describes how business activity is oriented towards making a profit by satisfying consumer needs. Several types of economic systems are also described. Chapter 2 presents a brief history of Canadian business and focuses on the different kinds of business ownership—sole proprietorships, partnerships, corporations, and cooperatives—that can be used to run a business. Chapter 3 describes how the interrelationship of business firms with consumers, the workforce, and government presents both challenges and opportunities for businesses. A major section of this chapter deals with business-government relationships. Chapter 4 describes the critical area of international business and free trade, and the importance of international business for Canada. The various levels of involvement in international business that are possible are also described. In Chapter 5, the impact of business ethics, social responsibility, and business law are discussed.

Part II: The Business of Managing

The chapters in this section focus on the general management activities that are necessary in business firms. Chapter 6 introduces the functions of management—planning, organizing, leading, and controlling—and the three basic types of management skills—technical, human relations, and conceptual. Chapter 7 focuses in detail on the planning and organizing functions. In Chapter 8, general management principles are applied to small business.

Part III: Understanding People in Organizations

The chapters in this section focus on the most important resource in business firms: people. Chapter 9 describes the activities that are necessary in order to recruit, hire, train, and compensate the company's human resources. Chapter 10 deals with managerial activities that are necessary to motivate and lead employees so that they are both satisfied and productive. Chapter 11 presents information on Canadian labour unions, and the way that unions affect management activity.

Part IV: Managing Operations

This section describes those managerial activities that are necessary to convert raw materials into finished products and services that are needed by consumers. Chapter 12 focuses on the production of goods, while Chapter 13 deals with the "production" of services. In Chapter 14, the crucial issue of productivity and quality is examined.

Part V: Managing Marketing

The chapters in this section explain the key activities that are carried out by marketing managers. Chapter 15 introduces the "4 Ps of marketing"—product, place, promotion, and price. Other activities—such as marketing research and the study of consumer behaviour—help marketing managers carry out the marketing function effectively. Chapter 16 looks in detail at the development and promotion of products, while Chapter 17 focuses on pricing and distributing goods and services.

Part VI: Managing Information

The chapters in this section describe the increasingly important activity of managing information for business success. Chapter 18 presents information on the dynamic and rapidly developing area of computers in business. The chapter focuses on how managers use information to make business decisions. Chapter 19 describes the accounting function and the financial statements that accountants develop for managers and investors.

Part VII: Managing Financial Issues

The chapters in this section introduce students to the key financial activities of business firms. Chapter 20 explores the nature of money, the various financial intermediaries that exist in Canada, and the role of the Bank of Canada. Chapter 21 looks at securities markets and the buying and selling of stocks, bonds, and other investments. Chapter 22 examines the reasons that business firms need funds, and the way they go about acquiring these funds. The role of the financial manager is also described.

Major Features of the Text

Each chapter in this text contains the following features to stimulate student interest in, and understanding of, the material that is being presented about business:

Part Opener

At the beginning of each of the seven parts of the book is a brief outline introducing the material that will be discussed in that part. By revealing the rationale for the structure of the part, it gives students a glimpse of the "big picture" as they head into a new area of the business world.

Chapter Materials

Each *chapter* contains several features that are designed to increase student interest and understanding of the material being presented. These features are as follows:

Opening case.   Each chapter begins with a one-page description of an incident that happened in a real Canadian company. The subject matter of this opening case is relevant to the material being presented in that chapter. This helps the student bridge the gap from theory to practice.

Learning objectives.   A list of learning objectives is found at the beginning of each chapter. These guide students in determining what is important in each chapter.

Boxed inserts.   Each chapter contains several boxed inserts describing activities in Canadian or international companies. These inserts are designed to clearly show students how theoretical concepts are put into actual practice by business firms. There are two types of boxes: "The Canadian Business Scene" (which focuses on Canadian businesses) and "International Report" (which focuses on examples of business activity from around the world).

Examples.   In addition to the boxed inserts, each chapter contains numerous examples of how businesses operate. These examples will further help students understand actual business practice in Canada and elsewhere.

Figures and tables.   The latest data available have been used to update Tables and Figures throughout the text. Our "Top 10" feature gives fascinating figures for top performers and issues.

Weblinks.   Internet addresses are supplied throughout the text for many of the organizations discussed.

End-of-Chapter Material

Several important pedagogical features are found at the end of each chapter. These are designed to help students better understand the material that was presented in the chapter. The features are as follows:

Summary of learning objectives.   The material in each chapter is concisely summarized to help students understand the main points that were presented in the chapter.

Key terms.   In each chapter, the key terms that students should know are highlighted and defined in the text, repeated in the margin, and listed at the end of the chapter (with page references).

Study questions and exercises.   There are three general types of questions here: questions for review (straightforward questions of factual recall), questions for analysis (requiring students to think beyond simple factual recall and apply the concepts), and application exercises (requiring students to visit local businesses or managers and gather additional information that will help them understand how business firms operate).

Building your business skills.   This feature is an in-depth exercise that allows students to examine some specific aspect of business in detail. The exercise may ask the student to work individually or in a group to gather data about some interesting business issue and then develop a written report or a class presentation based on the information that was gathered.

Exploring the Net.   This new feature gives students the opportunity to carry out interesting, business-related assignments by using the Internet. By doing so, students will gain important skills in locating and using information from Canadian and international Web sites.

Case studies.   Each chapter concludes with two case studies that focus on real Canadian or international companies. These cases are designed to help students see how the chapter material can be applied to a real company that is currently in the news. At the end of each case, there are several questions that guide students in their analysis. Classic cases from previous editions are included in the Instructor's Resource Manual.

End-of-Part Material

Each part concludes with several additional pedagogical features. These are designed to help the student master the material and think analytically about it.

CBC video cases.   There are two CBC video cases at the end of each part; each case is based on a recent episode of such CBC series as *Venture, The National Magazine*, or *Market Place*. The instructor can show the episode in class and then either have a class discussion using the questions at the end of the written case as a guideline, or ask students to turn in a written assignment which contains answers to the questions at the end of the case. This approach to teaching will add a major new dynamic to classes.

Lands' End video cases.   While the CBC videos described above deal with many different companies, the Lands' End videos at the end of most parts describe activity in the different functional areas of one company. This allows students to gain a better understanding of how the different areas of a business firm must work together in order for the organization to be successful.

Experiential exercise.   These exercises, which typically require one or two hours to complete, are positioned at the end of six of the text's seven Parts. They are set up so that students can "experience" a realistic business situation and thereby gain increased understanding of business.

Careers in business.   Students have a keen interest in the kinds of jobs they might take when they leave college or university. This new feature provides information about careers that are available, occupations which are in high demand, pointers on interviewing for jobs and preparing a resume, and other related career information. This should be of great practical use to students.

Supplementary Material

For the Instructor

Instructors Resource Manual with Cases, Video Guide and Web Exercise Answers. This supplement contains suggestions on how to use the text effectively. It also provides suggested lecture outlines and answers to end-of-chapter materials, including questions, cases, CBC video cases, and Exploring the Net exercises. Available in paper or on disk. (ISBN: 0-13-081103-3; disk: 0-13-081102-5)

Test Item File.   With approximately 75 multiple choice, 25 true/false, and 15 essay questions per chapter, this supplement provides a total of almost 2200 questions for class tests. Available in paper or on disk. (0-13-081112-2)

WIN PH Custom Test.   Prentice Hall's computerized test file uses a state-of-the-art software program that provides fast, simple, and error-free test generation. Entire tests can be previewed on-screen before printing. PH Custom Test can print multiple variations of the same test, scrambling the order of questions and multiple-choice answers. Tests can be saved to ASCII format and revised in your word-processing system. (ISBN: 0-13-081111-4)

CBC/Prentice Hall Video Library.   This dynamic collection of hand-picked CBC video clips includes segments from *Venture, The National Magazine*, and *Market Place*. Each clip is an average of eight minutes long and almost all have been replaced from the second edition to ensure students' access to the most current issues in Canadian business. Written summaries with questions are provided at the end of each Part in the text, and answers are discussed in the Instructor's Resource Manual. (Please contact your Prentice Hall sales representative for details. These videos are subject to availability and terms negotiated upon adoption of the text.)

Venture
http://www.tv.cbc.ca.venture

ON LOCATION! Lands' End Videos.   Prepared exclusively for Prentice Hall, these six video segments focus on Lands' End Inc., a major catalogue retailer. The purpose of these videos, which were shot on location and include interviews with managers and employees at Lands' End, is to anchor exercises focusing on the operations of a successful American company that deals with both goods and services on a global scale. Each segment is eight to 10 minutes long. Written summaries with questions are provided at the end of Parts 1 to 5 in the text, and answers are discussed in the Instructor's Resource Manual. (Please contact your Prentice Hall sales representative for details. These videos are subject to availability and terms negotiated upon adoption of the text.)

Transparency Resource Package.   Expanded and improved for the third edition, this supplement contains 20 slides per chapter in PowerPoint 4.0 plus lecture notes that include a summary, questions for discussion, and page references to the text. All slides and lecture notes have also been printed out as black-and-white masters for those who prefer to create their own acetates. (ISBN: 0-13-081107-6)

Colour Transparencies.   Also expanded and improved, this full-colour set of transparencies presents numerous graphic illustrations from the text. Lecture notes with a summary, questions for discussion, and page references to the text are included in the package. (Please contact your Prentice Hall sales representative for details.)

Companion Website with Online Study Guide.   Our exciting new Website includes a comprehensive online study guide with multiple choice and true/false review questions, as well as Internet destinations and search tools, CBC video case updates, and more. See **www.prenticehall.ca/griffin** and explore.

For the Student:

Study Guide.   The Study Guide enables students to review the introductory business concepts presented in the text and help them gain insight into the application of these concepts. (ISBN: 0-13-081104-1)

EZ Write Business Plan Software.   This exceptionally easy-to-use software, available on a 3.5-inch disk for IBM and compatibles, provides a template for a complete business plan, and includes examples of financial documents on Lotus templates.

Prentice Hall Canada
http://www.prenticehall.ca/griffin

Acknowledgements

We owe special thanks to Susan Broadhurst for her excellent copyediting; Kelly Dickson, Production Editor, for her efficient management of this project; and Susan Wallace-Cox for finding so many fine photo illustrations. Thanks are also due to Pat Ferrier, Publisher; Mike Ryan, Acquisitions Editor; Lesley Mann, Senior Developmental Editor; Ann Byford, Senior Marketing Manager; and all the members of the Prentice Hall sales team.

In addition, we would like to acknowledge the contribution of Todd Mercer, who prepared Canadian Exploring the Net exercises and compiled Weblinks for the text, and Reg Litz of the University of Manitoba for writing the CBC video cases.

We appreciate the insights and suggestions of the following individuals who reviewed the manuscript:

Richard F. Barnes, CGA
Chuck Bridges, Saint Mary's University
Edward V.G. Brown, Langara College
Patricia Draves, Seneca College
Richard H.G. Field, University of Alberta
Ibrahim Hayani, Seneca College
Les Lewchuk, Kwantlen College
John P. Logan, Ryerson Polytechnic University
Karen Murkar, DeVry Institute

Their comments were carefully considered and implemented wherever possible.

Frederick A. Starke
1998

TO STUDENTS

We started to call this section "How to Make an A." However, in this age of litigation, we decided to take a more conservative approach and instead explain how we think you can get the greatest value from this text.

First, it is important to recognize that business is a complex and dynamic field in which you are likely to encounter many new concepts and terms. You may find yourself disagreeing with some things. On the other hand, avoid the pitfall of believing that everything you find in this book—and in the study of business—is simply common sense. If this were the case, the statistics on business failure discussed in Chapter 8 would be quite different.

The starting point in any class is your instructor's course outline. Read it thoroughly and make sure you understand all the objectives and course requirements.

You should always read assigned chapters before coming to class. First read carefully through the chapter objectives and reflect on what the chapter will be about. Then, as you read the text, keep the objectives in mind (perhaps looking back at them occasionally) to see how they are being developed. Make notes about important points and anything you do not understand. Use the figures, tables, and photos to amplify the text material. Use the marginal notes to acquaint yourself with vocabulary.

When you reach the end of the chapter, read the summary carefully and make sure you understand all the things it lists. Use the review questions to test your recall of important points. And make sure you know the meanings of all the key terms. Use the cases as your instructor assigns.

When you go to class, listen carefully to what your instructor says about the assigned material. You might highlight ideas from the text as your instructor discusses them. Be sure to take notes on points covered in class that are not in the book.

As well, be sure to ask questions about any point you do not understand. All too often, students don't ask questions for fear of looking silly. In our opinion, there is no such thing as a silly question from someone who wants to learn.

After class, spend more time with the chapter. Read through it again, noting other things you are learning. And if there are still points you do not understand, see your instructor during her or his office hours.

Be aware, too, that you have access to the same kinds of information that most businesspeople use to manage their business lives. Publications such as *Canadian Business, The Globe and Mail, The Financial Post,* and *The Report on Business Magazine* contain valuable information about the nature of business in Canada. The CBC television series *Venture* also presents useful information about the dynamics of Canadian business activity. As you use this text and gain a sense of the workings of the business world, try to think about what you read and see and hear from the full range of information sources available to you.

Will all this work get you an A? Maybe, but regardless of the effect it has on your grade in the course, this process will greatly enhance your learning and get you off to a good start on your future career in business.

Canadian Business
http://www.canbus.com/

The Globe and Mail
http://www.GlobeAndMail.CA/

The Financial Post
http://www.canoe.ca/FP/

Venture
http://www.tv.cbc.ca/venture

Part One

Part One

INTRODUCING THE CONTEMPORARY BUSINESS WORLD

In Chapters 1–5, you will read about five situations that may seem at first glance to have little in common: the discovery of a large nickel deposit at Voisey's Bay, employee buy-outs at several Canadian companies, the downsizing trend among Canadian business firms, international sales efforts at Purdy's Chocolates, and socially responsible business behaviour at The Body Shop.

All of these situations, and many more that are described in this text, have a common thread: they all demonstrate the key elements of business as well as the excitement and complexity of business activity. Each case tells a part of the story of our contemporary business world.

Part One, Introducing the Contemporary Business World, provides a general overview of business today, including its economic roots, its legal structure, current trends and challenges, the globalization of business, and the ethical problems and opportunities facing business firms.

- We begin in **Chapter 1, Understanding the Canadian Business System**, by examining the role of business in the economy of Canada and other market economies.

- Then, in **Chapter 2, Setting Up Business in Canada**, we review the history of business development in Canada and examine the various forms of business ownership that have evolved.

- In **Chapter 3, Recognizing Business Trends and Challenges**, we consider the wide range of issues confronting businesses in Canada and elsewhere. Special attention is paid to business–government interactions.

- In **Chapter 4, Understanding International Business**, we look at why countries engage in international trade, how companies organize to operate internationally, the development of free trade agreements, and factors that help or hinder international trade.

- Finally, in **Chapter 5, Business Ethics, Social Responsibility, and Business Law**, we look at how individual ethics and corporate social responsibility develop and affect the firm's environment and its customers, employees, and investors. The legal system within which business firms must operate is also described.

1

Understanding the Canadian Business System

Field of Dreams

Here's a classic Canadian success story: In September 1993, Chris Verbisky and Al Chislett were flying in a helicopter over the rolling hills of northeast Labrador. Their company, Archean Resources Ltd., was doing diamond prospecting work for Vancouver-based Diamond Fields Resources (DFR) Inc. On that day, the two prospectors were returning from a three-month trip into the interior. Their search for diamonds had been completely unsuccessful, but their luck was about to change in a way that they never expected.

When they were only 10 kilometres from Voisey's Bay, they spotted a *gossan*—a rusty-coloured outcropping which is usually a good place to look for metals. This gossan was darker and more intense than usual. Since the helicopter was almost out of fuel, they couldn't land, but they did return two days later. As soon as they broke open the first rock, they knew they had stumbled onto something big. What they didn't know was that they had just discovered one of the world's richest base metals deposits.

Even though Verbisky and Chislett were impressed by their first "grab samples," it would still be 14 months before DFR really got interested in the discovery. In April 1994, DFR came up with $175 000 for a last-minute renewal of their option on the Voisey's Bay claim. It was not until October 1994 that the initial holes were drilled. Two sceptical engineers from a Toronto firm who came out to analyze the drill samples were dumbfounded at what they saw. The samples contained nearly 4 percent nickel content and 3 percent copper content (many mining companies are happy with 2 percent copper content).

In spite of the discovery, many people in the mining industry did not seem to take DFR seriously (there is lots of hype in this business). A few days after the analysis by the Toronto engineers, DFR made a brief announcement about a potentially significant base metals discovery at Voisey's Bay. But it still took some weeks before other companies began the rush to stake claims in the area. By the end of 1994, it was clear that DFR really had found something of immense value.

It is now estimated that the main body of ore contains reserves of about 150 million tonnes, which should translate into hundreds of millions of pounds of nickel annually and millions of pounds of copper. Annual revenues from this ore body alone will reach at least 400 million. Company profits will reach at least $150 million each year. The cost to develop the mine is expected to be about $500 million. Because the Voisey's Bay metals are very close to the surface and because the mine is close to Voisey's Bay, it should be very profitable.

The company's stock, which is listed on the Toronto Stock Exchange, has reflected the metal discovery. In October 1994, it was trading at about $4 per share. After the announcement of the discovery, the stock climbed steadily for the next few months, reaching $15 per share by early 1995. By April 1995, it had reached $33 per share.

The company finally gained instant credibility in April 1995 when Teck Corp. invested $108 million for a 10.4 percent share in DFR. That is more than DFR was worth before the Voisey's Bay discovery. Teck's investment has helped allay investor fears about the involvement of controversial mining promoter Robert Friedland, the co-chairman of DFR. In 1996 Inco bought controlling interest in DFR so that Inco would continue to be the dominant company in the world nickel mining industry. Inco paid $41 for each share of DFR stock.

What does all this mean for prospectors Verbisky and Chislett? They will receive a 3 percent royalty on any nickel, copper, and cobalt that is produced at the new mine. While that may not sound like much, they will probably become millionaires several times over.

The development will boost the economic growth of Newfoundland and Labrador by 15 to 25 percent. Of the 5 percent GDP growth that is predicted for the year 2003, a full percentage point will come as a result of the Voisey's Bay development. The development will also have a significant effect on the Innu and Inuit living in the area. But it is also a chance for DFR to do everything right—to respect the traditional lifestyles of the aboriginal people, to improve the economic well-being of local people, and to protect the environment.

Doing everything right may not be easy, however. Between March and November 1997, several things happened that caused Inco's stock price to drop 50 percent: declining world nickel prices, increased numbers of Inco shares (which were issued to pay for purchase of the property), and the company's decision to delay the development of Voisey's Bay because of political disputes in Labrador. ◆

The forces of supply and demand that play such an important role in the financial future of companies like Diamond Fields Resources and Archean Resources also dictate stories of success and failure for virtually every business enterprise. As you will see in this chapter, those forces define the Canadian market economy. You will also see that although the world's economic systems differ markedly, the standards for evaluating the success or failure of a system are linked to its capacity to achieve certain basic goals.

By focusing on the learning objectives of this chapter, you will better understand the Canadian business system and the mechanisms by which it not only pursues its goals but permits businesses large and small to pursue theirs. After reading this chapter, you should be able to:

LEARNING OBJECTIVES

1. Define the nature of Canadian *business* and its goals.

2. Describe different types of *economic systems* according to the means by which they control the *factors of production*.

3. Show how *demand* and *supply* affect resource distribution in Canada.

4. Identify the elements of *private enterprise* and explain the various degrees of *competition* in the Canadian economic system.

5. Explain the criteria for evaluating the success of an economic system in meeting its goals and explain how the federal government attempts to manage the Canadian economy.

The Idea of Business and Profit

What do you think of when you hear the word business? Does it conjure up images of huge corporations like Canadian Pacific and Alcan Aluminum? Smaller companies like your local supermarket? One-person operations like the barbershop around the corner? Indeed, each of these firms is a **business**—an organization that produces or sells goods or services in an effort to make a profit. **Profit** is what remains after a business's expenses have been subtracted from its revenues. Profits reward the owners of businesses for taking the risks involved in investing their money and time.

business
An organization that seeks to earn profits by providing goods and services.

profit
What remains (if anything) after a business's expenses are subtracted from its sales revenues.

The prospect of earning profits is what encourages people to open and expand businesses. Today businesses produce most of the goods and services that we consume, and they employ many of the working people in Canada. Profits from these businesses are paid to thousands of owners and shareholders. And business taxes help support governments at all levels. In addition, businesses help support charitable causes and provide community leadership.

In this chapter, we begin your introduction to Canadian business by looking at its role in our economy and society. Because there are a variety of economic systems found around the world, we will first consider how the dominant ones operate. Once you have some understanding of different systems, you can better appreciate the workings of our own system. As you will see, the effect of economic forces on Canadian businesses and the effect of Canadian businesses on our economy produce dynamic and sometimes volatile results.

Global Economic Systems

economic system
The way in which a nation allocates its resources among its citizens.

A Canadian business is different in many ways from one in China. And both are different from businesses in Japan, France, or Peru. A major determinant of how organizations operate is the kind of economic system that characterizes the country in which they do business. An **economic system** allocates a nation's resources among its citizens. Economic systems differ in who owns and controls these resources, known as the "factors of production."

Factors of Production

factors of production
The resources used to produce goods and services: natural resources, labour, capital, and entrepreneurs.

The basic resources a business uses to produce goods and services are called **factors of production**. They include natural resources, labour, capital, and entrepreneurs.[1] Figure 1.1 illustrates the factors of production.

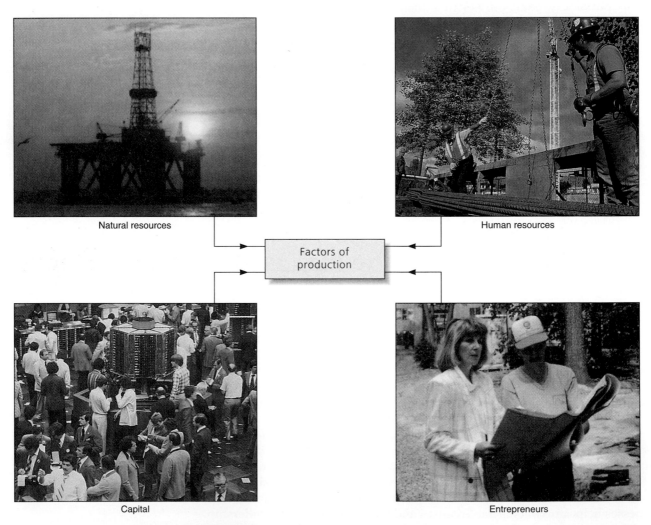

Natural resources

Human resources

Factors of production

Capital

Entrepreneurs

Figure 1.1
Factors of production are the basic resources a business uses to create goods and services. The four basic factors used are natural resources, labour, capital, and entrepreneurs.

Land, water, mineral deposits, and trees are good examples of **natural resources.** For example, Imperial Oil makes use of a wide variety of natural resources. It obviously has vast quantities of crude oil to process each year. But Imperial also needs the land where the oil is located, as well as land for its refineries and pipelines.

The people who work for a company represent the second factor of production, **labour**. Sometimes called *human resources*, labour is the mental and physical capabilities of people. Carrying out the business of such a huge company as Imperial requires a labour force with a wide variety of skills ranging from managers to geologists to truck drivers.

Obtaining and using material resources and labour requires **capital**, the funds needed to operate an enterprise. Capital is needed to start a business and to keep the business operating and growing. Imperial's annual drilling costs alone run into the millions of dollars. A major source of capital for most businesses is personal investment by owners. Personal investment can be made either by the individual entrepreneurs or partners who start businesses or by investors who buy stock in them. Revenues from the sale of products, of course, is another and important ongoing source of capital. Finally, many firms borrow funds from banks and other lending institutions.

Entrepreneurs are those people who accept the opportunities and risks involved in creating and operating businesses. They are the people who start new businesses and who make the decisions that allow small businesses to grow into larger ones. Murray Pezim, Conrad Black, and the Griffiths family are well-known Canadian entrepreneurs. The box "Raising Rhinos for Horns and Profit" describes the activities of entrepreneur Norm Travers.

natural resources
Items used in the production of goods and services in their natural state, including land, water, minerals, and trees.

Imperial Oil
http://www.imperialoil.ca

labour
The mental and physical training and talents of people; sometimes called human resources.

capital
The funds needed to operate an enterprise.

entrepreneur
An individual who organizes and manages natural resources, labour, and capital to produce goods and services to earn a profit, but who also runs the risk of failure.

Types of Economic Systems

Different types of economic systems manage the factors of production in different ways. In some systems, ownership is private; in others, the factors of production are owned by the government. Economic systems also differ in the ways decisions are made about production and allocation. A **command economy**, for example, relies on a centralized government to control all or most factors of production and to make all or most production and allocation decisions. In **market economies**, individuals—producers and consumers—control production and allocation decisions through supply and demand. We will describe each of these economic types and then discuss the reality of the *mixed market economy*.

command economy
An economic system in which government controls all or most factors of production and makes all or most production decisions.

market economy
An economic system in which individuals control all or most factors of production and make all or most production decisions.

Command Economies

The two most basic forms of command economies are communism and socialism. As originally proposed by the 19th-century German economist Karl Marx, **communism** is a system in which the government owns and operates all sources of production. Marx envisioned a society in which individuals would ultimately contribute according to their abilities and receive economic benefits according to their needs. He also expected government ownership of production factors to be only temporary: Once society had matured, government would "wither away" and the workers would gain direct ownership.

Most Eastern European countries and the former Soviet Union embraced communist systems until very recently. During the early 1990s, however, one country after another renounced communism as both an economic and a political system. Today, Cuba, North Korea, Vietnam, and the People's Republic of China are among the few nations with avowedly communist systems. Even in these countries, however, command economic systems are making room for features of the free-enterprise system from the lowest to the highest levels.

communism
A type of command economy in which the government owns and operates all industries.

International Report

Raising Rhinos for Horns and Profit

Norman Travers operates a game farm in Zimbabwe that contains a herd of endangered black rhinos. He does most of his business with tourists who pay to take photo safaris through his game farm. Some of his guests hunt game as well. Travers is part of an increasingly vocal African conservation movement that is driven by free-market thinking. He hopes someday to harvest rhino horns and sell them for profit. The removal of the horn does not hurt the animal and a new horn grows in to replace the old one. Travers can't do this yet because trading in rhino horns is banned by an international treaty designed to protect the dwindling rhino population. Travers and others argue that this approach to conservation is not working since poaching remains a serious problem. What is needed, he argues, is rhino ranching, which could supply the world demand for rhino horns while protecting the animals on game farms.

Travers is part of a growing group of game farmers who are privatizing and commercializing the wild game business in Africa. South Africa, for example, has 25 large private game reserves and many smaller ones. These game farms are so successful that animals such as buffalo, giraffe, impala, and wildebeest are regularly sold at animal auctions. All this activity provides jobs. The amount of land dedicated to game farming increased from 12 to 17 percent between 1986 and 1996.

In Zimbabwe, the Communal Areas Management Program for Indigenous Resources (CAMPFIRE) was started to help reduce complaints about marauding animals in villages that were close to national game parks. Indigenous residents were given permits to harvest game that came onto their lands. Villagers could either hunt the animals and use their meat, or sell their harvesting permits to safari operators who guided big-game hunters into the area. Either way, the villagers made money. Villages in north-

western Zimbabwe earned almost $500 000 in one three-year period under this program. Most striking, poaching in these areas dropped sharply, because the people living there now have an interest in preserving their local wildlife.

The move towards privatization has run into stiff opposition from Western conservation organizations and animal rights groups. They oppose the hunting of animals on moral grounds, and they object to reducing wild animals to simply an economic number. The CAMPFIRE program has been attacked by the Humane Society, which claims that CAMPFIRE is a stooge for safari operators and says that it is not necessary to kill animals in order to help the local people.

The clash of ideas is illustrated by the elephant situation in Zimbabwe. The government wants to repeal the international ban on trading in elephant ivory because there is a surplus of elephants and they want their poor rural populations to benefit from the selling of ivory. The country has about 64 000 elephants, but the government estimates that the carrying capacity of the land is only about 35 000. The "excess" elephants could be harvested, and their ivory and meat would be a big economic boost to the area.

Those who want the ivory ban lifted argue that groups like the Humane Society are simply practising "eco-colonialism." A game economist at the University of Zimbabwe says that it's easy for Westerners to view the problem from a distance and demand that elephants and other species be preserved, but that ignores the problems the people in the area are having. The economist asks this question: "Would citizens of industrialized countries choose the survival of, say, whales at the expense of their lives, or the education of their children, or their pensions?" Not likely. Yet that is what Westerners are asking Africans to do.

In Cuba, for example, special shops once reserved for diplomats are now patronized by Cubans from all walks of life. Here, they can buy goods that the severely troubled government system cannot supply. Moreover, they use money earned from a variety of free-market activities (which are, technically, illegal). For example, the stores themselves are surrounded by paid bicycle parking lots, carwashes, and stalls selling home-grown produce and home-made handicrafts. All of this street-corner commerce reflects a rapid growth in private enterprise as a solution to problems that a centralized economy has long been unable to solve.[2]

As the box "China Moves Warily Towards Capitalism" shows, the People's Republic of China is, in effect, abandoning its communist ideology in favour of a more capitalistic one, but it is doing so very quietly.[3]

In a less extensive command economic system called **socialism**, the government owns and operates only selected major industries. Smaller businesses such as clothing stores and restaurants may be privately owned.

socialism

A kind of command economy in which the government owns and operates the main industries, while individuals own and operate less crucial industries.

While we can identify different types of economies, the distinctions between them are becoming increasingly blurred. Previous command economies in Eastern Europe, for example, are moving towards a market system. The woman shown here is selling decorated eggs on the street. China still uses a command economy, but more and more elements of capitalism are becoming evident. In Canada, capitalism has always allowed farmers to decide what they would grow and how much to sell it for. Of course, capitalists aren't protected from failure, a concern that people in command economies seldom have to confront.

Although workers in socialist countries are usually allowed to choose their occupations or professions, a large proportion generally work for the government. Many government-operated enterprises are inefficient, since management positions are frequently filled based on political considerations rather than ability. Extensive public welfare systems have also resulted in very high taxes. Because of these factors, socialism is generally declining in popularity.[4]

In Israel, even the kibbutz concept is being questioned. In a kibbutz, members contribute their services in producing goods and then share equally in the resources that are generated. The emphasis is on teamwork and absolute equality. But at Kibbutz Ein Ziwan, a monument to socialist values, several historic practices (communal cars, central dining facilities) have been

International Report

China Moves Warily Towards Capitalism

China's province of Guangdong (formerly known as Canton) ranks fifth among China's 30 provinces in terms of population, but it ranks first in exports, industrial production, and foreign investment. Billboards tout Coke, Pepsi, and Head & Shoulders Shampoo. In the early 1980s, Guangdong became a laboratory for experiments with capitalism. Since then, hundreds of manufacturing firms in nearby Hong Kong have shifted some or all of their production to the province. The economic alliance of Chinese neighbours links the sophistication, management skills, and marketing know-how of Hong Kong's population with the low-cost production base of Guangdong's citizens. Labour costs are 80 percent lower in Guangdong than in Hong Kong.

China's experiments with capitalism came after years of disastrous attempts to put all production under government control. Communally run farms were the first organizations to be modified to provide incentives for individual farmers, and these formed the nucleus of China's return to small-scale private enterprise. In 1987, the country's southern coastal district was designated as a "scout" to explore new roads to an open, market-oriented economy.

Joint ventures with Western firms are very popular in Guangdong, with over 10 000 undertaken so far. Avon Products Inc. began selling cosmetics in China in 1990; its initial sales were four to six times its estimates.

But China's movement towards capitalism is not without problems. While free-enterprise experiments have been going on for about 15 years, state-owned enterprises still dominate, employing over 100 million workers and supporting pensions paid to another 20 million. The effort to integrate free enterprise into a command economy is plagued with problems. Consider conditions in Wuhan, a city of 7 million people.

While China has mostly deregulated cotton prices, it still maintains a quota system to support its huge textile industry. Under the quota system, Communist party managers can buy cotton for their textile mills at about $920 per metric ton. Critics charge, however, that buyers then underreport their purchases and sell the surplus on open world markets at about twice the price—$1800. Supplies are also diverted to small local cotton mills, where labour is cheaper and taxes go uncollected. Naturally, at the mills for which the cotton was originally intended, shortages become critical. The No. 1 Cotton Mill in Wuhan has been completely shut down for weeks at a time, and 9000 workers are often in danger of being unemployed for longer stretches. The director of the factory acknowledges that, ironically, the culprits are inspired by the profit motive: "This is the problem," he explains, "that you have in the transition from a planned to a market economy."

Meanwhile, 70 000 out of 90 000 workers at Wuhan Iron and Steel Co. have been shifted to jobs at smaller subsidiary firms. Once guaranteed salaries and pensions by the state, they have been informed that their futures now depend on the profitability of their new employers. "We are helping the workers mount a horse and leading it a short distance and hoping it will gallop," explains the president of Wuhan Steel.

In 1997, China became the new owner of the former British Crown Colony of Hong Kong. The success of the Hong Kong–Guangdong experiment, as well as other capitalist initiatives in China, will play a large part in determining how far China will go in its experiment with capitalism. The selection of the new Chinese premier in 1998 may push the move towards capitalism even further.

---

abandoned because they are no longer affordable. In addition, the kibbutz will soon take a dramatic step: paying people based on how productive they are, rather than on the equal-sharing basis of the past. Other kibbutzim are also considering taking this step.[5]

Market Economies

A *market* is a mechanism for exchange between the buyers and sellers of a particular good or service. To understand how a *market economy* works, consider what happens when a customer goes to a fruit stand to buy apples. Let's say that while one vendor is selling apples for $1 per kilogram, another is charging $1.50. Both vendors are free to charge what they want, and customers are free to buy what they choose. If both vendors' apples are of the same quality, the customer will buy the cheaper ones. But if the $1.50 apples are fresher, the customer may buy them instead. In short, both buyers and sellers enjoy freedom of choice.

Market economies rely on markets, not governments, to decide what, when, and for whom to produce. **Capitalism** provides for the private ownership of the factors of production. It also encourages entrepreneurship by offering profits as an incentive. Businesses can provide whatever goods and services and charge whatever prices they choose. Similarly, customers can choose how and where they spend their money.[6] Businesses that produce inefficiently or fail to provide needed or desired products will not survive. At least that is the theory in "pure" market economies.

capitalism

A market economy; an economic system in which markets decide what, when, and for whom to produce.

Mixed Economies

The economic systems we have described differ greatly from each other, but the fact is that no country in the world today has a purely communistic, socialistic, or capitalistic economy. As already noted, for example, the People's Republic of China has begun encouraging some entrepreneurial activity. Both England and France maintain government control of some industries but allow free market operations in others. Government planners in Japan give special assistance to "sunrise industries"—those expected to grow. In Canada, the federal government regulates many aspects of business, and many utilities are owned by provincial governments. Thus, most of the world's countries have a **mixed economy** in which one of the basic economic systems dominates but elements of the other systems are present as well.

mixed economy

An economic system with elements of both a planned economy and a market economy; in practice, typical of most nations' economies.

The Canadian Economic System

Understanding the complex nature of the Canadian economic system is essential to understanding Canadian businesses. In the next few pages, we will examine the workings of our market economy in more detail. Specifically, we look at markets, demand, supply, the business cycle, private enterprise, and degrees of competition.

Markets, Demand, and Supply

In economic terms, a **market** is not a specific place, such as a supermarket, but an exchange process between buyers and sellers. Decisions about production in a market economy are the result of millions of exchanges. How much of what product a company offers for sale and who buys it depend on the laws of demand and supply.

Basically, **demand** is the willingness and ability of buyers to purchase a product or service. **Supply** is the willingness and ability of producers to offer a good or service for sale. The **law of demand** states that buyers will purchase (demand) more of a product as its price drops. Conversely, the **law of supply** states that producers will offer more for sale as the price rises.

market

An exchange process between buyers and sellers of a particular good or service.

demand

The willingness and ability of buyers to purchase a product or service.

supply

The willingness and ability of producers to offer a good or service for sale.

law of demand

The principle that buyers will purchase (demand) more of a product as price drops.

law of supply

The principle that producers will offer (supply) more of a product as price rises.

Demand and Supply Schedule

To appreciate these laws in action, consider the market for pizza in your town. If everyone in town is willing to pay $25 for a pizza (a relatively high price), the town's only pizzeria will produce a large supply. But if everyone is willing to pay only $5 (a relatively low price), the restaurant will make fewer pizzas. Through careful analysis, we can in fact determine how many pizzas will be sold at different prices. These results, called a **demand and supply schedule**, are obtained from marketing research and other systematic studies of the market. Properly applied, they help managers better understand the relationships among different levels of demand and supply at different price levels.

demand and supply schedule

Assessment of the relationships between different levels of demand and supply at different price levels.

Demand and Supply Curves

demand curve
Graph showing how many units of a product will be demanded (bought) at different prices.

supply curve
Graph showing how many units of a product will be supplied (offered for sale) at different prices.

**market price
(or equilibrium price)**
Profit-maximizing price at which the quantity of goods demanded and the quantity of goods supplied are equal.

The demand and supply schedule can be used to construct demand and supply curves for pizza in your town. A **demand curve** shows how many products—in this case, pizzas—will be *demanded* (bought) at different prices. A **supply curve** shows how many pizzas will be *supplied* (cooked) at different prices.

Figure 1.2 shows the hypothetical demand and supply curves for pizzas in our illustration. As you can see, demand increases as price decreases; supply increases as price increases. When the demand and supply curves are plotted on the same graph, the point at which they intersect is the **market price**, or **equilibrium price**—the price at which the quantity of goods demanded and the quantity of goods supplied are equal. Note in Figure 1.2 that the equilibrium price for pizzas in our example is $10. At this point, the quantity of pizzas demanded and the quantity of pizzas supplied are the same—1000 pizzas per week.

Surpluses and Shortages

surplus
Situation in which quantity supplied exceeds quantity demanded.

shortage
Situation in which quantity demanded exceeds quantity supplied.

But what if the restaurant chooses to make some other number of pizzas? For example, what would happen if the owner tried to increase profits by making more pizzas to sell? Or what if the owner wanted to reduce overhead, cut back on store hours, and reduce the number of pizzas offered for sale? In either case, the result would be an inefficient use of resources—and perhaps lower profits. For example, if the restaurant supplies 1200 pizzas and tries to sell them for $10 each, 200 pizzas will not be purchased. The demand schedule clearly shows that only 1000 pizzas will be demanded at this price. The pizza maker will have a **surplus**—a situation in which the quantity supplied exceeds the quantity demanded. The restaurant will thus lose the money that it spent making those extra 200 pizzas.

Conversely, if the pizzeria supplies only 800 pizzas, a **shortage** will result: The quantity demanded will be greater than the quantity supplied. The pizzeria will "lose" the extra money that it could have made by producing 200 more pizzas. Even though consumers may pay more for pizzas because of the shortage, the restaurant will still earn lower profits than it would have if it had made 1000 pizzas. In addition, it will risk angering customers who cannot buy pizzas. To optimize profits, therefore, all businesses must constantly seek the right combination of price charged and quantity supplied. This "right combination" is found at the equilibrium point.

This simple example, of course, involves only one company, one product, and a few buyers. The Canadian economy is far more complex. Thousands of companies sell hundreds of thousands of products to millions of buyers every day. In the end, however, the result is much the same: companies try to supply the quantity and selection of goods that will earn them the largest profits.

The Business Cycle

business cycle
The fluctuation in the level of economic activity that an economy goes through over time.

General Motors
http://www.gmcanada.com

The **business cycle** is the fluctuation in the level of economic activity that an economy goes through over time.

The business cycle can be divided into four stages: peak, recession, trough, and recovery. The *expansionary* phases are peak and recovery. A new business like Sky Freight Express is more likely to be successful if it starts up during the expansionary phases of the business cycle. The *contractionary* stages are recession and trough. When the recession period lasts a long time or is particularly severe, it is called a depression. During recessions, companies cut back on items such as executive travel. At GM Canada, for example, employees have been told to travel less and use the phone more. At McDonald's

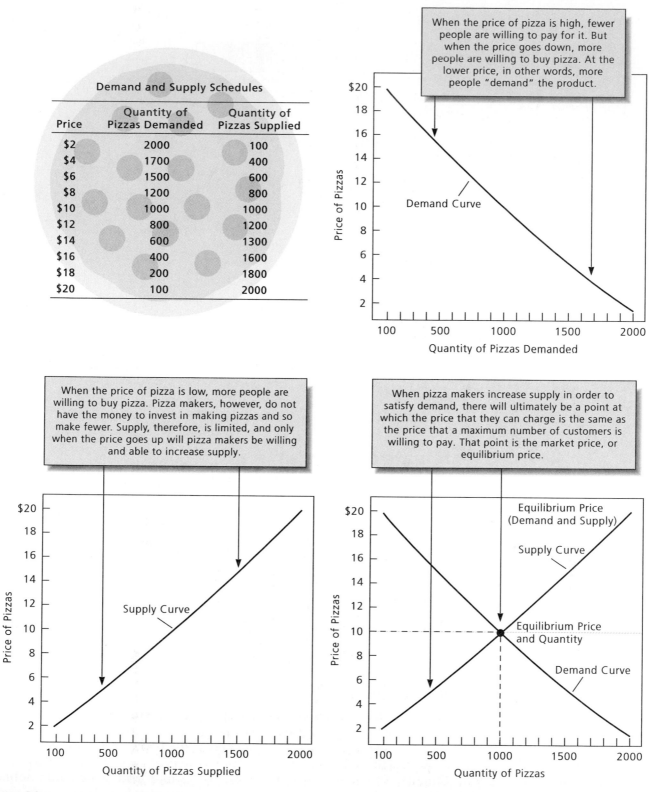

Figure 1.2
Demand and supply.

Restaurants, 300 managers travelled to a convention in Montreal in car pools rather than by air.[7]

Periods of expansion and contraction can vary from several months to several years. As shown in Figure 1.3, a slowdown need not result in a depression if the recovery gets underway before the economy tumbles too far down.

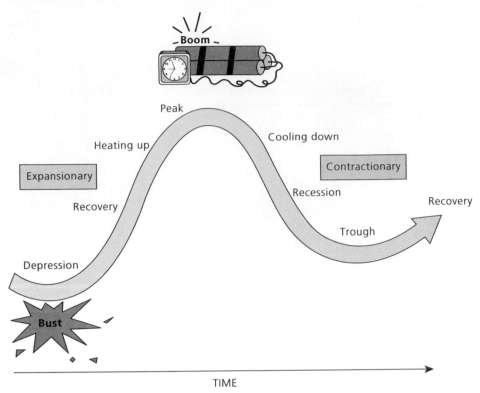

Figure 1.3
The business cycle.

Private Enterprise

In his book *The Wealth of Nations*, first published in 1776, economist Adam Smith argued that a society's interests are best served by **private enterprise** —allowing individuals within that society to pursue their own interests without governmental regulation or restriction. He believed that because of self-interests, the "invisible hand of competition" would lead businesses to produce the best products they could as efficiently as possible and to sell them at the lowest possible price. Each business would unintentionally be working for the good of society as a whole.

Market economies have prospered in large part due to private enterprise. As Adam Smith first noted, private enterprise requires the presence of four elements: (1) private property rights, (2) freedom of choice, (3) profits, and (4) competition.[8] These elements are shown in Figure 1.4.

private enterprise
An economic system characterized by private property rights, freedom of choice, profits, and competition.

Private Property

Smith maintained that the creation of wealth should be the concern of individuals, not the government. Thus, he argued that the ownership of the resources used to create wealth must be in the hands of individuals, not the government. Individual ownership of property is part of everyday life in Canada. You or someone you know has bought and owned automobiles, homes, land, or stock. The right to **private property**—to buy, own, use, and sell almost any form of property—is one of the most fundamental aspects of capitalism. Most of us take private property for granted. Yet, in some countries you could not own a business even if you had the money to pay cash.

private property
The right to buy, own, use, and sell an item.

Freedom of Choice

Freedom of choice means that you can try to sell your labour to whomever you choose. You can also choose which products to buy. Freedom of choice

freedom of choice
The right to choose what to buy or sell, including one's labour.

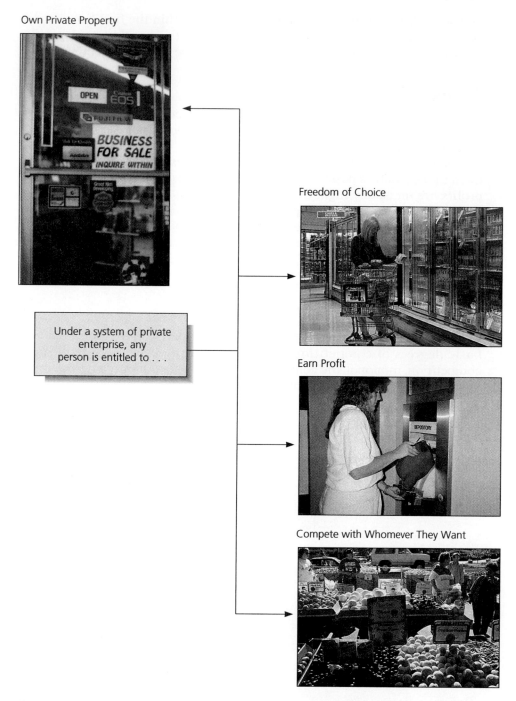

Own Private Property

Under a system of private enterprise, any person is entitled to . . .

Freedom of Choice

Earn Profit

Compete with Whomever They Want

Figure 1.4
A free enterprise system is based on four basic elements. In such a system, all people are entitled to own private property, to choose what to buy and sell, to earn profit, and to compete with whomever they want.

further means that producers of goods and services can usually choose whom to hire and what to make. Under normal circumstances, the government does not go to a manufacturing firm, for example, and tell it what kinds of products to make.

Profits

What a company chooses to produce will, by definition, be affected by the *profits* it hopes to make. A business that fails to make a profit must eventually close its doors. The majority of small businesses fail within the first five years of their existence.[9] But the lure of profits leads some people to give up the security of working for someone else and assume the risks of entrepreneurship.

Competition

competition
The vying among businesses in a particular market or industry to best satisfy consumer demands and earn profits.

If profits motivate individuals to start businesses, **competition** for resources and customers motivates individuals to operate their businesses efficiently. In order to gain an advantage over their competitors in the marketplace, businesses must produce their goods and services for as little as possible and sell them for as much as possible. However, if they are quite successful and their profits are unusually high, other firms will sense an opportunity and also enter the market. The ensuing competition between these firms will drive the prices down. To continue to make a profit, each business must constantly look for more efficient ways to make its products, as well as for new and/or improved products.

Degrees of Competition

Not all industries are equally competitive. Economists have identified four basic degrees of competition within a private enterprise system—pure competition, monopolistic competition, oligopoly, and monopoly. Figure 1.5 illustrates these four degrees of competition.

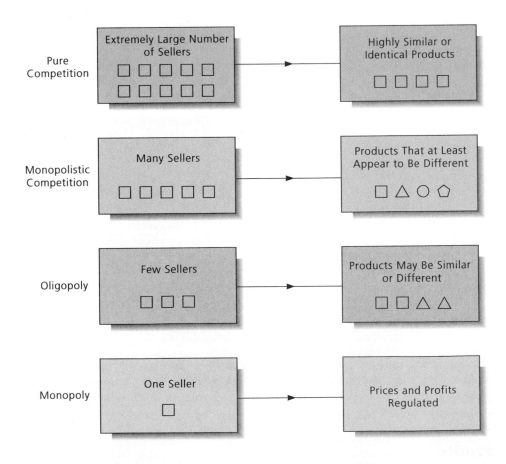

Figure 1.5
There are four basic degrees of competition in a private enterprise system.

Pure Competition

In order for **pure competition** to exist, firms must be small in size, but large in number. In such conditions, no firm is powerful enough individually to influence the price of its product in the marketplace.

First, in pure competition the products offered by each firm are so similar that buyers view them as identical to those offered by other firms. Second, both the buyers and sellers know the price that others are paying and receiving in the marketplace. Third, the firms involved in a purely competitive situation are small, which makes it relatively easy for a firm to go into or out of business.

Under pure competition, price is set exclusively by supply and demand in the marketplace. Sellers and buyers must accept the going price. Despite some government price-support programs, agriculture is usually considered to be a good example of pure competition in the Canadian economy. The wheat produced on one farm is essentially the same as wheat produced on another farm. Both producers and buyers are well aware of prevailing market prices. Moreover, it is relatively easy to get started or to quit producing wheat.

pure competition
A market or industry characterized by a very large number of small firms producing an identical product so that none of the firms has any ability to influence price.

Monopolistic Competition

In **monopolistic competition**, there are fewer sellers than in pure competition, but there are still many buyers. Sellers try to make their products at least appear to be slightly different from those of their competitors by tactics such as brand names (Tide and Cheer), design or styling (Ralph Lauren and Izod clothes), and advertising (as done by Coke and Pepsi).

Monopolistically competitive businesses may be large or small, because it is relatively easy for a firm to enter or leave the market. For example, many small clothing manufacturers compete successfully with large apparel makers. Product differentiation also gives sellers some control over the price they charge. Thus Ralph Lauren Polo shirts can be priced with little regard for the price of Eaton's shirts, even though the Eaton's shirts may have very similar styling.

monopolistic competition
A market or industry characterized by a large number of firms supplying products that are similar but distinctive enough from one another to give firms some ability to influence price.

Oligopoly

When an industry has only a handful of sellers, an **oligopoly** exists. As a general rule, these sellers are almost always very large. The entry of new competitors is restricted because a large capital investment is usually necessary to enter the industry. Consequently, oligopolistic industries (such as the automobile, rubber, and steel industries) tend to stay oligopolistic.

Oligopolists have even more control over their alternatives than do monopolistically competitive firms. However, the actions of any one firm in an oligopolistic market can significantly affect the sales of all other firms. When one reduces prices or offers some type of incentives to increase its sales, the others usually do the same in order to protect their sales. Likewise, when one raises its prices, the others generally follow suit. As a result, the prices of comparable products are usually quite similar.

Since substantial price competition would reduce every seller's profits, firms use product differentiation to attract customers. For example, the four major cereal makers (Kellogg, General Mills, General Foods, and Quaker Oats) control almost all of the cereal market. Each charges roughly the same price for its cereal as do the others. But each also advertises that its cereals are better tasting or more nutritious than the others.[10] Competition within an oligopolistic market can be fierce.

oligopoly
A market or industry characterized by a small number of very large firms that have the power to influence the price of their product and/or resources.

Monopoly

When an industry or market has only one producer, a **monopoly** exists. Being the only supplier gives a firm complete control over the price of its product.

monopoly
A market or industry with only one producer, who can set the price of its product and/or resources.

Consumers often buy products under conditions of monopolistic competition. For example, there are few differences between different brands of toothpaste, cold tablets, detergents, canned goods, and soft drinks.

natural monopoly

A market or industry in which having only one producer is most efficient because it can meet all of consumers' demand for the product.

Its only constraint is how much consumer demand will fall as its price rises. Until 1992, the long-distance telephone business was a monopoly in Canada, and cable TV, which has had a local monopoly for years, will lose it when telephone companies and satellite broadcasters are allowed into the cable business.[11]

In Canada, laws such as the *Competition Act* forbid many monopolies. In addition, the prices charged by "natural monopolies" are closely watched by provincial utilities boards. **Natural monopolies** are industries where one company can most efficiently supply all the product or service that is needed. For example, like most utilities, your provincial electric company is a natural monopoly because it can supply all the power (product) needed in an area. Duplicate facilities—such as two nuclear power plants, two sets of power lines, and so forth—would be wasteful.

Evaluating Economic Systems

Thus far we have noted that nations employ a variety of economic systems. We naturally think our economic system works better than those used in other countries. We point with pride to our high standard of living and to our general prosperity. Yet, leaders in other countries believe just as strongly that their systems are best. So how do we really know that our system works as well as we think? To assess the effectiveness of an economic system objectively, we must consider the society's goals, its record in meeting those goals, and the interaction of governmental and non-governmental forces within the economy.

Economic Goals

Nearly every economic system has as its broad goals stability, full employment, and growth. Economies differ in the emphasis they place on each and their approach to achieving them.

Stability

In economic terms, **stability** is a condition in which the balance between money available and goods produced remains about the same. As a consequence, prices for consumer goods, interest rates, and wages paid to workers change very little. Stability helps maintain equilibrium and predictability for business people, consumers, and workers.

The biggest threat to stability is **inflation**, a period of widespread price increases throughout the economic system. The most widely known measure of inflation is the **consumer price index**, which measures changes in the cost of a "basket" of goods and services that a typical family buys. Figure 1.6 shows how inflation has varied over the last 20 years in Canada. The box "Coping with Inflation" describes some of the difficulties that several countries have faced because of high inflation.

Yet inflation is not necessarily bad. Stability can cause stagnation and a decline in innovation. The onset of inflation is usually a sign of growth. Initially, higher prices cause businesses to expand, hire new workers, pump more dollars into advertising, and introduce new and exciting products and services. New businesses also start up to take advantage of the prosperity.

Inflation is not the only threat to economic stability. Suppose that a major factory in your town closes. Hundreds or even thousands of workers would lose their jobs. If other companies in the area do not have jobs for them, these unemployed people will reduce their spending. Other local businesses will thus suffer drops in sales—and perhaps cut their own workforces. The resulting **recession**, characterized by a decrease in employment, income, and production, may spread across the province and the nation. A particularly severe and long-lasting recession, such as the one that affected much of the world in the 1930s, is called a **depression**.

stability

A situation in which the relationship between the supply of money and goods, services, and labour remains constant.

inflation

A period of widespread price increases throughout an economic system.

consumer price index

Changes in the cost of a basket of goods and services that the typical family buys.

recession

The part of the business cycle characterized by a decrease in employment, income, and production.

depression

A particularly severe and long-lasting recession such as the one that affected the world in the 1930s.

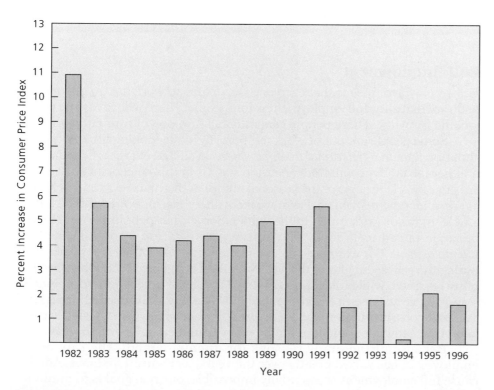

Figure 1.6
In the last few years the rate of price increases in Canada has dropped.

International Report

Coping with Inflation

For most of the 20th century, Canadians have taken for granted that inflation will not be a serious problem. While the annual inflation rate in Canada occasionally creeps up to 10 or 12 percent, this is nothing compared to the 500 percent experienced in Brazil in 1994, and the 4200 percent experienced in Argentina in 1989.

Argentina attempted to fight inflation by swapping its nearly worthless austral for a new peso valued at one to one with the U.S. dollar. By doing this, they hoped to develop a currency that Argentines could believe in. But conditioned as they were to high inflation, businesses initially continued to raise prices even after the new currency had been introduced. Over time, however, the inflation rate has gradually come down, and by 1994 was in the neighbourhood of 120 percent per year. Unfortunately, the new peso is overvalued by as much as 40 percent, and purchasing power is lower than it was before the plan was introduced. Many people who were formerly part of the middle class have been pushed into the lower class.

Brazil's annual inflation has exceeded 100 percent each year for the last decade. Recently, the rate has climbed even higher, exceeding 500 percent according to some indexes. These high rates have been caused primarily by chronic government deficits and excessive government spending. Individuals cope with these high rates using various strategies. One popular method is to pay by cheque and date the cheque as much as 10 days later. On the tenth day, the person takes the money from an interest-bearing account and puts it in an empty chequing account. But even these strategies may not help. Doctors note that the number of heart and stroke victims was up 20 percent in 1993, and they think that high inflation was the culprit because it increased the stress that people felt.

Like Argentina, Brazil is making a concerted effort to get inflation under control by introducing a new currency (the real, pronounced ray-AL) and tying it to the U.S. dollar. Unlike Argentina, there is no law guaranteeing convertibility of one real for one dollar, nor is there any law that forbids the central bank from printing money not backed by reserves. The expectations of Brazilians are crucial to the success of the plan. If they think the government will not back up the plan if the going gets tough, then the country is likely to experience a new round of inflation soon.

These stories of high inflation in other countries may come as a surprise to Canadians. Inflation in Canada dropped to very low levels in the early 1990s, and by the middle of 1994 *deflation*—a decline in price levels—was experienced for the first time since 1955, as consumer prices fell by 0.2 percent. Lowered prices were caused in part by reductions in government tobacco taxes, and by the invasion of retail discounters like Wal-Mart into Canada.

Full Employment

Full employment means that everyone who wants to work has an opportunity to do so. In reality, full employment is impossible. There will always be people looking for work. These people generally fall into one of four categories.

Some people are out of work temporarily while looking for a new job, a situation known as *frictional unemployment*. A skilled engineer who has just quit her job but who will find a new job soon is in this category. Other people are out of work because of the seasonal nature of their jobs, a situation known as *seasonal unemployment*. Farm workers and construction workers, for example, may not work much in the winter. Sometimes people are out of work because of reduced economic activity, a situation known as *cyclical unemployment*. For example, many oil field workers in Alberta lost their jobs during the petroleum glut of the late 1980s. Some regained their jobs when stability returned, while many others moved to jobs in other industries. Finally, some people are unemployed because they lack the skills needed to perform available jobs, a situation known as *structural unemployment*. A steel worker laid off in a town looking for computer programmers falls into this category.

Because of the many reasons for unemployment, the rate of unemployment has varied greatly over the years, as Figure 1.7 shows. And because full employment is essentially impossible, our real goal is to minimize unemployment. High unemployment wastes talent and is a drain on resources that must be allocated to unemployment-associated welfare programs. Higher welfare costs, in turn, result in higher taxes for everyone.

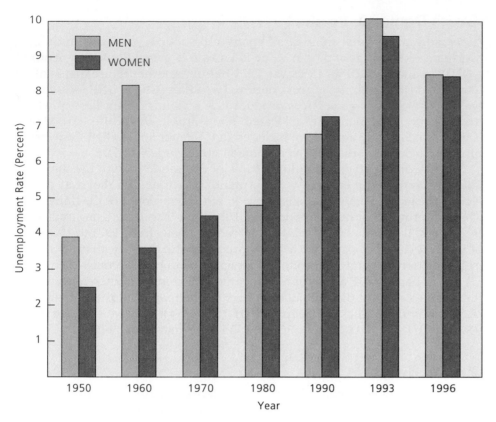

Figure 1.7
There has been a gradual upward trend in unemployment rates, with women having rates much closer to men in recent years.

Growth

A final goal of our economic system is **growth**, an increase in the amount of goods and services produced by our own resources. In theory, we all want our system to expand—more businesses, more jobs, more wealth for everyone. In practice, growth is difficult without triggering inflation and other elements of instability. However, an extended period of no growth may eventually result in an economic decline—business shutdowns, a loss of jobs, a general decrease in overall wealth, and a poorer standard of living for everyone.

For many decades, Canada experienced growth rates in excess of most nations. More recently, however, countries such as South Korea, Taiwan, Japan, and Germany all had higher growth rates than Canada, in part because they became increasingly more efficient at producing goods and services.[12]

growth
An increase in the amount of goods and services produced using the same resources.

Measuring Economic Performance

In order to judge how well an economic system is achieving its goals, economists use one or more of the following measures: standard of living, gross domestic product, productivity, the balance of trade, and national debt.

Standard of Living

The **standard of living** is a measure of a society's economic well-being. It helps us to observe the change in a society's well-being over time and to compare one society's well-being with that of another. Canadians have become used to expecting their living standards to increase as time goes on. But we may be entering a period when living standards will not increase at all. Infometrica, an Ottawa-based economic consulting firm, predicts that in real terms, consumer disposable income will show no increase at all for the 1990s.[13]

standard of living
A measure of a society's economic well-being.

Gross Domestic Product

gross domestic product (GDP)
The value of all goods and services produced in Canada during a one-year period.

If we add up the total value of all goods and services produced in Canada during a one-year period, that value is known as **gross domestic product (GDP)**. Canada's GDP in 1996 was $771 billion. Another figure that is often computed by economists is **gross national product (GNP)**. GNP includes the value of all goods and services produced by a country regardless of where the factors of production were located. For example, the profits earned by a Canadian company abroad are included in GNP, but not in GDP. Conversely, profits earned by foreign firms in Canada *are* included in GDP.

gross national product (GNP)
The value of all goods and services produced by a country regardless of where the factors of production were located.

GDP and GNP are useful measures of economic growth because they allow us to track our economy's performance over time. But they may distort economic growth figures because they do not take account of the things that "nature" provides for free. Consider the GDP of, say, Indonesia. Using traditional measures, Indonesia's GDP grew 7.1 percent annually from 1971 to 1984. But if we calculate what was taken from nature to achieve this growth (tree cutting, soil depletion, mineral depletion), Indonesia's growth rate was only 4 percent.[14]

per capita GDP
Allows comparison of GDP figures for different countries, taking into account population size.

Per capita GDP allows us to compare GDP figures for different countries, taking into account their population size. Of the major industrial countries, Japan has the highest per capita GDP ($40 734), followed by Germany ($29 304), the U.S. ($26 225), France ($25 817), and Canada ($18 919).[15]

Productivity

productivity
A measure of efficiency that compares how much is produced with the resources used to produce it.

As a measure of economic growth, **productivity** describes how much is produced relative to the resources used to produce it. That is, if Mind Computers can produce a personal computer for $1000 but Canon needs $1200 to produce a comparable computer, Mind is more productive. Chapter 14 provides a detailed look at productivity.

Balance of Trade

balance of trade
The total of a country's exports (sales to other countries) minus its imports (purchases from other countries).

Another commonly used measure of economic performance is the **balance of trade**, the total of a country's exports to other countries minus its imports from other countries. A positive balance of trade is generally considered to be favourable because new money flows into the country from the sales of exports. A negative balance is less favourable because money is flowing out of the country from the purchase of imports. Canada has enjoyed a favourable balance of trade since the mid-1970s, but the balance is favourable only because Canada exports so much to the United States. Our balance of trade with most other countries is unfavourable.

National Debt

Like a business, the government takes in revenues (primarily in the form of taxes) and has expenses (military spending, social programs, and so forth). For many years, the government of Canada incurred annual **budget deficits**, that is, the government spent more money each year than it took in. These accumulated annual deficits have created a huge **national debt**—the amount of money that Canada owes its creditors. We discuss this in more detail in Chapter 3.

budget deficit
The result of the government spending more in one year than it takes in during that year.

national debt
The total amount of money that Canada owes its creditors (presently over $550 billion).

Managing the Canadian Economy

fiscal policies
Policies by means of which governments collect and spend revenues.

The government manages the economic system through two sets of policies. **Fiscal policies** refer to the collection and spending of government revenues. Tax policies, for example, can function as fiscal policy to increase revenues. Similarly, budget cuts (for example, closing military bases) function as fiscal policy when spending is decreased.

Monetary policies focus on controlling the size of the nation's money supply. Working primarily through the Bank of Canada (the nation's central bank), the government can influence the ability and willingness of banks throughout the country to lend money. It can also influence the supply of money by prompting interest rates to go up or down. A primary goal in recent years has been to adjust interest rates so that inflation is kept in check.

monetary policies
Policies by means of which the government controls the size of the nation's money supply.

The Bank of Canada
http://www.bank-banque-canada.ca

Summary of Learning Objectives

1. **Define the nature of Canadian *business* and its goals.** *Businesses* are organizations that produce or sell goods or services to make a profit. *Profits* are the difference between a business's revenues and its expenses. The prospect of earning profits encourages individuals and organizations to open and to expand businesses. The benefits of business activities also extend to wages paid to workers and to taxes that support government functions.

2. **Describe different types of *economic systems* according to the means by which they control the *factors of production*.** An *economic system* is a nation's system for allocating its resources among its citizens. Economic systems differ in terms of who owns and/or controls the four basic *factors of production*: natural resources, labour, capital, and entrepreneurs. In *command economies*, the government controls all or most factors. In *market economies*, which are based on the principles of *capitalism*, individuals control the factors of production. Most countries today have *mixed market economies* that are dominated by one of these systems but include elements of the others.

3. **Show how *demand* and *supply* affect resource distribution in Canada.** The Canadian economy is strongly influenced by markets, demand, and supply. *Demand* is the willingness and ability of buyers to purchase a product or service. *Supply* is the willingness and ability of producers to offer goods or services for sale. Demand and supply work together to set a *market* or *equilibrium price:* the price at which the quantity of goods demanded and the quantity of goods supplied are equal.

4. **Identify the elements of *private enterprise* and explain the various degrees of *competition* in the Canadian economic system.** The Canadian economy is founded on the principles of *private enterprise: private property rights, freedom of choice, profits,* and *competition.* Degrees of competition vary because not all industries are equally competitive. Under conditions of *pure competition*, a large number of small firms compete in a market governed entirely by demand and supply. In an *oligopoly*, there are only a handful of sellers. A *monopoly* exists when there is only one seller.

5. **Explain the criteria for evaluating the success of an economic system in meeting its goals and explain how the federal government attempts to manage the Canadian economy.** The basic goals of an economic system are *stability, full employment,* and *growth.* Measures of how well an economy has accomplished these goals include *standard of living, gross domestic product, productivity, balance of trade,* and *national debt.* The government uses *monetary policies* to control the size of the nation's money supply and *fiscal policies* to manage the effects of its spending and revenue collection.

Key Terms

business, 5
profit, 5
economic system, 6
factors of production, 6
natural resources, 7
labour, 7
capital, 7
entrepreneur, 7
command economy, 7
market economy, 7
communism, 7
socialism, 8
capitalism, 11
mixed economy, 11

market, 11
demand, 11
supply, 11
law of demand, 11
law of supply, 11
demand and supply
   schedule, 11
demand curve, 12
supply curve, 12
market price, 12
surplus, 12
shortage, 12
business cycle, 12
private enterprise, 14

private property, 14
freedom of choice, 14
competition, 16
pure competition, 17
monopolistic competition,
  17
oligopoly, 17
monopoly, 17
natural monopoly, 18
stability, 19
inflation, 19
consumer price index, 19
recession, 19
depression, 19

growth, 21
standard of living, 21
gross domestic product
  (GDP), 22
gross national product
  (GNP), 22
per capita GDP, 22
productivity, 22
balance of trade, 22
budget deficit, 22
national debt, 22
fiscal policies, 22
monetary policies, 23

Study Questions and Exercises

Review Questions

1. What are the factors of production? Is one more important than the others? If so, which one? Why?
2. What are the major characteristics of a market economy? How does a market economy differ from a planned economy?
3. Explain the differences in the four degrees of competition and give an example of each. (Do not use the examples given in the text.)
4. Why is productivity important? Why is inflation both good and bad?

Analysis Questions

5. Select a local business and identify the basic factors of production that it uses. Now identify the factors used by your college or university. What are the similarities and differences?
6. In recent years, many countries have moved from command economies to market economies. Why do

you think this has occurred? Can you envision a situation that would cause a resurgence of command economies?
7. Identify a situation in which excess supply of a product led to decreased prices. Identify a situation in which a shortage led to increased prices. What eventually happened in each case? Why?

Application Exercises

8. Choose a locally owned and operated business. Interview the owner to find out what factors of production the business uses and its sources for acquiring them.
9. Visit a local shopping mall or shopping area. List each store you see and determine what degree of competition it faces in that environment. How do other businesses compete to market goods or services?
10. Go to the library and read about 10 different industries. Classify each according to degree of competition.

Building Your Business Skills

Goal

To encourage students to understand how the competitive environment affects a product's price.

Situation

Suppose that you open an ice-cream parlour in a community that has three other ice-cream shops within an area of four city blocks. During the first six months, you charge $1.50 for each ice-cream cone—the same price as your competitors. Just as summer begins, however, one competitor drops the price to $1.25. Within a week, the others follow suit. Your break-even price per cone is $1. You are thus concerned about getting into a price war that may destroy your business.

Method

Divide into groups of four or five people. The mission of each group is to develop a general strategy for handling the competitors' price changes. In your discussion, take the following factors into account:

- how the demand for your product is affected by price changes
- the number of competitors selling the same or a similar product
- the methods you can use—other than price—to attract new customers.

Analysis

Develop specific pricing strategies based on the following situations:

- Within a week after dropping the price to $1.25, one of your competitors raises the price back to $1.50.
- Two of your competitors drop their prices further— to $1 a cone. As a result, your business drops by 30 percent.
- On August 1, at the height of the summer season, one of the stores that dropped its price to $1 goes out of business. Of the remaining stores, one holds the price at $1 while the other sells cones for $1.25.

Follow-up Questions

1. How is it possible to create a demand for your product through inducements that are not price-related, including customer service, store environment, and location?

2. Is it always in a company's best interest to feature the lowest prices?

EXPLORING the Net

To learn more about the Disney Institute and its programs (see Concluding Case 1-2), log on to the following Web site:

http://www.disney.com/disneyworld/disneyinstitute/welcome.html

Read the material about the Disney Institute in Concluding Case 1-2 and then consider the following questions:

1. How much interest do you have in attending the Disney Institute?

2. Do you see the Institute as a program having real value in and of itself, or is it simply a marketing ploy to get more visitors to Disney World?

3. Which Institute programs do you think are likely to be the most popular? The least popular?

4. Are there other programs that you think Disney could offer at the Institute?

5. Construct a basic profile of the kind of person you think is most likely to attend the Institute.

6. Do you think Disney's Web site itself is a good marketing tool?

At Last! Hibernia Starts Up

In 1959, a research geologist at Mobil Oil began speculating that there might be oil off the coast of Newfoundland. Various wells were drilled over the next 20 years, but none were commercially viable. In 1979, however, a huge reserve of oil was discovered. Now, nearly 40 years after the first tentative exploration efforts, the Hibernia project has finally begun pumping oil. A consortium of companies, including Mobil, Chevron, and Petro-Canada, are involved in the drilling.

Two other megaprojects are also in the works in the same general area off the coast of Newfoundland. The Terra Nova project (Petro-Canada) could begin pumping oil as early as 1999, and the Whiterose project (Husky Oil) by 2002. By 2002, production from these three projects could be as high as 350 000 barrels of oil a day. That is more than the combined output of Syncrude Canada and Suncor in northern Alberta's tar sands.

Hibernia's three biggest enemies were nature, politics, and economics. Although the area was known to contain oil, it was avoided for years because of major storms, and because it is in "iceberg alley." In 1982, the Ocean Ranger drilling rig sank in a winter storm, killing all 84 workers on it. That disaster motivated engineers to build a heavy platform that is anchored to the sea bottom. This platform will be able to withstand iceberg hits as well.

Federal and provincial squabbling about who owned the mineral rights also created uncertainty. Newfoundland claimed that it owned the rights, but the federal government argued that Newfoundland gave up those rights when it joined Canada in 1949. Eventually, all royalty rights were given to Newfoundland after then–prime minister Brian Mulroney intervened. Mulroney also demanded that the oil companies give at least some of the construction work associated with the project to Newfoundland companies.

Fluctuating oil prices were also a problem. High prices in the late 1970s made the project look economically sound.

But by the late 1980s, oil prices had dropped to the point that the oil companies had decided to halt work on the project. The federal government then agreed to put up $1 billion in grants and $1.7 billion in loan guarantees to keep the project going. For its investment, the government received an 8.5 percent share in the project. In 1992, Gulf Canada suddenly pulled out of the consortium, creating another crisis. Gulf was replaced by Murphy Oil, which was also given loan guarantees by the federal government.

The federal government has adopted a policy that allows the companies in the consortium to recover some of their huge capital costs early; most royalties and corporate taxes won't come until some years later. It is doubtful whether the federal government will get any of the $1 billion in grant money back, but it does expect revenues from its 8.5 percent share.

The Hibernia project has made only a slight dent in Newfoundland's famous high unemployment rate. Critics say that the $1 billion grant translates into a cost of $172 400 for each of the 5800 jobs that were created during the peak construction time. Only about 650 workers will find permanent work because of Hibernia.

Case Questions

1. What is a "mixed economy"? How does the Hibernia project demonstrate Canada's mixed economy?

2. What incentives existed for oil companies to get involved in Hibernia? What incentives existed for the federal government to get involved?

3. Should the federal government have given $1 billion to the oil companies in order to keep them involved in the Hibernia project?

4. How did the forces of supply and demand affect the decisions of the oil companies and the federal government?

5. How are the factors of production evident in this case?

◆

CONCLUDING CASE 1-2

Tired of Mickey Mouse Vacations?

There's no getting around it: the baby boom generation is aging. The oldest of the 76 million baby boomers turned 50 in 1996, and in the next decade, the number of Canadians over 50 will increase sharply. Most are so-called "empty nesters"—couples whose children have left home. Many thrive on personal and even physical challenge, but—perhaps predictably—most have absolutely no interest in taking another Disney World vacation. To borrow an expression from Generation X, they've "been there, done that."

Creative minds at the Walt Disney Co. saw these demographic and mood shifts as a commercial challenge requiring a tailor-made solution: They had to find a way to attract 40- and 50-year-olds who were no longer as active or child-oriented as they once were and who wanted to return from their vacations with something more than a suntan.

Disney's answer is the Disney Institute, a 30-hectare resort within a resort. Located at Orlando's Disney World, the resort allows guests to try their hand at bird watching, cartoon animation, rock climbing, gourmet cooking, spiritual inquiry, and more. This U.S. $35 million solution—billed by Disney as "smart fun"—is pretty much like a summer camp for adults. Described in the official guide as "a unique resort with 80 different programs to expand your mind and challenge your body," the Disney Institute required that Disney build the equivalent of a new business from scratch.

The vision for the Disney Institute began to take shape when Disney CEO Michael Eisner visited the Chautauqua Institution, an adult-learning community located in upstate New York that holds classes on politics, philosophy, and the performing arts. Eisner's visit convinced him that Disney could create a similar environment "to enhance and improve quality of life in the Disney fashion." Marketing research revealed that this type of vacation alternative was particularly attractive to baby boomers. It also showed that baby boomers had money to spend and the willingness to spend it on themselves.

Eleven years after Eisner's visit to Chautauqua, the Disney Institute opened its doors. Not surprisingly, visitors found elements of the Disney they knew, including perky, uniformed staff and immaculate grounds. Missing, however, were Goofy, Mickey, Donald, and Pluto. Gone, too, were endless lines for rides and stores filled with stuffed animals. In their place were feel-good classes, like the one on "Culinary Technique." The Institute is also a recreational resort, with nightly entertainment and such features as a golf program created by legendary pro Gary Player.

The greatest challenge for Disney was to convince the public to try a venture that was so far afield from Disney's traditional mass-market resorts. It had to build a new market by slowly creating demand. Disney responded to this need in several ways:

■ By catering to the trend towards shorter vacations (the Disney Institute offers three-, four-, and seven-night packages)

■ By striking a balance between education and entertainment (although it offers a variety of unique "challenges," no one would ever accuse the Institute of being a grind)

■ By offering special introductory rates as part of its "First 100 Days of Discovery"

■ By relying on word of mouth as well as traditional advertising to build a base of support

■ By deciding that the Institute would be a long-term investment

Underlying all of these efforts was an appeal to the needs and wants of each individual customer in the target market. "Experience a vacation," beckons one ad, "where every day is different and every day is yours to design."

The Disney Institute is Disney's first attempt to enter the adult education market. As such, it is part of a much broader diversification strategy that includes theme parks, movie studios, a sports complex, the Mighty Ducks professional hockey team, cruise lines, and the City of Celebration, near its Disney World hub. The Disney Institute expects to attract about 100 000 visitors a year, far fewer than the 33 million people who visit Disney World each year.

Case Questions

1. How is the Disney Institute a good example of capitalism at work?

2. What role did changing market forces play in Disney's decision to create the Disney Institute?

3. Disney's strategy is to be patient in building the demand for spaces at the Disney Institute. As demand increases, are prices likely to drop, increase, or remain the same? What factors might affect Disney's pricing decisions?

4. If Warner Brothers, which owns Universal Studios, decides to open a competing institute in Orlando, how might the competition affect the operation and marketing of the Disney Institute?

5. Do you agree or disagree with the following statement: The Disney Institute would never have been created in a communist or socialist economy. Support your answer with specific reasons.

◆

2

Setting Up Business in Canada

Employee Buyouts—Good News and Bad News

During the past few years, the idea of employee buyouts has become increasingly popular in both Canada and the U.S. In the U.S., for example, several of the largest firms in the commercial airline industry—United, TWA, and Northwest—recently became employee-owned. At United, the pilots and machinists unions now own 53 percent of the company. In exchange, they made concessions like agreeing to a no-strike clause.

In Canada, there are several prominent examples of employee buyouts. The most famous is probably the buyout of the Temiscaming, Quebec, forest products plant in 1972. International Paper sold the mill to the Quebec government, which kept a 40 percent stake and sold the rest to managers and an investment company. The mill has been profitable ever since. In 1991, the Ontario government helped facilitate a deal that allowed workers to save the Kimberly-Clark mill at Kapuskasing, Ontario. The workers paid $12.5 million for 52 percent ownership. Skeptics doubted whether the deal would be as successful as Temiscaming, but they were proved wrong. In its first quarter of operations, the mill made a profit of nearly $500 000. At Algoma Steel, employees bought a 60 percent ownership in the company as part of a bailout deal by the Ontario government. In 1994, employees and managers at Pine Falls Paper Company in Manitoba bought the firm after Abitibi Price indicated that it was unwilling to spend the money necessary to upgrade the facility. In 1998, Tembec Inc. made an offer to acquire the employee-owned firm.

When Nova Corp. decided to shut down its division that manufactured magnetic bearings and gas seals, it gave several managers the chance to form a separate company to carry on the work. Each manager invested

between $80 000 and $100 000 in the new venture, called Revolve Technologies Inc. Eighteen former Nova employees have also joined the new firm and have contributed between $10 000 and $50 000 apiece. Individuals who once worked for a large firm are now owner-managers of a much smaller one, with all the benefits (and problems) that go along with ownership.

An interesting, but less well-known case, is that of Great Western Brewery. In 1990, Molson Cos. Ltd. decided to close the Carling O'Keefe brewery in Saskatoon. The company offered to transfer workers to other plants, but Don Ebelher, the maintenance chief at the brewery, and 14 other workers bought the plant because they felt they would have more job security working for themselves. Each person put up between $50 000 and $100 000 for the 25 percent equity required. The rest of the money came from a loan through Saskatchewan's Economic Development Corp. Ebelher is now Great Western's CEO.

In this employee-owned company, employee initiative is high, consultation and teamwork are facts of life, the management structure is very flat, and everyone takes pride in their work because they own the company. The firm still needs managers, but they behave quite differently than their predecessors. They work much more closely with production workers and often discuss methods to improve the way that work is done. In a traditional organization, this typically wouldn't happen. The marketing manager at Great Western, Jack White, says that consultation with employees has made him a better manager. The company has 4 managers instead of the 12 it had when it was owned by Molson. The total number of employees has dropped from 65 to 55.

(continued)

Problems exist in employee-owned firms, just as they do in traditionally owned businesses. At Great Western, for example, demand for the new company's product exceeded expectations, so workers felt they had to work long hours and scrape together left-over assembly line parts in order to increase production. Some employees routinely worked 60- or 70-hour weeks. But after these problems had been solved, the company's beer lost its novelty status in the marketplace, and its market share declined from its original 20 percent down to 8 percent. At present, the plant is operating at less than 50 percent capacity.

At Algoma Steel, bonuses for top executives were cancelled in 1994 even though the company made a $16 million profit for the first quarter. Workers had given up $3 an hour as part of the original employee buyout plan, and the president felt that it would be inappropriate for him to take a large bonus after the workers had made big sacrifices. So he gave up his $400 000 bonus. A recent employee survey strongly favoured limiting the compensation of top executives. However, if lowered compensation makes it harder for the firm to attract top quality executives, company performance may decline.

Companies that switch to employee ownership need time to reorganize, to change work processes, and to take advantage of greater employee participation and motivation. Interlink Freight Services Ltd. (formerly CP Express) was purchased by employees in 1994, just before a steep downturn in the trucking industry. The financial problems that resulted slowed the transition to real employee control. Unionized employees, who gave wage concessions with the expectation that their sacrifices would pay off with returns from profit sharing, have been disappointed because there have been no profits. ◆

C reative solutions to problems of business organization are becoming more common as firms struggle to enter markets or to remain competitive in rapidly changing markets. In this chapter, we examine the business structures that are used by both large and small businesses. By focusing on the learning objectives of this chapter, you will better understand the structural options open to Canadian businesses. After reading this chapter, you should be able to:

LEARNING OBJECTIVES

1. Trace the history of business in Canada.

2. Identify the major *forms of business ownership*.

3. Describe *sole proprietorships* and *partnerships* and explain the advantages and disadvantages of each.

4. Describe *corporations* and explain their advantages and disadvantages.

5. Describe the basic issues involved in creating and managing a corporation.

6. Identify recent trends and issues in corporate ownership.

A Brief History of Business in Canada

Canadian business has not always had a variety of complex structures. Indeed, a look at the history of business in Canada shows a steady development from sole proprietorships to the complex corporate structures of today. In this section, we will trace the broad outlines of the development of business in Canada. Table 2.1 highlights some of the specific events in Canadian business history.[1]

The Early Years

Business activity and profit from commercial fishing were the motivation for the first European involvement in Canada. In the late 1400s, ships financed

Table 2.1   **Some Important Dates in Canadian Business History**

1490	English fishermen active off the coast of Newfoundland	**1897-1899**	Klondike gold rush
1534	Account of first trading with native peoples written by Jacques Cartier	**1907**	First issue of *The Financial Post*
		1917-1922	Creation of Canadian National Railways
1669	*Nonsuch* returns to London with a cargo of furs from Hudson Bay area	**1920**	First ship-plate steel mill in Canada opens in Sydney, Nova Scotia
1670	Hudson's Bay Company founded	**1926**	U.S. replaces Great Britain as Canada's largest trading partner
1730-1740	Hat-making industry arises in Quebec and is stifled by French home officials	**1927**	Armand Bombardier sells first "auto-neige" (forerunner of the snowmobile)
1737	Compagnie des forges du St. Maurice formed to produce iron	**1927**	Canadian Tire begins operations in Toronto
1779	North West Company forms	**1929**	Great stock market crash
1785	Molson brewery opens	**1929-1933**	Great Depression
1805	First Canadian paper mill built at St. Andrew's, Quebec	**1930**	Canadian Airways Limited formed
1809	First steamboat (the *Accommodation*) put into service on the St. Lawrence River by John Molson	**1932**	Canadian Radio Broadcasting Corporation formed. (It became the CBC in 1936.)
1817	Bank of Montreal chartered	**1935**	Bank of Canada begins operations
1821	Hudson's Bay Company and North West Company merge	**1937**	Canadian Breweries Limited is formed
		1940	C.D. Howe appointed as Minister of Munitions and Supply
1830-1850	Era of canal building		
1836	First railroad train pulled by a steam engine	**1945**	Argus Corporation Limited formed
1850-1860	First era of railroad building	**1947-1951**	Early computer built at the University of Toronto
1855	John Redpath opens first Canadian sugar refinery in Montreal	**1947**	Leduc Number 1 oil well drilled in Alberta
1856	Railroad trains begin running between Toronto and Montreal	**1949**	A.V. Roe (Avro) makes Canada's first commercial jetliner
1857-1858	First oil well in Canada drilled near Sarnia, Ontario	**1964**	Volvo of Sweden begins assembling cars in Nova Scotia
1861	Toronto Stock Exchange opens	**1965**	Auto Pact signed with the U.S.
1869	Eaton's opens for business in Toronto	**1969**	Canada becomes world's largest potash producer
1879	National Policy implemented; raised tariffs on foreign goods to protect and encourage Canadian manufacturers	**1980-1986**	Dome, Canadair, and Massey-Ferguson receive financial assistance from the federal government
1880-1890	First western land boom		
1885	Last spike driven to complete the Canadian Pacific Railroad	**1989**	Free trade agreement with U.S. comes into effect
1896	First large pulp and paper mill in Canada opened at Sault Ste. Marie	**1993**	North American Free Trade Agreement comes into effect

by English entrepreneurs came to the coast of Newfoundland to fish for profit. By the late 1500s, the Newfoundland coast was being visited by hundreds of fishing vessels each year.

Beginning in the 1500s, French and British adventurers began trading with the native peoples. Items such as cooking utensils and knives were exchanged for beaver and other furs. One trading syndicate made over 1000 percent profit on beaver skins sold to a Paris furrier. Trading was aggressive and, over time, the price of furs rose as more and more Europeans bid for them. Originally the fur trade was restricted to eastern Canada, but by the late 1600s, *coureurs de bois* were travelling far to the west in search of new sources of furs.

European settlers who arrived in Canada in the 16th and 17th centuries initially had to farm or starve. Gradually, however, they began to produce more than they needed for their own survival. The governments of the countries from which the settlers came (notably England and France) were strong supporters of the mercantilist philosophy. Under *mercantilism*, colonists were expected to export raw materials like beaver pelts and lumber at low prices to the mother country. These raw materials were then used to produce finished goods like fur coats which were sold at high prices to settlers in Canada. Attempts to develop industry in Canada were thwarted by England and France who enjoyed large profits from mercantilism. As a result, Canadian manufacturing was slow to develop.

The Factory System and the Industrial Revolution

British manufacturing took a great leap forward around 1750 with the coming of the **Industrial Revolution**. This revolution was made possible by advances in technology and by the development of the **factory system**. Instead of hundreds of workers turning out items one at a time in their cottages, the factory system brought together in one place all of the materials and workers required to produce items in large quantities, along with newly created machines capable of **mass production**.

Mass production offered savings in several areas. It avoided unnecessary duplication of equipment. It allowed firms to purchase raw materials at better prices by buying large lots. And most important, it encouraged **specialization** of labour. No longer did production require highly skilled craftspeople who could do all the different tasks required to make an item. A series of semiskilled workers, each trained to perform only one task and supported by specialized machines and tools, greatly increased output.

In spite of British laws against the export of technology and manufacturing in North America, Canadian manufacturing existed almost from the beginning of European settlement. Modest manufacturing operations were evident in sawmills, breweries, grist mills for grinding grain, tanneries, woollen mills, shoemakers' shops, and tailors' shops. These operations were so successful that by 1800, exports of manufactured goods were more important than exports of fur.

With the advent of steam power in the early 1800s, manufacturing activity began to increase rapidly. By 1850, more than 30 factories—employing more than 2000 people—lined the Lachine Canal alone. Exports of timber to England in 1850 were 70 times greater than what they were in 1800. The demand for reliable transportation was the impetus for canal building in the mid-1800s and then the railroad-building boom in the mid- and late 1800s.

Industrial Revolution
A major change in goods production that began in England in the mid-18th century and was characterized by a shift to the factory system, mass production, and specialization of labour.

factory system
A process in which all the machinery, materials, and workers required to produce a good in large quantities are brought together in one place.

mass production
The manufacture of products of uniform quality in large quantities.

specialization
The breaking down of complex operations into simple tasks that are easily learned and performed.

The Entrepreneurial Era

One of the most significant features of the last half of the 19th century was the emergence of entrepreneurs willing to take risks in the hope of earning huge profits. Adam Smith in his book *The Wealth of Nations* argued that the government should not interfere in the economy, but should let businesses function without regulation or restriction. This *laissez-faire* attitude was often adopted by the Canadian government. As a result, some individuals became immensely wealthy through their aggressive business dealings. Some railway, bank, and insurance executives made over $25 000 per year in the late 1800s, and their purchasing power was immense. Entrepreneurs such as Joseph Flavelle, Henry Pellatt, and John MacDonald lived in ostentatious mansions or castles.

The size and economic power of some firms meant that other businesses had difficulty competing against them. At the same time, some business

In the 18th century, the home crafts industry provided our young nation with clothing and foodstuffs. During the 19th century, machinery such as the cotton gin changed the way the world worked. Today, automation continues to alter our work lives and the types of products that are available to us.

executives decided that it was more profitable to collude than to compete. They decided among themselves to fix prices and divide up markets. Hurt by these actions, Canadian consumers called for more regulation of business. In 1889, the first anti-combines legislation was passed in Canada, and legislation regulating business has increased ever since.

The Production Era

The concepts of specialization and mass production that originated in the Industrial Revolution were more fully refined as Canada entered the 20th century. The Scientific Management Movement focused management's attention on production. Increased efficiency via the "one best way" to accomplish tasks became the major management goal.

Henry Ford's introduction of the moving assembly line in the U.S. in 1913 ushered in the **production era.** During the production era, less attention was paid to selling and marketing than to technical efficiency when producing

production era

The period during the early 20th century when businesses focused almost exclusively on improving productivity and manufacturing methods.

goods. By using fixed work stations, increasing task specialization, and moving the work to the worker, the assembly line increased productivity and lowered prices, making all kinds of products affordable for the average person.

During the production era, large businesses began selling stock—making shareholders the owners—and relying on professional managers. The growth of corporations and improved production output resulting from assembly lines came at the expense of worker freedom. The dominance of big firms made it harder for individuals to go into business for themselves. Company towns run by the railroads, mining corporations, and forest products firms gave individuals little freedom of choice over whom to work for and what to buy. To restore some balance within the overall system, both government and labour had to develop and grow. Thus, this period saw the rise of labour unions and collective bargaining. We will look at this development in more detail in Chapter 11. The Great Depression of the 1930s and World War II caused the federal government to intervene in the economic system on a previously unimaginable scale.

Today, business, government, and labour are frequently referred to by economists and politicians as the three *countervailing powers* in our society. All are big. All are strong. Yet, none totally dominates the others.

The Sales and Marketing Eras

By the 1930s, business's focus on production had resulted in spectacular increases in the amount of goods and services for sale. As a result, buyers had more choices and producers faced greater competition in selling their wares. Thus began the so-called **sales era**. According to the ideas of this time, a business's profits and success depended on hiring the right salespeople, advertising heavily, and making sure products were readily available. Business firms were essentially production- and sales-oriented, and they produced what they thought customers wanted, or simply what the company was good at producing. This approach is still used by firms that find themselves with surplus goods that they want to sell (e.g., used-car dealerships).

Following World War II, pent-up demand for consumer goods kept the economy rolling. While brief recessions did occur periodically, the 1950s and 1960s were prosperous times. Production increased, technology advanced, and the standard of living rose. During the **marketing era**, business adopted a new philosophy on how to do business—use market research to determine what customers want, and then make it for them. Firms like Procter & Gamble and Molson were very effective during the marketing era, and continue to be profitable today. Each offers an array of products within a particular field (toothpaste or beer, for example), and gives customers a chance to pick what best suits their needs.

sales era
The period during the 1930s and 1940s when businesses focused on sales forces, advertising, and keeping products readily available.

Procter & Gamble
http://www.pg.com

marketing era
The period during the 1950s and 1960s when businesses began to identify and meet consumer wants in order to make a profit.

The Finance Era

In the 1980s, emphasis shifted to finance. In the **finance era** there was a sharp increase in mergers and in the buying and selling of business enterprises. Some people now call it the "decade of greed." As we will see in the next chapter, during the finance era there were many hostile takeovers and a great deal of financial manipulation of corporate assets by so-called corporate raiders. Critics charged that these raiders were simply enriching themselves and weren't creating anything of tangible value by their activity. They also charged that raiders were distracting business managers from their main goals of running the business. The raiders responded that they were making organizations more efficient by streamlining, merging, and reorganizing them.

finance era
The period during the 1980s when there were many mergers and much buying and selling of business enterprises.

The Global Era

The last few years have seen the continuation of technological advances in production, computer technology, information systems, and communication capabilities. They have also seen the emergence of a truly global economy. Canadians drive cars made in Japan, wear sweaters made in Italy, drink beer brewed in Mexico, and listen to stereos made in Taiwan. But we're not alone in this. People around the world buy products and services from foreign companies.

While it is true that many Canadian businesses have been hurt by foreign imports, numerous others have profited by exploring new foreign markets themselves. And domestic competition has forced many businesses to work harder than ever to cut costs, increase efficiency, and improve product and service quality. We will explore a variety of important trends, opportunities, and challenges of the global era throughout this book.

Types of Business Organizations

All business owners must decide which form of legal organization—a sole proprietorship, a partnership, a corporation or a cooperative—best suits them and their business. Few decisions are more critical, since the choice affects a host of managerial and financial issues, including income taxes and the owners' liability. In choosing a legal form of organization, the parties concerned must consider their likes, dislikes, and dispositions, their immediate and long-range needs, and the advantages and disadvantages of each form. Seldom, if ever, does any one factor completely determine which form is best.[2]

Sole Proprietorships

sole proprietorship

A business owned (and usually operated) by one person who is personally responsible for the firm's debts.

Eaton's
http://www.eatons.com/winter/home

As the very first legal form of business organization, **sole proprietorships** date back to ancient times. They are still the most numerous form of business in Canada. Despite their numbers, however, they account for only a small proportion of total business revenues in this country.

Because most sole proprietorships are small, often employing only one person, you might assume that all are small businesses. However, sole proprietorships may be as large as a steel mill or as small as a lemonade stand. Some of Canada's largest companies started out as sole proprietorships. Eaton's, for example, was originally a one-man operation founded by Timothy Eaton. One of Canada's biggest sole proprietorships is the Jim Pattison Group, with sales of $3 billion and 15 000 employees (see the boxed insert on page 222). Figure 2.1 summarizes the basic advantages and disadvantages of the sole proprietorship form of ownership.

Advantages

Freedom is the most striking feature of sole proprietorships. Because they alone own their businesses, sole proprietors need answer to no one but themselves. They can also maintain a high level of privacy, since they are not required to report information about their operations to anyone.

Sole proprietorships are simple to form. Sole proprietors often need only put a sign on their door in order to go into business for themselves. They are also easy to dissolve. Rock concerts or athletic events may be organized as sole proprietorships by individuals who then dissolve the business entity when the event is over.

Low start-up costs are yet another attractive feature of sole proprietorships. Legal fees are likely to be low, since some sole proprietorships

ADVANTAGES   DISADVANTAGES

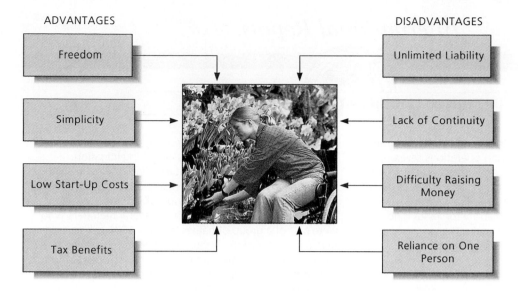

Freedom

Simplicity

Low Start-Up Costs

Tax Benefits

Unlimited Liability

Lack of Continuity

Difficulty Raising Money

Reliance on One Person

Figure 2.1
The most popular form of business ownership in Canada is the sole proprietorship. There are both advantages and disadvantages to this form of ownership.

need only register the business with the provincial government in order to make sure that no other business bears the same name. Some proprietorships do need to take out licences, however. For example, restaurants and pet shops need special licences.

Sole proprietorships also offer tax benefits for new businesses likely to suffer losses before profits begin to flow. Tax laws permit sole proprietors to treat the sales revenues and operating expenses of the business as part of their personal finances. Thus, a proprietor can cut taxes by deducting any operating losses from income earned from sources other than the business. Since most businesses lose money at the beginning, this tax situation is very helpful to entrepreneurs starting up.

Disadvantages

One major drawback of sole proprietorships is their **unlimited liability**. A sole proprietor is personally liable for all debts incurred by the business. Bills must be paid out of the sole proprietor's own pocket if the business fails to generate enough cash. Otherwise, creditors can step in and claim the proprietor's personal possessions, including a home, furniture, and automobile. (Actually, the law does protect some of the proprietor's assets, but many can be claimed.) The impact of unlimited liability is described in the box "Unlimited Liability at Lloyd's of London."

Another disadvantage is lack of continuity. A sole proprietorship legally dissolves when the owner dies. The business can, of course, be reorganized soon after the owner's death if a successor has been trained to take over the business. Otherwise, executors or heirs must **liquidate** (sell the assets of) the business.

Finally, a sole proprietorship is dependent upon the resources of a single individual. If the proprietor has unlimited resources and is a successful manager, this characteristic is not really a problem. In most cases, however, the proprietor's financial and managerial limits constrain what the organization can do. Sole proprietors often find it hard to borrow money not only to start up, but also to expand. Banks often reject such applications, fearing that they will not be able to recover the loan if the sole proprietor becomes disabled. Often, would-be proprietors must rely on personal savings and loans from family for start-up funds.

unlimited liability
A person who invests in a business is liable for all debts incurred by the business; personal possessions can be taken to pay debts.

Lloyd's of London
http://www.lloydsoflondon.co.uk

liquidate
Sell the assets of a business.

International Report

Unlimited Liability at Lloyd's of London

Lloyd's of London is one of the most famous insurance companies in the world. It began operations several centuries ago by insuring British merchant ships. The individuals who invest in Lloyd's are called "names." These names have unlimited liability, i.e., they are liable for any losses incurred by the company. Their liability for losses is not limited to their original investment, but rather to the amount of money they have. Thus, their personal property can be seized to pay off their liabilities.

Why would a person invest in a company like Lloyd's when they know they will have unlimited liability? Because historically such investments have yielded good returns. Traditionally, names have been wealthy people who could afford to take the occasional loss. But during the go-go 1980s, many new names were recruited who were not wealthy (but had dreams of wealth). When their involvement brought losses instead of profits, they lost everything they owned. The British press played up cases of names being forced to move out of expensive homes that had been in the family for generations, but many poorer people have also lost their homes.

Why has Lloyd's suddenly run into financial difficulty? The answer is that changing times are threatening the company. It is becoming clear that an insurance system designed in 1600 cannot cope with certain 20th-century realities—natural disasters, terrorism, pollution, industrial accidents, and a trend towards increasing litigation.

All of these factors have sent insurance claims sky-high. During the last three years, for example, Lloyd's lost a total of $12 billion. In that same period, the number of names has fallen from 27 000 to 19 000. Several members who were part of a group of names that lost $800 million committed suicide. Another group of names from Canada have sued the company, alleging fraud, to prevent Lloyd's from seizing their assets to make good on claims.

In April 1993, Lloyd's CEO David Rowland introduced a plan that would end the company's tradition of unlimited liability and allow corporations to become new members with limited liability. But existing names will continue to have unlimited liability. Late in 1994, the group suing Lloyd's won a lawsuit which said they had been the victims of negligence by professionals in the insurance market. In 1995, Lloyd's proposed a $6 billion settlement plan that was designed to end litigation and ensure the survival of the firm. The proposed settlement would forgive over $4 billion owed by names who simply can't repay it. In return, the names would be expected to drop their lawsuits against the company.

The deal was finally agreed to in September 1996. Past liabilities will be reinsured in a new company called Equitas Group.

Partnerships

A partnership is established when two or more individuals agree to combine their financial, managerial, and technical abilities for the purpose of operating a company for profit. The partnership form of ownership was developed to overcome some of the more serious disadvantages of the sole proprietorship. There are several different types of partnerships. (See Table 2.2.) Our discussion, however, focuses on the most common type—the **general partnership**.

general partnership

A business with two or more owners who share in the operation of the firm and in financial responsibility for the firm's debts.

Partnerships are often an extension of a business that began as a sole proprietorship. The original owner may want to expand, or the business may have grown too big for a single person to handle. Many professional organizations, such as legal, architecture, and accounting firms, are also organized as partnerships. Figure 2.2 summarizes the advantages and disadvantages of the partnership form of organization.

Advantages

The most striking feature of general partnerships is their ability to grow by adding talent and money. Partnerships also have a somewhat easier time borrowing funds than do sole proprietorships. Banks and other lending institutions prefer to make loans to enterprises that are not dependent on a single individual.

Like a sole proprietorship, a partnership is simple to organize, with few legal requirements. Even so, all partnerships must begin with an agreement of

Table 2.2   Types of Partnerships and Partners

Types of Partnerships	
General partnership	All partners have unlimited liability for the firm's debts.
Limited partnership	This partnership has at least one general partner and one or more limited partners. The latter's liability is limited to their financial investment in the firm.

Types of Partners	
General partner	Actively involved in managing the firm and has unlimited liability.
Secret partner	Actively participates in managing the firm and has unlimited liability. A secret partner's identity is not disclosed to the public.
Dormant partner	Does not actively participate in managing the firm. A dormant partner's identity is not disclosed to the public. Has unlimited liability.
Ostensible partner	Not an actual partner but his or her name is identified with the firm. Usually an ostensible partner is a well-known personality. Promotional benefits accrue from using his or her name for which the person is usually paid a fee. Has unlimited liability.
Limited partner	Liability is limited to the amount invested in the partnership.

some kind. It may be written, oral, or even unspoken. Wise partners, however, insist on a written agreement to avoid trouble later. This agreement should answer such questions as

- Who invested what sums of money in the partnership?
- Who will receive what share of the partnership's profits?
- Who does what and who reports to whom?
- How may the partnership be dissolved? In that event, how would left-over assets be distributed among the partners?
- How would surviving partners be protected from claims by surviving heirs if a partner dies?

Although it helps to clarify how partners relate to each other, the partnership agreement is strictly a private document. No laws require partners to file an agreement with some government agency. Nor are partnerships regarded as legal entities. In the eyes of the law, a partnership is nothing more than two or more persons working together. The partnership's lack of legal standing means that Revenue Canada taxes partners as individuals.

Disadvantages

As with sole proprietorships, unlimited liability is the greatest drawback of general partnerships. By law, each partner may be held personally liable for all debts incurred in the name of the partnership. And if any partner incurs a debt, even if the other partners know nothing about it, they are all liable if the offending partner cannot pay up. For example, right after two men formed a partnership to operate a car wash, their equipment severely damaged a customized van. The owner sued for damages. One partner lacked the funds to cover the loss, even though the partnership agreement specified that he was responsible for equipment liability claims. Fortunately, the other partner agreed to pay half the damages and to loan the money to his partner for the other half.

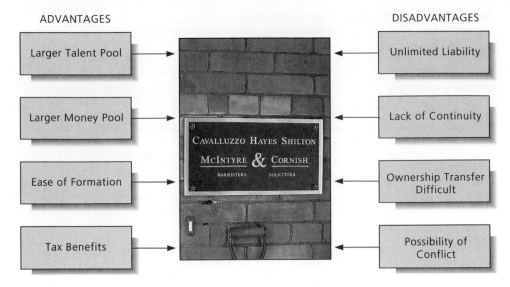

Figure 2.2
Partnerships are fairly common in professional organizations.

Another drawback is often lack of continuity. When one partner dies or pulls out, a partnership may dissolve legally, even if the other partners agree to stay. The dissolving of a partnership, however, need not cause a loss of sales revenues. If they wish, the surviving partners can quickly form a new partnership to retain the business of the old firm.

A related drawback is the difficulty of transferring ownership. No partner may sell out without the other partners' consent. Also, a partner who wants to retire or to transfer his or her interest to a son or daughter must receive the other partners' consent. Thus, the life of a partnership may depend on the ability of retiring partners to find someone compatible with the other partners to buy them out. Failure to do so may lead to forced liquidation of the partnership.

Finally, a partnership provides little or no guidance in resolving conflict between the partners. For example, suppose one partner wants to expand the business rapidly and the other wants it to grow slowly. If under the partnership agreement the two are equal, it may be difficult for them to decide what to do. Conflicts can involve anything from personal habits like smoking to hours of operation to managerial practices.

Corporations

corporation

A business considered by law to be a legal entity separate from its owners with many of the legal rights and privileges of a person; a form of business organization in which the liability of the owners is limited to their investment in the firm.

When you think of corporations you probably think of giant businesses like General Motors of Canada or BCE (see Table 2.3). The very word **corporation** suggests bigness and power. Yet, the tiny corner newsstand has as much right to incorporate as does a giant oil refiner. And the newsstand and oil refiner have the same basic characteristics that all corporations share: legal status as a separate entity, property rights and obligations, and an indefinite lifespan.

A corporation has been defined as "an artificial being, invisible, intangible, and existing only in contemplation of the law."[3] As such, corporations may

- Sue and be sued.
- Buy, hold, and sell property.
- Make and sell products to consumers.
- Commit crimes and be tried and punished for them.

Table 2.3 The Top 10 Corporations in Canada and the U.S., Ranked by Sales, 1996

Canada	
Company	Sales (in billions)
1. BCE Inc.	$28.1
2. General Motors of Canada	28.0
3. Ford Motor of Canada	25.5
4. Chrysler Canada	17.0
5. The Seagram Co. Ltd.	16.3
6. George Weston Ltd.	12.7
7. TransCanada Pipelines Ltd.	10.7
8. The Thomson Corp.	10.5
9. Alcan Aluminum Ltd.	10.3
10. Noranda Inc.	9.5

U.S.	
Company	Sales (in billions)
1. General Motors	$168.3
2. Ford Motor	146.9
3. Exxon	119.4
4. Wal-Mart Stores	106.1
5. General Electric	79.1
6. IBM	75.9
7. AT&T	74.5
8. Mobil	72.2
9. Chrysler	61.3
10. Philip Morris	54.5

Corporations can be found in both the private and the public sector in Canada, although our emphasis is on the private sector. We discuss Crown (government) corporations in Chapter 3.

Public Versus Private Corporations

Some corporations are public, others private. A **public corporation** is one whose stock is widely held and available for sale to the general public. Anyone who has the funds to pay for them can go to a stockbroker and buy shares of Brascan, George Weston, or Canadian Pacific. The stock of a **private corporation,** on the other hand, is held by only a few people and is not generally available for sale. The controlling group may be a family, employees, or the management group. Eaton's and Bata Shoes are private corporations.

Most new corporations start out as private corporations, because few investors will buy an unknown stock. As the corporation grows and develops a record of success, it may decide to issue shares to the public as a way to raise additional money. Apple Computer is just one example of a corporation that "went public." McCain Foods is a large private corporation that has been experiencing problems because of a feud between two of the McCain brothers, Wallace and Harrison. In 1994, they began serious discussions about how to take their company public.[4] Mutual Life Assurance Co. of Canada has also decided to go public, and several other Canadian life insurance companies are likely to do the same.[5] But some very large private corporations intend to stay private. For example, U.S. giant Cargill, with revenues of nearly $60 billion, intends to remain a private corporation. Because it does not have a lot of shareholders, it can invest in projects that show losses initially, but that might be very profitable in the long run. Shareholders might not be patient

public corporation

A business whose stock is widely held and available for sale to the general public.

private corporation

A business whose stock is held by a small group of individuals and is not usually available for sale to the general public.

enough to allow this strategy if Cargill was a public corporation.[6] The box "Going Public" describes one manager's experience with going public.

Just as companies can "go public," they can also "go private;" that is, a public corporation can be converted to a private corporation. In 1997, Jim Pattison, a well-known Canadian entrepreneur, was involved in negotiations to convert three companies to private corporation status: Westar Group Ltd., Great Pacific Enterprises Inc., and B.C. Sugar Refinery Ltd.[7]

Formation of the Corporation

The two most widely used methods to form a corporation are federal incorporation under the *Canada Business Corporations Act* and provincial incorporation under any of the provincial corporations acts. The former is used if the company is going to operate in more than one province; the latter is used if the founders intend to carry on business in only one province.

Except for banks and certain insurance and loan companies, any company can be federally incorporated under the *Canada Business Corporations Act*. To do so, Articles of Incorporation must be drawn up. These articles include such information as the name of the corporation, the type and number of shares to be issued, the number of directors the corporation will have, and the location of the company's operations. All companies must attach the word "Limited" (Ltd./Ltée) or "Incorporated" (Inc.) to the company name to indicate clearly to customers and suppliers that the owners have limited liability for corporate debts. The same sort of rules apply in other countries. British firms, for example, use PLC for "public limited company" and German companies use AG for "Aktiengesellschaft" (corporation).

Provincial incorporation takes one of two forms. In certain provinces (British Columbia, Alberta, Saskatchewan, Manitoba, Ontario, Newfoundland, Nova Scotia, and the two territories), the registration system or its equivalent is used. Under this system, individuals wishing to form a corporation are required to file a memorandum of association. This document contains the same type of information as required under the *Canada Business Corporations*

The Canadian Business Scene

Going Public

At the first annual meeting of DataMirror Corp. in 1997, CEO Nigel Stokes acquired some new bosses—shareholders. These shareholders are just some of the people that Stokes will have to deal with now that he is heading a public corporation. Bay Street analysts, institutional investors, reporters, and others are now much more likely to hold him accountable for actions that he takes.

The biggest pressure he will have to deal with is the "pressure to perform," that is, the pressure to regularly show growth and profitability to investors. Stokes, who formerly owned 60 percent of privately held Nidak Associates, says that many private firms are low-growth, "lifestyle" companies where owners take pretty easy profits and employees are not under a lot of pressure to perform. In a public corporation, much more is expected of both managers and workers. And in a public company, workers often own shares of stock, so they feel more pressure

to work harder in the hope that their shares will increase in value. Eighty percent of DataMirror employees bought stock in the company when it went public.

Stokes draws a relatively modest salary of $150 000. He hopes to make much more money from appreciation of the company's stock. DataMirror's stock price is already 50 percent higher than when it first began trading on the Toronto Stock Exchange in December 1996. Stokes believes in creating realistic expectations among investors so that when the company performs well the stock price will go up. In the company's first year, actual sales exceeded those forecast by 12 percent.

DataMirror
http://www.datamirror.com

Act. In the remaining provinces, the equivalent incorporation document is called the letters patent. In Quebec, a corporation may be formed either by issuing a letters patent or by drawing up articles of incorporation. The specific procedures and information required vary from province to province. The basic differences between these incorporation systems is that the registration system forms corporations by authority of parliament, while the letters patent system forms corporations by royal prerogative.

Corporate governance refers to the relationship between shareholders, the board of directors, and other top managers in the corporation. We discuss each of these groups in the following paragraphs.

corporate governance
The relationship between shareholders, the board of directors, and other top managers in the corporation.

Shares of Stock and Shareholders' Rights

Corporations can raise money by selling shares in the business—**stock**—to investors, who then are known as **shareholders.** Shareholders are the owners of a business. Business profits are distributed among shareholders in the form of **dividends.** Managers who run a corporation also serve at the discretion of the shareholders. The nature of the relationship between the shareholders, the board of directors, and management has been the focus of much recent discussion.[8]

stock
A share of ownership in a corporation.

shareholders
Those who own shares of stock in a company.

Why do corporations sell stock? Besides the obvious reason already noted—to raise money—stock makes for an easy transfer of ownership in a corporation. Shareholders can sell their shares to anyone who is willing to buy them (unless the stock certificates say that shareholders must offer to sell them to the corporation first).

dividend
A part of a corporation's profits paid out per share to those who hold its stock.

Corporate stock may be either preferred or common. **Preferred stock** guarantees those who own it a fixed dividend, much like the interest payment earned in a savings account. Preferred shareholders have priority, or preference, over common shareholders as to dividends and also to assets if a business liquidates, but usually do not have voting rights. Many major corporations issue preferred stock; few small corporations do.

preferred stock
Shares whose owners have first claim on the corporation's assets and profits but who usually have no voting rights in the firm.

In contrast, **common stock** usually pays dividends only if the corporation makes a profit. Holders of common stock have the last claim to any assets if the company folds. Dividends on common stock, like those on preferred stock, are paid per share. Thus, a shareholder with ten shares receives ten times the dividend paid a shareholder with one share. Unlike preferred stock, however, common stock *must* be issued by every corporation, big or small.

common stock
Shares whose owners usually have last claim on the corporation's assets (after creditors and owners of preferred stock) but who have voting rights in the firm.

There are two types of common stock—Class A and Class B. Class A common shares always have voting rights, but Class B common shares usually do not. Shareholder rights advocates argue that Class B common shares prevent democracy from working in companies because controlling shareholders hold most of the Class A stock and sell non-voting Class B stock to the general public. If Class B shareholders don't like what is going on in the company, they can't vote out the board of directors (see below).[9]

When investors cannot attend a shareholders' meeting, they can grant to someone who will attend authority to vote the shares. This procedure, called voting by **proxy**, is the way almost all individual investors vote.

proxy
A legal document temporarily transferring the voting rights of a shareholder to another person.

Ownership of common stock does not automatically give an individual the right to act for the corporation or to share in its management. (Many management personnel do own stock, however.) The only way that most shareholders can influence the running of a corporation is to cast their votes for the board of directors of the corporation once a year. In most cases, however, shareholders' votes are meaningless, since corporations offer only one slate of directors for election.

Even when shareholders have choices, the number of shareholders may mean little real power for individual owners. For example, Noranda has thousands of shareholders, but only a handful of them have enough votes to have any effect on the way the company is run.

The Board of Directors

By law, the governing body of a corporation is its **board of directors**. The directors choose the president and other officers of the business and delegate the power to run the day-to-day activities of the business to those officers. The directors set policy on paying dividends, on financing major spending, and on executive salaries and benefits. For example, the board of directors can fire the CEO if the board does not agree with the CEO's business decisions. However, in most cases a board of directors will support the CEO.

Large corporations tend to have large boards with as many as 20 or 30 directors. Smaller corporations, on the other hand, tend to have no more than five directors. Usually, these are people with personal or professional ties to the corporation, such as family members, lawyers, and accountants.

Many boards have outside as well as inside directors. **Inside directors** are employees of the company and have primary responsibility for the corporation. That is, they are also top managers, such as the president and executive vice-president. **Outside directors** are not employees of the corporation in the normal course of its business. Attorneys, accountants, university officials, and executives from other firms are commonly used as outside directors. The basic responsibility of both inside and outside directors is the same, however—to ensure that the corporation is run in a way that is in the best interests of the shareholders.

Directors also are legally responsible for corporate actions, and they are increasingly being held responsible for their actions (see the box "Hot Seats on the Board of Directors"). For example, a group of shareholders sued the entire board of Microsoft Corporation because the company's failure to meet its profit projections caused the price of its stock to plummet.[10] And directors of Loewen Group Inc. were hit with a lawsuit from U.S. investors because they rejected a takeover offer from a competing company; the investors felt that this decision caused the price of Loewen stock to be lower than if the company had accepted the offer.[11] Boards communicate with shareholders and other potential investors through the corporation's annual report, a summary of the company's financial health.

Corporations hold annual meetings with their shareholders. At such meetings, managers summarize what the corporation accomplished during the last year, announce plans for the coming year, and answer questions from individual shareholders. Shareholders also elect new members to the board of directors.

The Canadian Business Scene

Hot Seats on the Board of Directors

In former years, it was not uncommon for individuals to be appointed to the board of directors by the "old-boy network" to rubber-stamp decisions made by company executives. But those days are fast disappearing. Directors are increasingly chosen based on their background and for the ways they can contribute to the success of the firm. Board members are also involved in the decision-making process.

Korn/Ferry International, an executive search firm, conducted a survey of Canadian CEOs and found that 95 percent of them felt that if a board member is not doing an adequate job, the CEO should be able to ask for the board member's resignation. Causes listed included insufficient interest in the job, poor attendance at board meetings, inadequate contribution at board meetings, and a change in the person's business position during their term on the board.

Accepting a director's post in the 1990s means more hard work than in the past. There are typically four to six board meetings per year, and preparation for each one can take up to 24 hours of work. Because of this, directors are getting larger fees than they used to. Average annual compensation for many directors now exceeds $15 000.

Changes in board composition are also evident. A survey by the Conference Board of Canada shows that the percentage of women sitting on boards has more than doubled since 1984. However, it still stands at only 5.8 percent. Most women who are board members are outside directors, not employees of the company. This is consistent with the general trend away from appointing top-level executives to the board.

Many investors feel that board members are not independent enough to make objective decisions. Directors usually see themselves as being chosen by management (usually the CEO), so they feel a responsibility to management but not to the shareholders. If problems arise, board members often give managers only a slap on the wrist. They also seem reluctant to reduce management salaries when the firm is doing poorly. And when takeover bids come along, board members often reject them, even if the takeover would benefit the shareholders. Board members reject these bids so they can maintain their power and position.

The threat of liability suits from unhappy shareholders has forced board members to take their responsibilities more seriously. The collapse of the Canadian Commercial and Northlands banks in Alberta in the 1980s led to lawsuits totalling $1.5 billion against directors of those banks. Ontario's hazardous waste legislation puts the responsibility on directors to make sure that their corporation does not damage the environment. To counter this pressure, board members are asking corporations to provide liability insurance. A survey by the Conference Board of Canada revealed that 16 percent of the companies surveyed had experienced at least one legal action against their directors, and some had had as many as 15 legal actions. More than 70 percent of Canadian companies pay for liability insurance for their directors.

Shareholders have shown increased willingness to vote out board members if they feel a poor job is being done. At Sherritt Gordon Ltd., one shareholder group accumulated more than 5 percent of the company's stock and then made a bid to elect a new slate of directors. The group claimed that the board of directors had failed to take proper steps to deal with potential problems regarding oversupply in the Canadian fertilizer industry. At the special meeting, the dissident shareholders were successful in voting out the existing board members and installing their own people.

In other firms, board members have been sued, with shareholders claiming that the board members failed to fulfil their duties. For example, 10 ex-directors of Peoples Jewellers Ltd. are involved in a $35 million lawsuit that alleges that the directors failed to disclose risks associated with a bond issue that was sold to the public in 1990. The directors could be forced to pay out of their own pocket if the judgment exceeds the $10 million in liability insurance that covers them. Liability fears such as this have caused directors to leave financially troubled companies like PWA and Westar Mining Ltd.

All of these challenges come at a time when the role of the board of directors is more important than ever. In an era of intense global competition, strategic leadership is absolutely essential. This will mean that big changes will have to occur in the way that boards operate. The "old code" of keeping the board in the background and letting management set strategy and operate the company will have to be replaced with a "new code" that requires board members to be actively involved in confronting problems the firm is facing.

Officers

Although board members oversee the corporation's operation, most of them do not participate in day-to-day management. Rather, they hire a team of top managers to run the firm. As we have already seen, this team, called *officers*, is usually headed by the firm's **chief executive officer**, or **CEO**, who is responsible for the firm's overall performance. Other officers typically include a *president*, who is responsible for internal management, and *vice-presidents*,

chief executive officer (CEO)
The person responsible for the firm's overall performance.

who oversee various functional areas like marketing or operations. Some officers may also be elected to serve on the board, and in some cases, a single individual plays multiple roles. For example, one person might serve as board chairperson, CEO, and president. In other cases, a different person fills each slot.

Advantages of the Corporation

limited liability

Investor liability is limited to their personal investments in the corporation; courts cannot touch the personal assets of investors in the event that the corporation goes bankrupt.

Limited liability is the most striking feature of corporations. That is, the liability of investors is limited to their personal investments in the corporation. In the event of failure, the bankruptcy courts may seize a corporation's assets and sell them to pay debts, but the courts cannot touch the personal possessions of investors. Limited liability may be the main reason that many businesses incorporate, but limited liability is meaningless in some cases. For example, if all your personal assets are tied up in a business, then limited liability offers you little protection.

Another advantage of a corporation is continuity. Because it has a legal life independent of its founders, a corporation can continue to exist and grow long after the founders have retired or died. In theory, a corporation can go on forever.

Most corporations also benefit from professional management. In a sole proprietorship, a single person typically owns and manages the business. In most corporations, on the other hand, professional managers run the company but do not necessarily own any part of it.

Finally, corporations have a relatively easy time raising money. By selling more stock, they can expand the number of investors. In addition, the legal protections afforded corporations and the continuity of such organizations tend to make bankers more willing to grant loans.

Disadvantages of the Corporation

Ease of transferring ownership, one of the corporation's chief attractions, can also complicate the life of its managers. For example, one or more disgruntled shareholders in a small corporation can sell their stock to someone who wants to control the corporation and overthrow its top managers. Gaining control of a large corporation by this method is a complicated and expensive process, partially because of the large number of shareholders and partially because of the large sums of money involved. Amid the takeover environment of the 1980s, some shareholders of large firms succeeded. Philip Morris took over both General Foods and Kraft against their wishes and then combined them to form Kraft General Foods.[12] We discuss this interesting topic in more detail in Chapter 3.

Forming a corporation also costs more than forming either a sole proprietorship or a partnership. The main reason is that someone who wants to incorporate must meet all the legal requirements of the province in which it incorporates. Corporations also need legal help in meeting government regulations. Corporations are far more heavily regulated than are proprietorships and general partnerships.

double taxation

A corporation must pay taxes on its profits, and the shareholders must pay personal income taxes on the dividends they receive.

The greatest potential drawback of the corporate form of organization, however, is **double taxation**. A corporation must pay income taxes on its profits, and then shareholders must pay income taxes on the dividends they receive from the corporation. Unlike interest expenses, dividends are not tax deductible for corporations. They come out of after-tax profits. So, from the shareholder's point of view, this procedure amounts to double taxation of the corporation's profits. By contrast, sole proprietorships and partnerships are taxed only once, since their profits are treated as the owner's personal income. The advantages and disadvantages of the corporate form of ownership are summarized in Figure 2.3. Table 2.4 compares the various forms of business ownership, using different characteristics.

ADVANTAGES

DISADVANTAGES

Limited Liability

Continuity

Greater Likelihood
of Professional
Management

Easier Access
to Money

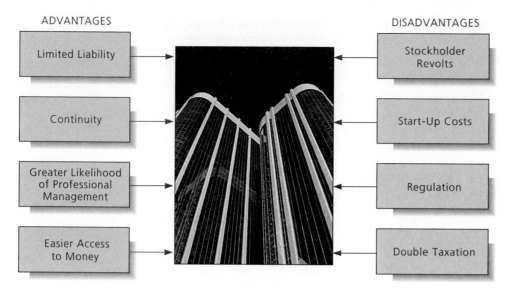

Stockholder
Revolts

Start-Up Costs

Regulation

Double Taxation

Figure 2.3

Corporations dominate the Canadian business system. Like sole proprietorships and
partnerships, the corporate form of ownership has several advantages and disadvantages.

Table 2.4   A Comparison of Three Forms of Business Ownership

Characteristic	Sole Proprietorship	Partnership	Corporation
Protection against liability for bad debts	low	low	high
Ease of formation	high	high	medium
Permanence	low	low	high
Ease of ownership transfer	low	low	high
Ease of raising money	low	medium	high
Freedom from regulation	high	high	low
Tax advantages	high	high	low

Cooperatives

A **cooperative** is an organization that is formed to benefit its owners in the
form of reduced prices and/or the distribution of surpluses at year-end. The
process works like this: suppose some farmers believe they can get cheaper
fertilizer prices if they form their own company and purchase in large volume.
They might then form a cooperative, which can be either federally or provincially chartered. Prices are generally lower to buyers and, at the end of the fiscal year, any surpluses are distributed to members on the basis of how much
they purchased. If Farmer Jones bought 5 percent of all co-op sales, he would
receive 5 percent of the surplus.

Voting rights are different from those in a corporation. In the cooperative,
each member is entitled to one vote, regardless of how many shares he or she
holds. This system prevents voting and financial control of the business by a few
wealthy individuals. Table 2.5 shows the top 10 Canadian cooperatives.

Some large cooperatives have recently decided to become publicly traded
companies. In 1994, SaskPool delegates voted 80 percent in favour of trading
their shares on the Toronto Stock Exchange, thus giving up their status as a
cooperative. United Grain Growers had made the same move a year earlier,

cooperative

*An organization that is formed to
benefit its owners in the form of
reduced prices and/or the distribution
of surpluses at year-end.*

Saskatchewan Wheat Pool

http://www.swp.com

Table 2.5   **The Top 10 Cooperatives in Canada, 1996**

Company	Sales (in billions)
1. Saskatchewan Wheat Pool	$4.1
2. Federated Co-operatives Ltd.	2.2
3. Alberta Wheat Pool	2.1
4. Cooperative fédérée de Québec	1.7
5. XCAN Grain Pool	1.3
6. Manitoba Pool Elevators	1.2
7. Agrifoods International Cooperative Ltd.	1.1
8. Agropur, Cooperative Agro-alimentaire	1.0
9. Calgary Cooperative Association	0.5
10. Co-op Atlantic	0.4

and it was able to raise $34 million in its first year as a corporation. Other grain cooperatives like Manitoba Pool Elevators may follow suit. The ability to sell shares of stock will give the grain companies extra capital to invest in food processing, but farmers say they will lose control of the grain companies, and that more and more power will fall into the hands of managers.[13]

Types of Cooperatives

There are hundreds of different cooperatives, but they generally function in one of six main areas of business:

■ Consumer cooperatives—These organizations sell goods to both members and the general public (e.g., co-op gasoline stations, agricultural implement dealers).

■ Financial cooperatives—These organizations operate much like banks, accepting deposits from members, giving loans, and providing chequing services (e.g., credit unions).

■ Insurance cooperatives—These organizations provide many types of insurance coverage, such as life, fire, liability (e.g., the Cooperative Hail Insurance Company of Manitoba).

■ Marketing cooperatives—These organizations sell the produce of their farm members and purchase inputs for the production process (e.g., seed and fertilizer). Some, like Federated Co-operatives, also purchase and market finished products.

■ Service cooperatives—These organizations provide members with services, such as recreation.

■ Housing cooperatives—These organizations provide housing for members, who purchase a share in the cooperative, which holds the title to the housing complex.

In numbers of establishments in Canada, cooperatives are the least important form of ownership. However, they are of significance to society and to their members; they may provide services that are not readily available or that cost more than the members would otherwise be willing to pay. The box "A Cowboy Cooperative" describes the formation of a cooperative.

International Report

A Cowboy Cooperative

Cattle farmers in two Canadian provinces and seven U.S. states are trying to raise $60 million to start a cooperative called Northern Plains Premium Beef. Two-thirds of this money will go towards construction of a high-tech meat packing plant that will slaughter 250 000 cattle each year. Cattle farmers want to get into meat packing because they think they can get their hands on some of the profits the meat packing industry is making. Cattle prices in the mid-1990s were so low that ranchers were losing about $30 on each calf that was sold. Meat packing houses, on the other hand, were making about $30 on each calf that was sold. Put another way, the farmers starting the cooperative want to "cut out the middleman."

But profits are not the new cooperative's only goal. Cattle ranchers also want to change beef from its "commodity" status to an item that can be branded (no pun intended). They point out that consumers pay extra for Starbucks coffee, Smithfield hams, and Butterball turkeys, so why not have a premium brand of beef as well? The marketing strategy for this new premium beef will include an interesting package, advertisements that emphasize that this beef comes from real cattle producers, and grocery store promotions by individuals dressed as cowboys. This strategy is based on the belief that the enduring John Wayne–type cowboy image will be very powerful in promoting consumption of premium beef.

To ensure high quality beef, the new meat packing plant will track each animal carcass as it is cut up so the co-op can reward ranchers who send high quality beef and dock those who send lower quality meat. Even though beef quality varies quite a bit, big meat packers like Cargill, IBP, and ConAgra Inc. usually pay similar amounts per kilogram. Northern Plains would distinguish between high and low quality beef and pay accordingly. To guarantee quality, cattle will have ear tags containing a microchip; this will allow the co-op to verify that the animal has been raised without antibiotics or artificial hormones.

Each co-op share a rancher buys will also be a contract to deliver one steer or heifer each year to the slaughterhouse. This will ensure that the big meat packers can't entice ranchers to sell their beef to them by raising the prices they are willing to pay.

Other Forms of Business Ownership

In recent years, several other forms of business ownership have become popular. Significant among these are employee-owned corporations, strategic alliances, subsidiary and parent corporations, and institutional ownership.

Employee-Owned Corporations

As we saw in the opening case, corporations are sometimes owned by the employees who work for them. While many smaller corporations are owned by the individuals who founded them, there is a growing trend today for employees to buy significant stakes of larger corporations. The current pattern is for this ownership to take the form of **employee stock ownership plans** or **ESOP**.

An ESOP is essentially a trust established on behalf of the employees. A corporation might decide, for example, to set up an ESOP to stimulate employee motivation or to fight a hostile takeover attempt. The company first secures a loan, which it then uses to buy shares of its stock on the open market. A portion of the future profits made by the corporation is used to pay off the loan. The stock, meanwhile, is controlled by a bank or other trustee. Employees gradually get ownership of the stock, usually on the basis of seniority. But even though they might not have physical possession of the stock for a while, they control its voting rights immediately.

employee stock ownership plan (ESOP)

An arrangement whereby a corporation buys its own stock with loaned funds and holds it in trust for its employees. Employees "earn" the stock based on some condition such as seniority. Employees control the stock's voting rights immediately, even though they may not take physical possession of the stock until specified conditions are met.

Strategic Alliances

strategic alliance
An enterprise in which two or more persons or companies temporarily join forces to undertake a particular project.

A **strategic alliance**, or joint venture, involves two or more enterprises cooperating in the research, development, manufacture, or marketing of a product. Companies might choose to engage in, say, a joint venture for several reasons. One major reason is that it helps spread the risk. For example, the national oil company of Nigeria and Chevron Oil were both interested in building a new type of drilling platform to search for oil in swampy areas. The platform was so expensive, however, that the companies were afraid to build it on their own. They decided to each contribute half the costs and share in its use. Thus, each firm decreased its own risks.

Another reason for joint ventures is that each firm thinks it can get something from the other. For example, Toyota and General Motors recently agreed to jointly own and manage an automobile assembly plant in California. General Motors had not been able to operate the plant profitably alone, and had actually shut it down. But they eventually realized that they could learn more about the Japanese approach to management by working with Toyota. And the Japanese, in turn, got access to an assembly plant in the U.S. without having to invest millions of dollars in a new one.

Subsidiary and Parent Corporations

subsidiary corporation
One that is owned by another corporation.

parent corporation
A corporation that owns a subsidiary.

Still another important trend in business ownership is the growing number of subsidiary and parent corporations, three of which are listed in Table 2.6. A **subsidiary corporation** is one that is owned by another corporation. The corporation that owns the subsidiary is called a **parent corporation**.

Institutional Ownership

institutional investors
Organizations such as mutual and pension funds that purchase large blocks of company stock.

Most individual investors do not own enough stock to exert any influence on the management of big corporations. In recent years, however, more and more stock has been purchased by **institutional investors** such as mutual funds and pension funds. Because they control enormous resources, these investors can buy huge blocks of stock. Occasionally, institutional investors may expect to be consulted on major management decisions. Mutual funds are discussed in Chapter 21.

Table 2.6   **Parent/Subsidiary Relations**

p = parent, s = subsidiary

p **Unilever**	p **Dylex**
s Lever Brothers	s Tip Top Tailors
s Lipton	s Harry Rosen
s Minnetonka	s Fairweather
s Chesebrough-Pond's	s Bi-Way
p Grand Met	s Thrifty's
s Pillsbury	
s Alpo	
s Heublein	

Summary of Learning Objectives

1. **Trace the history of business in Canada.** Modern business structures reflect a pattern of development over centuries. Throughout much of the colonial period, sole proprietors supplied raw materials to English manufacturers. The rise of the factory system during the Industrial Revolution brought with it mass production and specialization of labour. During the entrepreneurial era in the 19th century, huge corporations—and monopolies—emerged. During the production era of the early 20th century, companies grew by emphasizing output and production. During the sales and marketing eras of the mid-1900s, businesses began focusing on sales staff, advertising, and the need to produce what consumers want. The most recent development has been towards a global perspective.

2. **Identify the major *forms of business ownership.*** The most common forms of business ownership are the *sole proprietorship*, the *partnership*, the *corporation*, and the *cooperative*. Each form has several advantages and disadvantages. The form under which a business chooses to organize is crucial because it affects both long-term strategy and day-to-day decision making. In addition to advantages and disadvantages, entrepreneurs must consider their preferences and long-range requirements.

3. **Describe *sole proprietorships* and *partnerships* and explain the advantages and disadvantages of each.** *Sole proprietorships*, the most common form of business, consist of one person doing business. Although sole proprietorships offer freedom and privacy and are easy to form, they lack continuity and present certain financial risks. For one thing, they feature *unlimited liability*. The sole proprietor is liable for all debts incurred by the business. *General partnerships* are proprietorships with multiple owners. Partnerships have access to a larger talent pool and more investment money than do sole proprietorships but may be dissolved if conflicts between partners cannot be resolved.

4. **Describe *corporations* and explain their advantages and disadvantages.** *Corporations* are independent legal entities that are usually run by professional managers. In some corporations, stock is widely held by the public; in other firms, stock is held by individuals or small, private groups. The corporate form is used by most large businesses because it offers continuity and opportunities for raising money. It also features financial protection through *limited liability*: The liability of investors is limited to their personal investments. However, it is a complex legal entity subject to *double taxation*: In addition to taxes paid on corporate profits, investors must pay taxes on earned income.

5. **Describe the basic issues involved in creating and managing a corporation.** Creating a corporation generally requires legal assistance to file *articles of incorporation* and corporate *bylaws* and to comply with government regulations. Managers must understand shareholders' rights as well as the rights and duties of the *board of directors*.

6. **Identify recent trends and issues in corporate ownership.** Recent trends in corporate ownership include *strategic alliances* (in which two or more organizations collaborate); *employee stock ownership plans* (ESOPs) (by which employees buy large shares of their employer companies); *subsidiary and parent corporations* (where one corporation owns another); and *institutional ownership* of corporations (by groups such as mutual and pension funds).

Key Terms

Industrial Revolution, 31
factory system, 31
mass production, 31
specialization, 31
production era, 32
sales era, 33
marketing era, 33
finance era, 33
sole proprietorship, 34
unlimited liability, 35

liquidate, 35
general partnership, 36
corporation, 38
public corporation, 39
private corporation, 39
corporate governance, 41
stock, 41
shareholders, 41
dividend, 41

preferred stock, 41
common stock, 41
proxy, 41
board of directors, 42
inside directors, 42
outside directors, 42
chief executive officer (CEO), 43
limited liability, 44
double taxation, 44

cooperative, 45
employee stock ownership plan (ESOP), 47
strategic alliance, 48
subsidiary corporation, 48
parent corporation, 48
institutional investors, 48

Study Questions and Exercises

Review Questions

1. Why is it important to understand the history of Canadian business?
2. What are the comparative advantages and disadvantages of the three basic forms of business ownership?
3. What are the primary benefits and drawbacks to serving as a limited partner in a partnership?
4. Why might a corporation choose to remain private? Why might a private corporation choose to go public?
5. Are joint ventures limited to corporations, or can individuals also enter into joint ventures?

Analysis Questions

6. Locate two annual reports and review them. Identify the specific points in the reports that the board of directors are communicating to the shareholders.

7. Go to the library and identify four major joint ventures beyond those discussed in the text. Is one of the parties likely to benefit more than the other?
8. What steps must be taken to incorporate a business in your province?

Application Exercises

9. Interview a manager in a sole proprietorship or general partnership. Based on your talks, what characteristics of that business form led the owner to choose it?
10. Interview the principal shareholder of a corporation. Based on your talks, what characteristics of that business form led the shareholder to choose it?

Building Your Business Skills

Goal

To encourage students to evaluate the form of business ownership that is best for a specific small business.

Situation

Suppose that you want to open a business in a suburban community. You will provide music lessons to children and musical entertainment at parties and community events. You will also sell musical instruments and sheet music. Although you will run the business yourself, you need four additional employees to service customers and to maintain inventory and facilities. Although you naturally expect to succeed, you also expect to lose money during the first two years of operation.

Method

Working in groups of four or five, consider how the following factors would influence your decision to operate your business as either a sole proprietorship or a private corporation:

- treatment of taxable income
- liability for unpaid business debts
- liability for injury to customers (remember, most of your customers are children)
- legal steps required to set up the business.

Follow-up Questions

1. Suppose that the music store is very successful and that within five years you own a chain of 10 stores. How would your analysis of the preceding factors change as your business expands?

2. Were liability concerns or tax concerns more important in your choice of business structure?

3. If as a sole proprietor you decide to take in a partner, would you be more likely to form a partnership or a private corporation? What type of partnership would you choose?

To learn more about Employee Stock Ownership Plans, log on to the Web site maintained by the National Center for Employee Ownership (NCEO) at:

http://www.nceo.org:80

Examine several sections of this site, especially those under "Library," "Training," "Columns," and "International." Then consider the following questions:

1. How effectively does the material in this Web site characterize the advantages and disadvantages of ESOPs?

2. What parts of the Web site do you find most informative? Least informative?

3. Note that you can perform your own searches from within this Web site. What, for example, can you find out about ESOPs in other countries? What sort of "Publications" does the NCEO offer? What sort of "Internet Resources" does it make available? What sort of ESOP-related "Events" are held, and what purposes are they designed to serve?

4. Do you think that you would want to work for a firm that offered an ESOP? Why or why not?

5. What factors do you think probably led to the creation of the National Center for Employee Ownership?

6. Specifically, what value can this Web site have for employees and managers at companies that already have ESOPs? At companies that do not?

We've Got To Stop Meeting Like This

Public corporations in Canada are required by law to hold a shareholder meeting each year. These meetings are supposed to be occasions when shareholders find out how their company is doing, and where they can ask important questions about company operations. But this frequently does not happen. Instead, annual meetings are often a waste of time for everyone, and almost nothing is said or done that affects the corporation's activity.

The following problems are all too common at corporate annual meetings:

Poor shareholder questions. Shareholders often don't ask very insightful questions. Good questions include the following: What are the three biggest risks facing the company? What is the prospect for continued good performance? What does the future hold for the company?

The CEO's speech. The centrepiece of the annual meeting is the CEO's speech, and everyone wants it to go well. But this desire often creates an atmosphere of formalized and ritualized activity that stifles creativity and spontaneity. The meeting therefore becomes stilted and artificial.

The video. Videos recounting the corporation's recent activity are commonly shown at annual meetings, but it is difficult to see how the shareholders get any real benefit from a corporate mini-epic that costs thousands of dollars to make.

The script. Many annual meetings are carefully scripted. For example, it is often decided ahead of time who will make and second motions. Controversial motions (which are rare anyway) are usually decided ahead of time because investors who own large blocks of shares assign their proxies to one side or the other. Even the supposedly spontaneous questions that are asked during the question-and-answer period may be prearranged.

The gadflies. No matter how carefully someone tries to script an annual meeting, there are those rare occasions when dissident shareholders disrupt the meeting. In recent years, two issues have been the focus of dissidents: CEO pay, and environmental concerns. Typically, however, the dissidents do not get their way because they do not own enough shares to vote in their proposals. But sometimes they do. At the Petro-Canada annual meeting in 1992, shareholders were very unhappy with the performance of the company and with the declining value of the company's shares. During the question period, there was much hostility directed towards CEO Bill Hopper. A few months later he was fired.

Case Questions

1. Does the corporate annual meeting serve any purpose? Defend your answer.

2. Why do the problems noted above occur at so many annual meetings?

3. What suggestions can you make for solving these problems?

CONCLUDING CASE 2-2

Bargain Burials

When Rev. Eloi Arsenault came to Prince Edward Island to take over a Catholic parish, he was appalled at how much it cost a family to bury its loved ones. So, with help from the Knights of Columbus, a Catholic men's group, he set up the Palmer Road Funeral Co-operative. A local carpenter was hired to build simple caskets for $300. An embalming room was set up in the church basement, and bodies were moved using an old Ford station wagon. The goal was to provide funerals for about $1500, far less than the average price of $5000 being charged by the big funeral home chains.

Co-op interest in the death industry can be traced back to the 1930s, when "memorial societies" were first formed to get discounts for their members from local morticians. As the big funeral home chains began to dominate the industry, these memorial societies became more aggressive. In the past 10 years or so, their growth has been considerable, and this growth is not limited to P.E.I. Similar co-ops are also springing up in the U.S. and Great Britain.

There are two main reasons for the recent growth of co-ops in the death industry. First, there has been a major consolidation in the funeral home business during the last decade, with fewer and fewer organizations owning more and more funeral homes. Two funeral home organizations—Service Corp. International (U.S.) and Loewen Group (Canada)—have become very large; the former has over 2000 funeral homes and the latter has almost 1000. A lot of people feel these corporate giants do not offer enough "warmth" when providing funeral services.

Second, the cost of an average funeral is now about $5000, a 25 percent increase just since the early 1990s. And this price does not include the cost of the cemetery plot, monument, or flowers, which can add several thousand dollars more. Even though industry consolidation should have lowered prices, that hasn't happened; instead, surveys show that large chains like Service Corp. and Loewen actually charge higher rates than independent funeral homes.

Funeral co-ops often operate with volunteer staff and do very little advertising. Yet their share of the market has increased to about 17 percent since the first one was formed in the mid-1980s. Traditional funeral homes have taken notice, and have fought back. For example, in P.E.I. they tried to persuade the Catholic bishop to transfer Father Arsenault off the island. When that failed, they tried to convince a Quebec casket manufacturer to stop supplying caskets to co-ops on the island. But that backfired when other co-ops in Quebec threatened to stop ordering caskets from the company unless it continued to supply the P.E.I. co-ops.

But success has had its price for the co-ops. Some people are worried that co-op funeral homes are becoming just like the big chains. The co-op started by Father Arsenault has abandoned its basement embalming room and Ford station wagon in favour of a more traditional funeral home and a hearse. And prices are creeping up; a co-op in Summerside sells funerals for about $5000.

Case Questions

1. What are the main differences between cooperatives and the other three forms of business ownership (sole proprietorships, partnerships, and corporations)?

2. Do these differences imply anything about the possible success of cooperatives versus the other three forms of business ownership? Why did cooperatives develop in the funeral business?

3. Compared to a corporation, why might a cooperative seem like a more appropriate form of ownership for a funeral home?

4. Cooperatives seem to be an appealing form of ownership, yet there are relatively few cooperatives in Canada. Why would this be so?

◆

3

Recognizing Business Trends and Challenges

The Downsizing Craze

By now, everyone has heard of downsizing—restructuring an organization and cutting large numbers of jobs in an attempt to improve profitability and productivity. Until recently, most firms that downsized were in financial trouble and needed to do something drastic to recover. But increasingly, organizations that are perfectly healthy are also downsizing. Bell Canada reduced staff by 3200, Inco laid off 2000 people, and Petro-Canada cut 564 jobs.

Even firms that are making record profits are downsizing. In 1995, General Motors of Canada reported record profits, yet it cut 2500 jobs during the year. The five largest banks in Canada reported total profits of over $6 billion in 1996, but they cut nearly 3000 jobs.

Normally when a recession hits, companies lay off people and then hire them back when business improves. But since the recession of 1990–92, companies have shown an unusual determination not to let staff levels increase. Why? Largely because they are very uncertain about what the future holds, and because increased global and domestic competition is motivating them to increase productivity while reducing costs. The top managers of most companies think that this can best be achieved by laying off workers.

Consider what is happening at Maritime Telephone and Telegraph Company Ltd. It cut 13 percent of its staff in 1995 and plans to make further cuts in 1998. The reason is increasing competition in the long-distance market, which contributed to a profit decline of 33 percent in 1995. MT&T is relying on improved technology to provide better service to customers, even as it cuts its staff. In the maintenance department, for example, calls are now routed to a central computer that automatically tests

the customer's line while a service person talks to the customer. This has allowed the company to cut the maintenance department by 23 employees.

The American Management Association analyzed the performance of 700 companies that had downsized between 1989 and 1994. They found that productivity rose in about a third of the companies and fell in another 30 percent of the companies. Profits rose in half of the companies and declined in about a third. In the vast majority of companies, morale dropped.

Whether downsizing is good or bad depends on your perspective. Politicians don't like it because they want lower unemployment levels. Employees certainly don't like it. But these are not the only groups that business managers must answer to. Another group—institutional and individual shareholders—often have a very big say in what management does. They often have a very positive view of downsizing because they feel it will improve profits and increase the size of their dividend cheques. For example, the price of Petro-Canada stock rose from $8 per share in 1993 to $16.75 per share in 1996 after the company had cut 700 jobs.

Another example is Scott Paper Ltd. The company's low stock price had been causing complaints from the controlling shareholder (Scott Paper Co. of Philadelphia), so when Lee Griffith took over as president in 1995, he promised swift action to remedy the problem. Part of the strategy involved cutting jobs. During 1995, the stock price doubled.

One reason management is paying so much attention to shareholders is the increasing importance of pension and mutual funds. For example, the Ontario Teachers Pension Plan Board now holds about $12 billion in

Canadian shares. Managers of pension and mutual funds are under pressure to achieve high returns for the pensioners and workers who invest in these funds, so they put pressure on company management to increase share value. One way to do this is downsizing, but managers of pension and mutual funds often don't care about staff levels in a company; they are more interested in the stock price.

Shareholder pressure on company management to downsize was illustrated at the 1995 annual meeting of National Trustco Inc. An institutional shareholder said the company was the worst-performing financial services company in North America. He said that the company needed a dramatic restructuring to reduce overhead, and layoffs had to be considered as part of that restructuring. He made this comment despite the fact that the company had already cut 400 jobs. National Trustco president Paul Cantor said that improvements had to be made, but he wasn't sure that downsizing was the answer.

Canadian politicians are very concerned about downsizing in the private sector because government is itself in the process of downsizing. The government had hoped that private-sector business firms would create new jobs at a time when government jobs would be harder to find, but now that appears unlikely.

Industry Minister John Manley has expressed concern that the downsizing trend is focusing attention too narrowly on profits and shareholder returns. He thinks Canadians want business to reinvest earnings into expansion to create new jobs. He is worried that downsizing is going to reduce consumer confidence in the economy, and that future growth prospects will be affected. He also thinks that shareholder concern about stock prices places too much emphasis on the short-term, and not enough on the long-term health of the economy.

The trade-off between share value and job creation is a complicated question. One interesting study by the management consulting firm A.T. Kearney Inc. showed that 69 percent of U.S. managers considered share value a critical issue, but that only 43 percent of Canadian managers and 25 percent of European managers did. But employment has risen 7 percent in the United States since 1990, and only 5 percent in Canada. It has dropped 3 percent in Europe. Could it be that when all is said and done, downsizing creates more jobs than it destroys? Could it be that downsizing makes firms more profitable and productive, and that an economy made up of these healthier firms creates more new jobs? Perhaps, but this is little comfort to the thousands of individuals who have lost their jobs through downsizing and have had to cope with the trauma of finding a new place in the economy. ◆

Downsizing has been one of the most prominent trends of the 1990s. But it is only one of the many trends and challenges faced by business firms. Today, nearly every company must contend with continual shifts in its relationships with its competitors, the government, its workforce, and its customers. In this chapter, we will explore these trends and challenges.

By focusing on the learning objectives of this chapter, you will better understand the trends and challenges facing Canadian business, and how these trends and challenges can be used to advantage. After reading this chapter, you should be able to:

LEARNING OBJECTIVES

1. Describe five major *trends* that affect the nature of Canadian business today.

2. Explain how and why *government* regulates business in Canada.

3. Discuss changes in the *workforce*, and how these changes have affected Canadian business.

4. Describe changes in *consumer rights* and *demographics*, and their impact on Canadian business.

5. Identify and discuss six major business *challenges* at the start of the 21st century.

Business and Change

The trends that affect Canadian businesses come from both inside and outside the organization. The most influential of these trends are the growth of high technology, a shift in emphasis from manufacturing to information services, an increase in mergers and acquisitions, a move towards deregulation and privatization, and the downsizing trend.

The Growth of High Technology

high technology (high-tech)
As applied to businesses, a firm that spends more on research and development and employs more technical personnel than the average manufacturing firm.

One major trend that has affected virtually every aspect of business is the development and spread of high technology. A **high-technology (high-tech)** firm spends more on research and development and employs more technical employees than the typical manufacturing firm. The term "high-tech" may conjure up images of computers and robots. For example, high-tech robots produced by Fanuc Corporation, a Japanese firm, are used in virtually all automobile plants today. Firms that make these products are definitely high-tech. But so are firms in the aircraft, pharmaceuticals, biotechnology, and communications industries.

High-tech has not, however, been the utopia originally envisioned. It has not created the number of new jobs that many economists originally predicted. Some of the production jobs it has created have been in foreign factories. Many workers trained for industrial jobs have also been unable or unwilling to make the transition to high-tech jobs. Finally, many entrepreneurs who rushed into the high-tech area did so with poorly conceived plans and were unsuccessful. Even firms like IBM, Digital Equipment Corp., and Wang have had to cut staff and reorganize in the face of declining profits. Still, high-tech is clearly with us to stay and will have an increasingly important role in our economy.[1] We will have more to say about this important issue later in this chapter, as well as at several other points in the text.

From Manufacturing to Information Services

service economy
A reference to the growing importance of services, rather than products, as the major contributor to the Canadian economy.

Developments in high technology have also contributed to another change in the business world. In recent years, the manufacturing sector—long the backbone of Canada's economy—has decreased as an employer of workers, while the service sector has grown. This growth is clearly illustrated in Figure 3.1. In 1950, only 42 percent of Canadians were employed in services-producing industries; by 1993, the figure was over 72 percent. No wonder, then, many have begun to say that Canada has a **service economy**.

Whether they are producing a product or a service, high technology is increasingly affecting all business firms.

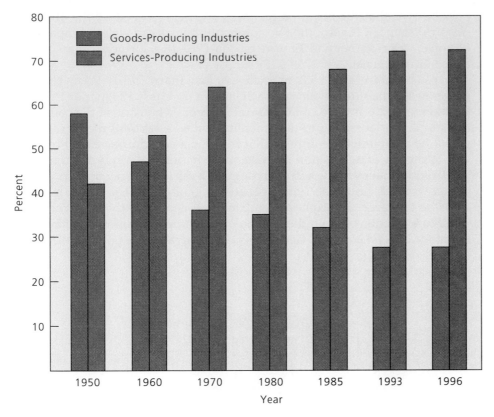

Figure 3.1
Proportion of employment in goods- and services-producing industries.

Not all service industries have grown as much as others, though. While employment in traditional service industries such as construction, restaurants, hotels, and repair services has grown as a percentage of total employment, **information services** is the area of greatest growth of late. Information services personnel include lawyers, accountants, data processors, computer operators, financial analysts, office personnel, and insurance agents—all those who spend their day working on or with information.

This sector has grown for many reasons. An increasing need to acquire and manage information in a highly competitive marketplace is a prime factor. Another reason is the increasing government regulation of business. With more government regulations, companies have had to hire more people to read the regulations and to construct and implement policies that comply with the regulations. Filling out government forms is another major task.

information services

Service industries that provide information in return for a fee. Examples include law, accounting, and computer processing.

The Rise of Mergers and Acquisitions

In Chapter 2, we saw that businesses today buy and sell other companies. In an **acquisition**, one firm—usually the larger—simply buys another firm—usually the smaller (e.g., Siemens AG acquired Relcon). The transaction is similar to buying a car that then becomes your property. In contrast, a **merger** is a consolidation of two firms. The firms are usually more similar in size, and the arrangement is more collaborative (e.g., Price Co. and Costco Wholesale Corp. merged their operations).

After a merger or acquisition, three things can happen. One possibility is that the acquired company will continue to operate as a separate entity. Even though Trilon Financial Corporation bought London Life Insurance, the insurance company has continued to operate autonomously. Another

acquisition

The purchase of a company by another, larger firm, which absorbs the smaller company into its operations.

merger

The union of two companies to form a single new business.

horizontal merger

A merger of two firms that have previously been direct competitors in the same industry.

vertical merger

A merger of two firms that have previously had a buyer-seller relationship.

conglomerate merger

A merger of two firms in completely unrelated businesses.

friendly takeover

An acquisition in which the management of the acquired company welcomes the firm's buyout by another company.

hostile takeover

An acquisition in which the management of the acquired company fights the firm's buyout by another company.

possibility is that the acquired business will be absorbed by the other and simply disappear. Finally, the two companies may form a new company. For example, when Warner and Time merged in 1989, they formed a new company called Time-Warner.

As shown in Figure 3.2, mergers can take many forms. When the companies are in the same industry, as when Ford purchased Jaguar or Price and Costco merged, it is called a **horizontal merger**. When one of the companies is a supplier or customer to the other, it is called a **vertical merger**. Finally, when the companies are unrelated, it is called a **conglomerate merger**.

A merger or acquisition can take place in one of several different ways. In a **friendly takeover**, the acquired company welcomes the acquisition, perhaps because it needs cash or sees other benefits in joining the acquiring firm. But in a **hostile takeover**, the acquiring company buys enough of the other company's stock to take control, even though the other company opposes the takeover. Philip Morris's takeovers of General Foods and Kraft were both hostile.[2]

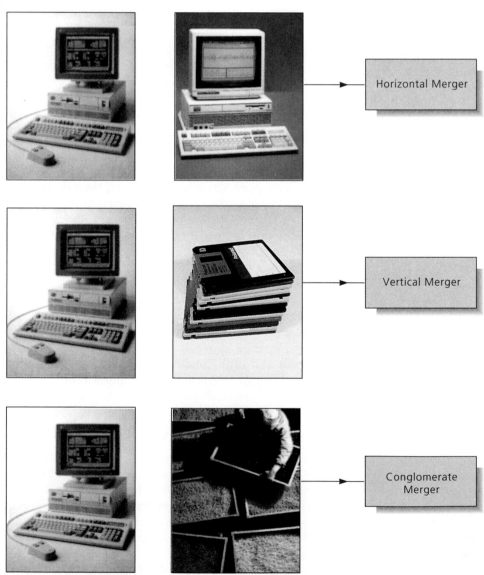

Figure 3.2
There are several different types of mergers. The three most common types are horizontal, vertical, and conglomerate mergers.

A **poison pill** is a defence management adopts to make a firm less attractive to a current or potential hostile suitor in a takeover attempt. The objective is to make the "pill" so distasteful that a potential acquirer will not want to swallow it. For example, a pill adopted by Inco gave shareholders the right to buy Inco stock or the acquirer's stock at a 50 percent discount if more than 20 percent of Inco stock were acquired by a group without approval of Inco's board of directors. As another example, United Grain Growers (UGG) threatened to sell millions of additional shares at far less than the market price if the Alberta and Manitoba Wheat Pools bought more than 15 percent of UGG's shares in any takeover attempt. After the Wheat Pools withdrew their takeover offer, UGG decided not to activate the poison pill after all.[3] The box "Poison Pills Are Back" describes several other examples of this tactic.

poison pill

A defence management adopts to make a firm less attractive to a hostile suitor in a takeover bid.

The Canadian Business Scene

Poison Pills Are Back

During the 1980s, terms like "corporate raider," "hostile takeover," and "poison pill" came into wide usage. In the late 1980s, for example, Garfield Emerson, a Canadian pioneer in poison pills, developed a takeover defence for Maclean-Hunter Ltd. that allowed its shareholders to buy more Maclean-Hunter stock at half price if another firm acquired more than 10 percent of Maclean-Hunter's stock. In the recession of the early 1990s, it seemed that these ideas were falling out of favour and that a more conservative business environment was returning. But there has been a resurgence of some 1980s-style activities such as poison pills. Consider the following cases.

When MDC Corp. of Toronto tried to take over Regal Greetings and Gifts Inc., Regal adopted a poison pill, or shareholder rights plan, that would allow Regal to flood the market with cheap shares of its stock. This would make it much more expensive for another company to take over Regal. When MDC heard of this ploy, it requested the Ontario Securities Commission to stop Regal from using its poison pill.

In a similar case, Pharma Patch PLC of Ireland tried to take over Cangene Corp. of Toronto. Cangene produces two biological products that are designed to detect and fight infections. Cangene introduced a poison pill that allowed its existing shareholders who were not sympathetic to the takeover bid to buy large numbers of cut-rate shares of Cangene's stock. This would make it much more difficult for Pharma Patch to acquire enough shares to gain control of Cangene.

Time-Warner Inc. adopted a poison pill defence to keep its largest shareholder, Seagram Co. Ltd., from acquiring more than 15 percent of Time-Warner's stock. The pill allowed Time-Warner shareholders to exercise lucrative stock rights if the 15 percent threshhold was exceeded by Seagram. Seagram later decided to sell its shares and invest elsewhere.

The most recent highly publicized poison pill case was the one in which Royal Oak Mines Inc. tried to take over Lac Minerals Ltd. When faced with this threat, Lac adopted a poison pill that allowed the directors of Lac to sell new shares at a 50 percent discount. This made it very expensive for Royal Oak to gain controlling interest, so they asked the Ontario Securities Commission to squelch the poison pill and threatened to withdraw their takeover offer if their request was not granted. In the end, all the maneuvering was irrelevant, because Lac finally agreed to a friendly takeover by American Barrick Resources.

As these cases demonstrate, poison pills are generally developed as a reaction to an outside takeover threat. But Nova Corp. proposed a poison pill to its shareholders, not because it was the target of a hostile takeover, but because it might be sometime in the future. Nova said the poison pill would protect shareholders, but Fairvest Securities Corp., a shareholder rights advocate organization, sent out a "shareholder alert" that argued that Nova's poison pill gave Nova's board of directors too much latitude in accepting or rejecting takeover offers. Nova put on a major public relations blitz and eventually got shareholders to agree to the poison pill.

At John Labatt Ltd., management proposed a poison pill that would have made it more difficult for an outsider to take over the company. But shareholders rejected the proposal at the 1994 annual meeting after an institutional money manager questioned the wisdom of management's expansion plans. Of the 57 poison pill proposals made by managers in Canadian companies, this is the first one to be rejected.

Opponents of poison pills argue that they are usually introduced to protect the current management of the company; they also say that poison pills hurt shareholders financially because they suppress the price of the company's stock. In 1996, the Ontario Securities Commission prevented Tarxien Corp. from introducing a poison pill. Tarxien was the target of a takeover by three different firms, and the Ontario Securities Commission ruled that the takeover attempt was fairly conducted, and that shareholders of Tarxien benefited from the right to choose which offer they preferred.

greenmail

A buyback of stock at a large profit to one or more investors who are threatening a hostile takeover of a firm.

A hostile takeover often involves the practice of paying **greenmail**. In this situation, investors (called *raiders*) acquire large blocks of stock, threaten a hostile takeover, then let the target company buy back their stock at a price that gives the raiders a substantial profit.

The Economic Council of Canada published a study showing that the profits of companies that have been targets of takeovers are as likely to rise as they are to fall. About 40 percent became more profitable after being taken over, while another 40 percent became less profitable.[4]

Because of the potential for monopolies to arise, the government has become increasingly vigilant regarding mergers and acquisitions. As you will see later in this chapter, this is but one of the areas where business is affected by the government.

The Move Towards Deregulation and Privatization

deregulation

A reduction in the number of laws affecting business activity.

In recent years government involvement in business has decreased through deregulation and privatization. **Deregulation** means a reduction in the number of laws affecting business activity and in the powers of government enforcement agencies. In most cases, deregulation frees the corporation to do what it wants without government intervention, thereby simplifying the task of management. Deregulation is evident in many industries, including airlines, pipelines, banking, trucking, and communications.

Deregulation of the Canadian airline industry has meant that the government no longer dictates how many airlines there will be and where and when they will be allowed to fly. After deregulation, demand increased 13 to 18 percent in most places, and up to 50 percent in some. Deregulation in pipelines freed prices and exports and encouraged direct contracts between producers and consumers. Because prices were freed in a period of oversupply, they fell. Banks have also been deregulated and are now selling government securities in their branches and offering a much wider array of financial services than previously. This same trend is evident in other countries as well. Deregulation in the trucking industry has forced many poorly run firms out of business. Those that remain must be very competitive if they are to survive. In the communications business, the historic decision by the Canadian Radio-television and Telecommunications Commission to allow competition among long-distance telephone companies has made long-distance calls cheaper, but it has also created some confusion for both business and residential customers.

privatization

The transfer of activities from the government to the public sector.

Privatization refers to the transfer of activities from the government to the private sector. The federal government has sold several corporations, including Air Canada, Teleglobe Canada, and Canadair Ltd. Provincial governments are also selling off businesses, for example, the Ontario Transportation Development Corp., Manitoba Oil and Gas Corp., Pacific Western Airlines (sold by the Alberta government), and Nova Scotia Power Inc. There is increasing talk about privatizing provincial hydroelectric utilities, particularly in Quebec and Newfoundland.[5]

Privatization does not only involve the selling of businesses. In some provinces, private business firms contract to manage hospitals and other health care institutions previously operated by government employees. Terminal Number 3 at Lester B. Pearson International Airport in Toronto, which opened in February 1991, was built and is operated by a private firm.

Privatization has had some unexpected outcomes. For example, executives at former Crown corporations have received some large wage increases because the government had put a ceiling on wages for various management positions. When the organization is privatized, salaries go up to reflect the average pay scale in the private sector. Another example of unexpected outcomes is contained in the box "It's a New World."

The Canadian Business Scene

It's a New World

For 70 years, the province of Alberta held a monopoly on the sale of liquor. The 202 stores in the province were neat, orderly, and boring. Alberta Liquor Control Board (ALCB) employees all wore tan shirts and brown pants. In 1993, the government suddenly announced that it was getting out of the retail liquor business. By doing so, it would save $65 million each year in salaries and operating costs; it would also get another $58 million from the sale or lease of the old government stores.

Within a year, 500 private stores had opened up, some leasing old ALCB sites. People from all walks of life have tried their hand at selling liquor, and almost 4000 private sector jobs have been created. But the Alberta Liquor Store Retailers Association (ALSRA) thinks a shakeout is coming. Competition is heating up, and price wars have pushed some owners to bankruptcy.

Consider the experience of Skip Bromley, who opened Calmar, Alberta's first retail liquor store. The old government store in the town averaged more than $900 000 in revenue annually, and Bromley figured he would do very well. Indeed, business was brisk for the first few weeks, but then a competitor popped up next door, then another one across the street. Bromley found himself working long hours to keep his business going; his profit margin also dropped as he was forced to reduce prices to cope with the competition. He closed up shop a few months later.

His story is not unusual. David Paulgaard also had big plans when he opened his store in Calgary. But within a short time, six competitors opened up shop within a five-kilometre radius. He says his markups are very low and profits are minimal.

The privatization of liquor sales was made without any public consultation. The day before privatization was an-

nounced, only a handful of people in the province knew it was coming. Within a few months, almost all of the former employees lost their jobs. The ALCB now restricts itself to the role of wholesaler, importer, and tax collector.

Considerable confusion accompanied privatization. A law was hastily passed that kept large grocery chains like Safeway from selling liquor in their stores. Instead, they were required to build stand-alone sites. This was the result of a fierce lobbying effort by ALSRA, which argued that privatization was supposed to benefit small business, not big business.

The new owners in the retail trade have a lot of complaints. Some say that they can't make a decent profit, even on sales of $7 to $8 million. They also say that customers notice that prices are higher than when the government ran the stores.

The retailers are not the only ones complaining. Local distillers and brewers say a new tax introduced by the province has cut into their profits, too. Drummond Brewing Co. managed to get a 9 percent share of the Alberta market by selling inexpensive beer. But the new tax has added 21 cents per litre to its price, and sales of the beer have dropped. The president of the firm says that privatization completely negated the firm's corporate strategy. Privatization also created a "one-way trade lane" into Alberta because producers in other provinces can ship their liquor to Alberta, but other provinces have maintained existing trade barriers keeping Alberta beer out.

Privatization forced Highwood Distillers Ltd. to expand its international focus, and its efforts are paying off. Prior to privatization, it exported about 1000 cases to foreign markets. After privatization, it shipped over 13 000 cases. Unfortunately, it also incurred the biggest loss in its history because of the one-way trade lane and the new government tax.

Canada is not the only country where privatization is taking place. In Mexico, for example, 900 of the 1200 state corporations have been privatized.[6] Telephone companies in Mexico, New Zealand, and Argentina have also been privatized. In France, the government is privatizing 21 key state-controlled companies in an attempt to reduce the deficit and energize the economy. And China plans to privatize 200 000 companies as it continues to move towards a more market-oriented economy. Privatization is a worldwide phenomenon, and it will lead to the dismantling of much of the government involvement in business that has developed during the 20th century. In 1996, governments in Western Europe sold off equity stakes worth about $43 billion.[7]

The Downsizing Trend

As we saw in the opening case, **downsizing** refers to the planned reduction in the scope of an organization's operations. It usually means cutting large numbers of employees and reducing the number and variety of products a

downsizing

The planned reduction in the scope of operations of a company, usually achieved by cutting large numbers of employees.

company produces. It may also mean that entire levels of management are eliminated. It has meant the loss of thousands of blue- and white-collar jobs in Canadian companies, including Air Canada, The Royal Bank, Northern Telecom, Bell Canada, Abitibi-Price, and the Canadian Imperial Bank of Commerce, to name just a few.

Although downsizing is a popular strategy, several serious problems have been noted: (1) it often does not achieve its goal of cost reduction; (2) productivity improvements often do not materialize; (3) profit often does not increase after it has taken place; (4) it has devastating effects on employee morale, productivity, and motivation; and (5) it may cause a decline in new product innovation.[8]

Is downsizing an effective strategy? If downsizing is done as a quick-fix, cost-cutting tactic, it is not likely to succeed. But if it is part of a carefully thought-out strategy to focus the firm's activities and to make it more competitive, downsizing can improve the organization's performance.[9] While the most dramatic examples of downsizing may now be complete, this trend will continue to affect business in the years to come.

Business and Government

Business and government have a complex, constantly evolving relationship. In this section, we briefly describe how the government of Canada works, the various roles that government plays in our society, and the ways in which business and government try to influence each other.

The Government of Canada

The government of Canada includes the Canadian federal government, the provincial (or territorial) governments, and nearly 5000 municipal governments. All three levels of government influence business activity.

The Canadian Parliamentary System

Canada's federal and provincial governments operate under a parliamentary system of government. There is an executive branch of government nominally headed by the monarch. The monarch's representative in Canada is the governor general. (See Figure 3.3.) The monarch's representative in each province is the lieutenant-governor. The positions of governor general and lieutenant-governor are largely ceremonial, but they do play a role in transferring power to a new government after an election. Federally, the prime minister and the cabinet are formally the monarch's advisors. In actual fact, they are the prime determiners of the Canadian government's policies. In the provinces, the provincial premier and the cabinet perform this function.

Both federally and provincially, the cabinet determines what executive actions the government will take. It also places legislative proposals before the House of Commons, Senate, or provincial legislatures.

The unit of local government is usually the municipality, normally incorporated as a city, town, village, district, or township. The powers and responsibilities of municipalities are delegated to them by the provincial governments.

distribution of government powers

The responsibility different levels of government hold for different matters.

The Structure of Government

Canada has a federal structure of government, outlined in *The Constitution Act, 1867*. The **distribution of government powers** means that different levels of government have responsibilities for different matters. The federal

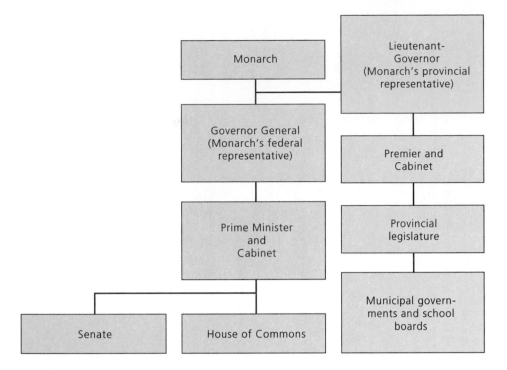

Figure 3.3
Structure of the Canadian parliamentary system.

government has legislative jurisdiction over all matters of general or common interest. Provincial governments have jurisdiction over all matters of local or common interest. The specific areas of jurisdiction for federal and provincial governments are described in Table 3.1.

The sharing of responsibilities between federal and provincial governments has been controversial. The tasks outlined in Table 3.1 sometimes overlap, as in the cases of agriculture, immigration, and old-age pensions. Social, technological, economic, and political developments have created new problems to be dealt with, including aviation, payment for medical services, telecommunications, energy shortages, provincial control of natural resources, broadcasting, and tax sharing.

Prime Minister Jean Chretien and his cabinet.

Table 3.1   Examples of Federal and Provincial Constitutional Responsibilities

Federal Government	Provincial Government
The legislative authority of parliament includes:	The legislature of each province may make laws in relation to the following:
• the amendment of the constitution of Canada	• amendment of the constitution of the province except as regards the lieutenant-governor
• the public debt and property	• direct taxation within the province
• the regulation of trade and commerce	• borrowing of money on the credit of the province
• employment insurance	• establishment and tenure of provincial offices and appointment and payment of provincial officers
• the raising of money by any mode or system of taxation	• the management and sale of public lands belonging to the province and of the timber and wood thereon
• the borrowing of money on the public credit	• the establishment, maintenance, and management of public and reformatory prisons in and for the province
• postal service	• the establishment, maintenance, and management of hospitals, asylums, charities, and eleemosynary institutions in and for the province, other than marine hospitals
• the census and statistics	• municipal institutions in the province
• militia, military and naval services, and defence	• shop, saloon, tavern, auctioneer, and other licences issued for the raising of provincial or municipal revenue
• the fixing of and providing for the salaries and allowances of civil and other officers of the government of Canada	• local works and undertakings other than interprovincial or international lines of ships, railways, canals, telegraphs, etc., or works which, although wholly situated within one province, are declared by the federal parliament to be for the general advantage either of Canada or of two or more provinces
• beacons, buoys, lighthouses, and Sable Island	• the incorporation of companies with provincial objects
• navigation and shipping	• the solemnization of marriage in the province
• quarantine and the establishment and maintenance of marine hospitals	• property and civil rights in the province
• seacoast and inland fisheries	• the administration of justice in the province, including the constitution, maintenance, and organization of provincial courts, both of civil and of criminal jurisdiction, including procedure in civil matters in these courts
• ferries between a province and any British or foreign country or between two provinces	• the imposition of punishment by fine, penalty, or imprisonment in enforcing any law of the province relating to any of the aforesaid subjects
• currency and coinage, banking, incorporation of banks, and the issue of paper money	• generally all matters of a merely local or private nature in the province
• savings banks	• education
• weights and measures	• agriculture and immigration
• bills of exchange and promissory notes—interest	
• legal tender	
• bankruptcy and insolvency	
• patents of invention and discovery	
• copyrights	
• native peoples and lands reserved for them	
• naturalization and aliens	
• marriage and divorce	
• the criminal law except the constitution of courts of criminal jurisdiction but including the procedures in criminal matters	
• the establishment, maintenance, and management of penitentiaries	
• agriculture and immigration	
• old-age pensions	

One of the major sources of revenue for local governments is property tax on agricultural, residential, and commercial property. This farmer pays property taxes but is also the recipient of federal aid to farmers.

The Process of Government Policy Formulation

One important type of interaction between business and government occurs when government policy is discussed and changed. **Government policy formulation** is the process by which changes are made in current government policies.

government policy formulation
The process by which changes are made in current government policies.

The process of changing government policy is long and complicated, but some general features can be identified. First, there are a number of stages. Second, there are usually a number of people involved who change at different stages of the process. Third, decisions will be made at each stage, which will depend on the power of the people involved in the given stage (see Figure 3.4).

No one person controls the process through all stages. The key people vary from politicians at the decision-to-proceed-with-legislation stage to civil servants at the drafting-of-legislation stage. Similarly, the opportunity to influence the decision makers varies from stage to stage.

Understanding the process of change in government policy is important for business managers who want to influence government policy. Business people should attempt to be influential at all stages of the process because decisions made at an early stage in the process can have a profound effect on the ultimate outcome.

The people who are involved at different stages must be identified, and the appropriate method by which to approach them must be considered. Recognizing the process of government policy formulation and thinking about the best way to participate at each stage can result in increased influence. Such influence is called lobbying, which is discussed later in this chapter.

Administration of Government Programs

For government programs to be effective, they must be put into practice and managed properly. **Administration of government programs** involves the day-to-day activities required to implement the programs. This creates the need for communication between business decision makers and those responsible for implementing government programs.

administration of government programs
The day-to-day activities required to implement the programs.

Stage of process	Outcome of stage	Primary determiner of outcome (decision maker)	Possible influencers
1. Societal need	The existence of a problem	Created by changes in technology or attitudes (economic or ecological)	
2. Perception of need	General awareness of a problem	Researchers, media, politicians	
3. Articulation of demand	Different groups with different ideas about what to do	Leaders of different groups: e.g., political parties, media, interest groups, businesses	Members of various groups
4. Decision to proceed with legislation	Government commitment to deal with the problem	Cabinet ministers	Political party members, civil servants, public, media, researchers, interest groups
5. Determination of the nature of the legislation	A decision about what type of legislation to introduce	Civil servant teams, cabinet	(Same influencers as for No. 4)
6. Drafting of legislation	A draft of new legislation	Public service drafting expert	Cabinet minister, civil servant study team
7. Legislative consideration	Royal assent to legislation	Parliament or legislative assembly	Party loyalties, pressure groups, media
8. Formulation of regulations	The completed set of regulations	Civil servants	Industry representatives, politicians, interest groups
9. Implementation	The new policy in practice	Civil servants	Groups being affected

Figure 3.4
The process of government policy formulation.

Government representatives need to understand business strategy and how it is formulated and implemented. They must also design efficient systems to comply with government regulations. Business managers, on the other hand, must have a thorough knowledge of government programs and how they are implemented. Then, business can deal effectively with government and keep its costs for this activity as low as possible.

The Role of Government in Our Economic System

We now turn our attention to the specific roles government plays in our economic system. These roles directly influence decisions made by business firms. Government can have the following roles:

- competitor
- economic administrator
- regulator
- taxation agent
- provider of incentive programs
- customer
- housekeeper

Government as a Competitor

The most obvious way that government competes with business is through Crown corporations. A **Crown corporation** is one that is accountable, through a minister, to parliament for the conduct of its affairs. The federal government has three types of Crown corporations: departmental corporations, agency corporations, and proprietary corporations (see Table 3.2).

Crown corporations exist provincially as well. The majority of the electricity in Canada is generated by provincial government utilities. A number of provinces own the telephone utilities within their borders. In addition, various provincial governments own and operate other types of businesses. The Manitoba, Saskatchewan, British Columbia, and Quebec governments own all or part of the provincial automobile insurance operations in their provinces. Government-owned and government-operated enterprises account for a significant amount of economic activity in Canada. (See Table 3.3.)

Crown corporation
One that is accountable through a minister to parliament for the conduct of its affairs.

Government as an Economic Administrator

Governments wishing to control business decisions have alternatives to Crown corporations. Governments can, for example, use administrative boards, tribunals, or commissions to screen decisions of private companies before they can be implemented.

Table 3.2   Types of Crown Corporations

Type of Corporation	Definition	Examples
1. Departmental	Responsible for administrative, supervisory, and/or regulatory government services	Atomic Energy Control Board, Employment Insurance Commission
2. Agency	Management of trading or service operations on a quasi-commercial basis	Atomic Energy of Canada Ltd., Lotto Canada, Royal Canadian Mint
3. Proprietary	Management of lending or financial operations; management of commercial or industrial operations	CBC, Central Mortgage & Housing Corp., St. Lawrence Seaway Authority

Table 3.3   The Top 10 Crown Corporations, Ranked by Revenues, 1996

Company	Revenues (in billions)
1. Ontario Hydro	$8.8
2. Hydro-Québec	7.6
3. The Canadian Wheat Board	5.8
4. Canada Post Corp.	4.9
5. B.C. Hydro & Power Authority	2.2
6. Loto-Québec	2.2
7. Ontario Lottery Corp.	2.1
8. Liquor Control Board of Ontario	1.8
9. Commission de la santé et de la sécurité du travail du Québec	1.7
10. Société des alcools du Québec	1.0

When Via Rail Canada provides passenger service, it is competing with other, private-sector firms such as bus lines and airlines.

Canadian Radio-television and Telecommunications Commission (CRTC)
Regulates and supervises all aspects of the Canadian broadcasting system.

The **Canadian Radio-television and Telecommunications Commission (CRTC)**, for example, regulates the Canadian broadcasting system. The CRTC issues broadcasting licences and renews licences of existing broadcasting outlets subject to certain conditions. For example, a licence may stipulate the type of programming, the power of the station, or the minutes of commercial messages that can be broadcast. The CRTC also decides on applications for rate changes submitted to it by federally regulated telecommunications carriers such as Bell Canada. In June 1992, the CRTC decided to end Bell Canada's long-standing monopoly on long-distance telephone service by allowing total competition in that market. As of January 1, 1998, cable television companies have been allowed to compete with phone companies in local markets. Likewise, telephone companies are also free to apply for broadcast licences.[10]

The advent of the much-publicized *information highway* has complicated the work of the CTRC. Hearings began in 1993 to determine how the convergence of telephone, television, cable, computer, and satellite technologies should be regulated. But this is a very difficult problem. Can the CRTC achieve a balancing act between promoting cultural sovereignty (with its Canadian content rules) on the one hand, and letting Canadian firms be competitive in a free-for-all, globalized market on the other hand? Many observers think this is not possible, and they question the usefulness of the CRTC.[11]

Canadian Transport Commission (CTC)
Makes decisions about route and rate applications for commercial air and railway companies.

The **Canadian Transport Commission (CTC)** makes decisions about route and rate applications for commercial air and railway companies. For example, before rail service can be expanded or contracted, the CTC must approve the change. The same holds true for other transportation activities (for example, trucking lines and airlines). Proposed changes in rates must also be approved.

National Energy Board (NEB)
Responsible for regulating the building and operation of oil and gas pipelines under the jurisdiction of the federal government.

The **National Energy Board (NEB)** is responsible for regulating the construction and operation of oil and gas pipelines under the jurisdiction of the Canadian government. This includes decisions about routes of pipelines and the size of pipe to be used in the lines. The NEB also decides on the tolls to be charged for transmission by oil and gas pipelines and levels of export and import of oil and gas. It issues guidelines on internal company accounting procedures and allowable rates of return. In recent years, deregulation has meant less control by the National Energy Board.

National Energy Board
http://www.neb.gc.ca

provincial boards
Consider and judge proposed decisions by private companies.

Certain **provincial boards** consider and judge proposed decisions by private companies, for example, provincial liquor boards or commissions. They authorize price changes by breweries within their province. Milk prices charged by farmers, dairies, and supermarkets are also regulated in a number of provinces. Other marketing boards for commodities such as pork, eggs, and vegetables have important roles in establishing prices and/or production levels of producers.

The power of marketing boards is likely to decrease in the coming years as free market ideas become more widely accepted. One of the most famous of all boards, the Canadian Wheat Board, came under fire in 1994 from farmers who wanted the freedom to sell their grain directly into the U.S. market instead of having to go through the Wheat Board.[12]

Government as a Regulator

As we saw earlier in this chapter, there has been a strong movement towards deregulation of industries such as banking, airlines, and trucking. However, government still regulates many aspects of business activity, and about one third of all federal and provincial statutes are regulatory. These statutes try to alter the economic behaviour of individuals in the private sector.

Four important areas of regulation are protecting competition, consumer protection, social goals, and ecological regulations.

Protecting competition. In 1992, Air Canada and Canadian Airlines International announced their intention to merge, but the federal government did not allow the merger for fear that domestic competition in the airline industry would cease to exist. As well, the government blocked the proposed merger of Maple Leaf Mills and Ogilvie Mills on the grounds that it would have substantially lessened competition in that industry. It also rejected the proposed merger of CN and CP east of Winnipeg because too much of Canada would have had only a single rail operator.

These examples show that a key reason government regulates business is to ensure that healthy competition exists among business firms. As we saw in Chapter 1, competition is crucial to a market economy. Without restrictions, a large company with vast resources could cut its prices so low and advertise so much that smaller firms would be forced out of the market.

Canada's competition policy has been the subject of much discussion—supporters argue it is necessary for a healthy economy and critics claim it is not effective. **Competition policy** seeks to eliminate restrictive trade practices and thereby stimulate maximum production, distribution, and employment through open competition.

The guidelines for competition policy are contained in the *Competition Act*, a comprehensive document that regulates the practices of Canadian business firms. It does not apply to labour unions. The box "The Competition Act" describes selected sections of the act.

Over the years, many business firms have been charged with activity illegal under the *Competition Act*. For example, it is illegal to refuse to supply buyers with the company's product. Chrysler Canada, Ltd. was charged with refusing to supply parts to R. Brunet Co. of Montreal. A major Canadian film distributor was charged for refusing to supply movies to Cineplex Odeon. And three gasoline companies were charged when they cut off gasoline supplies to a dairy company.[13]

Consumer protection. The Canadian government has implemented a number of government programs related to consumer protection, many of them administered by Consumer and Corporate Affairs Canada. The department initiates programs to promote the interests of Canadian consumers.

The *Hazardous Products Act* regulates two categories of products. The first comprises products that are banned because they are dangerous. Some examples are toys and other children's articles painted with coatings containing harmful amounts of lead or other chemical compounds, certain highly flammable textile products, and baby pacifiers containing contaminated liquids. The second category comprises products that can be sold but must be labelled as

Air Canada
http://www.aircanada.ca

Canadian Airlines International
http://www.cdnair.ca

competition policy
Tries to eliminate restrictive trade practices in order to stimulate maximum business activity.

Hazardous Products Act
Regulates banned products and products that can be sold but must be labelled hazardous.

The Canadian Business Scene

The Competition Act

Section 32. Prohibits conspiracies and combinations formed for the purpose of unduly lessening competition in the production, transportation, or storage of goods. Persons convicted may be imprisoned for up to five years or fined up to $1 million or both.

Section 33. Prohibits mergers and monopolies that substantially lessen competition. Individuals who assist in the formation of such a monopoly or merger may be imprisoned for up to two years.

Section 34. Prohibits illegal trade practices. A company may not, for example, cut prices in one region of Canada while selling at a higher price everywhere else if this substantially lessens competition. A company may not sell at "unreasonably low prices" if this substantially lessens competition. (This section does not prohibit credit unions from returning surpluses to their members.)

Section 35. Prohibits giving allowances and rebates to buyers to cover their advertising expenses, unless these allowances are made available proportionally to other purchasers who are in competition with the buyer given the rebate.

Section 36. Prohibits misleading advertising including (1) false statements about the performance of a product, (2) misleading guarantees, (3) pyramid selling, (4) charging the higher price when two prices are marked on an item, and (5) referral selling.

Section 37. Prohibits bait-and-switch selling. No person can advertise a product at a bargain price if there is no supply of the product available to the consumer. (This tactic baits prospects into the store, where salespeople switch them to higher-priced goods.) This section also controls the use of contests to sell goods, and prohibits the sale of goods at a price higher than the advertised one.

Section 38. Prohibits resale price maintenance. No person who produces or supplies a product can attempt to influence upward, or discourage reduction of, the price of the good in question. It is also illegal for the producer to refuse to supply a product to a reseller simply because the producer believes the reseller will cut the price.

Food and Drug Act

Prohibits the sale of food unfit for human consumption and regulates food advertising.

Tobacco Act

Prohibits cigarette advertising on billboards and in retail stores, and assigns financial penalties to violators.

Weights and Measures Act

Sets standards of accuracy for weighing and measuring devices.

Textile Labelling Act

Regulates the labelling, sale, importation, and advertising of consumer textile articles.

hazardous. Standard symbols that denote poisonous, flammable, explosive, or corrosive properties must be attached to certain products.

Food and drug regulations are designed to protect the public from possible risk to health, fraud, and deception in relation to food, drugs, cosmetics, and therapeutic devices. For example, the **Food and Drug Act** prohibits the sale of a food that contains any poisonous or harmful substances, is unfit for human consumption, consists in whole or in part of any rotten substances, is adulterated, or was manufactured under unsanitary conditions. The act also provides that no person can sell or advertise a food in a misleading or deceptive manner with respect to its value, quantity, composition, or safety.

In 1997, the **Tobacco Act** received royal assent. It prohibits cigarette advertising on billboards and in stores. Penalties of up to $300 000 or two years in jail can be assessed for violators. The law is designed to reduce the impact that advertising has on young people in encouraging them to start smoking.[14]

Regulations under the *Weights and Measures Act* complement the packaging and labelling regulations. The **Weights and Measures Act** sets standards of accuracy for weighing and measuring devices. The **Textile Labelling Act** regulates the labelling, sale, importation, and advertising of consumer textile articles. The *National Trade Mark and True Labelling Act* provides that products authorized under the regulations can be designated by the term "Canada Standard." A familiar application is children's garments that bear the Canada Standard trade mark.

Meeting social goals.   Another reason for the regulation of business is to help meet social goals. Social goals promote the general well-being of our society. In several areas, business activities and social goals overlap.

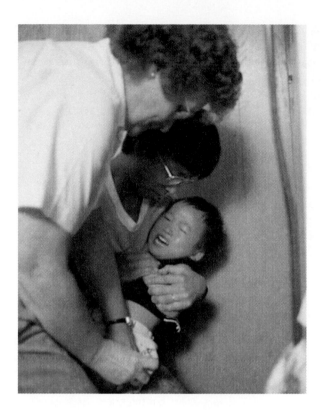

Meeting social goals is a continuing challenge to business. Immunization programs such as the one shown here are set up to help prevent the spread of diseases. Business often contributes to such programs and/or helps manage them.

In Canada, as in any market economy, consumers must have money to purchase goods and services. But our sense of fairness dictates that the ill should be treated, regardless of their ability to pay. Towards this end, Canada has maintained a public health-care system with wide access. Public immunization programs have inoculated millions of Canadians against TB, polio, and even the flu.

Another social goal—a safe workplace—has also generated extensive government regulation of businesses. Each province has workplace health and safety legislation to assure worker safety. In addition, worker compensation programs require businesses to contribute to a fund that pays workers who have been injured on the job.

Federal and provincial governments also regulate industrial pollution and countless other aspects of business in order to "protect" the public. Federal laws regulate banks, stock sales, and automotive emissions. Provinces license physicians, insurance salespeople, and barbers. And local ordinances establish where garbage can be dumped and who can serve liquor. Indeed, thousands of laws regulate every aspect of business in Canada today. When Michael Talker, the founder of Sky Freight Express, started an air courier service, he discovered that the company and its pilots had to be certified by Transport Canada before they were allowed to start operations.

Ecological regulations.   Most industrial sources of environmental pollution are subject to provincial regulation. The federal role is limited to areas in which there are interprovincial or international implications.

One of the major pieces of federal environmental legislation is the *Canada Water Act*. The federal government can control water quality in fresh and marine waters when there is a formal federal–provincial agreement, when federal waters are involved, or when there is sufficient national urgency to warrant federal action. The federal government handles the acid rain situation because international negotiation is necessary.

Two other important environmental regulations are the *Fisheries Act*, which controls the discharge of any harmful substance into any water, and the

Environmental Contaminants Act, which establishes regulations for airborne substances that are a danger to human health or the environment.

Many business managers in Canada feel that government regulates business too closely. They feel that government regulation inhibits business activity when it should be facilitating it. But, compared to the way that some foreign governments regulate business firms, the Canadian government seems quite orderly and reasonable (see the box "Business-Government Relations in Russia").

Government as a Taxation Agent

revenue taxes

Taxes whose main purpose is to fund government services and programs.

restrictive taxes

Levied to control certain activities that legislators believe should be controlled.

income tax

Tax paid by individuals and corporations on income received in a given tax year.

Taxes are imposed and collected by federal, provincial and local governments. **Revenue taxes** are taxes whose main purpose is to fund government services and programs. These represent the majority of taxes at all levels of government in Canada. **Restrictive taxes** are levied to control certain activities that legislative bodies believe should be controlled.

Revenue taxes.   The three main forms of revenue taxes are income taxes, property taxes, and sales taxes. **Income tax** is a tax paid by individuals and corporations on income received in a given tax year and is the primary taxing device federally. All three types are used in different combinations provincially and locally.

International Report

Business-Government Relations in Russia

Before the collapse of communism, entrepreneurial activity was illegal in Russia. The entire economic system was biased against thinking in entrepreneurial terms. Children were not encouraged to earn money. The parents of one child, who was collecting glass bottles and jars in order to get a small refund from a state store, were criticized by their neighbours for allowing such activity. One Russian banker says the problem with Russia is that "… no one ever had a paper route." Even though entrepreneurial activity is now legal, businesspeople are still known colloquially as *speculyant* (meaning speculator) or *zhulyik* (which means thief).

Evgeny Poletsky is one such speculator. In the 1980s, he was arrested for buying Scottish woollen scarves from sailors at the port of Tallinn and reselling them to gypsy traders in Novosibirsk. For his "crime," he was sentenced to two years hard labour in a steel mill. When Mikhail Gorbachev instituted major economic reforms a few years later, Poletsky decided to go into business for himself.

He started with a small construction business and parlayed that into a fishing fleet of five boats. He also bought a factory ship that the government was selling for scrap. He then borrowed money from a state-run poultry farm and promised to pay them back in fish meal (which can be used for animal feed). Since there is always a shortage of fish meal, Poletsky does not have money problems.

But he does have one big problem—government bureaucrats who demand "commissions" before they will approve the permits he needs. The Western media give a lot of coverage to the Russian Mafia (which kidnaps, bombs, and extorts money from businesspeople), but Poletsky says his biggest problem is poorly paid government bureaucrats who are trying to line their pockets at his expense.

In trying to run his fish meal processing business, Poletsky has discovered that government bureaucrats have a lot of power because he must get permission for all sorts of things—fishing quotas, fishing licences, opening a bank account, and even building a new fishing boat. His refusal to pay bribes to get these permissions has resulted in permit delays and many dirty tricks. For example, his factory ship was seized by the Azerbaijani government, an act Poletsky is convinced was engineered by Moscow bureaucrats. The entire fish meal cargo on the ship disappeared sometime after the boat was seized. Now he is trying to get restitution for his losses.

Like most entrepreneurs, Poletsky does not give up easily. He has ordered another five fishing boats from a shipyard that would have folded without his business. He feels that he has achieved a lot in the last few years, but says he would have achieved even more if he didn't have to fight with government bureaucrats all the time.

Both federal and provincial income taxes are examples of progressive taxes. A **progressive tax** is one levied at a higher rate on higher-income tax-payers and at a lower rate on lower-income taxpayers. A progressive income tax has the effect of increasing total consumption because poorer people spend more of their income than do richer people. Tax policy, however, must avoid being so progressive that little incentive remains for wealthy people to invest.

Most provinces have a sales tax that is paid through retail stores, which act as collection agents when they sell their merchandise. The rate of sales tax varies across provinces. It also applies to different groups of products in different areas. Food and drug sales are often exempted. A sales tax is an example of a regressive tax. A **regressive tax** causes poorer people to pay a higher percentage of income than richer people pay. All pay the same percent of the selling price. But poorer people spend a much higher percentage of their income in retail stores than middle-income and rich people do.

Restrictive taxes. Two major taxes are levied not just for their revenue. They are excise taxes on alcohol, tobacco, and gasoline, and import duties. Excise taxes serve both as a "deterrent to excesses"—to discourage what many regard as behaviour the government should curtail—and as a revenue source. Import duties were once a major revenue source as well as a kind of protection for home industries. The growth of free trade in the post–World War II era has resulted in a reduction of this revenue source.

Government as a Provider of Incentives

Federal, provincial, and municipal governments offer incentive programs that help stimulate economic development. **Incentive programs** are designed to encourage managers to make certain decisions and take certain actions desired by governments. For example, they are designed to encourage managers to locate in one (underdeveloped) region rather than another, to invest in new product development, or to engage in export activities. Because incentive programs can improve the pay-offs for a firm, they encourage a manager to choose that option.

One example of a grant incentive program is the Industrial and Regional Development Program (IRDP) offered by the federal Department of Regional Industrial Expansion. The IRDP is designed to deliver federal assistance to manufacturers throughout Canada. Four tiers of assistance are offered, with the greatest support (Tier IV) available for firms in the most disadvantaged areas of the country.

There are many other examples of grant programs. Some include municipal tax rebates for locating in certain areas, design assistance programs, and remission of tariffs on certain advanced technology production equipment. Government incentive programs may or may not have the effect intended.

Information on incentive programs is available from the various provincial and municipal governments. CCH Canadian Limited publishes a book entitled *Industrial Assistance Programs in Canada*, which is updated regularly.

Many people are critical of government incentive programs for business. They argue that private sector firms should have to make it on their own in a free market society. They also say that government money taken from taxpayers should not be given to business firms.

Government involvement at Hyundai Motor's plant in Bromont, Quebec, illustrates these concerns. Workers at the plant were paid $4.2 million in 1992 under a special unemployment insurance program; the company received another $682 000 to pay for training employees. That money is in addition to the $6.4 million that the federal and provincial governments gave Hyundai to build the plant in the first place. On top of all that, the government has forgiven over $28 million in customs duties on cars and parts imported from

progressive tax
A tax levied at a higher rate on higher-income taxpayers and at a lower rate on lower-income taxpayers.

regressive tax
A tax that causes poorer people to pay a higher percentage of income than richer people pay.

incentive programs
Programs to encourage managers to make certain decisions desired by governments.

South Korea. In 1993, Hyundai closed the plant and laid off the workers while it retooled the plant. In 1994, Hyundi announced that it was putting on hold any plans to reopen the plant, which has lost $400 million since it opened in 1988.[15]

Government services. Governments also offer incentives through the many services they provide to business firms. One example of such a program is the Trade Commissioner Service of the federal government. External Affairs Canada has approximately 300 trade commissioners in 70 countries. The Trade Commissioner Service responds to requests for assistance from Canadian exporters and helps foreign importers to find Canadian sources of supply for products they wish to buy. Trade commissioners also participate in developing programs to improve Canadian exports. This service includes identifying market opportunities.

The Export Development Corporation was designed to assist Canadian exports by offering export insurance against nonpayment by foreign buyers; long-term loans or guarantees of private loans to foreign buyers of Canadian products; and insurance against loss of or damage to a Canadian firm's investment abroad arising from expropriation, revolution, or war.

Energy, Mines and Resources Canada provides geological maps of Canada's potential mineral-producing areas. This service gives companies interested in mineral exploration much better geological information about Canada than is available about most other countries. Provincial governments also provide geological services to the mining industry.

Statistics Canada is yet another valuable government service to business firms. Its data and analysis describe almost every aspect of social and economic life in Canada, and provide information used in government policy formulation and decision making by the private sector. The Census of Population and Housing, taken every five years, is a high-profile Statistics Canada activity. This census produces a range of key social and economic data describing all Canadians. The Labour Force Survey, which monitors the labour force activities of Canadians, and the Consumer Price Index, which

Export Development Corporation

http://www.edc.ca

The federal and provincial governments provide a variety of services that facilitate business activities. The construction of roads, ports, and harbours, for example, helps business firms move goods that are vital to our economy.

measures price changes for consumer goods and services, are among the agency's other major programs.

Statistics Canada's information is available in publications, on microfiche and microfilm, on computer tape, and on the Internet through CANSIM, the agency's electronic data bank. Special tabulations and a considerable volume of unpublished data can be obtained on request.

Government as a Customer

Government spending for its own needs can also influence business decisions, such as where to locate or what type of product to produce. Government buys many services as well as products, ranging from paper clips and pencils to warships, helicopters, highways, and high-rise office buildings. Many firms and industries depend on government purchasing decisions, if not for their survival, at least for their level of prosperity. Examples include construction and architectural firms and companies in the aerospace industry. Government expenditure on goods and services amounts to billions of dollars per year.

Government as a Housekeeper

The federal, provincial, and municipal governments facilitate business activity through the wide variety of services they supply. The federal government provides highways, the postal service, the minting of money, the armed forces, and statistical data on which to base business decisions. It also tries to maintain stability through fiscal and economic policy.

Provincial and municipal governments provide streets, sewage and sanitation systems, police and fire departments, utilities, hospitals, and education. All these activities create the kind of stability that encourages business activity.

How Government Influences Business Decisions

A business decision has four elements: the decision maker(s), the options available to the decision maker(s), the criteria by which the options are judged, and the pay-offs for each option. Consider the case of Christine Beliveau, who has to choose one of two competing products to sell in her store. Her objective is to make as much profit on the product as possible. The criterion she will apply in judging the two brands will be the anticipated profitability of each. Based on her knowledge of the brand, image, price, quality of product, and sales in other stores, she estimates that she can sell 12 000 units of Product A at an average profit per unit of $2.73. She estimates that she can sell 15 000 units of product B at an average profit per unit of $1.68. Total profit from Product A would be $32 760. Total profit from Product B would be $25 200. Christine would therefore choose Product A (see Table 3.4).

The government can influence the way this decision is made. It can change the decision maker, the options available to the decision maker, the criteria used to make the decision, or the anticipated pay-offs from one or more of the decision options. Let's look at each of these possibilities.

Table 3.4   **Four Elements of the Decision About What Products to Sell**

The Decision Maker	The Options	The Criterion	The Anticipated Pay-Offs
Christine Beliveau	1. Product A	Profit for the	12 000 × $2.73 = $32 760
	2. Product B	store	15 000 × $1.68 = $25 200

Governments Can Change the Decision Maker

In the example above, Christine Beliveau is the only decision maker. This would change if, for example, a government decided to nationalize the sale of the product, as is done with liquor in most provinces. The decision maker in that case would not be Christine. She would simply be a representative of the government. The authority and responsibility to make the decision would shift from the private sector to the public sector.

The authority and responsibility for making the decision would also shift away from Christine if a government-appointed board or tribunal reviewed and approved decisions about what products could be sold. If this type of body existed, Christine would no longer be free to decide what product to sell. The government, through its board, would have control over the decision. When government control over the decision increases, so does government responsibility for the decision.

Governments Can Change Options

The options currently available to Christine Beliveau are to sell either Product *A* or Product *B*. Government action could make it illegal to sell one or the other or both of the products; this action might be taken if, for instance, the product was considered unsafe.

Governments Can Change Decision Criteria

Government actions can change the criteria applied to the making of economic decisions. This occurs when government becomes involved as a decision maker, either through Crown corporation ownership or through a regulatory board or tribunal.

Imagine a situation in which Christine went to a government agency and received a grant for hiring three new employees. After she hired them, some circumstance occurred that made it necessary to lay off two of the people and cancel the positions. Because the government grant had helped create the jobs, the employees cannot be laid off without at least considering the likely reaction from the relevant government agency that part of the grant may be revoked. On its own and without the government grant, the decision about how to handle the layoff is less complicated than it is when the government agency must also be taken into account.

Governments Can Affect Pay-Offs

Many government policies can affect the anticipated pay-offs from decision options, including taxes, incentive grants, and tariffs. Government purchasing decisions can also affect the anticipated pay-offs.

Let's assume that Product *B* was imported from France, and the federal government decided to impose an import tariff of $1.00 per unit on it. This would have the effect of reducing the profit per unit by $1.00, assuming the selling price was not raised by $1.00. This tariff would reduce the potential on Product *B* to $10 200. making it even less attractive in relation to Product *A* than it had previously been.

Assume that Christine has just received an order from the government for 12 000 units of Product *B* in addition to the initial 15 000 units she had estimated could be sold. Suppose also that she could make the same profit per unit on these 12 000 units as she could on the initial 15 000. She is also aware that the government will not buy Product *A*. Christine has to recalculate the estimated profitability of Product *B*. Instead of $1.68 × 15 000 units or $25 200, it is now $1.68 × 27 000 units or $45 360. This will make Product *B* more profitable than Product *A*, and Christine will decide to sell it if she wishes to maximize profits.

How Business Influences Government

As shown in Figure 3.5, businesses attempt to influence the government through lobbyists, trade associations, and advertising. A **lobbyist** is a person hired by a company or industry to represent its interests with government officials. The Canadian Association of Consulting Engineers, for example, regularly lobbies the federal and provincial governments to make use of the skills possessed by private sector consulting engineers on projects like city water systems. Some business lobbyists have training in the particular industry, public relations experience, or a legal background. A few have served as legislators or government regulators.

lobbyist
A person hired by a company or an industry to represent its interests with government officials.

The *Lobbyists Registration Act* came into effect in 1989. Lobbyists must register with the Registrar of Lobbyists so that it is clear which individuals are being paid for their lobbying activity. For many lobbying efforts, there are opposing points of view. The Canadian Cancer Society and the Tobacco Institute present very different points of view on cigarette smoking and cigarette advertising.

Employees and owners of small businesses that cannot afford lobbyists often join **trade associations**. Trade associations may act as an industry lobby to influence legislation. They also conduct training programs relevant to the particular industry, and they arrange trade shows at which members display their products or services to potential customers. Most publish newsletters featuring articles on new products, new companies, changes in ownership, and changes in laws affecting the industry.

trade association
An organization dedicated to promoting the interests and assisting the members of a particular industry.

Corporations can influence legislation indirectly by influencing voters. A company can, for example, launch an advertising campaign designed to get people to write their MPs, MPPs, or MLAs demanding passage—or rejection—of a particular bill that is before parliament or the provincial legislature. The box "Trading Places" describes a program designed to encourage the exchange of ideas between business and government.

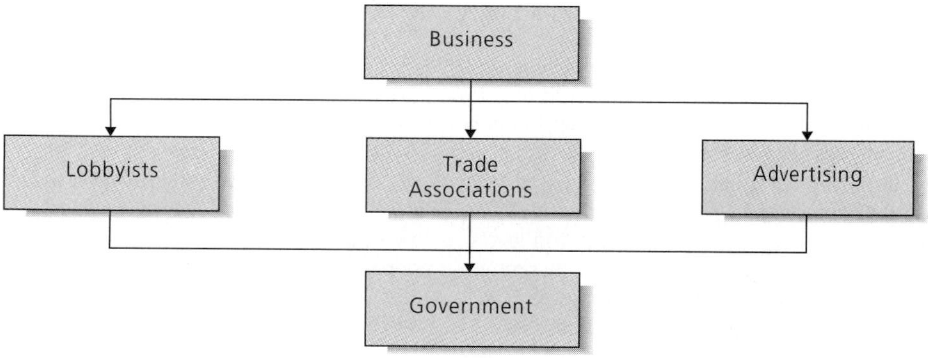

Figure 3.5
Business influences the government in a variety of different ways.

Business and the Workforce

Because workers are an important resource to every company, relations with the workforce are an important dimension of the contemporary business world.

Changing Demographics of the Workforce

The statistical makeup—the demographics—of the Canadian labour force has changed gradually over the years. As Figure 3.6(a) illustrates, the workforce has grown steadily throughout the 20th century.

The Canadian Business Scene

Trading Places

There is a program designed to prove that Pierre Trudeau's two solitudes—business and government—can, at least occasionally, reach out and touch each other. The goal of the Business-Government Executive Exchange program is to provide a place for an exchange of ideas and expertise between business and government. It places senior public servants in key private sector jobs for up to two years, and takes promising young private sector managers and gives them challenging government assignments.

Since its inception, 30 men and women have "graduated" from the program, and another 30 are currently enrolled. A program advisory committee made up of 17 industry chiefs and 10 federal deputy ministers coordinates the program. Senior government officials from the Treasury Board, Secretary of State, Supply and Services Canada, and the Department of Finance have gone to work for firms such as IBM, Coles Book Stores, DuPont, and the Royal Bank of Canada. Executives from IBM, Canadian Airlines International, DuPont, and Bell Canada have taken positions with the Department of National Defence, Transport Canada, and Revenue Canada.

Bob Weese, one of nine senior government officials currently in the program, is a typical program member. He had been an assistant deputy minister with Supply and Services Canada for six years and supervised a staff of 150. He was transferred to General Electric Canada as manager of corporate business development programs. He says the most striking difference between a large public organization and an even larger private sector one is the amount of paperwork. At General Electric, decisions on problems may be made based on a five- or six-page report, and it may take as little as one week to make the decision. In government, in contrast, such a decision would involve hundreds of people, thousands of pages of analysis, and perhaps years before the decision is reached.

Weese also notes that General Electric has reduced its workforce by 100 000 over the last five years. He does not think that kind of downsizing will ever happen in government. But Weese's private sector experience reinforces his belief that public sector managers are hard-working and conscientious. Unfortunately, they work in a rigid, bureaucratic system that frustrates them because it is too control-oriented.

But private sector firms have shortcomings, too. In Weese's view, General Electric has not done enough to convey to the public all the different business lines it is involved in. The company is the world's largest manufacturer of diesel locomotives and commercial aircraft engines, and GE Capital Canada is one of the fastest-growing, nonbank financial institutions in Canada. Weese is also surprised by the lack of women in private sector management. He is used to seeing women around the management table and was shocked when he attended a company meeting with 30 others, all of whom were men.

Another member of the program, Victor Shantora, found that, when he moved from government to a private sector firm, he had to live with the very regulations he had helped develop while in government. Shantora was a director with Environment Canada, and his staff developed environmental regulations affecting industry. He then moved to DuPont Canada as environmental affairs manager. He notes that the industry is responding to environmental concerns more favourably than it did in the 1960s and 1970s. For example, DuPont tackled the problem of chlorofluorocarbons by building a plant that now produces an alternative chemical.

Shantora experienced some culture shock when he went to DuPont. He says that objectives are much clearer in the private sector, and individuals know exactly what they are expected to do. When top management sets a goal, they expect it to be reached. When a government minister gives a direction, it may take an octopus to pull things together.

Russell Bula was production manager at DuPont before spending two years in Ottawa as a manager at Industry, Science, and Technology Canada. He too was impressed with the motivation and commitment of public servants—at least at the top levels. Below middle management, he saw too many uncommitted people. He discovered that the lines of communication between business and government were better than he had expected, but he also saw government taking excessive time to make decisions.

The Greying Workforce

As shown in Figure 3.6(b), the workforce has been getting older. In 1931, for example, the median age of the Canadian population was under 25 years; by 1996, it had risen to over 35 years. The median age continues to rise and could be as high as 50 by the year 2036. In 1981, the largest age bracket was the group between 15 and 24. Population projections show that by 2006 the largest group will be the 40–49 age bracket and by 2031 it will be the 70–74 age bracket. These are dramatic changes. Business firms will have to cope not only with slower population growth but also with people's changing needs as they age. This means increased emphasis on marketing research (see Chapter 15) and more sophisticated assessment of consumer needs as they move through the various stages of life. Care of the elderly is emerging as an important issue of the late 20th century.

Figure 3.6

(a) Canadian workforce, 1921–1996, selected years.

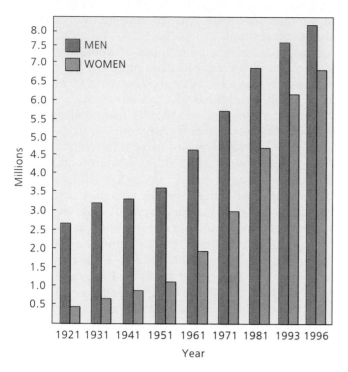

(b) Median age of the Canadian population, 1931–1996, selected years.

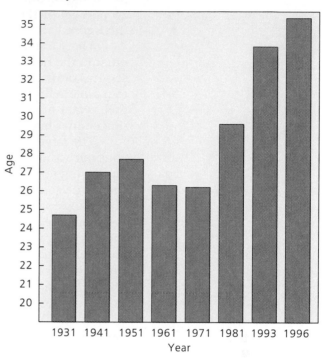

(c) Employment participation for men and women, 1931–1996, selected years.

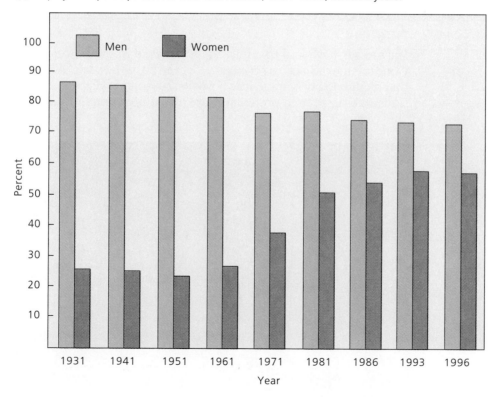

   Companies that produce baby food have already experienced problems because of the declining number of babies. In the future, companies that sell products to people in their twenties will find that market declining significantly. On the other hand, increased opportunities are available to firms selling goods and services to older people.

Women in the Workforce

The growing number of women in the workforce is another trend that has had a significant impact on business. As Figure 3.6(c) shows, in 1931 only 25 percent of the female population worked outside the home. By 1996, the figure had risen to almost 60 percent.

There are many reasons for the increased number of women working outside the home. Faced with rapid increases in the prices of goods and services during the 1970s, many couples found that they needed two incomes to maintain their standard of living. In addition, the women's movement and the greater number of women attending and graduating from colleges and universities have provided more career options for women.

The large percentage of women in all types of careers has had and will continue to have a major impact on business. For example, many companies are having to address the problem of child care in order to retain valuable trained personnel. Women working outside the home are also providing more marketing opportunities for business. For example, in recent years there has been increased demand for convenience foods that require little preparation, such as microwaveable dinners and frozen pizzas. Products such as telephone answering machines and home computers are now commonplace in homes because they assist the busy lifestyles of two-career families. Restaurants and home-cleaning services have benefited too. There has also been increased demand for professional "gear" for working women: business attire, briefcases, and the like. The fact that women are no longer caring for children full-time has even created a new industry—the day-care industry.

Business and Consumers

Businesses have had to adjust to an increase in the power of the consumer. Gone are the days of *caveat emptor,* "let the buyer beware." A business following that dictum today is apt to face boycotts, lawsuits, and government intervention. Consumer tastes and preferences are also more complex than in the past.

The increased number of women working outside the home has resulted in more demand for the services provided by day-care centres.

Activism on the part of consumers seeking better value from businesses—the **consumer movement**—has altered the way many businesses conduct themselves. While the consumer movement traces its roots back to the turn of the century, Ralph Nader's much-publicized attack on unsafe cars being produced by General Motors (*Unsafe at Any Speed,* 1965) really gave consumerism its momentum.

consumer movement
Activism on the part of consumers seeking better value from businesses.

Over the last decade, legislation has broadened **consumer rights** considerably. In particular, legislation now essentially guarantees consumers the right to choose the products they desire, the right to safety in the products they purchase, the right to be informed about what they are buying, and the right to be heard in the event of problems. As a result, most products today come with extensive instructions as to their use and, in the case of food products, a detailed list of their ingredients. Most products also have a guarantee or warranty, and many list telephone numbers, addresses, or Web sites to contact in the event of problems. We will consider these and related issues more fully in Chapter 15.

consumer rights
The legally protected rights of consumers to choose products, to safety when using products, to be informed about any potential risk from a product, and to be heard in the event of problems with a product.

Challenges at the Start of the 21st Century

Given the nature and complexities of today's business environment, it is not surprising that Canadian business faces a number of critical challenges. As Figure 3.7 shows, six of the most important challenges are productivity, the national debt, liberalized trade, environmental protection, technology, and preserving Canadian unity.

In Search of Higher Productivity

As we saw in Chapter 1, productivity is a measure of our economy's success. It is also the measure of a business's success, since it reflects the efficiency with which a company uses resources. A company that uses fewer resources (whether of materials, management, or labour) to make the same number of products as another firm is more efficient. While Canadian workers are very productive, intense domestic and foreign competition has caused managers to look closely at ways to improve productivity even further. The complex nature of the productivity problem and attempted solutions are discussed in Chapter 14.

The National Debt

A **federal deficit** occurs when federal government expenditures are greater than federal revenues in a given year. Defence, social welfare, and interest

federal deficit
The situation that occurs when federal expenditures are greater than federal revenues in a given year.

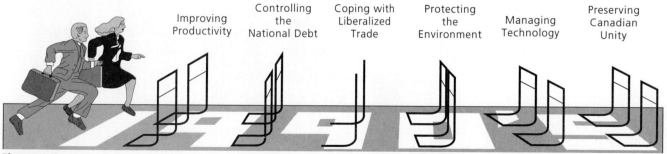

Improving Productivity · Controlling the National Debt · Coping with Liberalized Trade · Protecting the Environment · Managing Technology · Preserving Canadian Unity

Figure 3.7
Six basic challenges at the start of the 21st century.

on government debt are kinds of federal expenditures. Federal revenues come mostly from personal and corporate income tax. Figure 3.8 shows Canada's federal surpluses and deficits for recent years.

The series of annual deficits in the last 10 to 15 years has added up to a staggering total *federal debt*. The Canadian government owes its creditors over $550 billion. These creditors include Canadian and foreign citizens, as well as business firms. The cost of servicing the debt (interest payments) is the government's largest single expenditure and accounts for about one quarter of all federal government spending.

Until the mid-1990s, annual deficits and the total federal debt were increasing at an alarming rate. From Confederation (1867) to 1981, the *total* accumulated debt was only $85.7 billion, but in the period 1981–94, *annual* deficits were in the $20 to $40 billion range. Since 1994, however, annual deficits have been declining rapidly, and in 1997 there was actually a small budget surplus for the first time since 1970. The challenge now is deciding how to spend the surplus: on debt reduction or reduced taxes for Canadians?

If the surplus is not used to reduce the total debt, that debt will obviously remain, and it will affect both Canadian consumers and Canadian business firms because the government must borrow money to finance the debt. Canada borrowed money more often in international markets than any

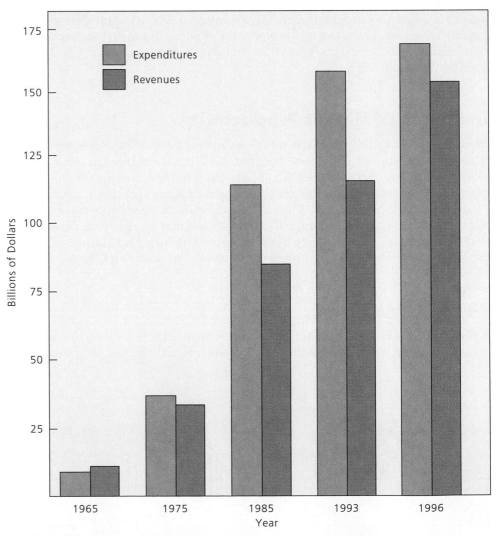

Figure 3.8
Federal government expenditures and revenues, 1965–1996, selected years.

other nation in the period 1989–94. Of all bonds issued in international markets during that period, Canada accounted for 31 percent of the total. The U.S. accounted for only 19 percent.[16] Because the supply of money available for lending at any given time is limited, the government finds itself competing with consumers, businesses, non-profit organizations, and local and provincial governments for borrowed money. This huge demand in the face of limited supply puts upward pressure on interest rates.

The debt also has an impact in other ways. If the government raises personal income taxes in an attempt to reduce the debt, this reduces consumer spending and business firms will sell less. If the government raises corporate taxes, business firms will have less profit to distribute to shareholders or to reinvest in the firm for future growth.

Coping with Liberalized Trade

In recent years there has been a rapid globalization of competition. In addition to the mature industrial economies of North America, Western Europe, and Japan, newly industrialized countries like South Korea, Singapore, Hong Kong, and Taiwan have become serious rivals for export sales. Canadian firms no longer can take domestic markets for granted because of this competition.

Why have so many foreign companies been more successful of late than their Canadian competitors? Some pay their employees lower wages. Some have employees who accomplish more in an equal amount of time. Lower safety standards and pollution controls in many foreign countries mean lower costs of producing goods. Fewer "paperwork" requirements means that foreign companies do not have to employ as many accountants and lawyers—a substantial savings.

Some countries fail to honour patents. Brazilian companies, for example, have copied computer designs and now sell these "clones" throughout Latin America. Even Japanese companies have copied computer circuits, although in the late 1980s they agreed to stop this practice. Like the former Soviet Union, Eastern European bloc nations actually employed spies to steal technology. In all these cases, the foreign companies did not have to spend money on research and development of the product, so they did not have to include that cost in the price of their product.

Many countries have complex rules that restrict the import of goods. Some impose tariffs (taxes) on our products. Others have complex "inspection" procedures that cost Canadian companies time and money.

The free trade agreement with the U.S., as well as NAFTA, have resulted in much new domestic competition for Canadian firms. They have also, however, resulted in competitive opportunities in the U.S. and Mexico that did not exist before.

As you can see, the international trade problem is a complex one. These and related issues of international business are explored more fully in Chapter 4.

The Continuing Challenge of Environmental Protection

Ecology is the relationship between living things and their environment. It includes conservation of resources, recycling of used resources, and pollution control. Pesticides, oil spills, smog, chemical dumping, solid wastes, noxious fumes, and radioactive waste all pollute our air, water, and land. **Pollution** is the contamination of the natural environment by the introduction of harmful substances that endanger our health and quality of life.

ecology
The relationship between living things and their environment.

pollution
The contamination of the natural environment by the introduction of harmful substances.

The activities of some business firms do pollute the environment. Water, air, and land pollution are all evident in Canada. Mercury emission in the English-Wabigoon and Spanish river systems in northern Ontario, acid rain, air pollution in the area surrounding Sudbury, and unsightly landfill sites around major cities are all examples of pollution.

In some cases we blame business for pollution that is caused by consumers. Because consumers demand convenient packaging of beverages, we have aluminum pop cans. But it is consumers, not businesses, who create litter through improper disposal of the used cans.

In other cases, the problem lies with the way the good or service is made. For example, chlorofluorocarbons are used as coolants in refrigerators and air conditioners and for making plastic foams. When they rise from the earth, they set off chemical reactions in the stratosphere that rapidly destroy ozone. It is the ozone layer that protects us from the sun's ultraviolet radiation.

The dilemma for business and government is that emphasizing pollution control in a single industry may result in that industry's output being non-competitive internationally. If other countries do not have the same pollution standards Canada has, their firms will have a lower cost structure; therefore they will be able to undercut the prices of Canadian firms. A similar situation exists for individual companies in an industry. If one company buys pollution control equipment and other companies do not, then the innovating company will have costs that are uncompetitively high.

Today we have laws covering air, solid waste, and water pollution. We also have laws against pollution by pesticides, noise, toxic substances, and hazardous wastes. It is becoming more and more obvious that pollution is a global problem that must be dealt with globally. The World Bank, which makes loans to countries for economic development, has established firm guidelines on how bank projects should avoid or minimize damage to tropical forests, watersheds, and wildlands.[17]

Increased concern about the ecology has also created numerous opportunities for new products. An entire industry has grown up to sell products that reduce air and water pollution. Devices to process smokestack emissions and waste before it is released into water sources are products for which markets have developed. We will explore the issue of pollution in more detail in Chapter 5.

Technology: Friend or Foe?

technology
The application of science that enables people to do entirely new things or perform established tasks in new and better ways.

Technology is the application of science that enables people to do entirely new things or perform established tasks in new and better ways. Consider the following examples:

- After studying the movement of the human foot in minute detail, Canstar Sports Inc. developed the Micron Mega skate, which is now worn by 70 percent of NHL players.[18]

- Improved technology in automobile engines by Honda and Mitsubishi has resulted in 20 percent increases in gas mileage with no loss of power. The engines also emit 20 to 30 percent less carbon dioxide. A Honda Civic, for example, will get 100 kilometres per 5.8 litres of gas in city driving.[19]

- Alcan has developed a ceramic and aluminum composite called Duralcan, which the company is confident will be widely used in automobile manufacturing by the year 2000. The material is already being used in mountain bikes to rave reviews; a bike built with Duralcan weighs less than half as much as a bike built with the standard steel frame.[20]

- Inco Ltd. and Ainsworth Electric Co. are cooperatively developing a new communications technology that may revolutionize mining. It will allow miners to operate heavy machinery to drill, load, and transport ore deep beneath the earth by punching keyboards on the surface. The first test of the system was at Inco's Copper Cliff North nickel mine in Sudbury; it increased productivity by 20 percent.[21]

■ Toyota Motor Corp. has demonstrated a new experimental car that monitors driver alertness with a pulse sensor worn on the wrist. The car sounds a chime to wake up a drowsy driver, and a voice urges the driver to pull over to the side of the road. If that doesn't work, the seat begins to vibrate rapidly.[22]

Business firms must embrace technological change so that their processes, products, and product features will not become obsolete. They must also be ready to respond to the competitive effect of such technology. If a firm is aggressive, it will be the first to introduce a new, cheaper way to make its Product X. It might also introduce Product X-Mark II with features that make a competitor's Product Y obsolete. Any of these objectives requires substantial investment in research and development (R&D). **R&D** refers to those activities that are necessary to provide new products, services, and processes. It usually requires a large investment in laboratories, equipment, and scientific talent.

Canada's R&D efforts have lagged behind those of other industrialized economies (see Figure 3.9). When we take into account the fact that the GDP of countries such as Japan, the U.S., and Germany is much higher than the GDP of Canada, it means that R&D spending (and employment) in Canada is only a fraction of what it is in other industrialized countries. Only a small number of firms do R&D in Canada, and the top 25 firms account for over half of all R&D.

research and development (R&D)

Activities that are intended to provide new products, services, and processes.

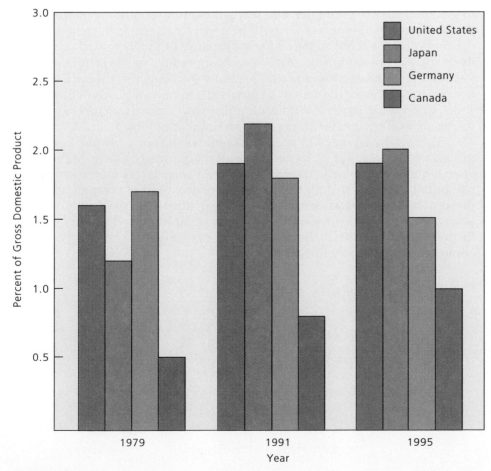

Figure 3.9
Gross expenditure for industrial R&D as a percentage of gross domestic product.

Technology and Social Problems

Dealing with technology and its role in modern society will continue to be a major business challenge as we enter the 21st century. Is high technology friend or foe to Canadians and Canadian businesses? Automated machinery has already replaced thousands of traditional jobs, but has also created thousands of new types of jobs that did not formerly exist. But a more depersonalized society now exists, in which people become numbers to a computer that receives telephone calls, handles banking transactions, maintains the temperatures in our homes, and even answers the doorbell.

Defenders of technology point to its promised benefits. New genetically engineered seeds that will increase agricultural production for a hungry world are now entering the market. New vaccines that may help win the battle against cancer and certain viruses are in development. And new employment opportunities in safer environments than the hot and dangerous steel mills of the past are a reality for many today.

Technology and Unemployment

Ever since machines became important in the production process, there has been concern that they would take over the work done by humans and that massive unemployment would result. Does automation cause unemployment? The best answer to this question is that automation does cause unemployment in the immediate area where it is applied but, overall, automation creates far more jobs than it takes away. The reasoning behind this conclusion is shown in Figure 3.10.

Competition motivates business firms to find better or cheaper ways to produce products. A company may introduce a new production technology to get the benefits of greater efficiency. This new technology will reduce production costs. Some workers will be needed to operate the new technology, but others will not be needed at all because of the increased productivity the new technology brings. With lower-cost production, the company is able to sell its products at a lower price. Generally speaking, the lower the price of a product, the greater the demand; increased demand for goods in general results in economic growth. With economic growth comes an increase in demand for workers and an increase in the number of jobs.

This is how automation affects unemployment society-wide, but it may not apply in a specific situation. Consider a company that is planning to open a highly automated factory with only 25 supervisory and maintenance personnel. The new factory will replace a nearly obsolete factory, which at present employs 300 workers. The company must face the problem of the unemployed workers. Economic theory says that improved technology will, in the long run, benefit the whole economy. But this theory gives little comfort to those who will be out of jobs.

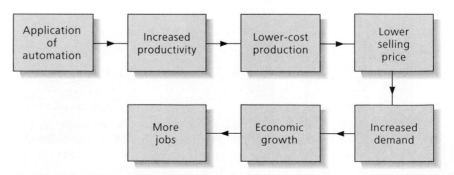

Figure 3.10
Automation and unemployment.

Preserving Canadian Unity

One of the greatest challenges facing Canada is the issue of unity. While this is not primarily a business issue, the unity debate and the uncertainty created by it does have a large impact on business activity and business firms. The threat of Quebec separation, for example, influences the value of the Canadian dollar, which in turn influences Canada's international business activities. As well, much has been written during the last couple of decades about business firms moving out of Quebec because of political uncertainty. Thus, political issues have a big effect on business firms.

Summary of Learning Objectives

1. **Describe five major *trends* that affect the nature of Canadian business today.** The most influential trends are the growth of high technology, a shift in emphasis from manufacturing to information services, an increase in the number of mergers and acquisitions, a move towards deregulation and privatization, and downsizing.

2. **Explain how and why *government* regulates business in Canada.** Government regulates business firms by passing various laws that prohibit certain activities, or by giving incentives that encourage businesses to carry out desirable activities. Government regulates business in order to encourage and protect competition, to protect consumers from unfair actions by businesses, to help meet social goals by promoting the well-being of our society, and to protect our natural environment from possible pollution.

3. **Discuss changes in the *workforce*, and how these changes have affected Canadian business.** The most notable changes are the aging of the workforce and an increase in the number of women in the workforce. These changes have presented both problems and opportunities; companies that sell products for babies and teens will have smaller markets, but those that cater to middle-aged or older people will have increasing opportunities. Women who are working outside the home are also providing more opportunities for business firms to cater to this type of consumer.

4. **Describe changes in *consumer rights* and *demographics*, and their impact on Canadian business.** Consumer rights activism has forced businesses to be more sensitive to consumer complaints. Legislation guarantees consumers the right to choose the products they desire, the right to safe products, the right to be informed when buying products, and the right to be heard if there are problems.

5. **Identify and discuss six major business *challenges* at the start of the 21st century.** The six challenges that must be faced by Canadian businesses are productivity, the national debt, liberalized trade, environmental protection, technology, and preserving Canadian unity.

Key Terms

high technology
   (high-tech), 56
service economy, 56
information services, 57
acquisition, 57
merger, 57
horizontal merger, 58

vertical merger, 58
conglomerate merger, 58
friendly takeover, 58
hostile takeover, 58
poison pill, 59
greenmail, 60
deregulation, 60

privatization, 60
downsizing, 61
distribution of
   government powers,
   62
government policy
   formulation, 65

administration of
   government programs,
   65
Crown corporation, 67
Canadian Radio-
   television and

Study Questions and Exercises

Review Questions

1. Identify three significant internal forces that businesses must now contend with.
2. Why does the government feel the need to regulate business?
3. In what ways do businesses attempt to influence government? What ethical implications can be drawn regarding these actions?
4. Why is productivity such an important issue today?
5. What are six major hurdles facing business at the start of the 21st century?

Analysis Questions

6. Using periodicals such as the *Globe and Mail* and *Canadian Business*, identify six recent mergers. Determine whether each was hostile or friendly. Also classify each as horizontal, vertical, or conglomerate.
7. Locate three examples of instances in which you believe business has been more responsive to consumer expectations recently than it was in the past.
8. What do you see as the appropriate role of technology in the future? In general, will it improve or harm our society? Should it be regulated? If so, how?

Application Exercises

9. Interview a local bank manager. Identify ways in which deregulation of the banking industry has made banking more risky and more profitable.
10. Visit a local manufacturing company. Identify ways in which it has been affected by high technology.

Building Your Business Skills

Goal

To increase student awareness and appreciation for the complexity of the relationship between business and government.

Situation

You are talking to two friends at a social gathering. One is a manager in a government regulatory agency, and the other is a marketing manager in a private sector business firm. These two friends are having a rather serious debate about the pros and cons of government regulation of business. The business manager argues that there is far too much government regulation of business and that this regulation is inhibiting business efficiency and effectiveness. The manager in the government regulatory agency argues that businesses must be regulated or they would do all sorts of things that are bad for the environment and bad for consumers.

Method

Divide the class into teams of three or four. Designate half of the teams as "government" teams and half as "business" teams. Have each of the government teams interview one manager working in a government regulatory agency. Have each of the business teams interview one marketing manager in a private sector firm. Both types of teams should get answers to the following questions:

1. Is it necessary for government to regulate business firms? Why or why not?
2. What are the costs associated with regulation of business firms? Give a specific example.
3. What are the benefits associated with regulation of business firms? Give a specific example.
4. What changes in regulations should be implemented in order to make the regulatory system more effective?

Follow-up Questions

1. For each of the four questions above, compare the answers of the government regulatory managers with those of the marketing managers in the private sector firms. What are the main differences? Is there any common ground where agreement exists?

2. Assuming that there is agreement that some form of government regulation is necessary, suggest ways to make this regulation positive for consumers and the environment without it being unduly restrictive for business firms.

To learn about an organization that acts as an economic administrator, visit the Canadian Radio-television and Telecommunications Commission (CRTC) Web site at:

http://www.crtc.gc.ca/

1. What mechanisms are in place for private citizens to have input into the CRTC decision-making process?

2. Think of how you use technology in a typical day. How do CRTC decisions affect you?

3. You and a group of friends are thinking of starting an alternative radio station. How would the CRTC affect your business decision to compete for an existing radio frequency? Consider the four elements of any business decision: the decision maker(s), the options available, the criteria by which options are judged, and the pay-offs for each option.

4. Based on information from the Web site, what are the advantages and disadvantages of having the CRTC?

5. Use your search engine to find Web sites for other Canadian government regulatory boards, commissions or tribunals mentioned in the text. What features do these Web sites have in common? Are there any differences in the user-friendliness of the Web sites? Explain.

CONCLUDING CASE 3-1

Two National Airlines or One?

Air Canada (AC) and Canadian Airlines International (CAI) have been engaged in a bruising competitive battle throughout the 1990s. What has been achieved? CAI continues to pile up losses while pursuing a market niche that industry analysts say is non-existent. In the period 1985–95, CAI never once made a profit; in that same period, AC made a profit only three times. Industry analysts say that CAI cannot survive in the long run because the domestic Canadian market is simply not big enough to accommodate two major airlines.

When deregulation came in the 1980s, it was supposed to lead to strong growth in air travel as lower prices attracted more flyers. But Canada's population, strung out as it is in a thin line along the U.S. border, has always been well-travelled, so the gains from deregulation were not as great as in the U.S., where a larger percentage of the population had never flown on a commercial airliner.

What has happened in post-deregulation Canada is that competition between AC and CAI has simply intensified. Given the finite number of Canadians who are available to buy airline tickets, this increased competition has meant that fewer seats are occupied on each flight that takes off. This is inefficient, and causes both major airlines to be less financially sound than they otherwise might be.

What is the solution? One suggestion is to merge the two airlines. The reduced overlap on domestic routes, it is argued, would allow the merged company to expand its overseas service, which tends to be more profitable. Combining AC's U.S. and European routes with CAI's Asian routes would also make Toronto a powerful transportation hub. The merged company would also enjoy cost savings on all other aspects of operations and would therefore get a better credit rating. This, in turn, would reduce borrowing costs and further increase profits.

But this is only one side of the issue. The Canadian Auto Workers Union fears that a merger would cause widespread layoffs. The union wants both airlines to continue operating. They feel that the government should "re-regulate" fares, routes, and new entrants into the industry. Supporters of re-regulation argue that it will mean fewer empty seats on airplanes, and this will lead to reduced fares for consumers.

Case Questions

1. Is a merger of Air Canada and Canadian Airlines International a good idea? Defend your answer.

2. If the two airlines merge, what would happen to domestic competition in the airline industry?

3. What role has government legislation played so far in this situation? What role should government have in the future? Defend your answer.

◆

CONCLUDING CASE 3-2

Mixing Business and Politics

On October 23, 1994, Pierre Desjardins was fired as CEO of Domtar by the firm's board of directors. Desjardins filed a $6.6 million wrongful dismissal suit which alleges that he was fired at the request of a Parti Québécois minister because of Desjardins's political views on Quebec separation (he opposes it), and because he led the leadership campaign of former Liberal premier Robert Bourassa. The charge is vehemently denied by the government of Quebec.

The dispute apparently stems from a long-standing disagreement between Jean Campeau, formerly the chairman of Domtar, and now a Parti Québécois Finance Minister. (Campeau is also a former head of the Caisse de dépôt et placement du Québec which, together with the Société Générale de Finance (SGF), controls 42 percent of Domtar.) When Campeau was at Domtar, he agreed to co-chair a commission on Quebec's constitutional future. Desjardins expressed concern that Campeau's activity might harm financial markets and negatively affect Domtar's sales and its reputation with its customers. Campeau quit Domtar in 1992 to campaign for Quebec independence.

The lawsuit alleges that Campeau gave the order that Desjardins be fired. The lawsuit further alleges that Desjardins was fired in a malicious and abusive way. Also fired was Chairman Paul Gobeil, a former Liberal minister in the Quebec cabinet. Desjardins says that he was told by certain board members that Campeau was the one who ordered his firing. Both Campeau and Domtar have refused comment on the case while it is before the courts.

The lawsuit alleges that two directors of Domtar met with Desjardins and at that meeting a handwritten statement was read which asked for Desjardins's resignation. No reason for the request was given. At the subsequent board meeting where the proposal was voted on, all the Caisse and SGF directors voted for it, while the independent directors voted against it. One independent director quit immediately thereafter, calling the incident a travesty.

The firing of Desjardins is interesting. He was originally hired in 1990 to save Domtar from bankruptcy. Under his leadership, Domtar went from staggering losses to record profits.

Case Questions

1. Assume for a moment that the allegations being made in the Desjardins lawsuit are true. Make the argument that an unethical decision was made in this case.

2. Again, assume that the allegations are true. Make the argument that this was not a case of unethical decision making.

◆

4

Understanding International Business

Purdy's Goes International

Purdy's Chocolates is a Vancouver-based gourmet chocolate maker that is run by Charles Flavelle and his daughter Karen. It is the largest manufacturer of chocolate in B.C., and has 30 stores there and 12 in Alberta. Sales revenues exceed $20 million a year, and the firm employs 600 people.

The Purdy brand is well-known in western Canada, but relatively unknown elsewhere. A couple of years ago Charles and Karen decided that they needed to break into some new markets if their firm had any hope of growing. They decided on Taipei, the capital of Taiwan, because the Taiwanese have a sweet tooth, and because Lei Mei How, a Taiwanese businesswoman, convinced them it would be a good idea.

Ms. How was so convinced that Purdy's Chocolates would be a hit in Taiwan that she paid for Neil Hastie, a vice-president at Purdy's, to fly to Taiwan and personally conduct some market research. Among other things, he discovered that there is a fascination with North American products in Taiwan, and a well-organized retail sector that does a good job of showcasing new products.

After hearing these positive comments, the Flavelles formed a partnership with Ms. How to set up shop in a high-end department store (Mitsukoshi) in Taipei. Purdy's began selling in October 1995, expecting first-year sales to be in the $200 000 to $250 000 range. But even that modest target wasn't reached because several unexpected roadblocks were encountered.

Purdy's discovered, for example, that getting chocolate onto store shelves in a tropical climate was a problem, particularly when the chocolate was melting in the cargo hold of a plane as it sat baking on the tarmac under the tropical sun. Hiring and managing staff from a distance was also a lot more difficult than it was close to the home base in Vancouver.

Purdy's also assumed that products that sold well to Asians in Vancouver would sell well in Taipei, but they found that was not the case. For example, ice cream dipped in chocolate and rolled in nuts wasn't nearly as popular in Taipei as it was in Vancouver.

They also discovered many "little" things that slowed them down. For example, the rectangular package that is so common for chocolate in Canada was not well received in Taipei. There, customers prefer packages that are circular or triangular, which necessitated changes in packaging.

These difficulties were serious enough that the profitability of the Asian venture was in serious doubt. The Flavelles decided they had to do something. Their solution was to sign an agreement with a distributor—Konig Foods Ltd. of Taipei. Konig arranges to have the product picked up at Purdy's factory and delivered to Konig's facility. Purdy's Chocolates now functions solely as a wholesaler and lets Konig deal with the retailers that sell Purdy's chocolate. ◆

L ike many other businesses. Purdy's is starting to adopt an international focus in its operations. Increasingly, Canadian firms will have to look beyond the domestic Canadian market in their business dealings.

By focusing on the learning objectives of this chapter, you will better understand the dynamics of international business management as well as some of the social, cultural, economic, legal, and political differences that make international trade a challenging enterprise. After reading this chapter, you should be able to:

1. Describe the rise of international business and identify the major world marketplaces.

2. Explain how different forms of *competitive advantage*, *import-export balances*, *exchange rates*, and *foreign competition* determine the ways in which countries and businesses respond to the international environment.

3. Discuss the factors involved in deciding to do business internationally and in selecting the appropriate *levels of international involvement* and *international organizational structure*.

4. Describe some of the ways in which *social*, *cultural*, *economic*, *legal*, and *political differences* act as barriers to international trade.

5. Explain how *free trade agreements* assist world trade.

6. Understand the *trade challenges* for Canadian businesses.

The Rise of International Business

globalization

The integration of markets globally.

imports

Products that are made or grown abroad and sold in Canada.

exports

Products made or grown in Canada that are sold abroad.

The total volume of world trade today is immense—around $7 trillion each year. As more and more firms engage in international business, the world economy is fast becoming a single interdependent system—a process called **globalization**. Even so, we often take for granted the diversity of goods and services available today as a result of international trade. Your television set, your shoes, and even the roast lamb on your dinner table may all be **imports**— that is, products made or grown abroad but sold in Canada. At the same time, the success of many Canadian firms depends in large part on **exports**— products made or grown domestically and shipped for sale abroad.

In this section, we examine some of the key factors that shape the global business environment. First, we identify and describe the major world marketplaces. Then we discuss some important factors that determine the ways in which both nations and their businesses respond to the international environment: the roles of different forms of *competitive advantage*, of *import-export balances*, and of *exchange rates*.

Major World Marketplaces

The contemporary world economy revolves around three major market-places: North America, the Pacific Rim, and Western Europe. But business activity is not limited to these three markets. The World Bank notes, for example, that 77 percent of the world's people live in so-called "developing" areas. Economies in those areas are expanding 5 to 6 percent annually. There are 300 million consumers in Eastern Europe and another 300 million in South America. In India alone, estimates of the size of the middle class run from 100 million to 300 million.[1]

North America

The United States dominates the North American business region. It is the single largest marketplace and enjoys the most stable and sound economy in the world. Many U.S. firms, such as General Motors and Procter & Gamble, have had successful Canadian operations for years, and Canadian firms like Northern Telecom and Alcan Aluminum are major competitors.

Mexico has also become a major manufacturing centre. Cheap labour and low transportation costs have encouraged many foreign firms to build plants in Mexico. Both Chrysler and General Motors, for instance, are building new assembly plants, as are suppliers like Rockwell International Corp. Nissan opened an engine and transmission plant in 1983 and a car-making plant in 1992. Mexican forecasters expect 200 000 workers to be in the automobile industry by 1998.

Western Europe

Europe is often divided into two regions. Western Europe, dominated by Germany, the United Kingdom, France, and Italy, has been a mature but fragmented marketplace for years. The evolution of the European Union in 1992 into a unified marketplace has further increased the importance of this marketplace. Major international firms like Unilever, Renault, Royal Dutch Shell, Michelin, Siemens, and Nestlé are all headquartered in this region.

Eastern Europe, which was until recently primarily communist, has also gained in importance, both as a marketplace and a producer. In May 1994, for example, Albania became the 197th country in which Coca-Cola is produced, as Coke opened a new $10 million bottling plant outside the capital city of Tirana. Meanwhile, Kellogg has opened a new plant in Riga, capital of the former Soviet republic of Latvia. Kellogg has also launched a vigorous campaign of television ads and in-store demonstrations to capitalize on one of the world's few remaining cereal frontiers.[2]

Foreign companies invested more than $8 billion in Poland in 1995–96, including $500 million from PepsiCo Inc. Also in 1995, Daewoo chose Poland as the centre of its new European operation, spending $1 billion for an auto plant near Warsaw.

The Pacific Rim

The Pacific Rim consists of Japan, the People's Republic of China, Thailand, Malaysia, Singapore, Indonesia, South Korea, Vietnam, Taiwan, Hong Kong, the Philippines, and Australia. Fueled by strong entries in the automobile, electronics, and banking industries, the economies of these countries grew rapidly in the 1970s and 1980s. Experts expect these countries to spend nearly $2 trillion on energy, transportation, and telecommunications by the year 2000. Today, the Pacific Rim is an important force in the world economy and a major source of competition for North American firms. Japan, led by companies like Toyota, Toshiba, and Nippon Steel, dominates the region. In addition, South Korea (with such firms as Samsung and Hyundai), Taiwan (owner of Chinese Petroleum and manufacturing home of many foreign firms), and Hong Kong (a major financial centre) are also successful players in the international economy. China, the most densely populated country in the world, continues to emerge as an important market in its own right. In fact, the International Monetary Fund concluded in 1993 that the Chinese economy is now the world's third largest, behind the U.S. and only slightly behind Japan.[3] More than 120 Canadian firms have set up offices in China and tried to cash in on its rapid growth. But most of them have found the going quite difficult. A 1996 survey of 20 Canadian firms that had invested in China showed that less than half of them were profitable.[4]

Forms of Competitive Advantage

No country can produce all the goods and services that its people need. Thus countries tend to export those things that they can produce better or less expensively than other countries. The proceeds are then used to import things that they cannot produce effectively. However, this very general principle does not fully explain why nations export and import what they do. Such decisions hinge, among other things, on whether a country enjoys an absolute or a comparative advantage in the production of different goods and services.[5]

An **absolute advantage** exists when a country can produce something more cheaply than any other country. Saudi oil and Canadian timber approximate absolute advantage, but examples of true absolute advantage are rare. A country has a **comparative advantage** in goods that it can make more cheaply or better than other goods. The United States has a comparative advantage in the computer industry because of technological sophistication. Canada has a comparative advantage in farming because of fertile land. South Korea has a comparative advantage in electronics manufacturing because of efficient operations and cheap labour.

absolute advantage

A nation's ability to produce something more cheaply or better than any other country.

comparative advantage

A nation's ability to produce some products more cheaply or better than it can others.

The Balance of Trade and the Balance of Payments

balance of trade

The difference in value between a country's total exports and its total imports.

A country's **balance of trade** is the difference in value between its total exports and its total imports. A country that exports more than it imports has a *favourable* balance of trade, or a surplus. A country that imports more than it exports has an *unfavourable* balance of trade, or a deficit.

Canada has enjoyed a favourable balance of merchandise trade since 1975 (see Figure 4.1). However, the trade balance is favourable only because Canada exports so much more to the U.S. than it imports from the U.S. Canada's trade balance with its other major trading partners (e.g., Japan, the U.K., and other EU countries) is unfavourable. Our trade balance with all remaining countries of the world taken together as a group is also unfavourable (see Table 4.1).

A recent study by the World Trade Organization (WTO) found that Canada's economic dependence on the U.S. is growing, and this trend leaves Canada vulnerable. The U.S. accounts for 80 percent of Canada's merchandise exports and two-thirds of its imports. What's worse, only 50 companies operating in Canada account for nearly half of all merchandise exports, and these companies are often U.S.-owned. Canada has too many of its eggs in one basket.[6]

Even if a country has a favourable balance of trade, it can still have an unfavourable balance of payments. A country's **balance of payments** is the

World Trade Organization

http://www.wto.org

balance of payments

The difference between money flowing into and out of a country as a result of trade and other transactions.

Table 4.1	Canadian Exports to, and Imports from, Selected Countries	
Country	**Exports to (billions)**	**Imports from (billions)**
United States	$142.4	$113.6
Japan	8.4	10.7
United Kingdom	2.8	4.4
Germany	2.4	3.5
South Korea	1.7	2.2
France	1.2	2.3
Taiwan	1.0	2.6
Mexico	0.8	3.6
Hong Kong	0.6	1.1

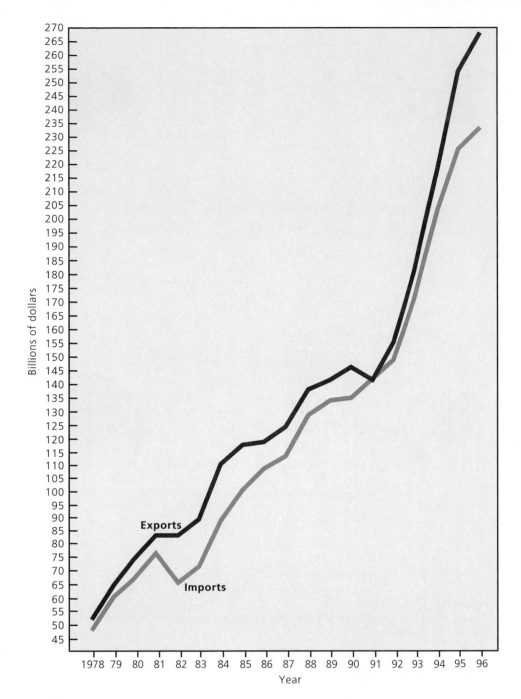

Figure 4.1
Canadian imports and exports of merchandise.

difference between money flowing into the country and money flowing out of the country as a result of trade and other transactions. An unfavourable balance means more money is flowing out than in. For Canada to have a favourable balance of payments for a given year, the total of our exports, foreign tourist spending in this country, foreign investments here, and earnings from overseas investments must be greater than the total of our imports, Canadian tourist spending overseas, our foreign aid grants, our military spending abroad, the investments made by Canadian firms abroad, and the earnings of foreigners from their investments in Canada. (See Figure 4.2.) Canada has had an unfavourable balance of payments for about the last 20 years.

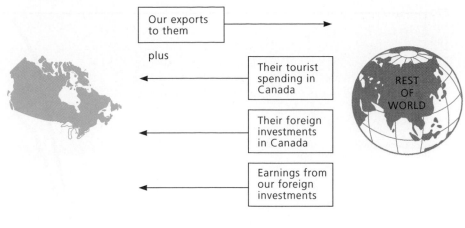

Total of above flows must be greater than

Figure 4.2
Requirements for Canada to have a favourable balance of payments. (The arrows indicate the direction of the flow.)

The Rate of Exchange

foreign exchange rate
The ratio of one currency to another.

The **foreign exchange rate** is the ratio of one currency to another; it tells how much a unit of one currency is worth in terms of a unit of another currency. Canada's exchange rate has a significant effect on imports and exports. If the exchange rate decreases (that is, the value of the Canadian dollar falls in relation to other currencies), two things happen: our exports become less expensive to other countries, so they will want to buy more of what we produce; and prices of the goods other countries export to Canada will become more expensive, so we will buy less of them. If the exchange rate increases (that is, the value of the Canadian dollar increases), two things also happen: our exports become more expensive to other countries, so they will want to buy less of what we produce; and prices of the goods other countries export to Canada will become less expensive, so we will buy more of them.

During the last 20 years, the value of the Canadian dollar has fluctuated a great deal in relation to the currencies of other countries, including the U.S. Since the U.S. is our biggest trading partner, the fluctuations of our currency compared to the U.S. dollar have a big impact on our economy. During the mid-1970s, the Canadian dollar was worth slightly more than the U.S. dollar. By the late 1970s, however, it started on a steady downward path that eventually led to a value of only $0.69 U.S. By 1990, it had risen substantially, and was worth about $0.89 U.S. In early 1998, the dollar declined to about $0.68 U.S. again, but when the Bank of Canada raised interest rates, the dollar moved up to nearly $0.71 U.S.

The fluctuations in the Canadian dollar are small compared to fluctuations that other countries have experienced (see the box "A Tale of Three Currencies"). In 1997 alone, the value of the Malaysian *ringgit*, the Philippine *peso*, and the Thai *baht* dropped sharply as concerns were expressed about the sustainability of those countries' economies.

International Report

A Tale of Three Currencies

Canadians pay a lot of attention to the fluctuations of the Canadian dollar against the U.S. dollar. But these fluctuations are minor compared to the changes in value that have occurred in the Czech *koruna*, the Russian *ruble*, and the Mexican *peso*.

The Czech Republic. Until recently, the Czech Republic has been a favoured place for investment in the eyes of Westerners. But in 1997, its image became tarnished because of poor economic performance and political wrangling. Economic growth fell far short of forecasts, and the country ran a large trade deficit with some of its trading partners. Industrial production also dropped. Scandals in Czech financial markets, bank failures, and looted investment funds have all worked together to cause a sharp decline in the value of the Czech koruna.

At the beginning of 1997, each koruna was worth about 3.75 cents U.S. Faced with heavy pressure from currency speculators, the Czech central bank gave up supporting the koruna. When the bank made this decision, the koruna had already declined to about 3.25 cents; in the next month it declined even further to 3.0 cents. The total loss in 1997 alone was nearly 25 percent of the value of the currency. The drop in the value of the koruna led to a run on banks and currency exchanges, as the people of the Czech Republic tried to get their hands on more stable Western currencies.

Russia. During the many years of the communist regime, the value of the ruble was artificially controlled by the government. Although the ruble was used by Russians in everyday business activities, no one outside Russia wanted rubles because the currency was seen as worthless. Since the fall of communism, the weaknesses in the Russian currency have come to light. In 1992, the ruble was trading at about 1000 to a U.S. dollar. By the end of 1994, it had declined to about 3000 to a U.S. dollar. Then the real decline started. In just one day, the value of the ruble fell 27 percent, going from 3081 to 3926 to the U.S. dollar. In six weeks, the ruble lost 78 percent of its value.

These changes have had a big impact on Russian consumers. In the time it took one shopper to pick out a telephone and take it to the checkout, its price had increased from 75 000 to 100 000 rubles. On Moscow's subway, a ride that cost five one-hundredths of a ruble for the last 40 years has now increased to 250 rubles.

To put all this in perspective, a McDonald's hamburger now costs about 4900 rubles, up from 3 rubles when the first McDonald's restaurant opened in 1990. That is the equivalent of a hamburger in Canada increasing from $2.00 in 1990 to well over $2000 in 1994.

Mexico. In early 1994, it took about 3.1 pesos to purchase a U.S. dollar. During the first 11 months of 1994, the peso gradually declined in value to about 3.7 to the dollar. The decline was caused by a variety of things, including excessive borrowing by Mexico in foreign markets, increasing interest rates, and a rebel uprising in a southern province.

By December 1994, speculative pressure on the peso had become so great that the Mexican government reversed its long-standing policy of supporting the peso. The value of the peso immediately dropped about 13 percent in relation to the U.S. dollar. In 1995, the value declined even further; it now took 7.7 pesos to buy one U.S. dollar. At this point, the value of the peso had declined by more than 50 percent in just one year. This would be the equivalent of the Canadian dollar dropping from $0.72 U.S. to $0.36 U.S.

In an attempt to reverse the decline, the Mexican government announced an austerity plan that involved big tax increases and reductions in government spending. This plan is necessary to restore the value of the peso, but it will inflict hardship on Mexican workers because prices will rise. The price of gasoline, for example, has increased by 35 percent, and electricity rates have risen 20 percent. Many small business owners have lost almost all their possessions since the austerity plan was introduced. Leaders of El Barzon (a political movement that has sprung up in response to the debt crisis) fear that unless the financial system is reformed, the middle class in Mexico will be eliminated. Until the currency fluctuations are brought under control, the climate for foreign investment will be uncertain in Mexico.

International Business Management

Wherever it is located, the success of any firm depends largely on how well it is managed. International business is so challenging because the basic management responsibilities—planning, organizing, directing, and controlling—are much more difficult to carry out when a business operates in several markets scattered around the globe.

It is not surprising, then, that business abounds with legends about managers who made foolish decisions because they failed to familiarize themselves with the foreign markets in which they hoped to do business. Estée Lauder, for example, launched an Italian cosmetics line with a picture of a model holding some flowers. The approach was conventional—and seemingly harmless. Unfortunately, the flowers chosen were the kind traditionally used at Italian funerals—hardly the image that Lauder intended to communicate.

Planning difficulties are compounded by difficulties in organizing, directing, and controlling. An organizational structure that works well in one country may fail in others. Management techniques that lead to high worker productivity in Canada may offend workers in Japan or the United Kingdom. Accounting and other control systems that are well-developed in Canada may be unsophisticated or even nonexistent in developing nations. The "internationalization" of a business also has an impact on individual managers, as the box "The Pleasures and Perils of International Business" shows.

International Report

The Pleasures and Perils of International Business

John Aliberti is a middle manager at Union Switch & Signal in Pittsburgh, Pennsylvania. He handles the nuts and bolts of updating computerized rail systems for American cities. Aliberti was born and raised in Pittsburgh and studied computer science at the University of Pennsylvania. After university, he was hired by Union Switch and moved steadily up the ranks. But he didn't feel his job was particularly exciting.

In 1992, Union Switch needed someone to go to China to drum up business. Aliberti volunteered because he had technical expertise in the area required by the Chinese. By his second trip to China, he was hooked on his new work. In 1996, he made 10 trips to China, where he is treated with respect bordering on awe. He loves this part of his new job.

When in Beijing, Aliberti stays at the plush Shangri-La Hotel. The clerks on the executive floor know him well, since he spent nearly six months there in 1996. On this day, he is flying to Shanghai to negotiate a contract his company has won for the city's new subway system. On the way, he reminisces about a previous trip to Nanchang, where Union was building a rail yard. When he arrived, the Chinese welcomed him with a large banner at the factory gate that said "Welcome, Foreign Expert John Aliberti." Once in Shanghai, Aliberti is picked up by a

chauffeur-driven limousine and taken to a meeting with Chinese railway officials. When he enters the room, they rise respectfully. They say they have been waiting two days for him because they can't go ahead without him. After the negotiations are successfully concluded, the Chinese put on a 10-course banquet for him.

Aliberti has tremendous status and power in China. In Pittsburgh, his job is two rungs below the vice-president, but in China he acts like a president. That turns him on. So does the knowledge that the rail systems his company is installing will dramatically improve the standard of living of the Chinese people. He feels that the same changes would hardly be noticed in Pittsburgh because the facilities are already so good there.

As more and more companies get involved in international business, managers like John Aliberti have tremendous opportunities for advancement in their companies. But opportunities are only part of the equation. As Aliberti's star rises at work, his ties to his family are becoming strained. His wife Cindy hates his trips to China because he is often gone at key family times: July 4, his daughter's birthday, Thanksgiving, just to name a few. Aliberti agrees, but he is drawn by the ground-breaking work he is doing in China. He sees himself as a pioneer, and that is exciting.

"Going International"

The world economy is becoming globalized, and more and more firms are conducting international operations. This route, however, is not appropriate for every company. For example, companies that buy and sell fresh produce and fish may find it most profitable to confine their activities to a limited geographic area because storage and transport costs may be too high to make international operations worthwhile.

As Figure 4.3 shows, several factors enter into the decision to go international. One overriding factor is the business climate of other nations. Even experienced firms have encountered cultural, legal, and economic roadblocks. (These problems are discussed in more detail later in this chapter.) In considering international expansion, a company should also consider at least two other questions: Is there a demand for its products abroad? If so, must those products be adapted for international consumption?

Gauging International Demand

Products that are seen as vital in one country may be useless in another. Snowmobiles, for example, are not only popular for transportation and recreation in Canada and the northern United States, but actually revolutionized reindeer herding in Lapland. But there would be no demand at all for this product in Central America. Although this is an extreme example, the point is quite basic to the decision to go international: namely, that foreign demand for a company's product may be greater than, the same as, or weaker than domestic demand.

Adapting to Customer Needs

If there is international demand for its product, a firm must consider whether and how to adapt that product to meet the special demands of foreign customers. For example, in Mexico, GM's Chevrolet division sells a Spanish-made

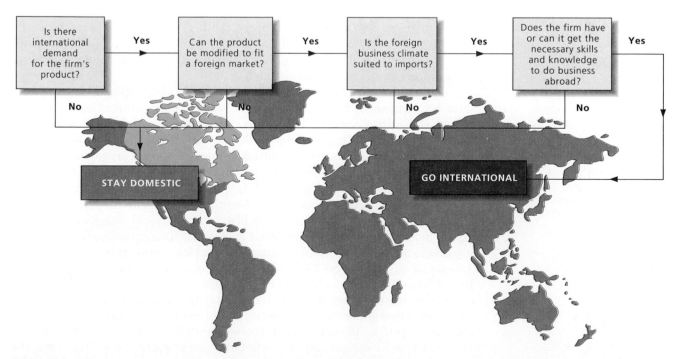

Figure 4.3
The decision to go international.

subcompact called the Joy. Chevy prices the Joy at $1500 to $2000 more than Volkswagen's old-fashioned Beetle, which still sells well in Mexico. GM has upped its price because it has found that in a country where 60 percent of the population is under 25, there is a huge market of younger buyers who will pay for stylish, more powerful vehicles. In the Czech Republic, however, GM markets the same car—known as the Opel Corsa—to potential buyers in their 30s. Here, says GM's director of sales for Central Europe, "younger buyers can't even afford bicycles."[7]

Levels of Involvement in International Business

Canadian business firms are involved in international business at many different levels, including importing and exporting goods and services, licensing agreements, establishing foreign subsidiaries, product mandating, strategic alliances, and as multinational firms. Each approach is discussed briefly in the following sections.

Exporting Goods and Services

Macmillan-Bloedel
http://www.mb-mdf.com

In 1996, almost 40 percent of all goods and services produced in Canada were exported. Canada ranks first among the G7 countries in the proportion of its production that is exported.[8] McCain Foods, for example, has become a formidable presence in Europe. It holds 75 percent of the "oven fries" market in Germany, and dominates the frozen french fry market in France and England.[9] MacMillan-Bloedel and Abitibi-Price sell newsprint and other forest products around the world. Small firms also export products and services. Seagull Pewter & Silversmiths Ltd., Magic Pantry Foods, and Lovat Tunnel Equipment Inc. have all recently won Canada Export Awards. Sabian Cymbals sells 90 percent of its products to 80 different countries outside Canada. Electrovert Ltd. does 95 percent of its business outside Canada. Other companies that export a high proportion of their output include Repap B.C. Inc. (95 percent), Pratt & Whitney Canada (86 percent), Noranda Inc. (86 percent), and General Motors of Canada (85 percent). These companies have little in common with firms that concentrate on the Canadian market and then unload what is left somewhere else.[10]

A Canadian firm may not even have to send salespeople to foreign countries because some foreign firms have set up international procurement offices (IPOs) in Canada. These IPOs buy Canadian parts and incorporate them into products they make and sell abroad. Horn Plastics Ltd. supplies plastic parts to IBM and Hewlett-Packard under an IPO arrangement.[11]

independent agent

A foreign individual, or organization, who agrees to represent an exporter's interests in foreign markets.

An **independent agent** is a foreign individual or organization that agrees to represent an exporter's interests in foreign markets. Independent agents often sell the exporter's products, collect payment, and make sure that customers are satisfied. They often represent several firms at once and usually do not specialize in any one product or market. Levi Strauss uses agents to market clothing products in many smaller countries in Africa, Asia, and South America. As a result of the Canada–Chile free trade agreement, the president of Ranpro Inc., a Canadian manufacturer of rainwear for commercial fishing companies, decided to use an agent in Chile to sell his company's products.[12]

Exporting increases sales volume and generates a flow of funds that can lead to profits. Exporting also reduces the unit cost of production because of the increased volume, allows for greater use of plant capacity, lessens the dependence on a single traditional market, offers some protection against a downturn in Canadian sales, and provides an opportunity to gain a knowledge of and experience with other products and potential markets. But there are also disadvantages to exporting, such as the expense required to develop export markets, the modifications to products necessary to meet government regulations, the acquisition of further financing, and the obligation to learn about the customs, culture, language, local standards, and government regulations of the new customers.

Improvements can be made in Canada's export record. Canada sells only 9 percent of its exports to developing countries. We export eight times as much to the U.S. alone as we do to *all* developing countries combined. In every developing area of the world, Canada ranks last among the G7 countries in exports.[13] Table 4.2 lists the top 10 importing and exporting countries of the world.

Importing Goods and Services

While many enterprises sell Canadian goods and services abroad, others are involved in buying goods and services in foreign countries for resale to Canadians. For example, Gendis Inc., a large Winnipeg-based corporation, distributes Sony electronic products throughout Canada. Locally, most large shopping malls have a retail outlet selling wicker goods, brass objects, carpeting, and similar products imported from India and various Far Eastern

Table 4.2   The Top 10 Importing and Exporting Countries

	Exporting		
Rank	**Country**	**$ Value (billions)**	**Share of World's Exports**
1	United States	584	11.7
2	Germany	511	10.2
3	Japan	443	8.8
4	France	286	5.7
5	Britain	242	4.8
6	Italy	231	4.6
7	Netherlands	195	3.9
8	**Canada**	**192**	**3.8**
9	Hong Kong	173	3.5
10	China	148	3.0
	All Others	2004	40.0
	Total	5009	100.0

	Importing		
Rank	**Country**	**$ Value (billions)**	**Share of World's Imports**
1	United States	771	15.6
2	Germany	448	9.1
3	Japan	335	6.8
4	France	275	5.6
5	Britain	265	5.4
6	Italy	204	4.1
7	Hong Kong	192	3.9
8	Netherlands	176	3.6
9	**Canada**	**168**	**3.4**
10	China	129	2.6
	All Others	1966	39.9
	Total	4929	100.0

countries. Canadian importing businesses employ buyers who travel around the world seeking out goods that can be sold here. Foreign suppliers might have salespeople or representatives based in Canada to market these products.

Licensing Agreements

licensing agreement
An agreement by an owner of a process or product to allow another business to produce, distribute, or market it for a fee or royalty.

Licensing agreements exist when the owner of a product or process allows another business to produce, distribute, or market the product or process for a fee or royalty. Such agreements can mean that a Canadian enterprise licenses another enterprise in a foreign country to produce, distribute, or market its products in that area. Or the agreement could work the other way, with foreign enterprises allowing Canadian firms to produce, distribute, and market their products in Canada. For example, Can-Eng Manufacturing, Canada's largest supplier of industrial furnaces, exports its furnaces under licensing agreements with Japan, Brazil, Germany, Korea, Taiwan, and Mexico.[14]

Licensing agreements are used when a company does not wish to establish a plant or marketing network in another country. They avoid the need to manage operations in foreign countries, and allow the owner of the product or process to concentrate on further technological research and development, financed, in part, from the royalties received.

Establishing Subsidiaries

If the volume of business to be conducted is large and ongoing, Canadian enterprises may choose to establish subsidiary or branch operations in foreign countries through which they can market goods and services. Other reasons for establishing a subsidiary are that a foreign government requires it, or it may increase sales because locally operated branches can respond more quickly to delivery and service requests. Sometimes branches are established by forming an operation where none previously existed. Another approach is to buy a business in the foreign country. Of course, this process works both ways, with foreign enterprises doing the same in Canada. The establishment of subsidiaries can lead to the sensitive issue of foreign ownership and the analysis of its benefits and drawbacks.

Product Mandating

When a business operates branches, plants, or subsidiaries in several countries, it may assign to one plant or subsidiary the responsibility for researching, developing, manufacturing, and marketing one product or line of products. This is known as **world product mandating**.

world product mandating
The assignment by a multinational of a product responsibility to a particular branch.

Northern Telecom
http://www.nortel.com

At Northern Telecom, for example, the company's Belleville, Ontario, plant was chosen as the one to produce a new business telephone system designed for the world market. The plant won out in a competition with two other Northern Telecom plants, one in Calgary and one in Santa Clara, California. The Belleville plant also has global mandates for several other product lines.

About 100 Canadian-based subsidiaries are now involved in some form of world product mandates. Some examples are the following:

- Pratt & Whitney Canada produces small gas turbine engines.

- Black and Decker Canada makes orbital sanders, the "Workmate" work bench, the "Workwheel" power stripper, and the "Workhorse" scaffold.

- Westinghouse Canada produces steam and gas turbines, airport lighting, and digital-video converters and displays.

Strategic Alliances

Strategic alliances involve two or more enterprises cooperating in researching, developing, manufacturing, or marketing a product. The relationship is more subtle than the usual supplier-customer relations, yet less formal than ownership. These relationships, which have become more popular in the last decade, take many forms and are also called cooperative strategies, joint ventures, strategic networks, and strategic partners. There are various reasons for entering into a strategic alliance, such as gaining access to new markets or customers, acquiring advanced or new technology, sharing the costs and risks of new ventures, obtaining financing to supplement a firm's debt capacity, and sharing production facilities to avoid wasteful duplication. Northern Telecom, for example, has strategic alliances with several firms, including Daewoo (Korea), Tong Guang (China), and Ascom Hasler (Switzerland).

strategic alliance
Two or more enterprises that cooperate in researching, developing, manufacturing, or marketing a product.

Multinational Firms

Multinational firms do not ordinarily think of themselves as having specific domestic and international divisions. Rather, planning and decision making are geared to international markets. Headquarters locations are almost irrelevant. Northern Telecom, Royal Dutch Shell, Nestlé, IBM, and Ford are well-known multinational firms.

multinational firm
Controls assets, factories, mines, sales offices, and affiliates in two or more foreign countries.

The British firm Imperial Chemical Industries (ICI) is one of the 50 largest industrial firms in the world, with nine major business units, four of which are headquartered outside of Britain. Until 1982, all 16 of its directors were British; today, the board includes two Americans, a Canadian, a Japanese, and a German. ICI has major operations in 25 different countries, and rather than managing businesses that are located and active within given countries, ICI managers are now in charge of business units that compete around the world.[15]

Fewer than 5000 of Nestlé Food Corp.'s 200 000-plus employees are stationed in its home country of Switzerland. The giant food-products company has manufacturing facilities in 50 countries and owns suppliers and distributors around the globe. Nestlé markets products worldwide by taking advantage of all possible levels of international involvement. In 1991, for instance, Nestlé entered a strategic alliance with the U.S. food-products company General Mills to create a new company called Cereal Partners Worldwide.

Northern Telecom's manufacturing plan in Mexico. Note the Canadian, Mexican and U.S. flags on the back wall of the plant.

General Mills initiated the joint venture with a European partner in an effort to cut into Kellogg's commanding lead in ready-to-eat cereals. For its part, Nestlé sees the venture as an opportunity to affirm its leadership in the European food industry.

Multinational firms have encouraged economic growth in many areas of the world by providing financing, technological expertise, and the managerial know-how to operate industry. Financing is not always available locally, and the multinational firms can provide funds from other sectors of their operations. They bring technological expertise to less developed areas. The management capabilities of multinational firms are also used to organize and operate business enterprises in parts of the world other than the corporation's home country. By facilitating international trade and the transfer of capital, technology, and managerial know-how, multinational firms further international economic development and cooperation.

Managers of multinational corporations face many challenges, but the greatest is the need to respond to criticisms. These criticisms include the multinational firm's alleged nonallegiance to the host country, transferring profits from the host country, failing to promote research and development activities, exporting jobs by not producing finished products, and not hiring local personnel.

Barriers to Trade

Whether a business is selling to just a few foreign markets or is a true multinational, a number of differences between countries will affect its international operations. How a firm responds to social, economic, and political issues will go a long way towards determining its success.

Social and Cultural Differences

Any firm involved in international business needs to understand something about the society and culture of the countries in which it plans to operate. Unless a firm understands these cultural differences—either itself or by acquiring a partner that does—it will probably not be successful in its international business activities.

Some differences are relatively obvious. Language barriers can cause inappropriate naming of products. In addition, the physical stature of people in different countries can make a difference. For example, the Japanese and French are slimmer and shorter on average than Canadians, an important consideration for firms that intend to sell clothes in these markets.

Differences in the average ages of the local population can also have an impact on product development and marketing. Countries with growing populations tend to have a high percentage of young people. Thus, electronics and fashionable clothing would likely do well. Countries with stable or declining populations tend to have more old people. Generic pharmaceuticals might be more successful in such markets.

In addition to such obvious differences, a wide range of subtle value differences can have an important impact on international business. For example, many Europeans shop daily. To Canadians used to weekly trips to the supermarket, the European pattern may seem like a waste of time. But for Europeans, shopping is not just "buying food." It is also meeting friends, exchanging political views, gossiping, and socializing. The box "Faux Pas in Foreign Lands" describes how North Americans can make embarrassing mistakes in both business and politics when they are in a foreign country.

International Report

Faux Pas in Foreign Lands

Politicians and business executives in both Canada and the U.S. frequently find it necessary to go to a foreign country to transact business. On occasion, these people fail to "do their homework" and do not learn enough about the country to which they are travelling. Then they do something that creates embarrassment.

When U.S. president Bill Clinton travelled to Russia in 1994, his trip was generally a hit with the media and the folks back home. But at the end of one town-hall style meeting, a beaming Clinton gave the audience the North American high-sign, a circle made with the thumb and forefinger. Oops! That gesture would likely have started a brawl in a Moscow pub, because in Russia it is the equivalent of our middle finger salute. Former U.S. president George Bush had the same problem when he visited Australia a few years earlier. There, he gave a "thumbs-up" sign, which unfortunately is the Australian equivalent of the same middle finger salute.

These gaffes are not limited to visiting politicians. Business executives also have to be aware of local etiquette and how this impacts business negotiations. Consider these examples:

- Crossing your legs in a business meeting in Saudi Arabia is considered an insult, because when you do that you are showing the sole of your foot; this is an insult to the other people in the room.
- In Portugal, it is considered rude to discuss business during dinner.
- In Taiwan, tapping your fingers on the table is a sign of appreciation for a meal.

Because the difference between proper and improper behaviour can be so subtle, some companies hire local individuals to make sure that negotiations go smoothly. One such company is Dominion Bridge, which successfully concluded a deal to supply a subway/light rail system, a hydroelectric power station, and a cement plant in Chengdu, China. Interestingly, the man that Dominion hired also was working for the city of Chengdu. This would be considered a blatant conflict of interest in Canada, but not in China.

Business negotiation in China is a finely tuned waltz of etiquette and politics, and if everything doesn't go just right, the deal will fall flat. It is therefore important to have someone orchestrating all of the activities leading up to the signing of the deal. The president of Dominion Bridge says that it would take 100 years for a Canadian to develop the subtle understanding of the Chinese culture that their Chinese business agent has.

What implications does this kind of shopping have for firms selling in European markets? First, those who go shopping each day do not need the large refrigerators and freezers common in North America. Second, the large supermarkets one sees in Canada are not an appropriate retail outlet in Europe. Finally, the kinds of food Europeans buy differ from those Canadians buy. While in Canada prepared and frozen foods are important, Europeans often prefer to buy fresh ingredients to do their own food preparation "from scratch." These differences are gradually disappearing, however, so firms need to be on the lookout for future opportunities as they emerge. The box "The Cavalier Attitude Towards Murky Tea" gives examples of companies that had problems in foreign markets.

Economic Differences

Although cultural differences are often subtle, economic differences can be fairly pronounced. In dealing with economies like those of France and Sweden, for example, firms must be aware of when—and to what extent—the government is involved in a given industry. The French government, for example, is heavily involved in all aspects of airplane design and manufacturing.

Similarly, a foreign firm doing business in a planned economy must understand the unfamiliar relationship of government to business, including a host of idiosyncratic practices. General Motors, which entered a $100 million joint venture to build pickup trucks in China, found itself faced with an

International Report

The Cavalier Attitude Towards Murky Tea

Quaker Oats and General Motors share a common set of woes. Recently, both companies introduced home-grown American products into the Japanese market, and both encountered cultural and business turbulence that turned the trip abroad into an unpleasantly bumpy ride.

For Quaker Oats, the global marketing debacle involved its Snapple Beverage division, which manufactures fruit and iced-tea flavoured beverages. (As a result of marketing and distribution features at home and abroad, Quaker sold Snapple in 1997—for $1.4 billion *less* than it had paid for it three years earlier.) Although Snapple's arrival in Japan was heralded by ads declaring that "The Snapple Phenomenon Has Landed," Japanese consumers disliked Snapple's sweet fruit juice flavourings and the trade mark bits of fruit and granules of tea that Snapple likes to leave in its bottles. "The iced tea," volunteered at least one Japanese taster, "was murky looking."

Quaker's miscalculation of Japanese tastes, coupled with its refusal to adapt Snapple's formula and a poorly conceived marketing program, resulted in a dramatic drop in sales from 2.4 million bottles a month just after introduction in 1995 to a mere 120 000 bottles a month in 1996. Quaker decided to cut its losses in 1996 and stopped shipping Snapple to Japan. "Japan," eulogized the *Wall Street Journal*, "has given Snapple the raspberry."

General Motors also had high hopes when the Chevrolet Cavalier hit Japanese showrooms early in 1996—all decked out with a Toyota nameplate. The Cavalier was the first American car that Toyota had agreed to market on Japanese soil, and it was heralded by both companies as a model of U.S.–Japanese cooperation. The initial reaction of Japanese consumers was good, as it had been for Snapple. Within three months, sales reached the monthly goal of 1667 vehicles. By May, however, sales had dropped to just 472 cars a month.

What went wrong? Problems began popping up when GM was forced to make 150 changes to meet the requirements of the Japanese market. Some changes—such as moving the gas pedal forward—were needed because Japanese drivers are shorter than Americans. Other changes—such as placing the steering column on the right—were obviously more fundamental. Still others—such as covering the steering wheel and handbreak with leather—were merely attempts to satisfy finicky buyers. Whatever the reasons, costly redesigns left GM frustrated and complaining that unnecessary expenses were making competition inside Japan all but impossible. Meanwhile, Toyota regarded GM's stance as mere resistance to change.

Toyota also found the Cavalier to be plagued by an alarmingly high defect rate. According to some reports, as many as nine out of ten cars needed at least one repair before being accepted for sale in Japan. "Their vehicle defect rate is about 50 times that of Japanese vehicles," explained Naoki Yamaguchi, president of a regional Japanese dealer network. "If they would just put a little more effort into production control...." GM denies the severity of Cavalier's quality problem and points instead to what it says is a well-known Japanese strategy, namely, keeping foreign goods out of the home market by finding excessive fault with them.

Clearly, both Quaker Oats and General Motors learned the hard way that marketing American goods in Japan is far from easy. Although both companies undoubtedly expected cultural and business problems, neither was prepared for what it got. Unfortunately, in the opinion of some analysts, both marketing ventures may have been doomed from the start.

economic system that favoured state-owned companies over foreign investors. So, while its Chinese suppliers passed on inflation-based price increases for steel and energy, GM could not in turn pass increases on to Chinese consumers. With subsidized state-owned automakers charging considerably less per truck, GM had no choice but to hold its own prices—and lose money on each sale.

Despite such problems, however, not all companies have had entirely negative experiences. For example, when Motorola opened a factory in China to manufacture paging devices, it planned to export most of the pagers because it forecasted limited internal demand. In a pleasant surprise, Motorola was forced to reassess the Chinese market after repeatedly selling out its weekly output of 10 000 units. This experience helped convince Motorola to build a $120 million plant in the northern port city of Tianjin to manufacture pagers, simple integrated circuits, and cellular phones. As part of the largest manufacturing venture in Canada, it will also involve Chinese technicians in the production process. Chinese designers and engineers will play key roles in creating an operation that integrates manufacturing, sales, research, and development.

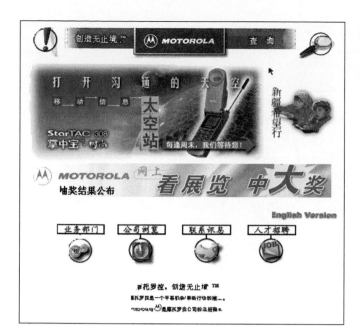

An advertisement for a Motorola paging device. Motorola hopes that advertisements like this one will help it to continue to exceed its sales goals for paging devices in China.

Legal and Political Differences

Closely linked to the structure of the economic systems in different countries are the legal and political issues that confront businesses as they try to expand internationally. These issues include tariffs and quotas, local-content laws, and business-practice laws. An awareness of differences in these areas can be crucial to a business's success.

Quotas, Tariffs, and Subsidies

Even free-market economies often use some form of quota and/or tariff that affects the prices and quantities of foreign-made products in those nations. A **quota** restricts the total number of certain products that can be imported into a country. It indirectly raises the prices of those imports by reducing their supply.

The ultimate form of quota is an **embargo**: a government order forbidding exportation and/or importation of a particular product—or even all the products—of a particular country. For example, many countries control bacteria and disease by banning certain plants and agricultural products.

In contrast, a **tariff** is a tax charged on imported products. Tariffs directly affect the prices of products, effectively raising the price of imports to consumers who must pay not only for the products but also for the tariff. Tariffs may take either of two forms. A **revenue tariff** is imposed strictly to raise money for the government. But most tariffs in effect today are **protectionist tariffs** meant to discourage the import of a particular product.

Governments impose quotas and tariffs for a wide variety of reasons. For example, the U.S. government restricts the number of Japanese automobiles that can be imported into that country. Italy imposes high tariffs on imported electronic goods. Consequently, Sony Walkmans cost almost $150, and CD players are prohibitively expensive. Canada also imposes tariffs on many imported goods.

The duties that Canadians must pay to Canada Customs after shopping in the U.S. yield revenue for the federal government and may also deter Canadians from buying some goods in the U.S. But if prices are low enough in the U.S., consumers will shop there. In the late 1980s, price differentials became so great that cross-border shopping increased dramatically. Canadian retailers lowered prices in response. When Cineplex Odeon reduced general

quota
A restriction by one nation on the total number of products of a certain type that can be imported from another nation.

embargo
A government order forbidding exportation and/or importation of a particular product.

tariff
A tax levied on imported products.

revenue tariff
A tariff imposed solely to raise money for the government that imposes it.

protectionist tariff
A tariff imposed at least in part to discourage imports of a particular product.

A Quebec customs official seizing illegal butter-coloured margarine. The dairy industry in Quebec has been successful in maintaining the legislation that makes it illegal to make margarine the same colour as butter.

admission prices, attendance went up substantially. And Bata Shoes announced in 1991 that it would match any U.S. price on a comparable brand.[16]

subsidy

A government payment to help domestic business compete with foreign firms.

A **subsidy** is a government payment to help a domestic business compete with foreign firms. Many European governments subsidize farmers to help them compete with U.S. grain imports. The U.S. argues that the Canadian government is actually subsidizing Canadian lumber companies by charging them unusually low fees to cut timber in certain areas.

protectionism

Protecting domestic business at the expense of free market competition.

Protectionism—the practice of protecting domestic business at the expense of free market competition—has both advocates and critics. Supporters argue that tariffs and quotas protect domestic firms and jobs. In particular, they protect new industries until they are truly able to compete internationally. Some claim that, since other nations have such measures, so must we. Still others justify protectionism in the name of national security. They argue that a nation must be able to produce goods needed for its survival in the event of war and that advanced technology should not be sold to potential enemies.

But opponents of protectionism are equally vocal. They note that protectionism reduces competition and drives up prices to consumers. They cite it as a cause of friction between nations. They maintain that, while jobs in some industries would be lost if protectionism ceased, jobs in other industries would expand if all countries abolished tariffs and quotas.

Local-Content Laws

local-content laws

Laws requiring that products sold in a particular country be at least partly made in that country.

A country can affect how a foreign firm does business there by enacting local-content laws. **Local-content laws** require that products sold in a particular country be at least partly made in that country. These laws typically mean that firms seeking to do business in a country must either invest directly in that country or have a joint-venture partner from that country. In this way, some of the profits from doing business in a foreign country are shared with the people who live there.

Many countries have local-content laws. In a fairly extreme case, Venezuela forbids the import of any product if a like product is made in Venezuela. Even when an item is not made in Venezuela, many companies choose to begin making their product in Venezuela both to drive out competitors and to prevent being forced out by local firms.

Local-content laws may even exist within a country; when they do, they act just like trade barriers. In Canada, for example, a low bid on a bridge in British Columbia was rejected because the company that made the bid was from Alberta. The job was given to a B.C. company. A New Brunswick window manufacturer lost a contract in Nova Scotia despite having made the lowest bid; the job went to a Nova Scotia company. Recognizing that these inter-provincial barriers are not helping Canada's international competitiveness, the federal government has committed itself to removing such barriers.

Business-Practice Laws

A final influence on how a company does business abroad stems from laws both abroad and in the firm's home nation. Sometimes, what is legal—and even accepted—business practice in one country is illegal in another. For example, in some countries it is legal to obtain business by paying bribes to government officials.

Transparency International, an organization devoted to stamping out global corruption, says that widespread bribery is devastating to developing countries. And the International Monetary Fund refused to lend money to Kenya until the government cleaned up its act.[17] In an attempt to create fairer competition among multinational companies, ministers from 29 member countries of the Organization for Economic Cooperation and Development (OECD) agreed in 1997 to criminalize bribery of foreign public officials.[18]

The formation of **cartels**—an association of producers whose purpose is to control supply and prices—gave the oil-producing countries belonging to the Organization of Petroleum Exporting Countries (OPEC) a great deal of power in the 1970s and 1980s. In 1994, the major aluminum producing countries, including Canada, worked out a deal to curb world production in an attempt to raise prices.[19] And in 1997, the 14-nation Association of Coffee Producing Countries (ACPC) agreed to extend their cartel-style export quotas to ensure that prices stayed up.[20] The diamond and shipping cartels have also been successful in keeping the prices they charge artificially high.[21]

But cartels have historically not been very effective. In the 1970s, Canadian uranium producers banded together to restrict supply, but the cartel was challenged in U.S. courts and defeated. The power of OPEC has declined in the 1990s because of internal dissension in that cartel. The only effective cartel at present is in diamonds.

Many countries forbid **dumping**—selling a product abroad for less than the comparable price charged at home. Antidumping legislation typically views dumping as occurring if

- products are being priced at "less than fair value," or

- the result unfairly harms domestic industry.

In 1997, the Canadian International Trade Tribunal renewed antidumping duties on bicycle imports from Taiwan and China. Canadian manufacturers argued that the Canadian industry was being damaged by cheap foreign bicycles, and that China and Taiwan would continue to "dump" bicycles on the Canadian market if the duties were not continued.[22]

cartel
Any association of producers whose purpose is to control supply of and prices for a given product.

dumping
Selling a product for less abroad than in the producing nation; illegal in Canada.

Overcoming Barriers to Trade

Despite the barriers described so far, world trade is flourishing. A number of world organizations and treaties have as their primary reason for being the promotion of international business.

Trade Agreements

Virtually every nation in the world has formal treaties with other nations regarding trade. One of the largest such treaties, the **General Agreement on Tariffs and Trade (GATT)**, was signed shortly after the end of the Second World War. But while the 92 countries that have signed GATT have agreed to

General Agreement on Tariffs and Trade (GATT)
An international trade accord in which the 92 signatories agreed to reduce tariffs; often ignored by signatories.

reduce taxes on imported goods to 5 percent, not all have complied. One of the worst offenders is the United States.

Other GATT signatories who often do not live up to the terms of this treaty include the members of the **European Union (EU).** The EU includes most Western European nations, most notably Belgium, Denmark, France, Greece, Ireland, Italy, Luxembourg, the Netherlands, the United Kingdom, and Germany. These nations continue to place quotas and high tariffs on goods imported from nonmember nations. But they have eliminated most quotas and set uniform tariff levels on products imported and exported within their group, encouraging intracontinental trade. In 1992, virtually all internal trade barriers were eliminated, making Western Europe the largest free marketplace in the world.

On January 1, 1995, the World Trade Organization (WTO) came into existence as the successor to GATT (often humorously referred to as the General Agreement to Talk and Talk). The WTO will oversee a one third reduction in import duties on thousands of products that are traded between countries. The reductions will be phased in over the next few years. Canada, the U.S., and the European Union are founding members of the WTO.[23]

Unlike GATT, the WTO's decisions are binding, and many people feared that it would make sweeping decisions and boss countries around. But the WTO is off to a slow start. It has not been very successful in toppling global barriers to trade in three critical areas—world financial services, telecommunications, and maritime markets—because political leaders from various countries are fearful of the consequences of freer trade.[24]

The Canada–U.S. Free Trade Agreement

On January 1, 1989, the far-reaching **Canada–U.S. Free Trade Agreement (FTA)** came into effect. The FTA has as its goal the elimination over time of tariffs on products and services that move between the two countries. By January 1, 1998, tariffs were eliminated on almost all goods and services traded between Canada and the U.S.

The FTA is the culmination of a long series of trade agreements made with the U.S. over the last 100 years. The first trade agreement was signed in 1854, and in 1935 a "most favoured nation" agreement came into effect with the U.S. In 1965, the Auto Pact provided for duty-free trade in cars, trucks, buses, and auto parts at the manufacturing level.

The North American Free Trade Agreement

On January 1, 1994, the **North American Free Trade Agreement (NAFTA)** took effect. The objective of NAFTA is to create a free trade area for Canada, the U.S., and Mexico. It eliminates trade barriers, promotes fair competition, and increases investment opportunities. Canada later signed a separate free trade agreement with Chile.

Surveys conducted during the early 1990s showed that the majority of Canadians were opposed to both the FTA and NAFTA. They feared that jobs would be lost to other countries, and that Canada would be flooded with products manufactured in Mexico, where wages are much lower than they are in Canada. Supporters of NAFTA argued that the agreement would open up foreign markets for Canadian products. Figure 4.4 lists the arguments that have been made for and against free trade agreements.

What has *actually* happened since NAFTA took effect? Canada is shedding its image as a country whose people are "hewers of wood and drawers of water" and is becoming an exporting powerhouse. Trade between the U.S. and Canada has risen 37 percent since 1994, and Canada enjoyed a $22 billion trade surplus with the U.S. in 1996. Before free trade, exports accounted for about one quarter of GDP, but now exports account for 40 percent. In the manufacturing

European Union (EU)

An agreement among Western European nations to eliminate quotas and keep tariffs low on products traded among themselves, but to impose high tariffs and low quotas on goods imported from other nations.

Canada–U.S. Free Trade Agreement (FTA)

An agreement to eliminate over time tariffs on goods and services that move between the two countries.

North American Free Trade Agreement (NAFTA)

A trade agreement signed by Canada, the U.S., and Mexico whose purpose is to create a free trade area.

Arguments in Favour of Free Trade	Arguments Against Free Trade
1. *Employment*. Canada needs open access to the U.S. market. To protect our employment we must get involved in free trade deals as other countries are doing. Canadian companies are already competing successfully with U.S. firms in industries in which there are no tariffs.	1. *Employment*. Canadian workers in a variety of industries will be laid off because U.S. firms will reduce their manufacturing activities here and simply send in goods from their duty-free U.S. plants.
2. *Social programs*. Canada already has over 200 agreements and understandings with the U.S. and none of these has ever threatened social services such as employment insurance and universal medical care. If Canada does not have a free trade deal with the U.S., the performance of our economy will be so poor that we will not be able to afford the current levels of social programs.	2. *Social programs*. Business firms in Canada will pressure the government to reduce social programs in order to lower their level of income tax. This will mean the end of universal access to services such as employment insurance and medicare.
3. *Takeovers*. Controls remain on foreign investment. Canada's corporate assets will remain subject to government approval before a takeover is allowed.	3. *Takeovers*. U.S. corporations can come into Canada and buy almost any Canadian company. Foreign ownership of Canada will increase.
4. *Energy*. There is nothing specific in the free trade agreement regarding energy or natural resources (e.g., water). There are, however, specific articles giving the Canadian government the right to act to protect health, safety, essential security, the environment, or consumer interest.	4. *Energy*. The free trade agreement will allow the U.S. to take the same percentage of our natural resources (e.g., oil) that they have taken in the past. If there is a shortage, Canadians will suffer.
5. *Effect on women*. Women are heavily employed in the service sector. Since many of the new jobs that will be created by the free trade deal will be in the service sector, women will benefit.	5. *Effect on women*. Women are heavily involved in the service sector. Since the free trade deal allows U.S. firms to deal in services, many of these jobs will be lost to the U.S.
6. *Environment*. Is not covered in the agreement. The federal government retains its right to take whatever actions are necessary to protect health, safety, essential services, the environment, and consumer interests.	6. *Environment*. Standards of all kinds must be harmonized with the U.S. This will mean that Canada will lose its right to control environmental standards.
7. *Culture*. The free trade agreement is about trade and tariffs. Canadian culture is not mentioned in the deal. European countries did not lose their culture when the Economic Community was formed, and Canada will not lose its culture because of a free trade deal with the U.S.	7. *Culture, sovereignty, and identity*. Because of all of the changes that will be required in the free trade deal, Canada will no longer be an independent country, but merely an economic subsidiary of the U.S.

Figure 4.4
Arguments for and against free trade.

sector, 60 percent of output is now exported, compared to just 30 percent in 1988. Canada is the most trade-intensive country in the G7 group. One job in three is now devoted to producing goods and services for export.[25]

Individual provinces are doing well, too. In the period 1990–96, for example, Manitoba's exports to the U.S. doubled to nearly $4.3 billion, and wheat is no longer its number one export. One Manitoba company—Digital Chameleon—colours and digitizes *Superman* comics for New York–based DC Comics. And Palliser Furniture, which used to export about 10 percent of its output to the U.S., is now exporting more than 50 percent. Nearly 2500 jobs have been created in Winnipeg alone.[26]

Many Canadian businesses did have problems adjusting to the "new world" of free trade, but as we shall see later in this chapter, Canada's international competitiveness has improved since NAFTA came into effect. The box "Canadian Magazines Tackle the U.S. Market" describes how one industry has reacted to NAFTA.

Canadians may be surprised to learn that there is now much more opposition to NAFTA in the U.S. than there is in Canada. A report issued in 1997

The Palliser furniture showroom in Winnipeg, Manitoba. Employment at Palliser has surged due to the company's success in exporting its products to U.S. markets.

by a coalition of U.S. labour and environmental groups says that NAFTA has been bad for the U.S. and good for Canada. The report claims that NAFTA has caused the loss of 420 000 U.S. jobs, an increasing trade deficit with Canada and Mexico, a flight of industry to Mexico, and a decline in the standard of living of U.S. citizens.[27] It is difficult to tell how much effect NAFTA has had compared to many other major changes that have occurred during the same time period—globalization, rapid changes in information technology, and the Bank of Canada's actions to stop inflation, to name just a few. One of the biggest concerns about free trade was what it would do to Canadian jobs. The latest evidence shows that factory employment as a proportion of all jobs in Canada has continued to drop (as it has for decades), but that there was little difference between industries affected most by NAFTA and those affected least.[28]

Other Free Trade Agreements in the Americas

The Canada–U.S. Free Trade Agreement and NAFTA are the most publicized trade agreements in the Americas, but there has recently been a flurry of activity among other countries as well. On January 1, 1995, a free trade agreement known as Mercosur went into effect between Argentina, Brazil, Uruguay, and Paraguay. By 2005, tariffs will be eliminated on 80 percent of the goods traded between those four countries. Brazil has proposed enlarging Mercosur into a South American Free Trade Area (SAFTA), which might eventually negotiate with NAFTA to form an Americas Free Trade Area (AFTA).

There are several other free trade areas already in existence in the Americas: The Andean Pact (Bolivia, Ecuador, Colombia, Peru, and Venezuela), The Central American Common Market (Costa Rica, El Salvador, Guatemala, Honduras, and Nicaragua), the G-3 group (Columbia, Mexico, and Venezuela), and The Caribbean Common Market (many of the island nations of the Caribbean).[29] The population of the various free trade areas of the Americas totals nearly 900 million. The economies of many of these nations are growing rapidly, and they will become increasingly important to Canada during the next decade.

Free Trade Agreements in Other Areas of the World

Free trade agreements are not restricted to the Americas. A high level of activity is evident around the world as groups of nations band together to form

International Report

Canadian Magazines Tackle the U.S. Market

Since the passage of NAFTA, much has been written about the importance of Canadian companies increasing their emphasis on export sales. Canada's trade publications industry is no exception. There are nearly 400 trade periodicals published in Canada, with a total circulation of over 60 million. These trade periodicals inform readers about key developments in specific industries such as mining, pulp and paper, and fish farming. There are over 1500 full-time employees engaged in the production of these periodicals.

The weekly newspaper *The Northern Miner* is typical of the increased emphasis on looking international. In March 1995 it began selling in the U.S. in an attempt to attract more readers and advertisers. The paper has opened an office in Denver, Colorado, and has added editorial features to make it relevant to both Canadian and U.S. readers. Publisher Doug Donnelly says that the paper's original reason for existence was to report on the activities of Canadian mining companies. As these companies have gone international, it makes sense for the industry trade paper to do so as well.

The Northern Miner is just the latest trade paper to tackle the U.S. market. Under NAFTA, the Canadian–U.S. border has grown fainter and multinational corporations are cutting costs by eliminating Canadian head offices. When they do that, they often take their advertising budgets with them. So, the trade magazines have an incentive to increase advertising revenues in the U.S. Already, nearly one quarter of *The Northern Miner*'s circulation is generated in the U.S., mostly by industry executives and investors who follow the Canadian stock market. Over 70 percent of the publication's newest subscriptions were gained in the U.S.

Mill Products News (formerly known as *Canadian Mill Products News*) has used this same approach. Its main advertisers are companies who sell products like saw blades and chippers to lumber mills. When these clients started moving to places like Atlanta, Georgia, to take advantage of the new mills being constructed there, publisher Heri Baum decided to follow them. He dropped "Canadian" from the tabloid's title and added 7000 U.S. names to his distribution list. Now the distribution of his magazine has increased to about 19 000 copies. *Northern Aquaculture* (formerly *Canadian Aquaculture*) made a similar decision after hard times hit Canada's fish farming industry.

Some trade papers have been doing fairly well in the U.S. for years. *Hockey News*, for example, sells about 60 percent of its 110 000 circulation in the U.S., and has done so since 1947. As hockey interest in the U.S. has grown, so has the circulation of *Hockey News*.

Industry experts say it can be difficult for Canadian trade papers to get a foothold in the U.S., especially when a U.S. publication already has a following there. Historically, Canadian journals stuck to Canadian coverage because it was a safe niche. Competition from U.S. journals wasn't a big problem because those journals often didn't talk about Canada very much. Government regulations also protected domestic trade publications. For example, advertising expenses in Canadian-owned magazines can be written off as a business expense, but advertising in foreign-owned magazines cannot. Regulations also require foreign magazines to have no more than 5 percent of their advertising directed at Canadians. This latter restriction does not apply to Canadian trade papers that are sold in the U.S.

---

regional trade associations for their own benefit. Some examples are the ASEAN Free Trade Area (Brunei, Indonesia, Malaysia, the Philippines, Singapore, Thailand, and Vietnam), the Asia-Pacific Economic Cooperation (many nations of the Pacific Rim, as well as the U.S., Canada, and Mexico), the Economic Community of Central African States (many nations in equatorial Africa), and the Gulf Cooperation Council (Bahrain, Kuwait, Oman, Qatar, Saudi Arabia, and United Arab Emirates).

Trade Challenges for Canadian Business

Many challenges confront Canadian companies as they become involved in international trade. Four areas where challenges must be met are

1. increasing the effectiveness of government involvement in promoting exports

2. improving Canadian competitiveness in world markets

3. meeting competitive challenges from other countries

4. monitoring the level of foreign investment in Canada.

Increasing the Effectiveness of Government Involvement

The federal and provincial governments recognize the importance of international trade for the Canadian economy. As a result, they are trying to encourage trade by helping those business firms that are interested. Table 4.3 lists some selected services that are available to businesses. Some provinces have trade offices similar to the federal government's trade services, and provincial premiers sometimes visit foreign countries to promote trade. In 1997, the "Team Canada" trade mission visited Southeast Asian countries in an attempt to increase trade between Canada and countries in that region. The mission included Prime Minister Chrétien and the provincial premiers.

While the government provides assistance in one way, it sometimes restricts international business in another. The government levies tariffs on imports and introduces nontariff barriers such as quotas and strict testing requirements to protect Canadian industry from foreign competitors. Canadian businesses wishing to import goods and services must sometimes pay duties and other charges that increase the price Canadians pay for these products. In some cases, imports are prevented from entering the country. Potential sales for businesses relying on foreign suppliers are therefore reduced.

Improving Canadian Competitiveness in World Markets

Canada's share of world trade is declining. This is partly caused by the increased competitiveness of other countries, as well as the decline in competitiveness of Canadian business firms. High-tech imports surpass exports, meaning that we rely on other countries for technological innovation. Canadian labour costs are also rising more quickly than elsewhere, and Canadian companies do not spend as much on either R&D or training employees as firms in many other countries. Some critics claim that Canada lacks a "competitive culture."

Canada's International Competitiveness

international competitiveness

The ability of a country to generate more wealth than its competitors in world markets.

International competitiveness refers to the ability of a country to proportionally generate more wealth than its competitors in world markets. Each year a global competitiveness index is published that ranks the international competitiveness of a large number of countries. In the period 1989–94, Canada steadily dropped in the rankings, going from fourth in 1989 to 14th in 1994. But by 1997, Canada was again ranked fourth (just behind the U.S.). Singapore and Hong Kong are at the top of the list, while Russia and Ukraine are at the bottom.[30]

The news is mixed regarding Canada's international competitiveness. The good news is that exports are up sharply since NAFTA was instituted. The bad news is that unemployment remains relatively high, wages are down

Table 4.3   **Examples of Government Assistance for Exports**

Program	Function
Program for Export Market Development	Assists in export promotion activities. Shares financial risks of entering new foreign markets.
Technology Inflow Program	Facilitates the flow of foreign technology into Canada. Helps Canadian scientists in gaining technological knowledge.
Trade Commissioner Service	Promotes export trade and represents and protects Canadian interests abroad.
Export Development Corporation	A Crown corporation that facilitates and develops Canada's export trade through provision of insurance, guarantees, and loans.

3 percent, the Canadian dollar has declined 16 percent since 1991, and the uncertainty over the future of Quebec is hurting Canada.[31]

Surveys of Canadian business executives show that Canada's strengths include healthy banks, a good legal system, a favourable exchange rate, good business schools, political stability, and an efficient transportation system. Weaknesses include a tax system that does not encourage competitiveness, inadequate R&D spending by business firms, labour unions with too much power, and social policies that discourage people from seeking work.

Meeting Competitive Challenges from Other Countries

Canadian business firms face aggressive competition from several economic entities, including the European Union, the Asian countries, the developing countries, and the former communist countries.

The European Union

The European Union means the economic integration of 15 nations: Austria, Belgium, Britain, Denmark, Finland, France, Germany, Greece, Ireland, Italy, Luxembourg, the Netherlands, Portugal, Spain, and Sweden. The EU comprises 320 million people, compared to the U.S.'s 250 million and Japan's 120 million, and has thus become a strong trading bloc.

The EU is based on the following premises:

- The removal of barriers through about 300 legislative actions to create one internal market allowing for the free movement of goods, services, people, and capital.

- The standardization and harmonization of national laws and regulations so that they no longer interfere with the free trade of goods and services within the community.

- The opening of government purchases to all companies within the community.

- Companies are free to develop cooperative arrangements with companies in other member states allowing industry to organize on a large scale.

- An attempt to harmonize consumer sales and excise tax rates.[32]

There has been much debate within the EU about the idea of a common currency (called the *euro*) for all members. Countries have the right to opt out of the common currency, but for those that opt in, the euro comes into effect on January 1, 1999, for non-cash transactions. On January 1, 2000, euro cash will start to circulate, and by January 1, 2002, all currencies from individual countries in the EU are supposed to disappear.

Many challenges for Canadian business emerge from this new trade bloc. The businesses within the EU that survive will be more efficient, more aggressive, and more likely to compete around the world, including in Canada. It has become more difficult for Canadian enterprises to export to the EU, unless they are already established in Europe, as there is protection for EU enterprises from "outsiders."

The Asian Countries

The Asian trading bloc is made up of Japan, Hong Kong, South Korea, Singapore, Taiwan, the ASEAN nations, and China.

Much has been written about Japanese business and how it operates.[33] Japanese enterprises have been very successful at exporting manufactured goods around the world, and have made huge inroads into Canadian markets. Japanese businesses have invested directly in Canadian business, including owning pulp and paper mills in Alberta and automobile plants in Ontario.

Canadian business enterprises face a formidable challenge when competing with the **keiretsu** companies of Japan.[34] These are loosely affiliated groups in industry and banking and can encompass hundreds of companies. A majority of the companies on the Tokyo stock exchange belong to a *keiretsu*, and the six major *keiretsu* companies account for 78 percent of the total capitalization of the exchange. The Mitsubishi *keiretsu* alone accounts for 11 percent of the capitalization. The main features of a *keiretsu* are

- The existence of cross-shareholdings. That is, companies own shares in each other, but no one company dominates ownership.
- The formation of a presidents' club. Top executives meet regularly to exchange information.
- Joint investment among member companies.
- *Keiretsu* member banks provide financing arrangements to member companies.
- Extensive buying and selling relationships exist among member companies.

Sometimes *keiretsu* companies are called cartels, that is, a group of companies that behave as a monopoly. They are hostile to outsiders, especially to foreign enterprises. They are demanding of new recruits, they extract special deals or cheap loans, and they expect obedience from all members. Their philosophy towards business differs from that of Western companies. Western multinationals emphasize profits, and shareholders are the most powerful stakeholders. With *keiretsu* companies, profits and the interests of shareholders are subordinate to long-range goals.

The rapidly developing nations of Asia present other challenges for Canadian business. Enterprises in these nations produce consumer goods, such as clothing and electronics, at much lower costs than can be achieved in Canada. In Indonesia, for example, workers who make running shoes are paid less than $10 a week. The government wants to keep labour costs down because it knows that foreign manufacturers will set up plants there if wages are low.

keiretsu

Loosely affiliated Japanese companies in industry and banking.

The Japanese have been very successful in the mass production of consumer electronic products like televisions, VCRs, and video cameras.

China is a huge market that is experiencing rapid change. Canada used to sell large amounts of grain to China but this market has been lost to other grain producers. Some companies are now making their first tentative moves into China. Manulife Financial, for example, began selling life insurance in China in 1995. China is potentially the world's largest market for life insurance, even though no insurance was sold there between 1947 and 1983.[35]

The Developing Countries

Canadian business cannot ignore developing countries as future markets. Approximately 77 percent of the world's population lives in these 142 nations, principally in South America, Africa, and Asia. These countries are buyers, suppliers, competitors, and capital users and are becoming increasingly important players in international business. They account for about 25 percent of the world's imports and 28 percent of exports.

The Former Communist Countries

With the emergence of more market-based economic systems in many Eastern European countries and the republics emerging from the former Soviet Union, Canadian business may have opportunities to conduct more trade with or to invest in business enterprises in these areas. One of the first Canadian enterprises to operate a business in the Soviet Union was McDonald's of Canada, which operates fast food outlets in Moscow and other Russian cities.

Glasnost and *perestroika* led to the demise of the command economy of the Soviet Union. The countries that made up the Soviet Union are experiencing rapid change as they move towards having more market-based economies. Some countries are moving more rapidly than others.[36] As we saw earlier in the chapter, much foreign investment is occurring in Poland, and it is now one of the strongest economies in Eastern Europe. While Canadian companies still can encounter bureaucratic red tape and political instability, opportunities abound in the former communist countries.

Doing business in Eastern Europe is also a challenge.[37] Not all the communist systems are changing at the same rate. East and West Germany are now integrated, and Poland and Hungary are introducing market mechanisms, but other countries are not as progressive.

Foreign Investment in Canada

Canada's manufacturing economy has developed behind a protective tariff barrier, which made it attractive for foreign firms to establish or acquire subsidiaries in Canada to supply the Canadian market. Foreign firms were able to supply goods to the Canadian market less expensively than by exporting to Canada and paying the tariff on the product. This situation is now changing rapidly as the free trade agreement takes effect.

Canada's rich natural resources—minerals and petroleum—also attracted money from abroad. Canada leads the world in the value of its mineral exports. It ranks first in the production of uranium, zinc, and nickel; second in asbestos, potash, sulphur, and gypsum; and third in gold, aluminum, and platinum.

Foreign firms that invested in Canada because of the tariff barriers often built small, inefficient plants to serve only the Canadian market. The cost of production, as well as the tariff barriers erected by other countries and the fact that head offices of foreign companies made most export allocations, made it difficult for these firms to compete actively as exporters.

The market size and the tendency for much technological development work done by foreign-owned companies to be conducted outside Canada means that Canadian subsidiaries do not do much new product development work. This, it has been argued, is one major disadvantage of the high degree of foreign ownership of Canadian corporations. The other side of the argument, of course, is that Canadian firms would have less access to technological developments were it not for foreign ownership.

Concern about foreign ownership in Canada has prompted several government studies. The first was the Gordon Commission Report in 1957. It pointed out that there were dangers to foreign investment, in particular, the possibility that U.S. subsidiaries in Canada, faced with a conflict between U.S. and Canadian positions, would choose to support the U.S. position. A key recommendation, subsequently acted on, was that financial intermediaries, such as banks, should be in Canadian hands.

extraterritoriality

The application of one country's laws to the subsidiaries of its companies in other countries.

The Watkins Report in 1968 dealt with **extraterritoriality**, that is, the application of one country's laws to the subsidiaries of its companies in other countries. Major recommendations of the Watkins Report were to create a government agency to survey multinational activities in Canada, to compel foreign subsidiaries to disclose more of their activities in Canada, to encourage nationalization of Canadian industry, to subsidize research and development and management education in Canada, to form the Canada Development Corporation, and to forbid the application of foreign laws in Canada.

The 1970 Wahn Committee investigation examined Canada–United States relations. Much of its work was based on the Watkins Report. One of its recommendations was that, over time, all foreign-owned firms in Canada should allow Canadians to own at least 51 percent of their shares.

The Gray Report in 1972, *Foreign Direct Investment in Canada*, attempted to determine the economic forces that promoted foreign investment and to measure its benefits and costs. The report saw the major benefits of foreign direct investment as access to new technology, resulting in increased productivity in Canada, and the introduction of new and improved products in Canada. The Gray Report recommended a foreign investment review agency to screen new foreign direct investments in Canada to determine their effect. As a result of that recommendation, the Liberal government of Canada established the **Foreign Investment Review Agency (FIRA)**. Its purpose was to ensure that significant benefits accrued to Canada from new foreign direct investment. In 1985, under a Conservative government, FIRA's title was changed to **Investment Canada**. The new federal organization is designed primarily to attract and facilitate foreign investment in Canada. During the 1970s and 1980s, in fact, U.S. ownership of Canadian assets declined steadily. Table 4.4 lists the largest foreign-owned firms in Canada.

Foreign Investment Review Agency (FIRA)

Established in 1973 to screen new foreign direct investment in Canada; supposed to ensure that significant benefits accrued to Canada.

Investment Canada

Replaced FIRA in 1985; designed primarily to attract and facilitate foreign investment in Canada.

Table 4.4   The Top 10 Foreign-Owned Companies in Canada, 1996

	Company	Sales (in billions)	Percent Foreign-Owned
1.	General Motors of Canada	$28.0	100
2.	Ford Motor of Canada	25.5	100
3.	Chrysler Canada Ltd.	17.0	100
4.	IBM Canada	9.5	100
5.	Imperial Oil Ltd.	9.2	82
6.	Amoco Canada Petroleum	6.2	100
7.	Shell Canada Ltd.	5.1	80
8.	Canada Safeway Ltd.	4.7	100
9.	Sears Canada	3.9	55
10.	Total Petroleum	3.5	55

Summary of Learning Objectives

1. **Describe the rise of international business and identify the major world marketplaces.** More and more business firms are engaged in international business. The term *globalization* refers to the process by which the world economy is fast becoming a single interdependent entity. The global economy is characterized by a rapid growth in the exchange of information and trade in services. The three major marketplaces for international business are *North America* (the United States, Canada, and Mexico), *Western Europe* (which is dominated by Germany, the United Kingdom, France, and Italy), and the *Pacific Rim* (where the dominant country, Japan, is surrounded by such rapidly advancing nations as South Korea, Taiwan, Hong Kong, and China).

2. **Explain how different forms of *competitive advantage, import-export balances, exchange rates,* and *foreign competition* determine the ways in which countries and businesses respond to the international environment.** With an absolute advantage, a country engages in international trade because it can produce a good or service more efficiently than any other nation. But more often countries trade because they enjoy comparative advantages, that is, they can produce some items more efficiently than they can produce other items. A country that exports more than it imports has a favourable balance of trade, while a country that imports more than it exports has an unfavourable balance of trade. If the exchange rate decreases (the value of the Canadian dollar falls), our exports become less expensive for other countries so they will buy more of what we produce. The reverse happens if the value of the Canadian dollar increases. Changes in the exchange rate therefore have a strong impact on our international competitiveness.

3. **Discuss the factors involved in deciding to do business internationally and in selecting the appropriate *levels of international involvement* and *international organizational structure.*** In deciding whether to do business internationally, a firm must determine whether a market for its product exists abroad, and if so, whether the firm has the skills and knowledge to manage such a business. It must also assess the business climates of other nations to make sure that they are conducive to international operations.

   A firm must also decide on its level of international involvement. It can choose to be an *exporter* or *importer*, to organize as an *international firm*, or to operate as a *multinational firm*. The choice will influence the organizational structure of its international operations, specifically, its use of *independent agents, licensing arrangements, branch offices, strategic alliances,* and *direct investment*.

4. **Describe some of the ways in which *social, cultural, economic, legal,* and *political differences* act as barriers to international trade.** *Social* and *cultural differences* that can serve as barriers to trade include language, social values, and traditional buying patterns. Differences in economic systems may force businesses to establish close relationships with foreign governments before they are permitted to do business abroad. *Quotas, tariffs, subsidies,* and *local-content laws* offer protection to local industries. Differences in *business-practice laws* can make standard business practices in one nation illegal in another.

5. **Explain how *free trade agreements* assist world trade.** Several *trade agreements* have attempted to eliminate restrictions on free trade internationally. The *General Agreement on Tariffs and Trade* (GATT) was instituted to eliminate tariffs and other trade barriers among participating nations. The *European Union* (EU) has eliminated virtually all trade barriers among the 12 principal Western European nations. The *North American Free Trade Agreement* (NAFTA) eliminates many of the barriers to free trade that exist among the United States, Canada, and Mexico.

6. **Understand the *trade challenges* for Canadian businesses.** Canadian businesses face four challenges: increasing the effectiveness of government involvement in promoting exports, improving Canadian competitiveness in world markets, meeting competitive challenges from other countries, and monitoring the level of foreign investment in Canada.

Key Terms

globalization, 92
imports, 92
exports, 92
absolute advantage, 94
comparative advantage, 94
balance of trade, 94
balance of payments, 94
foreign exchange rate, 96
independent agent, 100
licensing agreement, 102

world product mandating, 102
strategic alliance, 103
multinational firm, 103
quota, 107
embargo, 107
tariff, 107
revenue tariff, 107
protectionist tariff, 107
subsidy, 108
protectionism, 108

local-content laws, 108
cartel, 109
dumping, 109
General Agreement on Tariffs and Trade (GATT), 109
European Union (EU), 110
Canada–U.S. Free Trade Agreement (FTA), 110

North American Free Trade Agreement (NAFTA), 110
international competitiveness, 114
keiretsu, 116
extraterritoriality, 118
Foreign Investment Review Agency (FIRA), 118
Investment Canada, 118

Study Questions and Exercises

Review Questions

1. Explain the difference between a nation's balance of trade and balance of payments.
2. What are the possible ways that Canadian firms can be involved in international business?
3. What are the advantages and disadvantages of multinational corporations?
4. How does the economic system of a country affect foreign firms interested in doing business there?

Analysis Questions

5. Make a list of all the major items in your bedroom. Identify the country in which each item was made. Give possible reasons why that nation might have a comparative advantage in producing this good.
6. Do you support protectionist tariffs for Canada? If so, in what instances and for what reasons? If not, why not?
7. Is the Canada–U.S. Free Trade Agreement good for Canada? Give supporting reasons for your answer.

8. Do you think that a firm that is operating internationally is better advised to adopt a single standard of ethical conduct or to adapt to local conditions? Under what kinds of conditions might each approach be preferable?

Application Exercises

9. Interview the manager of a local firm that does at least some business internationally. Identify reasons why the company decided to "go international," as well as the level of the firm's international involvement and the organizational structure it uses for its international operations.
10. Select a product familiar to you. Using library reference works to learn something about the culture of India, identify the problems that might arise in trying to market this product to India's citizens.

Building Your Business Skills

Goal

To help students appreciate how high-context and low-context cultures influence global business communication. *Low-context cultures* use explicit written and verbal messages to communicate in business and other situations. Written agreements and written messages are important. *High-context cultures* communicate through both explicit messages and implicit context. Interpersonal relationships, and a high level of formality and etiquette, will affect the success of the communication.

Method

Step 1:

A continuum of world cultures as defined by anthropologist Edward T. Hall is shown below. Use this information to develop a strategy for conducting meetings with businesspeople in Switzerland and Japan.

Low	Swiss	Scandinavian	French	Italian	Latin American	Japanese	High
	German	North American		English Spanish	Arabian		

Step 2:

Working in groups of four or five students, answer the following questions for each country: What should you do before you arrive in the country in order to increase your chance of success? If your meeting time is 1:00 p.m. on Tuesday, when should you arrive in order to get the best results from your meeting? What title and position should you or another member of your team hold in order to achieve your business goals? How would your business style and the pace of your conversation differ in each country?

Follow-Up Questions

1. *Culture shock*—the inability to adapt to foreign cultures—is a problem that many Canadian businesspeople face when they work abroad. Based on this exercise, why do you think this is a problem?

2. How can management training seminars reduce *ethnocentrism*—the tendency to judge the cultures of foreign countries by Canadian standards?

3. Japan, Arab countries, and Latin American countries are high-context cultures. Do these countries share cultural patterns? How would you adapt your business style from country to country?

EXPLORING the Net

The Internet has immense potential value for anyone who is interested in the global environment of business. An excellent source of information regarding international business is a Web site called "Business Resources on the Web: International Business." Log on to this site at:

http://www.idbsu.edu/carol/busintl.htm

First, browse the site according to what interests you most. Then consider the following questions:

1. Select one country in each of the following areas: Asia and the Pacific Rim, Latin and South America, and Russia and Eastern Europe. Find out as much as you can about the social/cultural and legal/political factors affecting business.

2. Briefly review the textbook discussions of exporting and licensing. Identify two or three sites that might be especially relevant to someone considering these forms of international business.

3. Select one of the following sites:
   - "Go to Marketing, Finance, Small Business"
   - "Go to Economic Statistics, Government Statistics, Business Law"
   - "Go to Small Business"

   On the site that you explored, what further information is available to the Canadian businessperson who is interested in learning more about the global environment of business today?

CONCLUDING CASE 4-1

Even Wal-Mart Has Its Problems

When the first Wal-Mart store opened in Mexico City, big crowds showed up and sales were strong. But interest soon waned, and customers complained that the chain's prices were too high. Some Mexicans living near the U.S. border cross it to shop at Wal-Marts in the U.S. When Wal-Mart opened a store in Monterey, the local press soon was publicizing the fact that prices were 15 to 20 percent higher than at the Wal-Mart in Laredo, Texas (a two-hour drive to the north). Wal-Mart is now admitting that it has a long way to go in establishing itself in Mexico.

Wal-Mart's experience should serve as a warning to any retailer who is thinking about entering a foreign market as a result of the North American Free Trade Agreement (NAFTA). Industry analysts say that retail outlets in Mexico are growing far faster than the buying power of their potential customers. The big problem is that Mexico's middle class is not very large by Canadian or U.S. standards, and it will take 10 to 20 years for such a group of consumers to develop.

Wal-Mart faces the following problems in Mexico:

- It does not have the same clout with Mexican suppliers that it has with U.S. suppliers because it is not a major presence in Mexico.

- Distribution systems in Mexico are different—suppliers ship directly to stores rather than to retailer warehouses—thus nullifying Wal-Mart's efficient control of distribution.

- The appeal of well-known U.S. brand names is fading.

- Mexicans continue to shop for food at small neighbourhood shops, not at big discount stores, because they feel the food is fresher at local markets.

- Most Mexicans do not own cars, so the geographic "reach" of a particular store is limited.

Kmart, one of Wal-Mart's major competitors in the U.S. and Canada, is also operating in Mexico. Unlike Wal-Mart (which shipped a manager from the U.S. to Mexico), Kmart hired a Mexican who was formerly director of store development for a Mexican department store chain. Juan Suberville knows all about Mexican shopping habits and has used this knowledge to advantage. For example, Kmart stores have a bank inside so that customers can easily get cash (there are few credit sales in Mexico). Also, each Kmart has a walk-in refrigerator where customers can choose the cut of beef they want. Even hot dogs are wrapped in front of customers to convey a sense of freshness.

Case Questions

1. What social, cultural, and economic differences has Wal-Mart had to cope with while trying to enter the Mexican market?

2. What level of involvement in international business has Wal-Mart demonstrated in its move into Mexico?

3. Is Wal-Mart a multinational company? Explain.   ◆

CONCLUDING CASE 4-2

Microsoft Heads for the Wild, Wild East

There's a lot that Microsoft founder and CEO Bill Gates doesn't like about doing business in China—piracy, for example. Every year, factories in the People's Republic manufacture 54 million illegally copied software packages, robbing Microsoft and other firms of revenue that is rightfully theirs. So severe is the problem that a pirated version of Windows 95 was available months before the product's official launch—at just $5 a package.

Nevertheless, Microsoft views China as a huge marketing opportunity (and a 1996 U.S.–Chinese agreement banning the reproduction and sale of pirated intellectual property undoubtedly is helping to ease the company's concerns). With a population of 1.2 billion people, China is on the verge of mass computerization. Only 1 million computers were sold in 1995, but sales of 5 million are projected for the year 2000. Not surprisingly, Bill Gates is doing everything he can to make sure that these computers use Microsoft software.

Priming the Chinese computerization pump are government purchases. In Beijing, for example, officials are planning to levy new taxes and monitor their collection through a computerized network connected to a central database. The success of the plan depends on the purchase of 20 000 computers to link 3200 tax offices via Microsoft servers, Windows NT, and Windows 95. In another deal, the central bank of China is planning to install Windows-based PCs and servers in every one of its 10 000 branches. Thanks to purchases like these, Microsoft expects its annual sales in China of $20 million to skyrocket. "We're looking at 100-percent growth every year as far as we can see," beams Bryan Nelson, Microsoft's director for Greater China.

Forty-five percent of China's 1.2 billion population is under the age of 26. This younger generation of consumers is spending more than its parents on all consumer goods, including such electronic products as colour televisions, refrigerators, VCRs, telephones, and computers.

Tapping into this emerging consumer market requires that multinationals learn to deal effectively with local businesspeople and government officials, who often operate in distinctly non-Western ways. Microsoft learned the art of doing business in China the hard way when, in 1992, it contracted with a Taiwanese company to produce a Chinese-language version of Windows for use in mainland China. Government officials in Beijing rejected the product for various reasons. It was produced in Taiwan, which China does not recognize. The Chinese government also insisted that officials, rather than outsiders, define the standards for translating Chinese character fonts into computer language.

Microsoft's miscalculations were serious enough for the Chinese electronics industry to threaten a ban on the Taiwanese version of Windows. Bill Gates was advised that if he wanted to do business in China, he had better spend time there and "learn something from 5000 years of Chinese history." Gates did just that and, in the process, learned that Microsoft's success depends on a cooperative relationship with the Beijing government—one that sometimes places Microsoft in the back seat but that does ensure that it gets to go along for the ride.

Case Questions

1. To help control its exploding population, China enforces strict family planning. How do you think smaller families will affect consumer purchasing patterns in the emerging Chinese economy?

2. After its 1992 business miscalculation, Microsoft replaced its Chinese management team. Do you think this was a wise decision? Explain your answer.

3. The national average annual household income in China was just $684 in 1994. However, per capita income is rising at about 20 percent per year and is expected to reach $4000 by 2020. Why is Microsoft trying so hard to get a foothold in China if so few individuals and families can afford its products?

4. Why did the Chinese suggest that Microsoft's success depended on Bill Gates first-hand knowledge of their country?

◆

5

Business Ethics, Social Responsibility, and Business Law

The Body Shop and Social Responsibility

Margot Franssen is proud of the accomplishments of The Body Shop Canada, a company that she heads as president. Franssen opened The Body Shop's first Canadian store in 1979 and has since developed a chain of over 100 franchise and company-owned stores across Canada and seven northeastern U.S. states. Sales in Canada are over $100 million.

As a retailer of cosmetics, the company wanted to avoid the existing image of that industry. It was an industry thought to exploit women, torture animals during product development and testing, pollute the environment, and use misleading advertising. Instead, The Body Shop has sought to promote sustainable development, enhance social justice, and work towards a balanced environment. It is involved in helping developing economies, and is promoting trade, not aid.

The philosophy of the company is expressed in the following two quotations by Franssen:

> We believe that retailers should do more than simply sell products. At The Body Shop, we get involved with our customers and social issues, environmental concerns, and community projects.
>
> Business should do more than make money; we believe that companies should actually help solve major social problems and be a driving force for change.

Its efforts are well known and it is a leading example of a business enterprise with humanitarian and environmental ideals. It has been recognized many times for its efforts. For example, it received a *Financial Post* Environmental Award in the Green Product Category for its commitment to operating in an environmentally responsible manner. It has been named one of the "100 Best Companies to Work for in Canada" because of its high level of personal development, job satisfaction, promotion potential, and working atmosphere.

Social responsibility is reflected in everything The Body Shop does. The following are some examples:

- The Body Shop's cosmetics are all natural and are not tested on animals.
- The containers are recyclable and refillable.
- The company is attempting to have products made in the Third World and high-unemployment areas.
- The Body Shop features window displays that are given to "causes," for example, Friends of the Earth or the Wildlife Federation.
- Each store is involved in a community project to which staff must devote an aggregate of four paid hours a week.

Despite its social awareness and initiatives, The Body Shop was being criticized. Margot Franssen and Anita Roddick, founder and managing director of Body Shop International PLC, were puzzled by the criticisms. They were addressing many concerns of society, were aware of various stakeholders, practised good business ethics, respected the environment, and supported many charities and volunteer organizations.

The following are some examples of the criticisms:

- The cause-related marketing is merely a clever way to differentiate their soaps and appeal to a niche market of consumers.
- The company receives the benefit of free and largely favourable media coverage, reducing the need to pay for advertising.
- The ingredients used in many products were once tested on animals, although they no longer are.

(continued)

The Body Shop does not oppose testing new medicines on animals, but some of these products later become ingredients for their products. The company has changed their "Not tested on animals" slogan to "Against animal testing."

- The company claims that its products are natural, yet it uses off-the-shelf industrial recipes such as artificial colours, synthetic fragrances, and chemical preservatives as base ingredients.

- The Body Shop's products sometimes do not rank well in consumer product testing.

- Despite claims to be supporting Third World economies, purchases from these countries are small and the going wages are paid.

- The company's past donations record was questionable, although in recent years their record has been very good.

- The company claims not to trade with cruel, oppressive regimes, yet it bought baskets from China.

Although the criticisms are extensive, even the critics concede that The Body Shop is making more efforts to be socially responsible than most corporations.

In 1995, The Body Shop responded to the criticisms by having an independent social audit performed by an American professor of business ethics. The resulting Values Report was an independently verified assessment of the company's impact on society and the environment.

As a result of that audit, the company has been updating its policy on animal testing, subjecting its suppliers to the ISO 9000 quality standards, reassessing how to measure the company's social impact, and revising its environmental statement. Franssen concedes that being socially and ethically responsible is challenging, and worries that some people's perception of the company may differ from reality. Yet she continues to operate the business in as socially responsible a manner as possible. ◆

The Body Shop
http://www.think-act-change.com

In this chapter, we look closely at business ethics, social responsibility, and business law. At one time, these issues were not considered very important. But times have changed, and the practices of today's business firms are in the spotlight. As you will see, managers are faced with a variety of ethical dilemmas, and business firms must address many issues of social responsibility.

After reading this chapter, you should be able to:

LEARNING OBJECTIVES

1. Explain how individuals develop their personal *codes of ethics* and why ethics are important in the workplace.

2. Distinguish *social responsibility* from *ethics*.

3. Show how the concept of social responsibility applies to environmental issues and to a firm's relationships with customers, employees, and investors.

4. Identify three general *approaches to social responsibility* and describe the four steps that a firm must take to implement a *social responsibility program*.

5. Explain how issues of social responsibility and ethics affect small businesses.

6. Identify the *sources of law*.

7. Explain the requirements for a valid *contract* and the remedies for *breach of contract*.

8. Compare the *agency–principal* and *bailor–bailee* relationships.

9. Outline the main points of the *law of property*, including the role of *warranty*.

The Nature of Ethics in the Workplace

ethics

Individual standards or moral values regarding what is right and wrong or good and bad.

Just what is ethical behaviour in business? You will find as many answers as people you ask, because **ethics**—standards or morals regarding what is right and wrong or good and bad—are highly personal.

Ethics vary greatly from person to person and from situation to situation. They are based on our society's ideas of right and wrong. Ethics vary from culture to culture. And within our cultural standards, we all develop our own personal "code of ethics" that accommodates differences within societal standards. For example, Western society generally considers stealing or bribery as "wrong" and patriotism and giving as "right." In other cultures, however, different ethical standards exist. It is important to realize, then, that what constitutes ethical and unethical behaviour is determined partially by the individual and partially by the cultural context in which it occurs.

Because ethics are both personally and culturally defined, differences of opinion can genuinely arise as to what is ethical or unethical. For example, many people who would be appalled at the thought of shoplifting a candy bar from a grocery store routinely take home pens and pads of paper from their offices, seeing these items almost as a part of their pay. Other people believe that if they find money on the sidewalk it is okay to keep it. Still other people view themselves as law-abiding citizens but have no qualms about using radar detectors to avoid speeding tickets. In each of these situations, people will choose different sides of the issue and argue that their views are ethical.

Influences on Ethics

Aside from situational factors, what makes different people's codes of ethics vary so much? Figure 5.1 shows the most common influences on an individual's ethics and behaviour: family and peers (and the values they convey) and experiences.

Families—especially parents—have the first chance to influence a child's ethics. Parents usually put a high priority on teaching their children certain values. In many families, these values include religious principles. Most parents also try to teach their children to obey society's rules and to behave well towards other people. The so-called *work ethic*—the belief and practice that hard work brings rewards—is learned in the home. Children who see their parents behaving ethically are more likely to adopt high ethical standards for themselves than are the children of parents who behave unethically. Teenagers are particularly likely to reject the verbal messages of parents who do not practise what they preach.

As children grow and are exposed more to other children, peers begin to have more influence on ethical behaviour. Indeed, the values of the group may become far more important than those of the larger society. Although such beliefs and behaviour are most talked about in the case of juvenile delinquent gangs, they also apply to the business world. Many unethical (and even criminal) business behaviours are fostered by a company environment in which such practices are acceptable (at least until the company gets caught).

Finally, experiences can increase or decrease certain types of ethical behaviour and beliefs about what is right and wrong. A child punished for telling lies learns that telling lies is wrong. Likewise, a company president who goes to jail for misrepresenting the company's financial position will probably have a new understanding of business ethics. But the manager who gets away with sexually harassing an employee will be more likely to see nothing wrong with it and do it again.

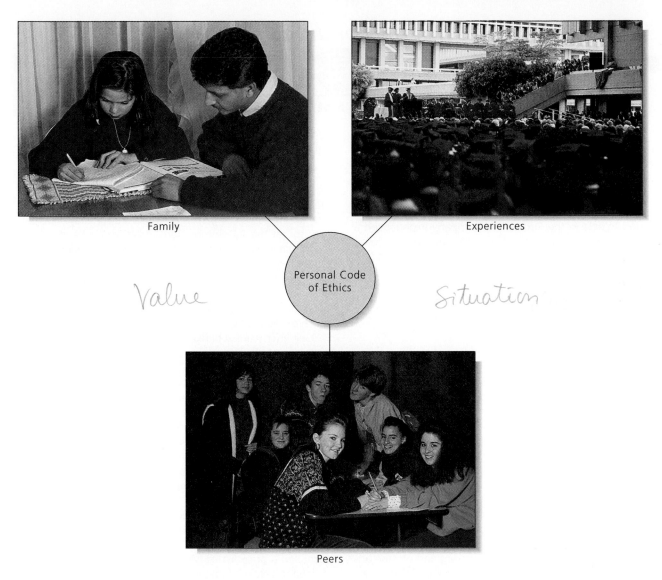

Value

Situation

Figure 5.1
An individual's ethics are determined by a number of different factors. Three of the most basic determinants are family, peers, and experiences.

Company Policies and Business Ethics

In recent years, the general public has become increasingly concerned about the behaviour of Canadian business leaders. A 1990 survey by Decima Research showed that 45 percent of Canadians consider business leaders unprincipled. The comparable figure 10 years earlier was 20 percent.[1] As illegal and/or unethical activities by managers have caused more problems for companies, many firms are taking steps to encourage their employees to practise more acceptable behaviour.[2]

Perhaps the single most significant thing a company can do is to demonstrate top management's support for ethical behaviour. The importance of top management support is demonstrated in the box "To Bribe or Not To Bribe." Many companies have adopted written codes of ethics that clearly state the firm's intent to conduct business ethically. Figure 5.2 (on p. 129) shows the code of ethics adopted by Great-West Life Assurance. Levi Strauss has an "aspiration statement" that spells out the company's values-based formula for earning profits and making the world a better place. It declares that management will set an example for ethical behaviour that others in the company must follow.

International Report

To Bribe or Not To Bribe

Business executives occasionally must make difficult decisions that have important ethical implications. Consider the following situations:

■ David Brink is the chairman of Murray & Roberts Holdings of South Africa. On one of its housing construction projects in the Sudan, the company experienced a problem when payments for work done didn't come through as expected. A government official indicated that he could start the money flowing again if the company would pay him a "commission." The company refused and took the matter to the World Court. Although it took 12 years to get a decision, the case was settled in the company's favour.

■ Jean-Pierre van Rooy is president of Otis Elevator Co. of Farmington, Connecticut. When mobsters in St. Petersburg, Russia, approached the Otis operation and asked for "protection" money, the company refused, even though they knew that several other companies—including Coca-Cola and Pepsi—had had their operations firebombed after refusing to pay. Otis has a strict company policy of not paying bribes, so it has simply tightened security around its St. Petersburg plant and is hoping for the best.

The experiences of Brink and van Rooy are not unusual in the world of international business. While speaking at a conference on business ethics, the secretary general of Interpol, the world police intelligence network, noted that the tolerance for dishonesty is increasing in both the advanced and developing countries of the world. Managers are therefore likely to be faced at some point in their career with demands that they pay bribes to someone in order to facilitate work. Since corruption is common in international business, the main fear among managers is that they will lose important business contracts if they take a tough stand against paying bribes or commissions. But both Brink and van Rooy don't accept that argument. Brink says that while his company has lost some contracts because they wouldn't pay bribes, they are better off without that business; van Rooy also feels that his company has not

suffered because of its strict anti-corruption policy.

Some observers estimate that U.S. business firms lost more than $400 billion worth of business because of strict anti-corruption laws there. The U.S. Foreign Corrupt Practices Act bans all commissions and bribes, but it applies only to U.S.-based companies. Attempts are currently underway to get the 24-member Organization for Economic Cooperation and Development to support a stronger anti-corruption agreement, but there is considerable resistance in other countries to imposing rules like those by which U.S. corporations have to abide. Other critics say such a measure will not work because corruption is so common in much of the world.

One international banker advises his clients that bribes are a way of life in Russia, and if they want to do business there they will have to go along with paying bribes. Corruption was common under the old communist regime in Russia. For example, people paid bribes to get their children into good schools or to jump the line to buy a refrigerator. Surprisingly, things have gotten worse since the collapse of communism. In the first 9 months of 1994, more than 70 000 bribery and extortion cases were opened. A presidential report said that one third of all retail trade earnings goes for corrupt purposes. Russian consumers therefore pay a 33 percent "tax" for bribery. Nearly half the respondents in a recent poll said they had been forced to pay a bribe to a government official. Bribery has become so common that the newspaper *Komsomolskaya Pravda* compiled a price list of Moscow bribes (e.g., the bribe needed to obtain a Moscow residency permit and the right to purchase an apartment is around $35 000).

The greatest hope in raising the level of ethical behaviour lies with individual managers, particularly those at the top management level. If the chief executive sanctions anything illegal, this will send the wrong message to the firm's employees. Conversely, if the chief executive is high-profile about being very ethical, this not only models correct behaviour to employees, it may actually discourage bribe requests from outsiders because they know where the company stands.

A 1997 survey by KPMG found that two-thirds of Canada's largest corporations have codes of ethics (90 percent of large U.S. firms do). More and more regulatory and professional associations in Canada are recommending that corporations adopt codes of ethics. The Canada Deposit Insurance Corp., for example, requires that all deposit-taking institutions have a code of conduct that is periodically reviewed and ratified by the board of directors. The Canadian Competition Bureau, the Canadian Institute of Chartered Accountants, and the Ontario Human Rights Commission all are pushing for the adoption of codes of ethics by corporations.[3]

A lively current debate concerns the degree to which business ethics can be "taught" in schools. Not surprisingly, business schools have been important participants in such debates. But companies also need to educate

Guiding Principles — The Great-West Life Assurance Company

1. Great-West Life's management recognizes that, to prosper, the company must serve its clients, staff members and sales representatives, shareholders, and the community at large, with integrity and according to the highest standards of conduct.

2. We will maintain an environment of trust in, and respect for, the dignity of the individual. We will strive to select superior people. We will build and maintain a dynamic organization through an open and participative style of management. We will give staff members and sales personnel every opportunity to make the most of their abilities and reward them according to their contribution to meeting our objectives.

3. We will distribute our products and services in the best interests of our clients through distribution systems that are contemporary, innovative, and socially responsible.

4. Our investment program will carefully balance the quality, terms, and rate of return on our investments. We will strive to achieve a consistently superior rate of return to meet our overall financial objectives and obligations to our clients.

5. We will find new and better ways to serve our clients by offering products and services that are both contemporary and innovative to satisfy their changing needs and desires. We will maintain their goodwill by meeting our commitments to them both in spirit and letter with particular emphasis upon the financial management and security of their funds.

6. We will work to increase the long-term value of shareholders' investment to maintain our reputation as a sound and growing financial institution.

Figure 5.2
Ethical principles at Great-West Life Assurance Co.

employees. More and more firms are taking this route, offering ethics training to their managers. Imperial Oil, for example, conducts workshops for employees that emphasize ethical concerns. Their purpose is to help employees put Imperial's ethics statement into practice.

The Nature of Social Responsibility

Ethics affect how an individual behaves within a business. But **social responsibility** affects how a business behaves as an entity on its own towards other businesses, customers, investors, and society at large. Like ethics, social responsibility is individualistic (for the firm, not a person), since it must attempt to balance different commitments. For example, in order to behave responsibly towards its investors, a company must try to maximize its profits. But a responsibility towards its customers means that it must produce safe goods or services. In their zeal to respond to investors, companies sometimes step over the line and act irresponsibly towards their customers. For example, Hertz Rent-A-Car was charged with overcharging its corporate customers and filing bogus insurance claims for damages.

Just as an individual's personal code of ethics is influenced by many factors, so is a firm's sense of social responsibility. To a large extent social responsibility depends on the ethics of the individuals employed by a firm—especially its top management. But social responsibility can also be forced from outside by government and consumers. How a firm behaves is also shaped by how other firms in the same country and industry behave and by the demands of investors.

social responsibility

A business's collective code of ethical behaviour towards the environment, its customers, its employees, and its investors.

Areas of Social Responsibility

In defining its sense of social responsibility—or having it defined—most firms must confront four issues. As Figure 5.3 shows, these issues concern an organization's responsibility towards its environment, its customers, its employees, and its investors.

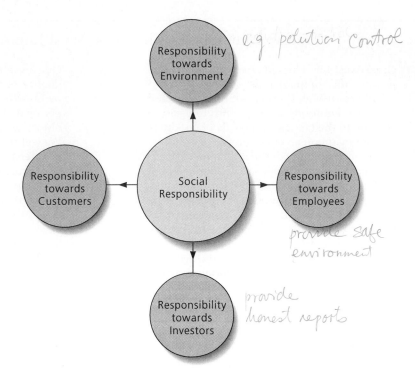

Figure 5.3
There are four basic areas of social responsibility.

Responsibility Towards the Environment

One critical area of social responsibility involves how the business relates to its physical environment. As noted earlier in Chapter 3, **pollution** has been and continues to be a significant managerial challenge. Although noise pollution is attracting increased concern, air pollution, water pollution, and land pollution are the subjects of most anti-pollution efforts by business and governments.[4] The Kyoto Summit in 1997 was an attempt by various governments to reach agreement on ways to reduce the threat of pollution.

Air Pollution

Air pollution results when a combination of factors converge to lower air quality. Large amounts of chemicals such as the carbon monoxide emitted by automobiles contribute to air pollution. Smoke and other chemicals emitted by manufacturing plants also help to create air pollution.

Legislation has gone a long way towards controlling air pollution. Under new laws, many companies have had to install special devices to limit the pollutants they expel into the atmosphere. Such clean-up efforts are not without costs, however. The bill to private companies for air pollution control devices runs into billions of dollars.

Even with these devices, however, acid rain remains a problem. **Acid rain** occurs when sulphur pumped into the atmosphere mixes with natural moisture and falls as rain. Much of the acid rain damage to forests and streams in the eastern United States and Canada has been attributed to heavy manufacturing and power plants in the midwestern United States.

Acid rain poses a dilemma in social responsibility for businesses. Current technologies to greatly reduce sulphur pollution are so costly that they would force many businesses to close. Such a move would cause major financial losses for investors and for laid-off employees, not to mention the loss of crucial services. The business challenge is to find ways to significantly re-

pollution

The injection of harmful substances into the environment.

acid rain

A form of pollution affecting the eastern United States and Canada as a result of sulphur expelled into the air by midwestern power and manufacturing plants.

duce the sulphur—and thus the acid rain—without incurring costs that are too high to bear.

Water Pollution

For years, businesses and municipalities dumped their waste into rivers, streams, and lakes with little regard for the effects. Thanks to new legislation and increased awareness on the part of businesses, water quality is improving in many areas. Millar Western Pulp Ltd. built Canada's first zero-discharge pulp mill at Meadow Lake, Saskatchewan. There is no discharge pipe to the river, no dioxin-forming chlorine, and next to no residue. Dow Chemical built a plant at Fort Saskatchewan that will not dump any pollutants into the nearby river.[5]

Dow Chemical
http://www.dow.com/homepage/index.html

Land Pollution

Two key issues are associated with land pollution. The first issue is how to restore the quality of land damaged and abused in the past. This issue is particularly important in areas where strip mining has jeopardized the safety of nearby residents.

A second, but no less important, issue is how to prevent such problems in the future. Changes in foresting practices, limits on types of mining, and new forms of solid waste disposal are all attempts to address this issue, although such changes are often opposed. A whole new industry—**recycling**—has developed as part of increased consciousness about land pollution. RBW Graphics, for example, uses a process that cleanses paper fibres and other impurities from ink recovered from printing presses. The system saves the company 35 000 kilograms of ink annually. This ink used to be transported to a dump. Instead, recycling saves the company $175 000 each year.[6]

recycling
The reconversion of waste materials into useful products.

Other business firms are also reducing what they send to city dumps. The Royal York Hotel in Toronto, for example, has installed machinery that extracts 70 percent of the moisture from organic waste. The hotel has reduced the amount it sends to the dump by 50 percent. Ramada Renaissance in Toronto has bought a refrigerator that stores waste which will ultimately become animal food. The hotel anticipates it will reduce its waste sent to the dump by

Toxic waste disposal and clean-up have become increasingly important areas of debate and concern in recent years.

toxic waste
Pollution resulting from the emission of chemical and/or radioactive byproducts of various manufacturing processes into the air, water, or land.

Greenpeace
http://www.greenpeacecanada.org

75 percent.[7] Bell Canada has reduced the amount of garbage it generates each day from 800 kilograms to 22 kilograms at its Etobicoke, Ontario, location.[8]

An especially controversial problem centres on toxic waste disposal. **Toxic wastes** are dangerous chemical and/or radioactive byproducts of various manufacturing processes. Because toxic waste cannot usually be processed into harmless material or destroyed, it must be stored somewhere. The problem is—where? Few people want a toxic waste storage facility in their town.

Various organizations aggressively monitor business activity that might lead to pollution. For example,

- Greenpeace sent a letter to 60 Canadian and foreign investment dealers making the case that the dealers should advise their clients not to invest in Canadian Mining and Energy Corp. because of environmental concerns.[9]

- A group of Canadian shareholders has criticized Placer Dome Inc. for its open pit copper mine on Marinduque Island in the Philippines.[10]

- The Task Force on the Churches and Corporate Responsibility (TFCCR) and Probe International have publicly criticized Canadian firms like Atomic Energy of Canada Ltd. (selling a food irradiator to Thailand), Petro-Canada (road building in the Ecuadorian rain forest), and Brascan Ltd. (exploration rights for tin in areas of Ecuador conflicting with Native land claims).[11]

- Because those who own the land can be forced to pay to clean it up, the Royal Bank refuses to lend money to some types of companies (e.g., waste oil firms) until an environmental audit has been carried out. When Dominion Barrel and Drum went bankrupt, for example, it left behind thousands of contaminated barrels on 21 hectares of land. The firm's creditor, the Federal Business Development Bank, decided not to foreclose on the land when it found that it would cost over $1 million—more than what the land was worth—to clean it up.[12]

Many business firms are now acting to reduce various forms of pollution. However, as the box "Living Up To Environmental Expectations" shows, the road to environmental purity is not easy. Under the Canadian and Ontario Environmental Protection Acts, liability for a business firm can run as high as $2 million per day. To protect themselves, companies must prove that they showed diligence in avoiding an environmental disaster such as an oil or gasoline spill.[13] The Environmental Choice program, sponsored by the federal government, licenses products that meet environmental standards set by the Canadian Standards Association. Firms whose products meet these standards can put the logo—three doves intertwined to form a maple leaf—on their products.[14]

Responsibility Towards Customers

Social responsibility towards customers generally falls into one of two categories: providing quality products and pricing those products fairly. As with the environment, firms differ in their level of concern about responsibility to customers. Yet unlike environmental problems, customer problems do not require expensive technological solutions. Most such problems can be avoided if companies obey the laws regarding consumer rights and illegal pricing practices.

Rights of Consumers

consumerism
A social movement that seeks to protect and expand the rights of consumers in their dealings with businesses.

Much of the current interest in business responsibility towards customers can be traced to the rise of consumerism. **Consumerism** is a form of social activism dedicated to protecting the rights of consumers in their dealings with businesses.

The Canadian Business Scene

Living Up To Environmental Expectations

Over the last few years, business firms have learned some hard lessons about the environmental movement in Canada. In spite of increased spending on pollution control equipment and greater sensitivity to environmental concerns, companies are finding that consumers and environmental groups can be difficult to satisfy. Chemical giant Dow Chemical and the fast-food wonder McDonald's are two firms that have experienced such frustrations.

Dow Chemical

Dow has long been a target of environmentalists, both because of the kinds of products it produces and because of some well-publicized chemical spills. One of the most famous occurred in 1985 when the company was responsible for a massive spill of perchloroethylene into the St. Clair River. That incident galvanized the company into aggressively confronting its pollution problem and, in the last few years, it has spent millions of dollars as part of its plan to drastically reduce pollution. At its Sarnia plant, for example, Dow has embarked on a 10-year, $100-million project to keep waste waters inside the plant. The company has also steadily increased environmental spending in general. It has pledged $20-$25 million to cut its air emissions in half by 1995. Teams of workers at its various plants systematically check equipment to assess the potential for leaks and spills before they happen.

But all this activity is not enough for environmental groups such as Pollution Probe, Greenpeace, and the Walpole Island First Nation Council. They want Dow to stop making certain chemicals altogether because ending their production will automatically solve the pollution problem. But "sunsetting" (stopping production of certain chemicals) is highly controversial. Dow makes considerable profits from manufacturing chemicals such as chlorine and is reluctant to stop producing it. Environmentalists, on the other hand, would like to see production of a whole range of chemicals ended almost immediately.

McDonald's

McDonald's has also had its share of environmental frustrations. Ironically, McDonald's is a company that has long been environmentally conscious. When McDonald's started operations in 1955, public health was a major concern and many fast-food restaurants were sanitary danger zones. McDonald's made a commitment to freshly prepared food of uniform quality wrapped in disposable paper. In the 1960s, environmentalists began to focus on litter. McDonald's pressured its franchisees to clean up all the garbage within a square block of each restaurant.

By the 1970s, legislation prompted McDonald's to address what type of disposable packaging it should use. Because environmentalists were concerned about the number of trees being cut down to fulfil its packaging needs, the firm adopted the plastic polystyrene foam container (the "clamshell"). But by the mid-1980s, environmentalists were denouncing polystyrene on three grounds: the manufacture of polystyrene creates harmful toxic emissions; the use of chlorofluorocarbons in the manufacturing process damages the ozone layer of the earth; plastic polystyrene is not biodegradable.

McDonald's responded to these concerns by changing the manufacturing process to eliminate the need for chlorofluorocarbons and to reduce the toxic emissions produced. In answer to the issue of biodegradability, McDonald's noted that polystyrene makes up only three-tenths of 1 percent of landfill by weight whereas paper and cardboard make up 35 percent of the total weight. Nonetheless, in spite of polystyrene's low impact on landfill sites, McDonald's stated that it wanted to be environmentally sound and so would recycle polystyrene.

The company committed over $5 million dollars to recycling, including building a recycling plant. Hoping to get a "green housekeeping" seal of approval, McDonald's signed a cooperation agreement with the Environmental Defense Fund (EDF) that gave the EDF complete access to McDonald's records. But, as McDonald's learned, the EDF was totally opposed to polystyrene in any form, recycled or not.

At about the same time, McDonald's began receiving large numbers of letters from consumers who didn't like the polystyrene clamshells. When the head of the EDF refused to join McDonald's senior environmental officer at a press conference, the company decided that its recycling plan just wasn't going to work. It replaced the clamshell with thin paper wrappers.

McDonald's seems to be in a no-win situation. Now the company is under fire from environmentalists who claim that paper waste is even worse than polystyrene. They accuse McDonald's of reneging on its commitment to recycling for public relations reasons rather than for environmental reasons. They also quote from a study McDonald's had used originally to defend polystyrene, a study that showed that greasy paper is almost impossible to recycle.

McDonald's decisions affect other businesses as well. When Lily Cups, the supplier of polystyrene, lost the clamshell business, it had to lay off 46 workers. It also had to scramble to buy paper-product machinery to fulfil its contract with McDonald's for coffee cups. McDonald's vice-president of environmental affairs says that the company is fed up with taking all the heat alone. He notes that other companies do less than McDonald's for the environment, yet they never get bad press.

The basic lesson that can be learned from McDonald's experience is that all the parties involved—government, business, environmentalists, suppliers—have to collaborate on environmental issues if the outcome is to be positive.

Consumers have several rights. First, they have the right to safe products. For example, when you buy a new paint sprayer, it must be safe to use for spraying paint. It must come with instructions on how to use it, and it must have been properly tested by its manufacturer. Dow Corning Corp. halted production of silicone breast implants after questions were raised about the product's safety. The box "What To Do in a Mad Cow Crisis" gives a detailed example of consumer safety.

Second, consumers have the right to be informed about all relevant aspects of a product. Food products must list their ingredients. Clothing must be labelled with information about its proper care. And banks must tell you exactly how much interest you are paying on a loan. Cereal companies have come under fire recently for some of the claims they have made about the oat bran content of their cereals, as well as its likely effects.

International Report

What To Do in a Mad Cow Crisis

The British public was jittery, and top executives at McDonald's and Burger King knew why. On March 21, 1996, the British government announced a possible link between bovine spongiform encephalopathy (BSE), or "mad cow disease," and Creutzfeld-Jakob disease, a fatal brain condition in humans. Fifty-five people in England had died from Creutzfeld-Jakob in 1994, including 10 people who had probably contracted the disease from beef contaminated with BSE. Coinciding with the increase in human deaths was a mad cow disease epidemic that had affected more than 162 000 animals since 1986.

To American fast-food restaurants doing business in Great Britain, the government announcement translated immediately into a business crisis. Customers' concerns about product safety and the need to maintain consumer confidence were uppermost on executives' minds. McDonald's was the first to act. Three days after the government announcement, the British division of the American fast-food giant suspended the sale of all British beef products. "Our customers expect us to take a lead and we have," declared Paul Preston, president of McDonald's United Kingdom division. "We believe that British beef is safe. However, we cannot ignore the fact that recent announcements have led to a growing loss of consumer confidence in British beef." McDonald's served nonburger selections for four days until its restaurants began receiving beef products from continental Europe.

Burger King acted seven days later to pull all British beef from its 382 restaurants. In making this decision, the firm cited the need to maintain consumer confidence in the safety of its products and the concern that it would be forced to close restaurants if it continued to use British beef. Burger King also announced that its burgers would be made from Italian, German, and French beef. The decision was well received. Burger King, confirmed company official Alan Randall, "has advertised extensively since this thing started and has been informing people that it imports all its meat. Because of that, our sales have not been hurt at all. People trust Burger King."

Many British food companies also took swift action. Bass Taverns, a chain of 2700 restaurants and pubs, withdrew all British beef and beef products from its menus four days after the crisis began. Monte's, an expensive private dining club in London, yielded to the concerns of diners who "can well afford the price of fine, imported cuts of meat." However, other British food companies took a different tack. Less concerned with consumer confidence than their U.S. counterparts, they continued to sell domestic beef and let customers make their own decisions about what not to eat. Many British firms seemed satisfied that the decision would not result in long-term sales drops. In fact, the first news of mad cow disease caused burger sales to decrease by half at restaurants, theme parks, and other food and beverage sellers. But, reports Maxine Donne, a food-service manager in Blackpool, "things quickly went back to normal. Everyone's aware of it now. I don't think anyone really cares." Colin Dawson, the managing director of a seaside resort park in Margate, agreed. "It's not that big a deal," argued Dawson. "The media has blown it out of proportion."

What influenced most the rapid decision of U.S. firms to pull British beef off their shelves? Was it an American culture that emphasizes health concerns? Or was it an equally American anxiety about litigation? No one can say for sure. It is certain, however, American fast-food chains placed great value on maintaining consumer confidence and trust. Perhaps the best indicator of whether these companies did the right thing is the collective reaction of their own consumers. If 20-year-old David Baker is typical, the choice to emphasize safety was on the mark: "I'm pretty wary of beefburgers now," volunteers Baker.

Third, consumers have a right to be heard. Many companies today have complaints offices. Retailers like Kmart offer a money-back guarantee if consumers aren't satisfied. On many of its products Proctor & Gamble puts a toll-free number that consumers can call if they have questions or complaints. When companies refuse to respond to consumer complaints, consumer protection agencies such as the Better Business Bureau and consumer interest groups such as the Airline Passengers Association may intervene.

Finally, consumers have a right to choose what they buy. Central to this right is free and open competition among companies. In times past, "gentlemen's agreements" were often used to avoid competition or to divide up a market so that firms did not have to truly compete against each other. Such practices are illegal today and any attempts by business to block competition can result in fines or other penalties.

Unfair Pricing

Interfering with competition can also mean illegal pricing practices. **Collusion** among companies—getting together to "fix" prices—is against the law. Polar Plastic Ltd. of Montreal pled guilty to conspiring to fix prices of disposable cups, glasses, and cutlery in the U.S. market. Although secret meetings and phone conversations took place between executives of competing companies as they tried to fix prices, the conspiracy was not successful.[15]

collusion
An illegal agreement among companies in an industry to "fix" prices for their products.

Responsibility Towards Employees

Organizations also need to employ fair and equitable practices with their employees. Later, in Chapter 9, we describe the human-resource management activities essential to a smoothly functioning business. These same activities—recruiting, hiring, training, promoting, and compensating—are also the basis for social responsibility towards employees. A company that provides its employees with equal opportunities for rewards and advancement without regard to race, sex, or other irrelevant factors is meeting its social responsibilities. Firms that ignore their responsibility to employees leave themselves open for lawsuits. They also miss the chance to hire better and more highly motivated employees.

Some progressive companies go well beyond these legal requirements, hiring and training the so-called hard-core unemployed (people with little education and training and a history of unemployment) and those who have disabilities. The Bank of Montreal, for example, sponsors a community college skills upgrading course for individuals with hearing impairments. The Royal Bank provides managers with discrimination awareness training. Rogers Cablesystems Ltd. has begun to provide individuals with mobility restrictions with telephone and customer-service job opportunities.[16] Bell Canada employs more than 1000 people with disabilities (2 percent of its permanent workforce). But, in Canada, over 50 percent of those with physical disabilities are still unemployed.[17]

In addition to their responsibility to employees as resources of the company, firms have a social responsibility to their employees as people. Firms that accept this responsibility make sure that the workplace is safe, both physically and emotionally. They would no more tolerate an abusive manager or one who sexually harasses employees than they would a gas leak.

Business firms also have a responsibility to respect the privacy of their employees. While nearly everyone agrees that companies have the right to exercise some level of control over their employees, there is great controversy about exactly how much is acceptable in areas like drug testing and computer monitoring. When Canadian National Railways instituted drug testing for train, brake, and yard employees, 12 percent failed. Trucking companies have found that nearly one third of truckers who have been involved in an accident are on drugs.[18]

Canadian National Railways
http://www.cn.ca

Employees are often unaware that they are being monitored by managers who are using new computer technology. Computer software firms even sell programs called "Spy" and "Peek" to facilitate monitoring. This type of monitoring increases employee stress levels because they don't know exactly when the boss is watching them. A lawsuit was brought against Northern Telecom by employees who charged that the firm installed telephone bugs and hidden microphones in one of its plants.[19]

Respecting employees as people also means encouraging ethical behaviour. Too often, individuals who try to act ethically find themselves in trouble on the job. This problem is especially true for **whistle-blowers**, employees who detect an unethical, illegal, and/or socially irresponsible action within the company and try to end it.

whistle-blower

An individual who calls attention to an unethical, illegal, and/or socially irresponsible practice on the part of a business or other organization.

For example, Ross Gray, formerly a vice-president at Standard Trustco Ltd., was dismissed from his position after he "blew the whistle" on illegal activities at the company. The company claimed that Gray had participated in the illegal activities. He filed a wrongful dismissal suit against the firm.[20]

In a socially responsible company, whistle-blowers can confidently report their findings to higher-level managers, who will act or forward the report to someone who can. However, in many firms, whistle-blowers are penalized for their efforts and find themselves demoted or even fired. A few of these individuals persist, taking their cases to the media or to government agencies. But employees in companies that discourage whistle-blowing more often choose to keep silent, to the loss of both business and society.

Responsibility Towards Investors

It may sound odd to say that a firm can be irresponsible towards investors, since they are the owners of the company. But if the managers of a firm abuse its financial resources, the ultimate losers are the owners, since they do not receive the earnings, dividends, or capital appreciation due them. The Bre-X stock market scandal (see Chapter 21) clearly shows how investors can be hurt when individuals in a business firm behave irresponsibly. This behaviour can take several forms.

Improper Financial Management

Occasionally, organizations are guilty of financial mismanagement. In other cases, executives have been "guilty" of paying themselves outlandish salaries, spending huge amounts of company money for their own personal comfort, and similar practices. Creditors can do nothing. Even shareholders have few viable options. Trying to force a management changeover is not only difficult, it can drive down the price of the stock, a penalty shareholders are usually unwilling to assign themselves.

Cheque Kiting

cheque kiting

The illegal practice of writing cheques against money that has not yet arrived at the bank on which the cheque has been written, relying on that money arriving before the cheque clears.

Other practices are specifically illegal. **Cheque kiting**, for instance, involves writing a cheque against money that has not yet arrived at the bank on which it is drawn. In 1993, E.F. Hutton and Co. was convicted of violating kiting laws on a massive scale: In a carefully planned scheme, company managers were able to use as much as $250 million every day that did not belong to the firm. Managers would deposit customer cheques for, say, $1 million into the company account. Knowing that the bank would collect only a percentage of the total deposit over the course of several days, they proceeded to write cheques against the total $1 million.

Insider Trading

Another area of illegal and socially irresponsible behaviour by firms towards investors is the practice of **insider trading**. Insider trading occurs when someone uses confidential information to gain from the purchase or sale of stocks. In the U.S., Ivan Boesky, a professional Wall Street trader, and Dennis Levine, an investment banker, worked together to make large profits. When Levine heard of an upcoming merger or acquisition, he passed the information along to Boesky. Boesky, in turn, bought and sold the appropriate stocks to make huge profits, which he then split with Levine. In one especially profitable instance, Boesky used Levine's information about Nestlé's plans to buy Carnation stock to earn over $28 million in profits.[21] Veronika Hirsch, a mutual fund manager for AGF Management Ltd., bought shares in a mining company for herself weeks before she also bought the stock—at double the price—for the mutual fund she was managing. This was technically not illegal, but when she failed to inform AGF officials that she had purchased some shares for herself, she violated the company's code of ethics and was removed from her job.

insider trading

The use of confidential information to gain from the purchase or sale of stock.

Misrepresentation of Finances

Irresponsible and unethical behaviour regarding financial representation is also illegal. All corporations are required to conform to generally accepted accounting practices in maintaining and reporting their financial status. Sometimes, though, managers project profits far in excess of what they truly expect to earn. When the truth comes out, investors are almost always bitter. Occasionally, companies are found guilty of misrepresenting their finances to outsiders.

Implementing Social Responsibility Programs

Thus far, we have discussed social responsibility as if a consensus exists on how firms should behave in most situations. In fact, dramatic differences of opinion exist as to the appropriateness of social responsibility as a business goal. As you might expect, some people oppose any business activity that cuts into profits to investors. Others argue that responsibility must take precedence over profits.

Even people who share a common attitude towards social responsibility by businesses may have different reasons for their beliefs. Some opponents of such activity fear that if businesses become too active in social concerns, they will gain too much control over how those concerns are addressed. They point to the influence many businesses have been able to exert on the government agencies that are supposed to regulate their industries. Other critics of business-sponsored social programs argue that companies lack the expertise needed. They believe that technical experts, not businesses, should decide how best to clean up a polluted river, for example.

Supporters of social responsibility believe that corporations are citizens just like individuals and therefore need to help improve our lives. Others point to the vast resources controlled by businesses and note that since businesses often create many of the problems social programs are designed to alleviate, they should use their resources to help. Still others argue that social responsibility is wise because it pays off for the firm.

Max Clarkson, formerly a top-level business executive, is now the director of the Centre for Corporate Social Performance and Ethics at the University of Toronto. He says that business firms that have a strong consciousness about ethics and social responsibility outperform firms that don't. After

The safety of workers is an important consideration for all organizations. The required use of hardhats, for example, is designed to protect workers from head injuries.

designing and applying a social responsibility rating system for companies, he found that companies that had the highest marks on questions of ethics and social responsibility also had the highest financial performance.[22]

Approaches to Social Responsibility

Given these differences of opinion, it is little wonder that corporations adopt a variety of postures when making decisions about social responsibility. Three common approaches are discussed below.

Social-Obligation Approach

social-obligation approach
A conservative approach to social responsibility in which a company does only the minimum required by law.

The **social-obligation approach** is consistent with the argument that profits should not be spent on social programs. The company that uses this approach does the minimum required by government regulation and standard business practices, but nothing else.

Tobacco companies exemplify this approach. They did not put health warnings on their packages and did not drop television advertising until forced to do so by the government. In other countries that lack such bans, Canadian and American tobacco companies still advertise heavily and make no mention of the negative effects of smoking.

Ronald McDonald House helps the families of children who are in hospital care. It is supported by McDonald's and is an excellent example of socially responsible behaviour by a business corporation.

Social-Reaction Approach

Firms using the **social-reaction approach** go beyond the bare minimums if specifically asked. For example, many companies will match employee contributions to approved causes. Others sponsor local hockey teams. But someone has to knock on the door and ask.

social-reaction approach
A moderate approach to social responsibility in which a company sometimes goes beyond the minimum required by law on request.

Social-Response Approach

Firms that adopt the **social-response approach** actively seek opportunities to contribute to the well-being of society. McDonald's, for example, has worked with children's hospitals and local communities to establish Ronald McDonald Houses to provide lodging for families of seriously ill children hospitalized away from home.

social-response approach
A liberal approach to social responsibility in which a company actively seeks opportunities to contribute to the well-being of society.

Donating money to different "causes" is one way that business firms try to show that they are socially responsible. Many groups that used to receive government funding (but no longer do because of government spending cuts) are increasingly seeking corporate support for their activities. More and more corporations are being asked to donate money to educational institutions, welfare agencies, service clubs, arts and culture groups, and athletic organizations.

A Decima Research survey found that 80 percent of Canadians think that business should give some its profits to social causes.[23] In another survey, Canadians expressed the opinion that business should provide 20 percent of the total money needed by various causes.[24] Corporations in Canada actually give about 10 percent of all money donated to charity; the typical corporation gives less than one half of 1 percent of pretax profits to charity. The top 10 corporate cash donors are listed in Table 5.1.

Most large business firms in Canada have clear procedures for dealing with requests for money from charities or other kinds of groups. The business firm first determines how much money it will give in total each year (usually a percentage of profit), and then decides which specific organizations will receive the money, and the amount each will receive. These decisions are made by the board of directors, usually after they receive a recommendation from a committee that has been set up by the business to consider charitable requests.

Table 5.1   **The Top 10 Corporate Givers in Canada, 1995–96**

	Company	Donation (in millions)
1.	Royal Bank of Canada	$16.0
2.	Canadian Imperial Bank of Commerce	9.0
3.	Bank of Montreal	6.5
4.	Imperial Oil Charitable Foundation	6.3
5.	Bank of Nova Scotia	5.0
6.	Glaxo Wellcome Inc.	4.7
7.	Bell Canada	4.7
8.	Seagram Co. Ltd.	4.0
9.	Nova Corp.	4.0
10.	Merck Frosst Canada Inc.	4.0

Includes companies that participated in the survey. Only covers cash donations; excludes gifts in kind and employee fund-raising.

Managing Social Responsibility Programs

Making a company truly socially responsible in the full sense of the social-response approach takes an organized and managed program. In particular, managers must take four steps to foster social responsibility, as shown in Figure 5.4.

First, social responsibility must start at the top. Without this support, no program can succeed. Top managers must make the decision that they want to take a stronger stand on social responsibility and develop a policy statement outlining their commitment.

Second, a committee of top managers needs to develop a plan detailing the level of support to be directed towards social responsibility. Some companies set aside a percentage of profits for social programs. Levi Strauss, for example, has a policy of giving 2.4 percent of its pretax earnings to worthy causes. Managers also need to set specific priorities. Should the firm train the hard-core unemployed or support the arts, for example?

Third, one specific executive needs to be given the authority to act as director of the firm's social agenda. Whether this is a separate job or an additional responsibility, this individual must monitor the program and ensure that its implementation is consistent with the policy statement and the strategic plan.

Figure 5.4
Establishing a social responsibility program involves four basic steps.

Finally, the organization needs to conduct occasional social audits. A **social audit** is a systematic analysis of how a firm is using funds earmarked for its social-responsibility goals. Consider the case of a company whose strategic plan calls for spending $100 000 to train 200 hard-core unemployed people and subsequently to place 180 of them in jobs. If at the end of one year the firm has spent $98 000, trained 210 people, and placed 175 into jobs, an audit will confirm the program as a success. But if the program cost $150 000, trained only 90 people, and placed only 10 of them in jobs, the audit will reveal the program's failure. A failure should signal the director and the committee to rethink the program's implementation and/or their choice of priorities.

social audit
A systematic analysis of how a firm is using funds earmarked for social-responsibility goals and how effective these expenditures have been.

Social Responsibility and the Small Business

Although many of the examples in this chapter illustrate responses to social responsibility and ethical issues by big business, small businesses face many of the same questions.

As the owner of a garden supply store, how would you respond to a building inspector's suggestion that a cash payment would expedite your application for a building permit? As the manager of a nightclub, would you call the police, refuse service or sell liquor to a customer whose ID card looks forged? Or as the owner of a small laboratory, would you actually call the board of health to make sure that it has licensed the company you want to contract with to dispose of the lab's medical waste? Is the small manufacturing firm justified in overcharging a customer by 5 percent whose purchasing agent is lax? Who will really be harmed if a small firm pads its income statement to help get a much-needed bank loan?

Can a small business afford a social agenda? Should it sponsor hockey teams, make donations to the United Way, and buy light bulbs from the Lion's Club? Is joining the Chamber of Commerce and supporting the Better Business Bureau too much or just good business? Clearly, ethics and social responsibility are decisions faced by all managers in all organizations, regardless of rank or size. One key to business success is to decide in advance how to respond to these issues.

The Role of Law in Canadian Society

Law is the set of rules and standards that a society agrees upon to govern the behaviour of its citizens. Both the British and the French influenced the development of law in Canada. In 1867, the *British North America (BNA) Act* created the nation of Canada. The *BNA Act* was "patriated" to Canada in 1982 and is known as the *Constitution Act*. As we saw in Chapter 3, this act divides legislative powers in Canada between the federal and provincial governments.

law
The set of rules and standards that a society agrees upon to govern the behaviour of its citizens.

Sources of Law

The law in Canada has evolved and changed in response to our norms and values. Our laws have arisen from three sources: 1) customs and judicial precedents (the source of common law), 2) the actions of provincial and federal legislatures (the source of statutory law), and 3) rulings by administrative bodies (the source of administrative law).

Common law is the unwritten law of England, derived from ancient precedents and judges' previous legal opinions. Common law is based on the principle of equity, the provision to every person of a just and fair remedy.

common law
The unwritten law of England, derived from precedent and legal judgments.

Canadian legal customs and traditions derive from British common law. All provinces except Quebec, which uses the French Civil Code, have laws based on British common law, and court decisions are often based on precedents from common law. That is, decisions made in earlier cases that involved the same legal point will guide the court.

statutory law

Written law developed by city councils, provincial legislatures and parliament.

Statutory law is written law developed by city councils, provincial legislatures, and parliament. Most law in Canada today is statutory law.

administrative law

Rules and regulations that government agencies develop based on their interpretations of statutory law.

Administrative law is the rules and regulations that government agencies and commissions develop based on their interpretations of statutory laws. For example, Consumer and Corporate Affairs Canada develops regulations on false advertising using federal legislation.

The Court System

In Canada, the judiciary branch of government has the responsibility of settling disputes among organizations or individuals by applying existing laws. Both provincial and federal courts exist to hear both criminal and civil cases. The Supreme Court of Canada is the highest court in Canada. It decides whether or not to hear appeals from lower courts.

Business Law

business law

Laws that specifically affect how businesses are managed.

Business firms, like all other organizations, are affected by the laws of the country. **Business law** refers to laws that specifically affect how business firms are managed. Some laws affect all businesses, regardless of size, industry, or location. For example, the *Income Tax Act* requires businesses to pay income tax. Other laws may have a greater impact on one industry than on others. For example, pollution regulations are of much greater concern to Inco than they are to Lawson Travel.

Business managers must have at least a basic understanding of eight important concepts in business law:

- contracts
- agency
- bailment
- property
- warranty
- torts
- negotiable instruments
- bankruptcy.

Contracts

contract

An agreement between two parties to act in a specified way or to perform certain acts.

Agreements about transactions are common in a business's day-to-day activity. A **contract** is an agreement between two parties to act in a specified way or to perform certain acts. A contract might, for example, apply to a customer buying a product from a retail establishment or to two manufacturers agreeing to buy products or services from each other. A valid contract includes several elements:

- *an agreement*—All parties must consciously agree about the contract.
- *consideration*—The parties must exchange something of value (e.g., time, products, services, money, etc.).
- *competence*—All parties to the contract must be legally able to enter into an agreement. Individuals who are below a certain age or who are legally insane, for example, cannot enter into legal agreements.

- *legal purpose*—What the parties agree to do for or with each other must be legal. An agreement between two manufacturers to fix prices is not legal.

The courts will enforce a contract if it meets the criteria described above. Most parties honour their contracts but, occasionally, one party does not do what it was supposed to do. **Breach of contract** occurs when one party to an agreement fails, without legal reason, to live up to the agreement's provisions. The party who has not breached the contract has three alternatives under the law in Canada: 1) discharge, 2) sue for damages, or 3) require specific performance.

An example will demonstrate these three alternatives. Suppose Barrington Farms Inc. agrees to deliver 100 dozen long-stemmed roses to the Blue Violet Flower Shop the week before Mother's Day. One week before the agreed-upon date, Barrington informs Blue Violet that it cannot make the delivery until after Mother's Day. Under the law, the owner of the Blue Violet can choose among any of the following:

breach of contract
When one party to an agreement fails, without legal reason, to live up to the agreement's provisions.

Discharge

Blue Violet can also ignore its obligations in the contract. That is, it can contract with another supplier.

Sue for Damages

Blue Violet can legally demand payment for losses caused by Barrington's failure to deliver the promised goods. Losses might include any increased price Blue Violet would have to pay for the roses or court costs incurred in the damage suit.

Require Specific Performance

If monetary damages are not sufficient to reimburse Blue Violet, the court can force Barrington's to live up to its original contract.

Agency

In many business situations, one person acts as an agent for another person. Well-known examples include actors and athletes represented by agents who negotiate contracts for them. An **agency–principal relationship** is established when one party (the agent) is authorized to act on behalf of another party (the principal).

The agent is under the control of the principal and must act on behalf of the principal and in the principal's best interests. The principal remains liable for the acts of the agent as long as the agent is acting within the scope of authority granted by the principal. A salesperson for IBM, for example, is an agent for IBM, the principal.

agency–principal relationship
When one party (the agent) is authorized to act on behalf of another party (the principal).

Bailment

Many business transactions are not covered by the agency–principal relationship. For example, suppose you take your car to a mechanic to have it repaired. Because the repair shop has temporary possession of something you own, it is responsible for your car. This is a **bailor–bailee relationship**. In a bailor–bailee relationship, the bailor (the car owner) gives possession of his or her property to the bailee (the repair shop) but retains ownership of the

bailor–bailee relationship
When a bailor, a property owner, gives possession of the property to a bailee, a custodian, but retains ownership of the property.

item. A business firm that stores inventory in a public warehouse is in a bailor–bailee relationship. The business firm is the bailor and the warehouse is the bailee. The warehouse is responsible for storing the goods safely and making them available to the manufacturer upon request.

The Law of Property

property
Anything of tangible or intangible value that the owner has the right to possess and own.

Property includes anything of tangible or intangible value that the owner has the right to possess and use. **Real property** is land and any permanent buildings attached to that land. **Personal property** is tangible or intangible assets other than real property. Personal property includes cars, clothing, furniture, money in bank accounts, stock certificates, and copyrights.

real property
Land and any permanent buildings attached to that land.

Transferring Property

personal property
Tangible or intangible assets other than real property.

From time to time, businesses and individuals need to transfer property to another person or business. A **deed** is a document that shows ownership of real property. It allows the transfer of title of real property.

deed
A document that shows ownership of real property.

A **lease** grants the use of an asset for a specified period of time in return for payment. The business or individual granting the lease is the lessor and the tenant is the lessee. For example, a business (the lessee) may rent space in a mall for one year from a real estate development firm (the lessor).

lease
A document that grants the use of an asset for a specified period of time in return for payment.

A **title** shows legal possession of personal property. It allows the transfer of title of personal property. When you buy a snowmobile, for example, the former owner signs the title over to you.

title
A document that shows legal possession of personal property.

Warranty

warranty
A promise that the product or service will perform as the seller has promised it will.

When you buy a product or service, you want some assurance that it will perform satisfactorily and meet your needs. A **warranty** is a promise that the product or service will perform as the seller has promised it will.

There are two kinds of warranties—express and implied. An **express warranty** is a specific claim that the manufacturer makes about a product. For example, a warranty that a screwdriver blade is made of case-hardened steel is an express warranty. An **implied warranty** suggests that a product will perform as the manufacturer claims it will. Suppose you buy an outboard motor for your boat and the engine burns out in one week. Because the manufacturer implies by selling the motor that it will work for a reasonable period of time, you can return it and get your money back.

express warranty
A specific claim that a manufacturer makes about a product.

implied warranty
An assumption that a product will perform as the manufacturer claims it will.

Because opinions vary on what is a "reasonable" time, most manufacturers now give limited time warranties on their products. For example, they will guarantee their products against defects in materials or manufacture for six months or one year.

Torts

tort
A wrongful civil act that one party inflicts on another.

A **tort** is a wrongful civil act that one party inflicts on another and that results in injury to the person, to the person's property, or to the person's good name. An **intentional tort** is a wrongful act intentionally committed. If a security guard in a department store suspects someone of shoplifting and uses excessive force to prevent him or her from leaving the store, the guard might be guilty of an intentional tort. Other examples are libel, embezzlement, and patent infringement.

intentional tort
A wrongful act intentionally committed.

Negligence is a wrongful act that inadvertently causes injury to another person. For example, if a maintenance crew in a store mops the floors without placing warning signs in the area, a customer who slips and falls might bring a negligence suit against the store.

negligence
A wrongful act that inadvertently causes injury to another person.

In recent years, the most publicized area of negligence has been product liability. **Product liability** means that businesses are liable for injuries caused to product users because of negligence in design or manufacturing. **Strict product liability** means that a business is liable for injuries caused by their products even if there is no evidence of negligence in the design or manufacture of the product. The box "McDonald's Brews Up a Lawsuit" describes an interesting case.

Negotiable Instruments

Negotiable instruments are types of commercial paper that can be transferred among individuals and business firms. Cheques, bank drafts, and certificates of deposit are examples of negotiable instruments.

The *Bills of Exchange Act* specifies that a negotiable instrument must

- be written
- be signed by the person who puts it into circulation (the maker or drawer)
- contain an unconditional promise to pay a certain amount of money
- be payable on demand
- be payable to a specific person (or to the bearer of the instrument).

Negotiable instruments are transferred from one party to another through an endorsement. An **endorsement** means signing your name to a negotiable instrument; this makes it transferable to another person or organization. If you sign only your name on the back of a cheque, you are making a *blank* endorsement. If you state that the instrument is being transferred to a specific person, you are making a *special* endorsement. A *qualified* endorsement limits your liability if the instrument is not backed up by sufficient funds. For example, if you get a cheque from a friend and want to use it to buy a new stereo, you can write "without recourse" above your name. If your friend's cheque bounces, you have no liability. A *restrictive* endorsement limits the negotiability of the instrument. For example, if you write "for deposit only" on the back of a cheque and it is later stolen, no one else can cash it.

Bankruptcy

At one time, individuals who could not pay their debts were jailed. Today, however, both organizations and individuals can seek relief by filing for **bankruptcy**—the court-granted permission not to pay some or all debts.

Thousands of individuals and businesses file for bankruptcy each year. Why do individuals and businesses file for bankruptcy? Cash-flow problems and drops in farm prices caused many farmers and small businesses to go bankrupt. In recent years, large enterprises such as Eaton's and Olympia & York have sought the protection of bankruptcy laws.

Three main factors account for the increase in bankruptcy filings:

1. The increased availability of credit
2. The "fresh-start" provisions in current bankruptcy laws
3. The growing acceptance of bankruptcy as a financial tactic

In some cases, creditors force an individual or firm into **involuntary bankruptcy** and press the courts to award them payment of at least part of what they are owed. Far more often, however, a person or business chooses to file for court protection against creditors. In general, individuals and firms whose debts exceed total assets may file for **voluntary bankruptcy**.

product liability

The liability of businesses for injuries caused to product users because of negligence in design or manufacture.

strict product liability

The liability of businesses for injuries caused by their products even if no evidence of negligence in the product's design or manufacture exists.

negotiable instrument

Types of commercial paper that can be transferred among individuals and business firms.

endorsement

Signing your name to a negotiable instrument making it transferable to another person or organization.

bankruptcy

Permission granted by the courts to individuals and organizations not to pay some or all of their debts.

involuntary bankruptcy

Bankruptcy proceedings initiated by the creditors of an indebted individual or organization.

voluntary bankruptcy

Bankruptcy proceedings initiated by an indebted individual or organization.

International Report

McDonald's Brews Up a Lawsuit

TORT

McDonald's serves up a *billion* cups of coffee each year. *Daily* revenue from coffee sales exceeds $1 million. Why does McDonald's sell so much coffee? For one thing, it serves its coffee the way most people like it: piping hot. For example, McDonald's heeds the recommendations of industry groups that coffee tastes best when brewed with water heated to 90 degrees Celsius and served at about 82 degrees. Temperatures that hot, of course, can cause serious burns, and in 1992, 81-year-old Stella Liebeck was scalded when she tried to remove the lid of a cup of coffee that she had purchased at the drive-through window of a McDonald's restaurant in Albuquerque, New Mexico. After McDonald's rejected Mrs. Liebeck's request for $800 U.S. to defray the cost of medical treatment, the injured woman hired a lawyer and sued. To the amazement of many observers, a jury sided with Liebeck and awarded her considerably more than $800—$2.9 million U.S., in fact.

quantify the damage

Should burns from a cup of coffee justify an award of that size? Liebeck's attorneys pointed out that her injuries were quite serious: She suffered third-degree burns and was hospitalized for seven days while undergoing skin grafts. After leaving the hospital and receiving no satisfaction from McDonald's, Liebeck met attorney Reed Morgan. Morgan had been involved in a 1986 lawsuit involving McDonald's coffee. Although that case had been settled for $27 500, Morgan remained convinced that McDonald's was wilfully serving coffee at a temperature that was both unnecessary and dangerous.

product liability

On Liebeck's behalf, Morgan filed a lawsuit contending that McDonald's coffee was "defective" because it was too hot. Originally, Morgan was willing to settle the case for $300 000, but McDonald's legal team refused the offer. Instead, it chose to defend the company's practice of brewing and serving piping-hot coffee. In fact, the defence team denied liability for Liebeck's injuries even after its own investigators had gathered data on coffee temperatures in other Albuquerque restaurants: McDonald's was indeed the hottest by a good margin.

As the trial opened, some jurors seemed skeptical about the merits of the suit. Then, however, they began to hear the evidence. Jurors were informed, for example, that McDonald's had received hundreds of complaints about coffee burns—and had in fact already paid more than $500 000 in settlements. In addition, the testimony of defence witnesses did little to help McDonald's cause. For example, a quality-assurance manager at the company admitted that McDonald's had never consulted burn experts about the possible dangers of extremely hot coffee. "There are," he explained, "more serious dangers in restaurants." Another expert witness called by the defence reported that, after all, the number of severe coffee scaldings was statistically insignificant in comparison to annual sales of a billion cups of coffee. Gradually, said one juror after the trial, it began to appear that McDonald's had, as the plaintiff charged, showed "a callous disregard for the safety of the people." The jury finally awarded $160 000 in compensatory damages and $2.7 million in punitive damages.

Although a New Mexico state court judge later reduced the punitive damages to $480 000, the parties ultimately settled out of court. For McDonald's, of course, the episode was costly not only in dollars but in negative publicity. For many firms—both large and small—it also serves as an object lesson on the possible impact of the legal system on business practices. The McDonald's case, however, has also focused the attention of many legal-system critics. In the fall of 1994, for example, the Republican "Contract with America" brought the U.S. legal system—especially negligence and product liability law—under close and official Congressional scrutiny. The size of the Liebeck award (indeed, the lawsuit itself) was cited to support the call for a "common sense" overhaul of personal-injury litigation. Business and trade associations have stepped up lobbying efforts for reform, and in May 1995, the U.S. Senate voted in favour of a bill that would apply a new formula for determining punitive damages: $250 000 or twice the combined amount of money awarded for pain and suffering, lost wages, and medical bills—whichever is greater.

Lining up against reform are consumer groups and the Association of Trial Lawyers. In reality, argue opponents of the pending legislation, juries seldom make outlandish personal-injury awards. Moreover, they point out, only one in four cases ever goes to trial; the vast majority are settled out of court. Finally, they contend that no new formulas are needed because many judges—like the one who adjusted the final Liebeck award—already adhere to a "three times compensatory" formula (that is, punitive awards that are no more than triple damages paid for injuries actually suffered).

Business Bankruptcy

A business bankruptcy may be resolved by one of three plans:

■ Under a *liquidation plan*, the business ceases to exist. Its assets are sold and the proceeds are used to pay creditors.

Mr. George Eaton announcing that Eaton's is seeking bankruptcy protection. The company eventually worked out a repayment plan that satisfied its creditors.

- Under a *repayment plan*, the bankruptcy company works out a new payment schedule to meet its obligations. The time frame is usually extended, and payments are collected and distributed by a court-appointed trustee.

- *Reorganization* is the most complex form of business bankruptcy. The company must explain the sources of its financial difficulties and propose a new plan for remaining in business. Reorganization may include a new slate of managers and a new financial strategy. A judge may also reduce the firm's debts to ensure its survival. Although creditors naturally dislike debt reduction, they may agree to the proposal, since 50 percent of what you are owed is better than nothing at all.

Summary of Learning Objectives

1. **Explain how individuals develop their personal *codes of ethics* and why ethics are important in the workplace.** Individual *codes of ethics* are derived from social standards of right and wrong. *Ethical behaviour* is behaviour conforming to generally accepted social norms concerning beneficial and harmful actions. The most common influences on ethics are situations, family and peers (and the values they convey), and experiences. Because ethics affect the behaviour of individuals on behalf of the companies that employ them, many firms are adopting formal statements of ethics. Unethical behaviour can result in loss of business, in fines, and even in imprisonment.

2. **Distinguish *social responsibility* from *ethics*.** *Social responsibility* refers to an organization's response to social needs, while ethics refers to an *individual's* perception of what is right and wrong or good and bad.

3. **Show how the concept of social responsibility applies to environmental issues and to a firm's relationships with customers, employees, and investors.** Social responsibility towards the environment requires firms to minimize pollution of the air, water,

and land. Social responsibility towards customers requires firms to price products fairly and to respect customers' rights. Social responsibility towards employees requires firms to respect workers both as resources and as people who are more productive when their needs are met. Social responsibility towards investors requires firms to manage their resources and to represent their financial status honestly.

4. **Identify three general *approaches to social responsibility* and describe the four steps a firm must take to implement a *social responsibility program*.** Companies approach social responsibility in many ways. The *social-obligation approach* emphasizes compliance with legal minimum requirements. Companies adopting the *social-reaction approach* go beyond minimum activities, if asked. The *social-response approach* commits a company to actively seeking to contribute to socially concerned projects. Implementing a *social responsibility program* entails four steps: (1) drafting a policy statement with the support of top management, (2) developing a detailed plan, (3) appointing a director to implement the plan, and (4) conducting social audits to monitor results.

5. **Explain how issues of social responsibility and ethics affect small businesses.** Managers and employees of small businesses face many of the same ethical questions as their counterparts at larger firms. Small businesses must confront the same areas of social responsibility and the same need to decide on an approach to social responsibility. The differences are primarily differences of scale.

6. **Identify the *sources of law*.** Common law grows out of previous judicial decisions and is based on precedent. Statutory law is codified, or written, law. It is enacted by city councils, provincial legislatures, and parliament. Administrative law is developed by government agencies and commissions. Business law is the body of law that pertains particularly to business actions.

7. **Explain the requirements for a valid *contract* and the remedies for *breach of contract*.** A contract is a mutual agreement between two or more people to perform or not perform certain acts. To be valid, a contract must include an agreement, consideration, competence of the parties to the contract, and a legal purpose. If there is a breach of contract, the remedies are discharge, suing for damages, and specific performance.

8. **Compare the *agency–principal* and *bailor–bailee* relationships.** The law of agency focuses on the legal duties of two parties who engage in an agency–principal relationship. The law of bailment is concerned with the surrender of personal property by one party to another with the expectation that the property will be returned in the future.

9. **Outline the main points of the *law of property*, including the role of *warranty*.** The law of property distinguishes between real property and personal property. In the sale of property the question of warranty often becomes important. The two kinds of warranty are express warranty and implied warranty.

Key Terms

Study Questions and Exercises

Review Questions

1. What factors influence the development of an individual's personal code of ethics?
2. What are the major areas of social responsibility that organizations need to be concerned about?
3. List the four rights of consumers.
4. What are the three basic approaches to social responsibility that an organization might choose to adopt?
5. Compare and contrast common, statutory, and administrative law.

Analysis Questions

6. What kind of wrongdoing would most likely prompt you to become a whistle-blower? What kind of wrongdoing would be least likely to prompt you? Why?

7. In what ways do you think your personal code of ethics might clash with the operations of some companies?
8. If you were a shareholder in a corporation, which of the approaches to social responsibility would you like to see applied by company management? Why?

Application Exercises

9. Develop and put into writing a code of ethics for use in the classroom. Your document should include guidelines for students, instructors, and administrators.
10. Find a newspaper or magazine account of a contract dispute between two parties. Identify the major issues in the dispute. How does the information in this chapter on contract law apply to the case?

Building Your Business Skills

Goal

To encourage students to apply general concepts of business ethics to specific business situations.

Situation

As the head of human resources of a large bank, you are in the process of developing a corporate code of ethics that will be issued to every bank employee. Among the major sections in the document are those that deal with the following sensitive topics:

- Discrimination against minority employees
- Discrimination against minority customers
- Sexual harrassment
- Conflicts of interest
- Accepting gifts from clients
- Privacy and confidentiality
- Accounting irregularities
- Lying to clients and fellow employees

Method

Step 1:
Working with four other students, determine your company's ethical stance on each of the topics listed above. This part of the project may require additional research. In your analysis, be certain to distinguish between your company's *ethical* and *legal* responsibilities.

...

For example, while discriminating against minority mortgage applicants on the basis of race is clearly illegal, lying to fellow employees may violate ethical, rather than legal, rules.

Step 2:

Using the information gathered in your research, draft a corporate code of ethics that explains the bank's position in each area. The code should define what the bank will do in each of the following situations:

■ A mortgage officer refuses to grant mortgages to qualified minority clients.

■ A female employee is sexually harassed by a male supervisor.

■ A lending officer grants a million-dollar loan to his wife's business associate even though the associate fails to meet appropriate qualifications.

■ A supplier of computer equipment receives special treatment after he gives gifts to bank employees in charge of computer purchases.

■ False data are included in accounting reports to stockholders.

■ Employees are regularly caught lying to clients and fellow employees in order to enhance their own positions in the company.

Follow-Up Questions

1. Do your responses to the ethics situations presented here have a common thread? If so, does this thread represent a values-based approach to corporate ethics? Explain.

2. What measures would you suggest for making your written code of ethics a living document that influences the way in which every employee conducts business?

3. In your opinion, is the need for corporate codes of ethics greater than it was five years ago? Explain your answer.

In this chapter, we note that some organizations develop codes of conduct or written statements that convey to interested parties how the firm views ethics and social responsibility. One firm, The Body Shop, is highly rated by sustainability for the United Nations Environmental Program. The Body Shop has drawn up written statements of its ethics and values. For a summary of the company's principles, visit its Web site at:

http://www.the-body-shop.com

1. Three business approaches to social responsibility are offered in the chapter. Which best describes The Body Shop? Explain.

2. Is The Body Shop's mission statement achievable? How could its success be measured?

3. What difficulties might The Body Shop have living up to company values and ethics when dealing with suppliers in less developed areas of the world? Research newspaper, magazines, or online sources to find out if any such problems have occurred for The Body Shop.

4. Based on the Web site, would you want to work for The Body Shop? Explain why or why not.

CONCLUDING CASE 5-1

Problems at the Better Business Bureau

Everyone has heard of the Better Business Bureau (BBB). Its mandate is to promote better business practices by warning consumers about everything from fly-by-night paving contractors to diamond mine scams.

The Toronto office has been the largest BBB in Canada for many years. Its president, Paul Tuz, worked tirelessly to build up the operation since he took the position in 1976. He pursued numerous business firms to become members of the BBB and got them to pay an annual membership fee. He became a member of the Order of Canada, and was an Ethnic Press Council man of the year. He was also a member of various charitable and hospital boards. In the mid-1980s, he helped out at the national BBB council when it ran out of money.

But problems began in the Toronto BBB's commission sales force in the late 1980s. These are the people who sign up the corporate memberships that are so critical to the BBB. One of the salespersons—a man by the name of James Peter Emms from Barrie, Ontario—eventually formed a group that challenged Tuz for leadership of the Toronto BBB.

Tuz originally praised Emms's sales skills. The average salesperson signs up four or five new members each week, but Emms signed up 14 per week on average. But Emms also had a talent for mobilizing dissent. Many people at the Toronto BBB had become so unhappy with Tuz that they wanted him out of the organization. Emms says that employees asked him to lead a task force to investigate complaints about the kind of money Tuz was taking out of the bureau.

During much of 1994, there were skirmishes between this task force (made up of several Barrie business firms) and the Toronto headquarters. Several of these were quite nasty. For example, Emms tried to get the Barrie police to investigate the BBB. Tuz retaliated by trying to have Emms arrested for parole violation (Tuz claimed that Emms came to the BBB after serving time in prison for fraud). Eventually, Tuz fired Emms.

By mid-1994, the task force was agitating to separate from the Toronto group. Then everyone started suing everyone else. A forensic accountant was hired to investigate task force complaints that Tuz had taken excessive pay and misappropriated money from the BBB. The accountant found that Tuz had been paid large sums of money, but that these payments had been approved by the BBB board.

When these findings hit the newspaper, the heat was turned up on the Toronto BBB, and they struck a deal with Emms and the Barrie task force. When *The Globe and Mail* obtained a copy of the agreement, it discovered that $325 000 had been paid by the Toronto BBB to Barrie; in return, the Barrie group agreed to drop Emms's wrongful dismissal lawsuits against the BBB and stop saying nasty things about Tuz. This was supposed to put an end to the infighting.

But in mid-1995, the national council said they would pull the Toronto bureau's licence unless its board of directors fired Tuz. Eventually Tuz resigned, as did the entire board. During this time, membership fees declined because good salespeople were leaving. The bureau ended up mortgaging its offices. It was also expelled from the Canadian Council of Better Business Bureaus.

In the view of his opponents, Tuz had one glaring weakness: he believed that he was indispensable to the BBB. The Toronto branch, which had logged 100 000 calls per year and had generated almost $2 million in membership fees, is now in shambles. The incident has raised questions about exactly what the BBB does, and, ironically, whether it has credibility as an organization.

Late in 1996, Tuz was arrested and charged with defrauding the BBB of $1.7 million. The charges dealt with issues about pay, pensions, expenses, and misappropriation of funds. Tuz has filed a defamation suit against BBB officials, but neither claims nor counterclaims have yet been proven.

Case Questions

1. What factors influence a person's ethical standards? What factor seems most prominent in influencing Paul Tuz?

2. How is it possible that an organization like the Better Business Bureau—which is committed to improving business practice—got itself into this kind of embarrassing situation?

3. Can business ethics be successfully taught in university or community college courses? Defend your answer. ◆

Better Business Bureau
http://www.bbb.org/index.html

Industrial Espionage

José Ignacio López de Arriortua did what millions of workers do each year—he changed jobs. But there was nothing ordinary about José López's job switch: Shortly after he left General Motors for Volkswagen, GM charged him with industrial espionage.

For nine months, López had headed GM's huge purchasing operation. Originally hired to slash $4 billion from GM's bill for automotive parts, he held a job that put him in the centre of key strategy decisions and financial forecasts. For one thing, José López handled on a daily basis the kind of top secrets that would in large part determine GM's success throughout the 1990s. Indeed, two days before announcing his resignation, López had attended an international strategy meeting at GM's Opel subsidiary in Germany. During the meeting, he was introduced to GM Europe's model plans, sales projections, and financial forecasts up to the year 2000. He also watched Opel prototypes being put through their paces on Opel's Dudenhofen track.

Fearing that López had taken confidential information away from the European strategy meeting, GM demanded written confirmation that López "had not taken any documents" with him "pertaining to [GM's] present and future corporate plans." Fueling GM's deepest fears were Volkswagen's subsequent efforts to lure away other GM employees. With López's help, Volkswagen had indeed tried to recruit more than 40 managers at Opel and GM, often enticing them with offers of doubled salaries. Before an injunction put a stop to its recruiting forays, VW had succeeded in hiring away seven key GM executives.

Although VW has denied allegations of industrial espionage and corporate raiding, the charges have left both López and the German carmaker under a legal and ethical cloud. That cloud became heavier when the district attorney of Darmstadt, Germany, discovered confidential GM documents at the home of a former GM executive who had, like López, defected to VW. At stake for Volkswagen is the public's perception of company ethics—an intangible factor that could affect the firm's sales. When a German polling organization asked 1000 Germans what they thought of the López affair, 65 percent believed that there was "something to" the allegations, while only 7 percent deemed them unfounded. Although Volkswagen hired López to cut costs and help return the company to profitability, it may have set itself up for failure if consumers react negatively to perceived unethical conduct. It may be a classic case, says Ian I. Mitroff, head of the crisis-management unit at the University of Southern California, where "the solution to one difficulty puts you into even worse problems." The potential problem for Volkswagen is fairly clear—the loss of public trust.

Finally, there is at least one more irony in the López affair. During his nine-month tenure at General Motors, López is charged with having leaked proprietary information from one supplier to another—actions that were in fact tolerated by GM. Suppliers who had been given blueprints of top-secret technology were able to underbid companies that had spent millions on research and development. As a result of these actions, 110 key automotive suppliers have ranked GM last among its industry peers in professionalism, cooperation, and communication. That vote constitutes an astounding fall for a purchasing department once considered the most professional and ethical in the auto industry.

GM filed a civil suit against Volkswagen claiming that López stole GM's plans for new cars, parts lists, price lists, and plans for a secret manufacturing plant. It claimed that VW used this information to lower its costs and to gain market share at GM's expense.

In early 1997, Volkswagen agreed to give GM $100 million in cash and to purchase $1 billion in parts from GM over the next seven years. López also resigned from VW, and GM agreed to drop their civil suit against VW. Both companies issued a statement expressing satisfaction that the disagreement had been settled.

Case Questions

1. As a result of López's resignation, GM CEO John F. Smith Jr. decided to require all top officers to sign formal contracts restricting their ability to work for a competing company for three years after leaving GM. How do you feel about this contract provision?

2. In your opinion, does an employee have an ethical responsibility to maintain the confidentiality of information gained on the job with one company when taking a job with a competing firm?

3. Should Volkswagen be concerned with the public's reaction to the López affair?

4. GM allowed López to reveal suppliers' proprietary information in order to elicit lower bids. In effect, says Carnegie Mellon management professor Gerald C. Meyers, "when it's used for GM, it's a boon. When it's used against them, it's a terrible thing." Considering its behaviour, did GM demonstrate a double standard in its reaction to the López affair?

5. The ethics of both VW and GM were called into question by the López affair. How will the ethical misjudgments of both companies affect their relationship with customers, suppliers, and employees?

"Foreign governments seeking to reduce the growing financial burden of social programs . . . pave the way for privatization and foreign investment."

—from a Liberty Mutual Annual Report

A very interesting sight awaits shoppers at the end of aisle 15 in one of Canada's new Wal-Mart stores, namely, a new private health insurance sales booth for U.S. company Liberty Health. As part of the insurance giant Liberty Mutual, Liberty Health finds its business exploding north of the U.S. border. According to company representatives, about one third of the costs of Canada's $24 billion health-care system are now covered by the private sector. This shift towards the private sector provides a real growth opportunity since, as Liberty Health's Gery Barry notes, "If you don't grow as an organization, you stop providing value." Liberty Health's parent company also sees Canada as a real growth opportunity, even mentioning it by name as a future growth market in a recent annual report.

Health-care consultant Michael Decter sees the possibility of substantial growth for companies such as Liberty Health. As medicare cuts back, it creates a real opportunity for the private sector to fill the gap in supplemental health coverage. Some observers are more cautious though, wondering if the trend to the private sector will also be accompanied by a shift towards increased pressures for cost savings. Private companies, notes industry observer Daphne Woolf, are motivated to reduce their liabilities in any way possible. Decter supports her assertion: "Managed care, as it's called in the U.S., is largely about costs, so it's really about squeezing costs, not about improving care."

Dan Smith, director of product design at Liberty Health, admits: "It is new to the Canadian marketplace where we don't just sit back and wait for the employee to go back to work. Traditionally, the marketplace has just let the employee get back to work. . . .We are working with the employee to force them back to work sooner." But some see Liberty Health's philosophy quite differently. Kathleen Connors, president of the Canadian Health Coalition, opposes the move towards privatization because health care is fundamentally different from "toasters or cars."

According to Connors, "It's about people and if we start treating people like commodities then the caring and compassion that has been the fundamental part of the Canadian system will get lost."

Study Questions

1. What are the different types of economic systems? Which is closest to the way health care has operated in Canada until recently? Which is closest to the way Liberty Health does business?

2. What is a parent corporation? Who is Liberty Health's parent corporation?

3. What is social responsibility? How does Liberty Health appear to view its social responsibilities?

* Source: This case was written by Professor Reg Litz of the University of Manitoba.
Video Resource: "Liberty Health," *Venture* #668 (November 11, 1997).

"Ultimately what a retailer does to us, that will put us out of business, they'll do to the next one, and the next one, and the one after that. And that's going to be your child, your husband, your relative that's going to be put out of work."

—Canadian manufacturer

Jack Berkovits looked up from his desk towards the wall in stunned disbelief. For over 20 years the Canadian retailer had served Zellers faithfully; in fact, the company had recently presented him with an award for excellence in service. The framed award hung on the wall a few feet from his desk. On his desk was another piece of paper from Zellers, however—this one quite intentionally not framed. It was a legal brief for a lawsuit Zellers was now filing against him and his company, D.G. Jewelry of Canada. As Zellers' sole ring supplier for over 20 years, he could not have even imagined the possibility of such a lawsuit only a few short years before. Recently Zellers had dictated new terms of sale to Jack—all stock would be brought in on consignment, rather than outright purchase, thus leaving the risk with Jack.

When $2 million of stock was subsequently returned, Jack decided that under these new terms he would have to look elsewhere, thus setting the stage for the Zellers suit. Even though the $2 million represented a comparatively minor inventory amount for a customer the size of Zellers, for a small firm such as D.G. Jewelry it represented life and death. As a result, Jack felt he had no choice but to look elsewhere for business. Now, to add insult to injury, his former "prized customer" was suing him!

The Zellers lawsuit signals a fundamental power shift in the Canadian marketplace. With a recent shake-out in Canadian retail, resulting in the closure of such firms as Consumers Distributing and Woodward's, only a half dozen large players remain. This shake-out only continues an earlier trend of consolidation in Canadian retail. From a high of 31 department stores in 1979, today there are but six; in the department store category, the "big three" of Eaton's, Sears, and the Bay dominate, while in the discount category, Zellers, Wal-Mart, and Kmart set the pace.

This allows the remaining retailers to place increased pressure on manufacturers to be faster and cheaper. More than one Canadian manufacturer has responded by simply going out of business. Other firms, with no choice but to "get along" in the new realities, find themselves increasingly integrated into a giant competitor's supply chain. Such "integration" includes using the retailer's computer system, and shipping quantity and quality according to the retailer's dictates, with the retailer having the option of shipping back if delivery specifications are violated in any way.

Perhaps most daunting for the small manufacturer is the prospect of penalties. When orders come in, the manufacturer must provide fast delivery, thus requiring the maintenance of huge inventories. If orders are not honoured, the supplier is vulnerable to huge penalties; being charged up to 10 percent for being two days late is not uncommon. The use of penalties was introduced by Wal-Mart and quickly embraced by other Canadian retailers. Some Canadian manufacturers wonder whether the penalties are viewed by the retailer as a profit centre, where a certain amount of penalty dollars are targeted for each quarter; retailers are quick to dismiss this as mere speculation.

Study Questions

1. What is profit? In what ways does the "power of the few" change who gets how much profit?

2. What are the different degrees of competition? How does this video case relate to the different degrees of competition?

3. What is a standard of living? What do the comments of some of the manufacturers suggest about the impact of the "power of the few" on the Canadian standard of living?

* Source: This case was written by Professor Reg Litz of the University of Manitoba.
  Video Resource: "Manufacturers Squeezed," *Venture* #666 (October 28, 1997).

Lands' End Video Case I-3

Lands' End, Inc.: A Brief History

LEARNING OBJECTIVES

The purpose of this video exercise is to help students

1. Become better acquainted with a specific company currently conducting business as a public corporation.
2. Understand the path to growth taken by a company that has been in existence for less than four decades.
3. Understand more about the operations of a company that deals in both consumer goods and services.

BACKGROUND INFORMATION

Lands' End is a *mail order* (or *catalogue marketing*) retailer based in Dodgeville, Wisconsin. From its headquarters, the company mails out catalogues featuring high-quality merchandise that is competitively priced and backed by an unconditional guarantee. Lands' End catalogues specialize in casual and tailored clothing but include a variety of other products, including shoes, accessories, luggage, and items for the bed and bath.

Founded in Chicago in 1963, Lands' End originally specialized in sailing equipment; the first black-and-white catalogue featured no clothing at all. By 1977, clothing and luggage dominated the catalogue, and by 1979—the year of the move to Dodgeville—Lands' End had already recruited personnel in such areas as fabrics and clothing manufacture. The company now works directly with fabric mills and clothing manufacturers who are contracted to make products according to Lands' End's own specifications.

Lands' End introduced the term "direct merchant" to describe itself in 1981. In 1994, when sales surpassed those of L.L. Bean, it became the largest specialty catalogue retailer in the U.S. Today more than 1000 phone lines handle 50 000 calls a day (about 100 000 calls a day in the weeks just before Christmas). Toll-free lines (both to sales and customer service operators) are open 24 hours a day. In-stock orders are usually shipped from the distribution centre the day after they are received. Within the continental United States, standard delivery usually requires two business days.

THE VIDEO

Video Source. "Lands' End, Inc.: A Brief History," *Prentice Hall Presents: On Location at Lands' End*. This video introduces Lands' End by tracing the company's history from its origins as a small Chicago outlet in 1963 to its current position as the largest specialty catalogue company in the United States. In describing the firm's current operations, the video focuses on the emphasis Lands' End places on customer service and distribution efficiency.

Discussion Questions

1. In general terms, describe the effect on Lands' End past, present, and/or future operations of each of the four factors of production (labour, capital, entrepreneurs, and natural resources).
2. In what ways do Lands' End's operations reflect patterns of demand and supply in its particular industry?
3. Lands' End operates in an industry characterized by pure competition. Which facets of the company's operations most clearly reflect conditions of pure competition? Which facets reflect the position currently enjoyed by Lands' End in its particular industry?
4. Lands' End became a public corporation in October 1986. In August 1987 and again in May 1994, shares were split two-for-one. If you were presented *today* with an opportunity to buy stock in Lands' End, would you buy some stock? Why or why not?

Follow-Up Assignment

To better understand the nature of Lands' End's industry and operations, familiarize yourself with the following concepts:

- Operations processes (Chap. 12)
- Service operations (Chap. 13)
- Quality control (Chap. 14)
- The marketing mix (Chap. 15)
- Pricing products (Chap. 17)
- Promoting products (Chap. 16)
- Direct mail (Chap. 17)
- Nonstore retailing (Chap. 17)
- Mail order marketing (Chap. 17)
- Physical distribution (Chap. 17)
- Distribution centre (Chap. 17)

For Further Exploration

Lands' End can be contacted on the Internet at
http://www.landsend.com

Lands' End Video Case I-4

Doing Business Abroad the Lands' End Way

LEARNING OBJECTIVES

The purpose of this video exercise is to help students

1. Appreciate the difficulties experienced by a company when it decides to go international.
2. Understand how Lands' End responded to customer needs in markets as diverse as the United Kingdom and Japan.
3. Understand how Lands' End dealt with social, cultural, and economic differences as it expanded into international markets.

BACKGROUND INFORMATION

International sales are nothing new to Lands' End, which began selling to Canadian customers through regular mailings in 1987. But in the early 1990s, overseas expansion threatened to be a completely different matter:

- The company's first overseas venture—to the United Kingdom—was undertaken less than 10 years ago. Surprisingly, one of the first challenges the company encountered was language. Lands' End's copywriters worked in American English, but its new British customers wanted to hear about products in British English—and said so. Adjustments were made to Lands' End copy and by 1993, operations in the United Kingdom had been moved to a new home-based facility just outside London.

- In Japan, operations began in 1993, with the first Japanese catalogue issued in August 1994. In Japan, the main challenge turned out to be advertising media and methods. Japanese customers are used to cluttered newspaper inserts; Lands' End has always worked to show individual products in the best possible light—a policy that doesn't lend itself to cluttered photography and advertising copy. Compromises were reached, and Lands' End discovered a formidable competitive tool in its iron-clad customer satisfaction guarantee.

THE VIDEO

Video Source. "Doing Business Abroad the Lands' End Way," *Prentice Hall Presents: On Location at Lands' End.* This video traces the history of Lands' End's foray into two overseas markets—the United Kingdom and Japan. Participants, including Vice-President for International Operations Frank Buettner, recount some of the key challenges that faced the company as it adapted its approach to catalogue retailing to the demands of foreign customers.

Discussion Questions

1. How would you describe Lands' End's level of international involvement? Which type of international organizational structure best applies to the company's approach to business in the United Kingdom and Japan?

2. List and describe some of the specific barriers to international trade that Lands' End has encountered. With which kinds of differences—social and cultural, economic, legal and political—does Lands' End seem to be most concerned? Why? In what ways have some of these differences affected Lands' End's international operations?

3. Why did Lands' End move so quickly to establish headquarters for its British operations inside the United Kingdom? What kinds of problems should be solved more easily because the company now has a "creative team of nationals" working at its home-based British facility?

4. Every company that markets its products in several countries faces a basic choice: (1) use a *decentralized approach* with a separate management for each country or (2) adopt a *global perspective* with a coordinated marketing program directed at one worldwide audience. Where would you place Lands' End on this spectrum? Is its approach primarily "decentralized"? Primarily "global"? If it reflects both options, why do you think this is so?

Follow-Up Assignment

At the conclusion of the video, Lands' End's three most important criteria for venturing into a foreign market are presented. All of these criteria concern a country's infrastructure: (1) the country must be economically stable, (2) it must have a good system for distributing goods, and (3) its telephone system must be dependable. You are also told that the company is now considering expansion into one of three countries—Germany, the Netherlands, or France. After your instructor has divided the class into groups of three to six people each, assign members to go to the library and gather current information on the infrastructure and economic conditions in these three countries. When each committee has collected its information, members should meet to compare notes and draw up a report that recommends that Lands' End select one country over the other two.

For Further Exploration

Lands' End can be contacted on the Internet at
http://www.landsend.com

EXPERIENTIAL EXERCISE:
Meeting the Challenge of Modern Business

OBJECTIVE

To help students understand the complexities facing businesses as they seek to act responsibly towards their shareholders, their employees, and their communities.

TIME REQUIRED

45 minutes
Step 1: Individual activity (to be completed before class)
Step 2: Small-group activity (25 minutes)
Step 3: Class discussion (20 minutes)

PROCEDURE

Step 1: Read the following case regarding the Wright Pen Company.

For over seven generations, the Wright Pen Company has been the proud maker of writing implements, beginning with quill pens. Today the firm makes fountain pens, ballpoint pens, rolling ball and felt-tipped pens, and refills for most of its pens. Since its founding by Jess Wright, the company has also prided itself on never having laid off its workers and on always being a good "corporate citizen." Funds from the Wright Pen Company have provided scholarships for local students, built the Wrightville Centre for the Arts, and supported a wide variety of local charities.

Now, however, the management at Wright Pen Company finds itself with a dilemma. For years, the firm has dumped the waste products from its ink-making operation into the Effluvia River, which runs alongside its plant. Unfortunately, recent studies show liver cancer rates five times higher among Wrightville residents than in the general population. Federal tests indicate that the water in the Effluvia River may be a contributing factor.

The options open to the Wright Pen Company are as follows:

Option 1: Make no changes in operations at this time. The evidence that has been presented is preliminary, and Wright Pen is not the only source of waste dumped into the river.

Option 2: Install a new waste-disposal system that would eliminate questionable substances from the waste being dumped by Wright Pen. As the chart indicates, however, this system would add to Wright's costs, forcing it to either reduce dividends to shareholders or to raise prices, which would lower sales and could force staff cutbacks.

Option 3: Close the ink-making plant and arrange to have these products made overseas where pollution controls are not as stringent and where labour costs are lower.

WHAT DO YOU THINK WRIGHT PEN COMPANY SHOULD DO?

Step 2: The instructor will divide the class into small groups. Each group is to complete the grid on the next page and decide on the best overall course of action for Wright Pen Company.

COSTS/PROFITS CHART

DECISION-MAKING GRID

	Under Current System	Under New Waste System
Cost of 1 ballpoint pen refill	.13	.23
Profit on one ballpoint pen refill 　at current $.29 ea. 　at $.39 ea.	.16 .26	.06 .16
Number of refills sold annually 　at current $.29 ea. 　at $.39 ea.	2 500 000 1 170 000	
Annual profits 　at current $.29 ea. 　at $.39 ea.	$400 000 $304 200	$150 000 $187 200

	Option 1	Option 2	Option 3
Probable effect on shareholders			
Probable effect on employees			
Probable effect on community			

Step 3: One member of each small group will present the group's conclusions to the class.

QUESTIONS FOR DISCUSSION

1. Why did different groups arrive at different answers? At the same answers?
2. How did your small group discussions reveal some of the problems partners face in making decisions for a partnership?

CAREERS IN BUSINESS
IT'S NOT JUST A JOB...

"What do you want to be?"

Throughout your life, you've probably heard this question over and over. Perhaps you already know the answer. But if you don't, you're not alone. Many people spend years searching for an answer, moving from job to job and working for company after company. Indeed, most people today wind up working for more than one firm and holding more than one position over the course of their career.

Most experts agree that the people with the most successful careers are those who make an effort to plan them. And just as a career is a lifelong progression, so career planning should not be limited to the search for your first job. Rather, it is a process that should occur throughout your working life. If you have not already begun to plan your career, now is the time to start.

One of the purposes of this book is to help you plan and manage your career. To that end, you will find a special two-page discussion at the end of each part of this text that addresses one or more aspects of careers and career planning. Since the first step in any sound planning process is the gathering of information, we begin by looking at the job market you will probably face when you graduate—which fields are expanding, which are shrinking.

OVERALL JOB OUTLOOK

During the 1960s and 1970s, many businesses grew rapidly. They built new facilities, hired new employees, and expanded their operations in many directions. In the 1980s, however, increased global competition forced many firms to cut back, a trend that continued with the recession of the early 1990s. Virtually every industry was affected to some extent—airlines and retailers, computer manufacturers and car makers all felt the pinch. Many shut down plants and laid off thousands of workers. Even firms such as IBM, which long had "no-layoff" policies, found themselves with no alternative. As a result, university and college graduates in the late 1980s and early 1990s faced an especially tight job market. As the economy has begun to bounce back, however, many companies are cautiously beginning to hire again.

JOB PROSPECTS BY FIELD AND OCCUPATION

Despite the general upturn, there remain important differences in job prospects. Table 1 categorizes job prospects by field as either good, fair, or poor for the next decade. Employment prospects are considered good when projections are for more job openings than candidates for those jobs. Jobs in business and health care are included in this category. Employment

---

Table 1 — Job Prospects by Field

Fields with Good Employment Prospects

Business—management, accounting, marketing, finance, operations

Computer and information sciences—systems analysis, programming

Engineering—chemical, mechanical, and civil engineering and drafting

Health care—medicine, nursing-home and hospital administration

Physical sciences—biology, chemistry

Fields with Fair Employment Prospects

Architecture and landscape design

Communication technologies—writing, broadcasting

Education—teaching and administration

Protective services—fire fighting, law enforcement

Fields with Poor Employment Prospects

Foreign languages

Parks and recreation

Public affairs

Social sciences—psychology, sociology, social work

Visual and performing arts

---

prospects are considered fair when the number of job openings is projected to be roughly the same as the number of candidates interested in those job openings. Careers in communications and architecture fall into this category. And employment prospects are considered poor when the number of job openings is expected to be smaller than the number of candidates for those jobs. Psychology and sociology are two fields with poor employment prospects.

Even within specific fields, prospects for some positions are brighter than they are for others. Table 2 illustrates projected growth in key managerial and professional jobs. Of the jobs listed, positions for mathematical and computer scientists are increasing the most rapidly, while employment for college and university teachers is increasing least rapidly. You may also be interested to know that one recent survey identified the 20 "hot track" careers for the 1990s and beyond as: international accountant, software developer, management consultant, environmental engineer, financial planner, health services administrator, human-resources director, corporate-bankruptcy lawyer, quality manager, international marketer, internist, fund-raising director, geriatric nurse, paralegal, chef, specialty store buyer, pharmaceutical representative, biomedical researcher, special education teacher, and recycling coordinator.

Table 2	Job Prospects by Occupation

Occupation	Rate of Increase, 1990–2005
Mathematical and computer scientists	73%
Registered nurses and other health therapists	43%
Lawyers and judges	34%
Primary, secondary, and special education teachers	30%
Health diagnosticians	29%
Executives, administrators, and managers	27%
Engineers	26%
Natural scientists	26%
Technical specialists	23%
College and university teachers	19%

JOB OUTLOOK FOR BUSINESS-RELATED FIELDS

In this text, we are naturally most concerned with the prospects for employment in the business sector. While business is included in the overall "good prospects" category, it is important to note that within the general field of business there are considerable variations in employment prospects. Table 3 lists specific employment prospects within business. While manufacturing jobs often pay better than service jobs, most growth in the business community of late has been—and is expected to continue to be—in the service sector, especially in business-to-business services and in the health-care industry.

INTERNATIONAL JOB PROSPECTS

Students today are increasingly interested in international job opportunities. Part of the allure of an international job is the prospect of travelling to exotic countries, living in interesting places, and dealing with different kinds of people. However, an "international" job sometimes means nothing more than working—in Canada—for a foreign-owned firm such as General Electric or IBM. Most entry-level international jobs fall into this category.

Table 3	Job Prospects in the Business World

Jobs with Good Prospects

Manufacturing or production management
Information systems
Quality management
Computer information technology
Tax accounting

Jobs with Fair Prospects

Public accounting
Auditing
General management
Marketing and sales
Human-resources management
Hotel and restaurant management
Retailing
Insurance
International management

Jobs with Poor Prospects

Banking
Advertising
Securities sales
Consulting
Retail buying
Financial administration
Administration of not-for-profit organizations

If you are committed to an international career, however, openings are available, and the number of truly international jobs—those involving extensive travel or even relocation to other nations—is expected to rise in the decades to come. In general, entry-level jobs in the arena include sales positions and export brokers and import merchants. Senior managers in many areas are also candidates for international reassignment—usually after they've mastered another tongue in which to talk business.

Part Two

Part Two

THE BUSINESS OF MANAGING

Loewen Group Inc., Canadian Pacific Ltd., and Zepf Technologies are three of the business firms you will read about in the opening cases of Chapters 6 to 8. Each of these firms must be effectively managed if they are to grow and prosper. Regardless of the size of the business, managers in all companies—indeed, in any kind of organization—must carry out the basic management functions of planning, organizing, leading, and controlling.

Part Two, The Business of Managing, provides an overview of business management today. It includes a look at the various types of managers that business firms need, the special concerns of managing small businesses, the ways in which managers set goals for their companies, and how a business's structure affects its management and goals.

■ We begin in **Chapter 6, Managing the Business Enterprise**, by describing how managers set goals and choose corporate strategies. The basic functions of management—planning, organizing, leading, and controlling—are examined, as are the different types and levels of managers that are found in business firms, and the corporate culture that is created in each firm.

■ In **Chapter 7, Organizing the Business Enterprise**, we look at the basic organizational structures that companies have adopted, and the different kinds of authority that managers can have. The impact of the informal organization is also analyzed.

■ Finally, in **Chapter 8, Understanding Entrepreneurship and Small Business**, we explore the role of small business and franchises in the Canadian economy—what they do, why they succeed or fail, and how they are owned and managed.

6

Managing the Business Enterprise

The Best-Laid Plans. . .

Most Canadians have heard that Americans seem to sue each other with great vigour, and how some of these lawsuits lead to very large payouts to the plaintiff. But one Canadian businessman found out first-hand how careful plans can go awry because of a lawsuit. Here is the story.

Ray Loewen is the founder and CEO of Loewen Group Inc., the second largest funeral home company in North America. Starting with one funeral home in Manitoba, he acquired another in Fort Frances, Ontario, and a third in New Westminster, BC. He then aggressively expanded operations across both the United States and Canada. The company now owns more than 750 funeral homes and employs 8000 people. Since 1987, the company has acquired more than 500 funeral homes in the United States.

Loewen's expansion plan typically involves buying a local funeral home, but keeping the former owners active in the business. Loewen does this because he recognizes that the funeral home business is very emotional; families often deal with one funeral home over several generations, and they do not like the idea of a cold, impersonal corporation burying their loved ones.

This strategy has served Loewen very well during its expansion period, but the company ran into trouble after it got into a seemingly minor legal wrangle. This occurred shortly after it had purchased Wright & Ferguson Funeral Homes in Mississippi. The legal dispute involved an insurance company that happened to be owned by a rival funeral home, the Bradford-O'Keefe Funeral Homes Inc., run by Jerry O'Keefe, a well-known local politician and a former mayor of Biloxi, Mississippi. The two sides initially agreed to settle the dispute by Loewen buying two

O'Keefe funeral homes, but when Loewen walked away from the deal after seeing the poor financial health of the O'Keefe operations, O'Keefe sued on the grounds that Loewen was trying to drive hime out of business.

Loewen's lawyers were confident the suit would not succeed. The plaintiff's strategy was developed by Michael Aldred, who portrayed Jerry O'Keefe as a good old local boy who was fighting for his life and his family. Another O'Keefe lawyer, Willie Gary (who has been featured on the television program *Lifestyles of the Rich and Famous*), focused on O'Keefe's family and his service record in World War II. Loewen, on the other hand, was portrayed as a greedy foreigner who took advantage of naive, small-town funeral-home operators when he bought them out. He then, it was claimed, tried to squeeze out any remaining competitors so he could raise prices. Overall, Loewen was painted as a person who was extracting money from grieving southern families.

After a seven-week trial, the jury awarded O'Keefe the amazing sum of $500 million in damages. The jurors came within one vote of giving O'Keefe $1 billion. Observers were astonished. Under Mississippi law, Loewen was required to post a $625-million bond before he could appeal the verdict to the Mississippi Supreme Court. When Loewen filed affidavits showing he couldn't afford that much, the amount was reduced to $125 million. Jerry O'Keefe appealed that ruling.

Loewen then developed contingency plans to cope with whatever outcome occurred. If the company was required to post the $625 million, it would have to file for bankruptcy. This threat caused the price of Loewen stock to drop from $40 per share to less than $30. Loewen's lawyers said they were confident that they would win the appeal.

(continued)

In January 1996 Loewen and O'Keefe reached an agreement in their dispute before it went through a formal appeal. Under the terms of the agreement, Loewen will pay Jerry O'Keefe $175 million in stock shares and cash over a 20-year period. O'Keefe received $50 million immediately, and will get $4 million per year for the next 20 years. O'Keefe will also receive 1.5 million shares of Loewen stock. The price of Loewen stock jumped $12.50 per share after the agreement was announced because the possibility of Loewen filing for bankruptcy was removed.

Ray Loewen had very mixed feelings about the settlement. On the one hand, the settlement was far less than the $500 million he might have had to pay. On the other hand, it was far more that the $5 million out-of-court settlement he was offered at one point in the dispute. But Loewen was happy that the uncertainty about the company had been removed. That uncertainty would have cost the company significantly.

Loewen said that the settlement would not have a big impact on the firm's financial performance for 1996. Spreading out the payments over 20 years also means that the settlement will not have a large long-term effect on the company. Loewen also said that the settlement would not hinder the company's future acquisition plans. Some analysts are skeptical, but others have been snapping up the company's stock.

The Mississippi experience has taught Loewen Group some big lessons. The company's board of directors will be much more careful in the future when it decides where to expand. It will also make sure that all future acquisition contracts have a clause stating that any disputes will be resolved through arbitration, not through the courts. ◆

Loewen Group
http://www.loewengroup.com

Ray Loewen is one of millions of managers worldwide. In this chapter, we explain how these managers differ from industrial engineers, accountants, market researchers, production workers, secretaries, and other people who work in business firms. Although we will focus on managers in business firms, managers are necessary in many other kinds of organizations—colleges and universities, charities, social clubs, churches, labour unions, and governments. The president of the University of Toronto, the prime minister of Canada, and the executive director of the United Way are just as much managers as the president of MacMillan Bloedel.

By focusing on the learning objectives of this chapter, you will better understand the nature of managing, the meaning of corporate culture, and the range of skills that managers like Ray Loewen need if they are to work effectively. After reading this chapter, you should be able to:

LEARNING OBJECTIVES

1. Explain the importance of setting *goals* and formulating *strategies* as the starting points of effective management.

2. Describe the four activities that constitute the *management process*.

3. Identify *types of managers* by level and area.

4. Describe the five basic *management skills*.

5. Describe the development and explain the importance of *corporate culture*.

Setting Goals and Formulating Strategy

The starting point in effective management is setting **goals**, objectives that a business hopes (and plans) to achieve. Every business needs goals, and we begin by discussing the basic aspects of organizational goal setting. However, deciding what it *intends* to do is only step one for an organization. A company's managers must also make decisions about actions that will and will not achieve its goals. From this perspective, *strategy* is the broad program that underlies those decisions; the basic steps in formulating strategy are discussed later in the chapter.

goals
Objectives that a business hopes and plans to achieve.

Setting Business Goals

Goals are performance targets, the means by which organizations and their managers measure success or failure at every level. In this section, we identify the main purposes for which organizations establish goals, classify the basic levels of business goals, and describe the process by which goals are commonly set.

The Purposes of Goal Setting

An organization functions systematically because it sets goals and plans accordingly. Indeed, an organization functions as such because it commits its resources on all levels to achieving its goals. Specifically, we can identify four main purposes in organizational goal setting:

1. *Goal setting provides direction, guidance, and motivation for all managers.* For example, each of the managers at Kanke Seafood Restaurants Ltd. is required to work through a goal setting exercise each year. Setting and achieving goals is the most effective form of self motivation.[1]

2. *Goal setting helps firms allocate resources.* Areas that are expected to grow, for example, will get first priority. Thus 3M allocates more resources to new projects with large sales potential than to projects with low growth potential.

3. *Goal setting helps to define corporate culture.* General Electric's goal, for instance, is to push each of its divisions to number one or number two in its industry. The result is a competitive, often stressful, environment and a culture that rewards success and has little tolerance for failure.

4. *Goal setting helps managers assess performance.* If a company sets a goal to increase sales by 10 percent in a given year, managers in units who attain or exceed the goal can be rewarded. Units failing to reach the goal will also be compensated accordingly.

Kinds of Goals

Naturally, goals differ from company to company, depending on the firm's purpose and mission. Every enterprise, of course, has a *purpose*—a reason for being. Businesses seek profit, universities work to discover and transmit new knowledge, and government agencies exist to provide service to the public. But every enterprise also has a mission and a **mission statement**—a statement of *how* it will achieve its purpose in the environment in which it conducts its business. By and large, a company's purpose is fairly easy to identify. Reebok, for example, attempts to make a profit by making and selling athletic shoes and related merchandise. IBM expresses the same purpose in selling computers and computer technology.

Consider the similarities and differences between Timex and Rolex. Both firms share a common purpose—to sell watches at a profit—yet they have very different missions. Timex sells low-cost, reliable watches in outlets ranging from department stores to corner drugstores. Rolex, on the other hand, sells high-quality, high-priced fashion watches through selected jewellery stores.

Regardless of a company's purpose and mission, every firm needs long-term, intermediate, and short-term goals:

■ **Long-term goals** relate to extended periods of time—typically five years or more into the future. American Express, for example, might set a long-term goal of doubling the number of participating merchants during the next 10 years. Similarly, Kodak might adopt a long-term goal to increase its share of the 35-mm film market by 10 percent during the next eight years.

---

mission statement

Organization's statement of how it will achieve its purpose in the environment in which it conducts its business.

long-term goals

Goals set for extended periods of time, typically five years or more into the future.

■ **Intermediate goals** are set for a period of one to five years into the future. Companies usually have intermediate goals in several areas. For example, the marketing department's goal might be to increase sales by 3 percent in two years. The production department might want to decrease expenses by 6 percent in four years. Human resources might seek to cut turnover by 10 percent in two years. Finance might aim for a 3 percent increase in return on investment in three years.

■ Like intermediate goals, **short-term goals**—which are set for one year or less—are developed for several different areas. Increasing sales by 2 percent this year, cutting costs by 1 percent next quarter, and reducing turnover by 4 percent over the next six months are all short-term goals.

intermediate goals
Goals set for a period of one to five years.

short-term goals
Goals set for the very near future, typically less than one year.

Who Sets Goals?

Within any company, managers at different levels are responsible for setting different kinds of goals. The firm's purpose is largely determined by the context in which it operates—that is, the environment in which it markets its products. The board of directors generally defines the firm's mission. Working in conjunction with the board, top managers then usually set long-term goals. These same managers typically work closely with middle managers to set intermediate goals. Finally, middle managers work with first-line managers to set and achieve short-term goals.

Formulating Strategy

Most managers must devote a great deal of attention (and creativity) to the formulation of business strategies—that is, ways of meeting company goals at all levels. **Strategy formulation** involves three basic steps:

1. setting strategic goals
2. analyzing the organization and its environment
3. matching the organization and its environment.[2]

strategy formulation
Creation of a broad program for defining and meeting an organization's goals.

Setting Strategic Goals

Strategic goals are long-term goals derived directly from the firm's mission statement. For example, one of the first things new CEO George Fisher did at Kodak was to set several strategic goals. One strategic goal called for renewed emphasis on film marketing and processing, one called for eliminating several peripheral businesses, and still another stressed the need to speed up the introduction of new technology.

General Electric Co. is one of the world's most successful companies, with 1996 revenues of nearly $80 billion and profits over $7 billion. Even so, the company is not resting on its laurels. Its chairman, Jack Welch, is pursuing four strategic goals in order to ensure continued success for the company: an emphasis on quality control, an emphasis on selling services and not just products, concentrating on niche acquisitions, and expansion globally.[3]

strategic goals
Long-term goals derived directly from a firm's mission statement.

General Electric
http://www.ge.com

Analyzing the Organization and Its Environment

Environmental analysis involves scanning the environment for threats and opportunities. New products and new competitors, for example, are both threats. So are new government regulations, imports, changing consumer tastes, and hostile takeovers. In formulating its new strategy, for instance, Kodak saw opportunities for growth in the film market and recognized that

environmental analysis
Process of scanning the environment for threats and opportunities.

organizational analysis
Process of analyzing a firm's strengths and weaknesses.

Kodak
http://www.kodak.com/
homePage.shtml

technology was changing so quickly that it had to get that technology to market much faster than planned. It also saw increased competition from its biggest rival, the Japanese firm Fuji.

Meanwhile, managers also must undertake an **organizational analysis** to understand a company's strengths and weaknesses better. Strengths might include surplus cash, a dedicated workforce, an ample supply of managerial talent, technical expertise, or little competition. The absence of any of these strengths could represent an important weakness. Kodak, for example, saw that although it was doing fine in research and development, translating technological breakthroughs into new products was taking a long time.

Matching the Organization and Its Environment

The final step in strategy formulation is matching environmental threats and opportunities with corporate strengths and weaknesses. The matching process is the heart of strategy formulation: More than any other facet of strategy, matching companies with their environments lays the foundation for successfully planning and conducting business.[4] Kodak managers, for example, decided that the firm needed to concentrate on its core business, photographic equipment and supplies. Thus it began selling its other businesses, such as a software manufacturer and a consumer-credit division.

A Hierarchy of Plans

Figure 6.1 shows how plans can be viewed on three general levels: *strategic* (SP), *tactical* (TP), and *operational* (OP). Each level reflects plans for which managers at that level are responsible. These levels constitute a hierarchy because implementing plans is practical only when there is a logical flow from one level to the next.

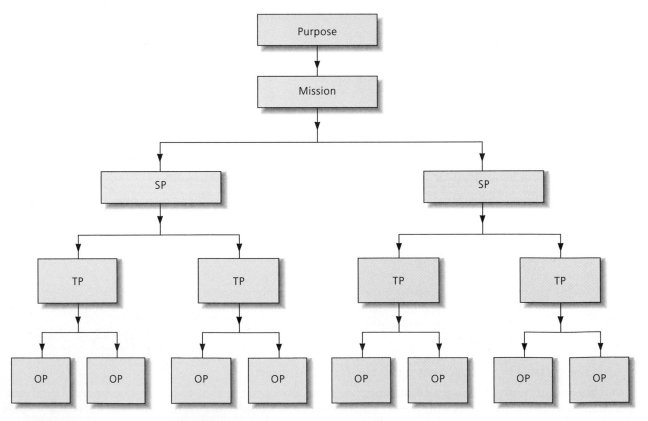

Figure 6.1
A hierarchy of plans.

■ **Strategic plans** reflect decisions about resource allocations, company priorities, and the steps needed to meet strategic goals. They are usually set by the board of directors and top management. Procter & Gamble's decision that viable products must be number one or number two within their respective categories is a matter of strategic planning.

■ **Tactical plans** are shorter-range plans concerned with implementing specific aspects of the company's strategic plans. They typically involve upper and middle management. Coca-Cola's decision to increase sales in Europe by building European bottling facilities is an example of tactical planning.

■ Developed by middle and lower-level managers, **operational plans** set short-term targets for daily, weekly, or monthly performance. McDonald's, for example, establishes operational plans when it explains precisely how Big Macs are to be cooked, warmed, and served.

strategic plans
Plans that reflect decisions about resource allocations, company priorities, and steps needed to meet strategic goals.

tactical plans
Generally, short-range plans concerned with implementing specific aspects of a company's strategic plans.

operational plans
Plans setting short-term targets for daily, weekly, or monthly performance.

Strategic Options

There are many strategic options a firm might choose. Several of the most well-known are described briefly below.

Generic Options

Generic strategies fall into one of three broad categories: cost leadership, differentiation, and focus.[5] **Cost leadership** occurs when an enterprise strives to have the lowest costs in the industry. Most enterprises in the resource industries base their strategies on cost leadership since the prices of the products are often established in markets over which they have no control. Canadian newsprint producers, for example, must control costs and find supplies of raw materials that will enable them to be cost leaders.

When pursuing a strategy of **differentiation**, an organization tries to provide goods or services that are distinctive from those of its competitors. Many consumer products firms try to differentiate, or distinguish, their products from others through distinctive advertising or packaging. Calvin Klein clothing is an example of a differentiated product.

When a **focus**, or niche, strategy is used, the business concentrates on serving a particular market segment, or niche. An enterprise choosing the focus strategy might be able to establish its niche on the basis of either cost leadership or differentiation.

cost leadership
Striving to have the lowest costs in the industry.

differentiation
Striving to provide products that are distinctive from those of competitors.

focus
Concentrating on serving a particular market segment.

Internal Growth Options

Market penetration occurs when an enterprise tries to increase the market share of its existing products or services in their present markets, usually through greater marketing efforts. By contrast, **market development** means introducing existing products into new geographic areas. Kodak has increased sales in foreign markets, including Japan, in an effort to develop new markets. **Product development** takes place when enterprises attempt to increase sales by improving or modifying their existing products or services for either existing or new customers.

market penetration
Seeking to increase market share in the firm's present market.

market development
Introducing existing products into new geographic areas.

product development
Improving existing products for current or new customers.

Integration Options

There are two basic integration options: vertical or horizontal. With **vertical integration** the corporation can seek ownership or control of a supplier, or it can seek ownership or control over a firm's distribution or retailers.

vertical integration
When a firm seeks ownership or control of its supplier or retailers.

horizontal integration
When a company buys or increases control of a competitor.

Horizontal integration occurs when a company purchases or increases control over another enterprise in the same business (i.e., a competitor).

Diversification Options

concentric diversification
Adding new but related products or services to an existing business.

Concentric diversification involves adding new but related products or services to an existing business. Both CP Rail and Canadian National diversified into trucking, an activity clearly related to railway operations.

conglomerate diversification
Adding unrelated products or services.

Adding unrelated products or services is called **conglomerate diversification**, or conglomerate merger. Bell Canada decided to diversify by forming BCE Inc., which acquired interests in such unrelated businesses as trust companies, pipelines, and real estate.

Cooperative Options

cooperative strategies
Joint ventures, alliances, networks, strategic partnering, and strategic networks.

Cooperative strategies, which may take the form of joint ventures, alliances, networks, strategic partnering, and strategic networks, have become more popular in the past decade. In each case, enterprises establish a collaborative arrangement for sharing or splitting managerial control in a particular undertaking.

stabilization
Maintaining revenues and profits.

Stabilization and Retrenchment Options

retrenchment
Increasing efficiency through asset reduction or cost cutting.

Strategic options do not always entail growth. The **stabilization** option is designed to maintain revenues and profits. Growth may occur but strategic decisions are only made gradually. In **retrenchment**, efforts are made to increase efficiency through asset reduction or cost cutting. **Liquidation** involves selling the enterprise's assets and ceasing to do business.

liquidation
Selling the enterprise's assets and ceasing to exist.

Contingency Plans and Crisis Management

Because things change—often with little warning or indication—most managers recognize that plans may not be achieved as expected and that alterations may be necessary. Two common methods of dealing with the unknown and unforeseen are *contingency planning* and *crisis management*.

Contingency Planning

contingency planning
Identifying aspects of a business or its environment that might entail changes in strategy.

Contingency planning takes into account the need to find solutions for specific aspects of a problem. By its very nature, a contingency plan is a hedge against changes that *might* occur. **Contingency planning**, then, is planning for change: It attempts to identify in advance important aspects of a business or its market that might change. It also identifies the ways in which a company will respond to changes. Today, many companies use computer programs for contingency planning.

Suppose, for example, that a company develops a plan to create a new business. It expects sales to increase at an annual rate of 10 percent for the next five years and develops a marketing strategy for maintaining that level. But suppose that sales have increased by only 5 percent by the end of the first year. Does the company abandon the business, invest more in advertising, or wait to see what happens in the second year? Any of these alternatives is possible. However, things will go more smoothly if managers have decided in advance what to do in the event of lower sales. Contingency planning can help them do exactly that.

Crisis Management

crisis management
An organization's methods for dealing with emergencies.

A crisis is an unexpected emergency requiring immediate organizational response. **Crisis management** involves an organization's methods for dealing

In the summer of 1996, there was concern that the *e. coli.* bacteria had gotten into some of the beef supply. This sign on a Burger King drive-through informed customers that it was not selling Whoppers or hamburgers while it carefully assessed the danger.

with emergencies. For example, when the oil tanker *Exxon Valdez* spilled millions of litres of oil off the coast of Alaska in March 1989, Exxon went into a crisis-management mode (albeit more slowly than some critics would have liked).

A highly publicized case of effective crisis management involved the nonaspirin pain reliever Tylenol. Johnson & Johnson (J&J), the maker of Tylenol, has been widely praised for its response to two incidents in which Tylenol products were found to be tainted with cyanide. As soon as the company learned of the poisonings, it removed all Tylenol capsules from grocery and drugstore shelves. J&J management also made itself available to the media and embarked on an education program to inform the public of the steps being taken to correct the problem.

To prepare for emergencies better, many organizations maintain crisis plans. These plans, designed to enable employees to cope when disasters do occur, typically outline who will be in charge in different kinds of circumstances, how the organization will respond, and so forth. In addition, they typically lay out plans for assembling and deploying crisis-management teams. Current estimates suggest that roughly half of the firms in the United States have crisis-management plans.[6]

Johnson & Johnson
http://www.jnj.com/homepage.htm

The Management Process

Management is the process of planning, organizing, leading, and controlling an enterprise's financial, physical, human, and information resources in order to achieve the organization's goals of supplying various products and services. Thus, the CEO of Walt Disney Productions, Michael Eisner, is a manager because he regularly carries out these four functions as films are being made. Actors like Bette Midler or Tom Selleck, while they may be the stars of the movies, are not managers because they don't carry out the four functions of management. The box "What Do Managers Actually Do?" gives some explanation of the dynamic nature of managerial jobs.

management
The process of planning, organizing, leading, and controlling a business's financial, physical, human, and information resources in order to achieve its goals.

The Canadian Business Scene

What Do Managers Actually Do?

Henry Mintzberg of McGill University conducted a detailed study of the work of five chief executive officers and found the following:

1. Managers work at an unrelenting pace.
2. Managerial activities are characterized by brevity, variety, and fragmentation.
3. Managers have a preference for "live" action, and emphasize work activities that are current, specific, and well-defined.
4. Managers are attracted to the verbal media.

Mintzberg believes that a manager's job can be described as 10 roles that must be performed. The manager's formal authority and status give rise to three **interpersonal roles**: 1) *figurehead* (duties of a ceremonial nature, such as attending a subordinate's wedding); 2) *leader* (being responsible for the work of the unit); and 3) *liaison* (making contact outside the vertical chain of command). These interpersonal roles give rise to three **informational roles**: 1) *monitor* (scanning the environment for relevant information); 2) *disseminator* (passing information to subordinates); and 3) *spokesperson* (sending information to people outside the unit).

The interpersonal and informational roles allow the manager to carry out four **decision-making roles**: 1) *entrepreneur* (improving the performance of the unit); 2) *disturbance handler* (responding to high-pressure disturbances, such as a strike at a supplier); 3) *resource allocator* (deciding who will get what in the unit); and 4) *negotiator* (working out agreements on a wide variety of issues like the amount of authority an individual will be given).

Insight into what managers actually do can also be gained by looking at the so-called *functions* of management (planning, organizing, leading, and controlling). Consider the work of Patrick Ferrier, who is the Publisher, College Division, at Prentice Hall Canada, a publisher of textbooks for universities, community colleges, and high schools. His job is to manage the activities that are necessary to acquire and develop books in business, economics, science, math, and medicine for the Canadian college and university market. His work is at times intense, fragmented, rewarding, frustrating, and fast-paced. In short, he is a typical manager.

Ferrier carries out the *planning* function when he drafts a plan for a new book. He is *organizing* when he develops a new organization chart to facilitate goal achievement. He is *leading* when he meets with a subordinate to discuss that person's career plans. And he is *controlling* when he checks sales prospects for a book before ordering a reprint.

Some of Ferrier's activities do not easily fit into this "functions of management" model. For example, it is not clear which function he is performing when he negotiates the size of a reprint run with the manager of the sales division, or when he talks briefly with the president of his division about recent events in Ferrier's area of responsibility.

The planning, organizing, leading, and controlling aspects of a manager's job are interrelated. While these activities generally follow one another in a logical sequence, sometimes they are performed simultaneously or in a different sequence altogether. In fact, any given manager is likely to be engaged in all these activities during the course of any given business day.

Planning

planning

That portion of a manager's job concerned with determining what the business needs to do and the best way to achieve it.

Determining what the organization needs to do and how to best do it or get it done means **planning**. Planning itself involves a series of steps, as shown in Figure 6.2.

Set Organizational Objectives

Goals are the results that an organization wants to achieve. (We use the terms "objectives" and "goals" synonymously.) Goals should have a time frame and

Figure 6.2
The planning process.

be specific, measurable, challenging, and accepted by the person who must achieve them. The goals of each company differ, depending on the company's purpose and mission.

To manage the planning process, many firms have adopted a **management by objectives (MBO)** approach.[7] MBO is a system of collaborative goal setting that extends from the top of the organization to the bottom. Managers meet with each of their subordinates individually to discuss goals. This meeting usually occurs annually and focuses on the coming year. The box "MBO at Investors" describes how this process works at a large Canadian company.

management by objectives (MBO)
An approach to management control and employee motivation in which a manager and an employee cooperatively establish goals against which the employee is later evaluated.

Determine the Gap Between Actual and Desired Positions

In the second step of the planning process, managers must determine how well organizational objectives are being achieved. The focus may be on the entire company, a department within the company, or an individual within a department. This step will be difficult to carry out if measuring performance creates fear and resentment in subordinates, or if objectives have not been stated clearly. Once these problems are overcome, managers can decide what plans are needed to close the gap between the desired and actual objective.

Develop Plans to Achieve Objectives

As we have seen, objectives focus on the results the organization wants to achieve. **Plans**, by contrast, focus on the activities that must be performed to achieve the objectives, on the person or group who will carry these activities out, and on the deadline for their completion. There are many types of plans, including strategic, tactical, and operational plans, single-use plans (for one-time projects), and standing plans (for regular corporate activities). Policies, procedures, and rules are all examples of standing plans.

plans
Activities that must be performed if goals are to be achieved.

Implement Plans

The steps that we have discussed so far—setting objectives, determining the gap between the desired and the actual, and developing plans to achieve objectives—all require managers to think about what is to be accomplished. At some point, however, this thinking must be converted into action. It is here that many managers encounter problems because implementing plans involves introducing change. And introducing any change, including new plans, is likely to meet with resistance from employees. Managers must address this opposition before the plans begin taking effect if they are to be successful in carrying out the planning function.

Evaluate Planning Effectiveness

A plan is effective if it helps an organization reach its objectives. Consider the issue of corporate policies. Suppose a firm has a policy that purchasing

The Canadian Business Scene

MBO at Investors Group Financial Services Inc.

Sales representatives at Investors Group Financial Services sell a wide range of financial services including mutual funds, investment certificates, insurance programs, pension plans, annuities, and tax-sheltered plans. The company has financial planning centres in every major metropolitan area of Canada, and employs over 3000 salespeople. It has the largest direct sales force of any company in the financial services sector.

Investors has used MBO since 1974 to motivate its sales force in selling financial services. The MBO process begins when the vice-president of sales develops general goals for the entire sales force. These goals may be based on last year's performance, or on a desired growth over last year's performance. This sets the stage for Planning Week, which is held annually in 73 regional centres across Canada during the first week of December. The purpose of Planning Week is to give salespeople a chance to (1) review their personal, career, and financial accomplishments, (2) relate their individual results to the goals of the whole company, and (3) think through personal, career, and financial goals for the coming year.

During Planning Week, sales reps meet with their division managers and set specific sales objectives for the next year. This process involves five steps:

1. *Determine franchise operating costs.* Since each sales rep in essence owns a franchise, the first step is to calculate what it will cost to operate the franchise during the upcoming year.

2. *Determine personal requirements.* Each salesperson decides how much money he or she needs to meet living expenses in the upcoming year.

3. *Determine total financial requirements.* The costs from steps 1 and 2, plus a profit requirement, determine the sales rep's total financial requirements for the year.

4. *Develop an activity plan.* The sales rep prepares a plan of action to reach the goals set in steps 1–3. This involves setting goals for the number of contacts and presentations the sales rep will have to make in order to reach the dollar sales goal.

5. *Measure productivity.* This involves completion of a detailed MBO summary sheet showing the sales rep's monthly production in the year just ended, as well as goals for each month's production in the upcoming year.

Once these five steps are completed, division managers meet with salespeople and come to a consensus about what the sales rep's goals will be. Each division manager then forwards the proposed objectives for his or her division to the appropriate regional manager. This process continues all the way up to the vice-president of sales, who gives final approval to the overall sales objectives of the company for the upcoming year.

On occasion, a salesperson will set a goal that a manager considers either too low or too high. When this happens, negotiation between the salesperson and the manager takes place to find a goal that is satisfactory to both. The company has found that resolving problems through negotiation early in the process helps to prevent serious disagreements later on.

Recognition and rewards are an important part of the MBO process. For example, sales production of $2 million per year qualifies the salesperson for the Millionaire plaque; sales of $8 million qualifies the person for a diamond ring. Most salespeople earn an award of some type, and they are publicly recognized for their achievement. Each salesperson feels that he or she is making a positive contribution to the company.

About 75 percent of Investors' salespeople conscientiously fill out the MBO forms, and it has made a noticeable difference in their sales performance. A few salespeople, however, view MBO as a game of paper shuffling, and for them, it is probably not very helpful. In such cases, managers try to "sell" MBO to their staff, rather than trying to force it on them.

Investors has found that MBO is well suited to its sales function. The goals of salespeople can be stated in quantitative terms, and the sales reps can easily tell whether they have reached their goals. The company has also found that salespeople often set much more challenging goals for themselves than they would have in the absence of MBO. All of this impacts favourably on the bottom line—Investors profitability continued uninterrupted right through the recession of 1991–93.

Managers usually work together to set goals and determine corporate strategy. These activities take a great deal of time but are critical to the success of any organization.

agents may not accept gifts from suppliers if those gifts unduly influence their purchasing behaviour. Such a policy is effective if it motivates purchasing agents to buy supplies that are best for the company. The plan is ineffective if it causes purchasing agents to spend time trying to figure out how to get around the policy.

Gauging the effectiveness of plans can be frustrating, especially if plans deal with the entire firm or have a long-term impact. It is easy to judge a plan intended to make the company the industry leader in sales, but it is much harder to measure the effectiveness of a plan to develop the most creative workforce in the industry.

Organizing

The second basic managerial activity, **organizing**, means determining how to best arrange resources and jobs to be done into an overall structure. Disney keeps each of its businesses somewhat independent and somewhat interdependent. Each business has its own management team, and the president of each business has considerable autonomy in running it. But many major decisions and those affecting several businesses (such as licensing Mickey Mouse T-shirts for sale at Disney World) are made at the corporate level. Groups such as the Imagineers also work for all Disney businesses. We will explore organizing in Chapter 7.

organizing
That portion of a manager's job concerned with structuring the necessary resources to complete a particular task.

Leading

The activities involving interactions between managers and their subordinates to meet the firm's objectives are known as **leading** (or directing). By definition, managers have the power to give orders and demand results. Leading, however, goes beyond merely giving orders. Leaders attempt to guide and motivate employees to work in the best interests of the organization. For example, Michael Eisner's plans for Disney require tens of thousands of people to execute them. We discuss leadership more fully in Chapter 10.

leading
That portion of a manager's job concerned with guiding and motivating employees to meet the firm's objectives.

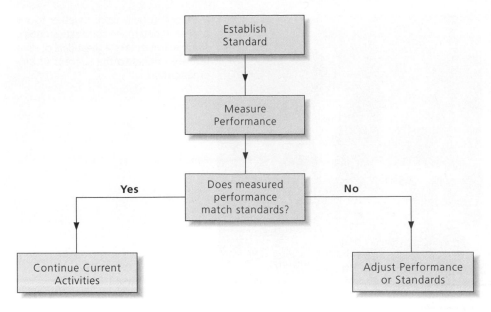

Figure 6.3
Steps in the control process.

Controlling

controlling

That portion of a manager's job concerned with monitoring the firm's performance and, if necessary, acting to bring it in line with the firm's goals.

The fourth basic managerial activity, **controlling**, means monitoring the firm's performance to make sure that it stays on track towards its goals. At Disney, Eisner's use of the Imagineers and the strategic management group and his decision to keep movie budgets low have kept the firm's profits growing.

Figure 6.3 shows the basic control process. The process begins with standards, or goals, the company wants to meet. For example, if the company wants to increase sales by 20 percent over the next 10 years, an appropriate standard might be an increase of around 2 percent each year. Managers must then measure actual performance regularly and compare this performance to the standard. If the two figures agree, the organization will continue its present activities. If they vary significantly, though, either the performance or the standard needs adjusting. For example, if sales have increased 2.1 percent at the end of the first year, things are probably fine. On the other hand, if sales have dropped by 1 percent, something needs to be done. The original goal may need to be lowered, more may need to be spent on advertising, and so forth.

Types of Managers

Although all managers plan, organize, lead, and control, not all managers have the same degree of responsibility for each activity. Moreover, managers differ in the specific application of these activities. Thus we can divide managers by their *level* of responsibility or by their *area* of responsibility.

Levels of Management

The three basic levels of management are top, middle, and first-line management. As Figure 6.4 shows, in most firms there are more middle managers

Top Management

Middle Management

First-Line Management

Figure 6.4
Most organizations have three basic levels of management.

than top managers and more first-line managers than middle managers. Moreover, as the categories imply, the power of managers and the complexity of their duties increase as we move up the pyramid.

Top Managers

The fairly small number of executives who guide the fortunes of most companies are **top managers**. Common titles for top managers include President, Vice-President, Treasurer, Chief Executive Officer (CEO), and Chief Financial Officer (CFO). Michael Eisner is a top manager for Disney, and Edgar Bronfman is a top executive for Seagram. Top managers are responsible to the board of directors and shareholders of the firm for its overall performance and effectiveness. They set general policies, formulate strategies, oversee all significant decisions, and represent the company in its dealings with other businesses and government.[8]

top managers
Those managers responsible for a firm's overall performance and effectiveness and for developing long-range plans for the company.

Middle Managers

Although below the ranks of the top executives, **middle managers** occupy positions of considerable autonomy and importance. Titles such as Plant Manager, Operations Manager, and Division Manager are typical of middle-management slots. The producer of a Disney film is a middle manager. In general, middle managers are responsible for implementing the strategies, policies, and decisions of the top managers. For example, if top management decides to bring out a new product in 12 months or to cut costs by 5 percent, middle management will have to decide to increase the pace of new product development or to reduce the plant's workforce. With companies increasingly seeking ways to cut costs, however, the job of middle manager has lately become precarious in many large companies. Labatt's laid off 120 middle managers when it developed a new corporate strategy. Air Canada also recently dropped 400 managers.[9]

middle managers
Those managers responsible for implementing the decisions made by top managers

First-line managers spend a considerable portion of their time supervising the work of operating employees. And a significant portion of this time may be devoted to training. For example, this supervisor is teaching an employee how to operate a new piece of equipment.

First-Line Managers

first-line managers

Those managers responsible for supervising the work of employees.

At the bottom of the management hierarchy are **first-line managers** who supervise the work of employees. First-line managers hold titles such as Supervisor, Office Manager, and Foreman. The supervisor of Disney's animation department is a first-line manager. First-line managers tend to spend most of their time working with and supervising the employees who report to them. Some have entered the firm without a college or university degree or have been promoted from within the company.

Areas of Management

Within any large company, the top, middle, and first-line managers work in a variety of areas including marketing, finance, operations, human resources, and information. Figure 6.5 illustrates this relationship.

Marketing Managers

marketing managers

Those managers responsible for developing, pricing, promoting, and distributing goods and services to buyers.

Marketing includes the development, pricing, promotion, and distribution of a product or service. **Marketing managers** are responsible for getting products and services to buyers. Marketing is especially important for firms dealing in consumer products, such as Procter & Gamble, Coca-Cola, and Sun Ice. These firms often have large numbers of marketing managers at various levels. For example, a large firm will probably have a vice-president for marketing (top manager), regional marketing managers (middle managers), and several district sales managers (first-line managers). A marketing person often rises to the top of this type of corporation.

In contrast, firms that produce industrial products such as machinery and janitorial supplies tend to put less emphasis on marketing and to have fewer marketing managers. However, these firms do not ignore marketing altogether. In recent years, law firms and universities have also come to recognize the value and importance of marketing. For a detailed look at marketing, see Chapters 15 to 17.

Financial Managers

financial managers

Those managers responsible for planning and overseeing the financial resources of a firm.

Management of a firm's finances, including its investments and accounting functions, is extremely important to its survival. Nearly every company has **financial managers** to plan and oversee its financial resources. Levels of

Operations Managers

Financial Managers

Human Resource Managers

Marketing Managers

Information Managers

Figure 6.5
Organizations require managers from a wide variety of areas to be effective. The most common areas are marketing, finance, operations, human resources, and information.

financial management may include a vice-president for finance (top), division controller (middle), and accounting supervisor (first-line). For large financial institutions like the Bank of Montreal, First City Trust, and Burns Fry, effective financial management is the company's reason for being. No organization, however, can afford to ignore the need for management in this area. Chapters 20 to 22 treat financial management in detail.

Operations Managers

A firm's operations are the systems by which it creates goods and services. **Operations managers** are responsible for production control, inventory control, and quality control, among other duties. Manufacturing companies like Steelcase, Bristol Aerospace, and Sony need operations managers at many levels. Such firms typically have a vice-president for operations (top), plant managers (middle), and foremen or supervisors (first-line). In recent years, sound operations management practices have also become increasingly important to service organizations, hospitals, universities, and the government. Operations management is the subject of Chapters 12 to 14.

operations managers
Those managers responsible for controlling production, inventory, and quality of a firm's products.

Human Resource Managers

Every enterprise uses human resources. Most companies have **human resource managers** to hire employees, train them, evaluate their performances, decide how they should be compensated, and, in some cases, deal with labour unions. Large firms may have several human resource departments, each dealing with specialized activities. Imperial Oil, for example, has separate departments to deal with recruiting and hiring, wage and salary levels, and labour relations. Smaller firms may have a single department, while very small organizations may have a single person responsible for all human resource activities. Chapters 9 to 11 address issues involved in human resource management.

human resource managers
Those managers responsible for hiring, training, evaluating, and compensating employees.

Information Managers

information managers
Those managers responsible for the design and implementation of systems to gather, process, and disseminate information.

A new type of managerial position appearing in many organizations is **information manager**. These managers are responsible for designing and implementing various systems to gather, process, and disseminate information. Dramatic increases in both the amount of information available to managers and in the ability to manage it have led to the emergence of this important function. While relatively few in number now, the ranks of information managers are increasing at all levels. Federal Express, for example, has a Chief Information Officer. Middle managers engaged in information management help design information systems for divisions or plants. Computer systems managers within smaller businesses or operations are first-line managers. Information management is discussed in Chapters 18 and 19.

Other Managers

Some firms have more specialized managers. Chemical companies like CIL have research and development managers, for example, whereas companies like Petro Canada and Apple have public relations managers. The range of possibilities is endless; the areas of management are limited only by the needs and imagination of the firm.

Basic Management Skills

While the range of managerial positions is almost limitless, the success that people enjoy in those positions is often limited by their skills and abilities. Effective managers must possess several skills: *technical, human relations, conceptual, decision making,* and *time management skills*.

Technical Skills

technical skills
Skills associated with performing specialized tasks within a firm.

Skills associated with performing specialized tasks within a company are called **technical skills**. A secretary's ability to type, an animator's ability to draw a cartoon, and an accountant's ability to audit a company's records are all technical skills. People develop their technical skills through education and experience. The secretary, for example, probably took a keyboarding course and has had many hours of practice both on and off the job. The animator may have had training in an art school and probably learned a great deal from experienced animators on the job. The accountant earned a university degree and, possibly, professional certification.

As Figure 6.6 shows, technical skills are especially important for first-line managers. Most first-line managers spend considerable time helping employees solve work-related problems, monitoring their performance, and training them in more efficient work procedures. Such managers need a basic understanding of the jobs they supervise.

As a manager moves up the corporate ladder, however, technical skills become less and less important. Top managers, for example, often need only a cursory familiarity with the mechanics of basic tasks performed within the company. Michael Eisner, for example, freely admits that he can't draw Mickey Mouse or build a ride for Disney World.

Human Relations Skills

Hyatt Hotels
http://www.hyatt.com

A few years ago, Hyatt Hotels checked 379 corporate employees into the chain's 98 hotels. They were not, however, treated as guests. Rather, they

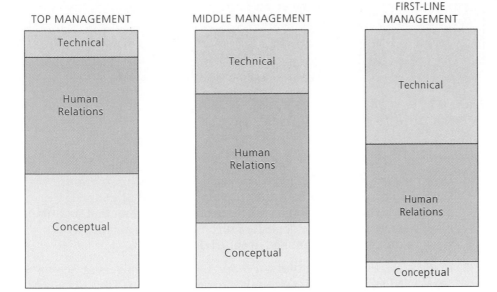

TOP MANAGEMENT

Technical

Human Relations

Conceptual

MIDDLE MANAGEMENT

Technical

Human Relations

Conceptual

FIRST-LINE MANAGEMENT

Technical

Human Relations

Conceptual

Figure 6.6
Different levels in an organization require different combinations of managerial skills.

were asked to make beds, carry luggage, and perform the other tasks necessary to make a big hotel function. Top management at Hyatt believes that learning more about the work of lower-level employees will allow executives to understand them better as human beings (and co-workers).

The Hyatt experiment was designed to test and improve the **human relations skills** of upper-level managers—that is, skills in understanding and getting along with other people. A manager with poor human relations skills may have trouble getting along with subordinates, cause valuable employees to quit or transfer, and contribute to poor morale.

While human relations skills are important at all levels, they are probably most important for middle managers, who must often act as bridges between top managers, first-line managers, and managers from other areas of the organization. Managers should possess good communication skills. Many managers have found that being able to understand others—and to get them to understand—can go far towards maintaining good relations in an organization.

human relations skills
Skills in understanding and getting along with people.

Conceptual Skills

Conceptual skills refer to a person's ability to think in the abstract, to diagnose and analyze different situations, and to see beyond the present situation. Conceptual skills help managers recognize new market opportunities (and threats). They can also help managers analyze the probable outcomes of their decisions. The need for conceptual skills differs at various management levels: top managers depend most on conceptual skills, first-line managers least. Although the purposes and everyday needs of various jobs differ, conceptual skills are needed in almost any job-related activity.

conceptual skills
Abilities to think in the abstract, diagnose and analyze different situations, and see beyond the present situation.

Decision-Making Skills

Decision-making skills include the ability to define problems and select the best course of action. Figure 6.7 illustrates the basic steps in decision making.

decision-making skills
Skills in defining problems and selecting the best courses of action.

Figure 6.7
The decision-making process.

1. *Define the problem, gather facts, and identify alternative solutions.* Current management at Schwinn recently realized that their predecessors had made some serious errors in assuming that mountain bikes were just a fad. The opposite proved to be true, and Schwinn's share of the bicycle market had dropped dramatically.

2. *Evaluate each alternative and select the best one.* Managers at Schwinn acknowledged that they had to take corrective action. They discussed such alternatives as buying a mountain bike maker, launching their own line of mountain bikes, or refocusing on other product lines. They chose to develop their own line of mountain bikes and did so in 1994.

3. *Implement the chosen alternative, periodically following up and evaluating the effectiveness of that choice.* Today Schwinn seems to be on track following its entry into the mountain bike market. Companywide sales and profits have begun to increase, and its new products are now attracting attention from the top mountain bike racers in the world.

Time Management Skills

time management skills
Skills associated with the productive use of time.

Time management skills refer to the productive use that managers make of their time. In one recent year, for example, IBM CEO Louis Gerstner was paid $12.4 million in salary and bonuses. Assuming that he worked 50 hours a week and took two weeks' vacation, Gerstner earned $4960 an hour—about $266 per minute. Any time that Gerstner wastes clearly represents a large cost to IBM and its stockholders. Most managers, of course, receive much smaller salaries than Gerstner. Their time, however, is valuable, and poor use of it still translates into costs and wasted productivity.

To manage time effectively, managers must address three leading causes of wasted time:

1. *Paperwork.* Some managers spend too much time deciding what to do with letters and/or reports. Most documents of this sort are routine and can be handled quickly. Managers must learn to recognize those documents that require more attention.

2. *The telephone.* Experts estimate that managers get interrupted by the telephone every five minutes. To manage this time more effectively, they suggest having a secretary screen all calls and setting aside a certain block of time each day to return the important ones.

3. *Meetings.* Many managers spend as much as four hours a day in meetings. To help keep this time productive the person handling the meeting should specify a clear agenda, start on time, keep everyone focused on the agenda, and end on time.

Management Skills for the 21st Century

Managers face some major challenges as they prepare to enter the 21st century. We will touch upon two of the most significant challenges: *global management* and *technology*.

Global Management Skills

Tomorrow's managers must equip themselves with the special tools, techniques, and skills necessary to compete in a global environment. They will need to understand foreign markets, cultural differences, and the motives and practices of foreign rivals.

On a more practical level, businesses will need managers who are capable of understanding international operations. In the past, most Canadian businesses hired local managers to run their operations in the various countries in which they operated. More recently, however, the trend has been to transfer Canadian managers to foreign locations. This practice helps firms better transfer their corporate cultures to foreign operations. In addition, foreign assignments help managers become better prepared for international competition as they advance within the organization.[10]

Management and Technology Skills

Another significant issue facing tomorrow's manager is technology, especially as it relates to communication. Managers have always had to deal with information. In today's world, however, the amount of information has reached staggering proportions. New forms of technology have added to a manager's ability to process information while simultaneously making it even more important to organize and interpret an ever-increasing wealth of input.

Technology has also begun to change the way the interaction of managers shapes corporate structures. Computer networking, for example, exists because it is no longer too expensive to put a computer on virtually every desk in the company. In turn, this elaborate network controls the flow of the firm's lifeblood—information. Information no longer flows strictly up and down through hierarchies. It now flows to everyone at once. As a result, decisions are made more quickly—and more people are directly involved. With e-mail, teleconferencing, and other forms of communication, neither time nor distance—nor such corporate "boundaries" as departments and divisions—can prevent people from working more closely together. More than ever, bureaucracies are breaking down, while planning, decision making, and other activities are beginning to benefit from group building and teamwork.

Becoming a Manager

The skills of management are not easily acquired by would-be managers. Nor can organizations easily identify people who possess these skills. As you will see in this section, both the training and the recruiting of managers are complex operations.

Preparing for Management

At one time, managers simply started at the "bottom" (in many cases, a plant or warehouse) and worked their way to the "top." While such a career path is still possible, the increasing complexity of management makes people who follow it a rare breed. Today more than ever before, managers are acquiring their skills and abilities through a cyclical process of education, experience, and then more education.

Education

The most common starting point for contemporary Canadian managers is a B. Comm. degree from a university or a college diploma in business administration. Many people leave school with this credential and start their careers. Their learning, however, is not complete. More and more people eventually return to school to get a masters of business administration (MBA) degree.[11] Even managers who do not earn an MBA usually go through corporate training programs. Many attend management development programs and seminars sponsored by universities, colleges, or private training companies. Learning is a lifelong process for most managers.

Experience

Education is not the only route into management. In some companies, managers—especially first-line managers—may have little or no advanced education. They have earned their positions strictly on the basis of experience. This pattern is common in heavy manufacturing industries such as steel and automobile production.

Experience is also necessary for those with degrees or diplomas who want to get ahead. After completing their degree(s) or diploma(s), most people today accept an entry-level position in a large company, go to work in a family-owned business, or start their own business. As their careers progress, they gain much valuable experience. In larger companies, for example, most management trainees go through formal training programs and work in a variety of areas to gain a broader perspective.

Where Organizations Find Managers

Just as there are different paths to management, companies acquire new managers in different ways. Firms have three basic sources of new managers: the academic world, the company itself, and other companies.

Recruiting from Colleges and Universities

Colleges and universities are a major source of new managers. Large firms such as Sears, the Bank of Montreal, Canadian Pacific, and Noranda hire hundreds of new graduates as managers every year. Often they start graduates from community colleges and universities as first-line managers. MBAs may be able to start at the lower levels of middle management.

The primary advantages of this source are that the managers are young and have been exposed to the latest ideas. On the other hand, they frequently lack experience and a proven track record. Businesses that adopt this strategy must invest in effective campus recruiting strategies and be prepared to develop future managers over a longer period of time.

Promoting from Within

Another common source of managers is the firm itself, especially one or two layers below where the new managers are needed. Promotion from within offers many advantages. Recognizing that they have a chance to advance within the company motivates lower-level employees to do their best. Employees

Most managers start learning their basic skills in university or college classrooms.

who are promoted from within also come with a track record. The firm has its own data on the individual's performance and accomplishments.

Of course, if someone from middle management is promoted to an executive position, someone else must be found to fill the middle-management position. Promotion from within tends to perpetuate current practices and ideas, giving less opportunity for innovation. In addition, these promotion decisions are sometimes seen as being too political, making other employees resentful, or damaging their morale.

Hiring Away from Other Organizations

Finally, some managers are hired away from other businesses. Contacts with talented managers willing to consider alternative opportunities can come from a manager's own network or through professional recruiting firms, commonly referred to as "headhunters."

As with the other options, hiring away from other firms has both advantages and disadvantages. The company may be able to get more talented people than are available internally. Already-trained managers mean a savings to the organization. Hiring from outside may inject fresh ideas and creativity. On the other hand, insiders passed over in favour of an outsider may feel resentful and leave. The newcomer may not fit into the company. Thus, the managers in charge of attracting human resources need to consider carefully the pros and cons of each source as they develop their human resource strategy.

Corporate Cultures

Recruiting new managers is a tricky business. Companies cannot rely solely on an individual's academic degrees and work experience in making a hiring or promotion decision. They must also consider the prospective manager's style and how it will fit into the company's culture.

Consider the following story, which details an interesting development in the relationship between employee behaviour and corporate values:

■ In 1989, Microsoft programmer Wes Cherry wrote a software program duplicating the game solitaire. Originally designed to amuse people as they learned Microsoft's new Windows software, Solitaire became such a hit that since 1990 the company has packaged it with nearly 50 million copies of Windows. To the consternation of many companies, however, Solitaire has become a nuisance and even a threat to productivity. According to one survey, about 42 percent of office computer users admit to playing games at their desks. Some organizations have banned game playing, and some have even removed programs from company-owned computers. Meanwhile, other companies actually endorse computer games. Managers in these offices see them as contributing to productivity because they help to reduce stress.[12]

This story shows that just as every individual has a unique personality, so every company has a unique identity—its corporate culture. **Corporate culture** is the shared experiences, stories, beliefs, and norms that characterize an organization. Various corporate cultures can be effective. What is important to managers is establishing and maintaining a strong, clear culture.[13]

At Toyota's Cambridge, Ontario, plant, for example, the corporate culture stresses values, principles, and trust. It also emphasizes customer satisfaction. For each employee, the next person down the production line is the customer. The culture is one of continuous improvement *(kaizen)*.[14]

corporate culture

The shared experiences, stories, beliefs, and norms that characterize a firm.

A company may consciously change its culture to improve its performance. Bata Shoes, long a traditional marketer, now stresses that it will not be satisfied with Canada's high prices to consumers. It advertises that its prices are as low as or lower than those in the U.S. The new corporate culture is also oriented to providing shoes to customers very quickly.

When two firms with different cultures merge, both have to adjust. For example, Baker-Lovick and McKim Advertising Ltd. were both purchased by BBDO Worldwide, a U.S. agency. But Baker-Lovick and McKim have completely different cultures. McKim is conservative and does not seek publicity, while Baker-Lovick loves the limelight. The new merged firm is likely to become more like Baker-Lovick in the future.[15]

Forces Shaping Corporate Culture

Apple Computer
http://www.apple.com

A number of forces shape corporate cultures. First, the values held by top management help set the tone of the organization and influence its business goals and strategies. For example, after Wozniak and Jobs founded Apple Computer, their laid-back approach and disdain for formality permeated the entire company. Even an older firm like Ford still bears traces of its founder. Most of Ford's top executives remain "car people," often engineers by training and background, rather than financial experts.

The firm's history also helps shape its culture. Championship banners line the Molson Centre, reinforcing the message that the Montreal Canadiens are winners. Maintaining a corporate culture draws on many dimensions of business life. Shared experiences resulting from norms sustain culture. Thus, working long hours on a special project becomes a shared experience for many employees. They remember it, talk about it among themselves, and wear it as a badge of their contribution to the company.

Stories and legends are also important. Walt Disney has been dead many years now, but his spirit lives on in the businesses he left behind. Quotations from Disney are affixed to portraits of him throughout the company's studios. And Disney's emphasis on family is still visible in corporate benefits such as paying for spouses to accompany employees on extended business trips. In fact, employees are often called "the Disney family."

Finally, strong behavioural norms help define and sustain corporate cultures. For example, a strong part of the culture at Hewlett-Packard Canada is that everyone wears a name tag and that everyone is called by his or her first name. And at Sony Corporation every employee wears a corporate smock.

Corporate culture is an important ingredient in organizational success. Japanese companies have been quite successful in building strong cultures by creating shared experiences and values among their employees. These executives are participating in a traditional purification ceremony at 4:30 in the morning. Later in the day they will remember this common experience as they work together.

Communicating the Culture

To use the corporate culture for the betterment of the organization, managers must accomplish several tasks that all depend on effective communication:

- Managers themselves must have a clear understanding of the culture.

- Managers must transmit the culture to others in the organization. Communication is thus one of the aims in training and orientation for newcomers. Another way of communicating the culture is to develop a clear and meaningful statement of the organization's mission.

- Managers can maintain the culture by rewarding and promoting those who understand it and who work towards maintaining it.

The box "Changing the Culture of a Manufacturing Plant" illustrates the importance of clearly communicating culture to employees.

The Canadian Business Scene

Changing the Culture of a Manufacturing Plant

James Bonini was only 33 years old when he was named manager of Chrysler Corp.'s van plant in Windsor, Ontario. His key responsibility was to prepare for the introduction of a new van model. But in order to do this successfully, he concluded that he was going to have to change the culture at the plant, which was unfortunately characterized by numerous quality problems, managers who acted like drill sergeants, and workers who were demoralized. Bonini knew that he would have to win support for his ideas from the 84 managers at the plant, Canadian Auto Workers officials, and the 1800 workers at the plant.

Although he had degrees from Princeton and the University of California at Berkeley, Bonini had very little manufacturing experience. Yet in one year, he managed to introduce a major change in the culture at the plant. How did he do it?

Bonini knew that the first thing he had to do was deal with the disappointed individuals who thought they should have been given the plant manager's job. He acknowledged that he was inexperienced, and said he needed their help to institute the changes that were going to be necessary to make the new model a success. He also conducted meetings with workers to get their ideas and hear their gripes. He met with union officals as well, who advised him to talk individually with workers, some of whom had never met a plant manager before.

Initially, Bonini spent a lot of time on the production floor; this impressed both workers and union officials. He also promised that he would try to boost the sale of vans by making sure the plant was responsive to special customer orders. The plant had the reputation of being reluctant to fill such special orders, so this was a major change. After several special orders were successfully filled, van sales began creeping up for the first time in years.

Bonini also overhauled the plant's manufacturing system. A new way of thinking was introduced: when things go wrong, don't automatically blame the workers. Instead, look at the production system to see if it makes sense. Consistent with this idea was the notion that workers should be involved in decision making about how the plant would operate. The plant's antiquated body shop, for example, was divided into teams of workers who were given the job of developing standard operating procedures. For the first time ever, workers decided how production processes would be carried out. In the end, about 70 percent of the plant's operations were changed.

Within a year of coming to Windsor, Bonini was asked to manage a new engine plant that Chrysler was building in Latin America. When the workers heard this, they expressed the concern that all the good things that had been started at the Windsor plant would be lost if Bonini left. But that hasn't happened; Bonini's successor says that the cultural change that Bonini introduced was very powerful, and that any outsider who came into the plant understood how things were going to be done.

Summary of Learning Objectives

1. **Explain the importance of setting *goals* and formulating *strategies* as the starting points of effective management.** *Goals*—the performance targets of an organization—can be *long-term, intermediate,* and *short-term.* They provide direction for managers, they help managers decide how to allocate limited resources, they define the corporate culture, and they help managers assess performance. *Strategies*—the methods that a company uses to meet its stated goals—involve three major activities: setting strategic goals, analyzing the organization and its environment, and matching the organization and its environment. These strategies are translated into *strategic, tactical,* and *operational plans.* To deal with crises or major environmental changes, companies develop *contingency plans* and plans for *crisis management.*

2. **Describe the four activities that constitute the *management process.*** *Management* is the process of planning, organizing, leading, and controlling an organization's financial, physical, human, and information resources to achieve the organization's goals. *Planning* means determining what the company needs to do and how best to get it done. *Organizing* means determining how best to arrange a business's resources and the necessary jobs into an overall structure. *Leading* means guiding and motivating employees to meet the firm's objectives. *Controlling* means monitoring the firm's performance to ensure that it is meeting its goals.

3. **Identify *types of managers* by level and area.** Managers can be differentiated in two ways: by level and by area. By level, *top managers* set policies, formulate strategies, and approve decisions. *Middle managers* implement policies, strategies, and decisions. *First-line managers* usually work with and supervise employees. Areas of managers include marketing, financial, operations, human resource, and information. Managers at all levels may be found in every area of a company.

4. **Describe the five basic *management skills.*** Most managers agree that five basic management skills are necessary for success. *Technical skills* are associated with performing specialized tasks ranging from typing to auditing. *Human relations skills* are associated with understanding and getting along with other people. *Conceptual skills* are the abilities to think in the abstract, to diagnose and analyze different situations, and to see beyond present circumstances. *Decision-making skills* allow managers to define problems and to select the best course of action. *Time management skills* refer to managers' ability to make productive use of the time available to them.

5. **Describe the development and explain the importance of *corporate culture.*** *Corporate culture* is the shared experiences, stories, beliefs, and norms that characterize an organization. A strong, well-defined culture can help a business reach its goals and can influence management styles. Culture is determined by several factors, including top management, the organization's history, stories and legends, and behavioural norms. If carefully communicated and flexible enough to accommodate change, corporate culture can be managed for the betterment of the organization.

Key Terms

goals, 165
mission statement, 166
long-term goals, 166
intermediate goals, 167
short-term goals, 167
strategy formulation, 167
strategic goals, 167
environmental analysis, 167
organizational analysis, 168
strategic plans, 169
tactical plans, 169
operational plans, 169
cost leadership, 169
differentiation, 169

focus, 169
market penetration, 169
market development, 169
product development, 169
vertical integration, 169
horizontal integration, 170
concentric diversification, 170
conglomerate diversification, 170
cooperative strategies, 170
stabilization, 170
retrenchment, 170

liquidation, 170
contingency planning, 170
crisis management, 170
management, 171
planning, 172
management by objectives (MBO), 173
plans, 173
organizing, 175
leading, 175
controlling, 176
top managers, 177
middle managers, 177
first-line managers, 178
marketing managers, 178

financial managers, 178
operations managers, 179
human resource managers, 179
information managers, 180
technical skills, 180
human relations skills, 181
conceptual skills, 181
decision-making skills, 181
time management skills, 182
corporate culture, 185

Study Questions and Exercises

Review Questions
1. Relate the basic managerial skills to the four activities in the management process. For example, which skill(s) is (are) most important in leading?
2. What are the major areas of management found in most organizations?
3. What are the three sources of new managers?
4. Why has the contingency approach become so important?

Analysis Questions
5. Select any group of which you are a member (company, family, club, etc.). Explain how planning, organizing, leading, and controlling are practised.
6. Identify managers by level and area at your college or university.
7. In what kind of company are technical skills for top managers more important than human relations or conceptual skills? Are there organizations in which conceptual skills are not important?

8. Why do companies recruit managers from various sources (e.g., colleges and universities, from within their own firms, and from other firms)?

Application Exercises
9. Interview a manager of a local company. Identify that manager's job according to the level and area of management. Show how planning, organizing, leading, and controlling are part of his or her job. Inquire about the manager's education and work experience. Which management skills are most important for this job?
10. Compare and contrast the corporate cultures of two businesses in your community in the same industry (for example, a Sears department store and a Costco warehouse).

Building Your Business Skills

Goal

To encourage students to understand the link between achieving organizational goals and managing the corporate culture.

Situation

Suppose that you are part of Taligent, an IBM/Apple Computer joint venture whose mission is to develop a new operating system to compete with Microsoft and Nexis. Besides formidable technical challenges, you must also find a way for the diametrically opposed corporate cultures from IBM and Apple to coexist. IBM, for example, is a hierarchical organization that moves ideas systematically up the corporate ladder, where they are approved and refocused before coming back down again in the form of strategic plans. Apple, on the other hand, has a collegial culture that empowers employees to make important decisions at all levels.

Method

Step 1:

Place yourself in the position of an IBM executive assigned to Taligent. What are the advantages and disadvantages that the IBM culture brings to the group in the following areas:

- *Decision making:* At IBM, the decision-making process is both crucial and deliberate, as is the collection and reporting of hard data.

- *Administrative support:* IBM executives are used to working with groups of dedicated support personnel who help them complete assignments but who also insulate them from the distractions of various events in the company.

- *Dress code:* Blue business suits are an IBM tradition.

Step 2:

Place yourself in the position of an executive from Apple Computer working on Taligent and perform the same analysis. What advantages and disadvantages does Apple's corporate culture bring to the project in the same areas:

- *Decision making:* While the pace of work is faster because decisions are made at all levels at Apple, the emphasis on empowerment over hierarchy can lead to anarchy—or at least to confusing communications. Moreover, decisions at Apple are often guided more by company folklore than by hard data.

- *Administrative support:* With fewer support personnel, Apple is a "leaner" organization than IBM.

- *Dress code:* The dress code at Apple is less formal and more relaxed than at IBM.

Step 3:

As a class, divide into groups of four or five. Discuss your analysis of the effects of the IBM and Apple corporate cultures on the success of Taligent.

Follow-up Questions

1. What cultural factors are likely to create the most serious problems for the joint venture?

2. How should team managers handle the cultural differences that will inevitably emerge among IBM and Apple employees?

To find out more about basic planning in and organization of a large company, visit the world and Canadian sites of Kodak at:

http://www.kodak.com

http://www.kodak.ca

1. What is the CEO's role in corporate structure as described in "Management Memos" and other Web site information?

2. What are some of the company's major goals as communicated in Web site press releases and other information? Which goals are long term? Which are short term?

3. How does the company indicate it will measure success in realizing management goals? What incentives are provided?

4. Based on your exploration of the main corporate and Canadian Kodak Web sites, what value do you think the company places on research and development? Explain.

CONCLUDING CASE 6-1

No Longer Leading the League

Until July of 1997, Paul Beeston was the CEO of the Toronto Blue Jays. His associates thought that, like Tom Hanks in the movie *Big*, he walked a fine line between crazy kid and top-notch executive. Beeston, who was legendary for his commitment to the organization, started as the team's first full-time accountant and rose through the ranks to become president in 1989. He arrived at work between 7 a.m. and 7:30 a.m. each day and didn't take a vacation for years.

Until 1994, Beeston worked closely with Pat Gillick, the executive vice-president and "master builder" of the club. Beeston handled the administration and balanced the books, while Gillick monitored the team's on-the-field performance. Big-name players like George Bell, Roberto Alomar, and Dave Winfield were signed to contracts. Beeston responded to fan concern about high player salaries by arguing that players need a good environment to work in.

Beeston was under constant pressure to win games and pennants. This is not a simple matter, since the club has 25 often temperamental ball players. It is necessary to continually find new players through the scouting system.

The ups and downs of professional sports franchises are well known. But until recently, the Toronto Blue Jays had been mostly up. From 1983 to 1993, the club had a winning record. It also won five divisional titles and, in 1992 and 1993, won back-to-back World Series titles. Attendance at Blue Jay games was high, the club was profitable, and the franchise was estimated to be worth nearly $200 million. Paul Beeston had indeed accomplished much as the club's CEO.

But since those good years, several problems have arisen. The baseball players strike in 1994 hurt all baseball teams, and in 1995 attendance at Blue Jay games dropped about 20 percent. These factors have caused a reduction in the salary budget. When the Jays won the World Series in 1993, the total salary payroll was a league-high $50 million. In 1996, it was just $30 million. The Blue Jays have also lost some personnel, including players and managers. Pat Gillick left to join a competing team, the Baltimore Orioles; several key players like Roberto Alomar and Paul Molitor also left to join other teams.

In 1995, Beeston sent a letter to season ticket holders asking for their continued support and patience while the team tried to rebuild. He noted that it was not fun running an organization with the kinds of problems the Blue Jays had recently experienced.

But Beeston was not the kind of person to give up when problems arose. In late 1996, the Blue Jays acquired several new players, including Roger Clemens, Benito Santiago, and Carlos Garcia. The Jays' salary budget for 1997 was approximately US$55 million. The Jays have once again become big spenders, and they hope to be a pennant contender with this new talent.

In July 1997, Paul Beeston was named president and chief operating officer of Major League Baseball. In his new job, Beeston will be responsible for all phases of the central offices in New York City.

Case Questions

1. What management skills does Paul Beeston need to be effective? How did these skills change as he has moved from accountant to CEO?

2. Briefly describe what each function of management involves in a position like Paul Beeston's.

3. Is being CEO of a baseball team much different from being CEO of a manufacturing firm? Explain.

◆

CONCLUDING CASE 6-2

Learning from Experience

The Canadian Forces and the U.S. Army have recently received some bad publicity because of the unprofessional behaviour of some of their members. But the two organizations are generally quite impressive in terms of their key function—military activity. They have achieved this success because they have carefully focused on learning lessons from experiences they have had.

The military has always had a fascination for "maneuvers," where soldiers practise various military tactics. Afterwards, the maneuver is analyzed to see what went right and what went wrong—in other words, what lessons can be learned. All of this is oriented towards increasing preparedness for the next real war.

A recent exercise by the U.S. Army near Death Valley, California, is typical. A reconnaissance aircraft intercepted a radio transmission that suggested that "enemy" soldiers were planning an attack by night. An unmanned, eight-metre model airplane carrying thermal-imaging cameras was dispatched to fly over the "enemy" camp and transmit precise targeting data. About one hour later, five enemy trucks moved out, but they were "destroyed" by simulated artillery, and all the enemy troops were marked as "killed." Later, the spy plane's role was explained to both sides in a debriefing session designed to clarify what had been learned during the maneuvers.

The "lessons-learned" mentality is particularly strong in the U.S. Army. The Bosnian peacekeeping mission has been ideal for refining this process. In Bosnia, the problems facing the troops are difficult and new, so there is much that can be learned. Rather than having each unit develop its own operational ideas, the U.S. commander required all military operations, even routine convoys, to be intensively reviewed afterwards. Lessons that were learned were then e-mailed to all units. For example: "Be careful of snow-covered roads where there are no tracks—they could be mined." And, "If you are caught in a minefield, don't turn around—back out the way you came." Every few days a new list of lessons learned is e-mailed to all the units.

Case Questions

1. Is the "lessons-learned" system of the military relevant to the management of business firms? How?

2. Are there any similarities between the "lessons-learned" system and the concept of continuous improvement currently used by some business firms?

3. In what kinds of business situations might the "lessons-learned" system be most useful? Explain the situation in enough detail so that your answer is clear.

◆

7

Organizing the Business Enterprise

Restructuring at Canadian Pacific

In November 1995, Canadian Pacific Ltd. announced a major restructuring. Under the plan, a new parent company will be set up, and it will wholly own six divisions: CP Rail System, CP Ships, PanCanadian Petroleum, Fording Coal, Marathon Realty, and Canadian Pacific Hotels. In the future, transportation and energy will be the two key elements in CP Ltd.'s overall corporate strategy.

As part of the reorganization, one of the six subsidiaries—CP Rail System Division—will move its headquarters from Montreal to Calgary. In the process, the division will cut 1450 management jobs and move another 730 jobs to Calgary. Most of the job losses will be felt in Montreal, although an eastern rail unit will still be located there. Shareholders must approve the proposed reorganization.

What motivated the move to Calgary? Since it was announced shortly after the Quebec referendum, some observers thought that it was politically motivated. But the CEO of CP Ltd., William Stinson, said that the referendum had nothing to do with the decision. He said it was strictly a business decision, and that it was necessary for railway management to be located where most of its revenues come from (80 percent of CP Rail Division revenues come from the west). Stinson also said that the reorganization would give CP Rail a better management style, lower costs, and would bring the company closer to the customer.

Under the new structure, CP Rail will have considerable autonomy, and may eventually become a publicly traded company in its own right. It will have access to capital markets, whereas previously it had to rely on the parent company for funding. CP Rail will also be able to merge with another firm if it desires, or get involved in a joint venture, or even institute some form of employee ownership.

Observers of the rail industry think that competitive factors were a big consideration in the reorganization decision. For example, the privatization of Canadian National Railways in 1995 makes it more likely that it will be a more aggressive competitor in the next decade. In spite of the fact that CP Rail is one of the largest railways in the world (1994 sales were $3.7 billion), it made only $43 million in profit in 1994. By contrast, CN earned over $200 million in 1994. To maintain its competitiveness, CP Rail will have to become more efficient, and this reorganization is designed to achieve that goal.

This latest reorganization gives parent company CP Ltd. quite a different look than it had as recently as 10 years ago. Then, it was involved in all sorts of diverse businesses, including mining (Cominco), forest products (Canadian Pacific Forest Products), airlines (Canadian Pacific Airlines), and communications (Unitel). All these business operations have been sold during the last decade.

Also as a result of the reorganization, the formerly 11 layers of management in the company will be compressed to six. As well, costs will be cut by reducing the scale of activities in various locations around North America, including Toronto, Vancouver, Minneapolis, and Albany, New York. The reorganization will save the firm $100 million each year in administrative costs. Overall, industry analysts think the reorganization will give CP Ltd. a much clearer corporate strategy. It will also give CP Rail a tighter focus and greater earning power. ◆

Canadian Pacific Ltd.
http://www.cprailway.com/

The need to fit structure to operations is common to all companies, large and small. Whether a company employs five people or 500 000, it needs organization to function. In this chapter, we consider the nature of business organization and the structures that firms have traditionally chosen. By focusing on the learning objectives of this chapter, you will better understand the importance of business organization and the ways in which both formal and informal aspects of its structure affect the decisions a business makes. After studying this chapter, you should be able to:

LEARNING OBJECTIVES

1. Discuss the elements that influence a firm's *organizational structure*.

2. Describe *specialization* and *departmentalization* as the building blocks of organizational structure.

3. Distinguish between *responsibility* and *authority* and explain the differences in decision making in *centralized* and *decentralized organizations*.

4. Explain the differences between *functional, divisional, project,* and *international organization structures*.

5. Define the *informal organization* and discuss *intrapreneuring*.

The Structure of Business Organizations

Exactly what do we mean by the term organizational structure? In many ways, a business is like an automobile. All automobiles have an engine, four wheels, fenders and other structural components, an interior compartment for passengers, and various operating systems including those for fuel, braking, and climate control. Each component has a distinct purpose but must also work in harmony with the others. Automobiles made by competing firms all have the same basic components, although the way they look and fit together may vary.

Similarly, all businesses have common structural and operating components, each of which has a specific purpose. Each component must fulfil its own purpose while simultaneously fitting in with the others. And, just like automobiles made by different companies, how these components look and fit together varies from company to company. Thus, **organizational structure** is the specification of the jobs to be done within a business and how those jobs relate to one another.

organizational structure
The specification of the jobs to be done within a business and how those jobs relate to one another.

Every institution—be it a for-profit company, a not-for-profit organization, or a government agency—must develop the most appropriate structure for its own unique situation. What works for Air Canada will not work for Revenue Canada. Likewise, the structure of the Red Cross will not work for the University of Toronto.

What accounts for the differences? An institution's purpose, mission, and strategy affect its structure. So do size, technology, and changes in environmental circumstances. A large manufacturing organization operating in a dynamic environment requires a different structure than a small service firm, such as a video rental store or barber shop.

organization chart
A physical depiction of the company's structure showing employee titles and their relationship to one another.

Most businesses prepare **organization charts** that illustrate the company's structure and show employees where they fit into the firm's operations. Figure 7.1 shows the organization chart for a hypothetical company. Each box represents a job within the company. The solid lines that connect the boxes define the **chain of command**, or the reporting relationships within the company. Thus, each plant manager reports directly to the vice-president for production who, in turn, reports to the president. When the chain of command is not clear, many different kinds of problems can result.

chain of command
Reporting relationships within a business; the flow of decision-making power in a firm.

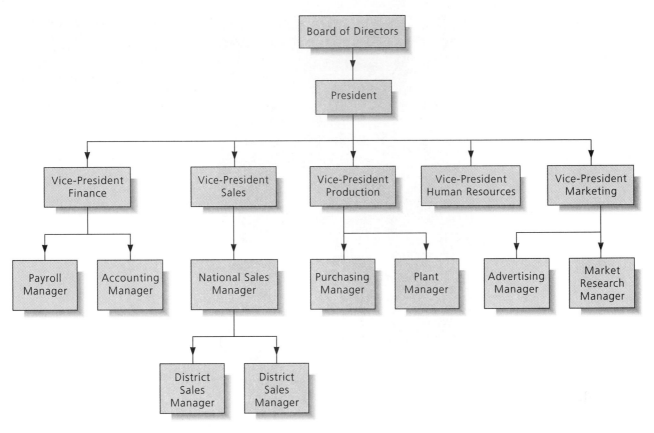

Figure 7.1
An organization chart shows key positions in the organization and interrelationships among them.

An actual organization chart would, of course, be far more complex and include individuals at many more levels. Indeed, because of their size, larger firms cannot easily draw a diagram with everyone on it.

The Building Blocks of Organizational Structure

The first step in developing the structure of any business, large or small, is twofold:

- *Specialization:* determining who will do what
- *Departmentalization:* determining how people performing certain tasks can best be grouped together

These two tasks are the basic building blocks of all business organization.

Specialization

The process of identifying the specific jobs that need to be done and designating the people who will perform them leads to **job specialization**. In a sense, all organizations have only one major "job"—say, making a profit by manufacturing and selling men's and boys' shirts. But this job, of course, is broken into smaller components. In turn, each component is assigned to an individual. Consider the manufacture of men's shirts. Because several steps

job specialization
The use of individuals with specialized skills to perform specialized tasks within a business.

Whether they are produced manually or digitally, the drawings that comprise a full-length Walt Disney cartoon are the result of highly coordinated job specialization. A lead animator, for example, may provide a rough pencil sketch that is then refined by one or more artists. Other teams scan clean drawings into a computer and colour them according to a plan devised by the art director. Finally, to achieve hand-drawn movement, a team of so-called "in-betweeners" completes all the drawings needed to give fluid motion to one or two key frames drawn by the lead animator.

are required to produce a shirt, each job is broken down into its component parts—that is, into a set of tasks to be completed by a series of individuals or machines. One person, for example, cuts material for the shirt body, another cuts material for the sleeves, and a third cuts material for the collar. Components are then shipped to a sewing room, where a fourth person assembles the shirt. In the final stage, a fifth person sews on the buttons.[1]

Specialization and Growth

In a very small organization, the owner may perform every job. As the firm grows, however, so does the need to specialize jobs so that others can perform them. To see how specialization can evolve in an organization, consider the case of Mrs. Fields Cookies. When Debbi Fields opened her first store, she did everything herself: bought the equipment, negotiated the lease, baked the cookies, operated the store, and kept the records. As the business grew, however, Fields found that her job was becoming too much for one person. She first hired a bookkeeper to handle her financial records. She then hired an in-store manager and a cookie baker. She herself concentrated on advertising and promotions. Her second store required another set of employees—another manager, another baker, and some salespeople. While Fields focused her attention on other expansion opportunities, she turned promotions over to a professional advertising director. Thus the job that she once did all by herself was increasingly broken down into components and assigned to different individuals.

Job specialization is a natural part of organizational growth. As the box "Di-Vine Madness" points out, it is neither a new idea nor limited to factory work. It carries with it certain advantages—individual jobs can be performed more efficiently, the jobs are easier to learn, and it is easier to replace people who leave the organization. On the other hand, if job specialization is carried too far and jobs become too narrowly defined, people get bored, derive less satisfaction from their jobs, and often lose sight of how their contributions fit into the overall organization.

Mrs. Fields Cookies
http://www.mrsfields.com

International Report

Di-Vine Madness

Once a year, for three days in November, the Burgundy region of France goes a little mad. These days, known as *Les Trois Glorieuses* (The Three Glorious Ones), are part of a traditional celebration marking the final harvesting of grapes. Over the course of the three days, pickers and chateau owners alike will make merry, eating wonderful food and, of course, drinking glass after glass of Burgundy wine.

Les Trois Glorieuses are just a taste of the full-bodied traditions surrounding French winemaking. Laws dating to the Napoleonic Era and a built-in aversion to change have left many aspects of the French wine industry virtually unaltered since Roman Catholic monks brewed the first modern wines centuries ago.

At the bottom of the social barrel are the *vendangeurs*—the pickers. In some areas of France, machines now pick the grapes. But in areas like Burgundy and Champagne, where plots are small and vines grow in close-set rows, handpicking is still necessary. Supervising the vendangeurs is the *vignon*. Typically a man with years of experience, the vignon also oversees all planting, weeding, and pruning of the vines throughout the year.

Unlike in Spain and Portugal, where workers still crush the grapes by stomping on them, French vineyards use machines to crush the grapes. Then, under the watchful eye of the *cellarer*, the juice (and skins in the case of red wines) is transferred into fermenting vats.

Left to its own devices, grape juice begins to ferment almost at once. Winemakers keep fermentation from changing the juice to vinegar by adjusting the oxygen supply and the temperature of the juice. At this point the chef de cave enters the picture in person. Traditionally, a *chef de cave* is a combination technical expert and chief operating officer. In addition to overall responsibility for the winery's operation, this is the person whose highly skilled palate dictates the ultimate taste of the wine.

Over the course of months, the chef de cave will taste the fermenting juice and test it for remaining sugar. At last the moment comes—it is time to end the fermentation. The juice is drawn off, leaving behind a fair amount of residue. But the wine is still clouded with sediment. To remove these "lees," vintners draw the wine through pipes to other casks in a process called "racking" that may be repeated several times. Gelatin, egg white, or a similar substance may be used to settle out remaining sediment, a process called "fining." Only then is the wine bottled.

Sparkling wines like champagne require a few extra steps—and specialists. After an initial fermentation, the unracked, unfined wine is placed in specially reinforced bottles with a small amount of sugar and yeast. The champagne will then lie on its side for months or even years. When the winery is ready to release the champagne for sale, it must clear out any residue. But because it is carbonated and already in bottles, ridding champagne of sediment is more complex than filtering still wines.

The process begins by placing the bottles in special racks. Each day a *remueur* turns each bottle a quarter of the way around and ever so slightly closer to upside down, until the neck is pointing almost straight down and the sediment has collected there. The neck of the bottle is then frozen. An expert *disgorgeur* quickly pops out the cork and removes the sediment. The disgorgeur's assistant tops off the bottle with some of the same champagne (and sometimes some sugar) and inserts a fresh cork, all in a matter of seconds.

At last the wine, be it still or sparkling, is ready to go to market. But no self-respecting chateau sells direct to any individual short of the Queen of England. Instead, France's wine houses go through intermediaries known as *courtiers* (wine brokers) and negotiants (wine wholesalers). *Courtiers* travel across the country, tasting and evaluating wines and establishing prices for them. Local *negotiants*, who ship French wines to the four corners of the globe, can place orders only through the courtiers, who get a 2 percent commission. Critics charge that the system is cumbersome and out-of-date. But one negotiant counters, "For years I've heard that we have an obsolete, dying system. The only problem is, no one has come up with anything better."

Departmentalization

After jobs are specialized, they must be grouped into logical units. This process is called **departmentalization.** Departmentalized companies benefit from the division of activities. Control and coordination are narrowed and made easier, and top managers can see more easily how various units are performing.

For example, departmentalization allows the firm to treat a department as a **profit centre**—a separate unit responsible for its own costs and profits. Thus, by assessing profits from sales in a particular area—say, men's clothing—Sears can decide whether to expand or curtail promotions in that area.

departmentalization
Process of grouping jobs into logical units.

profit centre
Separate company unit responsible for its own costs and profits.

Computer maker Hewlett-Packard Co. recently reorganized its structure to increase customer responsiveness and improve decision making. Most of the firm's operations are now handled by teams, each of which functions with a great degree of autonomy from the others. Indeed, individual teams are virtually business owners. In the network-server division, for instance, top managers are responsible for their unit's overall costs. "Our profit-and-loss statement," reports marketing manager Jim McDonnell, "is like any other small company." Similarly, managers have the authority to reinvest their profits back into their own operating units. As decision makers, they need not wait for budget requests to percolate to the top of the corporate hierarchy and then filter back down. At the same time, however, they are responsible for contributions to companywide operations—supporting the firm's general research unit, for example, and paying the CEO's salary.[2]

Managers do not group jobs randomly. They group them logically, according to some common thread or purpose. In general, departmentalization may occur along *customer, product, process, geographic,* or *functional* lines (or any combination of these).

Customer Departmentalization

customer departmentalization
Departmentalization according to types of customers likely to buy a given product.

Stores like Sears and The Bay are divided into departments—a men's department, a women's department, a luggage department, and so on. Each department targets a specific customer category (men, women, people who want to buy luggage). **Customer departmentalization** makes shopping easier by providing indentifiable store segments. Thus, a customer shopping for a baby's playpen can bypass Lawn and Garden Supplies and head straight for Children's Furniture. Stores can also group products in locations designated for deliveries, special sales, and other service-oriented purposes. In general, the store is more efficient and customers get better service—in part because salespeople tend to specialize and gain expertise in their departments.[3]

Product Departmentalization

product departmentalization
Departmentalization according to products being created.

Both manufacturers and service providers often opt for **product departmentalization**—dividing an organization according to the specific product or service being created. A bank, for example, may handle consumer loans in one department and commercial loans in another. On a larger scale, 3M Corp., which makes both consumer and industrial products, operates different divisions for Post-it brand Tape Flags, Scotch-Brite scrub sponges, and the Sarns 9000 perfusion system for open-heart surgery.

Process Departmentalization

process departmentalization
Departmentalization according to production process used to create a good or service.

Other manufacturers favour **process departmentalization**, in which the organization is divided according to production processes. This principle, for example, is logical for the pickle maker Vlasic, which has separate departments to transform cucumbers into fresh-packed pickles, pickles cured in brine, and relishes. Cucumbers destined to become fresh-packed pickles must be packed into jars immediately, covered with a solution of water and vinegar, and prepared for sale. Those slated for brined pickles must be aged in brine solution before packing. Relish cucumbers must be minced and combined with a host of other ingredients. Each process requires different equipment and worker skills.

Geographic Departmentalization

geographic departmentalization
Departmentalization according to the area of the country or world supplied.

Some firms may be divided according to the area of the country—or even the world—they serve. This is known as **geographic departmentalization.**

Many department stores are departmentalized by product. Concentrating different products in different areas of the store makes shopping easier for customers.

Concluding Case 7-2 at the end of the chapter describes a company that is structured along geographic lines.

Functional Departmentalization

Many service and manufacturing companies develop departments according to a group's functions or activities—a form of organization known as **functional departmentalization.** Such firms typically have production, marketing and sales, human resource, and accounting and finance departments. Departments may be further subdivided. For example, the marketing department might be divided geographically or into separate staffs for market research and advertising.

Because different forms of departmentalization have different advantages, larger companies tend to adopt different types of departmentalization for various levels. For example, the company illustrated in Figure 7.2 uses functional departmentalization at the top level. At the middle level, production is divided along geographic lines. At a lower level, departmentalization is based on product groups.

functional departmentalization
Departmentalization according to functions or activities.

Establishing the Decision-Making Hierarchy

A major question that must be asked about any organization is this: *Who makes which decisions?* The answer almost never focuses on an individual or even a small group. The more accurate answer usually refers to the decision-making hierarchy. The development of this hierarchy generally results from a three-step process:

1. *Assigning tasks:* determining who can make decisions and specifying how they should be made

2. *Performing tasks:* implementing decisions that have been made

3. *Distributing authority:* determining whether the organization is to be centralized or decentralized

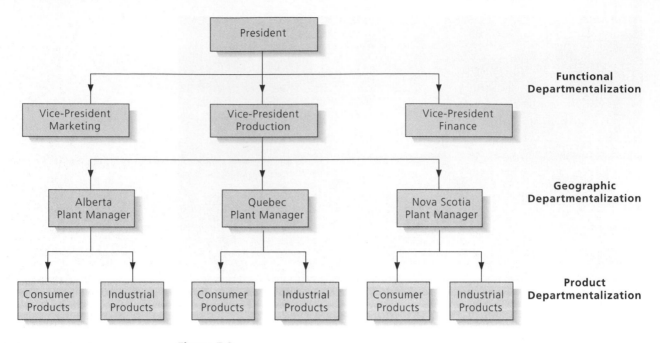

Figure 7.2
Most organizations use multiple bases of departmentalization. This organization, for example, is using functional, geographic, and product departmentalization.

Assigning Tasks

The question of who is *supposed* to do what and who is *entitled* to do what in an organization is complex. In any company with more than one person, individuals must work out agreements about responsibilities and authority. **Responsibility** is the duty to perform an assigned task. **Authority** is the power to make the decisions necessary to complete the task.

For example, imagine a mid-level buyer for The Bay who encounters an unexpected opportunity to make a large purchase at an extremely good price. Let's assume that an immediate decision is absolutely necessary—a decision that this buyer has no authority to make without confirmation from above. The company's policies on delegation and authority are inconsistent, since the buyer is *responsible* for purchasing the clothes that will be sold in the upcoming season but lacks the *authority* to make the needed purchases.

Performing Tasks

Trouble occurs when appropriate levels of responsibility and authority are not clearly spelled out in the working relationships between managers and subordinates. Here, the issues become delegation and accountability. **Delegation** begins when a manager assigns a task to a subordinate. **Accountability** falls to the subordinate, who must then complete the task. If the subordinate does not perform the assigned task properly and promptly, he or she may be reprimanded or punished, possibly even dismissed.

Subordinates sometimes cannot complete a task because their managers have not also delegated the necessary authority. Such employees face a dilemma: they cannot do what the boss demands, but that boss will probably still hold them accountable. Successful managers surround themselves with a team of strong subordinates and then delegate sufficient authority to those subordinates to get the job done. There are four things to keep in mind when delegating:

responsibility
Duty to perform an assigned task.

authority
Power to make the decisions necessary to complete a task.

delegation
Assignment of a task, a responsibility, or authority by a manager to a subordinate.

accountability
Liability of subordinates for accomplishing tasks assigned by managers.

This manager is using her *authority* to *delegate* work to a subordinate. The subordinate has a duty, or a *responsibility* to perform the task and is also *accountable* for the completed work.

- decide on the nature of the work to be done

- match the job with the skills of subordinates

- make sure the person chosen understands the objectives he or she is supposed to achieve

- make sure subordinates have the time and training necessary to do the task.

Distributing Authority

In every organization, management must decide how to distribute authority throughout the hierarchy. **Centralization** occurs when top management retains the right to make most decisions that need to be made. In a highly centralized organization, the CEO makes most of the decisions, and subordinates simply carry them out. For example, Cedric Ritchie, the CEO of the Bank of Nova Scotia, knew all the details of the bank's operations and made many decisions that CEOs of other banks delegated to subordinates.[4]

Decentralization occurs when top managers delegate the right to make decisions to the middle and lower levels of the management hierarchy. At General Electric's Bromont, Quebec, plant, for example, every effort has been made to get employees involved in a wide range of decision making.[5] Traditional jobs like supervisor and foreman do not exist at the plant, and all hiring is done by committees made up of workers. Some workers spend only 65 percent of their time on production work; the other 35 percent is spent on training, planning, and in meetings. At Hymac Ltée., a Laval, Quebec, producer of pulp processing machinery, managers encourage employees to meet with customers to determine how Hymac can serve them more effectively.[6]

centralization
Occurs when top managers retain most decision-making rights for themselves.

decentralization
Occurs when lower- and middle-level managers are allowed to make significant decisions.

Span of Control

The distribution of authority in an organization also affects how many people work for any individual manager. The number of people managed by one

span of control

The number of people managed by one manager.

supervisor is called the **span of control**. Employees' abilities and the supervisor's managerial skills help determine whether the span of control is wide or narrow. So do the similarity and simplicity of tasks performed under the manager's supervision and the extent to which they are interrelated. For example, by eliminating two layers of management, the president of the Franklin Mint recently increased his own span of control from 6 to 12.

When several employees perform either the same simple task or a group of interrelated tasks, a wide span of control is possible and often desirable. For instance, because all the jobs are routine, one supervisor may well control a whole assembly line. Moreover, each task depends on another: If one station stops, everyone stops. Having one supervisor ensures that all stations receive equal attention and function equally well. In contrast, when jobs are not routine, or when they are prone to change, a narrow span of control is preferable.

Not surprisingly, decentralized companies use wide spans of control and require few layers of management. The result is often called a *flat organizational structure*. On the other hand, centralized authority means that a firm relies on narrow spans of control, multiple layers of management, and a *tall organizational structure*.

Three Forms of Authority

In an organization, it must be clear who will have authority over whom. As individuals are delegated responsibility and authority in a firm, a complex web of interactions develops. These interactions may take one of three forms of authority: *line, staff,* or *committee and team*. In reality, like departmentalization, all three forms may be found in a given company, especially a large one.

Line Authority

line authority

Organizational structure in which authority flows in a direct chain of command from the top of the company to the bottom.

line department

Department directly linked to the production and sales of a specific product.

Line authority is authority that flows up and down the chain of command (refer back to Figure 7.1). Most companies rely heavily on **line departments**—departments directly linked to the production and sales of specific products. For example, Clark Equipment Corp. has a division that produces forklifts and small earth movers. In this division, line departments include purchasing, materials handling, fabrication, painting, and assembly (all of which are directly linked to production) along with sales and distribution (both of which are directly linked to sales).

Each line department is essential to an organization's success. Line employees are the "doers" and producers in a company. If any line department fails to complete its task, the company cannot sell and deliver finished goods. Thus, the authority delegated to line departments is important. A bad decision by the manager in one department can hold up production for an entire plant. For example, say that the painting department manager at Clark Equipment changes a paint application on a batch of forklifts, which then show signs of peeling paint. The batch will have to be repainted (and perhaps partially reassembled) before the machines can be shipped.

Staff Authority

staff authority

Authority that is based on expertise and that usually involves advising line managers.

staff members

Advisers and counsellors who aid line departments in making decisions but do not have the authority to make final decisions.

Most companies also rely on **staff authority.** Staff authority is based on special expertise and usually involves counselling and advising line managers. Common **staff members** include specialists in areas such as law, accounting, and human resource management. A corporate attorney, for example, may be asked to advise the marketing department as it prepares a new contract with the firm's advertising agency. Legal staff, however, do not actually make decisions that affect how the marketing department does its job. Staff members, therefore, aid line departments in making decisions but do not have the authority to make final decisions.

Suppose, for example, that the fabrication department at Clark Equipment has an employee with a drinking problem. The manager of the department could consult a human resource staff expert for advice on handling the situation. The staff expert might suggest that the worker stay on the job but enter a counselling program. But if the line manager decides that the job is too dangerous to be handled by a person whose judgment is often impaired by alcohol, that decision will most likely prevail.

Typically, the separation between line authority and staff responsibility is clearly delineated. As Figure 7.3 shows, this separation is usually shown in organization charts by solid lines (line authority) and dotted lines (staff responsibility). It may help to understand this separation by remembering that while staff members generally provide services to management, line managers are directly involved in producing the firm's products.

Committee and Team Authority

Recently, more and more organizations have started to use **committee and team authority**—authority granted to committees or work teams that play central roles in the firm's daily operations. A committee, for example, may consist of top managers from several major areas. If the work of the committee is especially important, and if the committee will be working together for an extended time, the organization may even grant it special authority as a decision-making body that goes beyond the individual authority possessed by each of its members.

At the operating level, many firms today are also using *work teams*—groups of operating employees empowered to plan and organize their own work and to perform that work with a minimum of supervision. As with permanent committees, the organization will usually find it beneficial to grant special authority to work teams so that they may function more effectively.[7]

committee and team authority

Authority granted to committees or work teams involved in a firm's daily operations.

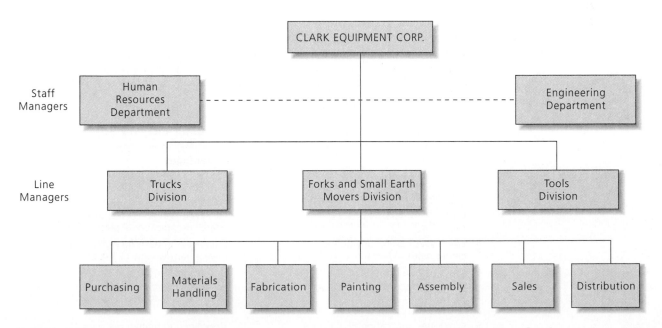

Figure 7.3
Line-and-staff organization: Clark Equipment Corp.

Business firms are increasingly using work teams and allowing groups of employees to plan and organize their own work with a minimum of supervision. This contributes to employee empowerment.

Basic Organizational Structures

A glance at the organization charts of many organizations reveals what appears to be an infinite variety of structures. However, closer examination shows that it is possible to identify four basic forms: functional, divisional, project, and international. These structures are described below.

The Functional Structure

functional structure

Various units are included in a group based on functions that need to be performed for the organization to reach its goals..

The functional structure is the oldest and most commonly used. In the **functional structure**, the various units in the organization are formed based on the functions that must be carried out to reach organizational goals. The functional structure makes use of departmentation by function. An example of a functional structure is shown in Figure 7.1. The advantages and disadvantages of the functional structure are summarized in Table 7.1.

Table 7.1   Advantages and Disadvantages of a Functional Structure

Advantages	Disadvantages
1. Focuses attention on the key activities that must be performed.	1. Conflicts may arise among the functional areas.
2. Expertise develops within each function.	2. No single function is responsible for overall organizational performance.
3. Employees have clearly defined career paths.	3. Employees in each functional area have a narrow view of the organization.
4. The structure is simple and easy to understand.	4. Decision making is slowed because functional areas must get approval from top management for a variety of decisions.
5. Eliminates duplication of activities.	5. Coordinating highly specialized functions may be difficult.

The Telus corporation (formerly Alberta Government Telephones) oversees the telecommunications activity of seven operating companies using a divisional organization structure.

The Divisional Structure

The functional structure's disadvantages can make it inappropriate for some companies. Many companies have found that the divisional structure is more suited to their needs. The **divisional structure** divides the organization into several divisions, each of which operates as a semi-autonomous unit and profit centre. In 1990, Alberta's Conservative government unveiled a new divisional structure and a new name for Alberta Government Telephones (AGT). The new organization is called Telus Corporation and is patterned after Montreal-based BCE. It oversees the telecommunications activity of seven operating companies, including AGT.

Divisions in organizations can be based on products, customers, or geography. Whatever basis is used, divisional performance can be easily assessed each year because the division operates as a separate company. Firms with this structure are often called *conglomerates*.

The advantages and disadvantages of the divisional structure are summarized in Table 7.2.

divisional structure

Divides the organization into divisions, each of which operates as a semi-autonomous unit.

Table 7.2   Advantages and Disadvantages of a Divisional Structure

Advantages	Disadvantages
1. Accommodates change and expansion.	1. Activities may be duplicated across divisions.
2. Increases accountability.	2. A lack of communication among divisions may occur.
3. Develops expertise in the various divisions.	3. Adding diverse divisions may blur the focus of the organization.
4. Encourages training for top management.	4. Company politics may affect the allocation of resources.

Project Organization

A typical line or line-staff organization is characterized by unchanging vertical authority relationships. It has such a setup because the organization produces a product or service in a repetitive and predictable way. Procter & Gamble, for example, produces millions of tubes of Crest Toothpaste each year using standardized production methods. The company has done this for years and intends to do so indefinitely.

But some organizations find themselves faced with new product opportunities or with projects that have a definite starting and end point. These organizations often use a project structure to deal with the uncertainty encountered in new situations. **Project organization** involves forming a team of specialists from different functional areas of the organization to work on a specific project.[8] A project structure may be temporary or permanent; if it is temporary, the project team disbands once the project is completed and team members return to their regular functional area or are assigned to a new project.

Project organization is used extensively by Canadian firms, for example, in the construction of hydroelectric generating stations like those developed by Hydro-Québec on La Grande River, and by Manitoba Hydro on the Nelson River. Once the generating station is complete, it becomes part of the traditional structure of the utility. Project organization has also proven useful for coordinating the many elements needed to extract oil from the tar sands. Project management is also used in other kinds of tasks, including shipbuilding, construction, military weapons, aerospace, and health care delivery.[9] The box "Project Management at Genstar" describes how this form of organization works, and how authority issues are decided.

Some companies use a **matrix organization**, which is a variation of project structure in which the project manager and the regular line managers share authority. When a project is concluded, the matrix is disbanded. IBM, for example, has a line-staff structure overall, but it used a matrix organization to develop the original PC. The matrix was disbanded when the PC succeeded.

A problem with the matrix structure is that employees have two bosses—their regular line boss *and* the project manager. Employees may therefore receive conflicting orders. These and other problems have caused some firms that used to like the matrix structure to move away from it. For example, Digital Equipment Company's president, Robert Palmer, announced in 1994 that "matrix management at our company is dead."[10]

project organization
An organization that uses teams of specialists to complete specific projects.

Hydro-Québec
http://www.hydro.qc.ca

Manitoba Hydro
http://www.hydro.mb.ca

matrix organization
A project structure in which the project manager and the regular line managers share authority until the project is concluded.

International Organization

Many businesses today manufacture, purchase, and sell in the world market. Thus a number of variations on basic organizational structure have emerged. Moreover, as competition on a global scale becomes more complex, companies often find that they must experiment with the ways in which they respond.

For example, at Club Méditerranée, an international French-based firm that provides vacation sites (called "villages") around the world, each village manager used to report both to a country manager and to a number of different directors. Directors worked out of company headquarters, and each director had primary responsibility for some facet of Club Med operations and marketing. This structure, however, proved less than satisfactory. Club Med prides itself on providing village arrangements that reflect various *local* atmospheres—a difficult feat for directors to achieve from remote locations. To solve this problem, the company adopted a different form of organization. A major component of the new structure involved sending operations and marketing staff to specific geographic regions.

The Canadian Business Scene

Project Management at Genstar Shipyards Ltd.

Genstar Shipyards Ltd. is a Vancouver firm that specializes in the custom building and repair of icebreakers, research vessels, ferries, tugs, and barges. In peak periods, it delivers a new ship every two months. The value of the ships varies from a low of about $2 million for a small tugboat to a high of nearly $60 million for a state-of-the-art icebreaker. Construction periods for ships range from four months to two years.

Project management is really the only structure that makes sense for shipbuilding. Since time is of the essence in every construction contract, and since costs must be closely monitored, a project structure is necessary.

The shipyard has an operations manager who is responsible for the overall shipbuilding activity. Two project managers (PMs) report to the operations manager. Each ship the company builds is treated as a project, and the two PMs are responsible for seeing that projects are finished on schedule, to specification, and within budget. Some projects employ up to 400 people, so the PM's job may have a major administrative component.

The PM is responsible for the development of a master schedule for each vessel's design and construction. He or she identifies personnel and equipment that are necessary to complete the job, and interacts with all departments involved in the project. Once the master schedule has been set, the PM is responsible for seeing that the schedule and the budget are met. After the ship is built and launched, the PM oversees its trial run and delivery to the owner.

The PM has the authority to decide the construction sequence on the project as well as the number of workers that will be assigned to each phase of the project. These decisions are made after consulting the project plans. Workers on the project report to a supervisor. If the PM and the supervisor disagree about who should be assigned to a project, the PM can appeal to the superintendent (the supervisor's boss). The PM usually prevails on staffing issues.

Other areas of potential disagreement also exist. For example, a supervisor might think work on some part of a ship's construction ought to be done in one way, while the PM thinks it should be done in some other way. If the disagreement is a question of sequencing of the work, the PM will usually prevail; if the disagreement is about specific trade practices, the supervisor will generally win out. As another example, a supervisor may try to assign more tradespeople to a project than the PM thinks are necessary. The supervisor may be trying to create a cushion in meeting the construction schedule. In these cases, the PM usually wins out because the total project schedule and budget must be kept in mind, whereas the supervisor may be thinking only of the work that a particular crew is doing.

The PM does not have the authority to hire, lay off, or fire workers; this is the responsibility of the supervisor. The PM works with the supervisor to determine when the workforce should be increased or decreased. The PM also has the authority to approve payment to outside sources from which the company has purchased materials.

To be effective, the PM requires interpersonal skills (the ability to instil enthusiasm in workers), administrative skills (the ability to keep the project on schedule and within budget), and technical skills (the ability to communicate with the technically skilled people who are working on the project).

For similar reasons, other firms have developed a wide range of approaches to international organizational structure. Whirlpool, for example, purchased the appliance division of the Dutch electronics giant N.V. Philips and as part of its international organization structure now makes the cooling coils for its refrigerators at its new plant in Trento, Italy.[11] Other companies, such as Levi Strauss, handle all international operations through separate international divisions. Still others concentrate production in low-cost areas and then distribute and market globally. Some firms, such as Britain's Pearson PLC (which runs such diverse businesses as publishing, investment banking, and Madame Tussaud's Wax Museum), allow each of their businesses to function autonomously within local markets. Finally, some companies adopt a truly global structure in which they acquire resources (including capital), produce goods and services, engage in research and development, and sell products in whatever local market is appropriate, without any consideration of national boundaries.

The Informal Organization

formal organization

The specified relationships between individuals, their jobs, and their authority, as shown in the company's organizational chart.

informal organization

A network of personal interactions and relationships among employees unrelated to the firm's formal authority structure.

grapevine

An informal communications network that carries gossip and other information throughout an organization.

mentor

A manager who guides the careers of subordinates by offering them advice, providing them with training and expanded responsibility, and otherwise assisting them in gaining promotions.

So far we have focused on the **formal organization** of businesses—the part that can be seen and drawn in chart form. But organization within any company is not limited to the organization chart and the formal assignment of authority. Frequently, the **informal organization**—the everyday social interactions among employees—alters a company's formal structure.

One of the most powerful informal forces in any firm is the grapevine. The **grapevine** is an informal communications network that carries gossip and other information throughout the organization. As the box "Heard It Through the Grapevine" notes, the grapevine can be a useful source of information—if you take it with a grain of salt.

When its reports are accurate, the grapevine can serve a company by supplying information more rapidly than formal channels can. For example, if employees see an ambulance pull up to the plant, they will use the grapevine to find out if someone has had an accident. Long before the personnel department can issue an announcement, the grapevine can supply the news that a pregnant worker had her baby early. Similarly, advance word of impending changes in the company's operations can help employees adjust mentally—and even physically (by getting a new job elsewhere, for example)—before the actual shift. The informal organization also facilitates networking and **mentoring**, which can enhance the career development of individuals and promote organizational effectiveness.

Some companies encourage the informal exchange of information.[12] For example, 3M sponsors clubs for 12 or more employees to try to enhance communication across departments. Other companies have physically arranged offices and other facilities to be more conducive to informal communications. One bank moved two departments to the same floor in an attempt to encourage intermingling of the employees. These companies believe informal communications can stimulate discussions that solve organizational problems.

The grapevine is a powerful informal communications network in most organizations. These workers may be talking about any number of things—an upcoming deadline on an important project, tonight's football game, the stock market, rumours about an impending takeover, gossip about forthcoming promotions, or the weather.

The Canadian Business Scene

Heard It Through the Grapevine

Faster than a speeding bullet—that's the office grapevine. But how accurate is it? Should you listen to it, or is it just so much gossip?

Today many experts advise tuning to the grapevine's message. They note that the grapevine is often a corporate early warning system. Ignoring this valuable source of information can leave you the last to know that you're about to get a new boss, or that you have a potentially fatal image problem. Even personal information about co-workers and superiors can be useful in helping you interact positively with these individuals.

Do consider both the source and the message carefully, though. Most office gossip has at least some kernel of truth to it. But as "facts" get passed down from person to person, they can get twisted out of shape. In other cases, those passing on news will deliberately alter it, either to advance their own goals or to submarine someone else's chances. Experts also warn that listening to and passing on information damaging to someone's reputation can backfire, harming your credibility and making you a target for similar gossip.

In general, the more detailed the information, the less likely it is to be true. Likewise, beware the hush-hush "don't quote me on this" rumour. (Cynics claim that the better the news, the less likely it is to be true, too.) But the higher the source, the greater the likelihood that the grapevine has the real story. Don't reject information from "lower" sources, however. Many an executive assistant can provide valuable insights into a corporation's plans.

An interesting phenomenon of office communication occurs when individuals responsible for formal information systems, such as newsletters, press briefings, and memoranda, spread a somewhat different story on the grapevine. Which should you believe? Today it is so common for a corporate executive to publicly deny rumours of layoffs one day and hand out pink slips the next that no one even raises an eyebrow. The grapevine, unconcerned with public image and long-range schemes, cuts to the heart of the matter.

The grapevine is not infallible, however. In addition to miscommunication and attempts by some people to manipulate it for their own ends, it may carry rumours with absolutely no basis in fact. Such rumours are most common when there is a complete lack of information. Apparently, human nature abhors such a vacuum and fills it. Baseless rumours can be very hard to kill, however.

On the down side, informal communications can also cause problems. They can play an instrumental role in office politics that put the interests of individuals ahead of those of the firm. Likewise, a great deal of harm can be caused if distorted or inaccurate information flows through the grapevine. For example, if the grapevine is carrying false information about impending layoffs, valuable employees may act quickly (and unnecessarily) to look for employment elsewhere.

Intrapreneuring

Sometimes organizations actually take steps to encourage the informal organization. They do so for a variety of reasons, two of which we have already touched on. First, most experienced managers recognize that the informal organization exists whether they want it or not. Second, many managers know how to use the informal organization to reinforce the formal organization. Perhaps more important, however, the energy of the informal organization can be harnessed to improve productivity.

■ To stimulate innovation, for example, 3M Corp. maintains a flat, decentralized organizational structure. As a rule, only a few levels of management bureaucracy are involved in approving new products. The corporate culture at 3M further supports innovation by encouraging researchers to spend 15 percent of their time exploring new ideas. Those who develop new products are rewarded both professionally and financially. As a result, 3M researchers usually develop about 200 new products each year. Among their most celebrated successes have been Post-it self-stick notes and a tape for mending broken bones.

3M
http://www.3M.com

Xerox
http://www.xerox.com

intrapreneuring
Process of creating and maintaining the innovation and flexibility of a small business environment within the confines of a large organization.

- Through Xerox Technology Ventures, Xerox Corp. allocates $30 million to fund companies like QuadMark Ltd., an electronics development firm in which Xerox has a 60 percent stake. The purpose of XTV is to nurture internal technological innovations that, for various reasons, do not receive adequate attention from the parent company's development centre. For example, QuadMark developed a battery-operated copier that fits inside a briefcase next to a laptop computer. Another XTV-funded start-up invented an advanced circuit board that could be inserted into an inexpensive PC and made to do the work of a $10 000 Xerox office workstation. Xerox deemed it wise to buy out the potential new competitor (for $15 million). Since 1989, XTV has generated 12 start-ups and now offers as much as 20 percent of the new companies' shares to successful founders.13

Both 3M and Xerox are supporting a process called **intrapreneuring**—creating and maintaining the innovation and flexibility of a small business environment within the confines of a large, bureaucratic structure. The concept is sound. Historically, most innovations have come from individuals in small businesses (see Chapter 8). As businesses increase in size, however, innovation and creativity tend to become casualties in the battle for more sales and profits. In some large companies, new ideas are even discouraged, and champions of innovation have even been stalled in mid-career. In companies like 3M and Xerox, however, intrapreneuring is seen as an effective way of remaining as innovative as smaller firms that specialize in new products that the larger firms can bring to market quickly.

Summary of Learning Objectives

1. **Discuss the elements that influence a firm's *organizational structure*.** Every business needs structure to operate. *Organizational structure* varies according to a firm's mission, purpose, and strategy. Size, technology, and changes in environmental circumstances also influence structure. In general, while all organizations have the same basic elements, each develops the structure that contributes to the most efficient operations.

2. **Describe *specialization* and *departmentalization* as the building blocks of organizational structures.** The building blocks of organizational structure are *job specialization* and *departmentalization*. As a firm grows, it usually has a greater need for people to perform specialized tasks (specialization). It also has a greater need to group types of work into logical units (departmentalization). Common forms of departmentalization are *customer, product, process, geographic,* and *functional*. Large businesses often use more than one form of departmentalization.

3. **Distinguish between *responsibility* and *authority* and explain the differences in decision making in *centralized* and *decentralized* organizations.** *Responsibility* is the duty to perform a task; *authority* is the power to make the decisions necessary to complete tasks. *Delegation* begins when a manager assigns a task to a subordinate; *accountability* means that the subordinate must complete the task. *Span of control* refers to the number of people who work for any individual manager. The more people supervised, the wider the span of control. Wide spans are usually desirable when employees perform simple or unrelated tasks. When jobs are diversified or prone to change, a narrower span is generally preferable.

In a *centralized organization*, only a few individuals in top management have real decision-making authority. In a *decentralized organization*, much authority is delegated to lower-level management. Where both *line* and *line-and-staff systems* are involved, *line departments* generally have authority to make decisions while *staff departments* have a responsibility to advise. A relatively new concept, *committee and team authority*, empowers committees or work teams involved in a firm's daily operations.

4. **Explain the differences between *functional, divisional, project,* and *international organization structures.*** In a *functional organization*, authority is usually distributed among such basic functions as marketing and finance. In a *divisional organization*, the various divisions of a larger company, which may be related or unrelated, operate in a relatively autonomous fashion. In *project organization*, in which individuals report to more than one manager, a company creates teams to address specific problems or to conduct specific projects. A company that has divisions in many countries may require an additional level of *international organization* to coordinate those operations.

5. **Define the *informal organization* and discuss *intrapreneuring.*** The informal organization consists of the everyday social interactions among employees that transcend formal jobs and job interrelationships. To foster innovation and flexibility, some large companies encourage *intrapreneuring*—creating and maintaining the innovation and flexibility of a small business environment within the confines of a large bureaucratic structure.

Key Terms

organizational structure, 194
organization chart, 194
chain of command, 194
job specialization, 195
departmentalization, 197
profit centre, 197
customer departmentalization, 198
product departmentalization, 198

process departmentalization, 198
geographic departmentalization, 198
functional departmentalization, 199
responsibility, 200
authority, 200
delegation, 200
accountability, 200

centralization, 201
decentralization, 201
span of control, 202
line authority, 202
line department, 202
staff authority, 202
staff members, 202
committee and team authority, 203
functional structure, 204
divisional structure, 205
project organization, 206
matrix organization, 206

formal organization, 208
informal organization, 208
grapevine, 208
mentor, 208
intrapreneuring, 210

Study Questions and Exercises

Review Questions

1. What is an organization chart? What purpose does it serve?
2. Explain the significance of size as it relates to organizational structure. Describe the changes that are likely to occur as an organization grows.
3. What is the difference between responsibility and authority?
4. How are product and customer departmentalization different?
5. Why is a company's informal organization important to its operations?

Analysis Questions

6. Draw up an organization chart for your college or university.
7. What kind of organizational structure might a small printing firm have? Describe the structural changes that might be necessary as the firm grows.

8. Compare the matrix and divisional approaches to organizational structure.

Application Exercises

9. Interview the manager of a local service business such as a fast-food restaurant. What types of tasks does this manager typically delegate? Is the appropriate authority also delegated in each case? How would you know?
10. Using books, magazines, or personal interviews, identify an individual who has succeeded as an intrapreneur. In what ways did the structure of the intrapreneur's company help this individual succeed? In what ways did the structure pose problems?

Building Your Business Skills

Goal

To encourage students to understand the role of the grapevine in business firms, and to learn how to deal with rumours that spread through the grapevine.

Situation

Suppose that as a department manager, you learn that a rumour is spreading through the grapevine that the company is planning to close your facility at the end of the month, thereby laying off dozens of employees. The rumour is not true. You want to stop it but are not sure what to do.

Method

Evaluate the pros and cons of the following strategies for stopping the rumour.

Strategy 1:

When you first hear the rumour, issue a formal memo denying everything but giving no additional information.

Strategy 2:

As you happen to see them in the office, talk with employees and reassure them that the rumour is false.

Rather than dealing with the rumour in detail, talk about it in general terms.

Strategy 3:

- When you first realize that a rumour is starting, try to track down its sources.
- Evaluate the damage being caused by the rumour.
- Plan a counterattack by gathering all the facts about the rumour and where it has spread.
- Confront the rumour by using concrete evidence to refute it; if necessary, bring in experts to support the refutation; directly state that the rumour is false and that spreading lies is damaging and unfair.

Follow-Up Questions

1. Which type of rumour is more difficult to contain—a rumour contained within an organization or one that has spread to competitors, customers, and other external groups?
2. Why do you think that the informal communication network holds such power in business organizations?

EXPLORING the Net

Chapter 7 describes the increasing importance of intrapreneurship in many organizations today. The following Web site is a useful starting point in learning more about this concept:

http://www.pinchot.com:80/

Browse this site, and then consider the following questions:

1. Review "The Intrapreneur's Ten Commandments." Do these principles seem reasonable to you? Which would be the most difficult for you personally to adopt?
   - What is your first reaction to the advice that you should "come to work each day willing to be fired"? What is your reaction upon further reflection?
   - If there is one theme that is more insistent than the others in this list, what is it?

2. Take the quiz entitled "Are You an Intrapreneur?" Basing your ideas on these questions, draw up a brief "personality profile" of someone who would make a good intrapreneur. To what extent do you fit this profile?

3. Review the feature entitled "Five People of Innovation" and draw up brief thumbnail sketches to characterize each of the five types described here. In what ways can people from these five groups be expected to work together successfully? In what ways might they encounter difficulties in working together?

4. Study the "Survey of the Climate for Innovation." Judging from the questions asked here, list five important characteristics of a climate that is conducive to innovation in an organization.

CONCLUDING CASE 7-1

United Airlines Gives Managers the Power to Manage

Are long ladders a sign of a successful corporate reorganization? At United Airlines they are. Long ladders symbolize the company's new approach to management—an approach that often depends on teamwork to solve problems. A case in point: a team made up of pilots, ramp workers, and managers sat down together—for the first time—to figure out how to power planes idling at the gate with electricity instead of jet fuel. Electricity would save money, but because their short working ladders prevented ramp workers from plugging electrical cables into the aircraft, using electricity was literally out of reach.

Not surprisingly, the solution—longer ladders—was a no-brainer for team members, and not simply because several of them actually knew the situation first hand. What *is* surprising, perhaps, was the failure of traditional managers to see that when the problem is short ladders, the solution is probably longer ladders. At United, it seems, managers far removed from the loading gates had no way of assessing even the simplest problem. Worse yet, a stringent top-down management style prevented them from consulting with the right people—in this case, ramp workers at loading gates. According to Robert M. Sturtz, United's top fuel administrator, the company was able to identify the real problem only when management resorted to teamwork. In this instance, the result has been an annual savings of $20 million in fuel costs.

In 1994, United's 80 000 employees bought the carrier, creating one of the country's largest *employee stock ownership plans (ESOP)*. Since then, United has been transformed from a top-driven hierarchical organization into one that values teamwork, initiative, and creativity. Chairman and CEO Gerald Greenwald has also reduced the number of management layers and removed many functional divisions in favour of a horizontal integration of resources that focuses on markets. "We are," he proclaims, "no longer a company that operates by command and control."

The key markets that now correspond to United's internal divisions are North America, international, cargo, shuttles, and new business development. Each division is headed by a senior vice-president who reports directly to President and Chief Operating Officer John A. Edwardson.

•••

United Airlines Gives Managers the Power to Manage

(continued)

In addition, all operational groups, including on-board services and flight operations, report to the president. In short, authority has been decentralized, and divisional managers have the power to run their businesses.

Reorganization has also increased the authority of divisional and mid-level managers. Previously, such functional operations as airport services and reservations were worlds unto themselves, with their own organizational structures and chains of command. Because members of different areas rarely communicated, airline operations often suffered. According to James E. Goodwin, Senior Vice-President for North America, United's Honolulu station nicely illustrated the poor coordination of the old system. "The sales organization," explains Goodwin, "reported to someone in Los Angeles, who then reported to someone in Chicago. The reservations function reported directly to Chicago. The airport manager reported to someone in San Francisco. In many cases, the people never even knew each other."

This arrangement led to open conflicts among departments. "The sales organization," recalls Goodwin, "would go out and make commitments to the customer that they couldn't deliver at the airport. All they could do is say, 'I only sell it. I don't make it.'" Worse yet, customer service problems had to be transferred to headquarters for resolution. When the new management discarded this function-based organizational structure, managers received both greater power and the resources needed to use it. To further speed decision making, unnecessary managerial levels were eliminated, thus creating a "flatter" organizational structure (the old one resembled a pyramid). Before that, recalls Edwards, "it wasn't uncommon to get a request for capital on my desk that had 13 to 14 signatures on it before it got to me."

What effect have these changes had on United's performance? Thanks in large part to improved productivity, United is taking market share away from rivals American and Delta and has solidified its position as America's number one air carrier. In addition, operating margins are fatter,

the stock price has climbed, and knowledgeable outsiders have formed a favourable view of United's improved performance. Reports one industry analyst at Merrill Lynch, "United has hard statistics that show the company is working differently than in the past."

One of the most obvious signs of organizational change at United Airlines is the increased authority of mid-level managers to spend money. Before decentralization, vice-presidents needed the president's approval for purchases over $4999—a situation that undermined their autonomy and their ability to make decisions.

John A. Edwardson learned of the spending limit about a week after he took over as United's President and Chief Operating Officer: He received a purchase request from a vice-president for $5000 worth of typing paper. Edwardson relates what happened next. "I walked over to his office and said, 'Is this a joke, or are you testing me?' And he said, 'I never test presidents, and I don't know you well enough to joke with you.'"

With the removal of United's rigid top-down organization, vice-presidents can now spend up to $25 000 without seeking approval and have authority over about 95 percent of their budgets.

Case Questions

1. How have organizational changes at United affected the company's decision-making hierarchy?

2. Why did United's function-based organization fail?

3. How did reorganization affect managers' accountability and span of control?

4. Was increasing the spending authority of vice-presidents a symbolic move, or did it have real organizational importance?

5. Why did a decentralized organizational structure work better at United than a top-down hierarchical structure?

◆

Corporate Structure at Bata Ltd.

Bata Ltd. has its headquarters in Toronto. It has 66 000 employees, 6300 shoe stores, and operates in 68 countries. Bata sells more than 1 million pairs of shoes each day. In an industry that must quickly sense and act upon footwear trends, Bata's enormous size means that it must work hard to be responsive to changes demanded by the market.

The company is departmentalized by territory, with divisions operating in Europe, Africa, the Far East, and South America. Each region is headed by a regional executive. In spite of its international operations, Bata has not been considered a global corporation in the usual sense of the term. It is not a vertically integrated production and marketing company. In fact, the company's products vary from region to region in accordance with the local population's wants and needs. The result is that the company is a "multidomestic" operation, with each subsidiary operating more or less autonomously.

The economics of the footwear industry have changed in recent years, and Bata has been running to keep up with companies such as Reebok International Ltd. and Nike. Reebok and Nike manufacture shoes in low cost areas like Korea, Taiwan, and China and then use a central office to market and distribute them. Bata, by contrast, operates factories around the world, gearing its production to the local population. This arrangement has led to poor integration of its operations.

Recognizing the need to change, the company has embarked on a major streamlining. Even though Bata has been highly decentralized, it still had excess layers of management at head office. The first step in revamping the operation was to flatten the organizational pyramid so that changes in the market could be responded to more quickly. The restructuring has meant great improvements, according to Tom Bata, Jr. He noted that having a series of executives in Toronto resulted in duplication and power struggles. The restructuring means that there is now just one layer of managers between top management and the managers in the various countries where Bata operates.

The shift has meant an increase in power and responsibility for the managers remaining in the hierarchy, and a decrease in the amount of time key figures spend politicking and selling their ideas to the entrenched hierarchy. Now, the four managers who make up the international head office are out of the country 60 to 70 percent of the time.

The company has evolved into a "horizontal corporation," a term used by Harvard Business School professor Michael Porter to describe corporations that must resolve both global and local interests. The horizontal corporation is based on the premise that the old-style multinational company is too rigid, too hierarchical, and too attuned to the interests of the "home country." Horizontal corporations stress lateral decision making and a common set of shared ideas, not the vertical chain of command.

Case Questions

1. On what basis is Bata departmentalized? What are the advantages and disadvantages of this type of departmentalization?

2. Contrast Bata's structure with its competitors' (Nike and Reebok). Why was Bata's structure disadvantageous for it?

3. Speculate on how the "horizontal corporation" idea might work in practice at Bata.

◆

8

*Understanding Entrepreneurship and Small Business**

Zepf Technologies Inc.

Zepf Technologies Inc. (ZTI) of Waterloo, Ontario, is a good example of a small family business that has grown and plans to continue growing. Lawrence Zepf started the business in 1972 as a machine shop making automated packaging equipment for high-speed production lines. It was truly a family business as all seven of Zepf's sons and three of his five daughters were involved in the business. Since machinists were critical in the early years, Zepf made sure that his sons obtained their machinist's papers in the local three-year community college program.

Eventually, the family business grew and transformed. Innovative software, calculated risks, and personal commitment changed the business from a machine shop to a competitor in the international packaging industry. According to Zepf, the company's development and use of innovative technology was the driving force behind its success. In 1986, working with control specialists from West Germany, ZTI developed a unique, multi-axis bi-directional cutting lathe, affectionately named RAMBO. It was the only one of its kind in the world.

ZTI also developed the software Feedscrew Design System (FDS), which enabled it to design feedscrews that were extremely sophisticated and durable, resulting in the superior packaging and faster output of products. The company's success in new products was attributable to its contributing 10 to 12 percent of annual sales to R&D, and to substantial expenditures on employee training. The Zepfs believed that good management skills are a factor in growth, and that training is the key to adapting to growth.

Rewarding employees is crucial, and in 1989 a profit sharing plan was introduced.

Recognizing the limited market in Canada, ZTI turned to European markets through a joint venture with a German firm to manufacture complete cams and specialty machinery. ZTI secured a contract in excess of $1 million with Jumex of Mexico to introduce the technology to that country. In 1989, the company won the Canada Awards for Business Excellence.

By 1992, the company had grown slowly to about $4 million in sales and 40 employees. It was a reasonable size, but Larry Zepf, Lawrence's son and now president and chief executive of ZTI (pictured), was considering whether the company should remain with the status quo or attempt to grow. He wondered what the implications of growth would be for his family business.

Larry Zepf decided to grow, but he faced several challenges. First, growth requires capital, and his bank was unwilling to extend more financing. Zepf went searching for a more understanding account manager and found one. He felt that the Bank of Montreal had trained their managers to understand export-oriented manufacturing, which needs financing during a period of rapid growth.

ZTI's commitment to R&D during the 1980s provided a good basis for growth in the 1990s. As a result, ZTI was able to stay ahead of its competitors in packaging technology, enabling them to enter export markets before their competitors. ZTI has grown internationally through exports sales, licensing agreements, and joint ventures in Scotland and the United States.

*Major sections of this chapter were written by Robert W. Sexty.

(continued)

The type of employees ZTI needs has also changed. In the beginning, machinists were crucial to success, whereas now technologists are needed who can operate CAD/CAM design equipment. In the 1980s, there were three employees on the factory floor to one designer. Now the ratio is two designers per production employee. ZTI has difficulty finding highly skilled technologists and finds it expensive to do the training itself.

As the business grew, so did the approach to management. In the past, family members were relied upon, but now professional managers from outside are being hired. The chief financial officer is not a family member, and others are likely to be hired to complement family talent. Even though financing was found through a bank, Zepf is now thinking about taking the company public, that is, selling shares to investors outside the family.

By 1995, ZTI had tripled sales to $11 million and employment had climbed to over 100. During this period, it experienced many challenges typical of growth in small businesses: family succession, the need for debt and equity financing, the change in type of employees, and the hiring of nonfamily managers.

◆

E very year, thousands of people like Lawrence Zepf launch new business ventures. These individuals, called entrepreneurs, are essential to the growth and vitality of the Canadian economic system. Entrepreneurs develop or recognize new products or business opportunities, secure the necessary capital, and organize and operate businesses.

In this chapter we first define the term "small business," describe the role of the entrepreneur, and note the advantages and disadvantages of owning a small business. Alternative approaches to becoming a small business owner (including franchising) are noted, as are the challenges facing entrepreneurs. The chapter concludes with a description of the various sources of assistance that are available to small business owners.

If you are aware of the challenges you will encounter as an entrepreneur, you are more likely to avoid the classic problems small business owners face. It is easy to start a business, but to operate one at a profit over a period of years requires the knowledge and application of the fundamentals of management. This chapter is designed to give you realistic expectations about small business management.

When you have completed this chapter, you should be able to:

LEARNING OBJECTIVES

1. Define *small business* and explain its importance to the Canadian economy.

2. Explain which types of enterprise best lend themselves to small business success.

3. Describe the start-up decisions made by small businesses.

4. Identify the advantages and disadvantages of *franchising*.

5. Identify the key reasons for the success and failure of small businesses.

6. Describe the sources of financial and management advice that are available to small businesses.

Small Business in Canada

The Canadian media pay considerable attention to the activities of large business enterprises but often neglect the fact that small businesses are thriving and are making a significant contribution to the economic well-being of Canadians. A small business may be a corporation, sole proprietorship, or a partnership. Small businesses include those operated by professionals, such as doctors, lawyers, and accountants, and self-employed owners, such as mechanics, television technicians, and restaurateurs. They are found in virtually every industry and are particularly prominent in the retail trade. In numbers, small business is the dominant type of business in Canada. According to Statistics Canada, small business enterprises account for about 98 percent of the 900 000 enterprises in Canada and for about 19 percent of total business revenue.

History has shown that major innovations are as likely to come from small businesses or individuals as from big businesses. Small firms and individuals invented the personal computer, the stainless-steel razor blade, the transistor radio, the photocopying machine, the jet engine, and the self-developing photograph. They also gave us the helicopter, power steering, automatic transmissions, air conditioning, cellophane, and the 19-cent ballpoint pen.

The degree of small business varies across different industries. As shown in Figure 8.1, small business firms are dominant in the construction and retailing industries, but not so dominant in manufacturing. About 6 out of every 10 Canadians employed in the private sector work in a firm with less than 500 employees.

During the past few years, small businesses have been net creators of jobs, while large firms have been net job destroyers. The value of small business to Canada's economy has been recognized by the federal and provincial governments with the establishment of small business departments and lending institutions catering to these enterprises. Government agencies sponsor awards to recognize entrepreneurs or enterprises that have performed in an outstanding manner. An example of one such award is the Canada Awards for Business Excellence. Begun in 1984 by the federal government, these awards were created to acknowledge exceptional business achievements, ones that contribute to Canada's competitiveness in national and international business. The awards are given each year to honour extraordinary performance in various categories of business activity including entrepreneurship and small business.

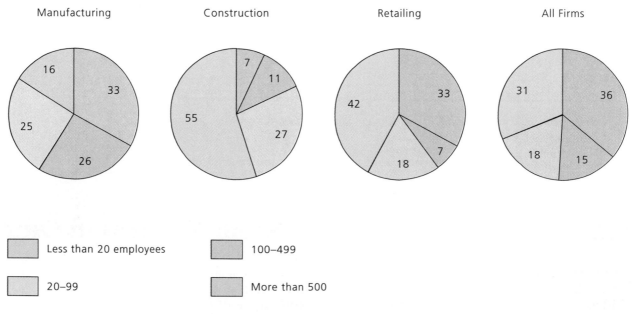

Figure 8.1
Employment distribution by enterprise size.

The Increase in Small Business Activity

The reasons for the increase in small business activity are as follows:

1. Big businesses offer less job security since layoffs are more likely. Growing numbers of employees are also dissatisfied with working for large organizations that are impersonal and where efforts of employees often go unrecognized.
2. Many large companies and government departments are being reduced in size, creating opportunities for subcontracting work and consulting services. Former employees often leave their employment and start businesses to provide these services.
3. For most of the past 15 years, it has been easier to start a small business than previously. The economy has grown, especially the service industries that require less investment to enter.
4. Persons who are self-employed earn almost 50 percent more on average than persons who are employees. Small business is financially attractive.[1]

Small Business Defined

There are almost as many definitions of small business as there are books on the topic. Two approaches will be used here to define a small business: one based on characteristics and the other based on size. A **small business** is one that is independently owned and operated and is not dominant in its field of operations. It possesses most of the following characteristics:

small business

An independently owned and operated business not dominant in its field of operations.

- Management of the firm is independent. Usually the managers are also the owners.

- An individual or a small group supplies the capital and holds the ownership.

- The area of operations is usually local, and the workers and owners live in the same community. However, the markets are not always local.

- The enterprise is smaller than others in the industry. This measure can be in terms of sales volume, number of employees, or other criteria. It is free of legal or financial ties to large business enterprises.

A common type of small business in Canada is the convenience store. It attracts customers from its immediate area with its long hours of operation and the product lines it carries.

■ The enterprise qualifies for the small business income tax rate under the Canada *Income Tax Act*.

The size of a small business and how the size should be measured are matters of debate. Two common measures are sales revenues and the number of employees. The Canadian government's Small Business Office in conjunction with Statistics Canada defines a small business as having less than $2 million in annual sales. Various government agencies also use numbers of employees to define small business. However, this number differs widely among government agencies: the federal Ministry of State for Small Business stipulates 50 or fewer, the Federal Business Development Bank says 75 or fewer, and Statistics Canada uses numbers ranging from 100 to 1500 for manufacturing industries, and 50 for service industries.

For our purposes, a small business is one that is independent and smaller than the main enterprises in an industry, generally employing 1 to 1500 people.

Entrepreneurship

Although the concepts of *entrepreneurship* and *small business* are closely related, there are some important, though often subtle, differences between them.

The Distinction Between Entrepreneurship and Small Business

entrepreneur

Businessperson who accepts both the risks and the opportunities involved in creating and operating a new business venture.

Many small businesspersons like to think of themselves as **entrepreneurs**—individuals who assume the risk of business ownership with the primary goal of growth and expansion. In reality, however, a person may be a small businessperson only, an entrepreneur only, or both. Consider an individual who starts a small pizza parlour with no plans other than to earn enough money from the restaurant to lead a comfortable lifestyle. That individual is clearly a small businessperson. With no plans to grow and expand, however, the person is not really an entrepreneur. In contrast, an entrepreneur may start with one pizza parlour and turn it into a national chain. Although this individual may have started with a small business, the growth of the firm resulted from entrepreneurial vision and activity.

Describing the Entrepreneur

Women Business Owners of Manitoba

http://www.wbom.mb.ca

The typical entrepreneur is about 42 years old, as compared with the typical employee, who is about 34 years old. An increasing number of women are becoming entrepreneurs. A Royal Bank of Canada study estimates that one quarter to one third of all businesses worldwide are owned by women, and women now account for half the increase in new businesses each year. Between 1991 and 1994, firms led by women created jobs four times faster than the average of all Canadian companies. Women are more conservative than men in running a small business, and their failure rate is lower than for men.[2]

Dozens of studies have identified common traits among entrepreneurs. A researcher at the University of Western Ontario compiled a list of many of the characteristics identified by these studies, including assertiveness, challenge seeking, charismatic, coping, creative, improvising, opportunistic, preserving, risk taking, self-confident, tenacious, venturesome, and oriented towards achievement and action.[3]

More and more women are starting and successfully operating their own small businesses; they now account for half all new businesses that are formed.

An Ontario government report, *The State of Small Business*, found that the main reasons entrepreneurs started businesses were:

■ The need to achieve or the sense of accomplishment. Entrepreneurs believe that they can make a direct contribution to the success of the enterprise.

■ The need to be their own boss and to control their time.

■ The perceived opportunity in the marketplace to provide a product or service.

■ The wish to act in their own way or have the freedom to adapt their own approach to work.

■ The desire to experience the adventure of independence and a variety of challenges.

■ The desire to make money.

■ The need to make a living.[4]

The motivations of successful entrepreneurs include having fun, building an organization, making money, winning in business, earning recognition, and realizing a sense of accomplishment.[5] The box "Jimmy Pattison—Canadian Entrepreneur Extraordinaire" describes the career of one of Canada's best-known entrepreneurs.

Costs and Benefits of Entrepreneurship

Entrepreneurship has both benefits and costs. On the positive side, entrepreneurs get a tremendous sense of satisfaction from being their own boss. They also enjoy successfully bringing together the factors of production (land, labour, and capital) to make a profit. Perhaps the greatest benefit, however, is that entrepreneurs can make a fortune if they have carefully planned what the business will do and how it will operate.

On the negative side, entrepreneurs can go bankrupt if their business fails. Customers can demand all sorts of services or inventory that small businesses cannot profitably supply. Entrepreneurs must work long hours and often get little in return in the first few years of operation. An entrepreneur

The Canadian Business Scene

Jimmy Pattison—Canadian Entrepreneur Extraordinaire

Most 65-year-old Vancouverites like to have a relaxed breakfast and read the newspaper. Not Jimmy Pattison, one of Canada's most famous entrepreneurs. It's 9 a.m., and he has been in his office since 6 a.m. He has already gone through his mail and phone messages, solved a potential crisis, and talked to a businessman from Thailand who wants to do a deal. In spite of his great wealth, Pattison has no intention of slowing down.

The Jim Pattison Group, one of Canada's largest sole proprietorships, employs 15 000 people and has sales in excess of $3 billion. Jimmy Pattison started out in the 1950s selling pots and pans door to door. He knew he could make enough money to live on if he sold just one set of pots and pans each day. He also learned that he could sell one set if he could just get three evening appointments to make his sales pitch. To get those three evening appointments, he had to knock on about 30 doors. Then he discovered that if he whistled while going door to door, he only had to make 22 house calls to get three appointments. So that's what he did.

In 1961, he began selling cars. Over the years he became involved in numerous other ventures. Now his one-man conglomerate owns 12 car franchises, a Caribbean bank, Ripley's Believe-It-Or-Not, Overwaitea food stores,

outdoor signs, Gold Seal fishery products, and Westar Group Ltd., to name just a few. The company's biggest investments in the next few years will be in B.C. and Alberta. Expansion into the U.S. is also planned. In the 1980s, the company did no business in the U.S., but now the U.S. accounts for 20 percent of company sales. He is also thinking of expanding into Mexico.

Pattison is obviously in charge of the company. His inner circle includes six executives specializing in law, tax, accounting, insurance/administration, cash management, and deal-making. He says being a private company allows him to take a long-run perspective. He says that as long as he keeps his banker happy, things run smoothly. One of Pattison's biggest recent challenges has been to "renew" the company by recruiting a younger generation to replace his colleagues. Most of the new top executives come from the operating divisions. One is only 29 years old.

Pattison says he has only sales skills, but those have served him well throughout his career. He notes that sales requires hard work, and it forces you to relate to people. Those two elements are crucial for success. He also learned in selling that having the door slammed in your face teaches you to handle setbacks and disappointments. He learned not to take no for an answer.

---

may find that he or she is very good at one particular aspect of the business—for example, marketing—but knows little about managing the overall business. This imbalance can cause serious problems. In fact, poor management is the main reason businesses fail.

Finding Information on Small Business

Many sources of information on small business are available. The following represent the main resources.

Small Business Textbooks

There are several Canadian textbooks on small business and entrepreneurship.[6] And of course, many others are written in other countries, especially the United States.

Books Profiling Canadian Entrepreneurs

Many books have been published on successful (and some unsuccessful) Canadian entrepreneurs. Examples include Gould's *The New Entrepreneurs:*

80 Canadian Success Stories, Barnes and Banning's *Money Makers: The Secrets of Canada's Most Successful Entrepreneurs*, and Fraser's *Quebec Inc.: French Canadian Entrepreneurs and the New Business Elite*.[7]

Magazines

Two Canadian publications are devoted to small business and entrepreneurship. *Profit: The Magazine for Canadian Entrepreneurs*, published nine times a year by CB Media Ltd., is a practical magazine oriented towards businesspeople. A more academic publication is the *Journal of Small Business and Entrepreneurship*, published quarterly by the Centre for Entrepreneurship, Faculty of Management, University of Toronto, for the International Council for Small Business Canada. In addition, there are many magazines and journals published in the United States.

Profit
http://www.profit100.com/1997/cover.html

Small Business Centres or Institutes

Dozens of centres and institutes, usually located at colleges or universities, provide assistance to small businesses. Examples are the P.J. Gardiner Small Business Institute at Memorial University of Newfoundland, the Centre for Entrepreneurship at the University of Toronto, and Business Consulting Services at the University of Saskatchewan.

Small Business Organizations

Several organizations have been formed to represent the interests of small business. The largest is the **Canadian Federation of Independent Business (CFIB)**, a non-profit, nonpartisan political action group, or lobby, representing the interests of small and medium-sized business to governments. The CFIB has about 75 000 members. Its stated objectives are to promote and protect a system of free competitive enterprise in Canada and to give the independent entrepreneur a voice in laws governing business and the nation. A similar organization is the Canadian Organization for Small Business, operating in western Canada. Numerous provincial groups also exist.

Canadian Federation of Independent Business (CFIB)
A non-profit, nonpartisan lobby group representing small and medium-sized businesses.

Government and Private Agencies

Information is also available from government and private bodies including small business departments in provincial governments, the "Small Business Network" in Willowdale, Ontario, and the Business Information Centre of the Federal Business Development Bank. The Canadian Youth Business Foundation (CYBF) is a non-profit, private-sector initiative to provide mentoring, business support, and loans to young entrepreneurs age 18 to 29 who are interested in starting a business. Many chartered banks have booklets and brochures on various topics related to small business.

Becoming a Small Business Owner

Most people become involved in a small business in one of four ways: they take over a family business, they buy out an existing firm, they start their own firm, or they buy a franchise. There are pros and cons to each approach.

Taking Over a Family Business

Taking over and operating one's own family business poses many challenges. There may be disagreement over which family member assumes control. If the parent sells his or her interest in the business, the price paid may be an

Martha Billes, the President of Canadian Tire. Ms. Billes' father and uncle co-founded Canadian Tire in 1927.

Canadian Tire
http://www.canadiantire.ca

issue. The expectations of other family members is typical of how managing such an organization can be difficult. Some may consider a job, promotion, and impressive title their birthright, regardless of their talent or training. Choosing an appropriate successor and ensuring that he or she receives adequate training, and disagreements among family members about the future of the business are two problem areas. Sometimes the interests of the family and those of the enterprise conflict. As a result, family enterprises often fail to respond to changing market conditions. The challenges faced in running such an organization are summarized in Figure 8.2.

A family business also has some strengths. It can provide otherwise unobtainable financial and management resources because of the personal sacrifices of family members; family businesses often have a valuable reputation or goodwill that can result in important community and business relationships; employee loyalty is often high; and an interested, unified family management and shareholders group may emerge.

Buying an Existing Enterprise

Because a family-run business and other established firms are already operating, they have certain advantages for the purchaser: the clientele is established, financing might be easier because past performance and existing assets can be evaluated, experienced employees may already be in place, and lines of credit and supply have been established. An entrepreneur who buys someone else's business, however, faces more uncertainty about the exact conditions of the organization than a person who takes over his or her family's operation.

The acquisition of an existing enterprise may have other drawbacks: the business may have a poor reputation, the location may be poor, and an appropriate price may be difficult to ascertain.

Starting a Business

This approach is likely the most challenging to becoming a small business owner, for there is no existing operation, no established customers, and no history in the form of financial or marketing records upon which to base

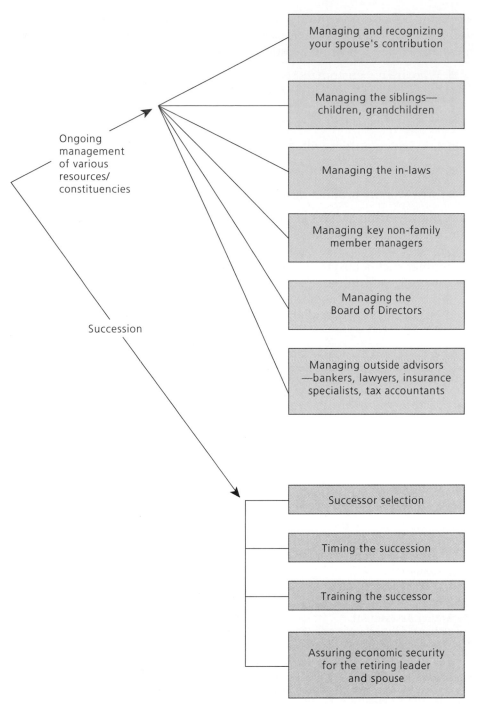

Figure 8.2
Family-owned business leader's key challenges.

decisions. Consequently, acquiring financing can be difficult; investors, either lenders or shareholders, have to be convinced of the enterprise's viability. Beginning a new enterprise usually means spending large amounts of money before sales or revenues materialize. Overall, new businesses pose a higher risk and greater uncertainty than established organizations since the business venture is unproven and the competence of the entrepreneur is most likely unknown. A business plan is essential for those individuals who wish to start a small business. The contents of a business plan are described in Table 8.1.

The risks of starting a business from scratch are, not surprisingly, greater than those of buying an existing firm. Success or failure depends on identifying a genuine business opportunity—a product for which many customers will pay well but which is currently unavailable to them. To find openings, entrepreneurs must answer the following questions:

- Who are my customers?
- Where are they?
- At which price will they buy my product?
- In what quantities will they buy?
- Who are my competitors?
- How will my product differ from that of my competitors?

microenterprise

An enterprise that the owner operates part-time from the home while continuing regular employment elsewhere.

Many new businesses start as **microenterprises**—enterprises operated from the home part-time while the entrepreneur continues to work as a regular employee of another organization (see the box "Starting as a Microenterprise). Sometimes such a business is operated in partnership with others. The obvious advantage of beginning as a microenterprise is that the entrepreneur can test his or her idea before quitting regular employment. This approach is being used increasingly by Canadians.

Table 8.1   A Business Plan

The contents of a business plan vary depending upon the information required by the financial institutions or government agencies. Some entrepreneurs develop plans as a personal guide to check on where they are or want to be. The following are the components that might be included in such a plan:

Cover Page
Contains the enterprise's name, address, telephone numbers, and key contacts.

Table of Contents

Executive Summary
A brief statement, usually about one page long, summarizing the plan's contents.

Background/History of the Enterprise
A concise outline of when and how the enterprise got started, the goods or services it sells, and its major suppliers and customers.

Management
Background information on the entrepreneur and other employees, especially other managers (if there are any).

Marketing Assessment
Descriptions of the products or a service profile, the results of any market research, a market description and analysis, an identification of competition, and an account of the marketing strategy.

Production Assessment
A brief description of the production process, the technological process employed, quality requirements, location and physical plant, and details of machinery and equipment.

Financial Assessment
A review of the capital structure and the money needed to finance the business. Usually includes a projected balance sheet, profit and loss statement, and a cash flow forecast. Lenders may also require details of loan collateral and a repayment proposal.

Research and Development (R&D)
For many enterprises, R&D is important and a statement of what is planned would be included. There may also be an assessment of the risks anticipated with any new products or ventures.

Basic Data
Data on the enterprise's bankers, accountants, lawyers, shareholders (if any), and details of incorporation (if applicable).

Appendices
The following might be attached to a plan: detailed management biographies, product literature, evaluation of assets, detailed financial statements and cash flow forecast, and a list of major contracts.

The Canadian Business Scene

Starting as a Microenterprise

Studies of entrepreneurship estimate that up to 50 percent of small businesses begin as "microenterprises." Two types of people start businesses with this approach: those with full-time employment outside the home who operate the business in off-hours and homemakers starting on a small scale to supplement a spouse's or partner's income. By the year 2000, it is estimated that 40 percent of the workforce will operate full-time from their homes, either by operating microenterprises or by telecommuting.

An example of a micro or home office business is Lori M Consulting in Toronto. It was formed by Lori Molmar, an executive with the Federation of Women Teachers' Association of Ontario. She left that job to set up a business in her home as an interior designer and environmental gerontologist. The cost of operating from her home was lower and she even built an addition to accommodate the business.

A key source of microbusiness opportunities is the increased use of outside services by business and government. Even small and medium-sized businesses are hiring consultants to provide some services, thus avoiding the obligations of hiring full-time employees. Microenterprises have also grown because of the overall growth in the service industry and the computerization and increased affordability of office equipment.

The principal benefits of microenterprises are the following: their start-up and operating costs are low; little financial risk is encountered if the business fails; the work environment is casual; family responsibilities can be accommodated; and the hours of operation can be tailored to an individual's schedule. But such businesses also have disadvantages: the owners may feel isolated, having little, if any, social interaction with others; family and friends may cause distractions and disruptions; a productive working environment may not be available; and self-discipline is required to keep working and not be distracted.

Home Inc.: The Canadian Home-Based Business Guide is a guide to microenterprises; the Canadian Federation of Independent Business has also studied the trend because it encourages entrepreneurship. The National Home Business Association has a database of over 10 000 home-based entrepreneurs from all over Canada. This association provides a package of services to members that includes group rates on health insurance, educational seminars, a referral service to promote members' services, and discounts from stationery and equipment suppliers.

Buying a Franchise

Contrary to popular belief, franchising did not begin with the 1950s boom in fast-food franchises like McDonald's. Rather, its beginnings date back to the early 1800s. Not until 1898, however, when General Motors began franchising retail dealerships, did modern franchising begin in earnest. Similar systems were created by Rexall (pharmacies) in 1902, Howard Johnson (restaurants and, later, motels) in 1926, and many oil, grocery, motel, and fast-food franchisers in the early 20th century.

One of the fastest ways to establish a business is to buy a franchise. Franchising has continued to increase in economic importance (see the box "Just Like Home"). **Franchising** involves drafting a contract between a manufacturer and a dealer that stipulates how the manufacturer's or supplier's product or service will be sold. The dealer, called a **franchisee**, agrees to sell the product or service of the manufacturer, called the **franchisor**, in return for royalties. Franchising organizations well-known in Canada include Holiday Inn, McDonald's, College Pro Painters, Weight Watchers, Kentucky Fried Chicken, Midas Muffler, and Canadian Tire.

franchising
A contract between a manufacturer and a dealer that stipulates how a product or service will be sold.

franchisee
The dealer who agrees to sell the product or service.

franchisor
The manufacturer of the product or service.

Advantages and Disadvantages of Franchising

Franchises offer many advantages to both sellers and buyers. Franchisors, for example, benefit from the ability to grow rapidly by using the investment money provided by franchisees. This strategy has enabled giant franchisors like McDonald's to mushroom into billion-dollar concerns in a relatively brief time.

International Report

Just Like Home

It could be any Canadian city. On one corner sits a McDonald's restaurant. On another is a Kentucky Fried Chicken shop. Down the street is a 7-Eleven convenience store. A Budget Rent-A-Car outlet sits next to a Holiday Inn. Yes, it could be anywhere in Canada. But it's not. It's Tokyo, Japan.

Despite its reputation as an insular culture, Japan has embraced a number of franchising overtures. Probably the most successful chain to franchise in Japan is 7-Eleven stores, thanks largely to its major Japanese franchisee, Ito Masatoshi. He now operates 3800 7-Eleven stores. A savvy marketer, Masatoshi appealed to single urban residents stranded by the early closing hours of traditional Japanese grocery stores.

Japan is just one of many nations providing new markets for the franchise concept. Today, more and more franchisors are selling or opening operations from Fiji to France, from Moscow to Malaysia. Canada has more franchises than any nation outside the United States and most of these franchises are with U.S. firms.

U.S. franchisors like Kentucky Fried Chicken and McDonald's have dominated international markets for years. But NAFTA has created opportunities for Canadian franchisors to move into Latin America. Yogenfruz (frozen yogurt), Ceiling Doctor (home repairs), Pizza Pizza Ltd., and Cara Operations Ltd. have already gained some success in Mexico.

A common language is not enough to ensure success for franchises. Cultural differences have kept sales in the United Kingdom low. For example, ComputerLand has sold only 20 of 60 planned franchises in the U.K. British residents simply do not impulsively buy computers they see in store windows as their North American cousins do. Fast-food franchises have fared especially badly because most Britons prefer not to spend their spare cash eating out in such places.

Undeterred, many firms are looking closely at continental Europe for franchising opportunities. The new European Community's rules will make it much easier for foreign firms to franchise their operations while still maintaining reasonable control over product offerings. The demise of communism in Eastern Europe and the dissolution of the Soviet Union also provide new areas for franchising. Formerly only joint ventures with the national governments were possible. Certainly franchising provides an excellent opportunity for citizens in these nations to gain expertise in marketing and other capitalist necessities. However, as some observers have noted, only the largest franchisors—those who can afford to accept a small initial fee and wait for the profits to come in—will be able to take advantage of this new franchising potential. Smaller franchisors will have to wait until the Eastern European countries develop stable economies, currencies, and individual entrepreneurs who have substantial cash to invest.

Those who have succeeded in international franchising offer a few basic rules. First, do your market research and make sure your product or service will fit into the culture. Gymboree, which franchises developmental play programs for preschoolers and their parents, has turned down Japanese investors because its centres require a great deal of space—something in short supply in Japan. Second, be patient. It may take 10 years for foreign stores to start showing a profit. Third, find a reliable partner. Toys 'R' Us entered into a joint venture with McDonald's to use the latter's expertise to open new toy stores in Japan. Finally, be prepared to be flexible. One frozen yoghurt maker found interest—and sales—picking up when it offered a green-tea flavour in Japan.

For the franchisee, the arrangement combines the incentive of owning a business with the advantage of access to big business management skills. Unlike the person who starts from scratch, the franchisee does not have to build a business step by step. Instead, the business is established virtually overnight. Moreover, because each franchise outlet is probably a carbon copy of every other link in the chain, the chances of failure are reduced.

There are, of course, disadvantages as well. Perhaps the most significant is the start-up cost. Franchise prices vary widely. While Fantastic Sam's hair salon franchise fees are only $20 000, a Gingiss Formalwear franchise can run as high as $100 000. Extremely profitable or hard-to-get franchises are even more expensive. A McDonald's franchise costs $610 000 to $700 000, and a professional sports team such as the Toronto Blue Jays can cost many millions of dollars. Franchisees may also have continued obligations to contribute percentages of sales to parent corporations.

Toronto Blue Jays
http://www.bluejays.ca

Franchising is very popular in Canada. It offers individuals who want to run their own business an opportunity to establish themselves quickly in a local market.

Buying a franchise also involves some intangible costs. For one thing, the small businessperson sacrifices some independence. A McDonald's franchisee, for example, cannot change the way hamburgers or milkshakes are made. Nor can franchisees create individual identities in their communities; for all practical purposes, the McDonald's owner is anonymous. In addition, many franchise agreements are difficult to terminate.

Finally, while franchises minimize risks, they do not guarantee success. Many franchisees have seen their investments—and their dreams—disappear because of poor locations, rising costs, or lack of continued franchisor commitment. Moreover, figures on failure rates are artificially low because they do not include failing franchisees bought out by their franchising parent companies. An additional risk is that the chain itself could collapse. In any given year, dozens—sometimes hundreds—of franchisors close shop or stop selling franchises. Concluding Case 8-1 describes some of these problems.

Challenges for the Entrepreneur

Starting and operating a business enterprise is challenging: financing must be obtained, the enterprise must be carefully managed, and assistance must often be found. The box "Entrepreneurship in the Former Soviet Union" describes some of the problems faced by entrepreneurs in formerly communist countries.

Financing the Small Enterprise

The amount of capital needed to start a small business prevents some people from becoming entrepreneurs. However, sources of funding are available, and a list is given in Table 8.2. It should be noted that some sources are more likely than others to provide money. Lenders may or may not lend money to entrepreneurs, depending upon whether the enterprise is just beginning or is ongoing.

Funds for Starting a Business

The most likely sources of financing are the personal funds of individuals, in particular, the entrepreneurs themselves. Some government agencies may provide assistance funds for startup and so may chartered banks if they think that the proposed business has promise.

International Report

Entrepreneurship in the Former Soviet Union

Malgorzata Daniszewska was an insider in communist Poland. Her husband was a government minister—the chief spokesman for the government of General Wojciech Jaruzelski. Although everyone expected her to espouse the party line, she never fully embraced the economic principles of communism. Therefore, it was not surprising that when the old regime crumbled, Daniszewska was ready to take on the risks and seek the rewards of capitalism. She was also in a position to spread the word to other would-be entrepreneurs in Poland. After buying *Firma*, a government-owned monthly business magazine, Daniszewska decided to deliver a strong pro-business message to the Polish populace. She chose to deliver her message symbolically: She set up a shoeshine stand—a symbol disdained by the communists as one of the worst forms of capitalist exploitation—on a Warsaw street. The public relations ploy—which made Daniszewska the first person to shine shoes in Warsaw since World War II—called attention to her serious capitalist theme: Private business is the future for Poland, and if it is good enough for an ex-bureaucrat's wife, it is good enough for other Poles who want to better their lives.

Daniszewska is one of the thousands of Polish entrepreneurs who are helping to transform their country's economy. Their efforts to establish a new private-enterprise system are moving in the right direction and, in the process, encouraging economic growth. While some other East European economies are actually shrinking, Poland's gross domestic product is modestly increasing, partly because of help from Western investment. Although this growth has been aided somewhat by Western investment, its backbone consists of small and medium-sized Polish businesses.

Poland's new generation of entrepreneurs has had to struggle to learn the basics of capitalism. Many who took off in the pursuit of profits before they understood the responsibilities of running businesses are already bankrupt. Admittedly, many failures were due not simply to lack of knowledge, but to a shortage of capital that has sent interest rates sky high.

Entrepreneurs are also active in other countries that used to be run by communists:

- In newly unified Germany, while a million East Germans have flooded into the wealthier, happier West, some 250 000 West Germans have headed to the "Wild East" for business opportunity. With backing from an investor-partner, for example, Albrecht Wendt leased 800 hectares of prime farmland from an elderly farmer who did not want to sign yet one more extension of a cooperative agreement left over from the communist era. Wendt has the land for 18 years, and his interest payments are subsidized by the government.

- In the city of Skoda in the Czech Republic, the most admired entrepreneur in town is Multi Dekor, who does a handsome business providing furnishings for the new shops of fellow entrepreneurs.

- In Saratov, Russia, where he has built a successful trucking business, rampant crime and police corruption require Vladimir Tyrin to employ 70 armed security guards among his 183 employees. In fact, Tyrin has now diversified: He hires out his private security force to other fledgling firms that cannot otherwise protect themselves. "You need connections, money, intellect, energy, and hard work," explains Tyrin. "We got the armoured personnel carrier just to be on the safe side."

- Arpad Kovacs runs a dress making shop in Budapest. He lives in relative luxury, but he has to cheat on his taxes in order to do so. He is supposed to pay 70 percent of his profits in taxes, but he understates his sales volume so that he ends up paying about 45 percent. Many entrepreneurs claim losses for their businesses even when the business makes a profit.

Funds for an Ongoing Business

After the enterprise has operated for some time, other services are more likely to be used, if a good financial reputation has been established. Sources include trade credit (that is, the delayed payment terms offered by suppliers), chartered banks, trust companies, and venture capitalists. Another source of funds is profits from the business. Entrepreneurs seldom pay themselves all the profits generated by the enterprise. Some profits are reinvested in the enterprise and are called **retained earnings.**

Managing Funds

In Table 8.2, each source is identified as debt or equity. **Debt** refers to borrowed funds that require interest payments and must be repaid. **Equity** refers

retained earnings
Profits reinvested in an enterprise.

debt
Borrowed funds that require interest payments and must be repaid.

equity
Money invested in the enterprise by individuals or companies who become owners.

Table 8.2 **Principal Sources of Funds for Small Business Enterprises**

Debt Sources

These are funds borrowed by the enterprise. They may come from:

The entrepreneur who may loan money to the enterprise

Private lenders, that is, individuals or corporations

Financial institutions such as banks, credit unions, trust companies, and finance companies. Such borrowing may be by the enterprise but guaranteed by the entrepreneur or secured against other nonbusiness assets of the entrepreneur

Trade credit, that is, the delayed payment terms offered by suppliers

Government agencies, for example, the Federal Business Development Bank

The selling of bonds or debentures (usually only done when the enterprise is larger)

Equity Sources

This money is invested in the enterprise and represents an ownership interest. It comes from:

The entrepreneur's personal funds

Partners, either individuals or corporations

Family and friends

Venture capitalists

Governments

The selling of shares to the public (usually only done when the enterprise is larger)

Employees who may participate in a stock purchase plan or simply invest in the enterprise.

Retained Earnings

Profits, that is, funds generated from the operation of the business, can be either paid to the owners in dividends or reinvested in the enterprise. If retained or reinvested, profits are a source of funds.

to the money, or capital, invested in the enterprise by individuals or companies who become owners, and to profits reinvested. In the case of small enterprises, the entrepreneur is often the sole owner. The challenge for entrepreneurs is to keep the amount of funds borrowed and funds invested in ownership in balance. If an enterprise relies upon debt too heavily, interest payments might become burdensome and could lead to the failure of the enterprise.

Investors who invest equity obtain ownership and have some influence on the firm's operations. If investors own 51 percent or more of the firm's equity, they could control the enterprise. As enterprises require funds to grow, this diminishing of control frequently cannot be avoided.

Transitions in Management

Changes in how a business is managed occur as the enterprise grows. Models of small business growth have been developed that help explain these changes in management.[8] Table 8.3, gives examples of the shift in management approaches necessary as a small enterprise develops.

The launch stage covers the preparatory activities as well as the actual startup, while the survival stage is the initial period of operation (up to five years) in which many enterprises fail. During expansion, the organization passes the break-even point, and success appears to be more likely. Finally, the maturity stage involves slowed or slight growth and might be referred to as a "comfort" stage where success is assured. Maturity is not necessarily the end of growth for a business. Expansion opportunities are still sought and diversification is considered, sometimes through taking over or merging with other enterprises.

Table 8.3   **Growth Model for Small Enterprises**

Characteristics	Launch	Survival	Expansion	Maturity
Key Issues	Development of business "idea" Raising funds Obtaining customers	Generating revenues Breaking even	Managing and funding growth Obtaining resources Maintaining control	Expense control Productivity Consideration of diversification and other expansion
Management Style	Entrepreneurial, individualistic, direct supervision	Entrepreneurial, allows others to administer but supervises closely	Delegation, coordinative, but still entrepreneurial Monitoring	Decentralization, reliance on others
Organizational Structure	Unstructured	Simple	Functional, centralized	Decentralized functional/ product
Product/Market	Single line and single market	Single line and market but increasing diversity	Wider product range and multiple markets	Several product lines, multimarket and channels
Main Sources of Funds	Owners, friends, and relatives	Owners, suppliers (trade credit), banks	Banks, new partners, retained earnings, secured long-term debt	Retained earnings, long-term debt, shareholders

During these stages, the firm changes from being entrepreneurial to being professionally managed. This change usually happens once the business employs between 50 and 100 people. That is, the entrepreneurial approach to management where one individual dominates shifts to a professional management style with several top, middle, and supervisory managers necessary to operate the enterprise.

The Survival of Small Business

Numerous statistics on the survival rate of small businesses have been compiled. The following data are representative:

- About 13 to 15 percent of all business enterprises disappear each year.

- One half of new businesses fail in the first three years. After that the failure rate levels off.

- After 10 years, only 25 percent of businesses are still in existence.

- The average life span of small enterprises is 7.25 years.

- Female entrepreneurs have a survival rate about twice as high as that of males.[9]

The low survival rate need not be viewed as a serious problem, since failures are natural in a competitive economic system. In some cases, enterprises are poorly managed and are replaced by more efficient and innovative ones. In recent years, more enterprises have started than have failed, indicating the resiliency of small business and entrepreneurs.

Reasons for Success

Four factors are typically cited to explain the success of small business owners:

1. *Hard work, drive, and dedication.* Small business owners must be committed to succeeding and be willing to put in the time and effort to make it happen. Long hours and few vacations generally characterize the first few years of new business ownership.
2. *Market demand for the product or service.* If the area around a college has only one pizza parlour, a new pizzeria is more likely to succeed than if there are already 10 in operation. Careful analysis of market conditions can help small businesspeople assess the reception of their products in the marketplace.
3. *Managerial competence.* Successful small businesspeople have a solid understanding of how to manage a business firm. They may acquire competence through training (by taking courses in small business management at a local college), experience (by learning the ropes in another business), or by using the expertise of others.
4. *Luck.* Luck also plays a role in the success of some firms. For example, after one entrepreneur started an environmental clean-up firm, he struggled to keep his business afloat. Then the government committed a large sum of money for toxic waste clean-up. He was able to get several large contracts, and his business is now thriving.

Reasons for Failure

Small businesses collapse for a number of reasons (see Table 8.4). The entrepreneur may have no control over some of these reasons (for example, weather, fraud, accidents), but he or she can influence most items on the list. This is the main reason an entrepreneur should learn as much as possible about management.

Table 8.4   Causes of Small Business Failure

Poor management skills
poor delegation and organizational ability
lack of depth in management team
entrepreneurial incompetence, such as a poor
    understanding of finances and business markets
lack of experience

Inadequate marketing capabilities
difficulty in marketing product
market too small, nonexistent, or declines
too much competition
problems with distribution systems

Inadequate financial capabilities
weak skills in accounting and finance
lack of budgetary control
inadequate cash flow forecasts
inadequate costing systems
incorrect valuation of assets
unable to obtain financial backing

Inadequate production capabilities
poorly designed production systems
old and inefficient production facilities and equipment
inadequate control over quality
problems with inventory control

Personal reasons
lost interest in business
accident, illness
death
family problems

Disasters
fire
weather
strikes
fraud by entrepreneur or others

Other
mishandling of large project
excessive standard of living
lack of time to devote to business
difficulties with associates or partners
government policies change

Assistance for Entrepreneurs and Small Business Enterprises

The Financial Post
http://www.canoe.ca/FP

In the Canadian economic system, the existence of small enterprises is considered desirable for a number of reasons, including the employment it provides, the innovations it introduces, and the competition it ensures. To help entrepreneurs through the hazards of starting up and operating a new business, substantial assistance is available. Government is the main source of assistance, but other sources are also available. Various sources of assistance are summarized in Table 8.5.

In spite of the numerous government assistance programs, small business owners are not happy with government involvement in small business. A 1993 *Financial Post* survey revealed that just 5 percent of small business owners felt that a government program had helped them start their business. By contrast, 46 percent felt that government policies and regulations (e.g., excessive paper work requirements and red tape) have caused them to cut back their business operations. Small business owners also said that government assistance programs are not as effective as they used to be. Small business owners rank managerial competence as most important in promoting growth. Government assistance is ranked last.[10]

Table 8.5   **Summary of Assistance for Small Business**

Government Assistance

Industry Canada is the department in the federal government responsible for small business and has many programs to promote entrepreneurship. Provincial governments also have numerous programs.

The National Entrepreneurship Development Institute was established as a non-profit organization to serve as a clearing house for information about entrepreneurship.

Taxation policy allows small business to pay lower levels of taxes than other enterprises.

The Federal Business Development Bank (FBDB) administers the Counselling Assistance for Small Enterprises (CASE) program, which offers one-on-one counselling by experienced people to thousands of entrepreneurs each year.

The *Small Business Loans Act (SBLA)* encourages the provision of term loan financing to small enterprises by private sector institutions by guaranteeing the loans.

The Program for Export Market Development shares the cost of efforts by business to develop export markets.

Incubators and technology centres operate across Canada. Incubators are centres where entrepreneurs can start their business with the assistance of counselling services. Federal government funds support technology centres that evaluate innovations under research and development.

Schools for Entrepreneurs funded by government but operated by the private sector prepare prospective entrepreneurs by training them in all aspects of small business. An example is the Regina Business and Technology Centre.

Private Sector

The Canada Opportunities Investment Network (COIN) is a computerized national investment match making service operated through Chambers of Commerce. This service brings potential entrepreneurs together with people who might be willing to supply them with capital.

Banks and other financial institutions not only lend money but also provide advice to entrepreneurs.

Venture capitalists finance high-risk enterprises to which others are unwilling to lend money. Business angels are a special category of private venture capitalists who invest in new, high-risk enterprises that they feel should be supported even though no one else will.

Consultants and numerous publications exist to answer questions.

The Canadian Federation of Independent Business (CFIB) is the largest of the organizations formed to protect the interests of small business. It is a non-profit, nonpartisan group, or lobby, that represents the interests of about 75 000 small and medium-sized enterprises.

Summary of Learning Objectives

1. **Define *small business* and explain its importance to the Canadian economy.** A *small business* is independently owned and managed and does not dominate its market. Small businesses are crucial to the economy because they create new jobs, foster *entrepreneurship* and *innovation*, and supply goods and services needed by larger businesses.

2. **Explain which types of enterprise best lend themselves to small business success.** Services are the easiest operations for small businesspeople to start because they require relatively low levels of resources. They also offer high returns on investment and tend to foster innovation. Retailing and wholesaling are more difficult because they usually require some experience, but they are still attractive to many entrepreneurs. New technology and management techniques are making agriculture profitable once again for small farmers. As the most resource-intensive area of the economy, manufacturing is the area least dominated by small firms.

3. **Describe the start-up decisions made by small businesses.** In deciding to go into business, the entrepreneur must choose between buying an existing business and starting from scratch. There are practical advantages and disadvantages to both approaches. A successful existing business, for example, has working relationships with other businesses and has already proved its ability to make a profit. New businesses, on the other hand, allow owners to plan and work with clean slates, but it is hard to make projections about the business's prospects.

4. **Identify the advantages and disadvantages of *franchising*.** *Franchising* has become a popular form of small business ownership because the *franchisor* (parent company) supplies the financial, managerial, and marketing assistance to the *franchisee*, who buys the right to sell the franchisor's product. Franchising also enables small businesses to grow rapidly. Finally, the risks in franchising are lower than those in opening a new business from scratch. However, the costs of purchasing a franchise can be quite high, and the franchisee sacrifices independence and creativity. In addition, franchises are no guarantee of success.

5. **Identify the key reasons for the success and failure of small businesses.** There are four key factors that contribute to small business failure: *managerial incompetence or inexperience; neglect; weak control systems;* and *insufficient capital.* Similarly, four key factors contribute to small business success: *hard work, drive, and dedication; market demand for the products or services being provided; managerial competence;* and *luck.* Among the *entrepreneurial characteristics* that are also important are resourcefulness, a concern for positive customer relations, a willingness to take risks, and a strong need for personal freedom and opportunity for the type of creative expression that goes with running one's own company.

6. **Describe the sources of financial and management advice that are available to small businesses.** Financial and management advice for small businesses is available from several private and government sources. The private sources include The Canada Opportunities Investment Network, banks, venture capitalists, the Federation of Independent Businesses, and the Canadian Youth Business Foundation. Government sources include Industry Canada, The Federal Business Development Bank, and incubators and technology centres.

Key Terms

small business, 219
entrepreneur, 220

Canadian Federation of
Independent Business
(CFIB), 223

microenterprise, 226
franchising, 227
franchisee, 227

franchisor, 227
retained earnings, 230
debt, 230
equity, 230

Study Questions and Exercises

Review Questions

1. Why has the number of small businesses in Canada increased?
2. What are the characteristics of a small business?
3. What are the characteristics of an entrepreneur?
4. What are the advantages and disadvantages of the following ways of becoming involved in a small business: taking over a family business, buying out an existing business, starting a business from scratch, and buying a franchise?
5. What are the causes of small business failure?

Analysis Questions

6. Why are small businesses important to the Canadian economy?
7. Why would a person want to become involved in a microenterprise instead of going into business full-time?

8. Why do small businesses fail despite all the assistance available? Should we be concerned about these failures?

Application Exercises

9. Interview a person who is involved in a family business to identify the management challenges he or she faces. Check your findings against the key challenges identified in Figure 8.2. Write the Canadian Association of Family Enterprises for more information at 10 Prince Street, 3rd Floor, Toronto, ON, M4W 1Z4.
10. Research a business that you are interested in and prepare a plan for starting it. Use the contents of a business plan listed in Table 8.1. Develop a complete, professional business plan using the EZ-Write Plan Writer disk that accompanies the *Study Guide* for this text or may be purchased separately.

Building Your Business Skills

Goal

To encourage students to appreciate the value of networking to small business success and to develop a practical approach to finding and questioning networking sources.

Situation

Suppose that you and three partners have just started a small publishing company specializing in ethnic cookbooks. All of you have publishing backgrounds, but none of you has ever owned a company or run a business. You decide that one of the best ways to learn what it takes to operate a successful small business is to seek the advice of others.

Method

Step 1:

Suggest six different networking sources—including professional and community organizations—that might be of value to a start-up publishing company. Choose each source based on its ability to help you in a special way. For example, while one organization might place you in contact with qualified editorial workers, another might help you learn everything you need to know about running a company in your town. Make a list of the sources and describe their value to you.

Step 2:

For each source, develop a list of questions, the answers to which might help your business in concrete ways. For example, in a networking meeting with the president of a professional editorial workers group, you might ask the following questions:

- Can I find copy editors and proofreaders through your organization?
- How much do they charge?
- Can you recommend an excellent photo researcher?

Step 3:

Now sit down with three or four other students in your class to compare and contrast your networking sources and questions.

Follow-Up Questions

1. What is the most valuable networking source on your list and on the lists of other group members? Describe the reasons for your choices.
2. Sources of networking help can be long-term, short-term, or both. How would you classify each of the sources you identified?
3. What factors were responsible for the different approaches to networking that you found in your small group?

A valuable information source for small businesspersons is the guide to Government of Canada services and support for small businesses. You can reach the Web site at the following address:

http://strategis.ic.gc.ca/SSG/mi02983e_pr201.sgml

1. Review the outline of a business plan in the text. Within the Web site, where would you find information to help you complete a business plan? For example, where in the Web site would you find information or tools to assist you in completing the market assessment section of a business plan?

2. Write down a type of business you'd like to start. In the "Financing" section of the Web site, investigate small business loan opportunities for your new business. List the loans you qualify for because of the nature of your proposed business, your geographic region, or other criteria.

3. Review the causes of small business failure. Assess your own weaknesses in the areas that are controllable (e.g., a weather disaster is beyond your control). What resources on the Web site could help you overcome these shortcomings?

4. What resources are available for someone wanting to start a home-based business? Evaluate the usefulness of the information.

CONCLUDING CASE 8-1

Bumps in the Franchising Road

Franchising is a very popular form of business in Canada. But in the last few years, a recurring theme has been evident: conflict between franchisees and franchisors. Consider the difficulties at three franchises: Subway, Grower Direct, and Pizza Pizza.

Subway. Chris Downer, the owner of a Subway franchise in Etobicoke, Ontario, arrived one day at his store and found the locks changed and a security guard inside. Subway Franchise Systems had repossessed his store because he had missed a royalty payment of $4800. Downer broke a window to get in and sent the security guard home. He paid the money four days later, but was then hit with a $4600 legal bill from Subway to cover costs they had incurred when trying to get him to pay up.

Some analysts feel that Subway has opened so many new outlets that existing franchisees are going to suffer. John Sotos, a Toronto franchise lawyer, fears that Subway's all-out expansion drive is putting franchisees at risk. He wonders what basis the Subway chain is using to reach the conclusion that it can sustain so many franchises. Ned Levitt, also a franchise lawyer, notes that the chain's low franchising fee ($10 000) may allow undercapitalized franchisees into the business. If they run into difficulty, these franchisees are more likely to be unable to keep up the necessary payments. Fred DeLuca, Subway's CEO, says the

chain does not open new stores without taking current franchisees' well-being into account. If the chain determines that the opening of a new outlet will have severe impact on an existing franchisee, the new outlet will not be opened. He notes that about one third of proposed new outlets are not opened because of objections from existing franchisees.

Grower Direct. This company is Canada's largest importer of roses, with sales of $25 million. It sells roses for $9.99 per dozen in stores across Canada. Owner Skip Kerr is able to sell roses at this low price because the firm is vertically integrated all the way back to the farm where the roses are grown. The company has grown rapidly by selling franchises for $20 000. In return, franchisees receive an exclusive territory.

While the franchising concept has allowed Grower Direct to rapidly increase its sales, there are problems. In Toronto and Vancouver, for example, several franchisees broke away from the company, claiming that they had to pay too much for their flowers from the franchisor and could buy them more cheaply in Toronto. But, as long as they were part of the franchise, they were forced to buy their flowers from Grower Direct.

Kerr agrees that franchisees can get flowers cheaper elsewhere, but he says these flowers are of much lower

...

Bumps in the Franchising Road

(continued)

quality. One Toronto franchisee discovered that she could buy flowers on the local market for about half the price that Grower Direct was charging her as a franchisee. She now owns a non-franchised store.

One franchisee who owns 11 Grower Direct franchise outlets says being a franchisee is very restricting. Franchisees often have ideas about how to improve the business, but they must operate the way the franchisor dictates. Other franchisees accept the restrictions because they want to run a business outlet where they can be their own boss.

Pizza Pizza. Darlene Thiele owned two Pizza Pizza franchises. Because she had an outstanding balance of $28 000 with the franchisor, she was fearful that her stores would be taken away. In order to prevent a situation like the one facing Chris Downer, she hired a locksmith to change the locks on her store, and she slept in the store overnight. The next morning the police arrived at the front door, accompanied by two managers from Pizza Pizza headquarters. Soon after, the chain filed a lawsuit against Thiele, alleging breach of the franchise agreement. Then they stopped deliveries to her store.

Thiele was not alone in her run-ins with the franchisor. In 1992, several franchisees who had experienced difficulties with Pizza Pizza formed the Southern Ontario Pizza Franchisee Association (SOPFA). The franchisees began to grow bolder as they recognized that others had the same concerns they had. They eventually hired a lawyer who filed a $7.5 million lawsuit against Pizza Pizza, demanding that it produce certain financial statements, stop interfering with the regular operations of franchisees, and stop terminating franchise agreements without cause.

The case was eventually turned over to an arbitrator in the spring of 1994. He handed down a decision that supported some of the franchisees' claims, but didn't go as far as they would have liked. Pizza Pizza was told it owed the franchisees a total of $821 495. It paid this out in the summer of 1995. But more than one third of the franchisees involved in the lawsuit were eventually terminated or bought out.

The province of Ontario introduced legislation in 1997 that will more closely regulate franchising. Alberta already has a law requiring franchisors to "deal fairly" with franchisees, and other provinces may follow suit. Lawyer Sotos says that regulation is needed prohibiting franchisors from doing things like increasing prices when they are the sole supplier, raising the amount of supplier rebates retained, discriminatory action against franchisees, and misuse of advertising funds.

Case Questions

1. Do franchisees really own their own businesses?

2. Do the benefits of being a franchisee outweigh the costs (e.g., restrictions put on franchisees by the franchisor)? Explain.

3. How might a franchisor address complaints from franchisees that they are being overly restricted in how they are allowed to operate?   ◆

Grower Direct
http://flowers.baynet.net/

Doll Maker Disarmed by Success

Hopes at the Georgetown Collection Inc. were high in the fall in 1995. The all-important Christmas selling season had arrived, and the company's 45-cm vinyl collection dolls, each accompanied by an illustrated novel telling the doll's own story, held great promise. The Magic Attic Club dolls, as the collectibles were known, were targeted at girls aged 6 through 11, who were too old for Barbies but still loved playing with dolls.

Research had already shown that there was a market for these dolls. The Pleasant Co., Georgetown's chief competitor, had sold more than 3 million American Girl collectibles since 1986, and there was room in the market for a company with a different approach to marketing a competing product. And a different approach, according to Gretchen Springer, Georgetown's Vice-President of Marketing, is precisely what Georgetown had. Whereas Pleasant dolls represent historical periods, Georgetown dolls are distinctly contemporary. "Pleasant Company," explains Springer, "has identified a whole new market, and we are trying to fill a gap in that market. Since our book characters and dolls are based on the present, we feel girls can relate to them more strongly. And the fantasy element of the books encourages girls to do more imaginative role-playing." Georgetown also enjoyed a major pricing advantage over Pleasant Co. While American Girl dolls sell for $82, their Magic Attic Club counterparts sells for only $59.

Georgetown's optimism, however, may have been premature. No sooner than it had bet its survival on the Magic Attic Club line, 40 000 dolls from a factory in China arrived at the company's Westbrook, Maine, headquarters with their arms falling off. With only six weeks left before Christmas, Georgetown's staff of 100 employees worked late into the nights to repair 80 000 doll arms—a process that took 20 minutes per doll. Even so, the arm fiasco was financially devastating, in large part because of the company's history of poor capitalization. Because it was seated on a very thin financial cushion, 1995 was a make-or-break year for Georgetown. "If Magic Attic had failed miserably," admits Georgetown president Jeffrey H. McKinnon, "we'd have bankrupted the business."

Georgetown's emergency repairs succeeded and the company survived. But profits fell victim to the emergency as overtime costs ate away the company's financial base. Looking to the future, however, Georgetown sees itself as poised for success and hopes to double its sales in the coming year. Still, company executives can't help but feel a little uncertain about the shifting sands on which small businesses are so often built, and they worry about their ability to perform without a secure financial safety net. In particular, they understand the increasing importance of financing their own success. In just a few months in 1995, for instance, burgeoning demand forced Georgetown to expand both its telephone order centre and its order-filling system. Moreover, in the midst of the bustling holiday season it was obliged to compete for qualified order takers with nearby L.L. Bean. "This is the point where companies grow or fail," says Springer. "We're at this point . . . where the company now has to *manage* its success and make the transition to the theoretical opportunity."

Demand for the Georgetown Collection's Magic Attic Club dolls is driven by the colourful catalogues in which the dolls are marketed and by the 17 books published by Magic Attic Press. The stories centre on the lives of four best friends—the doll characters Alison, Megan, Heather, and Keisha—who discover a trunk filled with elegant costumes and a magic mirror. When the girls don the costumes and look into the mirror, they are transported through time and space to encounter different adventures. "Each story," explains marketing VP Gretchen Springer, "leads the girls to a self-discovery, passing on to them a value lesson relating to something they are struggling with in real life."

Parents love the doll/book concept so much that 1.5 million books, priced at $5.95 each, are now in print. Says one mother, "I think it's great that my daughter is playing with these dolls so creatively. There isn't that much in the toy stores for girls. . . . Now suddenly the girls are into dressing up dolls, and it's so wonderfully old-fashioned."

Having found its marketing niche and overcome its 1995 production disaster, Georgetown's continuing challenge, according to Jill S. Krutick, an analyst with Smith Barney, is to attract the capital and resources that it needs to "take the business to a higher plane." But Georgetown, like many other small companies, finds itself in a chicken/egg situation. "It's hard to maintain consistency and credibility with banks without a long track record," admits Krutick, "and it's hard to achieve a track record without adequate capital." Assuming that Georgetown can find the capital it needs to expand, it is riding a crest in the toy industry—the phenomenal growth of the high-end doll-and-book category. "This category," reports one toy-industry consultant, "is very hot."

Case Questions

1. Why is Georgetown Collection Inc. an example of an entrepreneurial company?

2. What factors were responsible for Georgetown's problems in 1995, and how are these factors typical of those encountered by small businesses?

3. How do you assess Georgetown's chances for business success?

4. Why is an adequate financial cushion so important to a company like Georgetown? Your answer to this question should focus on both survival and growth.

5. What role have product and marketing innovation played in Georgetown's success so far?

Earth Buddy*

Thoughts of bankruptcy, scandal and personal disaster raced through Anton Rabie's mind as he faced the prospect that loomed before him. The buying office of the U.S. retail giant, Kmart, appeared to be having second thoughts about placing an order with Anton's fledging manufacturing company. The product Anton's company hoped to sell Kmart was a novelty product called Earth Buddy that Anton, together with four of his closest friends, had developed for the retail fad market.

The Earth Buddy was manufactured by stuffing sawdust and grass seed inside a nylon stocking. The stocking was then decorated with two eyes, glasses, a nose and mouth and placed in a colourful cardboard box. After purchasing an Earth Buddy the customer watered it and then watched as it sprouted its grassy toupee in the ensuing weeks.

To date Anton and his four business cohorts had sold thousands of Earth Buddies to several of the largest retail operations in Canada, including Zellers. Tremendous demand for the product had netted the company nearly $400 000 profit in only four short months of operation.

With this healthy momentum behind them, Anton and company had set their collective sights on even bigger targets south of border in the huge U.S. market. Combining persistence with panache, he had recently enticed Kmart U.S. to consider placing an order for 500 000 units. This order was several times larger than anything the company had handled to date.

The Kmart order was not without its problems, however. Foremost was Kmart's insistence on the order's timely delivery. This was a problem because of the comparatively small-scale runs the company was used to. Producing half a million buddies was almost inconceivable. Further complicating the demand for timely delivery was Kmart's unwillingness to make a firm written commitment to the order. This resulted in Anton's company having to begin the manufacture of the order on speculation that the written purchase order would be forthcoming.

Faced with these two uncertainties Anton and his friends decided to risk all and began manufacturing hundreds of thousands of Earth Buddies in the hope that the Kmart order would actually materialize. In order to realize their objective of 500 000 units, the company needed to produce about 16 000 units each day. This production objective required Michelle and Ben, the two manufacturing managers, to hire and train an additional 140 employees.

In the early weeks of manufacturing the order another problem had surfaced: raw material stockouts. Secure, sufficient, and balanced supplies of each of the key raw inputs were not always on hand. At one point, a shortage of sawdust had resulted in most of the company's production employees having to be sent home early and in a shortfall of several thousand finished buddies.

However, the worst problem associated with the Kmart order was its perpetual uncertainty. While Anton had been assured of a purchase order from the U.S. giant, he still had not received written confirmation of Kmart's commitment to the sawdust-based pals. With the majority of the order now complete, Anton felt both relieved and worried. What if the Kmart order fell through? Fresh out of business school, he had only limited experience in dealing with giant corporations and the giant orders they placed. What, if anything, could he do to secure the Kmart order?

Study Questions

1. What is a mission statement? How would you articulate the mission employed by the makers of Earth Buddy?

2. What is a contingency plan? How well do the makers of Earth Buddy appear to plan for possible contingencies?

3. What are the generic competitive strategies? Which of these best describes the Earth Buddy?

* Source: This case was written by Professor Reg Litz of the University of Manitoba.
Video Resource: "Earth Buddy," *Venture* #518 (December 11, 1994).

CBC Video Case II-2

Diversifying with Jimmy*

"If you take a longer-term view of the world, which we tend to do in a private company, then all we have to do is concentrate on the growth of the business, what's best for the business. We don't have to worry about the security analysts, or the P/E ratios, or what the market is doing today."

—Jimmy Pattison

Canadian business legend and free enterprise evangelist Jimmy Pattison has quietly amassed one of Canada's largest private fortunes. His empire, which began out of a car dealership, is currently assessed at $3.4 billion and includes hundreds of companies in a dozen different countries. Being a privately held concern is very important to Jimmy. With no public shareholders to be accountable to, Pattison is free to pursue his penchant for acquisitions as and when he sees fit. He appears to "see fit" quite often; he bought 21 companies in a one-year period, or one almost every two weeks.

Today's trip on his private jet takes him and his senior management team to Cedar Grove, New Jersey, where he meets with representatives from four of his packaging companies. At every meeting the routine is the same; the divisional management team under review sits along one side of the conference table, Pattison's top management team along the other.

Pattison both observes and participates in the discussion as senior team members volley question after question at each division's team. Some might think that such a large and diverse empire would be difficult to control, but Pattison's monthly and quarterly reporting systems assure that he is kept abreast of everything and anything that might potentially affect operating results. Such a system is crucial. With operations in industries as diverse as fish marketing, outdoor billboard advertising, broadcasting, food retailing, and magazine publishing, many would be overwhelmed by the complexity. But, diverse as it is, it all makes sense to Jimmy. His theory of diversification is simple: Buy businesses you can relate to. Pattison explains: "We can put ourselves in the position of a consumer. . . . When I walk into a grocery store and I get treated a certain way, I can understand how the customer feels if she or he doesn't get treated very good. I can't understand that sitting in a nuclear plant because I don't understand it."

Part of running a diversified empire is being willing to face the hard music of who's producing and who isn't. Pattison, who built his reputation on such practices as routinely firing his lowest-producing salesperson, keeps a watchful eye on key managers and how they deal with weak performers in his workforce of 17 000. He explains, "If people don't perform because they're either in the wrong spot in life, or they're lazy, or they lose interest, or they're better suited for something else, then we help them make up their mind."

He also demonstrates a realistic understanding of the seemingly unpredictable elements of business. He readily admits having "never owned a company that hasn't at some time . . . had some difficulties and had a winter season." Still, for all the bumps in the road, this self-made billionaire seems to know the art of managing.

Study Questions

1. What is the difference between conglomerate and concentric diversification? Which better describes Pattison's business?

2. What is the difference between vertical and horizontal integration? What evidence is there in the video case that Pattison pursues one, the other, or both?

3. What is the difference between corporate level and business unit level strategy? How easily can you apply these terms to Pattison's empire?

---

* Source: This case was written by Professor Reg Litz of the University of Manitoba.
  Video Resource: "The Gospel According to Jimmy," *Venture* #671 (December 2, 1997).

Planning in the Coming Home Division of Land's End

LEARNING OBJECTIVES

The purpose of this video exercise is to help students:

1. Appreciate the process whereby marketing managers develop practical plans to carry out the strategic decisions they make.

2. Understand the ways in which a specific company perceives its organizational strengths and uses them to seize marketplace opportunities.

3. Understand the relationship between product development and marketing as interrelated management areas.

BACKGROUND INFORMATION

The *Coming Home* catalogue, which specializes in products for bed and bath, was one of three specialty divisions launched by Lands' End in 1989. The decision to branch out into home textiles, says Managing Director Phil Young, came when marketers at Lands' End "recognized opportunity in the marketplace." Textile mills were either merging or closing, and those that stayed in business were stressing efficiency over quality. Lands' End thus saw an opportunity to enter the home-textiles market—especially in bedding—by introducing high-quality products backed by the company's unconditional guarantee and priced along its usual lines.

The process of developing such products as fitted sheets and folded baby blankets consists of several steps:

■ The product development team identifies a need or opportunity in the marketplace.

■ The strategy for designing the actual product reflects the company's mission—to develop the best product for the identified need.

■ The competition is analyzed and the input of potential customers is collected.

■ An appropriate supplier is selected.

■ The product is tested, both in-house and among customers.

Young characterizes this approach to strategic planning as *SWOT analysis*: matching internal organizational Strengths and Weaknesses with external Opportunities and Threats.

THE VIDEO

Video Source. "Planning in the Coming Home Division at Lands' End," *Prentice Hall Presents: On Location at Lands' End.* The video focuses on the planning that underpins the product development process at the Coming Home division, which specializes in home textile products for bed and bath. Merchandising manager Rob Hayes discusses the approach that Lands' End marketers take to developing products that both meet carefully researched customer needs and satisfy the company's established quality standards.

Discussion Questions

1. How would you characterize the overall approach of Lands' End management to the concept of matching the organization with its environment? Does it take risks, for example, or is it conservative?

2. According to Phil Young, the division's approach to the "'sheet that fits' . . . provides an edge for all Coming Home products—meeting the needs of the customer." How might this goal be translated into an item in the company's mission statement? Does the product development process described in the video suggest any particular strategic goals that might have been set by Lands' End management?

3. Judging from the management approach to product development at the Coming Home division, what can you say about the nature of managerial responsibility and organizational structure at Lands' End? Judging from the video, what can you say about corporate culture at Lands' End?

Follow-Up Assignment

At the conclusion of the video, the narrator poses the following question: *How does Lands' End fight against competitors using its ideas, like "the sheet that fits"?* To address this question, secure a *Coming Home* catalogue (phone, fax, or e-mail Lands' End). Next, consider the following comment made by Phil Young in 1996:

One issue is always the "edge." Our just-completed SWOT analysis indicated that our competitors were catching up—chipping away at the "edge." So to identify all the elements of the edge, we listed the strengths and weaknesses that we have and what we *needed to do* to reinforce that edge. Then we set some specific goals in order to address everything we had to do in order to stay ahead of the competition.

Your instructor will divide you into groups of five or six people, with each acting as a "product development team." Each team should examine the descriptions of several different products in the *Coming Home* catalogue. Which products seem to be promoted most effectively? To which products would you attach an apparent marketing "edge"—some benefit or feature that, as a result of product development planning, looks as if it might help a given product to "stay ahead of the competition"? As a team, make recommendations for giving an "edge" to two or three products that seem to be in need of a competitive boost.

For Further Exploration

Visit Lands' End on the Internet at
http://www.landsend.com

On the Web page, scroll down to "The Company" and then down to the link to "The Company Inside and Out." To get a better idea of the areas in which the company tries to develop its organizational strengths, look at such features as "At Lands' End the Word 'Value' Rings True" and "Quality in the Apparel Business. . . ." According to Lands' End, in what ways does attention to quality furnish an "edge" in the development of its products? What role should "value" play in formulating a mission statement for Lands' End?

EXPERIENTIAL EXERCISE:
Reorganizing for More Efficient Growth

OBJECTIVE

To help students see how changes in a company's business operations may require changes in its organizational structure.

TIME REQUIRED

45 minutes
   Step 1: Individual activity (to be completed before class)
   Step 2: Small-group activity (25 minutes)
   Step 3: Class discussion (20 minutes)

PROCEDURE

Step 1: Read the following case regarding the firm of T. Wilder Industries.

T. Wilder Industries was started 20 years ago with a mission of producing and selling moderately priced clothing for large and tall women. Initially, such clothing was the only product T. Wilder made. Also, like most clothing companies at the time, it sold its products through department and specialty stores. Then, 15 years ago, T. Wilder branched out and began making clothing for big and tall men. Ten years ago, the firm decided to offer a full range of sizes, from the smallest women's petites to the largest men's portly longs. Five years ago, the firm added a line of children's clothing. This year, the company opened a series of company-owned stores to sell its goods directly to the public.

As the organization grew, Thea Wilder, founder and chief executive officer of T. Wilder Industries, simply added new vice-presidents to the organizational structure she started with. Because all vice-presidents (see list on facing page) report directly to her, however, Wilder now finds this structure unwieldy. Not only must she directly manage too many people, but she is also forced to make far too many decisions. This problem will escalate if, as management plans, the company begins to manufacture and sell accessories for men and women five years from now.

HOW SHOULD T. WILDER INDUSTRIES BE ORGANIZED?

Step 2: The instructor will divide the class into small groups. Each group is to

   a. Decide on a new organizational structure for T. Wilder Industries.

   b. Develop a new organization chart for the firm.

   c. Identify each position as line or staff.

   d. Write a new mission statement for T. Wilder Industries.

Step 3: One member of each small group will present the group's proposal for reorganization to the class.

QUESTIONS FOR DISCUSSION

1. Which individuals would you expect to oppose your proposed reorganization most strongly and why?

2. How would your proposed reorganization work if T. Wilder Industries were to enter the home draperies market 10 years hence? What if it entered the consumer electronics market (televisions, VCRs, etc.) instead?

VICE-PRESIDENTS AND THEIR PERSONNEL

Vice-Presidents (Senior Mgmt.)	Middle Management	First-Line Mgmt./ Technicians	Others
Big & Tall Women's Design		2 designers	1 clerical
Big & Tall Women's Sales and Marketing	1 sales manager 1 marketing mgr.	30 sales reps 3 marketers	8 clerical
Big & Tall Women's Manufacturing		3 supervisors 2 schedulers	300 line 3 clerical
Big & Tall Men's Design		1 designer	1 clerical
Big & Tall Men's Sales and Marketing	1 sales manager 1 marketing mgr.	25 sales reps 3 marketers	6 clerical
Big & Tall Men's Manufacturing		2 supervisors 1 scheduler	200 line 2 clerical
Petite Women's Design		1 designer	1 clerical
Petite Women's Sales and Marketing	1 sales manager 1 marketing mgr.	15 sales reps 2 marketers	4 clerical
Petite Women's Manufacturing		2 supervisors 1 scheduler	150 line 2 clerical
Regular Women's Design		3 designers	2 clerical
Regular Women's Sales and Marketing	1 sales manager 1 marketing mgr.	40 sales reps 5 marketers	9 clerical
Regular Women's Manufacturing		5 supervisors 3 schedulers	450 line 4 clerical
Regular Men's Design		2 designers	2 clerical
Regular Men's Sales and Marketing	1 sales manager 1 marketing mgr.	30 sales reps 3 marketers	6 clerical
Regular Men's Manufacturing		3 supervisors 2 schedulers	300 line 3 clerical
Children's Design		1 designer	1 clerical
Children's Sales and Marketing	1 sales manager 1 marketing mgr.	25 sales reps 2 marketers	5 clerical
Children's Manufacturing		2 supervisors 1 scheduler	200 line workers
Retail Stores	4 district mgrs.	38 store mgrs.	175 clerks 5 clerical
Finance	2 supervisors	4 accountants	7 clerks
Computer Services		2 programmers/ analysts	20 order entry
Personnel		4 recruiters	5 clerical
Warehousing		5 supervisors	50 workers

CAREERS IN BUSINESS
REALITY CHECK

Combined with your studies in the classroom, real-world experience can both provide you with an excellent grounding for your working years and guide you in selecting the path that's right for you. Indeed, some professions—including medicine and public accounting—require "hands-on" training before an individual can be licensed.

But even if your chosen (or contemplated) occupation doesn't require practical experience, you are well advised to get some before seeking your first job. There are many ways in which you can gain experience. Some of your options include part-time work, volunteer work, internships, cooperative education, and getting to know people in your field (networking).

PART-TIME AND VOLUNTEER WORK

Many students have to work during the school year to make ends meet. Many others have the financial resources that allow them not to work. But the fact that you don't have to work doesn't mean that you can't work. Getting a part-time job during the school year and/or working summers is a great way to gain insights into different occupations.

The key is to find work now that is related to the work you think you'd like to do in the future. For example, if you think you might want to work in retailing, consider getting a part-time job in a local clothing, music, or sporting goods store. If you think you might want to be a lawyer, apply for a clerical job in a law office. If you think banking might be your forte, apply for a part-time job in a local bank. Even if you are doing only a routine clerical job, you will still gain some appreciation for what the people in that line of work do. If you are interested in a career in international business, take advantage of the summers to broaden your international horizons.

Volunteer work is another useful avenue for learning about different career paths. If you think the medical profession is your calling, volunteer at a local hospital. Serving as a teacher's aide in a local high school can help you gain insights into the teaching profession. Churches, charities, and museums also depend on volunteer assistance and can provide valuable career insights now and prepare you for a full-time, paid career in the future. For example, one woman who joined a neighbourhood association to help "sell" her partly restored neighbourhood to potential buyers found herself with multiple job offers to sell real estate—and the skills to earn a good living.

During the summer, if you need a paying job and can't find one in your chosen field, you might want to consider taking two jobs instead of one. That is, accept a part-time paying job outside your area of interest, but then put in unpaid time at a nonprofit or for-profit organization in your chosen field.

Besides helping you learn more about potential careers, part-time and volunteer work while you are in school will send a message to prospective employers later that you are industrious, inquisitive, and highly motivated. All of these traits are considered assets in potential employees. Moreover, learning to balance work and school will help you focus your energies, plan your time, and prioritize different tasks.

INTERNSHIPS

One special form of work/study deserves special mention: the internship. An internship is essentially a temporary full-time position in an organization. Most internships are set up for the summer months. The intern spends the summer working on special projects, as a member of a team, or as an assistant to a manager in the organization. For example, an accountant might work as an intern in an accounting firm, a finance student might work as an intern in a bank, and a restaurant management intern might work as an intern in a food services firm. Although some small firms offer internships, most internships are set up at large firms.

Internships come in a variety of forms. Some are set up by schools, while others are lined up by students, either on their own or with the help of the campus placement office. Some firms pay interns for their services. Others offer only the chance to learn.

If your school offers an internship program, visit the appropriate office and find out what's involved. If your school does not offer an internship program, contact firms in the appropriate industry and offer your services. Be sure to spell out what you are interested in learning and stress that the organization will receive something for its efforts (your work), all while contributing to your education.

Most organizations want to interview internship candidates before making their decision. During the interview, don't forget to find out as much about the organization and what you will be doing as an intern as you possibly can. Among the most important things to learn are:

- *Whom* will you work with? Will you spend much time working and interacting with other interns? Will you have any interactions with managers other than those to whom you will be assigned?
- *What* will your duties be? Will you be working on an ongoing project or a special project? What skills will you develop during the internship? What will be the outcome of your work? Will it be a report? A presentation to the managers?
- *Where* (in what city) will you be working? Will you be working in an office, a factory, a sales office? Will you be working in a single department or in several departments?
- *How* will you be compensated? Will you receive a formal evaluation at the end of the internship? Will you be paid? If so, how much? Will any of your expenses be paid? (This is an especially important consideration if you will incur significant commuting expenses.) Will

you receive any university or college credits for your internship? Will the organization consider hiring you later if you do a good job during your internship?

COOPERATIVE EDUCATION

Some colleges—and businesses—are so committed to the importance of internship that they have formalized it as an ongoing cooperative education program. In such programs, students complete some core courses, then alternate between semesters of full-time study and semesters of full-time work.

NETWORKING

Finally, you can get another perspective on—and possibly even a boost up into—a career path by networking, or making contacts with people who might be influential in helping you get a position later. You can establish such contacts in a variety of ways. Start by joining clubs or associations on campus like the Marketing Club or the Management Society. Also consider joining professional associations. Attend all local meetings of whatever associations you join.

Career fairs, which are usually sponsored by student organizations, also present excellent opportunities. At these fairs, companies send recruiters to campus to meet students and explain what their organizations do. Meeting such people can be of considerable help later. Attending campus speeches and talks by visitors from the business community is also a good way to meet people.

If you work part-time, volunteer, and/or land an internship, everyone you meet in that organization should become a part of your network. Even if your bosses during your internship cannot offer you a job later, they will pass your name on to their contacts if you have done a good job for them. As you seek contacts for your network, don't overlook your own classmates, who may be able to introduce you to others in your field. You may end up working with them later on down the line!

Part Three

Part Three

UNDERSTANDING PEOPLE IN ORGANIZATIONS

You will read about several timely and complex human resource management issues in the opening cases of the chapters in this section—the increasing success of women in top management positions at Ford and General Motors, attempts to achieve labour peace at MacMillan Bloedel, and the unionization of a Wal-Mart store. In the difficult circumstances in which many Canadian business firms have found themselves in the 1990s, it is even more important that the firm's human resources be managed effectively.

Part Three, Understanding People in Organizations, provides an overview of the relationship between managers and their employees, including managers' attitudes, the activities of managers responsible for human resource management, the special relationship between management and labour unions, and the role of the government in labour-management issues.

■ We begin in **Chapter 9, Managing Human Resources**, by exploring the activities of assessing employee needs and training, promoting, and compensating employees.

■ Then, in **Chapter 10, Motivating and Leading Employees**, we examine the reasons why firms should establish good relations with their employees and how managers' attempts to maintain productivity can affect their relations with employees.

■ Finally, in **Chapter 11, Understanding Labour-Management Relations**, we look at the development of the union movement in Canada, why and how workers organize, and how government legislation has affected workers' rights and abilities to organize.

9

Managing Human Resources

Breaking Through the Glass Ceiling

Much has been written about the "glass ceiling" that prevents women from achieving top jobs in industry. Historically, most top jobs in the private and public sector have been held by men, and women were concentrated in the lower-paying clerical and secretarial positions. But times are changing, and women are gradually occupying more and more senior management positions. Recently there have been some major breakthroughs by women who have achieved top ranking jobs in major industrial firms. In the Canadian automobile industry, for example, the CEOs of two of the three domestic manufacturers are now women.

General Motors of Canada. Maureen Kempston Darkes (pictured), the president of General Motors of Canada Ltd., heads a company with a workforce of 35 000 people and 10 assembly and component plants. Although GM has the biggest automotive market share, that share has dropped over the years to about 33 percent. In the early 1990s, GM lost billions from its North American operations. Kempston Darkes has undertaken the task of improving GM's performance.

Dealing with overall manufacturing and marketing problems is a new experience for Kempston Darkes, who started with GM in 1975 and worked her way up through the legal and government affairs side of GM Canada. Along the way, she spent two years in the treasurer's office in New York, then returned to Oshawa and moved up through positions like vice-president of public affairs and general counsel. Most CEOs at GM do not move up through this side of the business.

Ms Kempston Darkes's leadership style is to be accessible to subordinates. She is as likely to show up at a Pontiac/Buick dealership in Saskatoon as she is to be conducting a meeting in her office in Oshawa, Ontario. She has spent a great deal of time visiting dealerships across Canada. Sandy Williamson, the head of GM Canada's dealer council, says that she is by far the most accessible president that he can remember. One of her first acts as president was to personally write all of GM Canada's dealers and assure them that she supported the idea of a dealer-factory communication team that had been put together by her predecessor. The team's job is to keep the working relationships between dealers and GM smooth.

Kempston Darkes's management style appears to be flexible and collegial, but demanding. She has an open-concept office, and the sentries that usually guard a CEO's office are nowhere to be seen. When she visits one of the production plants, she drives herself to the site and unobtrusively walks in the front door like everyone else. She emphasizes that she is a team player.

Ford Motor of Canada Ltd. Bobbie Gaunt, the CEO of Ford Motor of Canada, was appointed in 1997. She heads a company that has 14 000 employees and several assembly and engine plants in Canada. Sales during 1996 were $25.5 billion. Gaunt is a 25-year veteran of Ford, and was formerly the director of marketing research for North American operations. She was also general sales manager for the Lincoln-Mercury division. She is considered to be a world-class marketer, and is expected to boost sales for Ford Canada.

Gaunt says that change is happening in the industry, but it hasn't gone far enough or proceeded fast enough. She says that an industry as old and as large as the automobile industry will require a very long time to change.

Other CEO appointments. The changes at GM and Ford are not unusual. The Canadian CEOs of Home Depot, Xerox, General Foods, EDS, and Kraft are all women. And in the U.S., Jill Barad is the CEO of Mattel Inc., and the first woman to take over as head of a major industrial corporation.

Other top-level jobs just below the level of CEO are increasingly held by women in both Canada and the U.S. Gail McGovern is the head of AT&T's $26 billion consumer business, and Lois Juliber is the head of North American and European operations for Colgate-Palmolive. Both these women have a chance to become CEOs in a few years.

In spite of these high-profile cases, there is general agreement that much work remains to be done since women still make up only a tiny proportion of senior executives in business firms. In the automotive industry in particular, the perception persists that the industry is still a "boys' club." Recent discrimination and harassment lawsuits against Magna International and Mitsubishi Motor Corp. illustrate the problems that remain. ◆

Ford Canada
http://www.ford.ca

The appointment of increasing numbers of women to top management jobs is no accident. Rather, it is the result of careful assessment of the human resources that a firm has available to it. The strategies used at Ford Canada and General Motors of Canada are typical of systems that businesses use to develop and maintain an effective workforce. These systems focus on defining the jobs that need to be done; ensuring that appropriate people are hired and oriented to their new jobs; training, appraising, and compensating employees; and providing appropriate human resource services to employees.

By focusing on the learning objectives for this chapter, you will better understand the key issues in contemporary human resource management. After reading this chapter, you will be able to:

LEARNING OBJECTIVES

1. Define *human resource management* and explain why businesses must consider job relatedness criteria when managing human resources.

2. Discuss how managers plan for human resources.

3. Identify the steps involved in *staffing* a company.

4. Describe ways in which managers can develop workers' skills and deal with workers who do not perform well.

5. Explain the importance of *wages and salaries, incentives,* and *benefits programs* in attracting and keeping skilled workers.

6. Describe how laws regarding *employment equity, pay equity,* and *worker safety* affect human resource management.

Foundations of Human Resource Management

Human resource management involves developing, administering, and evaluating programs to acquire and enhance the quality and performance of people in a business. Human resource specialists—sometimes called personnel managers—are employed by all but the smallest firms. They help plan for future personnel needs. They recruit, train, and develop employees. And they set up employee evaluation, compensation, and benefits programs.

But in fact all managers are personnel managers. Managers of production, accounting, finance, and marketing departments choose prospective employees, train new workers, and evaluate employee performance. As you will see in this section, all managers must be aware of the basis of good human resource management—job-relatedness and employee-job matching.

human resource management
The development, administration, and evaluation of programs to acquire and enhance the quality and performance of people in a business.

Job-Relatedness and Employee-Job Matching

job-relatedness
The principle that all personnel decisions, policies, and programs should be based on the requirements of a position.

According to the principle of **job-relatedness**, all personnel decisions, policies, and programs should be based on the requirements of a position. That is, all criteria used to hire, evaluate, promote, and reward people must be tied directly to the job they perform. For example, a policy that all secretaries be young women would not be job-related since neither youth nor femaleness is essential in performing secretarial work. Such a policy represents poor human resource management because the company loses the chance to hire more experienced help and to consider skilled men for the position. On the other hand, a policy of hiring only young women to model teenage girls' clothing would be job-related and would thus reflect sound human resource management.

Fundamental to the concept of job-relatedness—and to human resource management in general—is the idea of matching the right person to the right job. The direct result of good human resource management is the close match of people, skills, interests, and temperaments with the requirements of their jobs. When people are well matched to their jobs, the company benefits from high rates of employee performance and satisfaction, high retention of effective people, and low absenteeism. All personnel activities relate in some fashion to the employee-job match. Job matching may not be easy, as shown in the box "Mismatch in Jobs and Skills."

Planning for Human Resources

Just as planning for financial, plant, and equipment needs is important, so too is planning for personnel needs. As Figure 9.1 shows, such planning involves two types of activities by managers—job analysis and forecasting.

Job Analysis

job analysis
A detailed study of the specific duties in a particular job and the human qualities required for that job.

Job analysis is the detailed study of the specific duties required for a particular job and the human qualities required to perform that job. For simple, repetitive jobs, managers might ask workers to create a checklist of all the duties they perform and the importance of each of those duties for the job. In analyzing more complex jobs, managers might combine checklists with interviews

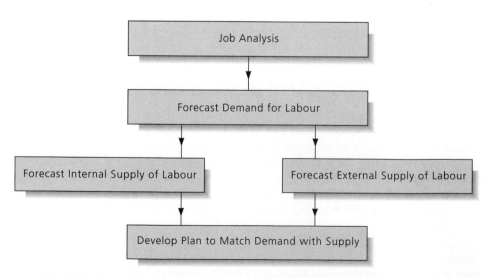

Figure 9.1
Planning for human resources.

The Canadian Business Scene

Mismatch in Jobs and Skills

There is a "mismatch" problem in Canada—people have skills the market no longer wants, and companies have needs that unemployed people cannot satisfy. The Canadian Labour Market and Productivity Centre estimates that 22 percent of the unemployed have skills that didn't match their former employers' needs. Interestingly, this figure is down from the 64 percent estimate in 1989. However, during the 1990s, the matching problem is likely to worsen again as companies become ever more demanding in what they want in employees.

The mismatch problem is obvious in a field like information technology. In an industry that relies almost solely on human brainpower and creativity, companies are in desperate need of computer programmers, software developers, and computer scientists. Canadian universities graduated one third fewer computer scientists in 1990 than they did in 1986. Yet some graduates had difficulty finding employment because they were not trained to deal with computer networks, servers, workstations, and other new developments. During this same period, university enrollment increased 12 percent, with the number of students studying history increasing 59 percent, and sociology 31 percent. Neither of these areas are promising in terms of available jobs.

Why have students not become interested in information technology? Attitudes and perceptions probably play a negative role. Computer experts are often portrayed as socially inept individuals who are "nerds" or "geeks." There is still something in Canadians that allows people to dismiss careers in technology as uninteresting.

But this is only part of the reason that a mismatch problem exists. There is also a growing recognition that we must change the way people are trained. Education should be a lifetime experience, not merely something that ends when a person graduates from some school. Pressure to change and adapt comes from the workplace as companies adopt new technologies to deliver new services. Employees who were hired in the 1960s or 1970s may not want to adapt to the new realities.

Honeywell Ltd. is just one firm that has had to come to grips with some unpleasant new realities. Its Toronto plant, which makes instrumentation for heating and cooling equip-

ment, found that customers were demanding that the firm be certified under the ISO 9000 international quality program. This meant that Honeywell would have to introduce just-in-time inventory, total quality management, and self-directed work teams. But when the company looked at its workforce, it found that only half had English as their first language, and that many had not finished high school.

Before the workers could cope with the new demands being imposed on the company, they needed to be trained. This gradually evolved into a "learning for life" program, which involved English, math, and computer courses. Employees were also trained in production and inventory management, total quality, and communication skills. Part of the training was provided at Humber College in Toronto. Each year, Humber sells about $30 million worth of education to private sector firms like Kodak Canada and John Labatt Ltd.

The mismatch problem will be solved when people on the job market have a total mix of characteristics—analytic abilities, practical skills, and flexibility—to encompass the full range of what companies are looking for. A recent Conference Board of Canada study asked employers what they were looking for in employees. Some of the things—teamwork, ability to think, ability to communicate—can be taught in school. But others—positive attitudes, responsibility, and adaptability—are more difficult to develop in educational programs.

One firm has taken advantage of this mismatch. Atlantic Computer Institute was founded on the idea that students often come out of universities over-educated and under-trained. The Institute trains them in computer technology in an intensive 11-month program. Graduates of the Institute find jobs in software writing, local-area network support, and writing technical manuals.

Another way to cope with potential mismatches is a co-op program. Under this system, university students alternate between taking classes and working for a business firm. The University of Victoria, for example, operates a year-round schedule, alternating "job semesters" with traditional classes. When students graduate, they are often hired by the firm they worked for during the co-op program.

---

of job holders to determine their exact duties. Managers might also observe workers to record the duties they perform.

Using the job analysis, human resource managers can develop **job descriptions**. A job description outlines the objectives, responsibilities, and key tasks in a job. It also describes the conditions under which the job will be done, the relationship of the job to other positions, and the skills needed to do the job. The skills, education, and experience necessary to fill a position make up the **job specification**.

Job analysis and the resulting job descriptions and specifications are the foundations of effective human resource management. They serve as tools

job description
The objectives, responsibilities, and key tasks of a job; the conditions under which it will be done; its relationship to other positions; and the skills needed to perform it.

job specification
The specific skills, education, and experience needed to perform a job.

in hiring personnel for specific positions, as guides in establishing training programs, and as sources of comparison in setting wages. But most important, by defining job requirements objectively, they allow managers to make personnel decisions in keeping with the principles of job-relatedness.

Forecasting

Once they have analyzed the nature of their needs, managers must forecast their needs. Managers need to forecast both their demand for employees of different types and the likely supply of such employees in the short term (less than one year), intermediate term (one to five years), and long term (over five years). Only then can they formulate specific strategies for responding to any potential employee surplus or shortage. As in any forecast, however, the manager's true purpose is to minimize major surprises, not to predict future needs exactly.

In forecasting *demand*, managers must take into account their businesses' plans for growth (if any). They must also figure in the normal rate of turnover and the number of older employees nearing retirement, among other factors. In forecasting *supply*, managers must consider the complexity of the job and which current employees could be promoted to fill higher positions. But they must also predict whether the labour market for a particular job will be in a state of surplus or shortage.

In an attempt to avoid layoffs, business firms are increasingly hiring contract workers to complete specific projects rather than hiring traditional full-time workers. When the project is over, the contract worker moves on to complete another contract at a different firm.

Part-time and contract workers are becoming more and more common. Between 1984 and 1994, for example, the hours worked by part-time employees at Canada Post tripled, while the hours worked by full-time workers dropped by 36 percent.[1]

Staffing the Organization

Canadian Federation of Independent Business
http://www.cfiba.ca

Once managers have decided what positions they need to fill, they must find and hire individuals who meet the job requirements. A 1996 study by the Canadian Federation of Independent Business found that the top three characteristics employers are looking for when they hire people are a good work ethic, reliability, and willingness to stay on the job.[2] Staffing of the corporation is one of the most complex and important aspects of good human resource management. In this section, we will consider how businesses fill positions from both outside and inside the organization. Sometimes personnel must be recruited and chosen from the outside. As well, decisions must be made about employee promotions to fill vacancies within the organization.

External Staffing

A new firm has little choice but to acquire staff from outside itself. Established firms may also turn to the outside to fill positions for which there are no good internal candidates, to accommodate growth, or as a way to bring in fresh ideas. Such external staffing can be divided into two stages: recruitment and selection.

Table 9.1   The Top 10 Employers in Canada, 1996

	Company	Number of Employees
1.	BCE Inc.	121 000
2.	Semi-Tech Corp.	100 000
3.	George Weston Ltd.	75 000
4.	McDonald's	68 000
5.	Laidlaw Inc.	66 000
6.	Canada Post Corp.	63 478
7.	Brascan Ltd.	60 000
8.	Imasco Ltd.	57 300
9.	Hudson's Bay Co.	57 000
10.	The Thomson Corp.	50 000

Recruitment

In the first step, the company needs to develop a pool of applicants who are both interested in and qualified for the open positions. The purpose of **recruitment** is to generate a large number of potential employees. Thus, successful recruitment focuses only on the most basic qualifications of a job.

For example, recruitment ads for a financial analyst might require applicants to hold an MBA degree with an emphasis on finance. But requiring a degree from a particular school will unnecessarily restrict the number of applicants. Recruitment specifications should always be clearly job-related.

Companies have many options in recruiting employees, depending in part on the nature of the job. As we will discuss in more detail later in this chapter, current employees may be recruited to fill openings within the firm. In seeking outside applicants, businesses may visit high schools, vocational schools, colleges, and universities. In some cases, labour agreements may specify that new employees be found using the labour union's membership rolls. Of course, many companies advertise in newspapers or trade publications or seek the help of public and private employment agencies. Word of mouth and personal recommendations are often factors in the hiring of top management personnel. Even unsolicited letters and resumes from job seekers can produce the right person for a job.

When recruiting, firms must be careful not to violate anti-discrimination laws. The key federal anti-discrimination legislation is the *Canadian Human Rights Act* of 1977. The goal of this act is to ensure that any individual who wishes to obtain a job has an equal opportunity to compete for it. The act applies to all federal agencies, federal Crown corporations, any employee of the federal government, and business firms that do business interprovincially. Thus, it applies to such firms as the Bank of Montreal, Air Canada, Telecom Canada, Canadian National Railways, and many other public and private sector organizations that operate across Canada. Even with such wide application, the act affects only about 10 percent of Canadian workers; the rest are covered under provincial human rights acts.

The *Canadian Human Rights Act* prohibits a wide variety of practices in recruiting, selecting, promoting, and dismissing personnel. The act specifically prohibits discrimination on the basis of age, race and colour, national and

recruitment
The phase in the staffing of a company in which the firm seeks to develop a pool of interested, qualified applicants for a position.

Canadian Human Rights Act
Ensures that any individual who wishes to obtain a job has an equal opportunity to apply for it.

An in-depth interview with a prospective employee is often part of the recruiting process, particularly for managerial jobs.

ethnic origin, physical handicap, religion, gender, marital status, or prison record (if pardoned). Some exceptions to these blanket prohibitions are permitted. Discrimination cannot be charged if a blind person is refused a position as a train engineer, bus driver, or crane operator. Likewise, a firm cannot be charged with discrimination if it does not hire a deaf person as a telephone operator or as an audio engineer.

These situations are clear-cut, but many others are not. For example, is it discriminatory to refuse women employment in a job that routinely requires carrying objects with a mass of more than 50 kilograms? Ambiguities in determining whether discrimination has occurred are sometimes circumvented by using the concept of "**bona fide occupational requirement**." An employer may choose one person over another based on overriding characteristics of the job in question. If a fitness centre wants to hire only women to supervise its women's locker room and sauna, it can do so without being discriminatory because it established a bona fide occupational requirement.

bona fide occupational requirement

When an employer may choose one applicant over another based on overriding characteristics of the job.

Even after referring to bona fide occupational requirements, other uncertainties remain. Consider three cases: Would an advertising agency be discriminating if it advertised for a male model about 60 years old for an advertisement that is to appeal to older men? Would a business firm be discriminating if it refused to hire someone as a receptionist because the applicant was overweight? Would a bank be discriminating because it refused to hire an applicant whom the human resources manager considered would not fit in because of the person's appearance?

We might speculate that the advertising agency is not discriminating, the business firm might or might not be discriminating, and the bank could probably be accused of discrimination, but we can't be sure. The human rights legislation cannot specify all possible situations; many uncertainties remain over what the law considers discriminatory and what it considers acceptable. Nevertheless, the spirit of the legislation is clear, and managers must try to abide by it.

Enforcement of the federal act is carried out by the Canadian Human Rights Commission. The commission can either respond to complaints from individuals who believe they have been discriminated against, or launch an investigation on its own if it has reason to believe that discrimination has occurred. During an investigation, data are gathered about the alleged discriminatory behaviour and, if the claim of discrimination is substantiated, the offending organization or individual may be ordered to compensate the victim.

Each province has also enacted human rights legislation to regulate organizations and businesses operating in that province. These provincial regulations are similar in spirit to the federal legislation, with many minor variations from province to province. All provinces prohibit discrimination on the basis of race, national or ethnic origin, colour, religion, sex, and marital status, but some do not address such issues as physical handicaps, criminal record, or age. Provincial human rights commissions enforce provincial legislation.

The ***Employment Equity Act of 1986*** addresses the issue of discrimination in employment by designating four groups as employment disadvantaged—women, visible minorities, aboriginal people, and people with disabilities. Companies covered by the act are required to publish statistics on their employment of people in these four groups.

> **Employment Equity Act of 1986**
>
> *Federal legislation that designates four groups as employment disadvantaged—women, visible minorities, aboriginal people, and people with disabilities.*

The Bank of Montreal recently became the first company outside the U.S. to win a prestigious award for promoting women's careers. Women represented over half of executive level promotions at the bank in 1993. The Bank of Montreal has introduced initiatives such as flexible working hours, a mentoring program, a national career information network, and a gender awareness workshop series.[3]

Companies are increasingly making provisions for disabled employees. At Rogers Cablevision, a division of Rogers Communications Inc., a large workplace area was completely redesigned to accommodate workers who were either visually disabled or in wheelchairs. Special equipment was also installed—a large print computer for workers with partial sight, and a device that allows blind workers to read printed materials.[4]

Selection

Once a pool of applicants has been identified, managers must sort through those individuals and select the best candidate for the job. **Selection** is by no means an exact science, since it is difficult to predict any given individual's behaviours and attitudes. Nevertheless, it is an important process. Hiring the wrong employee is costly to the firm and is unfair to that individual.

> **selection**
>
> *The process of sorting through a pool of candidates to choose the best one for a job.*

To reduce the element of uncertainty, personnel experts and other managers use a variety of selection techniques. The most common of these methods, as shown in Figure 9.2, are applications and resumes, screening interviews, ability and aptitude tests, reference checks, on-site interviews, and medical, drug, and polygraph tests. Each organization develops its own mix of selection techniques and may use them in any order.

The application form, used for almost all lower-level jobs, asks for information about the applicant such as background, experience, and education. A resume is a prepared statement of the applicant's qualifications and career goals, and is commonly used by people seeking managerial or professional positions.

In many cases, companies receive several applications or resumes for a job opening. Human resource personnel must narrow the field, first on the basis of the applications and then by holding screening interviews. In these ways, clearly unqualified individuals are weeded out, especially walk-in applicants for low-level jobs who simply do not have the required job skills. Line managers (those with hiring authority) then interview qualified applicants at greater depth. Other people in the hiring manager's department may also interview job candidates. In some companies, potential subordinates of the prospective employee are included in the interview process.

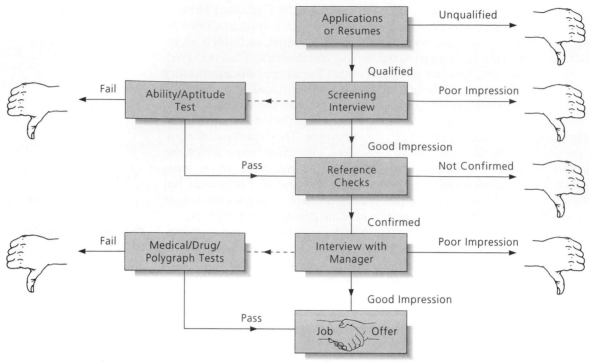

Figure 9.2
General steps in the selection process.

During both types of interviews, the interviewer asks questions about the applicant's background and qualifications. The interviewer must be careful to address only job-related issues. For example, a female applicant cannot be asked whether she plans to marry or have a family. Such questions can further sex discrimination. In addition to asking questions, interviewers also provide information about the company and answer any questions applicants may have.

For some positions, ability or aptitude tests may be part of the initial screening process.[5] When Toyota hired workers for its Cambridge, Ontario, plant, applicants were put through a series of tests to determine their math, verbal, and communication skills and their ability to work on a team. Even though most of the workers hired had never worked for an automobile firm before, they are now producing the highest-rated car in North America.[6] A new way to screen job applicants is described in the box "Screen Test."

Regardless of the type of test used, it must meet two conditions. First, the test must be job-related. A company cannot, for example, ask an applicant for a secretarial job to take a test on operating a forklift. It is clearly appropriate, however, to ask the person to take a typing test. The second requirement of an employment test is that it must be a valid predictor of performance. That is, there must be evidence that people who score well on the test are more likely to perform well in the job than are people who score poorly on the test. A test used for selection must not serve as a basis for discrimination against anyone for reasons unrelated to the job.

Another step used in employee selection is to check references. Reference checks often provide little useful information about an applicant's personality because applicants usually list as references only people likely to say good things about them. Even former employers may be reluctant to say negative things, fearing a lawsuit. But crosschecks can confirm information about an applicant's experience or education. For example, if you tell an interviewer that you graduated with a B. Comm. (Honours), a quick call to the student records office of your university can verify the truth of your statement.

Once a number of applicants have been interviewed and checked out, the manager will make a hiring decision. Before a job offer is actually made, however,

The Canadian Business Scene

Screen Test

Finding, screening, and hiring new employees can be a big expense for companies. It can cost $5000–$10 000 to hire a clerical person, and much more to hire a top manager. In this cost-conscious era, companies are always ready to consider alternatives to the traditional hiring techniques.

One such promising new technique is video assessment. Potential new hires view videos that show a series of realistic work situations (portrayed by actors). For example, one scenario shows an assistant to a department manager who is trying to convince the supervisor of the word-processing pool to give his job top priority because the boss wants some last-minute changes made in a report. The supervisor refuses and the assistant goes back to the boss asking him to intercede. At the end of each situation the viewers choose one of four courses of action to resolve the problem shown in the video. The test administrator then uses the computer to score candidate choices (much like a university or college instructor would grade student exams).

Video assessment is fast, reliable, cheap, and versatile. It also lets managers screen more extensively for jobs at the lower levels in the organization. Improving selection at entry level jobs should mean better customer service and greater chances for promotion from within. Video assessment can also give management greater insight into employee strengths and weaknesses before they are hired, and this can help the company solve long-standing problems like high turnover.

Video assessment evolved from assessment centres, which have been in use for more than 30 years (see the description later in this chapter). While assessment centres do get results, they are high-cost operations (up to $5000 for each person who is assessed). Videos are cheap by comparison. They take about an hour to complete and cost between $25 and $100. Canadian firms using video assessment include Weyerhaeuser, Reebok, Northern Telecom, Eaton's, and BC Hydro.

But care must be taken when using video assessment. If a company simply buys a ready-made video from a consulting firm it may get lax about doing its homework—stating the specific knowledge, skills, and motivation needed to do various jobs. Mindlessly using video assessment could, for example, cause a company to hire a salesperson who is good at "cold calls" when what they really needs is a salesperson who is good at maintaining existing accounts.

Another potential problem is that managers don't have a stake in selection criteria the way they do when they interview people. Some companies overcome these limitations by using multiple methods. Weyerhaeuser used both video assessment and an assessment centre to hire a supervisor for a sawmill. Some companies also use video assessment for ongoing training purposes. At Reebok, employees view the videos on a regular basis in training and development sessions.

---

some companies require an extra step—a physical exam, a polygraph test, and/or a drug test.[7] These tests are designed to protect the employer. For example, a manufacturer afraid of injuries from workers hurt on the job might require new employees to have a physical examination. The company gains some information about whether the employees are physically fit to do the work and what (if any) preexisting injuries they have. Polygraph (lie detector) tests are largely illegal now, and drug tests are also coming under fire. However, some companies still use one or both as insurance against theft or drug abuse by employees.

Internal Staffing: Promotions

No matter how careful it is, the selection process of new applicants cannot compare with a company's knowledge of its current employees. It is not surprising that many firms prefer to "hire from within"—to promote or transfer existing staff members—whenever possible.

Some firms that historically have practised promotion from within are rethinking that strategy. IBM, for example, has had only six CEOs in its history, all of whom were appointed after they had spent many years working their way up the hierarchy at IBM. But with the replacement of John Akers with outsider Louis Gerstner, the company will have an easier time breaking with tradition as it works to solve its problems.[8] Furthermore, promotion from within can cause disputes, especially in family-owned businesses.

IBM Canada
http://www.can.ibm.com

Jill Barad, the Chief Executive Officer of Mattel Inc., the company which makes the world-famous Barbie doll. Ms. Barad is the first woman to become the CEO of a major North American industrial firm.

Women often face a "glass ceiling" in their quest to get promoted. They can see what it is like in upper management, but they are not allowed to go there. Some recent evidence suggests that the glass ceiling is developing some holes. A growing number of women who started their careers in the 1970s are now beginning to land top jobs in corporations. The Opening Case in this chapter describes several women who have broken through the glass ceiling. Another is Irene Rosenfeld, who is president of Kraft Foods Canada. In 1997 alone, several other high-profile top management positions were earned by women: Jill Barad (appointed CEO of Mattel Inc.), Gail J. McGovern (appointed head of the $26 billion consumer business of AT&T), and Lois Juliber (appointed head of North American and European operations for Colgate-Palmolive).[9] But there is still a long way to go. A 1996 survey by Catalyst showed that just 2 percent of senior executives at large corporations are women.

closed promotion system

An internal promotion system in which managers choose the workers who will be considered for a promotion.

Handling of promotions and job changes varies from company to company. Some firms use **closed promotion systems** in which managers decide which workers will even be considered for a promotion. In such companies, promotion decisions tend to be made informally and subjectively and to rely heavily on the recommendations of an employee's supervisor. Closed systems remain popular, especially in small firms, because they minimize the time, energy, and cost of making promotion decisions.

open promotion system

An internal promotion system in which all employees are advised of open positions and may apply for those positions if they want.

Other firms maintain **open promotion systems** in which available jobs and their requirements are posted. Employees who feel they possess the qualifications fill out applications, take tests, and interview with managers, much as if they were outside applicants. Open systems allow individual employees to have more say in their career paths. The democratic nature of such systems may also contribute to higher employee morale. But an open system can be time-consuming and expensive. Resources must be spent processing, interviewing, and screening internal applicants.

In addition to open and closed systems, some promotions are determined in part by seniority. Employees with more years of service in the company receive the promotions. This pattern—a standard feature of many union contracts—assures that those promoted have experience. It does not guarantee promotion of the most competent candidate, however.

Developing the Workforce

One of the first things that newcomers participate in is their orientation to the organization. It then falls to personnel experts and other managers to maintain and enhance the employee-job match and employees' performance on the job. Towards this end, some companies have instituted training and development programs on many levels. In addition, every firm has some system for performance appraisal and feedback that helps managers and employees assess the need for more training.

Orientation

The purpose of the **orientation** is to help employees learn about and fit into the company. At one level, the orientation can focus on work hours, parking priorities, and/or pay schedules. People may simply watch films, read manuals, and be introduced to new co-workers. At another level, orientation can indoctrinate the worker into the corporate culture and provide valuable insights into how to succeed.

orientation
The initial acquainting of new employees with the company's policies and programs, personnel with whom they will interact, and the nature of the job.

Employee Training and Development

After orientation, the new employee starts to work. However, both old and new employees may receive training or be enrolled in a development program. Such training generally occurs for one of two reasons: to make up for some deficiency or to give the employee a chance to acquire skills needed for promotion. GM Canada, for example, recently spent $24 million on employee training as part of a program to increase quality levels at its Canadian plants.

Statistics Canada reports that 16 percent of Canadian adults cannot read the majority of written material they encounter in everyday life, and that 22 percent do not have the reading skills to deal with complex instructions. Companies like Northern Telecom and CCL Custom Manufacturing are finding that they have to train workers because the equipment they must use is increasingly complex.[10] A study by the Conference Board of Canada found that large companies spend an average of $475 per year on training employees. This amount is only half as much as American firms spend, and American companies, in turn, spend only a fraction of the amounts that Japanese firms spend.[11]

Many companies are reluctant to retrain older workers, fearing that they are uninterested in training or that the company will not recoup its training investment because the workers have only a few years left in their careers. But Kenworth, the heavy truck manufacturer, found that after it trained a group of older workers, productivity rose nearly 20 percent, and the time spent correcting manufacturing defects dropped from about 40 hours per truck to less than 10.[12]

The reasons for training and development differ, as do the methods used. The most common methods are on-the-job training, off-the-job training, management development programs, networking/mentoring, and assessment centres.[13]

On-the-Job Training

As the term suggests, **on-the-job training** is training that occurs while the employee is actually at work. Ford Motor trained 140 workers for a year to work in a new aluminum casting plant in Windsor, Ontario. Because workers need to know many jobs (e.g., melting aluminum and molding and

on-the-job training
Those development programs in which employees gain new skills while performing them at work.

cleaning engines), they needed a lot of training.[14] Much on-the-job training is unplanned and informal, as when one employee shows another how to use the new photocopier. Someone needs some help, so it is provided.

In other cases, on-the-job training is quite formal. For example, secretaries may learn to operate a new word-processing system at their desks. The advantages of on-the-job training are that it occurs in the real job setting and can be done over an extended period of time. The biggest disadvantage is that distractions on the job site may make training difficult.

Off-the-Job Training

off-the-job training

Those development programs in which employees learn new skills at a location away from the normal work site.

Second Cup

http://www.northernlife.com/second

In contrast, **off-the-job training** is performed at a location away from the work site. It may be at a classroom within the same facility or at a different location altogether. For example, refresher courses are offered for managers of McDonald's 600 Canadian restaurants at the Canadian Institute of Hamburgerology; training videotapes are also shown to restaurant workers.[15] Coffee College is a two-week cram course run by Second Cup Ltd., Canada's largest retailer of specialty coffee. During their stay at Coffee College, franchisees and managers learn how to hire workers, keep the books, detect employee theft, and boost Christmas sales.[16]

For many years, airline pilots and sea-tanker captains have spent time on simulators before actually taking control of planes and ships. Now, freshwater riverboat pilots are also going to be trained with a new simulator that was developed in 1997.[17]

The advantage of off-the-job training is that the instructor can focus intensively on the subject without interruption and in a controlled environment. On the other hand, many off-the-job locations are artificial and lack the realism necessary to really learn more about the job. Many companies therefore do both. The workers at Circo Craft Co. Inc., a maker of printed circuit boards, spent an average of 71 hours in training in 1993. Some of the training was on-the-job and some was off-the-job.[18]

A management trainee learns the ropes at Coffee College, the off-the-job training site run by Second Cup Ltd.

Management Development Programs

These programs are targeted specifically at current or future managers. In contrast to regular training, which focuses on technical skills, **management development programs** try to enhance conceptual, analytical, and problem-solving skills. Most large organizations have management development programs. Some programs are run in-house by managers or training specialists. Others take place at management development centres on university campuses. Still others require managers to get completely away from the workplace and study certain subjects intensively.

management development programs
Those development programs in which current and prospective managers learn new conceptual, analytical, and problem-solving skills.

Networking and Mentoring

In addition, some management development also takes place informally, often through processes known as networking and mentoring. **Networking** refers to informal interactions among managers for the purpose of discussing mutual problems, solutions, and opportunities. Networking takes place in a variety of settings, both inside and outside the office—for example, at conventions and conferences, meetings, business lunches, social gatherings, and so forth.

A mentor is an older, more experienced manager who sponsors and teaches younger, less experienced managers. The mentoring process helps younger managers learn the ropes and benefit from the experiences, insights, and successes (and failures) of senior executives. Networking and mentoring may be especially useful for female and/or minority managers: These individuals may have fewer role models and may be more likely to benefit from greater interaction with experienced managers.

networking
Informal interactions among managers for the purpose of discussing mutual problems, solutions, and opportunities.

Assessment Centres

An **assessment centre** is a series of exercises in which management candidates perform realistic management tasks under the watchful eyes of expert appraisers. Each candidate's potential for management is assessed or appraised.

assessment centre
A series of exercises in which management candidates perform realistic management tasks while being observed by appraisers.

Mentoring can take many forms. Here, two employees informally share information that will be helpful to them in their jobs.

A typical assessment centre might be set up in a large conference room and go on for two or three days. During this time, managers and potential managers might take selection tests, engage in management simulations, make individual presentations, and conduct group discussions. In a program like this the assessors look to see how each participant reacts to stress or to criticism by colleagues. They also watch to see which candidates emerge as leaders of the group discussions.

Performance Appraisal

performance appraisal

A formal program for comparing employees' actual performance with expected performance; used in making decisions about training, promoting, compensating, and firing.

Performance appraisals are formal evaluations of how well workers are doing their jobs. Every company assesses the performance of its employees in some way, even if it is only the owner telling the only employee, a receptionist, "Good job. You're getting a raise." In larger firms, the process is more extensive. A formal performance evaluation system generally involves a regularly scheduled written assessment. The written evaluation, however, is only one part of a multistep process.

The appraisal process begins when a manager makes job performance expectations clear to an employee. The manager must then observe the employee's performance. If the standards are clearly defined, a manager should have little difficulty with the next step—comparing expectations with actual performance. For some jobs, a rating scale like that illustrated in Figure 9.3 is useful. This comparison forms the basis for a written appraisal and for

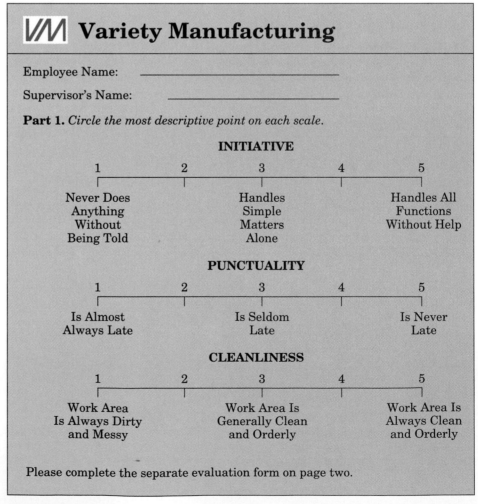

Figure 9.3
Graphic rating scales such as this one are common methods of performance appraisal.

decisions about any raise, promotion, demotion, or firing of the employee. The final step in the appraisal process is for the manager to meet with the employee to discuss the appraisal.

When job performance expectations are based on the actual requirements of the job, formal appraisals benefit both the company and workers. The company is protected from lawsuits charging unfair treatment. It also has a reasonably objective basis on which to compare individuals for promotions. Workers benefit from clear goals to work towards and knowledge of how well they are doing. They often feel that such systems are fairer than subjective evaluations. Performance appraisals pose some potentially significant problems for companies, as described in the box "Here We Go Again!"

Terminating and Demoting Workers

Written appraisals are especially important when a business must fire or demote employees either because of poor worker performance or because the firm

The Canadian Business Scene

Here We Go Again!

It sounds perfectly reasonable to say that employees should have their work appraised at regular intervals. Yet surveys of both managers and employees reveal that the process is frequently disliked. W. Edwards Deming, the quality guru, called performance appraisals the "deadly disease."

Performance reviews are supposed to benefit both employees and the company. If workers are informed of their weaknesses, the argument goes, they will be able to develop a plan to overcome them. After the weaknesses are overcome, workers will feel better about themselves and the company will benefit. In fact, it often doesn't work this way because people don't want to hear *anything* negative about their performance. Even when a performance review is generally positive, all the worker may remember is the few negative points that the boss made. And, if employees believe that their boss doesn't like them, they may be convinced that they will get a negative rating even if they're doing good work.

It isn't just subordinates that don't like performance appraisals—managers don't either. They particularly don't like giving negative feedback to subordinates because strained future relations often result. One study showed that 98 percent of managers who gave negative feedback encountered some form of hostility or aggression from employees. Most of this aggression is verbal, but there have been a number of well-publicized cases where subordinates killed their bosses after a negative performance review.

When managers dislike performance appraisals, it is likely that they will spend insufficient time working on them. Research suggests that the typical manager spends about one hour preparing for and giving feedback to an employee. An added problem is that managers aren't sure how to do performance appraisals because their firm has given them very little guidance about how to conduct a performance appraisal. Emphasis is placed on filling out

performance appraisal forms rather than on doing a meaningful performance appraisal.

Besides this basic human aversion to performance appraisals on the part of managers and workers, several other things have happened during the last decade that have caused performance appraisals to become problematic. First, as companies have downsized, managers have ended up with larger groups of subordinates to manage and appraise. These managers feel overwhelmed and overworked, and feel they don't have enough time to do performance appraisals. Second, as more emphasis is placed on work *teams,* managers wonder how they can evaluate *individuals.* Third, as companies move people around from job to job, performance appraisals are harder to carry out and interpret.

Do the problems with performance appraisals, and the suggestions for change mean that things are going to change anytime soon? Not likely. Companies will probably continue to carry out performance reviews because they do not see an easy alternative. As well, in an era when employees increasingly sue companies for wrongful dismissal, the documents generated during the performance appraisal process may provide a critical record of an employee's work so the firm can defend itself. Of course, if the record doesn't show substandard work by the employee, this may harm the company more than help it.

Some human resource management consultants think that the problems with performance appraisals are so significant that they should just be abandoned and replaced with an emphasis on goal setting and giving constant feedback to employees. This approach involves setting clear performance goals for employees and then giving them feeback on how well they are doing. Research has consistently demonstrated that these two activities increase employee productivity.

is reorganizing or is in economic trouble. Whether the worker or the company is the problem, demoting or firing employees is one of the duties a manager least wants to perform. For example, managers who dismiss subordinates as part of a downsizing may become very depressed themselves as they think about all the people whose jobs they terminated. The task may be made easier by writing a glowing recommendation or securing a good severance arrangement for an employee let go because of company changes. And when the employee is causing a problem, a systematic process can help the manager—and the employee.

Most companies with formal systems have a step-by-step process of warnings and punishments leading up to dismissal. For the first warning, the manager might talk informally to the employee, expressing disappointment over the problem—poor job performance or attendance, for example. To protect itself from lawsuits, many companies require managers to give the offending employee a written warning. An employee causing a problem can also expect to hear about it during a formal appraisal. At that time, the manager will specify certain changes that the employee must make or lose the job. This system not only protects the company, it also lets employees know that their jobs are in jeopardy and offers them a chance to do better.

If a problem persists, a manager may have little choice but to discipline, demote, or dismiss the employee. Disciplinary actions—such as suspending a worker from the job without pay for several days—are usually taken only when the employee's behaviour is dangerous or disruptive. For example, someone who strikes a fellow worker might be sent home to "cool off."

demotion

Reducing the rank of a person who is not performing up to standard.

Demotions are most often used when managerial personnel fail to meet expectations. For example, a sales manager who is performing poorly may be demoted to sales representative. Demoted managers are often humiliated by this downgrading and seek jobs elsewhere.

termination

Firing an employee who is not performing up to standard.

Finally, in extreme cases, outright **termination** of the employee may be the only recourse. For example, a salesperson who continually falls far short of the established quota may be a drag on corporate profitability. Although firing is never pleasant, managers of companies with sound human resource policies can take some solace in knowing that, by the time such a dismissal takes place, the employee should be expecting it.

Companies must now be extremely careful when dismissing employees. A general manager at Jumbo Video Inc., who was fired when he refused to take a large pay cut, was awarded more than $226 000 in damages. The manager had earlier signed a contract containing certain stipulations that the company later tried to void because of financial problems. The judge ruled that the company had reneged on the contract.[19] The box "The World of 'Unjust Dismissal'" gives further information on the issue of employee dismissal.

alternate dispute resolution

The employee and the company agree to submit their dispute to binding arbitration.

Employees and employers are beginning to use **alternate dispute resolution** (ADR) with increasing frequency. Suppose an employee is dismissed and feels that it is a wrongful dismissal. The employee and the company agree to submit the dispute to binding arbitration with no appeal of the decision possible. This saves both parties considerable time and money.[20]

Compensation and Benefits

compensation system

What a firm offers its employees in return for their labour.

A major factor in retaining skilled workers is a company's **compensation system**—what it offers employees in return for their labour. Wages and salaries are a key part of any compensation system, but most systems also include features such as incentives and employee benefits programs. We will explore each of these elements in this section. Bear in mind, however, that finding the right combination of elements is complicated by the need to make

The Canadian Business Scene

The World of "Unjust Dismissal"

Legislation on unjust dismissal was added to the *Canada Labour Code* in 1978. It covers nonunionized, nonmanagement employees in federally regulated industries such as banking, transportation, and telecommunications and is designed to provide a cheap, fast, and effective route for employees to appeal an unfair firing without having to go to court.

An employee who thinks he or she has been unjustly fired files a complaint with Labour Canada. If the complaint is judged worthwhile, the employer is contacted and asked to give the reason why the employee was fired. A Labour Canada inspector then reviews the case and tries to persuade the two parties to agree. If the parties cannot agree, the case is sent to an adjudicator who either upholds the dismissal or orders the employee reinstated. If either side disputes the judgment, it can request a judicial review.

The legislation requires that the employee be given the benefit of the doubt whenever possible. The company must prove it had "just cause" in firing the person. Since adjudicators do not have to base their decisions on precedent, it is difficult for a company to predict the outcome of a complaint.

Critics of the legislation point to cases in which they feel poor decisions were made. Consider the case of a Canadian Imperial Bank of Commerce employee who was fired because of her off-hours associations. Police burst into her apartment at precisely the time five men were dividing the loot from a robbery at a nearby CIBC branch. The Labour Canada adjudicator who reviewed the case ruled that the bank did not have "just cause" for firing her because she had not done anything wrong herself. CIBC was ordered to give her back pay. A supervisor at another bank got her job back even after she admitted that she had planned to steal customers' money. A consumer credit officer in another firm was reinstated despite his conviction on weapons charges.

Because of the time and risk involved, many employers settle before the adjudication stage. Nearly 75 percent of the 600 complaints that are brought annually are resolved before they get to adjudication and another 10 percent are resolved before the adjudicator's report. Critics of the legislation argue that the cost of the procedure and the potential for reinstatement give "daring" employees an incentive to complain. They would like to see more training of adjudicators, transcriptions of proceedings, and adjudicators given the right to award costs against a frivolous complaint.

Even prominent managers may go to court over wrongful dismissal. Robert Campeau, who took Campeau Corp. to the edge of bankruptcy, is asking for damages of $10 million from the company. He claims his employment was improperly terminated when he was fired as CEO of Campeau. When Joel Bell was fired as head of Canada Development Investment Corp., he received $3.3 million in a wrongful dismissal suit.

employees feel valued while simultaneously keeping company costs to a minimum. Thus, compensation systems are highly individualized, depending on the nature of the industry, the company, and the types of workers involved.

Wages and Salaries

Wages and salaries are the dollar amounts paid to employees for their work. **Wages** are dollars paid for time worked or for number of units produced. Workers who are paid by the hour receive wages. Canadian manufacturing workers are among the highest paid workers in the world. Only German workers receive higher wages.[21]

With the exception of the U.S., the compensation of Canadian CEOs does not appear to be out of line with what executives in other countries earn (Canadian CEOs earned about $438 000 per year, while their U.S. counterparts earned about $871 000). The average Canadian CEO earns 13 times the pay of the average Canadian worker. In Sweden, the multiple is 9, in the U.S. 24, in Singapore 38, and in Mexico 44. Canada ranks 16 out of 22 countries in CEO pay levels.[22]

Salary is the money an employee receives for getting a job done. An executive earning $100 000 per year may work five hours one day and fifteen the next. Such an individual is paid to get a job done rather than for the specific

wages

Dollars paid based on the number of hours worked or the number of units produced.

salary

Dollars paid at regular intervals in return for doing a job, regardless of the amount of time or output involved.

number of hours or days spent working. Salaries are usually expressed as an amount to be paid per year but are often paid each month or every two weeks.

In setting wage and salary levels, a company must consider several factors. First, it must take into account how its competitors compensate their employees. A firm that pays less than its rivals may soon find itself losing valuable personnel.

Within the company, the firm must also decide how wage and salary levels for different jobs will compare. And within wage and salary levels, managers must decide how much to pay individual workers. Two employees may do exactly the same job, but the employee with more experience may earn more, in part to keep that person in the company and in part because the experienced person performs better. Some union contracts specify differential wages based on experience. Note that the basis for differential pay must be job-related, however, not favouritism or discrimination.

Incentive Programs

incentive program

Any program in which a company offers its workers additional pay over and above the normal wage or salary level in order to motivate them to perform at a higher-than-normal level.

The term **incentive programs** refers to special pay programs designed to motivate high performance. The use of incentive programs increased in the 1980s, largely because of concern for productivity.

Sales bonuses are a typical incentive. Under such a program, employees who sell a certain number or dollar amount of goods for the year receive a special payment. Employees who do not reach this goal earn no bonus. Similarly, *merit salary systems* link raises to performance levels in non-sales jobs. For example, many baseball players have clauses in their contracts that pay them bonuses for hitting over .300, making the All-Star game, or being named Most Valuable Player. Executives commonly receive stock options and bonuses as an incentive. The box "Compensation at the Top" deals with the sometimes controversial issue of compensation levels of top executives.

gain-sharing plan

An incentive program in which employees receive a bonus if the firm's costs are reduced because of greater worker efficiency and/or productivity.

Some incentive programs apply to all employees in a firm. **Gain-sharing plans** distribute bonuses to all employees in a company based on reduced costs from working more efficiently. Palliser Furniture Ltd. introduced a gain-sharing plan that rewards employees for increasing production. Any profit resulting from production above a certain level is split 50-50 between the company and the employees.[23]

profit-sharing plan

An incentive program in which employees receive a bonus depending on the firm's profits.

Profit-sharing plans are based on profit levels in the firm. Profits earned above a certain level are distributed to employees. Stock ownership by employees serves as an incentive to lower costs, increase productivity and profits, and thus increase the value of the employees' stock.[24]

Comparable Worth

In spite of recent advances, the *average* woman still earns only about three-quarters of what the average man earns; *single* women, however, earn 99 percent of what single men earn. In 1969, women earned only 59 percent of what men earned. The most recent gains by women have occurred because men lost four of every five jobs that disappeared during the early 1990s. But most top jobs in the public and private sector continue to be held by men.[25]

comparable worth

A legal idea that aims to pay equal wages for work of equal value.

Comparable worth is a legal concept that aims at paying equal wages for jobs that are of comparable value to the employer. This might mean comparing dissimilar jobs, such as those of nurses and mechanics or secretaries and electricians. Proponents of comparable worth say that all the jobs in a company must be evaluated and then rated in terms of basic dimensions such as the level of skill they require. All jobs could then be compared

The Canadian Business Scene

Compensation at the Top

The average family income in Canada is about $54 000 per year. The chief justice of the Supreme Court of Canada and the president of the University of Toronto receive about $200 000 per year. Although a salary of $200 000 would be considered very comfortable by the average person, it is relatively insignificant compared to the compensation that top business managers receive. The following are examples of total compensation that some top Canadian CEOs received in 1996:

Laurent Beaudoin (Bombardier Inc.)	$19.1 million
Michael Brown (Thomson Corp.)	$11.3 million
Francesco Bellini (BioChem Pharma Inc.)	$9.9 million
William Holland (United Dominion)	$8.9 million
Gerald Schwartz (Onex Corp.)	$8.3 million
William Stinson (Canadian Pacific)	$8.3 million

Managers who earned $1 million did not even make it on the "top 50" list. Hundreds of other managers across Canada earn between $500 000 and $1 million per year.

In addition to getting high compensation when they are working for a company, executives may also receive large compensation when they leave. When Paul Stern resigned as president and CEO of Northern Telecom, the company came up with a severance package that totalled approximately $3 million. This included two years' salary and benefits, 10 years of credited service to his pension plan, and the purchase of his home.

Some business firms will end up paying large sums of money to executives after they retire. An executive who earned a large salary during his or her time with the company may represent a liability to the company of more than $5 million dollars (assuming that the executive lives for 15 years after he or she retires).

In spite of this, the compensation of top Canadian managers does not appear to be out of line in comparison with what executives in other countries are paid. While Canadian salaries are higher than those of top executives in Japan and Germany, they are much lower than those in the United States.

Besides the question of absolute salaries paid to top executives, there is the issue of whether their salaries should move up and down in relation to their company's performance. Does this happen? Sometimes, but it is not hard to find cases where executive salaries go up while company profit goes down. For example, Imperial Oil Ltd. where, in a year when profit fell 37 percent, Chairman Arden Haynes' total compensation package went up 12 percent. Similar situations were evident in other companies, including Bell Canada Enterprises, Canadian Occidental Petroleum, Canadian Pacific, and Westcoast Transmission Co. Ltd.

Recent Statistics Canada data show that the average hourly paid worker in Canada earns slightly more than $20 000 per year. Are the large differences in compensation between hourly workers and CEOs warranted? How do we determine what a top executive is worth? Those who defend large executive salaries suggest an instructive comparison with professional sports, where one superstar can make a team. A similar argument might be made that a certain CEO could make a company. As in professional sports, a business firm may have little alternative but to pay a seemingly large salary to a top manager.

A key issue in this debate is the determination of executive performance. Unlike a professional superstar—whose performance stats are objective and easily measured, a top executive operates in an environment of considerable uncertainty. How should executive performance be measured? Ideally, the board of directors should clearly indicate the goals they want the company to achieve (for example, a certain level of competitiveness or quality), and then reward the CEO for achieving those goals. Unfortunately, many boards do not have the confidence or insight to set such goals. They may also be reluctant to deal firmly with CEOs on the issue of salary.

But shareholders have no such reluctance, and they are increasingly demanding a say in executive compensation decisions. For example, there has recently been much lobbying for laws that force companies to disclose the salaries and benefit schemes of their executives. Under new rules imposed in 1993 in Ontario, most Canadian companies with public shareholders must state the dollar amounts that the CEO and the four top-paid people in the company earn.

To many critics, it is simply not right that top managers receive 20, 50, or even 100 times more than their workers receive. They argue that it is unethical to pay top executives $1 million or $5 million per year for what they do. Professor Henry Mintzberg of McGill University says that these salary levels send a terrible message to the average working person, particularly since many top managers frequently talk about how important employees are. Mintzberg says that real leadership qualities are shown by top managers who take salaries in the range of $250 000 to $500 000.

Is it unethical for top managers to receive such high salaries? What do you think?

based on a common index. People in different jobs that rate the same on this index would be paid the same. Experts hope that this will help to reduce the gap between men's and women's pay.

Critics of comparable worth object on the grounds that it ignores the supply and demand aspects of labour. They say, for example, that legislation forcing a company to pay people more than the open market price for their labour (which may happen in jobs where there is a surplus of workers) is another example of unreasonable government interference in business activities. They also say that implementing comparable worth will cost business firms too much money. A study prepared for the Ontario Ministry of Labour estimated that it would cost approximately $10 billion for the public and private sectors in Ontario to establish equitable payment for jobs of equal value. Yet the cost defence cannot be easily used. In one case, the Quebec Human Rights Commission ruled that 24 female office employees of the Quebec North Shore Paper Company were performing work of equal value to that done by male production workers. The company was required to increase the secretaries' salaries by $701 annually and give them over $1000 in back pay.[26]

There is one very interesting fact in this debate about comparable worth: Male earning power has been declining for decades. Young males who are now entering the labour market, regardless of their education, will likely earn dramatically less than their predecessors. Young, female university graduates, on the other hand, have recently earned more than their predecessors.[27]

Benefits Programs

A growing part of nearly every firm's compensation system is **benefits** programs—compensation other than wages and salaries. Benefits now often comprise over half a firm's total compensation budget. Most companies are required by law to provide workers' compensation, holiday pay, and Canada

Ontario Ministry of Labour
http://www.gov.on.ca/LAB/main.htm

benefits
What a firm offers its workers other than wages and salaries in return for their labour.

Benefits are an important part of most compensation programs. Some are provided by the employer while others are mandated by the government. A new parental leave provision allows either parent to take up to 10 weeks of paid leave after the birth or adoption of a child.

Pension Plan and employment insurance contributions. Most businesses also voluntarily provide extended health, life, and disability insurance. Many also allow employees to buy stock through payroll deductions at a slightly discounted price. In the 1980s, many firms began to provide vision care and dental benefits to employees. Some even provide free legal services to employees.

As the range of benefits has grown, so has concern about containing their cost. Businesses are experimenting with a variety of procedures to cut benefits costs, while maintaining the ability to attract, retain, and maintain the morale of employees.[28] One approach is the use of **cafeteria benefits**. These plans provide a set dollar amount in benefits and allow employees to pick among alternatives. Employees at Toyota's Cambridge, Ontario, plant are given the opportunity once each year to structure their benefits packages. For example, they can give more weight to dental coverage if they have young children, or to life insurance or disability coverage, depending on their circumstances.[29]

cafeteria benefits
A flexible approach to providing benefits in which employees are allocated a certain sum to cover benefits and can "spend" this allocation on the specific benefits they prefer.

Employee Safety and Health

Employee safety and health programs help to reduce absenteeism and labour turnover, raise productivity, and boost morale by making jobs safer and more healthful.

Government regulations about employee safety are getting stricter. Ontario, which loses more than 7 million working days yearly because of on-the-job injuries, has passed amendments to the Ontario *Occupational Health and Safety Act*. Officers and directors of companies are held personally responsible for workplace health and safety and are punishable by jail terms and fines for permitting unsafe working conditions.[30]

Some industrial work—logging, construction, fishing, and mining—can put workers at risk of injury in obvious ways. But other types of work—such as typing or lifting—can also cause painful injuries. **Repetitive strain injuries** (RSIs) occur when workers perform the same functions over and over again. These injuries disable more than 200 000 Canadians each year and account for nearly half of all work-related time loss claims.

repetitive strain injuries
Injuries that occur when workers perform the same functions over and over again.

In Canada, each province has developed its own workplace health and safety regulations. The purpose of these laws is to ensure that employees do not have to work in dangerous conditions. These laws are the direct result of undesirable conditions that existed in many Canadian businesses at the close of the 19th century. While much improvement is evident, Canada still has some problems with workplace health and safety. In one study of six Western industrialized nations, Canada had the worst safety record in mining and construction and the second worst record in manufacturing and railways.

The Ontario *Occupational Health and Safety Act* illustrates current legislation in Canada. It requires that all employers ensure that equipment and safety devices are used properly. Employers must also show workers the proper way to operate machinery. At the job site, supervisors are charged with the responsibility of seeing that workers use equipment properly. The act also requires workers to behave appropriately on the job. Employees have the right to refuse to work on a job if they believe it is unsafe; a legal procedure exists for resolving any disputes in this area.

In most provinces, the Ministry of Labour appoints inspectors to enforce health and safety regulations. If the inspector finds a sufficient hazard, he or she has the authority to clear the workplace. Inspectors can usually come to a firm unannounced to conduct an inspection.

Retirement

Some employees are ready for retirement earlier than others. But because many retirement plans are based on an employee's age, some workers who should retire earlier stay on the job while others, who are still useful workers, leave before they would like to. This policy is shortsighted. A compromise is to grant year-to-year extensions to productive employees who want to continue working past the traditional retirement age.

During the past decade, workers in several different locations across Canada have successfully challenged mandatory retirement rules. Their employers must therefore allow them to continue working, even though they are past the traditional retirement age of 65. Some executives are also deciding to work past age 65 because their companies need their expertise. Arthur Childs (CEO of Burns Foods), Sol Kanee (Soo Line Mills Ltd.), Vernon Aanenson (Old Dutch Foods), and Jack Diamond (Western Coast Reduction Ltd.) continued to work into their seventies and eighties.

In spite of these individual exceptions, Canadians generally are retiring earlier than they used to. In the period 1976–80, for example, the median retirement age in Canada was 64.9 years, but in the period 1991–95 that figure dropped to 62.3 years.[31] Two other interesting facts: Workers over age 65 are nearly four times as likely to die from work-related causes than younger workers, and older workers have double the health care costs that workers in their forties do.[32]

Other Services

Human resource departments also provide many other services, which vary widely among firms. These range from setting policies to deal with allegations of sexual harassment on the job to helping employees arrange car pools.

At Levac Supply Ltd. of Kingston, Ontario, one employee harassed another with derogatory remarks over a 14-year period. In spite of the fact that the Ontario *Human Rights Code* excludes companies from liability in the case of sexual harassment (as long as they make a reasonable effort to stop the harassment), a board of inquiry ruled that the company was jointly responsible with the employee who had actually done the harassing. The woman who was harassed was awarded $48 273 in a settlement.[33]

Time and circumstances greatly affect the nature of human resource work. For example, a firm may experience a big decrease in one department's workload and a big increase in another department's workload. The human resource department might help the two department managers to shift workers between departments, help arrange retraining if that is needed, or help to develop a plan for sharing the available work among employees—shorter work weeks for all workers or layoffs in order of seniority.

Summary of Learning Objectives

1. **Define *human resource management* and explain why businesses must consider job relatedness criteria when managing human resources.** Human resource management involves developing, administering, and evaluating programs to acquire and enhance the quality and performance of people in a business. Good managers always bear in mind the principle of job-relatedness—that human resource decisions and policies should be based on the requirements of a job. Managers who apply this principle and match the right employee to the right job produce satisfied, effective workers.

2. **Discuss how managers plan for human resources.** Planning for future human resource needs entails several steps. Conducting a job analysis enables managers to create detailed, job-related job descriptions and specifications. Managers must then forecast supply and demand for

the types of workers they will need. Only then can managers devise strategies to match supply with demand.

3. **Identify the steps involved in *staffing* a company.** Staffing a business may involve hiring from outside the company. Such external staffing requires the company first to recruit applicants and then to select from among the applicants. Companies must ensure that they do not discriminate against candidates during this phase of the process. The selection phase typically includes interviewing, testing, and checking the references of applicants. Whenever possible, however, many companies prefer to fill positions internally, by promoting existing personnel.

4. **Describe ways in which managers can develop workers' skills and deal with workers who do not perform well.** If a company is to get the most out of its workers, it must develop those workers. Nearly all employees undergo some initial orientation process. Many also acquire new skills through on-the-job training, off-the-job training, and/or management development programs. Performance appraisals help managers decide who needs training and who should be promoted. Appraisals also tell employees how well they are doing at meeting expectations. Employees who continually fail to meet performance or behaviour expectations may be disciplined, demoted, or terminated.

5. **Explain the importance of wages and salaries, incentives, and benefits programs in attracting and keeping skilled workers.** Compensation programs include wages and salaries, incentives, and benefits for workers. By paying its workers as well as or better than competitors do, a business can attract and keep qualified personnel. Incentive programs such as sales bonuses, gain-sharing, and profit-sharing can also motivate existing personnel to work more effectively. Benefits programs may increase employee satisfaction but are a major expense to businesses today.

6. **Describe how laws regarding *employment equity*, *pay equity*, and *worker safety* affect human resource management.** In hiring, training, compensating and/or firing workers, managers must obey many laws. Equal employment opportunity and equal pay laws forbid discrimination other than that based on legitimate job requirements. Controversy over what constitutes discrimination in paying men and women who hold different jobs is a current issue. Managers are also required to provide employees with a safe working environment.

Key Terms

human resource management, 251
job-relatedness, 252
job analysis, 252
job description, 253
job specification, 253
recruitment, 255
Canadian Human Rights Act, 255
bona fide occupational requirement, 256
Employment Equity Act of 1986, 257

selection, 257
closed promotion system, 260
open promotion system, 260
orientation, 261
on-the-job training, 261
off-the-job training, 262
management development programs, 263
networking, 263
assessment centre, 263

performance appraisal, 264
demotion, 266
termination, 266
alternate dispute resolution, 266
compensation system, 266
wages, 267
salary, 267
incentive program, 268
gain-sharing plan, 268

profit-sharing plan, 268
comparable worth, 268
benefits, 270
cafeteria benefits, 271
repetitive strain injuries, 271

Study Questions and Exercises

Review Questions

1. Why is a good employee-job match important? Who benefits more, the organization or the employee? Why?
2. Identify as many advantages and disadvantages as you can for internal and external staffing. Under what circumstances is each more appropriate?
3. Why is formal training so important? Why not just let people learn about their jobs as they do them?

Analysis Questions

4. How are overtime wages different from and similar to incentive program payments?
5. Select a job currently held by you or a close friend or relative. Draw up a job description and job specification for this position.
6. Did you have to take a test to be admitted to school? How valid do you think your score was as a predictor of academic success? Why?

7. What benefits do you consider most and least important in attracting workers? In keeping workers? In motivating workers?
8. Have you or anyone you know been discriminated against in a hiring decision? Was anything done about it?

Application Exercises

9. Interview a human resource manager at a local company. Select a position for which the firm is currently recruiting applicants and identify the steps in the selection process.
10. Obtain a copy of an employment application. Examine it carefully and determine how useful it might be in making a hiring decision.

Building Your Business Skills

Goal

To aid students in understanding the complexity of writing human resources regulations that affect employee behaviour in controversial areas.

Situation

As the human resource director of a manufacturing company with 400 employees, your mission is to revise sections of the employee handbook covering three of today's most important issues:

- sexual harassment
- diversity training
- drug testing of job candidates and current employees.

Method

Step 1:
Work with three other students to research each of these areas. Through library research and interviews with human resources executives in local companies, try to find out as much as you can in each of the following areas:

- Current laws and regulatory requirements

- What other corporations are doing in each area
- How employees are responding to increasingly stringent rules.

Step 2:
Working in groups, develop written guidelines for your company handbook. Try to be as specific as possible. Keep in mind that the handbook will be given to current employees and job candidates.

Step 3:
Compare your findings with those of other teams.

Follow-Up Questions

1. Based on your research, which of the three areas poses the most difficulty for employers? For employees? Why?

2. Given what you know about the difficulty that many companies have in eliminating sexual harassment and discrimination in the workplace, do you think that education (in the form of clear employee guidelines and diversity training) or disciplinary action (perhaps even demotions and dismissals) is the key to change? Explain your answer.

3. Support the position that pre-employment drug tests are fair to job candidates.

EXPLORING the Net

To find out what a real-world company would like you to know about its human resources policies and programs, log on to McDonald's, Careers, at:

http://www.mcdonalds.com./careers/index.html

After you have read the material, consider the following questions:

1. Which of the skills listed by McDonald's would you list under your own strong points? Under your weak points? Which one or two skills do you think you need to focus on most conscientiously?

2. Why do you think McDonald's puts so much emphasis on career advancement within the company? Why does it put so much emphasis on the awards earned by the company's training program? In what respects are these important criteria for you?

3. What do you think the word "opportunities" should mean in a slogan like "McDonald's Means Opportunities"?

CONCLUDING CASE 9-1

Up and Out

Donovan Retzlaffe, chairman and chief executive officer (CEO) of Lanark Products Ltd., announced on July 1, 1994, that he had reluctantly accepted the resignation of the firm's vice-chairman, Lorenzo Valli. In his announcement, Retzlaffe indicated that Valli had served the firm well and had been a "rock of Gibraltar" during the 49 years he had worked there.

The rise of Valli from mailroom clerk to vice-chairman is the stuff that legends are made of. Valli constantly said that there was nothing more important than loyalty to the firm. He joined Lanark in 1945 at the age of 19. He began working in the mailroom, and over the next 43 years gradually worked his way up the corporate ladder until he became vice-chairman in 1988. Valli fondly remembers the time that the company loaned him $4500 in 1963 to pay some legal bills that he had incurred. Valli was a no-nonsense, simple man. When he stepped down, he still lived in the same modest home that he had purchased in 1965.

Although the public announcement indicated that Valli had resigned, insiders at Lanark knew that he had actually been asked to leave because his management style was just too "abrasive" for the new image Lanark Products Ltd. was cultivating. It was also widely believed that there was a basic personality conflict between the CEO and Valli, even though the two had been working closely together for about 10 years. Some senior managers expressed the view

that the company should never have given Valli the position of vice-chairman if they thought his style was too abrasive.

The "resignation" of Valli had some industry observers worried because of other events at Lanark. Employment statistics in early 1994 showed that nearly half of Lanark's upper management personnel had been with the firm for less than two years. This was partially the result of rapid expansion of the firm's activities. There had also been a rather large number of middle level managers leaving the firm. Although the reasons weren't completely clear, there were indications that they were not happy with the new direction of the firm.

Case Questions

1. Do you think that Lanark Ltd. treated Valli fairly in asking him to resign after 49 years of service?

2. Was his dismissal handled properly? How would you have handled the situation?

3. If you were the CEO of Lanark Ltd., would you be concerned that nearly half the top managers had been with the firm for less than two years? If you were concerned, what would you do about it? How would you go about determining if there is a problem with the middle level of managers?

◆

CONCLUDING CASE 9-2

Freelancing

When people think about careers, they usually think of going to work full-time for a company and, if they like it, staying at that company for many years. In fact, until recently the notion of "lifetime employment" was touted as the wave of the future. Even if a person didn't stay at one firm, the idea still was that the person would work full-time for a company for at least a few years.

But times are changing. A growing number of workers are becoming freelancers—individuals who contract with a company for a set period of time, usually until a specific project is completed. After the project is completed, the freelancer moves on to another project in the firm, or to another firm. Statistics Canada estimates that 30 percent of working adults are doing non-standard work such as freelancing.

Why is this happening? The main reason is that competitive pressures are forcing firms to reduce their costs and increase their productivity. The current buzzword is "flexibility" and this can often be achieved by hiring freelancers to solve specific company problems. This allows a firm to maintain a minimum number of full-time workers and then supplement them with freelancers.

Some people freelance because they can't get full-time work with one company, but others freelance by choice. Accomplished freelancers can control their own destiny, make above-average incomes, and have a strong sense of flexibility and freedom. Typically, freelancers don't get paid company benefits like full-time workers do, but pressures are building to change this. In 1994, the province of Saskatchewan became the first in Canada to require companies to pay contract and part-time workers at least some benefits.

Many banks and insurance companies have trouble seeing the needs of contract workers. To them, it may appear that the contract worker is not really employed on a steady basis because they work for so many different companies. Creative Arts Management Service is a firm that fills this void. It offers business advice, financial planning, budgeting, and legal services for contract workers. The firm takes the view that freelancing, if properly planned and executed, is the best security in the new economy of the 1990s.

While the work of technical or professional employees is often contracted out to freelancers, the management of various functions may also be contracted out. The Halifax District School Board contracted out the management of custodial services for the district's 42 schools to ServiceMaster Canada Ltd. The school district expects to save more than half a million dollars each year. And Manpower Temporary Services manages a packaging department for a pharmaceutical firm that sometimes numbers up to 130 people, and sometimes as few as 70, depending on demand. A Manpower manager is on site at the pharmaceutical firm; she recruits the temporary workers, does some of the necessary training, conducts performance appraisals of temporary workers, and handles the payroll.

Management experts predict that freelancing will increase in importance. With the massive layoffs that have been evident in recent years, workers are beginning to realize that job security is not provided by large firms. Rather, security comes from having confidence in your own knowledge and skills, and marketing yourself in innovative ways. Freelancing has been facilitated by the recent advances in information technology, since workers do not necessarily have to be at the workplace in order to do their work.

There are both positive and negative aspects to the idea of non-standard work. From the worker's perspective, those with marketable skills will find that non-standard work will result in high pay and satisfying work. For those without marketable skills, non-standard work will likely mean part-time work in low-paying service jobs. Those individuals who lack either the ability or interest to capitalize on non-standard work will find that there is much uncertainty in their careers.

From the organization's perspective, a conclusion about the value of non-standard work means weighing the value of long-term employee loyalty and commitment against the benefits of the increased flexibility that is possible with part-time freelancers.

Case Questions

1. What kind of people are most likely to want freelance work?

2. What are the pros and cons of freelance work from the individual's perspective? From the organization's perspective?

3. Is it unethical to hire freelancers in order to avoid paying company benefits to them?

◆

10

Motivating and Leading Employees

Making Peace with the Workforce

In the 1980s, forestry giant MacMillan Bloedel went through a traumatic time of downsizing, closing mills, shutting down machines, and reducing its workforce by 25 000 people. Today it is a very 90s company—trim size, a big presence in the Japanese market, and many innovative products coming from its mills and laboratories. Despite all of its restructuring, however, the company still lost money in 1991 and 1992, and still suffers from competitive disadvantages. A Price-Waterhouse survey showed that the labour cost component of a tonne of pulp from the B.C. coast was $129, compared to $94 for eastern Canada and $84 for the southern U.S. And the company still suffers from outdated human resource practices, which hamper its drive to become more competitive.

Labour relations have never been particularly good at the company. On three different occasions in the 1980s the company experienced wildcat (unauthorized) strikes. Each time, the company sued the union for lost revenue, and each time they won cash awards and workplace concessions. The regional vice-president of the union says that there is not a lot of trust in the relationship between workers and the company. Further compounding the problem was a remark by the company's president in 1990 that the problems with the Canadian workforce meant that the company would be expanding operations only in the U.S.

To resolve its many problems, the company is embarking on a strategy to get its workers more involved in decision making. Several new ideas have been introduced by management, including the following:

- Production plans and financial data are now shared with workers at regular intervals.

- Division managers take union reps on trips to competing mills to show them just how competitive the market has become.

- Joint union/management committees encourage suggestions from workers on how productivity can be improved.

But much distrust remains. At the Port Alberni mill, management and workers struck a deal where the company would spend $5 million to extend early-retirement benefits, and the union would institute much more flexible working arrangements. For example, in the past, if a millwright wanted to work on a pump and needed pipes disconnected, the millwright had to wait for a pipefitter to disconnect the pipes. Now, a worker can do as much of a job as he or she is able to do. Unfortunately, the Port Alberni agreement is falling apart because of poor communication and misunderstood goals. The workers were supposed to "pay back" the $5 million in increased productivity, but when these goals were not reached, the company announced that it would lay off another 200 workers.

The agreement ran into difficulty because the workers thought they were going to get new investment in the plant and more jobs. The company thought the workers were agreeing to be more cooperative. Workers are now being warned that workplace reforms contain no guarantees. The union has responded by promising to be much less cooperative in the future.

There are still difficulties at Port Alberni. During a strike in 1994, the provincial labour board ruled that workers from TNL Construction should be allowed to cross the picket line. When they tried, a riot ensued. Union officials said the company "set up" the union and caused the trouble by contracting for TNL to do work for the company.

The company has been more successful at the Chemainus mill on Vancouver Island. There, employees are organized into work teams and meet with management each week to make suggestions for improving operations. A gain-sharing program was instituted and started paying out bonuses for productivity. In 1992, for example, each worker received an $11 500 bonus. Company management, concerned because the payout to workers reflected the falling Canadian dollar and skyrocketing lumber prices far more than it did increases in worker productivity, demanded that the plan be redesigned. If properly handled, a gain-sharing program can benefit both the company and workers. The company says that 30 percent of the division's sales increase in 1992 was caused by increased productivity.

Attitude adjustments are still necessary. While the company talks of teamwork and flexibility, it still threatened to sue the union for a one-day wildcat strike over company plans to discontinue bus service for workers. For its part, the union says it is willing to talk about increasing the company's competitiveness, but it interprets every initiative as a threat to the status quo. Perhaps the company has discovered the key to better employee relations—money. For people to produce more, they must see some personal benefit in doing so. ◆

Because a firm's human resources are its most important asset, managers must effectively motivate, lead, and satisfy employees. In this chapter, we will explore the reasons why satisfied employees are an asset to any company. We will also consider some of the approaches managers have taken to satisfy employees over the years. Increasingly, companies are looking for ways to enhance worker's job satisfaction and to develop managers with the leadership skills to meet both employee and corporate goals.

By focusing on the learning objectives of this chapter, you will better understand why employee morale and job satisfaction are important to businesses as large as MacMillan Bloedel and as small as the corner grocery. After reading this chapter, you should be able to:

LEARNING OBJECTIVES

1. Discuss the importance of *job satisfaction* and *employee morale* and summarize their roles in *human relations* in the workplace.

2. Identify and summarize the most important theories of employee *motivation*.

3. Discuss different managerial styles of *leadership* and their impact on human relations in the workplace.

4. Describe the strategies used by organizations to improve employee motivation and job satisfaction.

The Importance of Good Human Relations in Business

human relations

Interactions between employers and employees and their attitudes towards one another.

Human relations refers to the interactions between employers and employees and their attitudes towards one another. In this section, we will explore ways to define good human relations and some of the reasons they benefit businesses.

Job Satisfaction and Employee Morale

job satisfaction

The pleasure and feeling of accomplishment employees derive from performing their jobs well.

One way to assess human relations in a firm is by workers' job satisfaction. **Job satisfaction** is the pleasurable feeling experienced from doing your job well, whether you are a mail carrier, retail clerk, bus driver, or business executive. Employees with high job satisfaction are also likely to have high employee morale. **Morale** is the mental attitude that employees have about their workplace. It reflects the degree to which employees perceive that their needs are being met by the job.

morale
The generally positive or negative mental attitude of employees towards their work and workplace.

Why Businesses Need Satisfied Employees

When workers are enthusiastic and happy with their jobs the organization benefits in many ways. Because they are committed to their work and the organization, satisfied workers are more likely to work hard and try to make useful contributions to the organization. They will also have fewer grievances and are less likely to engage in negative behaviours (e.g., complaining, deliberately slowing their work pace, etc.). Satisfied workers are also more likely to come to work every day and are more likely to remain with the organization. So, by ensuring that employees are satisfied, management gains a more efficient and smooth-running company.

Just as the rewards of high worker satisfaction and morale are great, so are the costs of job dissatisfaction and poor morale. Dissatisfied workers, for example, are far more likely to be absent due to minor illnesses, personal reasons, or a general disinclination to go to work. Low morale may also result in high turnover. Some turnover is a natural and healthy way to weed out low-performing workers in any organization. But high levels of turnover have many negative consequences, including numerous vacancies, disruption in production, decreased productivity, and high retraining costs.

Empowerment of employees is the buzzword of the 1990s. It means motivating and energizing employees to create high-quality products and to provide bend-over-backwards service to customers so that the firm is more competitive. It means eliminating whole layers of traditional management that exist simply to control people. Properly used, it can reduce absenteeism and turnover and increase quality and productivity.[1]

empowerment
Motivating employees to produce high-quality products.

Job Satisfaction and Dissatisfaction Trends

The picture of Canadian industry shows mixed results when companies try to give employees what they want and to keep them on the job. Consider the following:

- A survey of 2300 workers by the Wyatt Co. of Vancouver found that three-quarters of Canadian workers are satisfied with the content of their job, but fewer than half are happy with the way they are managed. Workers felt that management did not show genuine interest in them and did not treat them with dignity. Managers, on the other hand, felt that they did treat workers with dignity. Perhaps most disconcerting of all, fewer than one third of those surveyed felt that promotions were based on merit. The longer they had been with a company, the more cynical they were about this issue.[2]

- Another survey of 1631 employees from 94 companies across Canada and the U.S. found that, while employees are optimistic and committed to their work, they also feel frustrated because they have no control over what happens in their job. Most employees feel that their abilities are not used to the fullest extent. They want direction and measurable goals.[3]

- Based on responses from 7000 private- and public-sector workers, a Conference Board of Canada survey found the following:

    One third of employees felt that caring for children or elderly parents limited their career advancement.

One eighth had left an employer because of family responsibilities.

Seventeen percent had turned down promotions.

Twenty-five percent had turned down transfers.

Women were four times as likely as men to report conflicts in home and work responsibilities.[4]

All categories of employees—professional, clerical, management, and hourly—feel less secure in their jobs than just a few years ago. This pattern stems in part from cutbacks and layoffs experienced throughout industry in recent years. Many large corporations have announced plant closings, putting thousands of employees out of work. Not surprisingly, workers are likely to feel decreased commitment and job satisfaction. Employees at small firms are generally more content with their lot, a situation explained in the box "When Good Things Come in Small Places." But it may be difficult to motivate some employees in family-owned firms—they know they will never control the firm because they are not part of the family.

Many workers are also dissatisfied with their salaries. Some, for example, do not think that pay is fairly distributed within their company. A large majority of nonmanagement employees do not believe that pay increases are linked directly to performance. Many workers think they are underpaid compared to people in other companies. The box "Workplace Blues" describes how many workers feel about their job and the company they work for.

The Canadian Business Scene

When Goods Things Come in Small Places

Most small companies do not pay as well as larger firms. They often cannot offer the benefits—especially pension plans—that are standard features at giant corporations. In many cases, they do not offer the chance for advancement to be found in a bigger company.

Why, then, do surveys consistently find that employees of small businesses are happier about their lot than corporate workers? The answer appears to lie in the old adage that "money isn't everything."

Chief among the reasons people give for enjoying their positions in small companies is the opportunity to make a difference. Especially in very small firms, virtually every employee has access to the top managers. With access comes the ability to take ideas for change and improvements to the people who can make them happen.

Many managers and employees of small businesses also enjoy the challenge of making a new business succeed. In place of the square-peg/square-hole jobs in larger companies, small firms welcome people with the ability and willingness to take on all sorts of projects.

The diversity of work attracts some managers away from large corporations, despite the lower pay at small firms. Increasingly, such managers are taking lateral (same job level) moves to smaller companies for the opportunity to gain broader experience. Then, with new skills, they return to the corporate world at higher levels and higher salaries.

People do differ in their satisfaction with small companies, however. Not surprisingly, satisfaction with a small company is often directly linked to an individual's position within that company. In general, the higher the level, the higher the satisfaction. Line workers, who tend to suffer the downside of low pay without getting the benefit of challenging work, are most apt to work for a small firm only because it is conveniently located.

At the other end of the scale, professional staff such as lawyers, accountants, and scientists enjoy the greatest challenges and feel the greatest satisfaction with their jobs. Salespeople, a positive breed by nature, fairly gush with enthusiasm for the flexibility of small companies. "If you have to change a policy to make a customer happy, it's easier," notes one sales representative for a small firm.

What about the managers? For many, small companies are a mixed blessing. Company owners who won't share decision-making power can be a source of frustration. Lack of opportunity for advancement—where do you go in a family-run firm with nine family members heading the departments?—drives many out. Managers at small companies are no less likely than their corporate counterparts to change jobs.

The Canadian Business Scene

Workplace Blues

Lately, many business journals have reported on the demoralization of business managers. The low morale reported by so many middle managers in the 1990s is the result of job losses, a vastly increased workload for those who remain on the job, and a feeling that their work world is completely beyond their control.

Middle managers increasingly perceive that top management has no "game plan" other than to draw enormous salaries for themselves (see the box on Executive Compensation in Chapter 9). The logical consequence is that many white-collar workers now have attitudes towards "the brass" that are more cynical than they were in the past.

"Loyalty between the corporation and its managers extends only as far as the next paycheque now," mourns one formerly committed manager. "In my career, I gave up a lot of personal plans—anniversary parties, vacations, and so on—for the sake of the company. I wouldn't do that today because I've realized all the loyalty and sacrifice was going one way only." Instead, more and more middle managers are turning to smaller companies, hoping not only to gain a real voice in operations, but also to escape the frenetic world of the large corporation.

Corporations benefit when demoralized managers move on. Low morale in the workplace has been linked to low productivity for reasons ranging from work avoidance (such as hanging out at the water cooler) to job avoidance (such as calling in sick) to sabotage (both physical sabotage of company property and "emotional" sabotage of other workers).

What can a company with low morale do? The buzzword in business today is "empowerment"—giving workers at all levels a feeling that they can control things, that they do make a difference. One of the quickest ways to empower employees is to make them part owners of the business, a route many companies (including such industry giants as Avis) have taken successfully. Giving teams of employees full authority over meaningful projects from start to finish can also build commitment to the firm. Conducting frequent surveys of employee attitudes, soliciting employee input, and—most importantly—acting on that input have given companies such as Hyatt an edge in attracting and keeping valued staff.

In the long run, though, rebuilding morale will require rebuilding both trust and communication between upper management and those below. Those searching for the source of the current morale problem need look no further than the one place where few seem to realize there is a morale problem: the executive suite. Despite widespread press reports of low morale, 91 percent of CEOs at major companies said morale among middle managers in their companies was "excellent" or "very good." Is anybody up there listening?

Motivation in the Workplace

Although job satisfaction and morale are important, employee motivation is even more critical to a firm's success. As we saw in Chapter 6, motivation is one part of the managerial function of directing. Broadly defined, **motivation** is the set of forces that cause people to behave in certain ways. For example, while one worker may be motivated to work hard to produce as much as possible, another may be motivated to do just enough to get by. Managers must understand these differences in behaviour and the reasons for them.

Over the years, many theories have been proposed to address the issues of motivation. In this section, we will focus on three major approaches to motivation in the workplace that reflect a chronology of thinking in the area: *classical theory* and *scientific management, behaviour theory*, and *contemporary motivational theories*.

motivation
The set of forces that causes people to behave in certain ways.

Classical Theory and Scientific Management

According to the so-called **classical theory of motivation**, workers are motivated solely by money. In his book *The Principles of Scientific Management* (1911), industrial engineer Frederick Taylor proposed a way for both com-

classical theory of motivation
A theory of motivation that presumes that workers are motivated almost solely by money.

The ideas of Frederick Taylor, the founder of Scientific Management, had a profound impact on the way manufacturing activities were carried out in the early 20th century. His basic ideas are still used today.

panies and workers to benefit from this widely accepted view of life in the workplace.[5] If workers are motivated by money, Taylor reasoned, then paying them more would prompt them to produce more. Meanwhile, the firm that analyzed jobs and found better ways to perform them would be able to produce goods more cheaply, make higher profits, and thus pay—and motivate—workers better than its competitors.

scientific management

Analyzing jobs and finding better, more efficient ways to perform them.

Taylor's approach is known as **scientific management**. His ideas captured the imagination of many managers in the early 20th century. Soon, plants across Canada and the U.S. were hiring experts to perform **time-and-motion studies**. Industrial-engineering techniques were applied to each facet of a job in order to determine how to perform it most efficiently. These studies were the first "scientific" attempts to break down jobs into easily repeated components and to devise more efficient tools and machines for performing them.

time-and-motion studies

The use of industrial-engineering techniques to study every aspect of a specific job to determine how to perform it most efficiently.

As for compensation, Taylor's *differential percent system* was a new twist on the standard **piecework system** by which a worker was paid a set rate per piece completed. For example, a worker in a garment shop might receive 25 cents for each sleeve stitched. Under Taylor's system, however, workers who fell below a specified quota were paid at a certain level—a different percent—per piece. Those who exceeded the quota got higher pay, not just for the extra pieces but for all the pieces they completed.

piecework system

Paying workers a set rate for each piece of work produced.

Taylor's approach enjoyed much initial success among manual labourers. In many heavy industries, management was willing to pay greater wages for significant increases in productivity. Henry Ford, for example, was eventually able to build cars more rapidly and cheaply than any other automaker, in large part by paying his workers *more than double* the usual wage. Ultimately, however, the scientific management system began to show flaws resulting from its failure to see that factors other than money often contribute to job satisfaction.

The Hawthorne Studies

One of the first challenges to the classical theory of human relations management came about by accident. In 1925, a group of Harvard researchers began a study at the Hawthorne Works of Western Electric. Their intent was to examine the relationship between changes in the physical environment and worker output, with an eye to increasing productivity.

The results of the experiment at first confused, then amazed, the scientists. Increasing lighting levels improved productivity but so did lowering lighting levels. And against all expectations, raising the pay of workers failed to increase their productivity. Gradually they pieced together the puzzle. The explanation for the lighting phenomenon lay in workers' response to attention. In essence, they determined that almost any action on the part of management that made workers believe they were receiving special attention caused worker productivity to rise. This result, known as the **Hawthorne effect**, had a major influence on human relations management, convincing many businesses that paying attention to employees is indeed good for business.

Hawthorne effect
The tendency for workers' productivity to increase when they feel they are receiving special attention from management.

But, as the scientists also found, the Hawthorne effect has limits. Even a pay raise is not enough to get people to work harder if they have an informal consensus that such behaviour is inappropriate. For example, they found that workers in a wiring room received constant criticism from their peers when they exceeded the group norm for output. Eventually, most got the message and decreased their production to the established level. This result has led businesses to pay greater attention to the informal organization within their companies (see Chapter 7) and to recognize that human relations management is not a perfect solution.[6]

Contemporary Motivation Theories

Following the Hawthorne studies, managers and researchers alike focused more attention on the importance of good human relations in motivating employee performance. Stressing the factors that cause, focus, and sustain workers' behaviour, most motivation theorists are concerned with the ways in which management thinks about and treats employees. The major motivation theories include the *human-resources model*, the *hierarchy of needs model*, *two-factory theory*, *expectancy theory*, *equity theory*, and *goal-setting theory*.

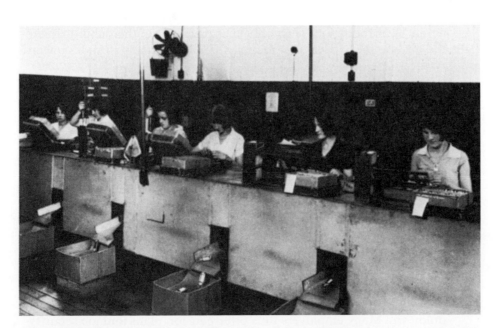

The Hawthorne studies were an important step in developing an appreciation for the human factor at work. These women worked under different lighting conditions as researchers monitored their productivity. To the researchers' amazement, productivity increased regardless of whether the light was increased or decreased.

The Human-Resources Model: Theories X and Y

In an important study, behavioural scientist Douglas McGregor concluded that managers had radically different beliefs about how best to use the human resources at a firm's disposal. He classified these beliefs into sets of assumptions that he labelled "Theory X" and "Theory Y."[7] The basic differences between these two theories are highlighted in Table 10.1.

Table 10.1   Beliefs about People at Work

Theory X and theory Y convey very different assumptions about people at work.

Theory X	Theory Y
1. People are lazy.	1. People are energetic.
2. People lack ambition and dislike responsibility.	2. People are ambitious and seek responsibility.
3. People are self-centred.	3. People can be selfless.
4. People resist change.	4. People want to contribute to business growth and change.
5. People are gullible and not very bright.	5. People are intelligent.

Theory X

A management approach based on the belief that people must be forced to be productive because they are naturally lazy, irresponsible, and uncooperative.

Theory Y

A management approach based on the belief that people want to be productive because they are naturally energetic, responsible, and cooperative.

Managers who subscribe to **Theory X** tend to believe that people are naturally lazy and uncooperative and must therefore be either punished or rewarded to be made productive. Managers who incline to **Theory Y** tend to believe that people are naturally energetic, growth-oriented, self-motivated, and interested in being productive.

McGregor generally favoured Theory Y beliefs. Thus he argued that Theory Y managers are more likely to have satisfied, motivated employees. Of course, Theory X and Y distinctions are somewhat simplistic and offer little concrete basis for action. Their value lies primarily in their ability to highlight and analyze the behaviour of managers in light of their attitudes towards employees.

Maslow's Hierarchy of Needs Model

Psychologist Abraham Maslow proposed that people have a number of different needs that they attempt to satisfy in their work. He classified these needs into five basic types and suggested that they are arranged in the hierarchy of importance shown in Figure 10.1. According to Maslow, needs are hierarchical because lower-level needs must be met before a person will try to satisfy those on a higher level.[8]

- *Physiological needs* are necessary for survival; they include food, water, shelter, and sleep. Businesses address these needs by providing both comfortable working environments and salaries sufficient to buy food and shelter.

- *Security needs* include the needs for stability and protection from the unknown. Many employers thus offer pension plans and job security.

- *Social needs* include the needs for friendship and companionship. Making friends at work can help to satisfy social needs, as can the feeling that you "belong" in a company.

GENERAL EXAMPLES   ORGANIZATIONAL EXAMPLES

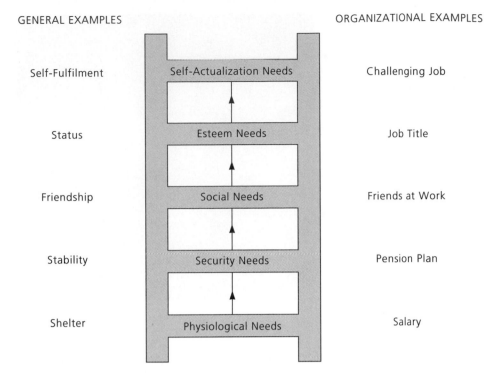

Figure 10.1
Maslow's hierarchy of human needs provides a useful categorization of the different needs people have.

- *Esteem needs* include the need for status and recognition as well as the need for self-respect. Respected job titles and large offices are among the things that businesses can provide to address these needs.
- Finally, *self-actualization needs* are needs for self-fulfilment. They include the needs to grow and develop one's capabilities and to achieve new and meaningful goals. Challenging job assignments can help satisfy these needs.

According to Maslow, once one set of needs has been satisfied, it ceases to motivate behaviour. This is the sense in which the hierarchical nature of lower- and higher-level needs affects employee motivation and satisfaction. For example, if you feel secure in your job, a new pension plan will probably be less important to you than the chance to make new friends and join an informal network among your co-workers. If, however, a lower-level need suddenly becomes unfulfilled, most people immediately refocus on that lower level. Suppose, for example, that you are seeking to meet your esteem needs by working as a divisional manager at a major company. If you learn that your division—and consequently your job—may be eliminated, you might very well find the promise of job security at a new firm as motivating as a promotion once would have been in your old company.

Maslow's theory recognizes that because different people have different needs, they are motivated by different things. Unfortunately, research has found that the hierarchy varies widely, not only for different people but across different cultures.

Two-Factor Theory

After studying a group of accountants and engineers, psychologist Frederick Herzberg concluded that job satisfaction and dissatisfaction depend on two factors: *hygiene factors*, such as working conditions, and *motivating factors*, such as recognition for a job well done.[9]

Rewards are an important determinant of employee motivation. Because this woman's outstanding performance was recognized and rewarded, she is likely to continue to work hard.

two-factor theory

A theory of human relations developed by Frederick Herzberg that identifies factors that must be present for employees to be satisfied with their jobs and factors that, if increased, lead employees to work harder.

According to **two-factor theory**, hygiene factors affect motivation and satisfaction only if they are *absent* or *fail* to meet expectations. For example, workers will be dissatisfied if they believe that they have poor working conditions. If working conditions are improved, however, they will not necessarily become *satisfied*; they will simply be *not dissatisfied*. On the other hand, if workers receive no recognition for successful work, they may be neither dissatisfied nor satisfied. If recognition is provided, they will likely become more satisfied.

Figure 10.2 illustrates two-factor theory. Note that motivation factors lie along a continuum from *satisfaction* to *no satisfaction*. Hygiene factors, on the other hand, are likely to produce feelings that lie on a continuum from *dis-*

Figure 10.2
According to two-factor theory, job satisfaction depends on two factors.

satisfaction to *no dissatisfaction*. While motivation factors are directly related to the work that employees actually perform, hygiene factors refer to the environment in which they perform it.

This theory thus suggests that managers should follow a two-step approach to enhancing motivation. First, they must ensure that hygiene factors—working conditions, clearly stated policies—are acceptable. This practice will result in an absence of dissatisfaction. Then they must offer motivating factors—recognition, added responsibility—as means of improving satisfaction and motivation.

Research suggests that two-factor theory works in some professional settings, but it is not as effective in clerical and manufacturing settings. (Herzberg's research was limited to professionals—accountants and engineers only.) In addition, one person's hygiene factor may be another person's motivating factor. For example, if money represents nothing more than pay for time worked, it may be a hygiene factor for one person. For another person, however, money may be a motivating factor because it represents recognition and achievement.

Expectancy Theory

Expectancy theory suggests that people are motivated to work towards rewards which they want *and* which they believe they have a reasonable chance—or expectancy—of obtaining.[10] A reward that seems out of reach, for example, is not likely to be motivating even if it is intrinsically positive. Consider the case of an assistant department manager who learns that a division manager has retired and that the firm is looking for a replacement. Even though she wants the job, she does not apply for it because she doubts that she would be selected. She also learns that the firm is looking for a production manager on a later shift. She thinks that she could get this job but does not apply because she does not want to change shifts. Finally, she learns of an opening one level higher—full department manager—in her own division. She may well apply for this job because she both wants it and thinks that she has a good chance of getting it.

Figure 10.3 shows a simplified expectancy model. As you can see, this theory holds that motivation leads to effort, whose success depends on both an employee's ability and the environment in which he or she is working. Effort also leads to various outcomes. The employee ultimately places a value on each of these outcomes—say, relatively desirable or undesirable. That value will determine the employee's level of motivation and the quality of the effort that he or she will put forth.

Expectancy theory also helps to explain why some people do not work as hard as they can when their salaries are based purely on seniority: Because they are paid the same whether they work very hard or hard enough to get by, there is no financial incentive for them to work harder. In other words, they ask themselves, "If I work harder, will I get a pay raise?" and conclude that the answer is no—that they expect not. Similarly, if hard work will result in one or more *undesirable* outcomes—say, a transfer to another location or a promotion to a job that requires travel—employees will not be motivated to work hard.

expectancy theory
The theory that people are motivated to work towards rewards which they want and which they believe they have a reasonable chance of obtaining.

Equity Theory

Equity theory focuses on social comparisons—people evaluating their treatment by the organization relative to the treatment of others. This approach says that people begin by analyzing what they contribute to their jobs (time, effort, education, experience, and so forth) relative to what they get in return (salary, benefits, recognition, security). The result is a ratio of contribution to return. Then they compare their own ratios to those of other employees. Depending on their assessments, they experience feelings of equity or inequity.[11]

equity theory
The theory that people compare (1) what they contribute to their job with what they get in return, and (2) their input/output ratio with that of other employees.

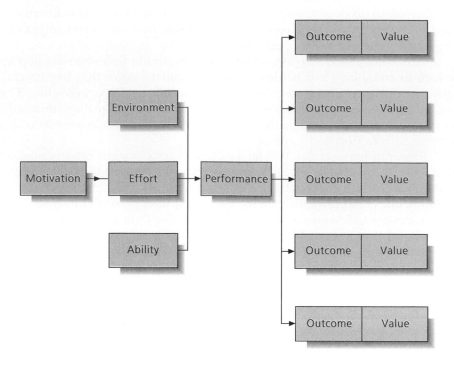

Figure 10.3
Expectancy theory suggests that obtainable rewards motivate people more than rewards that appear to be out of reach.

For example, suppose a new college graduate gets a starting job at a large manufacturing firm. His starting salary is $25 000 per year, he gets a compact company car, and he shares an office with another new employee. If he later learns that another new employee has received the same salary, car, and office arrangement, he will feel equitably treated. If the other newcomer, however, has received $30 000, a full-size company car, and a private office, he may feel inequity.

Note, however, that the two ratios do not have to be the *same*—they need be only *fair*. Let's assume, for instance, that our new employee has a bachelor's degree and two years' work experience. Perhaps he learns subsequently that the other new employee has an advanced degree and 10 years' experience. After first feeling inequity, our new employee may now conclude that his comparison person is actually contributing more to the organization. The other employee is equitably entitled, therefore, to receive more in return.

When people feel that they are being inequitably treated, they may do various things to restore fairness. For example, they may ask for raises, reduce their effort, work shorter hours, or just complain to their bosses. They may also rationalize their situation ("management succumbed to pressure to promote a woman"), find different people with whom to compare themselves, or leave their jobs altogether.

Good examples of equity theory at work can be found in professional sports. Each year, for example, rookies are signed to lucrative contracts. No sooner is the ink is dry than veteran players start grumbling about raises or revised contracts.

Goal-Setting Theory

goal-setting theory
The theory that people perform better when they set specific, quantified, time-framed goals.

Goal-setting theory describes the kinds of goals that better motivate employees. In general, effective goals tend to have two basic characteristics. First, they are moderately difficult: While a goal that is too easy does little to enhance effort and motivation, a goal that is too difficult also fails to motivate people. Second, they are specific. A goal of "do your best," for instance, does not motivate people nearly as much as a goal such as "increase profits by 10 percent." The specificity and clarity of this goal serves to focus attention and energy on exactly what needs to be done.[12]

An important aspect of goal setting is the employee's participation in the goal-setting process. When people help to select the goals that they are to work towards, they tend to accept them more readily and are more committed to achieving them. On the other hand, when goals are merely assigned to people with little or no input on their part, they are less likely to adopt them.

Managerial Styles and Leadership

In trying to enhance morale, job satisfaction, and motivation, managers can use many different styles of leadership. **Leadership** is the process of motivating others to work to meet specific objectives. Leading is one of the key aspects of a manager's job. In this section, we describe some of the basic features of and differences in managerial styles, and then focus on an approach to managing and leading that understands those jobs as responses to a variety of complex situations.

leadership
Process of motivating others to work to meet specific objectives.

Managerial Styles

Early theories of leadership tried to identify specific "traits" associated with strong leaders. For example, physical appearance, intelligence, and public-speaking skills were once thought to be "leadership traits." Indeed, it was once believed that taller people made better leaders than shorter people. The "trait" approach, however, proved to be a poor predictor of leadership potential. Ultimately, attention shifted from managers' traits to their behaviours, or **managerial styles**: patterns of behaviour that a manager exhibits in dealing with subordinates. Managerial styles run the gamut from *autocratic* to *democratic* to *free-rein*. Naturally, most managers do not clearly exhibit any one particular style. But these three major types of styles involve very different kinds of responses to human relations problems. Under different circumstances, any given one—or any combination—may prove appropriate:

managerial style
Patterns of behaviour that a manager exhibits in dealing with subordinates.

- Managers who adopt an **autocratic style** generally issue orders and expect them to be obeyed without question. The military commander, of course, prefers and usually needs the autocratic style on the battlefield. Because no one else is consulted, the autocratic style allows for rapid decision making. It may therefore be useful in situations testing a firm's effectiveness as a time-based competitor.

autocratic style
Managerial style in which managers generally issue orders and expect them to be obeyed without question.

- Managers who adopt a **democratic style** generally ask for input from subordinates before making decisions but retain final decision-making power. For example, the manager of a technical group may ask other group members to interview and offer opinions about job applicants. The manager, however, will ultimately make the hiring decision.

democratic style
Managerial style in which managers generally ask for input from subordinates but retain final decision-making power.

- Managers who adopt a **free-rein style** typically serve as advisors to subordinates who are allowed to make decisions. The chairperson of a volunteer committee to raise funds for a new library may find a free-rein style most effective.

free-rein style
Managerial style in which managers typically serve as advisers to subordinates who are allowed to make decisions.

Regardless of theories about the ways in which leaders ought to lead, the relative effectiveness of any leadership style depends largely on the desire of subordinates to share input or to exercise creativity. While some people, for example, are frustrated, others prefer autocratic managers because they do not want a voice in making decisions. The democratic approach, meanwhile, can be disconcerting both to people who want decision-making responsibility and to those who do not. A free-rein style lends itself to employee creativity—and thus to creative solutions to pressing problems. This style also appeals to employees who like to plan their own work. Not all subordinates, however, have the necessary background or skills to make creative decisions. Others are not sufficiently self-motivated to work without supervision.

Canadian vs. American Management Styles

The management style of Canadian managers might look a lot like that of Americans, but there are several notable differences. Most fundamentally, Canadian managers are more subtle and subdued than American managers. Canadian managers also seem more committed to their companies, less willing to mindlessly follow the latest management fad, and more open to different cultures because of the multicultural nature of Canada. All of these characteristics may be advantageous for Canadian companies that will increasingly be competing in global markets.[13]

The Contingency Nature of Leadership

Because each managerial style has both strengths and weaknesses, most managers vary their response to different situations. Flexibility, however, has not always characterized managerial style or responsiveness. For most of the 20th century, in fact, managers tended to believe that all problems yielded to preconceived, pretested solutions. If raising pay reduced turnover in one plant, for example, the same tactic would work equally well in another plant.

contingency approach

Approach to managerial style holding that the appropriate behaviour in any situation is dependent (contingent) on the elements unique to that situation.

More recently, however, managers have begun to adopt a **contingency approach** to managerial style. They have started to view appropriate managerial behaviour in any situation as dependent, or *contingent*, on the elements unique to that situation. This change in outlook has resulted largely from an increasing appreciation of the complexity of managerial problems and solutions. Pay raises, for example, may reduce turnover when workers have been badly underpaid. The contingency approach, however, recognizes that they will have little effect when workers feel adequately paid but ill-treated by management. This approach also recommends that training managers in human relations skills may be crucial to solving the problem in the latter situation.

The contingency approach also acknowledges that people in different cultures behave differently and expect different things from their managers. A certain managerial style, therefore, is more likely to be successful in some countries than in others. Japanese workers, for example, generally expect managers to be highly participative and to give them input in decision making. In contrast, many South American workers actually balk at participation and want take-charge leaders. The basic idea, then, is that managers will be more effective when they adapt their styles to the contingencies of the situation that they face.[14]

Strategies for Enhancing Job Satisfaction

Deciding what motivates workers and provides job satisfaction is only part of the manager's battle. The other part is to apply that knowledge. Experts have suggested—and many companies have instituted—a wide range of

These employees are part of a quality circle that is discussing ways to improve work methods and thereby increase productivity.

programs designed to make jobs more interesting and rewarding and the work environment more pleasant. In this section, we will consider five of the most common types of programs: reinforcement and punishment, management by objectives, participative management, job enrichment and re-design, and modified work schedules.

Reinforcement and Punishment

Many companies try to alter workers' behaviour through systematic rewards and punishment for specific behaviours. Rewards, or positive reinforcement, can be used to increase the frequency of desired behaviours. For example, paying large cash bonuses to salespeople who exceed their quotas will cause them to work even harder in the future to exceed their quotas again. Incentive reward systems at B.C. Tel, Drexis Inc., and the Toronto SkyDome all rely on positive reinforcement (see the box "Incentives and Motivation").

Punishment, on the other hand, is used to get people to change their behaviour by giving them unpleasant consequences. Employees who come to work late repeatedly may need to be suspended or have their pay docked to change their behaviour in the future. When the National Hockey League fines or suspends players found guilty of drug abuse, it is seeking to change their behaviour in the future.

Sometimes punishments may be necessary. Most managers dislike punishing unacceptable behaviour, in part because workers may respond with anger, resentment, hostility, or retaliation.

Extensive reinforcement works best when people are learning new behaviour, new skills, and new jobs. As they become more adept, rewards can become more infrequent. Managers generally like giving rewards and placing a positive value on a person's good behaviour, since these actions make for positive employer-employee relationships. Moreover, rewards are more likely to motivate workers and increase their job satisfaction than are punishments.

There are some limitations on using rewards to shape workers' behaviour. Rewards will only work if people:

B.C. Tel
http://www.education.bctel.com

SkyDome
http://www.skydome.com

The Canadian Business Scene

Incentives and Motivation

Canadian companies have begun to realize that offering incentives beyond the normal benefits can result in creative ideas as well as large increases in employee productivity. These incentives may be monetary or nonmonetary. Consider the following:

■ At B.C. Tel, a suggestion system was implemented that gives cash rewards to employees for ideas that generate revenue or save the company money. The employee receives 10 percent of the money saved or the revenue generated. Employees have received up to $20 000 for ideas.

■ Drexis Inc. recently flew 12 employees and their families to Disney World as a reward for increasing sales by over 100 percent in one year.

■ Proctor & Redfern Ltd., a consulting engineering firm, lets high achievers serve on committees with senior executives, represent the firm at outside functions, or enrol in development courses for which the company pays the bill.

■ Avatar Communications Inc. sent employees on a weeklong Outward Bound expedition into the wilderness. The trip had both reward and motivational components.

■ Pitney Bowes Canada Ltd. sent 60 of its top salespeople and their spouses to Hong Kong after they achieved 135 percent of their sales quota; salespeople who achieved 112 percent received a trip to San Diego.

■ At Cloverdale Paint, employees who come up with innovative ideas to improve customer service receive a personal letter from the president and a coffee mug or T-shirt bearing the company logo. The best idea submitted each quarter earns the originator a restaurant gift certificate worth $50. The employee who makes the best suggestion of the year receives $200 and an engraved plaque presented at a workplace ceremony.

■ Manitoba Telephone System instituted a suggestion system called IDEA$PLUS, which gives employees cash awards of up to $10 000 for good ideas.

■ Employees at the Toronto SkyDome are given coupons for exceptional service, such as finding a lost child or repairing a broken seat. The coupons can be used to accumulate points which can be redeemed for prizes.

■ Emery Apparel Canada Inc. conducts an annual "Oscar" awards ceremony. With great hoopla, the CEO asks for the envelope with the name of the winner of the top award. Last year, a 12-year employee won the award for figuring out (on her own time) how to satisfy a customer's difficult request.

■ At Ford Motor Company, workers are rewarded for suggestions that save the company money. For example, when a metal press operator found a way to save on the amount of sheet metal used in floor panels, the company gave back to the worker $14 000 of the $70 000 saved. A recent study shows that activity like this has an effect—it takes workers at Ford one third less time to build a car than workers at GM.

Incentives are important for top managers as well. The higher a manager is placed in a firm, the more likely it is that a good chunk of the manager's pay will be performance-based. A Conference Board of Canada study of executive compensation in Canada showed that up to 40 percent of top executives' total compensation comes in the form of incentives. For lower-level managers, the figure was 20 percent, and for other employees it was 10 percent. Top managers in the U.S. often receive up to 60 percent of their total compensation in the form of incentives. Most Canadian companies have set up some type of incentive plan for their senior executives.

Incentive systems must be carefully developed or they will not motivate employee behaviour in the desired direction. In addition to the usual sales and profit goals, firms are beginning to look at incentive systems that reward managers for achieving goals like effective downsizing, increasing environmental consciousness, and improving the corporate culture. A decision must also be made about whether the incentive system will be directed at individual employees or groups. Historically, incentives have been directed at individuals, but with the new emphasis on teamwork in organizations, this is changing. Now, a group may get an incentive if it gets a new product launched on time.

Incentive systems must be used with care because they may unintentionally motivate employees to engage in undesirable behaviour. For example, stockbrokers are often given bonuses for making sales of mutual funds. Super salespeople may be given trips to exotic locations in return for making their sales goals. This may motivate the salesperson to push a product or service that really doesn't meet the customers' needs.

Cloverdale Paint
http://www.cloverdalepaint.com

Manitoba Telephone System
http://www.mtd.mb.ca

■ believe they can perform better by making an effort.

■ believe that they will receive rewards for performing better.

■ want the rewards the company offers for performing better.

Management by Objectives

In Chapter 6, we described a technique for managing the planning process called *management by objectives,* or *MBO.* While MBO is mainly concerned with helping managers implement and carry out their plans, it can serve other purposes as well.

One very important benefit of using MBO is improved human relations. For example, when employees meet with their managers to set goals for the coming year, they learn more about the organization's goals, come to feel that they are an important part of the team, and see how they can improve the company's performance by working towards their own goals.

The year-end assessment of goal attainment and rewards can also improve human relations. Assuming managers are using the MBO system properly, employees should come away from these meetings understanding the value of their contributions and with a fair and equitable reward. Thus, MBO can help employees satisfy a variety of needs and can also facilitate their perceptions of fairness. Investors Syndicate has enjoyed considerable success with its MBO program (refer to the box on p. 174).

Participative Management

Another popular technique for promoting human relations is **participative management.** Simply stated, participative management involves giving employees a voice in how they do their jobs and how the company is managed. Such participation should make employees feel more committed to the goals of the organization because they help shape them.

> **participative management**
> *A method of increasing employees' job satisfaction by giving them a voice in how they do their jobs and how the company is managed.*

Some employees prefer a democratic, or supportive, leader. A survey at B.C. Telecom, for example, showed that people with a supportive boss missed less work, were less tense, felt more secure, and were more confident about their ability to get ahead in the company. Supervisors who got negative ratings usually were inflexible, supervised their workers too closely, and didn't communicate useful information to them.[15]

Japanese companies like Honda have been especially effective at practising participative management. And participative management has become more popular in recent years in Canada, partly from imitating the Japanese and partly as businesses and labour unions have become increasingly cooperative. At CP Express and Transport, for example, truck drivers were allowed to decide how to spend $8 million on new equipment.[16] The box "The Japanese Management System" describes some of the strong and weak points of that system.

At one level, employees may be given decision-making responsibility for certain narrow activities, such as when to take their lunch breaks, how to do their jobs, and so forth. At a broader level, employees are also being given a say in more significant issues and decisions. One popular technique to encourage participative management is the **quality circle,** a group of employees who meet regularly to consider solutions for problems in their work area. Great West Life, for example, has reported success with its quality circle program. Quality circles are explored in detail in Chapters 12 and 14.

> **quality circle**
> *A technique for maximizing quality of production. Employees are grouped into small teams that define, analyze, and solve quality and other process-related problems within their area.*

International Report

The Japanese Management System

In the 1980s, the Japanese management system was all the rage. At its most basic, the system contained the following elements:

1. *Lifetime employment.* Employees stay at one firm for their entire career instead of changing jobs as is common in Canada. Seniority is the basis for promotion.

2. *Temporary employees.* Large Japanese firms have many temporary employees, most of them female. If a downturn occurs, these employees are the first to be laid off. Women act as a buffer to protect men's jobs.

3. *Participative decision making.* When an important decision is to be made, everyone who will feel its impact is involved in the decision-making process. A decision is made only after a consensus is reached.

4. *Management training.* An emphasis on company loyalty underlies much management training in Japan. Training is oriented towards groups instead of individuals, and is designed to encourage team spirit.

5. *Other characteristics.* The Japanese management system also emphasizes daily exercise for employees at the work site, pep talks by supervisors, identical uniforms for workers and managers, no unions, nonspecific job classifications, and company outings for employees and their families.

This system has served Japan well over the years. In fact, until recently it was thought that this system made Japan a formidable competitor in world markets. But things have changed dramatically in just a few short years. The 1990s have not been a happy time for Japanese managers and workers. During 1992–94, Japan found itself in a major recession, and industrial output declined for 23 consecutive months, the longest decline on record. Consumer confidence is weak, unemployment is rising, GNP is declining, and the lifetime employment and seniority ideas are coming under fire.

And now, another problem has appeared. In the past, most of the emphasis in Japanese companies was on training factory workers to carry out their tasks in an efficient manner. But in the process, not enough attention was paid to the productivity of office workers. Only a few office workers have personal computers, and it is not unusual for four or five workers to share a phone. The sense of order that pervades the factory is absent in the office.

When times were good in the 1980s, the excess office staff was not noticeable. But the deep recession of the 1990s has made the problem very clear. Japanese managers are now realizing that no amount of economizing in the factory can make up for overstaffed offices. One management consultant estimates that Japan's big public companies have between 12 and 20 percent too many middle managers.

Japanese companies are beginning to address the problem of overstaffing. Many companies have reduced the hiring of college graduates, and are hoping that attrition will eventually solve the problem of overstaffing. Others are using the carrot-and-stick approach. At Honda Motors, for example, the seniority system is being replaced with a merit system. Employees will now be judged on the basis of how well they meet six-month goals set by their managers. Those who do not perform well will end up in lower paying jobs.

Toyota Motor is trying to shock its white-collar workers into being more productive. Each department has been asked to give up 20 percent of its employees to task forces that will identify new business opportunities and explore ways to improve white collar productivity.

Job Enrichment and Redesign

While MBO programs and participative management can work in a variety of settings, job enrichment and job redesign programs can increase satisfaction only if a job lacks motivating factors to begin with.

Job Enrichment Programs

job enrichment

A method of increasing employees' job satisfaction by extending or adding motivating factors such as responsibility or growth.

Based on the two-factor theory discussed earlier, **job enrichment** attempts to add one or more motivating factors to a situation. For example, job rotation programs add to growth opportunities by rotating an employee through various positions in the firm. Workers gain new skills and a broader overview of their work that allows them to contribute to the firm in more ways.

Other job enrichment programs focus on increasing responsibility or recognition. At one company, a group of eight typists worked in isolated cubicles. Their job involved taking calls from any of dozens of field sales representatives and typing up service orders. They had no client contact; if they had a question about the order, for example, they had to call the sales representative. They also received little performance feedback. Interviews with these workers suggested that they were bored with their jobs and did not feel valued. As part of a job enrichment program, each typist was paired with a small group of designated sales representatives and became a part of their team. Typists were also given permission to call clients directly if they had questions about the order. Finally, a new feedback system was installed to give the typists more information about their performance. As a result, their performance improved and absenteeism decreased markedly.[17]

Job Redesign Programs

In some ways an extension of job enrichment, **job redesign** is even more application-oriented and recognizes that different people want different things from their jobs. By restructuring work to achieve a more satisfactory person-job fit, job redesign can motivate individuals who have a high need for growth or achievement.[18] Three typical ways of implementing job redesign are to combine tasks, to form natural work groups, and to establish client relationships.

Combining tasks enlarges a job and increases its variety, making workers feel that their work is more meaningful. In turn, workers are more motivated. For example, the job done by a computer programmer who maintains computer systems might be redesigned to include some system design and development work. The programmer is then able to use additional skills and is involved in the overall system package.

People who do different jobs on the same project are good candidates for *natural work groups*. On the one hand, these groups help employees get an overview of their jobs and see their importance in the total structure. On the other hand, these groups help management, and the firm in general, because the

job redesign

A method of increasing employees' job satisfaction by improving the worker-job fit through combining tasks, creating natural work groups, and/or establishing client relationships.

One part of job redesign programs is to establish client relationships. This mechanic is explaining to a customer why she needs to have her air filter changed. Such personal contact often motivates employees to work harder because they can see how their work benefits customers.

people working on a project are usually the most knowledgeable about it and are thus able to solve problems related to it. Quality circles are natural work groups.

To see how natural work groups affect motivation, consider a group where each employee does a small part of the job of assembling radios. One person sees his job as attaching red wires while another sees hers as attaching control knobs. The jobs could be redesigned to allow the group to decide who does what and in what order. The workers can exchange jobs and plan their work schedules. Now they all see themselves as part of a team that assembles radios.

A third way of redesigning a job is to *establish client relationships*—to let employees interact with customers. This approach increases the variety of a job. It also gives workers greater feelings of control over their jobs and more feedback about their performance. Lotus Development Corp. uses this approach as a means of granting necessary independence to creative employees. Instead of responding to instructions from marketing managers on how to develop new products, software writers are encouraged to work directly with customers. Similarly, software writers at Microsoft watch test users work with programs and discuss problems with them directly rather than receive feedback from third-party researchers.

Modified Work Schedules

As another way of increasing job satisfaction, many companies are trying out different approaches to working hours and the work week. Several types of modified work schedules have been tried, including flextime, the compressed workweek, telecommuting, and workshare programs.

Flextime

flextime

A method of increasing employees' job satisfaction by allowing them some choice in the hours they work.

Some modifications involve adjusting a standard daily work schedule. **Flextime** allows people to pick their working hours. Figure 10.4 illustrates how a flextime system might be arranged and how different people might use it. The office is open from 6 a.m. until 7 p.m. Core time is 9 a.m. until 11 a.m.

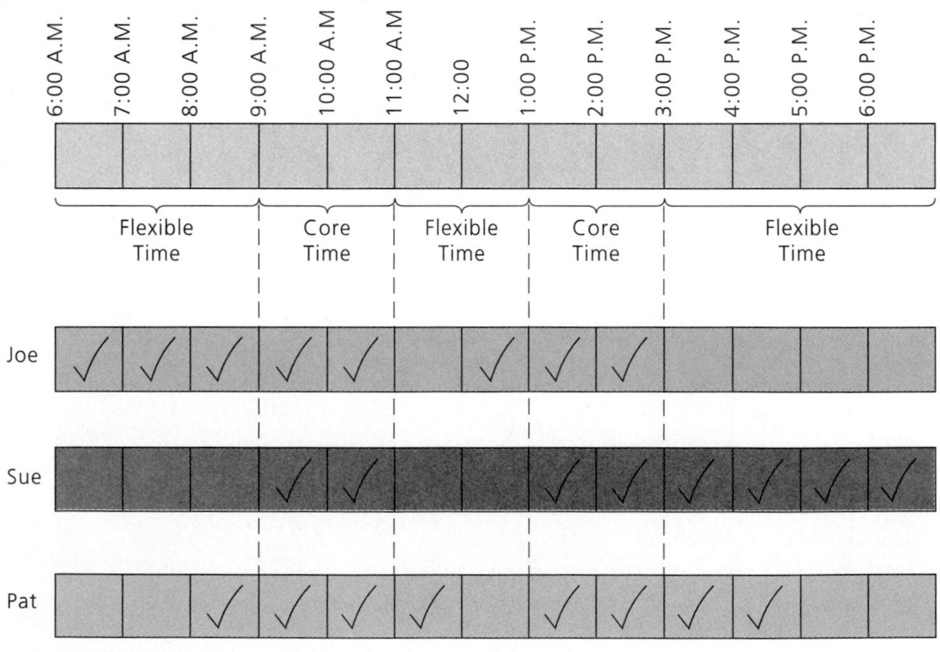

Figure 10.4
Flextime schedules include core time, when everyone must be at work, and flexible time, during which employees can set their own working hours.

and 1 p.m. until 3 p.m. Joe, being an early riser, comes in at 6 a.m., takes an hour lunch between 11 and 12, and finishes his day by 3 p.m. Sue, on the other hand, prefers a later day. She comes in at 9 a.m., takes a long lunch from 11 a.m. to 1 p.m., and then works until 7 p.m. Pat works a more traditional day from 8 a.m. until 5 p.m.

Flextime programs give employees more flexibility in their professional and personal lives. Such programs allow workers to plan around the work schedules of spouses and the school schedules of young children, for example. The increased feeling of freedom and control over their work life also reduces individuals' levels of stress.

Companies can also benefit from flextime programs. In large urban areas, flextime programs reduce traffic congestion that contributes to lost work time. Companies benefit from the higher levels of commitment and job satisfaction among workers in such programs. 3M Canada and National Cash Register are among the companies that have adopted some form of flextime. A survey of 1600 Canadian companies showed that nearly half of them had some type of flextime program.

The Compressed Workweek

In the **compressed workweek**, employees work fewer days per week, but more hours on the days they do work. The most popular compressed workweek is 4 days, 10 hours per day, but some companies have also experimented with 3 days, 12 hours per day. The "weekend worker" program at 3M Canada in London, Ontario, offers workers 12-hour shifts on Saturdays and Sundays only, and pays them the same wage as if they had worked normal hours Monday through Friday. There is a long waiting list to transfer to weekend work.[19]

compressed workweek
Employees work fewer days per week, but more hours on the days they do work.

Tellers at the Bank of Montreal in Oakville Place work long days (up to 14 hours), but enjoy a short work week. Some tellers work 7 a.m. to 9 p.m. Thursday and Friday, and 7:30 a.m. to 5:30 p.m. Saturdays. Others work Monday to Wednesday for 14 hours each day. Employees like the system because it allows them to do personal errands during the day on the weekdays they do not have to be at work.[20]

Telecommuting

A third variation in work design is **telecommuting**, which allows people to do some or all of their work away from their office. The availability of networked computers, fax machines, cellular telephones, and overnight delivery services makes it possible for many independent professionals to work at home or while travelling. More and more Canadian workers do a significant portion of their work outside their conventional offices.[21]

telecommuting
Allowing employees to do all or some of their work away from the office.

Telecommuting helps employees avoid driving a long way to work, but they often report feeling isolated and lonely. To avoid this problem, B.C. Tel and Bentall Development Inc. jointly developed a satellite telecommuting office in Langley, B.C. It allows workers who used to have to commute to Burnaby or Vancouver to reduce their travel time considerably and still be able to interact with other workers.[22]

But telecommuting may not be for everyone. Would-be telecommuters must ask themselves several important questions: "Can I meet deadlines even when I'm not being closely supervised? What will it be like to be away from the social context of the office five days a week? Can I renegotiate family rules, so my spouse doesn't come home expecting to see dinner on the table just because I've been home all day?"

Another obstacle to establishing a telecommuting program is convincing management that it will be beneficial for everyone involved. Telecommuters may have to fight the perception—from both bosses and co-workers—that if they are not being supervised, they are not working. Managers are often very suspicious about telecommuting, asking "How can I tell if someone is working when I can't see them?"

Workshare Programs

worksharing (job sharing)

A method of increasing employee job satisfaction by allowing two people to share one job.

NOVA Corp.
http://www.nova.ca

A fourth type of modified work schedule, **worksharing** (also called **job sharing**), benefits both employee and employer. This approach allows two people to share one full-time job. For example, Kim Sarjeant and Loraine Champion, who are staff lawyers for NOVA Corp. in Calgary, share a position advising the human resources department. Sarjeant works Monday through Wednesday, and Champion works Wednesday through Friday.[23] A Statistics Canada survey showed that 8 percent of all part-time workers in Canada share a job with someone. People who share jobs are more likely to be women, to be university educated, and to have professional occupations like teaching and nursing. In addition, job sharers earned more than regular part-time workers.[24]

Short-run worksharing programs can help ease experienced workers into retirement while training their replacements. Worksharing can also allow students in university co-op programs to combine academic learning with practical experience.

Long-run worksharing programs have proven a good solution for people who want only part-time work. For example, five people might decide to share one reservationist's job at Air Canada with each working one day a week. Each person earns some money, remains in the job market, and enjoys limited travel benefits.

Motivation and Leadership in the 1990s

Motivation and leadership remain critically important areas, but as times change, so do the ways that managers motivate and lead their employees.

On the motivation side, today's employees want rewards that are often very much different from those that earlier generations desired. Money, for example, may not be the prime motivator for most people. In addition, because businesses today cannot offer the degree of job security that many workers want, motivating employees to strive towards higher levels of performance requires skilful attention from managers.

The diversity inherent in today's workforce also makes motivating worker behaviour more complex for managers. The reasons for which people work encompass more goals than ever before, and the varying lifestyles of diverse workers means that managers must first pay closer attention to what their employees expect to get for their efforts and then try to link rewards with job performance.

Today's leaders are also finding it necessary to change their own behaviour. As organizations become flatter and workers more empowered, managers find it less acceptable to use the autocratic approach to leadership. Instead, many are becoming more democratic, functioning more as "coaches" than "bosses"; in other words, just as an athletic coach teaches athletes how to play and then steps back to let them take the field of competition, many leaders now try to provide workers with the skills and resources to perform at their best before backing off to let them do their work with less oversight and supervision.

Summary of Learning Objectives

1. **Discuss the importance of *job satisfaction* and *employee morale* and summarize their roles in *human relations* in the workplace.** Good *human relations*—the interactions between employers and employees and their attitude towards one another—are important to business because they lead to higher levels of *job satisfaction* (the degree of enjoyment that workers derive from their jobs) and *morale* (workers' overall attitude towards their workplace). Satisfied employees generally exhibit lower levels of absenteeism and turnover; they also have fewer grievances and engage in fewer negative behaviours.

2. **Identify and summarize the most important theories of employee *motivation*.** Views of employee motivation have changed dramatically over the years. The *classical theory* holds that people are motivated solely by money. *Scientific management* tried to analyze jobs and increase production by finding better ways to perform tasks. The *Hawthorne studies* were the first to demonstrate the importance of making workers feel that attention is being paid to their needs.

   The *human-resources model* identifies two kinds of managers: *Theory X managers*, who believe that people are inherently uncooperative and must be constantly reinforced, and *Theory Y managers*, who believe that people are naturally responsible and self-motivated to be productive.

   Maslow's *hierarchy of needs model* proposes that people have a number of different needs (ranging from physiological to self-actualization) that they attempt to satisfy in their work. People must fulfil lower-level needs before seeking to fulfil higher-level needs. *Two-factor theory* suggests that if basic *hygiene factors* are not met, workers will be dissatisfied; only by increasing more complex *motivating factors* can companies increase employees' satisfaction levels.

   Expectancy theory holds that people will work hard if they believe that their efforts will lead to desired rewards. *Equity theory* says that employees compare the treatment they receive from the organization to the treatment received by others. *Goal-setting theory* says that employees who set quantified, difficult goals will outperform employees who don't set such goals.

3. **Discuss different managerial styles of *leadership* and their impact on human relations in the workplace.** Effective *leadership*—the process of motivating others to meet specific objectives—is an important determinant of employee satisfaction and motivation. Generally speaking, managers practise one of three basic managerial styles. *Autocratic managers* generally issue orders and expect they will be obeyed. *Democratic managers* generally seek subordinates' input into decisions. *Free-rein managers* are more likely to advise than to make decisions. Managers need to assess situations carefully, especially to determine the desire of subordinates to share input or exercise creativity.

4. **Describe the strategies used by organizations to improve employee motivation and job satisfaction.** Managers can use several strategies to increase employee motivation and satisfaction. The principle of *reinforcement* holds that reward and punishment can control behaviour. *Rewards*, for example, are positive reinforcement when they are tied directly to desired or improved performance. *Punishment* (using

unpleasant consequences to change undesirable behaviour) is generally less effective. *Management by objectives* (a system of collaborative goal setting) and *participative management* (techniques for giving employees a voice in management decisions) can improve human relations by making employees feel like part of a team. *Job enrichment, job redesign,* and *modified work schedules* (including *flextime* and *workshare programs*) can enhance job satisfaction by adding motivating factors to jobs in which they are normally lacking.

Key Terms

human relations, 278
job satisfaction, 278
morale, 279
empowerment, 279
motivation, 281
classical theory of
  motivation, 281
scientific management,
  282

time-and-motion studies,
  282
piecework system, 282
Hawthorne effect, 283
Theory X, 284
Theory Y, 284
two-factor theory, 286
expectancy theory, 287
equity theory, 287

goal-setting theory, 288
leadership, 289
managerial style, 289
autocratic style, 289
democratic style, 289
free-rein style, 289
contingency approach, 290
participative
  management, 293

quality circle, 293
job enrichment, 294
job redesign, 295
flextime, 296
compressed workweek,
  297
telecommuting, 297
worksharing (job
  sharing), 298

Study Questions and Exercises

Review Questions
1. Do you think most people are satisfied or dissatisfied with their work? Why?
2. Compare and contrast the hierarchy of human needs and the two-factor theory.
3. How can participative management programs enhance employee satisfaction?
4. In what type of situations might a manager be primarily autocratic (boss-centred)? In what type of situations might a manager be primarily democratic (subordinate-centred)?

Analysis Questions
5. Some evidence suggests that people fresh out of college or university initially show high levels of job satisfaction. Their job satisfaction drops dramatically in their late twenties, but gradually increases again as they get older. What might account for this pattern?

6. As a manager, how could you apply each of the theories of employee motivation discussed in this chapter? Which would be easiest to use? Which would be hardest? Why?
7. Suppose you were an employee and realized one day that you were essentially dissatisfied with your job. Short of quitting, what might you do to improve things for yourself?
8. List five important Canadian managers of today who are also great leaders. Give reasons why you chose the five.

Application Exercises
9. Go to the library and research a manager and/or owner of a company in the early 20th century and a manager or owner of a company in the last decade. Compare and contrast the two in terms of their leadership style and their view of employee motivation.
10. Interview the manager of a local manufacturing company. Identify as many different strategies for enhancing job satisfaction at that company as you can.

Building Your Business Skills

Goal
To encourage students to think about the role that family-friendly strategies play in motivating students.

Situation
Business Week magazine recently published the results of a year-long study comparing the family-friendly strategies of some major corporations. Among strate-

gies defined as family-friendly are flexible scheduling, telecommuting, job sharing, child care and elder care assistance, and employee help lines. As part of the study, *Business Week* surveyed 7776 employees at 37 companies with established programs. The purpose of the study was to learn how employees perceive company policies and how these policies affect employees' ability to function both at work and at home.

...

Method

Step 1:

Join with three or four other students in your class. Ask each person in the group to identify relatives and friends who are currently working and who would agree to answer several of the questions posed in the *Business Week* survey. Make a list of these workers, their positions, and the companies for which they work.

Step 2:

Have each member of the group ask survey participants the following questions. Answers should fit into one of the categories listed below each question. The percentage that appears next to each answer reflects the response received in the *Business Week* survey.

■ What impact does your work have on your home life?
Negative impact	(42%)
Neutral	(26%)
Positive impact	(32%)

■ Does your company have high-quality programs for people who have to care for children or elder family members?
Not at all/Not much	(23%)
Somewhat	(26%)
Considerably/A great deal	(51%)

■ Can you have a good family life and still get ahead in your company?
Not at all/Not much	(22%)
Somewhat	(30%)
Considerably/A great deal	(48%)

■ Is your supervisor flexible when it comes to responding to your work/family needs?
Not at all/Not much	(8%)
Somewhat	(16%)
Considerably/A great deal	(76%)

Step 3:

Meet as a group to analyze responses. Specifically, determine how the responses that your group gathered compare with those in the *Business Week* survey.

Follow-Up Questions

1. How do family-friendly strategies affect employee motivation and productivity?

2. What do the responses to the *Business Week* survey tell you about the level of satisfaction or dissatisfaction people are experiencing at work as a result of their dual roles? Are workers satisfied that their companies are trying to help them balance their work/family responsibilities?

3. What do the differences and/or similarities in the responses reported by *Business Week* and those gathered by your own survey group tell you about the family-friendly strategies of the companies for which your survey subjects work?

This chapter stresses the fact that employee satisfaction and morale are important to any organization. However, it is also quite difficult for managers to know for sure just how satisfied and motivated their employees actually are. In most cases, managers interested in assessing satisfaction and/or morale do so with surveys. Employees are asked to respond to various questions about how they feel about their work, and their responses are scored to provide an indication of their satisfaction and morale. To examine such a survey, visit this Web site:

http://www.fdgroup.co.uk/neo/djassoc/dj_jdq.html

After you have examined the satisfaction questionnaire at this site, consider the following questions:

1. For whose use is this questionnaire geared? After studying the explanatory headnote, can you identify two or three key principles of instruments like this one?

2. At face value, how valid does this survey instrument seem to be? Is it likely to meet the objectives outlined in the headnote?

3. Fill out the survey yourself, and then analyze your responses.

4. What appear to be the biggest strengths and weaknesses of this particular survey? Assuming this questionnaire to be typical, what would you judge to be the strengths and weaknesses of job satisfaction surveys in general?

5. Try writing a survey yourself. Focus it on job satisfaction in your present job, in a previous job, or in this class. What information do you most want to elicit? What aspect of this information is hardest to elicit? Why?

CONCLUDING CASE 10-1

Motivating the Sales Force

Mary Kay Cosmetics was begun by Mary Kay Ash. Sales have increased from $198 000 in 1963 to $613 million in 1993. The company employs 300 000 salespeople, all but 2000 of whom are women.

The typical Mary Kay saleswoman starts at the bottom by buying a makeup kit for about $100. She then phones friends, organizes parties in her home, and sells them makeup for about twice what she paid for it. She also recruits new saleswomen and receives a percentage of what they sell. Each saleswoman buys direct from head office at the same price. There is no cap on how much a woman can make. The most successful make over $200 000 per year.

How does the company motivate these salespeople? By giving them recognition, not just cash. Each year thousands of Mary Kay Cosmetics saleswomen attend a three-day rally called Seminar. At this rally, saleswomen are recognized for their achievements in selling. They receive compliments and gifts ranging from small tokens to the legendary pink Cadillac. At this annual rally, the emphasis is on recognizing accomplishments. Emotional compensation is just as important as financial compensation. Company-paid trips are seen as particularly desirable. One group of winners won a trip to London. The high point of the trip came when Harrods was closed for an hour so the group could shop in private.

Recognition from Mary Kay Ash seems to be what many saleswomen crave the most. She personally crowns four Queens of Seminar—women who have excelled at sales or recruiting. She kisses the winners, pats their hands, and presents them with roses. She also tells her own life story of how she started out poor in 1937 and, after seeing how women were treated by business firms (a man received a promotion she should have received), she decided, at age 45, to start her own company that would treat women right.

Husbands are very much in evidence at the annual Seminar, and recently one salesman even received a pink Cadillac for his selling achievements. But it is clear that the event is for the saleswomen. The company stresses that the wife's business is a proprietorship, not a partnership. It belongs to her, not to the couple. At the Seminar, the general view is conveyed that the husband's responsibility is to support his wife's career. In a videotape directed to husbands, Mary Kay Ash stresses that woman was created to stand alongside man as his equal.

Case Questions

1. What is the relative emphasis on money vs. recognition as a motivational tool at Mary Kay Cosmetics?

2. Would the kind of recognition given at this company motivate workers in other kinds of business firms?

3. Are there any shortcomings in the way Mary Kay Cosmetics motivates salespeople? ◆

Mary Kay Cosmetics
http://www.marykay.com

CONCLUDING CASE 10-2

Teamwork or Dirty Work?

To proponents, it's a chance for Canadian firms to increase productivity and become competitive in global markets once more, and for workers to use their brains as well as their backs. But to opponents, it's just another management attempt to speed up production at the expense of workers' jobs, earnings, and health. It's the latest in Japanese imports: the team concept.

Actually, the idea of using teams of workers trained in all phases of constructing a product is not original to the Japanese. British, Swedish, and American firms have experimented with the team concept for over 40 years.

In a traditional assembly line, an individual worker performs only one specified task. Over the years, the worker builds up seniority and is then allowed to apply for better paying or easier jobs in the company. Assembly line workers are, in turn, supervised very closely by first-line managers.

In contrast, the team concept breaks down job distinctions. All members of a team are "cross-trained" to perform every necessary function to produce a good or service. Teams also solve minor problems as they arise. Individuals who show the most leadership within the team—not necessarily those with the most seniority—are promoted.

...

Teamwork or Dirty Work?

(continued)

These radical departures disturb both managers and workers in many companies. First and foremost on the minds of both groups is the issue of power. Managers in industries such as automobiles and steel—which are trying hardest to institute teamwork—are accustomed to giving orders and having them carried out. The need to share power and to ask for suggestions instead of issuing commands is difficult for many managers. First-line managers are particularly likely to resist such changes since, under the team concept, far fewer of such managers are needed.

On the other side of the fence, some workers see the team concept as transferring responsibility but not authority. In many places, managers of the team still dictate the problem to be solved and the parameters for solving it. Teams may be put in a position of choosing to increase production either by using less safe methods or by rejecting fewer flawed pieces.

Part of this problem no doubt stems from differences between Japanese and Canadian workers. Japanese workers do not expect a voice in management and the teamwork system devised in Japan makes no provision for it. To get Canadian workers to "buy into" working harder for their employers, companies have had to face worker demands for greater input into management. Any shift will take years to effect.

Even the job rotation aspect of the team concept has been called into question. Some workers like the chance to change assignments: "I used to switch jobs for half a day with one of my buddies just because we were bored. [Job rotation] makes the day go by faster." But others disagree sharply: "Being able to do six monotonous jobs is no more fulfilling than being able to do one," says one worker.

Although some labour unions support the team concept when management is willing to link it to guarantees of job security, a very vocal minority see it as another in a long series of union-busting attempts by industry. The Canadian Auto Workers, for example, opposes teamwork partnerships between labour and management. In particular, they dislike the fact that unions are being forced to bid against each other for jobs. They point to GM's decision to close a more productive non-team plant and keep open a less productive pro-team plant.

Case Questions

1. What are the differences between the new team concept and the old assembly-line concept?

2. What problems might a company encounter when it tries to implement the team concept?

3. Can labour and management ever really be a team, or is there a fundamental difference in goals between workers and managers?

4. Is the team concept just a gimmick to allow management to get more work out of workers or to "bust" unions? Even if it is a gimmick, might there be advantages for workers?

◆

11

Understanding Labour-Management Relations

What?! A Union at Wal-Mart?

Wal-Mart employees are supposed to be one big, happy family. And that family atmosphere is often cited as a key reason for Wal-Mart's phenomenal growth during the last decade (1996 sales were $93 billion). Wal-Mart has never had a union in any of its 2798 stores in the U.S., Canada, Argentina, Brazil, Mexico, or Puerto Rico. It has

been able to resist unions partly by promoting its family-like culture. The company argues that forcing employees to work under a collective agreement will reduce their motivation and damage the company's successful formula for keeping consumers happy. The company has also resisted unionization in more direct ways. For example, when it purchased 122 Woolco stores in Canada a few years ago, it pointedly did not buy the nine Woolco stores that were unionized.

But in 1997, the Ontario Labour Relations Board (OLRB) certified a United Steelworkers Union local as the bargaining agent for employees at Wal-Mart's Windsor, Ontario, store in spite of the fact that the union lost the certification vote. And Wal-Mart employees at the store have been squabbling ever since.

How did Wal-Mart, which is famous for keeping unions out, lose this battle? Apparently, problems began on April 26, 1996, the day that management heard that a union was approaching employees about joining. Mr. Tino Borean, the district manager, came to the Windsor store the next day and spoke to employees at the "morning meeting" (this meeting is held every day and includes activities such as the store cheer and a discussion about store performance). While Borean's speech was not a violation of the labour act, it appeared that the union's organizing drive began faltering soon afterwards.

A few days later, an anti-union employee gave a speech at the morning meeting exhorting her fellow employees not to join the union. Pro-union employees who asked to respond to her speech were denied the right to do so. On May 2, the union filed its application for certification.

Employees were encouraged by management to ask questions about the union drive, but then the company decided to adopt a policy of refusing to answer employee questions, particularly the one about whether the store would close if the union vote was successful. This strategy was carried out in spite of Wal-Mart's well-known practice of promptly answering employee questions about work-related matters.

On May 5, four days before the certification vote was held, the Windsor store manager told at least one employee that a union would mean a lot of changes at the store, and that employees might lose certain benefits that they currently had. When the certification vote was eventually held, the count was 151-43 against the union. This occurred in spite of the fact that the union had submitted 91 signed cards when it originally filed for certification. Since late April, support for the union had apparently dropped dramatically. The OLRB concluded that the company had violated the Ontario Labour Relations Act by giving employees the impression that the store would be closed if the union was certified, and decided to certify the union at Wal-Mart store 3115.

Since the OLRB ruling, a conflict has developed between Wal-Mart's pro- and anti-union workers, some of whom no longer speak to each other. The atmosphere at the store is also being threatened by many union mem-

(continued)

bers who refuse to be involved in the morning cheer and are also resisting other aspects of Wal-Mart's culture. The anti-union forces are pressing for a new vote, and have collected 130 signatures so far.

The attempt to unionize Wal-Mart is not an isolated phenomenon. A new wave of unionism may be about to sweep across Canada, and it may mean an increased presence for unions in service industries where they have historically had little representation. The movement may be fueled by young people (including university graduates) who fear they will be stuck in low-wage jobs, and who hope that unions can help them avoid that fate. In 1997, unions were certified at nine Starbucks Coffee locations, and an unsuccessful attempt was made to certify a union at McDonald's.

Other changes are also occurring, including the increased numbers of women as union members. In 1967, women accounted for less than 20 percent of union membership in Canada, but by 1997, they represented nearly half of all union workers. These unionized women are highly concentrated in the public sector, which provides jobs for only 19 percent of the workforce, but accounts for 43 percent of all union members. ◆

Many of the issues raised by the unionization of one Wal-Mart store highlight the key principles in contemporary labour-management relations. In this chapter, we will examine various aspects of labour-management relations in Canada. We will begin by considering how and why workers have chosen to band together in the past, as well as what laws regulate labour-management relations. We will then explore the interaction of worker organizations and management in areas such as compensation, employee performance, and workers' grievances. Fianlly, we will take a look at the future of labour organizations in Canada.

By focusing on the learning objectives for this chapter, you will better understand the formation of unions as a result of workers' fundamental concerns about workplace conditions, the legal and regulatory basis for labour-management relations, and the working of the collective bargaining process. After reading this chapter, you will be able to:

LEARNING OBJECTIVES

1. Explain why workers *unionize*.

2. Trace the development of *unionism* in Canada.

3. Describe the major *laws* governing labour-management relations in Canada.

4. Identify the steps in the *collective bargaining process*.

5. Discuss the future of unionism in Canada.

Why Workers Unionize

Over two thousand years ago, the Greek poet Homer wrote, "There is a strength in the union even of very sorry men."[1] Although there were no labour unions in Homer's time, his comment is an apt expression of the rationale for unions. **Labour unions** are groups of individuals working together to achieve job-related goals, such as higher pay, shorter working hours, and better working conditions.

Labour unions arose in this country as a way to force management to deal collectively with employees in a more humane and fair manner. In the 19th and early 20th centuries, working hours were long, pay was minimal, and working conditions were often unsafe. Workers had no job security and minimal benefits. Many companies employed large numbers of children and paid them poverty wages (see the box "Child Labour: Then and Now"). If people complained, they were fired.

labour unions

Groups of individuals who work together to achieve shared job-related goals.

The Canadian Business Scene

Child Labour: Then and Now

The employment of young children in factories and mines has been a problem since the Industrial Revolution began. In Canada, the U.S., and most Western European countries, child labour was a significant problem in the 18th and 19th centuries. Young children were hired to work in factories and mines at very low wages and under extremely poor working conditions. Because most of them were denied the chance to attend school, they remained unskilled all their life.

These problems took many years to resolve. The founding conference of the Canadian Labour Union in 1873 supported a resolution to prohibit the employment of children under age 10 in factories where machinery was used. In 1886, the *Ontario Factory Act* was passed. It prohibited the employment of boys under age 12 and girls under age 14, and set a limit of 60 hours of work per week for women and children.

During the 20th century, major advances have been made in the highly industrialized countries of the world. In Canada, the federal government and all provinces have passed child labour laws. The *Canada Labour Code* allows the employment of individuals under the age of 17, but only if they are not required to attend school under the laws of their province of residence and if the work is unlikely to endanger their health or safety. In addition, no one under age 17 is permitted to work between 11:00 p.m. and 6:00 a.m.

In the developing countries, significant child labour problems remain. In 1997, an international conference on child labour observed that 250 million children are still employed worldwide. Many of these children are working in industrial situations similar to those in Canada in the last century. But many others are forced into child labour of the worst kind—slavery, prostitution, and drug trafficking. The conference focused on the plight of these children, and called for action to immediately end this abuse. The point was also made that solving this problem will be difficult because the causes of child labour are complex, including poverty, social values, and even cultural complacency.

A Canadian teenager, Craig Kielburger, has founded an organization called Free the Children, which promotes children's rights around the world. In 1996, the organization won support from the World Council of Churches to establish a network linking youth organizations internationally so they can effectively bring pressure to bear on governments to ensure that children's rights are protected.

Free the Children
http://www.freethechildren.org/index.html

---

collective bargaining

The process through which union leaders and management personnel negotiate common terms and conditions of employment for those workers represented by the union.

Unions forced management to listen to the complaints of all workers rather than to just those few brave enough to speak out.[2] The power of unions comes from collective (group) action. **Collective bargaining** is a process through which union leaders and management personnel negotiate common terms and conditions of employment for those workers represented by the unions.

The Development of Canadian Labour Unions

The earliest evidence of labour unions in Canada comes from the maritime provinces early in the 19th century. Generally, these unions were composed of individuals with a specific craft (e.g., printers, shoemakers, barrelmakers). Most of these unions were small and had only limited success. However, they laid the foundation for the rapid increase in union activity that occurred during the late 19th and early 20th centuries.

A succession of labour organizations sprang up and just as quickly faded away during the years 1840–70. In 1873, the first national labour organization was formed—the Canadian Labour Union. By 1886, the Knights of Labour (a United States-based union) had over 10 000 members in Canada. The Canadian labour movement began to mature with the formation of the Trades and Labour Congress in 1886. The TLC's purpose was to unite all labour organizations and to work for the passage of laws that would ensure the well-being of the working class.

The growth of labour unions began in earnest early in the 20th century as the concept of organized labour gradually came to be accepted. Within the ranks of labour, various disputes arose that resulted in numerous splits in labour's ranks. For example, there was concern that United States-based unions would have a detrimental effect on Canadian unions. The Canadian Federation of Labour was formed in 1908 to promote national (Canadian) unions over U.S. unions. These and other disputes (such as how communists in the movement should be handled) often led to the creation of rival union organizations that competed for membership. By 1956, these disputes had been largely resolved, and the two largest congresses of affiliated unions—the Trades and Labour Congress and the Canadian Congress of Labour—merged to form the Canadian Labour Congress. This amalgamation brought approximately 80 percent of all unionized workers into one organization. Table 11.1 highlights some of the important events in Canadian labour history.

Canadian Labour Congress
http://www.clc-ctc.ca

Table 11.1   Some Important Dates in Canadian Labour History

1827	First union formed: boot and shoemakers in Quebec City
1840-1870	Many new unions formed; influenced by U.S. and British unions
1871	Formation of Toronto Trades Assembly; composed of five craft unions; went out of existence a few years later
1873	Canadian Labour Union formed; objective was to unite unions across Canada
1879	First coal miners union in North America formed in Nova Scotia
1881	The U.S.-based Knights of Labor enter Canada
1883	Canadian Labour Congress formed; lasted until 1886
1886	Canadian Trades and Labour Congress formed; later became known as the Trades and Labour Congress of Canada (TLC)
1902	Knights of Labor expelled from TLC
1902	Expelled unions form the National Trades and Labour Congress (became the Canadian Federation of Labour [CFL] in 1908); purpose was to promote national unions instead of international ones
1902-1920	Rapid growth of union membership in both major unions (TLC and CFL)
1919	One Big Union formed; organized in opposition to the TLC
1919	Winnipeg General Strike
1921	Canadian Brotherhood of Railway Employees (CBRE) expelled from TLC
1921	Confédération des Travailleurs Catholiques du Canada (CTCC) organized by the Roman Catholic clergy in Quebec; goal was to keep French-Canadian workers from being unduly influenced by English-speaking and American trade unions
1927	All-Canadian Congress of Labour (ACCL) formed; objective was to achieve independence of the Canadian labour movement from foreign control; made up of One Big Union, the CFL, and the CBRE
1939	TLC expels industrial unions; Canadian Congress of Industrial Organization (CIO) Committee formed
1940	ACCL and the Canadian CIO Committee unite to form the Canadian Congress of Labour (CCL)
1956	TLC and CCL merge to form the Canadian Labour Congress; remnants of One Big Union join new organization
1960	CTCC drops association with Roman Catholic Church and chooses a new name—Confédération des Syndicats Nationaux (CSN); in English, the Confederation of National Trade Unions (CNTU)
1960-1969	Rapid growth of CNTU in Quebec
1971	Centre for Democratic Unions formed as a result of secession from the CNTU by dissident members
1981	International building trades unions suspended from CLC
1982	Founding convention of Canadian Federation of Labour (CFL)
1985	Formation of United Auto Workers of Canada; formerly part of international UAW
1989	Merger of Candian Union of Postal Workers (CUPW) and Letter Carriers Union of Canada
1992	First-ever strike of NHL players
1994	Major league baseball players strike; no World Series played; NHL players also locked out, only half of hockey season played
1997	Strike of primary and secondary school teachers in Ontario

Unionism Today

The growth of unions has slowed since the mid-1970s (see Figure 11.1). What has caused this change? Revelations of leadership corruption in the 1950s and 1960s tarnished the appeal of some unions. As well, since that time, foreign competition has prompted many heavily unionized industries, such as automobile and steel manufacturing, to cut back their workforces. The makeup of the workforce has also changed. Most union members used to be

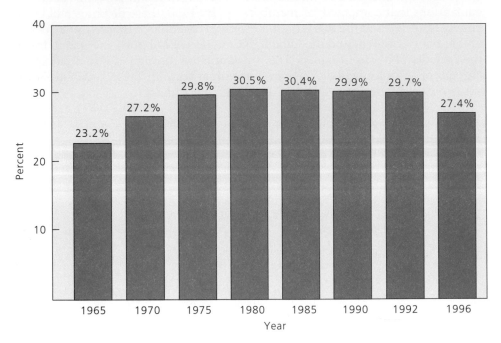

Figure 11.1
Union members as a proportion of the total workforce.

The Canadian Labour Congress (CLC), formed in 1956, brought the majority of unionized workers in Canada into one organization.

white men in blue-collar jobs. But the workforce is increasingly composed of women and minorities in white- or "pink"-collar (secretarial) positions.

At the same time, many nonunionized industries have developed strategies for avoiding unionization. Some companies have introduced new employee relations programs to keep their nonunionized facilities union free. Some work to create a "family feeling," setting aside company land for gardens, tennis courts, and other family activities. Some have used carefully managed campaigns to persuade workers not to form unions.

Even where union membership remains high, such as in the public sector, union power has declined. Growing international competition in certain private-sector industries has led employers to demand unprecedented concessions from unions. **Givebacks**, or sacrifices of previously won terms and conditions of employment, have become commonplace. These are turbulent times for unions and their leaders.

givebacks
Union sacrifices of previously won wages and benefits in return for increased job security.

Nevertheless, labour unions remain a major factor in Canadian business. The labour organizations in the Canadian Labour Congress and independent major unions, such as the International Brotherhood of Teamsters and the Canadian Union of Public Employees, can disrupt the economy by refusing to work. The votes of their members are still sought by politicians at all levels. And the concessions they have won for their members—better pay, shorter working hours, safer working conditions, and benefits such as extended health insurance—now cover nonunion workers as well. The box "Workers of the World, Reorganize!" describes the environment for labour unions in several different countries.

The Legal Environment for Unions in Canada

Political and legal barriers to collective bargaining existed until well into the 20th century. Courts held that some unions were conspirators in restraint of trade. Employers viewed their employees' efforts to unionize as attempts to deprive the employers of their private property. The employment contract, employers contended, was between the individual worker and the employer—not between the employer and employees as a group. The balance of bargaining power was very much in favour of the employer.

The employer/employee relationship became much less direct as firms grew in size. Managers were themselves employees. Hired managers dealt with other employees. Communication among owners, managers, and workers became more formalized. Big business had more power than workers. Because of mounting public concern, laws were passed to place the worker on a more even footing with the employer.

In 1900, government concern about labour disputes resulted in the passage of the *Conciliation Act*. The act was designed to help settle labour disputes through voluntary conciliation and was a first step in creating an environment more favourable to labour. A more comprehensive law, the 1907 **Industrial Disputes Investigation Act**, provided for compulsory investigation of labour disputes by a government-appointed board before a strike was allowed. However, this act was later found to violate a fundamental provision of the *BNA Act* (see below).

Industrial Disputes Investigation Act (1907)
Provided for compulsory investigation of labour disputes by a government-appointed board before a strike was allowed.

The current positive environment for labour did not come into being until 1943 when *Privy Council Order 1003* was issued. This order recognized the right of employees to bargain collectively, prohibited unfair labour practices on the part of management, established a labour board to certify bargaining authority, and prohibited strikes and lockouts except in the course of negotiating collective agreements. Approximately 45 years of dealings among labour, management, and government were required before the labour movement achieved its fundamental goal of the right to bargain collectively.

Privy Council Order 1003 (1943)
Recognized the right of employees to bargain collectively.

The Canadian Business Scene

Workers of the World, Reorganize!

A tidal wave of political change has washed across the globe since the late 1980s. As market economies flourish and trading relations among nations grow more friendly, the role of unions is changing in many parts of the world, including countries as diverse as China, Poland, Mexico, and South Africa. In China, for instance, the government's market-oriented policies have resulted in both double-digit growth and an economic catch-22. On the one hand, Beijing is trying to reduce labour abuse through laws and decrees designed to spur union organization and regulate child labour. On the other hand, strict regulation could make foreign investors nervous about labour problems and send them in search of joint ventures elsewhere. Urban unemployment in 1994 was up 25 percent from the previous year. Although the government promises reform, the restructuring of state-owned enterprises has not yet taken place.

There is strong evidence that China also needs serious labour reform. Foreign investment, for example, has resulted in the hasty construction of thousands of new factories where profit is a priority over worker safety. Factories are plagued by fires and job-related accidents that have killed hundreds of workers in just a few short months. Wang Yuxian, director of the International Liaison Department of the government-run All-China Federation of Labour Unions (ACFLU) blames Asian investors in Hong Kong and Taiwan, citing "their emphasis on profits and their cavalier disregard for safety." In turn, foreign labour leaders call the ACFLU a "yellow union" for bowing to government pressures. "Yellow unions are totally useless," reports one labour official from Hong Kong. "Whenever management negotiates with the union, the union agrees with management."

Poland is experiencing similar troubles in its transition from a controlled economy. Solidarity—the Polish labour union that brought about the fall of Communism in that country in 1988—is no longer the powerful agent for change that it was in the 1980s. As foreign investors moved in to take over state-run enterprises, management styles have changed and Solidarity has had a hard time making the transition. For example, a strike at Huta Warszawa steel works, a former state enterprise, put Solidarity in the position of negotiating wages rather than leading social upheaval. "Before," complains Maciej Jankowski, leader of the union's Warsaw chapter, "we worked on everything: economic, political, and social. Now everything is strictly wages." Of course, the union's most famous member, Lech Walesa, is now president of Poland. His popularity, however, has dropped, as has public support of Solidarity. Seventy percent of respondents to a poll taken in 1994 said that Solidarity, once in the forefront of progress in many aspects of Polish life, had deteriorated.

In Mexico, meanwhile, a unionization drive is being spearheaded by Americans opposed to the North American Free Trade Agreement (see Chapter 4). One goal is to increase pay in Mexico: For example, hourly wages for U.S. factory workers average $16, including benefits; Mexican workers' make about $8 per day. Another goal is leverage. Baldemar Velásquez, head of the Farm Labour Organizing Committee in the U.S., sees cross-border cooperation as a key to increased power among Mexican unions. "If we ever get into a big fight with a North American company that has operations in Mexico," says Velásquez, "I'm sure we're going to get good cooperation from the Mexican unions." Ironically, even though Mexican labour laws are more stringent than those in the United States, many of the large unions, like those in China, support official government positions rather than those of workers.

Finally, South African labour unions were instrumental in ending apartheid, and many observers expected Nelson Mandela's election in April 1994 to result in stronger unions: "It's our turn to be treated as human beings," announced Clara Monethi of the South African Clothing and Textile Workers Union. Unfortunately, economic realities are working against South African unions. Shortly after the election, for example, seven mills in the town of Kimberly were shut down by their Taiwanese owners, threatening to idle 1000 workers.

In addition, because South African workers had built up immense hostility towards employers during decades of white rule, post-apartheid unions pushed hard—and successfully—for higher and higher wages. Consequently, South African wage rates are now twice as high as those in Mexico and several times higher than wages in Thailand and China. Potential foreign investors are concerned that in addition to such high wages, South African unions are extremely powerful. The challenge, reports local labour expert Duncan Innes, is to make union members realize that a new era has begun: "They still see business as a kind of endless pot from which they can draw ever-increasing wages, and there is no end to the process."

Constitution Act, 1867
Divided authority over labour regulations between the federal and provincial governments.

The Constitution Act (originally the *BNA Act*), passed in 1867, has also affected labour legislation. This act allocated certain activities to the federal government (e.g., labour legislation for companies operating interprovincially) and others to individual provinces (labour relations regulations in general).

Thus, labour legislation emanates from both the federal and provincial governments but is basically a provincial matter. That is why certain groups of similar employees might be allowed to go on strike in one province but not in another.

Federal Legislation—The Canada Labour Code

The *Canada Labour Code* is a comprehensive piece of legislation that applies to the labour practices of firms operating under the legislative authority of parliament. The code is composed of four major sections:

Canada Labour Code
Legislation that applies to the labour practices of firms operating under the legislative authority of parliament.

Fair Employment Practices

This section prohibits an employer from either refusing employment on the basis of a person's race or religion or using an employment agency that discriminates against people on the basis of their race or religion. These prohibitions apply to trade unions as well, but not to non-profit, charitable, and philanthropic organizations. Any individual who believes a violation has occurred may make a complaint in writing to Labour Canada. The allegation will then be investigated and if necessary, an Industrial Inquiry Commission will be appointed to make a recommendation in the case. (Since 1982, fair employment practices have been covered by the *Canadian Human Rights Act*; they are also covered by the Canadian Charter of Rights and Freedoms.)

Standard Hours, Wages, Vacations, and Holidays

This section deals with a wide variety of mechanical issues such as standard hours of work (eight-hour day and 40-hour week), maximum hours of work per week (48), overtime pay (at least one and a half times the regular pay), minimum wages, equal wages for men and women doing the same jobs, vacations, general holidays, and maternity leave. The specific provisions are changed frequently to take into account changes in the economic and social structure of Canada, but their basic goal is to ensure consistent treatment of employees in these areas.

Safety of Employees

This section requires that every person running a federal work project do so in a way that will not endanger the health or safety of any employee. It also requires that safety procedures and techniques be implemented to reduce the risk of employment injury. This section requires employees to exercise care to ensure their own safety; however, even if it can be shown that the employee did not exercise proper care, compensation must still be paid. This section also makes provisions for a safety officer whose overall duty is to assure that the provisions of the code are being fulfilled. The safety officer has the right to enter any federal project "at any reasonable time."

Canada Industrial Relations Regulations

The final major section of the *Canada Labour Code* deals with all matters related to collective bargaining. It is subdivided into seven divisions:

- Division I—gives employees the right to join a trade union and gives employers the right to join an employers association.
- Division II—establishes the Canada Labour Relations Board whose role is to make decisions on a number of important issues (e.g., certification of trade unions).

- Division III—stipulates the procedures required to acquire or terminate bargaining rights.
- Division IV—establishes the rules and regulations that must be adhered to during bargaining; also presents guidelines for the content and interpretation of collective agreements.
- Division V—states the requirement that the Minister of Labour must appoint a conciliation officer if the parties in the dispute cannot reach a collective agreement.
- Division VI—stipulates the conditions under which strikes and lockouts are permitted.
- Division VII—a general conclusion giving methods that might be used to promote industrial peace.

Provincial Labour Legislation

Each province has enacted legislation to deal with the personnel practices covered in the *Canada Labour Code*. These laws vary across provinces and are frequently revised; however, their basic approach and substance is the same as in the *Canada Labour Code*. Certain provinces may exceed the minimum code requirements on some issues (e.g., minimum wage).

Each province also has a labour relations act. To give an indication of what these acts cover, the *Ontario Labour Relations Act* is briefly described below.

The Ontario Labour Relations Act

The *Ontario Labour Relations Act* is a comprehensive document dealing with the conduct of labour relations in that province. Some illustrative provisions of the Ontario law are noted below.

- A trade union may apply at any time to the Ontario Labour Relations Board (OLRB) for certification as the sole bargaining agent for employees in a company.
- The OLRB has the right to call for a certification vote. If more than 50 percent of those voting are in favour of the trade union, the board certifies the union as the bargaining agent.
- Following certification, the union gives the employer written notification of its desire to bargain, with the goal being the signing of a collective agreement. The parties are required to begin bargaining within 15 days of the written notice.
- On request by either party, the Minister of Labour appoints a conciliation officer to confer with the parties and to help achieve a collective agreement. On joint request, the Minister of Labour can appoint a mediator.
- The parties may jointly agree to submit unresolved differences to voluntary binding arbitration. The decision of the arbitrator is final.
- Employers are required to deduct union dues from the union members and remit these dues directly to the union.
- Every agreement must include a mechanism for settling grievances—differences between the parties arising from interpretation, application, or administration of the collective agreement.
- If a person objects to belonging to a labour union because of religious beliefs, he or she is allowed to make a contribution equal to the amount of the union dues to a charitable organization.
- If a trade union is not able to negotiate a collective agreement with management within one year of being certified, any of the employees in the union can apply to the OLRB for decertification of the union.

- No employer can interfere with the formation of a union. The employer is, however, free to express an opinion about the matter.

- No employer shall refuse to employ an individual because he or she is a member of a trade union.

The basic provisions of the *Ontario Labour Relations Act* are found in one form or another in the labour relations acts of all provinces, but the details and procedures vary from province to province. It is obvious that administering labour relations activity is complex and time-consuming. Company management, the union, and the government all expend much time and energy in an attempt to ensure reasonable relations between management and labour.

Union Organizing Strategy

A union might try to organize workers when a firm is trying to break into a new geographical area, when some workers in a firm are members and it wants to cover other workers, or when it is attempting to outdo a rival union. In some cases, a union might try to organize workers for purposes other than helping a group of employees to help themselves.

Management often becomes aware of a union organizing effort through gossip on the company grapevine. These rumblings may set off a countereffort by management to slow the drive. Management must know, however, what it can do legally. A do-nothing approach is rare today. An employer can exercise the right of free speech to present its side of the story to the workers.

In Quebec, McDonald's has been the target of union organizing drives at several of its restaurants. In 1998, the McDonald's restaurant in St. Hubert closed when it appeared that the teamsters union might be successful in getting certified as the bargaining agent for the employees. Critics immediately called for a government investigation into the possibility of unfair labour practices on the part of the company.[3]

Suppose that a union is trying to organize employees of a Manitoba company. If it can show that at least 50 percent of the employees are members of the union, it can apply to the Manitoba Labour Board (MLB) for certification as the bargaining agent for the employees.

A problem may arise regarding the right of different types of workers to join or not join the union. For example, supervisors may or may not be included in a bargaining unit along with nonmanagement workers. The **bargaining unit** includes those individuals deemed appropriate by the province. The MLB has final authority in determining the appropriateness of the bargaining unit. Professional and nonprofessional employees are generally not included in the same bargaining unit unless a majority of the professional employees wish to be included.

Once the MLB has determined that the unit is appropriate, it may order a **certification vote.** If a majority of those voting are in favour of the union, it is certified as the sole bargaining agent for the unit.

bargaining unit
Individuals grouped together for purposes of collective bargaining.

certification vote
A vote supervised by a government representative to determine whether a union will be certified.

Types of Unions

The two basic types of union are craft and industrial unions.

Craft unions are organized by crafts or trades—plumbers, barbers, airline pilots, etc. Craft unions restrict membership to workers with specific skills. In many cases, members of craft unions work for several different employers during the course of a year. For example, many construction workers are hired by their employers at union hiring halls. When the particular job for which they are hired is finished, these workers return to the hall to be hired by another employer.

craft unions
Unions organized by trades; usually composed of skilled workers.

Craft unions have a lot of power over the supply of skilled workers because they have apprenticeship programs. A person who wants to become a member of a plumber's union, for example, will have to go through a training program. He or she starts out as an apprentice. After the training, the apprentice is qualified as a journeyman plumber.

industrial unions

Unions organized by industry; usually composed of semiskilled and unskilled workers.

Industrial unions are organized according to industries, for example, steel, auto, clothing. Industrial unions include semiskilled and unskilled workers. They were originally started because industrial workers were not eligible to join craft unions. Industrial union members typically work for a particular employer for a much longer period of time than do craft union members. An industrial union has a lot of say regarding pay and human resource practices within unionized firms.

local union

The basic unit of union organization.

The **local union** (or local) is the basic unit of union organization. A local of a craft union is made up of artisans in the same craft in a relatively small geographical area. A local of an industrial union is made up of workers in a given industry or plant in a relatively small geographical area. Thus, plumbers in a local labour market may be members of the local plumbers' union. Truck drivers and warehouse workers in that same area may be members of a teamsters' local.

The functions of locals vary, depending not only on governance arrangements but also on bargaining patterns in particular industries. Some local unions bargain directly with management regarding wages, hours, and other terms and conditions of employment. Many local unions are also active in disciplining members for violations of contract standards and in pressing management to consider worker complaints.

national union

A union with members across Canada.

A **national union** has members across Canada. These members belong to locals affiliated with the national union. There are many national unions in Canada, including the Canadian Union of Public Employees, the National Railway Union, and the Canadian Airline Pilots Union.

international union

A union with members in more than one country.

An **international union** is a union with members in more than one country. One example is the United Steelworkers of America, made up of locals in the United States and Canada.

independent local union

One not formally affiliated with any labour organization.

An **independent local union** is one that is not formally affiliated with any labour organization. It conducts negotiations with management at a local level, and the collective agreement is binding at that location only. The University of Manitoba Faculty Association is an independent local union. Membership in local unions in 1996 was 3.4 percent of total union membership (see Table 11.2). Table 11.3 shows the 10 largest unions in Canada.

Union Structure

Just as each organization has its own unique structure, so too does each union create a structure that best serves its own needs. As Figure 11.2 shows, however, there is a general structure that characterizes most national and

Table 11.2 **Characteristics of National and International Union Membership, 1996**

Total Union Membership	4 032 989
Percentage in CLC/CTC	63.2
Percentage in AFL/CIO/CLC	24.2
Percentage in SCN/CNTU	6.2
Percentage in International Unions	29.4
Percentage in National Unions	65.7
Percentage in Independent Local Unions	3.4

Unionized workers can be found in both manufacturing and service businesses. Here, a unionized VIA Rail employee serves a customer on a cross-country passenger train.

Table 11.3   **The Top 10 Unions in Canada**

Union	Members (thousands)
1. Canadian Union of Public Employees	455.8
2. National Union of Public and General Employees	310.6
3. National Automobile, Aerospace, and Agricultural Implement Workers	205.0
4. United Food and Commercial Workers Union	185.0
5. Public Service Alliance of Canada	167.8
6. United Steelworkers of America	161.2
7. Communication, Energy, and Paperworkers Union of Canada	124.7
8. Confédération des affaires sociales (CSN)	97.0
9. International Brotherhood of Teamsters, Chauffeurs, Warehousemen, and Helpers of America	95.0
10. Service Employees International Union	80.0

international unions. A major function of unions is to provide service and support to both members and local affiliates. Most of these services are carried out by the types of specialized departments shown in Figure 11.2.

Officers and Functions

Each department or unit represented at the local level elects a **shop steward**—a regular employee who acts as a liaison between union members and supervisors. For example, if a worker has a grievance, he or she takes it to the steward, who tries to resolve the problem with the supervisor. If the local is very large, the union might hire a full-time **business agent** (or **business representative**) to play the same role.

shop steward

A regular employee who acts as a liaison between union members and supervisors.

business agent

In a large union, the business agent plays the same role as a shop steward.

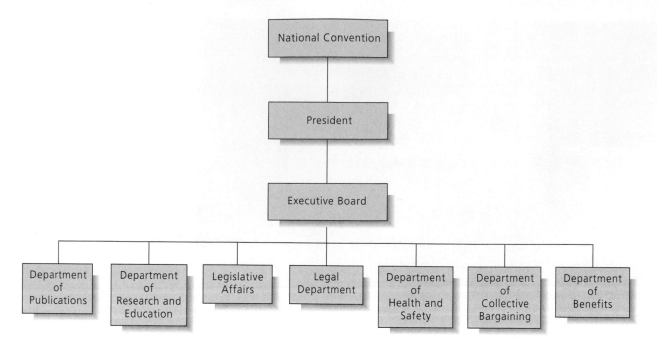

Figure 11.2
Organization of a large national union.

Within a given union, the main governing bodies are the national union (or international union when members come from more than one country) and its officers. Among their other duties, national and international unions charter local affiliates and establish general standards of conduct and procedures for local operations. For example, they set dues assessments, arrange for the election of local officers, sanction strikes, and provide guidance in the collective bargaining process. Many national unions also engage in a variety of political activities, such as lobbying. They may also help coordinate organizing efforts and establish education programs.

Given the magnitude of their efforts, it is little wonder that unions often take on many of the same characteristics as the companies for which their members work. For example, almost all large unions have full-time administrators, formal organizational structures (see Figure 11.2), goals and strategic plans, and so forth.

Union Security

The growing security consciousness of Canadian workers is reflected in union goals. The seniority provision in most contracts spells out the workers' rights when layoffs, transfers, and promotions occur. Employees are ranked by length of service. Those with longer service get better treatment.

Much conflict exists regarding seniority. For example, women and members of minority groups typically have less seniority and are the first to be laid off and the last to move up to higher jobs. These workers tend to oppose the tradition of seniority.

union security

The maintenance of a union's membership so that it can continue to meet the criteria for certification.

Union security refers to the means of ensuring the union's continued existence and the maintenance of its membership so that it can continue to meet the criteria for certification. There is always a danger—particularly in bad economic times—that the membership may drop below the required absolute majority. The union may then lose its certification.

The greatest union security is found in the closed shop. In a **closed shop**, an employer can hire only union members. For example, a plumbing or electrical contractor who hires workers through a union hiring hall can hire only union members.

In a **union shop**, an employer may hire nonunion workers even if the employer's current employees are unionized. New workers, however, must join the union within a stipulated period of time (usually 30 days).

In an **agency shop**, all employees for whom the union bargains must pay dues, but they need not join the union. This compromise between the union shop and the open shop is called the Rand Formula after the judge who proposed it. In the *Quebec Labour Code*, the Rand formula applies to all unions certified under this code.

In an **open shop**, an employer may hire union and/or nonunion labour. Employees need not join or pay dues to a union in an open shop.

Another union security issue is job security, especially in highly automated industries. The guaranteed annual wage reflects workers' concerns about job security. The **guaranteed annual wage** is a provision in a labour contract that maintains the workers' income level during a year. Most labour contracts with this guarantee provide the worker with a minimum amount of work during the contract period. This provision lends stability to the worker's employment. Some contracts provide for early retirement, lengthy vacations, or sabbatical leaves for employees.

The security of unions themselves is also in question. The most unionized industries—steel, auto, transportation—are automating rapidly. Prospects for new members are not attractive. Furthermore, the stronghold of unions—blue-collar labour—is diminishing as a percentage of the labour force. On the other hand, unions have found new areas, such as government workers and white-collar workers, to organize.

closed shop
An employer can hire only union members.

union shop
An employer can hire nonunionized workers but they must join the union within a certain period.

agency shop
All employees for whom the union bargains must pay dues but they are not required to join the union.

open shop
An employer may hire union or nonunion workers.

guaranteed annual wage
A provision in a contract that guarantees the workers' income level during a year.

Collective Bargaining

Too often, people associate collective bargaining with the signing of a contract between a union and a company or industry. In fact, collective bargaining is an ongoing process involving not only the drafting but also the administering of the terms of a labour contract.

Reaching Agreement on the Contract's Terms

The collective bargaining process begins with the recognition of the union as the exclusive negotiator for its members. The *bargaining cycle* begins when union leaders meet with management representatives to agree on a new contract. By law, both parties must sit down at the bargaining table and negotiate "in good faith." Each side presents its demands. Ultimately, they reach some compromise and the new agreement is submitted to the union's membership for a *ratification vote*.

Most of the time this process will go smoothly. Sometimes, however, the two sides cannot—or will not—agree. Such an impasse is not illegal. How quickly and easily it is resolved depends in part on the nature of the demands made, the willingness of each side to use the weapons at its disposal, and the prospect for mediation or arbitration.

Contract Demands

Contract negotiations may centre on any number of issues. One common point of negotiation is compensation. For example, unions frequently fight

cost-of-living adjustment (COLA)

A contract clause specifying that wages will increase automatically with the rate of inflation.

British Steel Corp.

http://www.britishsteel.co.uk

for clauses ensuring a **cost-of-living adjustment (COLA)**, especially during times of high inflation. Such a clause specifies that wages will increase automatically in proportion to increases in the cost of living, usually as reflected in the *consumer price index,* a measure of inflation.

Compensation was probably the dominant negotiation issue during the 1970s and 1980s. Business growth was producing large profits and labour wanted a portion of them. But as growth and inflation levelled off, compensation became a less critical part of most contract negotiations. The highly publicized strike of Ontario primary and secondary school teachers in 1997, for example, focused more on working conditions, layoff provisions, and classroom issues than it did on teacher compensation.

There is also a trend to reducing the workforce in return for job security. At British Steel Corp.'s Llanwern plant, the union agreed to a loss of 4454 jobs and the end of strict demarcations between jobs that prevented members of one union from doing the work of those in another union. In return, they received job security for the remaining workers at the plant. British Steel is now one of the lowest-cost producers of steel in the world.[4]

A final critical point of negotiation is management rights. Obviously, management wants as much control as possible over whom it hires, how it assigns work, and so forth. The union, on the other hand, often tries to limit management rights by specifying how hiring will be done, how work will be assigned, and other *work rules.* For example, at one automobile plant, the union contract specifies that three workers are to be used to change fuses in robots—a machinist to open the robot, an electrician to change the fuse, and a supervisor to oversee the process. Unions try to specify as many different job categories as possible. Workers in one category cannot perform work that falls into the domain of another category.

When Bargaining Fails

An impasse occurs when, after a series of bargaining sessions, management and labour fail to agree on a new contract or a contract to replace an agreement that is about to expire. Although it is generally agreed that both parties suffer when an impasse is reached and action is taken, each side can employ several tactics to support its cause until the impasse is resolved.

Members of the Ontario Teachers Federation demonstrate their displeasure with the process of collective bargaining during their 1997 dispute with the province of Ontario.

Union Tactics

Unions can take a variety of actions when their demands are not met. Chief among these tactics is the **strike**. Strikes triggered by impasses over mandatory bargaining items are called economic strikes, even if they occur over noneconomic issues such as working hours. Most strikes in Canada are economic strikes. The strike by National Hockey League players in 1992 and the lockout of players in 1994, as well as the strike by major league baseball players in 1994, were largely over economic issues.

During a strike, workers are not paid and the business is usually unable to produce its normal range of products and services. During this time, the union may try to convince the general public that the company is being unfair. For example, the United Steelworkers of America launched a global campaign against Bridgestone/Firestone to generate negative publicity about the company. After demonstrations and work stoppages were held in 26 different countries, the company agreed to a new contract.[5] As the box "Strike Was No Ball for Business" demonstrates, the impact of a strike goes far beyond the company and its employees.

After a strike is over, employees may exhibit low morale, anger, increased absenteeism, and decreased productivity. In these situations, care must be taken to improve communications between management and workers.[6]

Strikes may occur in response to an employer's unfair labour practices. A firm that refuses to recognize a duly certified union may find itself with a striking workforce and having to explain its refusal to the provincial labour relations board. Such strikes are rare, however.

Not all strikes are legal. The Ontario primary and secondary school teachers strike in 1997 against the province of Ontario was illegal because the teachers had not gone through the necessary steps prior to going out on strike. The teachers voluntarily returned to work after striking for only two weeks. *Sympathy strikes* (also called *secondary strikes*), where one union strikes

strike

A tactic of labour unions in which members temporarily walk off the job and refuse to work in order to win concessions from management.

Bridgestone/Firestone
http://www.bridgestone-firestone.com

Postal workers picket Queen's Park.

The Canadian Business Scene

Strike Was No Ball for Business

When the major league baseball players went on strike in 1994, many other organizations were affected. Brewing giant John Labatt Ltd. was particularly hard-hit. Labatt owns 90 percent of the Toronto Blue Jays, 41 percent of the SkyDome where the team plays, and TSN (which broadcasts the games). The SkyDome alone was losing more than $100 000 per day during the strike. The strike also threatened Labatt's main product—beer—because baseball is such a high-profile arena for advertising this product.

But Labatt wasn't the only organization that suffered because of the strike. Broadcasters, advertisers, retailers, and restaurants had to scramble to save what remained of the summer after the strike began on August 12. Overall, the strike could have cost Toronto-area businesses more than $50 million in lost revenues of one sort or another. Montreal businesses could have lost $20 million.

Bitove Corp. is a hospitality company that handles catering at the SkyDome; it also operates food services at nearby restaurants, including Wayne Gretzky's and the Hard Rock Cafe. The company incurred substantial losses when games that were originally scheduled ended up not being played because of the strike. Well over 2000 jobs were lost at the SkyDome and Olympic Stadium as a result of the strike.

At CTV, losses approached $10 million because the network did not get to televise any post-season play. The losses were high because advertising rates for special events like the World Series are much higher than rates for regular movies or dramatic programs that CTV had to substitute when there were no games to televise.

The bad news for baseball is sometimes good news for people operating other types of businesses. Video rental chains reported increases in sales after the strike began, and The Second City, a Toronto comedy club, played to a full house every night the week after the strike started. Formerly the club had experienced low turnouts whenever the Blue Jays played.

The lockout of National Hockey League players in 1994 caused the same kinds of problems as the baseball strike. Molson Cos. Ltd. owns the Montreal Canadiens, the Molson Centre, and the country's largest brewer, which advertises heavily at hockey games. Therefore they lost money on several ventures.

Maple Leaf Gardens also suffered during the strike. An entire season with no hockey would have resulted in a loss of $7 million. Layoffs and other cost-cutting measures would have been necessary, not only at Maple Leaf Gardens, but at every arena around the league.

The CBC was also hard hit because it had planned to start airing two hockey games instead of one in the fall of 1994 on Hockey Night in Canada. Saturday evening TV audiences, especially men, were down by as much as 50 percent during the lockout. While most of the money that was originally scheduled to be spent advertising hockey games was redirected, broadcasters worried that after the lockout ended they would have a tough time getting advertisers back.

Provincial governments stood to lose $75 million in profits because wagering on sports lotteries declined by as much as 50 percent during the hockey lockout. Ontario was the hardest hit because interest in sports betting is highest there. The Pro-Line lottery accounted for $65 million in 1993.

---

picketing

A tactic of labour unions in which members march at the entrance to the company with signs explaining their reasons for striking.

boycott

A tactic of labour unions in disputes with management in which members refuse to buy the products of the company and encourage other consumers to do the same.

slowdown

Instead of striking, workers perform their jobs at a much slower pace than normal.

lockout

A tactic of management in which the firm physically denies employees access to the workplace in order to pressure workers to agree to the company's latest contract offer.

in sympathy with strikes initiated by another labour organization, may violate the sympathetic union's contract. *Wildcat strikes,* strikes unauthorized by the union that occur during the life of a contract, deprive strikers of their status as employees and thus of the protection of labour laws.

As part of or instead of a strike, unions faced with an impasse may picket or launch a boycott. **Picketing** involves having workers march at the entrance to the company with signs explaining their reasons for striking. A **boycott** occurs when union members agree not to buy the product of the firm that employs them. Workers may also urge other consumers to shun their firm's product. Another alternative to striking is a work **slowdown**: Instead of striking, workers perform their jobs at a much slower pace than normal. A variation is the "sickout," during which large numbers of workers call in sick.

Management Tactics

Management can also respond forcefully to an impasse. To some extent, **lockouts** are the flip side of the strike coin. Lockouts occur when employers physically deny employees access to the workplace. Lockouts are illegal if they are used as offensive weapons to give the firm an economic advantage in the bargaining process. They might be used, for example, if management wants to avoid a buildup of perishable inventory or in similar circumstances. Lockouts, though rare today, were used by major league baseball team owners (without success) in 1990.

As an alternative to a lockout, firms faced with a strike can hire temporary or permanent replacements (**strikebreakers**) for the absent employees. When players in the National Football League went out on strike during the 1987 season, the team owners hired free agents and went right on playing. In 1992, National Hockey League owners planned to use minor league hockey players if they could not reach an agreement with striking NHL players. In extreme cases, management may simply close down a plant if they cannot reach agreement with the union. In 1997, Maple Leaf closed its Edmonton hog processing plant when the workers went on strike. This cost 850 workers their jobs.

More and more firms are contracting out work as a way to blunt their unions' effects. Instead of doing all the assembly work they used to do themselves, many firms now contract out work to nonunion contractors. This lessens the impact that the unions can have and results in fewer union workers.

Employers' associations are especially important in industries that have many small firms and one large union that represents all workers. Member firms sometimes contribute to a strike insurance fund. Such a fund could be used to help members whose workers have struck. They are similar in purpose to the strike funds built up by unions.

Employers are also increasingly using what unions refer to as "union-busting" consultants. These consultants assist management in improving their communications with the shop floor. They help management identify and eliminate the basic pressures that led to the pro-union vote in the first place.

The same law that grants employees the right to unionize also allows them to decertify. **Decertification** is the process by which employees legally terminate their union's right to represent them. In 1992, employees at Rogers Cablesystems Ltd. voted to decertify the union that has represented them since 1975. The union charged that management had induced workers to leave the union.[7]

Decertification campaigns do not differ much from certification campaigns (those leading up to the initial election). The union organizes membership meetings, house-to-house visits, and other tactics to win the election. The employer uses meetings, letters, and improved working conditions to try to obtain a decertification vote.

Mediation and Arbitration

Rather than using weapons on one another, labour and management can agree to call in a third party to help resolve the dispute. In **mediation**, the neutral third party (a mediator) can only advise—not impose—a settlement on the parties. In **voluntary arbitration**, the neutral third party (an arbitrator) dictates a settlement between two sides who have agreed to submit to outside judgment.

In some cases, arbitration is legally required to settle bargaining disputes. Such **compulsory arbitration** is used to settle disputes between government and public employees such as firefighters and police officers.

Administering the Contract's Terms

No matter how a contract is reached, once signed it must be administered and interpreted. Given the complexity of many contracts, this process can be difficult and controversial. To avoid recurring industrial conflicts over contract interpretations, unions and management typically negotiate grievance procedures

strikebreaker
An individual hired by a firm to replace a worker on strike; a tactic of management in disputes with labour unions.

National Hockey League
http://www.nhl.com

decertification
The process by which employees terminate their union's right to represent them.

mediation
A method of settling a contract dispute in which a neutral third party is asked to hear arguments from both the union and management and offer a suggested resolution.

voluntary arbitration
A method of settling a contract dispute in which the union and management ask a neutral third party to hear their arguments and issue a binding resolution.

compulsory arbitration
A method of settling a contract dispute in which the union and management are forced to explain their positions to a neutral third party who issues a binding resolution.

grievance

A complaint on the part of a union member that management is violating the terms of the contract in some way.

into final contracts. A **grievance** is a complaint by a worker that a manager is violating the contract. Figure 11.3 traces a typical grievance procedure.

The union generally promises not to strike over disputes about contract interpretation. In return, unions get the right to file grievances in a formal procedure that culminates in binding arbitration. Most grievance arbitrations take place over disputes regarding the discipline or discharge of employees, but safety issues are a cause for arbitration in some industries.

The Future of Unionism in Canada

The union movement began in a period when the excesses of early capitalism placed the average worker at the mercy of the employer. For decades unions sought to bargain at arm's length with employers. This goal was met through legislation and the collective-bargaining process.

Many people considered unionism to be a worthwhile cause through the 1930s. But some people became critical of unions towards the end of the 1940s, and criticism has continued to mount. Unions are increasingly aware that they must cooperate with employers if they are both to survive. Critics of unions contend that excessive wage rates won through years of strikes and hard-nosed negotiation are partially to blame for the difficulties of large corporations. Others argue that excessively tight work rules limit the productivity of businesses in many industries. More and more often, however, unions are working with organizations to create effective partnerships in which managers and workers share the same goals—profitability, growth, and effectiveness with equitable rewards for everyone.

The future of unions depends on their ability to cope with the economic and social trends that threaten the labour movement. Some of these trends are

- the decline of the smokestack industries (e.g., steel, meat packing, chemicals, metals)
- employment growth in the service industries
- deregulation
- a more competitive business environment
- technological changes
- free trade.

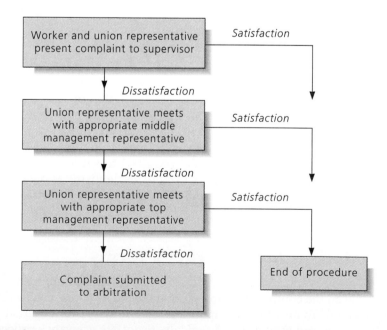

Figure 11.3
A typical grievance procedure.

The Decline of the Smokestack Industries

Competition from abroad is causing many of these industries to seek ways to become more productive. The drive to make Canadian firms competitive internationally is a deep concern for Canadian labour leaders. They believe that management inevitably asks for concessions in its attempt to become more competitive.

Employment Growth in the Service Industries

The majority of Canada's labour force is now employed in the service industries. Except for government employees, these workers have never been highly unionized. Many work part-time, and the typical firm is small. These factors make it harder and more costly for unions to organize them than to organize full-time workers in large factories. As we saw in the opening case, however, unions are beginning to make progress in the service industries.

Deregulation

Deregulation continues to have an impact on unions. Deregulation of the airline, railway, and trucking industries has forced firms to become more competitive. Mergers, layoffs, givebacks, and new nonunionized firms in these and other deregulated industries challenge unions. Just as these firms have to learn to survive under deregulation, so will their employees' unions.

The Business Environment

As domestic and international competition becomes more intense, management has introduced changes to increase corporate efficiency. But these changes have caused conflicts between labour and management. United Parcel Service, for example, has been trying to capture more of the light-trucking market, so it raised its maximum package weight from 32 kilograms to 68 kilograms. But unionized drivers and sorters revolted when asked to lift the increased weights without protective health and safety guarantees. Employees are also unhappy about the way the company is pressuring them to do more work.[8]

UPS
http://www.ups.com

Technological Change

Technology will continue to challenge labour unions. Some clerical and professional workers, for example, now work at home on computer terminals linked to their employers' office computers. Instead of having to commute to work by car, bus, or train, these workers telecommute. Some unions oppose the work-at-home concept because it makes organizing workers harder.

Free Trade

Finally, organized labour is concerned about the potentially negative impact of free trade agreements. Their fear is that products made in the U.S. or Mexico will be shipped tariff-free into Canada, and business firms will put pressure on Canadian workers to work for lower wages. At the worst, companies may simply move out of Canada altogether and do all their production in the U.S. or Mexico.

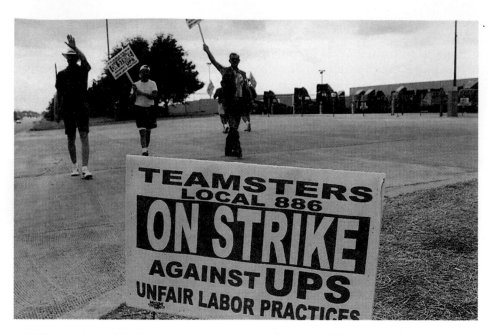

In 1997, members of the Teamsters union went on strike against United Parcel Service, claiming that the company was engaging in unfair labour practices. The strike disrupted the delivery of thousands of UPS packages, and forced customers to look to alternative companies to handle their deliveries.

In 1994, for example, unionized workers at H.J. Heinz in Leamington, Ontario, signed a new collective agreement that contained concessions such as a wage reduction of 50 cents per hour and a reduction in paid holidays. Workers agreed to this in return for a guarantee of job security. In 1998, workers at the Maple Leaf plant in Burlington, Ontario, agreed to a contract that cut their wages by 40 percent. In return, the company agreed to guarantee 900 jobs.

Summary of Learning Objectives

1. **Explain why workers *unionize*.** The Industrial Revolution and the emergence of a factory-based production system made many workers dependent on continuing factory employment. The treatment of labour as a raw material led to such abuses as minimal pay, long workdays, unsafe working conditions, and even child labour. Individuals had little recourse in rectifying problems. By organizing into labour unions, however, workers are able to act collectively to improve working conditions. Most important, acting as a group, they can engage in collective bargaining for higher wages, greater benefits, and better working conditions.

2. **Trace the development of *unionism* in Canada.** The first unions were formed early in the 19th century in the Maritimes. Many labour organizations sprang up and then faded away during the 19th century. In the 20th century, unions began to develop in earnest. In 1943, *Privy Council Order 1003* gave unions the right to collectively bargain with employers. The growth of unions has slowed dramatically in the last decade.

3. **Describe the major *laws* governing labour-management relations in Canada.** *Privy Council Order 1003* gave unions the right to collectively bargain in Canada. The *Constitution Act of 1867* means that the federal government passes legislation (e.g., the *Canada Labour Code*) dealing with labour legislation for companies that operate interprovincially, and the provincial governments pass legislation (e.g., the *Ontario Labour Relations Act*) dealing with companies that operate in only one province.

4. **Identify the steps in the *collective bargaining process*.** Collective bargaining is the process of negotiating a formal agreement between management and labour that spells out the terms and conditions of employment for the workers represented by the union. Labour's weapons during negotiations are the strike, picketing, and boycotts. Management's weapons include the lockout and using strikebreakers. If labour and management cannot agree on employment terms during negotiations, a strike or lockout may occur. Or the two parties may agree to call in a mediator, conciliator, or arbitrator to try to settle their differences.

5. **Discuss the future of unionism in Canada.** Several recent trends may have a significant impact on the union movement. These are: 1) the decline of the smokestack industries (unions' historical base of strength); 2) employment growth in the service industries where unions are not strongly entrenched; 3) deregulation (less government involvement in business); 4) a more competitive business environment, which causes management to be more aggressive in dealing with unions; 5) technological changes (automation threatens union jobs); and 6) free trade agreements (manufacturers may move out of Canada and union jobs will be lost).

Key Terms

labour unions, 305
collective bargaining, 306
givebacks, 309
Industrial Disputes Investigation Act (1907), 309
Privy Council Order 1003 (1943), 309
Constitution Act, 1867, 310
Canada Labour Code, 311

bargaining unit, 313
certification vote, 313
craft unions, 313
industrial unions, 314
local union, 314
national union, 314
international union, 314
independent local union, 314
shop steward, 315
business agent, 315

union security, 316
closed shop, 317
union shop, 317
agency shop, 317
open shop, 317
guaranteed annual wage, 317
cost-of-living adjustment (COLA), 318
strike, 319
picketing, 320

boycott, 320
slowdown, 320
lockout, 320
strikebreaker, 321
decertification, 321
mediation, 321
voluntary arbitration, 321
compulsory arbitration, 321
grievance, 322

Study Questions and Exercises

Review Questions

1. Why do workers in some companies unionize while workers in other companies do not?
2. Why did it take so many years for the union movement to mature in Canada? Describe some of the key events along the way.
3. The proportion of the Canadian workforce that is unionized has been constant for more than 15 years. Why hasn't the proportion increased or decreased?
4. Describe the kinds of employment issues that the Canada Labour Standards Code deals with.
5. How are craft and industrial unions different? How are international, national, and local unions different?

Analysis Questions

6. Workers at the Canadian plants of Ford, General Motors, and Chrysler are represented by the Canadian Auto Workers. Why are automobile workers at Toyota's Cambridge, Ontario, plant—who are doing exactly the same kind of work—not unionized?
7. Suppose you are a manager in a nonunionized company. You have just heard a rumour that some of your workers are discussing forming a union. What would you do? Be specific.
8. What are the implications for management of a closed shop, a union shop, and an agency shop?

Application Questions

9. Interview the managers of two local companies, one unionized and one nonunionized. Compare and contrast the wage and salary levels, benefits, and working conditions of workers at the two firms.
10. With your instructor playing the role of management and a student playing the role of a union organizer, role play the processes involved in trying to form a union.

Building Your Business Skills

Goal

To help students understand the types of labour-management issues affecting various businesses.

Situation

Suppose you are the human-resources manager at a midsized firm where there has been some unrest among the unionized workforce. At issue are such things as pay and mandatory overtime. The president of the company wants to know whether the firm's problems are unique or whether similar issues arise at other companies. The president has asked you to prepare a report surveying labour issues confronting management today.

Method

Working in groups of four or five, make arrangements to conduct interviews at businesses near your college or university. Speak to members of management as well as workers or workers' representatives. Try to cover as many different types of businesses as possible—union and nonunion, service and manufacturing, large and small, and so on. One group could conduct on-campus interviews with employees from your campus food service, physical plant, housekeeping, and clerical areas. In particular:

- At a union shop, interview a shop steward or the officer of a local union.

- Ask management whether the presence (or absence) of a union has an effect on company activities. If so, what kind of effects?

- Inquire about contract negotiations, personnel issues, pay issues, hiring and firing, and pressure from global competition.

- Ask what labour issues are facing the company in the next two to three years.

Circulate your findings to the other teams.

Follow-Up Questions

1. In your research, did you find that one particular labour-management issue showed up repeatedly?

2. What differences, if any, arise in unionized businesses as opposed to nonunionized ones? In service firms as opposed to manufacturing companies?

Labour-management issues play an important role in determining the business climate of Canada. The Ontario Secondary Teachers' Federation is an example of one labour organization. Visit their Web site at:

http://www.osstf.on.ca

The Canadian Union of Postal Employees (CUPW) is a major national union. Visit their Web site at:

http://www.cupw-sttp.org

---

1. What are the most important issues facing the Federation and its members? Where do you stand on these issues? Why?

2. Where in the Web site could you go to find the management (Ontario government) position on these issues? What is the management position?

3. What are the major issues affecting postal workers?

4. What do the statistics in "About CUPW" tell you about the union? About life as a postal employee?

CONCLUDING CASE 11-1

Labour Relations at Canada Post

Relations between Canada Post and the Canadian Union of Postal Workers (CUPW) have been troubled for nearly two decades. Canada Post wants to introduce technological improvements in the way work is done, and this action will reduce the number of employees it needs. CUPW has vigorously opposed these ideas from the start. During 1997, the long-simmering dispute between workers and management heated up again as the two sides tried to sign a new collective agreement.

Bargaining dragged on for many months without much progress. A mediator was then appointed in the hope that he could get the disputing parties to reach an agreement and avert a strike. But after a few days of talks, the mediator concluded that the two sides were not willing to bargain seriously, and he gave up. CUPW then went on strike, and its 45 000 members began walking the picket line.

Tensions were high, and during the strike CUPW workers delayed some commercial airline flights by preventing cargo and food from reaching the planes. They also snarled traffic in some locations, and picketed Preston Manning's official Ottawa residence to show their displeasure. Manning's Reform party viewed the postal service as "essential," and thought that strikes should not be allowed in essential services.

About two weeks after the strike started, the Liberal Minister of Labour, Lawrence MacAulay, introduced back-to-work legislation that forced the postal workers to return to work. The imposed agreement gave the workers a 5.15 percent wage increase over three years (they had been hoping for a 10 percent increase over two years). The legislation also levied fines of $1000 per day against workers who defied the back-to-work order. Union leaders could be fined up to $50 000 per day, and CUPW could face fines of up to $500 000 if it defied the back-to-work order.

MacAulay said he felt compelled to introduce the legislation since so many Canadians were suffering during the labour dispute. Many businesses and charities, for example, were being hurt by the strike since they could not carry on their usual activities without mail service. While MacAulay scolded both Canada Post and CUPW for failing to reach a new agreement, the Reform party criticized the Liberal government for not having acted sooner.

CUPW immediately condemned the legislation, and promised large-scale civil disobedience if the workers were forced back to work. Darrell Tingley, CUPW president, claimed that the Canadian Direct Marketing Association was putting pressure on the government to get the postal workers back on the job.

On December 4, 1997, the defiant postal workers grudgingly returned to work. Tingley suggested that postal workers disrupt normal Canada Post activities by purposely misdirecting business mail, and by sending mail through the system without stamps. Canada Post president Georges Clermont said that it was unbelievable that the postal workers would listen to advice like this, because it would mean hurting Canada Post's customers—the very people who are responsible for the workers having jobs in the first place. Clermont said that workers who followed Tingley's suggestions would be disciplined. But Tingley said that Canada Post can expect a campaign of workplace defiance for the remainder of the three-year agreement.

Case Questions

1. When the postal workers went on strike, many businesses and charities were hurt. Is this an argument for abolishing the right to strike for postal workers? Should postal workers have the right to strike? Defend your answer.

2. What is mediation? Why do you think mediation was not effective in this situation?

3. Read newspaper accounts of the postal strike and the events leading up to it (consult papers dated November 15 through December 5, 1997). How do these accounts illustrate how the collective bargaining process works?

◆

The New Job Title at United Airlines—"Owner"

In July 1994, United Airlines employees were finally successful in acquiring their employer through a $4.9 billion shareholder buyout. The action was hailed by many observers as perhaps a sign of a new era in labour-management relations. By the time the buyout was approved by the company's shareholders, United's unions—representing pilots, machinists and flight attendants—had been involved in a struggle with management for more than a decade.

The buyout process began in 1987, when union representatives of United pilots made two separate bids—both rejected by shareholders—to buy the company for more than $4 billion. In addition to two other unsuccessful employee buyout attempts, rumours of mergers, takeovers, and downsizing soon made the "United" company name a real contradiction. Divisions within the organization ran deeper than the traditional union-management schism.

At times, even relations between United's unions were strained. United's union employees are drawn from the 8700-member Airline Pilots Association (ALPA), the International Association of Machinists (IAM) (representing 24 000 mechanics and ground-service workers), and the Association of Flight Attendants. Within each union, there are still members who disagree with the buyout agreement and its results. For example, a dissident group of ALPA members circulated a survey claiming that 1250 of 1700 pilots surveyed opposed the buyout. In fact, although the IAM had voted to support the buyout, the final tally was a narrow vote of 54 to 46 percent. IAM members opposed to the buyout were in court at the last minute trying to prevent the deal from going through.

Also affected by the buyout are 28 000 employees who are not union members or are not covered by union contracts—for example, ticket agents, crew members, schedulers, and sales employees. These workers complain that they have been forced to accept an agreement on which they never had a vote. They are especially unhappy because the buyout deal subjected them to a 8.25-percent pay cut. (It also included a 23.5-percent cut for pilots and a 15.7-percent cut for IAM employees.)

Arnie Canham, a United employee since 1969, sums up the feelings of many of her colleagues: "There's a lot of unhappiness, a lot of anxiety and underlying resentment. Taking a pay cut is not good news; you can't sugar coat that. I'm afraid that a lot of people are still looking at the situation as us vs. them—management vs. labour, nonunion vs. union. There's a distinct emotional feeling among many people here," adds Canham, "that we don't need to be part of this deal, taking a pay cut.... Why are you taking 8.25 percent of my pay when I didn't contribute to this high-cost operation? That's a big hurdle for people like me to get over."

Supporters of the buyout admit that employees were required to make concessions—including pay cuts. They argue, however, that those concessions cut costs by about $5 billion. They also contend that job security is improved because the new contracts prevent management from laying off employees and from selling assets that could cut jobs. "For me," says James Kozar, a United mechanic since 1986, "it all comes down to job security. I got laid off at TWA after nine years, so I know what that's like. Basically, we are making a sacrifice, and that won't be easy. But we've got our jobs, and that means a lot these days."

The buyout also granted the unions' demand that United's top three executives, including CEO Stephen Wolf, be replaced. Gerald Greenwald, former vice-chairman at Chrysler, is taking over the top job. He has his work cut out for him. Among his biggest tasks will obviously be healing rifts not only between unions and management but among United's unions themselves. In order to keep shareholders and employee-owners happy with their new deal, Greenwald must also boost profitability. In 1994, the numbers were promising: United made a $100 million profit on $16 billion in revenues. Unfortunately, the money is needed to balance big losses in recent years—$50 million in 1993, nearly $1 billion in 1992, and $332 million in 1991.

Employees still differ in their views of what UAL will become as a result of the changes. Reservations agent Melody Sadlier counts herself among the company's "Proud Owners," to borrow a phrase from a button worn by CEO Greenwald. "I'm going to make the best of this thing," she says, "and maybe we are going to weed out all the negative people, the people who complain and crab all the time. If people don't like what's happening, they can always leave. I'm used to change, and I like learning new things. The nice thing about all this is that now I own part of this company. It's like if I own my own house, I want to make sure it looks nice and the grass looks good."

On the other hand, some flight attendants still harbour resentment leftover from their treatment in the past. Says Kevin Lum, head of the Association of Flight Attendants master executive council and a United attendant since 1979: "We've always been treated like angry children who don't deserve what they get. Upper management has been adversarial and confrontational with us for over 10 years now." He notes, for example, that attendants' hotels are frequently in less desirable locations than those of pilots who stay overnight. Attendants are also required to maintain their weight, while other groups of employees are not. "Attendants," charges Lum, "have always been singled out for this sort of treatment, and it has exacerbated our problems with management. The irony, of course, is that bosses ought to think a lot harder about how we feel if they want to keep their customers happy. We're the peo-

...

ple who spend all the time with the passengers. To the public, we are United."

Finally, flight attendants and management are not the only groups perceived to be feuding. "Mechanics and pilots," admits 737 captain Dave Sharp, "have always had a rift between them. That's a conflict as old as aviation history. Hopefully, we can work together in quality management groups or whatever to establish some trust." Labour-management relations may be another matter. "As for management," says Sharp, "I don't know if they can change their culture. There are a lot of power struggles over there, and they worry more about those than they do running the airline. [Gerry Greenwald] has a track record for employee relations, and this trust thing is the key to the whole future."

Case Questions

1. What were some of the most important circumstances that led to the buyout at United?

2. Why have there traditionally been differences and disagreements between the various unions at United? Why do they persist?

3. How do you think employee ownership will affect worker attitudes towards United?

4. What recommendations would you make to Gerald Greenwald as CEO—that is, chief manager—of an employee-owned company?   ◆

Question: For what reason, besides the love of skiing, would executives from across Canada take 10 days out of their busy schedules and pay $4000 to come to Banff, Alberta, in the middle of winter?

Answer: To attend the Banff School of Management, one of Canada's most innovative executive training programs.

The Banff School of Management, situated in Canada's beautiful Rocky Mountains, is fast achieving a national reputation for its creative approach to management development. Managers come from across the country in search of something "extra" in leadership training.

The school's director, Doug Macnamara, advises students to "expect an intense experience." Macnamara claims that the school's training helps make managers into better leaders. One of the ways the school accomplishes this is by emphasizing creativity. The focus is not altogether surprising, given the school's home in the Banff Centre of Creative Arts. Doug sees the school's mission as helping bring creativity back to business. According to one student, the emphasis on creativity is essential, since "Creativity is a tool that a lot of businesses have not enhanced . . . they've actually depressed it."

The focus on encouraging creativity calls for a different pedagogical approach, since, according to Macnamara, people "can't figure out how to be creative by lecture." The course typically involves a wide variety of hands-on exercises emphasizing teamwork and collaborative problem solving. One class began its session with a semi-structured orienteering exercise carried out in the middle of the night. The exercise was intended to replicate some key conditions of the workplace, including hidden goals and confusing directions, while encouraging cooperation and team-building.

Outdoor exercises comprise only part of the course though, with nearly half of it taking place in the classroom, where top-flight instructors from across the country provide a theoretical grounding for the practical side of management. Emphasis is on understanding personal behaviour, in this case both the student's and that of fellow team members, in order to understand basic principles of why people behave the way they do. Role playing is often used, as well as direct and sometimes confrontational feedback.

For some, the program is too "touchy-feely." This route should not be interpreted as a substandard teaching mode, however. According to Macnamara, the Banff School seeks to "push people beyond their envelope." The director continues, arguing that "the best learning happens when you're active in it."

The course's training exercises range from yoga and ceramics to interpretative dance and improvisation. One reason for the inclusion of such "artsy" activities arises from the on-site presence of some of Canada's leading artists. The school doesn't hesitate to co-opt the artists into the program, since they are an excellent resource for alternative ideas, insights, and paradigms. According to Macnamara, "An excellent leader and excellent artist are actually very, very close to the same type." Therefore, since "we are called to be creative starting at 8:30 in the morning until whenever," it only makes sense to stimulate the creative juices using whatever is inherently creative and, in this case, readily accessible.

Study Questions

1. What is the difference between on-the-job and off-the-job training? Which better describes the training that managers receive at the Banff School of Management?

2. What is empowerment? In what ways does the Banff School of Management seek to empower its students?

3. What is the difference between Theory X and Theory Y? Which theory better describes how the leaders of the Banff School of Management view their students?

*Source: This case was written by Professor Reg Litz of the University of Manitoba.
Video Resource: "The Banff Experience," *Venture* #637 (April 6, 1997).

"Nations of people become wise once they've exhausted all the other possibilities."

—Abba Eban, former Israeli foreign minister

Spirituality and religious faith are becoming increasingly important in the corporate workplace. While in many cultures the practice of spirituality and prayer within the workplace is nothing new, the long-standing dichotomy between church and state in such Western cultures as Canada and the United States shows signs of being bridged in an increasing number of organizational environments.

In locations as "spiritual" as the office towers of Toronto's King and Bay Streets, Christians gather for Bible study and prayer. For some, the time is well spent, representing "an oasis in the middle of the week." Seminar leader Ian Percy reports never seeing such a widespread increase of interest in religion. Part of the reason for this interest may be a reaction to the fierce and cutthroat realities of modern day competition. Part of the reason may also be faddish, though—just one more float in the endless parade of quick fixes such as total quality and management by objectives. However, with the realities of downsizings and restructuring upon them, people appear to want something that endures and provides a transcendent meaning beyond the immediate moment. Ted Wayman of Organization Change Consultants also reports people desiring ethical principles grounded in spiritual principles that help in "coming to grips with our morality." For many, religious faith offers such a perspective.

The increased interest in religion can also be understood in a historical context. Wilfrid Laurier University history professor David Menault notes that the late 1800s were a period of massive change. One way to deal with the social dislocation of the new century was to focus beyond the present to the enduring meaning offered by religious faith. While Menault wonders whether last century's interest was more rhetorical than real, for some in this century the interest may indeed be genuine and enduring.

One company demonstrating the reality of its rhetoric is Service Master. The first of this company's four objectives is to honour God, followed by people development, pursuit of excellence, and finally, profitable growth. The company, founded in 1947, has racked up sales of over $4.5 billion and a 25 percent growth rate while holding to its God-centred creed. According to company management, the Biblical standards allow them to be good and prosper.

Study Questions

1. What is Maslow's hierarchy of needs? How does the increased attention on spirituality relate to the hierarchy?

2. What is the difference between hygienes and motivators in Frederick Herzberg's two-factor theory? Which does the increased focus on spirituality relate to?

3. What is meant by the term "human relations"? How does it relate to the increased interest in spirituality?

*Source: This case was written by Professor Reg Litz of the University of Manitoba.
Video Resource: "Sprituality in Business," *Venture* #628 (February 2, 1997).

Lands' End Video Case III-3
Some Secrets of the Much-Envied Work Climate

LEARNING OBJECTIVES

The purpose of this video exercise is to help students

1. See how a specific company has implemented its human resources policies

2. Understand the relationship between a company's overall "culture" and its approach to human resources

3. Understand how specific strategies for enhancing job satisfaction and morale can affect the attitudes and performance of a company's employees

4. Appreciate the importance of training as an element in both job satisfaction and productivity

BACKGROUND INFORMATION

According to Kelly Ritchie, Vice-President for Human Resources at Lands' End,

> Turnover of our regular benefited group is in the single digits—very low for this industry. When people really like what they do, like who they do it with and for, work in facilities that are among the best around, and are fairly paid for their efforts, it would seem almost impossible not to be at least minimally satisfied.

In fact, Lands' End employees seem to be more than "minimally satisfied." Among the reasons is an 80,000-square-foot Activity Center that includes an Olympic-size swimming pool, a full-size gym, an indoor track, state-of-the-art exercise equipment, locker and shower rooms, and a not-for-profit cafeteria. The $8 million centre was donated by founder Gary Comer in 1987.

Lands' End employees also seem to be happy about the way their input is solicited during monthly feedback meetings and about the way CEO Michael Smith openly shares company information during all-company quarterly meetings. For its part, Lands' End considers its employees' job satisfaction a key element in one of its most important competitive strategies—keeping customers satisfied. Thus, the emphasis on what Ritchie describes as "our commitment to continuous, proactive training. . . . By spending the money up front," she reports, "we have much happier employees, we don't have to spend nearly as much money . . . on quality checks, and, most importantly, we have satisfied customers."

THE VIDEO

Video Source. "The Establishing and Maintaining of a Much-Envied Work Climate," *Prentice Hall Presents: On Location at Lands' End.* The video focuses on three aspects of human resources at Lands' End: the importance of open communications, both top-down and bottom-up; the importance of the Activity Center in maintaining job satisfaction and morale; and the importance of job training in maintaining a high level of customer service. Participants include Human Resources Manager Kelly Ritchie, who describes company policy, and two veteran phone operators, who talk about the practical effect of company policy.

Discussion Questions

1. What strategies for enhancing motivation are evident at Lands' End? What strategies for enhancing job satisfaction and morale do you see at work?

2. Judging from the video, what can you say about the role played by human resources management in Lands' End's efforts to fulfil its organizational mission?

3. How would you describe the managerial style of CEO Michael Smith?

4. In what respect does the brand of human resources management practised at Lands' End reflect thinking about motivation and leadership in the 1990s?

Follow-Up Assignment

At the end of the video, the narrator asks whether you think there might be "other tools" Lands' End could implement to improve its human resources "culture." To address this question, your instructor will divide the class into "advisory teams" of five or six students each. Each member of the team should use the Internet to contact the Office of the American Workplace (OAW) at **http://www. fed.org/uscompanies/labor/**

...

Here you will find detailed reports on the "best practices" of several high-performance companies singled out by the OAW. Each member of the team should examine the report on a specific company and provide the team with a brief overview of its human resources practices. Each team should then prepare a descriptive list of those practices that might be useful as "other tools" for human resources managers at Lands' End. The team should prepare a brief report summarizing its recommendations.

For Further Exploration

To find out more abut what Lands' End itself has to say about its people and about the relationship between its human resources philosophy and its corporate culture, contact the company on the Internet at **http://www.landsend.com**

From the Home page, click on "The Library" to reach "In Persons," or click on "The Company" and then "The Company Inside" to reach "Out Our Way."

EXPERIENTIAL EXERCISE:
Etablishing a Pay Policy

OBJECTIVE

To help students grasp the difficulties of creating an equitable system for paying employees and the inherent problems when the legality of such a system is questioned.

TIME REQUIRED

45 minutes
Step 1: Individual activity (to be completed before class)
Step 2: Small-group activity (25 minutes)
Step 3: Class discussion (20 minutes)

PROCEDURE

Step 1: Read the following case regarding Hildebrandt Clothing Stores.

Hildebrandt Clothing Stores, long noted for their selection of men's suits, have recently branched out into sales of women's and children's clothing as well. The company's management feels that customers for men's and women's clothing are more comfortable buying their clothes from salespeople of the same sex and that both sexes are more comfortable buying children's clothing from saleswomen. Thus all salespeople in the men's department are male and all salespeople in the women's and children's departments are female.

All salespeople at Hildebrandt's stores are paid a flat salary and receive no commissions on the goods they sell. However, pay rates differ by department. The management at Hildebrandt gives the following rationale for this difference: men's suits (the biggest seller in the men's department) sell for higher prices—and also generate higher profit margins—than do dresses (the biggest seller in the women's department) or children's clothes. Thus salesmen bring in more revenue per person than do saleswomen (see table).

Hildebrandt's female workers resent the policy and have begun talks with local union organizers. Their success at getting this company policy spotlighted in the local newspaper has also led to a partial boycott of the stores by enraged citizens of both sexes. In addition, they are contemplating a lawsuit for possible discrimination. Hildebrandt's lawyers have advised that the company has a 50 percent chance of winning a lawsuit regarding possible discrimination in its hiring practices. They further advise, however, that the firm has virtually no chance of winning a lawsuit regarding its pay practices.

SHOULD HILDEBRANDT CHANGE ITS POLICY?

Step 2: The instructor will divide the class into small groups as follows:

a. Female workers at Hildebrandt

b. Male workers at Hildebrandt

c. Hildebrandt's management (to include persons of both sexes)

d. Union organizers (to include persons of both sexes)

Group members will then decide on a plan of action to meet their goals, completing the Decision-Making Grid on the facing page.

Step 3: One member of each small group will present the group's conclusions to the class.

QUESTIONS FOR DISCUSSION

1. If each group follows through on its decision, what will be the overall outcome eventually?
2. Regardless of their legality, how would you assess the ethics of Hildebrandt's employment practices?

SALES AND PROFITS FOR A TYPICAL HILDEBRANDT CLOTHING STORE

	Men's Department	Women's Department	Children's Department	% Excess Male/Female
Average sales per year/department	$647 000	$523 000	$519 000	23.78%
Average gross profits per year/department	$305 000	$197 000	$195 000	54.8%
Average percent profit per year/department	47.2%	37.6%	37.5%	——
Average sales per hour/individual	$150.46	$85.74	$84.39	75.5%
Average gross profits per hour/individual	$70.93	$32.30	$31.71	119.6%
Average wage per hour/individual	$7.20	$5.50	$5.50	31%
Wages as a percent of profits/hour	9.9%	17.0%	17.3%	——

DECISION-MAKING GRID

Group	How Proposed Plan Will Affect
Male employees	
Female employees	
Unionization efforts	
Protesting customers	
Management authority	
Overall wage rates	
Profits at Hildebrandt	

THE WRITE STUFF

"The pen is mightier than the sword."

—Edward Bulwer-Lytton

No matter how well-conceived your career plan, how good your grades, or how much real-world experience you have, getting a job will take work…and a first-class cover letter and resume. A cover letter introduces you and your qualifications to an organization and explains that you are seeking a position. Your resume summarizes your qualifications.

PREPARING AN EFFECTIVE RESUME

A resume is probably the most important factor in landing an interview with a firm. A resume should be relatively brief (usually only a single page for applicants early in their careers), concise, clear, accurate, and professional.

Consider, for example, the sample resume for Lee Fairfield—which is only one page long (Figure 1). Most employers get dozens of resumes. If yours is too long, it is likely to be discarded. Of course, if your credentials warrant two pages, then by all means include them all. But make sure that the infor-

mation you include is relevant to the job you are seeking. *Never* exceed two pages.

The sample resume shown here is just one of many different forms that you might use. Most libraries and many bookstores have books that contain a variety of sample resumes. In all cases, though, remember that the basic purpose of your resume is to help you get a job. Thus, it should be structured to highlight your strengths while not calling undue attention to your weaknesses.

Regardless of its structure, most experts agree that your resume should include the following:

- Education, experience, honours and activities

In addition, experts recommend that you do not include:

- Age, marital status/children, height and weight, health, a photo of yourself

Expert opinion is divided on the inclusion of either a statement of employment objective or a summary. An employment objective (for example, "A sales position for a major pharmaceutical manufacturer") is useful if you know just what you are looking for. But vague statements designed to cover a vari-

Figure 1 Lee Fairfield's Resume

Lee Fairfield
1906 Meredith Lane
Toronto, Ontario
(416) 555-4239

EMPLOYMENT OBJECTIVE
A sales representative with a full-range consumer products firm.

EDUCATION
B. Comm., University of Toronto, 1997 (Marketing major)

EMPLOYMENT EXPERIENCE
Assistant manager for J. Riggins Clothing Store in Toronto (September 1996 to April 1997); assisted manager in scheduling sales clerks; supervised weekly ordering of merchandise; helped monitor inventory levels of basic merchandise lines.

Intern for Ensearch Corporation in Toronto (Summer 1996); assisted a team of five managers developing a new marketing strategy.

Sales clerk for The Varsity Shop in Toronto (September 1994 to August 1995); helped customers in selecting clothing, finding correct sizes, matching colours, and ringing up sales.

OTHER EXPERIENCE
Coached youth ringette program in Toronto on a volunteer basis (Summer 1995)

Worked as a United Way coordinator (1995)

HONOURS AND ACTIVITIES
Deans List (1996–97)
James Collin Scholarship (1995–96)
Vice-President of the Marketing Club (1996–97)
Member of the Marketing Club (1994–97)

Be as specific as possible in your objective (if you include one).

List education with your most recent degree first. (*Note*: After many years on the job, education should follow, not precede, experience.)

List most recent experience first. Be sure to include dates, locations, and specific duties/achievements. Note use of action verbs (e.g., "assisted," "supervised," "helped").

List other experiences that show your leadership qualities, level of commitment, and other skills of value to an organization.

Focus on items that show a connection to areas of concern for the organization to which you are applying. *Warning*: Too many activities may imply that you have no time (or energy) for work.

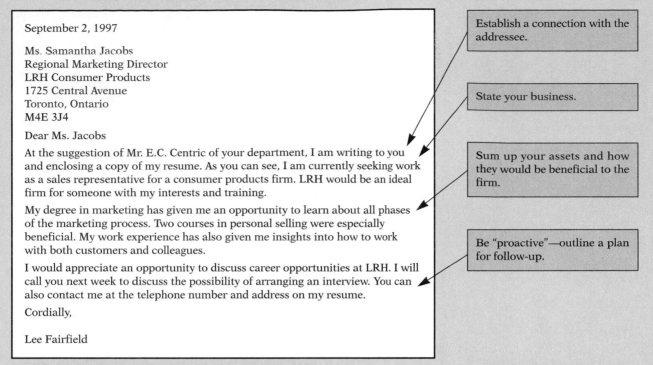

September 2, 1997

Ms. Samantha Jacobs
Regional Marketing Director
LRH Consumer Products
1725 Central Avenue
Toronto, Ontario
M4E 3J4

Dear Ms. Jacobs

At the suggestion of Mr. E.C. Centric of your department, I am writing to you and enclosing a copy of my resume. As you can see, I am currently seeking work as a sales representative for a consumer products firm. LRH would be an ideal firm for someone with my interests and training.

My degree in marketing has given me an opportunity to learn about all phases of the marketing process. Two courses in personal selling were especially beneficial. My work experience has also given me insights into how to work with both customers and colleagues.

I would appreciate an opportunity to discuss career opportunities at LRH. I will call you next week to discuss the possibility of arranging an interview. You can also contact me at the telephone number and address on my resume.

Cordially,

Lee Fairfield

Sidebar annotations:
- Establish a connection with the addressee.
- State your business.
- Sum up your assets and how they would be beneficial to the firm.
- Be "proactive"—outline a plan for follow-up.

Figure 2 Lee Fairfield's Cover Letter

ety of positions can do you more harm than good. Unless you plan to have several variations of your resume printed or have access to desktop publishing that makes such variations possible, you might want to skip an employment objective if you're flexible regarding what kind of job you'll accept. Those with a great deal of experience may choose to include a summary statement (for example, "An experienced marketing manager with a proven track record in developing and promoting new consumer products") instead.

Lee's resume includes the key elements in a concise and clear fashion. Note, for example, that she lists two jobs and one internship under employment experience. Each listing includes the dates, location, and basic activities performed. This information helps a prospective employer better assess the nature of Lee's experiences and how they relate to both her employment objective and the type of work the firm has to offer.

While it should be obvious that a resume must be accurate, some people exaggerate their accomplishments to make themselves look better. This tactic usually backfires. Prospective employers generally verify the content of resumes before making job offers. If they find a resume to contain misleading or downright false statements, they will almost certainly reject the applicant immediately. Don't hesitate to blow your own horn about your accomplishments—if you led a task force that figured out how to save your employer $100 000 a year, then say so. But don't identify yourself as Warehouse and Distribution Manager if your real job was carrying merchandise from a small stockroom to the sales floor!

Over the past two decades, the availability of desktop publishing has also fostered explosive growth in resume-writing services. Should you use one? Most experts say you shouldn't need to. But many people swear by their services for the help they offer in shaping a resume, ensuring that it looks professional, and offering encouragement to the struggling job hunter. If you opt for one of these services, don't abandon the basic principles of good resume writing and presentation. And don't leave the proofreading to anyone else.

PREPARING A COVER LETTER

A cover letter should always be included with your resume. The purpose of this letter is to introduce yourself, indicate your intentions, refer the reader to your resume, and suggest a course of action.

Note, for example, the structure of Lee's cover letter (Figure 2). It begins with a brief mention of a mutual acquaintance. (If you don't write at someone's suggestion, be sure to say how you heard about a possible opening.) Next, Lee states her reason for writing. The letter goes on to note ways in which Lee (and her experience) may fit well into this company. (Caution: Do not repeat too much information from the resume.) Be sure to phrase that fit in terms of what you have to offer the organization. Lee concludes her letter by describing the actions she will take—she will call the addressee, or the person receiving the letter can contact Lee first. If you ask the addressee to call you, ideally you should have an answering machine to take calls when you aren't there.

Cover letters should be brief. Unless you are sending your letter anzd resume to a "blind" ad (one that does not indicate the name of the organization involved), your letters should always be addressed to a specific individual, as opposed to "Director of Human Resources" or (even worse) "To Whom It May Concern." As with resumes, always proofread your cover letters carefully to prevent errors.

Four

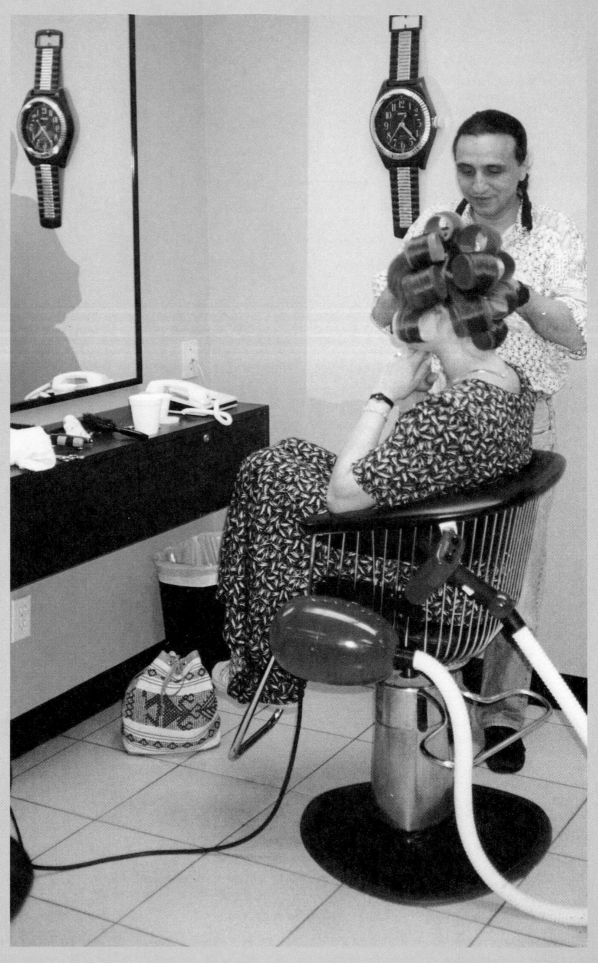

Part Four

MANAGING
OPERATIONS

Producing high quality goods and services is at the heart of all business operations. Business firms in Canada face increased international competition and the new reality of the North American Free Trade Agreement. The opening cases of the chapters in this section show how business firms like Dorel Industries, Western Star Trucks, Ipsco Inc., Mount Sinai Hospital, and Jaguar have responded to increased competition and ever-increasing consumer expectations about quality and productivity.

Part Four, Managing Operations, provides an overview of three aspects of business important to firms' existence: production of goods, production of services, and increasing productivity and quality.

■ We begin in **Chapter 12, Producing Goods**, by examining how firms manufacture goods, plan and schedule manufacturing processes, and control both the costs and quality of the final output.

■ Then, in **Chapter 13, Producing Services**, we explore the special nature of services and how their particular characteristics affect planning, scheduling, and quality control in service industries.

■ Finally, in **Chapter 14, Increasing Productivity and Quality**, we consider some of the ways by which companies can improve the productivity and the quality of their output, and thus their competitive position.

12
Producing Goods

The New Industrial Revolution

Canadians want a strong manufacturing sector because it makes us feel that we are more than simply hewers of wood and haulers of water. So, when jobs started to disappear from manufacturing in the early 1990s, everyone worried. In 1990 and 1991 in Ontario alone, more than 200 000 manufacturing jobs were lost to the U.S. after the Canada-U.S. Free Trade Agreement went into effect. Often the driving force behind the exodus was the promise of lower costs in the U.S. The average manufacturing wage in Tennessee, for example, was 30 percent lower than in Ontario. The cost of land, taxes, and transportation are also lower.

Firms like Tridon Ltd. and St. Lawrence Starch Co. were typical of firms that left. Tridon closed two auto parts manufacturing plants, putting 500 employees out of work. It moved to cope with its U.S. competitors, who had a lower cost structure. St. Lawrence Starch joined a strategic alliance with an Illinois firm because the Canadian government imposed a duty on U.S. corn, which also caused the price of Canadian corn to increase. The company said it couldn't pass the price increase on to consumers. So it moved to the U.S. and now ships its product into Canada under the provisions of the free trade agreement.

These and many other stories were a cause of deep concern just a few years ago. But the Canadian manufacturing sector is making a strong comeback. In 1992 and 1993, more than half of the growth in gross domestic product came from manufacturing. So did most of the growth in jobs. Manufacturing employment is now rising at five times the rate of Canadian business generally, and growth in Canadian manufacturing output has outpaced that of any other major industrial competitor.

Although the free trade agreement has indeed caused a "gutting" of the traditional manufacturing sector, for every firm that went out of business, another has rushed in to take its place. These new firms are building products that are more competitive and more suitable for the export market. In 1980, Canadian firms exported about 25 percent of their production to foreign markets; in 1993, the figure was almost 50 percent.

Consider these success stories. Dorel Industries Inc. of Montreal, a manufacturer of ready-to-assemble children's furniture, has quadrupled its sales by merging several Canadian companies and cracking the U.S. market. It now sells 70 percent of its output in the U.S. Ipsco Inc. recently achieved the highest profits in its history after adopting the latest technological improvements and selling its steel products in the U.S. Western Star Trucks Inc. is in the middle of a major expansion, and produces twice as many trucks per day as it did two years ago. SR Telecom, a manufacturer of microwave-telecommunications systems, sells its products in 73 countries and controls over 40 percent of the world market. Husky Injection Molding has increased its productivity by more than 65 percent since 1990, and exports 88 percent of its output.

In spite of these success stories, critics can still be found. They point to the fact that the share of the Canadian market accounted for by Canadian firms dropped from 67 percent in 1981 to 59 percent in 1991. But for the huge U.S./Canadian market combined, Canada's share went from 1.9 percent before the free trade agreement to 2.6 percent since. Because the U.S. market is so large, this more than makes up for any losses

(continued)

of market share in Canada. And Canadian manufacturing firms have also been gaining an increasing share of the growth in this combined market.

It is true that many jobs in manufacturing have been lost. Employment peaked in 1989 at 2.1 million production workers; by 1993, there were just 1.7 million. But this drop in employment is one of the key reasons for the manufacturing sector's recent success. Output is back up to pre-recession levels, even though employment is down by 19 percent. In the wood products industry, for example, sales increased by 8 percent even though employment dropped by 2 percent. The same trend is evident in automotive, electrical products, and chemical firms. The labour cost gap with the U.S., which had reached 21 percent, is now only 3 percent.

Canadian manufacturing firms are also more competitive because they have aggressively adopted new technologies. Increases in labour productivity have outstripped those in the U.S. for the first time since 1985. Canadian firms have also adopted aggressive pricing strategies; the average price for manufactured goods was the same in 1993 as it was in 1989.

The future looks bright for Canadian manufacturing. The gains made in the last few years may be just the beginning. After learning some very tough lessons in the 1980s, Canadian manufacturers are not likely to fritter away their new-found advantages. The increased emphasis on worker training and an increased commitment to quality are likely to become mainstays of Canadian manufacturing for the foreseeable future. ◆

The opening case gives some idea of just how complex and dynamic the Canadian manufacturing sector is. In this chapter, we will consider how firms involved in the production of goods deal with this complexity and with the rapid change with which they are continually faced. In the next chapter, we will do the same for the "production" of services, since many principles are common to both goods and services production. Both require management of the production process, including planning and control.

By focusing on the learning objectives of this chapter, you will better understand the complexity of production processes for physical goods. After reading this chapter, you will be able to:

LEARNING OBJECTIVES

1. Classify a business's *operations processes* in three ways and explain the role of the operations managers.

2. Identify five major areas of *operations planning* and two levels of *operations scheduling*.

3. Describe the activities in *materials management* and identify four tools for achieving *operations control*.

4. Characterize some of the major forms of *automation* currently used in production operations.

5. Explain the advantages and disadvantages of small and large production companies.

A Short History of Manufacturing

Before the Industrial Revolution began in England in the 18th century, the typical workplace was the small shop and the home. Leather and cloth were handmade, as were needles and other tools; clothing, harnesses, and other goods were made one at a time by craftspeople. In the late 1770s, however, a new institution emerged: Using machines, materials, industrial workers, and managers, the factory produced greater quantities of goods in an organized fashion. Throughout the 19th century, the factory remained the central institution for commerce. By then, it was using water, and then electricity, for power sources. The factory also relied on heavy machinery that was cumbersome, powerful, and often operated by children.

In the early 1900s in the U.S., two major developments took place: Frederick W. Taylor began his "scientific management" studies and Henry Ford revolutionized industry with the Ford "mass production" system. Production had become—at least in theory—the "science" of making products economically on a massive scale. Using specialization of labour for efficiency, the assembly line became the new tool for gaining economies of scale. Through the 1940s, the assembly line still depended heavily on human labour. By the 1960s, however, when mass production had reached its zenith, the factory culture had matured socially as well as commercially. As consumers continued to rely on access to the material goods that flooded from factories, attitudes towards production and production workers were changing. Children, of course, were no longer a part of the workforce, and such "radical" ideas as gender equality and ethnic diversity were soon to become accepted goals. Environmental concerns were also gaining in prominence.

More recently, other countries have joined the ranks of "developed" nations and benefited from new and better manufacturing methods. As a result, global competition has reshaped production into a fast-paced, challenging business activity. Although the factory remains the centrepiece for manufacturing, it is virtually unrecognizable when compared to its counterpart of even a decade ago. The noise, smoke, and danger have been replaced in many companies by glistening high-tech machines, computers, and "clean rooms" that are contaminant-free and carefully controlled for temperature.[1] Instead of the need to maintain continuous mass production, firms today face constant change. They must continually develop new technologies to respond to ever-changing consumer demands. They must produce varieties of different products at high quality levels. They must strive to design new products, get them into production, and deliver them to customers faster than their competitors.[2]

Creating Value Through Production

utility
The power of a product to satisfy a human want; something of value.

time utility
That quality of a product satisfying a human want because of the time at which it is made available.

place utility
That quality of a product satisfying a human want because of where it is made available.

ownership (possession) utility
That quality of a product satisfying a human want during its consumption or use.

form utility
That quality of a product satisfying a human want because of its form; requires raw materials to be transformed into a finished product.

operations (production) management
The systematic direction and control of the processes that transform resources into finished goods.

To understand the production processes of a firm, you need to understand the importance of products—both goods and services. Products provide businesses with both economic results (profits, wages, goods purchased from other companies) and noneconomic results (new technology, innovations, pollution). And they provide consumers with what economists call **utility**—want satisfaction.

Four basic kinds of utility would not be possible without production. By making a product available at a time when consumers want it, production creates **time utility**, as when a company turns out ornaments in time for Christmas. By making a product available in a place convenient for consumers, production creates **place utility**, as when a local department store creates a "Trim-A-Tree" section. By making a product that consumers can take pleasure in owning, production creates **ownership (possession) utility**, as when you take a box of ornaments home and decorate your tree.

But above all, production makes products available in the first place. By turning raw materials into finished goods, production creates **form utility**, as when an ornament maker combines glass, plastic, and other materials to create tree decorations.

Because the term *production* has historically been associated with manufacturing, it has been replaced in recent years by *operations*, a term that reflects both services and goods production. **Operations** (or **production**) **management** is the systematic direction and control of the processes that transform resources into finished goods and services. Thus production managers are ultimately responsible for creating utility for customers.

As Figure 12.1 shows, production managers must bring raw materials, equipment, and labour together under a production plan that effectively

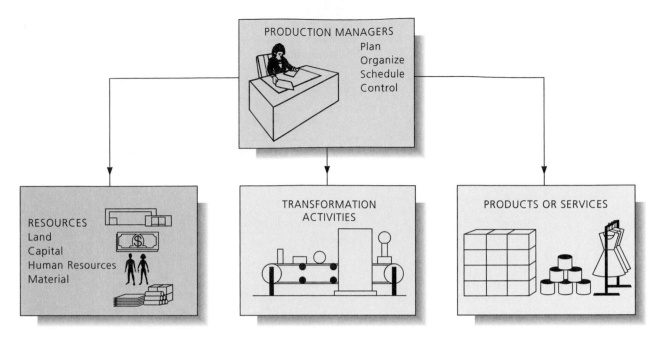

Figure 12.1
The transformation system.

uses all the resources available in the production facility. As demand for a good increases, they must schedule and control work to produce the amount required. Meanwhile, they must control costs, quality levels, inventory, and plant and equipment.

Not all production managers work in factories. Farmers are also production managers. They create form utility by converting soil, seeds, sweat, gas, and other inputs into beef cattle, tobacco, wheat, milk, cash, and other outputs. As production managers, farmers have the option of employing many workers to plant and harvest their crops. Or they may decide to use automated machinery or some combination of workers and machinery. These decisions affect farmers' costs, the buildings and equipment they own, and the quality and quantity of goods they produce. Table 12.1 shows examples of different types of production management.

Classifying Operations Processes

Whether they are independent farmers or employees of a multinational manufacturer, production managers must control the process by which goods are produced. We can classify production processes in four different ways:

- by the type of transformation technology used
- by whether the process is analytic or synthetic
- by the pattern of product flow during transformation
- by the extent of labour use

Any process can be classified in any of these ways. The point of these different classification systems is to help managers analyze new or unfamiliar production processes by comparing them with familiar ones.

Transformation Technology

Manufacturers use chemical, fabrication, assembly, transport, and clerical processes to transform raw materials into finished goods. In *chemical processes*, raw materials are chemically altered. Such techniques are com-

Table 12.1   Inputs, Transformation, and Outputs in Production Systems

Production System	Inputs	Transformation	Outputs
Farm	Land, tractors and equipment, labour, buildings, fertilizer, farmer's management skills	Cultivation of plants and livestock	Food products, profit for owner, jobs for farmer's family
Jewellery store	Fashion-conscious customers, merchandise, sales clerks, showroom, fixtures, and equipment	Exchange of merchandise between buyer and seller	Satisfied jewellery customers
Tire producer	Rubber and chemical compounds, blending equipment, tire molds, factory, and human skills	Chemical reactions of raw materials	Tires for autos, airplanes, trucks, trailers, and other vehicles
Furniture manufacturer	Wood-working equipment fabrics, wood, nails and screws, factory, woodworking skills	Fabrication and assembly of materials	Furniture for homes and offices

mon in the aluminum, steel, fertilizer, petroleum, and paint industries. In contrast, *fabrication processes* mechanically alter the basic shape or form of the product. Examples of fabrication abound in the metal-forming and machining industries, the wood-working industry, and the plastic-molding and plastic-forming industries.

As their name suggests, *assembly processes* involve putting together various components. These techniques are often used in the electronics, appliance, and automotive industries. *Transport processes*, in which goods acquire place utility by moving from one location to another, are also common in the appliance industry. For example, refrigerators are routinely moved from manufacturing plants to consumers through a series of regional warehouses and discount stores.

Finally, *clerical processes* transform information. Combining data on employee absences and machine breakdowns into a productivity report is a clerical process. One issue currently facing users of clerical transformation is whether too much information is being processed and presented. Methods for managing these information problems are discussed in Chapter 18.

Analytic versus Synthetic Processes

analytic process

Any production process in which resources are broken down.

A second way of classifying production processes is by the way resources are converted into finished goods. An **analytic process** breaks down the basic resources into components. For example, Alcan manufactures aluminum by extracting it from an ore called bauxite. The reverse approach, a **synthetic process**, combines a number of raw materials to produce a finished product such as fertilizer or paint.

synthetic process

Any production process in which resources are combined.

Product Flow Pattern

continuous process

Any production process in which the flow of transformation from resources to finished product is fairly smooth, straight, and continuous.

We can also classify production processes by how the plant is arranged and how the product moves through the plant.[3] In a **continuous process**, the flow is fairly smooth, straight, and continuous. A continuous-process pattern is usually found when a manufacturing operation is repetitive. Typically, such a plant turns out nearly identical finished products in production runs

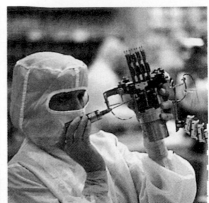

As these photos show, various industries utilize different transformation techniques: (from left, top) chemical, fabrication, assembly; (bottom) transport, clerical.

of several days, months, or even years. Toyota, Imperial Tobacco, and Labatt's all use continuous processes.

In contrast, material in an **intermittent process** flows through a plant in a stop-and-go fashion and a seemingly scattered arrangement of equipment and departments. The jumbled flows occur because such plants produce short runs of custom-made products, each requiring a unique set of operations. Printing shops are an example. As various jobs are routed through the necessary departments, machines are shut down frequently in order to set up for other jobs.

One other major characteristic of this process is that each job passes through specialized departments. Intermittent processes usually group similar machines—grinders in one department and milling machines in another, for example. But a continuous process would place grinders or mills wherever they are needed along an assembly line. Figure 12.2 illustrates some of the differences between continuous and intermittent processes.

intermittent process

Any production process in which the flow of transformation from resources to finished product starts and stops.

Labour Use

Finally, processes vary in the amount of human input they need. **Labour-intensive processes** depend more on people than on machines. They are most likely to be used when labour is cheap or when there is an artistic element to the work. Many kinds of farming are still highly labour intensive. Producing cherries or lettuce is much more labour intensive than producing wheat or sugar beets.

Capital-intensive processes are those in which investment in machinery is great. A huge petroleum refinery is a classic example of a capital-intensive process. A refinery that may cost hundreds of millions of dollars to build and equip may operate with fewer than 100 employees.

labour-intensive process

Any process that depends more on people than on machines.

capital-intensive process

Any process in which investment in machinery is great.

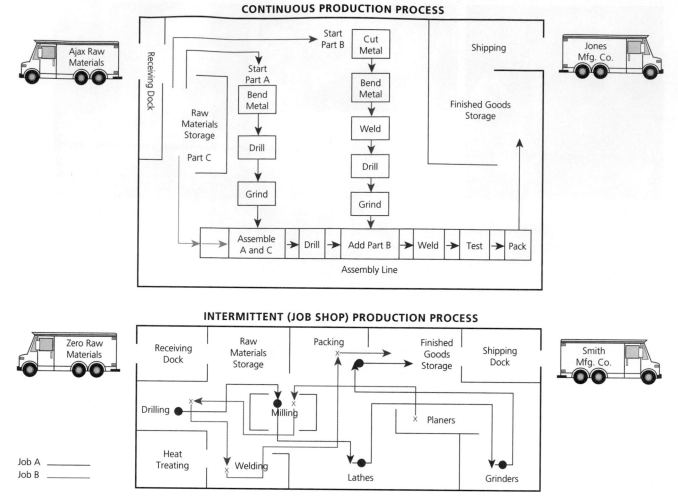

Figure 12.2
Continuous and intermittent processes.

Operations Planning

Managers from many departments contribute to decisions about production management. As Figure 12.3 shows, however, no matter how many decision makers are involved, the process can be described as a series of logical steps. The success of any firm depends on the final result of this logical sequence of decisions.

The overall business plan developed by a company's top executives guides operations planning. This plan outlines the firm's goals and objectives, including the specific products and services that it will offer in the upcoming years. In this section, we will survey each of the major components of the business plan that directly affect operations planning. First, we will describe *forecasting* and then we will discuss the key planning and forecasting activities that fall into one of five major categories: *capacity, location, layout, quality,* and *methods planning.*

Forecasting

forecasts

Estimates of future demand for both new and existing products.

In addition to the business plan, managers develop the firm's *long-range production plan* through **forecasts** of future demand for both new and existing

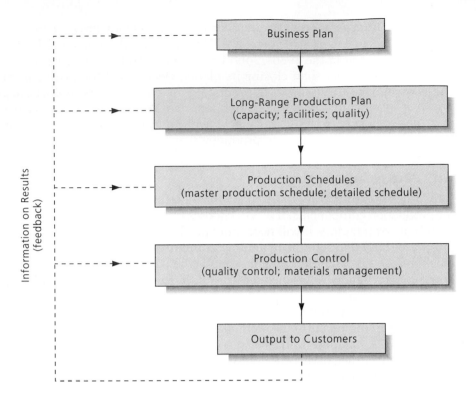

Figure 12.3
The steps in a production planning and control system ensure that production activities lead to customer satisfaction.

products. This plan covers a two- to five-year period. It specifically details the number of plants or service facilities, as well as labour, machinery, and transportation and storage facilities, that will be needed to meet demand. It also specifies how resources will be obtained.

Forecasting uses both qualitative and quantitative methods. *Qualitative forecasts* may come from an expert or group of experts who basically use judgment and experience. *Quantitative forecasts* are statistical methods to project future demand from past demand patterns. For example, in developing a new line of Memorex videotapes, Memtek Products might use quantitative methods to calculate demand three years hence at 4 million cassettes per year. Its long-range production plan might translate this demand into a need to build three new plants, lease another warehouse, acquire four new tape-filling machines, and hire 2500 new employees.

Capacity Planning

The amount of a product that a company can produce under normal working conditions is its **capacity**. A firm's capacity depends on how many people it employs and the number and size of its facilities. Long-range planning must take into account both current and future capacity.

Capacity planning means ensuring that a firm's capacity just *slightly* exceeds the normal demand for its product. To see why this policy is best, consider the alternatives. If capacity is too small to meet demand, the company must turn away customers—a situation that not only cuts into profits but alienates both customers and salespeople. If capacity exceeds demand, the firm is wasting money by maintaining a plant that is too large, by keeping excess machinery on line, or by employing too many workers.

capacity
The amount of a good that a firm can produce under normal working conditions.

John Deere
http://www.deere.com

When forecasts indicate a temporary business slowdown, companies plan for ways to use existing capacity. For example, when demand for farm machinery waned in the 1980s, John Deere found itself with excess production capacity. Rather than closing its plants, Deere used the extra capacity to make engines for companies producing air compressors and irrigation pumps as well as motor-home components for Winnebago. Capacity planning allowed Deere to use slack capacity while awaiting anticipated increases in demand for traditional farm products.[4]

Adjusting Capacity

Capacity adjustments are often made through the *make-versus-buy decision* for production components. If a firm chooses to manufacture (make) a needed item in its own facility, it will need *more* production capacity. If it chooses to purchase (buy) that item from another company, it will need *less* capacity. A clock maker, for example, can either make the hands for its products or buy hands already made by another company. If it decides to buy, it can adjust capacity downward.

Instead of expanding capacity to meet peak demand, companies sometimes use pricing to shift peak demand to nonpeak periods. Golf club manufacturers, for example, will offer seasonal discounts to retailers during the winter to encourage early ordering. This practice sustains production during the winter months (an otherwise slow production period) and helps reduce the peak demand for production in springtime.

Location Planning

Because facility location affects production costs and flexibility, sound location planning is crucial. Depending on the site of its facility, a company may either be capable of producing a low-cost product or may find itself at an extreme cost disadvantage. Such considerations weighed heavily on the decision-making process at Ford that resulted in the Mondeo—the so-called "world car" introduced in Europe in 1993 and (as the Ford Contour and Mercury Mystique) in the United States in 1994. Developed to be both manufactured and marketed around the world, the "world car" took advantage of design strengths in three separate engineering centres: Detroit (V-6 engine, automatic transmission, heating and air-conditioning units), London (4-cylinder engine, steering, suspension, electronics), and Cologne, Germany (basic structural engineering). To free its engineering workforce for other projects and facilities, Ford assigned a single 800-person team to design the Mondeo for both Europe and the United States and will employ identical production facilities to build the car at Genk, Belgium, and Kansas City, Missouri. By custom-building two production facilities on two continents, Ford has saved about 25 percent on customized factory machinery such as stamping dies and secured better prices for larger orders from its suppliers.[5]

As we can see from Ford's "world car" strategy, managers must consider many factors in location planning. Location attractiveness is influenced by proximity to raw materials and markets, availability of labour, energy and transportation costs, local and provincial regulations and taxes, and community living conditions.

Some location decisions are now being simplified by the rise of industrial parks. Created by cities interested in attracting new industry, these planned sites come with the necessary zoning, land, shipping facilities, utilities, and waste-disposal outlets already in place. Such sites offer flexibility, often allowing firms to open new facilities before competitors can get started in the same area. The ready-made site also provides faster construction start-ups because it entails no lead time in preparing the chosen site.

Layout Planning

Once a site has been selected, managers must decide on plant layout. Layout determines if a company can respond quickly and efficiently to customer requests for more and different products or if it finds itself unable to match competitors' production speed. Alternatives include *process, product, craft work, cellular,* and *fixed-position layouts*.

Process Layouts

In a **process layout**, equipment and people are grouped together according to function. In a custom-cake bakery, for instance, the blending of batters is done in an area devoted to mixing, baking occurs in the oven area, icing is prepared in the mixing area, and cakes are decorated on tables in a finishing area before boxing. The various tasks are each performed in specialized locations. Machine, woodworking, and dry cleaning shops usually feature process layouts.

    Process layouts are well suited to *job shops*—firms that specialize in custom work. These companies do a variety of jobs for different customers. They rely on general-purpose machinery and skilled labour to respond to the needs of individual customers. For example, your local bakery can accommodate both your request for a wedding cake and your friend's request for a birthday cake.

process layout
A way of organizing production activities such that equipment and people are grouped together according to their function.

Product Layouts

In a **product layout**, resources move through a fixed sequence of steps to become finished goods. Equipment and people are set up to produce only one type of good and are arranged according to its production requirements. Product layouts often use **assembly lines**—a partially finished product moves step by step through the plant on conveyor belts or other equipment, often in a straight line, until the product is completed. Automobile, food-processing, and computer-assembly plants use product layouts.

    Product layouts can be efficient and inexpensive because they simplify work tasks and use unskilled labour. They tend, however, to be inflexible because they require a heavy investment in specialized equipment that is hard to rearrange for new applications. In addition, workers are subject to boredom. Moreover, when workers at one end are absent or overworked, those farther down the line cannot help out.

product layout
A way of organizing production activities such that equipment and people are set up to produce only one type of good.

assembly line
A type of product layout in which a partially finished product moves through a plant on a conveyor belt or other equipment.

Craft Work

To address these problems, many Japanese companies have pioneered new ideas in job design on the assembly line. Both at home and in their Canadian and U.S. factories, NEC, Toyota, Sony, and other firms are finding alternatives to traditional conveyor belts and assembly lines. Instead of specialized jobs, workers are engaged in so-called "craft work" where each worker has the opportunity to assemble an entire product. Even when assembly lines are retained, as in automobile factories, employees are performing more tasks.

    Much of the impetus for changes in job design came from Toyota, which is widely credited with developing "lean production" techniques to improve efficiency. Even in situations where assembly lines have been retained, Toyota has expanded employee responsibilities. In the past, for example, an employee's job might have been to install wheels and tires. If he or she discovered a flaw, the production process continued: Finding and fixing problems was not the wheel installer's job. Those tasks were handled by two workers farther down the line: a quality-control checker and a repairperson. However, in a modern Toyota

Employees at the Toyota manufacturing plant in Cambridge, Ontario discuss a production problem. At this plant, employees are responsible not only for making automobiles, but also for monitoring quality control and for maintaining and cleaning the work area.

facility like the plant in Cambridge, Ontario, employee responsibilities also include maintaining equipment and cleaning the work area, as well as monitoring overall quality control. If a wheel installer finds a flaw, he or she pulls a cord, which lights up the quality-control board. A team leader will then stop the line to repair the problem. Because workers up and down the line are flexible enough to perform whatever task arises, it can be stopped as often as necessary. Costs are thus lower for two reasons. First, fewer workers, of course, mean lower costs. Second, defective parts can be replaced immediately—and with little waste—because they are either manufactured or purchased in small quantities. Consequently, because both parts and partially finished cars can be held in small batches, inventory costs are also lower.[6]

Cellular Layouts

cellular layouts

Used to produce goods when families of products can follow similar flowpaths.

Closely related to craft work are **cellular layouts** which are used when *families* of products can follow similar flowpaths. A clothing manufacturer, for example, may establish a "cell," or designated area, dedicated to making a family of clothing pockets—say, pockets for shirts, coats, blouses, trousers, and slacks. Although each type of pocket is unique in shape, size, and style, all go through the same production steps. Within the cell, therefore, various types of equipment (for cutting, trimming, sewing) are arranged close together in the appropriate sequence. All pockets pass, stage-by-stage, through the cell from beginning to end, in a nearly continuous flow. The cellular layout is similar to a product layout, except that product layouts usually are dedicated to single products instead of product families. Our clothing maker might also have cells for sleeves, collars, and so on. There may also be a separate area for final assembly.

Cellular layouts came into widescale use in the 1980s as an improvement over process layouts in some applications. They have several advantages. For example, because similar products require less machine adjustment, equipment setup time is reduced. Because flow distances are usually shorter, materials handling and transit time is more efficient. Finally, inventories of goods in-process are lower—and paperwork is simpler—because material flows are more orderly.[7]

Developments in Flexibility

In addition to variations on the product layout, many companies have experimented with ways to make standard production lines more flexible. Some firms, for example, have adopted **U-shaped production lines**: Rather than stretching out in a straight line, machines are placed in a narrow *U*-shape, with workers operating them from within the *U*. Because machines are close together, in slow periods one worker can complete all the tasks needed to make a product by easily moving from one side of the *U* to the other. In busier times, more workers can be added until there is one worker per machine.[8]

Another tool for production flexibility is the **flexible manufacturing system** (**FMS**)—using computer information systems, a single factory can produce a wide variety of products. Production is adapted rapidly to changes in customer demand, product-by-product, by integrating sales information with the factory's production activities.

Many Japanese companies already have FMS facilities on line. At Toshiba, for instance, workers can make 9 different desktop and 20 different laptop computers on adjacent assembly lines. At each post, a laptop screen displays a drawing and gives instructions for the appropriate product. The goal is to produce sufficient numbers of products that sell while avoiding overproduction of those that do not. "Customers," explains Toshiba president Fumio Sato, "wanted choices. We needed variety, not mass production." The key, says Sato, is shorter production runs of smaller lots. "Every time I go to a plant," he stresses, "I tell the people, 'Smaller lot!'"

Similarly, Japan's largest soap and cosmetics company, Kao Corp., maintains a remarkable information-delivery system: A single system links information on everything, ranging from production and purchasing data to daily figures recorded on cash registers and salespeople's hand-held computers. Information is fed back into the company's R&D and manufacturing facilities, where decisions on how to respond to inventory buildup or competitor activity can be made within a single day. When Kao introduces a new product, information collected at point-of-sale locations is routed immediately to a test-marketing system that compares the data with input collected from customer calls and focus groups—a process much quicker than waiting for market surveys. Ultimately, production-line workers learn from posted signs what they will turn out each day to serve 280 000 stores with customized deliveries of goods.

But flexible manufacturing may soon be replaced by an even newer development. **Soft manufacturing** emphasizes computer software and computer networks instead of production machines. Soft manufacturing recognizes that complete automation of production processes may not be advisable and that humans are better at certain things than machines are. The box "The Latest Revolution in the Factory" gives more details about soft manufacturing.

Fixed-Position Layouts

Sometimes, of course, the simplest layout is the most efficient. In a fixed-position layout, labour, materials, and equipment are brought to the work location. This layout is used in building ships, homes, skyscrapers, dams, and manufacturing facilities.

Quality Planning

In planning production systems and facilities, managers must keep in mind the firm's quality goals.[9] Thus any complete production plan includes systems for ensuring that goods are produced to meet the firm's quality standards. The issues of productivity and quality are discussed in detail in Chapter 14.

U-shaped production lines

Machines are placed in a U-shape rather than a straight line so that a single worker can complete all the necessary tasks.

flexible manufacturing system (FMS)

A production system in which automatic equipment produces small batches of different goods on the same production line.

Toshiba
http://www.toshiba.com

soft manufacturing

Emphasizes computer software and computer networks instead of production machines.

International Report

The Latest Revolution in the Factory

During the 1980s, much was written about how Japan and Germany were leading the way in new production technology. But an amazing thing has happened: American manufacturing has regained its No. 1 position in manufactured exports for the first time since the mid-1980s. How did it happen?

Part of the answer is something called "soft manufacturing" (SM), which involves an emphasis on computer software and networks rather than production machines, where robots play only a supporting role, and where human workers are back in unexpectedly large numbers. SM plants, which can turn out customized products at mass-production speeds, will stabilize or even increase the number of jobs available in manufacturing.

How quickly times have changed. Just a few years ago, there was great alarm about the future of North American manufacturing. Japan was feared because of its flexible manufacturing system (FMS). Such a system emphasized computer-controlled machines, robots, and remotely guided carts to deliver materials to the production line. FMSs were supposed to lead to automatic factories that would be able to operate with very few workers.

But it didn't work out that way. Companies discovered that too much automation actually caused losses because large, complex systems are inherently vulnerable to failure. Robots were a real disappointment; they couldn't do the fine work needed in mass production assembly.

Under SM, robots are used only in jobs at which they excel (for example, spot welding). Humans are used in jobs that require high dexterity and judgment, like dealing with odd-size components and tight tolerances. Consider what happens at a Motorola plant that makes pagers. Orders come in from Motorola salespeople via an 800 line or e-mail. The exact specifications desired for each pager (for example, colour, type of beeper tone, etc.) are digitized and sent to the assembly line. Robots pick out the components, and humans assemble the pagers. The order is often completed within 80 minutes, and the customer may receive the pager on the same day it was ordered.

IBM does much the same thing in taking orders for PCs. Sales reps take orders from customers on an 800 phone line and enter the specifications desired by the customer. Finished orders are sent electronically to a nearby assembly plant, where workers receive them on hand-held bar code readers. The worker picks the right combination of parts like hard disks and memory boards from parts bins, and when a complete kit has been gathered together, it is taken to an assembly station. The assembler makes the computer and sends it down the line to be tested and packaged. The customer receives it the next day by airborne express.

SM has helped U.S. manufacturers outdistance their foreign rivals in such crucial measures as time to market and manufacturing flexibility. Hewlett-Packard, for example, recently embarrassed its Japanese rival NEC by beating it to the market with an ink-jet colour printer. H-P's product was so good that the Japanese withdrew theirs a few months later.

Will the Japanese once again copy what the Americans are doing and beat them at their own game? Industry observers think not. They point out that Japanese business firms do not think in terms of customizing products for individual customers; rather, they emphasize the mass production of identical, high-quality items. Japanese business managers will have to make a major change in the way they think if they are going to be successful at SM.

Methods Planning

In designing production systems, managers must clearly identify every production step and the specific methods for performing them. They can then work to reduce waste and inefficiency by examining procedures on a step-by-step basis—an approach sometimes called *methods improvement*.

Improvement begins when a manager documents the current method. A detailed description, often using a diagram called *process flow chart*, is usually helpful for organizing and recording all information. It identifies the sequence of production activities, movements of materials, and the work performed at each stage as the product flows through production. The flow can then be analyzed to identify wasteful activities, sources of delay in production flows, and other inefficiencies. The final step is implementing improvements.

Mercury Marine, for example, used methods improvement to streamline the production of stern-units for power boats. Examination of the process flow from raw materials to assembly (the final production step) revealed numerous wastes and inefficiencies. Each product, for instance, passed through

Mercury Marine
http://www.mercurymarine.com

122 steps, travelled nearly 6.4 kilometres in the factory, and was handled by 106 people. Analysis revealed that in the 122 steps through the factory, only 27 steps involved production that actually added value to the product (for example, drilling, painting). The remaining steps included handling, counting, checking, storing, and record-keeping. Work methods were thus revised to eliminate non-productive activities. Mercury ultimately realized savings in labour, inventory, paperwork, and space requirements. Because production lead time was also reduced, customer orders were filled faster.

Operations Scheduling

Once plans identify the necessary resources and how to use those resources to reach a firm's quantity and quality goals, managers must develop timetables for acquiring the resources. This aspect of operations is called **scheduling**.

Scheduling occurs on many levels. A **master production schedule** shows which product(s) will be produced, when production will occur, and what resources will be used during the coming months. For example, the master schedule for Memtek might state that 70 000 Memorex tape cassettes should be produced in May, 60 000 in June, and 50 000 in July.

But this information does not tell the manufacturing people how many of the 70 000 cassettes in May should be standard videotapes, how many should be deluxe videotapes, or how many should be audio cassettes. Short-term *detailed schedules*, a type of tactical plan (see Chapter 6), answer questions of this kind on a daily or weekly basis. These schedules use incoming sales orders and weekly sales forecasts to determine what size and variation of cassettes to make in each of the next several days.

scheduling
Developing timetables for acquiring resources.

master production schedule
A general, rather than highly detailed, schedule of which product(s) will be produced, when production will occur, and what resources will be used in coming months.

Tools for Scheduling

Production managers must sometimes schedule special projects, such as plant renovations or relocations, that require close coordination and timing. In these cases, project scheduling is facilitated by special tools like *Gantt and PERT charts*.

Gantt Charts

A **Gantt chart** diagrams the steps to be performed in a project and specifies the time required to complete each step. The manager lists all activities necessary to complete the work and then estimates the time required for each activity. To control production, the manager then checks the progress of the project against the chart. If the project is ahead of schedule, some workers may be shifted to another project. If behind schedule, workers may be added or completion of the job may be delayed.

Figure 12.4 shows a Gantt chart that has been prepared for the renovation of a college classroom. It serves both to show progress to date and to schedule remaining work. The current date is 5/11. Note that workers are about one half week behind schedule in removing old floor tiles and reworking tables and chairs.

Gantt chart
A diagram laying out the steps in a production schedule along with the projected time to complete each step; used in production control.

PERT Charts

PERT—short for *Program Evaluation and Review Technique*—is useful in managing major customized projects whose success means coordinating numerous activities. Like Gantt charts, **PERT charts** break down one large project

PERT (Program Evaluation and Review Technique) chart
A method of diagramming the steps in the production schedule along with the projected time to complete each step, taking into account the sequence of steps and the critical path of those steps.

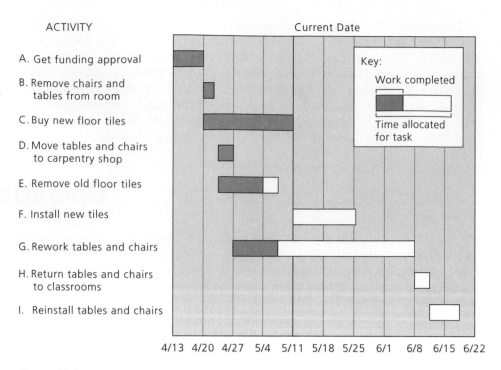

Figure 12.4
A Gantt chart for a classroom renovation shows the progress to date, as well as a schedule for the remaining work.

into its necessary steps and specify the time required to perform each step. Unlike Gantt charts, however, PERT not only shows the necessary sequence of activities but identifies the *critical path* for accomplishing project goals.

Figure 12.5, for example, shows a PERT chart for the classroom renovation that we visited above. The critical path consists of activities *A, B, D, G, H,* and *I.* It is "critical" because any delay in completing any activity on it will cause workers to miss their completion deadline (9 1/2 weeks after startup). First, no activity can be started until all preceding activities are finished. For instance, chairs and tables cannot be returned to the classroom (*H*) until after they have been reworked (*G*) and after new tiles are installed (*F*). Second, the chart clearly identifies activities that will cause delays unless special action is taken at the right time. By reassigning workers and equipment, for example, potentially late activities can be speeded up to keep the project on schedule.

Operations Control

operations control

Managers monitor production performance by comparing results with plans and schedules.

follow-up

Checking to ensure that production decisions are being implemented.

Once long-range plans have been put into action and schedules have been drawn up, the production manager's task is to control production activities so that they conform to plans. **Operations control** requires managers to monitor production performance, in part by comparing results with detailed plans and schedules. If schedules or quality standards are not met, corrective action is needed. **Follow-up**—checking to ensure that production decisions are being implemented—is an essential and ongoing facet of operations control.

Operations control features two major subareas: *quality control* and *materials management.* Both activities seek to ensure that schedules are met and that production goals are fulfilled, both in quantity and quality. In this section, we consider the nature of materials management and some important operations-control tools.

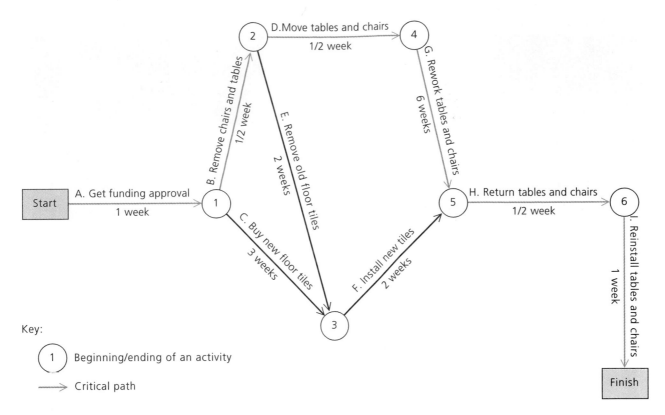

Figure 12.5

A PERT chart for a classroom renovation shows which activities must be completed before others can begin.

Materials Management

Both goods-producing and service companies use materials. For some manufacturing firms, materials costs account for 50 to 75 percent of total product costs. For goods whose production uses little labour, such as petroleum refining, this percentage is even higher. Thus companies have good reasons to emphasize materials management.

Materials management involves not just controlling but also planning and organizing the flow of materials. Even before production starts, materials management focuses on product design by emphasizing materials **standardization**: the use, where possible, of standard and uniform components rather than new or different components. Ford's engine plant in Romeo, Michigan, for instance, builds several different engine models. To save costs, the plant now uses common parts for several models rather than unique parts for each. One kind of piston, therefore, is now used in different engines. When components were standardized, the total number of different parts was reduced by 25 percent. Standardization also simplifies paperwork, reduces storage requirements, and eliminates unnecessary materials flows.

Once the product is designed, materials management purchases the necessary materials and monitors the production process through the distribution of finished goods. The four major areas of materials management are *transportation, warehousing, inventory control,* and *purchasing* (see Figure 12.6).

Transportation includes the means of transporting resources to the company and finished goods to buyers. *Warehousing* refers to the storage of both incoming materials for production and finished goods for physical distribution to customers. Because inventory control and purchasing are more specialized operations, we will explain each process in more detail.

materials management

Planning, organizing, and controlling the flow of materials from purchase through distribution of finished goods.

standardization

Using standard and uniform components in the production process.

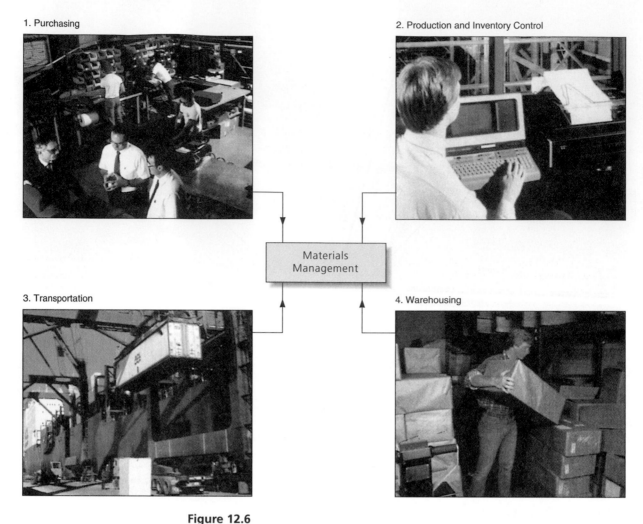

Figure 12.6
Materials management begins with newly purchased materials and continues during production, transportation, and warehousing.

Inventory Control

inventory control

The receiving, storing, handling, and counting of all resources, partly finished goods, and finished goods.

Inventory control includes the receiving, storing, handling, and counting of all raw materials, partly finished goods, and finished goods. Inventory control of raw materials and finished goods is primarily a warehousing task. Production managers generally spend more time and effort controlling *materials inventory*—the stock of items needed during the production process, which might include such items as small components to be used in final assembly. Inventory control ensures that enough materials inventories are available to meet production schedules.

Purchasing

Most companies have purchasing departments to buy proper materials in the amounts needed, both at reasonable prices and at the right time. The importance of purchasing can be seen in the relationship between buying practices and certain materials-management costs. For many years, purchasing departments practised *forward buying*: That is, they routinely purchased quantities of materials large enough to fill their needs for long periods. The practice was popular because it can save money by allowing a firm to purchase materials at quantity discounts. Thus it may be advantageous for a crate manufacturer to buy truckloads of nails to satisfy its need for several weeks.

At the same time, however, purchasing agents must balance the need to hold enough materials in stock with the need to avoid excess supplies. Excess supplies entail increased **holding costs**—the costs of keeping extra supplies or materials on hand. These include the real costs of storage, handling, insurance, and obsolescence of the inventory as well as *opportunity costs*—additional earnings that the company must pass up because of the funds tied up in inventory.

In response to today's rising holding costs, many purchasing departments have adopted a so-called *hand-to-mouth pattern*—placing small orders frequently. This practice also requires shorter **lead time**—that is, the gap between the customer's placement of an order and the seller's shipping of merchandise. For example, a radio maker who uses hundreds or thousands of standard components ranging from packaging materials to push buttons may significantly reduce holding costs by ordering only what it needs for the coming day or week.

Purchasing departments are responsible for **supplier selection**—finding and determining which suppliers to buy from.[10] Supplier selection typically follows a four-stage process. The purchaser first surveys possible suppliers. The purchaser then visits, evaluates, and narrows the list to the few suppliers who are best qualified to fill the company's needs. Purchaser and potential suppliers then negotiate terms of purchase, followed by the purchaser's final choice of a supplier. The fourth "stage" is actually an ongoing process: maintaining a continuing positive buyer-seller relationship. A good relationship ensures reliable and uninterrupted transactions that benefit both parties.

Obviously, maintaining relationships with multiple suppliers is expensive for the purchasing organization. It takes time to survey, inquire, communicate with, and evaluate potential suppliers and to build good purchaser-supplier relationships. Today, therefore, most purchasers are working hard to reduce the number of their suppliers or vendors. A 3M factory provides a typical example: In the first year of its vendor-reduction program, active vendors were trimmed from 2800 to 600, followed by another reduction to 300 the following year. Similarly, Wallace Co., a distributor of industrial valves, fittings, and repair parts, trimmed its supplier list from 2500 to 325.[11] When fewer in number, purchaser-supplier relationships become strengthened. As a rule, both parties work more cooperatively because they are mutually dependent.

holding costs

Costs of keeping currently unsaleable goods, or costs of money that could be otherwise invested.

lead time

The time between placing an order and actually receiving a shipment.

supplier selection

Finding and determining suppliers to buy from.

Tools for Operations Control

A wide variety of tools are available to help managers to make the necessary trade-offs for production control. Chief among these tools are just-in-time inventory systems, material requirements planning, and quality control.

Just-in-Time Inventory Systems

To minimize trade-offs between setup and holding costs, some production managers are using a **just-in-time (JIT) inventory system**. JIT brings together all materials and parts needed at each production step at the precise moment when they are required for the production process. At Toyota's Cambridge, Ontario, plant, delivery trucks constantly pull up at the plant to unload tires, batteries, steering wheels, seats, and many other items needed in the just-in-time production system.[12]

When the Oshawa assembly plant of General Motors of Canada needs seats for cars, it sends the order electronically to a local supplier. The supplier has four hours to make the seats and ship them to the plant. The supplier loads

just-in-time (JIT) inventory system

A method of inventory control in which materials are acquired and put into production just as they are needed.

the truck in reverse order so that the last seat loaded is the first one that will be used on the assembly line. The supplier knows, for example, that the plant will be making five 4-door Luminas and then six 2-door Monte Carlos.[13]

JIT saves money by replacing a stop-and-go production approach with a smooth movement. Everything flows from the arrival of raw materials to subassembly, final completion, and shipment of finished products. JIT reduces the number of goods *in process* (not yet finished) to practically nothing. It also helps to assure reliable quality levels.

Ironically, the problem of backlog orders has changed the minds of some production managers about the virtues of JIT. They have come to the conclusion that the JIT approach to lean inventories—both in terms of parts and finished goods—is not flexible enough to meet expanding orders. In some industries, therefore, inventory levels are creeping up again as insurance against such unexpected events as delays from key suppliers or the need to replace defective parts.

Winnebago Industries, the maker of recreational vehicles, has cyclical demand for its RVs; this means declining orders in the fall and winter. When it first moved to JIT, Winnebago cut its year-round full-time operations and hired workers and scheduled overtime only in the spring and summer. The result was disastrous: Parts were missing, poor fit meant leaks around windows and doors, and appliances inside the vehicles were often scratched. The costs of fixing items covered by warranty skyrocketed, and relations with dealers deteriorated. Finally, Winnebago abandoned JIT. It smoothed out production schedules over the course of the year, and now allows vehicle inventories to build up during the off season.

Winnebago
http://www.winnebagoind.com

material requirements planning (MRP)

A method of inventory control in which a computerized bill of materials is used to estimate production needs so that resources are acquired and put into production only as needed.

bill of materials

A "recipe" for production of a "batch" of a good that specifies the resources needed and the method of combining those resources.

MRP II (manufacturing resource planning)

An advanced version of MRP that ties together all parts of the organization into the company's production activities.

Material Requirements Planning

Like JIT, **material requirements planning (MRP)** also seeks to deliver the right amounts of materials to the right place at the right time. MRP uses a **bill of materials** that is basically a "recipe" for the finished product. It specifies the necessary ingredients (raw materials and components), the order in which they should be combined, and the quantity of each ingredient needed to make one "batch" of the product (say, 2000 finished telephones). The recipe is fed into a computer that controls inventory and schedules each stage of production. The result is fewer early arrivals, less frequent stock shortages, and lower storage costs. MRP is most popular among companies whose products require complicated assembly and fabrication activities, such as automobile manufacturers, appliance makers, and furniture companies.

Manufacturing resource planning, also called **MRP II**, is an advanced version of MRP that ties together all parts of the organization into the company's production activities. For example, MRP inventory and production schedules are translated into cost requirements for the financial management department and personnel requirements for the human resources department; information on capacity availability for new-customer orders goes to the marketing department.

Quality Control

quality control

The management of the production process so as to manufacture goods or supply services that meet specific quality standards.

Not all production-control tools focus on inventory control. Also important is **quality control**: the management of the production process so as to manufacture goods or supply services that meet specific quality standards. McDonald's, for example, has been a pioneer in quality control in the restaurant industry since the 1950s. The company oversees everything from the farming of potatoes for french fries to the packing of meat for Big Macs. Quality-assurance staffers even check standards for ketchup sweetness and french fry length.

In their quest for quality control, many businesses have adopted *quality-improvement teams* (patterned after the Japanese concept of *quality circles*): groups of employees from various work areas who define, analyze, and solve common production problems. Teams meet regularly to discuss problems and to keep management informed of the group's progress in addressing various issues.

Many companies report that improvement teams have not only raised quality levels but increased productivity and reduced costs. They have also improved job satisfaction. But improvement teams also involve risks. Not all employees, for example, want to participate. Moreover, management cannot always adopt group recommendations, no matter how much careful thought, hard work, and enthusiasm went into them. The challenge for production managers, then, is to make wise decisions about when and how to use quality-improvement teams. (Quality control and quality-improvement teams are discussed in more detail in Chapter 14.)

Completing the Operations Management Process: Feedback

Production management does not stop when the goods go out the door or even when they are purchased. Feedback from consumers, the final phase, influences every other part of production management. Comments from users may lead managers to plan smaller or larger production runs. Consumer enthusiasm may dictate a speed-up in master schedules that calls for opening new plants or hiring more workers. Negative criticism of quality may cause managers to seek new production methods and to tighten controls. Because it is consumers—and their "dollar votes"—who determine the success or failure of a company, managers have little choice but to heed customer feedback.

The Future of Operations Management

As Canadian businesses struggle to survive in fiercely competitive world markets, operations management becomes more and more crucial. As discussed in Chapter 3, lagging productivity put Canadian industries at a disadvantage in pricing their goods for world markets. In their battle for lower production costs, higher productivity, and higher quality, more and more managers are turning to mechanization and automation of the operations process, especially with computers.

Mechanization and Automation

Using machines to do work previously done by people is the process of **mechanization**. Its natural extension is **automation**, performing mechanical operations with either minimal or no human intervention. These techniques are not new, of course. The Industrial Revolution began with huge spinning and weaving machines that soon rendered handmade fabric obsolete. Nearly every company in the world uses some machinery in place of hand labour. Some of the most advanced firms are using sophisticated robots in production. Many small firms have automated at least to the degree that personal computer systems monitor production outcomes.

mechanization
The process of using machines instead of people to perform tasks.

automation
The process of performing mechanical operations with minimal or no human involvement.

Computers and Robotics

Computers stand at the forefront of modern automation. Companies use computers to construct detailed schedules, to monitor production, and to help determine raw material needs. In some firms, computers track customer orders as they move through the plant. Computers may also send production information to managers in various departments so that they know how much work is coming, what materials will be needed, and when each job must be completed. When Federal Express picks up a package, for example, the destination is read immediately by a portable scanner. This information then enters the Federal Express computer and is electronically transmitted to the central routing hub in Memphis. With this advance information, the facility can schedule its vehicles out of Memphis to other cities even before it receives incoming packages.

Robotics and Computer-Integrated Manufacturing

robotics
The use of computer-controlled machines that perform production tasks.

Although Japanese companies pioneered their use, Canadian firms are becoming increasingly interested in **robotics**, the construction, maintenance, and use of computer-controlled machines in manufacturing operations. Automobile plants use robots to weld, assemble, paint, and inspect cars. Aircraft manufacturing plants are also using robotics to build planes faster and at less cost than humans can. Still, as the box "Robots: Mixed Success" discusses, robots have not yet found acceptance in many firms.

computer-integrated manufacturing (CIM)
Computer systems that drive robots and control the flow of materials and supplies in the goods production process.

Robotics are only one part of a larger manufacturing automation system called **computer-integrated manufacturing (CIM)**. In addition to controlling robots, CIM can manage material requirements planning and just-in-time inventory systems.

Computer-Aided Design and Manufacturing

computer-aided design (CAD)
Computer analysis and graphics programs that are used to create new products.

The use of computers in manufacturing is not limited to robots and inventory control. Some of the most exciting uses of computers in production are in the areas of computer-aided design (CAD) and computer-aided manufacturing (CAM), known collectively as CAD/CAM.

As its name suggests, **computer-aided design** uses computers to design new products. Through the use of sophisticated analysis methods and graphics, CAD allows users to create a design and simulate conditions to test the performance of the design, all within the computer. Engineers use CAD to design planes and cars. CAD systems let designers see the result of changes in design without having to create costly prototype models and test them under real-world conditions.

computer-aided manufacturing (CAM)
Computer systems used to design and control all the equipment and tools for producing goods.

In a direct offshoot of computer-aided design, **computer-aided manufacturing** uses computers to design and control the equipment needed in the manufacturing process. For example, CAM systems can produce tapes to control all the machines and robots on a production line. Overall, CAD/CAM is useful for engineers in a manufacturing environment to design and test new products and then to design the machines and tools to manufacture the new product.

Decision Support Systems

decision support systems (DSS)
Computer systems used to help managers consider alternatives when making decisions on complicated problems.

A new development in the evolution of *management information systems*, which we will discuss in Chapter 18, has had an impact on manufacturing and production. Computer programs called **decision support systems (DSS)** give users easy access to decision models and data to help them make decisions on

The Canadian Business Scene

Robots: Mixed Success

Industrial robots are not the glamorous creations usually pictured in science fiction movies. Rather, they are machines that are programmed to repeat tirelessly the chores common in industry. At present, robots are used most frequently in the automobile industry for such tasks as welding, painting, and metalworking.

The first fully computerized robotic paint shop for railroad cars in North America was opened on October 5, 1988, at Canadian National Railways' Winnipeg Transcona shops. The system cleans and repaints CN's 11 500 covered hopper cars, which transport bulk commodities like grain and potash. The shops process about 1100 cars per year, four times more than under the old manual system.

Harber Manufacturing, a Fort Erie, Ontario, manufacturer of wood-burning stoves, uses several different types of robots in its manufacturing processes. Five arc-welding robot systems—each costing over $100 000—join metal seams together in a continuous weld. Programmable platforms are also used to move raw materials within the reach of the arc-welding robots.

Robots were supposed to revolutionize the workplace, performing all the mundane and dangerous tasks from welding bolts to handling radioactive isotopes. Yet today, Canadian and American businesses employ only a fraction of the number used in Japan. Why so few electronic helpers? The answer lies in three problems: cost, complexity, and technical limitations.

Cost has kept robots out of many smaller enterprises. A hydraulic robot from Unimation, the leader in robotics, runs $30 000 to $200 000. Even smaller, less powerful robots from Japan can cost up to $40 000 each. With a price tag of $25 000 each, a HelpMate nurse's aid robot from TRC will pay for itself in two and a half years—if it's used 24 hours a day, 7 days a week, 52 weeks a year.

Larger companies have often found that the initial purchase cost is the cheapest part of robotics. A company installing robotics needs computer scientists to program and reprogram robots. And before that, it needs to perform exhaustive studies to determine the precise task to be accomplished. Workers must be trained to operate and work with robots.

Human beings are still vastly superior to robots in a great many regards, especially in tasks requiring sensory input and adaptation. The most sophisticated robots today cannot read handwriting or pick a single right part out of a box of wrong ones. A few can recognize about 20 slightly different shapes as airplanes. Humans can identify thousands of slightly different shapes as planes. As one researcher notes, one human eye has about "100 million vision cells and four layers of neurons, all capable of doing about 10 billion calculations a second." In other words, the visual calculations of a one-eyed human being would take 100 000 supercomputers to imitate.

Perhaps one reason why Japanese businesses use more robots is that they expect less of them. In Japan, robots are used for the most simple, most mindless, most limited of tasks. The preponderance of such tasks in the auto industry (along with the enormous economic and technical resources of such companies) may explain why more than 50 percent of robots in use in Canada are in auto plants versus 10 percent in Japan.

The future of robotics in Canada may depend on recognizing where it can be most useful. Already, robots are making inroads into fields dangerous to humans. Submersible robots are replacing divers in offshore oil and gas operations. They toil for hours in areas of nuclear power plants where once humans worked in very short relays to minimize their exposure to radiation. Cyberworks Inc. is a Canadian manufacturer of robots. While the growth in demand for industrial robots has been slower than expected, the company believes robots will eventually be widely used in space exploration, undersea work, underground mining, and in nuclear waste facilities.

As they become more aware of the special capabilities of robots, more mundane businesses may be willing to take a chance. Robots never get a backache from stooping. Their arms and wrists can twist around completely. A robot watchguard with microwave vision can see through nonmetallic walls and spot an intruder 40 metres away in the dark. And those challenged had better give the right password. Robots still have no sense of humour.

complicated problems. DSS allows users to investigate conveniently "What if?" questions. "What if the company decides to order twice as much raw material as needed—will we need more warehousing space?" "What if the company purchases 10 additional robots—will we be able to cut some of our present workforce?" "What if the company adds more flexible automation—will sales go up?"

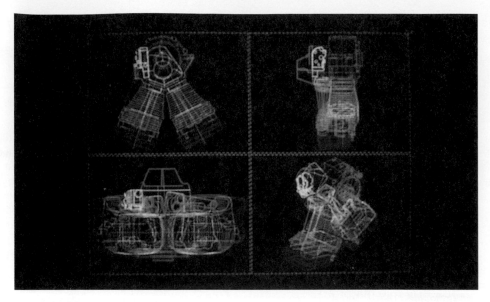

A CAD system displays four different views of this gasoline engine, allowing its design to be easily examined and modified.

Production and the Small Business Enterprise

As we noted in Chapter 8, manufacturing is the hardest industry for small businesses to break into because of the extensive resources it requires. But while large corporations continue to dominate this arena, small companies continue to enter—and succeed. Manufacturing giants increasingly find themselves overextended and close or sell off unprofitable companies. And small business people are moving in to fill market gaps and turn losing corporate subsidiaries into winners as independent small companies.

Precisely how do small companies succeed where larger ones have failed, in both goods and services production? Analysts cite the following advantages, among others:

- Many small firms offer higher product quality—a practice that makes them more competitive against foreign products than some bigger companies.
- Small businesses can frequently offer greater varieties of products because they have not committed themselves to the expensive, special-purpose equipment to which many large businesses have tied themselves.
- Small operations frequently offer more challenging work. They often give workers greater opportunities for advancing ideas and have better records in respecting and adopting those ideas. Indeed, surveys show that small businesses sometimes have a distinct competitive advantage because of favourable employee attitudes.

Of course, small businesses still face problems as manufacturers, especially with regard to equipment and inventories. Even general-purpose and small-volume equipment is expensive. And small businesses can more easily overextend themselves, both financially and with respect to the equipment's performance capabilities, than can large firms.

Inventories tend to be the single biggest problem area for small manufacturers. Too many resources on hand, rather than too few, is one of the most common and costly mistakes. Such surpluses can usually be traced to poor information about what and how many resources are on hand and what they will be used for. Since they have less capital than big companies, small manufacturers must maintain particularly close control over their inventories to succeed.

Summary of Learning Objectives

1. **Classify a business's *operations processes* in three ways and explain the role of the operations managers.** Operations processes can be classified by the type of *technology* used (*chemical*, *fabrication*, *assembly*, *transport*, or *clerical*) by whether products are submitted to *analytic* or *synthetic processes*, by the *pattern of product flow* (*continuous* or *intermittent*), and by the extent of *labour use*. Operations managers use these classifications to plan, organize, and control the operations process.

2. **Identify five major areas of *operations planning* and two levels of *operations scheduling*.** Many operations-planning activities are conducted by managers in different departments and fall into one of five major categories. *Capacity planning* deals with the amount of product that a firm can produce under various working conditions. In determining facility locations, *location planning* can affect a producer's costs and flexibility.

   Layout planning is concerned with the different ways in which products can be moved through facilities as they are being manufactured. Alternatives include: *process layouts*, whereby equipment and workers are grouped according to function; *product layouts*, which move raw and partially complete materials through a fixed sequence of steps; *craft work*, where each worker has the opportunity to assemble an entire product; *cellular layouts*, which are efficient in moving families of products through similar flow paths; and *fixed-position layouts*, whereby resources are brought to the work location.

   Quality planning includes systems for ensuring that goods meet a firm's quality standards. Finally, *methods planning* is designed to identify and, when necessary, improve the methods for performing each step in the production process.

   These plans are translated into two levels of *operations scheduling*. A *master production schedule* is drawn up to show which products will be produced, when production will occur, and what resources will be used within scheduled time periods. Short-range, detailed *production schedules* designate when, where, and how much of a specific good will be produced.

3. **Describe the activities in *materials management* and identify four tools for achieving *operations control*.** *Materials management* is the process of planning, organizing, and controlling the flow of materials through the operations process. It can be divided into four major areas. *Transportation* refers to the means of getting resources to the manufacturer and manufactured goods to customers. *Warehousing* refers to ways of storing both resources and goods.

   Inventory control includes the receiving, storing, handling, and counting of all raw materials, partly finished goods, and finished goods. Production managers are basically concerned with controlling *materials inventory* (the stock of items needed during the production process).

   Finally, *purchasing* refers to the process of buying proper materials in the right amounts, both at reasonable prices and at the right time. To control purchasing, production managers must decide whether to use a *forward-buying approach* (buying enough materials to satisfy long-term needs) or a *hand-to-mouth approach* (placing smaller orders frequently). To control inventory, they must balance *holding costs* (the costs of keeping extra inventory on hand) with setup costs. They must also establish and maintain positive relationship with suppliers.

Techniques like *just-in-time (JIT) production systems*, *material requirements planning (MRP)*, and *manufacturing resource planning (MRP II)* can assist managers in inventory control. All of these techniques are designed to deliver the right amounts of materials to the right place at the right time. The use of *quality-improvement teams* can assist in quality control, as can improved and continuous *worker training*.

4. **Characterize some of the major forms of *automation* currently used in production operations.** *Automation* is the process of performing mechanical operations with either minimal or no human involvement. It is changing the face of production operations in many areas. Computers drive robots that can perform many boring or dangerous tasks formerly requiring human labour in a process called *computer-integrated manufacturing (CIM)*. CIM also integrates *computer-aided design (CAD)* and *computer-aided manufacturing (CAM)*, which allow firms to send information back and forth between design engineers and production managers. *Decision support systems (DSS)* assist production managers in making decisions by allowing them to ask and answer "What if?" questions.

5. **Explain the advantages and disadvantages of small and large production companies.** Small businesses have an advantage over larger manufacturers because they can frequently offer customers higher quality and greater product flexibility. They can also offer their employees more challenge and a chance to make a difference in the company. However, they face greater problems with inventories and equipment because of their more limited funds.

Key Terms

utility, 342
time utility, 342
place utility, 342
ownership (possession) utility, 342
form utility, 342
operations (production) management, 342
analytic process, 344
synthetic process, 344
continuous process, 344
intermittent process, 345
labour-intensive process, 345
capital-intensive process, 345
forecasts, 346

capacity, 347
process layout, 349
product layout, 349
assembly line, 349
cellular layouts, 350
U-shaped production lines, 351
flexible manufacturing system (FMS), 351
soft manufacturing, 351
scheduling, 353
master production schedule, 353
Gantt chart, 353
PERT (Program Evaluation and Review Technique) chart, 353

operations control, 354
follow-up, 354
materials management, 355
standardization, 355
inventory control, 356
holding costs, 357
lead time, 357
supplier selection, 357
just-in-time (JIT) inventory system, 357
material requirements planning (MRP), 358
bill of materials, 358
MRP II (manufacturing resource planning), 358

quality control, 358
mechanization, 359
automation, 359
robotics, 360
computer-integrated manufacturing (CIM), robotics, 360
computer-aided design (CAD), 360
computer-aided manufacturing (CAM), 360
decision support systems (DSS), 360

Study Questions and Exercises

Review Questions

1. Explain how General Motors of Canada provides different forms of utility to its customers.
2. How does a process layout differ from a product layout? How does a fixed-position layout differ from a customer-oriented layout?
3. In what situations is forward buying most appropriate? In what situations is hand-to-mouth buying most appropriate?
4. What are the advantages of a flexible manufacturing system?
5. Why do small business people choose to go into manufacturing industries dominated by large companies?

Analysis Questions

6. Find examples of a synthetic production process and an analytic process. Then classify each according to whether it is chemical, fabrication, assembly, transport, or clerical. Explain your analysis.
7. In deciding to produce the first luxury minivan, the Town & Country, Chrysler had to develop long-range production plans. Outline as many of the major elements (production activities and resources) that they had to plan for as you can. Then, select any one of the elements and show the detailed aspects of it that would have to be investigated and considered before production could start.
8. Choose a simple project, such as giving a party, and draw a PERT chart that could be used to manage the project's progress.

Application Exercises

9. Select two manufacturers, a large one and a small one, in your community and compare the methods they use to get good quality in their products. Contrast the kinds of problems they face in assuring high product quality.
10. Interview the owner of a small manufacturing firm. Classify the firm's production processes, and then identify the major production problems of the firm and propose solutions for these problems.

Building Your Business Skills

Goal

To help students understand the just-in-time approach to inventory management of both components/raw materials and finished goods.

Situation

Suppose you work in the purchasing department at a manufacturing firm. Management is trying to decide whether just-in-time represents an approach that could help cut inventory costs and improve productivity. Your job is to find out what other companies are doing about JIT.

Method

Working in groups of four or five, make arrangements to conduct interviews at various manufacturing companies near your college or university. Try to speak to a company executive as well as someone in purchasing or sales. In particular:

■ Determine which inventory method is used.
■ Assess attitudes towards JIT and ask about its strengths and weaknesses.
■ Ask whether the company's suppliers and customers are using JIT and find out what their experiences have been.

Prepare a brief report to summarize your findings and exchange reports with the other teams in the class.

Follow-Up Questions

1. Did your research reveal strong feelings, pro or con, about JIT? In particular, what aspect of JIT caused these feelings?

2. Can you make any generalizations about companies that look favourably on JIT compared to those that do not?

At a time when rigorous competition has driven some Canadian companies out of the steel-making business, Dofasco has survived. To learn more about production operations, log on to the Dofasco Web site at:

http://www.dofasco.ca

1. How would you describe Dofasco's operations process? What type of transformation technology does it use?

2. What are the major inputs to the production process? What are its outputs?

3. What are Dofasco's traditional markets? What are some major emerging markets?

4. Using specific information from the Dofasco Web site, what can you conclude about this company's position on environmental issues? Are any environmental considerations evident in the company's production activities?

5. Visit the "Technology" section of the Web site. Summarize how the company is using computer technology to improve operational efficiency.

CONCLUDING CASE 12-1

Compaq Programs a Path to the Top

At the end of 1994, executives at Compaq Computer Corp. celebrated the achievement of an ambitious goal: Year-end industry data ranked Compaq number one among American manufacturers—ahead of IBM and Apple—in terms of personal computers built and shipped to customers. To achieve this goal, CEO Eckhard Pfeiffer had spent tens of millions of dollars on manufacturing improvements that yielded tremendous productivity gains. During the past three years, for example, Compaq had doubled the number of PCs produced per square foot of factory floor space. In 1994 alone, production had grown more than 50 percent, and output of finished computers per employee had increased 50 percent. Moreover, as production volume increased, Compaq had negotiated more favourable prices from vendors supplying such components as disk drives. The result was a 10-percent annual reduction in the costs of production materials.

Not content with these gains, Compaq decided that its next step would be a radical one: eliminating assembly lines in favour of three-person "cells" through which similar products would flow continuously from beginning of production to end of testing. In trials at a plant in Scotland, output increased 23 percent over the best assembly-line output, and output per square foot went up 16 percent. Moreover, cell manufacturing provides another benefit besides productivity: It will enable Compaq to engage in "mass customiza-

tion." In other words, machines like Compaq's popular ProLinea can be built as customer orders are received.

Perhaps more importantly, this approach reduces dependence on forecasts of market demand. In the computer industry especially, such forecasts are often unreliable because technology advances can inspire dramatic product changes in a matter of just a few months. "A computer maker today," observes one management consultant, "must be able to manufacture to customer order, not just put a machine on the shelf and hope that a customer buys it."

Greg Petsch, senior vice-president of manufacturing, was given the job of transforming Compaq's factories. His first challenge was to increase production without investing in more factory space. One option was closing plants in Scotland and Houston, Texas, and contracting out assembly work to low-wage countries in the Far East. Petsch realized, however, that the human-labour content in a PC is only about 15 minutes. Thus he opted instead for the diametrically opposite strategy: running Compaq's Houston factory around the clock. "We know we can build computers for North America cheaper here in Houston," he says confidently.

Another key decision involved producing some critical components in-house. Taking an opposite approach from arch rival Dell Computer, Compaq now has 13 new production lines turning out so-called "motherboards"—the semiconductor component housing a computer's main chip

...

and memory. This critical part accounts for about 40 percent of the cost of a PC, and Petsch discovered that Compaq could produce its own for $25 less than suppliers in the Far East. It could also save two weeks in shipping time. Obviously, the motherboard is also critical to the success of any plan that calls for flexible manufacturing and just-in-time inventory: "If you can delay the definition of the motherboard until the time you receive the order," explains Petsch, "you also save a great deal on inventory and obsolescence of parts."

Admittedly, Compaq's recent manufacturing successes have been offset somewhat by problems with notebook computers. Portables are important because they represent a fast-growing, highly profitable segment of a computer maker's market. Although Compaq actually began as a manufacturer of portable computers, it has recently lost ground to competitors like Toshiba. Lorie Strong, vice-president for portable-computer marketing, sums up the problems of her division as bluntly as possible: "We weren't delivering real consistently," she admits. For example, production of one portable business computer, the expensive LTE Elite, was delayed and then plagued by annoying bugs once it hit the market.

Industry observers also fault Compaq for sticking with popular products too long before offering improvements. For instance, Compaq's entry in the subnotebook category, the Aero, not only met with lukewarm acceptance but also was on the market for more than two years without an upgrade. However, now that the company is introducing both product improvements and price cuts, industry consultant Tim Bajarin believes that "Compaq is back on track. The mistakes they made cannot be duplicated again."

Case Questions

1. What type of transformation technology does Compaq use?

2. How did Greg Petsch tackle the issue of capacity planning? What factors influenced his decisions?

3. What is "mass customization"? What does Compaq hope to gain by adopting this approach?

4. What type of materials-handling issues are likely to be important at Compaq?

5. What must Compaq do to reassert itself in the portable-computer market?

◆

CONCLUDING CASE 12-2

Just-in-Time II

Just-in-time inventory systems were made famous by the Japanese in the 1980s. But in the 1990s, North American firms are carrying the concept even further.

When JIT II is used, manufacturing firms treat their suppliers almost like their own employees. At some companies, sales representatives from suppliers even have desks next to the factory floor in the company they are supplying. They can go wherever they choose in the factory, attend production meetings, wander around the research lab, and even check the company's sales forecast.

Consider the JIT II works at Honeywell's Golden Valley, Minnesota plant. There are 15 representatives from 10 different suppliers who have offices in the plant. They think like Honeywell employees and are constantly trying to trim purchasing costs. Some are even allowed to place orders on Honeywell's behalf with their own competitors. Inventory levels at the plant are now measured in days instead of weeks, and Honeywell employs 25 percent fewer purchasing agents than it used to.

But JIT II is not always easy to introduce. The biggest problem is developing trust between the vendor and the manufacturer. Historically, the relationship between suppliers and manufacturers has been one of hard-nosed bargaining over prices. A substantial amount of mistrust is not

uncommon. As a result, manufacturers are often not keen on the idea of letting one of their suppliers have confidential information about how the company operates.

For example, one purchasing manager at Honeywell, who oversees $180 million worth of purchases each year, didn't like the JIT II idea when it was initially proposed. She was concerned that Honeywell's suppliers would find out about each other's prices by overhearing conversations between Honeywell's managers. But now, five suppliers work closely with her 20 buyers and there have been very few problems.

Suppliers may also be reluctant to get involved in JIT II because *they* may have to reveal their own costs. Suppliers have always been concerned that if the manufacturer found out their costs, that they would try to take advantage of them.

Bose Corp., the manufacturer of radio and stereo speakers, screens potential in-plant suppliers and requires them to sign a confidentiality agreement and stipulates certain guidelines. Purchases over a certain amount require a signature from a Bose manager.

One potential problem with JIT II concerns termination of agreements. Ball Corp., a manufacturer of baby food jars, had a plant right next door to a Gerber Baby Foods manu-

•••

Just-in-Time II

(continued)

facturing plant. Ball always knew exactly how many jars to produce because workers from both plants interacted frequently. But when Gerber decided to shop around for a cheaper worldwide source of jars, it ended the relationship. Ball was forced to close its plant and lay off 350 workers.

Case Questions

1. Why have companies started to move to JIT II?

2. What are the advantages of JIT II? Be specific.

3. What are the possible disadvantages of JIT II? Be specific.

13

Producing Services

Just-in-Time to the Hospital

Mount Sinai Hospital in downtown Toronto buys about 600 different medical and surgical items from 60 different suppliers. Until recently, the narrow street behind the hospital was constantly clogged with suppliers' trucks delivering goods such as bandages, gloves, catheters, needles, and other supplies that hospitals use. These trucks caused traffic jams and interfered with cars bringing patients and visitors.

But things have changed dramatically. Now, one delivery truck comes to the hospital each evening at 11:00 p.m. This single delivery signifies the hospital's shift from the old system of keeping inventory to a new, stockless system of materials management.

Here's how it works. Individual suppliers no longer come to Mount Sinai to deliver the items they have sold the hospital. Rather, all suppliers deliver their products to Livingston Healthcare Services Inc. in Oakville. Livingston then stores these items and fills Mount Sinai's orders once each day. The orders are put into plastic boxes that are delivered to specific nursing stations at the hospital.

Formerly, the hospital spent about $33 million on supplies; of that, about 18 percent was for medical and surgical products. But only $28 million actually went to suppliers. The other $5 million was spent on salaries for hospital workers who managed the supplies once they got to the hospital.

A typical product, for example, was brought in, unpacked, and stored in the central store room. Then someone from one of the nursing stations would come to the store room, put the product on a cart, take it to the nursing station, unload it, and store it again. By the time the

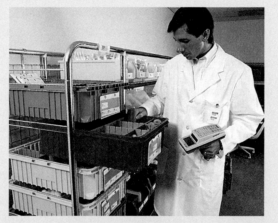

product was used on a patient, it might have been handled 20 times. The new system eliminates most of those steps. Now, all the items needed by a certain nursing station come in one bundle from Livingston.

The new system is highly computerized. Clerks carry scanners as they tour the stockrooms for each nursing station. Each product has a bar code and the computer indicates how many of that item are in stock. If more product is needed, the number is transmitted to the hospital's central computer. The computer assembles data from all the nursing stations and transmits a blanket order to Livingston's warehouse and distribution centre. If there is a crisis, Livingston can deliver within one hour.

How did Mount Sinai come up with the stockless system of materials management? Several years ago, when the hospital decided to overhaul its materials management system, it set up a committee to decide on a new system. That committee included everyone who was involved in ordering, handling, and paying for medical supplies—nurses, stockroom people, accountants, and ward clerks. The director of materials management says the new system was implemented smoothly because the people who had to use it had been involved in designing the system.

In the first year using the new system, Mount Sinai saved about $200 000. Seven full-time stocking employees were shifted to other work. The hospital also now has 5000 square feet of vacant space. This could mean additional savings of $750 000. The hospital is also looking at expanding the system to include food service, drugs, and laboratory testing. ◆

Mount Sinai Hospital is just one example of the increasingly important role that services play in business today.

By focusing on the learning objectives for this chapter, you will better understand the unique nature of services and the ways in which businesses deal with the special problems associated with the "production" of services. After reading this chapter, you will be able to:

LEARNING OBJECTIVES

1. Identify the characteristics that distinguish *service operations* from *goods production*.

2. Classify services according to the extent of *customer contact* and *similarity to manufacturing*.

3. Describe the major decisions in *service-operations planning* and *scheduling*.

4. Explain how managers can control the *quantity* and *quality* of services offered.

5. Identify ways to overcome the special problems of service operations management.

Service Operations: An Overview

service operations
Business activities that transform resources into services for customers.

Everywhere you go today, you encounter examples of **service operations**—business activities that provide services to their customers. You wake up in the morning to the sound of your favourite radio station. You stop at the newsstand on the corner for a newspaper on your way to the bus stop, where you catch the bus to work or school. Your instructors, the bus driver, the clerk at the 7-Eleven store, and the morning radio announcer are all examples of people who work in service operations. They provide you with tangible and intangible products: entertainment, transportation, education, and food preparation.

The Service Sector Explosion in Canada

Services are big business today. We saw in Chapter 3 that over 70 percent of employed Canadians work in service industries. Projections indicate that service sector employment will continue to grow at a faster rate than manufacturing sector employment. Much of the growth in the service sector is in the areas of finance, insurance, real estate, government, retailing, and health care.

Employment in service industries is also more stable than employment in manufacturing. Apparently, consumers will stop buying many goods before they will sacrifice such essential services as education, telephones, banking, and police and fire protection.

The perception that the manufacturing sector offers high-paid jobs, while the service sector offers only low-paid, dead-end jobs is not correct. The service sector includes high paid people like doctors, lawyers, movie stars, and architects. It is as varied as the manufacturing sector. And the gap in wages between service and manufacturing jobs is narrowing.

All businesses are service operations to some extent.[1] Consider General Motors of Canada, a company that to many people is the epitome of manufacturing. Certainly GM produces cars. But it is also heavily involved with repairs and maintenance, warranty fulfilment, installation advice, operator training, and, through GMAC, lending funds. Without its attendant services, GM's automobile sales would shrivel.

Differences in the Service Focus

Service operations have features in common with manufacturing operations. For example, both involve transforming raw materials into finished goods. But the raw materials in services are not glass or steel. Rather, they are people with unsatisfied needs and people's possessions, which may need various kinds of care or alteration. The finished products are not goods like cars or houses. Rather, they are people with needs met and possessions serviced. Table 13.1 shows some examples of inputs, transformations, and outputs in the service sector.

Service operations differ from manufacturing operations in important ways. Probably the most obvious is that goods are *produced*, while services are *performed*. The focus of service operations is more complex. And services are more *intangible*, *customized*, and *perishable* than most products. There is also a unique link between production and consumption in service operations. Finally, consumers evaluate services differently than goods.

Focus on Process and Outcome

Manufacturing operations focus on the *outcome* of the production process. But most services, because they are actually a combination of goods and services, focus on both the transformation *process* and its *outcome*. Thus, managing service operations requires some skills that differ from those required to manage manufacturing operations. For example, workers for a local gas company must possess interpersonal skills to calm and reassure frightened customers who have reported a leak. Their job is more than just repairing a problem with a pipe or valve. For factory workers installing gas pipes in mobile homes, in contrast, such interpersonal skills may not be important at all.

Intangibility

Services often cannot be touched, tasted, smelled, or seen. An important part of their value may be subconscious, value that the individual doesn't consciously consider. For example, when you rent a hotel room for the night,

Table 13.1   Examples of Service Operation Inputs, Transformations, and Outputs

Service Operation	Inputs	Transformations	Outputs
Airline	Cold person in Toronto, jet, fuel, pilot and crew	Air travel	Warm person in Florida
Home security	House, family with fear of theft, home security system, tools, installer	Installation of system	Safe house, peace of mind
Hospital	Sick and injured people, supplies, nurses, doctors, utilities	Medical care and treatment	Healthy people
Jail	Convicted criminals, guards, wardens, teachers, food, clothing, utilities	Punishment, education	Responsible members of society
Lawn service	Overgrown lawn, lawn mower, worker	Lawn mowing, yard work	Neat yard
Theatre	Expectant people, actors, costumes, sets, utilities	Theatrical production	Entertained people
TV repair shop	Inoperable television set, replacement parts, tools, skilled technician, utilities	Television repair	Operable television set
University	High-school graduates, tuition, books, professors	Education	University graduate

you are purchasing the intangible quality of shelter. You may also be purchasing something even more intangible—a safe, homey, comfortable feeling—whether or not you are actually aware of it. All services have some degree of intangibility.[2]

Actually, tangible goods also have intangible aspects. Although a sofa is certainly a tangible good, it also provides comfort, an intangible, and its appearance may be aesthetically pleasing, another intangible. Figure 13.1 places a number of products on a scale from most to least tangible. Note that most products contain both tangible and intangible elements.

Customization

Another characteristic of services is that they are typically *customized*. When you visit a therapist, you expect to be examined for the symptoms *you* are experiencing. Even a general diagnostic exam typically includes questions about your own unique problems. Similarly, when you buy insurance, get your favourite pet groomed, or have your hair cut, you expect these services to be customized to meet your needs.

Perishability

Services are typically characterized by a high degree of perishability. Services such as garbage collection, transportation, child care, and house cleaning cannot be produced ahead of time and then stored. If a service is not used when it is available, it is wasted.

Link Between Consumer and Service

Because services transform a customer or a customer's possessions, service operations must often contend with the fact that the customer is part of the production process. For example, unless you are a movie star or the prime minister, you must go to the barbershop or beauty salon to buy a haircut.

As part of the production process, consumers of services have a unique ability to affect that process. As the consumer, you expect the salon to be conveniently located, to be open for business at convenient times, to offer needed services at reasonable prices, and to provide prompt service. Accordingly, the manager adopts hours of operation, available services, and numbers of employees to meet the requirements of the customer.

Consumers of services also have an opportunity to comment on how well the service satisfies their needs. Indeed, managers of service operations often complain that everyone is an expert on services—or at least they think they are. Have you ever complained about the way your mail was delivered, the way checkout lines operated at the discount store, or the way your classes were taught? Probably. But have you given as much advice on how to manufacture

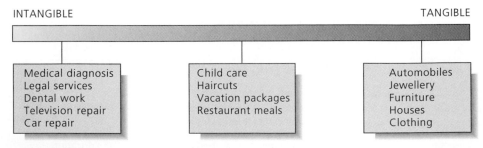

Figure 13.1
Tangible and intangible elements in services.

a product? Probably not. The box "Customer Service in the Retail Store" gives additional information on the importance of service to customers.

Differing Quality Considerations

Finally, consumers judge services on different bases than they do goods. Managers of service operations must understand that quality of work and quality of service are not necessarily synonymous. Your car could be flawlessly repaired, but if you had to wait a day past the time at which it was promised, you might feel that you had not received good service.

Consider the case of Ford's Parts and Service Division, which changed its name to Customer Service in June 1993. In a drive to improve service quality, it now focuses not on selling parts to dealers for profit but on acting as a consultant and technical trainer for Ford dealer repair staffs. The change is part of Ford's overall strategy to stress quality as "Job 1." Because gaps in *product* quality have been closed by all automakers, Ford's strategy is to transform its *service* operation into a more powerful competitive tool.[3]

The Canadian Business Scene

Customer Service in the Retail Store

The customer service revolution began in earnest a decade ago when books like *In Search of Excellence* were published. These books touted the importance of being obsessed with meeting customer needs. While this idea is undeniably correct, these books often fail to explain how companies can reconcile the conflicting demands of customer service, inventory control, employee efficiency, and profitability.

Consider the case of a clothing shop. It is now fashionable to stress customer service, and salesclerks are routinely sent to seminars to sharpen their skills in this area. At the same time, to counter theft, many shops have a rule that a customer cannot take more than two garments into the change room. Salesclerks spend excessive time watching the customers who are going in and out of change rooms and insufficient time with customers who have problems or want help.

Retail clerks are often caught in a catch-22 situation because exhortations about good service conflict with other rules of the business. In recessionary times, for example, retail stores may become less customer-oriented to improve the bottom line. Simultaneously, they are under pressure from competitors to improve customer service.

The retail sector must recognize that improving customer service requires a company-wide perspective, not just a focus on retail clerks. For example, Coopers & Lybrand Consulting Group created its Centre for Customer Satisfaction Excellence because it recognized the need for broad-based responses to customer demands. When a problem develops in customer service, resources from marketing, production, information technology, and human resources are involved to solve it.

Service excellence enthusiasts caution that the payoffs from improved service do not happen immediately, while the costs can be high. A full commitment to excellent service requires expenditures on employee training, incentive schemes, communications, and marketing. Excellence in service cannot overcome other weaknesses such as a poor product; rather, excellence in customer service is a potential competitive advantage.

Retail and Financial Consulting Services Inc. advises retailing firms on customer service and staff motivation programs. Their studies show that it is six times more expensive to attract a new customer to a store than it is to retain a current customer. Keeping the current customers is a matter of providing good service. To do that, staff enthusiasm is critical. Furthermore, by rewarding and recognizing staff properly, turnover is reduced. And when turnover is reduced, profits increase.

Toronto's SkyDome typifies the new emphasis on customer service. The 180 full-time and 500 part-time staff have to deal with as many as 68 000 people at once. To implement its philosophy of total guest satisfaction, the SkyDome requires 20 or more hours of training for each staff member. In 1991, "SkyDome U" was launched; each graduating class participates in a commencement ceremony. An employee incentive program has been set up to emphasize the goals of SkyDome's customer service strategy, and supervisors give out coupons to staffers who provide exceptional service to patrons. Lesley Chefero, human resources manager at Toronto Stadium Corp., says that none of this would have happened without the strong support of president Richard Peddie.

Classifying Service Operations

One way to classify service operations is according to how necessary it is for the customer to be a part of the system as the service is produced. A second way is based on how similar service operations are to a factory. Any service can be classified by either method. The point of classifications is to help managers determine the most appropriate strategy for managing services.

Extent of Customer Contact

A useful criterion for classifying service operations is the extent of customer contact.[4] Is it possible to provide the service without the customer being a part of the system?

Think of a public transit system. The service this business provides is transportation. It is impossible to provide transportation to a customer without the customer being a part of the system. The customer who purchases transportation must actually be on the bus. A public transit system is an example of a **high-contact system**. The customer must be a part of the system to receive the service. Other high-contact service providers include airlines, doctors, and car rental systems.

On the other hand, consider the cheque-processing operations at a bank. Workers sort the cheques that have been cashed that day and dispatch them to the banks on which they were drawn to receive a transfer of funds. This, too, is an example of a service operation. However, it is a **low-contact system**. Customers receive the service of having funds transferred to cover their cheques without ever setting foot in the cheque-processing centre. Other low-contact systems include gas and electric utilities, auto repair shops, and lawn care services.

In some systems in both groups—for example, automatic car washes, computer time-sharing, and automatic bank teller machines—machines provide the service. Substituting technology for the provider of the service may increase quality and efficiency (like the car wash). It can also lower consumer costs (computer time-sharing) or improve customer convenience (bank machines).

high-contact system

System in which the customer must be part of the system to receive the service.

low-contact system

System in which the customer need not be part of the system to receive the service.

A public transit system, which is an example of a high-contact system, provides the service of transportation.

As you can imagine, it is much harder to manage a high-contact system than it is to manage a low-contact system. Having the customer in the system can lead to a number of uncertainties. For example, customers can affect the *timing* of when services must be performed, as when a restaurant must cope with a lunch or dinner rush. Since high-contact services cannot be inventoried, they can become overloaded in rush periods but sit idle during slow periods. Customers can also affect the exact *nature* of the service. A physician cannot provide exactly the same service to every patient, regardless of symptom!

In low-contact systems, the customer's interaction with the service production system is infrequent or very brief. Thus, the customer does not have much impact on the system during the production process. It is much easier for the company to conduct its business without interference from customers. In the sorting department of a parcel delivery service, for example, the workers who sift through the packages have no contact with the customers. So long as their packages are delivered on time, customers don't care how the sorters get the job done. But, for better efficiency, sorters in Toronto might fill a plane bound for the West Coast before one for Winnipeg, a procedure that would have offended Winnipeg customers if they had been first in line in a high-contact system.

Similarity to Manufacturing

Another way to classify service operations is by their similarity to manufacturing operations, as shown in Table 13.2. **Pure services** are high-contact services, such as hair styling or surgery. They have no inventoriable products. **Quasimanufacturing** services are much lower-contact and are in many ways similar to manufacturing.[5] **Mixed services** share some characteristics of both pure services and quasimanufacturing and involve moderate contact levels.

A main post office is a good example of quasimanufacturing because it is a lot like a factory. Machines and conveyors sort mail and people perform routine tasks, such as key-punching postal codes, very efficiently. This post office is providing a service: information delivery. But this service is not nearly as subject to uncertainties as pure services are. Whereas a barber cannot predict the arrival of a customer, shipments of mail arrive on a predictable schedule and can be briefly held in inventory when there is an overload. Automation can be applied to routine processes, and a number of the

pure services
High-contact services in which the customer is part of the service production process.

quasimanufacturing
Low-contact services in which the customer need not be part of the service production process.

mixed services
Moderate-contact services in which the customer is involved in the service production process to a limited degree.

Table 13.2   **Classification of Services by Similarity to Manufacturing Operations**

Pure (High-Contact) Services	Mixed (Medium-Contact) Services	Quasimanufacturing (Low-Contact) Services
Medical clinics	Branch offices of banks and insurance companies	Home offices of banks and insurance companies
Schools		
Apartments	Real estate	Government
Taxicabs	Parcel delivery	Advertising agencies
Restaurants	Dry-cleaning stores	Mail-order services
Theatres	Home-cleaning services	News syndicates
Beauty parlours	Repair shops	Research labs
Prisons	Emergency departments Police Fire Ambulance	
	Moving companies	

same production management techniques that apply to goods can be used to improve the efficiency of the post office operation.

In contrast, a branch post office is a mixed service operation. Bags of mail arrive and are delivered on a predictable schedule. Inventories of stamps and mailing supplies are maintained. Although usually not automated, preliminary mail sorting is routine and efficient, as in quasimanufacturing. However, the branch office is more like a pure service operation when it comes to customer service. Many customers stop at the post office during their lunch breaks or at the end of the day, creating peak periods of demand. They also affect the nature of the service. One customer may buy a few stamps. The next may have questions about sending mail to several overseas locations. A third may want to ship several packages. Dealing with this variety of demands is anything but routine, making it harder for managers to develop efficient procedures.

Service Operations Planning and Scheduling

Now that you know something about what services are, you can better understand how they can be managed. As with production, service operations management can be divided into planning, scheduling, and control phases. The planning phase includes not only deciding on the service to offer but also capacity planning and designing and laying out the service operation.

Capacity Planning

In low-contact systems, the presence of inventory enables managers to set capacity at the level of average demand. Orders that arrive faster than expected can be temporarily placed in inventory to be processed during an upcoming slower period. If you were planning a main post office, for example, you would logically use average demand to figure capacity for at least the sorting area.

In contrast, in high-contact systems, managers must plan capacity to meet peak demand. Your local supermarket has far more cash registers than it needs on an average day. But on a Saturday morning or during the three days before Christmas, all registers will be running full speed.

Location Planning

In low-contact services, the service is usually located near the firm's resource supply, labour, or transportation. For example, the mail sorting and processing facility of the post office is usually located downtown in an urban area. In this way, it is close to much of its supply (mail from downtown businesses). It is also usually near a highway, making it convenient for deliveries from suburban branches and for outgoing transport of mail.

On the other hand, high-contact services need to be located near their customers, who must be a part of the system. Have you ever noticed how several banks will be located close to each other? This pattern is the result of careful research by the banks' planning divisions, who have analyzed traffic flows, other businesses and schools in the area, and income patterns of local residents.

Sometimes high-contact services take to the road, bringing service to the customer. At small and large factories across the nation, canteen trucks pull up at coffee breaks and mealtimes each day. A bloodmobile that travels to schools and places of employment makes it easier for people to donate blood. Pizza delivery trucks traverse Canada's cities and towns to help satisfy our cravings.

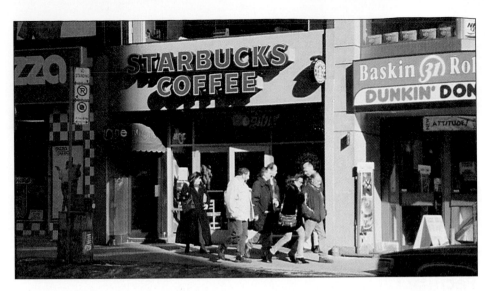

Location planning is an important part of service operations. Starbucks Coffee outlets are often located in areas close to competitors in order to take advantage of the high volume of consumer traffic.

The increasing globalization of business has led many service companies to consider international sites. Some foreign restaurants and banks, for example, have opened new facilities to serve customers in Canada. Similarly, many Canadian companies have expanded their services into international locations.

System Design

In a low-contact service system, the design process may resemble equipment planning in a manufacturing operation. The product is often a tangible item, such as a repaired television set, a legal document like a will, or a filled prescription.

In designing a high-contact service, managers must develop procedures that clearly spell out the ways in which workers interact with customers.[6] These procedures must cover information exchanges, delivery of material to and from the customer, exchanges of money, and physical contact. For example, people who work on patients in dental offices must follow strict procedures to avoid contact that can transmit disease. The next time you are at a dentist's office, notice that dental hygienists "scrub up" and wear disposable gloves. They also scrub after contact with a patient, even if they intend to work on equipment or do paperwork, and they rescrub before working on the next patient.

Service Flow Analysis

A useful way to design a service effectively is to develop a **service flow analysis**. Such analysis shows the flow of processes that make up the service and makes it easy to identify whether all the processes are necessary. Knowing what all the processes are also makes it easier to identify and isolate potential problems (known as *fail points*). Each process is a potential contributor to good or bad service.

A service flow analysis also makes scheduling easier. In the example in Figure 13.2, the shop manager has determined that the standard execution time for developing a roll of film is 48.5 minutes. Drive-in customers don't like to wait very long to get their finished photos from a "one-hour" photo finisher, but they will apparently tolerate up to a 90-minute wait before lowering their assessment of the quality of the service.

service flow analysis
A method of improving services by identifying the flow of processes that make up the service.

Standard execution
time: 48.5 minutes

1/2 minute	1 minute	45 minutes	2 minutes
Customer drive-in	Receive exposed film from customer	Develop film	Return film and collect payment

Total acceptable execution time:
90 minutes

Proper development

Fail point

Figure 13.2
Service flow analysis for quick photo-finishing.

Facility Layout

In a low-contact system, the arrangement of the facility should be designed to enhance the production of the service. A mail processing facility at Federal Express looks very much like a factory. Machines and people are arranged in the order in which they are used in the processing of mail.

High-contact service systems are arranged to meet customer needs and expectations. Consider the cafeteria layout shown in Figure 13.3. Families enter and immediately find an array of high chairs and baby beds with wheels, so that it is convenient to wheel their children through the line with them. Waitresses carry trays for elderly people and those pushing high chairs. Hungry customers must walk past the whole serving line before they can begin making selections. Not only does this layout help customers make up their minds, but it also tempts them to select more.

Applying Concepts from Goods Production Management

Some service industries lend themselves to the same techniques used in goods production management. Service operations can be carefully planned and controlled and sometimes even automated. They can be regularly reviewed for quality, performance improvement, and customer reaction.

McDonald's has done an outstanding job of treating the fast-food business as manufacturing, and many other fast-food franchisors have followed in its path. The byword at McDonald's is to substitute technology for discretion. By automating processes that otherwise would rely on judgment, McDonald's has been able to provide consistent service while using a staff with little specialized training.

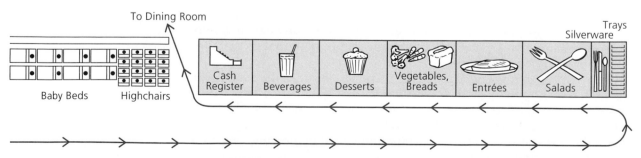

Figure 13.3
Layout of a cafeteria.

For example, the hamburger patties at McDonald's are carefully pre-measured and prepacked at a central supply house. Employees at a particular McDonald's outlet have no discretion in determining the size, shape, or quality of a hamburger patty. The drawers, shelves, and bins are designed to hold the ingredients for McDonald's standard product mix only. The scoop measures the same volume of french fries into each bag. Numerous trash cans in the parking lot remind customers where to dispose of their trash.

Sometimes, machines can substitute for employee discretion. For example, some hotels have a coffee machine in each guest's room. Guests feel they are getting something extra, while the coffee shop has more room for customers who want more than a cup of coffee for breakfast.

Scheduling Service Operations

Scheduling in service operations involves scheduling both work and workers. In a low-contact service, work scheduling is based on desired completion dates or on the time of arrival of orders. If a garage has several cars needing repairs and yours is not scheduled to be picked up until 5:00, it may sit idle for a while, even if it was the first to be dropped off. In such businesses, reservations and appointments systems can help to smooth demand.

On the other hand, in a high-contact service, the customer is in the system and must be accommodated. If a hospital emergency room is overloaded, patients cannot be asked to make an appointment to return at another time. Other high-contact systems such as airlines must also be able to quickly accommodate their customers. The box "A Scheduling Nightmare" describes this complex activity. In high-contact systems, orderly scheduling of services may be difficult.

In scheduling workers, managers must consider efficiency and costs. McDonald's, for example, guarantees workers that they will be scheduled for at least four hours at a time. To accomplish this goal without having workers idle, McDonald's uses *overlapping shifts*: The ending hours for some employees overlap the beginning hours for others. The overlap provides maximum coverage during peak periods. McDonald's also trains its employees to put off minor tasks, such as refilling napkin dispensers, until slow periods.

A 24-hour-a-day service operation, such as a hospital, can be an even greater scheduling challenge. Nurses must be on duty around the clock, seven days a week, yet few nurses want to work on weekends or during the wee hours of the morning. Enough nurses must be scheduled to meet emergencies, yet most hospitals are on a tight budget and cannot afford to have an overabundance of nurses. Incentives are often used to entice nurses to work at times they might not otherwise choose. For example, would you choose to work 12 hours a day, seven days a week? Probably not. But what if you were entitled to have every other week off in exchange for working such a schedule? A number of hospitals use just such a plan to attract nurses.

Service Operations Control

Is it possible to control the quantity and quality of services? Goods have constant, measurable characteristics. It is relatively easy to set a standard (for example, length or weight) and to measure items to determine whether that standard is being achieved. Services are more variable, and their quality is often in the eye of the beholder. Different customers want different services.

Because services are often performed by people, assuring a consistent quantity or quality of service may be difficult or impossible. Nevertheless every firm must have some standards and try to maintain some quality level.

The Canadian Business Scene

A Scheduling Nightmare

Air Canada's systems operations control (SOC) is the airline's nerve centre; it tracks all the company's aircraft from its headquarters in Toronto. On January 3, 1996, SOC personnel were hard at work on computers and telephones trying to forecast the impact of a storm that was brewing in the midwestern U.S. By January 5, it was clear that this was going to be a very bad storm that would disrupt air travel.

Ron Leradza, the general manager of SOC, talked constantly on his cellular phone to front-line employees—including those in reservations—who had the task of contacting customers before they went to airports. Airlines don't want to unnecessarily disrupt travellers' plans, but they also don't want travellers to go to an airport if their planes can't fly. The biggest challenge is to keep communication lines open between headquarters and workers in locations that are having problems.

By January 7, Air Canada had cancelled all its flights to snowed-in airports (one fifth of its total daily schedule). By January 9, Air Canada was in a scheduling mess, but it had acted fast enough to ensure that none of its aircraft were stranded at snowed-in airports. Since each plane is used about 10 hours a day, keeping planes at locations where they can be used is a top priority.

Canadian Airlines International (CAI) was also affected by the same storm, but to a lesser extent because it has fewer flights to the U.S. With good scheduling, CAI was also able to avoid having any of its planes stranded. To handle the larger number of passengers who were stuck in

Toronto and New York, CAI upgraded to aircraft with 270 seats instead of 112. CAI institutes a "ghost schedule" to cope with unexpected service interruptions.

American Airlines, the company that has poured millions into CAI, has a systems operations control centre that is staffed by meteorologists, flight dispatchers, crew schedulers, and financial analysts. The centre is used to quickly reroute passengers, redeploy planes, and shift schedules. Other major airlines such as Continental and Delta also have operation control centres. At all airlines, operations scheduling is viewed as a giant jigsaw puzzle, with the goal being to minimize customer disruption and maximize profit.

Weather isn't the only thing that can cause changes in schedules. When travellers were stranded in Caracas, Venezuela, after a diplomatic dispute with the U.S. government, American Airlines cancelled a flight from Guatemala to Miami and redirected that plane to Caracas to get all the travellers out. Airlines may also cancel lightly booked flights and put passengers on another plane, especially if there is one available within an hour or two.

American Airlines
http://www.americanair.com/aa_home

Managing Demand and Supply

In Chapter 12, we discussed how important inventory control is in goods production. Keeping a suitable amount of inventory can help a business to meet uneven demand. But since high-contact services cannot be stored, they cannot be inventoried. There are ways, however, in which managers of service operations can control demand for and/or supply of services.

Managing Demand

Some service operations use pricing to shift demand to nonpeak periods. This technique allows service-providing employees to be on a consistent schedule. Instead of hiring many employees to work a few hours a day or a few days a week, the company can hire fewer employees to work full-time schedules.

Examples of pricing to shift peak demand to nonpeak periods include matinee prices at movie theatres, weekday happy hours, and weekend rates at hotels frequented by business travellers. Evening and weekend long-distance telephone rates, peak-load pricing by utility companies, and two-for-one coupons at restaurants (good only Monday through Thursday) also represent demand shifting.

Special service offerings may also be used to stimulate demand during nonpeak periods. This approach is especially important for facilities with high

Pricing first-run movies at very low prices during the day is an attempt by theatre owners to shift peak demand to non-peak periods. People generally want to see a movie in the evening, but if the price is low enough, some people will be willing to go during the day. This allows the movie house to sell more tickets, since they can show a movie several times during a 24-hour period.

fixed costs and low variable costs. For example, supermarkets have increased the number of hours they are open for business and have promoted it heavily. The additional hours of operation help cover the high fixed costs of the facility (such as mortgage, taxes, and insurance) at a low variable cost (few additional employees). In recent years, ski resorts have offered low-cost summer vacation packages. Many even provide special summer convention planning assistance.

Offering complimentary services during peak periods can temporarily soothe customers who are awaiting the service they desire. For example, many cocktail lounges provide free "munchies" for customers who are waiting to be seated in a busy restaurant. A mirror in the central lobby of each floor allows hotel patrons to check their appearance while waiting for a busy elevator.

Reservation systems can also be effective in managing demand. By pre-selling capacity, reservations force incoming demand into a predictable rate and pattern. A reservation system can be used to deflect excess demand to another slot at the same facility, for example, a later flight on the same airline.

Excess demand may also be deflected to another facility owned by the same company. There are, for example, two Road King motels in Grand Forks, North Dakota, to capitalize on Canadian demand for cross-border shopping. If the one next to Columbia Mall is full, the customer can usually be booked at the other one, just a few minutes up the road.

Controlling Supply

Rather than trying to manage demand, some service organizations try to manage the supply of services available. For example, part-time employees can help meet variable demand. A company typically maintains a base of full-time employees to meet demand during nonrush periods and adds part-timers during peak demand periods. Part-time employees may be added during certain hours of the day (such as during the peaks at fast-food restaurants or transit services). They may also be added on certain days of the week (Fridays and Saturdays in a beauty parlour) or weeks of the month (the last week of each month at a bank). In some cases, companies even bring on part-time help for certain peak months of the year, such as income tax services during March and April.

Canadian Passport Office
http://www.ncf.carleton.ca:12345/
freeport/government/federal/
passport/menu

cross training

Training employees to perform a variety of jobs as a way of increasing the supply of services.

shared capacity

A way of increasing the supply of services by having several individuals or companies share equipment, office space, or personnel.

The Canadian Passport Office is focusing more on the needs of customers. Business hours have been extended, a new system has been introduced that will speed up the process of completing customer files, and some passport offices have been moved to suburban locations that have more parking.[7]

A careful analysis of the service delivery system may show ways in which efficiency can be improved for a system to get the most supply during peak periods.[8] For example, during peaks, only essential services should be provided. In lawn-care companies, fertilizing, seeding, and insecticide applications are critical during the spring and autumn months. Equipment maintenance can wait.

Training employees to perform many jobs—**cross training**—can increase supply when one part of the delivery system is temporarily overloaded. Lawn-care businesses train their workers so that during a busy time a manager can help with the truck driving, drivers can help apply the lawn treatments, and so forth. Cross training also provides variety in otherwise boring jobs. Rearranging the layout of a service system can also make it more efficient and increase its capacity. Supermarkets constantly rearrange their shelf displays to better use space, present more products, and increase sales.

Managers can also increase the supply of services by using **shared capacity**, especially when a major investment in equipment or labour is required. The executive suite concept is one example. A group of professionals—perhaps a lawyer, a psychologist, an accountant, and a public relations person—rent a group of offices together. They share a secretary, a duplicating machine, and a small computer. Because none of the professionals has enough work to justify a full-time secretary, this is a convenient arrangement. It may also free up funds for the lawyer to hire a paralegal aide, thereby increasing the supply of services within the law office.

Quality Control: Training Workers

An important factor to remember in service product design is that people deliver most services. Service system employees are both the producers of the product and the salespeople. Thus, human relations skills (see Chapter 6) are vital to anyone who has contact with the public.[9] In high-contact systems, the people are the service; your lawyer is the physical representation of the product you are receiving.

The wrong attitude from service employees can reduce sales of services. Conversely, the right attitude can increase sales, as the box "Beeg Maks" attests. Frequently, though, service employees receive low financial rewards, occupy low status positions in the organization, and receive little training. Some companies, however, remind top executives of the importance of the employee-customer relationship by having their executives perform the services. The president of Hyatt Hotels, for example, once worked as a doorman.

The Disney organization does a tremendous job of remembering that no matter what their jobs, all their service employees are links to the public. For example, Disney World has a team of sweepers constantly at work picking up bits of trash virtually as they fall to the ground. When visitors have questions about directions or time, they often ask one of the sweepers. Because their responses affect visitors' overall impressions of Disney World, sweepers are trained to respond appropriately. Their work is evaluated and rewarded based on strict performance-appraisal standards.

In low-contact service operations, the technical skills of workers are more important than their human relations skills. As a consumer, you are not terribly concerned about how personable the individual who repairs your watch or television set is. But in high-contact service operations, human relations skills are more important. A student's counselling session can be made much more enjoyable by a cheerful, pleasant academic advisor. A pleased customer is more likely to return.

International Report

"Beeg Maks" in Moscow

The first McDonald's outlet opened in Moscow in 1990, the brainchild of George Cohon, president of McDonald's Canada. In the beginning, the company faced four major difficulties. First, the quality and quantity of food supplies was uncertain. Local processors could not begin to meet McDonald's exacting standards for milk and beef, so the firm had to hire outside expertise to help improve the local supply. McDonald's ended up building a huge complex to do the necessary processing of food that serves as the input for its restaurants.

Second, ensuring that the food items were available at the right place and time was also a big problem. The most demanding job in the entire McDonald's empire probably was that of quality assurance manager in a country that had one of the worst-run agricultural sectors in the world. At one point, McDonald's workers had to be persuaded to go out and actually harvest potatoes. Rapid inflation added to the firm's difficulties. On top of all this, the company was operating in a country that had until recently ridiculed the idea of private enterprise (one critic of the Russian economic system said, "The trouble with Russia is that no one ever had a paper route.").

Third, Russian workers were not polite—let alone friendly—towards customers. In a land where shortages were the rule, the general attitude of shop workers was, "So do you want it or not?" Before McDonald's opened its doors in Moscow, its workers had to learn to smile, say please and thank you, and tell each customer "priyatnovo appetita," Russian for "enjoy your meal."

Fourth, when the company first set up shop in Moscow, it owned only 49 percent of the local restaurants, while the

city government owned the other 51 percent. This did not give the company much incentive to expand its operations.

But in the last couple of years, the outlook has suddenly brightened, and the original problems McDonald's faced have been largely resolved. Quality products are now supplied by 150 independent Russian businesses, and they are generally provided on time. Customers at McDonald's outlets are amazed at the friendly service and the quality of the food. The ownership arrangement with the city of Moscow has also been improved, with McDonald's now having an 80 percent ownership stake and the government 20 percent.

In September 1996, McDonald's opened its eighth restaurant in Moscow and its first outlet in St. Petersburg. Within a few years, there will be 18 or 19 outlets in Moscow, 8 or 9 in St. Petersburg, and several in Nizhny Novgorod, the third-largest city in Russia. The first drive-through McDonald's—called MakAuto—opened in Moscow in 1996.

A Big Mac is priced at $2.80, which doesn't sound too high until you consider that the average monthly wage of Russian workers is about $200. In spite of this, demand is high and profits are large. The McDonald's in Pushkin Square in Moscow is the busiest in the world, serving over 40 000 customers each day. The outlet on the Old Arbat is the second-busiest, serving 20 000 people per day. The three biggest restaurants in Moscow serve as much food as 30 average sized McDonald's in North America. The restaurants are so successful that a competitor recently opened its doors. How things have changed in the former Soviet Union!

Quality Control: Motivating Workers

In addition to selecting and training the right workers, managers of service operations need to motivate their workers to offer the appropriate quality level of service. Positive and publicized recognition, such as employee-of-the-month awards, can be very effective, especially when based on customer feedback. Marriott hotels have evaluation slips in each room that guests are asked to fill out, indicating if they have received especially good service from a particular employee.

Monetary incentives, such as a bonus for being named employee of the month, are also effective. But other types of incentives may be equally effective and less costly. Examples include an employee badge that says "Employee of the Month" or "Superior Service Award" and special baseball caps or T-shirts to indicate superior service.

Making the deliverer of the service more visible to the customer makes the employee more aware of quality. At Ichi Ban restaurants, customers are seated around a large grill where a costumed chef puts on an elaborate show as he prepares their meals. This showcase promotes consistently high quality, and chefs are rewarded with consistently high tips. Similarly, quality in a repair garage may be improved if customers are allowed to speak directly with the mechanic who works on their car.

Handling the Special Problems of Service Operations

Although the production of goods and the production of services are similar in many ways, as noted at the beginning of this chapter, services have unique characteristics. These traits—intangibility, customization, and perishability, as well as the presence of customers within the production process—cause special challenges. In this section, we will consider some techniques for meeting these challenges. As you will see, each of these characteristics creates special problems for service operations managers and affects service management.

Intangibility

The often intangible nature of services makes them difficult for customers to evaluate before buying. When the product is a physical good, customers can see, touch, or hear its **search qualities**. These qualities may be determined before customers buy. Similarly, customers can determine **experience qualities** of goods, such as taste, after they have made their purchases. But with services, customers sometimes find it impossible to evaluate the **credence qualities**—the value you believe the service delivered—even after purchase or consumption. For example, most people have a difficult time evaluating the quality of the legal or psychological counselling services they buy.

Most services have few search qualities, so customers rely more on experience and credence qualities to evaluate services. That is, customers use a different process to evaluate service products, such as a funeral, before buying than they do to evaluate goods before buying. Those charged with selling services thus have an interesting challenge.

One solution is to provide tangible evidence of the intangible, whenever possible. Lawyers and doctors display their diplomas on their office walls. Hotels provide evidence that the room has been specially cleaned and prepared for the new occupant: clean glasses in white paper bags, wrapped new bars of soap, a "sanitized" band across the toilet, a chocolate mint on the pillow.

search qualities

Qualities in a product that can be perceived before buying by sight, touch, or hearing.

experience qualities

Qualities in a product that can be perceived after buying by senses such as taste.

credence qualities

Qualities in a product that a purchaser believes exist but that are not subject to objective proof.

This highly skilled and diverting chef provides the quality food preparation and entertainment that keep customers coming back.

Customization

The customized nature of services often makes their scheduling difficult or impossible. This difficulty is one reason why you often have to wait at your doctor's or dentist's office, even though you have an appointment. Because the patients before you also bought customized services, the receptionist could not know exactly when your appointment would begin.

In some services, scheduling can be improved by shifting the level of customer contact. High-contact service systems are harder to schedule than are low-contact systems. Thus, some services try to shift the level of customer contact downward. One way to lower the level of contact is to handle routine transactions by telephone or mail and to handle only exceptions face-to-face. L.L. Bean and Cabela's have built phenomenally successful mail-order catalogue businesses. Mailed orders can be "inventoried" for a day or two without a major effect on delivery times. Imagine being asked to wait a day or two at a department store!

L.L. Bean
http://www.llbean.com

Cabela's
http://www.cabelas.com

Reservations or appointments-only systems can also help to reduce the level of customer contact. Only those customers who have an appointment are allowed into the system. These systems reduce the number of face-to-face contacts and simplify the scheduling of employees who have contact with customers.

Another strategy is to separate information-gathering from the provision of the service. For example, a well-run medical office will give you a medical history form to fill out while you wait. This system frees all the office personnel, including the doctor, for other duties.

Drop-off points away from the main facility also reduce the level of customer contact. Consider the success of automatic teller machines. Not only are they more convenient for the customer, but they also free bank tellers from processing routine deposits and withdrawals.

A final strategy for lowering the level of customer contact is to separate the high- and low-contact elements of a service. The purchase of some services may be divided into four phases: information, reservation, payment, and consumption. Often, the consumption phase must take place at a distant, specialized location, such as in an airplane or theatre. But the other three elements can be separated from consumption and treated as low-contact services.

You may be familiar with this strategy from the entertainment service of a hockey or football game. Teams distribute *information* by publishing schedules in the newspaper and by making free pocket schedules widely available. When you have chosen a game to attend, you can make your *reservation* by calling the arena or stadium ticket office or by calling or visiting a nearby ticket outlet. You then make *payment* through the mail or by using a credit card, and the tickets are mailed to you. Only for the *consumption* phase do you actually need to be a part of the system (at the arena or stadium).

Perishability

Earlier in this chapter, we noted that the perishability of services means there is potential for waste. This characteristic causes many hotels to schedule more customer reservations than they have rooms for a given night. If some of the customers fail to keep their appointments, the hotel's ability to provide rooms has not been wasted (although they risk offending customers who are turned away.) Likewise, many airlines overbook flights, knowing that there will usually be some "no shows."

Customer Involvement

We have already seen that having customers as part of the process complicates the production of services. But some managers have found a way to turn customer presence into an advantage. They actually get the customer more involved in the process. Direct long-distance dialling, for example, allows the customer to do the work that long-distance operators used to do. Some car washes provide the basic necessary equipment, but require the consumer to actually wash the car.

Shifting some of the productive effort to the customer frees employees for the tasks that require their special abilities. But some customers reject the idea of doing the work and paying for it too. This problem may be solved by offering financial incentives, such as reduced prices for self-service gasoline or bag-your-own groceries.

Summary of Learning Objectives

1. **Identify the characteristics that distinguish *service operations* from *goods production*.** Although the creation of both goods and services involves resources, transformations, and finished products, service operations differ from goods manufacturing in several important ways. While services are typically performed, goods are produced. Services are largely *intangible* and *perishable* and are more likely to be *customized* to meet the purchaser's needs. In addition, service production often requires the presence of the customer.

2. **Classify services according to the extent of *customer contact* and *similarity to manufacturing*.** In *high-contact systems*, the customer must be within the service system while the service is being performed. In *low-contact systems*, services may be performed independent of the customer, much as in manufacturing. *Quasimanufacturing* is the most like manufacturing, with low customer contact and products that can be inventoried (usually briefly). *Pure services* are the opposite, with high customer contact and products that cannot be inventoried. *Mixed services* have some of the characteristics of both pure services and quasi-manufacturing.

3. **Describe the major decisions in *service-operations planning* and *scheduling*.** Planning for service operations requires decisions on the *capacity*, *location*, *systems design*, and *layout* of the service facilities. In designing the system, managers must pay special attention to *service-flow activities*: By analyzing these activities, they can identify the components of the process and decide which are necessary. Scheduling the workforce in high-contact systems may involve *overlapping shifts* and other special scheduling strategies.

4. **Explain how managers can control the *quantity* and *quality* of services offered.** *Quantity control* in high-contact systems involves adjusting the demand for and the supply of services. *Reservations systems* and *price incentives* may smooth demand, while the use of *part-time employees*,

cross training, and *shared capacity* may smooth the supply of labour in service operations. To ensure quality control, managers must focus on human relations aspects of the operations, hiring the right types of workers and then motivating them for quality performance.

5. **Identify ways to overcome the special problems of service operations management.** To overcome the intangibility of services, managers need to provide as many tangible signs of quality as possible. To minimize the scheduling problems that result from customized high-contact services, managers may try to lower the level of contact. To avoid the waste of perishable services, managers may elect to use reservations systems and even to "overbook" some services. To deal with the presence of customers in the production of high-contact services, managers may choose to involve customers further, perhaps by running self-service operations.

Key Terms

service operations, 370	pure services, 375	service flow analysis, 377	search qualities, 384
high-contact system, 374	quasimanufacturing, 375	cross training, 382	experience qualities, 384
low-contact system, 374	mixed services, 375	shared capacity, 382	credence qualities, 384

Study Questions and Exercises

Review Questions
1. Why has employment in the service sector continued to grow, even during periods of overall unemployment and recession?
2. Identify pure services, quasimanufacturing services, and mixed services according to the degree of customer contact involved.
3. What factors must a manager consider when planning the layout of a service facility?
4. List three ways to deal with the unpredictable timing of demand in service organizations.
5. How does reducing the level of customer contact help managers schedule high-contact customized services?

Analysis Questions
6. What are the resources and finished products of the following services?
   - real-estate firm
   - child care facility

   - bank
   - municipal water department
   - hotel
7. Explain why the police department is a mixed service.
8. Develop a service flow analysis for some service you use frequently, such as buying lunch at a fast-food restaurant, having your hair cut, or riding a bus. Identify steps of potential quality or productivity failures in the process.

Application Questions
9. Interview the manager of a local service business, such as a laundry and/or dry-cleaning shop. Identify the major decisions that were involved in planning for its service operations. Suggest areas for improvement.
10. Select a high-contact industry. Write an advertisement to hire workers for this business. Draw up a plan for motivating the hired workers to produce high-quality services for the firm.

Building Your Business Skills

Goal

To encourage students to identify specific mechanisms for improving the service encounter in a high-contact service company.

Situation

As the director of training at a regional airline, you decide to initiate a program for all employees who come in contact with the public. The goal of the program is to improve the quality of the service encounter.

Method

Step 1:

Draft a memo to be distributed to all employees with customer contact. Your memo should outline the aims of your training program by addressing the following points:

- The implications of the high-contact nature of the airline business for customer service
- Specific procedures for improving the service encounter

- The "people" skills and attitudes that you want every employee to acquire
- The effect of technology on the nature of customer service

Step 2:

Meet with three or four other students to compare your drafts. Analyze points of agreement and disagreement. Once you have negotiated a version that everyone can agree on, write a final draft.

Follow-Up Questions

1. Identify the key points of your final draft, including the role played by employees in high-contact service businesses in improving the service encounter.

2. Would you have addressed the memo's key issues differently if you worked for a low-contact service business, such as a credit card company?

3. What steps can all service companies take to improve the quality of the service encounter? (Your answer should address the importance of employee training as well as other factors.)

In the chapter you learned about companies that offer services and the ways in which businesses deal with the problems associated with the "production" of services. Coopers and Lybrand is a consulting firm that offers a wide range of consulting services. Check out their Web site at:

http://www.ca.coopers.com

A business that offers a completely different service than Coopers and Lybrand is the Whistler Ski Resort. Check out their Web site at:

http://www.whistler.net

1. Visit the "Our Firm" section of the Coopers and Lybrand Web site. What are the inputs, transformations and outputs of the services Coopers and Lybrand provide?
2. Classify Coopers and Lybrand service operations in terms of the extent of customer contact.
3. Visit "The Centre of Excellence in Customer Satisfaction" on the Coopers and Lybrand Web site. Describe the level of customization the firm offers to its clients.
4. What are the inputs, transformations and outputs of the services that Whistler provides?
5. Classify Whistler's service operations in terms of the extent of customer contact and similarity to manufacturing.

CONCLUDING CASE 13-1

Hold the Line!

Toronto-based Delrina Inc. is one of the hottest software companies in North America. Its most well-known product is Winfax Pro 3, a fax software. Its revenue soared from less than $50 million in 1992 to over $100 million in 1993. But it was growing faster than its ability to handle questions from customers. When an article appeared in *Info World* claiming that Delrina's technical support left much to be desired, the company's management knew it had to do something fast. The future of the company was at stake.

The mission statement of the company said that Delrina measured its success by how satisfied its customers were. But the company was failing to meet these expectations. Technical support services were not well organized and the company was chronically short-staffed in this important area. Customers who phoned in with questions about the company's software were often put on hold for a long time. By the time customers got to talk to a representative, they were often very angry. The average time a customer spent on hold was 10 minutes.

Enter Jim Moore, who took over as director of technical support in April of 1993. He first set out to create the right mentality and culture for a support call centre. Because technical reps need to have a detailed understanding of software, Moore put a freeze on the transfer of anyone out of the technical support department until they had been there at least 9 months.

A more formal approach was adopted to get the right people into managerial positions. Previously, many people had just evolved into management positions based on their technical expertise, even if they had no managerial ability.

Moore also purchased a new Automatic Call Distribution (ACD) system to handle customer calls. The company now handles 2000 calls per day with the new system. A new customer management system was also installed. It keeps track of the kinds of questions and complaints that customers have and allows the new product development people to revise software quickly and accurately.

How successful has the company been in its attempts to improve customer satisfaction? The average time a customer was on hold in 1992 was 10 minutes; now it is less than 3 minutes. The ACD system has led to a reduction in the time it takes to get a revised version of software to the market; it has also led to a 40 percent reduction in the number of calls with complaints about revised software products. One customer was so delighted by the service level that he named his daughter Delrina.

Case Questions

1. What steps were taken at Delrina to ensure that customer satisfaction was actually achieved?

2. Explain how the factors of intangibility, customization, and perishability manifest themselves in this kind of service business.

3. Is this a high- or low-contact service? Explain.

4. How does Delrina deal with the management of supply and demand?

♦

CONCLUDING CASE 13-2

Being Efficient Isn't Enough

Each day, more than 122 000 boxy, brown delivery trucks from United Parcel Service hit the streets in Canada, the U.S., Puerto Rico, Germany, and many other countries. The company, which was started in 1907, delivers 11.5 million packages (750 000 by air) for 2 million different business customers each day. The company has 162 airplanes working out of more than 500 airports.

Perhaps the most distinguishing feature of the company is the rigid control that it maintains over every aspect of its operations. Time-and-motion studies have been conducted on virtually every task that workers do. For example,

delivery people are supposed to walk 1 metre per second, hold their key rings with their middle finger, and fold their money face up, sequentially ordered. Drivers are instructed to climb aboard their trucks with their left foot first to avoid wasted steps. Packages are arranged in a precise fashion in the trucks (which have overhead lights so the drivers can read the addresses better). Workers at sorting centres are carefully timed according to strict standards for each task. Drivers are closely timed also; each delivery is timed with a stopwatch. All trucks are washed every day, and they are kept on a strict maintenance schedule.

•••

Being Efficient Isn't Enough

(continued)

All these activities have resulted in a very efficient operation, and these efficiencies enabled UPS to achieve market success for more than 50 years.

Partly because of its emphasis on internal efficiency, UPS was reluctant to give discounts. Instead, it prided itself on charging the same rates to residential customers as it did for business customers. This policy alienated several large clients. Competitors who were willing to give discounts jumped in to fill the void. Roadway Package Systems Inc. began offering widespread discounts on large-volume shipments and now offers a package-tracking service to customers.

UPS's most formidable competitor is Federal Express, which gives volume discounts and tracks packages for customers. Federal controlled about 45 percent of the air cargo market in 1992, while UPS held about 25 percent.

After losing business to aggressive competitors like Federal Express and Roadway Package Systems, UPS has dramatically changed the way it does business. In 1990, CEO Kent Nelson ordered a sweeping examination of the company's business methods. The company's flaws were identified and fixed so that UPS could more effectively respond to competitive rivals.

The "we know what's best for the customer" attitude was one of the first casualties. Previously, UPS had the view that they knew what was best for their corporate customers. But in 1990, with Eastman Kodak thinking about dropping UPS because of its "bad attitude," things began to change. Now, UPS emphasizes customer satisfaction, offers flexible pickup and delivery times, customized shipment plans, and discount prices to volume shippers.

The head office marketing staff has been increased from 7 to 175, and face-to-face interviews have been conducted with 25 000 customers to find out what services they want. UPS increased its advertising budget from $75 000 in 1981 to $18 million in 1990. It is also trying to improve its image with the public. It launched a $35 million television advertising campaign (its first ever) focusing on the now well-known slogan "We run the tightest ship in the shipping business."

UPS has added to its air fleet and is matching technically advanced rivals with such devices as electronic scanners in its sorting centres and onboard computers in its delivery trucks. Between 1986 and 1991, UPS increased its spending on information technology almost tenfold, spending an average of $300 million per year. By 1996, the company will have spent an additional $3.2 billion on information technology. The company is in good shape financially, with only $114 million in debt, compared with $2.5 billion in employee equity.

In addition to its spending on advertising and equipment, UPS has also purchased a number of small foreign companies to get a foothold in the overseas package delivery market. It has also spent $1.4 billion on a system to efficiently track packages from door-to-door. A key part of the system is an in-house invention called a "dense code" which holds twice the information in a normal bar code. Scanners in the field and at sorting centres can read information on package origin, destination, and contents. The system is designed to leapfrog Federal Express's system. A system called GroundTrac has also been introduced; it allows shippers to get status reports on their ground packages 24 hours a day just by calling a toll-free number.

But with all of these changes, UPS is still committed to its emphasis on worker efficiency and commitment. That's the way the company achieved its success, and it will continue to bring new workers into a corporate culture where efficiency is a key word.

Case Questions

1. Explain how each factor that distinguishes services production from goods production affects UPS's operations.

2. How would you classify UPS in terms of the degree of customer contact and its similarity to manufacturing?

3. If you were a senior UPS manager, with which aspect of planning and scheduling would you be most concerned? Why?

4. In what ways does UPS's management currently seek to control the quality of its service? The quantity of its service?

◆

14

Increasing Productivity and Quality

Ford Seeks New Way to Skin a Cat at Jaguar

Superstitious or not, executives at Britain's Jaguar Cars Ltd. apparently believe that cats have nine lives. In any case, they are hoping that the cat's proverbial good fortune applies to the world-famous automobiles named for one of nature's most powerful and graceful felines. So far, history is on their side. After nearly dying in the early 1980s, Jaguar is clawing its way back through a concentrated program of increased productivity and quality improvement. Its chances for survival increased dramatically in 1989, when Ford Motor Co. bought Jaguar for $2.5 billion and then invested another $700 million to breathe new life into its acquisition.

Despite the revival, however, Jaguar is not entirely out of danger. Plagued by serious quality and productivity problems, the company at one time lost $18 000 on every car it sold, and quality remains such a problem that some industry observers still joke that "Jaguar owners need two cars: one to drive and one for spare parts." Although quality has improved considerably since Ford took over, Jaguar still lags behind competitors in this crucial area. While Lexus, for instance, has an average of 0.66 defects per car, Jaguar owners face an average of 1.67.

Indeed, many problems in quality seem to be built into the Jaguar line. Introduced in 1986, for example, the pricy XJ6 sedan requires 20 000 parts—many of which are fragile and troublesome. By contrast, the Lincoln Town Car made by Jaguar's parent company uses only 5000 parts. Known in the company as the "problem child," Jaguar's second offering—the sleek and elegant XJS coupe—has proved to be even more prone to trouble.

How did such a once renowned company manage to saddle itself with such a problematic product line? Most analysts agree that Jaguar's quality and productivity prob-

lems can be traced, at least in part, to a corporate culture that stifled initiative. Discouraged from speaking up, for instance, managers and engineers became part of a grossly inefficient manufacturing system whose break-even point required more income than could actually be generated by the number of cars that the company built. Bitter labour-management relations and restrictive union practices made matters worse. Prior to 1990, when a new contract was signed, workers who met their daily quotas simply stopped working. Aging production facilities in Coventry, England, added to the problem.

Despite Jaguar's troubled history, Ford is by most accounts turning the company around. Largely as a result of rigorous quality checking, assembly-line defects have been cut by about 80 percent. Each week, engineers test 25 new cars to detect motor and electrical problems, leaks, and even bothersome squeaks. When problems are detected, a special squad of 25 inspectors works to fix these specific problems on the next cars coming down the line. Recurrent defects are referred to engineering for redesign.

Meanwhile, productivity is also improving. In 1991, for example, Jaguar required 418.6 person-hours to assemble a car. Two years later, it needed only 251.9. By 1997, Ford hopes to reduce that number to 126. Not surprisingly, as the manufacturing process has become more efficient, the company's workforce has shrunk—from 12 000 to 6500 in three years. Perhaps more surprisingly, these reductions have also been accompanied by a new spirit of labour-management cooperation. "Our members," explains union leader Chris Liddell, "have a new realization that they are the company, that customer satisfaction starts inside the factory."

Today, the confidence of Ford executives is up. They have reason to believe that with improved quality and produc-

(continued)

tivity—plus design changes and exciting new models—consumers will be convinced to come back to Jaguar, a nameplate many still rank among the classiest on the road. For example, when the restyled XJ sedan was unveiled in the fall of 1994 with a base price of $53 450, Ford strategists predicted worldwide sales would rise by 7000 units the following year. Company forecasts call for Jaguar to sell 39 000 cars in 1995, although even a lower break-even point should allow Jaguar to eke out a slim profit on sales of $2.2 billion.

Ford also hopes to broaden its market base by introducing a lower-priced, entry-level model—possibly designed and built in Japan by Mazda. Whether or not the company implements such a radical plan, it is clear that Ford sees Jaguar as a long-term investment and is willing to bide its time as it works towards the payoff in productivity. As Jaguar CEO Nick Steele says of the new XJ, "This is our opportunity to show people that we are world-class." ◆

Under the guidance of Ford, Jaguar is undergoing the growing pains of a company learning to appreciate the costliest and most valuable lessons about productivity and quality. It is a painful but necessary process—without vast improvements in both areas, Jaguar may soon use up what's left of its nine lives. It is no secret that *productivity* and *quality* are the watchwords of the 1990s. Companies are not only measuring productivity and insisting on improvements, they are also insisting that quality means bringing to market products that satisfy customers, improve sales, and boost profits.

By focusing on the learning objectives of this chapter, you will better understand the increasingly important concepts of productivity and quality. After reading this chapter, you will be able to:

LEARNING OBJECTIVES

1. Describe the connection between *productivity* and *quality*.

2. Understand the importance of increasing productivity.

3. Explain *total* and *partial measures of productivity* and show how they are used to keep track of national, industrywide, and companywide productivity.

4. Identify the activities involved in *total quality management* and describe four tools that companies can use to achieve it.

5. List six ways in which companies can compete by improving productivity and quality.

The Productivity-Quality Connection

productivity

A measure of efficiency that compares how much is produced with the resources used to produce it.

productivity paradox

Despite massive investment in computers, the rate of productivity growth is now lower than it was before computers were introduced.

As we saw in Chapter 1, **productivity** is a measure of economic performance. It measures how much is produced relative to the resources used to produce it. The more we are able to produce the right things while using fewer resources, the more productivity grows and everyone—the economy, businesses, and workers—benefits.

There is a **productivity paradox** facing the industrialized nations of the world: In spite of the millions of dollars that have been invested in computers, the rate of productivity growth is much lower than it was in the years before computers were introduced. From 1961–73, productivity growth in 18 industrial countries averaged 2.4 percent a year. But from 1974–92, productivity growth averaged less than 1 percent a year.

Why would this be so? It is possible that productivity measures are not sophisticated enough to detect productivity growth because so much more economic activity is in the services area, where production is very hard to calculate. Or, it is possible that the productivity gains will just take a few more years to show up. It is even possible that the productivity gains will never arrive, because the importance of information technology has been exaggerated.[1]

Productivity considers both the amounts and the quality of what is produced. By using resources more efficiently, the quantity of output will be greater. But unless the resulting goods and services are of satisfactory quality (the "right things"), consumers will not want them. **Quality**, then, means fitness for use—offering features that consumers want.

The importance of quality in productivity cannot be overstated. Poor quality has created competitive problems for Canadian firms that have focused only on efficiency (quantity). Businesses in other countries have emphasized both efficiency and quality and consequently have increased productivity more rapidly than Canadian companies.

quality
A product's fitness for use in terms of offering the features that consumers want.

Meeting the Productivity Challenge

Productivity is an international issue with major domestic effects. A nation's productivity determines how large a piece of the global economic resource pie it gets. A country with more resources has more wealth to divide among its citizens. A country whose productivity fails to increase as rapidly as that of other countries will see its people's standard of living fall relative to the rest of the world.

Nations also care about domestic productivity regardless of their standing versus other nations. A country that makes more out of its existing resources (increases its productivity) can increase the wealth of all its inhabitants if it so chooses. But a productivity decline shrinks a nation's available resources so that any one person's increase in wealth can come only at the expense of others in the society. In addition, investors, suppliers, managers, and workers are all concerned about the productivity of specific industries, companies, departments, and individuals.

Productivity Trends

The United States remains the most productive nation in the world. In 1993, for instance, the value of goods and services produced by each U.S. worker was $46 500. This **level of productivity** was higher than that of any other country. In second place, French and Belgian workers produced $43 700 per worker, followed by Italian workers at $42 500. Canadian workers produced $42 000.[2]

level of productivity
The dollar value of goods and services produced versus the dollar value of resources used to produce them.

Slower Growth Rates

Many Canadians are alarmed by the slowdown in our **growth rate of productivity**—the annual increase in a nation's output over the previous year. Canadian productivity has also slowed in comparison with that of other countries. The Conference Board of Canada released a report in 1997 showing that output per person in the U.S., for example, was one third higher than output per person in Canada.[3] The report also noted that Canada's rate of productivity growth has been slow for 25 years.

growth rate of productivity
The increase in productivity in a given year over the previous year.

Difference Between the Manufacturing and Service Sectors

Manufacturing productivity is higher than service productivity. Thus, manufacturing is primarily responsible for recent rises in the nation's overall productivity. With services growing as a proportion of Canadian businesses, productivity *must* increase more rapidly in that sector in the years ahead if Canada is to keep its edge. The box "Suggestions for Improving Canada's International Competitiveness" gives additional ideas for productivity improvements for Canada's industry in general.

International Report

Suggestions for Improving Canada's International Competitiveness

In October 1991, Michael Porter, a business professor at Harvard University and an internationally recognized expert on competitiveness, released a report. In it he claims that Canada will have to stop living off its rich diet of natural resources and start emphasizing innovation and a more sophisticated mix of products if it hopes to be successful in international markets. He notes that one third of Canada's total exports in 1989 were unprocessed or semiprocessed natural resources. In other words, Canadian industry has not upgraded or extended its competitive advantage into processing technology and the marketing of more sophisticated resource-based products. The proportion of Canadian exports based on resources is higher than in many industrialized countries, including the U.S., Japan, Germany, Britain, Korea, and Sweden.

Porter points out that nostalgic thinking about the "good old days" before free trade is not productive, and that rescinding the Canada-U.S. Free Trade Agreement will not make everything better. He says there can be no turning back and that old attitudes and practices inconsistent with international competitiveness will have to go.

The study criticizes Canadian business, government, and labour for their failure to abandon outdated ways of thinking regarding productivity and innovation. Porter makes the following recommendations to these groups:

To Business

- Compete based on innovation and cost, not simply cost.

- Concentrate on products with a lasting competitive edge.
- Spend more money on employee training.
- Finance university research to ensure that more of it is relevant.
- Base employee compensation on corporate performance.
- Stop relying on government assistance.

To Government

- Provide more training for the unemployed.
- Set higher national education standards.
- Finance university programs that are oriented towards competitiveness.
- Introduce stricter product standards to force Canadian companies to meet world product standards.
- Expand apprenticeship programs.

To Labour

- Recognize that, in the long run, the best guarantee of good wages is competitive corporate activities such as productivity enhancement programs.
- Help company management identify and remove barriers to productivity.
- Support broadening workers' skills.
- Take a more collaborative approach to union-management relations.

Industry Productivity

In addition to differences between the manufacturing and service sectors, industries within these sectors differ vastly in terms of productivity. Agriculture is more productive in Canada than in many other nations because we use more sophisticated technology and superior natural resources. Technological advances have also given the computer industry a productivity edge in many areas. But investment in automated equipment—and thus productivity—in the automobile and steel industries has lagged behind that of other nations.

The productivity of specific industries concerns many people for different reasons. Labour unions need to take it into account in negotiating contracts, since highly productive industries can give raises more easily than can less productive industries. Investors and suppliers consider industry productivity when making loans, buying securities, and planning their own future production. Areas that have long depended on steel and auto plants have experienced economic and social devastation as a result of plant closings, layoffs, and closings of related businesses.

Company Productivity

High productivity gives a company a competitive edge because its costs are lower. As a result, it can offer its product at a lower price (and gain more customers), or it can make a greater profit on each item sold. Increased productivity also allows companies to pay workers higher wages without raising prices.

As a result, the productivity of individual companies is also important to investors, workers, and managers. Comparing the productivity of several companies in the same industry helps investors in buying and selling stocks. Employee profit-sharing plans are often based on the company's productivity improvements each year. And managers use information about productivity trends to plan for new products, factories, and funds to stay competitive in the years ahead.

Department and Individual Productivity

Within companies, managers are concerned with the productivity of various divisions, departments, workstations, and individuals. Improved productivity in any of these areas can improve a firm's overall productivity. An overemphasis on the performance of individuals and departments, however, tends to discourage working together as a team for overall company improvement. For this reason, many companies are cautious about using departmental and individual productivity measures.

Measuring Productivity

To improve productivity, we must first measure it. Otherwise, we will not be able to tell whether a program has increased productivity.

Total and Partial Measures of Productivity

Every productivity measure is a ratio of outputs to inputs. The outputs are the value of goods and services produced. The inputs are the value of the resources used to create the outputs. In selecting a productivity measure, managers must decide which inputs are most important for their business. The choice of inputs (factors) determines the specific measure.

In some cases, all inputs are equally important, so managers use a **total factor productivity ratio**, which can be expressed as

$$\text{Productivity} = \frac{\text{Outputs}}{\text{Labour} + \text{Capital} + \text{Materials} + \text{Energy inputs}}$$

total factor productivity ratio
A measure of a firm's overall productivity calculated as outputs divided by all inputs.

If an insurance company sold $10 million in policies and used $2 million of resources to do so, its total factor productivity would be 5.

Total factor measures can become complicated because of the different inputs involved. It is difficult to find comparable measures for energy consumption, capital, labour, and material. For some purposes, **partial productivity ratios**—which ignore some factors—may be best. For example, **materials productivity** (a partial productivity ratio) may be a fairly good measure of overall productivity in non-labour-intensive industries. Expenditures for equipment are also a more significant cost in many of these firms. Materials and equipment, not labour, constitute over 90 percent of operating costs in highly automated oil refineries, chemical companies, and manufacturing plants.

partial productivity ratio
A measure of a firm's overall productivity based on the productivity of its most significant input; calculated as total outputs divided by the selected input.

materials productivity
A partial productivity ratio calculated as total outputs divided by materials inputs.

An employee observes a robot's movements at a nuclear laboratory. Properly used, robots can perform dangerous tasks more safely than humans.

$$\text{Productivity} = \frac{\text{Outputs}}{\text{Materials}}$$

If a chemical plant uses eight tonnes of chemicals to produce two tonnes of insecticide, its materials productivity is 0.25.

National Productivity Measures

labour productivity

A partial productivity ratio calculated as total outputs divided by labour inputs for a company and as gross domestic product divided by the total number of workers for a nation.

At one time, partial ratios of labour productivity were the measure typically used by most nations. A country's **labour productivity** is usually calculated as

$$\frac{\text{Gross domestic product}}{\text{Total number of workers}}$$

The total number of workers in this equation represents the nation's total labour input. (Sometimes the total hours worked, not the number of workers, is used as the input in figuring labour productivity.) **Gross domestic product (GDP)**—the value of all goods and services produced in the economy—represents the nation's total output.

gross domestic product (GDP)

The value of all goods and services produced by an economy.

Labour productivity measures are popular because they are easy to calculate and compare. Most governments keep records on gross domestic product and adjust them for inflation. The resulting constant-dollar data permit reliable year-to-year comparisons of national and international productivity changes. But as labour-intensive industries become less important, other measures, such as materials productivity, capital productivity, and even total factor productivity are coming into wider use.

Sector and Industry Productivity Measures

In addition to national productivity measures, we need to determine the productivity of various sectors and industries in order to isolate and solve productivity problems.

The rise in labour productivity among manufacturing workers does not necessarily mean that they are working harder or better than service workers, whose productivity is stagnating. More often, labour productivity increases because other, nonlabour resources are added. The use of more capital—modernized trucks, machinery, and office equipment—often increases labour productivity by enabling fewer workers to accomplish more.

Is the additional capital investment worth the cost? To see, we need to look at capital productivity. **Capital productivity** is the ratio of outputs (the value of all goods and services) divided by the capital inputs for all firms.

capital productivity

A partial productivity ratio calculated as total outputs divided by capital inputs.

Company Productivity Measures

Many companies have established productivity measures for individual divisions, plants, departments, and even jobs. Goals for productivity improvements are set in the areas of greatest importance. They serve as guidelines for workplace changes and performance evaluations. For example, an automated, petroleum-fueled factory may place high priority on energy productivity. Its major goal, therefore, might be to raise the level of its sales per barrel of consumed fuel from $200 to $220. Employees would thus seek ways to conserve fuel while maintaining or increasing production and sales.

By contrast, a labour-intensive restaurant might use the dollar amount of food served per server as its main productivity measure. If it offers servers incentives to increase sales, they will encourage customers to order tempting (and highly profitable) specialties, drinks, and desserts.

Total Quality Management

It is no longer enough for businesses to simply measure productivity in terms of numbers of items produced. They must also take into account quality. But Canadian business has not always recognized the importance of quality.

In the decades after the Second World War, American business consultant W. Edwards Deming tried to persuade U.S. firms that they needed to improve quality at least as much as quantity. Like many a prophet, he was not honoured in his homeland. But his arguments won over the Japanese. Through years of meticulous hard work, Japan's manufacturers have changed "Made in Japan" from a synonym for cheap, shoddy merchandise into a hallmark of reliability.

Many of the quality assurance programs that are integral to the modern Japanese production system were Deming's brainchildren. And Japan's highest honour for industrial achievement is the Deming Award for Quality. It took the economic troubles of the 1970s and 1980s for Deming's ideas to gain acceptance in Canada and the United States.

In the automobile industry in the 1980s, Japanese firms held a big lead in quality. North American manufacturers have closed that gap, but the Japanese are ahead once again in the area of customer service. Nissan, for example, has formed a Satisfaction Department that coordinates training for their 4000 Canadian dealers, salespeople, and employees. It even determines bonuses based on customer satisfaction ratings rather than sales volume.[4]

European businesses have also recognized the importance of the quality message. In 1988, executives from Olivetti, Renault, and other companies established the European Foundation for Quality Management (EFQM). The stated mission of the organization is to increase quality awareness and to promote quality in goods and services throughout European enterprise. Today, EFQM has more than 160 member companies that all face the difficult challenge of producing high-quality products and services for customers across a continent with diverse languages, cultures, and economies.

W. Edwards Deming

Nissan
http://www.nissancanada.com

Emphasis on quality manufacturing in Canada is increasing, as is evidenced by the Gold Plant Quality Award given to the workers of Toyota's Cambridge, Ontario, plant in 1991 and 1995. This award honours the plant as the top quality producer of automobiles in North America. The award is proof of Toyota's emphasis on *kaizen* (the continual search for improvement) and *jidoka* (defect detection). But there is still room for improvement. In a recent survey of consumers in 20 different countries, Canada came in sixth in the overall quality of its products. Japan was first, Germany second, and the U.S. third.[5]

The perception of quality is also important. Canadian wines are turned back at European ports because the Economic Community maintains that Canada does not have a proper quality control system for its wines. This happens despite the recent prestigious award won by Inniskillen Wines Inc. at the Bordeaux Vin Expo against more than 4000 entries.[6]

Today, many Canadian companies recognize that quality products are a must. But they have found that producing quality goods and services requires an effort from all parts of the business. **Total quality management (TQM)** emphasizes that no defects are tolerable and that employees are responsible for maintaining quality standards. At Toyota's Cambridge, Ontario, assembly plant, for example, workers can push a button or pull a rope to stop the production line when something is not up to standard.[7] The box "TQM at Standard Aero" shows how the concept was introduced at one Canadian company.

Any activity necessary for getting quality goods and services into the marketplace is a part of **quality assurance** (sometimes called quality management). Quality assurance is the management of the firm's quality efforts. Like any other management function, it involves planning, organizing, leading, and controlling.

total quality management (TQM)

A concept that emphasizes that no defects are tolerable and that all employees are responsible for maintaining quality standards.

quality assurance

Those activities necessary to get quality goods and services into the marketplace; also called quality management.

Planning for Quality

Planning for quality should begin before products are designed or redesigned. Managers need to set goals for both quality levels and quality reliability in the beginning. **Performance quality** refers to the features of a product and how well it performs. For example, Maytag gets a price premium because its washers and dryers offer a high level of performance quality. Customers perceive Maytags as having more advanced features and being more durable than other brands. (Everyone knows that the Maytag repairman is a lonely and idle person.)

Performance quality may or may not be related to quality reliability in a product. **Quality reliability** refers to the consistency or repeatability of performance. Toyota's small cars may not equal the overall quality level or have the luxury features of Rolls Royce; consequently, Toyota's prices are much lower. But Toyotas have high quality reliability. The firm has a reputation for producing very few "lemons."

Some products offer both high quality reliability and high performance quality. Kellogg has a reputation for consistent production of cereals made of good-quality ingredients. To achieve any form of high quality, however, managers must plan for production processes—equipment, methods, worker skills, and materials—that will result in quality products, as discussed in Chapter 12.

performance quality

The overall degree of quality; how well the features of a product meet consumers' needs and how well the product performs.

quality reliability

The consistency of quality from unit to unit of a product.

Organizing for Quality

Perhaps most important to the quality concept is the belief that producing quality goods and services requires an effort from all parts of the organization. The old idea of a separate "quality control" department is no longer enough. Everyone from the chairperson of the board to the part-time clerk—purchasers, engineers, janitors, marketers, machinists, and other personnel—must work to assure quality. In Germany's Messerschmitt-Boelkow-Blohm

The Canadian Business Scene

TQM at Standard Aero Ltd.

In 1991, the U.S. Air Force visited Standard Aero in Winnipeg, Manitoba. Standard had submitted a bid to overhaul aircraft that undercut its competitors by more than 50 percent, and the Air Force wanted to see the firm's factory before it signed the contract. They must have liked what they saw, because Standard got the contract. What the Air Force didn't know was that the impetus for the bid came not from Standard's managers (who were concerned about the size of the contract), but from shop floor employees.

Standard Aero has made TQM work where other companies have failed because it is dedicated to an often overlooked tenet of TQM: the only definition of quality that really counts is "what the customer wants." Standard employees talk to customers to find out exactly what they expect from the firm's work. Top management is also committed to TQM, has spent $13 million on the program to date and has fired several top managers who would not commit to the program.

TQM became popular in the late 1980s, but has lately been greeted with increasing skepticism, with many companies being disappointed with the lack of fast results. Bob Hamaberg, CEO, says that there is nothing wrong with TQM; it has simply been applied badly in many companies.

The TQM process began at Aero in 1990 with the election of a "change council" consisting of Hamaberg and five senior managers. This council ensured that the TQM process received the money, equipment, and support necessary for success. A full-time "change manager" was appointed from within the company to make sure that the process didn't pull other managers from their regular duties.

Next, a nine-person task force was formed that consisted of employees who had done the full range of jobs on one of Standard's major overhaul contracts. Their first task was to find out what the customer wanted. To do this, the team designed a questionnaire and then visited customer plants around the world to gather information. Even though the cost of this part of the process was about $100 000, much new information was gathered and many old beliefs about customers were shattered. For example, Standard found that in spite of free trade some U.S. firms were reluctant to deal with them because of complex cross-border paperwork. So Standard now does the paperwork for the customer. As a result of these actions, the task force picked up $7 million in new business.

The task force also worked within Standard to determine exactly how the company did its aircraft overhaul work. After weeks of analysis, the team was able to reduce the flow and complexity of work dramatically. For example, one gearbox had previously required 213 steps as it moved through the plant; the task force reduced the distance travelled by 80 percent, and cut the number of times the component changed hands by 84 percent. Also, by reducing paperwork involved in tracking the item they saved the company $150 000 per year.

Training is a major feature of the TQM program. Workers receive training in technical areas like statistics and machine operation, as well as in team building. The price tag at Standard has been about $1.5 million per year. Getting workers to be enthusiastic about TQM was not easy at first. Hamaberg's pep talks were crucial in getting workers to try it.

Hamaberg says that implementing TQM has been very hard, but that the results have been impressive. The task force members worked 12 to 14 hours per day, and he was concerned that they would burn out. He also notes that you can't do TQM all at once; it must be implemented step by step because people can't handle large amounts of immediate change.

Standard Aero
http://www.standardaero.ca

---

aerospace company, for example, all employees are responsible for inspecting their own work. The overall goal is to reduce eventual problems to a minimum by making the product right from the beginning. The same principle extends to teamwork practice at Heinz Co., where teams of workers are assigned to inspect virtually every activity in the company. Heinz has realized substantial cost savings by eliminating waste and rework.

At Motorola, the concept of teamwork as a key to organizational quality has resulted in an international event called the Total Customer Satisfaction Team Competition. Teams are composed of Motorola employees and also include customers and outside suppliers. Teams are judged on their success not only in promoting productivity but in sharing innovative ideas with people both inside and outside the company.

Although everyone in a company contributes to product quality, responsibility for specific aspects of total quality management is often assigned to specific departments and jobs. In fact, many companies have quality assurance, or quality control, departments staffed by quality experts. These people may be called in to help solve quality-related problems in any of the firm's other departments. They keep other departments informed of the latest developments in equipment and methods for maintaining quality. In addition, they monitor all quality control activities to identify areas for improvement.

Leading for Quality

Too often, firms fail to take the initiative to make quality happen. Leading for quality means that managers must inspire and motivate employees throughout the company to achieve quality goals. They need to help employees see how they affect quality and how quality affects their jobs and their company. Leaders must continually find ways to foster a quality orientation by training employees, encouraging their involvement and tying wages to quality of work. If managers succeed, employees will ultimately accept **quality ownership**—the idea that quality belongs to each person who creates or destroys it while performing a job.

quality ownership
The concept that quality belongs to each employee who creates or destroys it in producing a good or service; the idea that all workers must take responsibility for producing a quality product.

General Electric Co. has recently embarked on a strong quality control initiative. Top management commitment to the program is assured by tying executive bonuses to actual implementation of the quality control program. The program involves training managers to be "Black Belts" in quality improvement. These Black Belts then spend their time in GE plants setting up quality improvement projects. Young managers have been told that they won't have much of a future at GE unless they become Black Belts. The company is investing millions in this project, and intends to have 10 000 Black Belts by the year 2000. The company is hopeful that the program can generate savings of $7 to $10 billion during the next decade.[8]

Controlling for Quality

By monitoring its products and services, a company can detect mistakes and make corrections. To do so, however, managers must first establish specific quality standards and measurements. Consider the following control system for a bank's teller services. Observant supervisors periodically evaluate transactions against a checklist. Specific aspects of each teller's work—appearance, courtesy, efficiency, and so on—are recorded. The results, reviewed with employees, either confirm proper performance or indicate changes that are needed to bring performance up to standards.

Tools for Quality Assurance

In managing for quality, many leading companies rely on assistance from proven tools. Often, ideas for improving both the product and the production process come from *competitive product analysis*. For example, Toshiba will take apart a Xerox photocopier and test each component. Test results help Toshiba's managers decide which Toshiba product features are satisfactory (in comparison to the competition), which product features need to be upgraded, or whether Toshiba's production processes need improvement.

Methods such as value-added analysis, statistical process control, quality/cost studies, quality circles, benchmarking, cause-and-effect diagrams, ISO 9000, and re-engineering provide different routes to quality. Each of these approaches is discussed briefly below.

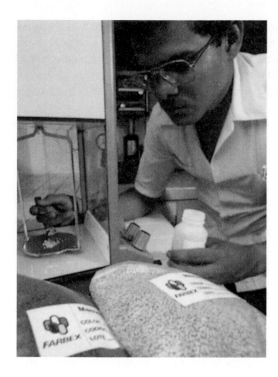

The quality control analyst at this plastics manufacturer is checking the weight of a sample of plastic pellets during the production process.

Value-Added Analysis

One effective method of improving quality and productivity is **value-added analysis**: the evaluation of all work activities, material flows, and paperwork to determine the value that they add for customers. Value-added analysis often reveals wasteful or unnecessary activities that can be eliminated without harming (and even improving) customer service. When Hewlett-Packard, for example, simplified its contracts and reduced them from 20 pages to as few as two pages for all customers, computer sales rose by more than 18 percent.

value-added analysis
The evaluation of all work activities, material flows, and paperwork to determine the value they add for customers.

Statistical Process Control

Every business experiences unit-to-unit variations in its products and services. Although every company would like complete uniformity in its outputs, this is an impossible quest. Companies can gain better control, however, by understanding the sources of variation. **Statistical process control (SPC)** methods—especially process variation studies and control charts—allow managers to analyze variations in production data.

statistical process control (SPC)
Statistical analysis techniques that allow managers to analyze variations in production data and to detect when adjustments are needed to create products with high quality reliability.

Process Variation

Variations in a firm's products may arise from the inputs in its production process. As people, materials, work methods, and equipment change, so do production outputs. While some amount of **process variation** is acceptable, too much can result in poor quality and excessive operating costs.

Consider the box-filling operation for Honey Nuggets cereal. Each automated machine fills two 400-gram boxes per second. Even under proper conditions, slight variations in cereal weight from box to box are normal. Equipment and tools wear out, the cereal may be overly moist, machinists make occasional adjustments. But how much variation is occurring? How much is acceptable?

process variation
Any change in employees, materials, work methods, or equipment that affects output quality.

process capability study

A statistical process control method in which samples of the product are measured to determine the amount of process variation; shows the outputs' conformity with or deviation from specification limits.

specification limits

Limits defining acceptable and unacceptable quality in production of a good or service.

Information about variation in a process can be obtained from a **process capability study.** Boxes are taken from the filling machines and weighed. The results are plotted, as in Figure 14.1, and compared with the upper and lower **specification limits** (quality limits) for weight. These limits define good and bad quality for box filling. Boxes with over 410 grams are a wasteful "giveaway." Underfilling has a cost because it is unlawful.

Looking at the results of the capability study, we see that none of machine A's output violates the quality limits. In fact, most of the boxes from machine A are very close to the desired weight of 400 grams. The shape of machine A's graph, high at the centre and dropping sharply at the margins, is typical of many production processes. Machine A, then, is fully capable of meeting the company's quality standards.

But machines B and C have problems. In their present condition, they are "not capable." They cannot reliably meet Honey Nuggets' quality standards. The company must take special—and costly—actions to sort the good from the bad boxes before releasing the cereal for shipment. Unless machines B and C are renovated, substandard production quality will plague Honey Nuggets.

Control Charts

control chart

A statistical process control method in which results of test sampling of a product are plotted on a diagram that reveals when the process is beginning to depart from normal operating conditions.

control limit

The critical value on a control chart that indicates the level at which quality deviation is sufficiently unacceptable to merit investigation.

Knowing that a process is capable of meeting quality standards is not enough. Managers must still monitor the process to prevent its drifting astray during production. To detect the beginning of bad conditions, managers can check production periodically and plot the results on a **control chart**. For example, several times a day a machine operator at Honey Nuggets might weigh several boxes of cereal together to ascertain the average weight.

Figure 14.2 shows the control chart for machine A, in which the first five points are randomly scattered around the centre line, indicating that the machine was operating well. However, the points for samples 5 through 8 are all above the centre line, indicating that something was causing the boxes to overfill. The last point falls outside the upper **control limit**, confirming that the process is out of control.

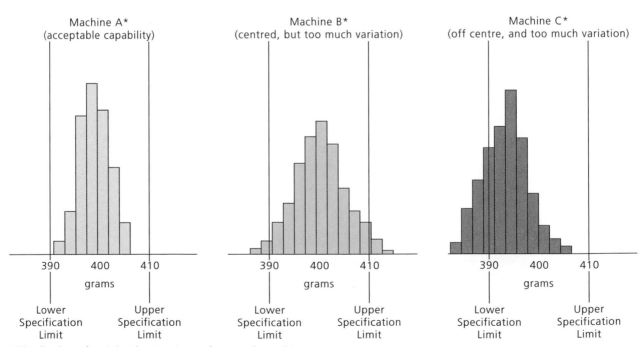

*Distribution of weights for 500 boxes from each machine

Figure 14.1

Process variation in box filling for Honey Nuggets cereal.

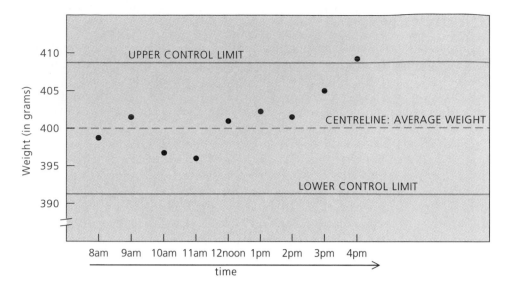

Figure 14.2
Honey Nuggets cereal process control chart for machine A.

At this point, the machine must be shut down so that a manager and/or the operator can investigate what is causing the problem—equipment, people, materials, or work methods. Control is completed by correcting the problem and restoring the process to normal.

Quality/Cost Studies for Quality Improvement

Statistical process controls help keep operations up to *existing* capabilities. But in today's competitive environment, firms must consistently *raise* quality capabilities. Any improvement in products or production processes means additional costs, however, whether for new facilities, equipment, training, or other changes. Managers thus face the challenge of identifying those improvements that offer the greatest promise. **Quality/cost studies** are useful because they not only identify a firm's current costs but also reveal areas with the largest cost-savings potential.

Quality costs are associated with making, finding, repairing, or preventing defective goods and services. All of these costs should be analyzed in a quality/cost study. For example, Honey Nuggets must determine its costs for **internal failures**. These are expenses—including the costs of overfilling boxes and the costs of sorting out bad boxes—incurred during production and before bad products leave the plant. Studies indicate that many manufacturers incur very high costs for internal failures—up to 50 percent of total costs.

Despite quality control procedures, however, some bad boxes may get out of the factory, reach the customer, and generate complaints from grocers and cereal eaters. These are **external failures** that occur outside the factory. The costs of correcting them—refunds to customers, transportation costs to return bad boxes to the factory, possible lawsuits, factory recalls—should also be tabulated in the quality/cost study.

The percentage of costs in the different categories varies widely from company to company. Thus every firm must conduct systematic quality/cost studies to identify the most costly—and often the most vital—areas of its operations. Not surprisingly, these areas should be targets for improvement. Too often, however, firms substitute hunches and guesswork for data and analysis.

quality/cost study
A method of improving product quality by assessing a firm's current quality-related costs and identifying areas with the greatest cost-saving potential.

internal failures
Expenses incurred during production and before bad product leaves the plant.

external failures
Allowing defective products to leave the factory and get into consumers' hands.

Quality Circles

As we noted in Chapter 12, one proven technique for improving quality is the use of **quality circles**, groups of employees who work in teams to improve their job environment. Meeting on company time in the facility, quality circles are a forum for quality improvement. Although the format varies in different companies, circle members are deeply involved in initiating changes in their work environment.

Quality circles organize their own efforts, choose a leader, and establish rules for discussion. Within the group, members identify aspects of their jobs that pose problems or are barriers to better quality and overall productivity. They gather data to evaluate the severity of problems and to identify improvement projects. The group's problem solving emphasizes brainstorming, group discussions, and tools such as process capability studies and cost analysis. Ultimately, the circle makes recommendations to management, identifying expected benefits, costs, and implementation timetables.

Perhaps the greatest benefit of quality circles, however, is not any direct cost savings, but their effect on employees' attitudes. Rather than viewing themselves as passive resources for production, employees develop a sense of self-worth and quality ownership. The talents and job knowledge of circle members are put to active, constructive use instead of lying dormant.

Benchmarking

An organization that uses **benchmarking** compares the quality of its output with the quality produced by the industry leaders. If differences are noted, the firm can figure out how the leaders are achieving their quality levels and then pursue the same strategy. Benchmarking can also be used to compare different departments or divisions in the same organization.

When Canon copiers first were sold in North America, they were priced below what it cost Xerox to make them. Canon could do this because it was far more efficient than Xerox. Xerox then embarked on a benchmarking exercise in order to regain its position as the most important company in the copier market. By using what it had learned about how other companies were making copiers, Xerox was able to cut its unit production cost in half and increase sales by 50 percent.[9]

Cause-and-Effect Diagrams

A **cause-and-effect diagram** summarizes the four possible causes of quality problems—materials, manpower, methods, and machines. For example, if car bodies are being produced with rippled paint, the problem might be thin paint (materials), poor training (manpower), a defective sprayer (machines), or a layer of paint that is too thick (methods). The cause-and-effect diagram is used to identify the source(s) of the problem. Once the source is identified, actions can be taken to resolve the problem.

ISO 9000

The International Standards Organization in Geneva, Switzerland, has developed a quality "scorecard" that is fast becoming a prerequisite for selling to the European Community. The aim of **ISO 9000** (pronounced ICE-O 9000) is to find the cause of product defects at the production line level. The North American automobile industry adopted the standard in 1994 in order to measure the performance of its suppliers. After Toronto Plastics was awarded the designation, defects fell to 15 000 parts per million, down from 150 000 parts per million. About 600 Canadian firms have received the designation.[10] More information is contained in the box "ISO 9000: Seeking the Standard in Quality."

Re-engineering

Re-engineering is the process of rethinking and redesigning business processes in order to achieve dramatic improvements in productivity and quality. In effect, those engaged in re-engineering ask, "If this were a new company, how would we run it?" The bottom line in every re-engineering process is redesigning systems to better serve the needs of customers.

A re-engineering process at IBM Credit Corp., a financing subsidiary of IBM, is typical. The firm exists to provide a service—financing computers and software. But each financing request had to go through a cumbersome series of steps, even though most customers needed an immediate answer. After two managers decided to "walk through" a typical request, they discovered that the actual approval work took only 90 minutes. The rest of the time was spent shuffling forms around between the various people who worked on the process. Their solution was to put one person in charge of all the steps. The result? A hundredfold increase in the number of requests handled.[11]

Re-engineering is also underway at Novacor Chemicals in Sarnia. Over the past 10 years, the company acquired four different businesses, each with its own style, technology, and processes. It is now rethinking how it produces about two million tonnes of petrochemicals each year. In the process, it is finding that it can save millions of dollars by having the four businesses operate in a coordinated fashion rather than as separate entities. For example, when plants were shut down for maintenance, each one hired its own maintenance teams. Now, one team is hired and rotated among the four plants.[12]

re-engineering

The process of rethinking and redesigning business processes in order to achieve dramatic improvements in productivity and quality.

International Report

ISO 9000: Seeking the Standard in Quality

ISO 9000 standards enable firms to demonstrate that they follow documented procedures for testing products, training workers, keeping records, and fixing product defects. To become certified, companies must document the procedures that workers follow during every stage of production. They must also show that they have incorporated mechanisms to ensure that workers actually follow accepted practices. Not surprisingly, this approach leads to more reliable products with fewer defects. The purpose of ISO 9000 is "to ensure that a manufacturer's product is exactly the same today as it was yesterday, as it will be tomorrow." The goal of standardization is to guarantee that "goods will be produced at the same level of quality even if all the employees were replaced by a new set of workers."

Companies seeking ISO 9000 certification are audited by an elite group of quality-systems "registrars." These registrars focus on 20 different functions including design control, contract review, purchasing, inspection and testing,

and training. For example, to pass order-processing requirements, a company must demonstrate procedures for guaranteeing on-time deliveries. Not surprisingly, the certification process is time-consuming and costly—it can take up to 18 months for a manufacturing plant employing 300 workers and cost more than $200 000.

Despite the interest in ISO 9000, however, it is not a cure-all for quality ailments. On the contrary, certification standards have little to do with customer satisfaction. Instead of imposing guarantee procedures, they focus on documenting a company's commitment to its *own* procedures. "With ISO 9000 you can still have terrible processes and products," complains Richard Buetow, director of corporate quality at Motorola. "You can certify a manufacturer that makes life jackets from concrete," says Buetow, "as long as those jackets are made according to the documented procedures and the company provides the next of kin with instructions on how to complain about defects. That's absurd."

In the mid-1990s, the re-engineering idea ran into difficulty, partly because it became too closely associated with downsizing.[13] What started out as a way to increase the efficiency of work processes ended up as a system that was used to rationalize downsizing. Some re-engineering efforts also failed because the changes that were introduced were not entrenched in the company's regular operations. As a result, after a few years it was hard to find any traces of the re-engineering that had supposedly been accomplished.[14]

Even major proponents of the idea such as Dr. Michael Hammer admit that somewhere along the way they lost sight of *people* and became too caught up in streamlining *processes*.[15] They also recognize that innovation comes from changing how people work, not simply from re-engineering.

Competing Through Productivity and Quality

While tools such as quality circles can help a firm improve product quality, they can enhance a company's ability to compete only when coupled with attention to all aspects of productivity. Both productivity and quality begin with attention to customers' needs. Also important are management's willingness to invest in innovation, its time perspective, its concern for quality of work life, how well it can streamline its service operations, and the size of the company.

Get Closer to the Customer

Many decaying businesses have lost sight of customers as the driving force for all business activity. With misplaced intentions, they waste resources designing products customers do not want. They ignore customers' reactions to existing products. They fail to keep up with changing consumer tastes, or they go beyond consumers' tastes. In contrast, the most successful businesses keep close to their customers and know what they want in the products they consume.

At Greyhound Lines of Canada, marketing and operations vice-president John Munro wanted to make a point about the importance of clean restrooms to customers. He warned regional managers that he would visit bus depots on one hour's notice to see if the restrooms were clean enough to eat dinner in them. Within weeks, photos of regional managers having dinner in the spotless restrooms began pouring into Munro's office.[16]

Greyhound
http://www.greyhound.ca

Invest in Innovation and Technology

Once companies know what their customers want, managers must find efficient ways to produce it. As we saw in Chapter 3, investment in research and development in Canada has lagged behind that in Europe and Japan. Rather than creating new products, more and more companies are choosing to copy innovations and market similar products to save innovation costs. Firms that have continued to invest in truly innovative technology have kept their productivity rising, along with their incomes. But firms that have merely copied the automation they see others using have not been as productive.[17]

For example, Caterpillar, which makes custom engines for truck makers and boat makers, adopted an innovative information technology. Formerly, customers ordering engines had to specify each component using Caterpillar's vocabulary and part-numbering system, which was cumbersome, error-prone, and frustrating. Now, using a computer connected to Caterpillar headquar-

Caterpillar
http://www.cat.ca

ters, customers simply order their engine preference—horsepower, displacement, and so forth—in plain English, which the computer translates into Caterpillar's part numbers. The electronic order is transmitted to the factory floor, where the computer shows workers the engine specifications and parts to be used. It even controls some of the automatic tools during assembly. In addition to pleasing the customer, this new technology allows Caterpillar to produce on only one work shift the same volume that formerly required two.[18]

Adopt a Long-Run Perspective

Part of the decline in innovation among Canadian firms reflects a common short-run perspective. Shareholders prefer short- and intermediate-term (less than five years), "sure thing" paybacks. Many companies reward managers with salaries and bonuses based on their quarterly or yearly performance. With owners and managers unwilling to wait for financial returns, many buildings, tools, and equipment have become old or obsolete. Canada is still a creative hothouse, but many businesses are shying away from long-term risks and are failing to convert their good new ideas into actual products.

By contrast, instead of emphasizing short-run results, many quality-oriented firms are committed to a long-run perspective for **continuous improvement**—the ongoing commitment to improving products and processes, step by step, in pursuit of ever-increasing customer satisfaction. Motorola is a good example of a company that emphasizes continuous, long-run improvement. In 1981, the firm adopted a five-year goal of a tenfold reduction of errors. In 1986, it extended that goal to a hundredfold reduction of errors by 1992. Despite initial hopes, however, Motorola missed its goal for 1992: At the start of that year, defects still ran at 40 per one million parts. Motorola managers had to be satisfied with the reminder that five years earlier, the defect rate had been 6000 per one million parts. Motorola continues to plan for still greater improvement. By 2001, say company officials, Motorola quality will be an unimaginable 1 defect per one *billion* parts. The focus on continuous improvement at another company is described in the box "SABRE-Toothed Tiger of the Skies."

continuous improvement
The ongoing commitment to improve products and processes, step by step, in pursuit of ever-increasing customer satisfaction.

Operators at Dofasco monitor the production of steel products with the latest in high-technology monitoring devices.

International Report

SABRE-Toothed Tiger of the Skies

SABRE is the computerized reservation service of American Airlines. Most Canadians first heard about it when American Airlines offered to invest $246 million in troubled Canadian Airlines International if CAI would become part of SABRE. However, CAI was already a partner with Air Canada in the Gemini reservation system; therefore, it needed approval to join SABRE because doing so would doom Gemini.

SABRE has over 85 000 terminals in 47 countries. It allows travel agents to make reservations on virtually any airline and to book hotel rooms, rental cars, and even theatre tickets in many places. The system is just the latest development in American's ongoing dedication to continuous improvement.

The system got its start in the late 1950s, when reservations for American's flights exceeded the old system's (file cards and blackboards) capacity to handle them. By 1963, the original SABRE was in place, handling 85 000 phone calls, 40 000 confirmed reservations, and 20 000 ticket sales in its first year. (Today the system handles nearly 2000 messages per second during peak season.) By keeping track of passengers and passenger miles, SABRE also enabled American to launch the first comprehensive "frequent flier" program in the industry. By the mid-1970s, the system was also tracking spare parts, scheduling crews, and developing flight plans. In addition, the system enables the firm to maximize its revenues by shifting fares on each flight as necessary.

In 1976, SABRE moved beyond American's offices and into the offices of travel agents, enabling them not only to make reservations instantly but also to provide their clients with seat assignments (and even boarding passes) prior to their flights. Before SABRE, less than 40 percent of airline tickets were booked through travel agents. Today 80 percent are. On an average day, 40 000 new or changed fares are entered into the system. When "fare wars" break out, that number zooms to 1.5 million per day!

American continued to make changes in SABRE throughout the 1980s. Some of these changes, such as making the screen formats of all airlines' listings the same so that American was not unfairly favoured, were the result of government regulations. But other changes—especially American's decision to sell copies of its software programs to anyone interested in buying them—came from within. Why? As the cost of developing and refining such software has risen, American wants to recoup some of its investment as quickly as possible. Moreover, the firm is convinced that it will still have an edge on its competition because it is better at interpreting and using the information that SABRE provides.

What lies ahead? Continued expansion worldwide is likely. But computer experts at American also argue that the current centralized system must be decentralized and that the system's reliance on the mainframe computer must be reduced if the system is to grow. American has also joined with a variety of other firms in the travel industry to create InterAAct, a system designed to list hotel and rental car options as methodically and comprehensively as SABRE does airline seats. If it succeeds, American will have another weapon against the competition.

Emphasize Quality-of-Work-Life Factors

Positive employee attitudes in small businesses have certainly made productivity growth better than it would otherwise have been. But big corporations represent so large a part of total national output that the reactions of their workers are central to improving productivity. Large firms can make their employees' jobs more challenging and interesting by enhancing their workers' physical and mental health through recreational facilities, counselling services, and other programs.

Many firms are replacing the environments of yesterday, based on management-directed mass production, with worker-oriented environments that foster loyalty, teamwork, and commitment. Firms using this approach have found success in the concept of **employee empowerment**: the principle that all employees are valuable contributors to a business and should be entrusted

employee empowerment

Principle that all employees are valuable contributors to business and should be entrusted with certain decisions regarding their work.

with certain decisions regarding their work. Such confidence in employee involvement contrasts sharply with the traditional belief that managers are the primary source of decision making and problem solving.

Employee Training

For employee involvement to be effective, it must be implemented with preparation and intelligence. Training is one of the proven methods for avoiding judgments and actions that can lead to impaired rather than improved performance. In a recent survey, for example, insufficient training was the most-mentioned barrier encountered by work teams.

Improve the Service Sector

As important as employee attitude is to goods production, it is even more crucial to service production, since employees often *are* the service. The service sector has grown rapidly but this growth has often come at a cost of high inefficiency. Many newly created service jobs have not been streamlined. Some companies operate effectively, but many others are very inefficient, dragging down overall productivity. As new companies enter these markets, however, the increased need to compete should eventually force service producers to operate more productively.

Quality begins with listening to customers in order to determine what services they want. Companies in the temporary-services industry, for example, have long emphasized the needs of clients for clerical and light-industrial employees. More recently, however, temp services have realized the need for high-skilled, specialized temps like nurses, accountants, and scientists.

In trying to offer more satisfactory services, many providers have discovered five criteria that customers use to judge service quality:[19]

- *Reliability*: Perform the service as promised, both accurately and on time.
- *Responsiveness*: Be willing to help customers promptly.
- *Assurance*: Maintain knowledgeable and courteous employees who will earn the trust and confidence of customers.
- *Empathy*: Provide caring, individualized attention to customers.
- *Tangibles*: Maintain a pleasing appearance of personnel, materials, and facilities.

Smaller Can Be Better than Bigger

One bright spot in the productivity picture is small business. Many giant corporations have found themselves overextended. One department does not know what another is doing. Unnecessary duplication leads to wasted resources. By offering their customers higher product quality and tailored services, smaller companies have improved their overall productivity and have become more competitive.

In terms of job satisfaction, small businesses offer features that large ones cannot. Employees in small firms lag well behind their corporate counterparts in pay and benefits. But small companies offer employees more challenging, interesting work than do big firms. They give their employees more respect and greater chances of having their ideas adopted.

Summary of Learning Objectives

1. **Describe the connection between *productivity* and *quality*.** *Productivity* is a measure of economic performance; it compares how much is produced with the resources used to produce it. *Quality* is a product's fitness for use. However, an emphasis solely on productivity or solely on quality is not enough. Profitable competition in today's business world demands high levels of both productivity and quality.

2. **Understand the importance of increasing productivity.** During the 1980s, the growth rate of Canadian productivity slowed down. In recent years, Canada's growth rate of productivity has lagged behind that of countries like Japan, South Korea, and France. It is important that Canadian business firms increase their rate of productivity growth so that they can be competitive in world markets. As the productivity of Canadian business firms increases, they will be able to produce a greater quantity of goods without using more resources.

3. **Explain *total* and *partial measures of productivity* and show how they are used to keep track of national, industrywide, and companywide productivity.** *Total factor productivity* includes all types of input resources: labour, capital, materials, energy, and purchased business services. *Partial productivity measures* do not use as many input factors. *Labour productivity* is the most common national productivity measure. Many companies develop their own measures for partial and total productivity.

4. **Identify the activities involved in *total quality management* and describe four tools that companies can use to achieve it.** *Total quality management* (*TQM*) refers to the planning, organizing, leading, and controlling of all the activities needed to get quality goods and services into the marketplace. Managers must set goals for and implement the processes needed to achieve high quality and reliability levels. *Value-added analysis* involves the evaluation of all work activities, materials flows, and paperwork to determine the value they add for customers. *Statistical process control* methods such as *process capability studies* and *control charts* can help keep quality consistently high. *Quality/cost studies*, which identify potential savings, can help firms improve quality. *Quality improvement teams* also can improve operations by more fully involving employees in decision making. *Bench-marking*—studying the best practices of other companies and using the knowledge to improve a company's own products and services—has become an increasingly common TQM tool. *Cause-and-effect diagrams* summarize the four possible causes of quality problems—materials, manpower, methods, and machines. *ISO 9000* is a quality scorecard whose aim is to find the cause of product defects at the production line level. *Re-engineering* is the process of rethinking and redesigning business processes in order to achieve improvements in productivity.

5. **List six ways in which companies can compete by improving productivity and quality.** A business must first and foremost stay close to customers to better know their needs and wants. To increase quality and productivity, businesses must invest in innovation and technology.

They must also adopt a long-run perspective for continuous improvement. In addition, they should realize that smaller can be better: Many smaller businesses have succeeded because they provide quality service and job satisfaction. Finally, placing greater emphasis on the quality of work life can also help firms compete. Satisfied, motivated employees are especially important in increasing productivity in the fast-growing service sector.

Key Terms

productivity, 392
productivity paradox, 392
quality, 393
level of productivity, 393
growth rate of productivity, 393
total factor productivity ratio, 395
partial productivity ratio, 395
materials productivity, 395

labour productivity, 396
gross domestic product (GDP), 396
capital productivity, 397
total quality management (TQM), 398
quality assurance, 398
performance quality, 398
quality reliability, 398
quality ownership, 400

value-added analysis, 401
statistical process control (SPC), 401
process variation, 401
process capability study, 402
specification limits, 402
control chart, 402
control limit, 402
quality/cost study, 403
internal failures, 403

external failures, 403
quality circle, 404
benchmarking, 404
cause-and-effect diagram, 404
ISO 9000, 404
re-engineering, 405
continuous improvement, 407
employee empowerment, 408

Study Questions and Exercises

Review Questions
1. What is the connection (relationship) between productivity and quality?
2. Why do labour unions care about the productivity of an industry?
3. How do total factor productivity ratios differ from partial factor ratios?
4. What activities are involved in quality assurance?
5. How do the purposes of statistical process controls and quality/cost studies differ?

Analysis Questions
6. How would you suggest the service sector increase productivity?
7. Some people argue that, while quality circles work well in Japan, Canadians lack the team orientation and management-labour trust to make them viable here. Do you agree or disagree? Why?

8. Re-engineering seems like a very good idea, yet it ran into difficulties in the 1990s. Why did difficulties arise, and what can be done to make it effective?

Application Exercises
9. Using a local company as an example, show how you would conduct a quality/cost study. Identify the cost categories and give some examples of costs in each category. Which categories do you expect will have the most and least costs? Why?
10. Select a company of interest to you and analyze it for productivity and quality improvements. Which of the "six suggestions for competing" detailed in the chapter apply to this company? What additional suggestions would you make to help this company improve its overall productivity?

Building Your Business Skills

Goal

To encourage students to evaluate the quality of the different goods and services they buy and to suggest ways to improve low-quality products.

Method

Step 1:

Working alone, think of a high-quality good and a high-quality service that you purchased recently. Then think of a good and a service with lesser quality. In each case, define the specific characteristics that led to your positive or negative assessment.

Step 2:

As a class, divide into groups of four or five and discuss your assessments. Where appropriate, try to focus on the following issues:

■ product reliability
■ process variation
■ customer service

Analysis

Choose one low-quality good and one low-quality service and analyze ways in which the following factors might be used to improve the final product. Some research may be needed to complete the analysis:

■ New production technologies: Can new or different technologies make a difference in product quality?
■ Improved quality of work life: Can an improved working environment improve employee performance and, ultimately, the quality of a good or service?

Follow-Up Questions

1. Is it possible for one consumer to consider a product to be of high quality and another to consider the same product inferior? What factors might be responsible for these differing perspectives?

2. Is it always in a firm's best interest to continue pursuing quality improvements?

The National Quality Institute (NQI) offers information on quality for Canada's private and public sectors. Visit their Web site at:

http://www.nqi.com/new_web/english/frames/frames.html

1. The NQI Web site provides statistics from many studies examining Canadian productivity and quality. What statistics surprised you? Which do you find alarming? Which do you find encouraging?

2. Look at historical information on the Web site. How has Canada's focus on quality changed?

3. According to Web site information, why is it important that a country be seen as representing quality?

End of an Era

The last cathode ray tube (CRT) manufacturing plant in Canada was in Midland, Ontario. It closed in September 1996, throwing 575 people out of work. Like many other manufacturing plants, it had rough going in the last few years—high product defect rates, strained labour relations, increased global competition, price wars, and a threatened plant closure. But the plant continued operating, thanks to a combination of Japanese management, Canadian engineering, and perseverance.

The plant was owned by Mitsubishi Electronics Industries Canada Inc., which shipped almost half its output to television-assembly plants in Japan. When Mitsubishi bought the plant in 1983, it embarked on a relentless pursuit of increased quality through automation and computerization. Because the plant was able to make far more CRTs than the Canadian market needed, the decision was made to ship tubes to Japan.

But reality soon hit home. When the Japanese plant rejected nearly a third of the Canadian plant's first shipment, management knew it had to make major changes in the way the plant operated. It decided that the top priority had to be the detection of defects *before* they left the plant. Assembly processes were therefore revised to prevent defects in the first place.

All of this required some high-powered new technology, which the plant decided to purchase locally. To "align" a tube, for example, the CRTs three electron guns must be aimed precisely at the tube's red, green, and blue phosphor dots. Formerly, workers walked around each tube with a microscope to do the aligning, which was very time-consuming. A computer monitor eventually was used to do the job, and it took only a fraction of the time. The plant also used robots to unload TV screen assemblies. Reduced handling saved more than $500 000 per year.

As a result of many changes, defect rates fell tenfold; production nearly doubled, even though the plant in 1996 employed only half as many workers as it used to.

But problems remained. Relations with the union were tense, partly because of the Japanese philosophy of *kaizen* (doing more with less). The plant eventually moved to a continuous operation with two 12-hour shifts each day, seven days a week. Union representatives say this caused lower morale and an increase in repetitive strain injuries. Workers felt that the Japanese model was imposed on them, except that workers were not allowed any input about operations.

Case Questions

1. What are some reasons that a firm may not pursue quality in its products?

2. What difficulties did the Midland plant experience as it pursued higher quality? Why did it experience these problems?

3. How were productivity and quality related at this company? ◆

When Is Enough Motorcycles Too Many Motorcycles?

Harley-Davidson represents a true riches-to-rags/back-to-riches story. Harley-Davidson motorcycles enjoyed decades of distinguished history as police bikes and dispatch vehicles during both world wars. (Of course, they also became notorious as the vehicles of choice for motorcycle "clubs" like the Hell's Angels.) At one time, Harley's competition included more than 140 companies. But when the Indian Motorcycle Co. of Springfield, Massachusetts, went out of business in 1953, Harley emerged the sole surviving American motorcycle manufacturer. Then, during the 1960s, as Honda and other aggressive Japanese competitors began exporting high-quality, low-priced motorcycles to Canada and the United States, Harley itself teetered on the brink of extinction.

In 1969, Harley-Davidson was acquired by American Machine and Foundry Inc., a recreational equipment conglomerate. AMF's strategy called for capitalizing on the explosion in market demand caused by Japan's successful marketing efforts. The new parent firm countered the competition by increasing production from 15 000 units to

●●●

When Is Enough Motorcycles Too Many Motorcycles?

(continued)

52 000 units per year. The plan failed: Among other consequences of stepped-up quantity, Harley's once touted quality began to plummet. About half of the motorcycles coming off the assembly line were actually missing parts, but problems with a new model, the Cafe Racer, best typified Harley's production woes: The first 100 Cafe Racers to roll off the assembly line required a total of $100 000 in rework before they could be shipped to dealers. Not surprisingly, Harley found itself at a distinct disadvantage in its road wars with the Japanese.

In 1981, Vaughn Beals, AMF's Harley division manager, led a successful management bid to buy the company back from AMF. Beals was determined to revamp Harley's image and marketing strategy. More importantly, he determined to improve reliability and quality—above even Harley's original standards. Even classic Harleys, for example, were legendary for leaking oil, and Harley had become the butt of such insider jokes as "What do hound dogs and Harleys have in common? They both like to ride in the back of a truck."

Beals understood, first of all, that many potential buyers lacked the backyard-mechanic skills traditionally needed to keep Harleys on the road. He thus instituted a number of internal changes. For example, quality circles and an employee-involvement program were established to improve product quality through employee input. A new inventory system called Materials as Needed (MAN) was instituted to reduce inventory costs, shorten manufacturing setup times, and contribute overall quality improvement. A third change involved training employees in problem solving and statistical methods for detecting defects on the assembly line.

Taken together, these steps soon produced significant results: a 36-percent reduction in warranty costs, a 46-percent increase in defect-free motorcycles delivered to dealers, and a 50-percent increase in employee productivity. CEO Richard Teerlink says that the turnaround resulted from a combination of improvements in operations and human resources: "If we can get people to focus on doing the right things and then doing the things right," he says, "we will be in good shape on the productivity issue." On the human resource front, Teerlink has recently turned his attention to Harley's organization chart. For instance, two executive positions—senior vice-presidents in marketing and operations—have been eliminated because "they didn't add value to our products. The people were auditors," explains Teerlink. "They were checkers. People would go up to one boss and that boss would go to another boss and he would go to still another boss. And we wondered why the Japanese beat us on the issue of time." Now Harley employees are organized into teams: A team to create demand, a production team, and a product-support team.

By improving quality and productivity, Harley-Davidson has become profitable once again. Its share of the super-heavyweight market, for example, has jumped to 64 percent from a low of 28 percent in 1985. Moreover, Harley has not only reclaimed its market position but has also experienced significant export growth. It seems that the cornerstones of Harley's image—ruggedness plus high quality—have great global appeal: In England, dealers put potential buyers on a six-month waiting list, and Harley is the best-selling import in Japan. The new Harley, however, carefully limits production increases in order to maintain Harley's hard-won reputation for quality—and, of course, to keep the product supply limited in relation to demand. Production is currently running at merely 350 units per day because, as one Harley executive puts it, "Enough motorcycles is too many motorcycles."

Case Questions

1. Identify some of the productivity and quality issues described in this case.

2. What role has employee empowerment played in Harley's comeback?

3. What specific tools of total quality management are integral to the quality/productivity effort at Harley?

4. Do you agree with Harley's strategy of intentionally limiting the supply of motorcycles that it produces? ◆

Harley-Davidson
http://www.harley-davidson.com

ISO 9000: Management Fad or New Competitive Reality?*

Global competition brings with it a whole new set of benefits and costs. Benefits include expanded markets for both supply and demand; costs include jet lag, making sure you get paid, and differences in quality standards across countries. One way to deal with the quality problem is to have a standard that is internationally recognized and conformed to. In recent years, for manufacturers that standard has been ISO 9000.

ISO 9000 is a certification process that involves being internationally recognized for conforming to certain standards of quality in all aspects of operation. Up front, the process seems rather simple—just satisfy the demands of an 11-page booklet of guidelines. Typically, the process involves documenting what the company does and how it does it with the help of a certified consultant. Once the documentation is complete, the company is audited by an ISO representative to see if it actually conforms to its own written standards. It is then either given a passing grade or rejected. Once the company successfully passes the audit, it is "in" as an ISO-certified company.

However, as the experiences of one Ontario company testify, the realities can be much more complex than might at first appear. Genesis Microchip, a small firm specializing in digital image manipulation, reports spending about $160 000 and a year and a half of company time in the certification process.

For some non-certified companies, the question of whether ISO certification really adds anything comes up frequently. Everyone aspires to quality, their line of reasoning goes, so what is added by going through the ordeal of certification? One respected quality-driven company, Motorola, supports this contrarian view. According to Vice-President for Quality Richard Budo, ISO 9000 in and of itself has had very little impact on the end product. Perhaps, he continues, ISO's biggest contribution is to bring the adherent's paperwork up to standard. Motorola has gone so far as to release a public statement indicating that Motorola is "critical of how ISO is being used and misrepresented." The suspicion also arises from the heavy reliance on consultants, who some see as getting into the ISO business as a way to make a quick buck. Recently, business cartoon Dilbert articulated this skepticism in a strip that satirized the ISO process as a sham.

One ISO advocate, Susan Lores, sees ISO differently. According to her, ISO is a reflection of the new global basis of competition. According to Lores, being ISO certified "enhances Canadian business competing in global markets." If you want to do business in a certain market, this line of counter-argument continues, you have to be ISO certified. This is particularly the case for Canadian businesses seeking to do business with firms in many European countries. ISO is dominant in Europe, where it emerged from a set of British standards. With 150 000 companies already registered worldwide, the trend towards registration has just hit Canada.

Study Questions

1. What is quality? How does ISO 9000 aid in achieving worldwide quality standards?

2. What is process variation? How can ISO 9000 aid in managing process variation?

3. What is quality ownership? Does ISO 9000 guarantee that quality ownership occurs?

*Source: This case was written by Professor Reg Litz of the University of Manitoba.
Video Resource: "ISO 9000," *Venture* #561 (October 8, 1995).

"The image we're working on here ... is not just about selling more product, but just about getting the image right."

Advertising is as much about selling a feeling as selling a product. For the advertising manager that means making a connection between a feeling—whether that feeling is freedom, happiness, or fear—and a client's product or service. One way that Regina photographer Douglas Alker has been able to make that connection is through the use of composite photography. Alker, referred to as the "king of image makers," has established himself on the forefront of this form of photographic imagery. He makes imaginative use of diverse and seemingly unrelated images.

Composite photography is a comparatively new technique. It involves blending digital photos into one overriding image. The technique is not cheap and can cost upwards of $10 000 per day. The high cost is a result of the nature of the technique, since finding the right image can potentially take the photographer almost anywhere.

The task of finding the "perfect" location recently took Alker to Hood River, Oregon, as he searched for the right image for an allergy-treatment product. His idea was to combine peach blossoms with a kayak race. His search took him to a peach orchard where the natural lighting at sunset was ideal. Alker's intent was to use the pollen-rich environment of the orchard to convey the "chained to a tissue box" sensation people feel when hit by a bout of allergic reactions.

The production schedule for this kind of shooting is extremely tight, both in terms of dollars and time. The day's shots get express-couriered to New York City, where they are scanned by the advertising agency that hired Alker. Given their final responsibility for the product, the New York agency screens, and either approves or rejects, Alker's daily production. Such tight control is part of the work package for Alker. Since he's really working for his client's client, its crucial that the intermediary, in this case the New York agency, be kept informed of what's happening and be happy with the results. Since Alker only works on about 20 campaigns each year, such close supervision doesn't present a problem.

On this particular shoot things apparently went well; the New York agency gave its approval the first time through. The next stop for the shoot was Hawaii. Alker's purpose? To find the right location for a surfer image that he might overlay on the Oregon peach orchard. After three nights, the background shot begins to emerge and shooting is scheduled to begin the next morning. Production recommences the next morning at 5 a.m.

Study Questions

1. What is utility? What are the different kinds of utility? What kind of utility is Alker providing his clients?

2. What are the different kinds of product layouts? Which of these best describes Alker's production system?

3. What is the difference between a high-contact and a low-contact service production system? Which best describes Alker's work?

*Source: This case was written by Professor Reg Litz of the University of Manitoba.
Video Resource: "Photo Boy," *Venture* #663 (October 7, 1997).

From a Functional to a Team Approach at Lands' End

LEARNING OBJECTIVES

The purpose of this video exercise is to help students:

1. Understand the purpose and function of formal team-work within a larger organizational structure
2. Assess the ways in which organizational structure can affect employee attitudes and productivity
3. Appreciate some of the factors that affect a company's decisions about how to organize its operations

BACKGROUND INFORMATION

In March 1994, certain key operations at Lands' End underwent a significant change. Up until then, different departments had been organized along *functional* lines: in other words, people who specialized in certain business functions—marketing, finance, quality control, and so on—were grouped with people performing "like" functions. But, says Joan Brown, Vice-President for Quality Assurance, "while we were expected to work together as teams, it really wasn't working very well." Consequently, Lands' End changed the operations of its product development personnel. It shifted from a functional to a truly team-oriented approach.

Reorganization, of course, meant upheaval, both physical and psychological. Work space was reconfigured to accommodate the team concept, and team members had to adjust their attitudes towards both work space and privacy. Although the precise benefits in effectiveness and efficiency cannot yet be measured, the new team approach appears to be addressing the three main problems that it was designed to address. "Time to bring a new product to market has been reduced," reports Brown, "and communication has significantly improved. Even more importantly, everyone associated with the product now has the same goals."

THE VIDEO

Video Source. "Product Development at Lands' End: From a Functional to a Team Approach," *Prentice Hall Presents: On Location at Lands' End*. The video focuses on the sleepwear and swimwear team to show how teamwork has been integrated into product development operations at Lands' End. Members of the team recall the adjustments they had to make in order to adapt to the new form of organization and explain the advantages that it has brought to them in their jobs.

Discussion Questions

1. Briefly describe what you understand to be the key responsibility of each member of the sleepwear and swimwear team (copywriter, inventory manager, art director, quality assurance specialist, team manager, and team assistant).
2. In what ways does the change from functional to team approach probably affect each member's level of responsibility and authority?
3. Of the three types of organizational change—structural, technological, and people—people change is generally regarded as the hardest to implement. Judging from the video, how would you assess the effectiveness of this change at Lands' End?
4. In what ways does team organization probably contribute to quality planning and quality control? To inventory control? To improvements in system design? To worker motivation and quality of work life? To overall productivity?

Follow-Up Assignment

"None of our goals blended," recalls Joan Brown. "Inventory's goal, for example, was to get the product in the building and out the door to the customer. Quality, on the other hand, would stop anything from going out that did not meet its expectations—which ran headlong against the inventory manager's goal."

Your instructor will divide the class into product development teams like the one described in the video. First, each team will decide on the consumer product that it is developing: it can be anything that is of interest to everyone. On each team, members will assume the following roles: inventory manager, copywriter, art director, quality assurance specialist, and team manager. Your quality assurance specialist will meet briefly with your instructor to identify some quality control problem in the team's selected product; he or she will then explain the problem to the team. One team member should be appointed to take minutes. With all members contributing, the team will work to find a solution to its problem. Working from the minutes of its meeting, each team will report to the class on its meeting and its solution to its problem.

For Further Exploration

Visit Lands' End on the Internet at
http://www.landsend.com

Scroll down from the "Home" page to the link to "The Company." From there, take a trip to the "Internet Store," where you can select from such product categories as "Kids," "Men's Casual," and "Women's." To get a better idea of how teamwork is ultimately reflected in the copywriter's description of company products, browse the descriptions of several products. In what ways does the copywriter promote quality as a key function of a given Lands' End product?

EXPERIENTIAL EXERCISE:
Computing for More Timely Production

OBJECTIVE

To give students insight into the manufacturing process and the role for computers therein.

TIME REQUIRED

45 minutes
   Step 1: Individual activity (to be completed before class)
   Step 2: Small-group activity (30 minutes)
   Step 3: Class discussion (15 minutes)

PROCEDURE

Step 1: Read the following case regarding the Hall Company. (Students should read Chapter 18 before doing this exercise.)

Management at Hall, which manufactures clocks, knows that the firm needs to upgrade its computer system. However, they also know that choosing a new system will be difficult and time-consuming, since each department has its own set of problems it expects the new system to solve. A partial list of these problems follows:

   Receiving Department: Currently logs in receipt of raw materials and shipment of finished goods by hand. Has trouble locating pertinent information when raw materials prove defective or finished goods are not received by the warehouse or a customer.

   Manufacturing Department: Pays many of its personnel by piecework, but one person may perform several functions, each paid at a different rate. Pay is calculated by adding up "job tickets" collected by workers on completing a task. Manual collection and entry of this information into the current computer system is time-consuming and has a high potential error rate. This department also has trouble tracking work in process, that stage between raw materials and finished products. Scheduling is currently done on microcomputers in the department, with printouts of final schedules distributed. Delays or more rapid progress in production is not reflected in revised schedules until floor supervisors advise schedulers of this change. Floor supervisors, schedulers, and purchasing staff all complain that the existing system is inadequate for MRP and/or JIT.

   Design Department: Current computer system allows reasonable CAD/CAM but does not hook into computer systems in other areas of the company. For example, the current system generates materials lists for new designs, but these must be printed out and manually sent to purchasing.

   Finance: Like scheduling, finance has its own microcomputers and its own software, none of which interfaces with the mainframe computer or with other microcomputers in the company. Financial personnel spend a great deal of time taking mainframe reports (for example, on sales), microcomputer reports (for example, on materials costs), and handwritten reports (for example, on goods received and shipped and on employee pay rates and hours worked) and re-entering this data.

   Sales and Marketing: Terminals hooked into the mainframe allow quick access to sales figures, but managers cannot currently tell whether or how much sales representatives have actually been paid without asking the finance department for this information.

   Warehousing: Current microcomputers do not interface with others in the company and cannot drive a roboticized system that automatically stores and ships bar-coded boxes on command.

   Customer Service: Records on customer payment must be rekeyed from reports issued by the finance department. Lack of interface with manufacturing and warehousing means promised delivery dates are not always accurate.

   Personnel Department: Current use of separate microcomputers means that information on employee earnings must be entered by hand.

WHAT DOES HALL COMPANY NEED IN ITS NEW COMPUTER SYSTEM?

Step 2: The instructor will divide the class into small groups and assign each group one or more departments in the Hall Company. Each group will complete the grid below with respect to its assigned department.

Department _____

Types of Software Needed: _____

Types of Hardware Needed: _____

Individuals To Be Questioned: _____

Type of Information Needed	Possible Source of Data	Process by Batch?	Other Depts. Involved

Type of system architecture recommended:

Centralized _____

Decentralized _____

Networked _____

Step 3: One member of each small group will present the group's conclusions to the class.

QUESTIONS FOR DISCUSSION

1. What problems do you foresee for the Hall Company as it chooses a new computer system?

2. What areas of conflict emerged from the various presentations? How might some of these be resolved so that everyone wins?

CAREERS IN BUSINESS
CAN WE TALK?

The greatest resume and the most persuasive cover letter in the world do not ensure that you will get the job. Rather, their purpose is to "get your foot in the door"—to get you an interview. Ultimately, it is the interview that will decide whether or not you get the job.

Interviewing for a job—whether it's your first or your twenty-first—is almost always a nerve-wracking experience. During an interview, recruiters and managers will talk to you, ask you questions, listen to your answers, and answer whatever questions you may have. They will then judge your qualifications based on this information. Because the interview is the basis on which most hiring decisions are made, it is very important that you understand how to prepare for an interview, how to handle yourself during an interview, and what to do after an interview.

PREPARING FOR AN INTERVIEW

The first step in preparing for an interview is to learn all you can about the company with which you'll be interviewing. Get a copy of the firm's annual report if time allows. Go to the library and check up on the company in business publications such as *Canadian Business* and the *Globe and Mail*. If such information is not available, prepare yourself by learning all you can about the industry or market.

The next step is to practise answering the questions you are likely to be asked. Friends or guidance counsellors can help you here. For example, you should know ahead of time what you'll say when asked about your prior experience, reasons for wanting a job change, reasons for wanting this job, ability to do the job, strengths, weaknesses, and future goals. Other common questions include:

- How would you describe the office politics in your current job and how do you handle them?
- What's your personal work ethic?
- How have you helped co-workers improve their productivity?
- Would you buy stock in your current firm?

Be prepared to answer these questions, but don't be complacent. If you interview with several people, the chances are good that someone will ask you something you never dreamt of. One man reports being asked, "What would your co-workers say about you if I met them at a bar late on a Friday night?"

The third step in preparing for an interview is to develop questions of your own to ask your interviewers. These questions serve two purposes. First, they show your interest in the firm. Second, the answers to them can help you decide whether you want to work there—if you are offered the job. Questions you might consider asking include:

- Does the company offer training for new employees, growth potential, and opportunities for advancement?
- When was my predecessor promoted?
- What skills and qualities do you believe are most important for this job?
- How would you describe a typical day in this job?
- What conditions in this job make it difficult to perform well?
- Do most supervisors or managers have advanced degrees?
- Are meetings an important part of the decision-making process on this job?

Warning: Do not ask about salary, benefits, or retirement plans until you are offered the job. Interviewers may interpret your concern as a desire to be comfortable—not productive.

Finally, assemble the materials you need to take with you: samples of your work (if appropriate), extra copies of your resume, and written recommendations (if you have them). Also contact those you plan to use as references and let them know about your upcoming interview. This way they will be prepared to answer questions about you.

PRESENTING YOURSELF AT AN INTERVIEW

Answers—and questions—set, you are now ready to present yourself at the interview. When going to your interview, allow plenty of time to get there a few minutes early. Some experts suggest that you even do a "dry run" in advance so you can be sure how much time it will take. It's best to arrive about five minutes early. Over 70 percent of interviewers admit that a late applicant has little chance of getting the job, regardless of qualifications.

Dress conservatively for the interview. A dark suit is your best bet for most professional jobs, regardless of your sex or age. But if you are applying for a creative position such as designer or advertising copywriter, you may do better by dressing with a bit more dash. Whatever you wear, make it the best quality you can afford—it will pay off in the long run. Shined shoes and a well-groomed look also impress interviewers.

HANDLING YOURSELF DURING THE INTERVIEW

When meeting the interviewer, try to project an air of competence and assurance. Relax and remain calm. When the interviewer introduces himself or herself, state your own name as well and extend your hand for a handshake. Speak clearly and directly as you are introduced. The interview will usually take place in a small room or office. Do not sit until the interviewer is ready to sit or at least indicates to you that you can sit. Sit up straight (do not slouch), but try not to be stiff. Likewise, don't fidget, but don't hold the arms of the chair in a death-grip either.

The interviewer will usually start by asking a few general questions, both to set the tone for the interview and to help you relax. When you answer questions, be honest, but don't bare your soul. Lies about what you have done probably won't get you the job, but never say you didn't get along with a previous boss. In fact, find something good to say about that person. If you were fired from a former job, admit it, but phrase it as a bad person-job fit—one you learned from.

Whatever the question, remember that your "job" at the moment is to sell yourself. Be upbeat and positive. Above all, try to present yourself as the right choice—the person who has:

- The skills to do the job.
- The commitment to do the job and to stay with the job.
- A personality that will enable you to get along with others on the job.
- The initiative to do the job—and even more than the job requires—without someone holding your hand.
- The ability to make the person who hired you look good.

Make your answers to the point, but don't be too brief—remember, the objective is to convey something about what you are like as a person. For example, if an interviewer asks you if you would consider relocating for a job, simply saying "Certainly" is not enough.

On the other hand, be careful not to talk too much. The old adage "Better to keep silent and be thought a fool than to open your mouth and remove all doubt" applies here. The more you talk, the better are the chances you'll say something that will disqualify you. For example, if asked whether you'd relocate, don't deliver a 30-minute travelogue about all the cities you would like to live in and why. Strike a happy medium: Indicate that you are willing to relocate and that you assume that an occasional move is necessary for advancement and to learn more about all aspects of the organization.

Some questions pose special problems. What if you are asked a question you don't know how to answer? If you are at all uncertain, ask the interviewer to clarify the question, but if you still don't know, *admit it.* Even more difficult is the situation in which an interviewer asks a question that is "out of bounds." Despite the fact that questions about a job applicant's age, ethnic background, religion, marital status, and personal life are illegal, a surprising number of interviewers continue to ask them. What should you do? You have two options: to answer or not to answer.

If it doesn't make you uncomfortable, you may choose to answer. Or you may respond with a "nonanswer" that shifts the topic back to job-related issues. For example, if asked whether you have a boy/girlfriend, you might try a nonanswer like the following: "I have many friends here, but I consider myself very adaptable and wouldn't expect to have difficulty making new friends wherever I was located. Would the job call for relocating me after the initial training session?"

What if you decide not to answer an illegal question? Certainly you risk losing the job if you point out to the interviewer that the question is inappropriate. You can report the firm, but you will need to prove that the purpose of the question was to discriminate against you—a difficult and time-consuming task indeed. And even if you win, you'll have to ask yourself whether you want to work for a company that supports such questioning. Turning the question back on the interviewer in the form of "Can you tell me how that question relates to this position?" may be some help, but the fact is that if you don't answer, or at least offer something resembling an answer, you probably won't get the job.

Regardless of how you perceive the interview to be going, remain calm and keep your sense of humour. Some interviewers may seem bored, others rude or distant. These attributes may have no bearing on how they are assessing you and your qualifications. The interviewer may be tired or cranky from travelling, or rudeness may just be her or his normal style. Some interviewers simply are not effective at what they do. A few interviewers may even push you a bit to see how you handle yourself under pressure. Remember that losing your temper will lose you the job for sure.

No matter how stressed you are and how much you want the job, try to keep things in perspective. The world will not end if the interview goes nowhere. In fact, having a sense of humour about the process can be a big asset. A vice-president of a major brokerage house was once asked at an interview what he knew about foreign exchange. "After some thought," he recalled, "I said, 'I can spell both words.'" He got the job.

The interviewer will usually indicate to you when the interview is over. But the interviewer will seldom tell you whether or not you will be offered the job. There may be several applicants for the job, or the interviewer may need to discuss your qualifications with other managers before making a decision. But the interviewer should explain what will happen next—when the company will be in contact with you, what the next step will be if the company remains interested in hiring you, and so forth. If this information is not offered, ask before you leave.

FOLLOWING UP AFTER THE INTERVIEW

After any interview, be sure to write a letter to each person with whom you spoke. These letters are an opportunity not only to restate your interest and qualifications but also to resolve one of life's common annoyances. Almost everyone thinks of something they should have said, hours after the interview. Here's your chance to say it.

If you have applied for a managerial position, you can also expect more interviews before you get the job. You may be invited to the company's headquarters or regional office for more interviews with managers. So when you get contacted for a second interview, remember two things: (1) you'll need to do it all again, and (2) you did a good job of it the first time through!

Part Five

*M*ANAGING
MARKETING

What is the first thing you think of when you hear the names Coffee Crisp, Post-It, Crest, and Eno? If you grew up in Canada, you probably didn't hesitate at all before picturing candy, little slips of paper with one sticky edge, toothpaste, and something to calm your stomach. Your rapid association of company names and the goods or services they provide is a tribute to the effectiveness of the marketing managers of the firms that produce these goods. These and many other names have become household words because companies have developed the right products to meet customers' needs, have priced those products appropriately, have made prospective customers aware of the products' existence and qualities, and have made the products readily available.

Part Five, Managing Marketing, provides an overview of the many elements of marketing, including developing, pricing, promoting, and distributing various types of goods and services.

■ We begin in **Chapter 15, Understanding Marketing Processes and Consumer Behaviour**, by examining the ways in which companies distinguish their products, determine customer needs, and otherwise address consumer buying preferences.

■ Then, in **Chapter 16, Developing and Promoting Goods and Services**, we explore the development of different types of products, the effect of brand names and packaging, how promotion strategies help a firm meet its objectives, and the advantages and disadvantages of several promotional tools.

■ Finally, in **Chapter 17, Pricing and Distributing Goods and Services**, we look at the strategies firms use to price their products. We also consider the various outlets business firms use to distribute their products, and we discuss the problems of storing goods and transporting them to distributors.

15

Understanding Marketing Processes and Consumer Behaviour

How Good Is Market Research Information?

Exactly how much confidence can companies place in the market research they purchase? Consider what happened in two interesting cases.

National Research Group Inc (NRG). This organization conducts consumer research for firms like Paramount, Twentieth Century Fox, MGM, TriStar, and Walt Disney. NRG recruits audiences to view soon-to-be-released films and then analyzes their reactions through the use of questionnaires. Summaries of audience reactions are sent to the movie studio, which can then alter the film or change the ending depending on what the market research shows. The movie studios pay NRG for developing this data.

In 1993, about two dozen former employees of NRG claimed that it was falsifying audience data about films, and that it prevented people who didn't like a film from being in focus groups that discussed it (see p. 441 for a discussion of focus groups). NRG also does phone surveys of moviegoers, and the former employees claim there are shady activities in this part of the business as well. For example, they claim that phone-room personnel routinely fill out unfinished questionnaires, and that test results are made up for movies when they can't find enough people to fill out questionnaires.

NRG disputes these claims and says that it would be impossible to falsify data because there is only a half hour between the time a test screening ends and the time preliminary data are conveyed to movie studio heads. The company also argues that if it were falsifying data, it would be much less accurate in its predictions of how much revenue a film will generate. NRG says its forecasts

of box office receipts are within 10 percent of those actually collected about 80 percent of the time.

Nielsen Media Research. This famous company has reported on the television viewing habits of North Americans for many years. In all that time, there seemed to be widespread acceptance that its market research was accurate. But suddenly in 1996, Nielsen reported a significant drop in the number of people watching television; as a result, broadcast networks might end up owing advertisers a lot of money because the networks are not delivering as large an audience as they promised when advertising rates were set.

How did the networks react to the latest Nielsen data? They claimed it was unreliable, and that the numbers were being generated from a sample of households that was different from those used in the past (Nielsen recently expanded the number of households it gathers data from).

It is a fact that gathering data on peoples' television viewing habits is becoming more difficult. In some markets, the system used involves an electronic meter attached to a TV set that determines what channel is being watched. A "people meter" is also part of this system; it tells *who* is watching. Viewers must punch in a preassigned number on their remote control whenever they start or stop watching. Critics say people forget to do this and so the data are inaccurate. In other markets, the classic "paper diary" is used to gather information. Viewers note their viewing habits for each quarter-hour, including the station they are watching, the channel number, and who is watching. This is a lot of work, and in some markets, less than one quarter of the targeted homes send in their diaries. Worse, one study showed that these diaries contained many errors.

Both NBC and Fox are considering a lawsuit against Nielsen after the ratings for NFL football dropped 7 percent. They also want changes made in their agreement with Nielsen before they renew it. Several networks are also spending $40 million to test a new market research system that will challenge Nielsen's within a few years. The work is being done by Statistical Research Inc., a company the networks have used in the past to check the accuracy of Nielsen's ratings.

◆

Certain businesses rely heavily on organizations like the National Research Group and Nielsen Media Research to provide data about their customers. But all businesses need information about their customers, and this important aspect of marketing will be explored in the next three chapters. We begin in this chapter by exploring the nature of marketing. As you will see, the marketing process is complex, requiring marketers to understand the nature of their product (and its place in the market) and the nature of their customers. The special problems of marketing internationally and of marketing for the small business are also addressed.

By focusing on the learning objectives of this chapter, you will gain a better understanding of such marketing activities and the ways in which marketing influences consumer purchases. After reading this chapter, you will be able to:

LEARNING OBJECTIVES

1. Define *marketing*.

2. Describe the five forces that constitute the *external marketing environment*.

3. Explain *market segmentation* and show how it is used in *target marketing*.

4. Explain the purpose and value of *market research*.

5. Describe the key factors that influence the *consumer buying process*.

6. Discuss the three categories of *organizational markets* and explain how *organizational buying behaviour* differs from consumer buying behaviour.

The Nature of Marketing

What do you think of when you think of marketing? If you are like most people, you probably think of advertising for something like detergent or soft drinks. But marketing is a much broader concept. **Marketing** is "the process of planning and executing the conception, pricing, promotion, and distribution of ideas, goods, and services to create exchanges that satisfy individual and organizational objectives."[1] In this section, we will dissect this definition to see what it encompasses.

marketing
Planning and executing the development, pricing, promotion, and distribution of ideas, goods, and services to create exchanges that satisfy both buyers' and sellers' objectives.

Marketing: Goods, Services, and Ideas

Marketing of tangible goods is obvious in our everyday life. You walk into a department store and a woman with a clipboard asks if you'd like to try a new cologne. A pharmaceutical company proclaims the virtues of its new cold medicine. Your local auto dealer offers an economy car at an economy

consumer goods
Products purchased by individuals for their personal use.

industrial goods
Products purchased by companies to use directly or indirectly to produce other products.

external environment
Outside factors that influence marketing programs by posing opportunities or threats.

price. These **consumer goods** are products that you, the consumer, buy for personal use. Firms that sell their products to the end user are engaged in *consumer marketing.*

Marketing is also applied to industrial goods. **Industrial goods** are items that are used by companies for production purposes or further assembly. Conveyors, lift trucks, and earth movers are all industrial goods, as are components and raw materials such as transistors, integrated circuits, coal, steel, and plastic. Firms that sell their products to other manufacturers are engaged in *industrial marketing.*

Marketing techniques can also be applied to services. *Service marketing* has become a major area of growth in the Canadian economy. Insurance companies, airlines, investment counsellors, clinics, and exterminators all engage in service marketing to consumers. Some firms market their services to other companies, for example, security guards, janitors, and accountants.

Finally, marketing can be applied to *ideas* as well as to goods and services. Television advertising and other promotional activities have made "participaction" a symbol of a healthy lifestyle.

The Marketing Environment

Marketing plans, decisions, and strategies are not determined unilaterally by any business—not even by marketers as experienced and influential as Coca-Cola and Procter & Gamble. Rather, they are strongly influenced by powerful outside forces. As you can see in Figure 15.1, any marketing program must recognize the outside factors that comprise a company's **external environment**. In this section, we will describe five of these environmental factors: the *political/legal, social/cultural, technological, economic,* and *competitive environments.*

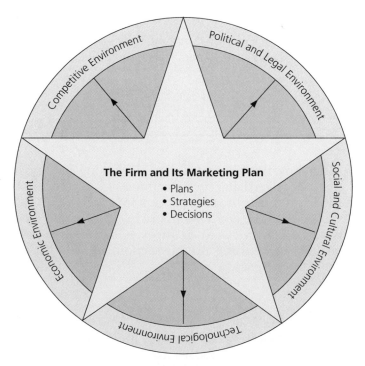

Figure 15.1
The external marketing environment.

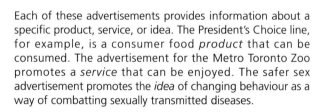

Each of these advertisements provides information about a specific product, service, or idea. The President's Choice line, for example, is a consumer food *product* that can be consumed. The advertisement for the Metro Toronto Zoo promotes a *service* that can be enjoyed. The safer sex advertisement promotes the *idea* of changing behaviour as a way of combatting sexually transmitted diseases.

Political and Legal Environment

Political activities, both foreign and domestic, have profound effects on business (refer back to Chapter 3 for a discussion of how government influences business).

To help shape their companies' futures, marketing managers try to maintain favourable political/legal environments in several ways. For example, to gain public support for their products and activities, marketing uses advertising campaigns for public awareness on issues of local, regional, or national importance. They also lobby and contribute to political candidates (although there are legal restrictions on how much they can contribute). Such activities sometimes result in favourable laws and regulations and may even open new international business opportunities.

Social and Cultural Environment

More women are entering the workforce, the number of single-parent families is increasing, food preferences and physical activities reflect the growing concern for healthful lifestyles, violent crimes are on the increase, and the growing recognition of cultural diversity continues. These and other issues reflect the values, beliefs, and ideas that form the fabric of Canadian society today. Obviously, these broad attitudes towards issues have direct effects on business. Today, for example, as we continue to insist on a "greener" Canada, we have seen the demise of freon in air conditioners and increased reliance on recycling materials in the goods that we consume.

By the same token, the need to recognize social values stimulates marketers to take fresh looks at the ways they conduct their business—say, developing and promoting new products for both consumers and industrial customers. Spalding, for example, has introduced a line of golf gear designed specifically for women. Naturally, such equipment requires new methods for advertising, promoting, and distributing products to meet the emerging preferences of women golfers.[2]

Technological Environment

Consider the phenomenon of DNA "fingerprinting." The O.J. Simpson trial and the Guy Paul Morin case, of course, have made just about everyone aware of its availability to law-enforcement officials. Bear in mind, however, that it is also the focal point of a new industry—one that involves biological science and laboratory analysis and instrumentation as well as criminology. DNA fingerprinting, then, is a product. Along with its technical developments, therefore, it involves marketing decisions—such as pricing and promotion. This has been the case with literally thousands of technological breakthroughs in such fields as genetics, electronics, aeronautics, medicine, information sciences, communications systems, and transportation.

New technologies affect marketing in several ways. Obviously, they create new goods (say, the satellite dish) and services (home television shopping). New products make some existing products obsolete (compact discs are replacing audiotapes), and many of them change our values and lifestyles. In turn, they often stimulate new goods and services not directly related to the new technology itself. Cellular phones, for example, not only facilitate business communication but free up time for recreation and leisure.

Economic Environment

Economic conditions determine spending patterns by consumers, businesses, and governments. Thus they influence every marketer's plans for product offerings, pricing, and promotional strategies. Among the more significant economic variables, marketers are concerned with inflation, interest rates, recession, and recovery. In other words, they must monitor the general business cycle, which typically features a pattern of transition from periods of prosperity to recession to recovery (return to prosperity). Not surprisingly, consumer spending increases as "consumer confidence" in economic conditions grows during periods of prosperity. Conversely it decreases during low-growth periods, when unemployment rises and purchasing power declines.

Traditionally, analysis of economic conditions focused on the national economy and the government's policies for controlling or moderating it. Increasingly, however, as nations form more and more economic connections, the "global economy" is becoming more prominent in the thinking of marketers everywhere. With pacts like the 1993 North American Free Trade Agreement and the 1994 General Agreement on Tariffs and Trade now in place, global economic conditions—indeed, conditions from nation to nation—will directly influence the economic fortunes of all trading partners (see Chapter 4). Certainly, marketers must now consider this new—and perhaps unpredictable—economic variable in developing both domestic and foreign marketing strategies.

Competitive Environment

In a competitive environment, marketers must convince buyers that they should purchase their products rather than those of some other seller. In a broad sense, because both consumers and commercial buyers have limited resources to spend, every dollar spent to buy one product is no longer available for other purchases. Each marketing program, therefore, seeks to make its product the most attractive; theoretically, a failed program loses the buyer's dollar forever (or at least until it is time for the next purchase decision).

By studying the competition, marketers determine how best to position their own products for three specific types of competition:

- **Substitute products** are dissimilar from those of competitors but can fulfil the same need. For example, your cholesterol level may be controlled with either a physical-fitness program or a drug regimen; the fitness program and the drugs compete as substitute products.

   substitute product
   Product that is dissimilar from those of competitors but that can fulfil the same need.

- **Brand competition** occurs between similar products, such as the auditing services provided by large accounting firms like Ernst & Young and KPMG Peat Marwick. The competition is based on buyers' perceptions of the benefits of products offered by particular companies.

   brand competition
   Competitive marketing that appeals to consumer perceptions of similar products.

- **International competition** matches the products of domestic marketers against those of foreign competitors—say, a flight on Swissair versus Air Canada. The intensity of international competition has been heightened by the formation of alliances like the European Union and NAFTA.

   international competition
   Competitive marketing of domestic against foreign products.

Planning and Executing Marketing Strategy

As a business activity, marketing requires management. Although many individuals also contribute to the marketing of a product, a company's **marketing managers** are typically responsible for planning and implementing all the marketing-mix activities that result in the transfer of goods or services to its customers. These activities culminate in the **marketing plan**: a detailed and focused strategy for gearing marketing activities to meet consumer needs and wants. Marketing, therefore, begins when a company identifies a consumer need and develops a product to meet it. One way of identifying those needs,

marketing managers
Responsible for planning and implementing all the marketing-mix activities that result in the transfer of goods or services to customers.

marketing plan
A detailed strategy for gearing the marketing mix to meet consumer needs and wants.

market research, is explored later in this chapter. Here, however, we begin by noting two important aspects of the larger market-planning process: developing the marketing plan and setting marketing goals.

Developing the Marketing Plan

Marketing managers must realize that planning takes time. Indeed, the marketing-planning process may begin years before a product becomes available for sale. For example, the Dutch electronics firm Philips (its major label is Magnavox) developed such products as VCRs and compact discs years before these products actually hit the market. And although Philips has recently invested $1 billion in the planning and development of advanced semiconductor memory chips, the company is not assured of success. Without such planning and preparation, however, the electronics line would have little or no chance of success in a highly competitive market.[3]

Setting Goals for Performance

Marketing managers—like all managers—must set objectives and goals and then establish ways to evaluate performance. An insurance company, for example, might establish the goal of increasing sales by 10 percent in its western and central Canadian sales districts. The district sales managers' performances will be evaluated against that goal. Or, a consumer products company might set a goal to reduce by 30 percent the time it takes to bring a new product to market.

The Marketing Concept

Increased competition and the growth of consumer discretionary income has given added impetus to an idea that had its beginnings early in the 20th century. This idea or philosophy, known as the **marketing concept**, means that the whole firm is coordinated to achieve one goal—to serve its present and potential customers and to do so at a profit. This concept means that a firm must get to know what customers really want and to follow closely the changes in tastes that occur. The various departments of the firm—marketing, production, finance, and human resources—must operate as a system, well coordinated and unified in the pursuit of a common goal—customer satisfaction.

The importance of customer satisfaction has been recognized at IBM, which introduced a scheme that influences the pay of 350 managers. Up to 15 percent of their pay is tied to how satisfied their customers are. Bell Canada has a similar scheme; team awards are based partly on customer satisfaction.[4] Japan Air Lines' 747s are equipped with video monitors in the armrests so that passengers may choose exactly what they want to watch from a movie library. At Air France, a passenger who purchases a first-class ticket to Paris can upgrade to the Concorde at no extra cost.[5]

The Marketing Mix

In planning and implementing their marketing strategies, managers rely on the four principal elements of marketing. These four elements, often called the Four Ps of marketing, are *p*roduct (including developing goods, services, and ideas), *p*ricing, *p*romotion, and *p*lace (distribution).[6] Together, these elements are known as the **marketing mix**, depicted in Figure 15.2.

There are many possible combinations of the four elements in the marketing mix. Price might play a large role in selling fresh meat but a very small role in selling newspapers. Distribution might be crucial in marketing

Philips
http://www.philips.com

marketing concept
The idea that the whole firm is directed towards serving present and potential customers at a profit.

marketing mix
The combination of product, pricing, promotion, and distribution strategies used in marketing a product.

Figure 15.2
Choosing the marketing mix for a business.

gasoline but not so important for lumber. Promotion could be vital in toy marketing but of little consequence in marketing nails. The product is important in every case but probably less so for toothpaste than for cars.

Product

Clearly, no business can undertake marketing activities without a **product**—a good, service, or idea that attempts to fulfil consumers' wants. The conception or development of new products is a continual challenge. Businesses must take into account changing technology, consumer wants and needs, and economic conditions, among other factors. A 1997 Statistics Canada study showed the percentage of Canadian households that owned the following items: VCR (85 percent), microwave oven (86.3 percent), compact disc player (25 percent), personal computer (33 percent), and dishwasher (48.5 percent). Most of these products did not even exist 25 years ago.[7]

Having the product that consumers desire may mean changing existing products. For example, in the clothing industry, manufacturers must be alert to changes in fashion, which often occur rapidly and unpredictably. And as computer technology changes, so must many computer products, such as application programs.

Manufacturers may also develop new products and enter markets in which they have not previously competed. Consumer food giants such as Kraft Inc., General Mills, Sara Lee, and Quaker Oats have entered the institutional and restaurant food-service markets. They have modified consumer food mixes for the mass production needed in prisons, hospitals, schools, and restaurants.

Producers may develop new or "improved" goods and services for the sake of product differentiation. **Product differentiation** is the creation of a product or product image that differs enough from existing products to attract consumers. Product differentiation does not always mean a change in how a product functions. But when successful, it always means a change in how customers react. For example, early kitchen and laundry appliances were available only in white. Frigidaire capitalized on this situation, offering comparably priced and performing appliances, but in colours. Procter & Gamble is a master at product differentiation, working to make its products not only different from those of other firms but also from its own competing goods.

Services can also be sources of differentiation. One company has developed a computer system so that its customers at retail home centres and lumber yards can custom-design decks and shelving. As a result, the company has differentiated its commodity two-by-fours by turning them into premium products. We discuss product development in Chapter 16.

Pricing

The second element of the marketing mix is the **pricing** of products. Deciding on the most appropriate price for the market is not easy. The price of the product must support the operating costs of the organization, administrative and research costs, and marketing costs such as advertising and sales salaries.

product
A good, service, or idea that satisfies buyers' needs and demands.

product differentiation
The creation of a product or product image that differs enough from existing products to attract consumers.

pricing
That part of the marketing mix concerned with choosing the appropriate price for a product to meet the firm's profit objectives and buyers' purchasing objectives.

Both low or high price strategies may be appropriate for a company under various situations. Low prices will generally lead to a larger volume of sales. High prices will usually limit the size of the market, but will increase a firm's profits per unit. In some cases, however, high prices may actually attract customers by implying that the product is especially good or rare. We will discuss pricing in more detail in Chapter 17.

Promotion

promotion

That part of the marketing mix concerned with selecting the appropriate technique for selling a product to a consumer.

advertising

Any promotional technique involving paid, nonpersonal communication used by an identified sponsor to persuade or inform a large number of people about a product.

personal selling

A promotional technique involving the use of person-to-person communication to sell products.

sales promotion

A promotional technique involving one-time direct inducements to buyers (such as coupons, sales displays, and contests) to purchase a product.

public relations

Any promotional activity directed at building good relations with various sectors of the population of buyers.

The most visible component of the marketing mix is **promotion**, those techniques designed to sell a product to consumers. Promotional tools include advertising, personal selling, sales promotions, and public relations. Chapter 16 explores the promotion of products in more depth.

In marketing terms, **advertising** is any form of paid, nonpersonal communication used by an identified sponsor to persuade or inform certain audiences about a good, service, or idea. Advertising may be done through television, radio, magazines, newspapers, billboards or any other type of broadcast or print media.

Automobiles, appliances, and stereo equipment are often promoted through the use of **personal selling**—person-to-person sales. However, the bulk of personal selling occurs with industrial goods. Purchasing agents and other members of a business who require information about a product's technical qualities and price are usually referred to the selling company's sales representatives.

Less expensive items are often marketed through the use of **sales promotions**. Sales promotions can take many forms. Premiums (gifts included with the product), trading stamps, coupons, and package inserts are all sales promotions meant to tempt consumers to buy more of a product. Free samples, exhibits, and trade shows give customers an opportunity to try the product or talk with company representatives. The prevalence of self-service retail outlets has led marketers to think about package design—the "silent seller"—as an important sales promotion.

Public relations includes all promotional activities directed at building good relations with various sectors of the population. Many public relations activities are good deeds paid for by companies. Sponsorship of softball

By providing both distribution and advertising for Levi's, this truck plays a dual role in the company's marketing.

teams, Special Olympics, and automobile racing teams are examples of public relations efforts. Companies may also use public relations activities to boost employee morale.

Publicity also refers to a firm's efforts to communicate to the public, usually through mass media. Publicity, however, is not paid for by the firm, nor does the firm control the content of publicity. Publicity, therefore, can sometimes hurt a business. For example, Dun & Bradstreet received considerable negative publicity when newspapers and magazines reported that it was billing its customers for financial reports they did not need.

publicity
A promotional technique that involves nonpaid communication about a product or firm and that is outside the control of the firm.

Place (Distribution)

Getting a product into a retail store requires transportation, decisions about direct sales, and a number of other **distribution** processes. Transportation options include moving merchandise by air, land, or pipeline, and, more specifically, by railroad, truck, air freight, or steamship.

Decisions about direct sales can affect a firm's overall marketing strategy. Many manufacturers sell their products to other companies who, in turn, distribute the goods to retailers. Some companies sell directly to major retailers such as Sears, Kmart, and Safeway. Still others sell directly to the final consumer. Chapter 17 presents more detail on distribution decisions.

distribution
That part of the marketing mix concerned with getting products from the producer to the buyer, including physical transportation and choice of sales outlets.

Target Marketing and Market Segmentation

Marketing managers long ago recognized that they cannot be "all things to all people." People have different tastes, different interests, different goals, different lifestyles, and so on. The marketing concept's recognition of consumers' various needs and wants led marketing managers to think in terms of target marketing. **Target markets** are groups of people with similar wants and needs.

Target marketing clearly requires **market segmentation**, dividing a market into categories of customer types or "segments." For example, Mr. Big-and-Tall sells to men who are taller and heavier than average. Certain special interest magazines are oriented towards people with specific interests (see Table 15.1). Once they have identified market segments, companies may adopt a variety of product strategies. Some firms decide to provide a range of products to the market in an attempt to market their products to more than one segment. For example, General Motors of Canada offers compact cars,

target market
Any group of people who have similar wants and needs and may be expected to show interest in the same product(s).

market segmentation
Dividing a market into categories according to traits customers have in common.

Table 15.1   Magazines with Specific Target Audiences

Accounting	**Fishing/Hunting**
CA Magazine	*Western Canada Outdoors*
CGA Magazine	*The Atlantic Salmon Journal*
CMA Update	*B.C. Outdoor Fishing Guide*
Agriculture	**Automotive**
Agro-Nouvelles	*Aftermarket Canada*
Canada Poultry	*Bodyshop*
Country Life in B.C.	*Canadian Automotive Trade*
Sports	**Boating**
B.C. Athletics Record	*Boating Business*
Canadian Squash	*Canadian Boating*
Athletics Canada	*Porthole Magazine*
Gardening	**Music**
Canadian Gardening News	*Billboard*
Prairie Landscape Magazine	*Guitar Player*
Landscape Ontario	*Rolling Stone*

Rolls-Royce
http://www.rolls-royce.com

positioning
The process of fixing, adapting, and communicating the nature of the product.

vans, trucks, luxury cars, and sports cars with various features and prices. Their strategy is to provide an automobile for nearly every segment of the market.

In contrast, some businesses restrict production to one market segment. Rolls-Royce understands that only a relatively small number of people are willing to pay $310 000 for exclusive touring limousines. Rolls, therefore, makes no attempt to cover the entire range of possible products; instead, it markets only to a very small segment of the total automobile buyers market.

Table 15.2 shows how the radio market might be segmented by a marketer of home-electronic equipment. Note that segmentation is a strategy for analyzing consumers, not products. The analysis in Table 15.2, for example, identifies consumer-users—joggers, commuters, travellers. Only *indirectly*, then, does it focus on the uses of the product itself. In marketing, the process of fixing, adapting, and communicating the nature of the product itself is called **positioning**.

Identifying Market Segments

By definition, the members of a market segment must share some common traits or behaviours that will affect their purchasing decisions. In identifying market segments, researchers look at geographic, demographic, psychographic, and product-use variables.

Geographics

In some cases, where people live affects their buying decisions. The heavy rainfall in British Columbia prompts its inhabitants to purchase more umbrellas than does Arizona's desert. Urban residents have less demand for four-wheel drive vehicles than do their rural counterparts. Sailboats sell better along both coasts than they do in the prairie provinces.

These patterns affect marketing decisions about what products to offer, at what price to sell them, how to promote them, and how to distribute them. For example, consider marketing down parkas in rural Saskatchewan. Demand will be high, price competition may be limited, local newspaper advertising may be very effective, and the best location may be one easily reached from several small towns.

Table 15.2 **Possible Segmentation of the Radio Market**

Segmentation	Product/Target Market
Age	Inexpensive, unbreakable, portable models for young children
	Inexpensive equipment—possibly portable—for teens
	Moderate-to-expensive equipment for adults
Consumer attitude	Sophisticated components for audio buffs
	All-in-one units in furniture cabinets for those concerned with room appearance
Product use	Miniature models for joggers and commuters
	"Boom box" portables for taking outdoors
	Car stereo systems for travelling
	Components and all-in-one units for home use
Location	Battery-powered models for use where electricity is unavailable
	AC current for North American users
	DC current for other users

Demographics

A variety of demographic characteristics are important to marketers. As we noted in earlier chapters, demographics include traits such as age, income, gender, ethnic background, marital status, race, religion, and social class. Many marketers, for example, have discovered that university and community college students are an important market segment. Students across Canada have discretionary income totalling $4 to $5 billion. Ford Motor of Canada has marketed to students since the mid-1980s, and gives graduates a $750 rebate on their first-time purchase of a car. Table 15.3 lists some demographic market segments. Note that these are objective criteria that cannot be altered. Marketers must work with or around them.

Demographics affect how a firm markets its product. For example, marketing managers may well divide a market into age groups such as 18–25, 26–35, 36–45 and so on. A number of general consumption characteristics that can be attributed to these age groups help marketing managers develop specific plans.[8] As a result, a community whose population is heavily dominated by young adults will most likely feature more fast-food restaurants and stores selling blue jeans and records than will a town with a high percentage of retirees. The box "Teenagers: An International Market Segment" describes similarities across countries in the 13–19 age group.

Psychographics

Members of a market can also be segmented according to **psychographic** (mental) traits such as their motives, attitudes, activities, interests, and opinions. Psychographics are of particular interest to marketers because, unlike demographics and geographics, they can be changed by marketing efforts. The box "Psychological Market Research" describes how consumers can be segmented by psychological variables.

Psychographics are particularly important to marketers because, unlike demographics and geographics, they can sometimes be changed by marketing

psychographics
A method of market segmentation involving psychological traits that a group has in common, including motives, attitudes, activities, interests, and opinions.

Table 15.3	Demographic Market Segmentation
Age	Under 5; 5–11; 12–19; 20–34; 35–49; 50–64; 65+
Education	Grade school or less; some high school; graduated high school; some college or university; college diploma or university degree; advanced degree
Family life cycle	Young single, young married without children; young married with children; older married with children under 18; older married without children under 18; older single; other
Family size	1, 2–3, 4–5, 6+
Income	Under $9000; $9000–$14 999; $15 000–$25 000; over $25 000
Nationality	Including but not limited to African, Asian, British, Eastern European, French, German, Irish, Italian, Latin American, Middle Eastern, and Scandinavian
Race	Including but not limited to Inuit, Asian, Black, and White
Religion	Including but not limited to Buddhist, Catholic, Hindu, Jewish, Muslim, and Protestant
Sex	Male, female
Language	Including but not limited to English, French, Inuktitut, Italian, Ukrainian, and German

International Report

Teenagers: An International Market Segment

We all know that trends spread rapidly through the ranks of teenagers. But that tendency is now accelerating internationally. Teens around the world have amazingly similar preferences for consumer products. BSB Worldwide, an advertising agency, videotaped teenagers' rooms in 25 different countries. From the items on display, it was hard to tell whether the room was in Mexico City, Tokyo, or Los Angeles.

The biggest beneficiary of this trend appears to be U.S. companies. The hot new trends in the U.S. often pop up in many other countries as well. Because the populations of Asia and Latin America are much younger than the population of North America, the teen market is big business. For example, the total number of 10- to 19-year-olds in Brazil, Argentina, and Mexico is 57 million; in the U.S., the total is only 35 million.

The most unifying force among teenagers is television. Satellite TV is helping to unify patchworks of domestic markets, and companies can mount Europe- or Asia-wide campaigns. No network is more popular than MTV, which is a monster hit in Europe and is watched by more households there than in the U.S. It broadcasts news and socially conscious programming, and is creating a Euro-language of simplified English.

MTV also promotes little-known European musicians and has the power to make them big stars in other countries. For example, it helped the Swedish group Ace of Base have a top 10 hit in Germany, Italy, Britain, and the U.S. MTV has a roster of 200 advertisers, including Levi Strauss, Procter & Gamble, Johnson & Johnson, Apple Computer, and Pepsi Cola. These firms advertise on MTV because it reaches the market segment they want.

MTV may cause a revolution in worldwide marketing. At present, it is difficult to sell the same products to 35-year-olds in different countries because they never were exposed to anything but products from the country where they were raised. Not so for the upcoming generation of teenagers. They see (and buy) products from various countries and will probably continue to do so as they get older. Two famous brand names, Coke and Pepsi, are already competing vigorously to attract international teens to use their product.

Fashion fads are also spreading around the world. Hip-hop, first popularized by African-Americans, means wearing loose-fitting urban street wear, baggy jeans, sweat shirts, hiking boots, athletic shoes, and baseball caps (worn backwards). Within this fashion category, certain brands have become very popular. Levi jeans, Nike or Reebok athletic shoes, and Timberland boots are some of the brands that have profited.

Sports is the other universal language of teenagers. Basketball stars like Michael Jordan and Shaquille O'Neal have high name recognition overseas. In a poll of Chinese students in rural Shaanxi province, Michael Jordan tied with former Chinese premier Zhou En-lai for the title "World's Greatest Man." Not surprisingly, testimonial advertisements by big-name sports stars have a big impact on potential buyers. It is not uncommon for students to own multiple pairs of Nike Air Jordans.

Teen tastes in consumer electronics are also similar across countries. Kodak is developing an advertising campaign directed specifically at teenagers in the hope that when they have their own children they will use Kodak products to take pictures of them. Teens are also more comfortable with personal computers than their parents are. So, even if the parents are buying the machine, the teen determines what brand is purchased.

MTV
http://www.mtv.com

---

efforts. For example, many companies have succeeded in changing at least some consumers' opinions by running ads highlighting products that have been improved directly in response to consumer desires. General Motors used this approach in the development and promotion of Saturns. GM gained an improved image by advertising its intended new design in conjunction with consumer-preferred features such as a one-price policy, careful selection of employees, high product quality, emphasis on quality, customer convenience during servicing, and extensive warranty coverage.

Product-Use Variables

This fourth way of segmenting looks at how group members use a good or service, their brand loyalty, and why they purchase the product. A woman's shoe maker, for example, might find three segments—athletic, casual, and dress shoes. Each market segment is looking for different benefits in a shoe. A woman buying an athletic shoe will probably not care much about its

The Canadian Business Scene

Psychological Market Research

Psychological researchers try to determine consumers' subconscious desires so that companies (or political parties) can develop products (or candidates) that will appeal to them. During the Ontario election campaign in 1990, the NDP conducted psychological research using focus groups (discussed on p. 441) which showed that the voters viewed their leader, Bob Rae, as a harmless-looking fellow. The research also showed that voters did not like the terms "the little man" or "the ordinary person." In response, the campaign avoided those terms and Rae developed a more commanding presence. The NDP won that election but was defeated in 1995.

Traditional market research focuses on quantitative data such as the number of people in certain age groups, the income levels of consumers, and structured responses from consumers about what they like or dislike. Qualitative research, on the other hand, is based on the assumption that consumers may be unwilling or unable to state exactly what it is about a product that attracts them (the product may calm their fears, increase their feelings of power or sexuality, make them feel competent, etc.).

Some of the techniques that marketers are currently using may seem strange. The most popular one at present is "let's pretend." Members of a focus group may, for example, be asked to pretend that a brand of beer is a car. They then state what car they think best represents the brand of beer. In one focus group, participants were asked to imagine that they were competing brands of dog food; they were then asked to come up with ways to entice the dog to eat the food they represented.

Although the techniques may seem bizarre, major companies including Lever Brothers Ltd., General Foods Inc., Sanyo Canada Inc., Procter & Gamble, Bell Canada, and Royal Trust have used them. It is estimated that marketers spend about $30 million per year in Canada on qualitative psychological research.

A typical success story of psychological research comes from Campbell's Soup. Campbell's was steadily losing market share. To counteract this trend, the company tried to develop a snappy image that stressed convenience. However, qualitative psychological research revealed that parental concern for children was a more promising theme. When advertisements began running that showed a loving mother preparing soup for her child, sales turned around.

---

appearance, but she will care a great deal about arch support, traction offered by the sole, and sturdiness. In contrast, a woman buying a casual shoe will want it to look good but be comfortable, while a woman buying a dress shoe may require a specific colour or style and accept some discomfort and a relatively fragile shoe.

Market Segmentation: A Caution

Segmentation must be done carefully. A group of people may share an age category, income level, or some other segmentation variable, but their spending habits may be quite different. Look at your friends in school. You may all be approximately the same age, but you have different needs and wants. Some of you may wear cashmere sweaters while others wear sweatshirts. The same holds true for income. University professors and truck drivers frequently earn about the same level of income. However, their spending patterns, tastes, and wants are generally quite different.

In Canada, the two dominant cultures—English and French—show significant differences in consumer attitudes and behaviour. Researchers have found, for example, that compared to English Canadians, French Canadians are more involved with home and family, attend ballet more often, travel less, eat more chocolate, and are less interested in convenience food. Obviously, prudent marketers should take these differences into account when developing marketing plans. This is, however, easier said than done.

It is one thing to know that consumers in Quebec buy large quantities of certain products; it is quite another to capitalize on these differences. One problem is that differences may not continue over time. Change is continually occurring in consumption patterns across Canada, and data may quickly become outdated. Another problem is that consumption patterns differ from region to region in Canada even where culture is not the main cause. The buying behaviour of Quebec and Ontario consumers may be more similar than the behaviour of British Columbia and Newfoundland consumers.

Market Research

market research

The systematic study of what buyers need and how best to meet those needs.

Market research can greatly improve the accuracy and effectiveness of market segmentation.[9] **Market research**, the study of what buyers need and how best to meet those needs, can address any element in the marketing mix. One marketer might study how consumers respond to an experimental paint formula. Another might explore how potential buyers will respond to a possible price reduction on calculators. Still another marketer might check audience response to a proposed advertising campaign with a humorous theme. A company manager might also try to learn whether customers will be more likely to buy a product in a store, a mall, or a special discount shop. But market research is no guarantee of success.

Most companies will benefit from market research, but they need not do the research themselves. O-Pee-Chee Co. Ltd. of London, Ontario (the bubble gum and candy manufacturer), does no market research and no product testing, yet it continues to be successful in a market where products change at a dizzying pace. By signing a licensing agreement with two U.S. giants, O-Pee-Chee simply has to look at what's hot in the U.S. and then start manufacturing those lines in Canada.[10]

The importance of selling products in today's international markets is expanding the role of market research into new areas. For example, when companies decide to sell their goods or services in other countries, they must decide whether to standardize products or to specialize them for new markets.

Consider the case of Pepsico when it entered a joint venture to market Cheetos in Guangdong province, China. Originally, Cheetos—crispy cheese puff snacks—did not "test well" in China. The Chinese, it seems, do not eat cheese and did not care for Cheetos' cheesy taste. Pepsico tested more than 600 flavours (including Roasted Cuttlefish) on more than 1000 Chinese consumers before arriving at two—Savoury American Cream and Zesty Japanese Steak. Chinese packaging will bear the Chinese characters "qui duo," pronounced "CHEE dwaugh." "Luckily," explains the general manager of Pepsico Foods International, "the translation is 'new surprise,' instead of some phrase that might offend people."

The box "Romancing the Profits" describes the experience of Harlequin Enterprises in doing market research on customers in foreign countries.

The Research Process

Market research can occur at almost any point in a product's existence. Most commonly, however, it is used when a new or altered product is being considered. To see why, you need to understand the steps in performing market research illustrated in Figure 15.3 on page 440.

The process begins with a *study of the current situation*. In other words, what is the need and what is being done to meet it at this point? Such a study should note how well the firm is or is not doing in meeting the need.

The second step is to *select a research method*. As you will see shortly, marketing managers have a wide range of methods available. In choosing a method, marketers must bear in mind the effectiveness and costs of different methods.

secondary data

Information already available to market researchers as a result of previous research by the firm or other agencies.

The next step is to *collect data*. **Secondary data** are information already available as a result of previous research by the firm or other agencies. For example, Statistics Canada publishes a great deal of data that are useful for business firms.

The Canadian Business Scene

Romancing the Profits

The largest romance publisher on earth occupies an uninspired office building in Toronto. Harlequin Enterprises Ltd., which started in Winnipeg in 1949, now has sales revenue exceeding $400 million annually. Its profits accounted for 83 percent of the total profits of its parent, Torstar Corp., the publisher of the *Toronto Star*. With the emergence of the women's liberation movement in the 1970s, skeptics predicted that romance novels were finished, but it hasn't worked out that way. Romance novels now account for 44 percent of all mass-market paperbacks sold in North America, and Harlequin controls 80 percent of that market.

The company also has a strong presence in overseas markets. By 1995, it will sell 45 million books in Eastern Europe alone; it also plans to start selling romances in China. Harlequin offers translations in 24 languages, and prints its books in 16 regions around the world. Interestingly, the book covers remain pretty much the same worldwide, including the emphasis on Caucasians.

When deciding whether to enter a foreign country, Harlequin looks for three things: First, there must be a distribution system already in place because it is prohibitively expensive to set one up. Second, there must be access to TV and print media so that demand can be stimulated through advertising. Third, the company must be able to convert the money it receives for books into dollars. The company has been reluctant to enter Russia because it does not really satisfy any of these criteria. In China, however, where the free market system is growing daily, the company has big plans.

How has Harlequin managed to achieve such success? A major reason is its emphasis on market research. The average reader is around 40, and half have a college education. Over half are employed. Research has shown that readers abroad have the same interests as North American readers. Focus groups and major surveys of North American consumers are a key part of Harlequin's strategic planning.

Readers of romance novels are not a demographic group to be trifled with. They want plot-driven books with lots of action. In all the romance books, the focal couple first meet, then have a misunderstanding, and then make up by the end of the book. Readers know there will be no violence and there will always be a happy ending.

The company has experienced some frustrations in gathering market research data. Because bookstores and other retail outlets take books on consignment, they can return any they don't sell. Thus, the publisher may ship products to retailers, but there is no guarantee of sales. Worse, it takes many months to determine how well a book is doing, and if it is selling particularly well or poorly. Executives at Harlequin say that if book sales could be accurately counted from week to week, Harlequin's books would take all 10 spots on the *New York Times* bestseller list.

Harlequin is developing new products by expanding into TV. For many years, film companies have courted the company, hoping to tap into its library and exploit its loyal readers. Now, the firm has signed a 50-50 partnership agreement with Alliance Communications Corp., Canada's largest independent film producer. Harlequin will supply the editorial work, and Alliance will produce the films. Six movies will be made in the first year of the arrangement, with 26 eventually being made each year. Eventually, the goal is to have a "Harlequin Night of the Week" on TV. The second part of the deal begins after several movies have been made. Then, Harlequin and Alliance will jointly market the movies on videocassettes.

Harlequin Enterprises Ltd.
http://www.romance.net

Using secondary data can save time, effort, and money. But in some cases secondary data are unavailable or inadequate, so **primary data**—new research by the firm or its agents—must be obtained. Hostess Frito-Lay, the maker of Doritos, spent a year studying how to best reach its target market—teenagers. The researchers hung around shopping malls, schools, and fast-food outlets to watch teenagers.[11]

Once data have been collected, marketers need to *analyze the data*. As we shall see in Chapter 18, data are not useful until they have been organized into information.

Marketing personnel then need to share their analysis with others by *preparing a report*. This report should include a summary of the study's methodology and findings. It should also identify alternative solutions (where appropriate) and make recommendations for the appropriate course of action.

primary data

Information developed through new research by the firm or its agents.

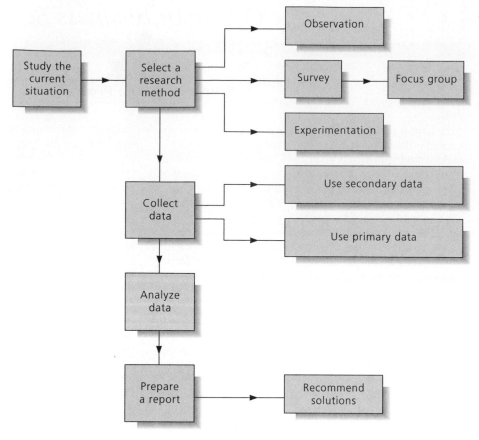

Figure 15.3
Steps in performing market research.

Research Methods

The four basic types of methods used by market researchers are observation, survey, focus groups, and experimentation. Probably the oldest form of market research is simple **observation** of what is happening. A store owner notices that customers are buying red children's wagons, not green. The owner re-orders more red wagons, the manufacturer's records show high sales of red wagons, and marketing concludes that customers want red wagons. Today, computerized systems allow marketers to "observe" consumers' preferences rapidly and with tremendous accuracy. For example, electronic scanners in supermarkets enable store owners to see what is and is not selling without having to check the shelves. Observation is also a popular research method because it is relatively low in cost, often drawing on data that must be collected for some other reason, such as reordering, anyway.

Sometimes, however, observation of current events is not enough. In many cases, marketers need to ask questions about new marketing ideas. One way to get answers is by conducting a **survey**. The heart of any survey is a questionnaire that is mailed to individuals for their completion or is used as the basis of telephone or personal interviews. Surveys can be expensive to carry out and may vary widely in their accuracy. Because no firm can afford to survey everyone, marketers must be careful to get a representative group of respondents. They must also construct their questions so that they get honest answers that address the specific issue being researched.

Some companies have their workers contact consumers directly to get information about how they feel about the company's product. Honda's "E.T. Phone Home Project" involved factory workers calling over 47 000 owners to

observation

A market research technique involving viewing or otherwise monitoring consumer buying patterns.

survey

A market research technique based on questioning a representative sample of consumers about purchasing attitudes and practices.

Focus groups, used by many firms, bring people together to talk about a product or service. This market research technique allows selected issues to be discussed in depth.

find out if they were happy with the car and to get ideas for further improvements. The changes that were suggested appeared in the 1995 and 1996 Honda Accords. At Hewlett-Packard, every bit of customer feedback is assigned to an "owner" who must act on the information and report back to the consumer who called. For example, if a complaint about a printer is received, an employee checks the company's database to see if the complaint is widespread and what the company is doing about it.[12]

Many firms also use **focus groups**, where six to 15 people are brought together to talk about a product or service. A moderator leads the group's discussion, and employees from the sponsoring company may observe the proceedings from behind a one-way mirror. The people in the focus group are not usually told which company is sponsoring the research. The comments of people in the focus group are taped, and then researchers go through the data looking for common themes.

Union Gas Ltd. and Levi Strauss have set up focus groups to ask employees about their needs. John Deere uses focus groups of farmers to discuss its tractors. From these discussions have come many specific suggestions for changes in the product (for example, turning off the tractor with a key, different ways to change the oil filter, and making the steps up to the tractor cab wider).[13]

At their best, focus groups allow researchers to explore issues too complex for questionnaires and can produce creative solutions. But because a focus group is small, its responses may not represent the larger market. Focus groups are most often used as a prelude to some other form of research.

The last major form of market research, experimentation, also tries to get answers to questions that surveys cannot address. As in science, **experimentation** in market research attempts to compare the responses of the same or similar individuals under different circumstances. For example, a firm trying to decide whether or not to include walnuts in a new candy bar probably would not learn much by asking people what they thought of the idea. But if it made up some bars with nuts and some without and then asked people to try both, the responses could be very helpful. Experimentation is, however, very expensive. In deciding whether to use it or any other research method, marketers must carefully weigh the costs against the possible benefits.

focus group

A market research technique involving a small group of people brought together and allowed to discuss selected issues in depth.

experimentation

A market research technique in which the reactions of similar people are compared under different circumstances.

Understanding Consumer Behaviour

Market research in its many forms can be of great help to marketing managers in understanding how the common traits of a market segment affect consumers' purchasing decisions. Why do people buy VCRs? What desire are they fulfilling? Is there a psychological or sociological explanation for why consumers purchase one product and not another? These questions and many others are addressed in the area of marketing known as consumer behaviour. **Consumer behaviour** focuses on the decision process by which customers come to purchase and consume a product or service.

consumer behaviour

The study of the process by which customers come to purchase and consume a product or service.

Influences on Consumer Behaviour

According to the not-so-surprising title of one classic study, we are very much "social animals."[14] To understand consumer behaviour, then, marketers draw heavily on the fields of psychology and sociology. The result is a focus on four major influences on consumer behaviour: *psychological, personal, social,* and *cultural.* By identifying the four influences that are most active, marketers try to explain consumer choices and predict future purchasing behaviour:

- *Psychological influences* include an individual's motivations, perceptions, ability to learn, and attitudes.

- *Personal influences* include lifestyle, personality, economic status, and life-cycle stage.

- *Social influences* include family, opinion leaders (people whose opinions are sought by others), and reference groups such as friends, co-workers, and professional associates.

- *Cultural influences* include culture (the "way of living" that distinguishes one large group from another), subculture (smaller groups, such as ethnic groups, with shared values), and social class (the cultural ranking of groups according to criteria such as background, occupation, and income).

All these factors can have a strong impact on the products that people purchase—often in complex ways.

The purchase of some products is not influenced by psychosocial factors. Consumers with high brand loyalty are less subject to such influences—they stick with the brand of their preference. However, the clothes that you wear, the food that you eat, and the dishes you eat from often reflect social and psychological influences on your consuming behaviour.

The Consumer Buying Process

Researchers who have studied consumer behaviour have constructed models that help marketing managers understand how consumers come to purchase products. Figure 15.4 presents one such model. At the base of this and similar models is an awareness of the psychosocial influences that lead to consumption. Ultimately, marketing managers use this information to develop marketing plans.

Problem Recognition

The buying process begins when a consumer becomes aware of a problem or need. After strenuous exercise, you may recognize that you are thirsty and need

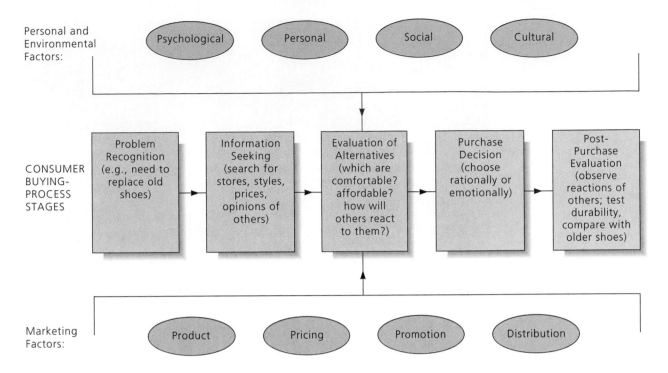

Figure 15.4
A model of the consumer buying process.

refreshment. After the birth of twins, you may find your one-bedroom apartment too small for comfort. After standing in the rain to buy movie tickets, you may decide to buy an umbrella.

Need recognition also occurs when you have a chance to change your purchasing habits. For example, the income from your first job after graduation will let you purchase items that were too expensive when you were a student. You may also discover a need for professional clothing, apartment furnishings, and cars. Visa and The Bay recognize this shift and market their credit cards to graduates.

Information Seeking

Having recognized a need, consumers seek information. This search is not always extensive. If you are thirsty, you may ask where the soda pop machine is, but that may be the extent of your information search. Other times you simply rely on your memory for information.

Before making major purchases, however, most people seek information from personal sources, marketing sources, public sources, and experience. For example, if you move to a new town, you will want to find out who is the best local dentist, physician, hair stylist, butcher, or pizza maker. To get this information, you may check with personal sources such as acquaintances, co-workers, and relatives. Before buying an exercise bike, you may go to the library and read the latest *Consumer Reports*—a public source of consumer ratings—on such equipment. You may also ask market sources such as the salesclerk or rely on direct experience. For example, you might test ride the bike to learn more before you buy.

Some sellers treat information as a value to be added to their products. For example, Body Shop International, a cosmetics manufacturer and retailer with no marketing or advertising department, has nevertheless been cited as a model of how to sell in the 1990s. The company's philosophy includes

Consumer Reports
http://www.Consumer-Reports.org

What information is this shopper looking for to decide on his purchase? Marketers would like to know how and why he makes his choices.

giving the customer product information rather than the traditional sales pitch. What makes this strategy work? The typical Body Shop customer is a skeptical consumer who generally distrusts advertising and sales hype, demands more product information, and is loyal to companies that, like the Body Shop, are perceived to be socially and environmentally responsible.[15]

Evaluation of Alternatives

The next step in the consumer decision process is to evaluate your alternatives. If you are in the market for a set of golf clubs, you probably have some idea of who produces clubs and how they differ. You may have accumulated some of this knowledge during the information-seeking stage and combined it with what you knew before. Based on product attributes such as colour, taste, price, prestige, quality, and service record, you will decide which product meets your needs most satisfactorily.

Purchase Decision

rational motives

Those reasons for purchasing a product that involve a logical evaluation of product attributes such as cost, quality, and usefulness.

emotional motives

Those reasons for purchasing a product that involve nonobjective factors.

Ultimately, you make a purchase decision. You may decide to defer the purchase until a later time or you may decide to buy now. "Buy" decisions are based on rational and emotional motives. **Rational motives** involve a logical evaluation of product attributes: cost, quality, and usefulness. **Emotional motives** can lead to irrational decisions. Many spur-of-the-moment decisions are emotionally driven, though not all irrational decisions are sudden. Emotional motives include fear, sociability, imitation of others, and aesthetics. You might buy mouthwash to avoid ostracism. You might buy the same brand of jeans as your friends. And you might buy a chocolate milkshake because you like the taste.

Note that by "irrational" we do not mean insane or wrong, merely a decision based on nonobjective factors. Gratifying a sudden urge for ice cream may not require much thought and may produce lots of enjoyment. But in some cases, irrational decisions are bad. We have all purchased items, taken them home, and then wondered, "Why in the world did I buy this thing?"

Body Shop International, which has no marketing or advertising department, is viewed by its loyal customers as socially and environmentally responsible.

Post-Purchase Evaluations

Marketing does not stop with the sale of a product or service, but includes the process of consumption. What happens *after* the sale is very important. A marketer wants consumers to be happy after the consumption of the product so that they will buy the product again. In fact, since consumers do not want to go through a complex decision process for every purchase, they often choose a product they have used and liked.

Not all consumers are satisfied with their purchases, of course. Dissatisfied consumers may complain, file a lawsuit, or publicly criticize the product and the company. They are unlikely to purchase the product again. In addition, dissatisfied customers are much more likely to speak about their experience with a product than are satisfied customers. Dissatisfied customers can have a very negative impact on a company's marketing effort. In fact, word-of-mouth can be the most influential marketing tool and also the most devastating, since businesses cannot control it.[16]

Doubts about the rationality of a purchase decision can cause **purchase anxiety**, sometimes called buyer's remorse. If you feel purchase anxiety after remodelling your home, you probably will not buy the services of the same interior designer again. Doing so would only perpetuate your anxiety. Reduction of purchase anxiety is important to marketers, particularly for expensive items such as furniture and major appliances.

purchase anxiety
A fear on the part of people who have made a purchase that their selection was wrong.

Organizational Marketing and Buying Behaviour

Buying behaviour is observable daily in the consumer market, where marketing activities, including buying-selling transactions, are visible to the public. Equally important, however, but far less visible, are *organizational* (or *commercial*) *markets*—organizations that buy goods and services to be used in creating and delivering consumer products. Marketing to these buyers must deal with different kinds of organizational markets and with buying behaviours that are quite different from those found in consumer markets.

Organizational Markets

Organizational or commercial markets fall into three categories: *industrial, reseller,* and *government/institutional markets.*

Industrial Market

industrial market
Businesses that buy goods to be converted into other products that will be sold to ultimate consumers.

The **industrial market** includes businesses that buy goods falling into one of two categories: goods to be converted into other products and goods that are used up during production. This market includes farmers, manufacturers, and some retailers. For example, Seth Thomas purchases electronics, metal components, and glass to make clocks for the consumer market. The company also buys office supplies, tools, and factory equipment—items never seen by clock buyers—to be used during production.

Reseller Market

reseller market
Intermediaries like wholesalers and retailers who buy finished products and resell them.

Before products reach consumers, they pass through a **reseller market** consisting of intermediaries, including wholesalers and retailers, who buy the finished goods and resell them (wholesalers and retailers are discussed in Chapter 17). Retailers like department stores, drug stores, and supermarkets buy clothing, appliances, foods, medicines, and other merchandise for resale to the consumer market. Retailers also buy such services as maintenance, housekeeping, and communications.

Government and Institutional Market

institutional market
Nongovernment organizations such as hospitals, churches, and schools.

Federal, provincial, and municipal governments purchase millions of dollars worth of computer equipment, buildings, paper clips and other items. The **institutional market** consists of nongovernmental organizations, such as hospitals, churches, museums, and charitable organizations, that also comprise a substantial market for goods and services. Like organizations in other commercial markets, these institutions use supplies and equipment, as well as legal, accounting, and transportation services.

Organizational Buying Behaviour

In many respects, industrial buying behaviour bears little resemblance to consumer buying practices. For example, industrial product demand is stimulated by demand for consumer products and is less sensitive to price changes. Other differences include the buyers' purchasing skills, their decision-making activities, and buyer-seller relationships.

Differences in Demand

derived demand
Demand for industrial products caused by (derived from) demand for consumer products.

inelasticity of demand
Exists when a price change for a product does not have much effect on demand.

Recall our definition of *demand* in Chapter 1: the willingness and ability of buyers to purchase a good or service. There are two major differences in demand between consumer and industrial products: *derived demand* and *inelasticity of demand.* The term **derived demand** refers to the fact that demand for industrial products often results from demand for related consumer products (that is, industrial demand is frequently *derived from* consumer demand). **Inelasticity of demand** exists when a price change for a product does not have much effect on demand. Take, for instance, the demand for cardboard used to package file cabinets. Because cardboard packaging is such a small part of the manufacturer's overall cabinet cost, an increase in cardboard prices will not lessen the demand for cardboard. In turn, because cabinet buyers will see little price increase, demand for filing cabinets—and for their accompanying cardboard packaging—will remain at about the same level.

Differences in Buyers

Unlike most consumers, organizational buyers are professional, specialized, and expert (or at least well-informed):

- As *professionals*, organizational buyers are trained in arranging buyer-seller relationships and in methods for negotiating purchase terms. Once buyer-seller agreements have been reached, industrial buyers also arrange for formalized contracts.

- As a rule, industrial buyers are company *specialists* in a line of items. As one of several buyers for a large bakery, for example, you may specialize in food ingredients like flour, yeast, butter, and so on.

- Industrial buyers are often *experts* about the products that they are buying. On a regular basis, organizational buyers learn about competing products and alternative suppliers by attending trade shows, reading trade magazines, and conducting technical discussions with sellers' representatives.

Differences in Decision Making

Recall that we illustrated the five stages in the consumer buying process in Figure 15.4. The organizational buyer's decision process differs in three important respects—*developing product specifications, evaluating alternatives,* and *making postpurchase evaluations.*

Following problem recognition, the first stage of the buying process, industrial buying takes an additional step—developing product specifications: A document is drawn up to describe the detailed product characteristics that are needed by the buyer and must be met by the supplier. These specifications are then used in the information-seeking stage, when buyers search for products and suppliers capable of meeting their specific needs.

In evaluating alternatives, buyers carefully measure prospective suppliers against the product specifications developed earlier. Only suppliers that can meet those requirements are considered further. Only thereafter are prospective vendors evaluated according to other factors, such as price, reliability, and service reputation.

The final stage, post-purchase evaluation, is more systematic in organizational buying than in consumer buying. The buyer's organization examines the product and compares it, feature-by-feature, for conformance to product specifications. Buyers retain records on product and service quality received from suppliers as the basis for evaluating suppliers' performance. These performance ratings become important considerations for selecting suppliers in the future.

Differences in the Buyer-Seller Relationship

Consumer-seller relationships are often impersonal and fleeting—short-lived one-time interactions. In contrast, industrial situations often involve frequent, enduring buyer-seller relationships. Accordingly, industrial sellers emphasize personal selling by trained representatives who can better understand the needs of each customer. Through extensive interaction with numerous buyers, sellers are better prepared to make suggestions for improving products and services that will benefit their customers.

The International Marketing Mix

Marketing products internationally means mounting a strategy to support global business operations. Obviously, this is no easy task. Foreign customers, for example, differ from domestic buyers in language, customs, business practices, and consumer behaviour. When they decide to go global, marketers must thus reconsider each element of the marketing mix: product, pricing, promotion, and place.

International Products

Some products, of course, can be sold abroad with virtually no changes. Budweiser, Coca-Cola, and Marlboros are exactly the same in Toronto, Tokyo, and Timbuktu. In other cases, firms have been obliged to create products with built-in flexibility—for instance, electric shavers that adapt to either 115- or 230-volt outlets.

At times only a redesigned—or completely different—product will meet the needs of foreign buyers, however. To sell the Macintosh in Japan, for example, Apple had to develop a Japanese-language operating system. Whether they are standard domestic products or custom-made products for foreign markets, however, the most globally competitive products are usually reliable, low-priced products with advanced features.

International Pricing

When pricing for international markets, marketers must handle all the considerations of domestic pricing while also considering the higher costs of transporting and selling products abroad. Some products cost more overseas than in Canada because of the added costs of delivery. Due to the higher costs of buildings, rent, equipment, and imported meat, a McDonald's Big Mac that sells for $2.99 in Canada has a price tag of over $10 in Japan. In contrast, products like jet airplanes are priced the same worldwide because delivery costs are incidental; the huge development and production costs are the major considerations regardless of customer location.

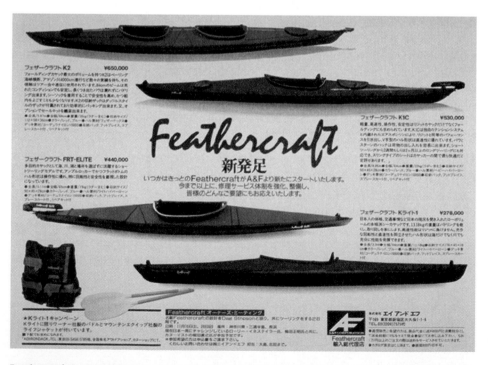

Feathercraft is a small British Columbia manufacturer that has been successful selling kayaks in the Japanese market.

International Promotion

Some standard Canadian promotional devices do not always succeed in other countries. In fact, many Europeans believe that a product must be inherently shoddy if a company does *any* advertising.

International marketers must also be aware that cultural differences can cause negative reactions to products that are advertised improperly. Some Europeans, for example, are offended by television commercials that show weapons or violence. Advertising practices are regulated accordingly. Consequently, Dutch commercials for toys do not feature the guns and combat scenes that are commonplace on Saturday morning television in North America. Meanwhile, liquor and cigarette commercials that are banned from Canadian and U.S. television are thriving in many Asian and European markets.

Symbolism, too, is a sometimes surprising consideration. In France, for instance, yellow flowers suggest infidelity. In Mexico, they are signs of death—an association made in Brazil by the colour purple. Clearly, product promotions must be carefully matched to the customs and cultural values of each country. The box "Pitfalls in Global Promotion" describes some difficulties companies have had when promoting their product in foreign markets.

International Distribution

Finally, international distribution presents several problems. In some industries, delays in starting new distribution networks can be costly. Therefore,

International Report

Pitfalls in Global Promotion

Marketing products internationally can provide big pay-offs to those who do their homework. As many firms have learned, careful research of both idiomatic nuances and cultural norms is critical to global success.

Some early attempts by Chinese marketers underscore this point. China had several products it wanted to market in the United States. But, as the manufacturers learned too late, brand names such as White Elephant batteries, Maxipuke playing cards, and Pansy brand men's underwear did not attract many U.S. customers.

But even careful research is not a guarantee of success. Japan's giant Toyota ran afoul in China with a marketing campaign targeted specifically to Chinese culture. Toyota launched an advertising campaign based on the old Chinese proverb, "When you get to the foot of the mountain, a road will appear." Toyota added "Wherever there is a road, there is a Toyota." In China, however, truth in advertising is taken very seriously. The Chinese hold to this tenet in their own advertising and expect foreign companies to do the same. A year after the slogan was used in print and TV ads, Chinese authorities told Toyota that it constituted false advertising. Toyota had to drop the campaign.

Ads sometimes backfire from miscalculating a country's sense of humour. Take the case of Luis Nasr, creative director of an ad agency in Ecuador, who designed an ad for a hairgrowth product called Regenal Forte. The ad featured a picture of Mikhail Gorbachev with the caption, "He didn't use Regenal Forte in time." The Russian ambassador was not amused. The uproar soon subsided, however, and the ad subsequently won a prize at the New York Print Festival.

Marketing managers are trying to avoid these kinds of problems with *global advertising*, a strategy in which the same basic ad campaign—with minor alterations from country to country—is used throughout the world. Peter S. Sealey, senior vice-president and director of global marketing for Coca-Cola, puts it this way: "There is global media now, like MTV. And there is a global teenager. The same kid you see at the Ginza in Tokyo is in Picadilly Square in London, in Pushkin Square, at Notre Dame." So why not create an advertisement that will appeal to the universal teenager (or universal parent or universal businessperson)?

companies with existing distribution systems often enjoy an advantage over new businesses. Several companies have gained advantages in time-based competition by buying existing businesses. Procter & Gamble, for example, saved three years of start-up time by buying Revlon's Max Factor and Betrix cosmetics, both of which are well established in foreign markets. P&G can thus immediately use these companies' distribution and marketing networks for selling its own brands in the United Kingdom, Germany, and Japan.

Other companies contract with foreign firms or individuals to distribute and sell their products abroad. Foreign agents may perform personal selling and advertising, provide information about local markets, or serve as exporters' representatives. But having to manage interactions with foreign personnel complicates a marketing manager's responsibilities. In addition, packaging practices in Canada must sometimes be adapted to withstand the rigours of transport to foreign ports and storage under conditions that differ radically from domestic conditions.

Given the need to adjust the marketing mix, success in international markets is hard won. Even experienced firms can err in marketing to other countries. International success requires flexibility and a willingness to adapt to the nuances of other cultures. Whether a firm markets in domestic or international markets, however, the basic principles of marketing still apply. It is only the implementation of those principles that changes.

Small Business and the Marketing Mix

As we noted in Chapter 8, far more small businesses fail than succeed. Yet many of today's largest firms were yesterday's small businesses. McDonald's began with one restaurant, a concept, and one individual (Ray Kroc) who had foresight. Behind the success of many small firms lies a skilful application of the marketing concept and careful consideration of each element in the marketing mix.

Small Business Products

Some new products—and firms—are doomed at the start simply because few consumers want or need what they have to offer. Too often, enthusiastic entrepreneurs introduce products that they and their friends like, but they fail to estimate realistic market potential. Other small businesses offer new products before they have clear pictures of their target segments and how to reach them. They try to be everything to everyone, and they end up serving no one well. In contrast, sound product planning has paid off for many small firms. "Keep it simple" is a familiar key to success—that is, fulfil a specific need and do it efficiently.

Small Business Pricing

Haphazard pricing that is often little more than guesswork can sink even a firm with a good product. Most often, small business pricing errors result from a failure to project operating expenses accurately. Owners of failing businesses have often been heard to utter statements like "I didn't realize how much it costs to run the business!" and "If I price the product high enough to cover my expenses, no one will buy it!" But when small businesses set prices by carefully assessing costs, many earn very satisfactory profits—sometimes enough to expand or diversify.

Small Business Promotion

Many small businesses are also ignorant when it comes to the methods and costs of promotion. To save expenses, for example, they may avoid advertising and rely instead on personal selling. As a result, too many potential customers remain unaware of their products.

Successful small businesses plan for promotional expenses as part of start-up costs. Some hold down costs by taking advantage of less expensive promotional methods. Local newspapers, for example, are sources of publicity when they publish articles about new or unique businesses. Other small businesses have succeeded by identifying themselves and their products with associated groups, organizations, and events. Thus a custom-crafts gallery might join with a local art league and local artists to organize public showings of their combined products.

Small Business Distribution

Problems in arranging distribution can also make or break small businesses. Perhaps the most critical aspect of distribution is facility location, especially for new service businesses. The ability of many small businesses—retailers, veterinary clinics, gourmet coffee shops—to attract and retain customers depends partly on the choice of location.

In distribution, as in other aspects of the marketing mix, however, smaller companies may have advantages over larger competitors, even in highly complex industries. They may be quicker, for example, in applying service technologies. Everex Systems Inc. sells personal computers to wholesalers and dealers through a system the company calls "Zero Response Time." Phone orders are reviewed every two hours so that the factory can adjust assembly to match demand.

Summary of Learning Objectives

1. **Define *marketing*.** *Marketing* is the process of planning and executing the conception, pricing, promotion, and distribution of ideas, goods and services to create exchanges that satisfy individual and organizational objectives.

2. **Describe the five forces that constitute the *external marketing environment*.** The *external environment* consists of the outside forces that influence marketing strategy and decision making. The *political/legal environment* includes laws and regulations, both domestic and foreign, that may define or constrain business activities. The *social/cultural environment* is the context within which people's values, beliefs, and ideas affect marketing decisions. The *technological environment* includes the technological developments that affect existing and new products. The *economic environment* consists of the conditions, such as inflation, recession, and interest rates, that influence both consumer and organizational spending patterns. Finally, *the competitive environment* is the environment in which marketers must persuade buyers to purchase their products rather than their competitors'.

3. **Explain *market segmentation* and show how it is used in *target marketing*.** *Market segmentation* is the process of dividing markets into categories of customers. Businesses have learned that marketing is more successful when it is aimed towards specific *target markets*—groups of consumers with similar wants and needs. Markets may be segmented by *geographic, demographic, psychographic,* or *product-use variables*.

4. **Explain the purpose and value of *market research*.** *Market research* is the study of what buyers need and of the best ways to meet those needs. This process involves a study of the current situation, the selection of a research method, the collection of data, the analysis of data, and the preparation of a report that may include recommendations for action. The four most common research methods are *observation*, *surveys*, *focus groups*, and *experimentation*.

5. **Describe the key factors that influence the *consumer buying process*.** A number of personal and psychological considerations, along with various social and cultural influences, affect consumer behaviour. When making buying decisions, consumers first determine or respond to a problem or need and then collect as much information as they think necessary before making a purchase. *Postpurchase evaluations* are also important to marketers because they influence future buying patterns.

6. **Discuss the three categories of *organizational markets* and explain how *organizational buying behaviour* differs from consumer buying behaviour.** The *industrial market* includes firms that buy goods falling into one of two categories: (1) goods to be converted into other products and (2) goods that are used up during production. Farmers and manufacturers are members of the industrial market. Members of the *reseller market* (mostly wholesalers) are intermediaries who buy and re-sell finished goods. Besides governments and agencies at all levels, the *government and institutional market* includes such nongovernmental organizations as hospitals, museums, and charities.

   There are four main differences between consumer and organizational buying behaviour. First, the nature of *demand* is different in organizational demands: It is often *derived* (resulting from related consumer demand), *inelastic* (largely unaffected by price changes), or both. Second, organizational buyers are typically professionals, specialists, or experts. Third, organizational buyers develop product specifications, evaluate alternatives more thoroughly, and make more systematic post-purchase evaluations. Finally, they often develop enduring buyer-seller relationships.

Key Terms

marketing, 425
consumer goods, 426
industrial goods, 426
external environment, 426
substitute product, 429
brand competition, 429
international competition, 429
marketing managers, 429
marketing plan, 429

marketing concept, 430
marketing mix, 430
product, 431
product differentiation, 431
pricing, 431
promotion, 432
advertising, 432
personal selling, 432
sales promotion, 432
public relations, 432
publicity, 433

distribution, 433
target market, 433
market segmentation, 433
positioning, 434
psychographics, 435
market research, 438
secondary data, 438
primary data, 439
observation, 440
survey, 440
focus group, 441

experimentation, 441
consumer behaviour, 442
rational motives, 444
emotional motives, 444
purchase anxiety, 445
industrial market, 446
reseller market, 446
institutional market, 446
derived demand, 446
inelasticity of demand, 446

Study Questions and Exercises

Review Questions

1. What are the similarities and differences between consumer marketing and industrial marketing?
2. Explain how and why market segmentation is used in target marketing.
3. Identify the steps in the consumer buying process.
4. What elements of the marketing mix may need to be adjusted to market a product internationally? Why?

Analysis Questions

5. Using examples of everyday products, explain why marketing plans must consider the marketing mix.
6. Pick an everyday product such as books, dog food, or shoes. Using your product as an example, show how different versions of it are aimed towards different market segments. Show how the marketing mix differs for each of the segments.

7. Select a readily available product and describe the steps you would expect to find in the consumer decision process about buying that product.
8. If you were starting your own new small business, what are the major pitfalls you would try to avoid as you put together your marketing plans?

Application Questions

9. Interview the owner of a local retail business. Determine if the store has a clear market segment it is trying to appeal to, and what that market segment is.
10. Select a product made by a foreign company and sold in Canada. Compare it to a similar product made domestically in terms of its product features, price, promotion, and distribution. Which one of the two products do you believe will be more successful with Canadian buyers? Why?

Building Your Business Skills

Goal

To encourage students to assess how their own buying behaviour differs for major and minor purchases and to understand how their buying behaviour compares with that of others.

Method

Step 1:

Keep a diary of the purchases you make during the next two weeks. Include both small purchases (a toothbrush, for example, or a can of tennis balls) and large ones (a computer, a mountain bike, a leather jacket). If you make no major purchases during this period, think back to several purchases you have made recently (perhaps within the past six months). In thinking about each purchase, identify and describe the steps involved in each—recognizing a problem or need, seeking information about competing products, evaluating alternative products, making the decision to purchase a specific product, and evaluating the purchase after it has been made.

Step 2:

Pair off with another student and take turns analyzing the five stages in each other's purchasing decisions.

Follow-Up Questions

1. Looking at your own consumer buying process, how would you say that it differs for major and minor purchases? Conduct the same analysis for your partner's purchases.

2. List and explain the important differences between the ways you and your partner handle the consumer purchase process.

3. What factors influenced the different ways in which you and your partner approached consumer purchases? Analyze the effects of psychological, economic, social, and cultural differences.

4. For minor purchases—a new cap, for example—were the information-seeking and evaluation of alternatives steps always performed quickly? If not, analyze why they took longer than the purchase probably warranted.

EXPLORING the Net

To find out about some of the marketing methods used by a world-class company, log on to the following Web site:

> http://www.ge.com

After you have browsed the various pages and reports posted by General Electric (GE), think about the following questions pertaining to the company's marketing processes:

1. From a marketing perspective, why do you suppose GE separates its Web site into two product/service categories: "At Home with GE" and "In Business with GE"?

2. Identify some examples of *consumer goods marketing* at GE. What are the specific goods and services that you found?

3. Identify some examples of *industrial marketing* at GE. What are some of the specific goods and services that you found?

4. From the Web site, can you identify any examples of *idea marketing* by GE?

5. Based on the full range of its products and customers, what challenges do you think GE's marketing managers face in their *political* and *legal* environments? In their *economic* environment? In their *social* and *cultural* environments?

CONCLUDING CASE 15-1

The Art and Science of Aisle-Traffic Control

There is nothing accidental about where products are placed on supermarket shelves. In fact, new marketing techniques are making aisle and shelf assignments more of a science than an art. Today's marketers use combinations of high-technology surveillance equipment and old-fashioned stakeouts to learn what they can about the aisles that shoppers travel and those they avoid. Naturally, they are adjusting product placement according to what they learn. The goal is to influence purchase decisions by placing *high-margin products*—those that produce the most revenue per unit sold—in high-traffic areas. Some stores also encourage sales through customized in-store video and audio ads, which direct consumers to specific products.

Executives at one supermarket knew that some items were moving faster than others, but they didn't really know how shoppers' habits affected purchase decisions. To gather some hard data, they placed a surveillance team on store catwalks. The team's mission: to observe the traffic patterns of 1600 shoppers. For one thing, they discovered that most shoppers were attracted to the periphery of the store—the produce, dairy, and meat aisles—but tended to avoid the store's centre (the area consuming the greatest store space). So the store installed video monitors on the

outskirts of the store to broadcast commercials for items shelved in the store's centre. The theory is that after viewing a commercial for Quaker Oats cereals or Little Friskies cat food, shoppers venture into less-travelled aisles.

Another surveillance study showed that although greeting cards are high-volume items, fewer than one in five shoppers ever walk down the greeting-card aisle. When the cards were moved to a part of the store that regularly draws 62 percent of the traffic, quarterly sales jumped 40 percent. Undoubtedly, being next to the peanut butter and jelly helped boost sales. "We're no longer guessing if location really matters," explains Richard Blatt, executive director of the Point-of Purchase Advertising Institute. "We now have statistical proof."

Other analysts have found that audio ads supplied by Muzak also encourage purchase decisions. Some supermarket chains use audio advertising to pitch specific products to a captive audiences of shoppers. Moreover, nearly half of all regional chains and independent supermarkets promote products through a series of three 20-second point-of-purchase audio ads sandwiched between eight minutes of background music. Messages can be geared to local markets and even to specific stores.

...

However, although attempts to influence purchasing decisions have been largely successful, retailers face some built-in dangers. For example, harried shoppers who are used to finding items in specific places may balk when different, unrelated items are combined. According to food-retail consultant Willard Bishop, "a crazy-quilt pattern isn't consumer-friendly." Moreover, many consumers find audio ads intrusive and annoying and may decide not to buy promoted products because of the assault on their senses.

For marketers, of course, the bottom line is whether such techniques actually influence shoppers to make specific purchases. A recent incident involving Muzak advertising demonstrates that, at the very least, in-store messages are being heard. Using Muzak, one grocer broadcast a tip on how to tell the difference between fresh and stale eggs. However, instead of saying that fresh eggs sink in water, the announcer told shoppers that fresh eggs float. When large groups of customers began returning newly purchased eggs, Muzak marketers realized their mistake and pulled the ad. The incident was embarrassing, of course, but it showed that people were actually listening and, more importantly, acting on what they heard.

Case Questions

1. When marketers watch shoppers' behaviour, they are using the oldest form of market research—observation. Because marketers can use inventory data to determine what is selling and what is not, why is it important to observe the routes that shoppers take as they navigate a store?

2. Does observing shoppers without their knowledge raise any ethical concerns?

3. Because point-of-purchase advertising is trying to influence purchasing decisions in the moments before they are made, are marketers assuming that shoppers wait to the last minute to evaluate alternatives and decide what they want?

4. How do you feel about attempts by marketers to influence your supermarket purchasing decisions? Are you likely to be annoyed or grateful? ◆

CONCLUDING CASE 15-2

Which Washer Is Best?

There are basically two types of washing machines—top loaders and front loaders. The former dominate the market in Canada and the U.S., and the latter dominate the market in Europe. In front loaders, clothes spin around a horizontal axis, with the clothes tumbling in and out of a pool of detergent-rich water. The clothes are rinsed repeatedly. By contrast, North American top loaders swirl clothes around in a tub of water that dilutes the detergent.

Europeans argue that front loaders are better because:

- they get clothes cleaner
- they use less water and are more energy-efficient
- they are easier on clothes because there is no centre shaft for the clothes to hit during the wash cycle
- they spin more water out of the clothes during the wash cycle, which means that the time in the dryer is reduced

North Americans see several disadvantages of front loaders:

- they take three times as long to complete the wash cycle
- they are much more expensive than top loaders because they must have watertight doors
- clothes cannot be added during the wash cycle as they can in top loaders
- front loaders don't have the capacity of top loaders
- front loaders are not as easy to load as top loaders

In spite of these back-and-forth arguments, front loaders may be getting a foothold in North America. In 1997, both Maytag and Amana announced that they would begin producing front loaders. At the moment, front loaders have only a 2 percent market share in North America. The key reasons are price (front loaders sell for as much as $3000, while top loaders often go for as little as $500) and efficiency (front loaders take much longer to complete the wash cycle).

The marketing strategy used by Europeans is to tout their washers as upscale products like fancy cars. Producers often try to get home builders to install them as a home is being built, and then the homeowner adds the price to the mortgage.

Case Questions

1. Consider the detailed activities that must be carried out when washing clothes. What would the typical consumer find attractive about front loaders? About top loaders?

2. What would the typical consumer find unattractive about front loaders? About top loaders?

3. What kind of consumers in Canada and the U.S. are likely to purchase a front-loading washing machine?

4. How can the perceived (and real) disadvantages of front loaders be overcome by manufacturers? Be specific. ◆

16

Developing and Promoting Goods and Services

Developing a New Product for a Small Market

When you think of new product development, you often think of toothpaste, computers, or automobiles. But how about airplanes? Two new airplanes, aimed at the most elite market in the world will be flying before the year 2000. They are long-range corporate jets, and they will be able to carry eight passengers from New York to Tokyo in 13 hours without refueling. Only 350 to 800 of these planes will be sold, likely at a price of about $30 million each. The customers are multinational companies, a few billionaires, and a few heads of state.

Only two companies are developing this new product. One is a world-famous U.S. firm (Gulfstream) and the other is Bombardier Inc. of Montreal. This is going to be a David and Goliath struggle, but there is a big surprise: the Goliath is Bombardier. With annual sales of nearly $5 billion, 36 500 employees, manufacturing operations in eight countries, and markets in more than 60, Bombardier is the sixth largest aviation company in the world, and a major force in international transportation. The company has grown from its beginnings as a maker of snowmobiles to its present size by acquiring several firms, including Canadair, Learjet, Short Brothers PLC, and de Havilland. By contrast, Gulfstream is a small player and makes only top-of-the-line corporate jets. Its new jet is called the Gulfstream V.

In a football field-size room at its Montreal headquarters, a team of 250 Bombardier engineers sit at computer screens designing the new plane (called the Global Express). Part of the team is responsible for the wings and fuselage. Another part is building the engine. Next door, in a building so big its corridors have street names so that workers won't get lost, other parts of the new product development plan are being carried out.

The idea for an intercontinental business jet costing $30 million dollars started in 1989 when CEO Laurent Beaudoin called vice-president John Holding from his car phone and suggested that they leapfrog the competition. Bombardier's strategy has been to be a leader in selected market niches, and company executives agreed that with the increasing globalization of business, a global business jet was needed. In spite of the increased emphasis on electronic communication and corporate efficiency, Bombardier is betting that it will continue to be necessary to conduct business face-to-face, particularly when new international deals are being put together. Hence, it will market the new jet on the basis that it economizes on the executive's most precious commodity—time.

Bombardier conducted market research on the new product by asking potential customers which pair of cities they most frequently travelled between. They found that New York-Tokyo was the key. Bombardier next asked customers if they would pay $28 million for a plane that could travel 12 000 kilometres at 850 kilometres per hour. They said yes. By the end of 1993, the company had 30 orders in hand, so the final go-ahead was given. Bombardier will break even when it sells the 100th plane.

At present, no corporate jet can match the speed of a commercial 747-400, which can fly from New York to Tokyo nonstop. But the Global Express will be able to fly the route in 13 hours nonstop *and* allow the executive to carry on business while in the air. Since executives on private jets move through customs much faster than those travelling on scheduled airlines, this will save further time.

Bombardier is shielded from a lot of financial risk in this new product venture because it isn't trying to carry the

(continued)

whole project. Although the total cost of the project is $1 billion, Bombardier has invested less than half that amount. It has generated the remaining funds by forming partnerships with several other firms like Mitsubishi and BMW Rolls Royce.

Compared to the Gulfstream V, the Global Express has the edge. It will be faster, enabling it to get to Tokyo an hour sooner. And it is roomier inside, with a higher, wider cabin that has 19 percent more floor area. The Gulfstream's advantage is that it will be on the market two years sooner. Because this is a critical new product for Gulfstream's future success, it is already aggressively competing against the Global Express. In late 1993, it took out a full page advertisement in *The Wall Street Journal* offering a $250 000 discount on its new plane to anyone who cancelled an order for the Global Express. But nobody took up the offer.

What other new products might Bombardier be introducing in the future? The most obvious is a supersonic corporate jet that could cut the flying time from New York to Tokyo to less than 6 hours. It's already technically feasible, but the product won't be developed until it makes financial sense. Bombardier always keeps in mind its two main goals: to make great aircraft, and to make money doing so. ◆

Bombardier Inc.
http://www.bombardier.com

In the last chapter, we introduced the four components of the marketing mix: product, promotion, price, and distribution. In this chapter, we will look at the complex issue of what a *product* is and how it can best be *promoted* to customers. The opening case shows that developing a new product is a risky and time-consuming activity, but it must be done if a company is to survive and prosper in the long run.

By focusing on the learning objectives of this chapter, you will better understand new product development and promotion. After reading this chapter, you should be able to:

LEARNING OBJECTIVES

1. Identify a *product* and distinguish between *consumer* and *industrial products*.

2. Trace the stages of the *product life cycle* and explain the *growth-share matrix*.

3. Discuss the importance of *branding* and *packaging*.

4. Identify the objectives of *promotion* and discuss the considerations involved in selecting a *promotional mix*.

5. Describe the various *advertising media* available to marketing managers.

6. Identify the different types of *sales promotions* and explain the uses of *publicity* and *public relations*.

What Is a Product?

In developing the marketing mix for any products—whether ideas, goods, or services—marketers must consider what consumers really buy when they purchase products. Only then can they plan their strategies effectively. We will begin this section where product strategy begins—with an understanding of product *features* and *benefits*. Next, we will describe the major *classifications of products*, both consumer and industrial. Finally, we will discuss the most important component in the offerings of any business—its *product mix*.

Features and Benefits

Customers do not buy products simply because they like the products themselves—they buy products because they like what the products can *do* for them, either physically or emotionally. As one marketing expert has observed, "Consumers don't buy quarter-inch drills; they buy quarter-inch holes." This observation goes to the heart of any effort to analyze products and product success: Companies must base the approach to products (quarter-inch drills) on providing consumers with products that *do* what customers want *done* (drill quarter-inch holes).

To succeed, then, a product must include the right features and offer the right benefits. Product features are the qualities, tangible and intangible, that a company "builds into" its products, such as a 12-horsepower motor on a lawn mower, an improved accounting system, pH balance in a shampoo, or a 60-40 fibre blend in a shirt. To be saleable, however, a product's features also must provide *benefits*: The mower must provide an attractive lawn; the accounting system, better information for making decisions; pH balance, clean and healthy hair; and a 60-40 blend, a good-looking, easy-care shirt.

Obviously, features and benefits play extremely important roles in the pricing of products. Products are much more than just *visible* features and benefits. In buying a product, consumers are also buying an image and a reputation. The marketers of Swatch Chrono watch, for example, are well aware that brand name, packaging, labelling, and after-purchase service are also indispensible parts of their product. Advertisements remind consumers that such "real" features as shock and water resistance, quartz precision, and Swiss manufacture come hand-in-hand with Swatch's commitment to three "concept" features: young and trendy, active and sporty, and stylistically cool and clean.

Classifying Goods and Services

One way to classify a product is according to expected buyers. Buyers fall into two groups: buyers of *consumer* products and buyers of *industrial* products. As we saw in Chapter 15, the consumer and industrial buying processes differ significantly. Not surprisingly, then, marketing products to consumers is vastly different from marketing them to other companies.

Classifying Consumer Products

Consumer products are commonly divided into three categories that reflect buyers' behaviour: convenience, shopping, and specialty products.

convenience goods/services

Relatively inexpensive consumer goods or services that are bought and used rapidly and regularly, causing consumers to spend little time looking for them or comparing their prices.

shopping goods/services

Moderately expensive consumer goods or services that are purchased infrequently, causing consumers to spend some time comparing their prices.

specialty goods/services

Very expensive consumer goods or services that are purchased rarely, causing consumers to spend a great deal of time locating the exact item desired.

- **Convenience goods** (such as milk and newspapers) and **convenience services** (such as those offered by fast-food restaurants) are consumed rapidly and regularly. They are relatively inexpensive and are purchased frequently and with little expenditure of time and effort.

- **Shopping goods** (such as stereos and tires) and **shopping services** (such as insurance) are more expensive and are purchased less frequently than convenience goods and services. Consumers often compare brands, sometimes in different stores. They may also evaluate alternatives in terms of style, performance, colour, price, and other criteria.

- **Specialty goods** (such as wedding gowns) and **specialty services** (such as catering for wedding receptions) are extremely important and expensive purchases. Consumers usually decide on precisely what they want and will accept no substitutes. They will often go from store to store, sometimes spending a great deal of money and time to get a specific product.

Classifying Industrial Products

Depending on how much they cost and how they will be used, industrial products can be divided into two categories: *expense items* and *capital items*.

Expense items are any materials and services that are consumed within a year by firms producing other goods or supplying services. The most obvious expense items are industrial goods used directly in the production process, for example, bulkloads of tea processed into tea bags. In addition, *support materials* help to keep a business running without directly entering the production process. Oil, for instance, keeps the tea-bagging machines running but is not used in the tea bags. Similarly, *supplies*—pencils, brooms, gloves, paint—are consumed quickly and regularly by every business. Finally, *services* such as window cleaning, equipment installation, and temporary office help are essential to daily operations. Because these items are used frequently, purchases are often automatic or require little decision making.

Capital items are "permanent"—that is, expensive and long-lasting— goods and services. All these items have expected lives of more than a year— typically up to several years. Expensive buildings (offices, factories), fixed equipment (water towers, baking ovens), and accessory equipment (computers, airplanes) are capital goods. Capital services are those for which long-term commitments are made. These may include purchases for employee food services, building and equipment maintenance, or legal services. Because capital items are expensive and purchased infrequently, they often involve decisions by high-level managers.

expense items
Relatively inexpensive industrial goods that are consumed rapidly and regularly.

capital items
Expensive, long-lasting industrial goods that are used in producing other goods or services and have a long life.

The Product Mix

The group of products a company has available for sale, be they consumer or industrial, is known as the firm's **product mix**. Black and Decker, for example, makes toasters, vacuum cleaners, electric drills, and a variety of other appliances and tools. 3M makes everything from Post-Its to laser optics.

Most companies begin with a single product. Over time, successful companies may find that the initial product does not suit all consumers shopping for the product type. So they often introduce similar products designed to reach other consumers. Apple computer introduced the first successful personal computer. Shortly thereafter, Apple produced a range of personal computers for various applications—for example, the Apple 2C, 2E, 2GS, Macintosh Plus, and Macintosh SE. A group of similar products intended for a similar group of buyers who will use them in similar fashions is known as a **product line**.

Companies may also extend their horizons and identify opportunities outside of their existing product line. The result—multiple (or diversified) product lines—is evident in firms like Procter & Gamble. This firm began by making soap, but it now also produces paper products, foods, coffee, and baby products. Multiple product lines allow a company to grow more rapidly and minimize the consequences of slow sales in any one product line.

product mix
The group of products a company has available for sale.

product line
A group of similar products intended for a similar group of buyers who will use them in a similar fashion.

Developing New Products

To expand or diversify product lines—indeed, just to survive—firms must develop and successfully introduce streams of new products. Faced with competition and shifting consumer preferences, no firm can count on a single successful product to carry them forever. Even basic products that have been widely purchased for decades require nearly constant renewal. Consider the unassuming facial tissue. The white tissue in the rectangular box has been joined (if not replaced) by tissues of many different colours and patterns.

They arrive in boxes shaped and decorated for nearly every room in the house, and they are made to be placed or carried not only in the bathroom but in the purse, the briefcase, and the car.

Finding a market for a new product may be difficult. Terry Knight and Al Robinson, the owners of Inuktun Services Ltd., developed small, submersible, remotely operated vehicles (ROVs) equipped with lights and a video camera. The idea was that boat owners could guide these devices down into the water and view the bottom of their boat on a TV monitor. Boat owners weren't interested, but the nuclear industry was. Now Inuktun's ROVs travel up and down stairs, around corners, over obstacles, in water up to 30 metres deep, and through ducts and pipes as little as 15 cm in diameter.[1]

The New Product Development Process

In January 1990, General Electric announced its five-year program for the revolutionary GE90, a cleaner, quieter jet engine. GE has already spent its $2 billion development budget and, in December 1993, celebrated the maiden flight of its test engine. Still, GE has no advance assurances that the engine will be certified in time for commercial service later in the decade. That is the basic risk. The opportunity, however, is also great. If completed on time and certified, the GE90 will dominate the commercial jet market for years while other engine manufacturers are still working to develop competing engines.[2] The issue of how to predict the success of new products is addressed in the box "Predicting the Success of New Products."

The Canadian Business Scene

Predicting the Success of New Products

What does it take to make a new product or service successful? Why do certain products or services flop, while others are wildly successful? Although predictions about which new product ideas will be successful are somewhat risky, there are certain "success factors" that are helpful in predicting success. The more success factors a product or service has, the higher the probability that it will be demanded by consumers.

Some of these success factors are as follows:

1. *Time*—if the product idea helps consumers save time or control time, it is more likely to be successful. The four new product champions of recent times—fax machines, VCRs, microwave ovens, and automatic teller machines (ATMs)—all save customers time.

2. *Convenience*—if a product makes it easier to do something, consumers will want it. Cellular phones and the appearance of ATMs in shopping malls are examples of this factor.

3. *Government regulation*—if regulations help a product, it is more likely to be successful; if not, it is more likely to fail. For example, U.S. and European governments have refused to approve the technical standards necessary for high definition television (HDTV). Thus, Japanese TV manufacturers have been unable to make much progress in selling HDTV sets.

4. *Existing technology*—the technology used to produce regular TV picture resolution is much cheaper than the technology needed for HDTV. And the picture that is produced is pretty good. It is therefore unlikely that consumers would pay a lot more money for HDTV.

5. *Human nature*—new products that require people to change the way they behave are less likely to be successful than those that don't. Personal computer usage in homes grew slowly during the 1980s because they required large behavioural changes in people. The use of debit cards, on the other hand, has increased rapidly because they are easy to use.

6. *Cost*—the less a product costs, the more likely people are to buy it. Car phones cost $4000 in the early 1980s and there weren't many buyers. Now they cost less than $100 and demand is skyrocketing.

Companies that develop new product and service ideas that maximize these success factors are more likely to achieve success than companies that ignore these factors.

Product development is a long and complex (and expensive) process. Companies do not dream up new products one day and ship them to retailers the next. In fact, new products usually involve carefully planned—and sometimes risky—commitments of time and resources.

Product Mortality Rates

Typically, new products move through a series of stages, beginning with the search for ideas and culminating in introduction to consumers. At each stage of this process, potential products fall from further consideration as the company pursues more attractive alternatives. In fact, it is estimated that it takes 50 new product ideas to generate one product that finally reaches the marketplace. Even then, of course, only a few of those survivors become *successful* products. Many seemingly great *ideas* have failed as *products*. Indeed, creating a successful new product has become more and more difficult.

Speed to Market

A product's chances for success are also better if it beats its competition to market. The principle applies to products in every industry:

- A classic example of the advantage of getting a competitive head start is Miller Lite beer. Miller dominated the light beer market for years because it established itself with consumers before its competitors even got started. Miller was one year ahead of Schlitz Light, two years ahead of Anheuser-Busch Natural Light, and three years ahead of some 22 other brands. (In 1994, after years of expensive advertising, Bud Light finally made up lost ground to take the lead in market share.)

- Similarly, Hewlett-Packard recently devastated Japanese rival NEC with speedy development of a new line of inkjet colour printers. NEC introduced its competing line only after H-P was entrenched in the market. Never able to make up for lost time, NEC abandoned its product after just four months of trying to sell it.[3]

- At Boeing, the time it takes to design and build each order of 747s and 767s has been reduced from 18 months in 1992 to just 10 months in 1994. Buyers, therefore, are now taking much less of a risk when they place orders for planes. Because airlines can order and receive planes while the business cycle is still on the upswing, new planes can generate revenues quickly. Formerly, longer lead times meant that planes might not be available from Boeing until the downside of the cycle was being felt; buyers often failed to earn the revenues needed to cover the costs of new planes.[4]

The principle reflected in these three cases is simple: The more rapidly a product moves from the laboratory to the marketplace, the more likely it is to survive. By introducing new products ahead of competitors, companies quickly establish market leaders. They become entrenched in the market before being challenged by late-arriving competitors. How important is **speed to market**— that is, a firm's success in responding to customer demand or market changes? One study has estimated that a product that is only three months late to market (that is, three months behind the leader) sacrifices 12 percent of its lifetime profit potential. A product that is six months late will lose 33 percent.

speed to market
Strategy of introducing new products to respond quickly to customer and/or market changes.

The Seven-Step Development Process

To increase their chances of developing a successful new product, many firms adopt some variation on a basic seven-step process (see Figure 16.1).

Figure 16.1
The new product development process.

1. Product ideas. Product development begins with a search for ideas for new products. Product ideas can come from consumers, the sales force, research and development people, or engineering personnel. The key is to actively seek out ideas and to reward those whose ideas become successful products.

2. Screening. This second stage is an attempt to eliminate all product ideas that do not mesh with the firm's abilities, expertise, or objectives. Representatives from marketing, engineering, and production must have input at this stage.

3. Concept testing. Once ideas have been culled, companies use market research to solicit consumers' input. In this way, firms can identify benefits that the product must provide as well as an appropriate price level for the product.

4. Business analysis. This stage involves developing an early comparison of costs versus benefits for the proposed product. Preliminary sales projections are compared with cost projections from finance and production. The aim is not to determine precisely how much money the product will make but to see whether the product can meet minimum profitability goals.

5. Prototype development. At this stage, product ideas begin to take shape. Using input from the concept-testing phase, engineering and/or research and development produce a preliminary version of the product. Prototypes can be extremely expensive, often requiring extensive hand crafting, tooling, and development of components. But this phase can help identify potential production problems.

6. Product testing and test marketing. Using what it learned from the prototype, the company goes into limited production of the item. The product is then tested internally to see if it meets performance requirements. If it does, it is made available for sale in limited areas. This stage is very costly, since promotional campaigns and distribution channels must be established for test markets. But test marketing gives a company its first information on how consumers will respond to a product under real market conditions.

7. Commercialization. If test-marketing results are positive, the company will begin full-scale production and marketing of the product. Gradual commercialization, with the firm providing the product to more and more areas over time, prevents undue strain on the firm's initial production capabilities. But extensive delays in commercialization may give competitors a chance to bring out their own version.

The development of services (both for consumers and industrial buyers) involves many of the same stages as goods development. Basically, Steps 2, 3, 4, 6, and 7 are the same. There are, however, some important differences in Steps 1 and 5:

- *Service Ideas*. The search for service ideas includes a task called **definition of the service package**, which involves identification of the tangible and intangible features that define the service (see Chapter 13).[5] This definition includes *service specifications*. For example, a firm that wants to offer year-end cleaning services to office buildings might commit itself to the following specifications: "The building interior will be cleaned by midnight, January 5, including floor polishing of all aisles, carpets swept free of all dust and debris, polished washbowls and lavatory equipment, with no interruption or interference to customer."

definition of the service package
Identification of the tangible and intangible features that define the service.

- *Service Process Design*. Instead of prototype development, services require a **service process design**. This step involves selecting the process, identifying worker requirements, and determining facilities requirements so that the service can be provided as promised in the service specifications. *Process selection* identifies each step in the service, including the sequence and the timing. *Worker requirements* specify employee behaviours, skills capabilities, and interactions with customers during the service encounter. *Facilities requirements* designate all the equipment that supports delivery of the service. All three of these areas must be coordinated.[6]

service process design
Selecting the process, identifying worker requirements, and determining facilities requirements so the service can be effectively provided.

The Product Life Cycle

Products that reach the commercialization stage begin a new series of stages known as the product life cycle. **Product life cycle (PLC)** is the concept that products have a limited profit-producing life for a company. This life may be a matter of months, years, or decades, depending on the ability of the product to attract customers over time. Strong products such as Kellogg's Corn Flakes, Coca-Cola, Ivory soap, Argo corn starch, and Caramilk candy bars have had extremely long productive lives.

product life cycle (PLC)
The concept that the profit-producing life of any product goes through a cycle of introduction, growth, maturity (levelling off), and decline.

Stages in the Product Life Cycle

The product life cycle is a natural process in which products are born, grow in stature, mature, and finally decline and die. The life cycle is typically divided into four states through which products pass as they "age" on the market:

1. *Introduction*. The introduction stage begins when the product reaches the marketplace. During this stage, marketers focus on making potential consumers aware of the product and its benefits. Because of extensive promotional and development costs, profits are nonexistent.
2. *Growth*. If the new product attracts and satisfies enough consumers, sales begin to climb rapidly. During this stage, the product begins to show a profit. Other firms in the industry move rapidly to introduce their own versions.
3. *Maturity*. Sales growth begins to slow. Although the product earns its highest profit level early in this stage, increased competition eventually leads to price cutting and lower profits. Towards the end of the stage, sales start to fall.
4. *Decline*. During this final stage, sales and profits continue to fall. New products in the introduction stage take away sales. Companies remove or reduce promotional support (ads and salespeople) but may let the product linger to provide some profits.

Figure 16.2 shows the four stages of the cycle—not yet complete—for VCRs. The product was introduced in the late 1970s and is, of course, widely used today. (Notice that profits lag behind sales because of the extensive costs of developing new products.) If the market becomes saturated, sales will begin to decline. Sales will also fall if new products, such as laser discs, send the VCR the way of the eight-track audio player.

Service products also have life cycles. Consider the management advice offered by consulting firms. Most major companies purchase advice for designing and implementing new management practices. For example, advice on appropriate wage-incentive systems flourished through the 1950s and then went into decline by the 1970s. Advice on how to implement "Management by Objectives" (see Chapter 6) was introduced in the 1960s, passed through the maturity stage during the 1970s, and today is in the decline stage. A more recent product, advice on "Total Quality Management" (see Chapter 14), has been introduced for firms that want assistance in implementing TQM.

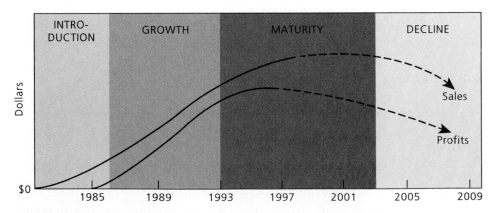

Figure 16.2
The product life cycle for VCRs. Note that profits lag behind sales due to the extensive development costs to create the new product.

Adjusting Marketing Strategy During the Life Cycle

As a product passes from stage to stage, marketing strategy changes, too. Each aspect of the marketing mix—product, price, promotion, place (distribution)—is re-examined for each stage of the life cycle. Changes in strategy for all four life-cycle stages are summarized in Table 16.1.

Extending Product Life

Not surprisingly, companies wish they could maintain a product's position in the maturity stage for longer periods of time. Many creative companies have successfully and profitably achieved this feat.[7] Cheez-Whiz experienced a rapid increase in sales when its maker used the popularity of microwave ovens to promote it as a "one-minute cheese sauce." Sales of television sets have been revitalized time and time again by introducing changes such as colour, portability, and stereo capability.

The beginning of a sales downturn in the maturity stage is not necessarily the time to start abandoning a product. Often, it is a time to realize that the old approach is starting to fade and to search for a new approach.

The Growth-Share Matrix

Companies with multiple product lines typically have various products at each point in the PLC. To decide how best to market each product, many marketers rely on the growth-share matrix, which classifies products according to market share and growth potential. Figure 16.3 shows the four categories into which products may be grouped: *question marks*, *stars*, *cash cows*, and *dogs*.

■ Most products start as *question marks*—low market share, high growth potential—because they are entering new markets that may grow but have not yet captured consumers' attention.

■ During the growth stage, products often become *stars* with high market share and high growth potential. Stars have large shares of still-growing markets.

Table 16.1   Marketing Strategy over the Life Cycle

Stage	Introduction	Growth	Maturity	Decline
Product Strategy	Develop market for product	Increase market share of product	Defend market share of product	Maintain efficiency in exploiting product
Pricing Strategy	High price, unique product/cover introduction costs	Lower price with passage of time	Price at or below competitors	Set price to stay profitable or decrease to liquidate
Promotion Strategy	Mount sales promotion for product awareness	Appeal to mass market; emphasize features, brand	Emphasize brand differences, benefits, loyalty	Reinforce loyal customers; reduce promotion expenditures
Place Strategy	Distribute through selective outlets	Build intensive network of outlets	Enlarge distribution network	Be selective in distribution; trim away unprofitable outlets

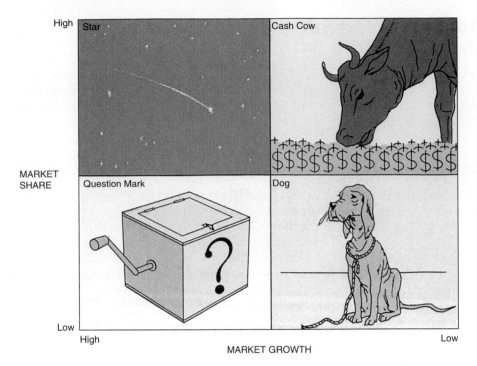

Figure 16.3
Growth-share matrix.

- In the maturity stage, products serve as *cash cows*—high market share, low growth potential—because their large market share makes them profitable even while market growth slows.

- Products in the decline stage are *dogs*—low market share, low growth potential—whose profits and sales signal that the life cycle is nearly complete.

When developing marketing plans, managers must consider not only the product's location on the growth-share matrix but also the direction in which it is moving. For example, while a question mark with increasing market share may be headed for stardom, a question mark with decreasing market share may require major changes or elimination.

In addition, companies always seek balance and continuity in the product mix. A company loaded with cash cows, for example, has a great present but may have a questionable future. Because they require a lot of attention, a firm loaded with stars may be focusing its managers' energies too narrowly. On the other hand, a firm with mostly cash cows and stars, some question marks, and a couple of unavoidable dogs has developed a strong product pipeline and a balanced product mix.

Identifying Products

As noted earlier in the chapter, developing the features of a product is only part of a marketer's battle. Identifying that product in consumers' minds through the use of brand names, packaging, and labelling is also important.

Branding Products

brand names

Those specific names of products associated with a manufacturer, wholesaler, and/or retailer that are designed to distinguish products from those of competitors and are promoted as part of the product.

An especially important component of product development is deciding on a name for the product. **Brand names** were introduced to try to simplify the process of product selection for consumers. Customers try a product, remember its name, and go back to it next time. Millions of dollars have been spent developing names like Noxzema, Prudential, and Minute Maid and attaching meaning to them in consumers' minds.

Managers have to be concerned not only about the brand names of the *products* they sell, but also about the name they choose for their *company*. With so many companies jostling for attention, it is not surprising that companies are choosing attention-getting names like Gadzooks, Wet Seal, Noodle Kidoodle, Koo Koo Roo, and Ugly Duckling.[8]

The key in coming up with a brand name for a product is to keep the name simple. As few letters and numbers as possible make the name sound "good" and easy to remember. The brand must also be consistent with current lifestyles. Post recently changed the name of Sugar Smacks to Honey Smacks and its mascot from Sugar Bear to Honey Bear. In today's health conscious market, a honey cereal is viewed more favourably than a sugar-coated one.

An issue of growing importance in branding strategy is faced by firms that sell products internationally. They must also consider how product names will translate in various languages. In Spanish, for example, the name of Chevrolet's now-defunct Nova simply became *no va*—"it does not go." Sales were particularly poor in South America. Similarly, Rolls-Royce was once going to name a new touring car "Silver Mist." Rolls changed the name to "Silver Shadow" when it discovered that *mist* is German for "manure."[9] Naturally, foreign companies hoping to sell in Canada must be equally careful. The box "Building Brands at Nestlé" describes that company's brand strategy.

Types of Brands

Virtually every product has a brand name of some form. However, different types of brand names tell the alert consumer something about the product's origin.

National Brands

Brand name products that are produced and distributed by the manufacturer are called **national brands**. These brands, such as Scotch tape, are often widely recognized by consumers because of large national advertising campaigns. The costs of developing a positive image for a national brand are high, so some companies use their national brand on several related products. Procter & Gamble now markets Ivory shampoo, capitalizing on the widely recognized name of its soaps.

national brands
Products distributed by and carrying a name associated with the manufacturer.

Licensed Brands

More and more nationally recognized companies and personalities have sold other companies the right to place their names on products, which are **licensed brands**. Licensing has become big business. Coca-Cola Company and Hard Rock Cafe will make millions on licensed apparel sales this year. Free advertising from T-shirts and sweatshirts worn primarily by young people—an age group in which cola consumption is heavy—is just an added bonus.

Tie-ins with movies and other entertainment vehicles are popular forms of licensing. In 1994, the surprise hit *Forrest Gump*, for instance, climbed to number five on the all-time box-office list. In the process, it generated nearly 30 different licensing agreements, with products ranging from T-shirts and baseball caps to a line of shrimp foods from the Bubba Gump Seafood Co. The movie's owner, Viacom Inc., will be paid anywhere from 5 to 12 percent of the wholesale price of every licensed item.[10]

licensed brands
Selling the right to use a brand name, a celebrity's name, or some other well-known identification mark to another company to use on a product.

International Report

Building Brands at Nestlé

Nestlé is the world's most successful international food company. It is the market leader in instant coffee in Australia (71 percent), France (67 percent), Japan (74 percent), and Mexico (85 percent). In powdered milk, it is the leader in the Philippines (66 percent) and Brazil (58 percent). In Chile, Nestlé has 73 percent of the cookie market and 70 percent of the soups and juices market.

Although Nestlé is a global company, it lives on local brands. It achieves much of its growth in the developing countries simply by getting there before other companies do. Once in a country, it builds both a manufacturing and a political presence. Nestlé already gets one quarter of its worldwide sales from the Far East and Latin America. About one third of company profits come from products sold outside the developed countries.

Nestlé owns nearly 8000 brands worldwide, but you won't see hundreds of their brands in a store near you. Only about 750 are registered in more than one country, and only 80 brands are registered in more than 10 countries. Nestlé thus rejects the "one-world, one-brand" school of marketing thought that companies like Coca-Cola and Pepsico embrace.

In the developed world, Nestlé pursues a strategy of acquiring well-known brands. For example, it owns Stouffer's, Perrier, and Carnation. In the developing countries, it grows by building up brand loyalty to a local brand— for example, Bear Brand condensed milk in Asia. By developing only a few brands in each country, Nestlé is able to highly focus its advertising money and thereby achieve big market shares. The executive vice-president in charge of marketing says the company does not believe in life cycles for brands; he says that a well-managed brand will outlive any manager.

Nestlé's experience selling coffee in Thailand demonstrates their attitude towards brand development. How does a Swiss company sell a hot beverage in the tropics? The general manager of Nestlé Thailand decided that coffee was the perfect product to capitalize on the growth that Thailand was experiencing in the late 1980s. He and his team decided to forget advertising coffee based on traditional taste and aroma. Instead, the advertisements emphasized coffee as a stress reducer and as a promoter of romance. When one of the team members saw a Nestlé promotion on cold coffee from Nestlé Greece, they quickly adopted that idea. Coffee sales jumped from $25 million in 1987 to $100 million in 1994.

An extreme example of Nestlé's strategy of local brand development is found in China. After 13 years of talks, Nestlé was finally invited into China in 1987 because the government wanted to increase milk production. Nestlé opened a powdered milk plant in 1990, but then it had a tough choice to make: use the overburdened local network of trains and roads to collect milk, or build its own roads. It chose the latter, even though it was very costly. Farmers now follow Nestlé's "milk roads" when they bring their milk to the chilling centres for weighing and analysis.

Nestlé pays the farmers promptly, something the government didn't always do, so farmers now have an incentive to produce more milk (the district cow population has increased 50 percent in the last 18 months). Nestlé also brought in experts to train farmers in animal health and hygiene. In its first year, the factory produced 316 tonnes of powdered milk; by 1994 it produced 10 000 tonnes. Nestlé now has exclusive rights to sell the product across China for 15 years. The company predicts that sales will reach $700 million by the year 2000.

Private Brands

private brands

Products promoted by and carrying a name associated with the retailer or wholesaler, not the manufacturer.

Cott Corp.
http://www.cott.com

When a wholesaler or retailer develops a brand and has the manufacturer place that brand name on the product, the resulting product name is a **private brand**. One of the best-known purveyors of private brands is Sears, with its Craftsman tools and Kenmore appliances.

J. Sainsbury PLC, the largest supermarket chain in Britain, recently introduced its own private brand of cola in a can that looks strikingly like the one used by Coke. The two products are stocked side by side on store shelves, and Sainsbury's offering is noticeably cheaper than Coke. The product is made by Cott Corp. of Toronto, which has successfully won market share from Coca-Cola in Canada.[11] The story is much the same in North America. Under the Sam's American Choice label, Cott sells a billion cans of soft drinks each year at Wal-Mart.

Loblaw Cos. Ltd., owned by George Weston, has created a line of upscale private brands called *President's Choice*. Clever advertising, fancy labels, and exotic product names differentiate the line and draw consumer attention to items like peanut butter and cookies. Another Weston-owned company, Holt

The Toronto Raptors benefit both from the licensing fees they receive as well as from the free advertising whenever these products are used.

Renfrew, is also planning to put more emphasis on its private brand. A stylish Prada suit sells for $2000 to $4000, but the Holt Renfrew equivalent will be priced at only $300 to $700.[12]

Private brands are causing difficulties for U.S. firms in foreign markets. After Dole, Tropicana, and other American orange juice brands went on sale in Japan, the Daiei supermarket chain immediately launched its own Savings line of private label juices. Daiei's products include juice made from Brazilian oranges and are priced 40 percent below American brands. A pint of Daiei's premium ice cream sells for half the price of Lady Borden. Daiei buys its ice cream from the same supplier and packages it in cartons quite similar to Lady Borden's.

Generic Products

"No-name" products in very plain packages with black lettering describing the contents were first introduced in the 1970s. For a while their lower prices attracted consumers. Supermarkets began devoting entire aisles to **generic products** such as paper towels, green beans, and shampoo. But concern over consistent product quality has resulted in a de-emphasis of generic products in recent years.

generic products
Products carrying no brand or producer name and sold at lower prices.

Trade Marks, Patents, and Copyrights

Because brand development is very expensive, a company does not want another company using its name and confusing consumers into buying a substitute product. Many companies apply to the Canadian government and receive a **trade mark**, the exclusive legal right to use a brand name. Trade marks are granted for 15 years and may be renewed for further periods of 15 years, but only if the company continues to protect its brand name.

trade mark
The exclusive legal right to use a brand name.

Just what can be trade marked is not always clear, however. If the company allows the name to lapse into common usage, the courts may take away protection. Common usage occurs when the company fails to use the ® symbol for its brand. It also occurs if the company fails to correct those who do not acknowledge the brand as a trade mark. Recently Windsurfer (a popular brand of sailboards by WSI Inc.) lost its trade mark. Like the trampoline, yo-yo, and thermos, the brand name has become the common term for the product and can now be used by any sailboard company. But companies like Xerox, Coke, Jello, and Scotch tape have successfully defended their brand names.

patent

Protects an invention or idea for a period of 20 years.

Companies want to be sure that both product brands *and* new product ideas are protected. A **patent** protects an invention or idea for a period of 20 years. The cost is $1000 to $1500; it takes nine months to three years to secure a patent from the Canadian Patent Office.[13]

Copyrights give exclusive ownership rights to the creators of books, articles, designs, illustrations, photos, films, and music. Computer programs and even semiconductor chips are also protected. Copyrights extend to creators for their entire lives and to their estates for 50 years thereafter. Copyrights apply to the tangible expressions of an idea, not to the idea itself. For example, the idea of cloning dinosaurs from fossil DNA cannot be copyrighted, but Michael Crichton, the author of *Jurassic Park*, could copyright his novel because it is the tangible result of the basic idea.

Brand Loyalty

brand loyalty

Customers' recognition of, preference for, and insistence on buying a product with a certain brand name.

Companies that spend the large amount of money it takes to develop a brand are looking for one thing from consumers: **brand loyalty**. That is, they want to develop customers who, when they need a particular item, will go back to the same brand and buy the company's products.

Brand loyalty is measured in three stages. First, the company wants *brand recognition*. By putting the brand in front of consumers many times and associating it with a type of product, the producer hopes that consumers will become aware of its existence.

Recognition is not enough, however. The owner of the brand wants consumers to start showing *brand preference* when they make a purchase. Brand preference requires not only awareness that the brand exists but also a favourable attitude towards the ability of the brand to provide benefits.

Finally, because a brand may be unavailable in a store from time to time, companies seek *brand insistence*. Brand insistence is highly valued by brand owners, but it is very difficult to achieve. For all convenience and many shopping products, consumers will freely substitute another brand when they need a product. Usually, only specialty products have much potential for developing brand insistence in a large group of consumers. For example, a family wanting to buy or sell a home might insist on using a trusted local realtor.

Packaging Products

packaging

The physical container in which a product is sold, including the label.

With a few exceptions, including fresh fruits and vegetables, structural steel, and some other industrial products, products need some form of **packaging** in which to be carried to the market. A package also serves as an in-store advertisement that makes the product attractive, clearly displays the brand, and identifies product features and benefits.

A growing number of companies are shifting their promotional spending from advertising to packaging. The trend is to lighter, brighter colours that stand out more on grocery store shelves. The package is the marketer's last chance to say "buy it" to the consumer.[14]

Packaging reduces the risk of damage, breakage, or spoilage, and it increases the difficulty of stealing smaller products. But once a product is opened and used, expensive packaging may become waste.

The year 1982 marked a turning point for the packaging industry. In that year seven people were killed when they took Tylenol that had been contaminated with cyanide after the capsules left the factory. In response to this and other incidents, consumers have begun to demand product packaging that provides some safety insurance. The packaging industry has responded with tamper-resistant package designs.

Labelling Products

Every product has a **label** on its package. Packaging and labelling can help market the product. The information on package labels is regulated by the federal government. The ***Consumer Packaging and Labelling Act*** has two main purposes: the first is to provide a comprehensive set of rules for packaging and labelling of consumer products, and the second is to ensure that the manufacturer provides full and factual information on labels. All prepackaged products must state in French and English the quantity enclosed in metric and imperial units. The name and description of the product must also appear on the label in both French and English.

In recent years labels have begun to display the Universal Product Code (UPC) bar code. This series of bars of various lengths and widths and spaces helps identify and keep track of merchandise. It also enables retailers to speed up the check-out process by using special bar-code scanners.

label
That part of a product's packaging that identifies the product's name and contents and sometimes its benefits.

Consumer Packaging and Labelling Act
A federal law that provides comprehensive rules for packaging and labelling of consumer products.

Promoting Products and Services

It is no secret to anyone who watches television, reads magazines, or even surveys the urban landscape that businesses rely on advertising, publicity, and other techniques in the battle to attract the attention of customers and maintain their loyalty. In many businesses, promotion can be the key either to establishing a new product or keeping an established product in the public eye.

The Importance of Promotion

Let's begin our look at promotion by observing how one company responded to threats in its marketing environment. For years, Burger King had declined to follow industry leaders McDonald's and Wendy's in introducing discounted products like "value meals." Like many franchisers, BK feared that discounting would cut into profit margins. But profits languished anyway, and in October 1993, new CEO James B. Adamson rolled out the "value menu," which offers breakfast, lunch, and dinner specials at 99¢, $1.99, and $2.99. He also informed the company's ad agency that he was putting the account up for review and seeking a refreshing campaign to replace the MTV-modelled "BK Tee Vee" spots that had alienated longtime customers. Finally, Adamson redistributed BK's advertising expenditures: Whereas the company customarily spent about $180 million of its $250 million annual marketing budget on TV and radio spots, Adamson reduced the amount to 40 percent and earmarked the rest for national discounts and local-market promotions.[15]

Burger King perceived its problem to lie in its *communications mix*—the total message that it was sending to consumers about its product. In particular, the company reacted to competitive pressures by adjusting its promotional practices, relying less on advertising and more on two other elements of marketing strategy: pricing and sales promotions.

As we noted in Chapter 15, *promotion* is any technique designed to sell a product. As part of the communications mix designed for products, promotional techniques—especially advertising—must communicate the uses, features, and benefits of products. Sales promotions, however, also include various programs that add further value beyond the benefits inherent in the product. It is nice, for example, to get a high-quality product at a reasonable price but even better when the seller offers, say, a rebate or a bonus pack with "20 percent more FREE." In promoting products, then, marketers have an array of tools at their disposal.

In free market systems, a business uses promotional methods to communicate information about itself and its products to consumers, industrial buyers, or both. The purpose, of course, is to influence purchase decisions. From an *information* standpoint, promotions seek to accomplish four things with potential customers:

- make them *aware* of products
- make them *knowledgeable* about products
- *persuade* them to like the products
- persuade them to *purchase* products.

Successful promotions provide communications about the product and create exchanges that satisfy both the consumer's and organization's objectives. At the same time, however, because promotions are expensive, choosing the best promotional mix becomes critical. The promotional program, then, whether at the introduction stage (promoting for new product awareness) or maturity stage (promoting brand benefits and customer loyalty) can determine the success or failure of a product.

Developing a promotional plan requires making decisions about promotional objectives, promotional strategies, and the promotional mix. These decisions are summarized in Figure 16.4 and discussed below.

Promotional Objectives

The ultimate objective of any promotion is to increase sales. However, marketers also use promotion to communicate information, position products, add value, and control sales volume.[16]

Communication of Information

Consumers cannot buy a product unless they have been informed about it. Information can advise customers about the availability of a product, educate them on the latest technological advances, or announce the candidacy of someone running for a government office. Information may be communicated in writing (newspapers and magazines), verbally (in person or over the telephone), or visually (television, a matchbook cover, or a

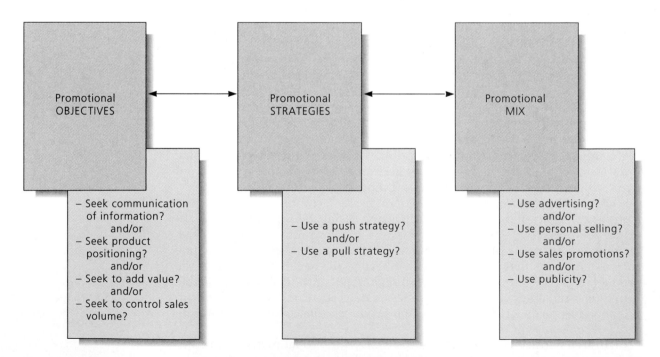

Figure 16.4
Developing the promotional plan.

billboard). Today, the communication of information regarding a company's products or services is so important that marketers try to place it wherever consumers may be. If you are an average consumer, you come in contact with approximately 1500 bits of promotional communication a day![17]

Product Positioning

Another objective of promotion, **product positioning**, is to establish an easily identifiable image of a product in the minds of consumers. For example, by selling only in department stores, Estée Lauder products have positioned themselves as more upscale than cosmetics sold in drugstores. With product positioning, the company is trying to appeal to a specific segment of the market rather than to the market as a whole.

Adding Value

Today's value-conscious customers gain benefits when the promotional mix is shifted and when it communicates value-increased products. Earlier we saw how Burger King shifted its promotional mix by cutting back on advertising and using those funds instead for customer discounts. Similarly, Compaq Computer countered increased pressure from low-priced competitors by introducing its own lower-priced desktop computers with enhanced capabilities.[18]

Customers must be given information about the value-adding characteristics—say, warranties, repair contracts, and after-purchase service—by which a product provides greater value than its competitors. Lexus, for example, prides itself on adding value by providing superb treatment of customers. Sales representatives don't pry, solicit, or hover over buyers in the showroom. The first two scheduled maintenances are free. Waiting customers can use offices, desks, or phones and can borrow cars or get rides.

Controlling Sales Volume

Sales volume control is also an objective of promotions. Many companies, such as Hallmark Cards, experience seasonal sales patterns. By increasing its promotional activities in slow periods, the firm can achieve a more stable sales volume throughout the year. As a result, it can keep its production and distribution systems running evenly.

Promotional Strategies

Once a firm's promotional objectives are clear, it must develop a promotional strategy to achieve these objectives. Promotional strategies may be of the push or pull variety. A company with a **push strategy** will aggressively "push" its product through wholesalers and retailers, who persuade customers to buy it. In contrast, a company with a **pull strategy** appeals directly to customers, who demand the product from retailers, who in turn demand the product from wholesalers. Advertising "pulls" while personal selling "pushes." In rare cases, a company may purposely do very little promotion of its products (see the box "There Are Always Exceptions to the General Rule").

Makers of industrial products most often use a push strategy, and makers of consumer products most often use a pull strategy. Many large firms use a combination of the two strategies. For example, General Foods uses advertising to create consumer demand (pull) for its cereals. It also pushes wholesalers and retailers to stock these products.

The Promotional Mix

As we noted in Chapter 15, there are four basic types of promotional tools: advertising, personal selling, sales promotions, and publicity and public relations.

product positioning
The establishment of an easily identifiable image of a product in the minds of consumers.

push strategy
A promotional strategy in which a company aggressively pushes its product through wholesalers and retailers, who persuade customers to buy it.

pull strategy
A promotional strategy in which a company appeals directly to customers, who demand the product from retailers, who demand the product from wholesalers.

International Report

There Are Always Exceptions to the General Rule

Talk to marketing executives today and they will tell you that there is fierce competition among the competing brands in every product class, and that companies must aggressively promote their products or they will be run out of business by their competitors. That's true generally, but there are always exceptions to the general rule.

Consider Langlitz Leathers, a Portland, Oregon, firm that makes leather jackets. The company was founded in the 1930s by Ross Langlitz, a motorcycle racing enthusiast. He was unimpressed with the leather jackets that were available at the time, so he quit his job at a leather-glove factory and began producing his own. The designs he created eventually set a standard for the industry (wide collar, shiny zippers, etc.).

Langlitz jackets are worn by rebels like Hell's Angels members, rockers like Bruce Springsteen, actors like Sylvester Stallone, and lots of business executives. The jackets can cost as much as $800. If you want one, you have to

place an order and then wait for seven months. The wait would be even longer if impatient customers didn't just leave and buy elsewhere. Langlitz steers these frustrated customers down the street to one of its competitors, Leatherworks Inc. The owner of that store is grateful.

Langlitz is not a well-known company, even to its direct competitors. But it has a cult-like following among bikers, police officers, and movie stars (Clark Gable wore a Langlitz). Part of the mystique of the product is the fact that you have to wait so long to get it. The company employs 15 people and makes just six leather jackets each day, the same number they have made for the last 40 years. The Langlitz leather jacket is the Rolls Royce of leather jackets, and the company simply refuses to expand production. Low production means that the high quality of the product can be maintained, and a relaxed atmosphere is created in the workplace.

---

promotional mix

That portion of marketing concerned with choosing the best combination of advertising, personal selling, sales promotions, and publicity to sell a product.

Figure 16.5 shows the relative usage of these tools by consumer- and industrial-goods businesses.

The best combination of these tools—the best **promotional mix**—depends on many factors. The company's product, the costs of different tools versus the promotions budget, and characteristics in the target audience all play a role. Figure 16.6 shows different combinations of products, promotional tools, and target consumers.

The Product

The nature of the product being promoted affects the mix greatly. For example, advertising can reach a large number of widely dispersed consumers. It is used by makers of products that might be bought by anyone, such as sun-

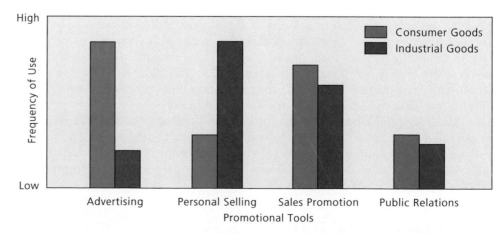

Figure 16.5
The relative importance of promotional tools.

Goods Promotion: House
(real estate)
Tool: Personal selling
Consumer: House buyer

Organizational Promotion:
Boy Scouts of Canada
Tool: Publicity
Consumer: Young men

Service Promotion: Weight-loss program
Tool: Sales promotion (coupon)
Consumer: Overweight person

Event Promotion: Rock
concert
Tool: Advertising
Consumer: Cheering fan

Person or Idea Promotion: Candidate for Prime Minister
Tool: Publicity/advertising/personal sales
Consumer: Voter

Figure 16.6
Each promotional tool should be properly matched with the product being promoted and the target customer.

glasses, radios, and snack foods. Companies introducing new products also favour advertising because it reaches a large number of people quickly and can repeat a message many times. Personal selling, on the other hand, is important when the product appeals to a specific audience, such as piping or pressure gauges for industrial customers.

Cost of the Tools

The cost of communication tools is important. Because personal selling is an expensive communication tool, it is most appropriate in marketing high-priced goods such as computers for industrial customers and homes for consumers. In contrast, advertising reaches more customers per dollar spent.

A promotional mix that is good for one company may not be good for another. A large firm can afford to spend millions of dollars on national advertising, but a local firm must rely on personal selling and publicity to promote its products.

Promotion and the Buyer Decision Process

Another consideration in establishing the promotional mix is the stage of the buyer decision process that customers are in. As noted in Chapter 15, customers must first recognize the need to make a purchase. At this stage, marketers need to make sure the buyer is aware that their products exist. Thus, advertising and publicity, which can reach a large number of people quickly, are important.

At the next stage, customers want to learn more about possible products. Advertising and personal selling are important because they both can educate the customer about the product.

During the third stage, customers will evaluate and compare competing products. Personal selling is vital at this point because sales representatives can demonstrate their product's quality and performance in direct relation to the competition's product.

Next, customers decide on a specific product and buy it. Sales promotion is effective at this stage because it can give consumers an incentive to buy. Personal selling can also help by bringing the product to convenient locations for the consumer.

Finally, consumers evaluate the product after buying it. Advertising, or even personal selling, is sometimes used after the sale to remind consumers that they made wise and prudent purchases. Figure 16.7 summarizes effective promotional tools for each stage of the consumer buying process.

The Promotional Mix Decision

Choosing the promotional mix begins by determining the promotional budget—one of the marketing manager's most difficult decisions. The budget specifies how much of the firm's total resources will be spent on promotions. The combined costs of personal selling, advertising, sales promotion, and public relations must fall within the budgeted amount. Moreover, the elements of the mix, collectively, must be *balanced* if they are to have the desired effect on attitudes and purchasing decisions.

The stage in the product's life cycle influences the promotional balance. New product introductions, for instance, may call for expensive personal sales promotions concentrated on a limited audience of early adopters and dealers. Personal sales may also be combined with direct mail to instil product awareness in the selected audience. The maturity stage, on the other hand, may call

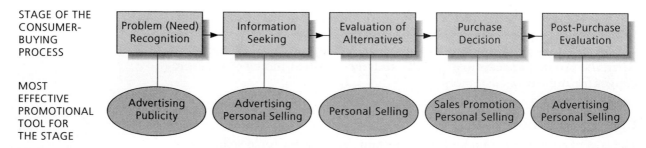

Figure 16.7
The promotional mix and the consumer buying process.

for mass-media advertising that emphasizes brand features and lower prices. Advertising may be used with sales promotions—say, coupons to get buyers to try the seller's product instead of competitors'.

Now that you have a general understanding of promotional tools, let's look more closely at each.

Advertising Promotions

What candy bar is "a nice light snack"? What soap is "99 and 44/100% pure"? What is the store where "the lowest price is the law"? What product is "only available in Canada? Pity"? If you are like most Canadians, you can answer these questions because of advertising. (The answers are Coffee Crisp, Ivory Soap, Zellers, and Red Rose Tea.) Figure 16.8 shows the top 10 advertisers in Canada.

Advertising Strategies

Advertising strategies most often depend on which stage of the product life cycle their product is in. During the introduction stage, **informative advertising** can help develop an awareness of the company and its product among buyers and can establish a primary demand for the product. For example, before a new textbook is published, instructors receive direct-mail advertisements notifying them of the book's contents and availability.

informative advertising
An advertising strategy, appropriate to the introduction stage of the product life cycle, in which the goal is to make potential customers aware that a product exists.

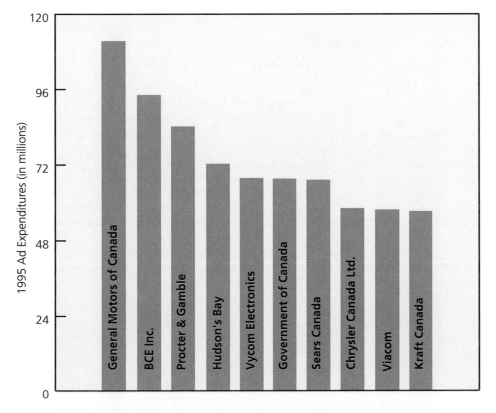

Figure 16.8
The top 10 advertisers in Canada.

persuasive advertising

An advertising strategy, appropriate to the growth stage of the product life cycle, in which the goal is to influence the customer to buy the firm's product rather than the similar product of a competitor.

comparative advertising

An advertising strategy, appropriate to the growth stage of the product life cycle, in which the goal is to influence the customer to switch from a competitor's similar product to the firm's product by directly comparing the two products.

reminder advertising

An advertising strategy, appropriate to the latter part of the maturity stage of the product life cycle, in which the goal is to keep the product's name in the minds of customers.

As products become established, advertising strategies must change. During the growth stage, **persuasive advertising** can influence consumers to buy the company's products rather than those of its rivals. Persuasive advertising is also important during the maturity stage to maintain the product's level of sales. **Comparative advertising** involves comparing the sponsoring company's brand name with a competitor's brand name in such a way that the competitor's brand looks inferior. For example, Procter & Gamble aired advertisements claiming that its Bounty brand had more absorbency than Scott Paper's competing product. Scott retaliated by producing an advertisement which said that Scott Clean Ultra was 60 percent more absorbent than P&G's Bounty.[19] The box "Battery Giants Get a Jolt" describes a recent example of comparative advertising in Canada.

In many countries (for example, Japan), advertisements that knock a competitor's product are frowned on. But not so in Canada or the U.S. In the European Union comparative advertising became legal in 1993, but advertisers must meet several limiting conditions.[20]

During the latter part of the maturity stage and all of the decline stage, **reminder advertising** keeps the product's name in front of the consumer.

Whatever the product's life cycle stage, advertising strategies must consider *timing*. Should the organization advertise continually throughout the year or seasonally? Companies such as banks space ads evenly throughout the year. In contrast, H&R Block Inc. runs advertisements in one major spurt during the tax season.

The Canadian Business Scene

Battery Giants Get a Jolt

Just before Christmas in 1994, Pure Energy Battery Corp. of Mississauga launched high-profile TV advertisements that compared their new Pure Energy Rechargeable alkaline battery with the batteries made by the two market leaders (Duracell Canada and Eveready Canada). The advertisements showed an animated battery taunting "Mr. Duracell" and "Mr. Energizer" to "move over" and make room for Canada's first mercury-free alkaline battery. The advertisement went on to say that Pure Energy's battery had "at least 25 times more life" than the other two batteries.

Eveready (the one with the pink bunny it its advertisements) had a lawyer's letter sent to Pure Energy, threatening legal action over the advertisement. And Duracell (the copper-top battery) launched a complaint with the Canadian Advertising Foundation, an industry self-regulatory group, claiming that the advertisement was misleading. Pure Energy then changed its claim to "up to 25 times more life," but that was still not acceptable to Duracell.

The president of Duracell said that he was not upset that the Duracell name was used in the advertisement, because the company appreciates the free publicity. Rather, he said that the claim Pure Energy made for its battery is physically and mathematically impossible. The vice-president of sales and marketing for Pure Energy (a former Duracell employee) says the claims can be documented.

Disputes between companies about comparative advertising are not new. Earlier in 1994, an Ontario court ordered Robin Hood Multifoods Inc. to stop airing comparative advertisements naming Tenderflake and Gainsborough pie crusts by name. These products are made by rival Maple Leaf Foods.

Pure Energy Battery
http://www.bti.ca/pur.htm

Advertising Media

In developing advertising strategies, marketers must consider the best **advertising medium** for their message. IBM, for example, uses television ads to keep its name fresh in consumers' minds. But it also uses newspaper and magazine ads to educate consumers on products' abilities and trade publications to introduce new software.

An advertiser selects media with a number of factors in mind. The marketer must first ask: Which medium will reach the people I want to reach? If a firm is selling hog breeding equipment, it might choose *Playboar*, a business magazine read mostly by hog farmers. If it is selling silverware, it might choose a magazine for brides. If it is selling toothpaste, the choice might be a general audience television program or a general audience magazine such as *Reader's Digest* (or *Sélection*, for exposure to a similar audience of francophones).

Each advertising medium has its own advantages and disadvantages. The relative importance of different media is shown in Figure 16.9.

advertising medium
The specific communication device—television, radio, newspapers, direct mail, magazines, billboards—used to carry a firm's advertising message to potential customers.

Newspapers

Newspapers remain the most widely used advertising medium. They offer excellent coverage, since each local market has at least one daily newspaper, and many people read the paper every day. This medium offers flexible, rapid coverage, since ads can change from day to day. It also offers believable coverage, since ads are presented side by side with news. However, newspapers are generally thrown out after one day, often do not print in colour, and have poor reproduction quality. Moreover, newspapers do not usually allow advertisers to target their audience well.

Television

Television allows advertisers to combine sight, sound, and motion, thus appealing to almost all the viewer's senses. Information on viewer demographics for a particular program allows advertisers to promote to their target audiences. National advertising is done on television because it reaches more people than any other medium.

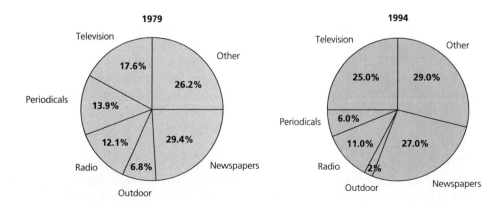

Figure 16.9
Relative importance of various media; 1979 and 1994.

Pepsi Cola
http://www.pepsi.com

In 1991, Pepsi Cola Canada Ltd. asked for amateur videos for the best rendition of its jingle: "Diet Pepsi: You Got The Right One Baby, Uh-Huh" (a takeoff on the Ray Charles commercial for regular Pepsi). After judging 500 videos, the company awarded the $10 000 first prize to the firefighters of Cole Harbour, Nova Scotia. Their video showed them walking over cans of Diet Coke to save a Diet Pepsi machine from a burning building.[21] The video was then shown as part of a television advertising campaign.

One disadvantage of television is that too many commercials cause viewers to confuse products. Most people, for example, can't recall whether a tire commercial was sponsored by Firestone, Goodyear, or B.F. Goodrich. In addition, VCR viewers often fast-forward past the ads of TV shows that they have recorded. Moreover, because "commercial spots" last only a short time (usually 30 seconds), the impact of the commercial is lost if the viewer is not paying attention. The brevity of TV ads also makes television a poor medium in which to educate viewers about complex products. Finally, television is the most expensive medium in which to advertise. A 30-second commercial during the NFL Super Bowl costs about $1 000 000.

Direct Mail

direct mail
Printed advertisements, such as flyers, mailed directly to consumers' homes or places of business.

Direct mail involves fliers or other types of printed advertisements mailed directly to consumers' homes or places of business. Direct mail allows the company to select its audience and personalize its message. Although many people discard "junk mail," targeted recipients with stronger-than-average interest are more likely to buy. Although direct mail involves the largest advance costs of any advertising technique, it does appear to have the highest cost effectiveness. Particularly effective have been "fax attacks," in which advertisers send their "mail" messages electronically via fax machines and get higher response rates than they would if they used Canada Post.

The rise of mailing lists and the high cost of developing them have led to a thriving industry: the swapping and selling of mailing lists and consumer data among businesses for use in direct-mail advertising. Such practices present an ethical question for many businesses, whose customers resent having their names and addresses bought and sold or their fax machines tied up. As a result of consumer protests, many companies now promise not to sell the customer's name if the customer asks them not to.

Radio

A tremendous number of people listen to the radio each day, and radio ads are inexpensive. In addition, since most radio is programmed locally, this medium gives advertisers a high degree of customer selectivity. For example, radio stations are already segmented into listening categories such as rock and roll, country and western, jazz, talk shows, news, and religious programming.

Like television, however, radio ads are over quickly. And radio permits only an audio presentation. As well, people tend to use the radio as "background" while they are doing other things, paying little attention to advertisements.

Magazines

The many different magazines on the market provide a high level of consumer selectivity. The person who reads *Popular Photography* is more likely to be interested in the latest specialized lenses from Canon than is a *Gourmet* magazine subscriber. Magazine advertising allows for excellent reproduction of photographs and artwork that not only grab buyers' attention but may also convince them of the product's value. And magazines allow advertisers plenty of space for detailed product information. Magazines have a long life and tend to be passed from person to person, thus doubling and tripling the number of exposures. The latest gimmick in print advertising is to catch the reader's eye by having the top half of an advertisement printed right side up and the bottom half upside down.[22]

One problem with magazine advertising is that ads must be submitted well in advance to be included in a certain issue. Often there is no guarantee of where within a magazine an ad will appear. Naturally, a company prefers to have its advertisement appear near the front of the magazine or within a feature article.

Outdoor

Outdoor advertising—billboards, signs, and advertisements on buses, taxis, and subways—is relatively inexpensive, faces little competition for customers' attention, and is subject to high repeat exposure. Unfortunately, companies have little control over who will see their advertisements. Because roadside billboards are prohibited on some major Ontario arteries, Moving Impressions Inc. has introduced "rolling billboards"—advertisements attached to the sides of large freight trucks. The truck companies get a piece of the action.[23]

Word-of-Mouth

Consumers form very strong opinions about products as a result of conversations with friends and acquaintances. If **word-of-mouth** says that a product is good, higher product sales are very likely. Of course, word-of-mouth will also spread bad news about a product.

Some companies rely heavily on word-of-mouth advertising. Big Rock Brewery does no advertising, but relies on word-of-mouth to expand its market share. It already has a 7 percent share of Alberta's draft beer market, and its exports to the U.S. are increasing rapidly.[24]

word-of-mouth
Opinions about the value of products passed among consumers in informal discussions.

Electronic Commerce

A new and rapidly growing approach to advertising involves the Internet. **Electronic commerce** refers to the buying and selling of goods through electronic means. Consumers can log on to various Web sites, examine the products available, and then decide which ones to purchase.

Internet shopping is beneficial to both the buyer and the seller. The company does not have to maintain a physical outlet with all its accompanying costs, yet it is able to reach a global market. The consumer understands that Internet shopping is an efficient way to gather information and make comparisons among competing products. But Internet advertising has limitations. Unless Web sites are very interesting, most consumers probably will not pay much attention to them. Consumers may also be reluctant to wade through thousands of electronic pages looking at details on hundreds of different products. This type of advertising will develop rapidly in the next few years, and time will tell exactly what form and importance electronic commerce will eventually assume.

electronic commerce
The buying and selling of goods through electronic means.

Other Advertising Channels

A combination of many additional media, including catalogues, sidewalk handouts, *Yellow Pages*, skywriting, telephone calls, special events, and door-to-door communications, make up the remaining advertisements that Canadians are exposed to. Bell Canada has introduced a "smart phone" called Direct Access that allows businesses to advertise on telephone screens; it also allows customers to shop, bank, and scan the news on the phone screen.[25] Each of these media is specialized and used selectively, often locally by small businesses, political campaigners, and special-interest groups.

The combination of media that a company chooses to advertise its products is called its **media mix**. Although different industries use different mixes, most depend on multiple media to advertise their products and services (see Table 16.2).

media mix
The combination of media through which a company chooses to advertise its products.

Table 16.2   Media Mix by Industry

Industry	Magazines	Newspapers	Outdoor	Television	Radio
Retail stores	4.2%	61.1%	1.9%	27.8%	5.0%
Industrial materials	29.3	7.8	0.3	52.8	9.8
Insurance and real estate	11.1	53.5	2.2	29.3	3.9
Food	14.9	0.7	0.3	80.5	3.6
Apparel	50.5	1.8	0.5	45.8	1.4

Types of Advertising

brand advertising

Advertising that promotes a specific brand-name product.

product advertising

A variation on brand advertising that promotes a general type of product or service.

advocacy advertising

Advertising that promotes a particular viewpoint or candidate.

institutional advertising

Advertising that promotes a firm's long-term image, not a specific product.

retail advertising

Advertising by retailers designed to reach end-users of a consumer product.

cooperative advertising

Advertising in which a manufacturer together with a retailer or wholesaler advertise to reach customers.

trade advertising

Advertising by manufacturers designed to reach potential wholesalers and retailers.

industrial advertising

Advertising by manufacturers designed to reach other manufacturers' professional purchasing agents and managers of firms buying raw materials or components.

Regardless of the media used, advertisements fall into one of several categories. **Brand advertising** promotes a specific brand, such as Kodak 126 film, Air Canada, or Nike Air Jordan basketball shoes. A variation on brand advertising, **product advertising** promotes a general type of product or service such as milk or dental services. **Advocacy advertising** promotes a particular candidate or viewpoint, as in ads for political candidates at election time and antidrug commercials. **Institutional advertising** promotes a firm's long-term image rather than a specific product.

In consumer markets, local stores usually sponsor **retail advertising** to encourage consumers to visit the store and buy its products and services. Larger retailers, such as Kmart and The Bay, use retail advertising both locally and nationally. Often retail advertising is actually **cooperative advertising**, with the cost of the advertising shared by the retailer and the manufacturer.

In industrial markets, to communicate with companies that distribute its products, some firms use **trade advertising** publications. For example, a firm that makes plumbing fixtures might advertise in *Hardware Retailer* to persuade large hardware stores to carry its products. And to reach the professional purchasing agent and managers at firms buying raw materials or components, companies use **industrial advertising**.

Make the mix that makes the party.

HOW TO BE A LOCAL HERO

BE PICKY Do you ever feel overwhelmed by all the good causes that ask for donations? You'd like to help every one, but it's just not possible. Local Heroes know that the answer is to be picky. Review the causes you already support and be sure that your experience with each of them is rewarding. Then think about other issues you feel are critical to you and your community. Now look for the organizations that work in these areas. Call them up, visit their offices, or write for their brochures and find out all you can about what they do. The more involved you get, the more satisfaction you'll get back. Nobody expects you to say yes all the time, but you can be a Local Hero by making some causes, "Your Causes". So be picky. And be a Local Hero.

IMAGINE
A New Spirit of Giving

A national program to encourage giving and volunteering.

The Kellogg's advertisement is an example of brand advertising because it promotes a specific brand. The Imagine advertisement is an example of advocacy advertising because it promotes a particular viewpoint about charitable giving.

Advertising Agencies

An **advertising agency** is a firm that specializes in planning, producing, and placing advertisements in the media for clients. Ad agencies work together with the client company to determine the campaign's central message, create the detailed message content, identify the ad media, and negotiate media purchases. The advantage that ad agencies offer is expertise that many clients do not possess on their own staffs—expertise in developing ad themes, message content, and artwork, as well as expertise in coordinating ad production and advising on relevant legal matters.

Agencies are normally paid a 15 percent commission based on the dollar amount of advertising placed in the media. (See Table 16.3 for a list of the top 10 advertising agencies in Canada.)

The globalization of business has impacted advertising agencies, both in Canada and elsewhere. In 1994, IBM abandoned its practice of using over 40 different advertising agencies around the world and replaced them with one single agency—Ogilvy & Mather. Since IBM spends over $400 million on advertising each year, this was a major windfall for Ogilvy & Mather. Other large U.S.-based multinational advertisers such as Ford and Coca-Cola have also dropped Canadian agencies. By giving all their advertising business to one agency, these firms hope to cut costs and deliver a uniform global message about their products.[26]

The box "Making It on Madison Avenue" describes how several Canadians have made it to the top of advertising.

The 18-member Association of Quebec Advertising Agencies says that big U.S. companies often bypass Montreal-based advertising agencies when they are developing advertising campaigns for Quebec. The group says that it is pointless to try to simply translate into French a campaign that is developed by a New York or Toronto agency for the rest of Canada. As an example of the right way to do it, consider advertisements for Pepsi. In the rest of English-speaking North America, big name singers and movie stars were used to promote the product, but in Quebec, successful commercials featured popular local comedian Claude Meunier to make Pepsi the number one soft drink in the province.[27]

advertising agency
A firm that specializes in creating and placing advertisements in the media for clients.

Personal Selling Promotions

Virtually everyone has done some selling. Perhaps you had a lemonade stand or sold candy for the drama club. Or you may have gone on a job interview, selling your abilities and service as an employee to the interviewer's company. In per-

Table 16.3   **The Top 10 Advertising Agencies in Canada, Ranked by Revenues, 1996**

Company	Revenues (in millions)
1. BBDO Canada	$56.0
2. Cossette Communication-Marketing	55.8
3. MacLaren McCann	41.2
4. Young & Rubicam Group	36.8
5. Leo Burnett Co. Ltd.	28.7
6. Ogilvy & Mather Canada Ltd.	27.0
7. FCB Canada Ltd.	26.5
8. Vickers & Benson Advertising Ltd.	20.9
9. Palmer Jarvis Inc.	19.3
10. DDB Canada	17.8

The Canadian Business Scene

Making It on Madison Avenue

Frank Anfield was born in Alert Bay, B.C. and is now the CEO of Young & Rubicam, a large advertising agency located in New York. He is one of many Canadians who are making their mark on Madison Avenue, the home of the major advertising agencies in the U.S. Six months before Anfield went to New York, Lintas Worldwide named Tony Miller (former CEO at MacLaren Lintas Inc. in Toronto) as CEO of its prestigious New York office. Two months after that, Peter Mills, who had been president of Baker Lovick, was named chief operating officer of BBDO North America. And finally, Allan Kazmer, the creative director of DDB Needham Ltd. of Toronto, was named international creative director at DDB Needham Worldwide Inc.

Why are Canadians so popular in U.S. advertising agencies? Part of the reason is the globalization of the world's advertising business. A more homogenous business world has resulted in more managers moving from country to country, and some Canadian managers are going to the U.S. Another reason is Canada's closeness to the U.S. and the increasing control of Canadian advertising firms by foreign companies. Just 10 years ago, seven of the top 10 advertising agencies in Canada were Canadian-owned; now only one is. Canada is a great place to work because it is possible for someone who is ambitious and wants to move up to head office to get noticed.

But the most important reason for the success of Canadian advertising executives is the challenging business climate in Canada. Peter Georgescu, president of Young & Rubicam, thinks that managers benefit from working in Canada because it's harder to succeed here. Those managers who do well have finely honed their business skills.

Steve Brown, a Toronto native who became executive management director at J. Walter Thompson in 1992, noted that he has a 20-person research unit that he can call on to develop data about a client's brand. But in Canada he had no such resource, so he had to become more entrepreneurial to get the job done. Peter Mills says that Canadian managers are expected to produce the same results as their American counterparts with budgets one tenth the size. Finding ways to do so develops their skills to a high level.

Julian Clopet spent 15 years at Ogilvy & Mather Canada before he was appointed president of Ogilvy & Mather's North American operations. He says that anyone who succeeds in Canada is an "all-rounder" with a wide breadth of experience. In Toronto, he was in charge of three major accounts, while in New York he was given only a portion of one account. He didn't even meet the client until six months after he was assigned to the account.

Canadians are also perceived as having a more wordly outlook than Americans. The experience with a bilingual culture, for example, is seen as a plus for agencies that are pursuing cross-cultural and global marketing strategies. Ironically, Canada's much lamented "branch plant economy" has helped managers here because Canada is seen as a great training ground for the best and brightest.

Will the continuing exodus of talented Canadians be bad for the advertising business in Canada? Apparently not. The same sort of business climate that developed Anfield, Mills, Kazmer, and Miller will continue to bring new faces to the forefront. And if that doesn't work, Canadian firms can hire Americans. Kazmer says he gets at least three calls a week from people in the U.S. who want to know about working in Canada.

---

sonal selling, a salesperson communicates one-to-one with a potential customer to identify the customer's need and match that need with the seller's product.

Personal selling—the oldest form of selling—provides the personal link between seller and buyer. It adds to a firm's credibility because it provides buyers with someone to interact with and to answer their questions. Because it involves personal interaction, personal selling requires a level of trust between the buyer and the seller. When a buyer feels cheated by the seller, that trust has been broken and a negative attitude towards salespeople in general can develop.

Personal selling is the most expensive form of promotion per contact because presentations are generally made to one or two individuals at a time. Personal selling expenses include salespeople's compensation and their overhead, usually travel, food, and lodging. The average cost of an industrial sales call has been estimated at nearly $300.[28]

telemarketing

The use of the telephone to carry out many marketing activities, including sales and research.

Such high costs have prompted many companies to turn to **telemarketing**: using telephone solicitations to carry out the personal selling process. Telemarketing can be used to handle any stage of the personal selling process or to set up appointments for outside salespeople. Because it saves the cost of personal sales visits to industrial customers, telemarketing is growing in importance.

Types of Personal Selling Situations

Managers of both telemarketing and traditional personal salespeople must always consider how personal sales are affected by the differences between consumer products and industrial products that we discussed earlier in this chapter. **Retail selling** involves selling a consumer product for the buyer's own personal or household use. **Industrial selling** deals with selling products to other businesses, either for manufacturing other products or for resale. For example, Levi's wholesales its jeans to the retail clothing operation The Gap (industrial selling). Consumers purchase these jeans at one of The Gap's stores (retail selling).

Each situation has its own distinct characteristics. In retail selling the buyer usually comes to the seller. The industrial salesperson almost always goes to the prospect's place of business. The industrial decision process also may take longer than a retail decision because more money, decision makers, and weighing of alternatives are involved. And industrial buyers are professional purchasing agents accustomed to dealing with salespeople. Consumers in retail stores, on the other hand, may be intimidated by salespeople.

Sales force management means setting goals at top levels of the organization, setting practical objectives for salespeople, organizing a sales force that can meet those objectives, and implementing and evaluating the success of the overall sales plan. Obviously, then, sales management is an important factor in meeting the marketing objectives of any large company.

retail selling
Selling a consumer product for the buyer's own personal or household use.

industrial selling
Selling products to other businesses, either for manufacturing other products or for resale.

sales force management
Setting goals at top levels of an organization; setting practical objectives for salespeople; organizing a sales force to meet those objectives; implementing and evaluating the success of a sales plan.

Personal Selling Tasks

Improving sales efficiency requires marketers to consider salespeople's tasks. Three basic tasks are generally associated with selling: order processing, creative selling, and missionary selling. Sales jobs usually require salespeople to perform all three tasks to some degree, depending on the product and the company.

Order Processing

At selling's most basic level, **order processing**, a salesperson receives an order and sees to the handling and delivery of that order. Route salespeople are often order processors. They call on regular customers to check the customer's supply of bread, milk, snack foods, or soft drinks. Then, with the customer's consent, they determine the size of the reorder, fill the order from their trucks, and stack the customer's shelves.

order processing
In personal sales, the receiving and follow-through on handling and delivery of an order by a salesperson.

Creative Selling

When the benefits of a product are not clear, **creative selling** may persuade buyers. Most industrial products involve creative selling because the buyer has not used the product before or may not be familiar with the features and uses of a specific brand. Personal selling is also crucial for high-priced consumer products, such as homes, where buyers comparison shop. Any new product can benefit from creative selling that differentiates it from other products. Finally, creative selling can help to create a need.

creative selling
In personal sales, the use of techniques designed to persuade a customer to buy a product when the benefits of the product are not readily apparent or the item is very expensive.

Missionary Selling

A company may also use **missionary selling** to promote itself and its products. Drug company representatives promote their companies' drugs to doctors who, in turn, prescribe them to their patients. The sale is actually made at the drugstore. In this case, the goal of missionary selling is to promote the company's long-term image rather than to make a quick sale.

missionary selling
In personal sales, the indirect promotion of a product by offering technical assistance and/or promoting the company's image.

The Personal Selling Process

Although all three sales tasks are important to an organization using personal selling, perhaps the most complicated is creative selling. It is the creative salesperson who is responsible for most of the steps in the personal selling process described here.

Prospecting and Qualifying

prospecting
In personal sales, the process of identifying potential customers.

qualifying
In personal sales, the process of determining whether potential customers have the authority to buy and the ability to pay for a product.

To sell, a salesperson must first have a potential customer or *prospect*. **Prospecting** is the process of identifying potential customers. Salespeople find prospects through past company records, customers, friends, relatives, company personnel, and business associates. Prospects must then be **qualified** to determine whether they have the authority to buy and the ability to pay.

Approaching

The first few minutes that a salesperson has contact with a qualified prospect are called the *approach*. The success of later stages depends on the prospect's first impression of the salesperson, since this impression affects the salesperson's credibility. Salespeople need to present a neat, professional appearance and to greet prospects in a strong, confident manner.

Presenting and Demonstrating

Next, the salesperson must *present* the promotional message to the prospect. A presentation is a full explanation of the product, its features, and its uses. It links the product's benefits to the prospect's needs. A presentation may or may not include a *demonstration* of the product. But it is wise to demonstrate a product whenever possible, since most people have trouble visualizing what they have been told.

Handling Objections

No matter what the product, prospects will have some *objections*. At the very least, prospects will object to a product's price, hoping to get a discount. Objections show the salesperson that the buyer is interested in the presentation

These customers have raised some questions that the salesperson is answering before they reach an agreed price for closing the sale of this car.

and which parts of the presentation the buyer is unsure of or has a problem with. They tell the salesperson what customers feel is important and, essentially, how to sell them.

Closing

The most critical part of the selling process is the **close**, in which the salesperson asks the prospective customer to buy the product. Successful salespeople recognize the signs that a customer is ready to buy. For example, prospects who start to figure out monthly payments for the product are clearly indicating that they are ready to buy. The salesperson should then attempt to close the sale.

Salespeople can ask directly for the sale or they can indirectly imply a close. Questions such as "Could you take delivery Tuesday?" and "Why don't we start you off with an initial order of 10 cases?" are implied closes. Such indirect closes place the burden of rejecting the sale on the prospect, who will often find it hard to say no.

closing
In personal sales, the process of asking the customer to buy the product.

Following Up

The sales process does not end with the close of the sale. Most companies want customers to come back again. Sales *follow-up* activities include fast processing of the customer's order and on-time delivery. Training in the proper care and use of the product and speedy service if repairs are needed may also be part of the follow-up.

Sales Promotions

Sales promotions are short-term promotional activities designed to stimulate consumer buying or cooperation from distributors, sales agents, or other members of the trade. They are important because they increase the likelihood that buyers will try products. They also enhance product recognition and can increase purchase size and amount. For example, soap is often bound into packages of four with the promotion, "Buy three and get one free."

To be successful, sales promotions must be convenient and accessible when the decision to purchase occurs. If Harley-Davidson has a one-week motorcycle promotion and you have no local dealer, the promotion is neither convenient nor accessible to you, and you will not buy. But if The Bay offers a 20-percent-off coupon that you can save for use later, the promotion is convenient and accessible.

sales promotion
Short-term promotional activities designed to stimulate consumer buying or cooperation from distributors and other members of the trade.

Types of Sales Promotions

The best known sales promotions are coupons, point-of-purchase displays, purchasing incentives (such as free samples, trading stamps, and premiums), trade shows, and contests and sweepstakes.

Coupons

Any certificate that entitles the bearer to a stated savings off a product's regular price is a **coupon**. Coupons may be used to encourage customers to try new products, to attract customers away from competitors, or to induce current customers to buy more of a product. They appear in newspapers and magazines and are often sent through direct mail. Coupons are very popular with consumers. When Procter & Gamble decided to end all coupons in three

coupon
A sales-promotion method featuring a certificate that entitles the bearer to a stated savings off a product's regular price.

New York cities on a test basis, it was surprised by the aggressive negative reaction from consumers. P&G ended the test in 1997 and began giving out coupons again.[29]

Point-of-Purchase Displays

point-of-purchase (POP) display

A sales-promotion method in which a product display is so located in a retail store as to encourage consumers to buy the product.

To grab customers' attention as they walk through a store, some companies use **point-of-purchase (POP) displays**.[30] Displays located at the end of the aisles or near the checkout in supermarkets are POP displays. POP displays often coincide with a sale on the item(s) being displayed. They make it easier for customers to find a product and easier for manufacturers to eliminate competitors from consideration. The cost of shelf and display space, however, is becoming more and more expensive.[31]

Purchasing Incentives

Purchasing incentives such as free samples, trading stamps, and premiums are used by many manufacturers and retailers. Free samples allow customers to try a product for a few days without any risk. They may be given out at local retail outlets or sent by manufacturers to consumers via direct mail.

Although the use of free samples is commonplace in Canada, it is very unusual in some other countries, especially those that are changing over to free-market economies. Procter & Gamble's marketing team was greeted with thanks and even tears when it gave free shampoo samples to grateful shoppers in Warsaw, who were stunned at getting a valued product without having to pay for it or even wait in a long line.[32]

premium

A sales-promotion method in which some item is offered free or at a bargain price to customers in return for buying a specified product.

Some retail outlets offer trading stamps as a bonus for patronizing a particular store. Finally, **premiums** are gifts, such as pens, pencils, calendars, and coffee mugs, that are given away to consumers in return for buying a specified product. Retailers and wholesalers also receive premiums for carrying some products.

Trade Shows

trade shows

A sales-promotion method in which members of a particular industry gather for displays and product demonstrations designed to sell products to customers.

Periodically, industries sponsor **trade shows** for their members and customers. Trade shows allow companies to rent booths to display and demonstrate their products to customers who have a special interest in the products or who are ready to buy. Trade shows are relatively inexpensive and are very effective, since the buyer comes to the seller already interested in a given type of product. International trade shows are becoming more important.

Contests and Sweepstakes

Customers, distributors, and sales representatives may all be persuaded to increase sales of a product through the use of contests. Distributors and sales agents may win a trip to Hawaii for selling the most pillows in the month of March. Although sweepstakes cannot legally require consumers to buy a product to enter, they may increase sales by stimulating buyers' interest in a product.

Publicity and Public Relations

publicity

Information about a company that is made available to consumers by the news media; not controlled by the company, but it does not cost the company any money.

Much to the delight of marketing managers with tight budgets, **publicity** is free. Moreover, because it is presented in a news format, consumers see publicity as objective and highly believable. Thus, it is an important part of the promotional mix. However, marketers often have little control over publicity.

For example, in 1995 Silken Laumann and her rowing teammates were stripped of their gold medals at an international competition because

Laumann had inadvertently used a little-known product called Benadryl that contained a banned substance. The maker of Benadryl, Warner Wellcome, suddenly saw its product mentioned prominently on national newscasts, and it didn't have to pay a cent for the advertising. However, the company is not sure that it wants its product to be associated with an unfortunate incident.[33]

The Miss Canada International organization also received negative publicity when the 1996 beauty contest winner was stripped of her title after being involved in a fight with a woman in a Newfoundland bar. Then, the first runner-up was denied the title because the pageant's organizer claimed she was not performing her duties. The first runner-up disputed these claims and accused the pageant's organizer of lying about her. All of this negative publicity was widely reported in newspapers across Canada.[34]

On a more positive note, the hottest-selling toy in 1996 was Tickle Me Elmo, a doll that says, "That Tickles" when you press on its chest. The craze started partly because a publicist at Freeman Public Relations sent one of the dolls to the son of TV personality Rosie O'Donnell. Two hundred Elmos were also sent to the show's producers. One day on her show, O'Donnell said she would toss an Elmo into the audience each time one of her guests used the word "wall." After that publicity, retail sales of the doll skyrocketed, and Tyco sold more than twice as many Elmos as they had predicted.[35]

In contrast to publicity, **public relations** is company-influenced publicity. It attempts to establish a sense of goodwill between the company and its customers through public-service announcements that enhance the company's image. For example, a bank may announce that senior citizens' groups can have free use of a meeting room for their social activities.

public relations
Public-service announcements by the company designed to enhance the company's image.

Most large firms have a department to manage their relations with the public and to present desired company images. As well, company executives may make appearances as guest speakers representing their companies at professional meetings and civic events. They may also serve as leaders in civic activities like the United Way campaign and university fundraising. Through PR offices, many companies produce audio-visual materials about company activities and make them available to interested groups, other companies, or the general public.

Companies can also take steps to exercise some control over publicity by press releases and press conferences. A *press release* is a written announcement sent to news agencies describing a new product, an event, or information about the company that may be of interest to the general public. In a *press conference*, a firm's representative meets face-to-face with the press to communicate information that the media may then publish or broadcast publicly.

International Promotional Strategies

As we saw in Chapter 4, recent decades have witnessed a profound shift from "home-country" marketing to "multi-country" and now to "global" marketing. Nowhere is this rapidly growing global orientation more evident than in marketing promotions, especially advertising.

Growth of Worldwide Advertising

In the mid-20th century, companies began exporting to other countries when domestic sales stagnated. Advertising played a key role in these efforts because it was the best tool for creating product awareness in each country—that is, for stimulating sales by explaining a product's benefits to new consumers.

Today, worldwide advertising is a large part of many companies' promotional expenditures. Collectively, the 50 top advertisers spend more than $15 billion annually for worldwide advertising. For example, taking advantage of advertising's broad cross-cultural reach, the Anglo-Dutch firm Unilever advertises soap and health-care products in more than 25 countries in the Middle East, South America, Europe, North America, Asia, Central America, and South Africa. Included in the top-50 list of global ad spenders are 29 Japanese companies and 10 from the United States, along with several European firms.

Emergence of the Global Perspective

global perspective

Company's approach to directing its marketing towards worldwide rather than local or regional markets.

Every company that markets its products in several countries faces a basic choice: use a *decentralized approach* with separate marketing management for each country or adopt a *global perspective* with a coordinated marketing program directed at one worldwide audience. The **global perspective**, therefore, is actually a company philosophy that directs marketing towards a worldwide rather than a local or regional market.

The truly global perspective means designing products for multinational appeal—that is, genuinely *global products*. Brands like Coca-Cola, McDonald's, Revlon, Rolex, and Xerox, which are approaching global recognition in a huge variety of countries and cultures, are thus becoming truly *global brands*. Not surprisingly, then, globalization is affecting many firms' promotional activities. In effect, they have already posed the question "Is it possible to develop global advertising?" Certainly one universal advertising program would be more efficient and cost-effective than developing different programs for each of many countries. For several reasons, however, global advertising is not feasible for most companies. There are four factors that make global advertising a difficult proposition: *language differences*, *product variations*, *cultural receptiveness*, and *image differences*.

Language Differences

Perhaps the most obvious barrier to the global ad is language. Compared with those in other languages, for example, ads in English require less print space and air time because English is an efficient language with greater precision of meaning than most. More importantly, translations from one language to another are often inexact and lead to confusion and misunderstanding.

Product Variations

Even if a basic product has universal appeal, at least modest *product variations*—slightly different products—are usually preferred in different cultures. In order to communicate product variations and their features (and of course their advantages), advertising must reflect these differences. For example, MasterCard International has created a worldwide TV ad with video "windows" placed at three strategic points at which regional marketers could insert footage appealing to local tastes in credit card agreements.[36]

Cultural Receptiveness

Another variable is cultural receptiveness to alien ideas and products. For example, there is considerable difference across nations regarding the acceptability of mass advertising for "sensitive" products or those that cause social discomfort (for instance, underwear, condoms, feminine-hygiene products), not to mention those for which advertising may be legally restricted (pharmaceuticals, alcohol, cigarettes). Generally speaking, European countries have more liberal advertising environments than countries in North America, Asia, the Middle East, and Latin America. For worldwide advertising, magazines are the most popular medium for sensitive products because clear messages can be demographically targeted.

Image Differences

Each company's overall *image* can vary from nation to nation, regardless of any advertising appeals for universal recognition and acceptance. For example, a recent study comparing well-known global brands in the United States and the United Kingdom found that American Express, IBM, and Nestlé had higher-ranking images in the U.S. than in the U.K. In contrast, Heinz, Coca-Cola, and Ford had higher-ranking images in the U.K.[37]

Firms that are concerned about image and visibility use advertising to present desirable corporate images and to boost public awareness of them. For example, Philips Electronics, the Dutch firm, has embarked on a worldwide campaign to make a more prominent connection between its product brands and its corporate name. Similarly, following two years of market research, Texas Instruments Inc. decided on some image updating. In order to inform consumers of its diversified operations and products and to overcome its traditional image as a semiconductor-chip maker, TI launched a $10 million worldwide advertising campaign in seven languages.[38]

Promotional Practices in Small Business

From our discussion so far, you might think that only large companies can afford to promote their goods and services. Although small businesses generally have fewer resources, cost-effective promotions can improve sales and enable small firms to compete with much larger firms.

Small Business Advertising

Advertising in non-prime-time slots on local television or cable TV offers great impact at a cost many small firms can afford. More commonly, though, small businesses with a local market use newspaper and radio advertising and, increasingly, direct mail. Billboards are beyond the means of many small businesses, but outdoor store signs can draw a strong response from passers-by.

The timing of advertising can be critical for generating revenues for a small business. For year-round advertising, the *Yellow Pages* are a widely used medium for advertising both industrial and consumer products in local markets. However, many small businesses, especially those selling to consumer markets, rely more on seasonal advertising. Retail stores advertise for the holidays; ads for lawn care and home maintenance services begin to appear in the early spring; and ads for tax preparation services become more visible at the beginning of the year.

Television, radio, and newspapers are seldom viable promotional options for reaching international markets because of their high costs and their limited availability. The market research needed to determine the best message and style for reaching the target audience is costly. Additional costs are incurred in developing broadcast and newsprint advertisements with the necessary variations in language and cultural appeal. Limited availability—the inaccessibility of the intended audience—is a problem in nations that have underdeveloped mass media or high illiteracy rates, or that place severe restrictions on advertising by private companies. In these situations, broadcast and newsprint media will not be feasible options for the international advertising mix. Instead, most small firms find direct mail and carefully targeted magazine advertising the most effective promotional tools.

The Role of Personal Selling in Small Business

Some small firms maintain a sales force to promote and sell their products locally. Your local newspapers and television and radio stations, for example, use personal selling to attract advertisements by individuals and businesses. As part of the personal selling process, they provide complete information about the audiences ads will reach. Other small firms prefer not to do their own selling, but instead contract with a sales agency—a company that handles the products of several companies—to act on their behalf. Insurance agents who sell insurance for several different companies are sales agencies.

Because of the high costs of operating a national sales force, many small companies have established telemarketing staffs. By combining telemarketing with a catalogue or other educational product literature, small companies can sell their products nationally and compete against much larger companies.

Most small companies cannot afford to establish international offices, though some entrepreneurs, such as Art de Fehr of Palliser Furniture, do visit prospective customers in other countries. However, for most small businesses, even sending sales representatives overseas is expensive. Thus many small companies have combined telemarketing with direct mail in order to expand internationally.

Small Business Promotions

Small companies use the same sales promotion incentives that larger companies use. The difference is that larger firms tend to use more coupons, POP displays, and sales contests. Smaller firms rely on premiums and special sales, since coupons and sales contests are more expensive and more difficult to manage. For example, some automobile dealerships offer fishing reels at a bargain price if you just "come on down and road-test" a new four-wheel-drive vehicle. Gas stations use premiums by offering a free car wash with each fillup. Special sales prices are commonly offered by many service companies, including martial arts centres, remodelling companies, and dry cleaners.

Small Business Publicity

Publicity is very important to small businesses with local markets. Small firms often have an easier time getting local publicity than do national firms. Readers of local papers like to read about local companies, so local papers like to write about such businesses. However, fierce competition for coverage in national and international publications limits the access small businesses have to those markets.

Summary of Learning Objectives

1. **Identify a *product* and distinguish between *consumer* and *industrial* products.** *Products* are a firm's reason for being: *Product features*—the tangible qualities that a company builds into its products—offer *benefits* to buyers whose purchases are the main source of the company's profits. In developing products, firms must decide whether to produce *consumer goods* for direct sale to consumers or *industrial goods* for sale to other firms. Marketers must recognize that buyers will pay less for common, rapidly consumed *convenience goods* than for less frequently purchased *shopping* and *specialty goods*. In industrial markets, *expense items* are generally less expensive and more rapidly consumed than such *capital items* as buildings and equipment.

2. **Trace the stages of the *product life cycle* and explain the *growth-share matrix*.** New products have a life cycle that begins with *introduction* and progresses through states of *growth*, *maturity*, and *decline*. Profits rise through the early maturity period; sales rise through the late maturity period. In the *growth-share matrix*, products are classified according to market share and growth potential. *Question marks* are new products with low market share but high potential. *Stars* have both high market share and high potential, while *dogs* rate low in both categories. *Cash cows* are mature products with high market share but low potential.

3. **Discuss the importance of *branding* and *packaging*.** Each product is given an identity by its brand and by the way it is packaged and labelled. The goal in developing *brands*—symbols to distinguish products and to signal their uniform quality—is to increase the preference consumers have for a product with a particular brand name. *Trade marks* grant exclusive legal rights to a brand name. *Packaging* provides an attractive container and advertises features and benefits.

4. **Identify the objectives of *promotion* and discuss the considerations involved in selecting a *promotional mix*.** The chief objectives of *promotion* are communicating information about products, positioning products, and controlling sales volume. To meet these objectives, marketers must choose a *push strategy* (marketing aggressively to channel members) or a *pull strategy* (appealing directly to consumers). They must also select the best combination of tools—advertising, personal selling, sales promotion, and/or publicity and public relations—for the *promotional mix*.

5. **Describe the various *advertising media* available to marketing managers.** Marketers may use various *advertising media*, or specific communication devices for transmitting a seller's message to potential buyers. The most common media—*newspapers, television, direct mail, radio, magazines*, and *outdoor advertising*—differ in their cost and their ability to segment target markets. The combination of tools chosen by a company is called the *media mix*.

6. **Identify the different types of *sales promotions* and explain the uses of *publicity* and *public relations*.** *Sales promotions*—such as *coupons, point-of-purchase (POP) displays, free samples, trading stamps, premiums, trade shows*, and *contests*—increase the chances that customers will recognize or try products. *Publicity*—general mass media information about a company or product—differs from other types of promotions in being free (although often uncontrollable) and is useful in ensuring the broad dissemination of a message. *Public relations* is company-influenced publicity.

Key Terms

convenience goods/services, 458

shopping goods/services, 458

specialty goods/services, 458

expense items, 459

capital items, 459

product mix, 459

product line, 459

speed to market, 461

definition of the service package, 463

service process design, 463

product life cycle (PLC), 463

brand names, 466

national brands, 467

licensed brands, 467

private brands, 468

generic products, 469

trade mark, 469

patent, 470

brand loyalty, 470

packaging, 470

label, 471

Consumer Packaging and Labelling Act, 471

product positioning, 473

push strategy, 473

pull strategy, 473

promotional mix, 474

informative advertising, 477

persuasive advertising, 478

comparative advertising, 478

reminder advertising, 478

advertising medium, 479

direct mail, 480

word-of-mouth, 481

electronic commerce, 481

media mix, 481

brand advertising, 482

product advertising, 482

advocacy advertising, 482

institutional advertising, 482

retail advertising, 482

cooperative advertising, 482

trade advertising, 482

industrial advertising, 482

advertising agency, 483

telemarketing, 484

retail selling, 485

industrial selling, 485

sales force management, 485

order processing, 485

creative selling, 485

missionary selling, 485

prospecting, 486

qualifying, 486

closing, 487

sales promotion, 487

coupon, 487

point-of-purchase (POP) display, 488

premium, 488

trade shows, 488

publicity, 488

public relations, 489

global perspective, 490

Study Questions and Exercises

Review Questions

1. What are the various classifications of consumer and industrial products? Give an example of a good and a service for each category different from the examples given in the text.

2. List the seven stages of the product development process. Give an example showing how or why a new product can fail or succeed at each stage.

3. Distinguish between national brands, licensed brands, and private brands. Give examples of at least two competing products for each type of brand.

4. Describe the differences between the push and pull promotional strategies. Why would a company choose one rather than the other?

5. Compare and contrast the advantages and disadvantages of the different advertising media.

6. What is the advantage of personal selling over the other communication tools?

7. How do creative and missionary selling differ? Give three examples of products for which each might be used, other than those listed in the chapter.

8. Is publicity more or less readily available to small firms than to large ones? Why?

Analysis Questions

9. How would you expect the naming, packaging, and labelling of convenience, shopping, and specialty goods to differ? Why? Give examples to illustrate your answers.

10. Take a look at some of the television advertising that is being done by small local businesses in your area. What differences can you see between those commercials and the ones done by large national companies?

11. Pick a consumer product and trace the steps in the personal selling process for this item. Do the same for an industrial product.

12. Find some examples of publicity about some local and national businesses. Do you think the publicity had positive or negative consequences for the businesses? Why?

Application Exercises

13. Interview a manager of a local manufacturing firm. Identify the company's products according to where they stand in the product life cycle.

14. Check out your college or university's Web site and determine how effective it is as a tool for promoting your school.

15. Choose a product sold nationally. Identify as many media used in its promotion as you can. Which medium is used most? Why? Do you believe the promotion is successful? Why or why not?

16. Interview the owner of a local small business. Identify the promotional objectives and strategies of the firm as well as the elements in the promotional mix. What (if any) changes would you suggest? Why?

Building Your Business Skills

Goal
To encourage students to evaluate advertising from the standpoint of industry professionals.

Situation
Bob Garfield is the advertising critic for *Advertising Age* magazine, which should be available in your college or local library. (An electronic edition can be found on Prodigy). He discusses various advertising issues and evaluates new ads, awarding ratings that range from one star (*) to four stars (****). Garfield has recently discussed ads for Magnavox (27-inch colour TV infomercial), IBM ("Solutions for a Small Planet"), and Coors (Coors Light Channel).

Method

Step 1:
Working individually or in small groups, identify one of the campaigns criticized by Bob Garfield (your instructor may provide them for you, or you may get the information through library research).

Step 2:
Evaluate and critique one or more ad campaigns individually or with a group. How would you rate a given ad?

Analysis
Compare your critique with Garfield's. What factors did you take into consideration when you evaluated the campaign? What was the rationale for your rating compared with Garfield's?

Follow-Up Questions

1. In evaluating an ad, what issues appear to be most important to Garfield? How do they compare with the criteria you used in your evaluation?

2. Were you surprised by some of the information contained in Garfield's reviews, such as the size of the budgets for individual advertising campaigns? Why? Did such information prompt you to rethink your opinion about a campaign?

Shopping at home by means of electronic media is a relatively recent development. Electronic shopping involves all aspects of marketing—strategy, product development, pricing, promotion, distribution—aimed at the consumer market. To find out more about marketing in the world of electronic home shopping, log on to the following Web site:

http://www.qvc.com

After you have explored the various pages and reports posted on the QVC Web site, think about the various ways in which the principles of marketing apply to electronic shopping by considering the following questions:

1. What is the "product" being offered under the *iQVC* label? What are the *features* and *benefits* of this product?

2. What are the important *marketing variables* that had to be considered in designing the *iQVC* product?

3. At which stage of the *life cycle* is *iQVC*'s "product" now situated? Explain your answer according to the information you obtained from this Web site.

4. Can you identify any features in *iQVC*'s Web site that are designed to encourage *brand loyalty* for its product?

5. Compare *iQVC*'s *price-setting* methods with those of its nonelectronic competitors. In what ways are they the same? In what ways do they differ?

6. Evaluate the *promotional methods* that *iQVC* uses at its Web site. What are some of those methods, and how effective do you believe them to be? Can you offer any suggestions for making them more effective?

Charting the Air Jordan Route

With a 37-percent share of the nearly $7 billion worldwide sneaker market, Nike is the clear winner in the race to dominate the athletic footwear market. Nowhere is Nike's dominance more evident than in the marketing strategy it uses to sell its biggest single product—Air Jordan sneakers. Endorsed by basketball superstar Michael Jordan, 12 different versions of Air Jordans have enjoyed the power of Nike's marketing muscle since 1985. The result, according to John G. Horan, publisher of *Sporting Goods Intelligence*, is that "over time, there's been nothing even remotely close to the Air Jordan. It's that extra zing that Michael Jordan brings to the party."

Not surprisingly, the introduction of a new Air Jordan product has the power to ignite the action at athletic footwear retailers. Fueling this ignition is Nike's deliberate, carefully crafted marketing strategy: control supply and increase demand while at the same time generating enough excitement among target customers—teenagers—to convince them to pay $115 (U.S.) a pair. Because of this strategy, customers are willing to pay for the Michael Jordan name—and, of course, state-of-the-art sneakers with carbon-fibre spring plates, herringbone traction inserts, air insoles, and 16 stitching-reinforced lace eyelets.

The strategy is implemented by means of hype, which begins when the company issues a release date for a new Air Jordan model. In Step 2, Nike deliberately manufactures too few shoes to meet expected demand. Customers learn of the release date not through advertising, but through a word-of-mouth network that connects them with shoe salespeople. The result of this combination of hype and operations control is a kind of self-perpetuating demand for Air Jordan sneakers. And make no mistake about it—demand issues from the star power of the Michael Jordan name. The Chicago Bulls superstar regularly wears the latest Air Jordan in one or two National Basketball Association play-off games, but Nike's advertising strategy is otherwise decidedly low key.

By stark contrast, there is nothing low key about the scene at stores on opening day for retail sales. Teenage customers arrive hours before the store opens, and many buy the latest Air Jordans even if they own six other Air Jordan models in good condition. Why? Because the sneakers are Jordans and because the shoes give them status among their peers. Because Nike's marketing strategy does not include meeting current demand, the unlucky may have little choice but to wait for the next Air Jordan model and the next bout of hype and purchasing frenzy.

Riding high on the sale of Air Jordan sneakers and propelled by a marketing strategy that limits supply in the face of increasing demand, Nike's relationship with small, independent retailers is often strained. For one thing, these outlets receive their product shipments after national chains. Even so, they realize that they are getting an eminently saleable product, and despite some frustration, many small retailers believe that late inventory shipments cost them relatively little in lost sales of Air Jordans. As one retailer explains, "I know I can sell them—before the [release] date or after." At the same time, however, Nike's practice of maintaining strict control over product allocation makes small retailers nervous, especially when products not related to Jordan are involved. "Nobody," volunteers one store owner, "likes to be told that they can't maximize their business."

With its astounding success, of course, Nike has little reason to change its marketing strategy. "When we stop producing the best product, then it will be the retailer's decision to stop selling Nike," says Nike president Tom Clarke. Until then, the marketing ball clearly remains in Nike's possession.

Case Questions

1. Air Jordan sneakers continue in the growth stage of the product life cycle. Is this trend likely to continue after Michael Jordan retires from basketball? (Research the impact on sneaker sales during Jordan's temporary retirement in 1994–95.)

2. The latest Air Jordan model does not have the Nike *swoosh* symbol emblazoned on its side. How do you think the decision to remove it will affect brand recognition? Why do you think Nike decided to market a sneaker without the company's trade mark symbol?

3. Describe the elements in Nike's promotion of Air Jordan sneakers. Why is advertising such a small part of the promotional mix?

4. Why is Michael Jordan's endorsement so important to product success? ◆

Nike
http://www.nike.com

CONCLUDING CASE 16-2

Cott vs. Coke

Coca-Cola is one of the most famous brands in the world. For many years it has been number one in the cola wars, closely followed by Pepsi. But in the early 1990s, Cott Corp. of Toronto began causing trouble for both Coke and Pepsi by making private brand cola for a variety of supermarkets.

Cott was started in the 1950s and sold its own branded cola with the slogan "It's Cott to be Good." But it wasn't very successful. In 1991, the company struck a deal with Royal Crown Cola (another also-ran in the cola wars) to buy its concentrate. Now Cott uses that concentrate to make private label pop that sells throughout North America. At Safeway, for example, Cott's private label is called "President's Choice," at A&P it is called "Master Choice," and at Wal-Mart it is called "Sam's American Choice." At one point, Cott had signed up 60 major U.S. retailers and controlled 2 percent of the $30 billion soft drink market. Sales revenue in 1994 was over $600 million, and profits were over $9 million. The company's goal was to achieve 5 percent of the market and sales revenue of $1.5 billion.

The most dramatic threat to Coke occurred when J. Sainsbury PLC, Britain's largest supermarket chain, introduced its own private brand cola, made by Cott, in a can that was strikingly similar to Coke's can. What caught the media's attention was the fact that Cott's quality was high enough and its packaging similar enough to be mistaken for the "Real Thing." Sainsbury stocked its private brand label (simply labelled "cola") right next to Coca-Cola, and priced it at only three-quarters the price of Coke.

But the threat to Coke seems to have been short-lived. In 1995, Cott began experiencing its own problems. In this David-and-Goliath story, the Goliaths (Coke and Pepsi) are now winning. Cott has been forced to freeze its international growth, lay off staff, and cut back operations.

What did Coke and Pepsi do to stop Cott? Quite simply, they trimmed expenses, cut staff, and developed more efficient operations. They lowered their price to be competitive with Cott, improved their packaging, and introduced easier-to-carry cases for cans. And they helped retailers display their products better by installing new refrigerated cases near the cash register.

Cott will still be able to make money in Canada and the U.S. because it is still the house label for the very large retail chains noted earlier. In fact, in Ontario during some months of 1995, Cott's market share exceeded Coke's.

However, industry observers note that several high-ranking Cott executives sold almost half a million of the shares they owned between July and September 1995. They received somewhere around $14 per share. The price of Cott's stock was down to just over $8 per share by November 1995. At its peak in 1993, it was almost $50 per share. By mid-1997, however, the company's stock price had again risen to over $15 per share. Sales revenue for the first quarter of 1997 was $358 million, a 16 percent increase over 1996.

Case Questions

1. What type of consumer good is cola?

2. Discuss each of the four elements in the promotion mix as they relate to the promotion of cola.

3. In what stage of the product life cycle is cola? How does the stage in the life cycle influence promotional strategy?

4. How important is brand loyalty in the sale of cola? Why have private brands been more successful recently? ◆

Pricing and Distributing Goods and Services

Big Changes at Canada's Most Famous Retailer

Timothy Eaton immigrated to Canada from Ireland in the 19th century and built a retailing empire by promising to refund money if the customer found the goods to be unsatisfactory. In that era, such a guarantee was unheard of. But it worked, and over the next few decades, Eaton's prospered. By the 1950s, Eaton's accounted for more than half of all department store spending in Canada.

Eaton's is a company that is rich in family tradition. Timothy Eaton passed the presidency on to his son John Craig Eaton, who was in turn succeeded by his cousin Robert Young Eaton. John David Eaton (John Craig's son) became president in 1942 and dominated the firm until the 1970s. John Craig Eaton II is the great-grandson of Timothy—a fourth-generation Eaton.

Their emphasis on tradition has, on occasion, led to an inability to change in response to changing markets. In the 1970s, for example, Eaton's refused to get rid of its in-store drug sections in spite of strong evidence that competitors like Shoppers Drug Mart had stolen this market from them. As well, suggestions that some small-town stores should be closed because they were a drain on the company's profitability were ignored.

Massive changes in Canadian retailing during the last decade (including the entry of large U.S. competitors) have caused a sharp decline in Eaton's fortunes. Because Eaton's is a private corporation, it is not required to publish its financial statements and has been famous for being tight-lipped about its financial condition. In response to speculation about the company's financial state, John Craig Eaton II had said only that it was making money. However by the early 1990s, the first rumours were heard that Eaton's was in trouble. A 1996 article in

Canadian Business speculated that Eaton's was in a tough race to see if it could cut costs fast enough to stay ahead of plunging sales. From 1992–97, annual sales revenue declined from $2.1 billion to $1.6 billion. The firm lost $80 million in 1995, and $120 million in 1996.

All the speculation ended in February 1997 when Eaton's shocked the industry by announcing that it was seeking bankruptcy protection under the *Companies' Creditors Arrangement Act* (CCAA). This act gives judges a lot of discretion as they seek ways to save the company. Filing for bankruptcy under the CCAA has become a fashionable alternative to the *Bankruptcy and Insolvency Act* (BIA), because the CCAA doesn't contain as many financial requirements. For example, if a company files for bankruptcy under the BIA, any dividends paid out a year or less before the filing can be taken back if the company was insolvent at the time (Eaton's paid out $10 million in dividends late in 1996).

The changes that are sweeping through retailing in the 1990s are going to make it difficult for Eaton's to prosper. Competition is coming from the so-called big-box stores like Price-Costco, from the so-called category killers like ToysЯUs, from television shopping, and from stores like Wal-Mart, Kmart, and Zellers. Each of these competitors is going to pose a significant problem for Eaton's.

It is unclear how committed the Eaton family is to maintaining its presence in retailing. At one time, the company controlled real estate worth about $1 billion, but it sold much of that in 1995. It also launched a takeover bid for Baton Broadcasting in January 1996. But the firm has maintained that it will continue to be a presence in retailing. Its commitment to retailing can be seen in its expenditures on store facelifts, upgrades in technology, and improved logistics.

In 1992, the Eaton's warehouse outside Toronto was operating with outdated equipment and procedures. As a result, deliveries to Eaton's retailers across Canada were often held up. Distribution managers were bluntly told that they weren't meeting the needs of customers and that things had to change. In just a few years, major changes were introduced. The warehouse is now a modern distribution facility. Arriving goods are taken off trucks and moved through the warehouse on an automated conveyor system. Bar-code readers scan labels and automatically send products down conveyers to trucks that take them to the appropriate Eaton's store. Now, a customer who orders a mattress will have it within 48 hours. In 1992, items were kept in a warehouse for an average of eight days.

Eaton's also changed the way it deals with suppliers, who must now comply with packaging, labelling, and shipment accuracy rules. For example, the company now deals with only four suppliers of brand-name ladies wear, whereas it formerly dealt with 20. Each of the four suppliers is rewarded with bigger sales volume.

But is all this change enough to ensure Eaton's place in retailing? The JC Williams Group, a retail consultant, estimates that Sears now controls 41 percent of the department store market, The Bay, 31 percent, and Eaton's, 28 percent. Eaton's sales are still edging downward, and the firm continues to cut costs and lay off personnel.

The Eaton family is looking at possible new frontiers. One of the most interesting is in broadcasting. The company already has a long history in this field as the majority owner of Baton Broadcasting. With money from the sale of its real estate holdings, Eaton's can buy up additional television stations. Perhaps retailers like Eaton's will one day sell merchandise through "virtual stores" that consumers will browse through via cable-TV channels.

In September 1997, Eaton's creditors approved a $419 million restructuring plan that may allow the company to return to profitability by the year 2000. The company may also start selling shares to the public if it becomes profitable again. ◆

In this chapter, we complete our look at the marketing function by examining the role of pricing and distribution. The opening case describes how one Canadian retailer is trying to meet the challenges of competition and changes in consumer tastes.

The first part of the chapter examines the pricing objectives of business firms, as well as the various methods they use to decide what to charge for the goods and services they produce. The second part of the chapter describes how producers get their goods and services into consumers' hands. Should the company sell directly to consumers? Or should some type of intermediary like a retailer be used? How will the merchandise be moved from the factory to the consumer?

By focusing on the learning objectives of this chapter, you will consider questions like these and better understand the importance of distribution in the marketing process. After reading this chapter, you should be able to:

LEARNING OBJECTIVES

1. Identify the various *pricing objectives* that govern pricing decisions and describe the tools used in making these decisions.

2. Discuss *pricing strategies* and tactics for existing and new products.

3. Identify the different *channels of distribution* and explain different *distribution strategies*.

4. Explain the differences between *merchant wholesalers* and *agents/brokers*.

5. Identify the different types of *retail stores*.

6. Describe the major activities in the *physical distribution process*.

7. Compare the five basic forms of *transportation* and identify the types of firms that provide them.

Pricing Objectives and Tools

Price is becoming an increasingly important part of the marketing mix. During the last 10 years, companies have increased their emphasis on quality, so quality across products is now very similar. As a result, consumers now focus more on price as a way to decide which products to buy. Consider these examples:

- In grocery stores, private brands are increasingly successful because they sell for 15 to 40 percent less than brand-name products.

- Wal-Mart has adopted an "everyday low price" (EDLP) policy.[1]

- McDonald's announced early in 1997 that they were dropping prices to keep competitors like Burger King from stealing market share from them.[2]

pricing
Deciding what the company will receive in exchange for its product.

In **pricing**, managers decide what the company will receive in exchange for its products. In this section, we first discuss the objectives that influence a firm's pricing decisions. Then we describe the major tools that companies use to meet those objectives.

Pricing to Meet Business Objectives

Companies often price products to maximize profits. But other objectives can also be involved. Some firms, for example, are more interested in dominating the market or securing high market share than in maximizing profits. Pricing decisions are also influenced by the need to survive in competitive marketplaces, by social and ethical concerns, and even by corporate image.

Profit-Maximizing Objectives

Pricing to maximize profits is tricky. If prices are set too low, the company will probably sell many units of its product. But it may miss the opportunity to make additional profit on each unit—and may indeed lose money on each exchange. Conversely, if prices are set too high, the company will make a large profit on each item but will sell fewer units. Again, the firm loses money. In addition, it may be left with excess inventory and may have to reduce or even close production operations. To avoid these problems, companies try to set prices to sell the number of units that will generate the highest possible total profits.

In calculating profits, managers weigh receipts against costs for materials and labour to create the product. But they also consider the capital resources (plant and equipment) that the company must tie up to generate that level of profit. The costs of marketing (such as maintaining a large sales staff) can also be substantial. Concern over the efficient use of these resources has led many firms to set prices so as to achieve a targeted level of return on sales or capital investment.[3]

Market-Share Objectives

market share
A company's percentage of the total market sales for a specific product.

In the long run, of course, a business must make a profit to survive. Nevertheless, many companies initially set low prices for new products. They are willing to accept minimal profits—even losses—to get buyers to try products. In other words, they use pricing to establish **market share**: a company's percentage of the total market sales for a specific product. Even with established products, market share may outweigh profits as a pricing objective. For a product like Philadelphia Brand Cream Cheese, dominating a market means that consumers are more likely to buy it because they are familiar with a well-known, highly visible product.

Other Pricing Objectives

Profit-maximizing and market-share objectives may not be appropriate in some instances. During difficult economic times, many firms go out of business. Loss containment and survival replace profit maximization when a company in distress attempts to right itself. In the mid-1980s, John Deere priced its agricultural equipment for survival in a depressed farm economy.

Social and ethical concerns may also affect pricing for some types of products. In 1987, drugmaker Burroughs Wellcome received approval to begin selling AZT, the first drug shown to help in combating AIDS. A storm of protest erupted when Burroughs announced that a year's supply of AZT would cost $10 000. After months of relentless pressure, Burroughs reduced the price to about $3000.[4]

Pricing decisions may also reflect a company's image. Retailers such as Braemar's and Holt-Renfrew will not sell a $10 shirt or $20 dress, and Kmart will not carry $500 men's suits, regardless of quality.

Price-Setting Tools

Whatever the company's pricing objective, managers must measure the business impact before they can set prices. Three basic tools are used for this purpose: economic demand-supply comparisons, cost-oriented pricing, and break-even analysis. Rarely is one of these tools sufficient. Most often, they are used together to identify prices that allow the company to reach its objectives.

Economic Demand-Supply Comparisons

Economic theory helps firms maximize profits. This approach looks at the total market for a product, identifying the amount that consumers will demand and producers will supply at various prices.

Figure 17.1 compares demand for and supply of movie tickets at various prices. As prices go up, the number of tickets sought goes down, causing the

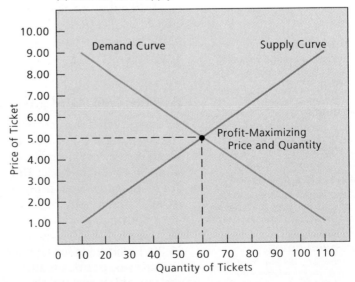

(a) Demand and Supply Schedules for Movie Tickets

(b) Demand and Supply Curves for Movie Tickets

Price (dollars)	Quantity Tickets Demanded	Quantity Tickets Supplied
$1.00	108	10
3.00	80	32
5.00	60	60
7.00	35	87
9.00	10	110

Figure 17.1
Demand and supply schedules for movie tickets (a) and demand and supply curves for movie tickets (b).

downward-sloping demand curve. But theatre owners would be willing to supply more tickets when prices are higher, as shown in the upward-sloping supply curve.

Considering the two curves together tells us the best (profit-maximizing) price for movie tickets: $5.00. At this price, the number of tickets demanded and the number of tickets supplied are the same. According to economic theory, in the long run, the market price will *always* settle where the demand and supply curves meet.

Cost-Oriented Pricing

The major weakness of the demand-and-supply approach to pricing is that it focuses entirely on identifying a market price for a product. It does not consider whether companies can make money at this price. As well, it treats the products of all suppliers as identical, which is not always true. In contrast, cost-oriented pricing takes into account the firm's need to cover its costs of producing the product.

A music store manager would begin using the cost-oriented approach to pricing records by calculating the cost of making compact discs (CDs) available to shoppers. Included in this figure would be store rent, sales clerks' wages, utilities, CD displays, insurance, and the cost of the CDs. Assume that the cost of a CD comes to $9.00. If the store sold the CD for this price, it would not make any profit. The manager must add in an amount for profit called **markup**. A markup of $6.00 over cost in this case would result in a selling price of $15.00.

Profit is usually evaluated based on a percentage of the selling price. The manager calculates the markup percentage as follows:

$$\text{Markup percentage} = \frac{\text{Markup}}{\text{Sales price}}$$

$$\text{Markup percentage} = \frac{\$6.00}{\$15.00} = 40.0\%$$

That is, out of every dollar taken in, 40 cents will be gross profit for the store. However, out of this profit still must come store rent, utilities, insurance, and all those other costs.

Another way to express the markup is as a percentage of cost instead of a percentage of sales price. The $6.00 markup is 66.7 percent of the $9.00 cost of a CD ($6.00 ÷ $9.00). Some retailers prefer to express the markup using this cost-based method. Others, however, prefer the sales-price approach.

Break-Even Analysis: Cost-Volume-Profit Relationships

A company that uses cost-oriented pricing can count on covering its **variable costs** (materials and labour primarily) for each item sold. It will also make some money towards **fixed costs** such as equipment, rent, management salaries, and insurance. But without a **break-even analysis**, the company does not know how many units it must sell before all its fixed costs are covered and it truly begins to make a profit.

Continuing on with the music store example, suppose the variable costs for each CD (basically, the cost of buying the CD from the producer) are $8.00. Fixed costs for keeping the store open for one year are $100 000. The **break-even point**, the number of CDs that must be sold to cover both fixed and variable costs and thus for the store to start to make some profit, will be 14 286 CDs, calculated as follows:

markup

The amount added to the cost of an item to earn a profit for the retailer or wholesaler.

variable costs

Those costs that change with the number of goods or services produced or sold.

fixed costs

Those costs unaffected by the number of goods or services produced or sold.

break-even analysis

An assessment of how many units must be sold at a given price before the company begins to make a profit.

break-even point

The number of units that must be sold at a given price before the company covers all its variable and fixed costs.

$$\text{Break-even point (in units)} = \frac{\text{Total fixed costs}}{\text{Price} - \text{variable cost}}$$

$$= \frac{\$100\ 000}{\$15.00 - \$8.00}$$

$$= 14\ 286\ \text{CDs}$$

Figure 17.2 shows the break-even point graphically. Note that if sales are below 14 286 CDs, the store loses money for the year. If sales exceed 14 286 CDs, profits grow by $7.00 for each CD sold.

In reality, managers calculate break-even points for each of several possible price levels. As the price per CD increases, the number of units that must be sold before the break-even point is reached decreases. As prices fall, the number of units that must be sold before the break-even point is reached increases. Table 17.1 shows this relationship for a variety of prices. Prices below $8.00 are not considered because, if the price does not exceed the item's variable cost, the break-even point will never occur.

The music store owner would certainly like to hit the break-even quantity as early as possible so that profits will start rolling in. Why not charge $20.00 per CD, then, and reach break-even earlier? The answer lies in the downward-sloping demand curve we discussed earlier. At a price of $20.00 per CD, CD sales at the store would drop. In setting a price, the manager must consider how much CD buyers will pay and what the store's local competitors charge.

Pricing Strategies and Tactics

The pricing tools discussed in the previous section provide a valuable guide for managers trying to set prices on specific goods. But they do not provide general direction for managers trying to set a pricing philosophy for their company. In this section, we discuss *pricing strategy*—that is, pricing as a planning activity that affects the marketing mix. We then describe some basic *pricing tactics*—ways in which managers implement a firm's pricing strategies.

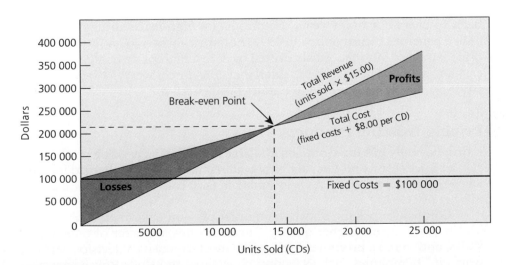

Figure 17.2
Break-even analysis: 14 286 CDs is the break-even point.

Table 17.1   **Comparison of Break-Even Quantities for Various Price Levels**

Price ($)	Number of CDs for Break-Even Quantity	Total Cost and Revenue at Break-Even Quantity
$ 8.00	*	*
$10.00	50 000	$500 000
$12.00	25 000	$300 000
$14.00	16 667	$233 340
$15.00	14 286	$214 290
$16.00	12 500	$200 000
$18.00	10 000	$180 000
$20.00	8 333	$166 660

*Does not exist at this price.

Pricing Strategies

Let's begin this section by asking two questions. First: Can a manager really identify a single "best" price for a product? The answer is: probably not. For example, a study of prices for popular nonaspirin pain relievers (such as Tylenol and Advil) found variations of 100 percent.[5] In this market, in other words, some products sold for *twice* the price of other products with similar properties. Granted, such differences may reflect some differences in product costs. The issue, however, is a little more complex. Such wide price differences reflect differing brand images that attract different types of customers. In turn, these images reflect vastly different pricing philosophies and strategies.

Our second question is this: Just how important is pricing as an element in the marketing mix? As we have already seen, it is a mistake to try to isolate any element in the marketing mix from the others. Nevertheless, because pricing has a direct and visible impact on revenues, it is extremely important to overall marketing plans. Moreover, it is a very flexible tool. It is certainly easier to change prices than to change products or distribution channels. In this section, we will focus on the ways in which pricing strategies for both new and existing products can result in widely differing prices for very similar products.

Whatever price strategy a company is using, it must be clearly communicated to buyers. Wal-Mart clearly communicates a low price strategy to consumers, but Eaton's strategy, with all its recent difficulties, has not been so clear. For many years, Eaton's had a high-price strategy, coupled with a generous return policy. In 1991, Eaton's switched to an "everyday low price" strategy, but then slowly drifted back to a high-price strategy with occasional sales. Industry experts think that consumers were confused by this strategy, and that this added to Eaton's problems.[6]

Pricing Existing Products

A firm basically has three options available in pricing its existing products. It can set prices for its product above prevailing market prices charged for similar products. It can set prices below market. Or it can set prices at or near the market price.

Companies pricing above the market play on customers' beliefs that higher price means higher quality. Curtis Mathes, a maker of televisions, VCRs, and stereos, promotes itself as the most expensive television set "but worth it." Companies such as Godiva chocolates and Rolls Royce have also succeeded with this pricing philosophy.

In contrast, both Budget and Discount car rental companies promote themselves as low-priced alternatives to Hertz and Avis. Ads for Suave hair-care

Curtis Mathes
http://www.curtismathes.com

products argue that "Suave does what theirs does—for a lot less." Pricing below the prevailing market price can succeed if the firm can offer a product of acceptable quality while keeping costs below those of higher-priced options.

A company can use different strategies for different customers. Airlines, for example, use a technique called *yield management* to predict precisely how many last-minute business travellers will want to get on a flight and be willing to pay a very high price. As a result, prices for leisure travel (which must be booked weeks in advance) are much lower than prices for business travel.[7] The price of a last-minute ticket from Chicago to Phoenix, for example, is $1404 while a "cheap seat" booked in advance costs only $238. This type of pricing system has allowed airlines to boost their profits significantly.

Finally, in some industries, a dominant firm establishes product prices and other companies follow along. This is called **price leadership**. (Don't confuse this approach with *price fixing*, the illegal process of producers agreeing among themselves what prices will be charged.) Price leadership is often evident in products such as structural steel, gasoline, and many processed foods. These products differ little in quality from one firm to another. Companies compete through advertising campaigns, personal selling, and service, not price.

price leadership
The dominant firm in the industry establishes product prices and other companies follow suit.

Pricing New Products: Skimming and Penetration Pricing

Companies introducing new products into the market have to consider two contrasting pricing policy options: coming in with either a very high price or a very low one. The former is known as a **price-skimming strategy** and the latter is a **penetration-pricing strategy**.

Skimming may allow a firm to earn a large profit on each item sold. This cash is often needed to cover product development and introduction costs. But skimming is possible only as long as the company can convince consumers that the product is truly different from existing products on the market. Eventually, the initial high profits will attract competition. Microwave ovens, calculators, and VCRs were introduced at comparatively high prices and prices fell as new companies entered the market.

On the other hand, the low initial prices of a penetration-pricing strategy seek to generate consumer interest and stimulate trial purchases of the new product. New food products—convenience foods, cookies, and snacks—are often promoted at special low prices that stimulate brisk early sales of the product. Penetration pricing provides for minimal, if any, profit. This strategy can only succeed if the company can raise its price as consumer acceptance grows. Such price increases must be managed carefully to avoid alienating future customers.

price-skimming strategy
The decision to price a new product as high as possible to earn the maximum profit on each unit sold.

penetration-pricing strategy
The decision to price a new product very low to sell the most units possible and to build customer loyalty.

Pricing Tactics

No matter what philosophy a company uses to price existing or new products, its managers may adopt one or more pricing *tactics* such as price lining, psychological pricing, or discounting.

Price Lining

Companies selling multiple items in a product category use price lining. For example, a department store carries literally thousands of products. To set a separate price for each brand and style of suit, plate, or couch would take many hours. By using **price lining**, the store can predetermine three or four price points at which a particular product will be sold. For men's suits, the price points might be $175, $250, and $400. All men's suits in the store will be priced at one of these three points. Buyers for the store must choose suits that can be purchased and sold profitably for one of these three prices.

price lining
The practice of offering all items in certain categories at a limited number of predetermined price points.

psychological pricing

The practice of setting prices to take advantage of the nonlogical reactions of consumers to certain types of prices.

odd-even psychological pricing

A form of psychological pricing in which prices are not stated in even dollar amounts.

threshold pricing

A form of psychological pricing in which prices are set at what appears to be the maximum price consumers will pay for an item.

discount

Any price reduction offered by the seller in order to persuade customers to purchase a product.

cash discount

A form of discount in which customers paying cash, rather than buying on credit, pay lower prices.

seasonal discount

A form of discount in which lower prices are offered to customers making a purchase at a time of year when sales are traditionally slow.

trade discount

Discount given to firms involved in a product's distribution.

quantity discount

A form of discount in which customers buying large amounts of a product pay lower prices.

Psychological Pricing

Another pricing tactic, **psychological pricing**, takes advantage of the fact that customers are not completely rational when making buying decisions.[8] **Odd-even psychological pricing** proposes that customers prefer prices that are not stated in even dollar amounts. That is, customers see prices of $1000, $100, $50, and $10 as much higher than prices of $999.95, $99.95, $49.95, and $9.95, respectively. One common explanation for this widely recognized process is that the consumer looks at the whole dollar figure, ignores the cents, and rounds down.

Closely related to odd-even pricing, **threshold pricing** argues that consumers set maximum prices they will pay for a particular item. Many gift shops, for example, will carry a supply of gifts in the $20-or-under price range. The feeling is that gift-givers often place an upper limit of $20 on gifts they buy.

Discounting

The price that is eventually set for a product is not always the price at which all items are sold. Many times a company has to offer a price reduction—a **discount**—to stimulate sales. Cash, seasonal, trade, and quantity discounts are the most common forms.

In recent years, **cash discounts** have become popular, even at retail stores. Stores may offer **seasonal discounts** to stimulate the sales of products during times of the year when most customers do not normally buy the product. Travellers can find low prices on summer trips to tropical islands and July shoppers can get sale prices on winter coats thanks to seasonal discounts. **Trade discounts** are available only to those companies or individuals involved in a product's distribution. Thus, wholesalers, retailers, and interior designers pay less for fabric than the typical consumer does. Related to trade discounts are **quantity discounts**—lower prices for purchases in large quantities. Case price discounts for motor oil or soft drinks at retail stores are examples of quantity discounts.

These teens are as concerned with the price tag as with the style of the clothing they might buy on this shopping trip.

The Distribution Mix

We have already seen that a company needs an appropriate product mix. But the success of any product also depends in part on its **distribution mix**: the combination of distribution channels that a firm selects to get a product to end users. In this section, we will consider some of the many factors that enter into the distribution mix. First, we will explain the need for *intermediaries*. We will then discuss the basic *distribution strategies*. Finally, we will consider some special issues in channel relationships—namely, conflict and leadership.

distribution mix

The combination of distribution channels a firm selects to get a product to end users.

Intermediaries and Distribution Channels

Once called *middlemen*, **intermediaries** are the individuals and firms who help to distribute a producer's goods. They are generally classified as *wholesalers* or *retailers*. **Wholesalers** sell products to other businesses, who resell them to final consumers. **Retailers** sell products directly to consumers. While some firms rely on independent intermediaries, others employ their own distribution networks and sales forces. The decision normally hinges on three factors:

- the company's target markets
- the nature of its products
- the costs of maintaining distribution and sales networks.

We examine these factors more closely below by describing some of the distribution decisions that go into the marketing of consumer products.

intermediary

Any individual or firm other than the producer who participates in a product's distribution.

wholesalers

Intermediaries who sell products to other businesses, who in turn resell them to the end-users.

retailers

Intermediaries who sell products to the end-users.

Distribution of Consumer Products

Figure 17.3 shows six primary **distribution channels** aimed at different target audiences and product types. Note that *all* channels *must* begin with a manufacturer and end with a consumer or an industrial user. Channels 1 through 4 are most often used for the distribution of consumer goods and services.

distribution channel

The path that a product follows from the producer to the end-user.

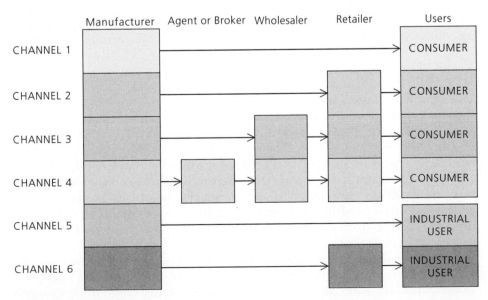

Figure 17.3
Channels of distribution: How the product travels from manufacturer to consumer.

Channel 1

In this **direct channel**, the product travels from the producer to the consumer with no intermediaries. Companies such as Avon, Fuller Brush, Tupperware, and many encyclopedia distributors use this channel. Direct channel distribution is also popular with craftspeople who sell their wares through word-of-mouth reference or from booths at local flea markets or craft shows. Roadside vegetable stands also use the direct channel. Dell and Gateway 2000 have captured one fifth of the personal computer market by selling direct to both industrial and ultimate consumers.

Channel 2

In Channel 2, manufacturers distribute products through retailers. Companies such as Goodyear and The Limited maintain their own systems of retail outlets. Liz Claiborne, on the other hand, relies on more than 9300 retailers to sell its apparel worldwide. Similarly, most firms in the perfume and fragrance industry use sales forces to sell products to retailers, who then sell them over the counter to consumers.

Channel 3

Until the mid-1960s, Channel 2 was a widely used method of retail distribution. But that channel requires a large amount of floor space both for storing merchandise and for displaying it in retail stores. As the cost of retail space rose, retailers found that they could not afford to buy space to store goods. Thus wholesalers have increasingly entered the distribution network. They have taken over more and more of the storage service. A good example of this philosophy in practice is convenience food/gas stores. Approximately 90 percent of the space in these stores is devoted to merchandise displays. Only about 10 percent is used for storage and office facilities.

Wholesalers have always played a role in distributing some products. Many manufacturers only distribute their products in large quantities. Small businesses that cannot afford to purchase large quantities of goods rely on wholesalers to hold inventories of such products and to supply them on short notice. For example, a family-owned grocery store that sells only 12 cases of canned spinach in a year cannot afford to buy a truckload (perhaps 500 cases) in a single order. Instead, it orders one case a month from a local wholesaler, which buys large lots of spinach and other goods from the makers, stores them, and resells them in small quantities to various retailers.

Channel 4

This complex channel uses **sales agents**, or **brokers**, who represent manufacturers and sell to wholesalers, retailers, or both. They receive commissions based on the price of goods they sell. Agents generally deal in the related product lines of a few producers, serving as their sales representatives on a relatively permanent basis. Travel agents, for example, represent the airlines, car-rental companies, and hotels. In contrast, brokers are hired to assist in buying and selling temporarily, matching sellers and buyers as needed. This channel is often used in the food and clothing industries. The real estate industry and the stock market also rely on brokers for matching buyers and sellers.

Indirect distribution channels do mean higher prices to the end consumer. The more members involved in the channel, the higher the final price to the purchaser. After all, each link in the distribution chain must charge a markup or commission to make a profit. Figure 17.4 shows typical markup growth through the distribution channel.

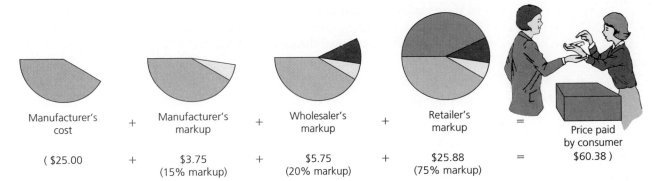

Manufacturer's cost	+	Manufacturer's markup	+	Wholesaler's markup	+	Retailer's markup	=	Price paid by consumer
($25.00	+	$3.75 (15% markup)	+	$5.75 (20% markup)	+	$25.88 (75% markup)	=	$60.38)

Figure 17.4
Where your dollar goes in the distribution channel for an electronic calculator.

Ernst & Young conducted a study of the competitiveness of distribution channels that showed that Canada often has an extra layer of wholesale distribution compared to American distribution channels and higher markups at the retail level. But the Canadian retail sector is becoming more like the U.S., with larger stores, more items, and fewer intermediaries.[9]

Intermediaries add to the visible dollar cost of a product but, in many ways, they save the consumer time and thus money. A manufacturer would not sell you one calculator for the same price it charges wholesalers who buy truckloads of them. In other ways, intermediaries actually save you money.

Consider Figure 17.5, which illustrates the problem of making chili without an intermediary—the supermarket. You would probably spend a lot more time (and a lot of money on gas) if you had to get all the necessary ingredients on your own. In fact, intermediaries can add form, place, and time utility by making the right quantities available where and when you need them.

Distribution of Industrial Products

Industrial channels are important because each company is itself a customer that buys other companies' products. The Kellogg Co. buys grain to make breakfast cereals, Stone Container Corp. buys rolls of paper and vats of glue to make corrugated boxes, and Victoria Hospital buys medicines and other supplies to provide medical services. **Industrial distribution**, therefore, refers

industrial distribution
The network of channel members involved in the flow of manufactured goods to industrial customers.

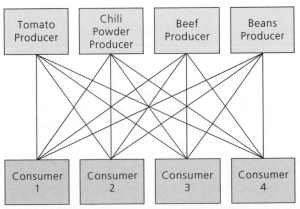

PURCHASE OF GOODS WITHOUT INTERMEDIARIES

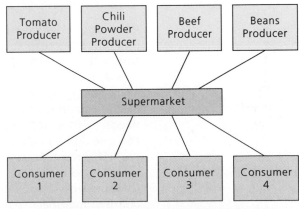

PURCHASE OF GOODS WITH INTERMEDIARIES

Figure 17.5
Advantages of intermediaries.

to the network of channel members involved in the flow of manufactured goods to industrial customers. Unlike consumer products, industrial products are traditionally distributed through Channels 5 or 6 (refer back to Figure 17.3).

Channel 5

sales offices

Offices maintained by sellers of industrial goods to provide points of contact with their customers.

Most industrial goods are sold directly by the manufacturer to the industrial buyer. For example, Lawless Container Corp. produces packaging containers that are sold directly to such industrial customers as Fisher-Price (toys), Dirt Devil (vacuum cleaners), and Mr. Coffee (coffee makers). As contact points with their customers, manufacturers maintain **sales offices**. These offices provide all services for the company's customers and serve as headquarters for its salespeople.

Steel, transistors, and conveyors are all distributed through Channel 5. Because such goods are usually purchased in large quantities, intermediaries are often unnecessary. In some cases, however, brokers or agents may enter the distribution chain between manufacturer and buyer.

Channel 6

Wholesalers function as intermediaries between manufacturers and users in only a very small percentage of industrial channels. Brokers and agents are even rarer. Channel 6 is most often used for accessory equipment (computer terminals, office equipment) and supplies (floppy disks, copier paper). While manufacturers produce these items in large quantities, companies buy them in small quantities. Few companies, for example, order truckloads of paper clips. As with consumer goods, then, intermediaries help end users by representing manufacturers or by breaking down large quantities into smaller sales units.

In some areas, however, relationships are changing. In the office-products industry, for instance, Channel 6 is being displaced by the emergence of a new channel that looks very much like Channel 3 for consumer products: Instead of buying office supplies from wholesalers (Channel 6), many users are shopping at office discount stores such as Staples and Office Depot. Warehouselike superstores target small- and medium-sized businesses, which generally buy supplies at retail stores, much as they target retail consumers. In these new "discount stores for industrial users," customers stroll down the aisles behind shopping carts, selecting from 7000 items at prices 20 to 75 percent lower than manufacturers' suggested prices.

Distribution Strategies

Choosing a distribution network is a vital consideration for a company. It can make the firm succeed or fail. The choice of distribution strategy determines the amount of market exposure the product gets and the cost of that exposure.

The appropriate strategy depends on the product class. The goal is to make a product accessible in just enough locations to satisfy customers' needs. Milk can be purchased at many retail outlets (high exposure). But there is only one distributor for Rolls Royce in a given city.

intensive distribution

A distribution strategy in which a product is distributed in nearly every possible outlet, using many channels and channel members.

Different degrees of market exposure are available through intensive distribution, exclusive distribution, and selective distribution. **Intensive distribution** means distributing a product through as many channels and channel members (using both wholesalers and retailers) as possible. For example, as Figure 17.6 shows, Caramilk bars flood the market through all suitable outlets. Intensive distribution is normally used for low-cost, consumer goods such as candy and magazines.

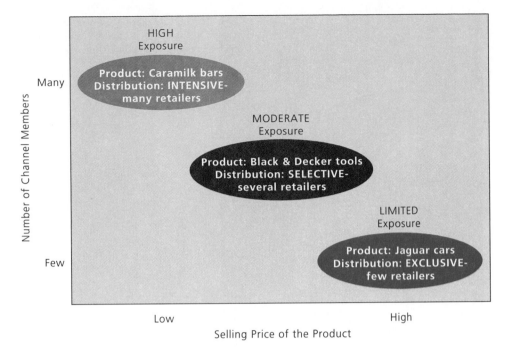

Figure 17.6
Amounts of market exposure from three kinds of distribution.

In contrast, **exclusive distribution** occurs when a manufacturer grants the exclusive right to distribute or sell a product to one wholesaler or retailer in a given geographic area. Exclusive distribution agreements are most common in high-cost, prestige products. For example, Jaguar automobiles are sold by only a single dealer servicing a large metropolitan area.

Selective distribution falls between intensive and exclusive distribution. A company that uses this strategy carefully selects only wholesalers and retailers who will give special attention to the product in terms of sales efforts, display position, etc. Selective distribution policies have been applied to virtually every type of consumer product. It is usually embraced by companies like Black & Decker whose product lines do not require intense market exposure to increase sales.

exclusive distribution

A distribution strategy in which a product's distribution is limited to only one wholesaler or retailer in a given geographic area.

selective distribution

A distribution strategy that falls between intensive and exclusive distribution, calling for the use of a limited number of outlets for a product.

Channel Conflict and Channel Leadership

Manufacturers can choose to distribute through more than one channel or wholesaler. They can also choose to make new uses of existing channels. Similarly, most retailers are free to strike agreements with as many producers as capacity permits. In such cases, *channel conflict* may arise. Conflicts are resolved when members' efforts are better coordinated. A key factor in coordinating the activities of independent organizations is *channel leadership*. Another strategy for improving coordination is known as the *vertical marketing system*.

Channel Conflict

Channel conflict occurs when members of the channel disagree over the roles they should play or the rewards they should receive. John Deere, for example, would no doubt object if its dealers began distributing Russian and Japanese tractors. Similarly, when a manufacturer-owned factory outlet store discounts the company's apparel or housewares, it runs the risk of alienating the manufacturer's retail accounts. Channel conflict may also arise if one

The intense competition between IBM and Apple has led to rapid technological advances in personal computers.

member has more power than the others or is viewed as receiving preferential treatment. Needless to say, such conflicts defeat the purpose of the system by disrupting the flow of goods to their destinations.

Consider the case of IBM, which sells both through wholesalers and retailers and directly to major corporations. When IBM makes a direct sale, its dealers point out that they have lost a chance to earn money by making the sale themselves. If this pattern repeatedly frustrates one particular dealer, that dealer may take action—switching, for example, from IBM to Apple products.[10]

Channel Leadership

channel captain

The channel member that is the most powerful in determining the roles and rewards of organizations involved in a given channel of distribution.

Usually, one channel member is most powerful in determining the roles and rewards of other members. That member is the **channel captain**. Often, the channel captain is a manufacturer, particularly if the manufacturer's product is in high demand. In some industries, an influential wholesaler or a large retailer like Wal-Mart or Sears may emerge as channel captain because of large sales volumes.

Vertical Marketing Systems

vertical marketing system

A system in which there is a high degree of coordination among all the units in the distribution channel so that a product moves efficiently from manufacturer to consumer.

To overcome problems posed by channel conflict and issues of channel leadership, the **vertical marketing system (VMS)** has emerged. In a VMS, separate businesses join to form a unified distribution channel, with one member coordinating the activities of the whole channel. There are three types of VMS arrangements:

- In a *corporate VMS*, all stages in the channel are under single ownership. The Limited, for example, owns both the production facilities that manufacture its apparel and the retail stores that sell it.

- In a *contractual VMS*, channel members sign contracts agreeing to specific duties and rewards. The Independent Grocers' Alliance (IGA), for example, consists of independent retail grocers joined with a wholesaler who contractually leads—but does not own—the VMS. Most franchises are contractual VMSs.

IGA

http://www.igainc.com

■ In an *administered VMS*, channel members are less formally coordinated than in a corporate or contractual VMS. Instead, one or more of the members emerge as leader(s) and maintain control as a result of power and influence. Although the administered VMS is more fragile than the corporate and contractual forms, it is more unified than channels relying on independent members.

Wholesaling

Now that you know something about distribution channels, we can consider the broader role played by intermediaries. Wholesalers provide a variety of functions for their customers, who are buying products for resale or for business use. In addition to storing products and providing an assortment of products for their customers, wholesalers offer delivery, credit, and information about products. Not all wholesalers provide all of these functions. The specific services they offer depend on the type of intermediary involved: merchant wholesalers or agents/brokers.

Merchant Wholesalers

Most wholesalers are independent operators who derive their income from sales of goods produced by a variety of manufacturers. All **merchant wholesalers** take title to merchandise. That is, merchant wholesalers buy and own the goods they resell to other businesses. They usually provide storage and a means of delivery.

A **full-service merchant wholesaler** provides credit, marketing, and merchandising services. Approximately 80 percent of all merchant wholesalers are full-service wholesalers.

Limited-function merchant wholesalers provide only a few services, sometimes merely storage. Their customers are normally small operations that pay cash and pick up their own goods. One such wholesaler, the **drop shipper**, does not even carry inventory or handle the product. Drop shippers receive orders from customers, negotiate with producers to supply goods, take title to them, and arrange for shipment to customers. The drop shipper bears the risks of the transaction until the costumer takes title to the goods.

Other limited-function wholesalers, known as **rack jobbers**, market consumer goods—mostly nonfood items—directly to retail stores.[11] Procter & Gamble, for example, uses rack jobbers to distribute products like Pampers diapers. After marking prices, setting up display racks, and displaying diapers in one store, the rack jobber moves on to another outlet to check inventories and shelve products.

Agents and Brokers

Agents and brokers serve as sales forces for various manufacturers. They are independent representatives of many companies' products. They work on commissions, usually about 4 to 5 percent of net sales. Unlike merchant wholesalers, they do not take title to—that is, they do not own—the merchandise they sell. Rather, they serve as the sales and merchandising arms of manufacturers who do not have their own sales forces.

The value of agents and brokers lies primarily in their knowledge of markets and their merchandising expertise. They also provide a wide range of services, including shelf and display merchandising and advertising layout. Finally, they maintain product saleability by removing open, torn, or dirty packages, arranging products neatly, and generally keeping them attractively displayed. Many supermarket products are handled through brokers.

merchant wholesaler
An independent wholesaler who buys and takes legal possession of goods before selling them to customers.

full-service merchant wholesaler
A merchant wholesaler who provides storage and delivery in addition to wholesaling services.

limited-function merchant wholesaler
An independent wholesaler who provides only wholesaling—not warehousing or transportation—services.

drop shipper
A type of wholesaler who does not carry inventory or handle the product.

rack jobber
A full-function merchant wholesaler specializing in nonfood merchandise who sets up and maintains display racks of some products in retail stores.

Trends in Intermediary-Customer Relationships

Like so many relationships in today's environment, intermediary-customer relationships are undergoing a variety of changes. Two emerging trends are the use of fewer intermediaries and more customer-supplier partnerships. In some industries, intermediaries are losing sales because customers with access to new information sources are locating new channels for the products they want. Travel agents, for example, still sell about four-fifths of all U.S. air-travel tickets (a service for which they are paid by airlines). This service, however, is now threatened with displacement by consumers who have such services as Prodigy and CompuServe, which give them direct computer access to airline reservations systems.[12]

Likewise, readers can order books factory-direct by fax or toll-free telephone. Buyers of electronics products, too, now have direct access to sellers via 800 lines and e-mail. Orders received electronically can be transmitted to the factory floor, where each unit can actually be earmarked for a specific customer. At its Erskine, Scotland, plant, for example, Compaq Computer is testing an automatic restocking system: For some customers, Compaq will build to order instead of producing ahead and placing products in inventory to await buyer demand. Similarly, telephone orders for Motorola pagers and IBM PCs can be placed for made-to-order customers.[13]

Even in industries where intermediaries are still thriving, new information technologies are altering relationships with industrial customers. For example, Bailey Controls, an Ohio manufacturer of control systems for factories, has close team relationships with two distributors that supply it with parts. One distributor, Future Electronics in Montreal, is electronically connected with Bailey: When Bailey's parts supply drops below a certain level, a laser scanner instantly notifies Future to send replacements at once. Bailey stocks only enough inventory to meet immediate needs and relies on quick service from Future.

Retailing

You probably have had little contact with merchant wholesalers, merchandise brokers, or manufacturers. If you are like most Canadians, you buy nearly all the goods and services you consume from retailers. Most retailers are small operations, often consisting of just the owners and part-time help. But there are a few very large retailers, and these account for billions of dollars of sales each year (see Table 17.2 for a top-10 listing of retailers in Canada).

Table 17.2   The Top 10 Retailers in Canada, 1996

Company	Sales Revenue (in billions)
1. George Weston Ltd.	$12.7
2. The Oshawa Group Ltd.	6.3
3. Hudson's Bay Co.	6.0
4. Provigo Inc.	5.8
5. Canada Safeway Ltd.	4.7
6. Sears Canada Inc.	3.9
7. Canadian Tire Corp. Ltd.	3.9
8. Metro-Richelieu Inc.	3.2
9. Empire Co. Ltd.	2.9
10. Price Costco Canada Inc.	2.7

In the past few years, U.S. retailers have become very aggressive in expanding into Canada and Europe. This has created problems for retailers in those countries, but bargains for consumers (see the box "U.S. Discounters Making Waves in Canada and Europe").

Types of Retail Outlets

The major categories of retail stores are department, speciality, discount (bargain), convenience, supermarkets, warehouse clubs, and hypermarkets. Some retailing is also done without stores.

Department Stores

As the name implies, **department stores** are organized into specialized departments—shoes, furniture, appliances, etc. Department stores began in the 1800s and were initially located in downtown districts, although most

department stores
Large retail stores that offer a wide variety of high-quality items divided into specialized departments.

International Report

U.S. Discounters Making Waves in Canada and Europe

During the 1990s, several U.S. retail giants have invaded the Canadian market. Why has this happened now? Most U.S. executives say that the Canada-U.S. Free Trade Agreement had a lot to do with it. Large U.S. retailers feel that the Canadian retail industry is five to ten years behind the U.S. in terms of purchasing, distribution, and technology. Since Canada is no longer a protected market, these retailers see good profit possibilities in Canada.

Since 1985, Price/Costco has opened 47 stores in Canada. Wal-Mart purchased 122 stores from Woolco and opened them as Wal-Marts in 1994. The Gap expanded from 34 outlets to 64. Home Depot, which came to Canada in 1994, plans to open 50 stores by 2000. One Canadian retail consultant predicts that only half of all Canadian retailers will survive to 2000.

Because high prices are the rule rather than the exception in Europe, U.S. discounters like Price/Costco, Toys 'R' Us, and Kmart are also starting to compete there. Bargain-hungry Europeans are welcoming these discounters with open arms. For example, at the grand opening of England's first factory outlet mall, 25 000 people showed up (some having travelled great distances) to pay discount prices for apparel by Wrangler, Benetton, and Pierre Cardin.

These changes are very threatening to European retailers, and some have already gone out of business. Some have gone to court in an attempt to defend their turf. The three largest grocery chains in Britain took legal action to keep Price/Costco out (they failed). In both Germany and France, merchants have banded together to oppose changes—like late-night hours—that American discounters bring with them. But these responses simply highlight the vulnerability of retail outlets that are not responsive to consumer needs.

U.S. discounters feel that the European market is a place where they can deliver bargains to consumers and in the process make fat profit margins for themselves.

Canadian retailers have also pursued a strategy of entering foreign markets, particularly in the U.S. Unfortunately, their success has been limited. Consider these examples:

- Canadian Tire tried twice to enter the retail market (once with Auto Source in the north-central U.S., and once with White Stores in Texas). The company lost over $300 million in the two ventures.

- Imasco, the owner of Shopper's Drug Mart, purchased Peoples Drug Stores in the U.S. The stores did not do well and were sold off.

- Dylex operates several well-known retail stores in Canada (Tip Top Tailors, Big Steel Man, Bi-Way). It also operated Foxmoor Specialty Stores in the U.S., but had to file for bankruptcy on those stores.

A study team at the University of Western Ontario found that fewer than one third of Canadian retailers who tried to enter the U.S. market were successful. By contrast, nearly all of the U.S. retailers who entered Canada were successful. Why? The research suggested four reasons. First, the U.S. firms were larger and therefore had more clout in the market place. Second, U.S. retailers provide more service and selection. Third, CEOs of U.S. retailers were older, more experienced, and had more education than Canadian CEOs. Finally, the competitive environment is tougher in the U.S. For example, the typical response of a U.S. retailer to foreign competition is to drive it out of business.

now have suburban branches. Generally, department stores are quite large and handle a wide range of goods. They usually offer a variety of services as well, such as generous merchandise return policies, credit plans, and delivery. The largest department stores—Hudson's Bay and Sears—have combined annual sales over $9 billion.

Specialty Stores

specialty stores

Small retail stores that carry one line of related products.

In sharp contrast to department stores are **specialty stores**, small stores that carry one line of related products. These stores serve a carefully defined market segment by offering a full product line in a narrow product field, along with knowledgeable sales personnel. For example, most golf courses have a pro shop that carries golf clubs, as well as apparel, shoes, and other accessories for golfing. Other examples of specialty stores are The Fishin' Hole, Radio Shack, and Jiffy Lube.

Particularly in the apparel industry, the 1980s were the decade of the specialty store. Between 1980 and 1990, retailers like The Gap, The Limited, and Ann Taylor spearheaded the growth spurt of a multi-billion dollar industry in stylish upscale clothing. More apparel manufacturers are entering the retail industry. Companies like Timberland (outdoor wear), Tommy Hilfiger (casual clothing), OshKosh B'Gosh (children's clothes), and Speedo (swim and athletic wear) have all opened showcase outlets in specialty shopping centres and large malls.

category killers

Retailers who carry a deep selection of goods in a narrow product line.

Retailers who carry an extremely deep selection of goods in a relatively narrow product line and hire technical experts to give customers advice are called **category killers**. They are so named because they carry virtually everything within a certain category. Home Depot, which recently purchased 75 percent of Aikenhead's Home Improvement Warehouse from Molson, is an example of a category killer. It sells building materials, lawn and garden supplies, and home improvement products.

This furniture shopper has chosen a specialty store that carries a complete line of furnishings and offers interior decorating services.

Discount Houses

After the Second World War, some retailers began offering discounts to certain customers. These **discount houses** sold items such as televisions and other appliances at substantial reductions in price in order to sell large volumes of products. As name-brand items became more plentiful in the early 1950s, discounters offered better assortments to customers while still embracing a basic philosophy of low-rent facilities and cash-only sales. But as discount houses became more firmly entrenched in the marketplace, they began moving to better locations, improving in-store decor and selling better quality merchandise at higher prices. They also began offering some of the services of a department store, such as credit plans and noncash sales. Kmart, Zellers, and Wal-Mart are discount stores. The box "The Wal-Mart Invasion" describes how this much publicized retailer operates.

discount houses
Bargain retail stores that offer major items such as televisions and large appliances at discount prices.

Catalogue showrooms mail catalogues with colour pictures of products, product descriptions, and prices to customers' homes and businesses. In the showroom, customers view samples on display, place orders, and wait briefly while clerks retrieve their orders from the warehouse attached to the showroom. Consumers Distributing has many such catalogue showrooms.

catalogue showrooms
Bargain retail stores in which customers place orders for items described in a catalogue and pick up those items from an on-premises warehouse.

Factory outlets sell merchandise directly from the factory to consumers, thereby avoiding wholesalers and retailers. The first factory outlets featured products such as apparel, linens, food items, and furniture. Located next to the factories in warehouse-like facilities, their distribution costs were very low. Consequently, they could offer their products at lower costs.

factory outlets
Bargain retail stores that are owned by the manufacturers whose products they sell.

Convenience Stores

While selection is the lure of department stores and price the lure of discount stores, **convenience stores**, as their name implies, offer ease of purchase. They stress an easily accessible location with parking, extended store hours (in many cases 24 hours), and fast service. Neighbourhood gasoline/food retailers like 7-Eleven and Circle K stores are convenience stores.

convenience stores
Retail stores that offer high accessibility, extended hours, and fast service on selected items.

Supermarkets

Beginning in the last half of the 1930s, a radical shift began to occur in the grocery business from the small corner grocery store to supermarkets. Like department stores, **supermarkets** are divided into departments of related food and household paper and cleaning products. The emphasis is on low prices, self-service, and wide selection. The largest supermarkets are chain stores such as Safeway, Loblaws, and Provigo.

supermarkets
Large retail stores that offer a variety of food and food-related items divided into specialized departments.

Warehouse Clubs

One of the newer innovations in retailing is the **warehouse club** (also called wholesale clubs). These are huge, membership-only, combination retail-wholesale operations that sell all kinds of brand-name merchandise. They carry groceries, appliances, tires, clothing, and countless other items at very low prices.

warehouse clubs
Huge, membership-only, combined retail-wholesale operations that sell brand-name merchandise.

Traditional retailers such as Canada Safeway generate 80 percent of their sales from just 20 percent of the products they carry. By contrast, warehouse clubs stock only the 20 percent and sell huge volumes of it at low margins. Supermarkets carry about 20 000 items, but warehouse clubs carry only about 3500. The typical warehouse club margin is 8 percent, while at more traditional discount stores the margin can be up to 40 percent. By carrying only the top-selling brands, warehouse clubs have been able to expand their product lines into non-grocery items like appliances, consumer electronics, tools, and office supplies.

The Canadian Business Scene

The Wal-Mart Invasion

Big, bad Wal-Mart has come to Canada. While Canadian retailers are worried, retailing experts say that in the long run everyone will benefit. They point to the experience of the domestic automobile industry in the 1980s when Japanese firms invaded North America in a big way. Eventually General Motors, Chrysler, and Ford stopped complaining about foreign competition, pulled up their socks, and became more competitive. Now, domestic automobiles are a better value (and are selling better) than Japanese cars. The same thing is going to happen in the retail business.

In the short-run, however, Wal-Mart's entrance into Canada has a lot of people worried. It will change a lot of things in Canada, including manufacturing and distribution processes. And it will shake up an industry that is still in turmoil after the recent recession. It will probably cause a lot of little retailers to go under, and perhaps a national chain as well. But it will not destroy Canadian retailing, just mediocre retailers. In short, Wal-Mart (and other innovations like warehouse clubs) will do to Canadian retailing what the Japanese threat did to automobile manufacturing.

Wal-Mart gives consumers what they want: low prices, convenience, good selection, no stock-outs, and fast in-and-out time. But Wal-Mart is not alone in changing the face of Canadian retailing. Warehouse clubs and "category killers" like Office Depot and Home Depot are also challenging traditional retailing and distribution practices.

Each of these three kinds of retailers has a slightly different strategy. Warehouse clubs keep prices low by offering minimal service, limited selection, and no guarantee that the same brand will be available next week. They pursue high volume and are content with low margins. Category killers offer a deep selection of a narrow range of goods and have higher margins, which allows them to provide much more customer service. Wal-Mart, Kmart, and Zellers lie somewhere in between these two formats, providing a wide range of products at low prices.

The success of these three retailing formats shows just how much Canadian consumers have changed over the years. In the 1960s, Canadian families spent more than 80 percent of their income on consumption; now it is 72 percent. Real disposable income has been falling and is now down to the level it was in 1980. Because of this, consumers are very price-conscious. They are also time-conscious; one study showed that shoppers now spend 20 minutes less on the average trip to a shopping mall than they did in 1982.

The success of Wal-Mart bears looking into. Its annual sales revenue of over $100 billion is five times greater than the total of all Canadian department and discount stores combined. How does it achieve this? Wal-Mart has figured out how business operates and how consumers think, and it successfully manipulated both of these. A large part of its success is attributed to its inventory and distribution systems. Check-out scanners feed information to distribution centres where products move on high speed conveyers. Most of its stores are within a day's drive of a distribution centre, and many stores are replenished daily. It is really just-in-time retailing. Information technology allows Wal-Mart's suppliers to better plan their production schedules because they know almost instantaneously what is going on at the retail level.

The system ensures that products will not be out of stock and that they will be the lowest price possible, a big advantage in an industry where small margins are the rule. Wal-Mart has a policy of everyday low prices; it has no sales except on items that are being closed out. But its big advantage comes with the use of something called variable pricing—maintaining unusually low prices on goods like motor oil, paper towels, and laundry detergent that are frequently purchased by customers. Local Wal-Mart managers have authority to lower prices on these goods to below that of their competitors. Because of the low prices on these sensitive goods, customers often think that Wal-Mart has the lowest prices on everything (it doesn't). Wal-Mart stores have sales of about $300 per square foot, which is about 50 percent higher than discount competitors like Kmart and Zellers.

Some Canadian retailers are in denial about the changes that are coming in retailing. They say that Wal-Mart, the warehouse clubs, and the category killers won't be able to achieve really low prices here because doing business in Canada is simply a higher cost proposition because of a smaller population, a large country, and higher taxes. But this is wishful thinking. New era retailers don't have to offer absolutely low prices; they simply have to beat the prices charged by the traditional Canadian retailers. And it won't stop there. The new retailers will also cause reductions in the activity of wholesalers by dealing directly with manufacturers. The new retailers even will change manufacturing as they continually question whether manufacturers are producing goods at the lowest possible cost.

Some traditional retailers have also experimented with the "warehouse format." Canadian Tire, for example, opened a warehouse format store in St. Hubert, Quebec, in 1991. The company's strategy is to convince consumers that it can match the low prices at warehouse clubs such as Price/Costco.[14]

Hypermarkets

Hypermarkets are also large institutions with broad merchandise offerings, but they have somewhat higher prices than warehouse clubs. Hypermarkets may also include service departments such as cafeterias and beauty salons. Meijer's Thrifty Acres near Detroit and Hypermarché Laval near Montreal are examples of hypermarkets. These firms practise **scrambled merchandising**, carrying any product—whether similar or dissimilar to the store's original product offering—they feel will sell.

Other retail variations exist. Liquidation World, with locations in Calgary, Edmonton, and Surrey, B.C., does not carry a standard product line. Instead, it gets deals on merchandise from insurance companies, receivers, and bankruptcy trustees and then sells the products at low prices. And McDonald's opens a mobile outlet during the summer months in Grand Bend, Ontario. The company is thinking of using mobile units at special events such as concerts.[15]

Nonstore Retailing

Not all goods and services are offered for sale in stores. In fact, some retailers sell all or most of their products without stores. Examples of nonstore retailing include mail order, vending machines, video marketing, telemarketing, electronic shopping, and direct selling.

Mail Order

Firms that sell by **mail order** typically send out splashy catalogues describing a variety of merchandise. Singer-actress Cher calls her catalogue "a coffeetable book you can order from." Called *Sanctuary*, it features a medieval theme—lamps with chain mail shades, wrought-iron bedsteads, and velvet pillows with Gothic church designs.[16]

Some firms sell solely through the mail. Others such as Sears have a combination marketing strategy and distribute merchandise through both catalogue sales and retail outlets. Although mail-order firms have existed for a long time, computer technology and telephone-charge transactions have helped this industry boom in recent years.

Vending Machines

Certain types of consumer goods—most notably candy, soft drinks, and cigarettes—lend themselves to distribution through **vending machines**. Vending machine sales in Canada were nearly $400 million in 1995, yet they represent only a small proportion of total retail sales.[17]

Video Marketing

More and more companies have begun using television to sell consumer commodities such as jewellery and kitchen accessories. Many cable systems now offer **video marketing** through home shopping channels that display and demonstrate products and allow viewers to phone in orders. One weekend in 1993, Ivana Trump's appearance on the Home Shopping Club netted $2 million in orders for her high-fashion apparel.

hypermarkets
Large institutions with broad product offerings but with somewhat higher prices than warehouse clubs.

scrambled merchandising
The retail practice of carrying any product expected to sell well, regardless of whether it fits into the store's original product offering.

mail order
A form of nonstore retailing in which customers place orders for merchandise shown in catalogues and receive their orders via mail.

vending machine
Machine that dispenses mostly convenience goods such as candy, cigarettes, and soft drinks.

video marketing
Selling to consumers by showing products on television that consumers can buy by telephone or mail.

Telemarketing

Telemarketing is the use of the telephone to sell directly to consumers. WATS (Wide Area Telephone Service) lines can be used to receive toll-free calls from consumers in response to television and radio advertisements. Offering live or automated dialling, message delivery, and order taking, tele-marketers can use WATS lines to call consumers to promote products and services. Telemarketing is used for both consumer and industrial goods, and it is experiencing rapid growth in Canada, the U.S., and Great Britain.

Electronic Shopping

Electronic shopping is made possible by computer information systems that allow sellers to connect into consumers' computers with information about products and services. The member's computer video display shows the available products, which range from plane reservations to consumer goods. Viewers can examine detailed product descriptions, compare brands, send for free information, or purchase by credit card—all at home. Prodigy, a joint venture of IBM and Sears, is the largest of the home networks.

Direct Selling

The oldest form of retailing, **direct selling** is still used by companies that sell door-to-door or through *home-selling parties*. Most of us have talked with salespeople from World Book, Avon, or Fuller Brush as they make their door-to-door sales calls.

Direct selling is also common in the wholesaling of such industrial goods as commercial photocopying equipment. Although direct selling is convenient and gives customers one-on-one attention, prices are usually driven up by labour costs (salespeople often receive commissions of 40 to 50 cents on every sales dollar). Worldwide, 9 million direct salespeople now generate annual sales of $35 billion. In Japan alone, for instance, 1.2 million distributors have made Amway Corp. second only to Coca-Cola as the most profitable foreign retailer.[18]

Some door-to-door firms use **multi-level marketing**, which attracts both buyers and sellers. The company convinces people to sell the product to anyone they can. In return the salesperson gets a commission. Salespeople also get a commission on the sales of any person they recruit to work for the business. Amway and Mary Kay Cosmetics are two of the most well-known multi-level marketing firms.

Changes in Retailing: The Wheel of Retailing

The **wheel of retailing** concept shows how retail stores evolve over time. The "wheel" works like this: A new retailer emerges primarily because existing stores have become overpriced. The new retailer initially keeps prices down by providing fewer services, selling unknown brands, or locating in a low-rent area. But as the new retailer gets a foothold in the market, it wants to expand its market share. So it begins to offer more services, sells name-brand merchandise, and upgrades its stores facilities. But this increases costs, so it begins charging higher prices to consumers. This, in turn, creates a gap in the low-price end of the market, and even newer retailers move in to fill that gap.

Kmart is a good example of the wheel of retailing concept. It initially offered low-priced products in converted warehouses. But over the years it built new stores, remodelled others, and began offering higher-quality merchandise. In response, a large number of "bargain barns" have sprung up to fill the gap that was created as Kmart moved up.

Physical Distribution

Physical distribution refers to the activities needed to move products efficiently from manufacturer to consumer. The goals of physical distribution are to keep customers satisfied, to make goods available when and where consumers want them, and to keep costs low. Thus physical distribution includes *customer-service operations* such as order processing, as well as *warehousing* and *transporting operations*.

physical distribution
Those activities needed to move a product from the manufacturer to the end consumer.

Customer-Service Operations

Often the customer's only direct contact with the seller is to place an order. Thus **order processing**—filling orders as they are received—strongly affects how customers view the firm's efficiency and cooperation. The behaviour of order-entry personnel can make or break a firm's reputation.

order processing
In a product's distribution, the receiving and filling of orders.

To please customers and assure repeat business, companies need to offer fast, convenient, and polite service. Bass Pro Shops' (offering a complete line of fishing and recreational products) catalogue sales has a toll-free number that is answered quickly by courteous, knowledgeable employees. They offer customers different methods of paying for purchases and indicate when and how an order will arrive.

Many companies set standards for order-cycle times. **Order-cycle time** is the total amount of time from when the order is placed to when the customer receives the goods. Companies that can achieve rapid order-cycle times may have a competitive edge over less efficient firms. Some customers are willing to pay extra to receive their purchases faster, rather than having to wait.

order-cycle time
The total amount of time from order placement to when the customer actually receives the order.

Warehousing Operations

Storing or **warehousing** products is a major function of distribution management. In selecting a warehousing strategy, managers must keep in mind the characteristics and costs of warehousing operations.

warehousing
That part of the distribution process concerned with storing goods.

Types of Warehouses

There are two basic types of warehouses: private and public. Within these categories, we can further divide warehouses according to their use as storage sites or as distribution centres.

The first type, **private warehouses**, are owned by and provide storage for just one company, be it a manufacturer, a wholesaler, or a retailer. Most are used by large firms that deal in mass quantities and need storage regularly.

private warehouses
Warehouses owned and used by just one company.

Public warehouses are independently owned and operated. Companies that use these warehouses pay for the actual space used. Public warehouses are popular with firms that need such storage only during peak business periods. They are also used by manufacturers who want to maintain stock in numerous locations in order to get their products to many markets quickly.

public warehouses
Independently owned and operated warehouses that store the goods of many firms.

Storage warehouses provide storage for extended periods of time. Producers of seasonal items, such as agricultural crops, most often use this type of warehouse. In contrast, **distribution centres** store products whose market demand is constant and quite high. They are used by retail chains, wholesalers, and manufacturers that need to break large quantities produced or bought into the smaller quantities their stores or customers demand.

storage warehouses
Warehouses used to provide storage of goods for extended periods of time.

distribution centres
Warehouses used to provide storage of goods for only short periods before they are shipped to retail stores.

Warehousing Costs

All warehouse types involve costs. These costs include obvious expenses such as storage space rental or mortgage payments (usually computed by square foot), insurance, and wages. They also include the costs of inventory control and materials handling. **Inventory control** is a vital part of warehouse operations. It goes beyond keeping track of what is on hand at any time and involves planning to ensure that an adequate supply of a product is in stock at all times—a tricky balancing act.

Materials handling is the transportation, arrangement, and orderly retrieval of goods in inventory. Most warehouse personnel are employed in materials handling. Keeping materials handling costs down requires managers to develop a strategy for storing a company's products that takes into account product locations within the warehouse. One strategy for managing materials is **unitization**, a method that standardizes the weight and form of materials and makes storage and handling more systematic. To reduce the high costs of materials handling, more and more warehouses are automating. Computerized systems can move, store, and retrieve items from storage in the warehouse.

inventory control
The part of warehouse operations that keeps track of what is on hand and ensures adequate supplies of products in stock at all times.

materials handling
The transportation and arrangement of goods within a warehouse and orderly retrieval of goods from inventory.

unitization
A materials-handling strategy in which goods are transported and stored in containers with a uniform size, shape, and/or weight.

Transportation Operations

Transportation, for both passengers and freight is big business, with the top 50 transportation companies generating over $400 billion in sales revenue each year. The major transportation modes are rail, water, truck, air, and pipelines. In the early part of the 20th century, railroads dominated the Canadian transportation system, but by the 1970s, truck and air transportation had become much more important.

Cost is a major factor when a company chooses a transportation method. The difference in cost among the various transportation modes is directly related to the speed of delivery. The higher the speed of delivery, the greater the cost. But cost is not the only consideration. A company must also consider the nature of its products, the distance the product must travel, timeliness, and customers' needs and wants. A company shipping orchids or other perishable goods will probably use air transport, while a company shipping sand or coal will use rail or water transport.

Trucks

The advantages of trucks include flexibility, fast service, and dependability. Nearly all sections of Canada, except the far north, can be reached by truck. Trucks are a particularly good choice for short-distance distribution and more expensive products. Large furniture and appliance retailers in major cities, for example, use trucks to shuttle merchandise between their stores and to make deliveries to customers. Trucks can, however, be delayed by bad weather. They also are limited in the volume they can carry in a single load.

More and more manufacturers are using **expedited transportation**, which involves paying a higher-than-normal fee for truck delivery in return for guaranteed delivery times. Even this higher fee is still cheaper than air freight.[19]

expedited transportation
Paying a higher-than-normal fee for truck delivery for guaranteed delivery times.

Planes

Air is the fastest available transportation mode. In Canada's far north, it may be the only available transportation. Other advantages include greatly reduced costs in packing, handling, unpacking, and final preparations necessary for sale to the consumer. Also, inventory-carrying costs can be reduced by eliminating the need to store certain commodities. Fresh fish, for example, can

A container train crosses the Salmon River bridge in New Brunswick.

be flown to restaurants each day, avoiding the risk of spoilage that comes with packaging and storing a supply of fish. However, air freight is the most expensive form of transportation. In recent years a whole new industry has evolved to meet the customer's need to receive important business papers and supplies "overnight."

Railroads

Railroads have been the backbone of our transportation system since the late 1800s. Until the 1960s, when trucking firms lowered their rates and attracted many customers, railroads were fairly profitable. They are now used primarily to transport heavy, bulky items such as cars, steel, and coal.

Water Carriers

Of all the transportation modes, water transportation is the least expensive. Unfortunately, water transportation is also the slowest way to ship. Boats and barges are mainly used for extremely heavy, bulky materials and products (like sand, gravel, oil, and steel) for which transit times are unimportant. Manufacturers are beginning to use water carriers more often because many ships are now specially constructed to load and store large standardized containers. The St. Lawrence Seaway is a vital link in Canada's water transportation system.

Water transportation is particularly important in Canada's far north. Northern Transportation Co. Ltd. has 90 barges, nine seagoing tugboats, and 250 employees. The company uses barges to deliver commodities such as fuel oil to various isolated hamlets along the western edge of Hudson's Bay during the summer months. Each barge has a capacity of 4000 tonnes.[20]

Pipelines

Like water transportation, pipelines are slow in terms of overall delivery time. They are also completely inflexible, but they do provide a constant flow of the product and are unaffected by weather conditions. Traditionally, this delivery system has transported liquids and gases. Lack of adaptability to other products and limited routes make pipelines a relatively unimportant transportation method for most industries.

Intermodal Transportation

intermodal transportation
The combined use of different modes of transportation.

Intermodal transportation—the combined use of different modes of transportation—has come into widespread use. For example, shipping by a combination of truck and rail ("piggy-back"), water and rail ("fishy back"), or air and rail ("birdyback") has improved flexibility and reduced costs.

containerization
The use of standardized heavy-duty containers in which many items are sealed at the point of shipment and opened only at the final destination.

To make intermodal transport more efficient, **containerization** uses standardized heavy-duty containers in which many items are sealed at points of shipment and opened only at final destinations. On the trip, containers may be loaded onto ships for ocean transit, transferred onto trucks, loaded on railcars, and delivered to final destinations by other trucks. The containers are then unloaded and returned for future use. International Cargo Management Systems has developed a device that is attached to the inside of containers being shipped. The device pulls in signals from global positioning satellites to determine the container's latitude and longitude. The device then transmits this information to computers at a tracking centre. Customers can call the tracking centre to determine where their package is at any moment.[21]

Companies Specializing in Transportation

The major modes of transportation are available from one or more of four types of transporting companies: common carriers, freight forwarders, contract carriers, and private carriers. Table 17.3 shows the top 10 transportation companies in Canada.

common carriers
Transportation companies that transport goods for any firm or individual wishing to make a shipment.

The nation's **common carriers** transport merchandise for any shipper—manufacturers, wholesalers, retailers, and even individual consumers. They maintain regular schedules and charge competitive prices. The best examples of common carriers are truck lines and railroads.

In 1897, the *Crow's Nest Pass Agreement* established the rate that railways could charge for hauling grain. This agreement was essentially a freight subsidy that helped prairie farmers pay some of their transportation costs to distant ports. But in 1995, the Liberal government abolished the Crow subsidy. Freight rates increased for prairie farmers, which caused them to reduce their emphasis on growing wheat and increase their emphasis on raising livestock.[22] Since the Crow rate was eliminated, livestock production and agricultural processing have increased on the prairies. In Manitoba, for example, the value of processed food and beverages leaving the province increased by 13 percent from 1995 to 1996.[23]

freight forwarders
Common carriers that lease bulk space from other carriers and resell that space to firms making small shipments.

Not all transportation companies own their own vehicles. A **freight forwarder** is a common carrier that leases bulk space from other carriers,

Table 17.3   The Top 10 Transportation Companies in Canada, 1996

Company	Sales (in billions)
1. Air Canada	$4.80
2. Canadian National Railway Co.	4.10
3. Laidlaw Inc.	3.10
4. Canadian Airlines Corp.	3.00
5. Trimac Ltd.	0.73
6. PCL Courier Holdings Inc.	0.73
7. Fednav Ltd.	0.68
8. British Columbia Railway Co.	0.41
9. VIA Rail Canada	0.39
10. CHC Helicopter Corp.	0.33

such as railroads or airlines. It then resells parts of that space to smaller shippers. Once it has enough contracts to fill the bulk space, the freight forwarder picks up whatever merchandise is to be shipped. It then transports the goods to the bulk carrier, which makes delivery to an agreed-on destination, and handles billing and any inquiries concerning the shipment.

Some transportation companies will transport products for any firm for a contracted amount and time period. These **contract carriers** are usually self-employed operators who own the vehicle that transports the products. When they have delivered a contracted load to its destination, they generally try to locate another contract shipment (often with a different manufacturer) for the return trip.

A few manufacturers and retailers maintain their own transportation systems (usually a fleet of trucks) to carry their own products. The use of such **private carriers** is generally limited to very large manufacturers such as Kraft Foods and Canada Safeway.

contract carriers

Independent transporters who contract to serve as transporters for industrial customers only.

private carriers

Transportation systems owned by the shipper.

Distribution as a Marketing Strategy

Distribution is an increasingly important way of competing for sales. Instead of just offering advantages in product features and quality, price, and promotion, many firms have turned to distribution as a cornerstone of their business strategies. This approach means assessing and improving the entire stream of activities—wholesaling, warehousing, transportation—involved in getting products to customers. Its importance is illustrated at Compaq Computer, which registered a loss of nearly $1 billion in sales for 1994 because products were unavailable when and where customers wanted them. To correct the problem, Compaq has placed distribution at the top of its list as the competitive strategy for the future. This commitment entails reworking the company's whole supply chain of distributors and transportation.

A key tool in contemporary distribution strategy is technology. Computers, for example, allow manufacturers to be electronically connected to specific customers. Even while in production, then, every unit in the factory can be already earmarked for a specific destination. This procedure streamlines the supply chain and allows it to be more efficient. The process for filling each customer's order can be customized and unnecessary steps eliminated more easily. Unnecessary waiting is reduced, and in some cases, the need for intermediaries in the distribution network is also eliminated. Because it speeds up delivery times, customers do not go elsewhere for products. Finally, it reduces inventories in the supply chain, thereby lowering inventory costs and freeing up funds for other uses.

Another approach to streamlining is the use of **hubs**—central distribution outlets that control all or most of a firm's distribution activities. This approach, which has emerged in the manufacturing sector, sees distribution from a *systems* perspective instead of focusing on the *separate steps* in the distribution network. Three types of distribution centres have emerged from this approach: *supply-side* and *"pre-staging," supplier-coordinated*, and *distribution-side hubs*.

hub

Central distribution outlet that controls all or most of a firm's distribution activities.

Supply-Side and "Pre-Staging" Hubs

Supply-side hubs make the most sense when large shipments of supplies flow regularly to a single industrial user, such as a large manufacturer. They are used, for example, by automobile factories, where thousands of incoming supplies can arrive by train, truck, and air. The chief job of the hub is to coordinate the customer's materials needs with supply-chain transportation. If the hub is successful, the factory's inventories are virtually eliminated, storage-space requirements are reduced, and long-haul trucks, instead of lining up at the customer's unloading dock, keep moving.

Supplier-Coordinated Hubs

The reverse practice occurs when a factory's suppliers, rather than the factory itself, set up their own coordinated hub. This is the system that supplies all the components for Compaq Computer's factories in Houston, Texas. Thirty-five suppliers store parts in a warehouse 20 kilometres away and coordinate their trucking so that parts arrive just when needed at Compaq.

Distribution-Side Hubs

While supply-side hubs are located near industrial customers, *distribution-side hubs* may be located much farther away—especially if customers are geographically dispersed. National Semiconductor, one of the world's largest chip-makers, is an example. National's finished products, silicon microchips, are produced in plants throughout the world and shipped to customers such as IBM, Toshiba, Siemens, Ford, and Compaq at factory locations around the globe. National airfreights its microchips worldwide from a single distribution centre in Singapore.

Summary of Learning Objectives

1. **Identify the various *pricing objectives* that govern pricing decisions and describe the tools used in making these decisions.** A firm's pricing decisions reflect the pricing objectives set by its management. Such objectives as profit maximization and a variety of market share goals may thus be relevant to those decisions. Cost-oriented pricing (recognizing the need to cover costs) and break-even analysis (determining the price level at which profits will be generated) can then be used as tools in determining prices.

2. **Discuss *pricing strategies* and tactics for existing and new products.** Either a price-skimming (pricing very high) or a penetration-pricing strategy (pricing very low) may be effective for new products. Depending on other elements in the marketing mix, existing products may be priced at, above, or below prevailing prices for similar products. Guided by a firm's pricing strategies, managers set prices using tactics such as *price lining* (offering items in certain categories at a limited number of prices), *psychological pricing* (appealing to buyers' perceptions of relative prices), and *discounting* (reducing prices to stimulate sales).

3. **Identify the different *channels of distribution* and explain different *distribution strategies.*** In selecting a *distribution mix*, a firm may use all or any of six distribution channels. The first four are aimed at getting products to consumers, and the last two are aimed at getting products to industrial users. Channel 1 involves direct sales to consumers. Channel 2 includes a *retailer*. Channel 3 involves a retailer and a *wholesaler*, while Channel 4 includes an *agent* or *broker* who enters the system before the wholesaler and a retailer. Channel 5 involves a direct sale to an industrial user. Channel 6, which is used infrequently, entails selling to industrial users through wholesalers. Distribution strategies include *intensive*, *exclusive*, and *selective distribution*, which differ in the number of products and channel members involved and in the amount of service performed in the channel.

4. **Explain the differences between *merchant wholesalers* and *agents/brokers*.** *Wholesalers* act as distribution intermediaries. They may extend credit as well as store, repackage, and deliver products to other members of the channel. *Full-service* and *limited-service merchant wholesalers* differ in the number and types of distribution functions they offer. Unlike wholesalers, *agents* and *brokers* never take legal possession of the product. Rather, they function as sales and merchandising arms of manufacturers that do not have their own sales forces. They may also provide such services as advertising and display merchandising.

5. **Identify the different types of *retail stores*.** Retailers can be described according to two classifications: product-line retailers and bargain retailers. *Product-line retailers* include department stores, supermarkets, hypermarkets, and specialty stores. *Bargain retailers* include discount houses, off-price stores, catalogue showrooms, factory outlets, warehouse clubs, and convenience stores. These retailers differ in terms of size, services and products offered, and pricing. Some retailing also takes place without stores. *Nonstore retailing* may use direct-mail catalogues, vending machines, direct selling, telemarketing, or video marketing.

6. **Describe the major activities in the *physical distribution process*.** *Physical distribution* refers to all the activities needed to move a product from manufacturer to consumer, including warehousing and transportation of products. *Warehouses* may be *public* or *private* and may function either as long-term *storage warehouses* or as *distribution centres*. In addition to storage, insurance, and wage-related costs, the cost to warehouse goods also includes *inventory control* (maintaining adequate but not excessive supplies) and *materials handling* (transporting, arranging, and retrieving supplies).

7. **Compare the five basic forms of *transportation* and identify the types of firms that provide them.** *Trucks*, *railroads*, *planes*, *water carriers* (boats and barges), and *pipelines* are the major transportation modes used in the distribution process. They differ in cost, availability, reliability of delivery, speed, and number of points served. Air is the fastest but most expensive mode; water carriers are the slowest but least expensive. Since transport companies were deregulated, they have become more cost-efficient and competitive by developing such innovations as *intermodal transportation* and *containerization*. Transportation in any form may be supplied by *common carriers*, *freight forwarders*, *contract carriers*, or *private carriers*.

Key Terms

Study Questions and Exercises

Review Questions

1. List five objectives a firm might have in setting its prices.
2. Identify four types of discounting and give an example for each that is different from the examples in the text.
3. From the manufacturer's point of view, what are the advantages and disadvantages of using intermediaries to distribute a product? From the end buyer's view?
4. How do the six distribution channels cited in the chapter differ from one another?
5. How do manufacturer-owned, merchant, and agent wholesalers differ? How are they the same?
6. Compare and contrast the five types of bargain stores listed in the text. Give an example of each in your town or city.

Analysis Questions

7. Suppose that a book company selling to book distributors has fixed operating costs of $600 000 per year and variable costs of $3.00 per book. How many books must the firm sell to break even if the selling price is $6.00? If the company expects to sell 50 000 books next year and decides on a 40 percent markup, what will the selling price be?
8. Under what competitive conditions would you price your existing product at the prevailing market price for similar products? Above the prevailing price? Below the prevailing price?
9. Give three examples (other than those in the chapter) of products that use intensive distribution. Do the same for products that use exclusive distribution and selective distribution. For which category was it easiest to find examples? Why?
10. If you could own a firm in the business of transporting products, what type of firm would you prefer to own (truck, air, shipping, etc.)? Why?

Application Exercises

11. Interview the manager of a local manufacturing firm. Identify the firm's distribution strategy and the channels of distribution it uses. Where applicable, describe the types of wholesalers and/or retail stores the firm uses to distribute its products.
12. Choose any consumer item at a supermarket and trace the chain of physical distribution activities that brought it to the store's shelf.

Building Your Business Skills

Goal
To encourage students to analyze the special requirements of catalogue retailers.

Situation
You and three partners have decided to go into business as catalogue retailers of kitchen supplies. Included in your product line are dishes, cutlery, pots and pans, decorative china, and specialty kitchen appliances.

Method

Step 1:
Join with three other students and assume the roles of partners.

Step 2:
Choose one of two target markets for your catalogue—either high-income consumers of gourmet products or low-budget, price-conscious shoppers. Then brainstorm ways of reaching your chosen market. Specifically, analyze how you would handle the following marketing issues:

- *Catalogue size and design.* How important is the look of the catalogue to your company's success? Would you include photos and extra attractions, like specialty recipes, to increase its appeal?

- *Merchandise price levels.* Would you include top-of-the-line, moderate, or low-priced merchandise, or merchandise combinations?

- *Shipping policy.* How quickly will "normal" items be delivered? Will overnight shipping be an option?

- *Staffing of customer service lines.* How important is it for customers to receive rapid attention? What is the price of putting customers on hold?

- *Purchase of mailing lists.* When dealing with companies that sell mailing lists to catalogue retailers, what criteria would you use to pinpoint your target market?

- *Return policy.* How liberal will your returns policy be? Will the customer or retailer pay for return postage?

Step 3:
Write up your analysis in the form of a working plan for your business. Make sure that each element of the plan is designed to help you reach your target market.

Follow-Up Questions

1. Based on your analysis, identify and explain the most critical elements for reaching your target market.

2. Based on your analysis, how would each element of your plan change if your target market changed?

To compare the distribution strategies and practices of firms in different industries, especially differences in their choices of distribution channels and their physical distribution methods, log on to the following two Web sites. QVC Inc., *i*QVC Shop, at:

http://www.qvc.com

Chaparral Steel Company at:

http://www.chaparralsteel.com

After you have browsed both sites, consider the following questions:

1. Compare the channels of distribution for Chaparral Steel's products with the channels used for the merchandise offered by *i*QVC. How would you describe each of those channels? How do they differ?

2. Compare the physical distribution activities at Chaparral Steel and *i*QVC. What are their similarities and differences?

3. With respect to the geographic location of their target markets, how do the distribution strategies differ for Chaparral Steel and *i*QVC? What do you suspect are the reasons behind each firm's decision about geographic range?

4. How do these companies compare regarding the modes of transportation they use for getting products from producer to customer? Explain the reasons for each company's primary transportation mode.

5. Are intermediaries involved in the distribution mix for products sold by *i*QVC? For products sold by Chaparral Steel? If so, identify the types of intermediaries, describe the services they provide, and explain the value they add for each firm's customers.

6. Which of the two companies is likely to have the larger warehousing operation? Explain the rationale for your answer, including a description of the types of warehousing activities you would expect to see at *i*QVC and at Chaparral Steel.

CONCLUDING CASE 17-1

The New Logistics General at Sears

Retired U.S. General Norman Schwarzkopf has declared that William G. "Gus" Pagonis did a "magnificent" job for him during the Persian Gulf War. Then a three-star Army general, Pagonis managed the largest military logistics operation in history while fighting firestorms, extreme weather conditions, and cultural confusion. Operating under nearly impossible wartime demands, Pagonis was in charge of distributing 122 million meals, 5.9 billion litres of fuel, 12 000 tanks and other combat vehicles, 363 million kg of ammunition, and 29 000 tonnes of mail. As much as any single person, Pagonis made the U.S. war effort possible.

The remarkable logistics achievements of the Persian Gulf War convinced Arthur Martinez, CEO of Sears, to offer the retired general a job as Sears' logistics czar—the person in charge of moving goods at the giant retailer from one

place to another. Pagonis has now held this job for more than three years, and by all accounts, he has been as successful in retailing as he was in war. In 1993, skeptics doubted whether Pagonis' background had prepared him to handle the goods at Sears—3 billion kg of merchandise a year carried by 600 000 truck-load shipments from 160 warehouses and distribution centres to 800 stores. There are no longer any doubts. Indeed, at a critical time in Sears' history—with its customers deserting in droves and analysts dismissing it as a "dinosaur"—Pagonis cut in half the time it takes to move merchandise from suppliers to stores and cut overall logistics costs by $45 million a year. His efforts have helped turn the company around.

Once called "the stepchild of the retail industry," *logistics*—or distribution management—involves moving goods from supplier to warehouse to store to customer. It

...

also entails managing the flow of supplies to increase efficiency and cut costs, and it means improving customer service. When Pagonis took charge at Sears, he found gross inefficiencies. Moreover, no single person was in charge—a fact that already disturbed Martinez. "It was very clear to me," the CEO recalls, "that getting costs out and getting a rational network could only happen if we had one executive in charge."

Pagonis attacked the status quo with military zeal. He reduced the number of channels used by store managers to order products from twelve to four and increased the average load carried by delivery trucks leaving Sears' distribution centres from 60 percent to 90 percent. Pagonis also coordinated the diverse operational functions. "You have to worry about all the elements working together," he explains. "Even in the Gulf War, if I had for a minute started worrying [only] about food, then nobody would have any tanks for the battlefield. . . . If I only thought about ammunition, what about the clothing? Some people say no, I just want the ammunition. But what about the poor soldier? It was 140 degrees when we arrived. When we went to war, it was freezing. If we hadn't ordered more than 5 million sets of long underwear, our troops would have suffered. If I allow myself to concentrate on just one area, the stores suffer, the consumer suffers. I just don't let that happen. I always look at total systems."

Under Pagonis' leadership, distribution functions have changed in ways that are noticeable to customers. In many parts of the country, for example, consumers can now choose among morning, afternoon, and evening deliveries, and next-day delivery—even on Sunday—is possible in seven out of ten markets. The need for speed applies to everything from appliances to fashion merchandise. For instance, it now takes seven days instead of 14 to ship apparel from suppliers to stores. This increased speed is vital in a market that often gains momentum from sudden fashion trends. If merchandise is in the stores when customers look for it, sales are made.

Faster deliveries from suppliers to stores have enabled Sears to reduce inventories and thus lower inventory financing costs. With smaller inventories in each store, Sears has converted 800 000 square feet of store storage space into selling space and reduced inventory costs by $10 million.

As the success of Gus Pagonis shows, a rapid, efficient distribution system is vital to retailing success. Indeed, by cutting distribution costs, a company can gain an important competitive edge. Among domestic retailers, Sears now has one of the lowest ratios of general and administrative expenses as a percentage of domestic sales. Moreover, the $45 million in cost savings achieved by Pagonis has helped boost annual profits from continuing operations to $1.03 billion.

Distribution management has everything to do with a retailer's image, and Sears' Gus Pagonis would be the first to explain the connection. "Logistics," he argues, "is concerned about image just as much as other parts of the team. If you walk into a Sears store, and if the hanging garments are wrinkled, [the store's image suffers]. We deliver those garments on hangers. They go right off the truck, right onto the floor. If you order a product and it's not delivered to your home properly or the guys walk in tracking mud—if those drivers are not courteous and concerned about the image of Sears, [then Sears loses]."

Pagonis' concern for image and customer service makes it natural for him to treat the 800 stores in the Sears chain as customers. Thus, when stores are in need of merchandise—when they are out of air conditioners in a heat wave, for example—Pagonis restocks store inventories within a day, not within the weeks that it used to take. To get an early jump on problems, for example, he started a system of "ghostbusters"—troubleshooters who visit stores and distribution centres and ride trucks.

Pagonis' concern for the customer comes in part from the numerous moves he made during his military career. "I've moved 30 times in 29 years," he says. "So when I have a couple of scratches on an old table, that's normal. But when someone buys a new piece of furniture, they want it delivered to their home scratch-free, and that's understandable. We provide that service to them. So we work with the vendor to make sure the production line is good, that the product they're sending us is of quality, and then we have to make sure we don't damage it as we take it through the system."

Case Questions

1. What qualities made Gus Pagonis a superb candidate for the job as logistics czar at Sears?

2. Why is achieving a low ratio of general and administrative expenses as a percentage of domestic sales so important to Sears' management?

3. Why are retailers becoming increasingly dependent on rapid, efficient distribution?

4. How does distribution management affect inventory?

5. Is improving customer service and store image a "natural" function of distribution managers, or do you think that Gus Pagonis is unusual in his approach? ◆

Sears
http://www.sears.com

CONCLUDING CASE 17-2

New Ways to Buy a Car

You know the routine: You walk into a car dealership, find a car that looks interesting, and then start negotiating with a salesperson. But you feel terribly insecure because you really have no idea of what constitutes a "good deal." Even if you are able to reach an agreement about which car to purchase and what you are willing to pay, there is always that nagging feeling that you paid too much. Is there a solution to this problem?

In the mid-1980s, the Saturn division of General Motors implemented a revolutionary pricing strategy. Saturn would take the hassle and heartache out of the dealer-consumer relationship by selling vehicles for a fixed low price that would make negotiation unnecessary. Pricing experts believed that this "no-haggle" approach to auto pricing would appeal to consumers who hated to dicker and who believed that traditional dealers maximized commissions by keeping prices high. Meanwhile, salespeople working for fixed-price dealers would be paid by the sale, not by a sliding scale commission linked to profit.

Unfortunately, not all good ideas work in the marketplace, and many auto dealers now believe that the fixed-price approach has some basic flaws. For example, although thousands of consumers have embraced the fixed-price concept, many more continue to seek dealers who are willing to negotiate price.

According to a recent survey, 89 percent of customers who visit fixed-price dealers, rather than buying from them, use their quoted prices as starting points from which to negotiate with traditional dealers. This practice, of course, leaves fixed-price dealers with two types of customers—those who are too busy to shop around and want the convenience of one-stop shopping and those who know so little about car buying that they might have been willing to pay more than the averaged fixed price.

Moreover, no-haggle dealers found themselves squeezed by competitors willing to undercut close-to-the-bone fixed prices in order to make sales and reduce inventories. The most aggressive competition is in cities where consumers routinely comparison shop at several dealers. Fixed-price dealers do best in areas—mostly rural—where they face few rivals. The reality, explains Chrysler CEO Robert J. Easton, is that "one price works better when you don't have dealerships selling the same product quite so close together."

A recent survey conducted by the marketing research firm of Dohring Co. found a sharp increase in the number of consumers who want to negotiate prices. According to Dohring's report, "Automotive consumers need to feel that they get a good deal when they purchase a vehicle, and, for most, the only way [to accomplish this] is through negotiation." As a result, the number of haggle-free new car dealerships in the U.S. has plummeted in recent years. From a total of nearly 2000 in 1994, the number had dropped to fewer than 1200 in 1996.

What is the situation in Canada? The Saturn one-price idea has been tried at various places in Canada. For example, you can visit a one-price dealership in Richmond Hill, Ontario. The North York Chevrolet Geo Oldsmobile dealership began offering one-price selling after its general manager visited a one-price dealership in Michigan. When the new system was implemented, the two top salespeople at the dealership left for greener pastures. And sales staff have let some people walk out the door because they were as little as $8 apart on the price. Sales numbers have not risen since the new system was implemented. But the dealership does get a lot fewer calls from dissatisfied customers after the sale is made.

If you want to take a high-tech approach, you can purchase a no-haggle car on the Internet from Auto-By-Tel. You simply click onto Auto-By-Tel's Web site and make a purchase order. Within 48 hours, one of the 90 Canadian Auto-By-Tel dealers phones you with a no-haggle price. The system requires that consumers know exactly what they want, but most of those who use this system do know.

In the U.S., there are several Internet sites that give consumers two pieces of crucial information that they need to get a good deal: (1) the dealer's cost to buy the car from the factory, and (2) how much profit a dealer needs to make on each car. Once this information becomes more widely available in Canada, consumers will have much more power when they are buying.

Case Questions

1. What are the various objectives a business might be pursuing when it prices its products? What objective(s) are automobile dealers pursuing when they price their products?

2. What are the advantages and disadvantages of the one-price system for buying automobiles?

3. Would you prefer to buy an automobile from a one-price dealer or from a traditional dealer? Explain the reasons for your choice. ◆

Chrysler
http://www.chrysler.com

Auto-By-Tel
http://www.autobytel.com

End in Sight for Eaton's?*

"The strong family connection . . . is always a problem. You can't always necessarily make the best business decisions because so much is tied up with the family name."

—Richard Talbot, Thomas Consultants International

Canadians have treasured the traditions, parades, and guarantees of retail giant Eaton's for generations. Such intergenerational trust and treasuring may, however, be a thing of the past. Eaton's, one of the touchstones of Canadian living for almost 130 years, recently admitted that it was in dire financial straits. The company's announcement stunned many longtime customers. For some, the thought of shopping elsewhere was tantamount to "deserting family." While the company was an early industry leader, pioneering such retail practices as catalogue shopping for Canada's rural community, it appears to have not kept pace with a changing world.

Part of the near-demise is attributable to basic shifts in the retail marketplace. According to business historian and University of Toronto professor Michael Bliss, the traditional department store has become a retail dinosaur. While department stores controlled close to half of retail spending in the 1950s, their market has been "eroded at top end by specialty stores and at bottom end by discount semi-department stores," leaving mid-line department stores in a retail endgame. In the past the company refused to dicker on price, inviting customers who wished to squabble to simply go elsewhere; in the 1990s, many former customers have done exactly that.

Prospects for change, and hence survival, are undeniably complex. For a national, privately held concern such as Eaton's, attempting large-scale change is equivalent to trying to make a U-turn with the *Queen Mary*. The core challenge any move must address, however, is how to consistently deliver superior customer value. Another complicating factor is location, with many of Eaton's stores located in the formerly bustling downtown hubs of Canada's cities. With downtown retail environments already battered by the flight of countless retail dollars to suburban discounters such as Wal-Mart, Zellers, and Kmart, any turnaround strategy faces a severe set of operating constraints.

In a recent interview, Eaton's family representative George Eaton admitted that some of the company's retail strategies, such as Every Day Value Pricing, have simply not worked. In an effort to keep the company's customers, landlords, and suppliers informed of its plans during this tumultuous time, Eaton stated the family business plans to focus on new formats that emphasize fashion and service. The company also plans to put major dollars into renovating its facilities. The new cost-conscious formats of such players as Wal-Mart affected the traditional U.S. department store in the late 1980s, Eaton also observed. It is only now, 10 years later, that the impact is being felt north of the border. On a hopeful note, Eaton concluded the interview by observing that many U.S. department stores, including J.C. Penney and Sears, are now re-emerging with strong prospects for a new retail era.

Study Questions

1. What is marketing? How well did the managers at Eaton's appear to market their company?

2. What is the external environment? How well did Eaton's managers appear to understand and respond to the external environment?

3. What are the different types of consumer products? Which of these best describes the products sold by Eaton's?

---

* Source: This case was written by Professor Reg Litz of the University of Manitoba.
Video Resource: "Eaton's Tape," *The National Magazine* (February 27, 1997).

"There was an entertainment void in this market!"
—hockey promoter Tim Berryman

Lafayette, Louisiana, is a long way from the National Hockey League. Located in the "bayou" of the deep south, this Louisiana city is about as climactically different as could be imagined from the frozen Canadian rivers where hockey originated. However, these long-standing weather barriers show signs of being all but eliminated with the recent expansion of professional hockey into the southern United States.

Enter the Louisiana Ice Gators. The team is but one of several new minor league teams that have formed in the wake of the NHL's southward expansion. The Louisiana franchise plays in the East Coast Hockey League that includes teams from Florida to Pennsylvania. The Ice Gators' roster is made up of players from Ontario and Quebec who want a shot at professional hockey. Operating out of Lafayette's Cajundome, the team is managed by the Berryman brothers. Both brothers are no strangers to professional sports; at one time, Tim played linebacker for the Toronto Argonauts, while Dave once ranked second in Canadian tennis.

The franchise, admittedly a risky venture, became a reality when a number of factors came together at just the right time. First was Lafayette's underused Cajundome. Sitting empty too much of the time, the facility's management was highly motivated to find a tenant. Next came the brothers Berryman. They believed that hockey could compete with basketball even though the locals didn't know a puck from a power play. "There was an entertainment void in this market," Tim observes. The final ingredient was money; and it came in two parts. First was the $1.5 million franchise fee arranged through the help of several venture capitalists—a lawyer and a couple of oil tycoons from California. With the outside financiers contributing 75 percent, Tim and Dave were still able to maintain a 25 percent interest in the team. Second was sponsorship money—$1 million from Pepsi.

One of the Berrymans' priorities is to keep the sponsors happy, which means filling the seats. How? Get the kids in the arena and the parents will follow. Going after families means pricing the evening right. At about $25 for a night of entertainment, the package seems to work. Part of the formula means featuring more than just hockey—in this case, product giveaways and lots of spontaneous off-ice happenings.

The Berrymans' formula appears to be working; the Ice Gators are the league's biggest draw, outdrawing even some NHL teams. The Cajundome wins, too, with concession sales of $800 000 as part of their cut, a figure they hope to double very soon. The future could bring another increase in cash flow—but this one flowing out. The team's players, earning an average salary of only $380 per week, are interested in getting a bigger piece of the action, which could mean a possible unionization drive.

Study Questions

1. What are the different kinds of consumer products and services? How would you categorize the product or service offered by the Louisiana Ice Gators?

2. What is a promotional mix? How does the concept apply to marketing the Ice Gators?

3. What is the difference between a cash, seasonal, trade, and quantity discount? Which, if any, of these discounts is the Ice Gators' management using?

* Source: This case was written by Professor Reg Litz of the University of Manitoba.
Video Resource: "Louisiana Hockey," *Venture* #630 (February 16, 1997).

Getting the Product Out at Lands' End

LEARNING OBJECTIVES

The purpose of this video exercise is to help students:

1. See how a specific company conducts its physical distribution operations

2. Understand the interaction of human and technological resources in the design and control of a company's distribution process

3. Appreciate the roles played by customer service and quality assurance in the design and control of a company's distribution process

BACKGROUND INFORMATION

The flow chart accompanying this case outlines the operations that take place at Lands' End's distribution centre. This process enables Lands' End to get products to customers in only two business days (or three if an order needs embroidering or monogramming). The key, according to Phil Schaecher, Senior Vice-President for Operations, is the fact that "LE's distribution centre is staffed by the best people available working together with some of the most sophisticated technology in the industry."

In each major step—receiving, active bins, picking, packing, and shipping—every item is tracked by a bar code pre-

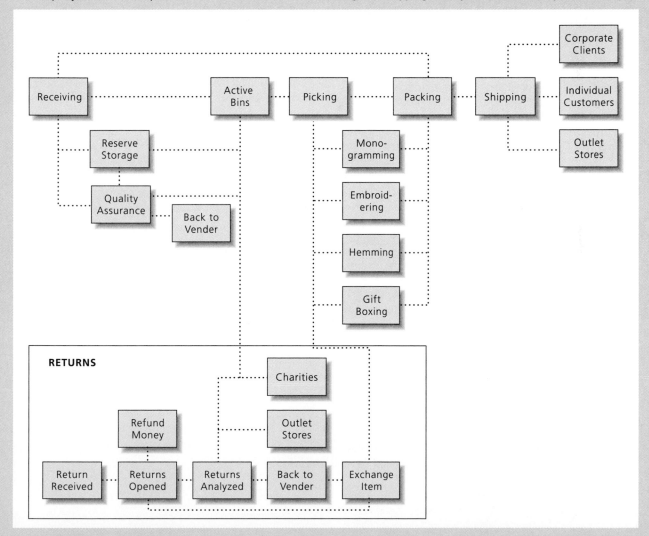

pared the night before it is received at the centre. This bar code enables a computer system to track the item throughout the building. The computer, for example, uses data on current demand to direct merchandise to active bins, quality assurance, shipping, or (as in most cases) reserve storage. The computer also prints out the "pick tickets" used by order-fillers to take items from active bins, which store items that will be needed in the immediate future. Because the bar code on the pick ticket also serves as the packing ticket, all items destined for the same packing bin bear the same three-digit code and are thus delivered by the computer to the same packing bin.

THE VIDEO

Video Source. "Lands' End: Getting the Product Out," *Prentice Hall Presents: On Location at Lands' End*. The video describes in step-by-step detail the computerized operations that enable Lands' End to distribute products to customers within two days of receiving an order. The flow chart accompanying the case is followed carefully as each step in the company's distribution process is illustrated with scenes of the Dodgeville distribution centre at work. Senior Vice-President for Operations Phil Schaecher and veteran packer Bill Gantenbein explain how various steps in the system work.

Discussion Questions

1. Why is Lands' End's physical distribution process particularly appropriate for a mail order retailer?

2. In what areas do you see activities in the video that can be classified as operations management? As operations control?

3. Which activities depicted in the video pertain to the control of warehousing costs? To inventory control? To materials handling?

4. As the video shows, Lands' End attaches considerable importance to *order processing* (the filling of orders as they are received) and *order-cycle times* (the total time elapsed between the customer's placement and receipt of an order). In what respects does the Lands' End approach to these processes reflect its mission and competitive strategy?

5. In what ways is *total quality management* integrated into Lands' End's distribution operations?

Follow-Up Assignment

At the end of the video, the narrator asks, *"With so much technology in place, why does Lands' End place such a high value on employees who work in the warehouse?"* One way to address this question might be to find out exactly why other companies value employees as part of high-tech operations. Contact the Office of the American Workplace (OAW) at **http://www.fed.org/uscompanies/labor**

Using the directories labelled "A-M" and "N-Z," go to the entries on one or more of the following companies:

- ■ Davis Vision Inc.
- ■ Motorola Inc.
- ■ Rhino Foods
- ■ White Storage and Retrieval Systems

By examining each company's description of its activities and goals under such headings as "Employee Participation," "Organizational Structure," "Product/Service Quality," and "Strategic Integration of Business," you should be in a position to draw up an informed answer to the question posed above.

For Further Exploration

Contact Land's End at **http://www.landsend.com**

At the Web page, scroll down to the icon labelled "Site Map." From here, you can access the company's description of the various "Services," including "Sizing," "Hemming Info," "Monogramming," "Gift Boxing," and "Care Info," that it offers between the "Picking" and "Packing" operations outlined in the flow chart above. In particular, the feature labelled "Let's Talk" might shed some light on the importance that Lands' End attaches to customer service operations as a component of its distribution process.

EXPERIENTIAL EXERCISE:
Setting Up a Promotional Plan

OBJECTIVE

To give students experience in using promotional strategies to overcome drawbacks in sales of new products and to make the most of the new products' assets.

TIME REQUIRED

45 minutes
- Step 1: Individual activity (15 minutes)
- Step 2: Small-group activity (15 minutes)
- Step 3: Class discussion (15 minutes)

PROCEDURE

Step 1: Read the following case regarding Supershop.

The Supershop Company owns a chain of successful supermarkets in eastern Canada. Managers at Supershop headquarters are currently contemplating a startling proposal from the marketing department: drive-through service.

As proposed, this system would require a sophisticated new computer system. Customers with personal computers at home or at work would be able to use them to tap directly into Supershop's system. Others would simply phone in their orders to store employees who would enter the specified items into the store's computer. The computer would generate a list—and a receipt. Other store employees would take the lists, pull the items from the shelves, and bag them. Customers would then pull into a special area at one end of the store and pay their bill at a drive-through window while their groceries were being loaded into the car.

Proponents of the new plan argue that it has several virtues:

a. The service would meet the needs of the two-career couples with families, who are the mainstay of Supershop's business. These individuals are typically attracted to services that save them time. At the same time, it should attract individuals more likely to shop at convenience stores and fast food restaurants.

b. The service would distinguish Supershop's offerings from those of its competition and give it a promotional advantage.

c. A fee of 2 percent of the total order would not deter most of Supershop's customers but would cover ongoing costs of the new system.

d. Customers could put in their orders hours ahead of time (with a one-hour minimum). Employees could pull nonperishable items from the shelves during slack times, increasing labour productivity. Placing items directly into bags as they were gathered would further improve productivity and efficiency.

e. If the service does well, eventually it could be run from a warehouse-type structure, mechanization of which would increase productivity and efficiency still further.

Opponents of the new plan argue that it has several drawbacks:

a. Glitches in the computer system and human error in picking items by store employees could result in customer dissatisfaction with Supershop in general. In particular, employee selection of fresh fruits and vegetables poses a high risk of customer dissatisfaction.

b. Start-up costs for the computer system and customer pick-up would be high—too high to be covered by a 2 percent fee.

c. The stores would lose "impulse sales," since customers would not be trapped in line near, or even just pass by, displays of high-profit items.

d. The plan could create trouble with the union workers employed by Supershop. Union representatives would probably fight the new job classifications that would be necessary and would probably strike over any reduction in employees due to greater productivity.

e. Producers of new goods, beverages, etc., might object that consumers are not exposed to and thus will not buy these items. They might in turn refuse to sell to Supershop at the highest discount rate, which would drive up costs and drive away customers.

HOW CAN SUPERSHOP USE PROMOTION TO MAKE THE MOST OF THIS PLAN'S VIRTUES AND MINIMIZE ITS DRAWBACKS?

Step 2: The instructor will divide the class into small groups and will assign each group one strong point and one weak point of the plan. Each group will then develop an advertising slogan to stress the strength and downplay the weakness. Each group should also complete the following grid, rating possible promotional tools from 1 (very effective at reaching/persuading target market) to 5 (very ineffective at reaching/persuading target market) and divide a promotions budget of $1 million among these tools.

Promotional Tool	1	2	3	4	5	$ Allocated
Advertising:						
Newspapers						
Television						
Direct mail						
Radio						
Magazines						
Billboards						
Personal Selling						
Sales Promotions:						
Coupons						
Premiums						
Contests						
Publicity/Public Relations						

Step 3: One member of each small group will present the group's conclusions to the class.

QUESTIONS FOR DISCUSSION

1. Would you or members of your family consider using a drive-through service like the one proposed by Supershop's marketing staff? Why or why not?

2. What do you consider to be the greatest virtue of the proposed service? What do you consider to be the greatest drawback? Overall, do you think Supershop would be wise to go ahead with this plan?

THE CHOICE IS YOURS

"The difficulty in life is the choice ... The wrong way always seems the more reasonable."

—George Moore, "The Bending of the Bough"

You did it! You got the job offer! Despite the tight job market, your impressive combination of sound coursework (and good grades), practical experience, and successful interviewing has garnered you not one but several job offers. You are now faced with the problem many job seekers would like to have—how to select one of these offers.

There are five major considerations to take into account when making your choice:

- Job responsibilities.
- Person-job fit.
- Quality of training and development.
- Career opportunities.
- Compensation.

Of course, all people will have additional factors to consider, and each individual will weigh each factor differently.

JOB RESPONSIBILITIES

The first question that will cross your mind as you evaluate various job offers will probably be: Which job will I enjoy most? As a general rule, you should avoid signing on with any company that thrusts too much responsibility on new managers too quickly. In these types of organizations, lack of both experience and the necessary job-specific skills will probably doom you to failure. Organizations that overextend newcomers may do so because they want to "stretch" them, because they are understaffed, or because they don't truly understand the strengths and weaknesses of new managers. You should also stay away from firms that tend to underutilize new managers, assigning them menial and/or routine assignments. Such practices may reflect a lack of trust in the capabilities of new managers or a lack of meaningful work in the organization.

What you should be looking for, clearly, is a balanced approach—one that will give you a chance to gain experience, but one that will also utilize your existing skills while giving you the opportunity to master new ones. The ideal assignment in this regard is one that has well-defined boundaries in a setting in which you can get advice and assistance from others in the organization.

PERSON-JOB FIT

Another factor to take into account when selecting among job offers is the fit between your own interests, aspirations, and preferences and the requirements and opportunities of the jobs you are considering. For example, if you have always wanted a career in retailing, then you will probably have no trouble choosing The Bay over Dofasco. But if you prefer a career in manufacturing, you are likely to find Dofasco a better fit.

The job itself is only one part of the person-job fit story, however. Other considerations include:

- *Location.* Will one job require you to live in a big city and another in a small town? If cities make you claustrophobic, you'd probably be better off taking the job in Regina instead of the one in Toronto. But if your favourite forms of entertainment are art museums, opera, major-league baseball, and ethnic restaurants, you should probably head for Toronto instead. Many single people also prefer urban locations because of the greater opportunities they provide for meeting people and developing romantic relationships.

- *Ambiance.* Did you feel more comfortable with the people and/or physical environment at one firm than you did at the other? Remember, you'll be spending between a quarter and a third of your life at work. Those hours can be miserable or pleasant, depending on how well you fit in.

- *Travel required by the job.* Some people look forward to the chance to travel, while others prefer to stay close to home. Do the jobs offered differ in their travel requirements? If the difference is a substantial one, give this factor serious consideration. You won't be happy for long if you're constantly on the go and hate being on the road . . . or if you're tied to a desk but itching to get out of the office.

- *Family consideration.* Children, spouses, other relations, and close friendships may also influence your ultimate choice. It is essential that you take into account the quality of the local schools for your children and the local job market for your spouse or "significant other." It's hard to be happy at work—and to do your best work—if you're worrying about things at home. If you have elderly parents, you may find it less stressful to live where you can be on hand in case of emergency. On the other hand, you may view a cross-country move as an opportunity to explore new aspects of your life and personality far away from the place where everyone knows everything about you.

QUALITY OF TRAINING AND DEVELOPMENT

Especially when choosing a first job, but also throughout your career, you should seriously weigh the value of the training and development that a firm offers its new employees. Although anecdotes from established managers about "How I survived in a 'sink or swim' situation" may be amusing, trial by fire is frequently frustrating, often counterproductive, and always stressful.

Your education is providing you with the fundamental information and skills you will need to succeed in the business world. But because each organization is unique, and because each values and expects different things from its employees, most large firms provide a systematic program to help them become more effective in performing their jobs.

Large firms like Proctor & Gamble, General Foods, IBM, and General Mills are all known to have outstanding training programs. Indeed, some firms actively seek to hire people who have successfully completed the training programs of these and similar firms. Although smaller firms generally do not offer such structured programs, at these organizations you may benefit greatly from the opportunity to work directly with upper-level management and from exposure to many areas of the firm's operations.

Finally, be sure to weigh the company's attitudes towards further education. Some companies pay all or part of tuition costs for those who take technical and/or advanced college courses and underwrite the costs of taking professional certification examinations. Some firms will even give you a paid "sabbatical" after a number of years on the job so that you can complete an advanced degree. Remember that in this fast-changing world, to stand still is to be left behind. To stay ahead, you must constantly sharpen your skills.

CAREER OPPORTUNITIES

Clearly, career opportunities and prospects with each of your potential employers will play a major role in your decision. Where will you go in a firm that has just laid off hundreds of managers? Will you be subject to the same degree of job insecurity? If another firm is hiring hundreds of new people each year but provides advancement opportunities for only a few, what are your chances of succeeding?

Most large organizations have clearly formulated career paths to help people understand where they can expect to be at different points in their career. Be wary if a large firm has not given consideration to these issues. But also be wary if its career paths are highly programmed and regimented. Ideally, your new employer will have several clear, well-developed career paths but still offer sufficient flexibility for you to pursue new opportunities.

COMPENSATION

Finally, give careful consideration to the compensation package that you are offered. You can get salary data for comparative purposes from your campus placement office, your friends, and similar sources. Most firms know what others are paying, so there probably will not be wide variation in the salary offers you receive. If you have excellent grades, a strong resume, and solid references, you may be able to start at a somewhat higher salary than someone with average grades, a mediocre resume, and weak references.

What if you like everything about the job—the fit, the location, the responsibilities, the prospects—except the pay? You may try to negotiate a higher salary, but experts agree that attempting to negotiate too much on salary can backfire. Most firms have a predefined salary structure for new employees and may react negatively to a request for a higher salary. If the company you really want to work for is offering less than the other firms, you might subtly point out the differences and ask if there is any *flexibility* in the offer. But always be both honest and discreet. If you tell your preferred employer that another firm has offered you $10 000 more than it really has, you might be advised to take the other job!

Finally, don't get too hung up on the starting salary itself. You also need to factor in such items as the value of benefits (such as insurance, retirement plans, etc.), perks (car, office, etc.), the cost of living where you will be working, and prospects for salary increases. Look at the *whole* package—and the *whole* job—before you say "Yes."

Part Six

Part Six

MANAGING
INFORMATION

The Opening Cases for the chapters in this section deal with an increasingly important aspect of business operations—managing the large amount of information that must be available for managers so they can make sound decisions. This information ranges from satellite-based ship location information to information about a company's operating costs. These and many other information-based situations are the focus of the chapters in this section.

Part Six, Managing Information, provides an overview of the important activity of information management, including the types of information that are needed, how that information is gathered, and how it is used by managers in business firms.

- We begin in **Chapter 18, Managing Information Systems and Communication Technology**, by describing how different types of computers have evolved to help managers carry out the information-management function. We explain the different kinds of computer systems, computer application programs for business, and how information and communications technology work together.

- In **Chapter 19, Understanding Accounting Issues**, we examine the role of accountants in gathering, assembling, and presenting financial information about a firm. We also look at the tools accountants use and the statements they prepare to report a firm's financial standing.

Managing Information Systems and Communication Technology

Information Processing Under Pressure

The ore carrier *Nanticoke*, owned by Canadian Steamship Lines (CSL), was working its way through the dangerous American Narrows on the St. Lawrence River when it suddenly encountered a fog bank. The fog was so dense that Captain Joe Sahni couldn't see the bow of the boat just 200 metres ahead. How could he stay in the narrow, safe channel and avoid running aground?

The answer was the ship's new Canadian designed and developed Electronic Chart Precise Integrated Navigation System (ECPINS). The system displayed the *Nanticoke*'s position on a computer screen showing the Thousand Islands waterway. The ship's position was updated twice a second using the U.S. military's global positioning satellite. This allowed Captain Sahni to determine where he was within five metres. The system provided so much detail that Sahni could actually see the bow of the ship change position on the screen as the ship drifted sideways. The ship successfully navigated the fog bank.

The next day, Captain Sahni phoned the director of navigation for the company and told him the investment in ECPINS had just paid for itself. The *Nanticoke* was the first ship outfitted with the system, which is produced by Offshore Systems International Ltd. of Vancouver. Now, Canadian Steamship Lines has installed ECPINS on 11 more of its ships that sail the Great Lakes and the eastern seaboard. CSL also plans to outfit its deep-ocean vessels with the system. Each unit costs about $100 000.

Massive changes are taking place in the shipping business. Raymond Johnston, who became CEO of CSL in 1991, moved into high-tech information processing initially to cut costs and to keep customers happy. But the changes that were eventually implemented weren't lim-

ited to ship navigation. Johnston also made the management decision that control over spending should be in the hands of the ships' masters rather than the financial and accounting people in Montreal.

Under the old system, a ship would order more supplies than it needed because orders were regularly cut by head office and delivery was unreliable. The solution to this problem lay in computers, not just for guiding ships through fog, but for a whole list of important functions. Now, ships order electronically directly from their suppliers, payroll is completed on board, and maintenance plans are computerized.

These major changes have had to be carefully introduced. Many of the people working on the ships did not have much experience with computers, and some of them were quite apprehensive about this new way to process information. The changes have also required CSL to invest in computer hardware and employee training. So far, the company has spent about $3 million on hardware and about $1.5 million on training and software.

But the new system is paying off. In tandem with traditional radar, ECPINS should help avoid collisions and running aground, two common problems ships face. In the first two years using ECPINS, CSL has had no significant groundings or collisions. This has saved about $2 million annually. Additional savings are evident because ships that cost $35 000 per day to operate don't have to wait at anchor for fog to clear. The time lost to breakdowns and accidents used to be about 2 percent of total fleet operating time; now it is less than one half of 1 percent. Computers and the ECPINS system are turning sea dogs into information workers. ◆

In today's complex business environment, the need to manage information efficiently and quickly is crucial. Information can take many forms: information about customers' locations and order patterns, information about supplies and finished goods on hand, information about workers' pay and productivity, information about products in development, and information about competitors and customers.[1]

By focusing on the learning objectives of this chapter, you will better understand why the list is so long—and getting longer all the time. You will also appreciate the role of the computer at the forefront of contemporary information management. After reading this chapter, you should be able to:

1. Show why businesses must manage information and show how computers have revolutionized *information management*.

2. Identify and briefly describe the main elements in a computer system.

3. Identify the role played in computer systems by *databases* and describe four important types of *business-application programs*.

4. Classify *computer systems* by size and structure.

5. List some trends in the application of computer technology to business-information management.

Information Management: An Overview

People in business today are bombarded with facts and figures. Modern communications enable businesses to hear from plants, branches, or sales offices at remote locations daily—or even more often. Despite predictions of paperless offices, managers are receiving more and more computer-generated reports and memos. One president of an electronics firm says he receives 97 reports a month![2] How can a manager sift through all the reports, memos, magazines, and phone calls to find the information needed to make critical decisions? How can businesses get useful information to the right person at the right time?

Most businesses regard their information as a resource and an asset that they plan, develop, and protect. It is not surprising that companies have **information managers**, just as they have production, marketing, and finance managers. As you will see in this chapter, information management is one of the operations that determines how well a business performs.

information manager
The manager responsible for the activities needed to generate, analyze, and disseminate information that a company needs to make good decisions.

Data versus Information

Although businesspeople often complain that they receive too much information, they usually mean that they get too much data. **Data** are raw facts and figures. **Information** is based on data, but it is a meaningful, useful interpretation of that data (see Figure 18.1).

Consider the following data: 50 million tubes of toothpaste were sold last year; the birth rate is rising; 35 million tubes of toothpaste were sold the year before last; advertising for toothpaste increased 57 percent; a major dentists' group recently came out in favour of brushing three times a day. If all these data can be put together in a meaningful way, they may produce *information* about what sells toothpaste and whether manufacturers should build new plants. The challenge for businesses is to turn a flood of data into information and to manage that information to their best advantage.

data
Raw facts and figures.

information
A meaningful, useful interpretation of data.

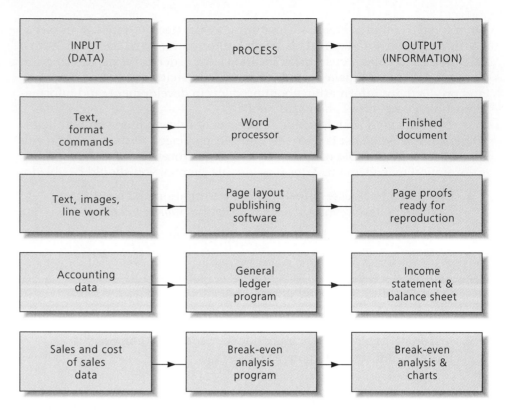

Figure 18.1
From data to information and knowledge.

Management Information Systems

management information system (MIS)

An organized method of transforming data into information that can be used for decision making.

One response to this challenge has been the growth of **management information systems (MIS)** designed to transform data into information that can be used for decision making. Those charged with the company's MIS services must determine what information will be needed, then gather the data and provide ways to convert them into the desired information. They must also *control* the flow of information so that only those who need or are entitled to certain information receive it. Information supplied to employees and managers varies, depending on the functional area in which they work (such as accounting or marketing) and on their level in management.

Levels of Management

First-line managers need information for the day-to-day operations of the business. Middle managers need summaries and analyses to help them set intermediate- and long-range goals and to plan strategies for reaching these goals. Top management needs even more sophisticated analyses to meet its responsibilities for long-range and corporate planning.

Consider the needs of various managers of a flooring manufacturer. Sales managers (first-line managers) supervise salespeople, assign territories to the sales force, and handle customer-service and delivery problems. To do their job well, they need current and accurate information on the sales and delivery of flooring products to customers in their branches. Regional managers (middle managers) set sales quotas for each sales manager, prepare budgets, and plan staffing needs for the next year. They need total monthly sales by product and by branch, as opposed to an itemized sales report. Finally, top management will need sales data summarized by product, customer type, and geographic region, and analyzed in comparison to previous years' and competitors' sales. Environmental (external) information such as consumer behaviour patterns, the competition's record, and related economic forecasts are as important as internal operations information.

Figure 18.2 illustrates the need for information at the different levels of management. As you can see, information is increasingly condensed and summarized as it moves up through the management hierarchy.

Top management may turn to outside companies to manage the firm's information systems. This is called *outsourcing*. Andersen Consulting provides a service that allows clients to modify, enhance, and maintain their existing MIS. Kodak Canada has such an arrangement with IBM. Businesses outsource because they lack the technical expertise to deal with rapid changes in computer technology.

Figure 18.2
Different information needs at various managerial levels.

Management information systems are becoming increasingly important as managers try to cope with the flood of data they are confronted with.

The Computer Revolution

Today, more than ever before, information management requires managing computers as an information tool. Changes in computer technology have revolutionized the way businesses manage information. As little as 15 years ago, automated banking machines were virtually unheard of. Now national banking networks like Circuit, Interac, and Cirrus mean that a customer of a Toronto bank can run out of cash in Caesar's Palace in Las Vegas and withdraw money from a teller machine in the hotel lobby.

Computers also offer businesses a wide range of capabilities. Airlines use reservation systems not only to book flight reservations but also to plan marketing programs for frequent travellers and airplane maintenance schedules. On a smaller scale, companies like the Artists' Frame Service, a custom picture framer, may use a computer to keep track of customers' addresses and also to decide when to order more framing materials.

The Outaouais Regional Community Transit Commission has equipped buses in Hull, Gatineau, and Aylmer with a special microprocessor that transmits information on the location of all 150 buses every 20 seconds. It also monitors important operational characteristics such as brakes, air and oil pressure, and engine temperature. The driver of a bus with a potential problem can be notified before a breakdown occurs.[3]

Diamond Taxi of Toronto has equipped its cabs with computers. The computer lets each driver know when a fare is waiting, and it displays the name and address of the fare on a small screen. The company is now responding about 20 percent faster to calls than it did before.[4]

The areas in which computers can help improve operations are almost endless. The box "The Paper Chase" describes how the computer helps manage information at the Canadian Patent Office.

Why are computers having such an impact on business? Although it is really nothing more than a machine, the computer boasts four features that make it especially useful:

- *Speed of Processing*. The computer is fast—very fast. Calculations requiring several lifetimes if done by hand can be performed in less than one second by today's most powerful computers.

- *Accuracy of Processing*. Modern computers have built-in error-checking ability that allows them to perform billions of literally error-free calculations.

- *Ability to Store Programs*. One of the most important breakthroughs of the computer revolution is the *stored-program concept*: Computers store and handle not only the data that need processing, but also the instructions (program) needed to process the data.

- *Ability to Make Comparisons*. Although computers cannot yet "think," they can make comparisons. More important, based on the results of those comparisons, they can take different courses of action—that is, they can execute a huge variety of programmed instructions.

Remember, however, that, for all its virtues, the computer is far from perfect. Unfortunately, the computer can and will process incorrect data just as quickly and accurately as it can process correct data. The accuracy of what you receive from the computer depends on the accuracy of what you put in. People in the computer field have coined a term for this phenomenon—*GIGO: Garbage In, Garbage Out*. In other words, if the computer is given the wrong data to process, it is likely to give you back the wrong answer. An additional problem with computers is described in the box "Can You Believe It?"

The Canadian Business Scene

The Paper Chase

The Canadian Patent Office receives a steady flow of patent applications for everything from cattle fences to computer anti-piracy devices. These applications are on top of the 1.3 million patents it has already granted since 1920. Paper files now occupy 12 kilometres of shelf space in various buildings around the Ottawa area.

How does the patent office know if the application it just received duplicates some idea that is already patented? Someone at the patent office has to do a lot of searching through files to see if something similar is already patented. Since this is a very time-consuming activity, the patent office spent $76 million putting all of its files, abstracts, diagrams, and chemical formulas on the computer.

Under the old system, when a patent application was received, an examiner filled out a form requesting files of previous designs in a certain area. The examiner then had to wait while a clerk found the relevant files. With the new computerized system, the examiner uses the computer to rapidly find the needed information. For example, when an examiner like Isaac Ho receives an application file labelled CO7K, he knows (based on an international coding system) that the application deals with a chemical formula. He then uses the computer to determine how many patents have been filed in that chemical field (the answer is 2289). He then uses different search terms to narrow the field down to just a handful of applications. Next he examines these few files to determine if the most recent application is breaking new ground. The process is complete when he decides whether or not a patent should be issued.

Inventors of ideas that are granted patents must supply a write-up of how their invention was created, and this information is made available to the public. Under the old system, interested parties had to come to the patent office to read the information, but with computerization, the information will be widely available. This may stimulate further creativity and more valuable patents. It will also help inventors avoid re-inventing the wheel.

Elements of a Computer System

The computer is a powerful electronic machine. But it is only part of the **computer system**. Every computer system has five parts: (1) hardware (2) software (3) people (4) control and (5) data. All five components must be present and properly coordinated for a computer system to function properly.

Hardware

Figure 18.3 shows the various systems and components that make up the **hardware** of a computer system. The functioning of a computer's hardware is not as complicated as it might look. To get a bird's-eye view of how it works, suppose you are a very simple piece of data—the number "3."

Inputting

To get into the computer, you must be entered by an **input device**. A punch card, magnetic tape, and a "mouse" are all input devices (see Figure 18.4), but let's assume that you are entered by a friend using the most common input device, a keyboard. When your friend presses the number "3" on the keyboard, an electronic signal is sent to the computer's **central processing unit (CPU)**, where the actual processing of data takes place.

Bits and Bytes

Actually, the CPU does not receive a signal that *is* "3." Rather, it receives a special code that *stands for* "3." This code consists of eight binary digits—**bits**—

computer system
An electronic method of turning data into information; its five parts are hardware, software, people, control, and data.

hardware
The physical components of a computer system.

input device
Hardware that gets data into the computer in a form the computer can understand.

central processing unit (CPU)
Hardware in which the actual transforming of data into information takes place; contains the primary storage unit, the control unit, and the arithmetic logic unit.

bit
A way of representing data in a computer as one of two digits (0 or 1); abbreviation for binary digit.

The Canadian Business Scene

Can You Believe It?

An interesting and, to some, unbelievable problem has arisen in computer systems. It seems that the arrival of the year 2000 will cause a lot of companies serious problems. Most computers use only the last two digits in a year to keep track of dates (e.g., "98" for 1998). They do this because in the bygone days of punched-card computer programs, which had only 80 columns for data, using only the last two digits saved space. When more modern software was developed, the issue was never revisited, perhaps because nobody thought that programs written back then would still be in use today. But they are, and when the year 1999 ends and the year 2000 begins, computers will become very confused.

Some computers will assume that "00" means 1900, while others will pick a year at random. Still others will not know what to do and will do nothing. Organizations that do calculations in which dates are critical will be most affected. For example, banks (interest rates), government agencies (employment insurance), insurance companies (insurance policies), and utilities (monthly bills) will all have this problem. Paul Raymond of CGI Information Systems in Montreal says that a person could conceivably get a telephone bill for 100 years when the century turns.

To appreciate the magnitude of this problem, consider these facts: large organizations have an average of 8000 computer programs, and each program averages 1500 lines of code. Assuming a cost of $1 per line to revise codes, it will cost a large organization about $12 million to solve this problem. At Allstate Insurance, for example, there are 100 full-time programmers working on the problem. The company will eventually spend $40 million to make its computers ready for the year 2000. A company that started working on the problem in 1996 would have had to allocate 27 full-time people to fix all of its codes before the year 2000. The Gartner Group, a technology research firm, estimates that worldwide expenditures could total $600 billion.

Insurance companies encountered the problem first. In 1993, they discovered that they could not compute the maturity date of seven-year policies. They resolved the problem by entering seven-year policies as six-year policies and doing the remaining year's calculations on paper. In 1994, they entered seven-year policies as five-year policies and did paper calculations for the last two years. But this system is becoming unworkable as the year 2000 approaches. Banks discovered the problem in 1994 when they realized that it was the last year for which they could calculate five-year mortgage rates.

The problem is significant enough that some organizations are already working on resolving it. Laurentian Bank spent six months fixing their mortgage system, just one of many systems the bank has. The trick is to develop software that recognizes that the year 2000 immediately follows 1999. To the average person, this may sound easy, but it is not.

Perhaps the biggest problem at the moment is getting management to recognize that a problem exists. Banks and insurance companies understand the date problem because they are already experiencing it, but many other firms are not yet aware of the difficulties they will face. These companies may discover the problem in 1999 and find that they simply do not have enough time to fix it. Various studies have shown that large software development projects are almost always problematic. One quarter of such projects are cancelled before they are finished, and three-quarters do not work as planned. If these findings hold true, businesses that wake up to the problem in 1999 may find that their very existence is threatened.

This problem is not limited just to business firms. A 1997 report by the Auditor-General warned that crucial government public services like search and rescue operations, employment insurance payments, and commercial cargo clearance could be severely disrupted unless the federal government takes immediate and aggressive action to solve the problem.

A crisis for one organization may be an opportunity for another. Those who will capitalize on this opportunity are technology consultants and computer programmers. Ottawa-based Progestic International Inc. has developed a system for fixing the year 2000 problem without having to tamper with the software programs in a computer system. It was chosen by the province of Ontario as one of the firms that will help solve its year 2000 problems.

Bob Bemer, the man who created the "escape sequence" (the "Esc" button on your computer keyboard) is now working on a way to solve the year 2000 problem. Basically, his approach is to attack the problem at the fundamental level where computers operate in ones and zeros (called machine code). His method is too complex to describe here, but expert programmers that have looked at his patented material agree that it will work for many companies. However, they think it is very risky because it requires tampering with source code and stored data, and that simply isn't done. But as time runs out, it may be the only alternative available to businesses who have waited until the last minute.

Progestic International
http://www.progestic.com/index.htm

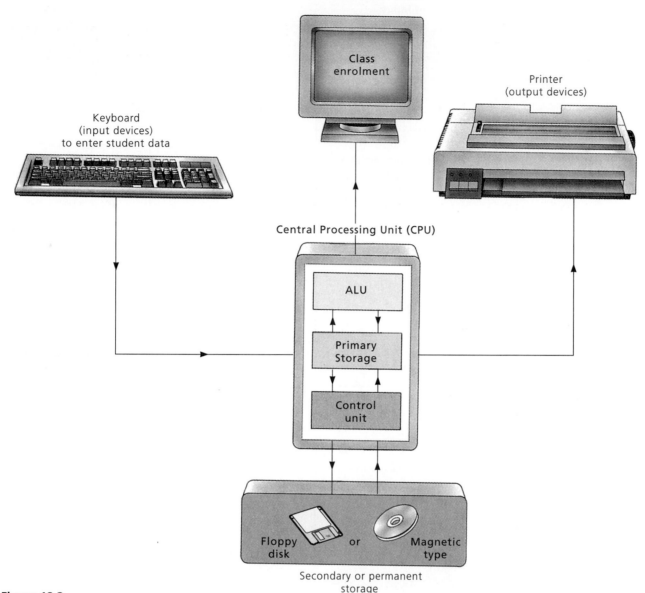

Figure 18.3
Components of a computer system.

which together form a **byte**. A bit is either the digit *0* or the digit *1*. To un-derstand how bits and bytes work, remember that the earliest computers had mechanical switches, much like the on/off light switches in your home. Although modern computers have no mechanical switches, the principle re-mains the same: The electronic signals tell the computer to set a particular switch in one of two positions (*binary* means *two*)—"on" or "off." In a com-puter, these two positions represent the flow—or lack of flow—of electricity.

Obviously, however, we need to signal many different letters, digits, and other symbols. A single "switch" (bit), therefore, is not enough. Taken to-gether, a series of eight bits—a single byte—can represent any character on the computer keyboard. As the number "3," for example, you would be sent to the computer as a command to turn bits *1, 2, 3, 4, 7,* and *8* "on" and bits *5* and *6* "off." The binary code for "3" thus works out as *11110011*.

byte
A series of eight bits that, together, represent a character in a computer.

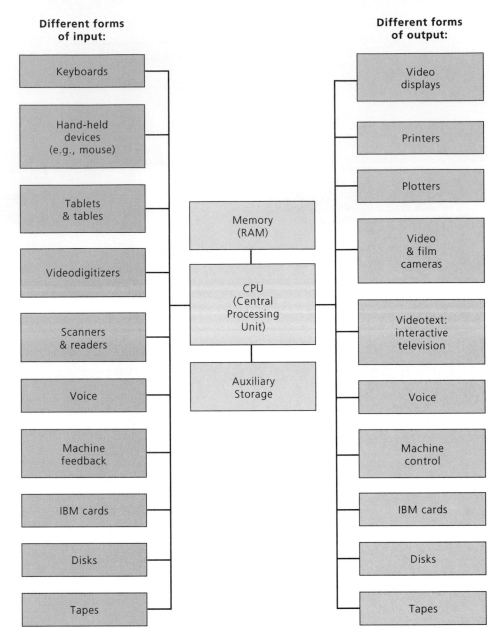

Figure 18.4
An overview of input and output.

---

primary storage

That part of the computer's central processing unit that houses the computer's memory of those items it needs to operate.

control unit

That part of the computer's central processing unit that locates instructions, transfers data to the arithmetic logic unit for processing, and transmits results to an output device.

program

Any sequence of instructions to a computer.

arithmetic logic unit (ALU)

That part of the computer's central processing unit that performs logical and mathematical operations such as addition, subtraction, multiplication, and division.

Primary Storage

You are now inside the CPU in a form that the computer can handle. Now what happens? If you look around the inside of the CPU, you will find three major objects: the computer's primary storage, its control unit, and its arithmetic logic unit. As a piece of data, you must go first to **primary storage**—the part of the computer's CPU that houses its memory of those items that it needs in order to operate.

Programs

At this point, the computer's **control unit** searches through its memory for instructions—**programs**—on what to do with you. Using the appropriate instructions, it then sends you to the **arithmetic logic unit (ALU)**, where (as the name implies) logical functions and calculations (addition, subtraction, multiplication, and division) take place. When the ALU is done with you, the control unit again takes over. It sends the results into one or more **output devices**—a cathode ray tube (CRT) more appropriately known as a *video display terminal (VDT)* and/or a printer.

output device

That part of a computer's hardware that presents results to users; common forms include printers and cathode ray tube (CRT)/video display terminals (VDTs).

Secondary Storage

If someone turned off the computer at this point, it would "forget" both the data (you) and information that resulted. Why? The computer's active memory is a short-term form of memory that lasts only as long as the computer stays on. This short-term memory is the main memory that is active when the computer does its work. It is also called **random-access memory (RAM)** because any part of it can be called upon for processing at any time. For long-term memory, however, we need **secondary storage**. Magnetic tape, hard disks, and floppy disks can all be used for secondary storage. Digital data can be written into storage and retrieved (that is, "read") from storage by the user.

random-access memory (RAM)

The computer's short-term active memory that lasts only as long as the computer stays on.

secondary storage

Any medium that can be used to store computerized data and information outside the computer's primary storage mechanism; magnetic tape, floppy disks, and hard disks are common forms.

Disks and ROM

Hard disks are rigid metal disks permanently enclosed in the computer. **Floppy disks** are portable and can be easily inserted and removed. Another kind of data storage uses **read-only memory (ROM)**: a portion of computer memory that can hold instructions that have been *read* by the computer but that does not accept instructions *written* into that memory.

CD-ROM disks (for *compact disk—read-only memory*) look just like music CDs and can hold as much data as 400 regular floppy disks. They are convenient for storing sound and video data but do not allow users to write new data onto them. Popular CD-ROMs include library materials, encyclopedias, and specialized scientific, medical, and technical tutorials that can be activated on newer PCs. For example, Microsoft's *Encarta* disc contains the complete text of the 29-volume Funk & Wagnall's New Encyclopedia.

Now that you have an inside view of computer hardware operations, let's look at things from the outside. Suppose you have a part-time job in the registrar's office at your school. Let's say that a student requests information about an introductory accounting class. You insert a floppy disk and type the request on your keyboard—your link to the CPU. Although the keyboard does no processing itself, it lets you "talk" with the CPU.

Inside the CPU, the control unit takes over. It issues an electronic command that finds data about accounting classes in secondary storage and copies it into primary storage. Note that information is available for use *only after it has been transferred into primary storage*, never while it is in secondary storage. Also moved to primary storage is a program that tells the computer how to search through course listings. The control unit then instructs the ALU to locate the necessary data in primary storage and search through it for the introductory course requested by the student.

Finally, the control unit transfers the results to primary storage and then to your VDT. In a matter of seconds, you can tell the student that the class meets at 8:30 a.m. every day and that three seats are still open.

hard disks

Rigid metal disks permanently enclosed in the computer.

floppy disks

Portable disks that can be easily inserted into and removed from the computer.

read-only memory (ROM)

A portion of computer memory that can hold instructions that have been read by the computer; does not permit instructions to be written in.

CD-ROM disks

Look like music CDs but can hold as much data as 400 regular floppy disks.

Software

While hardware is a vital component of a computer system, it is useless without the other components. As you have just seen, hardware needs programs—**software**—to function. Canada's software industry made profits of about $500 million in 1991, but it may also have lost as much as $200 million to software pirates—people who make illegal copies of computer software. The problem is that, with millions of individuals copying software, it is hard to know the magnitude of the problem or to catch anyone.[5]

software

Programs that instruct the computer in what to do and how to do it.

system program
A program that tells a computer what resources to use and how to use them.

application program
A program that actually processes data according to a particular user's specific needs.

object-oriented technology
Reduces the complexity of writing software programs by dividing the programs into reusable chunks with standard interfaces.

There are basically two types of programs: system programs and application programs. **System programs** tell the computer what resources to use and how to use them. For example, an operating system program tells the computer how and when to transfer data from secondary storage to primary storage and return information to the user. You have probably heard of DOS, the *d*isk *o*perating *s*ystem used by the IBM PC and its clones.

In contrast, **application programs** actually process data according to the special needs of the particular user. A computer system usually has only one operating system program, but it may use many application programs. Application programs run payroll, act as word processors, and play games. Programs such as Lotus 1-2-3 and WordPerfect are application programs. (See Figure 18.5 for an example.) We will consider the types of application programs most often used in business later in this chapter.

Writing software programs requires painstaking work and thousands of lines of commands. As software programs have become more complex, the time needed to write all these commands is becoming excessive. **Object-oriented technology** reduces these demands by dividing programs into

Application Program:	Electronic Spreadsheet (ESS)
What is it?	A program for creating, editing, and producing spreadsheets for comparing numeric data, making projections, and conducting "what if" analyses.
Examples.	Multiplan, Lotus 1-2-3, Excel, Jazz, Symphony, Framework, Crunch, and many others. Some of the products listed here are integrated with other applications including word processing, file or database management, and presentation graphics. Integrated systems are discussed in the chapter.
Cost?	$100 to $500
How?	Data are entered into a matrix of rows and columns displayed on the screen. The rows and columns are labelled by the user. For example, the columns could represent years, and the rows sales, cost of sales, and other expenses. The ESS would compute and display profit or loss over the years.
Metaphor.	Imagine the screen of the computer as a large sheet of grid paper with many rows and columns. The ESS would allow rapid movement to any location on the grid; you can enter and edit column and row names, data in the body of the matrix, and formulas that define relationships among rows and columns.

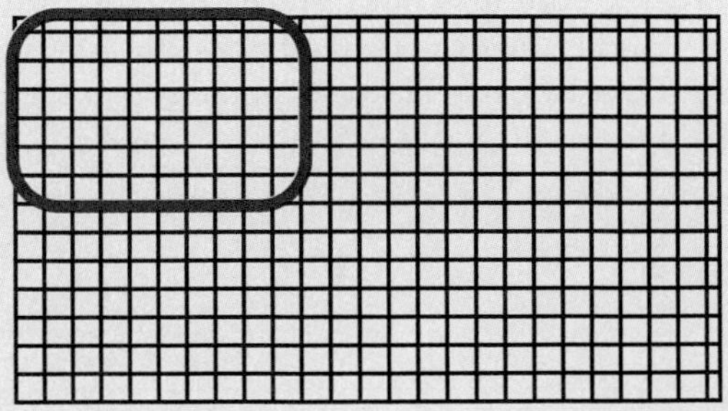

Figure 18.5
Creating spreadsheets with applications software.

small, reusable chunks of code (objects) with standard interfaces. Programmers can fit the objects together in different configurations as they write different programs. It's like building a house with Lego blocks instead of doing it molecule by molecule.[6]

Graphic User Interface

One of the most popular software developments in recent years is the **graphic user interface (GUI)**—the user-friendly visual display that helps users select from among the many possible applications on the computer. Typically, the screen displays numerous bright boxes with animated characters representing such choices as Word Processing, Graphics, DOS, Fax, Printing, or Games. A pointing device (usually an arrow) is moved around the screen to activate the desired box. Colourful printed text presents simple instructions for using activated features.

Before the Macintosh first popularized the GUI, new users were often frustrated in their attempts to *interface* with computers—that is, in figuring out how to copy a disk, write a program in a given language, create graphs, or use the computer's many other capabilities. Prior to GUI, interfaces were standard letters, numbers, and keyboard symbols that appeared on the video screen. For most people, they required long hours of computer practice and extensive reading of users manuals to become familiar with computers. Today, just one of the GUI software packages, Microsoft Windows, has found millions of customers because it simplifies computer use while actually making it fun.

graphic user interface (GUI)
The user-friendly display that helps users select from among the many possible applications of the computer.

People

We think—and speak—of computer systems as if they were only hardware and software. In large part, however, a computer system is a function of the people who construct and use it. The people in a computer system can be divided into three categories: *programming personnel, operations personnel,* and *end-users*.

Programming Personnel

Programming personnel include both systems analysts and applications or systems programmers:

- *Systems analysts* deal with the entire computer system. They work with users to learn their requirements and then design systems to meet them. Generally, they decide upon the type of computer, its size, and how to link it to all the users who will use the system.

- Using various language programs, *programmers* write the instructions that tell computers what to do. *Applications programmers*, for example, write the instructions to address particular problems. *Systems programmers* ensure that a system can handle the requests made by various applications programs.

Operations Personnel

Individuals who run the computer equipment are called *operations personnel*: They make sure that the right programs are run in the correct sequence and monitor equipment to ensure that it is operating properly. Many organizations also have *data-entry clerks* who key data into the system for processing.

End-Users

Finally, *end-users* employ the system to obtain information needed for their jobs. For example, a marketing manager who needs weekly reports on expenses for personal selling promotions is an end-user of a company's system. As we noted earlier, many programmers today realize that effective systems can be created only if intended users play a part in designing them.

Although programming personnel, operations personnel, and end-users are the people inside the computer system, other people benefit from computers. For example, you benefit when your bank teller can tell you your balance quickly. And individuals who service computers benefit from the employment.

Control

The fourth component of a computer system is control. *Control* ensures that the system is operating according to specific procedures and within specific guidelines. These procedures include guidelines for operating the system, the responsibilities of the personnel involved with it, and plans for dealing with system failure. For example, a key aspect of information management is controlling two groups of individuals: those who have access to input or change its data and those who receive the output from it. Thus most firms limit access to salary information. Control procedures are usually detailed in company manuals and often designate protected "passwords" for gaining system access.

Problems of Privacy

"Breaking and entering" no longer refers merely to physical intrusions into one's home or business. Today, it applies to computer-system intrusions as well. In this section, we will describe the three most common forms of computer intrusion: *privacy invasion, viruses,* and *piracy.* We will also discuss some of the methods that companies use to provide security for their information systems.[7]

privacy invasion
Intruders gain unauthorized access to computers in order to steal information or tamper with data.

In the computer world, **privacy invasion** occurs in two forms. First, intruders gain unauthorized access, either to steal information, money, or property or to tamper with data. We have all read, for instance, about computer "hackers" who have gained access to school systems to change grades. Others have invaded government databases to sabotage data, and still others have broken into stock brokerage databases to access the private transaction records of individual clients. One high school student stole more than $1 million in software from AT&T's computer system, and it is estimated that billions of dollars are embezzled electronically every year by intruders who alter data and shift funds from corporate and government accounts. One such intruder illegally transferred $10 million from one bank to another. Other intruders have been convicted of taking unauthorized information from computers and selling it to other governments and companies.

viruses
Harmful programs created and spread by vandals seeking to destroy or disrupt computer operations.

A second form of intrusion involves passing a computer "virus" into the system. **Viruses** are harmful programs created and spread by vandals seeking to destroy or disrupt computer operations. In effect, the virus is an unwanted "disease" that spreads from computer to computer, damaging data, programs, and even hardware.

While some viruses erase databases or programs immediately, others spread slowly like a cancer. Some may even lie dormant for weeks before suddenly activating. Viruses can be transmitted electronically from one system to another and can be distributed by virus-infected disks. Today, virus-protecting software is widely available for scanning incoming computer disks before they are introduced into a user's system.

Piracy

Computer piracy is the unauthorized copying of software. Nearly half of all the software used in the world is pirated.[8] A common form of piracy occurs when users simply ignore the law, illegally copying programs for friends and family, who then do not have to purchase the software. One firm, which had sold only two registered copies of a software package in Russia, found to its dismay that hundreds of thousands of copies were illegally circulating a short time later. One study showed that legal software accounted for less than 1 percent of the software in countries like Pakistan, Thailand, and Indonesia.[9] A Canadian company has developed an anti-piracy technology called SoftCop that works by "thumbprinting" the software to the authorized user's computer so that it will not run on another computer.[10]

A second form of piracy involves proprietary software for special applications. For example, one company's computer staff may develop its own program for computer-aided design. Piracy occurs when it is stolen from the developer company and illegally sold to other firms. A third form of piracy occurs when a buyer distributes unauthorized copies of software throughout the company. Most software suppliers offer **site-license agreements** that authorize companywide use of software in return for a fee.

computer piracy
The unauthorized copying of software programs.

site-license agreement
Authorizes companywide use of a software package in return for a fee.

Security

Security measures for protection against intrusion and piracy are a constant challenge for many firms. To prevent unlawful modification of software, codewords allowing access to it can be changed periodically. The activities of users can also be monitored, and some procedures require second-person confirmation before any one person can make changes in software programs.

Protection for data files and databases is not foolproof and typically involves making backup copies to be stored outside the computer system, usually in a safe. Thus if system files are damaged, they can be replaced by backup. Data communications can be intercepted during transit from one location to another. To prevent interception, transmission signals can be *scrambled* so that only those with deciphering codes can read them. The most common measure for virus protection is a program called a *vaccine*.

Finally, the most important factor in communications security is the *people* in the system. At most firms, therefore, procedures carefully control access to the system's components. Personnel are trained in the responsibilities of computer use and often apprised of the penalties for violating system security. For example, each time the computer boots up, a notice displays the warning that software and data are protected and spells out penalties for unauthorized use.

Data

Chunks of data—numbers, words, and sentences—are stored in fields, records, and files. Figure 18.6 presents the various levels of data as they might be structured for customers of Artists' Frame Service. All the files together are the **database**—a centralized collection of related data.

Once data are entered into the database, they can be *processed*—manipulated, sorted, combined, and/or compared. Data can be processed in a batch mode or a real-time mode. Neither mode is generally superior to the other. The "better" mode depends on the characteristics of the particular problem to be solved. In fact, many companies use both modes at different times.

database
A centralized, organized collection of related data.

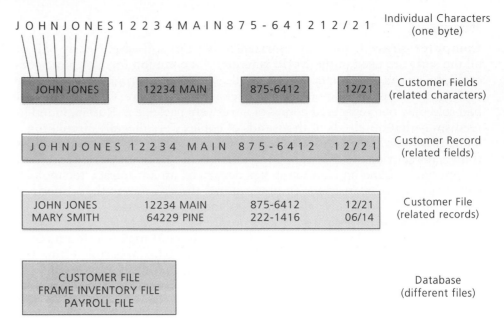

Figure 18.6
Levels of data for a database.

batch processing
A method of transforming data into information in which data are collected over a period of time and then processed as a group or batch.

In **batch processing**, operations personnel collect data over some time period and then process that data as a group or batch. The key aspect of batch processing is that the data are not processed at the time they are collected. For example, payroll is usually run in a batch mode. Few of us get paid the same hour or even the same day we earn the money. Rather, we get paid weekly, biweekly, or monthly. The data (hours) are accumulated over the pay period and processed all at one time. Batch processing was the only mode available on early computers and is still widely used.

Today, however, companies have choices about processing modes. Instead of batch processing, they can use a real-time (on-line) system. End-users feed data into the computer in **real-time processing**, and the data are processed instantly. Real-time processing is always used when the results of each entry affect subsequent entries. For example, if you book seat F6 on Air Canada flight 253 on December 23, the computer must thereafter keep other passengers from booking the same seat.

real-time processing
A method of transforming data into information in which data are entered and processed immediately.

Computer Application Programs for Business

Increasingly inexpensive equipment and software have made computers an irresistible option for businesses of all types and sizes. Programs are available for a huge variety of business-related tasks. Some of these programs address such common, long-standing needs as accounting, payroll, and inventory control. Others have been developed for application to an endless variety of specialized needs. Most applications programs used by businesses fall into one of four categories: *word processing, spreadsheets, database management,* and *graphics*. Seventy percent of all PC software applications are designed for the first three types of programs.[11]

Word Processing Programs

Many companies use **word processing**, which allows the computer to act as a sophisticated typewriter. Word processing programs make it easy to correct mistakes or revise quickly. Sentences or paragraphs can be added or deleted without retyping or restructuring the entire document. Word processing has greatly increased productivity in many companies.

Word processing also means that mailing lists and form letters can be prepared quickly and easily. As a result, you and millions of other consumers now get letters from advertisers that appear to be directed specifically at you. Word, WordPerfect, and DisplayWrite are three popular word processing programs.

word processing
Application programs that allow the computer to act as a sophisticated typewriter to store, edit, and print letters and numbers.

Spreadsheet Programs

Worksheets called **electronic spreadsheets** spread across and down a page in columns and rows. The user enters data, including formulas, at row and column intersections, and the computer automatically does the calculations. Balance sheets, income statements, and a host of other financial reports can be prepared using these programs.

Spreadsheets are also a useful planning tool, because they allow managers to see how changing one item will affect other related items. For example, as Figure 18.7 shows, a manager can insert various operating cost percentages, tax rates, or sales revenues. The computer will automatically recalculate all of the other figures and determine net profit.

Since they are helpful for investigating changes, spreadsheets can be used in building *decision support systems* (see Chapter 12). Popular spreadsheet packages include Lotus 1-2-3 and Excel.

electronic spreadsheet
Application programs that allow the user to enter categories of data and determine the effect of changes in one category (e.g., sales) on other categories (e.g., profits).

Database Management Programs

As the name implies, **database management** programs can keep track of all relevant data in a business. They can sort and search through data and integrate a single piece of data into several files. For example, Figure 18.8 illustrates a small database integrating customer picture-framing orders and an inventory file for Artists' Frame Service.

database management
Application programs that keep track of and manipulate the relevant data of a business.

	A	B
1	EXPENSES %	60
2	TAX %	20
3	SALES $	300.00
4		
5	SALES $	300.00
6	EXPENSES $	180.00
7	INCOME $	120.00
8	TAX $	24.00
9	NET PROFIT $	96.00

	A	B
1	EXPENSES %	70
2	TAX %	20
3	SALES $	300.00
4		
5	SALES $	300.00
6	EXPENSES $	210.00
7	INCOME $	90.00
8	TAX $	18.00
9	NET PROFIT $	72.00

Figure 18.7
This spreadsheet shows what happens to income, taxes, and net profit if operating expenses rise from 60 to 70 percent of sales.

Some books on current computer application programs.

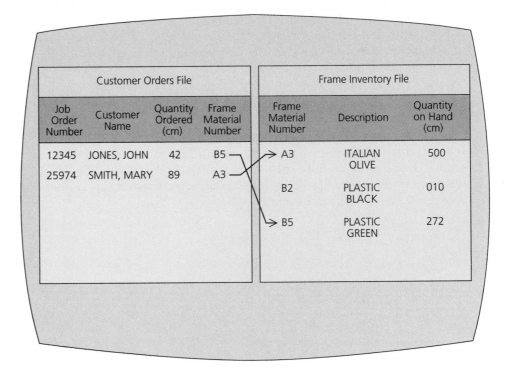

Figure 18.8
The two files are integrated in the database. New customer orders reduce the on-hand inventories of frame materials.

In addition to producing standardized reports, database management programs can supply answers to one-time questions such as "What are the names of the students who failed English Composition last term?" or "What was our most popular product last year?" Examples of database management programs include DBase IV and RBase System V for personal computers and Total and IMS for mainframes.

In addition to "home grown" or *primary databases*, a company may decide to use external, or *secondary databases*. Secondary databases can be broad or narrow. Nexis is a secondary database of news and financial information that draws on over 100 newspapers, newsletters, magazines, and wire services such as Associated Press. Lexis is a secondary database that deals solely with legal materials. Dow Jones News/Retrieval offers business and economic news headlines, including highlights from *The Wall Street Journal*.

The popularity of secondary databases has grown because they are easy to use and can provide information on factors outside the company. Using a personal computer with a **modem**, a computer-to-computer link via telephone lines, a user can search for articles based on key words. A restaurant chain, for example, could query Nexis to locate information on consumer preferences for Mexican food.

The Wall Street Journal
http://www.wsj.com

modem
A hardware device permitting the user of a personal computer to link up with other computer systems via telephone lines.

Graphics

Computer-graphics programs convert numeric and character data into pictorial information such as charts and graphs. These programs make computerized information easier to use and understand in two ways. First, graphs and charts summarize data and allow managers to detect problems, opportunities, and relationships more easily. Second, graphics are valuable in creating clearer and more persuasive reports and presentations.

Some of the latest software for **desktop publishing** combines word processing and graphics capability in producing typeset-quality text from personal computers. Quark XPress, for example, is able to manipulate text, graphics, and full-colour photographs. Desktop publishing eliminates costly printing services for reports and proposals, and Quark is also used by advertising agencies where computer-generated designs offer greater control over colour and format.

Two of the most common graphics displays are the pie chart and the bar graph. As Figure 18.9 shows, both types of graphics can convey different kinds of information—in this case, the type of framing materials that should be ordered by a picture-framing shop like Artists' Frame Service. Both types of graphs are more likely to help a manager make decisions than the stack of numbers on which they are based.

computer-graphics programs
Application programs that convert numerical and character data into pictorial forms.

desktop publishing
Combines word processing and graphics capability in producing typeset-quality text from personal computers.

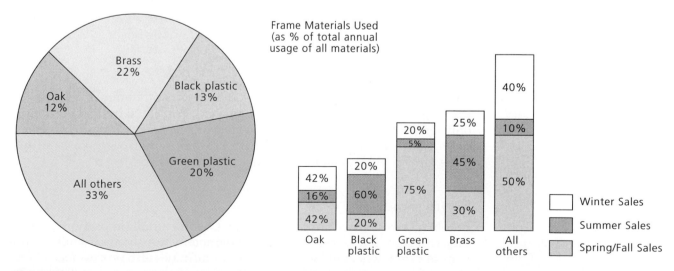

Figure 18.9
Both the pie chart and the bar graph show that four frame materials are the most used, but the bar graph also shows that brass and oak are most popular in winter.

Computer graphics capabilities extend beyond mere data presentation. They also include stand-alone programs for artists, designers, and special effects designers. Everything from simple drawings to fine art, television commercials, and motion-picture special effects are now created by computer graphics-software.[12] The realism of the dinosaurs in *Jurassic Park* and the physical appearance of the legless Vietnam veteran in *Forrest Gump* are special effects created with computer graphics.

Types of Computer Systems

Although all computer systems share the common elements of hardware, software, control, people, and data, not all computer systems are alike. Computer systems vary dramatically in their overall size, capacity, and cost, as well as in how their elements are put together.

Categorizing Computer Systems by Size

One way of grouping computer systems is by their cost, capacity, and capability. This approach results in four basic categories of computer systems: microcomputers, minicomputers, mainframes, and supercomputers.

Microcomputers

microcomputer (or personal computer)
Smallest, slowest, least expensive form of computer.

Most of the computers that you see sitting on desks are **microcomputers** (also called **personal computers**). The convenience and power of microcomputers such as IBM PC and Apple Macintosh have shifted the balance of computing power to smaller systems. Smaller, portable PCs include *laptops*, *notebooks*, and *palmtops*. Light in weight, ranging from a few grams (palmtops) to 7 kg (laptops), portables have external power sources (such as rechargeable batteries) and many, but not all, of the features of desktops. Notebooks and palmtops, for example, have more limited keyboards and smaller memories, and palmtops have very small monitors. Their advantages—they are lightweight, transportable, and storable (some are small enough for your pocket)—make them attractive timesavers for commuters and travellers. More information on microcomputers is contained in the box "A Different Type of Downsizing."

Minicomputers

minicomputer
A computer whose capacity, speed, and cost fall between those of microcomputers and mainframes.

Larger, faster, and more sophisticated than microcomputers, **minicomputers** range in cost from around $25 000 upward. While micros typically process only tens of thousands of instructions per second, minis can process over a million instructions per second (MIPS). Minis can also support multiple users and provide much more storage than micros do.

Mainframes

mainframe
A computer whose capacity, speed, and cost fall between those of minicomputers and supercomputers.

Still bigger and faster are **mainframes**. Costing a million or more dollars, they can store and access billions of characters, not the thousands or millions of characters in micros and minis. Mainframes also process tens of millions of instructions per second. Because of their speed and capacity, mainframes are most often found in banks, other large commercial organizations, and universities where large volumes of data must be processed.

The Canadian Business Scene

A Different Type of Downsizing

In a way, you could view the history of computers as an "incredible shrinking story." The earliest computers, despite their limited abilities, were huge—about the size of an average house. But over the years, machines have become smaller and smaller, and many companies have moved from mainframes to minicomputers to the microcomputers (PCs) found on desks in most companies.

Yet the trend towards "downsizing" continues, with the latest crop of computerized wonders making the standard PC look like an elephant. First came the *laptops*, computers weighing between 3.5 and 9 kg and about the size of a small briefcase. With laptops, businesspeople could for the first time literally take their offices with them. Sales staff could hook into their firms' main computers via modem and get the latest prices and place orders.

Laptops had barely begun to get a foothold in the market when the next wave of even smaller machines hit. Called *notebooks*, these variations on the microcomputer are about the size of a notebook—approximately 21.5 by 28 cm—and weigh 2 to 3 kg. Despite the difficulties of typing on a somewhat smaller keyboard, many businesspeople have embraced notebook computers, thrilled to be able to tuck the units into a briefcase and avoid carrying an extra piece of luggage on trips.

The future appears to be even smaller. Consider the latest in computer miniaturization—*palmtops*. As the name implies, these mini-minicomputers fit into the palm of your hand, measuring as little as 20 cm by 10 cm by 2.5 cm thick and weighing in at only 300 to 540 *grams*. Yet these miniature marvels offer standard (albeit tiny) 25-line-by-80-character screens. They come with 512 RAM, hard drives, and a host of built-in programs (including the popular Lotus 1-2-3). And with the aid of special connecting cables, palmtops can be connected to other computers, printers, and modems. While their miniature keyboards make touch typing impossible, palmtops can be tucked into a jacket pocket and taken anywhere—from the oil fields to the board room—and can be used to make notes, revise spreadsheets, and check important data on the spot. Fold-up keyboards are now available which allow the computer to be very small, but which still permit standard touch typing once the keyboard is unfolded.

Can computers get much smaller? Improvements in computer chips mean that some further reductions in the size of the processing operation may be possible, even as tiny computers become more and more powerful. Furthermore, the introduction of pen-based technologies—in which users just "write" information into the computer—may banish keyboard size as an issue. Screens probably cannot be made much smaller (though they may get thinner and lighter), but with scientists at work teaching computers to accept spoken commands and data, perhaps someday the computer will simply talk back.

Supercomputers

The largest, fastest, and most expensive of all computers are the **supercomputers**. They are used mainly in scientific applications where large numbers of complex calculations need to be performed quickly. In part because of their cost—over 5 million dollars—fewer than 150 of these systems are currently in actual operation.

supercomputer
The largest, fastest, and most expensive form of computer available today.

Systems Architecture

While differences in computer capacity and ability are shrinking, systems *architecture* has remained a fairly constant feature. **Systems architecture** refers to the location of the various parts of the system—its data-entry and

systems architecture
The way in which a computer system's data entry, data processing, database, data output, and computer staff are located.

data-processing operations, database, data output, and computer staff. System architecture is classified according to the organization of a system's parts.

Centralized Systems

In a **centralized system**, most of the processing is done in one location. For example, all of a bank's branch teller machines need the same information. Thus they are all hooked up to the main-office mainframe, which houses all customer-information files in a central database. Centralized systems do have drawbacks: For example, when the central computer fails or communication lines to it go down, all the branches also go down.

Decentralized Systems

In a **decentralized system**, each location determines the needs of its own system—physical components, programs, databases, personnel. Locations are independent of centralized mainframes, and there are no communication links between locations. A drawback arises when different locations independently adopt incompatible components and/or programs. It may then become difficult or impossible for systems at separate locations to share important data.

Networks

At the same time, however, *networking* now allows computers to exchange data quickly and easily. A **computer network** is a group of interconnected systems that can exchange information among several different locations. Networks may link computers statewide or even nationwide through telephone wires or satellites, as in **wide area networks**. Wal-Mart stores, for example, invested more than $20 million in a satellite network that links more than 2000 retail stores to its headquarters.

Internal networks may link computers through cables, as in **local area networks (LANs)**. The computers in internal networks share processing duties, software, storage areas, and data. On television's *Home Shopping Network*, for example, hundreds of operators seated at monitors in a large room are united by a LAN for entering call-in orders from customers. This arrangement allows the use of a single computer system with one database and software system.

Combination systems using local and wide area networks are also possible. For example, separate plants or offices might handle orders locally while electronically transmitting sales summaries to a corporate office. Computer networks thus give companies the advantages of both centralized and decentralized processing.

Server-Client Systems

Over the years, components and features were simply added on to mainframe systems, increasing capacity without meeting the need for greater flexibility. Consequently, many companies now find their old mainframe systems outmoded. In addition, systems have become overcustomized, and reprogramming mainframes to respond to new formats is expensive and time-consuming. In order to construct systems that will support such innovative management techniques as just-in-time inventory and total quality management, many companies are thus "downsizing"—switching from mainframe to more adaptable, cost-effective LANs systems.

Although some LANs systems are specialized, they are shared to avoid costly, unnecessary duplication. Any component that can be shared by LAN users is called a **server**. The powerful minicomputer at the network hub, for example, may be the server for the surrounding **client PCs** in the network.

More specifically, it may act as either a *file server* or a *print server*. As a file server, the mini has a large-capacity disk for storing the programs and data shared by all the PCs in the network. It will thus contain customer files plus the database, word processing, and spreadsheet programs that may be called upon when needed by clients. As a print server, the mini controls the printer, stores printing requests from client PCs, and routes jobs to the printer as it becomes available. Only one main memory and one printer, therefore, are needed for an entire system.

Miniaturization

The year 1971 witnessed the first commercial introduction of the **microprocessor chip**. This chip, the size of a small paper clip, contains the computer's central processing unit. Prior to 1971, computers had specialized chips for logic, programming, and so forth. Intel Corp.'s development of the microprocessor made it possible to put all the computer's functions on a single chip. Today, many cars, watches, and televisions also use microprocessors.

Continued miniaturization has made it possible to put even more circuits on a single chip. The result is known as *large-scale integration (LSI)* and *very-large-scale integration (VLSI)*. Today's "super chips" have room for thousands of miniature transistors on a space no thicker than a human hair.

LSI and VLSI permit software and printers to react more quickly with each other and with the computer. Coupled with improvements in software, the latest computers are faster and easier for nonprogrammers to use. In addition, the microprocessor made possible microcomputers, which have revolutionized the role of computers in business.

Although no one is sure what the next generation of computing will be like, the continuing miniaturization of transistor circuits is creating—almost daily—new possibilities in both speed and storage capacity. A microprocessor's speed determines how fast it can process software instructions. Smaller circuit sizes mean that more transistors can be placed on a single silicon chip. They can also be placed closer together, and reduced distance means faster processing. If downsizing continues at current rates, even today's transistor sizes of less than a *micron* (one-millionth of a metre) will be goliaths compared to those expected in the future.

microprocessor chip
Single silicon chip containing a computer's central processing unit.

Intel Corp.
http://www.intel.com

Table 18.1   The Top 10 Information Technology Companies in Canada, 1996

	Company	Sales Revenue (in billions)
1.	IBM Canada Ltd.	$9.50
2.	Digital Equipment of Canada Ltd.	2.30
3.	SHL Systemhouse Inc.	1.80
4.	Hewlett-Packard Canada Ltd.	1.30
5.	Xerox Canada Inc.	1.20
6.	Bell Sygma Inc.	0.84
7.	DMR Consulting Group Inc.	0.65
8.	ATI Technologies Inc.	0.46
9.	EDS Canada	0.45
10.	Corel Corp.	0.45

With miniaturization, the transistor circuits in memory chips are also smaller. More circuits per chip means much larger memory capacity. While today's capacities are measured in *megabits* (millions of bits), chip technology is fast approaching the *gigabit* (billion-bit) range. The 486-class chip that was common in PCs in the mid-1990s had about 100 million transistors, making it more powerful than the mainframes of 1985. It is just one product of a computer-power "explosion" that has been growing by a factor of four every three years since 1979: In other words, the performance of this year's PC is about four times that of the PC of just three years ago. And today's PC is priced lower.[13]

The Marriage of Information and Communications Technology

Although the next generation of computing has not yet arrived, some of its foundation elements are here: *artificial intelligence, natural language dialogue between computers and users, expert systems, office automation*, and *executive information systems*. However, the most powerful vehicle for exploiting these elements to their full potential is the marriage of computers to communications technologies. Thanks to lower-cost, higher-capacity networks, the joining of computers, communications, and the mass media is already in its first stages.

This marriage promises to change the future face of business—indeed, of society itself. "Personal computing," observes Microsoft's Bill Gates, "was qualitatively a very, very different thing than the computing that came before. The advances in communication likewise will create new ways of using communication for learning, education, and commerce that go far beyond anything done to date." Thus both independently and through joint ventures, companies like Microsoft, AT&T, Oracle Corp., and Telecommunications Inc. are pursuing such products as personal digital assistants, digital TVs, and devices for tapping into high-band-width networks, multimedia information, and online services.[14] In this section, we will briefly discuss the progress of some of these projects that are already realities.

Artificial Intelligence

artificial intelligence

The construction and/or programming of computers to imitate human thought processes.

Artificial intelligence (AI) is the construction and programming of computers to imitate human thought processes. In developing components and programs for artificial intelligence, computer scientists are trying to design computers capable of reasoning so that computers, instead of people, can perform useful activities.

Robotics is just one category of AI. For example, IBM's Tape Library Dataserver, which is designed to serve giant companies that must store immense amounts of information, stores 42 trillion bytes of data. Data requests can be made from terminals in various departments. Cameras mounted on each robotic "hand" locate one out of almost 19 000 numbered tape cartridges. The robot then loads the cartridge into a reader that projects the information on the personal computer screen of a manager needing data on inventory, transactions, employees, or customers.[15]

With their "reasoning" capabilities, such robots can "learn" repetitive tasks such as painting, assembling components, and inserting screws. Furthermore, they avoid repeating mistakes by "remembering" the causes of past mistakes and, when those causes reappear, adjusting or stopping until adjustments are made.

Computer scientists are also designing AI systems that possess sensory capabilities (vision with lasers, as well as hearing and feeling). In addition, when machines are ultimately able to process natural languages, humans will be able to give instructions and ask questions without learning special computer languages. In fact, Oracle Corp., the leading supplier of database software for minicomputers and servers, has already introduced software, called ConText, that understands such natural-language instructions as "Get my broker on the phone." When machines learn to reason on the basis of natural-language inputs, they may even be able to learn from experience and apply their learning to solve new problems.[16]

AND Corp. of Toronto has developed a software program—called HNet— that closely mimics how the human brain works. The software can, for example, learn to recognize faces. This may seem like a simple thing, but millions of dollars had been spent on this problem without success until AND Corp. developed the software. The system could be used to improve airport security and to track terrorists.[17]

Oracle Corp.
http://www.oracle.com

Expert Systems

A special form of artificial intelligence programs, **expert systems** try to imitate the behaviour of human experts in a particular field. Expert systems thus make available the rules that an expert applies to specific types of problems. In effect, they supply everyday users with "instant expertise."

Many firms already use expert systems for training and analysis:

- The Digital Equipment sales force, for example, uses a system called Xcon to match customer needs with the most appropriate combination of computer input, output, and memory devices. Almost as if they were accompanied by expert sales advisors, salespeople receive one-of-a-kind equipment suggestions that the system has tailored to each customer's specific requirements.[18]

- Northern Telecom uses a system called Engineering Change Manager to simplify and speed up product design changes. The system considers such factors as a component's strength requirements, shape, appearance, and cost. It then creates the suggested redesigns to meet all the requirements. The new designs are then given to engineers, who can compare them to their own designs for better, faster product improvements.[19]

expert system
A form of artificial intelligence in which a program draws on the rules an expert in a given field has laid out in order to arrive at a solution for a problem.

IBM's Tape Library Dataserver stores 42 trillion bytes of data.

Office Automation

Office automation refers to the computer-based devices and applications whose function is to enhance the performance of general office activities.[20] In this section, we will survey three of the most solidly entrenched innovations in today's automated office: *fax machines, voice mail,* and *e-mail.*

Fax Machines

fax machine

A machine that can quickly transmit a copy of documents or graphics over telephone lines.

Fax machines (short for *facsimile-transceiver machines*) can transmit text documents (and even drawings) over telephone lines in a matter of seconds, thus permitting written communication over long distances. Fax machines are popular with both large and small firms because of speed and low cost.

Voice Mail

voice mail

A computer-based system for receiving and delivering incoming telephone calls.

Voice mail is a computer-based system for receiving and delivering incoming telephone calls. Incoming calls are never missed when the phone owner is absent because a voice responds to the caller and invites a message, stores it, and delivers it when instructed to do so by the callee. A company with voice mail has each employee's phone networked for receiving, storing, and forwarding calls.

Voice mail consists of software that links the communications device (telephone) with the computer. The input from the telephone is sent to the computer, which digitizes the voice data and stores it on a disk. The employee can then call the voice-mail centre to retrieve from storage a recording of waiting calls and voice messages.

E-Mail

electronic mail (e-mail)

Electronic transmission of letters, reports, and other information between computers.

An **electronic mail** (or **e-mail**) system electronically transmits letters, reports, and other information between computers, whether in the same building or across the country. Thus they substitute for the flood of paper and telephone calls that threatens to engulf many offices. They are, however, expensive and generally found only in large, technically sophisticated companies. Some potential problems with e-mail are described in the box "Information Overload."

groupware

System that allows two or more individuals to communicate electronically between desktop PCs.

A new type of software—called **groupware**—is changing the nature of personal computing. The simplest and most familiar groupware is e-mail, but more sophisticated groupware programs function like an electronic conference room where many people can converse at once. Groupware allows people from all levels in the organization to "talk" together, and people may be judged more on what they say than on their rank in the hierarchy. Groupware may therefore end up changing corporate culture and reducing the impact of the classic organizational hierarchy.[21]

Executive Information Systems

executive information systems (EIS)

Easy-access information clusters especially designed for instant access by upper-level managers.

Executive information systems (**EIS**) are quick-reference, easy-access information clusters especially designed for instant access by upper-level managers. Business planning, strategy sessions, and competitive evaluations depend on retrieving information conveniently by senior-level managers who, typically, are not computer-oriented and do not possess technical computer skills. An EIS is easily accessible with simple, unintimidating keyboard strokes or even voice commands. The system predetermines and prepares for access the types of data of special interest to the senior manager—for instance, sales summarized by geographic regions and company divisions, competitive sales trends, market shares among different product lines, and costs of operation in various profit centres.

The Canadian Business Scene

Information Overload

A recent study of 972 workers at large companies revealed that the average person received 178 messages each day. These messages came via completed phone calls, e-mail, voice mail, fax, post-it notes, courier packages, traditional mail, and telephone message slips. This barrage of messages has left increasing numbers of workers frustrated and feeling overwhelmed.

E-mail has received the most recent negative publicity. Because e-mail messages can be easily constructed and then copied to just about anybody with a single stroke of a key, the amount of information that is being electronically sent is escalating dramatically. More and more managers and workers are spending more and more time reading and responding to an increasing number of e-mail messages, many of which are either trivial or, worse, have nothing to do with their work.

Andrew Grove, CEO of Intel Corp., has told employees to stop broadcasting non-essential memos such as notices of softball practice or pets for sale. And Bill Gates, CEO of Microsoft, fired an employee who used his Microsoft e-mail address to complain about Ukrainian communists. After the firing, Gates (who is an avid e-mail person) was bombarded with e-mail protests about his actions. Charles Wang, CEO of Computer Associates International, no longer sends or reads e-mail, even though his company sells an e-mail package. He shuts down the company's e-mail system for five hours each day so employees can get their work done.

The introduction of e-mail was supposed to increase workplace democracy by giving everyone increased access to important information. And so it has. But here's the rub: In hierarchical organizations, this may be threatening to those near the top of the hierarchy who are used to being more isolated from those who are lower in the hierarchy. To counter this problem, some top executives use a "bozo filter," which is special software that culls e-mail from strangers and puts it into an electronic archive where it sits, unread. Maybe corporations aren't ready for democracy yet.

A final problem concerns the impersonality of e-mail. The ease of sending messages motivates some people to conduct much of their communication through the e-mail system. This is efficient and can be positive, at least up to a point. But the written word can easily be misinterpreted, and nasty disputes have broken out between workers who fire written salvos back and forth on e-mail instead of walking down the hall and talking through the problem face-to-face. E-mail has also been used by subordinates to criticize managerial competence, especially in companies that are going through downsizing. Managers can retaliate by snooping on an employee's e-mail, even after it has supposedly been erased from the system.

Upon retrieval, EIS data are organized into menus allowing for selective access and manipulation. You might, for example, retrieve data on geographic sales and then instruct the computer to provide a further breakdown year-by-year for each competing firm. With fingertip access, the manager can request needed information in the midst of executive sessions, when new questions arise, as plans are being developed, or at the time decisions are being made.

Manufacturing Information Systems

As we saw in Chapter 12, computer technology is already having a major impact on manufacturing through the use of *computer-aided design* (*CAD*), *computer-aided manufacturing* (*CAM*), and *computer-integrated manufacturing* (*CIM*). In their competition for world markets, companies are continuing to develop more sophisticated variations of these computer systems in order to increase productivity.[22]

Multimedia Communications Systems

Today's information systems include not just computers, but **multimedia communications systems**: connected networks of communications appliances such as faxes, televisions, sound equipment, printing machines, and

multimedia communications systems

Connected networks of communications appliances such as faxes, televisions, sound equipment, printing machines, and photocopiers that may also be linked with mass media such as TV.

photocopiers that may also be linked with such mass media as TV and radio broadcast programming, news and other print publications, and library collections. Not surprisingly, the integration of these elements is changing the way we live our lives and manage our businesses.

Data Communications Networks

data communications networks

Global networks that permit users to send electronic messages quickly and economically.

Also gaining popularity on both home and business computers are public and private **data communications networks**: global networks that permit users to send electronic messages, documents, and other forms of video and audio information quickly and economically. Internet is the largest public network, serving thousands of computers in North America with information on business, science, and government and providing communications flows with certain private networks, including CompuServe and MCI Mail.[23] (See the box "Surfing the Internet" for more information.)

Communications Channels

Communications channels refer to the media that make all these transmissions possible. These include coaxial and fibre-optic cable and infrared, microwave, and

The Canadian Business Scene

Surfing the Internet

The popularity of the Internet (or "the Net," for short) has skyrocketed in recent years. Originally commissioned by the Pentagon in the U.S. as a communication tool for use during war, the Internet allows personal computers in virtually any location to be linked together by means of large computers known as network servers. The Net has gained in popularity because it makes available an immense wealth of academic, technical, and business information. Another major attraction is the Net's capacity to transmit electronic mail, or e-mail. In addition, such popular on-line services as Prodigy and CompuServe provide e-mail gateways to the Net.

For thousands of businesses, therefore, the Net is joining—and even replacing—the telephone, the fax machine, and express mail as a standard means of communication. In 1994, the number of Net users doubled, to 15 million, with links to more than 138 countries.

Moreover, thanks to a subsystem of 7000 computers known as the World Wide Web (WWW, or simply "the Web"), the Internet is easier to use than ever before. "The Web," explains investment analyst Stephen Franco, "has made the Internet usable to a general audience, rather than the technical users who had been the only ones using it for years and years." The computers linked by the Web are known as "Web servers"; they are owned by corporations, colleges, government agencies, and other large organizations. The individual user can connect with the Web by means of so-called "browser" software, such as Mosaic. The user must simply "point and click," and ex-

perts predict that as more people become familiar with "browsers," the number of Net users will grow by 10 to 15 percent a month.

The Net's power to change the way business is conducted has already been amply demonstrated. Digital Equipment Corp., for instance, is a heavy Internet user: With more than 31 000 computers connected to the network, DEC's monthly e-mail volume has jumped to an average of 700 000 messages. DEC has also linked its new Alpha AXP high-speed business computer to the Internet so that potential buyers and software developers can spend time using and evaluating it. Gail Grant, the Internet administrator at DEC, reports that in just a few months, 2500 computer users in 27 countries have taken advantage of the opportunity to explore the Alpha AXP.

The Net has also benefited small companies. For example, one florist shop has used the Net to establish an international presence. Its owner reports that the Net now generates nearly as many orders as FTD.

Of course, the advent of such services has accelerated to a fairly heady pace by the mid-1990s. What can the average company do to keep up with constant, sometimes dramatic changes in the Internet era? For one thing, seminars and workshops provide uninitiated members of the business community with in-depth looks at the Net and its potential applications. A 1994 Internet conference in New York attracted 1750 attendees and 40 vendors; in 1992, the same conference attracted only 600 people and 13 vendors.

satellite transmission. In particular, the use of satellite channels is increasing to meet the growing demand for wireless transmission. For example, Teledesic Corp. plans to create a major global wireless telephone network by launching 840 satellites. One new application for wireless systems is electronic terminals installed on seatbacks of airplanes so that you can access your e-mail during business travel.[24]

Most of us, of course, use communications channels when we use some type of telephone system. Even today, however, the bulk of telephone transmissions are data, not conversations. Fax data, for instance, account for 90 percent of all telephone signals between North America and Japan.

"Smart" Software

Software for many multimedia components actually permits them to perform some activities automatically. "Smart" modems, for example, perform such functions as dialling, answering the phone, and transmitting. "Smart" TVs remember your program preferences, make suggestions for your viewing pleasure, and remind you of upcoming programs. Similar software is available for watches, ovens, automobiles, airplanes, and air conditioners. New software is also emerging to integrate the activities of the multimedia hardware. Microsoft at Work, for example, can be installed in office equipment hardware—phones, fax machines, copiers—so they can all be controlled by PCs.[25]

Changing Lifestyles: The Virtual Office

The impact of communications technologies on lifestyles is nowhere more evident than in the so-called "virtual office"—the mobile office-like working environment that is replacing the traditional, fixed-location office housing hundreds of employees side-by-side. Are you one of the growing number of employees who want to work more at home? Today, the technology is available for more and more people to communicate electronically with the office, lab, or factory by means of their home PCs. On the road, a portable computer can communicate with either the PC at home or the mainframe at headquarters. Wireless faxes can transmit written communications from computer to computer, while voice mail and e-mail provide most of the work-related interaction with headquarters that is ever needed by many employees.

The Use of Computers in Small Businesses

In the past, retail stores, medical offices, restaurants, and farms had manual systems or used a data processing service bureau. Today, many of these businesses own their own computer systems. Personal computer systems offer small businesses the advantage of better inventory control, more accurate sales analysis, and improved financial planning. Several new software programs are aimed specifically at the needs of emerging businesses.[26] The Quattro Pro spreadsheet, for example, is available for less than $50. Quicken, the personal-finance software that tracks cheques, bills, credit-card accounts, and anything else that passes through a wallet or cash register, is already used in more than 5 million homes and businesses.[27]

Computer ownership, of course, is not without challenges. For example, many small business owners and managers have trouble choosing programs. In addition, they may lack the time and expertise needed to set up programs to handle such data as payroll records, customer payment schedules, and inventory control. An alternative approach is using programs developed for specific applications. General accounting packages like Dac-Easy Accounting and the IBM Accounting Assistant Series are designed for small businesses and contain programs for all of the major accounting functions.

A business such as a real estate company or a medical office may be able to buy even more specific software designed for its industry. A real estate office package will maintain client lists, keep sales records, and hook into a multiple-listing service for the city. A medical office package will schedule patients and create and maintain a database for patient medical records. Small businesses have also found the combination of database and word processing programs valuable for mailing list management. Advertisements and notices of special sales or new merchandise can be targeted to specific clientele by using an appropriate customer database.

Summary of Learning Objectives

1. **Show why businesses must manage information and show how computers have revolutionized *information management*.** Because businesses today are faced with an overwhelming amount of data and information about customers, competitors, and their own operations, the ability to manage this information can mean the difference between success and failure. Because of their *speed, accuracy, storage capabilities,* and *ability to make comparisons*, computers have emerged as a powerful tool for information management.

2. **Identify and briefly describe the main elements in a computer system.** *Hardware* is a computer's physical components. It consists of an input device (such as a keyboard), a central processing unit (CPU), internal or external disk drives, floppy disks for data storage, and output devices (such as video monitors and printers). *Software* includes the computer's operating system and applications such as spreadsheets and programs for word processing and desktop publishing.

   People are also part of the computer system. Systems analysts, for example, design systems, and programmers write instructions. Operations personnel run the computers, and end-users log onto computers to obtain and manipulate the data needed to perform their jobs. *Control* is important to ensure not only that the system operates correctly but also that data and information are transmitted through secure channels to people who really need them. *Data* such as numbers, words, and sentences are stored in fields, records, and files in the computer. All of the files together are called the database.

3. **Identify the role played in computer systems by *databases* and describe four important types of *business-application programs*.** Through computer sequences of instructions called *programs*, computers are able to process data and to perform specific functions. Once *data* (raw facts and figures) are centralized and organized into meaningful *databases*, they can be manipulated, sorted, combined, and/or compared according to program instructions.

   Four major types of application programs for businesses are *word processing* (which allows computers to act like sophisticated typewriters), *electronic spreadsheets* (which enter data in rows and columns and perform calculations), *database management* (which organizes and retrieves a company's relevant data), and *graphics* (which convert numeric and character data into pictorial information).

4. **Classify *computer systems* by size and structure.** Computers can be classified according to cost, capacity, and capability. The smallest, slowest, and least expensive computers are *microcomputers.* The largest, fastest, and most expensive are *supercomputers. Minicomputers* and

mainframes fall in between, but all these distinctions are beginning to blur. In contrast, computer systems differ sharply in architecture. In *centralized systems*, most processing is done from one location, using a centralized database. In *decentralized systems*, each location handles its own processing from its own database. Computer *networks* allow branch computers to communicate, offering some of the advantages of both centralized and decentralized systems.

5. **List some trends in the application of computer technology to business-information management.** The fifth generation of computers promises exciting developments in information management. Recent advances already include *artificial intelligence* (programming computers to imitate human thought processes), *expert systems* (which try to imitate the behaviour of experts in a given field), *office automation* (which includes machine technology—fax machines, e-mail, and the like—that streamlines communications), *executive information systems* (which provide upper-level managers with easy access to information), and *manufacturing information systems* (which increase productivity). All of these technologies offer businesspeople assistance in making decisions and solving problems.

Multimedia communications systems link connected networks of communications appliances (such as faxes) with such mass media as print publications and TV programming. New technology for multimedia has made on-line informations services available, and electronic discussion groups and interactive on-screen dialogue are now possible. *Data communications networks* such as the Internet permit users to send electronic messages and video and audio information quickly and economically. The emergence of the *virtual office* means that mobile office-like working environments are replacing traditional, fixed-location workplaces.

Key Terms

information manager, 545
data, 545
information, 545
management information system (MIS), 546
computer system, 549
hardware, 549
input device, 549
central processing unit (CPU), 549
bit, 549
byte, 551
primary storage, 552
control unit, 552
program, 552
arithmetic logic unit (ALU), 552
output device, 553
random-access memory (RAM), 553

secondary storage, 553
hard disks, 553
floppy disks, 553
read-only memory (ROM), 553
CD-ROM disks, 553
software, 553
system program, 554
application program, 554
object-oriented technology, 554
graphic user interface (GUI), 555
privacy invasion, 556
viruses, 556
computer piracy, 557
site-license agreement, 557
database, 557
batch processing, 558

real-time processing, 558
word processing, 559
electronic spreadsheet, 559
database management, 559
modem, 561
computer-graphics programs, 561
desktop publishing, 561
microcomputer, 562
minicomputer, 562
mainframe, 562
supercomputer, 563
systems architecture, 563
centralized system, 564
decentralized system, 564
computer network, 564
wide area network, 564

local area network (LAN), 564
server, 564
client PCs, 564
microprocessor chip, 565
artificial intelligence, 566
expert system, 567
fax machine, 568
voice mail, 568
electronic mail (e-mail), 568
groupware, 568
executive information systems (EIS), 568
multimedia communications systems, 569
data communications networks, 570

Study Questions and Exercises

Review Questions

1. Why does a business need to manage information as a resource?
2. Describe the components of a computer system. Explain how each part is related to the others.
3. Rank microcomputers, minicomputers, mainframes, and supercomputers according to their cost, speed of processing, and capacity.
4. Describe the four categories of applications programs used by business firms.
5. How can an e-mail system increase office productivity and efficiency?

Analysis Questions

6. Give two examples not in this chapter for each of the four major types of application programs used in businesses.

7. Describe the types of work or activities for which a local department store might choose to use batch processing. Do the same for real-time processing.
8. Choose a simple, everyday problem and prepare an artificial intelligence system to help solve it.

Application Exercises

9. Describe the computer system at your college or university. Identify the components of the system (including specific examples of some of the fields, records, and files in its database), the capacity/speed of the system, and its architecture.
10. Visit a small business in your community to investigate how it uses computers and how it plans to use them in the future. Prepare a report to present to your class.

Building Your Business Skills

Goal

To help students understand how organizations use technology and information systems in their day-to-day operations.

Method

Visit a small business in your community—perhaps an insurance agency, a travel agency, or an auto-parts dealer. Determine the various organizational activities linked to the company's information system. Ask employees about the particular uses to which they put the system in order to do their jobs. Ask them whether they have experienced any difficulties using the system. Ask them to describe any significant changes that have occurred in the company's operations since the installation or last upgrade of the system.

Follow-up Questions

1. What information is available on the computer system that you examined? Is it available to everyone in the company?
2. To what extent is the computer system that you examined linked to other computers (for example, to a database at the home office of an insurance company)?

A major technological challenge facing Canadian business is the year 2000 computer problem. To find out more about what Canada is doing to address this dilemma, check out the Year 2000 Web site at:

http://www.strategis.ic.gc.ca/sos2000

1. Look at the Statistics Canada information on Canada's preparedness for the year 2000 computer problem. What statistics or information surprised you? Which are the most alarming? Explain.
2. What business sectors will be hardest hit by the year 2000 problem?
3. What industries have led the way in tackling the year 2000 problem? Why do you think this is so?
4. Consider the businesses and government departments you regularly deal with. How could you be affected by this technology problem?
5. What can a business person with a single personal computer do to prepare himself or herself for the year 2000 problem?

Computerized Cattle

What comes to mind when you hear the phrase "cattle auction?" A bunch of bawling steers in a smelly corral? Think again, because the computer revolution has come to the cattle business. Calgary Stockyards Ltd. conducts most of its business on the "open range of cyberspace" instead of the confined space of the old auction barn.

In the 1970s, the stockyards sold all their cattle at a complex of corrals, loading pens, and barns along the CPR track in Calgary. By 1994, two-thirds of the cattle were marketed by modem from places like Douglas Lake, B.C. Cattle are moved by an on-line system called TEAM (The Electronic Auction Method).

Here's how it works: A single PC is connected by phone lines and modems to buyers in various locations. Buyers get a detailed description of the cattle for sale, but they don't actually see the cattle. Don Danard, president of Calgary Stockyards, sets the starting price, which drops every five seconds until someone makes a bid by hitting the ENTER key. When that happens, the price rises one quarter of a cent with every bid. After 15 seconds have passed without another bid, the seller can accept or reject the last offer on the screen.

As you can imagine, this type of auction is a lot quicker and quieter than the old-fashioned kind. At one recent computer auction, 3600 cattle were sold in two hours; a "live auction" at nearby Strathmore took eight hours to sell just 2500 cattle.

There are other advantages as well. Under the old system, a rancher had to pay to transport cattle to a live auction without knowing what price the cattle would fetch. Now ranchers know the price they will get before their cattle are moved. The system has also allowed large ranchers to avoid rounding up the 2000 or so cattle needed for on-ranch auctions (a practice that caused the animals

stress and reduced the prices they would bring). Now, ranchers can sell smaller lots of cattle—normally 300 to 500—when conditions are right and a good price can be obtained. The rancher rounds up cattle only if a sale is made. Small ranchers also benefit because their cattle are exposed to a larger number of buyers in a computer auction than they would be in a live auction. Another advantage: On a day when it's minus twenty degrees, cattle buyers would rather be looking at a computer screen in a comfortable room than standing out in a corral with a cold wind blowing down their neck.

Some buyers are still suspicious of computer auctions. They feel that buying cattle this way is risky because the person writing up the computer description of the cattle may exaggerate. The operators of TEAM deal with this concern by constantly weeding out individuals who write exaggerated descriptions of their cattle. Other cattle markets are not happy with Calgary Stockyards because they fear the company will take away their business with its new technology. Some of these smaller markets got together and formed the Canadian Satellite Livestock Auction. It shows video clips of cattle to prospective buyers who phone in their bids.

Case Questions

1. What type of computer hardware and software is used in computer auctions?

2. What kinds of attitudes towards computer technology might exist in the minds of cattle buyers? How might these attitudes affect acceptance of the new computer buying system?

3. Summarize the advantages and disadvantages of computer auctions as noted in the case study. What other advantages and disadvantages might exist? ◆

CONCLUDING CASE 18-2

Computing Flower Power

G.A. Vantreight & Sons has grown daffodils on Vancouver Island's Saanich peninsula since the 1930s. Each spring, about 12 million yellow daffodils are picked by seasonal labourers. Vantreight's sells about half of its daffodils to the Canadian Cancer Society, which uses them for its Daffodil Day fundraiser that kicks off its annual April campaign. Other flowers grown by Vantreight are sold to Canada Safeway, wholesale florists, and other retailers.

As serene and slow moving as this business might seem, it has been changed dramatically by computers in the last few years. The big change is a recently-introduced automated payroll system that tracks each worker's production in the field. With the new system, the average worker's output has doubled, labour and production costs have declined, and profits are up.

The system uses 12 portable, hand-held computers, bar-coded packaging tags, bar-coded employee identification badges, and a customized software package called FieldManager designed especially for the company. Under the old system, the names of workers were scribbled on notepads before they were sent to various fields to pick. Errors in keeping track of workers were common. And when it rained (which was often), the notepads got soaked. At the end of the day, the notepads were turned in to the office staff so they could figure out how much each worker should get paid.

With the new system, most of these problems have disappeared. Supervisors now record the output of each worker right in the field by scanning each worker's bar-coded identification that is attached to each bunch of flowers the worker picks. By 3 p.m. each day, the company knows how many flowers have been picked that day. Under the old system, all the company could do was make an educated guess.

The new system has also meant a change in the way workers are paid. Workers, who used to receive a flat $6.50 per hour, are now paid 14 cents for each bunch of 10 flowers they pick. A fast worker can pick enough flowers to earn the equivalent of $11.50 per hour, a big improvement over the flat wage amount. This payment system has reduced the number of pickers employed, but those that do work are much more productive. It has also reduced the farm's unit costs—from 22 cents per bunch to 18 cents per bunch.

The use of computers is just beginning at Vantreight's. The next step is to start tracking bulb production and relate it to actual flower production.

Case Questions

1. How has computerization improved productivity and profits at Vantreight's?

2. From the workers' perspective, what are the disadvantages of the new computer system?

3. What kinds of attitudes towards computer technology might exist in the minds of field workers as they consider the introduction of the new computer system? What attitudes might supervisors and office workers have? How will these attitudes facilitate or inhibit the acceptance of the new system?

◆

19

Understanding Accounting Issues

Accounting for Costs

Traditional cost accounting methods used by Canadian business firms are based on the idea that the primary value in a product is generated by the direct labour of production workers. To determine costs, accountants add together the cost of materials, labour, and overhead (things like R&D, rent, administration expense, etc.) to get a total cost figure. To determine unit cost, total costs are divided by the number of units that are produced.

That accounting system worked well when labour was the biggest part of cost. But today, overhead can be as much as 70 percent of the total cost of a product. The primary value in the product is now usually generated by knowledge workers, not production line workers. Whereas direct labour used to be as high as 35 percent of the cost of goods sold, it is now often less than 10 percent.

A new cost accounting system called *activity-based costing* (ABC) has been developed to help managers figure out how much it actually costs to make specific products or services. Here's how it works: First, all the activities that are necessary to get the product from the raw materials stage to the shipping dock are identified. After the list of activities is developed, ABC focuses on the events that stimulate the activity. For example, an event may be the number of invoices issued, the number of people supervised, the number of sales calls completed, or the number of pallets loaded onto a truck. Then data are gathered on these events and plugged into computer software like NetProphet II. The "bottom line" stays the same, but previously unknown information about costs usually emerges.

To see how ABC works, consider a production line where two kinds of pens are being made—black in high volume and purple in low volume. The total cost includes supplies (which are the same for both kinds of pens), the direct labour of the production line workers who make the pens, and overhead. The most significant overhead cost is the time it takes to switch over from making black to purple or purple to black. Under traditional cost accounting systems, if 10 times as many black pens are made as purple pens, then 10 times the cost of each changeover will be allocated to the black pens. But this obviously understates the cost of producing the low-volume pens. ABC, on the other hand, recognizes the importance of the change-over activity, and charges it against each batch of pens that is made, regardless of the size of the production run. This will clearly yield a higher unit cost for the low volume purple pens.

The ABC system can generate information that causes managers to agonize over some tough decisions. One bakery found that 86 percent of its output was purchased by just 16 percent of its customers. Deliveries to small, owner-operated stores were costing the bakery a fortune. An ABC analysis showed that if the bakery dropped 84 percent of its customers, its profits would triple. But this might not be a wise move strategically. The bakery has not yet decided what to do about this information generated by ABC.

Other firms, faced with the same type of dilemma, have taken decisive action. When Northern Telecom discovered that making a red telephone with French-language packaging cost four times what it thought, it did not stop making the product. Rather, it took action to reduce activity costs. In the process, the company discovered that purchasing 20 percent of the plant's raw materials ate up 80 percent of the purchasing budget. So they decided to pay a little more and get everything from one supplier, thus saving about half a million dollars a year on purchasing activities.

Thorlo Inc. is another company that changed its work processes after an ABC analysis showed that it was losing money on 80 percent of its customers. But Thorlo was loyal to its customers and didn't want to stop selling to them. So, it revised its procedures for dealing with small customers, including the setting up of an entirely separate warehouse that is designed to efficiently deal with small orders. After introducing this system, profits rose 40 percent in one year. ◆

s the 21st century approaches, business firms are facing intense competition, both domestically and internationally. The opening case demonstrates that business firms must be able to accurately compute their business costs or they will not be able to compete. Accounting occupies a central place in the determination of these costs.

Of all the business disciplines, probably none has the universal reach of accounting, which is found in nearly every community in the world. Within most businesses, accountants play a role in virtually all activities. By focusing on the learning objectives of this chapter, you will become acquainted with accountants: who they are, what they do, what concepts and rules they apply, and how these rules are formulated. You will also understand more about the most important part of accounting—the basic financial reports of economic activity that are the primary reason for accounting. After reading this chapter, you should be able to:

LEARNING OBJECTIVES

1. Explain the role of accountants and distinguish between the kinds of work done by *public* and *private accountants*.

2. Explain how the following three concepts are used in *record-keeping*: *accounting equations*, *double-entry accounting*, and *T-accounts* for debits and credits.

3. Describe the three basic *financial statements* and show how they reflect the activity and financial condition of a business.

4. Discuss the importance of *budgets* in internal planning and control.

5. Explain how computing key *financial ratios* can help in analyzing the financial strengths of a business.

6. Explain some of the special issues facing accountants at firms that do international business.

What Is Accounting?

accounting

A comprehensive system for collecting, analyzing, and communicating financial information.

Accounting is a comprehensive information system for collecting, analyzing, and communicating financial information. As such, it is a system for measuring business performance and translating those measures into information for management decisions. Accounting also uses performance measures to prepare performance reports for owners, the public, and regulatory agencies. To meet these objectives, accountants keep records of such transactions as taxes paid, income received, and expenses incurred, and they analyze the effects of these transactions on particular business activities. By sorting, analyzing, and recording thousands of transactions, accountants can determine how well a business is being managed and how financially strong it is.

bookkeeping

Recording accounting transactions.

Bookkeeping, a term that is sometimes confused with accounting, is just one phase of accounting—the recording of accounting transactions. Clearly, accounting is much more comprehensive than bookkeeping because accounting involves more than just the recording of information.

accounting system

An organized procedure for identifying, measuring, recording, and retaining financial information so that it can be used in accounting statements and management reports.

Because businesses engage in many thousands of transactions, ensuring consistent, dependable financial information is mandatory. This is the job of the **accounting system**: an organized procedure for identifying, measuring, recording, and retaining financial information so that it can be used in accounting statements and management reports. The system includes all the people, reports, computers, procedures, and resources for compiling financial transactions.[1]

Users of Accounting Information

There are numerous users of accounting information:

- *Business managers* use accounting information to set goals, develop plans, set budgets, and evaluate future prospects.
- *Employees and unions* use accounting information to get paid and to plan for and receive such benefits as health care, insurance, vacation time, and retirement pay.
- *Investors and creditors* use accounting information to estimate returns to stockholders, to determine a company's growth prospects, and to decide if it is a good credit risk before investing or lending.
- *Taxing authorities* use accounting information to plan for tax inflows, to determine the tax liabilities of individuals and businesses, and to ensure that correct amounts are paid in a timely fashion.
- *Government regulatory agencies* rely on accounting information to fulfil their duties; the provincial securities commissions, for example, require firms to file financial disclosures so that potential investors have valid information about a company's financial status.

Who Are Accountants and What Do They Do?

At the head of the accounting system is the **controller**, who manages all the firm's accounting activities. As chief accounting officer, the controller ensures that the accounting system provides the reports and statements needed for planning, controlling, and decision-making activities. This broad range of activities requires different types of accounting specialists. In this section, we will begin by distinguishing between the two main fields of accounting, *financial* and *managerial*. Then we will discuss the different functions and activities of *chartered accountants* and *private accountants*. The box "Certification Programs in Accounting and Finance" describes the various careers open to students interested in these areas.

controller
The individual who manages all the firm's accounting activities.

A financial report is an integral component of the financial accounting system.

The Canadian Business Scene

Certification Programs in Accounting and Finance

Not too long ago, a professional certificate in accounting meant the CA or Chartered Accountant. To become a CA, a person must earn a university degree, complete an accounting-oriented education program, and then pass a national exam. About half of all CAs work in public accounting firms (CA firms). These firms give external opinions on their clients' financial statements. The other half work in business, government, and non-profit organizations. The main emphasis in CA work is on financial accounting, auditing, and taxation accounting.

In recent years, accounting and financial skills have become increasingly specialized. In addition to the CA, the following certification programs are now available.

■ *Certified General Accountant (CGA).* To become a CGA, a person must complete an education program and pass a national exam. To be eligible, a person must have an accounting job with a company. There are fewer CGAs than CAs, and in some provinces they are not allowed to give opinions on financial statements of publicly held companies. Almost all CGAs work in private companies, but there are a few CGA firms. Some CGAs work in CA firms.

■ *Certified Management Accountant (CMA).* The goal of the CMA program is to train accountants for industry. To become a CMA, a person must have an accounting position with a company and must complete an education program. Unlike CAs, CMAs have management accounting as their focus. That is, they are concerned about internal uses of accounting data rather than their external uses, as are CAs.

■ *Certified Financial Analyst (CFA).* To earn the CFA designation, a person must complete a three-year self-study program and pass a series of three national exams of increasing difficulty. These exams deal with securities regulations, investments, and related topics.

The CFA designation is granted only to people who hold jobs in the securities industry (e.g., investment bankers, stock brokers, securities analysts, etc.).

■ *Certified Financial Planner.* This is a two-year course of studies that is relevant for those who will be advising clients with respect to retirement planning, tax planning, and the setting up of investment programs. There are six courses at six levels that must be taken. There is an exam at the end of each course, as well as a national exam at the end of the six courses. Courses can be taken by correspondence or in-class.

■ *Canadian Securities Course (CSC).* The CSC is a mandatory licensing requirement for people training to become investment advisors. Courses are offered by correspondence for people in the financial services industry (e.g., mutual fund salespeople, financial planners, bank employees, etc.). The course is designed to increase the competency levels of people working in the securities and financial services industry. To complete the one-year course, students must pass a three-hour exam.

■ *Registered Financial Planner.* This designation is offered by the Canadian Association of Financial Planners, and is relevant for individuals who are helping people with financial planning needs. The course, which is open only to individuals who are members of the Association, is a self-study course. A six-hour exam must be passed before the designation is granted. There are no formal classes required, but the Association does offer a series of financial planning seminars that are helpful in studying for the exam. The time required to earn the designation varies depending on how much experience and knowledge the person has.

Financial and Managerial Accounting

In any company, two fields of accounting—financial and managerial—can be distinguished by the different users they serve. As we have just seen, it is both convenient and accurate to classify users of accounting information as users outside the company and users inside the company. This same distinction allows us to categorize accounting systems as either *financial* or *managerial*.

financial accounting system
The process whereby interested groups are kept informed about the financial condition of a firm.

Financial Accounting

A firm's **financial accounting system** is concerned with *external* users of information—consumer groups, unions, shareholders, and government agencies.

It prepares and publishes income statements and balance sheets at regular intervals. All of these documents focus on the activities of *the company as a whole*, rather than on individual departments or divisions.

In reporting data, financial accountants must conform to standard reporting formats and procedures imposed by both the accounting profession and government regulatory agencies. This requirement helps ensure that users can clearly compare information, whether from many different companies or from the same company at different times. The information in such reports is mostly *historical*: That is, it summarizes financial transactions that have occurred during past accounting periods.

Managerial Accounting

In contrast, **managerial** (or **management**) **accounting** serves *internal* users. Managers at all levels need information to make decisions for their departments, to monitor current projects, and to plan for future activities. Other employees, too, need accounting information. Engineers, for instance, want to know costs for materials and production so they can make product or operations improvements. To set performance goals, salespeople need data on past sales by geographic region. Purchasing agents use information on materials costs to negotiate terms with suppliers.

managerial accounting
Internal procedures that alert managers to problems and aid them in planning and decision making.

Reports to these users serve *the company's individual units*, whether departments, projects, plants, or divisions. Internal reports may be designed in any form that will assist internal users in planning, decision making, and controlling. Furthermore, as *projections and forecasts* of both financial data and business activities, internal reports are an extremely important part of the management accounting system: They are forward-looking rather than historical in nature.

Public Accountants

Although public accountants are not the most common type of accountants, they are probably the best known. **Chartered accountants** (CAs) derive their name from the fact that they are members of firms who offer their accounting services to the public. They are also licensed provincially based on the results of a rigorous examination.[2] The Canadian Institute of Chartered Accountants prepares the CA examination. It also provides technical support to its members and discipline in matters of professional ethics.

chartered accountant (CA)
An individual who has met certain experience and education requirements and has passed a licensing examination; acts as an outside accountant for other firms.

While some CAs work as individual practitioners, many join with one or more other CAs in a partnership. Table 19.1 lists the 10 largest CA firms in Canada.

Virtually all CA firms—whether they boast 10 000 employees and 100 offices or just one person in a tiny office—provide three types of services: audit services, tax services, and management services. The larger CA firms earn about 60 to 70 percent of their revenue from audit services. Smaller firms typically earn most of their income from tax and management services.

Auditing

In an **audit**, the accountant examines a company's accounting system to determine whether the company's financial reports fairly present its financial operations. Companies normally must provide audited financial reports when applying for loans or when selling stock.

audit
An accountant's examination of a company's financial records to determine if it used proper procedures to prepare its financial reports.

The audit will determine if the firm has controls to prevent errors or fraud from going undetected. Auditors also examine receipts such as shipping

Table 19.1   The Top 10 Accounting Firms in Canada, Ranked by Revenues, 1996

Company	Revenues (in millions)
1. KPMG	$524.7
2. Deloitte & Touche	499.0
3. Ernst & Young	415.0
4. Coopers & Lybrand	333.5
5. Andersen Worldwide Canada	300.0
6. Price Waterhouse	279.0
7. Doane Raymond Grant Thornton	202.9
8. BDO Dunwoody	132.0
9. Richter, Usher & Vineberg	62.0
10. Collins Barrow	31.1

forensic accountant

An accountant who tracks down hidden funds in business firms, usually as part of a criminal investigation.

generally accepted accounting principles (GAAP)

Standard rules and methods used by accountants in preparing financial reports.

Canadian Institute of Chartered Accountants

http://www.cica.com

documents, cancelled cheques, payroll records, and cash receipts records. In some cases, an auditor may physically check inventories, equipment, or other assets, even if it means descending 200 metres underground in a lead mine.

Forensic accountants are special types of accountants who track down hidden funds in business firms. Because white-collar crime is on the increase, the number of forensic accountants has increased in recent years. They were used to unravel the Daiwa Bank and Barings Bank scandals. They are also examining Swiss bank accounts for assets deposited by victims of Nazi persecution during World War II.[3]

One of the auditor's responsibilities is to make sure the client's accounting system adheres to generally accepted accounting principles. **Generally accepted accounting principles** (**GAAP**) are a body of theory and procedure developed and monitored by the Canadian Institute of Chartered Accountants (CICA), a professional accounting organization. At the end of an audit, the auditor will certify whether or not the client's financial reports comply with GAAP.

Some large accounting firms—particularly the so-called "Big Six" in the U.S.—are beginning to reject audit clients that they deem to be high risk. The accounting firms say that they have been sued so often in recent years over allegedly faulty audits that they are now spending more than 15 percent of their audit revenue on liability insurance premiums. Since 1994, the Big Six firms have dropped a total of 275 clients.[4] The box "Who Can We Blame for This Mess?" describes some additional problems in auditing.

Recently, some non-profit organizations such as churches and universities have said that they felt pressured by their auditors to use GAAP. They argue, however, that GAAP principles are designed for profit-seeking business firms, not non-profit organizations. Non-profits should be judged on how well they meet their goals—for example, helping people—rather than on a financial criterion like profit.[5]

Tax Services

Tax services include helping clients not only with preparing their tax returns but also in their tax planning. Tax laws are complex. A CA's advice can help a business structure (or restructure) its operations and investments and save millions of dollars in taxes. To best serve their clients, of course, accountants must stay abreast of changes in tax laws—no simple matter.

The Canadian Business Scene

Who Can We Blame for This Mess?

The accounting profession has come under increased pressure during the 1990s, partly as a result of fallout from the unexpected failures of the Canadian Commercial Bank and the Northland Bank. It now seems that every time a business firm fails, there is talk of suing the CA firm that audited its books. The average person simply does not understand how a business firm can suddenly fail right after it has just been audited by a CA firm, particularly after the CA firm certifies that the business adhered to generally accepted accounting principles.

Some people think that auditors should expand their reports or clarify their language so that readers of financial statements will have a better idea of how a company is doing before they invest in it. Others suggest that auditors should give more consideration to the users of financial statements, and perhaps provide specific financial reporting for different user groups. Perhaps auditors should be charged with detecting fraud and reporting it when they find it.

Individuals in the accounting profession recognize that there is a "chummy" relationship between CA firms and their clients. There is also considerable elasticity in the application of generally accepted accounting principles. Some critics argue that business firms should be required to change their auditors every five years to prevent these relationships from developing.

Because of several visible business failures in Canada and the U.S., liability insurance premiums have risen sharply, coverage has been reduced, and deductability limits have been increased. Interestingly, the smaller accounting firms have not faced big increases, mainly because they do not generally audit the books of large firms (the ones who get sued for megabucks).

Big firms attract big clients, and when a big firm is sued, the suit frequently names the firm's auditor as well. At the end of 1992, for example, outstanding claims against the six biggest accounting firms in the U.S. totalled $30 billion. The most notable Canadian case involved Coopers & Lybrand, with claims against that firm totalling $500 million.

In 1993, the Canadian Life & Health Insurance Compensation Corp. (better known as Comp-Corp.), which was set up to protect holders of policies issued by insolvent companies, sued the CA firm of Mallette Maheu for negligence. It claimed Mallette made errors that forced Comp-Corp. to pay over $93 million in claims to policyholders of Les Cooperants, the failed insurance company. Comp-Corp. claimed that Mallette employees made errors that allowed Les Cooperants Insurance Group to report a profit of over $3 million in 1989, whereas the company actually lost $21 million. Mallette Maheu said the suit was frivolous and unfounded.

There are interesting legal ramifications of these lawsuits. In the simplest case, both a corporation and its auditor may be sued. But even if they are both found negligent, and if the courts decide that the auditor is 20 percent responsible, the accounting firm may have to pay the entire bill if the business firm has no money (which is likely, since it went bankrupt). And its gets worse. In theory, since accounting firms are partnerships, the partners have unlimited liability. In a big settlement, the partners' personal assets could be seized to pay the legal judgment.

Management Services

Management services range from personal financial planning to planning corporate mergers. Other services include plant layout and design, marketing studies, production scheduling, computer feasibility studies, and design and implementation of accounting systems. Some CA firms even assist in executive recruitment. Small wonder that the staffs of CA firms include engineers, architects, mathematicians, and even psychologists.

Private Accountants

To assure the fairness of their reports, CAs must be independent of the firms they audit. They are employees of accounting firms and provide services for many clients. But businesses also hire their own **private accountants** as salaried employees to deal with the company's day-to-day accounting needs.

Private accountants perform a variety of accounting jobs. An internal auditor at Petro-Canada, for example, might fly to the Hibernia site to confirm the accuracy of oil-flow meters on the offshore drilling platform. But a supervisor responsible for $200 million in monthly accounts payable to ven-

private accountant
An accountant hired as a salaried employee to deal with a company's day-to-day accounting needs.

This advertisement by the chartered accountant and management consulting firm of Deloitte & Touche is directed towards services that will help small businesses that are managed by their owners.

Deloitte & Touche
http://www.deloitte.ca

dors and employees may travel no further than the executive suite. The nature of the accounting job thus depends on the specific business and the activities needed to make that business a success.

Large businesses employ specialized accountants in such areas as budgets, financial planning, internal auditing, payroll, and taxation. Each accounting area has its own challenges and excitement. In small businesses, a single individual may handle all accounting tasks—and approve credit terms, too!

The box "Is There a 'Preparation Gap' in Accounting?" describes some concerns about the training that accountants receive.

Tools of the Accounting Trade

All accountants, whether public or private, rely on record-keeping. Private accountants use journals and ledgers to enter and keep track of business transactions for their company. Underlying these records are the two key concepts of accounting: the accounting equation and double-entry bookkeeping.[6]

Record-Keeping with Journals and Ledgers

As Figure 19.1 shows, record-keeping begins with initial records of the firm's financial transactions. Examples include sales orders, invoices for incoming materials, employee time cards, and customer payments on instalment purchases. Large companies receive and process tens of thousands of these documents every day. But unless they are analyzed and classified in an orderly fashion, managers cannot keep track of the business's progress.

Notations of the sorted records are entered into a journal, an intermediate form of record, as the initial records are received. A **journal** is just a chronological record of financial transactions along with a brief description of the transaction. Some companies keep only a single (general) journal. Others keep specialized journals for cash receipts, sales, purchases, and the

journal
A chronological record of a firm's financial transactions along with a brief description of each transaction.

International Report

Is There a "Preparation Gap" in Accounting?

Here is a pertinent question: Are university and college students learning the right things in their accounting courses? Not according to a report issued by the Institute of Management Accountants and the Financial Executives Institute. The report charges that "a preparation gap exists between the needs of today's lean, global, technologically savvy corporations and the accounting graduates." After surveying hundreds of financial executives, Professor Gary Siegel reports that "few college courses focus enough on business budgeting, cost accounting, and how to manage working capital, which is what companies need." Instead, says Siegel, too many college courses emphasize auditing, taxes, and other studies that would be most useful to someone preparing for a career with a public accounting firm. In reality, however, only about one third of accounting students end up working for such firms.

Steven R. Berlin, senior vice-president of finance at Citgo Petroleum Corp., agrees with Siegel. "Today's accounting students," he says, "don't hit the ground running. We need students who are more imaginative at seeing the strategic direction our business is taking." To deal with the problem, many firms are taking the initiative. At pharmaceutical giant Johnson&Johnson, for instance, newly hired accounting staffers are urged to take evening MBA courses or to study for the CPA exam (the U.S. equivalent to the CA exam). "Most accounting graduates," complains J&J finance executive Clark H. Johnson, "just aren't well-prepared for business."

Meanwhile, what, if anything, are colleges and universities doing to address the problem? Internships that provide students with real-world accounting experience can help. Another option is a seminar that requires each student to work with a local business to identify an actual accounting problem and propose a solution by semester's end. A graduate seminar at the University of Georgia focuses on corporate accounting policy. The objective, according to Professor James Don Edwards, "is to help students go beyond the traditional 'correct-solution' mentality and acquire the multidimensional mindset that decision makers need when using financial statements." At California State University, emphasis is placed on coordinating accounting with other functional areas (such as marketing and information systems) and understanding the environmental factors that affect a business or industry. The Faculty of Management at the University of Manitoba is also testing a new way of teaching accounting patterned on the California State University idea.

Institute of Management Accountants
http://www.rutgers.edu/Accounting/raw/ima/ima.htm

Financial Executives Institute
http://www.fei.org

ACCOUNTING is a comprehensive system for

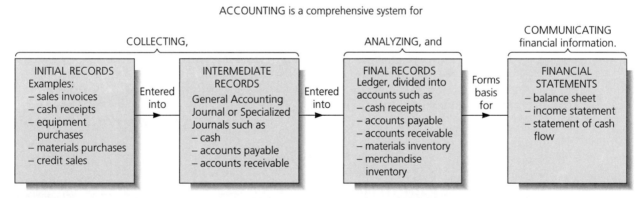

Figure 19.1
Accounting and record-keeping.

---

like. For centuries, journals were kept by hand but, today, many firms use computers for their record-keeping.

Transactions from a company's journal(s) are brought together and summarized, usually monthly, in final records called **ledgers**. Ledgers are divided into categories (accounts) similar to those of specialized journals. Unlike journals, accounts in a ledger contain only minimal descriptions of transactions. But they do contain an important additional column, labelled "Balance," as shown

ledger
Summations of journal entries, by category, that show the effects of transactions on the balance in each account.

in Figure 19.4 (see page 588). (We will explore the meaning of the debit and credit columns shortly.) Because of this column, ledgers enable managers to tell at a glance where the company stands. If the balance is unexpectedly high or low, accountants and other managers can track backward to the corresponding journal entry to see what has caused the unexpected balance.

Finally, at the end of the year, accountants total up all the accounts in a firm's ledger and assess the business's financial status. This summation is the basis for annual financial reports. With the preparation of financial reports, the old *accounting cycle* ends and a new cycle begins.

To clarify this record-keeping process, consider Figure 19.2, which illustrates a portion of the process for Perfect Posters Inc. Notice how the cheque from Eye Poppers (an initial record) has been entered in the firm's general accounting journal (an intermediate record). As you can see, this entry eventually turns up in Perfect Poster's ledgers (a final record). And as we will discuss in the next section, these ledger entries are ultimately reflected in the financial reports that Perfect Posters needs for its shareholders and bank.

The Accounting Equation

At various points in the year, public and private accountants balance the data in journals and ledgers by using the following accounting equation:

$$\text{Assets} = \text{Liabilities} + \text{Owners' equity}$$

To understand why this equation is important, you must first understand what accountants mean by assets, liabilities, and owners' equity.

You are probably familiar with the first two terms in their general sense. Charm and intelligence are often said to be "assets." Someone who cannot swim may be a "liability" on a boat trip. Accountants apply these terms more narrowly, focusing on items with quantifiable value. Thus an **asset**, in the accounting sense, is anything of economic value owned by the firm. Examples include land, buildings, equipment, inventory, and payments due the company. In contrast, a **liability** is a debt owed by the firm to others.

Finally, you may have heard people speak of the "equity" they have in their home, meaning the amount of money they would get if they sold the house and paid off the mortgage. Similarly, **owners' equity** refers to the

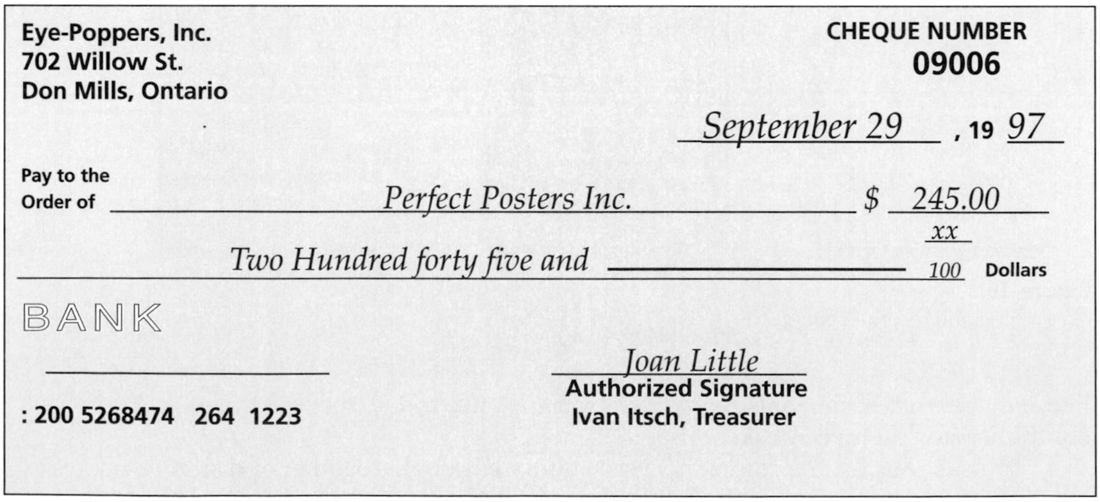

asset
Anything of economic value owned by a firm or individual.

liability
Any debt owed by a firm or individual to others.

owners' equity
Any positive difference between a firm's assets and its liabilities; what would remain for a firm's owners if the company were liquidated, all its assets sold, and all its debts paid.

Eye-Poppers, Inc.	**CHEQUE NUMBER**
702 Willow St.	**09006**
Don Mills, Ontario	

September 29 , 19 _97_

Pay to the
Order of _____ _Perfect Posters Inc._ _____ $ _245.00_

Two Hundred forty five and _____ xx / 100 **Dollars**

BANK

: 200 5268474 264 1223

_____ _Joan Little_
Authorized Signature
Ivan Itsch, Treasurer

Figure 19.2
Record-keeping at Perfect Posters Inc. traces the path of every financial transaction, such as this cheque from a customer, showing how it affects each financial category.

amount of money a firm's owners would receive if they sold all the company's assets and paid off all its liabilities (*liquidated* the company). We can rewrite the accounting equation to show this definition:

$$Assets \ - \ Liabilities \ = \ Owners' \ equity$$

If a company's assets exceed its liabilities, owners' equity is positive: If the company goes out of business, the owners will receive some cash (a gain) after selling assets and paying off liabilities. If liabilities outweigh assets, however, owners' equity is negative: There are insufficient assets to pay off all debts. If the company goes out of business, the owners will get no cash and some creditors will not be paid. Finally, owners' equity is also a meaningful number of both investors and lenders. For example, before lending money to owners, lenders want to know the amount of owners' equity existing in a business.

Owners' equity consists of two sources of capital:

- the amount that the owners originally invested
- profits earned by and reinvested in the company.

For example, when a company operates profitably, its assets increase faster than its liabilities. Owners' equity, therefore, will increase if profits are kept in the business instead of paid out as dividends to shareholders. Owners' equity can also increase if owners invest more of their own money to increase assets. However, owners' equity can shrink if the company operates at a loss or if the owners withdraw assets.

Double-Entry Accounting

If your business purchases inventory with cash, you do *two* things: (1) decrease your cash and (2) increase your inventory. Similarly, if you purchase supplies on credit, you (1) increase your supplies and (2) increase your accounts payable. If you invest more money in your business, you (1) increase your cash and (2) increase your owners' equity. In other words, *every transaction affects two accounts*. Accountants thus use a **double-entry accounting system** to record the *dual effects* of financial transactions.

Recording dual effects ensures that the accounting equation always balances. As the term implies, the double-entry system requires at least two bookkeeping entries for each transaction. This practice keeps the accounting equation in balance.

double-entry accounting system
A bookkeeping system, developed in the 15th century and still in use, that requires every transaction to be entered in two ways—how it affects assets and how it affects liabilities and owners' equity—so that the accounting equation is always in balance.

Debits and Credits: The T-Account

Another accounting tool uses *debits* and *credits* as a universal method for keeping accounting records. To understand debits and credits, we first need to understand the **T-account**. The format for recording transactions takes the shape of a **T** whose vertical line divides the account into two sides. The **T** format for Perfect Posters' General Accounting Journal is shown in Figure 19.3.

T-account
An accounting format that divides an account into a debit and a credit side.

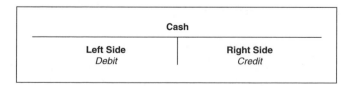

Figure 19.3
This unnumbered/unlabelled general accounting journal T format divides an account into two sides.

In bookkeeping, *debit* and *credit* refer to the side on which account information is to be entered: The left column of any T-account is called the *debit* side, and the right column is the *credit* side:

$$debit = left\ side$$

$$credit = right\ side$$

debit

In bookkeeping, any transaction that increases assets or decreases liabilities or owners' equity; always entered in the left column.

credit

In bookkeeping, any transaction that decreases assets or increases liabilities or owners' equity; always entered in the right column.

When an asset increases, it is entered as a **debit**. When it decreases, it is entered as a **credit**. Thus when Perfect Posters received payment from Eye-Poppers, it received more cash—an asset. It thus debited the General Accounting Journal (Figure 19.4) by placing $245 on the left side of that T-account.

Figure 19.5 shows how the rules of the T-account are consistent with the terms of the accounting equation. Debits and credits provide a system of checks and balances. Every debit entry in a journal must have an offsetting credit entry elsewhere (not shown here). If not, the books will not balance because some error (or deliberate deception) has been introduced in the record-keeping. To ensure accurate financial records, accountants must find and correct such errors.

The double-entry system, therefore, provides an important method of accounting control: At the end of the accounting cycle, debits and credits must balance. In other words, total debits must equal total credits in the account balances recorded in the general ledger. An imbalance indicates improper accounting that must be corrected. "Balancing the books," then, is a control procedure to ensure that proper accounting has been used.

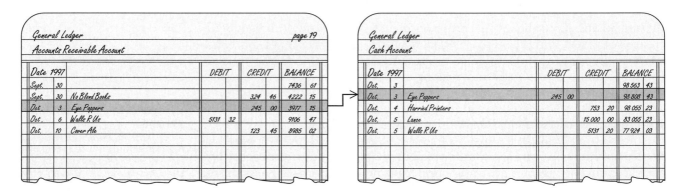

Figure 19.4
Under the double-entry accounting system, this cheque from a customer increases the Cash Balance and decreases the Accounts Receivable Balance.

Accounting Equation Rules of the T-Account	Assets		=	Liabilities		+	Owner's Equity	
	Debit for Increase	Credit for Decrease		Debit for Decrease	Credit for Increase		Debit for Decrease	Credit for Increase

Figure 19.5
In both the T-account and the accounting equation, debits and credits provide a system of checks and balances.

Financial Statements

As we noted earlier, the primary purpose of accounting is to summarize the results of a business's transactions and to issue reports that can help managers and others make informed decisions. Some of the most important reports, called **financial statements**, fall into several broad categories: balance sheets, income statements, and statements of cash flows. Balance sheets are sometimes called statements of financial position because they show the financial condition of a firm at one time. Other financial statements summarize the economic activities that have occurred during a specified period, usually one year. Together, these statements provide a picture of a business's financial health: what it is worth, how much it earns, and how it spends its resources.[7] Misleading financial statements can be very costly to investors.

financial statement
Any of several types of broad reports regarding a company's financial status; most often used in reference to balance sheets, income statements, and/or statements of cash flows.

Balance Sheets

At one time, the only financial statement released to external users (such as shareholders and lenders) was the **balance sheet**. Early balance sheets provided sketchy information. Today, balance sheets supply a considerable amount of information including detailed, technical descriptions of complex accounts and transactions. Balance sheets present the accounting equation factors: a company's assets, its liabilities, and its owners' equity. Figure 19.6 shows a balance sheet for Perfect Posters.

balance sheet
A type of financial statement that summarizes a firm's financial position on a particular date in terms of its assets, liabilities, and owners' equity.

Assets

Most companies have three types of assets from an accounting standpoint: current, fixed, and intangible. **Current assets** include cash and assets that can or will be converted into cash in the following year. They are normally listed in order of **liquidity**, which refers to how quickly they can be converted into cash or used up. Business debts normally can be satisfied only through payments of cash. A company that cannot generate cash easily as needed (in other words, a company that is not liquid) may be forced to sell assets at sacrifice prices or even to go out of business.

Cash is, by definition, completely liquid. Marketable securities are slightly less liquid but can be sold quickly if there is a need for additional cash. Stocks or bonds of other companies and government securities such as treasury bills are all marketable securities. **Accounts receivable** are amounts due from customers who have purchased goods on credit. Most businesses expect to receive payment within 30 days of a sale.

Following accounts receivable is **merchandise inventory**, the cost of merchandise that has been acquired for sale to customers but is still on hand. Merchandise inventory is two steps removed from cash: first the inventory must be sold, generating accounts receivable, and then the accounts receivable must be collected to obtain cash.

The final current asset listed is **prepaid expenses**. Included in this category would be supplies on hand and rent paid for the period to come. In all, Perfect Posters's current assets as of December 31, 1997, totalled $57 210.

Normally, the next major balance sheet classification is **fixed assets**. Items in this category have long-term use or value, for example, land, buildings, and equipment. Because buildings and equipment do eventually wear out or become obsolete, however, the accountant has depreciated them.

current assets
Cash and other assets that can be converted into cash in the following year.

liquidity
The ease and speed with which an asset can be converted to cash; cash is said to be perfectly liquid.

accounts receivable
Amounts due to the firm from customers who have purchased goods or services on credit; a form of current asset.

merchandise inventory
The cost of merchandise that has been acquired for sale to customers but is still on hand.

prepaid expense
Includes supplies on hand and rent paid for the period to come.

fixed assets
Assets that have long-term use or value to the firm such as land, buildings, and machinery.

Perfect Posters, Inc.
555 Riverview, Toronto, Ontario

Perfect Posters, Inc.
Balance Sheet
As of December 31, 1997

Assets

Current Assets:

Cash		$7,050
Marketable securities		2,300
Accounts receivable	$26,210	
Less: Allowance of doubtful accounts	(650)	25,560
Merchandise inventory		21,250
Prepaid expenses		1,050
Total current assets		**$57,210**

Fixed Assets: Land		18,000	
Building	65,000		
Less: Accumulated depreciation	(22,500)	42,500	
Equipment	72,195		
Less: Accumulated depreciation	(24,815)	47,380	
Total fixed assets			**107,880**

Intangible Assets:

Patents	7,100	
Trademarks	900	
Total intangible assets		**8,000**
Total assets		**$173,090**

Liabilities and Owners' Equity

Current liabilities:

Accounts payable	$16,315	
Wages payable	3,700	
Taxes payable	1,920	
Total current liabilities		**$21,935**

Long-term liabilities:

Notes payable, 8% due 2001	10,000	
Bonds payable, 9% due 2005	30,000	
Total long-term liabilities		**40,000**
Total liabilities		**$61,935**

Owners' Equity

Common stock, $5 par	40,000	
Additional paid-in capital	15,000	
Retained earnings	56,155	
Total owners' equity		**111,155**
Total liabilities and owners' equity		**$173,090**

Figure 19.6
Perfect Posters, Inc. balance sheet as of December 31, 1997.

depreciation

Distributing the cost of a major asset over the years in which it produces revenues; calculated by each year subtracting the asset's original value divided by the number of years in its productive life.

intangible assets

Nonphysical assets such as patents, trade marks, copyrights, and franchise fees, that have economic value but whose precise value is difficult to calculate.

current liabilities

Any debts owed by the firm that must be repaid within the year.

accounts payable

Amounts due from the firm to its suppliers for goods and/or services purchased on credit; a form of current liability.

Depreciation means calculating the useful life of the asset, dividing its worth by that many years, and then subtracting the resulting amount each year. That is, the asset's remaining value on the books goes down each year. In Figure 19.6, Perfect Posters has fixed assets of $107 880 after depreciation.

Despite their name, intangible assets are not without monetary value, although their worth is hard to set. **Intangible assets** usually consist of the cost to obtain rights or privileges such as patents, trade marks, copyrights, and franchise fees. Another intangible asset, *goodwill*, can be recorded only when a business is being bought. It is the amount paid for an existing business over and above the value of its other assets because the firm has a particularly good reputation or good location. Perfect Posters has intangible assets of $8000 in patents for specialized equipment it designed to store posters vertically in the warehouse and for trade marks it owns.

Liabilities

Like assets, liabilities are separated into different categories, in this case, current liabilities and long-term liabilities. **Current liabilities** are debts that must be paid within the year. They include unpaid bills to suppliers for materials (**accounts payable**) as well as wages and taxes that will have to be paid in the coming year. Note in Figure 19.6 that Perfect Posters has current liabilities of $21 935.

Debts that are not due within one year are called **long-term liabilities**. They normally represent borrowed funds on which the company must pay interest. Perfect Posters's long-term liabilities are $40 000.

long-term liabilities
Any debts owed by the firm that need not be repaid within the year.

Owners' Equity

The final section of the balance sheet shows owners' equity broken down into common stock, paid-in capital, and retained earnings. When Perfect Posters was formed, the declared legal value of stock was $5 per share. By law, this $40 000 ($5 × 8000 shares) cannot be distributed as dividends. **Paid-in capital** is additional money invested in the firm by the owners.

paid-in capital
Any additional money invested in the firm by the owners.

A company's net profits less dividend payments to shareholders are its **retained earnings**. Retained earnings accumulate when profits, which could have been distributed to shareholders, are instead kept for use by the company. Perfect Posters has total paid-in capital of $55 000 (from common stock plus additional paid-in capital) and retained earnings of $56 155.

retained earnings
A company's net profits less any dividend payments to shareholders.

Income Statements

Perhaps the most popular form of financial statement is the **income statement**. It is sometimes called a **profit-and-loss statement** because its description of a company's revenues and expenses results in a figure of the firm's profit or loss. That is,

income (profit-and-loss) statement
A type of financial statement that describes a firm's revenues and expenses and indicates whether the firm has earned a profit or suffered a loss during a given period.

$$\text{Revenues} - \text{Expenses} = \text{Profit (or Loss)}$$

An income statement enables the reader to assess how effectively management is using the resources entrusted to it. Figure 19.7 shows an income statement for Perfect Posters.

Revenues

The first major category shown on an income statement is revenues. **Revenues** are the value of the resources that flow into a business from selling products or providing services. The $250 a law firm receives for preparing a will and the $65 a supermarket receives from a customer for groceries are both revenue. Perfect Posters reported revenues of $256 425 from the sale of the art prints and other posters it supplies to retailers.

revenues
Any monies received by a firm as a result of selling a good or service or from other sources such as interest, rent, and licensing fees.

Fixed assets at this Coca-Cola bottling plant include the building and equipment that fills the bottles and moves them through production.

```
□□□□□□□□□□□□□    Perfect Posters, Inc.
                       555 Riverview, Toronto, Ontario
```

Perfect Posters, Inc.
Income Statement
Year ended December 31, 1997

Revenues (gross sales)		**$256,425**
Costs of goods sold:		
Merchandise inventory,		
January 1, 1997	$22,380	
Merchandise purchases		
during year	103,635	
Goods available for sale		$126,015
Less: Merchandise inventory,		
December 31, 1997		21,250
Cost of goods sold		104,765
Gross profit		**151,660**
Operating expenses:		
Selling and repackaging expenses:		
Salaries and wages	49,750	
Advertising	6,380	
Depreciation-warehouse and		
repackaging equipment	3,350	
Total selling and repackaging		
expenses		59,480
Administrative expenses:		
Salaries and wages	55,100	
Supplies	4,150	
Utilities	3,800	
Depreciation-office equipment	3,420	
Interest expense	2,900	
Miscellaneous expenses	1,835	
Total administration expenses		71,205
Total operating expenses		**130,685**
Income before taxes		20,975
Income taxes		8,390
Net income		**$12,585**

Figure 19.7
Perfect Posters, Inc. income statement for year ended December 31, 1997.

Cost of Goods Sold

cost of goods sold

Any expenses directly involved in producing or selling a good or service during a given time period.

The next section of the income statement details expenses involved in producing goods—the **cost of goods sold**. This category shows the costs of obtaining materials to make the products that were sold during the year. Perfect Posters, for example, started the year with posters valued at $22 380 in the warehouse. During the year it bought $103 635 more of these posters for a total of $126 015 worth of merchandise available to sell during 1997. By the end of the year it had sold all but $21 250 of the posters, which remained as "merchandise inventory" on December 31. So the firm's cost to obtain the goods it sold was $104 765.

gross profit (gross margin)

A firm's revenues (gross sales) less its cost of goods sold.

Subtracting cost of goods sold from revenues gives us **gross profit** (or **gross margin**). Perfect Posters's gross profit was $151 660 ($256 425–$104 765).

Operating Expenses

In addition to costs directly related to acquiring the goods it sells, every company has general operating expenses, ranging from erasers to the president's salary. Like cost of goods sold, **operating expenses** are resources that must flow out of a company for it to earn revenues. Perfect Posters had operating expenses of $59 480 in selling and repackaging expenses and $71 205 in administrative expenses for a total of $130 685.

Subtracting operating expenses and income taxes from gross margin yields **net income** (also called **net profit** or **net earnings**). As Figure 19.7 shows, in 1997, Perfect Posters's net income was $12 585. Remember that the net income figure can only be computed after many assumptions have been made and much data analyzed.

operating expenses

Costs incurred by a firm other than those included in cost of goods sold.

net income (net profit or net earnings)

A firm's gross profit less its operating expenses and income taxes.

Statement of Changes in Cash Flows

A balance sheet and an income statement are the only financial reports some companies prepare. But a third report, a **statement of cash flows**, is also important. This statement describes a company's cash receipts and cash payments for the year. Since it provides the most detail about the company's ability to generate and use cash, some investors and creditors consider it the most important statement of all. A statement of cash flows, like that in Figure 19.8 for Perfect Posters, shows the effects on cash of three aspects of the business: operations, investing, and financing.

statement of cash flows

A financial statement that describes a firm's generation and use of cash during a given period.

❑❑❑❑❑❑❑❑❑❑❑❑❑ **Perfect Posters, Inc.**
555 Riverview, Toronto, Ontario

Perfect Posters, Inc.
Statement of Cash Flows
Year ended December 31, 1997
Increase (Decrease) in Cash

Cash flows from operating activities:		
Net income		$12,585
Adjustments to reconcile net income to		
net cash provided by operating activities:		
Depreciation	$ 6,770	
Decrease in merchandise inventory	1,130	
Increase in accounts receivable	(2,165)	
Increase in accounts payable	3,215	
Total adjustments		8,950
Net cash provided by		
operating activities		**21,535**
Cash flows from investing activities:		
Payment for purchase of land	(10,000)	
Payment for purchase of equipment	(13,495)	
Net cash used in investing activities		**(23,495)**
Cash flows from financing activities		
Proceeds from issuance of long-term note	10,000	
Dividends paid	(6,000)	
Net cash provided by financing		
activities		**4,000**
Net increase in cash		2,040
Cash at beginning of year		5,010
Cash at end of year		**$ 7,050**

Figure 19.8
Perfect Posters, Inc. statement of cash flows for year ended December 31, 1997. Increase (decrease) in cash.

Cash Flows from Operations

The first section of the statement is concerned with the firm's main operating activities—cash transactions in buying and selling goods and services. Perfect Posters's main operations provided cash of $21 535.

Cash Flows from Investing

This section reports net cash used in or provided by investing. It includes cash receipts and payments from buying and selling stocks, bonds, property, equipment, and other productive assets. Perfect Posters's purchases of land and equipment used $23 495 of net cash in 1997.

Cash Flows from Financing

This final section reports the net cash from all financing activities. It includes cash inflows from borrowing or issuing stock as well as outflows for payment of dividends and repayment of borrowings. Perfect Posters received $10 000 from issuing long-term notes. Dividend payments used $6000.

The overall *change* in cash from the three sources—operations, investing, and financing—is an increase of $2040 for the year. This amount is added to the beginning cash (from the 1996 balance sheet) to arrive at 1997's ending cash position of $7050.

The Budget: An Internal Financial Statement

budget

A detailed financial plan for estimated receipts and expenditures for a period of time in the future, usually one year.

In addition to financial statements, managers need other types of accounting information to aid in internal planning, controlling, and decision making. Probably the most crucial *internal* financial statement is the budget. A **budget** is a detailed statement of estimated receipts and expenditures for a period of time in the future. Although that period is usually one year, some companies also prepare budgets for three- or five-year periods, especially when considering major capital expenditures.

Budgets are also useful for keeping track of weekly or monthly performance. Procter & Gamble, for example, evaluates all its business units monthly by comparing actual financial results with monthly budgeted amounts. Discrepancies in "actual versus budget" totals signal potential problems and initiate action to get financial performance back on track.

Although the accounting staff coordinates the budget process, it requires input from many people in the company regarding proposed activities, needed resources, and input sources.[8] Figure 19.9, for example, is a sample sales budget. In preparing such a budget, the accounting department must obtain from the sales group both its projections for units to be sold and expected expenses for each quarter of the coming year. Accountants then draw up the final budget, and throughout the year, the accounting department compares the budget to actual expenditures and revenues.

Analyzing Financial Statements

The financial statements discussed above present a great deal of information. But what does it all mean? How can these statements help investors decide what stock to buy or managers to decide whether to extend credit to another firm? By using statistics and ratios, we can analyze and compare financial statements from various companies and help answer these questions. We can also check a firm's progress by comparing its current and past statements.

			Perfect Posters, Inc.
			555 Riverview, Toronto, Ontario

Perfect Posters, Inc.
Sales Budget
First Quarter, 1998

	January	February	March	Quarter
Budgeted sales (units)	7,500	6,000	6,500	20,000
Budgeted selling price				
per unit	$3.50	$3.50	$3.50	$3.50
Budgeted sales revenue	**$26,250**	**$21,000**	**$22,750**	**$70,000**
Expected cash receipts:				
From December sales	$26,210[a]			$26,210
From January sales	$17,500[b]	$8,750		26,250
From February sales		14,000	$7,000	21,000
From March sales			15,200	15,200
Total cash receipts:	**$43,710**	**$22,750**	**$22,200**	**$88,660**

[a] This cash from December sales represents a collection of the Account Receivable appearing on the December 31, 1997, Balance Sheet.
[b] The company estimates that two-thirds of each month's sales revenues will result in cash receipts during the same month. The remaining one third is collected during the following month.

Figure 19.9
Perfect Posters, Inc. sales budget, First Quarter 1998.

A **key ratio** is a value obtained by dividing one value on a financial statement by another value. A business firm's financial condition can be assessed by comparing several important key ratios of items from its financial statements with key ratios for similar types of firms. Dun & Bradstreet Canada publishes key ratios for a variety of industries, including retail trade, wholesale trade, manufacturing, construction, services, and so on.

Ratios are normally grouped into four major classifications based on what they measure. As summarized in Table 19.2, these groups are (1) short-term solvency ratios, (2) long-term solvency ratios, (3) profitability ratios, and (4) activity ratios. Solvency ratios estimate risk; profitability ratios measure potential earnings; and activity ratios reflect management's use of assets. Depending on the types of decisions to be made, a user may apply none, some, or all the ratios in a particular group.

key ratio
A value obtained by dividing one value on a financial statement by another value.

Short-Term Solvency Ratios

In the short run, a company's survival depends on its ability to pay its immediate debts. As noted earlier, such payments require cash. Short-term solvency ratios measure a company's relative liquidity. The higher a firm's **liquidity ratios**, the lower the risks involved for investors. The two most commonly used liquidity ratios are the current ratio and the quick (or acid-test) ratio.

liquidity ratios
Measures of a firm's ability to meet its immediate debts; used to analyze the risks of investing in the firm.

Current Ratio

This ratio has been called the bankers' ratio because it is used by those concerned with a firm's creditworthiness. By dividing current assets by current liabilities, the **current ratio** measures a company's ability to meet its current obligations out of its current assets. It reflects a firm's ability to generate cash

current ratio
A form of liquidity ratio calculated as current assets divided by current liabilities.

Table 19.2   **Financial Ratios**

Overall Type	What Measured	Specific Types	Formula
Short-Term Solvency (Liquidity Ratios)	Potential Risk	Current Ratio	$\dfrac{\text{Current assets}}{\text{Current liabilities}}$
		Quick (Acid-test) Ratio	$\dfrac{\text{Quick assets}}{\text{Current liabilities}}$
Long-Term Solvency (Debt) Ratios	Potential Risk	Debt-to-Owners'-Equity Ratio	$\dfrac{\text{Debt}}{\text{Owners' equity}}$
Profitability Ratios	Potential Rewards	Return on Sales	$\dfrac{\text{Net income}}{\text{Sales}}$
		Return on Investment	$\dfrac{\text{Net income}}{\text{Total owners' equity}}$
		Earnings Per Share	$\dfrac{\text{Net income}}{\text{Number of common shares outstanding}}$
Activity Ratios	Efficient Use of Resources	Inventory Turnover Ratio	$\dfrac{\text{Cost of goods sold}}{\text{Average inventory}}$

to meet obligations through the normal, orderly process of selling inventories and collecting accounts receivable.

As a rule of thumb, a current ratio of 2:1 is satisfactory. A larger current ratio may imply that assets are not being used productively and should be invested elsewhere, rather than in current assets. A smaller current ratio may indicate that a company will have difficulty paying its bills.

How does Perfect Posters measure up? Judging from its current assets and liabilities at the end of 1997, we see that

$$\frac{\text{Current assets}}{\text{Current liabilities}} = \frac{\$57\ 210}{\$21\ 935} = 2.61$$

The firm may be holding too much cash, but it is a good credit risk.

Working Capital

working capital

Difference between a firm's current assets and current liabilities.

A related measure is **working capital**—the difference between the firm's current assets and its current liabilities. Working capital indicates the firm's ability to pay off short-term debts (liabilities) that it owes to outsiders. At the end of 1997, Perfect Posters's working capital was $35 275—that is, $57 210 – $21 935. Because current liabilities must be paid off within one year, current assets are more than enough to meet current obligations.

Quick (Acid-Test) Ratio

quick ratio (acid-test ratio)

A form of liquidity ratio calculated as quick assets (cash plus marketable securities and accounts receivable) divided by current liabilities.

The current ratio represents a company's ability to meet expected demands for cash. In contrast, the **quick ratio**, or **acid-test ratio**, which divides quick assets by current liabilities, measures a firm's ability to meet emergency demands for cash. *Quick assets* include cash and assets just one step removed from being converted into cash: marketable securities and accounts receivable. Inventory is excluded from this measure because it can be liquidated quickly only at sacrifice prices. Thus, the quick ratio is a more stringent test than is the current ratio. As a rule of thumb, a quick ratio of 1.0 is satisfactory.

If we again consider Perfect Posters's position at the end of 1997, we see that

$$\frac{\text{Quick assets}}{\text{Current liabilities}} = \frac{\$7050 + 2300 + 26\ 210 - 650}{\$21\ 935} = 1.59$$

In an emergency, the firm apparently can pay off all current obligations without having to liquidate its inventory.

Long-Term Solvency Ratios

If a company is to survive in the long run, it must be able to meet both its short-term (current) and long-term liabilities. These debts, as we have seen, usually involve interest payments. A firm that cannot meet these payments is in serious danger of collapse or takeover—a risk that makes creditors and investors alike very cautious. To measure this risk, we use long-term solvency ratios—**debt ratios**—like the debt-to-equity ratio.

debt ratios
Measures of a firm's ability to meet its long-term debts; used to analyze the risks of investing in the firm.

The Debt-to-Owners'-Equity Ratio

Calculated as debt (total liabilities) divided by owner's equity, the **debt-to-owners'-equity ratio** describes the extent to which a firm is financed through borrowings. This ratio is commonly used in industry financial statistical reports so that a reader can compare a company's ratio with industry averages. Companies with debt-to-equity ratios above 1 are probably relying too much on debt.

In the case of Perfect Posters, this ratio works out to

$$\frac{\text{Debt}}{\text{Owners' equity}} = \frac{\$61\ 935}{\$111\ 155} = 0.56$$

debt-to-owners'-equity ratio
A form of debt ratio calculated as total liabilities divided by owners' equity.

If this firm developed disastrous business difficulties and had to liquidate, all of the creditors would be protected. The owners' equity is more than sufficient for meeting all debts.

Sometimes, however, a fairly high debt-to-owners'-equity ratio may be not only acceptable but desirable. Borrowing funds gives companies or individuals **leverage**, the ability to make a purchase they otherwise could not afford. You have probably read about a "leveraged buyout" (LBO) in the newspapers. In these instances, firms have borrowed (taken on debt) in order to buy out another company. When the purchased company allows the buying company to earn profits that exceed the cost of the borrowed funds, leveraging makes sound financial sense, even if it raises the debt-to-owners'-equity ratio. Unfortunately, many LBOs have gotten into financial trouble when actual profits fell short of anticipated levels or interest payments ballooned due to rising rates.

leverage
Using borrowed funds to make purchases, thus increasing the user's purchasing power, potential rate of return, and risk of loss.

Profitability Ratios

Although it is important for investors to know that a company is solvent in both the long and short term, safety or risk alone is not an adequate criterion for investment decisions. To decide which company's stock to buy, investors also need to have some measure of what returns they can expect. Return on sales, return on investment, and earnings per share are three commonly used **profitability ratios**.

profitability ratios
Measures of a firm's overall financial performance in terms of its likely profits; used by investors to assess their probable returns.

Return on Sales

return on sales (net profit margin)
A form of profitability ratio calculated as net income divided by net sales.

Also called the **net profit margin**, **return on sales** is calculated as net income divided by sales. It indicates the percentage of income that is profit to the company. There is no single right net profit margin. The figure for any one company must be compared to figures for other firms in the industry to determine how well a business is doing. Typical returns on sales ratios are 1 percent for meat-packing plants, 3 percent for wholesalers such as Perfect Posters, and 6 percent for machinery manufacturers.

In the case of Perfect Posters, return on sales for 1997 was

$$\frac{\text{Net income}}{\text{Sales}} = \frac{\$12\ 585}{\$256\ 425} = 0.049 = 4.9\%$$

That is, the business realized a 4.9 cent profit on each dollar of sales. Thus, if someone shoplifted a $15.00 item from the warehouse, $306 in sales would be required ($15.00/0.049) to make up the loss.

Return on Investment

return on investment (return on equity)
A form of profitability ratio calculated as net income divided by total owners' equity.

Owners are interested in how much net income the business earns for each dollar invested by the owners. **Return on investment** (sometimes called **return on equity**) gives them the desired measure by dividing net income by total owners' equity.

For Perfect Posters, the ratio in 1997 was

$$\frac{\text{Net income}}{\text{Total owners' equity}} = \frac{\$12\ 585}{\$111\ 155} = 11.3\%$$

Is this figure good or bad? There is no set answer. If the firm's ratio for 1994 is higher than for previous years, then owners and potential investors should be encouraged. But if 11.3 percent is lower than the ratios of other companies in the same industry, they should be concerned.

Earnings per Share

earnings per share
A form of profitability ratio calculated as net income divided by the number of common shares outstanding.

This ratio is one of the most quoted financial statistics. Defined as net income divided by the number of shares of common stock outstanding, **earnings per share** determines how large a dividend a company can pay its shareholders. It also indicates how much the company can reinvest in itself instead of paying dividends—that is, how much it can grow. Investors watch this ratio and use it to decide whether to buy or sell the company's stock. Often, a company's stock will lose market value when its latest financial statements report a decline in earnings per share.

If we assume that Perfect Posters has only one class of stock, we can calculate its earnings per share as

$$\frac{\text{Net income}}{\substack{\text{Number of common} \\ \text{shares outstanding}}} = \frac{\$12\ 585}{8000} = \$1.57 \text{ per share}$$

Earnings per share is easy to calculate in the abstract. But in real life the computation is quite complex, in part because of the many classes of stock available.

Activity Ratios

activity ratios
Measures of how efficiently a firm uses its resources; used by investors to assess their probable returns.

Obviously, the efficiency with which a firm uses resources is linked to profitability. As a potential investor, then, you want to know which company "gets more mileage" from its resources. **Activity ratios** measure this efficiency. For example, say that two firms use the same amount of resources or assets. If Firm A generates greater profits or sales, it is more efficient and thus has a better activity ratio.

By the same token, if a firm needs more resources to make products comparable to its competitors', it has a worse activity ratio. The consulting firm of Harbour & Associates Inc. released a study showing that in order to match Ford's efficiency, General Motors would have to cut 20 000 workers. According to the report, production inefficiency at its plants costs GM $2.2 billion annually in excess labour costs. On the upside, however, GM is making substantial progress. A similar report issued two years earlier had concluded that GM needed to cut 70 000 workers because excess labour costs were $4 billion.[9]

Inventory Turnover Ratio

Perhaps the most widely used typical activity ratio is the **inventory turnover ratio**. This ratio measures the average number of times inventory is sold and restocked during the year. It is expressed as the cost of goods sold divided by the average inventory. A high ratio means efficient operations—a smaller amount of investment is tied up in inventory. The company's funds can then be put to work elsewhere, earning greater returns.

Inventory turnover rates must be compared with earlier years and with industry averages. An inventory turnover rate of 5 might be excellent for an auto-supply store, but it would be disastrous for a supermarket, where a ratio of about 15 is common.

Perfect Posters's inventory turnover ratio for 1997 was

$$\frac{\text{Cost of goods sold}}{\text{Average inventory*}} = \frac{\$104\ 765}{(\$21\ 250 + \$22\ 380)/2} = 4.8 \text{ times}$$

Average Inventory is the average of inventory value on January 1, 1997, and December 31, 1997.

The firm's new merchandise replaces old merchandise every 76 days (365 days/4.8). This ratio of 4.8 is below the average of 7 for comparable wholesaling operations, indicating that the business is slightly inefficient. So, although Perfect Posters is highly profitable and low risk, it is not truly a "perfect" company!

inventory turnover ratio
An activity ratio that measures the average number of times inventory is sold and restocked during the year.

International Accounting

More and more companies are buying and selling goods and services in other countries. Accounting for foreign transactions is therefore increasing in importance. One of the key activities in international accounting is translating the values of the currencies of different countries.

The value of any country's currency is subject to occasional change. Political and economic conditions, for instance, affect the stability of a nation's currency and its value relative to the currencies of other countries. The Swiss franc, for example, has a long history of stability, while the Brazilian real has a history of instability.

Any currency's value is determined by market forces—what buyers and sellers are willing to pay for it. The resulting values are called *foreign-currency exchange rates*. These rates can be very volatile. The Mexican peso, for example, began a disastrous plunge in December 1994. The peso is thus regarded as a *weak currency*. On the other hand, the Japanese yen is a *strong currency* because its value is rising in comparison to the Canadian dollar. As exchange rate changes occur, they must be considered by accountants for their firm's international transactions.

International Purchases

Accounting for international transactions involves two steps: (1) translating from one currency to another and (2) reflecting gains or losses due to exchange-rate changes. Let's explain these two steps by using an illustration. Suppose that on March 7, an American firm called Village Wine and Cheese Shops imports Bordeaux wine from Pierre Bourgeois in France. The price is 32 000 francs, and the exchange rate on March 7 is $0.18 per French franc.

The first step for Village's accountant is to translate the price of the transaction into U.S. dollars:

$$\text{price in French francs} = 32\ 000\ \text{Fr}$$
$$\text{price in U.S. dollars} = (32\ 000\ \text{Fr}) \times (\$0.18) = \$5760$$

Next, the transaction must be recorded in Village's books. Assume that Village purchases on credit and that Bourgeois requires payment within 30 days. Village's accounting records will then appear as follows:

		Debit	Credit
March 7	Inventory	5760	
	Accounts		
	payable		5760

Then, on April 1 when Village pays Bourgeois, the payment entry will appear this way:

		Debit	Credit
April 1	Accounts		
	payable	5760	
	Cash		5760

Thus far, our bookkeeping has been straightforward because Village's accountants have assumed a constant exchange rate of $0.18 per franc. The above entries, then, are correct *if the exchange rate for francs on April 1 is the same as it was on March 7* ($0.18 per franc). However, because exchange rates rise and fall daily, some change will no doubt occur during the month in question.

Let's say, for example, that on April 1 the value of the French franc has fallen below $0.18. Village Cheese, therefore, will enjoy a *foreign-currency transaction gain*: It can pay its debt with fewer dollars. Suppose that the franc has fallen to $0.17 by the time Village pays Bouregois on April 1. The payment entry, therefore, will appear as follows:

		Debit	Credit
April 1	Accounts		
	payable	5760	
	Cash		
	(32 000 × $0.17).......		5440
	Foreign-currency		
	transaction gain........		320

In other words, when the value of the franc decreased, Village needed only $5440 to pay the original account payable of $5760. Of course, had the franc *increased* to a value above $0.18, Village would have paid more than the original $5760. It would have suffered a *foreign-currency transaction loss*.

International Sales

Sales made to customers in other countries can also be recorded to reflect both translations from foreign currency and changes in currency exchange rates. Suppose, for instance, that on June 1, Motorola sells some cellular phones on credit to the Japanese distributor Hirotsu. The total price of the phones is 50 million yen, and the exchange rate is $0.01 per yen. Motorola's transaction is thus recorded as follows:

		Debit	Credit
April 1	Accounts receivable		
	(50 000 000 × $0.01)	500 000	
	Sales revenue		500 000

Let's suppose that when Hirotsu pays Motorola—say, on June 30—the exchange rate has fallen to $0.0095 per yen. Motorola, therefore will receive *fewer* dollars than were recorded in its June 1 accounts-receivable entry. It will suffer the foreign-currency transaction loss shown in the following entry:

		Debit	Credit
June 30	Cash (50 000 000 × $0.0095) ...	475 000	
	Foreign-currency		
	transaction loss	25 000	
	Accounts receivable		500 000

At the end of an accounting period, all exchange rate gains and losses are combined to reveal a net gain or loss. This net gain or loss can then be shown on the income statement as "other revenue and expense."

Summary of Learning Objectives

1. **Explain the role of accountants and distinguish between the kinds of work done by *public* and *private accountants*.** By collecting, analyzing, and communicating financial information, accountants provide business managers and investors with an accurate picture of the firm's financial health. *Chartered accountants (CAs)* are licensed professionals who provide auditing, tax, and management advisory services for other firms and individuals. *Public accountants* who have not yet been certified perform similar tasks. *Private accountants* provide diverse specialized services for the specific firms that employ them.

2. **Explain how the following three concepts are used in *record-keeping*: *accounting equations*, *double-entry accounting*, and *T-accounts* for debits and credits.** The *accounting equation* (assets = liabilities + owners' equity) is used to balance the data in both *journals* and *ledgers*. *Double-entry accounting* acknowledges the dual effects of financial transactions and ensures that the accounting equation always balances. Using the *T-account*, accountants record financial transactions in the shape of a *T*, with the vertical line dividing the account into *debit* and *credit* columns. These tools enable accountants not only to enter but to track transactions.

3. **Describe the three basic *financial statements* and show how they reflect the activity and financial condition of a business.** The *balance sheet* summarizes a company's assets, liabilities, and owners' equity at a given point in time. The *income statement* details revenues and expenses for a given period of time and identifies any profit or loss. The *statement of cash flows* reports cash receipts and payments from operating, investing, and financing activities.

4. **Discuss the importance of *budgets* in internal planning and control.** To ensure the overall efficient use of resources, accountants and other managers develop *budgets*. A budget shows where funds will be obtained (the sources) and where they will be spent (the uses). Throughout the year, the budget is monitored to ensure that costs are not exceeding revenues.

5. **Explain how computing key *financial ratios* can help in analyzing the financial strengths of a business.** Drawing upon data from financial statements, ratios can help creditors, investors, and managers assess a firm's finances. The *liquidity*, *current*, *quick* (or *acid test*), and *debt-to-equity ratios* all measure solvency—a firm's ability to pay its debt in both the short and the long run. *Return on sales*, *return on investment*, and *earnings per share* are all ratios that measure profitability. *Inventory turnover ratios* show how efficiently a firm is using its funds.

6. **Explain some of the special issues facing accountants at firms that do international business.** Accounting for foreign transactions involves some special procedures. First, accountants must consider the fact that the *exchange rates* of national currencies change. Accordingly, the value of a foreign currency at any given time—its *foreign currency exchange rate*—is what buyers are willing to pay for it. Exchange rates will affect the amount of money that a firm pays for foreign purchases and the amount that it gains from foreign sales. Canadian accountants, therefore, must always translate foreign currencies into the value of the dollar. Then, in recording a firm's transactions, they must make adjustments to reflect shifting exchange rates over time. Shifting rates may result in either *foreign-currency transaction gains* (a debt, for example, may be paid with fewer dollars) or *foreign-currency transaction losses*.

Key Terms

accounting, 578
bookkeeping, 578
accounting system, 578
controller, 579
financial accounting system, 580
managerial accounting, 581
chartered accountant (CA), 581
audit, 581
forensic accountant, 582
generally accepted accounting principles (GAAP), 582

private accountant, 583
journal, 584
ledger, 585
asset, 586
liability, 586
owners' equity, 586
double-entry accounting system, 587
T-account, 587
debit, 588
credit, 588
financial statement, 589
balance sheet, 589
current assets, 589
liquidity, 589

accounts receivable, 589
merchandise inventory, 589
prepaid expense, 589
fixed assets, 589
depreciation, 590
intangible assets, 590
current liabilities, 590
accounts payable, 590
long-term liabilities, 591
paid-in capital, 591
retained earnings, 591
income (profit-and-loss) statement, 591
revenues, 591

cost of goods sold, 592
gross profit (gross margin), 592
operating expenses, 593
net income (net profit or net earnings), 593
statement of cash flows, 593
budget, 594
key ratio, 595
liquidity ratios, 595
current ratio, 595
working capital, 596
quick ratio (acid-test ratio), 596

Study Questions and Exercises

Review Questions

1. Identify the three types of services that CAs perform.
2. How does the double-entry system reduce the chances of mistakes or fraud in accounting?
3. What are the three basic financial statements and what major types of information does each contain?
4. Identify the four major classifications of financial statement ratios and give an example of one ratio in each category.
5. In what ways does an electronic spreadsheet simplify the budgeting process?

Analysis Questions

6. Suppose Inflatables Inc., makers of air mattresses for swimming pools, has the following transactions one week:
   - Sale of three deluxe mattresses to Al Wett (paid cash—$75) on 7/16
   - Received cheque from Ima Flote in payment for mattresses bought on credit ($90) on 7/13
   - Received new shipment of 200 mattresses from Airheads Mfg. (total cost $2000) on 7/17
   Construct a journal for Inflatables Inc.
7. If you were planning to invest in a company, which of the three types of financial statements would you most want to see? Why?

8. Dasar Company reports the following data in its September 30, 1997, financial statements:

■ Gross sales	$225 000
■ Current assets	40 000
■ Long-term assets	100 000
■ Current liabilities	16 000
■ Long-term liabilities	44 000
■ Owners' equity	80 000
■ Net income	7 200

   a. Compute the current ratio.
   b. Compute the debt-to-equity ratio.
   c. Compute the return on sales.
   d. Compute the return on owners' equity.

Application Exercises

9. Interview an accountant at a local manufacturing firm. Trace the process by which budgets are developed in that company. How does the firm use budgets? How does budgeting help its managers plan business activities? How does budgeting help them control business activities? Give examples.
10. Interview the manager of a local retail or wholesale business about taking inventory. What is the firm's primary purpose in taking inventory? How often is it done?

Building Your Business Skills

Goal

To encourage students to understand the purpose of financial statements and to understand the functions of each of the three broad categories of financial statements.

Method

At the library, look through the financial statements of a local company or of some well-known company. For each category listed below, list the company's main item and its dollar amount from its financial statements. From which financial statement did you obtain each item?

Follow-Up Questions

1. Which financial statement provides the most complete picture of the company's finances?

2. How are the various financial ratios—solvency, profitability, and activity ratios—used in the financial statements that you examined?

Financial Statement			
Category	Item	Dollar Amount	From which Financial Statement
Current assets			
Fixed assets			
Intangible assets			
Revenues			
Expenses			
Current liabilities			
Long-term liabilities			
Owners' equity			

To get a feel for real-world accounting activity using a computerized system, log on at the following Web site:

http://www.ccas.com/CCASDoc/ccasdoc0.html

Specifically, you are seeking access to the following features offered at the site:

■ Online User's Guide and Procedures Documentation
■ The CCAS Demo

You can gain access to the Demo without purchasing the software. You must, however, obtain a "UserID" and a "Password" by following the instructions at the Web site. After obtaining the UserID and Password, you do not actually have to download the demo to perform this exercise. In order to view CCAS Online Documentation, select "Here" under "Downloading." A little patience will reward you with an informative adventure.

The purpose in examining this software demo is to see the contents of a real-world accounting software system, to recognize the wide range of accounting activities that it handles, to experience the detailed level of information required for such a system, and to appreciate how the various accounting activities are interrelated with one another within the system.

Begin by scrolling down to "User's Guide and Procedures Documentation: Table of Contents." From there, click on "CCAS Reports Available" and then on "Closing and Maintaining Your Books."

After examining the material in this section, consider the following questions:

1. On the page entitled "The CCAS and NewsViews Relationship," a graphic is presented that "illustrates the CCAS concept." It shows "Accounting Transactions" as the input to the system and several reports that come out of the system. Based on this graphic and the various reports available from the system, would you classify CCAS as a *management accounting* system or as a *financial accounting* system? Why?

2. What information does the "Bank Accounts" report contain? How might that information be useful in managing the firm's activities?

3. What is the purpose of the "Fixed Asset Report"? What information does it contain?

4. How is the "Professional Time Report (PT)" related to the "Payroll Records (PR)" report? What is the purpose of the flow of data between these two reports?

5. What is the function or purpose of the "ADDEMP" procedure? Explain how it relates to the "Payroll Records (PR)" report.

6. Explain the contents of the "PDIST—Payroll Distribution Entry" procedure. How does this procedure relate to the "Professional Time Report (PT)"?

7. How much time and effort do you suspect would be involved in first-time implementation of the CCAS system by a user company? What types of skills do you expect would be needed for system implementation?

CONCLUDING CASE 19-1

There's No Business Like Show Business

When Ethel Merman belted out the famous refrain, "There's no business like show business," she wasn't singing about the business of accounting in Hollywood. But she probably should have been. That's because the accounting rules in Hollywood are like no other accounting rules in the world. According to critics, the rules make it difficult—if not impossible—for investors to determine the *real* financial condition of movie studios and their products.

Under existing rules, for example, studios can treat advertising costs as an *asset* (an economic resource) instead of an *expense*. This practice enables studios to inflate both assets and short-term profits. Studios can also choose to add to a film's costs millions in studio "overhead" charges and millions more in start-up costs of unrelated failed projects. Like advertising costs, these costs can be treated as assets and depreciated over a given number of years from the studio's balance sheet.

The following illustration (adapted from an article in *Business Week*) demonstrates how Hollywood's accounting system works. Using the unique system suggested above, studios manipulate balance sheet entries to paint a rosy financial picture that leaves investors in the dark about expenses and profits.

1. Let's say that Bigwig Pictures makes *Violent Death*, spending $50 million to acquire the story, hire actors, and film the movie.

2. The studio spends another $40 million to advertise and release *Violent Death*. This money is added to the movie's reported cost. This cost, moreover, climbs when Bigwig adds another $10 million to cover expenses from other films that were never released—plus costs related to everything from Bigwig salaries to paper clips. The total cost of *Violent Death* now stands at $100 million.

3. Now let's thicken the plot (albeit in a perfectly plausible way). Let's say that Bigwig is facing a depressed stock price and investor pressure to raise the value of shares by improving its performance. Bigwig management thus decides to project that *Violent Death* will bring in $1 billion over the next 20 years. This revenue will come not only from the film's theatrical release, but from its release to home video, to pay and regular TV, and to laser disks, not to mention licensing in foreign markets. Because the studio states that *Violent Death* will be making money for 20 years, Bigwig can take the full two decades to subtract the film's bloated $100 million cost from its books.

4. Let's now say that *Violent Death* does well, taking in $200 million in box office and video revenue in the first year of its release. After deducting $20 million—that year's share of expenses—Bigwig shows an immediate profit of $180 million. Naturally, the studio's earnings—and stock price—jump. What about the remaining $80 million that the studio spent on the film? That sum remains on Bigwig's books for years—as an asset, not a liability.

Studios argue that this system makes sense. Because a movie has value that lasts long beyond the year in which it's made, it is reasonable to estimate profit margins *over the lifetime* of a movie. Profits, meanwhile, can be reported as such *as soon as box office dollars begin rolling in*. Why is this bookkeeping mechanism so important in the movie-making business? Studio executives point out that even a runaway hit has virtually no chance of making money *during its first distribution year*. In most cases, *first-year box office receipts* cannot cover the average $65 million cost required to make and market a Hollywood film. (For one thing, only 40 percent of the box office gross goes to the studio, with the remaining 60 percent going to theatres.)

However, this unique accounting system makes it extremely difficult for people with a so-called "net profit" interest in a movie to make any money from that interest. *Net profits* are the revenues that big studios agree to distribute among writers, actors, and others *after expenses, including salaries and distribution fees, have been paid*. Net profit arrangements are typically negotiated as part of individual contracts. Interestingly, however, only 5 to 20 percent of all films pay any net profits. "For most films," charges Philip Hacker, a consultant to plaintiffs in lawsuits against studios, "net profit participants don't receive anything." Thus, even though the blockbuster *Forrest Gump* grossed approximately $650 million, it has paid no money to anyone with a net profit interest in the film. So, too, with such successful releases as *JFK*, *Coming to America*, and *Batman*.

The estate of Jim Garrison, the late New Orleans prosecutor whose book was the basis for the 1991 Warner Brothers movie *JFK*, has initiated a federal class-action suit over the net profit issue. Joining in the suit are thousands of people who signed net profits contracts with movie studios since 1988. All the studios involved, including Disney, Universal, Warner Brothers, 20th Century Fox, Paramount, Columbia-TriStar, and MGM-UA, use the same accounting practices. If successful, the Garrison-*JFK* suit could force payments of more than $1 billion and redefine Hollywood's approach to accounting.

A task force reporting to the Financial Accounting Standard Board (FASB) is now taking a close look at the way Hollywood studios determine their balance sheets. Its goal is to reform many of the unorthodox practices that give investors a distorted view of studio finances. The toughest practice to change involves the capitalizing of advertising costs (treating them as assets rather than expenses). The FASB, which determines the accounting rules by which U.S. companies must generally live, objects to this practice. The movie industry, however, is determined to maintain the status quo. "Most of us think that how we do the accounting makes sense," says Peter Cyffka, a task

...

There's No Business Like Show Business

(continued)

force member and the senior vice-president of finance at Twentieth Century Fox Film Corp.

Even if the task force succeeds in changing Hollywood's accounting practices, its reforms will not affect the disbursement of net profits to those who help create movies. Any change in the studios' net profit system must come from the studios themselves in the process of contracting with creative artists. Dreamworks, the production company founded by Steven Spielberg, Jeffrey Katzenberg, and David Geffen, was the first studio to initiate a change. Screenwriters, animators, and other artists working for Dreamworks now sign contracts guaranteeing that they will share in the success of the films they help create.

Case Questions

1. In your opinion, are Hollywood's current accounting practices fair to investors?

2. What changes would you suggest to make Hollywood's accounting system fair to both studios and investors?

3. Why is the contractual agreement to share in a film's net profits usually an empty agreement?

4. If you were a screenwriter, what accounting-related questions would you ask before agreeing to a movie deal?

5. Why is the Financial Accounting Standards Board involved in reforming Hollywood's accounting practices? ◆

Twentieth Century Fox Film Corp.

http://www.fox.com/white.html

CONCLUDING CASE 19-2

Who's To Blame Here?

When it went bankrupt in 1991, Standard Trustco Ltd. was Canada's eighth largest trust company. Several members of the board of directors of Standard Trustco are now suing the CA firm of Peat Marwick Thorne (the firm's auditors), accusing the accountants of negligence and of failing to disclose that the firm was insolvent two years before it actually collapsed. Chairperson Helen Roman-Barber maintains that Standard's board would have taken immediate action had the auditing firm warned the directors that financial problems existed. She says that a review of corporate financial statements has convinced the directors that Peat Marwick Thorne failed to convey appropriate warnings to the directors. A spokesperson for Peat Marwick says the firm was blameless; he is confident the auditing firm will be vindicated.

The directors launched their lawsuit against Peat Marwick one day after the Ontario Securities Commission (OSC) concluded a probe of Standard Trustco. The OSC accused Mrs. Roman-Barber and several other directors of issuing a misleading news release in 1990 which failed to state that federal regulators had concerns about the firm. The release painted a rosy picture of the firm and claimed it was profitable. Later, an audited statement showing extremely large losses replaced this unaudited one.

At the hearings, the OSC said the directors either knew of the firm's problems or they were wilfully blind to them. It noted that Standard had made loans on construction projects for condominiums, and that the directors knew these were riskier than loans on single-family houses. The OSC also pointed out that Michael Mackenzie, the Superintendent of Financial Institutions, had conveyed serious reservations about some of the firm's accounting policies. He believed the company would experience a cash shortfall, and that the firm was understating loan losses. The board of Standard did nothing about these concerns.

But Standard's directors place the blame for their inaction on Peat Marwick. They claim that the auditor failed to tell the company to set aside adequate amounts to cover loan losses on its deteriorating real estate loans. The directors argue that, if Peat Marwick had taken this action, it would have been obvious in 1988 that Standard Trustco was insolvent.

Case Questions

1. What kind of evidence is needed to show that a CA firm has been negligent? Do you think there is such evidence in this case?

2. What kind of evidence is needed to show that members of a firm's board of directors have been negligent? Do you think there is such evidence in this case? ◆

"Anne of Green Gables never changes," sang Matthew Cuthbert in the closing scene of the musical *Anne of Green Gables*. However, as the efforts of the Fredericton, New Brunswick, enterprise Renaissance attest, Anne of Green Gables may be changing in ways the heroine's creator, Lucy Maud Montgomery, never imagined. Company president Mike Morrisey and friends Trevor and Dave Marks have developed a new Anne CD-Rom. The product was developed to be ready for the opening of the new Confederation bridge linking Prince Edward Island and mainland Canada.

Morrisey and company were able to secure the interactive rights to take Anne digital as a result of their technical competence and their willingness to share proceeds with the P.E.I. government. By blending pictures with sounds, the company has developed a computerized version of the classic story of the red-haired orphan adopted by the elderly sibling couple of Matthew and Mirilla Cuthbert.

As marketing of the product proceeded, the company encountered an immovable deadline—the opening of the "Span of Green Gables," more specifically the Confederation Bridge. This required the company to labour away around the clock during the days before the bridge's opening. Trying to get the CD ready stretched the trio in every way possible. Financially, the group put up every last dollar available, even to the point of holding off on a much-needed oil change for their company van. This also meant living off bagels, donuts, and coffee, and wearing the same clothes for days on end. After getting only scattered hours of sleep, the three entrepreneurs were so exhausted they missed the ferry exit when delivering the final product. It was essential that their project be completed by the opening of the new bridge. With over 400 000 visitors expected to go through the special visitor centre, sales were projected to reach as high as 10 000 units.

The bridge launch was only a first step, however. After completing the opening, the trio hoped to go after an even bigger target, the North American video game market. Hoping to sign a software publishing deal with a major firm that could vault them into larger volumes—and larger profits—the three friends headed off to the Atlanta Expo. The show was famous as a hangout for the big guns of the interactive and educational software industry.

The nature of the Anne product put Renaissance into a very specialized niche. Less than 1 percent of interactive and educational software product is estimated to be targeted at girls. This is because girls play differently; rather than trying to "blast opponents into smithereens," girls are much more cooperative and less adversarial. In addition, Anne's non-superhero status could mean that Renaissance will have its work cut out for it. In a market where 4000 to 5000 products compete for only 900 spots of retail shelf space, Anne of Green Gables could be an orphan once again.

Study Questions

1. What is computer piracy? Under what conditions would computer piracy be relevant in this case?

2. What are the different kinds of disks? What kind of disk is Renaissance attempting to develop?

3. What are the different kinds of computers? Is Renaissance trying to put out a product for all of these different types of computers or for only one type?

http://www.tv.cbc.ca/venture/archives/anne_of_cd_971104/index.html

*Source: This case was written by Professor Reg Litz of the University of Manitoba.
Video Resource: "Anne of Green Gables CD," *Venture* #667 (November 4, 1997).

Five years ago computer crime was barely a statistic worth reporting. Today the story is quite different, as computer theft has become as pervasive as computers themselves. According to police statistics, theft involving computers and computer chips has become Canada's fastest-growing crime. And the problem is anything but unique to Canada, with a worldwide "grey" market for computer parts emerging, aided in large part by the Internet. As a result, law enforcement officials are calling "hot" computers the "dope of the 90s."

A recent example of this new type of crime occurred at Digital Canada's offices in Kanata, near Ottawa. A trailerload of computers, worth millions of dollars, was stolen while in transit. Small business is also a target. One small business manager, Dino Georgio, had his computer stolen and was left without any backup copies of his company's data.

Sometimes computers are stolen to simply get the microchips within them. In one recent incident, police tracking some thieves concluded that this was their motive after seeing the highway littered with discarded computer bodies that were intact, except for the valuable operating microchips.

In some cases, gangs appear to be involved; in other cases, solo operators carry out the crimes. One solo operation involved a "gym bag" thief who simply walked into a large office area at the lunch hour. Aided by his duffel bag, he proceeded to pick up selected computer equipment and walk out unchallenged.

Unfortunately, the Internet has facilitated these crimes. "Fences" place "orders" for specific parts; these are then located, stolen, stripped, and shipped through points of departure such as the port of Vancouver. Other times, the order is domestic, with stripped parts being reassembled inside new products that re-enter the Canadian market undetected. Rarely are the culprits caught. One notable exception involved the previously mentioned Digital case, where stolen components were detected during a FedEx courier shipment.

One of the challenges companies have to face is the embarrassment of having been robbed. At a recent meeting of businesspeople, Tom Cornwell of Chubb Insurance advised those present to "stop treating it [computer theft] as a corporate embarrassment and face up to the problem. [Computer theft] is increasingly a global venture with computers stolen in one area of the world showing up in other parts of the world."

People don't seem to act until they've been hit, even though there are several simple precautions they could take. These would include taking an inventory of what you have and asking why it might be wanted and how it might be stolen. Other more action-oriented steps could involve getting a protective cable to, at the very least, slow the thieves down. In short, experts advise, "treat your components as if they were gold."

Study Questions

1. What are some of the privacy-related problems of computers the textbook mentions? In what way is computer theft different from the problems mentioned in the textbook?

2. What is the difference between microcomputers, minicomputers, mainframes, and supercomputers? Which of these would seem particularly vulnerable to the kinds of crime described in this video case?

3. What is the difference between computer hardware and software? Which types of computer hardware appear to be of least interest in computer crime?

*Source: This case was written by Professor Reg Litz of the University of Manitoba.
Video Resource: "Computer Crime," Venture #630 (February 16, 1997).

STARTING OVER

"All is flux, nothing stays still ... Nothing endures but change."

The Greek philosopher Heraclitus wrote these words nearly 2500 years ago, but they remain as true today as they were then. If anything, the rate of change in our modern world seems to be accelerating continually.

If you are like most of your classmates, the chances are very strong indeed that you will change jobs—even change professions—at some point in your career. In this section, we consider some of the reasons people change jobs and offer some suggestions on how to go about it.

WHY CHANGE JOBS?

During your career, you may find yourself changing what you do and where you do it for a variety of reasons. As the vast number of Baby Boomers reach the "upper-executive" years, the number of upper-management jobs is sure to fall short of demand, a trend that may well drive some managers in pursuit of better opportunities. Moreover, in today's uncertain economic climate, many people have found themselves out of a job as their firms cut back or went under. The demand for some positions is growing, while demand for others is declining. And, increasingly, people are opting for self-employment, setting up as consultants, and opening the new small businesses that are projected to be the major source of growth in the 21st century.

The most common reason of all, however, is an inappropriate person-job fit. Though many people find their first job interesting, challenging, and rewarding, many others find their first jobs to be much different than they expected. Some experts estimate that as many as 20 percent of all new graduates change jobs within 12 months of starting their careers.

People sometimes find that they chose the wrong job because they did not truly understand their own interests and abilities. The young man who got into sales after enjoying jobs as a paperboy and counterman at McDonald's may find that what he really liked was the independence of being a paperboy and the camaraderie of working with schoolmates at McDonald's—neither of which is part of selling cosmetics to Kmart. The young woman who chose her job because she wanted the highest possible salary, because she did not want to be too far away from home, or because her father worked for the company before he retired may find that the high salary carries with it too many unpleasant working conditions or that she would actually prefer to live farther from home.

SHOULD YOU CHANGE JOBS?

If you have just taken your first job and find yourself unhappy with it—for whatever reason—experts have a few words of advice: HANG IN THERE. No organization is perfect, nor is any job.

And no matter how well you thought you understood what you would be doing, there will always be some surprises in store. Moreover, it may not be the job that's making you unhappy. The upheaval and stress of being independent and coping with the myriad problems of everyday life may be partially to blame for your frustration.

Resist moving too quickly; try to last at least a year. Why a year? Because leaving much earlier than that can be interpreted as a sign of impatience, or a lack of commitment or maturity, on your part. One year is usually perceived to be a long time for a person to make an informed and professional decision about staying or leaving. A year will also give you a chance to reassess what you like and don't like about the job while giving you valuable experience that can help you in your next job.

Even if it's not your first job, experts recommend that you stay at least a year—or even two—so as not to create an impression of instability. While employers today are much more open to hiring individuals who have worked for several companies, a job hopper's resume is more likely than most to hop into the circular file.

HOW TO LOOK FOR A NEW JOB

If you are sure that you made the wrong decision in selecting an occupation or employer, or if changes in the organization are simply too great for your comfort, you may very well decide to look for another job. If you do decide to look around, you should keep several things in mind. Remember, you are not starting over, but simply making a change. You made a decision, it turned out to be the wrong one, and now you want to correct it.

Spend some time thinking about why you want to change jobs. Is it because of location? Or pay? Or company policies? Or is it the actual work you are doing? Make sure that a new job will actually correct the problems you are experiencing. Table 1 lists some of the right—and wrong—reasons for changing careers.

Second, compile a list of your strengths and weaknesses, goals, and aspirations. Also develop a list of the things you like and don't like about your current job. Why do you want to keep it and why do you want to leave it? Use this information to determine exactly what kind of new job you want.

Third, revise your resume and start job-hunting. If you graduated from college or university less than five years ago, your campus placement office may still be willing to assist you. If you want to stay in the same line of work, contact the companies you interviewed with before—especially any firm that offered you a job. Use personal contacts, the local newspaper, employment agencies—anything and anyone you can think of to turn up leads on job openings.

The library can be an excellent source of leads for job hunters. Scan the newspapers of other cities in which you might like to work. And don't forget to look in trade publications and journals in your field for positions that are open.

Prospective new employers will be very interested in why you want to leave your current job. Be honest, but don't wear your heart on your sleeve. Don't blame your current employer—doing so may make you look like a complainer or malcontent. But don't blame yourself too much either. Explain why you made a mistake in taking the job, then explain that you are now trying to correct it.

What should you tell your current employer when you decide it's time to go? Some experts recommend that you advise your employer of your unhappiness and your plans to seek employment elsewhere. You should be aware, however, that by doing so you are effectively "giving notice." Some firms may make an effort to find a different position for you, but most will start looking for someone else to fill your job. Thus, many people choose to keep the job-hunting activities a secret until they have found a new position. Whichever way you choose to handle the situation, be sure to give your current employer adequate notice—it's the professional thing to do, and it can influence the references you get from that employer in years to come.

EXCELSIOR! (ONWARD AND UPWARD)

Job hunting is never easy, but it can be highly profitable. Many studies have found that changing jobs offers the best chance for middle-level managers to improve their positions and salaries. As Figure 1 shows, moving is essential to career development in some careers, so if you don't like your job or don't see a future in it—go for a change.

Table 1 Reasons to Change—and Not to Change—Careers

Reasons to Change	Reasons Not to Change
■ Your job or industry is becoming obsolete because of changes in technology. ■ The personal costs of your job—long hours, too much travel—outweigh its benefits. ■ You've been fired because you were not well suited for the work. ■ Your financial needs have changed. ■ You feel bored or burned-out. ■ You don't fit in.	■ Eyeing your friend's profitable career without giving any thought to the day-to-day activities involved. ■ Considering a field where job security or money is the only plus. ■ Entering a field because it's what your father, mother, sister, or brother does. ■ Hearing that a certain field is growing, but ignoring that it doesn't fit you.

Figure 1 Optimal Time in Job, by Occupation

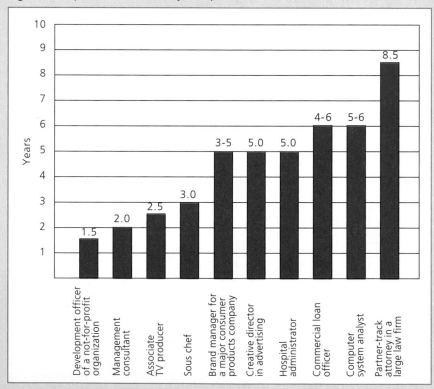

Part Seven

*M*ANAGING FINANCIAL ISSUES

Management of the financial transactions of a business firm are absolutely critical to its survival. Whether it involves raising money to start a new firm, having an accurate view of the riskiness of the firm's investments, or monitoring the firm's activities in securities markets, financial management is a key business activity. The opening cases of the chapters in this section are diverse, yet they all deal specifically with the important function of financial management.

Part Seven, Managing Financial Issues, provides an overview of business finance, including how firms raise and manage money, how they define and manage risk, and how they use Canadian and international securities markets to meet their financial needs.

■ We begin in **Chapter 20, Understanding Money and Banking**, by exploring the nature of money, its creation through the banking system, and the role of the Bank of Canada in the nation's financial system. We also describe other important financial services organizations.

■ Next, in **Chapter 21, Understanding Securities and Investments**, we consider the markets in which firms raise long-term funds by examining how these markets operate and how they are regulated.

■ Finally, in **Chapter 22, Financial Decisions and Risk Management**, we look at three reasons businesses need funds and how financial managers raise both long- and short-term funds. We also examine the kinds of risks businesses encounter and the ways in which they deal with such risks.

20

Understanding Money and Banking

What's the New Price?

If you want to find out how much the Iraqi *dinar* is worth, don't check with the Central Bank or the Ministry of Finance. Instead, check the Shorja outdoor market in Baghdad and watch how the black market for the Iraqi currency operates. Exchange rates here are affected by international events that Iraqis hear about on their short-wave radios. A rumoured new missile strike by the U.S., for example, will send the dinar plunging, but a visit to Baghdad by a U.N. weapons-inspection team might send it up if the report is positive (the report usually isn't). There are thousands of illegal money changers in the streets of Baghdad, and their assessment of international news has a big effect on how much the dinar is worth.

The dinar fluctuates so much because its value is determined by the country's oil exports. After the Gulf War of 1991, the UN imposed sanctions on Iraq, limiting the amount of oil it could export. Before the war, the Iraqi government was loaded with cash it received from selling oil, and the official exchange rate was three U.S. dollars per dinar. But in late 1996 on the black market, it took 1190 dinars to buy *one* dollar. The average Iraqi earns only 5000 dinars a month, and one kilogram of flour costs hundreds of dinars. Thus, there is great economic hardship in Iraq.

Because the dinar's value is so heavily influenced by the actions of foreign governments, retailers operate under almost impossible conditions. The value of the currency changes by the hour (or by the minute if a crisis develops). Retailers have therefore been forced to become experts in international politics. Retailers call money changers numerous times each day to determine the latest value of the dinar. The standard question is: What's the new price? They also spend a lot of time listening to short-wave radio broadcasts in the hope of hearing some important international news that will help them determine whether the dinar is going up or down in value.

Retailers aren't the only people who have problems. Consumers are also driven to distraction by price changes. One man who wanted to buy two automobile tires noticed a price of 98 000 dinars at the first shop he visited. Thinking that was too high, he kept looking but all he could find was another shop offering the tires for 110 000 dinars. He returned to the first shop to buy the tires, but found that while he was gone, the price there had gone up to 120 000 dinars.

The government of Saddam Hussein has not tried to do away with the black market. Rather, it has set up licensed exchange offices around Iraq to compete with the black market money changers. But the black market still thrives, especially when big transactions are involved or when people who are trading don't want others to know who they are. The official exchange-office managers keep in touch with the black market traders so they know what exchange rates they should charge. These managers may also do some trading on the black market themselves. Generally, the black market offers better rates than either the government's exchange offices or the banks. ◆

The opening case shows just how important money is to each of us as we go about our daily lives. Money is also important to business firms, and in this chapter we describe what money is, the different definitions of the money supply, and why money is essential for every business. We also describe the major financial institutions in Canada, and the way they facilitate business activity. The failures of firms such as Bargain Harold's, Olympia & York, Royal Trustco, and Canadian Commercial Bank underscore the importance of stability in Canada's economic system.

By focusing on the learning objectives of this chapter, you will better understand the environment for banking in Canada, and the different kinds of financial institutions that are important. After reading this chapter, you should be able to:

1. Define *money* and identify the different forms it takes in the nation's money supply.

2. Describe the different kinds of *financial institutions* that make up the Canadian financial system and explain the services they offer.

3. Explain how banks create money and identify the means by which they are regulated.

4. Explain the functions of the *Bank of Canada* and describe the tools it uses to control the money supply.

5. Identify ways in which the banking industry is changing.

Money

When someone asks you how much money you have, what do you say? Do you count the bills and coins in your pockets? Do you mention the funds in your chequing and savings accounts? What about stocks, bonds, your car? Taken together, the value of everything you own is your personal *wealth*. Not all of it, however, is *money*. In this section, we will consider what money is and what it does.

What Is Money?

The bills and coins you carry every day are money. So are U.S. dollars, British pound notes, French francs, and Japanese yen. Modern money often takes the form of printed paper or stamped metal issued by a government. But over the centuries, items as diverse as stone wheels, salt, wool, livestock, shells, and spices have been used as money. **Money** is any object generally accepted by people as payment for goods and services.

Thousands of years ago, people began to accept certain agreed-upon objects in exchange for goods or services. As early as 1100 B.C., the Chinese were using metal money that represented the objects they were exchanging (for example, bronze spades and knives). Coins probably came into use sometime around 600 B.C. and paper money around 1200 A.D.

money
Any object generally accepted by people as payment for goods and services.

Desirable Characteristics of Money

Any object can serve as money if it is portable, divisible, durable, and stable.[1] To understand why these qualities are important, imagine using as money something valuable that lacks them—a 35 kilogram salmon, for example.

Throughout the ages, humans have used many monetary devices. Two interesting ones that were in common circulation are the Iroquois wampum belt (early 19th century) from eastern North America and this ancient Greek coin (circa 375 B.C.).

Portability

If you wanted to use the salmon to buy goods and services, you would have to lug a 35 kilogram fish from shop to shop. Modern currency, by contrast, is lightweight and easy to handle.

Divisibility

Suppose you wanted to buy a hat, a book, and some milk from three different stores—all using the salmon as money. How would you divide the fish? First, out comes a cleaver at each store. Then, you would have to determine whether a kilogram of its head is worth as much as a kilogram from the middle. Modern currency is easily divisible into smaller parts with fixed value for each unit. In Canada, for example, a dollar can be exchanged for 4 quarters, 10 dimes, 20 nickels, 100 pennies, or any combination of these coins. It is easy to match units of money with the value of all goods.

Durability

Fish seriously fail the durability test. Each day, whether or not you "spend" it, the salmon will be losing value (and gaining scents). Modern currency, on the other hand, does not spoil, it does not die, and, if it wears out, it can be replaced with new coins and paper money.

Stability

Fish are not stable enough to serve as money. If salmon were in short supply, you might be able to make quite a deal for yourself. But in the middle of a salmon run, the market would be flooded with fish. Since sellers would have many opportunities to exchange their wares for salmon, they would soon have enough fish and refuse to trade for salmon. While the value of the paper money we use today has fluctuated over the years, it is considerably more stable than salmon.

The Functions of Money

Imagine a successful fisherman who needs a new sail for his boat. In a *barter economy*—one in which goods are exchanged directly for one another—he would have to find someone who not only needs fish but who is willing to exchange a sail for it. If no sailmaker wants fish, the fisherman must find someone else—say, a shoemaker—who wants fish and will trade for it. Then the fisherman must hope that the sailmaker will trade for his new shoes. Clearly, barter is quite inefficient in comparison to money. In a money economy, the fisherman would sell his catch, receive money, and exchange the money for such goods as a new sail.

In broad terms, money serves three functions:

- *Medium of exchange*. Like the fisherman "trading" money for a new sail, we use money as a way of buying and selling things. Without money, we would be bogged down in a system of barter.

- *Store of value*. Pity the fisherman who catches a fish on Monday and wants to buy a few bars of candy on, say, the following Saturday. By then, the fish would have spoiled and be of no value. In the form of *currency*, however, money can be used for future purchases and so "stores" value.

- *Unit of account*. Finally, money lets us measure the *relative* values of goods and services. It acts as a unit of account because all products can be valued and accounted for in terms of money. For example, the concepts of "$1000 worth of clothes" or "$500 in labour costs" have universal meaning because everyone deals with money every day.

The Money Supply: M-1

For money to serve as a medium of exchange, a store of value, or a unit of account, buyers and sellers must agree on its value. The value of money, in turn, depends in part on its supply, that is, how much money is in circulation. When the money supply is high, the value of money drops. When the money supply is low, the value of money increases.

Unfortunately, it is not easy to measure the supply of money, nor is there complete agreement on exactly how it should be measured. The "narrow" definition of the money supply is called M-1. **M-1** counts only the most liquid forms of money: currency and demand deposits (chequing accounts) in banks.

M-1
Only the most liquid forms of money (currency and demand deposits).

Currency

Currency is paper money and coins issued by the Canadian government. It is widely used to pay small bills. Canadian currency states clearly: "This note is legal tender." Legal tender is money the law requires a creditor to accept in payment of a debt.

currency
Paper money and coins issued by the government.

Demand Deposits

The majority of Canadian households have chequing accounts against which millions of cheques are written each year. A **cheque** is an order instructing the bank to pay a given sum to a specified person or firm. Although not all sellers accept cheques in payment for goods and services, many do. Cheques enable buyers to make large purchases without having to carry large amounts of cash. Sellers gain a measure of safety because the cheques they receive are valuable only to them and can later be exchanged for cash. Money in chequing accounts, known as **demand deposits**, is counted in M-1 because such funds may be withdrawn at any time without notice.

cheque
An order instructing the bank to pay a given sum to a specified person or firm.

demand deposit
Money in chequing accounts; counted as M-1 because such funds may be withdrawn at any time without notice.

The Money Supply: M-2

M-2 includes everything in M-1 plus items that cannot be spent directly but that are easily converted to spendable forms: *time deposits*, *money market mutual funds*, and *savings deposits*. M-2 accounts for nearly all the nation's

M-2
Everything in M-1 plus savings deposits, time deposits, and money market mutual funds.

money supply. It thus measures the store of monetary value that is available for financial transactions. As this overall level of money increases, more is available for consumer purchases and business investment. When the supply is tightened, less money is available; financial transactions, spending, and business activity thus slow down.

Time Deposits

time deposit

A deposit that requires prior notice to make a withdrawal; cannot be transferred to others by cheque.

Unlike demand deposits, **time deposits** require prior notice of withdrawal and cannot be transferred by cheque. On the other hand, time deposits pay higher interest rates. Thus the supply of money in time deposits—such as *certificates of deposit* (CDs) and *savings certificates*—grew rapidly in the 1970s and 1980s as interest rates rose to levels never before seen in Canada.

Money Market Mutual Funds

money market mutual funds

Funds operated by investment companies that bring together pools of assets from many investors.

Money market mutual funds are operated by investment companies that bring together pools of assets from many investors. The fund buys a collection of short-term, low-risk financial securities. Ownership of and profits (or losses) from the sale of these securities are shared among the fund's investors.

These funds attracted many investors in the 1980s because of high pay-offs and because they often allow investors to write cheques against their shares. Mutual funds pay higher returns than most individuals can get on their own because:

1. Funds can buy into higher-paying securities that require larger investments than most individuals can afford.
2. They are managed by professionals who monitor changing investment opportunities.

Savings Deposits

In the wake of new, more attractive investments, traditional savings deposits, such as passbook savings accounts, have declined in popularity.

Credit Cards

Although not included in M-1 or M-2, credit—especially credit cards—has become a major factor in the purchase of consumer goods in Canada. The use of MasterCard, Visa, American Express, Discover, and credit cards issued by individual businesses has become so widespread that many people refer to credit cards as "plastic money." Nevertheless, credit cards do not qualify as money. Rather, they are a *money substitute*; they serve as a temporary medium of exchange but are not a store of value. The box "To Catch a Credit-Card Thief" describes an interesting development in credit-card fraud detection.

Credit cards are big business for two reasons. First, they are quite convenient—and about to become both more convenient and more reliable:

Visa
http://www.visa.com

MasterCard
http://www.mastercard.com

- Visa, for instance, has already modified the software used at its processing centres and can now attach a special "transaction identifier" to every transaction. This digital code stays with the transaction from the time the consumer uses the card until the time everyone in the system has been paid. Visa says that the number of erroneous charges has already been greatly reduced.

- MasterCard is experimenting with real-time auditing of charges filed by merchants: Every transaction will be completed as soon as it is made rather than, as now, at the end of the day with 20 million others. Merchants will be paid more quickly, and chances of both error and fraud will be reduced significantly.[2]

The Canadian Business Scene

To Catch a Credit Card Thief

Imagine a computer technology that could find relationships among hundreds of unrelated variables and, in the process, recognize patterns, make associations, generalize about new problems, and even learn from the experience. This technology, which roughly mimics the activity of the human brain, is currently operational in the form of *neural networks*. Not surprisingly, companies that have incorporated these networks into their computer systems are already experiencing significant productivity gains.

Neural network chips will soon be part of all computers. Over the next five years, neural network chips not only will be integrated into every PC but will also control the ordinary tasks of everyday life, including microwave cookery (the oven will know how long to cook a chicken without being told) and balancing the shifting load in a washing machine.

Meanwhile, banks and other credit-card issuers are already using neural networks to detect credit-card fraud. Before the development of neural networks, companies relied on specialized computer programs to detect sudden, obvious changes in cardholders' spending patterns. For example, a cardholder who normally purchased no more

than $500 at a time would be notified if thousands of dollars in jewellery and furs were suddenly charged to the account. The relatively crude nature of these early systems often created more problems than solutions, however. Computers often flagged innocent cardholders as well as those who had lost their cards. Consumers who may have altered their spending habits even slightly were notified, a practice that annoyed many and wasted the time and resources of fraud detectors.

Faced with an inefficient system, one bank began using a neural network. Its old system had alerted it to as many as 1000 potential frauds each day (many of which were false alarms), but the neural network flagged only about 100—each of which was likely to signal an actual case of fraud. Using the neural network, bank personnel can now focus on fewer cases and complete investigations within hours rather than days. In one case, the bank notified a customer that her credit card had been stolen only hours after the theft had taken place and before she realized that it was gone.

Second, credit cards are extremely profitable for issuing companies. Profits derive from two sources:

1. Some cards charge annual fees to holders. All charge interest on unpaid balances. Depending on the issuer, cardholders pay interest rates ranging from 11 to 20 percent.
2. Merchants who accept credit cards pay fees to card issuers. Depending on the merchant's agreement with the issuer, 2 to 5 percent of total credit-sales dollars goes to card issuers.

Credit cards are used to purchase very diverse products. They are profitable for the companies that issue them, and they are convenient for consumers.

Annually, more than 25 million cards are used in Canada, 28 million in the United Kingdom, and over 1 billion in the U.S. The accompanying problems are international in scope. The number of cards issued in Japan, for instance, doubled (to 166 million) from 1985 to 1990—and so did the number of delinquencies. Many younger Japanese have incurred large debts by using credit cards to purchase high-ticket items like travel packages and automobiles. In South Korea, because heavy spending by young people is contributing to higher inflation, the Finance Minister has actually curbed the issuance of credit cards: No more cards can be issued to college students, to people younger than 20, or to workers holding jobs less than one year.[3]

The Canadian Financial System

The financial system is central to business firms in Canada. A financial system is made up of organizations and individuals who are sources and users of funds, and/or who help funds flow from sources to users. (See Figure 20.1.) People or organizations with surplus funds will want to earn a return on them. An individual may put his or her money into a savings deposit, buy a bond or a life insurance policy, or invest in the stock market. A business firm may deposit its money in a bank in the short term, buy treasury bills, or buy long-term securities. Charitable organizations and governments may also have surplus funds they wish to invest for certain periods of time.

All people and organizations are users of funds. Sometimes they are unable to raise all the funds they require from personal or internal sources. Money must then be raised from other people or institutions that have surplus funds. Individuals borrow money for certain purposes. Business firms raise money to finance projects, as do governments.

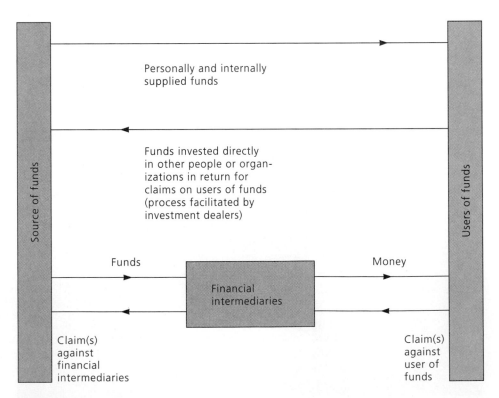

Figure 20.1
Sources of funds, users of funds, financial intermediaries, and investment dealers.

Financial institutions facilitate the flow of funds from sources to users. Their services are important both to organizations that have surplus funds to invest and to those that are in a deficit position and must raise funds.

Financial Intermediaries

There are a variety of financial intermediaries in Canada. They vary in size, in importance, in the types of sources they appeal to, in the form of the claim they give to sources of funds, in the users they supply credit to, and in the type of claim they make against the users of funds.

Until recently, the financial community in Canada was divided rather clearly into four distinct legal areas. Often called the "four financial pillars," they were: (1) chartered banks; (2) alternate banks, such as trust companies and *caisses populaires* or credit unions; (3) life insurance companies and other specialized lending and saving intermediaries, such as factors, finance companies, venture capital firms, mutual funds, and pension funds; and (4) investment dealers. We will discuss the role of these four financial divisions in a moment, but it is important to understand that so many changes have taken place in the financial services industry that the differences across the four divisions are now very blurred.

The crumbling of the four financial pillars began in 1980 when several changes were made to the *Bank Act*. The process accelerated when additional changes were made in 1987 and 1992. Canadian banks, for example, are now permitted to own securities dealers (in 1996, the Royal Bank purchased investment dealer Richardson Greenshields); they are also permitted to sell commercial paper and to own insurance companies (although they are not allowed to sell insurance in their own bank branches). Banks have also established subsidiaries to sell mutual funds.

The changes to the *Bank Act* have also allowed subsidiaries of U.S. banks to set up business in Canada, and over 40 of them have done so. In 1997, legislation was changed again to allow *branches* of U.S. banks to conduct business in Canada.

Trust companies have declined in importance during the last few years, and many smaller trust companies have been bought by banks or insurance companies. The largest trust company—Canada Trust—now offers services that are similar to those offered by banks. Insurance companies are facing increased challenges since banks can now sell insurance. The mutual fund business is booming and has created many new jobs during the last decade.

All these significant changes must be kept in mind as we now turn to a discussion of the four financial pillars of the Canadian economy.

Financial Pillar #1—Chartered Banks

A **chartered bank** is a privately owned, profit-seeking firm that serves individuals, nonbusiness organizations, and businesses as a financial intermediary. Chartered banks offer chequing and savings accounts, make loans, and provide many other services to their customers. They are the main source of short-term loans for business firms.

Chartered banks are the largest and most important financial institution in Canada. They offer a unique service. Their liability instruments (the claims against their assets) are generally accepted by the public and by business as money or as legal tender. Initially, these liability instruments took the form of bank notes issued by individual banks. The *Bank Act* amendments of 1944 removed the right to issue bank notes.

chartered bank
A privately owned, profit-seeking firm that serves individuals, nonbusiness organizations, and businesses as a financial intermediary.

Canada has a branch banking system. Unlike the United States, where there are hundreds of banks, each with a few branches, in Canada there are only a few banks, each with hundreds of branches. The largest chartered banks in Canada are shown in Table 20.1.

The 1980 *Bank Act* requires Schedule A banks to be Canadian-owned and have no more than 10 percent of voting shares controlled by a single interest. It also permits Schedule B banks, which may be domestically owned banks that do not meet the 10 percent limit or may be foreign-controlled. Schedule B banks are initially limited to one main office and one branch. Since the passing of the act, several foreign banks have set up Schedule B subsidiaries. The act limits foreign-controlled banks to deposits that do not exceed 8 percent of the total domestic assets of all banks in Canada.

The five largest Schedule A banks account for about 90 percent of total bank assets. Some of them also have branches in other countries. There are thousands of branch bank offices in Canada, about one for every 3300 people.

Services Offered by Banks

The banking business today is a highly competitive industry. No longer is it enough for banks to accept deposits and make loans. Most, for example, now offer bank-issued credit cards and safe-deposit boxes. In addition, many offer pension, trust, international, and financial advice, and electronic money transfer.

Pension Services

Most banks help customers establish savings plans for retirement. Banks serve as financial intermediaries by receiving funds and investing them as directed by customers. They also provide customers with information on investment possibilities.

Trust Services

trust services

The management of funds left in the bank's trust.

Many banks offer **trust services**—the management of funds left "in the bank's trust." In return for a fee, the trust department will perform such tasks as making your monthly bill payments and managing your investment portfolio. Trust departments also manage the estates of deceased persons.

International Services

The three main international services offered by banks are *currency exchange*, *letters of credit*, and *banker's acceptances*. Suppose, for example, that a Canadian

Table 20.1   The Top 10 Banks in Canada, Ranked by Revenues, 1996

Bank	Revenues (in billions)
1. Royal Bank of Canada	$16.7
2. Canadian Imperial Bank of Commerce	14.8
3. Bank of Montreal	13.0
4. Bank of Nova Scotia	12.4
5. Toronto-Dominion Bank	9.0
6. National Bank of Canada	4.1
7. Hongkong Bank of Canada	1.7
8. Laurentian Bank of Canada	1.0
9. Province of Alberta Treasury Branches	0.8
10. Citibank Canada	0.4

company wants to buy a product from a French supplier. For a fee, it can use one or more of three services offered by its bank:

1. It can exchange Canadian dollars for French francs at a Canadian bank and then pay the French supplier in francs.
2. It can pay its bank to issue a **letter of credit**—a promise by the bank to pay the French firm a certain amount if specified conditions are met.
3. It can pay its bank to draw up a **banker's acceptance**, which promises that the bank will pay some specified amount at a future date.

A banker's acceptance requires payment by a particular date; letters of credit are payable only after certain conditions are met. The French supplier, for example, may not be paid until shipping documents prove that the merchandise has been shipped from France.

letter of credit
A promise by a bank to pay money to a business firm if certain conditions are met.

banker's acceptance
Promises that the bank will pay a specified amount of money at a future date.

Financial Advice

Many banks, both large and small, help their customers manage their money. Depending on the customer's situation, the bank may recommend different investment opportunities. The recommended mix might include guaranteed investment certificates, mutual funds, stocks, and bonds. Today, bank advertisements often stress the role of banks as financial advisers.

Electronic Technologies

Chartered banks and some other financial institutions now use electronic funds transfer (EFT) to provide many basic financial services. **Electronic funds transfer** combines computer and communication technology to transfer funds or information into, from, within, and among financial institutions. Examples include the following:

electronic funds transfer (EFT)
A combination of computer and communications technology that transfers funds or information into, from, within, and among financial institutions.

- Automated teller machines (ATMs), or 24-hour tellers, are electronic terminals that let you bank at almost any time of day or night. Generally, you insert a special card and enter your own secret identification number to withdraw cash, make deposits, or transfer funds between accounts.

- Pay-by-phone systems let you telephone your financial institution and instruct it to pay certain bills or to transfer funds between accounts merely by pushing the proper buttons on your phone.

- Direct deposits or withdrawals allow you to authorize in advance specific, regular deposits and withdrawals. You can arrange to have paycheques and social assistance cheques automatically deposited and recurring expenses, such as insurance premiums and utility bills, automatically paid.

- Point-of-sale transfers let you pay for retail purchases with your debit card. A **debit card** is a type of plastic money that immediately reduces the balance in the user's bank account when it is used. For example, if you use a debit card at a grocery store, the clerk simply runs the card through the machine and asks you to punch in a personal identification number on a keypad next to the cash register. The price of the groceries is then deducted electronically from your chequing account, and money moves from your chequing account to the grocery store's account.

debit card
A type of plastic money that immediately on use reduces the balance in the user's bank account and transfers it to the store's account.

- The so-called **smart card** is a credit card-sized computer that can be programmed with "electronic money." Also known as "electronic purses" or "stored-value cards," smart cards have existed for nearly a decade. Shoppers in Europe and Asia are the most avid users, holding the majority of the 33 million cards in circulation at the beginning of 1995.[4]

smart card
Credit card-sized computer that can be programmed with "electronic money."

Automated Teller Machines (ATMs) have revolutionized the way we do our banking. Now we have access to our money almost everywhere we go—shopping malls, grocery stores, even roadside "minibanks."

Why are smart cards increasing in popularity today? For one thing, the cost of producing them has fallen dramatically—from as much as $10 to as little as $1. Convenience is equally important, notes Donald J. Gleason, president of Electronic Payment Services' Smart Card Enterprise division. "What consumers want," Gleason contends, "is convenience, and if you look at cash, it's really quite inconvenient."[5]

Smart cards can be loaded with money at ATM machines or, with special telephone hookups, even at home. After using your card to purchase an item, you can then check an electronic display to see how much money your card has left. Analysts predict that in the near future, smart cards will function as much more than electronic purses. For example, travel industry experts predict that people will soon book travel plans at home on personal computers and then transfer their reservations onto their smart cards. The cards will then serve as airline tickets and boarding passes. As an added benefit, they will allow travellers to avoid waiting in lines at car rental agencies and hotel front desks.

E-cash

Money that moves among consumers and businesses via digital electronic transmissions.

■ A new, revolutionary world of electronic money has begun to emerge with the rapid growth of the Internet. Electronic money, known as **E-cash**, is money that moves along multiple channels of consumers and businesses via digital electronic transmissions. E-cash moves outside the established network of banks, cheques, and paper currency. How does E-cash work? Traditional currency is used to buy electronic funds, which are downloaded over phone lines into a PC or a portable "electronic wallet" that can store and transmit E-cash. E-cash is purchased from any company that issues (sells) it, including banks. When shopping online—say, to purchase jewellery—a shopper sends digital money to the merchant instead of using traditional cash, cheques, or credit cards. Businesses can purchase supplies and services electronically from any merchant that accepts E-cash. E-cash flows from the buyer's into the seller's E-cash funds, which are instantaneously updated and stored on a microchip.

Although E-cash transactions are cheaper than handling cheques and the paper records involved with conventional money, there are some potential problems. Hackers, for example, may break into E-cash systems and drain them instantaneously. Moreover, if the issuer's computer system crashes, it is conceivable that money "banked" in memory may be lost forever. Finally, regulation and control of E-cash systems remains largely nonexistent; there is virtually none of the protection that covers government-controlled money systems.[6]

Figure 20.2 summarizes the services that chartered banks offer. Banks are chartered by the federal government and are closely regulated when they provide these services. As the box "Promoting Banking Services" describes, banks have recently begun to promote their services more actively.

Bank Deposits

Chartered banks provide a financial intermediary service by accepting deposits and making loans with this money. Banks make various types of loans to businesses. When applying for a business loan, it is wise for the manager to remember that the banker is interested in making money for the bank through the loan. The banker is also interested in how the loan will be repaid and how it will be secured. A brief written statement accompanied by a cash-flow analysis is a useful approach when applying for a loan.

One type of deposit a customer can make in a bank is a chequable, or demand, deposit. A **chequable deposit** is a chequing account. Customers who deposit coins, paper currency, or other cheques in their chequing accounts can write cheques against the balance in their accounts. Their banks must honour these cheques immediately; this is why chequing accounts are also called demand deposits.

chequable deposit
A chequing account.

The other type of deposit a customer can make in a chartered bank is a term deposit. A **term deposit** is one that remains with the bank for a period of time. Interest is paid to depositors for the use of their funds. There are two types of term deposits. The most popular is the regular passbook savings account. Although banks can require notice before withdrawals can be made, they seldom do. These accounts are intended primarily for small individual savers and non-profit organizations.

term deposit
Money that remains with the bank for a period of time with interest paid to the depositor.

Another type of term deposit is the guaranteed investment certificate. This deposit is made for a specified period of time ranging from 28 days to

Figure 20.2
Examples of services provided by many chartered banks and trust companies.

The Canadian Business Scene

Promoting Banking Services

Years ago, banks did virtually no advertising. Apparently their managers held the view that advertising was somehow inconsistent with the image of stability and security that banks wanted to project. During the last couple of decades, banks became more involved in advertising but always with a conservative, tasteful, business-like approach. All this is changing as banks turn away from some of the commercial activities that have occupied their minds for the last decade (for example, loaning money to high-risk developing countries and building major office complexes) and begin to refocus on the consumer.

As the competition for the small consumer's business intensifies, banks are beginning to spend large sums of money on advertising, sales promotion, and market research. Their goal is to increase customer loyalty; they do this through "relationship banking" (emphasizing a renewed commitment to personal service) and by giving incentives to customers who remain with one bank.

At Toronto-Dominion, the emphasis is on customer service. More than 7000 of TD's front-line staff are taking a customer-service workshop designed to sensitize them to customers' feelings.

The Bank of Montreal is combining television advertisements designed to improve the bank's image with practical innovations at the branch level. For example, mortgagees no longer automatically get a nasty letter when they miss a payment. Instead, a staff member phones and tactfully asks if there is a problem with the payment. The overall goal is to empower branch staff to manage customer relationships better.

Banks are trying to target more precise market segments. The Royal Bank's seniors banking centre in Toronto is located next to a senior citizens' home. It features a push-button door opener, sit-down service, and large-print withdrawal slips. Staff at the centre make house calls on shut-ins, and generally keep an eye out for their clients, many of whom live alone.

Mass advertising plays a role at many banks as part of their overall strategy of increasing customer loyalty:

- CIBC advertisements show bank personnel talking to customers about how the bank can deliver a better product or service than the competition can.

- National Trust developed commercials that spoof the frustrating situations consumers encounter at an unnamed rival financial institution. The ads stress that National Trust never forgets whose money it is they are working with.

- The Bank of Montreal has developed a series of advertisements that features the slogan "We pay attention."

All of these campaigns are aimed at reducing the "bank-as-bad-guy" image that Canadian banks have. Bank-bashing is the second-most popular sport in Canada after politician-bashing. Consumers feel that banks are making record profits, but they have done a poor job of listening to customers' concerns and of caring about their financial problems.

Research shows that the main reason Canadians close a bank account is poor service. So banks are responding with the above-noted advertising campaigns, as well as other promotions designed to convince Canadians that things are going to change. Skeptics point out that certain problems remain. For example, banks have not addressed some long-standing, high-profile irritants. They still charge high interest rates on credit cards for their supposedly important customers.

---

several years. These certificates are available to all savers. The interest rate paid on a guaranteed investment certificate is higher than that paid on a regular savings account, but many GICs cannot be cashed in before their maturity dates, so they are less flexible than a savings account.

Bank Loans

Banks are the major source of short-term loans for business. Although banks make long-term loans to some firms, they prefer to specialize in providing short-term funds to finance inventories and accounts receivable.

A *secured* loan is backed by collateral such as accounts receivable or a life insurance policy. If the borrower cannot repay the loan, the bank sells the collateral. An *unsecured* loan is backed only by the borrower's promise to repay it. Only the most creditworthy borrowers can get unsecured loans.

Borrowers pay interest on their loans. Large firms with excellent credit records pay the prime rate of interest. The **prime rate of interest** is the lowest rate charged to borrowers. This rate changes constantly owing to changes in the demand for and supply of loanable funds as well as to policies of the Bank of Canada. The so-called "Big Six" Canadian banks (Royal Bank, CIBC, Bank of Montreal, Bank of Nova Scotia, Toronto-Dominion, and National Bank of Canada) typically act in concert with respect to the prime rate.

prime rate of interest
The lowest rate charged to borrowers.

Banks as Creators of Money

In the course of their activities, financial institutions provide a special service to the economy—they create money. This is not to say that they mint bills and coins. Rather, by taking in deposits and making loans, they *expand the money supply*. We will first look at how this expansion process works, assuming that banks have a **reserve requirement**, that is, that they must keep a portion of their chequable deposits in vault cash or as deposits with the Bank of Canada. (This reserve requirement was dropped in 1991, and the implications of this change are described later.)

reserve requirement
The requirement (until 1991) that banks keep a portion of their chequable deposits in vault cash or as deposits with the Bank of Canada.

Suppose you saved $100, took it to a bank, and opened a chequing account. Some portion of your $100 is likely to stay in your account, so your bank can earn interest by lending some of it to other borrowers. Let's assume that there is a reserve requirement, and that it is 10 percent. Your bank must therefore keep $10 of your $100 deposit in reserve, so it has only $90 to lend.

Now suppose a person named Jennifer Leclerc borrows $90 from your bank. She now has $90 added to her chequing account. Assume that she writes a cheque for $90 payable to Canadian Tire. Canadian Tire's bank ends up with a $90 deposit, and that bank is also required to keep $9 in reserve. It therefore has $81 to lend out to someone else.

This process of deposit expansion can continue as shown in Figure 20.3. As you can see, your original deposit of $100 could result in an increase of $1000 in new deposits for all banks in the system. But, what happens if there is no reserve requirement? At the extreme, it means that banks could (theoretically) create infinite amounts of money because they don't have to keep any in reserve. But banks will not do this because it is risky. So, in practice, the dropping of the reserve requirement simply means that banks will be able to create more money than they did when there was a reserve requirement.

Why was the reserve requirement changed? Partly because banks claimed that in the new, deregulated financial services industry it was going to be difficult for them to compete with trust and insurance companies, who have no reserve requirements.

Even though the reserve requirement has disappeared, the chartered banks must still keep clearing balances with the Bank of Canada, which can increase or decrease these balances and thereby continue to influence interest rates as before.

The change in reserve requirements could cost the federal government millions of dollars each year in lost interest; it will also lead to increased bank profits or lower loan rates to consumers, or some combination of both.[7]

Other Changes in Banking

Fundamental changes in addition to those already described are taking place in banking. For example, deregulation has caused banks to shift away from their historical role as intermediaries between depositors and borrowers. Canada's banks are diversifying to provide a wider array of financial products to their clients. Training bankers to be effective in this environment is necessary. For

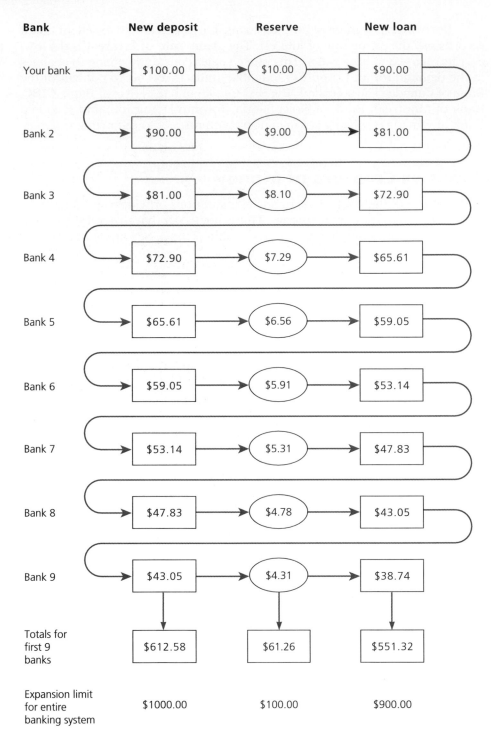

Figure 20.3
How the chartered banking system creates money.

example, over 100 executives at Toronto-Dominion Bank attended a Harvard University course that taught them to think like investment bankers. The Bank of Montreal conducted a similar course for over 400 executives.

In the last few years, large companies have reduced their use of bank loans. To compensate for this loss, banks are setting up money market operations. For example, until deregulation, only securities firms were allowed to sell commercial paper (see Chapter 22), but banks expect to dominate in this area before too long. (Commercial paper is usually issued by blue-chip companies that pay a fee to investment dealers or banks to sell the security.) Banks have been allowed to sell commercial paper since June 1987, when deregulation opened up this possibility. The Bank of Montreal and the Toronto-Dominion Bank have been the most active in this market.

In Canada, about 200 companies have a credit rating good enough for commercial paper. Banks want to use commercial paper more because they do not have to keep capital reserves on hand for commercial paper as they do for acceptances.

Changes are also taking place in banking because consumers are no longer content to simply keep money in a bank when they can get more for it elsewhere. Banks are responding by selling a growing array of corporate and government securities through their branches.

All of this activity is transforming the profit base of banks. In the past, they made most of their money from the spread between interest rates paid to depositors and the rates charged on loans. Investment banking, on the other hand, is fee-based. Banks are making a larger proportion of their profits from fees, and this is blurring the traditional boundary between banks and securities firms.

Another change concerns international banking. Because U.S. and other foreign banks are now allowed to do business in Canada, Canada's Big Six banks are going to experience increased competition. They are responding to this threat with a variety of tactics, including cooperating to spread their fixed costs. Syncor Services, for example, is a joint venture between three of the Big Six banks that provides cheque-clearing services across Canada.[8] The competitive threat from one foreign bank is described in the box "Discount Banking: Will It Work?"

International Report

Discount Banking: Will It Work?

International Nederlanden Groep (ING) is a large Dutch firm (1996 profits of $2.38 billion) that has decided to use Canada as a test market for a new concept: discount banking. One of its banking subsidiaries, called ING Direct, is off to a good start. It hopes to have 35 000 customers and more than $250 million in deposits in its first year.

How does ING propose to achieve these goals? By paying higher interest on deposits than its competitors, by not levying fees or service charges as the Big Six Canadian banks do, and by charging lower rates on loans than traditional banks do. How can it do all these things and still earn a profit? By using *branchless banking*, and by relying on the latest information processing technologies to serve customers.

A study by the Canadian Imperial Bank of Commerce showed that the cost of paying a bill in person at a bank branch is $1.29; paying the same bill by Internet costs $0.15. If ING has no branches, it may be able to develop a huge cost advantage over Canadian banks. In simple terms, ING is a high-volume, low-margin bank—the Wal-Mart of banking, if you will.

How can ING be sure that Canadians will do business with a bank that has no branches? They can't, but they know that Canadians are famous for their willingness to embrace new technologies such as e-mail, debit cards, and automated teller machines. They are banking on this willingness (no pun intended) to be competitive in the Canadian market. ING's customers will be able to carry out banking transactions with ING without having to go to a bank branch.

If ING can make it in Canada, that will mean that other foreign financial institutions may also get interested. So, Canadian banks aren't concerned just about ING. They are also going to have to contend with giant U.S. financial companies such as Wells Fargo Bank, which offers small business loans to Canadians even though it has no branches in Canada. All the necessary work to complete the transaction is done by direct mail, the Internet, and telemarketing.

Will the new technologies allow foreign banks to enter Canada and put real pressure on the Big Six Canadian banks? Time will tell.

The Bank of Canada

Bank of Canada
Canada's central bank; formed in 1935.

The **Bank of Canada**, formed in 1935, is Canada's central bank. It has a crucial role to play in managing the Canadian economy and in regulating certain aspects of chartered bank operations.

The Bank of Canada is managed by a board of governors composed of a governor, a deputy governor, and 12 directors appointed from different regions of Canada. The directors, with cabinet approval, appoint the governor and deputy governor. The deputy minister of finance is also a nonvoting member of the board. Between meetings of the board, normally held eight times a year, an executive committee acts for the board. This committee is composed of the governor, the deputy governor, two directors, and the deputy minister of finance. The executive committee meets at least once a week.

Operation of the Bank of Canada

The Bank of Canada plays an important role in managing the money supply in Canada. (See Figure 20.4.) If the Bank of Canada wants to increase the money supply, it can buy government securities. The people selling these bonds deposit the proceeds in their banks. These deposits increase banks' reserves and their willlingness to make loans. The Bank of Canada can also lower the bank rate; this action will cause increased demand for loans from businesses and households because these customers borrow more money when interest rates drop.

If the Bank of Canada wants to decrease the money supply, it can sell government securities. People spend money to buy bonds, and these withdrawals bring down banks' reserves and reduce their ability to make loans. The Bank of Canada can also raise the bank rate; this action will cause decreased demand for loans from businesses and households because these customers borrow less money when interest rates rise.

Member Bank Borrowing from the Bank of Canada

The Bank of Canada is the lender of last resort for chartered banks. The rate at which chartered banks can borrow from the Bank of Canada is called the

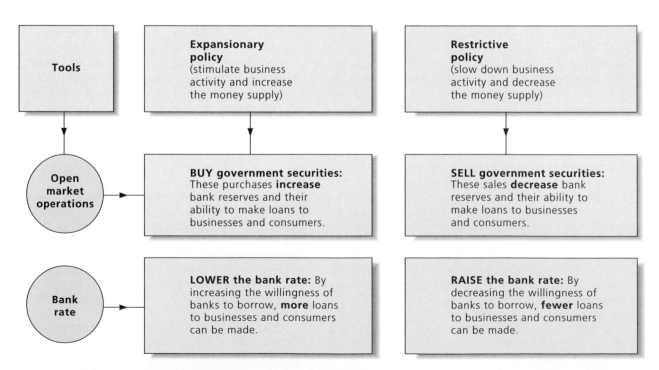

Figure 20.4
Bank of Canada monetary policy actions.

bank, or rediscount, **rate**. It serves as the basis for establishing the chartered banks' prime interest rates. By raising the bank rate, the Bank of Canada depresses the demand for money; by lowering it, the demand for money increases. In practice, chartered banks seldom have to borrow from the Bank of Canada. However, the bank rate is an important instrument of monetary policy as a determinant of interest rates.

bank rate
The rate at which chartered banks can borrow from the Bank of Canada.

Financial Pillar #2—Alternate Banks

Trust Companies

Another financial intermediary that serves individuals and businesses is the alternate, or near, bank: the trust company. A **trust company** safeguards property—funds and estates—entrusted to it; it may also serve as trustee, transfer agent, and registrar for corporations and provide other services.

A corporation selling bonds to many investors appoints a trustee, usually a trust company, to protect the bondholders' interests. A trust company can also serve as a transfer agent and registrar for corporations. A transfer agent records changes in ownership of a corporation's shares of stock. A registrar certifies to the investing public that stock issues are correctly stated and comply with the corporate charter. Other services include preparing and issuing dividend cheques to shareholders and serving as trustee for employee profit-sharing funds. Trust companies also accept deposits and pay interest on them. The box "A Classic Case of Mismanagement" describes the collapse of Royal Trustco, one of Canada's largest trust companies.

trust company
Safeguards funds and estates entrusted to it; may also serve as trustee, transfer agent, and registrar for corporations.

The Canadian Business Scene

A Classic Case of Mismanagement

Royal Trustco Ltd., the holding company for Canada's second-largest trust company, disintegrated in 1993. Its brewing troubles became evident in 1990, when it incurred its first loss ever. Much of the blame is put on CEO Michael Cornelissen, who took three specific actions that later came back to haunt him: he acquired the financial services holdings of Dow Chemical, made major investments in the U.S. savings and loan industry, and moved into the British mortgage market. All of these initiatives caused big problems for Royal Trust.

When Cornelissen became CEO at Royal Trustco in 1983, he introduced major changes in the laid-back way the firm operated. He expected all executives to arrive at 7 a.m., and left nasty notes on the desks of executives who didn't comply. He berated people publicly in front of others and called his new colleagues "turkeys." He was impatient with the slow pace of decision making at management meetings.

Not surprisingly, many managers who had been with the firm for years decided to leave. Cornelissen then brought in new people more to his liking. He tried to make Royal Trustco an entrepreneurial, decentralized organization, an objective that clashed with the culture of most banks, which are bureaucratic and hierarchical. No one questioned his commitment and hard work, and there was strong loyalty to him within his new top management team. But he received little

sympathy in financial circles, partly because he had a short fuse and because some people he dealt with considered him arrogant. And industry analysts expressed concern that Royal Trustco's emphasis on entrepreneurialism would lead to a lack of discipline and the financial controls that are critical in a financial institution.

Their fears were well founded. In 1993, the company disintegrated from superficial good health to near collapse and was sold to the Royal Bank of Canada (Cornelissen had already left as CEO). At the company's annual meeting in June 1993, company officials gave shareholders a humble presentation explaining how things had gone so wrong and why they had decided to sell the company's best assets to the Royal Bank. In a nutshell, the company had made too many real estate loans in markets such as London, Los Angeles, and Toronto. When those markets collapsed, loan losses began. Once that happened, investor confidence declined and the company started losing depositors.

The shareholders at the meeting were not impressed. Today, these investors are left holding shares in Gentra Inc., the renamed company that was left behind after most of Royal Trustco's assets were sold. The shares are trading for about 40 cents (Royal Trustco's shares were trading for $36 in 1986).

Credit unions (caisses populaires) are cooperative saving and lending organizations that loan money to both consumers and businesses.

Credit Unions/Caisses Populaires

credit union

Cooperative savings and lending association formed by a group with common interests.

Credit unions (called *caisses populaires* in Quebec) are also alternate banks. They are important to business because they lend money to consumers to buy durable goods such as cars and furniture. They also lend money to businesses. **Credit unions** and *caisses populaires* are cooperative savings and lending associations formed by a group with common interests. Members (owners) can add to their savings accounts by authorizing deductions from their paycheques or by making direct deposits. They can borrow short-term, long-term, or mortgage funds from the credit union. Credit unions also invest substantial amounts of money in corporate and government securities. The largest credit unions in Canada are listed in Table 20.2.

Table 20.2   The Top 10 Credit Unions in Canada, 1996

Credit Union	Revenues (in millions)
1. Caisse centrale Desjardins	$409.6
2. Vancouver City Savings Credit Union	377.8
3. Surrey Metro Savings Credit Union	151.7
4. Richmond Savings Credit Union	136.7
5. Pacific Coast Savings Credit Union	116.8
6. First Heritage Savings Credit Union	72.5
7. Capital City Savings and Credit Union	71.3
8. Civil Service Cooperative Credit Society	69.6
9. Niagara Credit Union Ltd.	62.1
10. HEPCOE Credit Union	60.5

Financial Pillar #3—
Specialized Lending and Savings Intermediaries

life insurance company

A mutual or stock company that shares risk with its policyholders for payment of premiums.

Life Insurance Companies

An important source of funds for individuals, nonbusiness organizations, and businesses is the life insurance company. A **life insurance company** is a mutual or stock company that shares risk with its policyholders in return for payment of a premium. It lends some of the money it collects from premiums to borrowers. Life insurance companies are substantial investors in real estate mortgages and in corporate and government bonds. Next to chartered banks, they are the largest financial intermediaries in Canada. We discuss insurance companies in more detail in Chapter 22.

Factoring Companies

An important source of short-term funds for many firms is factoring companies. A **factoring company** (or factor) buys accounts receivable (amounts due from credit customers) from a firm. It pays less than the face value of the accounts but collects the face value of the accounts. The difference, minus the cost of doing business, is the factor's profit.

A firm that sells its accounts receivable to a factor without recourse shifts the risk of credit loss to the factor. If an account turns out to be uncollectable, the factor suffers the loss. However, a factor is a specialist in credit and collection activities. Using a factor may enable a business firm to expand sales beyond what would be practical without the factor. The firm trades accounts receivable for cash. The factor notifies the firm's customers to make their overdue payments to the factor.

factoring company
Buys accounts receivable from a firm for less than their face value, and then collects the face value of the receivables.

Financial Corporations

There are two types of financial corporations: sales finance companies and consumer finance companies.

A major source of credit for many firms and their customers is the sales finance company. A **sales finance company** specializes in financing instalment purchases made by individuals and firms. When you buy durable goods from a retailer on an instalment plan with a sales finance company, the loan is made directly to you. The item itself serves as security for the loan. Sales finance companies enable many firms to sell on credit, even though the firms could not afford to finance credit sales on their own.

General Motors Acceptance Corporation (GMAC) is a sales finance company. It is a captive company because it exists to finance instalment contracts resulting from sales made by General Motors. Industrial Acceptance Corporation is a large Canadian sales finance company.

Sales finance companies also finance instalment sales to business firms. Many banks have instalment loan departments.

An important source of credit for many consumers is the consumer finance company. A **consumer finance company** makes personal loans to consumers. Often the borrower pledges no security (collateral) for the loan. For larger loans, collateral may be required, such as a car or furniture.

These companies do not make loans to businesses but they do provide the financing that turns many people into actual paying customers. Household Finance Corporation is an example of a consumer finance company.

sales finance company
Specializes in financing instalment purchases made by individuals or firms.

consumer finance company
Makes personal loans to consumers.

Venture Capital or Development Firms

A **venture capital firm**, or development firm, will provide funds for new or expanding firms thought to have significant potential. Venture capital firms obtain their funds from initial capital subscriptions, from loans from other financial intermediaries, and from retained earnings.

Venture capital firms may provide either equity or debt funds to firms. Financing new, untested businesses is risky, so venture capital firms want to

venture capital firm
Provides funds for new or expanding firms thought to have significant potential.

earn a higher-than-normal return on their investment. The ideal situation is an equity investment in a company that becomes very successful and experiences substantial increases in its stock value.

Pension Funds

pension fund

Accumulates money that will be paid out to plan subscribers in the future.

A **pension fund** accumulates money that will be paid out to plan subscribers at some time in the future. The money collected is invested in corporate stocks and bonds, government bonds, or mortgages until it is to be paid out. Pension funds are discussed in more detail in Chapter 21.

Financial Pillar #4—Investment Dealers

Investment dealers (called stockbrokers or underwriters) perform two important financial functions. First, they are the primary distributors of new stock and bond issues (underwriting). Second, they facilitate secondary trading of stocks and bonds, both on stock exchanges and on over-the-counter stock and bond markets (the brokerage function). These functions are discussed in more detail in Chapter 21. The 10 largest investment dealers are shown in Table 20.3.

Table 20.3 **The Top 10 Investment Dealers in Canada, Ranked by Revenues, 1996**

Company	Revenues (in millions)
1. CIBC Wood Gundy Securities Inc.	$2436
2. RBC Dominion Securities Ltd.	1390
3. The Nesbitt Burns Group	958
4. Scotia Capital Markets	790
5. TD Securities Inc.	781
6. Midland Walwyn Inc.	723
7. Levesque Beaubien Geoffrion Inc.	345
8. Fahnestock Viner Holdings Inc.	291
9. First Marathon Inc.	259
10. Yorkton Securities	144

Other Sources of Funds

Government Financial Institutions and Granting Agencies

In Canada, a number of government suppliers of funds are important to business. In general, they supply funds to new and/or growing companies. However, established firms can also use some of them.

Industrial Development Bank (IDB)

A subsidiary of the Bank of Canada created to make loans to business firms.

Federal Business Development Bank (FBDB)

Took over operation of the IDB in 1975; particularly active in lending money to small businesses.

The **Industrial Development Bank (IDB)**, a subsidiary of the Bank of Canada, was created to make loans to business firms. The **Federal Business Development Bank (FBDB)** took over operation of the IDB in 1975. The IDB was set up to make term loans, primarily to smaller firms judged to have growth potential but unable to secure funds at reasonable terms from traditional sources. Its services were expanded by providing proportionally more equity financing and more management counselling services. The FBDB has been especially active in providing loans for small businesses.

A variety of provincial industrial development corporations provide funds to developing business firms in the hope that they will provide jobs in the province. These were discussed in Chapter 8.

The federal government's Export Development Corporation can finance and insure export sales for Canadian companies. The Canada Mortgage and Housing Corporation (CMHC) is involved in providing and guaranteeing mortgages. The CMHC is particularly important to the construction industry.

A number of federal and provincial programs are specifically designed to provide loans to agricultural operators. Most of these, with the exception of farm improvement loans which guarantee bank loans to farmers, are long-term loans for land purchase.

In addition to these activities, governments are involved in providing grants to business operations. For example, the federal government, through the Department of Regional Industrial Expansion (DRIE), gives grants for certain types of business expansion in designated areas of the country. Other federal government grants are available for activities such as new product development.

Canada Mortgage and Housing Corporation
http://www.cmhc-schl.gc.ca

International Sources of Funds

Not all of the financing requirements of Canadian businesses and governments are met from within Canada. Foreign sources of funds are also important. The financial institutions of Canada play a role in facilitating the flow of funds into the country.

The Canadian capital market is one part of the international capital market. Canadian provinces borrow extensively in foreign markets such as those in London and in New York. Canadian corporations likewise find it attractive to borrow in foreign markets.

Foreign sources of funds have been significant to the economic development of Canada. Although many groups and individuals have expressed concern about foreign ownership of Canadian firms, projections of Canada's future capital requirements indicate that it will continue to need foreign sources of funds. Canadian financial institutions will continue to play a large role in making these funds available.

International Banking and Finance

Each nation tries to influence its currency exchange rates for economic advantage in international trade. The subsequent country-to-country transactions result in an *international payments process* that moves money among buyers and sellers on different continents.

Exchange Rates and International Trade

As we saw in both Chapters 4 and 19, every country's currency exchange rate affects its ability to buy and sell on the global market. The value of a given currency—say, the Canadian dollar—reflects the overall supply and demand for Canadian dollars both at home and abroad. This value, of course, changes with economic conditions. Worldwide, therefore, firms will watch those trends. What, for example, is the current exchange rate between their own currencies and that of Canada? Decisions about whether or not to do business in Canada will be affected by more or less favourable exchange rates. How do firms determine when rates are favourable?

The Law of One Price

When a country's currency becomes *overvalued*, its exchange rate is higher than warranted by its economic conditions. Its high costs make it less competitive. Because its products are expensive to make and buy, fewer are purchased by other countries. The likely result is a *trade deficit*. In contrast, an *undervalued* currency means low costs and low prices. It attracts purchases by other countries, usually leading to a *trade surplus*.

law of one price

The principle that identical products should sell for the same price in all countries.

How do we know if a currency is overvalued or undervalued? One method involves a simple concept called the **law of one price**: the principle that identical products should sell for the same price in all countries. In other words, if the different prices of a Rolex watch in different countries were converted into a common currency, the common-denominator price should be the same everywhere.

But what if prices are not equal? In theory, the pursuit of profits should equalize them: Sellers in high-priced countries will have to reduce prices if they are to compete successfully and make profits. As prices adjust, so, too, should the exchange rates between different currencies until the Rolex can be purchased for the same price everywhere.

A simple example that illustrates over- and undervalued currencies is the "Big MacCurrencies," an index published in the British magazine *The Economist*. The "identical product" here is always McDonald's Big Mac, which is made locally in 68 countries. The first two columns in Table 20.4 list several countries and Big Mac prices in terms of local currencies. Each country's price is then converted into U.S. dollars (based on recent exchange rates). As you can see, while the Swiss price (SFr5.70) is most expensive, the Chinese yuan is the cheapest.

According to the Big Mac index, then, the Swiss franc is the most overvalued currency (against the U.S. dollar), while the Chinese yuan is the most undervalued. In theory, this means that you could buy Big Macs in China (using yuan) and resell them in Switzerland (for Swiss francs) at a handsome profit. In China, therefore, the demand for burgers would increase, driving the price up towards the higher prices in the other countries. In other words, the law of one price would set in. The index also indicates that the exchange rates of Greece, Taiwan, Chile, and Canada are slightly overvalued or undervalued against the U.S. dollar.[9]

Table 20.4   The "Big Mac" Currency Index

Country	Big Mac Prices in Local Currency	Big Mac Prices in Equivalent U.S. Dollars	Local Currency Overevaluation (+) or Undervaluation (–)
United States	**$2.30**	**$2.30**	
Switzerland	5.70 francs	3.96	+72%
Denmark	25.75 krone	3.85	+67
Argentina	3.60 pesos	3.60	+57
Belgium	109 francs	3.10	+35
S. Korea	2300 won	2.84	+24
Greece	620 drachma	2.47	+8
Taiwan	$62 Taiwanese	2.35	+2
Chile	948 pesos	2.28	-1
Canada	**$2.86 Canadian**	**2.06**	**-10**
Australia	$2.45 Australia	1.72	-25
Poland	3100 zloty	1.40	-40
China	9.00 yuan	1.03	-55

Government Influences on Exchange Rates

What happens when a currency becomes overvalued or undervalued? A nation's economic authorities may take action to correct its balance-of-payments conditions. Typically, they will *devalue* or *revalue* the nation's currency. The purpose of *devaluing*—as Mexico did in 1994—is to cause a decrease in the home country's exchange value. It will then be less expensive for other countries to buy the home country's products. As more of its products are purchased, the home country's payment deficit goes down. The purpose of revaluation is the reverse: to increase the exchange value and reduce the home country's payment surplus.

The International Payments Process

Now we know why a nation tries to control its balance of payments and what, at least in part, it can do about an unfavourable balance. Exactly how are payments made? Transactions among buyers and sellers in different countries are simplified through the services provided by their banks. For example, payments from buyers flow through a local bank that converts them from the local currency into the foreign currency of the seller. Likewise, the local bank receives and converts incoming money from the banks of foreign buyers. The *payments process* is shown in Figure 20.5.[10]

Step 1. A Canadian olive importer withdraws $1000 from its chequing account in order to buy olives from a Greek exporter. The local Canadian bank *converts* those dollars into Greek drachmas at the current exchange rate (230 drachmas per dollar).

Step 2. The Canadian bank sends the cheque for 230 000 drachmas (230 × 1000) to the exporter in Greece.

Steps 3 and 4. The exporter sends olives to its Canadian customer and deposits the cheque in its local Greek bank. While the exporter now has drachmas that can be spent in Greece, the importer has olives to sell in Canada.

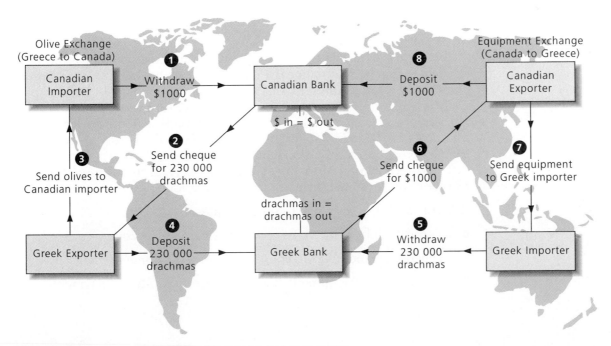

Figure 20.5
The international payments process.

At the same time, a separate transaction is being made between a Canadian machine exporter and a Greek olive oil producer. This time, the importer/exporter roles are reversed between the two countries: The Greek firm needs to *import* a $1000 olive oil press from Canada.

Steps 5 and 6. Drachmas (230 000) withdrawn from a local Greek bank account are converted into $1000 Canadian and sent via cheque to the Canadian exporter.

Steps 7 and 8. The olive oil press is sent to the Greek importer, and the importer's cheque is deposited in the Canadian exporter's local bank account.

In this example, trade between the two countries is *in balance*: Money inflows and outflows are equal for both countries. When such a balance occurs, *money does not actually have to flow between the two countries*. Within each bank, the dollars spent by local importers offset the dollars received by local exporters. In effect, therefore, the dollars have simply flowed from Canadian importers to Canadian exporters. Likewise, the drachmas have moved from Greek exporters to Greek importers.

Interbank Trading

To get a true picture, however, we must multiply this simple illustration by the huge number of daily transactions that take place between countries. Obviously, this system of trade involves banks (or other financial institutions) that buy and sell foreign currencies for their customers. Among these currency trades, the U.S. dollar was by far the most active currency, being involved in 89 percent of all transactions. Next most active were the German mark (34 percent), the Japanese yen (23 percent), and the British pound (9 percent).

International Bank Structure

There is no worldwide banking system that is comparable, in terms of policy-making and regulatory power, to the system of any single industrialized nation. Rather, worldwide banking stability relies on a loose structure of agreements among individual countries or groups of countries.

The World Bank and the IMF

Two United Nations agencies, the World Bank and the International Monetary Fund, help to finance international trade. Unlike true banks, the **World Bank** (technically the International Bank for Reconstruction and Development) actually provides only a very limited scope of services. For instance, it funds national improvements by making loans to build roads, schools, power plants, and hospitals. The resulting improvements eventually enable borrowing countries to increase productive capacity and international trade.

The **International Monetary Fund (IMF)** is a group of some 150 nations that have combined their resources for the following purposes:

■ To promote the stability of exchange rates

■ To provide temporary, short-term loans to member countries

■ To encourage members to cooperate on international monetary issues

■ To encourage development of a system for international payments

World Bank
http://www.worldbank.org

International Monetary Fund
http://www.imf.org

World Bank
United Nations agency that provides a limited scope of financial services, such as funding national improvements in undeveloped countries.

International Monetary Fund (IMF)
United Nations agency consisting of about 150 nations who have combined resources to promote stable exchange rates, provide temporary short-term loans, and serve other purposes.

Summary of Learning Objectives

1. **Define *money* and identify the different forms it takes in the nation's money supply.** Any item that is portable, divisible, durable, and stable satisfies the four basic characteristics of *money*. Money also serves three functions: it is a medium of exchange, a store of value, and a unit of account. The nation's money supply is often determined by two measures: *M-1* includes liquid (or spendable) forms of money: currency (bills and coins), demand deposits, and other "chequable" deposits (such as chequing accounts and ATM withdrawals). *M-2* includes M-1 plus items that cannot be directly spent but which can be easily converted to spendable forms: time deposits, money market funds, and savings deposits. *Credit* must also be considered as a factor in the money supply.

2. **Describe the different kinds of *financial institutions* that make up the Canadian financial system and explain the services they offer.** The financial intermediaries that form the "four financial pillars" in Canada are chartered banks, alternate banks, specialized lending and savings intermediaries, and investment dealers. The chartered banks, which are at the heart of our financial system, are the most important source of short-term funds for business firms. The chartered banking system creates money in the form of expanding demand deposits. The four kinds of financial institutions offer services like financial advice and brokerage services, electronic funds transfer, pension and trust services, and lending of money.

3. **Explain how banks create money and identify the means by which they are regulated.** By taking in deposits and making loans, banks create money, or more accurately, they expand the money supply. The overall supply of money is controlled by the Bank of Canada.

4. **Explain the functions of the *Bank of Canada* and describe the tools it uses to control the money supply.** The Bank of Canada manages the Canadian economy, controls the money supply, and regulates certain aspects of chartered banking operations. If the Bank of Canada wants to increase the money supply, it can buy government securities or lower the bank rate. If it wants to decrease the money supply, it can sell government securities or increase the bank rate.

5. **Identify ways in which the banking industry is changing.** The clear divisions between the activities of the "four financial pillars" are becoming less obvious. For example, deregulation has allowed banks to begin selling commercial paper. Other financial intermediaries are also beginning to get involved in new financial activities. For example, life insurance companies are starting to take over trust companies so they can get a foothold in the trust business. *Electronic technologies* offer a variety of new financial conveniences to customers. *Debit cards* are plastic cards that permit users to transfer money between bank accounts. *Smart cards* are credit card-sized computers that can be loaded with "electronic money" at ATMs or over special telephone hookups. *E-cash* is money that can be moved among consumers and businesses via digital electronic transmissions.

Key Terms

money, 615
M-1, 617
currency, 617
cheque, 617
demand deposit, 617
M-2, 617
time deposit, 618
money market mutual
    funds, 618
chartered bank, 621
trust services, 622

letter of credit, 623
banker's acceptance, 623
electronic funds transfer
    (EFT), 623
debit card, 623
smart card, 623
E-cash, 624
chequable deposit, 625
term deposit, 625
prime rate of interest, 627
reserve requirement, 627

Bank of Canada, 630
bank rate, 631
trust company, 631
credit union, 632
life insurance company,
    632
factoring company, 633
sales finance company,
    633
consumer finance
    company, 633

venture capital firm, 633
pension fund, 634
Industrial Development
    Bank (IDB), 634
Federal Business
    Development Bank
    (FBDB), 634
law of one price, 636
World Bank, 638
International Monetary
    Fund (IMF), 638

Study Questions and Exercises

Review Questions
1. What is money? What are its ideal characteristics?
2. What are the components of M-1? Of M-2?
3. Describe the structure and operation of the Bank of Canada.
4. List and describe the sources of short-term funds for business firms.

Analysis Questions
5. What kinds of changes in banking are shifting banks away from their historical role?
6. Do we really need all the different types of financial institutions we have in Canada? Could we make do with just chartered banks? Why or why not?

7. Should credit cards be counted in the money supply? Why or why not?
8. Should chartered banks be regulated or should market forces be allowed to set the money supply? Defend your answer.

Application Exercises
9. Interview several consumers to determine which of the new banking services and products they use (debit cards, ATMs, smart cards, etc.). If interviewees are using these services, determine the reasons. If they are not, find out why not.
10. Interview the manager of a local chartered bank. Identify the ways in which the Bank of Canada helps the bank and the ways in which it limits the bank.

Building Your Business Skills

Goal
To help students evaluate the risks and rewards associated with excessive credit card use.

Situation
Suppose that you've been out of school for a year and are now working in your first job. Your annual $30 000 salary is enough to support your apartment, car, and the basic necessities of life, but the luxuries are still out of reach. You pay cash for everything until one day you get a preapproved credit card solicitation in the mail, which offers you a $1500 line of credit. You decide to take the offer and begin charging purchases. Within a year, five other credit card companies have contacted you, and you accumulate a total credit card line of $12 000.

Method
Step 1:
Working with three or four classmates, evaluate the advantages and dangers inherent in this situation, both to the consumer and to credit card issuers. To address this issue, research the current percentage of credit card delinquencies and rate of personal bankruptcies. Find out, for example, how these rates compare with those in previous years. In addition, research the profitability of the credit card business.

Step 2:
Evaluate the different methods that credit card companies use to attract new customers. Specifically, look at the following practices:

...

- Sending unsolicited, preapproved credit card applications to consumers with questionable and even poor credit
- Offering large credit lines to consumers who pay only monthly minimums
- Lowering interest rates on accounts as a way of encouraging revolving payments
- Charging penalties on accounts that are paid in full at the end of every billing cycle (research the GE Rewards MasterCard)
- Sending card holders catalogues of discounted gifts that can be purchased with their charge cards
- Linking credit card use to a program of rewards— say, frequent flier miles linked to amounts charged.

Step 3:
Compile your findings in the form of a set of guidelines designed for consumers receiving unsolicited credit card offers. Your guidelines should analyze the advantages and disadvantages of excessive credit card use.

Follow-Up Questions

1. If you were the person in our hypothetical example, how would you handle your credit situation?
2. Why do you think credit card companies continue to offer cards to people who are financially overextended?
3. What criteria can you suggest to evaluate different credit card offers?
4. How do you know when you have enough credit?

Many banks have introduced or are introducing electronic banking. The major challenge of implementing these new systems is educating customers. Many bank Web sites have demonstration sections. Here potential customers can preview on-line services. Below are demonstration sites for the Bank of Nova Scotia, the Bank of Montreal, and the Royal Bank:

http://www.pcbanking.scotiabank.ca/entrust_demo

http://www.mbanx.com/candam/ex.html

http://www.royalbank.com/english/online/signin.html

1. Explore all of the above sites. What are the common banking features and services? What features and services are unique to each?
2. What are the advantages and disadvantages to the bill payment functions in each bank's electronic system?
3. As a credit card customer, which electronic banking service provides the best way for keeping track of transactions and amounts owing? How do the electronic records compare with paper account information?
4. What advantages and disadvantages would you expect to encounter in using the electronic transfer of funds? Which bank has the best electronic transfer services? Explain.

Accounting for South Africa's "Unbanked"

When South Africa's 35 million blacks experienced the miracle that ended apartheid, they witnessed a sea change in the politics of their nation that transferred control from a white minority government to a representative government headed by President Nelson Mandela and the African National Congress. They watched in amazement as world governments accepted South Africa back into the fold of nations after years of ostracism for its racist policies. Yet none of these monumental changes prepared South Africa's poor black population for a practice that nearly every Canadian adult takes for granted—opening a personal bank account. "A bank here? I never dreamed of such a thing," exclaimed Mrs. Ntombizanele King, who recently opened an account at the E Bank affiliate of Standard Bank of South Africa, the country's second-largest bank.

King is in the forefront of a banking revolution that is attempting to reach the so-called "unbanked" of South Africa—impoverished, illiterate blacks who were virtually ignored as potential customers in the old South Africa. Today, E Bank, Peoples Bank (a division of Nedcor Bank), and other financial institutions see opportunity in serving this vast, untapped market, which represents approximately 80 percent of the country's entire population. "You cannot be a national bank and not bank the masses," explains E Bank general manager Bob Tucker, who believes that the poor black customers of today will become the middle-class savers of tomorrow.

Bankers like Tucker realize that although their institutions will earn little from each new account, there is money to be made by serving the *community* of customers. Collectively, the domestic workers, peddlers, and day labourers who make up South Africa's informal economy control millions of dollars in cash. These potential customers need basic services in the form of cash card debit-and-savings accounts that provide an easy way to deposit and withdraw money. E Bank thus offers an account that requires no minimum balance and pays interest on average daily balances higher than the equivalent of about $60. Deposits are free, and cash withdrawals cost anywhere from a nickel to a quarter.

Having access to banking services offers poor South African blacks peace of mind. Gloria Mvunyiswa, a domestic worker who lives in a shack 32 km east of Cape Town, has been robbed numerous times by knife-wielding thieves as she walked to the homes of relatives whom she helps to support. Now she deposits her wages in a bank ATM near her home, and her relatives withdraw what they need from the ATM in their own village. "It's much better now," she says, "because I draw only the money I need for the week's groceries and hide it in my bra until I get to the shop. The rest is safe in the bank."

By 1996, E Bank had 31 branches, serving 175 000 clients around South Africa. Two years earlier, there were probably no more than a few hundred blacks in all of South Africa with bank accounts. Moreover, as part of a five-year government program to move about a million families out of shacks and into houses, E Bank has begun reinvesting some of its new capital into home loans for poor black customers.

Not surprisingly, these changes have had important social consequences. As poor blacks open bank accounts for the first time, they are seen as individuals with money of their own. Says Henry Jackelen, an adviser with the United Nation's Development Program who helped E Bank develop its banking program: "It brings people into the institutional fabric of the society."

Bank clerks who speak native dialects help new customers fill out simple computerized account applications. An ATM card is then issued and the customer watches the clerk insert the card into the slot. Using a numeric keyboard, the clerk punches in account information and then instructs the customer to make a choice—to deposit or withdraw money. This process is time consuming but necessary. "We will help customers as long as they need it," explains Loyiso Maggaza, area manager for Standard Bank's E Bank operation. "But the whole purpose is to try to educate our customers to help themselves."

With labour being the bank's largest single operating cost, ATM technology promises to keep expenses down. E Bank is also trying out more advanced technologies that may be even easier for illiterate customers to use. One device currently being tested reads the customer's fingerprints and foregoes the need to enter a secret code. After inserting the bank card, the customer places a thumb on the fingerprint reader and watches as account information pops onto the screen.

South African banks now realize that, ironically, technology gives them the ability to market to poorly educated consumers. They understand, too, that success depends on a simple approach. The key, according to E Bank general manager Bob Tucker, is the fact that "you can work our machines without even being able to read and write."

Case Questions

1. For poor South African blacks, what is the relationship between opening a bank account and becoming part of their nation's emerging economy?

2. Why are South African banks courting poor black consumers?

3. Why are banks relying on ATMs as their customer service centrepiece?

4. With so many black South African consumers now using ATM technology, do you think these same consumers would be willing to use debit cards at retail stores? What factors might stand in the way of implementing a debit card system?

5. Why do you think this population of banking customers shows little interest in chequing accounts or investments like certificates of deposit?

6. What can Canadian banks learn from the experience of South African banks?

◆

Dollar Fluctuations: Good or Bad News for Canada?

For most of the 1980s, the Canadian dollar declined sharply. It dropped as low as $.69 (U.S.), but rebounded to a high of $.89 by 1991. More recently, the dollar has been trading at around $.70. When the dollar began its decline, some analysts claimed a low dollar was good for Canada while others claimed it was bad.

One school of thought argues that a high dollar is good. It means lower prices for imports, lower interest rates, faster growth, and more jobs. A low dollar is bad because it increases the price of imports, boosts inflation, deflates income, and harms Canadian competitiveness. Holders of this view stress that Canada's relentless attack on inflation during the 1980s impressed money managers in foreign countries and convinced them that Canada was a good place to invest, even though our economy was not doing very well.

Those who argue for a cheaper Canadian dollar, such as David West of DRI/McGraw-Hill, say that the dollar's sharp increase in the late 1980s caused the decline of Canada's international competitiveness. These opponents of a high dollar argue that an inflated dollar causes demand for our exports to drop. They also argue that, if the dollar were to be at $.80 (U.S.) rather than climbing higher, our competitiveness relative to the U.S. would be higher.

Other analysts at DRI/McGraw-Hill considered two scenarios for the Canadian dollar: one at $.75 (U.S.) and one at $.95. With the dollar at $.75, Canada will sell more abroad, but imports will also cost more. Since imports constitute 25 percent of gross domestic product, inflation will increase. Capital spending will go down because of the increased cost of imported machinery. As a result, productivity will also decline. Annual growth will be less than 3 percent.

If the Canadian dollar is at $.95, our exports will be more expensive to foreigners, so we will sell less abroad.

However, our imports will be much cheaper. Capital spending will go up, as will productivity. Inflation will be down because of the lower price of imported goods. In this scenario, inflation will be beaten because the Canadian economy will become more efficient. Annual growth will be about 4 percent.

So who is right? In the middle of 1990, David West predicted that the Canadian dollar would decline to $.81 (U.S.) by the end of 1990. This obviously did not happen. In fact, the dollar rose to $.91 by late 1991. But it did happen by the fall of 1992. Like a company's stock, the value of a country's currency depends on a variety of factors that are hard to pin down. A big factor is consumer confidence, in this case foreign consumers, that is hard to measure. Perhaps we can comfort ourselves with this fact: During the last 20 years, the Canadian dollar has fluctuated widely and much has been written about the benefits and costs of a high or a low dollar. Yet our economic system continues to function.

Case Questions

1. What are the benefits of a "high" Canadian dollar? The drawbacks?

2. What are the benefits of a "low" Canadian dollar? The drawbacks?

3. Compare the level of the Canadian dollar over the last 15 years with Canada's pattern of imports and exports. Is there any relationship among imports, exports, and the level of the Canadian dollar? (The *Bank of Canada Review* contains the information you need to answer this question.)

4. Should the government of Canada intervene to influence the level of the Canadian dollar? Defend your answer.

◆

21

Understanding Securities and Investments

A Whopper of a Fraud

David Walsh started a company called Bre-X in the basement of his Calgary home in 1988. He readily admitted that he was looking for the pot of gold at the end of the rainbow. But he had to continually scramble to put deals together and to stay ahead of creditors.

Bre-X was eventually listed on the Alberta Stock Exchange, and the company acquired various mineral claims in the Northwest Territories. But Walsh had trouble raising exploration capital and the company was going nowhere. During this period, the price of Bre-X stock was about 27 cents a share.

In 1993, good fortune descended on David Walsh when John Felderhof, a mining friend, told him about some interesting mining properties in Indonesia, particularly a place called Busang. To get the money he needed to explore the site, Walsh convinced some friends to invest in Bre-X. He was able to raise $200 000 this way.

In September 1993, Bre-X did its first test drilling at the Busang site. Felderhof was convinced that there was about 2 million ounces of recoverable gold there. Eventually, Walsh struck a deal with the Toronto brokerage firm of Loewen Ondaatje McCutcheon Ltd. and received $4.5 million to continue exploration of Busang. By now Bre-X stock was trading at about $2 per share.

Late in 1994, the geologists found what they claimed was a large gold-laden dome of rock containing perhaps 10 million ounces of gold. When this news hit the stock market, the value of Bre-X stock soared to nearly $15 per share. Over the next few months, estimates of the amount of gold at Busang increased to 100 million ounces, and by early 1996, Bre-X stock had rocketed to $150 per share. The company was now listed on the Toronto Stock Exchange. In May 1996, Bre-X shares split 10-for-1, and the price immediately moved up to $28 per share (a pre-split equivalent of $280 per share).

The good news continued unabated until early 1997, at which time disturbing rumours started circulating that there might not be as much gold as originally thought at the Busang site. What happened, so the rumour said, was that drilling samples had been "salted" (tampered with) to make it appear as if there was significant gold in the samples. This tampering could have easily been achieved by one or two people adding gold to sample bags. As this rumour spread during the next few weeks, the price of the stock gradually dropped from about $28 per share to $3 to $4 per share.

Eventually, an independent study of the Busang core samples was carried out by Strathcona Minerals Services. When that study showed that the Busang samples really had been salted, a panic ensued on the stock market. In one day, the price of the stock dropped from $3 per share to 8 cents per share as frantic investors sold off their holdings.

But most investors couldn't sell their shares at anything close to what they had been worth even the day before, and total losses were in the millions. Losses ranged widely: One investor from Vancouver learned a cheap lesson while losing only $100, but the City of Edmonton's pension fund lost $745 000. Karl Zetmeir, an investor who owned 200 000 shares of Bre-X when it was worth over $28 per share, hung in until the bitter end and lost $5.2 million. And First Marathon Inc., a sophisticated investment company, lost $4.5 million. Some companies actually profited from the debacle. New York–based Oppenheimer & Co. made $100 million by betting that the price of Bre-X was going to fall sharply.

On May 8, 1997, the Toronto Stock Exchange delisted Bre-X, saying that it no longer met the required listing standards. The wild ride was over.

Although sensational, the Bre-X scam is not an isolated case. In early 1996, Timbuktu Gold Corp. stock was trading for $30 per share (up from 30 cents a share the year before), when it was revealed that core samples had been salted and that the gold strike was phoney. And, just a couple of weeks after the Bre-X fiasco, Delgratia Mining Corp. said that promising core samples from a Nevada property that it owned were also salted.

Thousands of Canadians regularly invest their money in stocks and bonds. As the opening case demonstrates, this can be risky for investors, especially when they are basing their purchasing decisions on faulty information. By focusing on the learning objectives of this chapter, you will better understand the importance of the marketplaces in which securities are traded, the nature of investment vehicles such as stocks and bonds, mutual funds, and commodities, and the reasons for government regulation of securities markets.

After reading this chapter, you should be able to:

LEARNING OBJECTIVES

1. Explain the difference between *primary* and *secondary securities markets*.

2. Discuss the value of *common stock* and *preferred stock* to shareholders and describe the secondary market for each type of security.

3. Distinguish among various types of *bonds* in terms of their issuers, safety, and retirement.

4. Describe the investment opportunities offered by *mutual funds* and *commodities*.

5. Explain the process by which securities are bought and sold.

6. Explain how securities markets are regulated.

What Are Securities Markets?

Stocks and bonds are both known as **securities** because they represent a secured (asset-based) claim on the part of investors. But while stocks are a claim on all the assets of a corporation (because they represent a part-ownership of the business), bonds are strictly a financial claim on the business. Collectively, the market in which stocks and bonds are sold is called the *securities market*.

securities
Stocks and bonds (which represent a secured-asset-based claim on the part of investors) that can be bought and sold.

Primary and Secondary Markets for Securities

Primary securities markets handle the buying and selling of new stocks and bonds by firms or governments. New securities are sometimes sold to one buyer or a small group of buyers. These so-called private placements allow the businesses that use them to keep their plans confidential. But because such offerings cannot be resold, buyers demand higher returns from them.

Most new stocks and some bonds are sold to the wider public market. To bring a new security to market, the issuing corporation must obtain approval from a provincial securities commission. It also needs the services of an investment banker. **Investment bankers** serve as financial specialists in issuing new securities. Such well-known firms as RBC Dominion Securities and Wood Gundy provide three types of investment banking services. They

primary securities market
The sale and purchase of newly issued stocks and bonds by firms or governments.

investment banker
Any financial institution engaged in purchasing and reselling new stocks and bonds.

advise the company on the timing and financial terms for the new issue. By *underwriting* (buying) the new securities, investment bankers bear some of the risk of issuing the new security. And, finally, they create the distribution network that moves the new securities through groups of other banks and brokers into the hands of individual investors.

New securities represent only a small portion of securities traded, however. The market for existing stocks and bonds, the **secondary securities market**, is handled by organizations like the Toronto Stock Exchange. We will consider the activities of these markets later in this chapter, after you know more about stocks and bonds and who buys them.

secondary securities market

The sale and purchase of previously issued stocks and bonds.

Who Invests in Securities Markets?

A variety of investors, ranging from average working citizens to huge cash-rich institutions, buy and sell securities. **Institutional investors**—organizations that invest for themselves and their clients (for example, a mutual fund)—may have the greatest influence on securities markets. But individual investors hold a substantial portion of the stock in Canadian companies.

institutional investors

Organizations whose investments for themselves and their clients are so large that they can influence prices on securities markets.

All investors, large and small, have unique motives and goals that affect their investment *portfolios* (the mix of securities they hold). Young people may be saving for college or university, a car, or a first house. They want relatively safe investments that will preserve their accumulated savings. They also want investments with some liquidity, so that the necessary funds are available when needed.

But people also have long-term goals, such as preparing for retirement. Such individuals are most interested in maximizing their wealth during the next 20 or 30 years. They are largely unconcerned about the ups and downs of investments in any particular year.

Personality differences, too, affect investment decisions. Some people are uncomfortable about taking chances with money, while some *speculators* thrive on the excitement of large gains and losses. Thus, the best types of investments differ depending on investors' goals and attitudes towards the need for safety, income, and growth. As you will see, each type of security offers its own mix of these traits.

Stocks

Each year, financial managers, along with millions of individual investors, buy and sell the stocks of thousands of companies. This widespread ownership has become possible because of the availability of different types of stocks and because markets have been established for conveniently buying and selling them. In this section, we will focus on the value of *common* and *preferred stock* as securities. We will also describe the *stock exchanges* where they are bought and sold.

Common Stock

Individuals and other companies buy a firm's common stock in the hope that the stock will increase in value, affording them a capital gain, and/or will provide dividend income. But what is the value of a common stock? Stock values are expressed in three different ways: as par value, as market value, and as book value.

Par Value

The face value of a share of stock, its **par value**, is set by the issuing company's board of directors. But this arbitrary accounting value has almost nothing to do with the real value of the share.

Market Value

The real value of a stock is its **market value**, the current price of a share in the stock market. Because it reflects buyers' willingness to invest, market value depends on a firm's history of dividend payments as well as expectations of **capital gains**, profits from selling the stock for more than it cost. Investors are primarily concerned with a stock's market value. Attempts are often made to influence the price of a stock (see the box "The Art of Influencing a Company's Stock Price").

par value
The arbitrary value of a stock set by the issuing company's board of directors and stated on stock certificates; used by accountants but of little significance to investors.

market value
The current price of one share of a stock in the secondary securities market; the real value of a stock.

capital gains
Profits from the sale of an asset (such as stock) for a higher price than that at which it was purchased.

The Canadian Business Scene

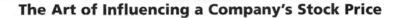

The Art of Influencing a Company's Stock Price

What determines the price of a company's stock? There are some obvious financial things such as a company's sales and earnings, or the number of promising new products it is bringing to the market. But other factors like stock market rumours, investor relations, and the activities of individual stockbrokers can also play a part.

Rumours One of the most well-known stock exchanges in Canada is the Vancouver Stock Exchange, not because it is large or successful, but because numerous charges have been made that stock swindles and market manipulations are not adequately controlled. Overall, the exchange is viewed by many as a place where highly speculative stocks are traded, where rumour and speculation abound, and investors have a good chance of losing their shirt. This is especially true for the so-called "penny mine" stocks—those that cost less than a dollar per share and are very high risk. A 1994 report (one of several that have been critical of the exchange) recommended that investors be given more information about the market, that stock promoters be more tightly regulated, and that more restrictions should be placed on traders' activities.

Investor Relations This is the art of disseminating information about a company's financial condition through activities like annual meetings, corporate reports, road shows, site tours, contacts with stock analysts, and properly timing the release of financial information. While public relations tries to make the company look good to the general public, investor relations tries to play up the positive aspects of a company's finances to a sophisticated audience of stockbrokers, financial analysts, and financial institutions.

There is a fine line between investor relations and mere hype. Done poorly, it can cause the price of the company's stock to decline, which in turn impacts on the earnings of company executives, since part of their compensation package is made up of stock options. A reduced stock price also makes it harder for the firm to raise funds.

American Barrick Resources Corp. is a Toronto-based company that is well-known for its investor relations. The company's CEO meets with financial analysts over a lunch buffet to spread the good word about his company. He communicates openly with the financial community and conducts a question-and-answer period at the end of the lunch. In addition, the company publishes a detailed account of its various gold mining operations and also conducts site tours for interested analysts.

Stockbrokers Individuals who buy and sell stock for their clients are also part of the equation that determines stock prices. Positive recommendations to customers can increase the demand for certain stock, and negative recommendations can reduce it. The brokerage industry has something of an image problem at the moment, due in part to the insider trading scandals of the late 1980s.

The general public has always worried that stockbrokers will put their own financial interests ahead of their customers'. Most brokers receive a combination of percentage of gross commissions (usually 30 to 45 percent) plus transaction size. A broker who grosses $150 000 annually in commissions with an average commission of $100 is lucky to take home $45 000. Because of these pressures, many brokers are not interested in customers with less than $20 000 in their account. To increase their earnings, brokers may be tempted to pursue a "churn and burn" strategy (buying and selling stocks frequently) to increase their commissions.

Customers who have large accounts may be able to negotiate discounts. A full-service broker (one that buys and sells stocks and performs other services such as conducting research on companies) will charge an average of 2 percent of the total share price per trade. But a good customer could ask for a 10 percent discount on a $10 000 transaction, and a 20 percent discount on a $50 000 transaction. Discount brokers (those who provide few services beyond buying and selling shares of stock) charge about $40 per transaction.

Book Value

Another commonly cited value, **book value**, represents shareholders' equity divided by the number of shares of common stock. Shareholders' equity is the sum of all common stock, retained earnings, and additional paid-in capital. While book value is often published in financial reports, its usefulness is also limited.

Investment Traits of Common Stock

Common stocks are among the riskiest of securities. When companies have unprofitable years, they cannot pay dividends. Shareholder income—and perhaps share price too—drops. Even companies with solid reputations sometimes have downturns. IBM is an example. Cash dividends have been paid continuously to shareholders every year since 1916. Revenues per share grew steadily from the 1970s to 1990, then began falling until 1993, when IBM showed a financial loss rather than a profit. Along with lower earnings per share during 1990–93, IBM paid smaller dividends to shareholders each year. During this period, IBM's stock price fell steadily, from a 1990 high of $123 per share to a 1993 low of $41.[1] But by mid-1997, IBM's stock reached its all-time high of $175 per share as a result of a major restructuring that had been instituted a few years earlier and that had improved the company's market performance.

Common stocks generally offer high growth potential for investors. In particular, the common stocks of pollution control, medical technology, natural gas, financial services, and high-technology firms can yield high returns. And the "blue-chip" stocks of some well-established firms such as General Electric and Imperial Oil offer investors a history of secure income.

Preferred Stock

Preferred stock is usually issued with a stated par value, such as $100. Dividends paid on preferred stock are usually expressed as a percentage of the par value. For example, if a preferred stock with a $100 par value pays a 6 percent dividend, shareholders would receive an annual dividend of $6 on each share.

Some preferred stock is *callable*. The issuing firm can require the preferred shareholders to surrender their shares in exchange for a cash payment. The amount of this cash payment, known as the *call price*, is specified in the agreement between the preferred shareholders and the firm.

Investment Traits of Preferred Stock

Because of its preference on dividends, preferred stock's income is less risky than the common stock of the same company. Moreover, most preferred stock is cumulative. With **cumulative preferred stock**, any dividend payments the firm misses must be paid later, as soon as the firm is able. Typically, the firm cannot pay any dividends to its common shareholders until it has made up all late payments to preferred shareholders. If a firm with preferred stock having a $100 par value and paying a 6 percent dividend fails to pay that dividend for two years, it must make up the arrears of $12 per share before it can pay dividends to common shareholders.

Nevertheless, even the income from cumulative preferred stock is not as certain as the corporate bonds of the same company. The company cannot pay dividends if it does not make a profit. The purchase price of the preferred stock can also fluctuate, leading to a capital gain or loss for the shareholder. And the growth potential of preferred stock is limited due to its fixed dividend.

Stock Exchanges

Most of the secondary market for stocks is handled by organized stock exchanges. In addition, a so-called "dealer," or the over-the-counter, market handles the exchange of some stocks. A **stock exchange** is an organization of individuals formed to provide an institutional setting in which stock can be bought and sold. The exchange enforces certain rules to govern its members' trading activities. Most exchanges are non-profit corporations established to serve their members.

To become a member, an individual must purchase one of a limited number of memberships—called "seats"—on the exchange. Only members (or their representatives) are allowed to trade on the exchange. In this sense, because all orders to buy or sell must flow through members, they have a legal monopoly. Memberships can be bought and sold like other assets.

stock exchange
A voluntary organization of individuals formed to provide an institutional setting where members can buy and sell stock for themselves and their clients in accordance with the exchange's rules.

The Trading Floor

Each exchange regulates the places and times at which trading may occur. Trading is allowed only at an actual physical location called the *trading floor*. The floor is equipped with a vast array of electronic communications equipment for conveying buy and sell orders or confirming completed trades. A variety of news services furnish important up-to-the-minute information about world events as well as business developments. Any change in these factors, then, may be swiftly reflected in share prices.

On April 23, 1997, the Toronto Stock Exchange trading floor closed after 145 years of operation. Buy and sell orders are now placed through computers. At its heyday in the 1980s, over 400 traders worked on the floor.[2]

One oft-cited cause of the 1987 panic on the Toronto Stock Exchange is **program trading**—the purchase or sale of a group of stocks valued at $1 million or more, often triggered by computerized trading programs that can be launched without human supervision or control.[3] As market values change during the course of a day, computer programs are busy recalculating the future values of stocks. Once a calculated value reaches a critical point, the program automatically signals a buy or sell order. Program trading could conceivably cause the market to spiral out of control. One way to avoid this is to set up "circuit breakers" that suspend trading for a preset length of time (for example, one hour). The interruption provides a "cooling-off" period that slows down trading activity and allows computer programs to be revised or shut down.

program trading
The purchase or sale of stocks by computerized trading programs that can be launched without human supervision or control.

Brokers

Some of the people working on the trading floor are employed by the exchange; others trade stocks for themselves. But a large number of those working on the trading floor are brokers. A **broker** receives buy and sell orders from those who are not members of the exchange and executes the orders. In return, the broker earns a commission from the order placer.

More and more investors are starting to bypass brokers and buy stocks on the Internet. The box "The Brave New World of Cyberspace Brokerage" describes this trend.

broker
An individual licensed to buy and sell securities for customers in the secondary market; may also provide other financial services.

The Toronto Stock Exchange

The largest stock exchange in Canada is the Toronto Stock Exchange (TSE). It is made up of about 100 individual members who hold seats. The securities of most major corporations are listed here. A company must pay a fee before it can list its security on the exchange. In addition to the TSE, there are stock exchanges in Winnipeg, Calgary, Vancouver, and Montreal.

International Report

The Brave New World of Cyberspace Brokerage

People who trade securities are in it to make money. Therefore, it should come as no surprise that thousands of computer-savvy investors are trying to maximize profits by doing business with discount brokers on the Internet. The following figures tell a story about how much investors can save by executing their own buys and sells in cyberspace.

■ Merrill Lynch, a full-service broker offering extensive investment research, personal service, and order execution, charges $100 to $1100 to trade 100 to 5000 shares of stock.

■ Fidelity Investments, a traditional discount broker that executes orders over the phone but provides no research, charges between $55 and $270 for the same trade.

■ E*Trade Securities, an electronic discount broker that lets customers handle their own account activities, charges a flat $15 to $20 for most trades.

Ed Harrison, a small investor from Santa Clarita, California, makes several trades a week on the Internet and sees cyberspace investing as an opportunity to save money. "My broker was so nice, but boy, he was robbing me," reports Harrison. "All he ever did was place my trades. I can do that for myself." And he can do it simply. "Anyone who feels comfortable picking up the phone and telling a broker, 'Buy me 100 shares of such and such' would find this just as easy," maintains Frederick Roehm, a Portland, Oregon student.

Although investors are happy doing business with Internet-based discount brokers, full-service brokers are worried that this newest investment trend may undermine their customer base. As investors realize that they can tap into investment research sites on the Web, obtain stock quotes and mutual fund rankings, and execute orders via an Internet broker at any time of the day or night, they are likely to question whether full-service brokers are worth premium prices.

This skepticism is likely to become more pronounced as Internet brokers add a variety of services to help guide investment decisions. Lombard Institutional Brokerage, for example, offers graphs showing the movement of stocks and options as well as a free quotation service that gives investors the ability to track, via their own computers, the movement of up to 50 stocks. By the middle of 1996, more than one million investors had visited Lombard's Web site, and activity in the company's 7000 Internet accounts tripled in a three-month period.

The pressure from Internet brokers is already changing traditional brokers. For the first time, Prudential is allowing customers to access their accounts on the Web, although trades are not yet permitted. Fidelity Investments will allow individuals to review their personal retirement accounts on the Web and plans to implement its own electronic trading system some time in the near future.

How do investors reach Web-based brokers? Here are three addresses:

E*Trade
http://www.etrade.com

Lombard Institutional Brokerage Inc.
http://www.lombard.com

Pawws Financial Network
http://www.pawws.com

The New York Stock Exchange

New York Stock Exchange
http://www.nyse.com

For many people, "the stock market" means the New York Stock Exchange (NYSE). Founded in 1792 and located at the corner of Wall and Broad Streets in New York City, the largest of all U.S. exchanges is in fact the model for exchanges worldwide. With an average of 345 million shares changing hands each day, about 45 percent of all shares traded on U.S. exchanges are traded there.

Only firms meeting certain minimum requirements—earning power, total value of outstanding stock, and number of shareholders—are eligible for listing on the NYSE. In 1995, about 2700 listings were traded on the NYSE with a total market value of about $3.1 trillion. Exxon Corp.'s common shares had the highest value in 1995—$145 billion. NYSE trading volume in 1995 was over 87 billion shares.[4]

The Toronto Stock Exchange is one of several in Canada where shares of stock in Canadian companies are bought and sold.

The Montreal Stock Exchange

In recent years, the Montreal Exchange has been aggressively promoting itself and improving its trading systems. It now accounts for nearly 24 percent of the combined Montreal-Toronto trading value. The Montreal Exchange has a sizeable market share in many of Canada's blue-chip companies. It handles more than 50 percent of the shares traded in companies like Bombardier, Provigo, Memotec Data, and Power Corporation.

Montreal Exchange
http://www.me.org

Foreign Stock Exchanges

In 1980, the U.S. stock market accounted for over half the market value of the world market. In 1975, the equity of IBM alone was greater than the national market equities of all but four countries! Market activities, however, have shifted as the value of shares listed on foreign exchanges continues to grow. The annual dollar value of trades on exchanges in London, Tokyo, and other cities is in the trillions. In fact, the London exchange exceeds even the NYSE in number of stocks listed; in market value, transactions on U.S. exchanges are now second to those on Japanese exchanges.

New exchanges are beginning to flourish in cities from Shanghai, China, to Warsaw, Poland. Founded in 1991, for example, the Chinese exchange now trades about $350 million in shares on a good day—more than the bustling Hong Kong exchange on a slow day. China now has about 2 million shareholders in various companies, with the number growing about 50 000 every week.

Meanwhile, many analysts currently regard the Polish exchange as the world's strongest-performing market. Although it lists only 22 stocks, the Polish index increased in volume by 700 percent in 1993. In countries like both China and Poland, thriving stock exchanges have contributed, among other things, to more efficient, profit-conscious companies (many of them once or still state-owned).[5]

Foreign stock exchanges have become increasingly important to portfolio managers. Foreign exchanges allow investors to *diversify* (spread investable funds among a variety of investments to reduce risk). Astute managers have also been able to achieve higher returns by investing internationally.

The Over-the-Counter (OTC) Market

over-the-counter (OTC) market
A complex of dealers in constant touch with each other who trade stocks and bonds of some smaller corporations and all fixed-income securities (bonds and debentures).

Many securities are not listed on any of the organized securities exchanges. Making a market in these securities is one of the functions of investment dealers. These securities are traded in the over-the-counter (OTC) market. (In reality, it is an over-the-telephone market.) The **over-the-counter market** is a complex of dealers in constant touch with one another. Stocks and bonds of some smaller corporations are traded on the OTC market as well as all fixed-income securities, including bonds and debentures.

Security dealers in the OTC market often buy securities in their own names. They must maintain an inventory of securities to make a market in them. They hope to sell them to their clients at a higher price. These dealers also buy shares at the request of their clients for a commission. Dealers selling to one another charge a wholesale price and sell to their customers at a retail price.

Bonds

bond
A written promise that the borrower will pay the lender, at a stated future date, the principal plus a stated rate of interest.

A **bond** is a written promise that the borrower will pay the lender, at some stated future date, a sum of money (the principal) and a stated rate of interest. Bondholders have a claim on a corporation's assets and earnings that comes before the claims of common and preferred shareholders. Bonds differ from one another in terms of maturity, tax status, and level of risk versus potential yield (the interest rate). Potential investors must take these factors into consideration to evaluate which particular bond to buy.

To help bond investors make assessments, several services rate the quality of bonds from different issuers. Table 21.1 shows ratings by three principal rating services: Standard & Poor's, Moody's, and the Canadian Bond Rating Service. The rating measures the bond's *default risk*—the chance that one or more promised payments will be deferred or missed altogether.

Table 21.1   Bond Ratings

	High Grade	Medium Grade (Investment Grade)	Speculative	Poor Grade
Moody's	Aaa Aa	A Baa	Ba B	Caa to C
Standard & Poor's	AAA AA	A BBB	BB B	CCC to D
Canadian Bond Rating Service	A++	B++	C	B

Although all corporations issue common stock, not all issue bonds. Shareholders provide equity (ownership) capital, while bondholders are lenders (although they are also considered "investors" as far as the securities market is concerned). Stock certificates represent ownership, while bond certificates represent indebtedness. Federal, provincial, and city governments as well as non-profit organizations also issue bonds.

Canada Savings Bonds
http://www.cis-pec.gc.ca/english/csb-rrsp.htm

Government Bonds

Government bonds—for example, Canada Savings Bonds—are among the safest investments available. However, securities with longer maturities are somewhat riskier than short-term issues because their longer lives expose

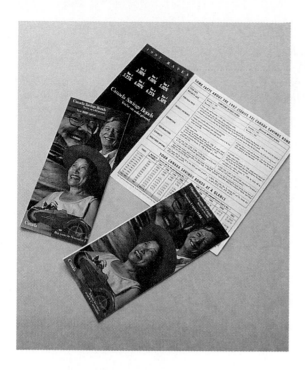

Private corporations are not the only organizations that issue bonds. The government of Canada issues Canada Savings Bonds to finance its debt.

them to more political, social, and economic changes. All federal bonds, however, are backed by the Canadian government. Government securities are sold in large blocks to institutional investors who buy them to ensure desired levels of safety in portfolios. As their needs change, they may buy or sell government securities to other investors.

Provincial and local governments also issue bonds (called municipal bonds) to finance school and transportation systems and a variety of other projects. The most attractive feature of municipal bonds is the fact that investors do not pay taxes on interest received. Banks invest in bonds nearing maturity because they are relatively safe, liquid investments. Pension funds, insurance companies, and private citizens also make longer-term investments in municipals.

Corporate Bonds

Corporate bonds are a major source of long-term financing for Canadian corporations. They have traditionally been issued with maturities ranging from 20 to 30 years. In the 1980s, 10-year maturities came into wider use. As with government bonds, longer-term corporate bonds are somewhat riskier than shorter-term bonds. Bond ratings of new and proposed corporate issues are published to keep investors informed of the latest risk evaluations on many bonds. Negative ratings do not preclude a bond's success, but they do raise the interest rate that issuers must offer.

Corporate bonds may be categorized in one of two ways: (1) according to methods of interest payment and (2) according to whether they are *secured* or *unsecured*.

Interest Payment: Registered and Bearer Bonds

Registered bonds register the names of holders with the company, which simply mails out cheques. Certificates are of value only to registered holders. **Bearer** (or **coupon**) **bonds** require bondholders to clip coupons from certificates and send them to the issuer in order to receive payment. Coupons can be redeemed by anyone, regardless of ownership.

registered bond
Names of holders are registered with the company.

bearer (coupon) bond
Require bondholders to clip coupons from certificates and send them to the issuer in order to receive interest payments.

Secured Bonds

secured bonds
Bonds issued by borrowers who pledge assets as collateral in the event of nonpayment.

Borrowers can reduce the risk of their bonds by pledging assets to bondholders in the event of default. **Secured bonds** can be backed by first mortgages, other mortgages, or other specific assets. If the corporation does not pay interest when it is due, the firm's assets can be sold and the proceeds used to pay the bondholders.

Unsecured Bonds

debentures
Unsecured bonds.

Unsecured bonds are called **debentures**. No specific property is pledged as security for these bonds. Holders of unsecured bonds generally have claims against property not otherwise pledged in the company's other bonds. Accordingly, debentures have inferior claims on the corporation's assets. Financially strong corporations often use debentures.

The Retirement of Bonds

Maturity dates on bonds of all kinds may be very long. But all bonds must be paid off—*retired*—at some point. Most bonds are callable, but others are serial or convertible.

Callable Bonds

callable bond
A bond that may be paid off by the issuer before the maturity date.

Many corporate bonds are callable. The issuer of a **callable bond** has the right at almost any time to call the bonds in and pay them off at a price stipulated in the bond indenture (contract). Usually the issuer cannot call the bond for a certain period of time after issue, but some are callable at any time.

Issuers are most likely to call in existing bonds when the prevailing interest rate is lower than the rate being paid on the bond. But the price the issuer must pay to call in the bond, the *call price*, usually gives a premium to the bondholder. For example, a bond might have a $100 face value and be callable by the firm for $108.67 anytime during the first year after being issued. The call price and the premium decrease annually as the bonds near maturity.

A Notice of Redemption calls for certain bonds to be turned in and paid off by the issuer. The accrual of interest on the selected bonds stops upon the redemption date.

Sinking Funds

sinking-fund provision
A clause in the bond indenture (contract) that requires the issuing company to put enough money into a special bank account each year to cover the retirement of the bond issue on schedule.

Bonds are often retired by the use of a **sinking-fund provision** in the bond indenture. This method requires the issuing company to put a certain amount of money into a special bank account each year. At the end of a number of years, the money in this account (including interest) is sufficient to redeem the bonds. Failure to meet the sinking-fund provision places the bond issue in default. Bonds with sinking funds are generally regarded as safer investments than bonds without them.

Serial and Convertible Bonds

serial bond
A bond issue in which redemption dates are staggered so that a firm pays off portions of the issue at different predetermined dates.

As an alternative to sinking funds, some corporations issue serial or convertible bonds. In a **serial bond** issue, the firm retires portions of the bond issue at different predetermined dates. In a $100 million serial bond issue maturing in 20 years, for example, the company may retire $5 million of the issue each year.

Convertible bonds can be paid off in (converted to) common stock of the issuing company, at the option of the bondholder, instead of in cash. Since bondholders have a chance for capital gains, the company can offer lower interest rates when issuing the bonds. However, since bondholders cannot be forced to accept stock in lieu of money, conversion will work only if the corporation is considered a good investment.

To draw a clearer picture of how convertible bonds work, let's consider the following example. In 1993, Lowe's Companies Inc. sold a $250 million issue of 4 1/2 percent convertible bonds. The bonds were issued in $1000 denominations; they mature in 2003 and are called after 1996. At any time before maturity, each debenture of $1000 is convertible into 19 1/8 shares of the company's common stock. Between October 1993 and March 1994, the stock price ranged from a low of $28 to a high of $67. In that time, then, 19 1/8 common shares had a market value ranging from $535 to $1281.[6] In other words, the holder could have exchanged the $1000 bond in return for stock to be kept or sold at a possible profit (or loss).

> **convertible bond**
> *Any bond that offers bondholders the option of accepting common stock instead of cash in repayment.*

Secondary Securities Markets for Bonds

Unlike stocks, nearly all secondary trading in bonds occurs in the over-the-counter market rather than on any organized exchange. As a result, precise statistics about annual trading volumes are not recorded.

Like stocks, however, market values and prices of bonds change from day to day. Prices of bonds with average risks tend to move up or down until the interest rate they yield generally reflects the prevailing interest rate of the economy. That is, the direction of bond prices moves opposite to interest rate changes—as interest rates move up, bond prices tend to go down. The prices of riskier bonds fluctuate more than those of higher-grade bonds and often exceed the interest rate of the economy.

Other Investments

Although stocks and bonds are very important, they are not the only marketable securities for businesses. Financial managers are also concerned with investment opportunities in mutual funds, commodities, and options.

Mutual Funds

Companies called **mutual funds** pool investments from individuals and other firms to purchase a portfolio of stocks, bonds, and short-term securities. Investors are part-owners of this portfolio. For example, if you invest $1000 in a mutual fund that has a portfolio worth $100 000, you own 1 percent of the portfolio. Mutual funds usually have portfolios worth many millions of dollars.

Mutual funds are a rapidly growing sector of the financial services industry. In February 1997 alone, $10 billion of new money was invested in mutual funds. In 1996, the value of assets under management by mutual funds was $232 billion, up from less than $5 billion in 1981. Two of the biggest companies—Investors Group and Trimark—account for nearly $50 billion.[7]

Like stocks and bonds, there are many types of mutual funds. Investors in **no-load funds** are not charged a sales commission when they buy into or sell out of the mutual fund. **Load funds** carry a charge of between 2 and 8 percent of the invested funds. Some potential problems with mutual funds are described in the box "A Review of the Mutual Fund Business."

> **mutual fund**
> *Any company that pools the resources of many investors and uses those funds to purchase various types of financial securities, depending on the fund's financial goals.*

> **no-load fund**
> *A mutual fund in which investors are not charged a sales commission when they buy into or sell out of the fund.*

> **load fund**
> *A mutual fund in which investors are charged a sales commission when they buy into or sell out of the fund.*

The Canadian Business Scene

A Review of the Mutual Fund Business

During the last few years, many Canadians have invested their money in mutual funds. Billions of dollars have flooded into mutual funds in spite of the fact that buyers don't know very much about the fund managers who invest their money or about the risks and rewards of such investing. By the end of 1996, assets in mutual funds exceeded $232 billion.

In an attempt to keep up with the rapid increase in mutual fund investment, the Ontario Securities Commission appointed Glorianne Stromberg to conduct a review of the mutual fund industry. Her report commented on a variety of concerns, including (1) disclosure laws, (2) soft-dollar transactions, and (3) reciprocal commissions.

Disclosure Laws   Under provincial securities rules, individuals and companies must reveal when they own 10 percent or more of a company's stock. But mutual fund managers argue that this law shouldn't apply to them because they hold the shares in several funds, and the 10 percent limit is exceeded only on an aggregate basis. The OSC is now deciding whether to require fund managers to stick to the 10 percent guideline.

The problem with the current lack of disclosure is that a fund manager could make the fund's performance look good by buying large blocks of shares in companies with only a small number of shares on the market. This type of buying could drive up the price of the stock and make the fund look good. But it is also risky, because if there is a downturn in the market, the fund manager will have difficulty selling so much stock from one company. Investors in the fund would then be stuck with a poorly performing fund.

Soft-Dollar Transactions   In these deals, brokerage firms play the role of intermediary between various kinds of money managers, including mutual fund managers. For example, a mutual fund manager may purchase a consulting report and then pay for it by routing trading commissions through a brokerage firm. The brokerage firm may get a substantial markup over the actual cost of the report.

The problem here is that the cost of these "soft-dollar" deals is borne by the investor (through commissions paid by the mutual fund). There is potential for abuse here because investors don't know what funds are buying with soft dollars and whether or not these expenses should rightfully be charged to the fund.

Reciprocal Commissions   This occurs when a stockbroker recommends that a client invest in a certain mutual fund. The mutual fund manager then buys and sells securities through the same broker. What is essentially happening is that the mutual fund manager is channelling commissions to the broker in return for the broker "pushing" the mutual fund. Critics point out that "sweetheart" deals like this work to the detriment of investors by raising the cost of doing business.

In its report issued on February 1, 1995, the Ontario Securities Commission made the following recommendations about the operation of mutual funds:

■ provide more information to buyers of mutual funds so they will better understand what they are buying

■ create an industry self-regulation organization that would be responsible for setting rules and monitoring conduct

■ eliminate controversial practices such as reciprocal transactions and soft-dollar transactions

■ increase training for mutual fund managers and introduce an apprenticeship program.

In December 1995, a voluntary sales code was drawn up by the Investment Funds Institute of Canada (IFIC). It prohibits, for example, "trailer fees" that kick in only after brokers have sold a minimum dollar amount of a fund. This provision may formerly have motivated brokers to direct clients to a fund in order for the broker to reach the minimum dollar amount. The IFIC report also bans the practice of funnelling trading commissions to a particular broker in return for that broker selling fund units. The IFIC cannot enforce these new rules because it has no disciplinary powers, but Glorianne Stromberg welcomed the report as a sincere effort by responsible people.

In July 1996, the Ontario Securities Commission banned incentives that mutual fund companies had been giving to brokers, fund dealers, and financial planners. Because the IFIC code was voluntary, some brokers were not abiding by it. The OSC therefore felt compelled to introduce binding rules immediately.

Stromberg's activities have not been appreciated by everyone. In 1997, she was asked to vacate the office she had been using at the OSC, and she was asked to stop communicating with OSC staff. Her crusade for tougher rules and more enforcement of the funds industry has served as a reminder of just how far regulation of the securities business has to go.

Mutual funds vary by the investment goals they stress. Some stress safety. The portfolios of these mutual funds include treasury bills and other safe issues that offer immediate income (liquidity). Short-term municipal bond funds emphasize tax-exempt, immediate income.

Other funds seek higher current income and are willing to sacrifice some safety. Long-term municipal bond mutual funds, corporate bond mutual funds, and income mutual funds (which invest in common stocks with good dividend-paying records) all fall into this category.

Still other funds stress growth. Examples include balanced mutual funds, which hold a mixture of bonds, preferred stocks, and common stocks. Growth mutual funds stress common stocks of established firms. Aggressive growth mutual funds seek maximum capital appreciation. To get it, these funds sacrifice current income and safety. They invest in stocks of new companies, troubled companies, and other high-risk securities.

Mutual funds give small investors access to professional financial management. Their managers have up-to-date information about market conditions and the best large-scale investment opportunities. The box "Are Pension and Mutual Funds Too Powerful?" describes a potential problem in this area.

The Canadian Business Scene

Are Pension and Mutual Funds Too Powerful?

Institutional investors such as pension and mutual funds invest money in the stock market for themselves and for their clients. During the past decade, the activities of institutional investors have increased so much that by early 1995 they accounted for 72 percent of the volume on the Toronto Stock Exchange. In the mid-1980s, the figure was less than 60 percent.

Why has this shift taken place? Because mutual funds are growing in popularity with investors who want professionals to invest their money. The stock market crash in October 1987 drove many individual investors from the market, and they have not returned. Observers of the stock market worry that with so few organizations dominating the daily trading on the exchange, an oligopoly effectively exists and this is not consistent with traditional ideas about stock markets.

In order to work efficiently, a stock market should have many small investors, each investing in a variety of companies. But in the current situation, there are relatively few investors, so the market is not very "liquid." This may make it difficult to determine what the real value of a stock is. It also makes it difficult for smaller firms to obtain equity capital because stock market analysts focus all their concern on the bigger firms.

The recent activities of the Ontario Teachers Pension Plan Board (OTPPB) illustrate the concerns that many observers have about the impact of institutional investors on the stock market. The OTPPB invests pension contributions from over 200 000 Ontario teachers. The market value of its investments is currently about $35 billion.

The power of the OTPPB can be seen if we consider the move by Wallace McCain (recently ousted from McCain Foods) to convince Hillsdown Holdings PLC to sell him a controlling stake in Maple Leaf Foods Inc. While McCain did take the usual contingent of investment bankers to the takeover discussions, he also took along George Engman, the vice-president of Ontario Teachers. Engman was at the meeting because he was carrying a commitment from Teachers to invest $150 million in the Maple Leaf Foods bid. Without this commitment, McCain would probably have found it difficult to interest banks in lending money for the takeover. (The strategy worked and McCain now owns Maple Leaf Foods.)

Pension funds became more active in the stock market after the province of Ontario relaxed the strict investment rules that had formerly applied to pension funds. The OTPPB set up a merchant banking team, which oversees the pension fund's purchases of shares to help acquirers finance corporate takeovers or restructuring. In just a few years, the OTPPB has spent about $500 million on corporate acquisitions; more than $1 billion of additional money is authorized.

This active involvement in acquisitions by pension funds is a new development. Some large U.S. pension funds *indirectly* finance acquisitions by investing in acquisition funds, but they are not directly involved in this kind of activity. The Ontario Municipal Employees Retirement Board (OMERS) has also directly invested some of its $21 billion in acquisitions, but most of those are low-profile ventures.

The activities of some mutual funds can create distortions in the market. For example, in 1993 and 1994, a mutual fund named Altamira Management Ltd. accounted for half of the trading volume in the stock of Dorset Exploration. Because Altamira had no legal obligation to disclose that it was heavily involved in trading Dorset stock, very few people knew. But they probably concluded that Dorset was a "hot" stock because there was so much trading activity. Altamira was fined $75 000 by the Ontario Securities Commission for its trading activities.

Commodities

Individuals and businesses can buy and sell commodities as investments. **Futures contracts**—agreements to purchase specified amounts of commodities at given prices on set dates in the future—can be bought and sold in the **commodities market**. These contracts are available not only for stocks but also for commodities including coffee beans, hogs, propane, and platinum. Because selling prices reflect traders' estimates of future events and values, futures prices are volatile and trading is risky.

To clarify the workings of the commodities market, let's look at an example. On April 29, 1996, the price of gold on the open market was U.S. $392.40 per ounce. Futures contracts for October 1996 gold were selling for $397.10 per ounce. This price reflected investors' judgment that gold prices would be higher the following October. Now suppose that you purchased a 100-ounce gold futures contract in April for $39 710 ($397.10 x 100). If in June 1996 the October gold futures sold for $422.10, you could sell your contract for $42 210. Your profit after the two months would be $2500.

Margins

Usually, buyers of futures contracts need not put up full purchase amounts. Rather, the buyer posts a smaller amount—the **margin**—that may be as small as $3000 for contracts up to $100 000. Let's look again at our gold futures example. As we saw, if you had posted a $3000 margin for your October gold contract, you would have earned a $2500 profit on that investment of $3000 in only two months.

However, you also took a big risk involving two big *ifs*:

1. If you had held onto your contract, and
2. if gold had dropped to a value of only $377 in October 1996,

you would have lost $2010. If you had posted a $3000 margin to buy the contract, you would receive only $990. In fact, between 75 and 90 percent of all small-time investors lose money in the futures market. For one thing, the action is fast and furious, with small investors trying to keep up with professionals ensconced in seats on the major exchanges. Although the profit potential is also exciting, experts recommend that most novices retreat to safer stock markets. Of course, as one veteran financial planner puts it, commodities are tempting: "After trading commodities," he reports, "trading stocks is like watching the grass grow."[8]

Most investors in commodities markets never intend to take possession of the commodity in question. They merely buy and sell the futures contracts. But some companies buy futures to protect the price of commodities important to their businesses, as when Canada Packers trades in hog futures.

More than 400 "commodity exchanges" have opened up in the former Soviet Union. These exchanges bring together buyers and sellers of many different types of goods. Although they call themselves commodity exchanges, they are in fact far more primitive than commodity exchanges in Canada and the U.S. One trader says they are more like flea markets than commodity exchanges.[9]

Stock Options

Trading in stock options has become a popular investment activity. A **stock option** is the right to buy or sell a stock. More specifically, a **call option** gives its owner the right to *buy* a particular stock at a certain price, with that right lasting until a particular date. A **put option** gives its owner the right to *sell* a particular stock at a specified price, with that right lasting until a particular date. These options are traded on several stock exchanges.

futures contract

Agreement to purchase specified amounts of a commodity at a given price on a set future date.

commodities market

Market in which futures contracts are traded.

margin

The percentage of the total sales price that a buyer must put up to place an order for stock or a futures contract.

Gold is one of the many commodities for which futures contracts can be bought.

stock option

The purchased right to buy or sell a stock.

call option

The purchased right to buy a particular stock at a certain price until a specified date.

put option

The purchased right to sell a particular stock at a certain price until a specified date.

Suppose you thought the price of Alcan (which sold for $37 5/8 on April 5, 1995) was going to go up. You might buy a call option giving you the right to buy 100 shares of Alcan anytime in the next two months at a so-called strike price of $55. If the stock rose to $65 before June, you would exercise your call option. Your profit would be $10 per share ($65 – $55) less the price you paid to buy the option. However, if the stock price fell instead of rising, you would not exercise your call option because Alcan would be available on the open market for less than $55 per share. You would lose whatever you paid for the option.

In contrast, if you thought the price of Alcan would fall below $37 5/8 sometime during the two months after April 5, 1995, you might buy a put option. This option would give you the right to sell 100 shares for $42 5/8 per share anytime before June 1995. If the stock price fell to $32 5/8, your profit would be $10 per share ($42 5/8 – $32 5/8), less whatever you paid for the option. Assume that the price of a put option was $2 3/4 per share at that time. If the stock price increased, you would not exercise your option to sell, and you would lose what you paid for the put option. The daily prices of put and call options are listed in the financial press.

Buying and Selling Securities

The process of buying and selling stocks, bonds, and other financial instruments is complex. To start, you need to find out about possible investments and match them to your investment objectives. Then you can select a broker and open an account. Only when you have a broker can you place different types of orders and make different types of transactions.

Using Financial Information Services

Have you ever looked at the financial section of your daily newspaper and found yourself wondering what all those tables and numbers mean? If you cannot read stock and bond quotations, you probably should not invest in these issues. Fortunately, this skill is easily mastered. More complicated but also important is some grasp of market indexes.

Stock Quotations

Figure 21.1 shows the type of information newspapers give about daily market transactions of individual stocks. The corporation's name is shown along with the number of shares sold (expressed in board lots). Prices are quoted in dollars and fractions of a dollar ranging from 1/8 to 7/8. A quote of 50 5/8 means that the price per share is $50.625.

Bond Quotations

Bond prices also change from day to day. These changes form the *coupon rate*, which provides information for firms about the cost of borrowing funds.

Prices of domestic corporation bonds, Canadian government bonds, and foreign bonds are reported separately. Bond prices are expressed in terms of 100, even though most have a face value of $1000. Thus, a quote of 85 means that the bond's price is 85 percent of its face value, or $850.

A corporation bond selling at 155 1/4 would cost a buyer $1552.50 ($1000 face value × 1.5525), plus commission. The interest rate on bonds is also quoted as a percentage of par, or face, value. Thus "6 1/2s" pay 6.5 percent of par value per year. Typically, interest is paid semiannually at half of the stated interest or coupon rate.

	Company	Sales	High	Low	Close	Change
■ *Stock* **Inco (Name of Company)**	H Bay Co	347 106	34.500	32.000	32.250	-2.500
	Humbird	196 310	50.250	47.250	48.850	-2.900
■ *Sales* 376 030 Total number of shares traded on this date. There were 376 030 shares sold.	Hy Zels	1 500	4.700	4.700	4.700	-0.100
	IBEX T	3 500	5.600	5.250	5.400	-0.200
	IITC A	7 000	1.000	1.000	1.000	0.000
■ *High* *Low* 29.150 28.500 During the trading day, the highest price was $29.15 and the lowest price was $28.50.	IPL eng	38 329	53.000	52.000	52.650	+0.150
	ISG Tech	6 583	4.050	3.900	3.950	-0.150
	Imasco L	439 447	44.800	44.000	44.250	-0.500
	Imax	46 058	35.000	34.000	35.000	+0.500
■ *Close* 28.600 At the close of trading on this date, the last price paid per share was $28.60.	Imp Metal	22 879	1.630	1.530	1.590	-0.020
	Imperial Oil	311 141	87.700	84.750	87.100	+1.100
	Inco	**376 030**	**29.150**	**28.500**	**28.600**	**-0.400**
■ *Net Change* -0.400 Difference between today's closing price and previous day's closing price. Price decreased by $0.40.	Indochin o	6 100	5.700	5.500	5.500	-0.100
	Inex Ph o	8 800	5.250	5.000	5.250	-0.100
	Infocorp o	24 400	0.750	0.660	0.740	-0.010
	Innova T o	15 000	0.870	0.870	0.870	-0.030
	Insulpro	12 000	1.180	1.080	1.130	+0.020

Figure 21.1
How to read a stock quotation.

The market value (selling price) of a bond at any given time depends on its stated interest rate, the "going rate" of interest in the market, and its redemption or maturity date.

A bond with a higher stated interest rate than the going rate on similar quality bonds will probably sell at a premium above its face value—its selling price will be above its redemption price. A bond with a lower stated interest rate than the going rate on similar quality bonds will probably sell at a discount—its selling price will be below its redemption price. How much the premium or discount is depends largely on how far in the future the maturity date is. The maturity date is shown after the interest rate. When more than one year is given, the bond is either retractable or extendible.

Figure 21.2 shows the type of information daily newspapers give about bond transactions.

Bond Yield

Suppose you bought a $1000 par-value bond in 1977 for $650. Its stated interest rate is 6 percent, and its maturity or redemption date is 1997. You therefore receive $60 per year in interest. Based on your actual investment of $650, your yield is 9.2 percent. If you hold it to maturity, you get $1000 for a bond that originally cost you only $650. This extra $350 increases your true, or effective, yield.

market index
A measure of the market value of stocks; provides a summary of price trends in a specific industry or of the stock market as a whole.

Market Indexes

Although they do not indicate how particular securities are doing, **market indexes** provide a useful summary of trends in specific industries and the stock market as a whole. Such information can be crucial in choosing

	Issuer	Coupon	Maturity	Price	Yield	Change
	GOVERNMENT OF CANADA					
■ *BC Tel*	Canada	4.00	Mar 15-99	100.175	3.865	+0.158
Company name is British	Canada	7.75	Sep 1-99	105.627	4.514	+0.124
Columbia Telephone.	Canada	5.50	Feb 1-00	101.897	4.600	+0.155
■ *Coupon*	Canada	8.50	Mar 1-00	108.417	4.648	+0.164
The annual rate of interest	Canada	7.50	Sep 1-00	107.122	4.780	+0.199
at face value is 9.65 percent.						
	PROVINCIALS AND GUARANTEED					
■ *Maturity*						
The maturity date is April	Alta	8.00	Mar 1-00	107.242	4.673	+0.130
8, 2022.	BC	9.00	Jan 9-02	114.729	5.046	+0.250
■ *Price*	Hy Que	7.00	Jun 1-04	108.100	5.514	+0.460
On this date, $138.48 was	Man	7.75	Sep 14-00	107.604	4.868	+0.172
the price of the last trans-	Ont Hy	7.75	Nov 3-05	114.086	5.546	+0.493
action.	PEI	8.50	Oct 27-15	123.663	6.285	+0.845
■ *Yield*						
This is computed by divid-	**CORPORATE**					
ing the annual interest paid						
by the current market price.	Bell	8.80	Aug 24-04	119.790	5.491	+0.490
■ *Change*	BC Tel	9.65	Apr 8-22	138.489	6.488	+1.118
The closing price on this	Cdn Util	8.43	Jun 1-05	117.385	5.583	+0.475
day was up $1.11 from the	Nova Gas	8.30	Jul 15-03	113.508	5.503	+0.386
closing price on the previ-	Royal Bk	5.40	Sep 7-02	100.461	5.289	+0.297
ous day.	Suncor	6.10	Aug 7-07	100.959	5.967	+0.515

Figure 21.2
How to read a bond quotation.

appropriate investments. For example, market indexes reveal bull and bear market trends. **Bull markets** are periods of upward-moving stock prices. The years 1981 to 1989 and 1995 to 1998 featured a strong bull market. Periods of falling stock prices, such as 1972 to 1974, are called **bear markets**.

The most widely cited market index is the **Dow Jones Industrial Average**. The "Dow," as it is sometimes called, is the sum of market prices for 30 of the largest industrial firms listed on the NYSE. By tradition, the Dow is an indicator of blue-chip stock price movements. Because of the limited number of firms it considers, however, it is a limited gauge of the overall stock market.

The Dow has been very volatile during the mid-1990s. On February 23, 1995, it topped 4000 for the first time ever. On April 24, it went over 4300. On November 20, 1996, it broke the 6400 barrier for the first time, and on February 13, 1997, it topped 7000. In July 1997, the index rose above 8000, by March 1998 it rose above 8600 and by April 1998 it rose above 9000.

Why was there such optimism on the part of investors? What does the Dow's performance say about attitudes towards the economy? Though unable to pinpoint one single reason for the Dow's performance, experts cite three factors that have been important: continued growth in corporate profits, continued merger and acquisition activity, and continued low inflation and low interest rates.

But with the Dow rising so far so fast, experts also expect that there will be some major downturns. In October 1997, for example, the Dow dropped over 550 points in one day. That was an all-time record drop. The next day, however, the Dow rebounded by over 300 points.

Standard & Poor's Composite Index is a broader report than the Dow. It consists of 500 stocks: 400 industrial firms, 40 utilities, 40 financial institutions, and 20 transportation companies. Other widely publicized indexes are the NYSE Index, the TSE 300 Index, and the Tokyo Index.

bull market
A period of rising stock prices; a period in which investors act on a belief that stock prices will rise.

bear market
A period of falling stock prices; a period in which investors act on a belief that stock prices will fall.

Dow Jones Industrial Average
An overall market index based on stock prices of 30 of the largest industrial, transportation, and utility firms listed on the New York Stock Exchange.

Selecting a Broker

In choosing a broker, you must consider what services you need. All brokerages execute customers' orders for securities purchases and sales. **Discount brokerage houses** do little beyond this minimum. But their low commissions make them popular with some investors.

In contrast, **full-service brokerages** offer a variety of services, including investment advice to meet individuals' financial goals. They suggest the best mix of debt versus equity for corporate investors. One service that some brokerages use as a tool in competing with other houses is research. Firms that offer research services provide clients with assessments on the quality and investment prospects of different industries, companies, and securities. Such reports are supplied free of charge, but brokerage fees are higher at these houses.

discount brokerage house
A stock brokerage that charges a minimal fee for executing clients' orders but offers only limited services.

full-service brokerage
A stock brokerage that offers a variety of services, including investment advice, to help clients reach their financial goals.

Placing an Order

Based on your own investigations and/or recommendations from your broker, you can place many types of orders. A **market order** requests the broker to buy or sell a certain security at the prevailing market price at the time. For example, your broker would have sold your Alcan stock for between $37.62 and $38.00 per share on April 5, 1995. When you gave the order to sell, however, you did not know exactly what the market price would be.

In contrast, both limit and stop orders allow for buying and selling of securities only if certain price conditions are met. A **limit order** authorizes the purchase of a stock only if its price is less than or equal to a given limit. For example, a limit order to buy a stock at $80 per share means that the broker is to buy it if and only if the stock becomes available for a price of $80 or less. Similarly, a **stop order** instructs the broker to sell a stock if its price falls to a certain level. For example, a stop order of $85 on a particular stock means that the broker is to sell it if and only if its price falls to $85 or below.

You can also place orders of different sizes. A **round lot** order requests 100 shares or some multiple thereof. Fractions of a round lot are called **odd lots**. Trading odd lots is usually more expensive than trading round lots, because an intermediary called an odd-lot broker is often involved, which increases brokerage fees.

market order
An order to a broker to buy or sell a certain security at the current market price.

limit order
An order to a broker to buy a certain security only if its price is less than or equal to a given limit.

stop order
An order to a broker to sell a certain security if its price falls to a certain level or below.

round lot
The purchase or sale of stock in units of 100 shares.

odd lots
The purchase or sale of stock in units other than 100 shares.

Financing Securities Purchases

When you place a buy order of any kind, you must tell your broker how you will pay for the purchase. You might maintain a cash account with your broker. Then, as stocks are bought and sold, proceeds are added into the account and commissions and costs of purchases are withdrawn by the broker. In addition, as with almost every good in today's economy, you can buy shares on credit.

Margin Trading

As with futures contracts, you can buy stocks on *margin*—putting down only a portion of the stock's price. You borrow the rest from your broker, who, in turn, borrows from the banks at a special rate and secures the loans with stock.

Margin trading offers clear advantages to buyers. Suppose you purchased $100 000 worth of stock in Alcan, paying $50 000 of your own money and borrowing the other $50 000 from your broker at 10 percent interest. If, after one year, the shares have risen in value to $115 000, you could sell them, pay your broker $55 000 ($50 000 principal plus $5000 interest), and have $60 000 left over. Your original investment of $50 000 would have earned a 20 percent profit of $10 000. If you had paid the entire price of the stock from your own funds, your investment would have earned only a 15 percent return.

Brokerages benefit from margin trading in two ways. First, it encourages more people to buy more stock, which means more commissions to the brokerage. And, second, the firm earns a profit on its loans, since it charges buyers a higher interest rate than it pays the bank.

Short Sales

In addition to money, brokerages also lend buyers securities. A **short sale** begins when you borrow a security from your broker and sell it (one of the few times it is legal to sell what you do not own). At a given time in the future, you must restore an equal number of shares of that issue to the brokerage, along with a fee.

short sale
Selling borrowed shares of stock in the expectation that their price will fall before they must be replaced, so that replacement shares can be bought for less than the original shares were sold for.

For example, suppose that in June you believe the price of Alcan stock will soon fall. You order your broker to sell short 100 shares at the market price of $38 per share. Your broker will make the sale and credit $3800 to your account. If Alcan's price falls to $32 per share in July, you can buy 100 shares for $3200 and give them to your broker, leaving you with a $600 profit (before commissions). The risk is that Alcan's price will not fall but will hold steady or rise, leaving you with a loss.

Securities Regulation

Canada, unlike the United States with its Securities and Exchange Commission (SEC), does not have comprehensive federal securities legislation or a federal regulatory body. Government regulation is primarily provincial and there is a degree of self-regulation through the various securities exchanges.

In 1912, the Manitoba government pioneered in Canada laws applying mainly to the sale of new securities. Under these "**blue-sky laws**," corporations issuing securities must back them up with something more than the blue sky. Similar laws were passed in other provinces. Provincial laws also generally require that stockbrokers be licensed and securities be registered before they can be sold. In each province, issuers of proposed new securities must file a prospectus with the provincial securities exchange. A **prospectus** is a detailed registration statement that includes information about the firm, its operation, its management, the purpose of the proposed issue, and any other data helpful to a potential buyer of these securities. The prospectus must be made available to prospective investors.

blue-sky laws
Laws regulating how corporations must back up securities.

prospectus
A detailed registration statement about a new stock filed with a provincial securities exchange; must include any data helpful to a potential buyer.

Ontario is regarded as having the most progressive securities legislation in Canada. The *Ontario Securities Act* contains disclosure provisions for new and existing issues, prevention of fraud, regulation of the Toronto Stock Exchange, and takeover bids. It also prohibits **insider trading**, which is the use of special knowledge about a firm to make a profit in the stock market.

insider trading
The use of special knowledge about a firm to make a profit on the stock market.

The Toronto Stock Exchange provides an example of self-regulation by the industry. The TSE has regulations concerning listing and delisting of securities, disclosure requirements, and issuing of prospectuses for new securities.

Summary of Learning Objectives

1. **Explain the difference between *primary* and *secondary securities markets.*** *Primary securities markets* involve the buying and selling of new securities, either in public offerings or through *private placements* (sales to single buyers or small groups of buyers). *Investment bankers* specialize in trading securities in primary markets. *Secondary markets* involve the trading of existing stocks and bonds through such familiar bodies as the New York and Toronto Stock Exchanges.

2. **Discuss the value of *common stock* and *preferred stock* to shareholders and describe the secondary market for each type of security.** *Common stock* affords investors the prospect of capital gains, dividend income, or both. Common stock values are expressed in three ways: as *par value* (the face value of a share when it is issued), *market value* (the current market price of a share), and *book value* (the value of shareholders' equity compared with that of other stocks). Market value is the most important value to investors. *Preferred stock* is less risky than common stock; for example, cumulative preferred stock entitles holders to receive missed dividends when the company is financially capable of paying. It also offers the prospect of steadier income than common stock. Shareholders of preferred stock must be paid dividends before shareholders of common stock.

   Both common and preferred stock are traded on *stock exchanges* (institutions formed to conduct the trading of existing securities) and in *over-the-counter (OTC) markets* (dealer organizations formed to trade securities outside stock exchange settings). "Members" who hold seats on exchanges act as *brokers*—agents who execute buy-and-sell orders—for nonmembers. Exchanges include the New York Stock Exchange, the Toronto Stock Exchange, and regional and foreign exchanges. In the OTC market, licensed traders serve functions similar to those of exchange members.

3. **Distinguish among various types of *bonds* in terms of their issuers, safety, and retirement.** The safety of bonds issued by various borrowers is rated by such services as Moody's and the Canadian Bond Rating service. *Government bonds* are the safest investment because they are backed by the federal government. *Municipal bonds*, which are offered by provincial and local governments to finance a variety of projects, are also usually safe, and the interest is frequently tax-exempt. *Corporate bonds* are issued by businesses to gain long-term funding. They may be *secured* (backed by pledges of the issuer's assets) or unsecured (*debentures*) and offer varying degrees of safety. *Serial bonds* are retired as portions are redeemed at preset dates; *convertible bonds* are retired by conversion into the issuer's common stock. Government and corporate bonds are *callable*; that is, they can be paid off by the issuer prior to their maturity dates.

4. **Describe the investment opportunities offered by *mutual funds* and *commodities.*** Like stocks and bonds, *mutual funds*—companies that pool investments to purchase portfolios of financial instruments—offer investors different levels of risk and growth potential. *Load funds* require investors to pay commissions of 2 to 8 percent; *no-load funds* do not charge commissions when investors buy in or out. *Futures contracts*—agreements to buy specified amounts of commodities at given prices on preset dates—are traded in the *commodities market*. Commodities traders often buy on *margins*, percentages of total sales prices that must be put up to order futures contracts.

5. **Explain the process by which securities are bought and sold.** Investors generally begin with some homework to study such *financial information services* as newspaper stock, bond, and OTC quotations. *Market indexes* such as the Dow Jones Industrial Average and Standard & Poor's Composite Index provide useful summaries of trends, both in specific industries and in the market as a whole. Investors can then place different types of orders. *Market orders* are orders to buy or sell at current prevailing prices. Because investors do not know exactly what prices will be when market orders are executed, they may issue *limit orders* or *stop orders* that are to be executed only if prices rise to or fall below specified levels. *Round* and *odd lots* are purchases ordered, respectively, in multiples or fractions of 100 shares. Securities can be bought on margin or as part of *short sales*—sales in which investors sell securities that are borrowed from brokers and returned at a later date.

6. **Explain how securities markets are regulated.** To protect investors, provincial securities commissions regulate the public offering of new securities and enforce laws against such practices as *insider trading* (using special knowledge about a firm for profit or gain). Many provincial governments prosecute the sale of fraudulent securities and enforce *blue-sky laws* that require dealers to be licensed and registered where they conduct business.

Key Terms

securities, 645
primary securities market, 645
investment banker, 645
secondary securities market, 646
institutional investors, 646
par value, 647
market value, 647
capital gains, 647
book value, 648
cumulative preferred stock, 648
stock exchange, 649

program trading, 649
broker, 649
over-the-counter (OTC) market, 652
bond, 652
registered bond, 653
bearer (coupon) bond, 653
secured bonds, 654
debentures, 654
callable bond, 654
sinking-fund provision, 654
serial bond, 654
convertible bond, 655

mutual fund, 655
no-load fund, 655
load fund, 655
futures contract, 658
commodities market, 658
margin, 658
stock option, 658
call option, 658
put option, 658
market index, 660
bull market, 661
bear market, 661
Dow Jones Industrial Average, 661

discount brokerage house, 662
full-service brokerage, 662
market order, 662
limit order, 662
stop order, 662
round lot, 662
odd lots, 662
short sale, 663
blue-sky laws, 663
prospectus, 663
insider trading, 663

Study Questions and Exercises

Review Questions
1. What are the purposes of the primary and secondary markets for securities?
2. Which of the three measures of common stock value is most important? Why?
3. What is the difference between callable and convertible bonds?
4. How might an investor lose money in a commodities trade?
5. How do the provincial securities commissions regulate securities markets?

Analysis Questions
6. Which type of stock or bond would be most appropriate for your investment purposes at this time? Why?
7. Which type of mutual fund would be most appropriate for your investment purposes at this time? Why?

8. Choose from a newspaper an example listing of a recent day's transactions for each of the following: a stock on the NYSE; a stock on the TSE; an OTC stock; a bond on the NYSE. Explain what each element in the listing means.

Application Exercises
9. Interview the financial manager of a local business or your school. What are the investment goals of this organization? What mix of securities does it use? What advantages and disadvantages do you see in its portfolio?
10. Contact a broker for information about setting up a personal account for trading securities. Prepare a report on the broker's requirements for placing buy/sell orders, credit terms, cash account requirements, services available to investors, and commissions/fees schedules.

Building Your Business Skills

Goal

To encourage students to understand how a company's internal and external environment affects the price of its common stock.

Method

Step 1:
Research the activity of *one* of the following common stocks during 1997. In addition, research the internal and external events that affected the company during the year:

- IBM
- Canadian National Railway
- Bank of Montreal
- Viacom
- General Motors of Canada
- Air Canada
- Apple Computer
- Borden

Step 2:
Based on your analysis, answer the following sets of questions:

- What happened to the stock price during the period? What was the high during the year? What was the low?
- What events affected the stock price?
- Which of these events involved internal changes—say, reorganizations, layoffs, a new CEO, a new labour contract, dramatic changes in sales? What were the effects of these events?
- Which of these events involved external factors—say, changes in the competitive environment or an economic downturn? What were the effects of these events?

Follow-up Questions

1. What were the main factors that influenced the company's stock price?

2. Based on what you learned, can you predict how well the stock will perform over the coming year?

Because stock market action can be fast and furious, up-to-date information is a must for most investors. To see the types of information available on the Internet, access the Web site maintained by the Toronto Stock Exchange at the following address:

http://www.tse.com

In order to observe the process and results of a day's actual trading activity, be sure to access the Web site when the market is open. On the Toronto Stock Exchange Web site, visit the "Express Menu" and examine both the "Glossary" and the "FAQ"(Frequently Asked Questions) sections. Now consider the following questions:

1. Use the "Glossary" feature to explain in your own words the following terms: "average down," "Best Price Guarantee," "Canadian Dealing Network," "limit up," "naked writer," Ontario Securities Commission," "Responsible Registered Trader," "Toronto 35 Index."

2. Use the "FAQ" to find out how the TSE is equipped to detect insider trading.

3. Find a stock quote for Rogers Cantel. What was the highest price paid that day? What is the difference between today's closing price and the previous day's closing price?

4. Using the "News" option, can you find a news release that might influence investors to buy or sell the stock of a particular company? An item that might influence investors to trade the stocks of a company in a particular industry?

Wham! Bang! Pow! The Marvel of Going Public

In 1991, Marvel Comics announced plans to sell 3.5 million common shares at $14 to $16 each. Before the shares could even get to market, demand was so great that the company decided instead to issue 4.2 million shares at $16 to $17 each. The stock promptly sold out, grossing $69.3 million for the comic-book company. About one third of the money went to pay down the $70 million debt incurred during the 1989 takeover by financier Ronald Perelman. In the form of special dividends, the rest went to various other Perelman enterprises. By early 1992, the price of the stock had skyrocketed to $65 per share.

Was everybody happy? Not by a long shot. In mid-February 1992, *Barron's* magazine ran an article highly critical of Marvel. Among the potential pitfalls noted:

- Roughly 85 percent of the firm's revenues come from publishing; 80 percent of publishing revenues come from comic books.

- Because of rising prices and the general economic downturn, comic-book sales have been levelling off.

- Recent increases in Marvel revenues can be traced largely to price increases, which are now meeting resistance from both consumers and retailers.

- Collector interest in comic books is waning, further depressing the company's ability to raise more money from comic-book sales.

- The recession of 1991–93 hit many of the U.S.'s specialty comic-book stores—which account for 73 percent of sales. This loss is especially troubling because these stores (unlike newsstands) buy comics with no option to return unsold copies. (Each month, newsstands return about two-thirds of their orders for refunds.)

- The remaining 15 percent of Marvel's revenues come from licensing its characters—a revenue source that may have reached the saturation point.

- Marvel's biggest licensing opportunity is an agreement with Carolco Pictures to produce a Spiderman movie. But with the movie studio in financial trouble of its own, the film may not get made. If so, licensed manufacturers will not produce Spiderman dolls and costumes—or, of course, pay licensing fees to Marvel.

- Although dominant with 45 percent of the $400 million annual market, Marvel faces serious challenges. Number-two DC Comics, for example, can look both to such popular characters as Batman and to its affluent parent company, Time Warner, for resources. Moreover, many small companies are cutting into the market with innovative characters and artwork.

The stock market responded quickly to the *Barron's* analysis: After a one-day New York Stock Exchange holiday, Marvel's stock fell from $66 to $54.625. Marvel executives criticized the article, arguing that the company would be free from debt by year's end and that its prospects for growth remained high. One day later, however, the company had to deal with the announcement that eight of its key writers and illustrators were leaving to join competitor Malibu Graphics.

Unfortunately, the concerns expressed in the *Barron's* article turned out to be real: On December 27, 1996, Marvel filed for bankruptcy protection in the U.S. The stock closed at $2.38 per share that day. What happened to Marvel? One answer is this: As collector interest declined and competition increased, the financial situation at Marvel worsened. Infighting began between Perelman and Carl Icahn, the noted corporate raider. Icahn is a creditor of Marvel, and he objected to Perelman's idea to merge Marvel with a company called Toy Biz Inc. in an attempt to resolve the company's financial problems. Icahn claimed that the deal would give Perelman a windfall profit that he didn't deserve. When Perelman declared bankruptcy, Icahn called the action "unconscionable."

The future for Marvel is suddenly very uncertain.

Case Questions

1. Who do you think were the major investors in Marvel's 1991 stock offering? Why?

2. If you had purchased Marvel stock in 1991, how would you have felt about its use of the monies raised in the offering?

3. Because of the flood of sell orders, the New York Stock Exchange initially delayed trading of Marvel stock following the *Barron's* article. Do you think this action was justified?

4. Not all brokers advised against purchasing Marvel stock following the appearance of the *Barron's* article. Why might some have recommended buying instead? ◆

Marvel Comics
http://www.marvel.com

Institutional Investors Are Getting More Demanding

A fundamental power struggle is being fought between management and the agents who invest the savings of millions of Canadians. The capital pool controlled by organizations such as Jarislowsky Fraser & Co., Canadian National Pension Trust Fund, and the Ontario Municipal Employees Retirement System (OMERS) keeps growing. It now totals over $1 trillion. Because takeovers and mergers have reduced the number of companies they can invest in, institutional investors have taken to watching their investments very closely.

The institutions win some fights and lose others. OMERS holds 6 percent of the common shares of Xerox Canada Inc. When the U.S. head office decided to exchange one common share of the U.S. company for three of the Canadian company, OMERS complained that the price was too low. The plan was approved anyway and OMERS sued Xerox. Since then, the OSC has developed more stringent rules on directors' responsibilities to shareholders during takeovers.

The same general trend is evident in the U.S. The California Public Employees' Retirement System (CalPERS), with $97 billion in assets to invest, has been very active in trying to get corporations to listen to shareholders. It has tried, for example, to talk to the management of eight publicly traded small- and medium-sized companies whose performance has been weak. But most of the companies ignored their request. The deputy executive officer of CalPERS says that the corporate governance movement hasn't yet reached smaller companies, and that they just don't understand that shareholders have a right to talk with management.

Sometimes institutional investors have had their representatives elected to the board of directors of companies they are concerned about. Royal Trust Energy Corp. nominated two of its officials to sit on the board of the near-bankrupt Oakwoods Petroleum Ltd. When it became clear that two pension funds—CN's and Central Trust's—would support the Royal Trust nominees, two incumbent management-supported nominees withdrew their names.

Major battles between pension funds and company management often shape up over the issue of poison pills.

Poison pills usually give shareholders the right to buy company stock at a below-market price if a would-be purchaser's holdings go beyond a certain level. Management favours poison pills, but institutional investors usually oppose them. In the case of Inco, the institutional investors were major losers when the company persuaded shareholders to adopt the poison pill by offering them a $10 dividend if they would approve the plan.

Management often resents institutional investors, arguing that they do not know how a specific company should be run yet they insist on input anyway. They want institutional investors simply to pick stocks for their clients, not try to tell company management what to do. They point out that institutions generally have no positive advice to offer; rather, they just veto management plans. When the pension funds of CBC and Investors Group torpedoed a restructuring plan at Unicorp Canada Ltd., they did not offer an alternative. Instead they insisted that the company come up with proposals for them to accept or reject. Unicorp finally abandoned the restructuring.

Pension fund managers counter by stressing that they are preventing company management from taking advantage of small investors. Companies, they argue, too often view small shareholders as a source of cheap money rather than as equal partners in the enterprise.

Case Questions

1. What motivates pension fund managers to try to influence the management decisions of companies they hold stock in?

2. What are the pros and cons of pension fund managers trying to influence management decisions of the companies the pension fund holds stock in?

3. Why do institutional investors such as pension funds oppose "poison pills"?

4. Imagine that you are a top manager in a company whose stock is often bought by institutional investors. What kinds of complaints about institutional investors are you likely to have?   ◆

22

Financial Decisions and Risk Management

What Happened to Bramalea?

For 37 years, Bramalea was one of Canada's largest and most respected builders and property developers. At its peak, it controlled assets worth $6 billion. But it got into trouble in the late 1980s for the same reason so many other firms did—greed and leverage. In 1990, Marvin Marshall was brought in to solve the problems that were developing.

The problems were more serious than most people knew. Bramalea had, for example, bought $1.5 billion of land at highly inflated late 1980s prices. It had also layered debts on every asset the company owned. Insiders knew the firm would need large amounts of new capital if it was to survive. But the Olympia & York failure had made it almost impossible to get that money from public capital markets.

Marshall and his team, therefore, came up with a plan to sell $1.5 billion in assets between 1993 and 1998. They would use this money to repay the company's outstanding loans. The plan was based on the assumption that the market for commercial space would recover and that investors would once again start buying real estate stocks. Many people at Bramalea were skeptical about the feasibility of the plan, but since there didn't seem to be any alternative, they supported it. Several large banks also went along with the plan because they had taken a big hit when Olympia & York failed, and they hoped they could somehow get their money back by keeping Bramalea afloat.

For a while, things seemed to be going according to plan. In late 1993, while addressing a gathering of pension fund managers and investment funds, Marshall noted that interest rates were low, the company had a positive cash flow, and its stock price had increased.

But apparently this was not enough for Bramalea. The company was determined to grow, in spite of its high debt levels. To accomplish this, several lenders were persuaded to defer interest which was due on loans they had made to Bramalea. This allowed Bramalea to buy still more land and build more new houses. It also allowed the company to tell shareholders that the company was operating according to plan. This was technically true since the lenders had agreed to the plan, but it obscured the fact that Bramalea was still badly in need of money. In the fall of 1994, rumours started circulating that Bramalea management had been sighted in meetings with firms with large amounts of money to invest in real estate. The thought was that the company was trying to get its hands on a lot more cash than the banks would lend it. After numerous complicated discussions with various financiers, no deal could be arranged that would give Bramalea the money it needed. This situation, coupled with the rumours, started the "death spiral" of Bramalea's stock, which lost half its value in one week.

When it became clear that no one was willing to lend Bramalea the amount of money it needed, the company sought the bankruptcy protection that led to its demise. Bramalea had hoped that demand for real estate would increase to the point that it could sell its assets to pay off its debts. When that didn't happen, it gambled that it could build and sell new houses fast enough to generate the money it needed to pay off its loans. It lost.

Industry experts estimate that it is costing about $5 million each month in professional fees for liquidators. That means that approximately $75 million was spent between August 1994 and November 1995 alone. And there are still more bills to come. Peat Marwick Thorne Inc., which is handling the liquidation for the Federal Office of the Superintendent of Financial Institutions, estimates that the process will take at least two or three years from start to finish. The costs of liquidation will eventually show up in higher premiums to customers of other insurance companies who have had to pay in to an industry fund that protects consumers when companies collapse.

♦

A s the Bramalea case shows, how a company handles its finances can mean the difference between life and death for the firm. It can also affect the level of interest that investors show in the firm. These fundamental facts apply to both established firms and those which are just starting up.

In this chapter, we will examine the role of financial managers and show why businesses need financial management. We will discuss the sources of short-term funds and how they are put to use, as well as sources and uses of long-term financing. By focusing on the learning objectives in this chapter, you will see how risks arise when companies deploy their funds and how financial managers work to protect their firms from unnecessary financial loss.

After reading this chapter, you should be able to:

LEARNING OBJECTIVES

1. Describe the responsibilities of a *financial manager*.

2. Identify four sources of *short-term financing* for businesses.

3. Distinguish between the various sources of *long-term financing* and explain the risks entailed by each type.

4. Show how financial *returns* to investors are related to *risks* they take.

5. Explain how risk affects business operations and identify the five steps in the *risk-management process*.

6. Describe the basic workings of the *insurance industry* and explain how insurers make profits.

7. Distinguish among the different types of *business insurance*.

The Role of the Financial Manager

We have seen that production managers are responsible for planning and controlling the output of goods and services. We have noted that marketing managers must plan and control the development and marketing of products. Similarly, **financial managers** plan and control the acquisition and dispersal of the company's financial assets.

The business activity known as **finance** (or **corporate finance**) typically entails four responsibilities:

■ determining a firm's long-term investments

■ obtaining funds to pay for those investments

■ conducting the firm's everyday financial activities

■ helping to manage the risks that the firm takes.

financial managers

Those managers responsible for planning and overseeing the financial resources of a firm.

finance

The business function involving decisions about a firm's long-term investments and obtaining the funds to pay for those investments.

Objectives of the Financial Manager

The overall objective of financial managers is to increase the value of the firm and thus to increase shareholder wealth. To reach this goal, financial managers must ensure that the company's earnings exceed its costs—in other words, that the company earns a profit. For a proprietorship or partnership, profits translate into an increase in the owners' wealth. For a corporation, profits translate into an increase in the value of its common stock.

The various responsibilities of the financial manager in increasing a firm's wealth fall into three general categories: *cash flow management, financial control*, and *financial planning*.

Cash Flow Management

To increase a firm's value, financial managers must ensure that it always has enough funds on hand to purchase the materials and human resources that it needs to produce goods and services. At the same time, of course, there may be funds that are not needed immediately. These must be invested to earn more money for a firm. This activity—**cash flow management**—requires careful planning. If excess cash balances are allowed to sit idle instead of invested, a firm loses the cash returns that it could have earned.

cash flow management

Managing the pattern in which cash flows into the firm in the form of revenues and out of the firm in the form of debt payments.

Financial Control

Because things never go exactly as planned, financial managers must be prepared to make adjustments for actual financial changes that occur each day. **Financial control** is the process of checking actual performance against plans to ensure that the desired financial status occurs. For example, planned revenues based on forecasts usually turn out to be higher or lower than actual revenues. Why? Simply because sales are unpredictable. Control involves monitoring revenue inflows and making appropriate financial adjustments. Excessively high revenues, for instance, may be deposited in short-term interest-bearing accounts. Or they may be used to pay off short-term debt. Otherwise earmarked resources can be saved or put to better use. In contrast, lower-than-expected revenues may necessitate short-term borrowing to meet current debt obligations.

financial control

The process of checking actual performance against plans to ensure that the desired financial status is achieved.

Budgets are often the backbone of financial control. The budget provides the "measuring stick" against which performance is evaluated. The cash flows, debts, and assets not only of the whole company but of each department are compared at regular intervals against budgeted amounts. Discrepancies indicate the need for financial adjustments so that resources are used to the best advantage.

Financial Planning

The cornerstone of effective financial management is the development of a **financial plan**. A financial plan describes a firm's strategies for reaching some future financial position. In constructing the plan, a financial manager must ask several questions:

financial plan

A description of how a business will reach some financial position it seeks for the future; includes projections for sources and uses of funds.

- What amount of funds does the company need to meet immediate plans?
- When will it need more funds?
- Where can it get the funds to meet both its short- and long-term needs?

To answer these questions, a financial manager must develop a clear picture of *why* a firm needs funds. Managers must also assess the relative costs and benefits of potential funding sources. In the sections that follow, we will examine the main reasons for which companies generate funds and describe the main sources of business funding, both for the short and long term.

Why Businesses Need Funds

Every company needs money to survive. Failure to make a contractually obligated payment can lead to bankruptcy and the dissolution of the firm. But the successful financial manager must distinguish between two different kinds of financial outlays: short-term operating expenditures and long-term capital expenditures.

Short-Term (Operating) Expenditures

A firm incurs short-term expenditures regularly in its everyday business activities. To handle these expenditures, financial managers must pay attention to accounts payable and receivable and to inventories.

Accounts Payable

In drawing up a financial plan, financial managers must pay special attention to accounts payable, for it is the largest single category of short-term debt for most companies. But they must rely on other managers for accurate information about the quantity of supplies that will be required in an upcoming period. Financial managers also need to consider the time period in which they must pay various suppliers. For example, a financial manager for *Maclean's* magazine needs information from production about both the amount of ink and paper needed to print the magazine and when it will be needed. Obviously, it is in the firm's interest to withhold payment as long as it can without jeopardizing its credit rating.

Accounts Receivable

A sound financial plan requires financial managers to project accurately both the amounts buyers will pay to the firm and when they will make those payments. For example, a manager at Kraft Foods needs to know how many dollars worth of cheddar cheese Safeway supermarkets will order each month and how quickly it pays its bills. Because they represent an investment in products on which the firm has not yet received payment, accounts receivable temporarily tie up some of the firm's funds. It is in the firm's interest to receive payment as quickly as possible.

Given that it is in the self-interest of buyers to delay payment as long as possible, how can a financial manager predict payment times? The answer lies in the development of a *credit policy*, the set of rules governing the extension of credit to customers. The credit policy sets standards as to which buyers are eligible for what type of credit. Financial managers extend credit to customers who have the ability to pay and honour their obligations to pay. They deny credit to firms with poor repayment histories.

The credit policy also sets payment terms. For example, credit terms of "2/10; net 30" mean that the selling company offers a 2 percent discount if the customer pays within 10 days. The customer has 30 days to pay the regular price. Thus, on a $1000 invoice, the buyer would have to pay only $980 on days 1 to 10 but all $1000 on days 11 to 30. The higher the discount, the more incentive buyers have to pay early. Sellers can thus adjust credit terms to influence when customers pay their bills. Often, however, credit terms can be adjusted only slightly without giving competitors an edge.

inventory
Materials and goods currently held by the company that will be sold within the year.

Inventories

Between the time a firm buys raw materials and the time it sells finished products, it has funds tied up in **inventory**, materials and goods that it will sell within the year. There are three basic types of inventories: raw materials, work-in-process, and finished goods.

The basic supplies a firm buys to use in its production process are its **raw materials inventory**. Levi Strauss's raw materials inventory includes huge rolls of denim. **Work-in-process inventory** consists of goods partway through the production process. Cut out but not yet sewn jeans are part of the work-in-process inventory at Levi's. Finally, the **finished goods inventory** is those items ready for sale. Completed blue jeans ready for shipment to dealers in Levi's jeans are finished goods inventory.

Failure to manage inventory can have grave financial consequences. Too little inventory of any kind can cost the firm sales. Too much inventory means that the firm has funds tied up that it cannot use elsewhere. In extreme cases, too much inventory may force a company to sell merchandise at low profits simply to obtain needed cash.

raw materials inventory
That portion of a firm's inventory consisting of basic supplies used to manufacture products for sale.

work-in-process inventory
That portion of a firm's inventory consisting of goods partway through the production process.

finished goods inventory
That portion of a firm's inventory consisting of completed goods ready for sale.

Long-Term Expenditures

Companies need funds to cover long-term expenditures for fixed assets. As noted in Chapter 19, fixed assets are items that have a lasting use or value, such as land, buildings, and machinery. The Hudson Bay Oil and Gas plant in Flin Flon, Manitoba, is a fixed asset.

Because they are so crucial to business success, long-term expenditures are usually planned more carefully than are short-term expenditures. But long-term expenditures pose special problems for the financial manager because they differ from short-term expenditures in several ways. First, unlike inventories and other short-term assets, they are not normally sold or converted into cash. Second, their acquisition requires a very large investment in funds. Third, they represent an ongoing tie-up of the company's funds. All these features influence how long-term expenditures are funded.

Short-Term Sources of Funds

Just as firms have many short-term expenditures, so they can call on many short-term sources for the funds to finance day-to-day operations and to implement short-term plans. These sources include trade credit, secured and unsecured loans, commercial paper, and factoring accounts receivable.

Trade Credit

Accounts payable are not merely an expenditure. They are also a source of funds to the company, which has the use of both the product purchased and the price of the product until the time it pays its bill. **Trade credit**, the granting of credit by one firm to another, is effectively a short-term loan. Trade credit can take several forms.

- The most common form, **open-book credit**, is essentially a "gentlemen's agreement." Buyers receive merchandise along with invoices stating credit terms. Sellers ship products on faith that payment will be forthcoming.

- When sellers want more reassurance, they may insist that buyers sign legally binding **promissory notes** before merchandise is shipped. The agreement states when and how much money will be paid to the seller.

trade credit
The granting of credit by a selling firm to a buying firm.

open-book credit
Form of trade credit in which sellers ship merchandise on faith that payment will be forthcoming.

promissory note
Form of trade credit in which buyers sign promise-to-pay agreements before merchandise is shipped.

trade draft

Form of trade credit in which buyers must sign statements of payment terms attached to merchandise by sellers.

trade acceptance

Trade draft that has been signed by the buyer.

secured loan

A short-term loan in which the borrower is required to put up collateral.

collateral

Any asset that a lender has the right to seize if a borrower does not repay a loan.

■ The **trade draft** is attached to the merchandise shipment by the seller and states the promised date and amount of payment due. To take possession of the merchandise, the buyer must sign the draft. Once signed by the buyer, the document becomes a **trade acceptance**. Trade drafts and trade acceptances are useful forms of credit in international transactions.

Secured Short-Term Loans

For most firms, bank loans are a vital source of short-term funding. Such loans almost always involve a promissory note in which the borrower promises to repay the loan plus interest. In **secured loans**, banks also require the borrower to put up **collateral**—to give the bank the right to seize certain assets if payments are not made as promised. Inventories, accounts receivable, and other assets may serve as collateral for a secured loan.

Perhaps the biggest disadvantage of secured borrowing is the paperwork and administrative costs. Agreements must be written, collateral evaluated, and the terms of the loans enforced. But secured loans do enable borrowers to get funds when they might not qualify for unsecured credit. And even creditworthy borrowers benefit by borrowing at lower rates than with unsecured loans.

Inventory Loans

When a loan is made with inventory as a collateral asset, the lender loans the borrower some portion of the stated value of the inventory. Inventory is more attractive as collateral when it provides the lender with real security for the loan amount: For example, if the inventory can be readily converted into cash, it is relatively more valuable as collateral. Other inventory—say, boxes full of expensive, partially completed lenses for eyeglasses—is of little value on the open market. Meanwhile, a thousand crates of boxed, safely stored canned tomatoes might well be convertible into cash.

The inventory in this auto parts warehouse is good collateral because it is neatly stored, accessible, can be readily evaluated, and is quickly disposable.

Accounts Receivable

When accounts receivable are used as collateral, the process is called **pledging accounts receivable**. In the event of nonpayment, the lender may seize the receivables—that is, funds owed the borrower by its customers. If these assets are not enough to cover the loan, the borrower must make up the difference. This option is especially important to service companies such as accounting firms and law offices. Because they do not maintain inventories, accounts receivable are their main source of collateral.

Typically, lenders who will accept accounts receivable as collateral are financial institutions with credit departments capable of evaluating the quality of the receivables. Loans are granted only when lenders are confident that they can recover funds from the borrower's debtors. (We will discuss the companies that specialize in these loans, called *factors*, later in the chapter.)

pledging accounts receivable

Using accounts receivable as collateral for a loan.

Unsecured Short-Term Loans

With an **unsecured loan**, the borrower does not have to put up collateral. In many cases, however, the bank requires the borrower to maintain a *compensating balance*: The borrower must keep a portion of the loan amount on deposit with the bank in a non-interest-bearing account.

The terms of the loan—amount, duration, interest rate, and payment schedule—are negotiated between the bank and the borrower. To receive an unsecured loan, then, a firm must ordinarily have a good banking relationship with the lender. Once an agreement is made, a promissory note will be executed and the funds transferred to the borrower. Although some unsecured loans are one-time-only arrangements, many take the form of *lines of credit*, *revolving credit agreements*, or *commercial paper*.

unsecured loan

A short-term loan in which the borrower is not required to put up collateral.

Lines of Credit

A standing agreement with a bank to lend a firm a maximum amount of funds on request is called a **line of credit**. With a line of credit, the firm knows the maximum amount it will be allowed to borrow if the bank has sufficient funds. The bank does not guarantee that the funds will be available when requested, however.

For example, suppose the Toronto-Dominion Bank gives Sunshine Tanning Inc., a $100 000 line of credit for the coming year. By signing promissory notes, Sunshine's borrowings can total up to $100 000 at any time. The bank may not always have sufficient funds when Sunshine needs them. But Sunshine benefits from the arrangement by knowing in advance that the bank regards the firm as creditworthy and will loan funds to it on short notice.

line of credit

A standing agreement between a bank and a firm in which the bank specifies the maximum amount it will make available to the borrower for a short-term unsecured loan; the borrower can then draw on those funds, when available.

Revolving Credit Agreements

Revolving credit agreements are similar to bank credit cards for consumers. Under a **revolving credit agreement**, a lender agrees to make some amount of funds available on demand to a firm for continuing short-term loans. The lending institution guarantees that funds will be available when sought by the borrower. In return, the bank charges a *commitment fee*—a charge for holding open a line of credit for a customer even if the customer does not borrow any funds. The commitment fee is often expressed as a percentage of the loan amount, usually one half to 1 percent of the committed amount.

For example, suppose the Toronto-Dominion Bank agrees to lend Sunshine Tanning up to $100 000 under a revolving credit agreement. If Sunshine borrows $80 000, it still has access to $20 000. If it pays off $50 000 of the debt, reducing its debt to $30 000, then it has $70 000 available to it. Sunshine pays interest on the borrowed funds and also pays a fee on the unused funds in the line of credit.

revolving credit agreement

A guaranteed line of credit for which the firm pays the bank interest on funds borrowed as well as a fee for extending the line of credit.

Commercial Paper

commercial paper
A method of short-run fundraising in which a firm sells unsecured notes for less than the face value and then repurchases them at the face value within 270 days; buyers' profits are the difference between the original price paid and the face value.

Some firms can raise funds in the short run by issuing commercial paper. Since **commercial paper** is backed solely by the issuing firm's promise to pay, it is an option for only the largest and most creditworthy firms.

How does commercial paper work? Corporations issue commercial paper with a face value. Companies that buy commercial paper pay less than that value. At the end of a specified period (usually 30 to 90 days but legally up to 270 days), the issuing company buys back the paper—*at the face value*. The difference between the price the buying company paid and the face value is the buyer's profit.

For example, if Noranda needs to borrow $10 million for 90 days it might issue commercial paper with a face value of $10.2 million. Insurance companies with $10 million excess cash will buy the paper. After 90 days, Noranda would pay $10.2 million to the insurance companies.

Commercial paper offers those few corporations able to issue it several advantages. Its cost is usually lower than prevailing interest rates on short-term loans. And it gives the issuing company access to a wide range of lenders, not just financial institutions.

Factoring Accounts Receivable

factoring
Selling a firm's accounts receivable to another company for some percentage of their face value in order to realize immediate cash; the buyer's profits depend on its ability to collect the receivables.

One way to raise funds rapidly is **factoring**, that is, selling the firm's accounts receivable. In this process, the purchaser of the receivables, usually a financial institution, is known as the *factor*. The factor pays some percentage of the full amount of receivables to the selling firm. The seller gets money immediately.

For example, a factor might buy $40 000 worth of receivables for 60 percent of that sum ($24 000). The factor profits to the extent that the money it eventually collects exceeds the amount it paid. This profit depends on the quality of the receivables, the costs of collecting the receivables, the time until the receivables are due, and interest rates.

Sources of Long-Term Funds

Just as firms need short-term sources of funds to cover their short-term expenditures, so they need long-term sources to finance long-term expenditures for fixed assets. Firms need funds for buildings and equipment necessary for conducting their business. Companies may seek long-term funds from outside the firm (debt financing), or they may draw on internal financial sources (equity financing).

Debt Financing

debt financing
Raising money to meet long-term expenditures by borrowing from outside the company; usually takes the form of long-term loans or the sale of corporate bonds.

Long-term borrowing from outside the company—**debt financing**—is a major component of most firms' long-term financial planning. The two primary sources of such funding are long-term loans and the sale of bonds.

Long-Term Loans

In some respects, a long-term loan is like a short-term loan. The major difference is that a long-term loan extends for three to ten years, while short-term loans must generally be paid off in a few years or less. Most corporations get their long-term loans from a chartered bank, usually one with which the firm has developed a long-standing relationship. But credit companies, insurance companies, and pension funds also grant long-term business loans.

Interest rates on long-term loans are negotiated between borrower and lender. Although some bank loans have fixed rates, others have *floating rates* tied to the prime rate (see Chapter 20). A loan at "1 percent above prime," then, is payable at 1 percentage point higher than the prime rate. This rate may fluctuate—"float"—because the prime rate itself goes up and down as market conditions change.

Long-term loans are attractive to borrowers for several reasons:

- Because the number of parties involved is limited, loans can often be arranged very quickly.

- The firm need not make public disclosure of its business plans or the purpose for which it is acquiring the loan. (In contrast, the issuance of corporate bonds requires such disclosure.)

- The duration of the loan can easily be matched to the borrower's needs.

- If the firm's needs change, loans usually contain clauses making it possible to change terms.

Long-term loans also have some disadvantages. Large borrowers may have trouble finding lenders to supply enough funds. Long-term borrowers may also have restrictions placed on them as conditions of the loan. They may have to pledge long-term assets as collateral. And they may have to agree not to take on any more debt until the borrowed funds are repaid.

Corporate Bonds

Like commercial paper, a **corporate bond** is a contract—a promise by the issuing company or organization to pay the holder a certain amount of money on a specified date. Unlike commercial paper, however, bond issuers do not pay off quickly. In many cases, bonds may not be redeemed for 30 years from the time of issue. In addition, unlike commercial paper, most bonds pay the bondholder a stipulated sum of interest semiannually or annually. If it fails to make a bond payment, the company is in default.

The terms of a bond, including the amount to be paid, the interest rate, and the **maturity** (payoff) **date**, differ from company to company and from issue to issue. They are spelled out in the bond contract, or *bond indenture*. The indenture also identifies which of the firm's assets, if any, are pledged as collateral for the bonds.

Corporate bonds are the major source of long-term debt financing for most corporations. Bonds are attractive when companies need large amounts of funds for long periods of time. The issuing company gets access to large numbers of lenders through nationwide bond markets and stock exchanges.

But bonds involve expensive administrative and selling costs. They also may require very high interest payments if the issuing company has a poor credit rating.

corporate bond
A promise by the issuing company to pay the holder a certain amount of money on a specified date, with stated interest payments in the interim; a form of long-term debt financing.

maturity date
The date on or before which a company must pay off the principal of a particular bond issue.

Equity Financing

Although debt financing has strong appeal in some cases, looking inside the company for long-term funding is preferable under other circumstances. In small companies, the founders may increase their personal investment in the firm. In most cases, however, **equity financing** takes the form of issuing common stock or of retaining the firm's earnings. As you will see, both options involve putting the owners' capital to work.

equity financing
Raising money to meet long-term expenditures by issuing common stock or by retaining earnings.

Common Stock

As noted in Chapter 2, when shareholders purchase common stock, they seek profits in the form of both dividends and appreciation. Overall, shareholders hope for an increase in the market value of their stock because the firm has profited and grown. By selling shares of stock, the company gets the funds it needs for buying land, buildings, and equipment.

For example, suppose Sunshine Tanning's founders invested $10 000 by buying the original 500 shares of common stock (at $20 per share) in 1994. If the company used these funds to buy equipment and succeeded financially, by 1996 it might need funds for expansion. A pattern of profitable operations and regularly paid dividends might allow Sunshine to raise $50 000 by selling 500 new shares of stock for $100 per share. This additional paid-in capital would increase the total shareholders' equity to $60 000, as shown in Table 22.1.

It should be noted that the use of equity financing via common stock can be expensive because paying dividends is more expensive than paying bond interest. Why? Interest paid to bondholders is a business expense and, hence, a tax deduction for the firm. Stock dividends are not tax-deductible.

Table 22.1   Shareholders' Equity for Sunshine Tanning Inc.

Common Shareholders' Equity, 1994:

Initial common stock (500 shares issued @ $20 per share, 1994)	$10 000
Total shareholders' equity	$10 000

Common Shareholders' Equity, 1996:

Initial common stock (500 shares issued @ $20 per share, 1994)	$10 000
Additional paid-in capital (500 shares issued @ $100 per share, 1996)	50 000
Total shareholders' equity	$60 000

Retained Earnings

Another approach to equity financing is to use retained earnings. As we saw in Chapter 19, these earnings represent profits not paid out in dividends. Using retained earnings means that the firm will not have to borrow money and pay interest on loans or bonds. A firm that has a history of eventually reaping much higher profits by successfully reinvesting retained earnings may be attractive to some investors. But the smaller dividends that can be paid to shareholders as a result of retained earnings may decrease demand for—and thus the price of—the company's stock.

For example, if Sunshine Tanning had net earnings of $50 000 in 1996, it could pay a $50-per-share dividend on its 1000 shares of common stock. But if it plans to remodel at a cost of $30 000 and retains $30 000 of earnings to finance the project, only $20 000 is left to distribute for stock dividends ($20 per share).

Financial Burden on the Firm

If equity funding can be so expensive, why don't firms rely instead on debt capital? Because long-term loans and bonds carry fixed interest rates and represent a fixed promise to pay, regardless of economic changes. If the firm defaults on its obligations, it may lose its assets and even go into bankruptcy.

Because of this risk, debt financing appeals most strongly to companies in industries that have predictable profits and cash flow patterns. For example, demand for electric power is steady from year to year and predictable from month to month. So provincial electric utility companies, with their stable stream of income, can carry a substantial amount of debt.

Hybrid Financing: Preferred Stock

Falling somewhere between debt and equity financing is the *preferred stock* (see Chapter 2). Preferred stock is a hybrid because it has some of the features of corporate bonds and some features of common stocks. As with bonds, payments on preferred stock are for fixed amounts, such as $6 per share per year. Unlike bonds, however, preferred stock never matures. It can be held indefinitely, like common stock. And dividends need not be paid if the company makes no profit. If dividends are paid, preferred shareholders receive them first in preference to dividends on common stock.

A major advantage of preferred stock to the issuing corporation is its flexibility. It secures funds for the firm without relinquishing control, since preferred shareholders have no voting rights. It does not require repayment of principal or the payment of dividends in lean times.

Choosing Between Debt and Equity Financing

Part of financial planning involves striking a balance between debt and equity financing to meet the firm's long-term need for funds. Because the mix of debt versus equity provides the firm's financial base, it is called the *capital structure* of the firm. Financial plans contain targets for the capital structure, such as 40 percent debt and 60 percent equity. But choosing a target is not easy. A wide range of debt-versus-equity mixes is possible.

The most conservative strategy would be to use all equity financing and no debt. Under this strategy, a company has no formal obligations for financial payouts. But equity is a very expensive source of capital. The most risk-filled strategy would be to use all debt financing. While less expensive than equity funding, indebtedness increases the risk that a firm will be unable to meet its obligations and will go bankrupt. Magna International, for example, has had a high debt to equity ratio in the recent past. Industry analysts believe increased demand for automobiles will allow the firm to make large profits and pay off much of the debt, causing its debt/equity ratio to fall.[1] Somewhere between the two extremes, financial planners try to find a mix that will maximize shareholders' wealth. Figure 22.1 summarizes the factors management must take into account when deciding between debt and equity financing.

Magna International
http://www.magnaint.com

Indexes of Financial Risk

To help understand and measure the amount of financial risk they face, financial managers often rely on indexes for various investments. *Financial World*, for example, publishes independent appraisals of mutual funds (see Chapter 21) using ratings of 1 to 5. A fund rated "1" is least volatile (stable price), while a "5" has the greatest volatility (a highly fluctuating price) compared to all others. Similarly, Standard & Poor's has volatility indexes for mutual funds and for stocks that are available for purchase by financial managers.[2] By using these indexes, financial managers can determine how stable a particular investment is compared to other investment opportunities.

Firms go into debt (both long- and short-term) in the hope of being able to pay the interest and principal out of earnings. If this does not work out over the period of indebtedness, the firm is in trouble. A firm that cannot meet its maturing financial obligations is insolvent. If, in addition, its liabilities are greater than its assets, the firm is said to be in **bankruptcy**.

Under voluntary bankruptcy, a person or firm files a petition in court claiming inability to pay debts because the debts exceed available assets. This petition asserts willingness to make all assets available to creditors under the supervision of a court-appointed trustee.

Under involuntary bankruptcy, a person or firm's creditors seek to have a debtor declared bankrupt by proving that the debtor committed one or more acts of bankruptcy as defined in the law. Once a defendant is declared

bankruptcy

When a firm's liabilities exceed its assets and it cannot meet its maturing financial obligations.

Debt financing 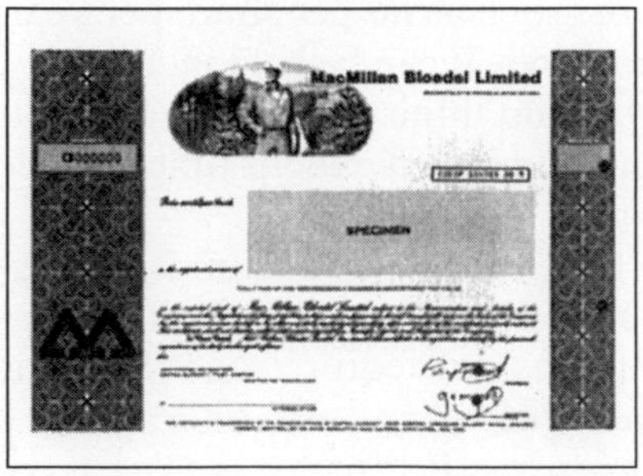	Equity financing 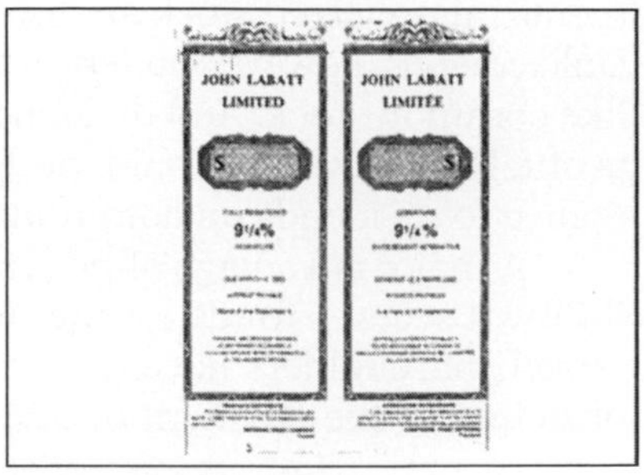

When must it be repaid?

Fixed deadline	No limit

Will it make claims on income?

Yes, regular and fixed	Only residual claim

Will it have claims on assets?

In liquidation, creditors come first	In liquidation, shareholders must wait until creditors are paid and preferred equity precedes common equity

Will it affect management control?

No	May cause challenge for corporation control

How are taxes affected?

Bond interest is deductible	Dividends are not deductible

Will it affect management flexibility?

Yes, many constraints	No, few constraints

Figure 22.1
Comparing debt and equity financing.

bankrupt by a court, the procedure is the same as for voluntary bankruptcy. The box "Bankruptcy at Olympia & York" describes a well-known Canadian example.

The Risk-Return Relationship

While developing plans for raising capital, financial managers must be aware of the different motivations of individual investors. Why, for example, do some individuals and firms invest in stocks while others invest only in bonds? Investor motivations, of course, determine who is willing to buy a given company's stocks or bonds. Everyone who invests money is expressing a personal preference for safety versus risk. Investors give money to firms and, in return, anticipate receiving future cash flows.

The Canadian Business Scene

Bankruptcy at Olympia & York

Olympia & York Developments Ltd. is a real estate and natural resources conglomerate that sought bankruptcy protection under the *Companies' Creditors Arrangement Act* in May 1992. O & Y had been hailed in the mid-1980s as a pioneer in new financial techniques when it issued short-term debt (commercial paper) to finance some of its office buildings. The firm believed it could issue short-term debt during the double-digit inflation of the early 1980s and replace it with lower-cost, long-term debt later.

In adopting this strategy, O & Y departed from the industry's traditional practice of paying for skyscrapers with 20- or 30-year mortgages. By 1990, O & Y had borrowed more than $1 billion in short-term financial instruments such as commercial paper as well as an additional $1 billion in five- and ten-year bonds. O & Y's major mistake, according to investment bankers, was to finance long-term assets with short-term debt.

When the recession caused a steep decline in real estate prices in 1991, investors began to back away from buying further commercial paper from O & Y. The company was left short of cash to pay the interest on other loans it had taken out from nearly 100 banks worldwide. In turn, investors threatened to seize O & Y's assets for nonpayment of interest. Eventually, the cracks in the O & Y empire became so great that the firm had to file for protection under bankruptcy laws. Had O & Y used long-term bonds to finance its real estate activities, it might have averted many of its difficulties.

A brief summary of the events leading to O & Y's bankruptcy is presented below.

February 1992
- Dominion Bond Rating Service downgrades its rating on O & Y's bonds.
- Bank stocks decline as investors worry about bank exposure to O & Y loans.
- CIBC and Royal Bank each have more than $500 million in outstanding loans to O & Y.
- Rumours begin to circulate that O & Y is in danger of collapse. The $7 billion Canary Wharf project in London, England, is seen as the big drain on the company.

March 6, 1992
- O & Y retreats further from the commercial paper market.
- O & Y denies it is headed for bankruptcy.

- O & Y sells its interest in Interprovincial Pipeline Inc. for $665 million and begins retiring $500 million in commercial paper.

March 25, 1992
- Thomas Johnson replaces Paul Reichmann as president of O & Y; he is hired to work out restructuring on debt of $14.3 billion.
- O & Y discusses the possibility of loan guarantees from the federal government.

March 28, 1992
- Albert Reichmann personally buys O & Y's interest in Damdev Corp. (the former Campeau Corp.).
- Company executives meet with bankers to begin discussions on restructuring; lenders asked to extend deadlines on debt falling due.

April 23, 1992
- O & Y states that it has no intention of applying for bankruptcy protection in Britain, the U.S., or Canada.

May 1992
- O & Y has a difficult series of meetings with bankers. They finally agree to lend enough money to keep the Canary Wharf project going for just one month.

May 14, 1992
- U.S. court rules that O & Y must pay Morgan Stanley International $231 million for its building at Canary Wharf; if O & Y does not make the payment, Morgan Stanley can seize the asset.
- Investors threaten to seize O & Y's First Canadian Place in Toronto unless the company pays $17 million in interest due.

May 15, 1992
- O & Y files for bankruptcy protection in Canada and the U.S. as it continues to try to restructure $14.9 billion in debt; investors increasingly threaten to seize O & Y's assets because the firm failed to make interest payments on loans.
- Documents show the company's assets equal its liabilities; under bankruptcy, O & Y must develop a plan for restructuring and talk with investors about its plan.

Paul Reichmann, one of the principals at Olympia & York Developments Ltd. The company bought real estate with short-term debt instead of long-term mortgages, but then ran into difficulty when the real estate market declined.

risk-return relationship

Shows the amount of risk and the likely rate of return on various financial instruments.

Some cash flows are more certain than others. Investors generally expect to receive higher payments for higher uncertainty. They do not generally expect large returns for secure investments such as government-insured bonds. Each type of investment, then, has a **risk-return relationship**. Figure 22.2 shows the general risk-return *relationship* for various financial instruments. High-grade corporate bonds, for example, rate low in terms of risk on future returns but also low on size of expected returns. The reverse is true of junk bonds, those with a higher risk of default.

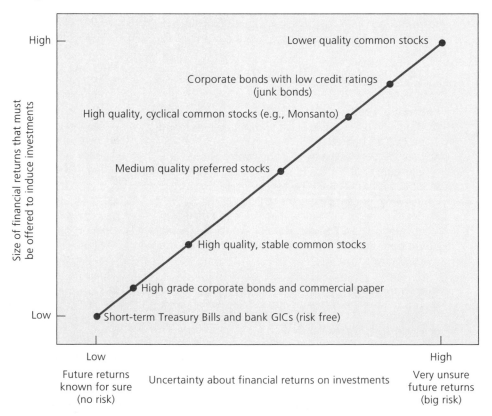

Figure 22.2
Investors expect a chance at greater financial returns for riskier investments.

Risk-return differences are recognized by financial planners, who try to gain access to the greatest funding at the lowest possible cost. By gauging investors' perceptions of their riskiness, a firm's managers can estimate how much it must pay to attract funds to their offerings. Over time, a company can reposition itself on the risk continuum by improving its record on dividends, interest payments, and debt repayment.

Financial Management for Small Businesses

Most new businesses have inadequate funding. An Ontario government report stated that the average investment needed to start a new enterprise was about $58 000, but that more than half of all new companies have less than $15 000 invested.[3] Another study of nearly 3000 new companies revealed a survival rate of 84 percent for new businesses with initial investments of at least $50 000. Unfortunately, those with less funding have a much lower survival rate.[4] Why are so many startups underfunded? For one thing, entrepreneurs often underestimate the value of establishing *bank credit* as a source of funds and use *trade credit* ineffectively. In addition, they often fail to consider *venture capital* as a source of funding, and they are notorious for not *planning cash-flow needs* properly.

Establishing Bank Credit and Trade Credit

Banks differ greatly in willingness to assume risk, ability to give professional advice, loyalty to customers, and maximum size of loans offered.[5] Some have liberal credit policies. Some offer financial analysis, cash-flow planning, and suggestions based on experience with other local small businesses. Some provide loans to small businesses in bad times and work to keep them going. Others do not.

Credit-seekers must be prepared to show they are worthy of the bank's help. A sound financial plan, a good credit history, and proven capability on the part of the entrepreneur can all convince bankers and other potential financiers that the business can succeed.

Once it has obtained a line of credit, the small business can then attempt to gain more liberal credit policies from other businesses. Sometimes, suppliers will give customers longer credit periods, such as 45 or 60 days net rather than 30 days. Such liberal trade credit terms with suppliers let the firm increase its own short-term funds and avoid additional borrowing from banks.

Planning Cash for Requirements

Although all businesses should plan for their cash flows, it is especially important for small businesses to do so. Success or failure may hinge on anticipating times when cash will be short and when excess cash is expected.

Figure 22.3 shows possible cash inflows, cash outflows, and net cash position (inflows minus outflows), month by month, for Slippery Fish Bait Supply. In this highly seasonal business, bait stores buy heavily from Slippery during the spring and summer months. Revenues outpace expenses, leaving surplus funds that can be invested. During the fall and winter, expenses exceed revenues. Slippery must borrow funds to keep going until sales revenues pick up again in the spring. Comparing predicted cash inflows from sales with outflows for expenses shows the firm's monthly cash-flow position.

By anticipating shortfalls, a financial manager can seek funds in advance and minimize their cost. By anticipating excess cash, a manager can plan to put the funds to work in short-term, interest-earning investments.

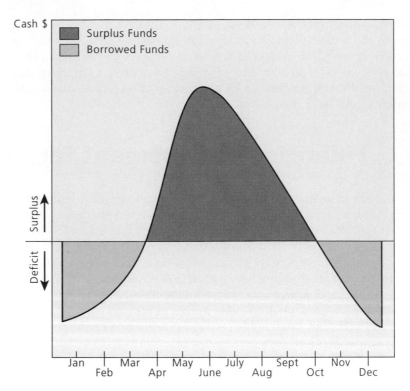

Figure 22.3
Cash flow for Slippery Fish Bait Supply Company.

Emcor Treasury Consultancy Inc. advises corporate and government clients on financial risk management. For example, if a client has money under a previously arranged credit deal but does not currently have a use for the money, the consultants ensure that the client earns a profit from the money until suitable assets are found as an investment.[6]

Risk Management

Financial risks are not the only risks faced every day by companies (and individuals). In this section, we will describe various other types of risks that businesses face and analyze some of the ways in which they typically manage them.

risk
Uncertainty about future events.

speculative risk
An event that offers the chance for either a gain or a loss.

pure risk
An event that offers no possibility of gain; it offers only the chance of a loss.

risk management
Conserving a firm's (or an individual's) financial power or assets by minimizing the financial effect of accidental losses.

Coping with Risk

Businesses constantly face two basic types of **risk**—that is, uncertainty about future events. **Speculative risks**, such as financial investments, involve the possibility of gain or loss. **Pure risks** involve only the possibility of loss or no loss. Designing and distributing a new product, for example, is a speculative risk: The product may fail or it may succeed and earn high profits. The chance of a warehouse fire is a pure risk.

For a company to survive and prosper, it must manage both types of risk in a cost-effective manner. We can thus define the process of **risk management** as "conserving the firm's earning power and assets by reducing the threat of losses due to uncontrollable events."[7] In every company, each manager must be alert for risks to the firm and their impact on profits. The risk-management process usually entails the five steps outlined in Figure 22.4.

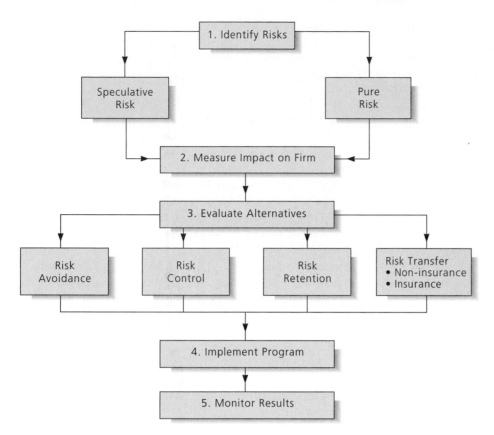

Figure 22.4
The risk-management process.

Step 1: Identify Risks and Potential Losses

Managers analyze a firm's risks to identify potential losses. For example, a firm with a fleet of delivery trucks can expect that one of them will eventually be involved in an accident. The accident may cause bodily injury to the driver or others, may cause physical damage to the truck or other vehicles, or both.

Step 2: Measure the Frequency and Severity of Losses and Their Impact

To measure the frequency and severity of losses, managers must consider both past history and current activities. How often can the firm expect the loss to occur? What is the likely size of the loss in dollars? For example, our firm with the fleet of delivery trucks may have had two accidents per year in the past. If it adds trucks, however, it may reasonably expect the frequency of accidents to increase.

Step 3: Evaluate Alternatives and Choose the Techniques That Will Best Handle the Losses

Having identified and measured potential losses, managers are in a better position to decide how to handle them. With this third step, they generally have four choices: *risk avoidance, control, retention,* or *transfer.*

A firm opts for **risk avoidance** by declining to enter or by ceasing to participate in a risky activity. For example, our firm with the delivery trucks could avoid any risk of physical damage or bodily injury by closing down its delivery service. Similarly, a pharmaceutical maker may withdraw a new drug for fear of liability suits.

risk avoidance

Stopping participation in or refusing to participate in ventures that carry any risk.

By definition, risk avoidance is always successful. It is not, however, always practical. A manager who avoids a certain risk may be acting inconsistently with the firm's strategic direction. For example, if a speedy, centrally controlled delivery system gives our company a competitive edge, risk avoidance may be the wrong choice.

risk control

Techniques to prevent, minimize, or reduce losses or the consequences of losses.

When avoidance is not practical or desirable, firms can practice **risk control**—say, the use of loss-prevention techniques to minimize the frequency of losses. A delivery service, for instance, can prevent losses by training its drivers in defensive-driving techniques, mapping out safe routes, and conscientiously maintaining its trucks.

Unfortunately, loss-prevention techniques cannot guarantee that losses will not occur. Rather, they concede that losses may occur while trying to minimize their severity. Seat belts or air bags, for example, can minimize injuries to truck drivers when accidents do happen. Many firms use fire extinguishers, fire alarms, or burglar alarms to reduce loss.

All risk-control techniques involve costs. The risk manager's job, therefore, is to find techniques whose benefits exceed their costs. For example, a new sprinkler system may cost $100 000. However, if it reduces fire losses by $150 000, it is money well spent.

When losses cannot be avoided or controlled, firms must cope with the consequences. When such losses are manageable and predictable, they may decide to cover them out of company funds. The firm is thus said to "assume" or "retain" the financial consequences of the loss: hence the practice known as **risk retention**. For example, the firm with the fleet of trucks may find that vehicles suffer vandalism totalling $100 to $500 per year. Depending on its coverage, the company may find it cheaper to pay for repairs out of pocket rather than to submit claims to its insurance company.

risk retention

The covering of a firm's unavoidable losses with its own funds.

Some large organizations choose to build up their own pools of funds as a reserve to cover losses that would otherwise be covered by commercial insurance. This type of coverage is called **self-insurance**.

self-insurance

Occurs when a company chooses to build up a pool of its own funds as a reserve to cover losses that would otherwise be covered by insurance.

The primary motive for self-insurance is to avoid the high cost of buying coverage from private insurers. For example, part of a firm's paid premiums go to cover the insurer's administrative, advertising, and sales costs. Self-insurance avoids these costs. Suppose, for instance, that an athletic club pays $100 000 in premiums annually but experiences average losses of only $20 000. Let's say, however, that the club decides instead to set up its own reserve fund of $50 000 annually. If it also establishes efficient procedures for handling damages and other losses, it might achieve comparable coverage through self-insurance *and* save $50 000 in annual premiums.

As a practical matter, self-insurance is not a reasonable alternative for smaller or new companies (even large ones) that have not yet built up sizeable reserves. What would happen if our athletic club suffers a $1 million fire loss when its reserve fund has grown to only $100 000? It may be forced to close. Had its previous commercial coverage been in effect, however, the entire loss might have been covered. Then it could have resumed operations after the club was renovated.

risk transfer

The transfer of risk to another individual or firm, often by contract.

When the potential for large risks cannot be avoided or controlled, managers often opt for **risk transfer**: They transfer the risk to another firm—namely, an insurance company. In transferring risk to an insurance company, a firm pays a sum called a *premium*. In return, the insurance company issues an **insurance policy**—a formal agreement to pay the policyholder a specified amount in the event of certain losses. In some cases, the insured party must also pay a **deductible**—an agreed-upon amount of the loss that the insured must absorb prior to reimbursement. Thus, our delivery service may buy insurance to protect itself against theft, physical damage to trucks, and bodily injury to drivers and others involved in an accident. Similarly, retail stores buy protection in case customers are injured on their premises. (We discuss insurance more fully later in this chapter.)

insurance policy

A written contract between an individual or firm and an insurance company transferring financial liability in the event of some loss to the insurance company in return for a fee.

deductible

A previously agreed-upon amount of loss the insured must absorb before reimbursement from the insurer.

Losses are reduced or prevented when this security specialist uses electronic surveillance (below), when valuables are stored under lock and key (top right), and when workers are reminded to wear safety gear at this construction site (bottom right).

Step 4: Implement the Risk-Management Program

The means of implementing risk-management decisions depends on both the technique chosen and the activity being managed. For example, risk avoidance for certain activities can be implemented by purchasing those activities from outside providers, such as hiring delivery services instead of operating delivery vehicles. Risk control might be implemented by training employees and designing new work methods and equipment for on-the-job safety. For situations in which risk retention is preferred, reserve funds can be set aside out of revenues. When risk transfer is needed, implementation means selecting an insurance company and buying the right policies.

Step 5: Monitor Results

Because risk management is an ongoing activity, follow-up is always essential. New types of risks, for example, emerge with changes in customers, facilities, employees, and products. Insurance regulations change, and new types of insurance become available. Consequently, managers must continually monitor a company's risks, re-evaluate the methods used for handling them, and revise them as necessary.

The Contemporary Risk-Management Program

Virtually all business decisions involve risks having financial consequences. As a result, the company's chief financial officer, along with managers in other areas, usually has a major voice in applying the risk management process. In some industries, most notably insurance, the companies' main line of business revolves around risk-taking and risk management for themselves and their clients.

Today, many firms are taking a new approach to risk management.[8] The key to that approach is developing a program that is both comprehensive and companywide. In the past, risk management was often conducted by different departments or by narrowly focused financial officers. Now, however, more and more firms have not only created high-level risk-management positions, but, at the same time, stressed the need for middle managers to practice risk management on a daily basis.

Why Insurance Companies Exist—and Thrive

The reason why companies often find insurance appealing is clear—in return for a sum of money, they are protected against certain potentially devastating losses. But why are insurance companies willing to accept these risks for other companies?

Like all firms, insurance companies are in business to make a profit (see Table 22.2 for a list of the 10 largest life insurance companies in Canada). They do so by taking in more premiums than they pay out to cover policyholder losses. They profit because they have many policyholders paying them for protection against the same type of loss, yet not all policyholders will experience a loss.

The Statistical Basis of Insurance

For example, consider a town with 5000 insured houses. Based on past history, insurers know that about 50 of these will be involved in a fire each year and that damages will average $40 000 per house involved. That is, insurance companies can expect to pay $2 000 000 ($40 000 x 50) to cover their policyholders. By charging each household in the town $500 a year for fire insurance the company effectively spreads out the risk. It also earns a gross profit of $500 000 ($2 500 000 in premiums versus $2 000 000 in damages). This is the insurer's gain for providing risk-spreading services.

law of large numbers
The statistical principle that the larger the number of cases involved, the more closely the actual rate will match the statistically calculated rate.

To earn a profit, insurance companies must know the likelihood of a particular loss. The more they know, the better their predictions and the fairer the rates they set will be. Insurance companies also benefit from a statistical principle called the **law of large numbers**. As the number of people who

Sun Life Assurance Co. of Canada

http://www.sunlife.com

	Table 22.2	The Top 10 Life Insurance Companies in Canada, Ranked by Revenues, 1996

	Company	Revenue (in billions)
1.	Sun Life Assurance Co. of Canada	$10.7
2.	Manulife Financial	9.8
3.	Great-West Life Assurance	5.8
4.	London Life Insurance Group	5.6
5.	The Canada Life Insurance Co.	5.0
6.	The Mutual Group	3.9
7.	Desjardins-Laurentian Life Group	2.0
8.	Industrial-Alliance Life Insurance	1.4
9.	Metropolitan Life Insurance Co.	1.4
10.	Crown Life Insurance Co.	1.3

seek insurance rises, so does the chance that the actual loss rate will be the same as the statistically calculated rate.

To help them properly price insurance policies, insurers use a system of classification that rates possible losses based on certain characteristics. The frequency of loss from an automobile accident varies with the number of kilometres driven per year, whether the driving is done in a rural or urban area, and the driver's experience. An individual driving under 5000 kilometres per year on uncongested roads with many years of experience will probably have fewer accidents than someone in the opposite situation. Therefore, individuals with a lower probability of accidents as determined by these classification characteristics should pay a relatively lower premium. If insurance companies did not try to make rates equitable, so few customers might buy policies that the insurance company could not cover its costs.

The ultimate purpose of insurance is to *indemnify* policyholders. That is, policyholders should be brought back to their financial position before the loss. No policyholder should gain financially from insurance. To remain financially viable, an insurance company must be sure never to pay for losses not covered by the policy nor to pay too much for each loss.

Insurable versus Uninsurable Risks

Like every business, insurance companies avoid certain risks. Towards this end, insurers divide potential sources of loss into insurable risks and uninsurable risks and issue policies only for insurable risks. While some policies provide certain exemptions, in general, to qualify as an insurable risk, the risk should be predictable, outside the control of the insured, spread geographically, and verifiable. As the box "Entertainment Insurance" indicates, some insurable risks are quite interesting.

Predictable

The insurance company must be able to use statistical tools to forecast the likelihood of a loss. For example, the insurer needs information about the number of car accidents in the past year to estimate the expected accidents for the following year. Translating the expected level of accidents into expected dollar losses helps to determine the premium.

Outside the Control of the Policyholder

The loss must result from an accident, not from an intentional act by the policyholder. Insurers do not have to cover the damages if a policyholder deliberately sets fire to an office building. To avoid paying in cases of fraud, insurers may refuse to cover losses when they cannot determine whether the policyholder's action contributed to the loss.

Spread Over a Large Geographic Area

One insurance company would not want to have all of the hail coverage in Saskatchewan or all of the earthquake coverage in Vancouver. Through selective underwriting of risks, the insurance company can dilute its chances of a large loss.

Verifiable

Did an employee develop emphysema due to a chemical he worked with in his job or because he smoked two packs of cigarettes a day for 30 years? Did the policyholder pay the renewal premium *before* the fire destroyed her home? Were the goods stolen from company offices or the president's home? What was the insurable value of the destroyed inventory?

International Report

Entertainment Insurance

The business of insuring entertainment productions and entertainers is very entertaining. Consider the experiences of Chubb Corp. and American Insurance Group.

Chubb Corp. This company is the lead insurer for the Broadway musical "Titanic." The producers of the show paid about $400 000 for insurance to cover things such as a member of the audience being hit by a flying deck chair, or a cast member being injured during the performance. Interestingly, Chubb also covered the real *Titanic*, the one that sank on April 15, 1912, claiming 1523 lives. That real disaster cost the insurance company $100 000, but if the Broadway *Titanic* sinks, Chubb could be out as much as $14 million.

Chubb's man on the scene is Jim Titterton, who has a degree in fire science and experience as a fire inspector. His first experience with theatre insurance came when he was asked to do a loss-control inspection for the Stephen Sondheim musical "Into the Woods." When Titterton does an inspection, he looks for anything that might cause injury to the actors or the audience. In the Titanic production, for example, powerful motors beneath the stage raise sections of the ship high above the stage, and in the most dramatic moment of the production, these motors tilt the ship just like the real *Titanic* tilted moments before it sank. It is at this point that the actors are in the greatest danger of injury.

Titterton's work is not just an idle exercise. A few years ago, a worker on the set of "Phantom of the Opera" was injured when he was knocked into the orchestra pit by a swinging light fixture. That settlement cost Chubb Corp. well into six figures to settle.

American Insurance Group Inc. (AIG) The producers of the musical "Victor/Victoria" purchased an insurance policy on Julie Andrews. The policy premium—$157 985—insured the producers of the show for up to $2 million if Andrews missed some performances, and up to $8.5 million if she had to leave the show. AIG shared the risk with several other insurance companies, but it was the lead underwriter.

Producers routinely buy this kind of insurance because if a star is unable to perform on a given night, many patrons who have bought tickets want their money back. As it happened, Andrews missed many performances because of various illnesses, and an unusually large number of patrons requested refunds. Total losses to the producers exceeded $1 000 000.

But when the producers tried to collect their money from the insurance companies, the companies refused to pay, arguing that Andrews had given false answers to questions about her medical history. AIG rescinded the policy on Andrews, and has filed a suit against her, claiming that she gave misleading answers on the insurance policy covering her for the production of "Victor/Victoria."

Chubb Corp.
http://www.chubb.com

American Insurance Group
http://www.aig.com

Types of Insurance Companies

Insurance firms can be either private or public (government).

Private Insurance Companies

stock insurance company

Any insurance company whose stock is held by members of the public, who may or may not be policyholders of the company.

mutual insurance company

Any insurance company that is owned by its policyholders, who share in its profits.

Private insurers may be shareholder-owned or mutually owned. **Stock insurance companies**, as the former are known, are like any other corporation. They sell stock to the public, which hopes to earn a profit on its investment. Shareholders can be, but do not have to be, policyholders of the insurance company.

Mutual insurance companies are owned by their policyholders, for whom they seek to provide insurance at lower rates. As *cooperative* operations, they divide profits among policyholders, either by issuing dividends or by reducing premiums. In other words, the company's profits are generated for the direct benefit of policyholders rather than for outside shareholders. As nonprofit operations, they divide any profit among policyholders at the end of the year.

Two of the most important activities of private insurers are the underwriting and marketing of insurance offerings. **Underwriting** involves two basic tasks:

1. determining which applications for insurance to accept and which ones to reject
2. deciding what rates the insurer will charge.

These decisions are made by *underwriters*—experts who gather information and tabulate data, assess loss probabilities, and decide which applications will be accepted. The purpose of all these functions, of course, is to maximize the insurer's profits.

Agents and brokers are the people who market insurance. An **insurance agent** represents and is paid a commission by an insurance company. The agent, then, represents the insurance seller. An **insurance broker**, on the other hand, is a freelance agent who represents insurance buyers rather than sellers. Brokers work for clients by seeking the best coverage for them. They are then paid commissions by the insurers whom they recommend to their clients. Some brokers also offer risk-management advice for clients.

underwriting
Determining which applications for insurance to accept and deciding what rates the insurer will charge.

insurance agent
A person who markets insurance and is paid a commission by the insurance company.

insurance broker
A freelance agent who represents insurance buyers rather than insurance sellers.

Public Insurers

Most insurance that businesses buy is written by private insurance companies. But some—and a great deal of individual insurance—is issued by government agencies.

Provincial governments administer workers' compensation insurance and the federal government administers the employment insurance program. Employers, employees, and the government share the cost of these programs. The federal government also operates the Social Insurance program. It has become an important part of our economic life and is a major means of protecting older, disabled, and poor citizens from economic hardship.

Insurance Products to Meet Diverse Needs

Insurance companies are often distinguished by the types of insurance coverage they offer. While some insurers offer only one area of coverage—life insurance, for example—others offer a broad range. In this section, we describe three major categories of business insurance: *liability*, *property*, and *life*. Each of these broad categories includes a wide variety of coverage plans and options.

Liability Insurance

As we saw in Chapter 5, *liability* means responsibility for damages in case of accidental or deliberate harm to individuals or property. Who, for example, might be financially responsible—liable—for the medical expenses, lost wages, and pain and suffering incurred by an individual temporarily or permanently disabled because of another's actions? **Liability insurance** covers losses resulting from damage to people or property when the insured party is judged liable. The box "The Fraud Squad" describes some interesting problems with liability insurance.

liability insurance
Insurance covering losses resulting from damage to persons or property of other people or firms.

General Liability

General liability policies protect business policyholders in cases involving four types of problems:

The Canadian Business Scene

The Fraud Squad

It's a good thing that the vast majority of people who buy insurance are honest. If they weren't, insurance companies couldn't stay in business. In spite of this, insurance industry experts say that between $10 and $15 of every $100 you pay in insurance premiums goes to cover fraud losses.

How do people defraud insurance companies? Consider this scam: A person goes to a junk yard and buys a wrecked late-model car simply to get the all-important vehicle identification number (VIN). After a few weeks, the person calls the police and says the car has been stolen. Some people even claim that their stolen car was full of gifts they had just purchased, or that the car was loaded with expensive stereo equipment. (People who do this have the sales slip to prove they bought the merchandise. Once they get reimbursed for the car, they return the merchandise to the store for a full refund.)

Another scam is the "staged accident." The swindler purposely (but carefully) runs into a telephone pole, and then everyone in the car claims "whiplash." After the accident is reported, the insurance company contacts the car occupants and sends them accident benefit packages. Sometimes people who aren't even insured are paid benefits because they use counterfeit "proof of insurance" cards.

When swindlers find a scam that works, they tend to repeat it—and this is when they sometimes get caught. Insurance companies may just get lucky in apprehending swindlers, but training of insurance investigators can pay off, too. Carolyn Ericson, a claims manager for H.B. Group Insurance Management, has a Class A mechanic's license. When she arrived at the scene of an accident to investigate, the tow truck was already there, and the cars were still in their original positions. As she lifted the hood of one car, she discovered it had no engine—it had been towed there by the tow truck.

Insurance companies are banding together in an attempt to reduce losses caused by fraud. The Canadian Coalition Against Insurance Fraud (CCAIF) estimates that insurance fraud costs insurers $1.3 billion each year. Because government regulations prohibit insurance companies from simply raising rates to cover fraud losses, they cannot be treated as just another cost of doing business.

One solution that has been suggested to reduce automobile insurance fraud is to take the VIN numbers of wrecked cars out of circulation. The industry is also fighting the perception that insurance fraud is a victimless crime—fraud costs money, and the people who pay are the honest policyholders. In Ontario, the CCAIF is working with Crimestoppers; it offers a reward to tipsters whose information leads to the discovery of fraud.

The major companies in the industry also fund the Insurance Crime Prevention Bureau. In 1994, $55 million was saved through disallowed fraudulent insurance claims.

---

personal liability

For a business, responsibility for certain actions of those who work for the business.

professional liability

For a business or a business person, responsibility for an individual's actions in working at the business or profession.

product liability

For a business, responsibility for the actions of its products.

premises liability

For a business, responsibility for occurrences on its premises.

■ **Personal liability** coverage would protect a firm if one of its truck drivers runs over a customer's foot.

■ **Professional liability** coverage would protect a surgeon who leaves a pair of scissors inside a patient.

■ **Product liability** coverage would protect the maker of a new hair conditioner that causes users' hair to fall out.

■ **Premises liability** coverage would protect a firm if a customer slips on a wet floor and suffers a severe concussion.

Selected Types of Liability Coverage

Businesses often choose to purchase comprehensive general liability policies, which provide coverage for all these problems and more. In this section, we will focus on three types of such coverage: *umbrella policies, automobile policies,* and *workers' compensation.*

Umbrella Policies

umbrella insurance

Insurance that covers losses over and above those covered by a standard policy as well as losses excluded by a standard policy.

Because the dollar value of a liability loss can be huge, many insurers will write coverage only up to a certain limit. Moreover, many liability contracts exclude certain types of losses. To cover financial consequences that exceed the coverage of standard policies, some businesses buy **umbrella insurance**: insurance intended to cover losses in addition to or excluded by an underlying policy.

For example, suppose that a business has an automobile policy with the following coverage:

- a limit of $500 000 for bodily injury and property damage
- a premises liability policy with a limit of $500 000
- a product liability policy with a limit of $750 000.

Figure 22.5 shows how an umbrella policy might double the coverage in each area. Another umbrella policy might extend product liability coverage to items not covered by the firm's existing policy.

Automobile Policies

A firm that owns and maintains automobiles for business use needs a *business automobile policy*. This policy will protect it against liability for bodily injury and property damage inflicted by its vehicles. Typically, such policies provide the following types of coverage:

- *Bodily injury and property damage*. Coverage that pays the firm if it is held legally liable for bodily injury or property damage.
- *Medical*. Coverage that pays for medical expenses incurred by persons in an insured vehicle.
- *Uninsured motorists*. Coverage that pays bodily-injury expenses when injury to an insured driver is caused by an uninsured motorist, a hit-and-run driver, or a driver whose employer is insolvent.

Workers' Compensation

A business is liable for any injury to an employee when the injury arises from activities related to occupation. When workers are permanently or temporarily disabled by job-related accidents or disease, employers are required by law to provide **workers' compensation** coverage for medical expenses, loss of wages, and rehabilitation services.

workers' compensation
A business's liability for injury to its employee(s) resulting from any activities related to the occupation.

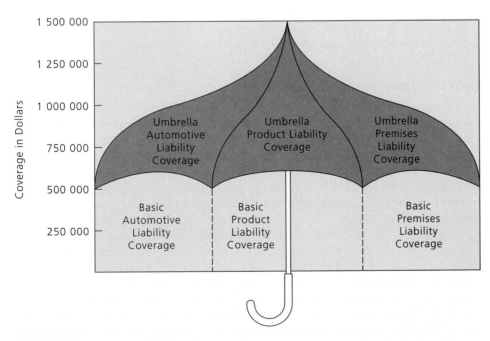

Figure 22.5
Umbrella insurance coverage.

Machines and people sometimes don't mix well, as this employee discovered when his wrist was caught in a conveyor sleeve. Industrial accidents are an undesirable risk.

Property Insurance

property insurance

Insurance covering losses resulting from physical damage to real estate or personal property.

Firms purchase **property insurance** to cover injuries to themselves resulting from physical damage to or loss of real personal property. Property losses might result from fire, lightning, wind, hail, explosion, theft, vandalism, or other destructive forces. Many different forms of property insurance exist to cover the many types of property losses.

Fire and Allied Lines

The typical fire insurance policy covers damage to specified property caused by fire, lightning, or theft. Coverage can be extended to cover other perils such as windstorm, hail, riot, smoke, aircraft, vehicles, explosion, vandalism, malicious mischief, and sonic boom. Some policies also include special provisions insuring the firm's property against sprinkler leakage, earthquake, or flood.

Marine Insurance

marine insurance

A form of transportation insurance covering both the act of transportation (by water, land, or air) and the transported goods.

Another area of property insurance is **marine insurance**, a form of transportation insurance. Marine insurance includes two distinct areas: ocean marine and inland marine. *Ocean marine insurance* has been around for more than 500 years. Medieval shippers used a system of insurance to protect their cargoes from loss. As commerce grew, so did the need for specialized services to guarantee financial solvency in the face of navigation disasters.[9] Today's ocean marine insurance covers the liability and loss of or damage to ships and their cargo.

Waterborne commerce was the most important method of transporting goods for centuries. As industry moved inland, land transportation of cargo became important and the *inland marine policies* were created. Although inland marine insurance sounds like a contradiction in terms, it is truly an extension of the ocean marine form, since it covers transportation (whether by truck, rail, or plane) and transported property. There are four main categories of inland marine insurance: property in transit (such as parcel post), bailee liability (such as dry cleaners), instrumentalities of transportation (such as bridges), and mobile property (such as farm animals).

Title Insurance

When real property is purchased, it is customary to research the *title* (ownership) of that property to determine whether it is free of defects such as tax liens. The easiest way for a purchaser to verify that the seller has a clear legal right to convey the property is through the purchase of **title insurance**. A title insurance company will search a variety of sources and guarantee that the seller is the proper owner and that there are no unknown debts or liens against the property. For instance, if the person selling the property owned it with a former spouse, a title search would verify whether the seller has the legal right to sell the property. If the title insurance company erroneously indicates that the title is free of defects and the policyholder subsequently suffers a loss, then the insurance company must reimburse the insured to an amount specified in the policy.

title insurance
Insurance that guarantees a seller has clear title to a property.

Business Interruption Insurance

In some cases the loss to property may be minimal in comparison to the loss of income suffered as a result of the property damage. A manufacturer may be required to close down for an extended period of time while repairs are being completed. During that time the company is not generating income. However, certain expenses—taxes, insurance premiums, and salaries for key personnel—may continue to accrue. The company may also need to keep running advertisements to make customers aware that repairs are progressing so they do not take their business elsewhere permanently. To cover these potential losses a firm may buy **business interruption insurance**.

business interruption insurance
Insurance to cover potential losses incurred during times when a company is unable to conduct its business.

Credit Insurance

In addition to protecting its physical assets, a firm may also purchase **credit insurance** to protect its financial assets. If a customer does not pay its bills to the business, the selling company loses the value of the goods or services that it sold to the customer on credit. Linda Lingerie Inc. (LLI) bought credit insurance when it heard rumours that Eaton's was in financial trouble. The premium was high—$200 000—but LLI's president, Carolyn Farha, says it gave her peace of mind knowing that her firm would not lose money if Eaton's went bankrupt and was unable to pay its bills to suppliers.[10]

credit insurance
Insurance to protect against customers' failure to pay their bills.

Coinsurance

Because a total loss of property is not likely, property owners have traditionally bought less than the total value in coverage. This practice results in coverage of losses on all parts of the property, but the insurer receives a premium for only a fraction of the property's value. To counter this problem, policies include a coinsurance provision requiring policyholders to insure to a certain minimum percentage of the total value of the property. If the policyholder fails to insure to the required percentage, the insurance company's payment will not cover the entire loss. Instead, insurance pays a smaller amount, as determined by the following formula:

$$\frac{\text{Amount of insurance owned}}{\text{Amount of insurance required}} \times \text{Amount of property loss} = \text{Insurance company's payment}$$

If, for example, a building has a replacement value of $80 000 and the insurance policy has an 80 percent coinsurance requirement, the required amount of insurance coverage is $64 000 ($80 000 × .80). If the owner carries $64 000 worth of insurance coverage, then a $25 000 loss will be paid in full, as will any other loss up to $64 000. However, if the owner carries only $50 000 of insurance coverage, the insurance company will pay only $19 531.25 of the $25 000 loss, as the following calculation shows:

$$\frac{\$50\ 000}{\$64\ 000} \times \$25\ 000 = \$19\ 531.25$$

The policyholder bears the remainder of the loss ($25 000 − $19 531.25 = $5468.75), in effect, a penalty for underinsuring the property.

Multi-Line Policies

Because companies have many risks, they may need many kinds of insurance. Rather than purchasing many separate policies, firms may elect to buy one of the *multi-line package policies* now offered. These policies combine coverage for property losses with coverage for liability losses. Examples of multi-line policies include the Special Multi-Peril Policy (SMP) for owners of large businesses and the Business Owners Policy (BOP) designed for small- to medium-sized retail stores, office buildings, apartment buildings, and similar firms.

Life Insurance

life insurance

Insurance that pays benefits to survivors of a policyholder.

beneficiary

The person to whom benefits of a life insurance policy are paid.

Insurance can protect not only a company's physical and capital assets but its labour assets as well. As part of their benefits packages, many businesses buy **life insurance** for their employees. Life insurance companies accept premiums from policyholders in return for the promise to pay a **beneficiary** after the death of the policyholder. A portion of the premium is used for current losses and expenses. The remainder is invested in various types of financial instruments such as corporate bonds and stocks. A portion of the investment income generated offsets the premium paid by the policyholder. Therefore, an insurance company with a high investment return theoretically should charge less than one with a lower investment return, assuming that both companies have similar loss experience and expenses.

Life insurance is a profitable business in Canada. In 1994, the top 10 insurance companies received over $28.9 billion in premiums from policyholders; net profit for the top 10 firms combined was almost $1.4 billion.[11] Among the many products life insurance companies offer are whole life, term insurance, endowment, and universal life policies.

Whole Life Insurance

whole life insurance

Insurance coverage in force for the whole of a person's life, with a build-up of cash value.

In **whole life insurance**, a business or individual pays a sum that is sufficient to keep the policy in force for the whole of the person's life. This sum can be paid every year for life or for a stated period of years (such as 20 years). For example, Evita Guard may pay $115 each year and be assured that her beneficiary, her husband, will receive the stated face value upon her death. Alternatively, she could pay $198 each year for 20 years and receive the same benefit. In both cases, the policy is said to be paid-up.

Whole life policies have an internal build-up called a *cash value*. This value can never be forfeited even if the policyholder chooses to stop paying the premium. In some cases, the policyholder can borrow against this value. Or a policyholder can surrender (discontinue) the insurance policy and receive its cash value from the insurance company. Cash value makes whole life policies attractive to some insurance purchasers.

term insurance

Insurance coverage for a fixed period of time, often one, five, ten, or twenty years.

Term Insurance

As its name suggests, **term insurance** provides coverage for a term (a temporary time period) stated in the policy. The term can be for one, five, ten or twenty years. Term insurance has no cash value and is less expensive than any of the other forms discussed in this section. A policyholder receives maximum death protection for the premium paid. An individual who has a limited insurance budget but a significant need for death protection should consider term insurance. Term insurance is also the form of life insurance companies supply most often to their employees.

Endowments

A type of policy called an **endowment** pays the face value of the policy whether the policyholder is dead or alive. The purpose of an endowment is to allow accumulation of a fund. For example, a father might buy a $20 000, 10-year endowment in order to accumulate $20 000 within a 10-year period for his daughter's university education. If he dies before the 10 years are up, the insurance company will pay his beneficiary (his daughter). However, if the father lives to the tenth year, the company turns the accumulated $20 000 over to him. Table 22.3 compares these three policies with regard to premiums, benefits, and use.

endowment

Insurance that pays face value after a fixed period of time whether the policyholder is alive or dead.

Table 22.3   Comparison of Basic and Common Life Insurance Contracts

Basic type	Protection period	When benefits are payable	Approximate costs for $10 000 at age 20*	How long premiums are paid	Uses
1. Whole Life	Permanent	At death, any time	—	—	Combination of moderate savings and protection
a. Straight or ordinary life	"	"	$115	Throughout life	"
b. 20-payment life	"	"	$198	For 20 years	Paying up premiums during working life
c. Life paid up at 65	"	"	$127	To age 65	
2. Term	Temporary	At death, only during term	—	—	Protection only
a. Yearly renewable term	"	"	$25 increasing each year	Varies—can be to age 60-70	Maximum protection
b. Five-year level term (renewable and convertible)	"	"	$53	5 years	Very high protection for limited period
3. Endowment	Temporary or long term	At death, or if living, at end of endowment period	—	—	Combination of higher savings and protection
a. 20-year endowment	"	"	$426	20 years	"
b. Retirement income at 65	"	"	$177	To age 65	"

*Costs are necessarily approximate for such general comparisons. Participating policies would be slightly higher, with net costs reduced by annual dividends. Nonparticipating policies would be somewhat lower. Smaller policies under $10 000 will be slightly higher; those over this amount may have a lower rate per $1000. Those insuring women will also be somewhat lower in cost. Extra policy features such as waiver of premium, accidental death benefits, and so on, would increase these estimates.

Universal Life Insurance

The life insurance industry was very profitable for many years selling only the three policies described above. Whole life was the backbone of the industry. But as interest rates spiralled in the 1960s and 1970s, many policyholders became disillusioned with the very low rate of interest they earned in whole life and endowment policies. Policyholders began surrendering their policies and investing their funds in higher yielding instruments such as guaranteed investment certificates. This withdrawal of funds, coupled with the difficulty of selling new policies, caused serious problems for life insurance companies. They responded by developing a new product to lure policyholders back to buying insurance: **universal life policies**.

Universal life policies combine a term insurance product with a savings component. Although this product may require a high initial premium, premium payments are flexible and interest earned on the savings component is competitive with other money market instruments.

universal life policy

A term insurance policy with a savings component.

Variable Life Insurance

Another new form of life insurance is a modified form of whole life insurance. **Variable life insurance** (**VLI**) allows flexibility regarding the minimum face value of the policy, the types of investments supporting it, and even the amount and timing of the premiums.

How does VLI work? Instead of buying a whole life policy with a fixed face value of $100 000, a policyholder may choose a variable life policy with a $100 000 *minimum* face value. The actual face value can exceed the minimum, depending on the market performance of the VLI investment portfolio. VLI policyholders can stipulate the portfolio mix, choosing among a variety of investment instruments such as common stocks, short-term bonds, and high-yield money market securities. The increase in the policy's face value depends on the success of the underlying investments. VLIs are a growing segment of the insurance market because they offer more flexibility than traditional policies.

variable life insurance (VLI)

A modified form of life insurance where the policyholder chooses the minimum face value of the policy.

Group Life Insurance

Most companies buy **group life insurance**, which is underwritten for groups as a whole rather than for each individual member. The insurer's assessment of potential losses and its pricing of premiums are based on the characteristics of the whole group. Johnson & Johnson's benefit plan, for example, includes group life coverage with a standard program of protection and benefits—a master policy purchased by J&J—that applies equally to all employees.

group life insurance

Life insurance written for a group of people rather than an individual.

Key Insurance

Many businesses choose to protect themselves against the loss of the talents and skills of key employees. If a salesperson who brings in $2.5 million in sales every year dies or takes a new job elsewhere, the firm will suffer loss. Moreover, the firm will incur recruitment costs to find a replacement and training expenses once a replacement is hired. *Key person insurance* can offset the lost income and the additional expenses. The box "Risky Rappers" describes the importance of key insurance in the music industry.

A related matter is who takes control of a business when a partner or associate dies. At issue is whether the surviving business partners are willing to accept an inexperienced heir as a management partner in the business. Business continuation agreements are traditionally used to plan for this situation. The business owners can plan to buy the ownership interest of the deceased associate from his or her heirs. The value of the ownership interest is determined when the agreement is made. Special business insurance policies can provide the funds needed to make the purchase.

International Report

Risky Rappers

Well-known rap artists like Snoop Doggy Dogg can earn more than $50 000 per night on a multi-city concert tour. But national tours by rap artists have been virtually non-existent since the late 1980s. Why? Because stabbings and gunfire were becoming all too common at these shows. Even when occasional live shows were staged, violence often erupted. Most rap artists have therefore had to rely on videos and radio-station promotions to sell their records and to keep their name prominently before their fans.

All this was supposed to change in 1997, when many rappers planned to take their acts on the road. Bad Boy Entertainment, the record label for rapper Biggie Smalls (also known as Notorious B.I.G.), planned a national tour of up to 30 cities starting in May 1997. But in March, Biggie Smalls was killed in a gangland-style hit. This killing occurred only six months after rapper Tupac Shakur was also gunned down.

Reliance National Insurance is one of the largest underwriters of music events. It also insures many concerts by crooners and rappers. When musicians perform live,

insurance costs are usually shared by the performer, the concert promoter, and the arena where the event is being held. Music companies also take out "key man" insurance on musicians. With the killings of Smalls and Shakur, insurance premiums on concerts are expected to skyrocket.

Insuring an all-rapper concert, particularly a "gangsta rap" concert, is seen by industry experts as being nearly impossible, given the violence that has occurred in the past. Eric Wilson, the president of Famous Artists Agency, says that insurance is either impossible to get or so expensive that it is difficult to make a profit on a concert. Some rap bands like the Fugees are seen as more insurable because they perform "feel-good rap."

In the wake of the killings of Smalls and Shakur, record companies are trying to convince rap artists to beef up their security. Insurance companies say they will have to raise premiums if concert promoters don't improve security. Metal detectors at entrances, security guards (one for every 100 people), and reserved seating may all be required before insurance can be purchased for rap concerts.

Summary of Learning Objectives

1. **Describe the responsibilities of a *financial manager*.** The job of the *financial manager* is to increase a firm's value by planning and controlling the acquisition and dispersal of its financial assets. This task involves two key responsibilities: (1) *cash-flow management*—making sure that a firm has enough available money to purchase the materials it needs to produce goods and services; and (2) *financial planning*—devising strategies for reaching future financial goals.

2. **Identify four sources of *short-term financing* for businesses.** To finance short-term expenditures, firms rely on *trade credit*—credit extended by suppliers—and on loans. *Secured loans* require *collateral*: the legal interest in assets that may include inventories or accounts receivable. *Unsecured loans* may be in the form of *lines of credit* or *revolving credit agreements*. Some very large firms issue *commercial paper*—short-term promises to pay. Smaller firms may choose to *pledge accounts receivable*—that is, sell them to financial institutions.

3. **Distinguish between the various sources of *long-term financing* and explain the risks entailed by each type.** Long-term sources of funds include debt financing, equity financing, and the use of preferred stock. *Debt financing* uses long-term loans and *corporate bonds* (promises to pay holders specified amounts by certain dates), both of which obligate the firm to pay regular interest. *Equity financing* involves the use of owners' capital, either from the sale of common stock or from retained earnings.

Preferred stock is a "hybrid" source of funding that has some of the features of both common stock and bonds. Financial planners must choose the proper mix of long-term funding. *All-equity financing* is the most conservative, least risky, and most expensive strategy. *All-debt financing* is the most speculative option.

4. **Show how financial *returns* to investors are related to *risks* they take.** Financial managers and investors must consider *risk-return relationships*: the risks involved in generating returns from different investments. If future return is certain, investors are willing to accept lower returns. But if the return is uncertain, they typically demand greater potential return before investing. For financial managers, the problem is to secure the greatest possible funding at the least possible cost. They work, then, to reduce the riskiness of investing in their company by compiling a good record of dividend, interest, and debt payment.

5. **Explain how risk affects business operations and identify the five steps in the *risk-management process*.** Businesses operate in an environment pervaded by risk. *Speculative risks* involve the prospect of gain or loss. *Pure risks* involve only the prospect of loss or no loss. Firms manage their risks by following some form of a five-step process: identifying risks, measuring possible losses, evaluating alternative techniques, implementing chosen techniques, and monitoring programs on an ongoing basis. There are generally four methods of handling risk: *risk avoidance*, *control*, *retention*, and *transfer*.

6. **Describe the basic workings of the *insurance industry* and explain how insurers make profits.** Insurance companies earn profits by charging customers *premiums* that, on average, exceed the losses that they cover and pay out to policyholders. Although many buyers will take out protection against the same type of loss, not all buyers will suffer that loss. To minimize their risk, insurers will provide coverage only for risks that meet four criteria: they are generally predictable; they occur beyond the control of the insured; they occur randomly and independently of other losses; and they are verifiable as to cause, time, place, and amount. Companies may be organized as *private insurers*, which may be owned by stockholders or policyholders, or *public insurers*, which are government agencies that write policies.

7. **Distinguish among the different types of *business insurance*.** *Liability insurance* covers losses resulting from damage, whether accidental or deliberate, to individuals or property. *Property insurance* covers losses to a firm's own buildings, equipment, and financial assets. *Life insurance* pays benefits to a policyholder's survivors.

Key Terms

financial managers , 670
finance, 670
cash flow management, 671
financial control, 671
financial plan, 671
inventory, 672
raw materials inventory, 673
work-in-process inventory, 673
finished goods inventory, 673
trade credit, 673
open-book credit, 673
promissory note, 673
trade draft, 674
trade acceptance, 674
secured loan, 674
collateral, 674

pledging accounts receivable, 675
unsecured loan, 675
line of credit, 675
revolving credit agreement, 675
commercial paper, 676
factoring, 676
debt financing, 676
corporate bond, 677
maturity date, 677
equity financing, 677
bankruptcy, 679
risk-return relationship, 682
risk, 684
speculative risk, 684
pure risk, 684
risk management, 684
risk avoidance, 685

risk control, 686
risk retention, 686
self-insurance, 686
risk transfer, 686
insurance policy, 686
deductible, 686
law of large numbers, 688
stock insurance company, 690
mutual insurance company, 690
underwriting, 691
insurance agent, 691
insurance broker, 691
liability insurance, 691
personal liability, 692
professional liability, 692
product liability, 692
premises liability, 692

umbrella insurance, 692
workers' compensation, 693
property insurance, 694
marine insurance, 694
title insurance, 695
business interruption insurance, 695
credit insurance, 695
life insurance, 696
beneficiary, 696
whole life insurance, 696
term insurance, 696
endowment, 697
universal life policy, 698
variable life insurance (VLI), 698
group life insurance, 698

Study Questions and Exercises

Review Questions

1. What questions must a financial manager answer when constructing a financial plan?
2. In what ways do the two sources for debt financing differ from each other? How do they differ from the two sources of equity financing?
3. What is the main source of credit for small businesses? Why?
4. Describe the risk-management process. What role does the risk manager play in the firm?
5. What requirements must a risk meet to be considered insurable?

Analysis Questions

6. Which of the life insurance products described in the chapter would you buy for yourself? Why?

7. How would you decide the best mix of debt and equity financing for a company?
8. If you were a financial manager for a large firm, what types of short-term funding would you use most? Why?

Application Exercises

9. Interview the owner of a local small business. Identify the types of short-term and long-term funding used by the firm. As well, ask the owner to describe the risk management process he or she uses in the business. Determine the reasons behind both these decisions.
10. Choose two well-known firms in different industries and compare their financial structures. Using public records and financial reports, determine each company's short-term debt, long-term debt, common equity, and preferred stock funding.

Building Your Business Skills

Goal
To encourage students to gain a better understanding of the major financial and risk-management issues that have faced large companies in the mid-1990s.

Method
In 1994, all of the following companies reported financial problems relating to risk management:

- Gibson Greetings
- Procter & Gamble
- Federal Paper Board
- Chemical Bank
- Metallgesellschaft AG

Step 1:
Working alone, research one of the companies listed above to learn more about the financial risks that were reported in the news.

Step 2:
Make sure that you can explain in your own words the risks and financial-management issues that were faced by the firm that you researched.

Step 3:
Join in teams with students who researched other companies and compare your findings.

Follow-Up Questions

1. Were there common themes in the "big stories" in financial management?

2. What have the various companies done to minimize future risks and losses?

Many tools and resources are available on Canadian business Web sites to help business managers improve financial decision making. One such Web site is the Federal Business Development Bank of Canada (FBDB). Check out their Web site at:

http://www.bdc.com

1. What types of financing sources are available through the Federal Business Development Bank?

2. Visit the "Tools" section of the Web site. Here you will find the "Ratio Calculator." What types of businesses would benefit most from this type of analysis tool? Why?

3. What does a "quick ratio" mean? Why and when would it be useful?

4. Which ratio(s) might be of most concern to an investor? A company sales manager? A company's creditors? A company's suppliers? The company's operations manager? An insurance underwriter? The company financial manager? Explain.

5. Evaluate the ratios as tools for making financial decisions. What are their strengths? What are their limitations?

CONCLUDING CASE 22-1

Barings Trader's Big Bet Breaks Bank

Twenty-eight-year-old Nicolas Leeson had certainly contributed his share to the bottom line of Barings PLC, the venerable British merchant bank. In less than two years as manager of Barings' futures-trading subsidiary in Singapore, Leeson had boosted profits from $1.2 million in 1992 to $30 million by the first seven months of 1994. Leeson's job involved buying and selling futures contracts, particularly investments known as *derivatives*. His specialties were trades in three markets: the Japanese stock index, known as the Nikkei 225; the futures market in Osaka, Japan; and the Singapore International Monetary Exchange (Simex). For example, Leeson exploited small price differences by buying contracts on Simex and selling them for slightly higher prices in Osaka. He was not, however, engaging in these trades on behalf of Barings' clients; rather, his trades were in-house transactions using the bank's own money. Many of Barings' 4000 employees enjoyed the fruits of Leeson's labours. In 1994, for example, a bonus pool of more than $160 million was paid out. Leeson's own 1994 bonus was more than half a million dollars, twice what he had received in 1993.

As one might expect for a British investment bank founded in 1762, Barings was widely regarded as a conservative institution. Indeed, its clients include the Queen herself. Thus the financial world was astounded in February 1995, when it was revealed that Leeson had incurred staggering trading losses of nearly $1 billion. In the aftermath of the disclosure, the Bank of England refused to come to the rescue by providing financial backing. Barings had no alternative but to declare bankruptcy. The problem, experts agreed, was a lack of internal risk-management controls. As one British banking official put it: "I always feared that the biggest danger to the banking system would be a rogue derivatives trader, but I never believed it could be on this scale."

What did happen to Barings? Over a three-week period, Leeson apparently bought $27 billion in futures contracts. In doing so, he wagered—very heavily—that the sluggish Japanese stock market would stage a rally. If the Nikkei 225 rose as he predicted, Leeson would cash in and profit. How? The contract price on which he had originally agreed would be lower than the actual level of the index when the contract came due. He would profit by the amount of the difference. In fact, however, the Nikkei fell *below* Leeson's contract price—whereby Barings was obligated to *pay* the difference. The young trader tried desperately to reverse his losses, but he was forced to put up cash for margin calls. In other words, he had to pay to maintain a certain percentage of the daily value of his contract—which was dropping along with the Nikkei.

Where did Leeson get the money? Investigators believe that he convinced Barings officials back in London to advance him more cash by claiming that he was trading on behalf of a client who would soon be depositing funds with the bank. The ploy failed. After leaving a note saying simply, "I'm sorry," Leeson disappeared. Several days later, he was apprehended by German police.

How could a single trader have racked up such losses? After all, Leeson's activities were subject to oversight by risk-management officials at Barings. Indeed, computers could have provided a warning when Leeson's trades exceeded preset amounts (as one financial expert notes, "There's widely available software for this type of risk management"). Barings officials, however, were slow to catch on, partly because Leeson was, in essence, supervising and settling his own trading activities. Despite warnings about lax controls over Leeson's trading following an internal audit in mid-1994, recommended changes were not made. For one thing, the same audit stressed Leeson's indispensability to the firm: "Without Leeson," advised internal auditors, Barings' Singapore operations "would lack a trader with the right combination of experience in trading sizeable lots, a detailed appreciation of trading strategies, familiarity with local traders' limits and practices, and contacts among traders and officials."

Another reason may have been internal rivalries and turf battles pitting Barings' London-based banking operations against the company's trading divisions in other parts of the world. In the weeks following Leeson's arrest, there was a flurry of accusations regarding which Barings executive should have been responsible for preventing the fiasco. "The great shame," lamented one Barings official, "is that we're very conservatively run. The one thing that we were trying to minimize—risk-taking—is what blew us out of the water."

Ultimately, the fate of Barings PLC was determined within a matter of days. A Dutch banking and insurance company, Internationale Nederlanden Groep NV (ING), paid a nominal sum of one British pound in exchange for all of Barings' liabilities and assets. The purchase came after ING officials carefully inspected Barings' books. "Don't forget, we're Dutch, after all," explained a spokesperson for ING. "We've got a well-deserved reputation for caution and thriftiness." Still, ING announced that it would provide an immediate cash infusion of more than $1 billion to allow Barings to continue its operations.

What happened to Nick Leeson? After being arrested in Germany, he was kept in jail while awaiting extradition to Singapore. In late 1995, after a trial in Singapore, he was sentenced to six and a half years in prison.

Case Questions

1. Discuss Leeson's trading activities in terms of the risk-return relationship.

2. Explain the type of risk that Leeson was facing in his financial dealings.

3. The Bank of England might have intervened to prevent Barings from falling into bankruptcy. What did Bank of England officials hope to achieve by not coming to the rescue?

4. Using the framework developed in the chapter, explain how a proper risk-management plan could help a financial institution prevent a disaster of the magnitude described in this case.

5. What are some of the risks and challenges ING might face as the new owner of Barings?

◆

CONCLUDING CASE 22-2

Lake Trout Ltd.

Don Braden was an avid fisherman. While pursuing his favourite sport, he experimented with many different fishing lures, always trying to find the ideal one. But he gradually came to the conclusion that what was available in tackle stores just wasn't quite right.

After some years of frustration, he began to think about making his own lures. His first efforts were rather crude but, because he was highly motivated and had some mechanical skill, he eventually produced three first-rate fishing lures. Initially, he concentrated on developing lures for pickerel (walleye) and lake trout because he was interested in catching them. During a couple of fishing seasons, he gave some of his new lures to several fishing buddies.

Although Don never intended to start a business, he soon began receiving inquiries about where his lures could be purchased. Because of this "natural demand," he began to think about getting into serious production of his products. In 1982, Don Braden decided to go full-time into the production and marketing of the three fishing lures he had developed. In 1985, he also got involved in the manufacture and sale of fishing rods. To date, the company's performance has exceeded his expectations. It has expanded dramatically and now has 28 employees. He has hired a production supervisor, and Don now concentrates on finance and marketing.

There are five shareholders in the firm. Don owns 65 percent of the company's shares. Three other investors each own 10 percent of the shares, and Don's sister owns 5 percent. Sales in 1989 were $4 600 000. This figure represents sales of about 400 000 fishing lures at an average price of $4.00 each, plus 100 000 fishing rods at an average price of $30 each. Demand continues to exceed the company's ability to supply it.

Lake Trout Ltd. has a good credit rating, and an analysis of its financial statements by a local CA firm indicates that it is a good prospect for further growth if it can obtain the capital it needs for expansion. Bonds currently outstanding total $1 million, with one quarter of that amount coming due within one year. Including the retirement of the maturing bonds and capital needed for expansion, Don estimates that Lake Trout Ltd. will need about $2 million in long-term capital funds over the next five years.

Don's sister recently proposed that the way to get this money was to issue $1 million in 12 percent bonds maturing in 20 years, and to sell 40 000 shares of stock at $25 per share. (This would double the number of shares outstanding.) Don is concerned about this proposal because he does not have sufficient funds to maintain majority ownership under such a plan. But he also sees the advantages of the plan. The three investors who each own 10 percent have indicated that they would be interested in purchasing 10 000 additional shares each. Financial advisors whom Don has talked to have indicated that he could probably sell up to $2 million in 12 percent bonds.

Case Questions

1. Assume that you are Don Braden. Would you oppose your sister's plan? Why or why not?

2. What are the advantages of the proposed stock plan? The disadvantages?

3. What are the advantages of selling $2 million in bonds?

4. What market information is needed before making this decision?

◆

Mutual Funds, Mutual Problems?*

"We've got a number of people who started a business about nine years ago from nothing . . . they've built it up to something that is extremely valuable."

—Peter Brewster,
editor of *Canadian Mutual Fund Advisor*

A few years ago, Andrew Gates began saving for his future by stashing his money away in Altamira mutual funds. The 34-year-old was attracted by the company's no-load policy. The absence of fees, Gates reasoned, meant higher returns for investors. For several years, his expectations were validated, with the mutual fund company providing its investors, which included over 300 000 Canadians, with industry-leading returns.

Lately, however, the story has been quite different, with Altamira's senior management enmeshed in intense internal political infighting. The fighting appears to have come at a price. With attention increasingly pulled away from the market and redirected towards a Toronto courtroom, returns have slumped, with the company recently winding up in twelfth spot within the industry. After working together for years to develop one of the country's hottest investment companies, the founders are now more intent on directing their competitive prowess against each other.

The key issue is whether the senior partners will hold or sell the company. One of the company's principals, Altamira's chief executive officer Ronald Bead, wants to cash out. He has initiated discussions with Canada's five chartered banks to see if any of them might be interested. His overtures produced one serious offer; the Toronto-Dominion Bank offered almost $800 million for control of the company. However, the company's other senior partners want to continue working there. The tragedy of cases such as this one is that the same forces that built the company could now tear it apart.

Part of Altamira's drop in performance may also be attributable to its large size. In its earlier years, it was comparatively less conservative and cautious. Now, with all the expectations that go along with investors looking to the fund for solid and reliable returns, it seems sentenced to a more conservative investment strategy. Some predict that the company may never lead the pack again. The infighting and general maturation of the company haven't resulted in Andrew Gates taking money out of the company . . . yet. Conversely, he hasn't invested more money.

Study Questions

1. What is the difference between par value and market value? Are both, only one, or neither of these affected by the political infighting going on at Altamira?

2. What is a mutual fund? What is the difference between a no-load and a load fund? Which is Altamira?

3. What is book value? How is the book value of Altamira being affected by the internal politics there?

Altamira
http://www.altamira-group.com

---

* Source: This case was written by Professor Reg Litz of the University of Manitoba.
  Video Resource: "Altamira," *Venture* #633 (March 9, 1997).

> **"If I can get out of this by writing out a cheque for $10 000, it's easier than spending $5000 to investigate."**
>
> —Allan Wood, insurance company executive

Insurance company executives report that questionable auto insurance claims are on the rise. The "crash for cash" mentality involves people intentionally staging minor automobile accidents in order to rake in cash from insurance companies that would rather settle out of court than fight in court. The strategy involves staging a low, or even no, speed fender bender, with little, if any, damage to either vehicle or occupants. The incident later gets reframed as a "major accident." In Alberta alone, the "auto lotto" pay-out arising from such accidents was estimated at $125 million in 1995.

Why does this happen? Part of the problem, insurance investigators report, is a "got nothing to lose" mentality. Part is also attributable to the incentive structure of the legal system. The use of contingency fee-based lawyering means that attorneys only get paid if their clients do, which means either winning their case in court or settling out of court. Part is also related to the system's acceptance of difficult-to-substantiate "soft tissue" injuries. What makes the increase of these cases particularly interesting, however, is that the number of collisions appears to be actually declining.

In one case, an alleged victim was driving a van along an Edmonton street. Suddenly, he stopped for no apparent reason, only to suffer a low speed rear-end collision from the car behind. The van received only minor damages. The driver, however, sued for chronic pain to his neck and lower back. Complicating the lawsuit further, the driver's wife sued for permanent disabilities to neck, back, shoulder, and lower jaw areas, even though it was later determined that only the husband and his four-year-old had been in the van at the time of the accident. An investigator later claimed it was impossible for the driver to have suffered the type and degree of injuries claimed.

The eventual settlement ordered the driver to stay away from manual labour; later, he was observed working as a machine operator and operating a vehicle while displaying a range of movement in his neck. Likewise, the driver's wife was seen lifting heavy bags of groceries, hoisting boxes, and cleaning their van. The claimants of this accident seem particularly suspect, however, by virtue of the sheer volume of accidents they seem to find themselves involved in; the husband reports involvement in no fewer than three other accidents, while his spouse reported being involved in five accidents in three years.

To be alert to the possibility of being taken for a ride on the "auto lotto," insurance companies recommend that people keep a disposable camera and notebook in their vehicle. Immediately after an accident, take notes and pictures of the accident and all apparent damage. Second, ask the other driver(s) about their previous insurance claim history. Finally, pressure the insurance company to investigate the accident thoroughly rather than just cave in to get out of the "auto lotto" game.

Study Questions

1. What is the difference between speculative and pure risk? How do they apply to the "auto lotto"?
2. What is risk control? How does it relate to the tactics of the insurance companies?
3. What is risk avoidance? What could an insurance company do if it wanted to practise risk avoidance regarding the "auto lotto"?

* Source: This case was written by Professor Reg Litz of the University of Manitoba.
 Video Resource: "Insurance Fraud," *Marketplace* #24 (March 25, 1997).

EXPERIENTIAL EXERCISE:
Going to Bat for Financing

OBJECTIVE

To help students understand how many aspects of a company's operations contribute to its financial standing and its access to capital.

TIME REQUIRED

45 minutes
   Step 1: Individual activity (15 minutes)
   Step 2: Small-group activity (15 minutes)
   Step 3: Class discussion (15 minutes)

PROCEDURE

Step 1: Read the following case regarding the Hickory Sport Company.

The Hickory Sport Company, manufacturer of aluminum baseball bats, has been doing a booming business. In each of the last five years, company sales and profits have risen by at least 20 percent:

Year	Sales	Profits
1993	$231 000	$29 000
1994	$307 000	$40 000
1995	$456 000	$59 000
1996	$610 000	$88 000
1997	$772 000	$106 000

Dan Bowers, cofounder and owner of Hickory Sport, is pleased with the growth of his business and expects it to grow further still. One element hampering his growth, however, is a loan limit of $200 000 at his bank, Batch National Bank. In considering his application for a $500 000 line of credit, the bank investigated Bowers and Hickory Sport thoroughly and learned the following:

Company History. The firm was founded by Bowers and his sister. In late 1993, Bowers bought his sister's share in the business for $150 000, mortgaging the firm's plant to raise part of the money needed. He is now the sole proprietor of the company.

Personal History. Bowers, now 37 years old, has a B.A. in economics and an MBA. A long-time sports enthusiast, he received a full athletic scholarship for playing baseball and played local softball after university. Over the last five years, however, he has given up softball and put in long hours at Hickory Sport. His suppliers and current bankers think highly of his knowledge of the business and willingness to do whatever needs to be done—typing and filing or running a lathe. His personal assets are limited to a $150 000 home with a $100 000 mortgage.

Employees. Bowers has a well-trained assistant who has been with the company since its inception, as well as three other office employees. His hard work and upbeat attitude have contributed to high productivity and a low turnover rate among the firm's 25 employees.

Financial Management. The company has a reputation for wise use of capital. Before Bowers bought out his sister, the firm paid its bills within the discount period. Since that time, mortgage payments and loan limits have forced Hickory Sport to delay payments to an average of 45 days. A recent financial report appears on the following page.

```
                        Hickory Sport Company
                            Balance Sheet
                        As of December 31, 1997

Current Assets
   Cash                                          21 150
   Accounts receivable                           86 600
   Merchandise inventory                         63 750
   Prepaid expenses                               3 150

Fixed Assets
   Land                                          54 000
   Building                                     195 000
   Equipment                                    216 585
   (Less depreciation)            141 945
      Total assets                                              498 290

Current Liabilities
   Accounts payable               48 945
   Wages payable                  11 100
   Taxes payable                   5 760

Long-term Liabilities
   Notes payable, 11.25% due 1999 120 000

Owner's Equity
   Retained Earnings                            312 485

Total Liabilities and Owner's Equity                           498 290
```

SHOULD THE BANK APPROVE A LINE OF CREDIT FOR HICKORY SPORT?

Step 2: The instructor will divide the class into small groups, each of which will complete the following grid ranking Hickory Sport from 1 (highly favourable in loan-making) to 5 (highly unfavourable), and decide whether the bank should extend a $500 000 line of credit to Hickory Sport.

DECISION-MAKING GRID

Characteristic	1	2	3	4	5
Form of ownership					
Qualities of owner					
Quality of employees					
Management of assets					
Current financial health					
Future prospects					

Step 3: One member of each small group will present the group's conclusions to the class.

QUESTIONS FOR DISCUSSION

1. What factor most influenced your decision to approve or not to approve a new credit line for Hickory Sport?

2. If turned down by the bank, what other methods of financing might Dan Bowers use to fund future growth at Hickory Sport?

REALITY CHECK

Landing a job is a major accomplishment. But keeping one—and advancing in the organization—is no less important and often considerably more difficult. While no one can guarantee you success on the job, following these seven guidelines can put you on the inside track to career success.

- Be a problem solver.
- Pay attention to details.
- Be a team player.
- Impress your peers.
- Do your own thing.
- Know how you're doing.
- Find a mentor.

BE A PROBLEM SOLVER

It's easy to identify and point out problems—sales are going down; turnover is too high; too many customers are complaining; quality is poor; productivity is low. It is much more difficult to be a constructive problem solver—one who not only points out problems but also identifies new, creative, and effective ways to remedy those problems.

After you have identified a problem, go ahead and solve it yourself—if you have the responsibility and authority. But don't go too far. If you don't have the responsibility and authority, write your boss a memo explaining the problem and recommending a solution. Even if the boss does not accept your recommendations, she or he will still be impressed by your initiative.

PAY ATTENTION TO DETAILS

It is important that you pay close attention to the "little things," the details. For example, when you submit your first report to your boss, check, double-check, and then check again to make sure that all calculations are correct and that there are no errors in your report. Also eliminate any misspelled words and/or grammatical errors.

Likewise, if you are making a presentation—whether to a group of managers, investors, or customers—don't allow mistakes to distract from your message. Be sure that your slides or overhead transparencies are just as error-free as that first report you submitted. If time permits, set the room up yourself. (At least give it a quick once-over before anyone else arrives.) Is the volume on the microphone correctly adjusted? Are your slides in the correct order? Is the projector properly focused? How do you dim the lights? Is there a spare bulb for the projector? If you will be operating the projector or any other mechanical device, make sure you can run the equipment flawlessly and smoothly. Always rehearse every element of your presentation several times.

BE A TEAM PLAYER

In school you will probably be awarded at least a few grades that are higher than you deserve. But overall, everything will equal out. The same is true on the job. You will no doubt have some great ideas for which others will be given credit. But you will sometimes get credit for other people's ideas.

Today's organizations want people who will be part of the team. Work hard at getting along with others in the organization—your boss, your peers, and your subordinates. And spread the credit around to everyone. Remember that organizations are most likely to succeed when people work together. Take joy and pride in the success of others, and recognize that no organization can function if people don't work together.

What if someone else claims credit for your ideas? If that someone is your boss, pat yourself on the back—if your boss rises because of your work, chances are good that you'll rise with that individual. If a peer deliberately misleads others and takes credit for your idea, you are likely to feel anger and resentment. Keep your mouth closed and keep doing your best. Chances are that over time your boss and everyone else in the organization will see who is really pulling the weight. As Figure 1 illustrates, a sour attitude can put a damper on your career faster than any rival can.

IMPRESS YOUR PEERS

Closely related to teamwork is the idea of impressing your peers. Obviously, it is important to impress your boss. But if you ignore your co-workers, downgrade their abilities and accomplishments, and work only to advance yourself, you will eventually become an outcast in the organization.

You will be far better served if you can earn the respect, trust, and support of your co-workers. Working well with them is sure to pay you dividends in the future. If you find yourself as their boss one day, you will have already earned their respect. And if one of them should someday become your boss, he or she will still respect you.

DO YOUR OWN THING

While it's important to be a team player and to get along with your peers, don't get dragged blindly into the herd. Part of the reason the company hired you is that you are you. Your job may dictate that you dress and behave in certain ways. But don't be a robot—be your own person.

Your success in the business world (or whatever career path you take) will depend in great measure on your abilities to determine what you are good at and to build a career around those skills. Are you good with statistics, or do your talents lie in more artistic directions? The answer may indicate whether you would be better off in the financial department or the advertising division. Are you adept at getting groups of people to work well together, or are you happier completing a project on your own? One path leads to management, while the other takes you to a more "technical" career. You chose your major at least in part because you were interested in the subject. Now that you're on the job, remember your love for that subject and try to use it every day in what you do.

Figure 1 Attitudes That Can Sabotage Your Career

Attitude	Example	Solution
"They owe me."	Deprived of a promised raise because of a financial pinch, you decide to stay at the best hotels and eat in the best restaurants while travelling—and put it all on your expense account.	Speak to your manager about your disappointment with a small raise. Get a commitment for another review soon or start hunting for a new job.
"I'm too good for them. They don't deserve me."	Assigned to write a two-page press release on a new bug spray, you, a *summa cum laude* graduate, write a memo on why such a release was a waste of time, then reject advice from a colleague on how to format it.	Remember that everyone has to start somewhere and that you still have a lot to learn. Ask a peer for advice—it could be the start of a lifelong friendship and/or working relationship. Use the opportunity to learn about the firm's products so you can talk about them intelligently in meetings.
"Why should I help *you*?"	When your assistant notes for the fifth time that he just can't get that spreadsheet of yours to run, you dismiss him curtly, saying, "Never mind, I'll do it myself."	Helping others in the organization, whether above or below you, is part of your job. Show your assistant how to use the spreadsheet again—and make arrangements for him to take a course in using computers.
"Now I can coast a little."	After months of 60-hour weeks to launch a new advertising campaign, you start routinely coming in a little late and taking long lunches to "recapture" the extra hours you put in earlier.	Never make it a habit to come in late, leave early, or take long, nonworking lunches. Keep up the appearance of hard work by being visible—just slow down the pace of what you do on the job when the situation doesn't call for haste.

KNOW HOW YOU'RE DOING

It's important for you to know at all times how the organization rates your efforts and achievements. A formal performance appraisal is one key source of feedback. Pay close attention to your boss's comments and suggestions at this time, don't get defensive, and work hard to improve in those areas in which you are perceived to be deficient.

In addition to the formal performance appraisal, you should seek actively your supervisor's feedback on other daily activities. When you submit your first report, ask your boss to critique it for you. When you solve your first problem, ask your boss if you handled it right. And after you make that first presentation, ask people who attended for their reactions. (One note of caution: Assuming all goes well with your first report, presentation, etc., do not seek constant reassurance. This may cause you to be viewed as insecure, not effective.)

Also pay attention to more subtle forms of feedback. Suppose you are given a routine project and complete it in what you think is a satisfactory manner. If your next several assignments are equally routine, your boss may not be as impressed with your work as you thought. If you sense that you are "falling behind" others who entered the organization at the same time as you, again seek feedback from your boss and co-workers and ask for suggestions on how you can improve your performance.

FIND A MENTOR

A final bit of advice: Find a mentor. As we noted in the text, a mentor is a senior person in the organization who is willing to help you with your career. In looking for a mentor, try to identify someone who has succeeded in the organization and who is respected by others. Things will be easier if the individual is someone you both respect professionally and like personally.

Start establishing a relationship with your prospective mentor by getting to know him or her. You don't want to waste anyone's time, but do drop by occasionally to ask advice and seek council. Be open, but not pushy, in your quest for a mentor. You will be able to detect fairly early if the person you've chosen is too busy or is not interested in helping you—in which case you should start looking for someone else.

Once you have found a mentor, she or he will be a valuable source of information throughout your career. You can ask for technical advice and career advice, or just talk about problems and opportunities. In addition, your mentor can be a champion for your interests in the organization by pointing out your positive qualities and recommending you to others.

NOTES, SOURCES, AND CREDITS

Reference Notes

Chapter 1

1. Larry Peppers and Dale G. Gails, *Managerial Economics: Theory and Applications for Decision Making* (Englewood Cliffs, NJ: Prentice-Hall, 1987).
2. Howard W. French, "On the street, Cubans fondly embrace capitalism," *The New York Times*, February 3, 1994, p. A4.
3. Robert Stone, "China's old guard holds on to power as the system slowly changes," *Winnipeg Free Press*, November 13, 1991, p. A7.
4. Richard I. Kirkland, Jr., "The death of socialism," *Fortune*, January 4, 1988, pp. 64-72.
5. Patrick Martin, "Cash-strapped kibbutz jettisons socialist values," *The Globe and Mail*, September 14, 1992, pp. A1-A2.
6. Page Smith, *The Rise of Industrial America* (New York: Viking Penguin, 1990).
7. Marina Strauss, "Business travel comes down to earth," *The Globe and Mail*, March 21, 1991, pp. B1-B2.
8. Adam Smith, *The Wealth of Nations* (New York: Modern Library, 1937; originally published in 1776).
9. Nicholas C. Siropolis, *Small Business Management*, 4th ed. (Boston: Houghton Mifflin, 1990).
10. "Big G is growing fat on oat cuisine," *Business Week*, September 18, 1989, p. 29.
11. John Partridge and Lawrence Surtees, "Rogers faces assault from Telcos," *The Globe and Mail*, March 28, 1994, pp. B1-B2.
12. "Where global growth is going," *Fortune*, July 31, 1989, pp. 71-92.
13. Peter Cook, "Nation's living standards under growing pressure," *The Globe and Mail*, August 31, 1991, pp. B1-B2.
14. Andrew Nikiforuk, "Putting a Price Tag on the Planet," *Canadian Business*, August 1997, p. 83.
15. *World Development Report 1997*, pp. 215, 237.

Chapter 2

1. Madelaine Drohan, "Ottawa targets interprovincial barriers," *The Globe and Mail*, May 14, 1991, p. B5.
2. U.S. Small Business Administration, "Selecting the legal structure for your firm," *Management Aid No. 6.004* (Washington, D.C.: U.S. Government Printing Office, 1985).
3. Quoted in Lowell B. Howard, *Business Law* (Woodbury, NY: Barron's Woodbury Press, 1965), p. 332.
4. John Heinzl, "The battling McCain's show signs of softening," *The Globe and Mail*, August 27, 1994, p. B1.
5. Dennis Slocum, "Mutual Life Goes Public," *The Globe and Mail*, December 9, 1997, pp. B1, B6.
6. Scott Kilman, "Giant Cargill Resists Pressure to Go Public As It Pursues Growth," *The Wall Street Journal*, January 9, 1997, pp. A1, A4.
7. Ann Gibbon, "Pattison Keeps Deals Spinning," *The Globe and Mail*, June 9, 1997, pp. B1, B5.
8. See "A seat on the board is getting hotter," *Business Week*, July 3, 1989, p. 72.
9. John Heinzl, "Dual Share Structures Targeted," *The Globe and Mail*, January 9, 1997, pp. B1, B10.
10. "A seat on the board is getting hotter." See note 3.
11. Brian Milner, "Loewen Directors Sued," *The Globe and Mail*, October 2, 1996, pp. B1, B7.
12. Stratford P. Sherman, "How Philip Morris diversified right," *Fortune*, October 23, 1989, pp. 120-128.
13. Bill Redekop, "Co-op withers as pool goes public," *Winnipeg Free Press*, July 15, 1994, p. 1.

Chapter 3

1. See Daniel McCarthy, Francis C. Spital, and Milton C. Lauenstein, "Managing growth at high-technology companies: A view from the top," *Academy of Management Executive*, August 1987, pp. 313-322, for an overview of high-tech companies and their management.
2. "Beyond Marlboro country," *Business Week*, August 8, 1988, pp. 54–58.
3. Bill Redekop, "UGG set to Poison Pools' Bid," *Winnipeg Free Press*, February 22, 1997, p. B12; also Bill Redekop, "UGG Rebottles Poison Pill," *Winnipeg Free Press*, March 21, 1997, p. B8; also Bill Redekop, "Court Ruling Ends Hostile Bid for UGG," *Winnipeg Free Press*, March 19, 1997, pp. A1–A2.
4. Alan Freeman, "Takeovers no cure," *The Globe and Mail*, June 13, 1991, p. B13.
5. Barrie McKenna, "The heat is on for Hydro Quebec," *The Globe and Mail*, November 24, 1993, pp. B1, B9.

6. John Stackhouse, "Missing the market," *Report on Business Magazine*, January 1992, p. 38; also Karen Lynch, "Wave of privatization sweeps the globe," *The Financial Post*, November 11, 1991, p. 42.
7. Silvia Ascarelli, "European Sell-Offs Set Record in '96; No Letup in Sight," *The Wall Street Journal*, January 2, 1997, p. A8.
8. A. Bennett, "Downsizing Doesn't Necessarily Bring an Upswing in Corporate Profitability," *The Wall Street Journal*, June 6, 1991, pp. B1, B4; also R. Henkoff, "Getting Beyond Downsizing," *Fortune*, January 10, 1994, p. 58; also W. McKinley, A.G. Schick, H.L. Sun, and A.P. Tang, "The Financial Environment of Layoffs: An Exploratory Study," working paper, Southern Illinois University, 1994; also Deborah Dougherty and Edward B. Bowman, "The Effects of Organizational Downsizing on Product Innovation," *California Management Review*, Summer 1995, pp. 28–44.
9. Garry Gruton, J. Keels, and Christopher Shook, "Downsizing the Firm: Answering the Strategic Questions," *Academy of Management Executive*, May 1996, pp. 38–45.
10. Lawrence Surtees, "CRTC Rings in New Telco Era," *The Globe and Mail*, May 2, 1997, pp. B1, B11.
11. Douglas Bell, "What Good *Is* the CRTC?" *The Financial Post Magazine*, December 1996, pp. 36–44.
12. Ashley Geddes, "Marketing boards under fire," *The Financial Post*, October 9, 1993, p. 6.
13. John Kohut, "Chrysler facing federal tribunal for refusing to supply car parts," *The Globe and Mail*, December 16, 1988, p. B5.
14. Karen Unland, "Tobacco Makers Lose Bid to Suspend Law," *The Globe and Mail*, April 30, 1997, p. B5.
15. Barrie McKenna, "Hyundai gorged on federal funds," *The Globe and Mail*, March 25, 1994, p. B3.
16. Dan Lett and John Douglas, "Too often to the well," *Winnipeg Free Press*, February 17, 1995, p. B10.
17. Eduardo Lachina, "Saving the earth: U.S. asks World Bank to make safeguarding environment a priority, " *Wall Street Journal*, July 3, 1987, p. 1.
18. Bruce McDougall, "Driven by design," *Canadian Business*, January 1991, pp. 49-53.
19. "Engine efficiency boosted," *The Globe and Mail*, July 31, 1991.
20. Barrie McKenna, "Alcan aims to be No. 1 with a 'bullet'," *The Globe and Mail*, July 31, 1991.
21. Victor Fung, "New system aims to revolutionize mining," *The Financial Post*, July 29, 1991, p. 5.
22. Robert L. Simison, "Test Cars Shake the Drowsy, Avert Crash," *The Globe and Mail*, April 17, 1997, p. B1.

Chapter 4

1. Bill Saporito, "Where the global action is," *Fortune*, Autumn/Winter 1993, pp. 62-65.
2. John Tagliabue, "Coca-Cola reaches into impoverished Albania," *New York Times*, May 20, 1994, pp. D1, D3; Joseph B. Treaster, "Kellogg seeks to reset Latvia's breakfast table," *New York Times*, May 19, 1994, pp. D1, D8.
3. Brenton R. Schlender et al., "Special Report/Pacific Rim: The battle for Asia," *Fortune*, November 1, 1993, pp. 126-156; Philip Shenon, "Missing out on a glittering market," *New York Times*, September 12, 1993, Sec. 3, pp. 1, 6; Steven Greenhouse, "New tally of world's economies catapults China into third place," *New York Times*, May 20, 1993, pp. A1, A8.
4. John Heinzl, "Conference Board Warns of Pitfalls in Chinese Ventures," *The Globe and Mail*, November 5, 1996, p. B8.
5. Michael Porter, "Why nations triumph," *Fortune*, March 12, 1990, pp. 94-108.
6. Madelaine Drohan, "Dependency on U.S. Leaves Canada 'Vulnerable:' WTO," *The Globe and Mail*, November 20, 1996.
7. Anthony DePalma, "G.M. gives Mexico its own 'Chevy'" *The New York Times*, May 12, 1994, pp. D1, D6; James B. Treece et al., "New worlds to conquer," *Business Week*, February 28, 1994, p. 51.
8. "Exports, Eh?" *Canadian Business*, January 1997, p. 21.
9. Peggy Berkowitz, "You say potato, they say McCain," *Canadian Business*, December 1991, pp. 44-48.
10. Daniel Stoffman, "Cross-border selling," *Report on Business Magazine*, November 1991, pp. 61-68.
11. "Cracking world markets without leaving home," *Canadian Business*, January 1992, pp. 13-14.
12. Elizabeth Church, "Rain-Gear Maker Casts Its Line in Chile," *The Globe and Mail*, November 18, 1996, p. B6.

13. John Stackhouse, "Missing the market," *Report on Business Magazine*, January 1992, p. 38.
14. "In hot pursuit of international markets," *Innovation*, Summer 1990, pp. 11–13.
15. Jeremy Main, "How to go global—and why," *Fortune*, December 17, 1990, pp. 70–73; see p. 72.
16. Randall Litchfield, "The pressure on prices," *Canadian Business*, February 1992, pp. 30-35.
17. Peter Cook, "Can Anyone Anywhere Ban Bribery?" *The Globe and Mail*, October 1, 1997, p. B2.
18. Nicholas Bray, "OECD Ministers Agree to Ban Bribery As Means for Companies to Win Business," *The Wall Street Journal*, May 27, 1997, p. A2.
19. Barrie McKenna, "Aluminum Producers Whispering Dirty Word," *The Globe and Mail*, March 5, 1994, pp. B1, B5.
20. Jalil Hamid, "Coffee Rally Reignited," *The Globe and Mail*, May 22, 1997, p. B9.
21. Anna Wilde Mathews, "As U.S. Trade Grows, Shipping Cartels Get a Bit More Scrutiny," *The Wall Street Journal*, October 7, 1997, pp. A1, A8.
22. "Bike Makers Win Dumping Case," *The Globe and Mail*, December 11, 1997, p. B6.
23. "New global trade regulator starts operations tomorrow," *Winnipeg Free Press*, December 31, 1994, p. A5.
24. Helene Cooper and Bhushan Bahree, "World's Best Hope for Global Trade Topples Few Barriers," *The Wall Street Journal*, December 3, 1996, pp. A1, A8.
25. Andrew Purvis, "Super Exporter," *Time*, April 28, 1997, p. 36.
26. *Ibid.*, p. 36.
27. Robert Russo, "NAFTA Report Calls Canada a Winner," *Winnipeg Free Press*, July 12, 1997, p. B24; also "NAFTA 'Bad Thing' for United States," *Winnipeg Free Press*, June 27, 1997, p. A11.
28. Bruce Little, "Free Trade 10 Years Later: Who Won?" *The Globe and Mail*, October 3, 1997, pp. B1, B6.
29. Peter Cook, "Free trade free-for-all causes confusion," *Globe and Mail*, December 5, 1994, p. B7.
30. "Canada Moves Up the Competitiveness Scale," *Winnipeg Free Press*, May 21, 1997, p. B8; also "A Glance at the Winners and Losers," *The New Straits Times*, June 3, 1996, pp. B1, B2.
31. Alan Swift, "Economy Gets Mixed Review," *Winnipeg Free Press*, June 13, 1996, p. B9.
32. Herman Daems, "The strategic implications of Europe 1992," *Long Range Planning*, 23, No. 3, 1990, pp. 41-48.
33. For example, see James C. Abegglen and George Stalk, *Kaisha: The Japanese Corporation* (New York: Basic Books, 1986).
34. See Edith Terry's series on *keiretsu* in *The Globe and Mail*: "The land of the rising cartels," September 22, 1990, pp. B1–B2; "The ties that bind," September 24, 1990, pp. B1, B4; and "Looking in from the outside," September 25, 1990, pp. B1–B2.
35. Michael Bociurkiw, "Manulife braces for push into China," *The Globe and Mail*, March 10, 1994, p. B3.
36. For a discussion of doing business in the (former) Soviet Union, refer to Carl H. McMillan, "Eastward ho! Tackling the last frontier," *Canadian Business Review*, Summer 1990, pp. 17–26.
37. For a discussion of practical ideas and useful information on surviving and succeeding in Eastern Europe, refer to Tarif Korabi and David G. Grieve, "Doing business in Eastern Europe: A survival guide," *Canadian Business Review*, Summer 1990, pp. 22–25.

Chapter 5

1. Michael Stern, "Ethical standards begin at the top," *The Globe and Mail*, November 11, 1991, p. B4.
2. Richard P. Nielsen, "Changing unethical organizational behavior," *Academy of Management Executive*, May 1989, pp. 123–130.
3. Mark Schwartz, "Heat's on to Get an Effective Code," *The Globe and Mail*, November 27, 1997, p. B2.
4. Jeremy Main, "Here comes the big new cleanup," *Fortune*, November 21, 1988, pp. 102-118.
5. Catherine Collins, "The race for zero," *Canadian Business*, March 1991, pp. 52-56.
6. Charles Davies, "Strategy session 1990," *Canadian Business*, January 1990, p. 48.
7. "Room service and the recyclable rubber chicken," *Canadian Business*, May 1991, p. 19.
8. Casey Mahood, "Bell zeros in on waste," *The Globe and Mail*, May 4, 1992, p. B1.
9. Martin Mittelstaedt, "Greenpeace takes on Cameco shares," *The Globe and Mail*, June 10, 1991, p. B10.
10. John Fox, "No eluding the enviro-sleuths—not even abroad," *The Financial Post*, April 8, 1991, p. 5.
11. See note 10.
12. Bruce Livesey, "Stuck with the cleanup," *Canadian Business*, February 1991, pp. 92-96.
13. Geoffrey Scotton, "Cleanups can hurt, companies warned," *The Financial Post*, June 25, 1991, p. 4.
14. Marc Huber, "A double-edged endorsement," *Canadian Business*, January 1990, pp. 69-71.

15. John Saunders, "Polar plastic plot flops," *The Globe and Mail*, June 10, 1994, p. B1.
16. Shona McKay, "Willing and able," *Report on Business*, October 1991, pp. 58-63.
17. "Why business is hiring the mentally abled," *Canadian Business*, May 1991, p. 19.
18. J. Southerst, "In pursuit of drugs," *Canadian Transportation*, November 1989, pp. 58-65.
19. G. Bylinsky, "How companies spy on employees," *Fortune*, November 4, 1991, pp. 131-140.
20. Michael McHugh, "Blowing whistle on company can be a risky venture," *The Financial Post*, August 26, 1991, p. 2.
21. "Is Ivan Boesky just the tip of the insider iceberg?" *Dun's Business Month*, January 1987, p. 22.
22. Daniel Stoffman, "Good behavior and the bottom line," *Canadian Business*, May 1991, pp. 28–32.
23. Tom Kierans, "Charity Begins at Work," *Report on Business Magazine*, June 1990, p. 23.
24. *Intersector: A Newsletter for IMAGINE'S Community Partners*, Canadian Centre for Philanthropy, Vol. 1, No. 2, p. 1.

Chapter 6

1. Robert Williamson, "Motivation on the Menu," *The Globe and Mail*, November 24, 1995, p. B7.
2. Charles W.L. Hill and Gareth Jones, *Strategic Management: An Analytical View*, 2nd ed. (Boston: Houghton Mifflin, 1992).
3. William Carley, "To Keep GE's Profits Rising, Welch Pushes Quality-Control Plan," *The Wall Street Journal*, January 13, 1997, pp. A1, A8.
4. Dave Ulrich and Dale Lake, "Organizational Capability: Creating Competitive Advantages," *The Academy of Management Executive*, February 1991, pp. 77–83.
5. Michael Porter, *Competitive Strategy: Techniques for Analyzing Industries and Competitors* (New York: The Free Press, 1980).
6. J. Carey, "Getting Business to Think About the Unthinkable," *Business Week*, June 24, 1991, pp. 104–07.
7. Stephen Carroll and Henry L. Tosi, *Management by Objectives* (New York: Macmillan, 1973).
8. Alex Taylor III, "How a top boss manages his day," *Fortune*, June 19, 1989, pp. 95–100.
9. John Lorinc, "Managing when there's no middle," *Canadian Business*, June 1991, pp. 86-94.
10. See Kamal Fatehi, *International Management: A Cross-Cultural and Functional Perspective* (Upper Saddle River, NJ: Prentice Hall, 1996), pp. 5–8, 153–64.
11. "MBAs are hotter than ever," *Business Week*, March 9, 1987, pp. 46-48.
12. Terrence Deal and Allen Kennedy, *Corporate Cultures: The Rites and Rituals of Corporate Life* (Reading, MA: Addison-Wesley, 1982).
13. Bruce McDougall, "The thinking man's assembly line," *Canadian Business*, November 1991, pp. 40-44.
14. Paul M. Eng and Evan I. Schwartz, "The games people play in the office," *Business Week*, October 11, 1993, p. 40.
15. Marina Strauss, "Baker's brassy style may rub off on McKim," *The Globe and Mail*, January 27, 1992, pp. B1, B6.

Chapter 7

1. See John A. Wagner and John R. Hollenbeck, *Management of Organizational Behavior* (Englewood Cliffs, NJ: Prentice Hall, 1992), pp. 563-565.
2. Alan Deutschman, "How H-P Continues to Grow and Grow," *Fortune*, May 2, 1994, pp. 99–100; Stratford Sherman, "Secrets of H-P's 'Muddled' Team," *Fortune*, March 18, 1996, pp. 116–20.
3. Jay Diamond and Gerald Pintel, *Retailing*, 6th ed. (Upper Saddle River, NJ: Prentice Hall, 1996), pp. 83–84.
4. Jacquie McNish, "A chairman with worries lots of others would like," *The Globe and Mail*, April 14, 1990, p. B6.
5. Peter Larson, "Winning strategies," *Canadian Business Review*, Summer 1989, p. 41.
6. Ian Allaby, "The search for quality," *Canadian Business*, May 1990, pp. 31-42.
7. Donna Fenn, "The Buyers," *Inc.*, June 1996, pp. 46–48+.
8. J. Galbraith, "Matrix organization designs: How to combine functional and project forms," *Business Horizons*, 1971, pp. 29-40; also H.F. Kolodny, "Evolution to a matrix organization," *Academy of Management Review*, 4, 1979, pp. 543-553.
9. Lawton R. Burns, "Matrix management in hospitals: Testing theories of matrix structure and development," *Administrative Science Quarterly*, 34, 1989, pp. 48-50.
10. Glenn Rifkin, "Digital dumps matrix management," *The Globe and Mail*, July 21, 1994, pp. B1, B4.
11. Barnaby J. Feder, "The Tech exec who also brings home the bacon," *New York Times*, August 21, 1994, Sec. 3, p. 4.
12. Thomas Peters and Robert Waterman, *In Search of Excellence* (New York: Harper & Row, 1982).
13. Shawn Tully, "Why to Go for Stretch Targets," *Fortune*, November 14, 1994, pp. 145–46+; Larry Armstrong, "Nurturing an Employee's Brainchild," *Business Week*, Enterprise 1993, p. 196.

Chapter 8

1. *The State of Small Business 1989, Annual Report on Small Business in Ontario* (Toronto: Ministry of Industry, Trade and Technology, 1990), pp. 3-4.
2. Gayle MacDonald, "War Stories from the World's Top Female Owners," *The Globe and Mail*, May 2, 1997, p. B9; also Murray McNeill, "Women Step Out on Their Own," *The Winnipeg Free Press*, December 8, 1994, p. C10.
3. Alan M. Cohen, "Entrepreneur and Entrepreneurship: The Definition Dilemma," Working Paper Series No. NC89-08, National Centre for Management Research and Development, The University of Western Ontario, London, February 1989.
4. *The State of Small Business*, pp. 24-27. See note 1.
5. *The State of Small Business*, p. 29. See note 1.
6. Recent Canadian textbooks include D. Wesley Balderson, *Canadian Small Business Management: Text, Cases and Incidents* (Homewood, IL: Richard D. Irwin, 1990); Raymond W.Y. Kao, *Entrepreneurship and Enterprise Development* (Toronto: Holt, Rinehart and Winston of Canada, 1989); Andrew J. Szonyi and Dan Steinhoff, *Small Business Management Fundamentals*, 3rd Canadian ed. (Scarborough, Ont.: McGraw-Hill Ryerson, 1987); K. Gersick, *Generation to Generation: Life Cycles of the Family Business* (Boston: Harvard Business School, 1997); and L. Shaw, *100 Ways to Market Yourself and Your Small Business* (New York: Berkeley Publishing, 1997).
7. Allan Gould, *The New Entrepreneurs: 80 Canadian Success Stories* (Toronto: Seal Books, 1986); also Kenneth Barnes and Everett Banning, *Money Makers: The Secrets of Canada's Most Successful Entrepreneurs* (Toronto: McClelland and Stewart, 1985); Matthew Fraser, *Quebec Inc.: French-Canadian Entrepreneurs and the New Business Elite* (Toronto: Key Porter Books, 1987); J.B. Miner, *The Four Routes to Entrepreneurial Success* (Barrett-Koehler Publishing, 1996); and D.L. Sexton and R.W. Smilor, *Entrepreneurship 2000* (Chicago: Upstart Publishing, 1997).
8. Many models of organizational growth have been developed. One that is often described in management books is in Larry E. Greiner, "Evolution and revolution as organizations grow," *Harvard Business Review*, 50, No. 4, July/August 1972, pp. 37-46. One example of a growth model developed for small business is Mel Scott and Richard Bruce, "Five stages of growth in small business," *Long Range Planning*, 20, No. 3, 1987, pp. 45-52.
9. The statistics in this section are from *Small Business in Canada: Growing to Meet Tomorrow* (Ottawa: Supply and Services Canada), Cat. No. C28-12 1989E; D.P. Moore and E.H. Buttner, *Women Entrepreneurs: Moving Beyond the Glass Ceiling* (Thousand Oaks, CA: Sage Publishing, 1997); also *The State of Small Business*, see note 1.
10. Paul Waldie, "Small business hits out," *The Financial Post*, September 4-6, 1993, pp. 1, 10-11.

Chapter 9

1. Margot Gibb-Clark, "Juggling Jobs a '90s Necessity," *The Globe and Mail*, July 28, 1997, pp. B1, B3.
2. Elizabeth Church, "Store Owners Struggle with Staffing," *The Globe and Mail*, November 25, 1996, p. B6.
3. John Partridge, "B of M lauded for promoting women's careers," *The Globe and Mail*, January 7, 1994, p. B3.
4. Vivian Smith, "Breaking down the barriers," *The Globe and Mail*, November 17, 1992, p. B24.
5. "More firms use personality tests for entry-level blue collar jobs," *Wall Street Journal*, January 16, 1986, p. 25.
6. Bruce McDougall, "The thinking man's assembly line," *Canadian Business*, November 1991, p. 40.
7. "Testing for drug use: Handle with care," *Business Week*, March 28, 1988, p. 65.
8. Jacquie McNish, "Akers out as IBM CEO," *The Globe and Mail*, January 27, 1993, pp. B1-B2.
9. Joseph B. White and Carol Hymowitz, "Watershed Generation of Women Executives Is Rising to the Top," *The Wall Street Journal*, February 10, 1997, pp. A1, A6.
10. Jane Allan, "Literacy at work," *Canadian Business*, February 1991, pp. 70-73.
11. Harvey Enchin, "Employee training a must," *The Globe and Mail*, May 15, 1991, p. B6.
12. John Southerst, "Kenworth's gray revolution," *Canadian Business*, September 1992, p. 74.
13. I.L. Goldstein, *Training in Organizations: Needs Assessment, Development, and Evaluation*, 2nd ed. (Monterey, CA: Brooks/Cole, 1986).
14. Jerry Zeidenberg, "Extra-curricular," *Canadian Business*, February 1991, pp. 66-69.
15. Charles Davies, "Strategy session 1990," *Canadian Business*, January 1990, p. 50.
16. Scott Feschuk, "Phi Beta Cuppa," *The Globe and Mail*, March 6, 1993, pp. B1, B4.
17. Michael J. McCarthy, "Now Riverboat Pilots Go to Shoal School in Paducah, Kentucky," *The Wall Street Journal*, May 27, 1997, pp. A1, A9.

18. Ann Gibbon, "How training primed the pump," *The Globe and Mail*, November 16, 1993, p. B26.
19. Margot Gibb-Clark, "Alternate mechanism solves work disputes," *The Globe and Mail*, November 7, 1994, pp. B1-B2.
20. Thomas Claridge, "Fired jumbo boss awarded $226,000," *The Globe and Mail*, May 31, 1993, p. B5.
21. "Well-paid workers, low-paid bosses?" *Canadian Business*, December 1992, p. 17.
22. Janet McFarland, "Higher U.S. Pay Triggers Concern," *The Globe and Mail*, November 5, 1996, p. B17.
23. David Roberts, "A long way from Cambodia," *The Globe and Mail*, July 5, 1994, p. B18.
24. C.D. Fisher, L. Schoenfeldt, and B. Shaw, *Personnel/Human Resources Management* (Boston: Houghton-Mifflin, 1990).
25. Bob Cox, "Women gaining on men's wages," *The Globe and Mail*, January 18, 1994, p. B4.
26. Gordon Pitts, "Equal pay issue: Business uneasy," *The Financial Post*, August 31, 1985, pp. 1-2.
27. Bruce Little, "Male Earning Power Wanes," *The Globe and Mail*, September 18, 1997, pp. B1, B4.
28. "Ouch! The squeeze on your health benefits," *Business Week*, November 20, 1989, pp. 110-116.
29. McDougall, "The thinking man's assembly line." See note 6.
30. Ted Kennedy, "Beware of health and safety law: It could bite you," *Canadian Business*, December 1990, p. 19.
31. "Canadians Are Retiring Earlier," *Winnipeg Free Press*, June 12, 1997, p. B12.
32. Michael Moss, "For Older Employees, On-the-Job Injuries Are More Often Deadly," *The Wall Street Journal*, June 17, 1997, pp. A1, A10.
33. Margot Gibb-Clark, "Harrassment cases can also hurt employees," *The Globe and Mail*, September 16, 1991, p. B4.

Chapter 10

1. Michael Stern, "Empowerment empowers employees," *The Globe and Mail*, December 9, 1991, p. B4.
2. Margot Gibb-Clark, "Canadian workers need some respect," *The Globe and Mail*, September 4, 1991, pp. B1, B6.
3. Margot Gibb-Clark, "Frustrated workers seek goals," *The Globe and Mail*, May 2, 1991, p. B7.
4. Margot Gibb-Clark, "Family ties limit workers," *The Globe and Mail*, January 22, 1991, pp. B1-B2.
5. Frederick W. Taylor, *Principles of Scientific Management* (New York: Harper and Brothers, 1911).
6. Fritz J. Roethlisberger and William J. Dickson, *Management and the Worker* (Cambridge, MA: Harvard University Press, 1939).
7. Douglas McGregor, *The Human Side of Enterprise* (New York: McGraw-Hill, 1960).
8. Abraham Maslow, "A theory of human motivation," *Psychological Review*, July 1943, pp. 370-396.
9. Frederick Herzberg, Bernard Mausner, and Barbara Bloch Snydeman, *The Motivation to Work* (New York: Wiley, 1959).
10. Victor Vroom, *Work and Motivation* (New York: Wiley, 1964); Craig Pinder, *Work Motivation* (Glenview, IL: Scott, Foresman, 1984).
11. J. Stacy Adams, "Toward an understanding of inequity," *Journal of Abnormal and Social Psychology*, Vol. 75, No. 5 (1963), pp. 422-36.
12. Edwin Locke, "Toward a theory of task performance and incentives," *Organizational Behavior and Human Performance*, Vol. 3 (1968), pp. 157-89.
13. Madelaine Drohan, "What Makes a Canadian Manager?" *The Globe and Mail*, February 25, 1997, p. B18.
14. Gregory Moorhead and Ricky W. Griffin, *Organizational Behavior*, 3rd ed. (Boston: Houghton and Mifflin, 1992).
15. Margot Gibb-Clark, "BC Telecom managers get an overhaul," *The Globe and Mail*, July 23, 1994, p. B3.
16. Wilfred List, "On the road to profit," *The Globe and Mail*, July 10, 1991, pp. B1, B3.
17. Ricky Griffin, *Task Design* (Glenview, IL: Scott, Foresman, 1982).
18. Richard J. Hackman and Greg Oldham, *Work Redesign* (Reading, MA: Addison-Wesley, 1980).
19. Robert White, "Changing needs of work and family: A union response," *Canadian Business Review*, Autumn 1989, pp. 31-33.
20. Margot Gibb-Clark, "Banks' short work week improves service," *The Globe and Mail*, September 23, 1991, p. B4.
21. "Escape from the office," *Newsweek*, April 24, 1989, pp. 58-60.
22. Margot Gibb-Clark, "Satellite office a hit with staff," *The Globe and Mail*, November 18, 1991, p. B4.
23. "Slaves of the New Economy," *Canadian Business*, April 1996, pp. 86-92.
24. Dawn Walton, "Survey Focuses on Job Sharing," *The Globe and Mail*, June 10, 1997, p. B4.

Chapter 11

1. Homer, *The Iliad*, Book XIII, Line 237.
2. Gary Dessler, *Personnel Management*, 4th ed. (Englewood Cliffs, NJ: Prentice-Hall, 1988).

3. Sarah Binder, "McDonald's Store Closes, Union Wails," *The Globe and Mail*, February 14, 1998, p. B23.
4. Madelaine Drohan, "Steel hands try velvet gloves," *The Globe and Mail*, p. B26.
5. Emily Nelson, "Anatomy of a Long, Bitter Labor Fight," *The Wall Street Journal*, November 6, 1996.
6. Margot Gibb-Clark, "Wounds left by strike require healing," *The Globe and Mail*, September 30, 1991, p. B4.
7. Margot Gibb-Glark, "Rogers workers abandon union," *The Globe and Mail*, January 22, 1992, p. B7.
8. Robert Frank, "UPS and downs," *The Globe and Mail*, June 7, 1994, p. B24.

Chapter 12

1. Gene Bylinsky, "The digital factory," *Fortune*, November 14, 1994, pp. 92–96+.
2. Christopher Farrell, "A wellspring of innovation," *Business Week*, Enterprise 1993, pp. 57–62.
3. Roger G. Schroeder, *Operations Management: Decision Making in the Operations Function*, 3rd ed. (New York: McGraw-Hill, 1989), pp. 234–64.
4. John R. Dorfman, "Deere's stock is attractive to those who see farmers about to splurge on new equipment," *Wall Street Journal*, July 1, 1991, p. C2; Steven Weiner, "Staying on top in a tough business in a tough Year," *Forbes*, May 27, 1991, p. 38.
5. Alex Taylor III, "Ford's $6 billion baby," *Fortune*, June 28, 1993, pp. 76-77+; Richard W. Stevenson, "Ford sets its sights on a world car," *New York Times*, September 27, 1993, pp. D1, D4; James B. Treece, "Motown's struggle to shift on the fly," *Business Week*, July 11, 1994, pp. 111-112.
6. Michael Williams, "Back to the past: Some plants tear out long assembly lines, switch to craft work," *Wall Street Journal*, October 24, 1994, pp. A1, A4; Doron P. Leven, "Toyota plant in Kentucky provides a font of ideas for U.S. manufacturers," *New York Times*, May 5, 1992, Sec. 3, pp. C1, C6.
7. Richard J. Schonberger and Edward M. Knod, Jr., *Operations Management*, 5th ed. (Burr Ridge, IL: Irwin, 1994), Chapter 11.
8. Hirano Hiroyuki and J.T. Black, *JIT Factory Revolution* (Cambridge, MA: Productivity Press, 1988), p. 126; James B. Dilworth, *Production and Operations Management*, 5th ed. (New York: McGraw-Hill, 1993), p. 567.
9. Don Marshall, "Time for just in time," *P&IM Review*, June 1991, pp. 20-22. See also Gregg Stocker, "Quality function deployment: Listening to the voice of the customer," *APICS: The Performance Advantage*, September 1991, pp. 44-48.
10. Schonberger and Knod, *Operations Management*, Chapter 11. See note 7.
11. Roy L. Harmon, *Reinventing the Factory II* (New York: Free Press, 1992), p. 126; Michael Barrier, "Overcoming Adversity," *Nation's Business*, June 1991, pp. 25–29.
12. Bruce McDougall, "The thinking man's assembly line," *Canadian Business*, November 1991, p. 40.
13. Alan Freeman, "Why firms avoid taking inventory," *The Globe and Mail*, December 12, 1994, pp. B1, B4.

Chapter 13

1. Richard B. Chase and Warren J. Erickson, "The service factory," *Academy of Management Executive*, August 1988, pp. 191–96.
2. Theodore Levitt, "Marketing intangible products and product intangibles," *Harvard Business Review*, May-June 1981, pp. 94–102.
3. Shawn Tully et al., "Twenty Companies on a Roll," *Fortune*, Autumn-Winter 1993, pp. 28–29.
4. Richard B. Chase, "Where does the customer fit in a service organization?" *Harvard Business Review*, November-December, 1978, pp. 137–42.
5. Theodore Levitt, "Production-line approach to service," *Harvard Business Review*, September-October 1972, pp. 41–52.
6. Richard B. Chase, "The 10 commandments of service system management," *Interfaces*, 15(3), pp. 68–72.
7. Alan Freedman, "Passports to profits," *The Globe and Mail*, December 14, 1993, p. B24.
8. Stanley Harris, "Improving customer support," *Management Today*, August 1986, pp. 67–90.
9. G.M. Hostage, "Quality control in a service business," *Harvard Business Review*, July-August 1975, pp. 98–106.

Chapter 14

1. Bruce Little, "Productivity Paradox Puzzles Experts," *The Globe and Mail*, April 14, 1997, pp. B1, B7.
2. Estimated from *Monthly Labor Review* (Washington, DC: U.S. Dept. of Labor, October 1994), p. 87; *Survey of Current Business* (Washington, DC: U.S. Dept. of Commerce, February 1994), p. 9; Carl G. Thor, *Perspectives '94* (Houston: American Productivity and Quality Center, 1994), p. 17.

3. Bruce Little, "Canada Seen Lagging in Productivity Race," *The Globe and Mail*, October 17, 1997, pp. B1, B22.
4. Bruce McDougall, "The next battleground," *Canadian Business*, February 1992, pp. 52-57.
5. Marina Strauss, "Canada rated 6th in quality of its manufactured goods," *The Globe and Mail*, February 10, 1994.
6. "A feisty domestic with a chip on its shoulder," *Canadian Business*, November 1991, p. 15.
7. Bruce McDougall, "The thinking man's assembly line," *Canadian Business*, November 1991, p. 40.
8. William Carley, "To Keep GE's Profits Rising, Welch Pushes Quality-Control Plan," *The Wall Street Journal*, January 13, 1997, pp. A1, A8.
9. Jeremy Main, "How to steal the best ideas around," *Fortune*, October 19, 1992, pp. 102-106; also Otis Port and Geoffrey Smith, "Beg, borrow—and benchmark," *Business Week*, November 30, 1992, pp. 74-75; also Howard Rothman, "You need not be big to benchmark," *Nation's Business*, December 1992, pp. 64–65.
10. Gordon Pitts, "Stepping on the quality ladder," *The Globe and Mail*, June 30, 1992, p. B20; also Timothy Pritchard, "Big three adopt new standard," *The Globe and Mail*, March 28, 1994, p. B3.
11. Michael Hammer and James Champy, "The promise of reengineering," *Fortune*, May 3, 1993, pp. 94-97; also Thomas A. Stewart, "Reengineering: The hot new managing tool," *Fortune*, August 23, 1993, pp. 41-48; also Ronald Henkoff, "The hot new seal of quality," *Fortune*, August 23, 1993, pp. 116-118.
12. Cathryn Motherwell, "How to fix a model of a muddle," *The Globe and Mail*, November 22, 1994, p. B30.
13. Janet McFarland, "How a Business Fad Went Wrong," *The Globe and Mail*, January 31, 1996, p. B13.
14. John Kotter, "Leading Change: Why Transformation Efforts Fail," *Harvard Business Review*, March-April 1995, p. 66.
15. Joseph White, "Re-Engineering Gurus Take Steps to Remodel Their Stalling Vehicles," *The Wall Street Journal*, November 26, 1996, pp. A1, A13.
16. "Customer service you can taste," *Canadian Business*, July 1991, pp. 19–20.
17. *Business Week*, Special 1989 Issue: "Innovation in America," p. 177.
18. Magnet, "The Productivity Payoff Arrives," pp. 82, 84.
19. Leonard L. Berry, A. Parasuraman, and Valarie A. Zeithaml, "Improving service quality in America: Lessons learned," *Academy of Management Executive*, Vol. 8, No. 2, 1994, pp. 32–45.

Chapter 15

1. From "AMA board approves new marketing definition," *Marketing News*, March 31, 1985, p. 1, published by the American Marketing Association.
2. Ricardo Sookdeo, "Golfing Gear for Women," *Fortune*, November 14, 1994, p. 257.
3. Jonathan Kapstein, Thaine Peterson and Lois Therrien, "Look out world, Philips is on a war footing," *Business Week*, January 15, 1990, pp. 44–45.
4. Margot Gibb-Clark, "Customers have a say on IBM managers' pay," *The Globe and Mail*, April 1, 1991, p. B4.
5. "Above the crowd," *Canadian Business*, April 1990, p. 76.
6. Philip Kotler, *Marketing Management: Analysis, Planning, Implementation, and Control*, 7th ed. (Englewood Cliffs, NJ: Prentice-Hall, 1991).
7. "Microwaves, VCRs Seen as Comforts of Home Now," *Winnipeg Free Press*, March 20, 1998, p. A15.
8. Charles D. Scheive, "Effective communication with our aging population," *Business Horizons*, January-February 1989, pp. 19–25.
9. John Morton, "How to spot the really important prospects," *Business Marketing*, January 1990, pp. 62–67.
10. Paul Sutter, "How to succeed in bubble gum without really trying," *Canadian Business*, January 1992, pp. 48–50.
11. Marina Strauss, "First you have to get their attention," *The Globe and Mail*, July 12, 1991, p. B1.
12. Terence Pare, "How to find out what they want," *Fortune*, Autumn/Winter 1993, pp. 39–41.
13. Oliver Bertin, "John Deere reaps the fruits of its labors," *Globe and Mail*, September 2, 1991, pp. B1, B3.
14. Stephen Barr, "Trading places: Barter re-enters corporate America," *Management Review*, August, 1993, p. 30; John J. McDonald, "Barter can work," *Chief Executive (U.S.)*, June 1994, p. 40.
15. William J. Stanton, Michael J. Etzel, and Bruce J. Walker, *Fundamentals of Marketing*, 10th ed. (New York: McGraw-Hill, 1994), Chapter 5.
16. Thomas Russell, Glenn Verrill, and W. Ronald Lane, *Kleppner's Advertising Procedure*, 11th ed. (Englewood Cliffs, NJ: Prentice-Hall, 1990); also James Engel, Martin Warshaw, and Thomas Kinnear, *Promotional Strategy*, 6th ed. (Homewood, IL: Richard D. Irwin, 1987).

Chapter 16

1. Patricia Lush, "From pipe dream to profit," *The Globe and Mail*, December 12, 1994, p. B6.

2. Todd Vogel, "Will GE's new jet engine ever get off the ground?" *Business Week*, February 4, 1991, pp. 98–99; Tim Smart et al., "Clash of the flying titans," *Business Week*, November 22, 1993, pp. 64–66.

3. David Greising, "Quality: How to Make It Pay," *Business Week*, August 8, 1994, p. 58.

4. Lohn Labate, "Companies to Watch: Daka International," *Fortune*, November 14, 1994, p. 258.

5. Richard Chase and Nick Aquilano, *Production and Operations Management*, 6th ed. (Homewood, IL: Irwin, 1992), Chapter 4.

6. Leonard E. Berry, A. Parasuraman, and Valerie A. Zeithaml, "Improving service quality in America," *Academy of Management Executive*, Vol. 8, No. 2, 1994, pp. 37–38.

7. Joel Baumwell, "Life cycle for brands? Forget it!" *Advertising Age*, March 17, 1986, p. 18.

8. Eileen Kinsella, "Corporate Names Go Quirky," *The Globe and Mail*, May 20, 1997, p. B12.

9. Cyndee Miller, "Little relief seen for new product failure rate," *Marketing News*, June 21, 1993, p. 1; Nancy J. Kim, "Back to the drawing board, *The Bergen (New Jersey) Record*, December 4, 1994, pp. B1, B4.

10. Stuart Elliott, "'Gump' sells, to Viacom's surprise," *New York Times*, October 7, 1994, pp. D1, D16.

11. Madelaine Drohan, "British await Coke's reply to grocer's look-alike cola," *The Globe and Mail*, April 29, 1994, p. B5.

12. Marina Strauss, "Holt Renfrew Brands a Strategy," *The Globe and Mail*, March 20, 1997, p. B13.

13. David Square, "Mouse Pad Gets Oodles of Nibbles," *The Winnipeg Free Press*, July 26, 1997, p. B10.

14. Marina Strauss, "Packaging is a marketer's last chance to say 'Buy me'," *The Globe and Mail*, September 17, 1991, p. B4.

15. Gail Degeorge with Julia Flynn, "Turning up the gas at Burger King," *Business Week*, November 15, 1993, pp. 62, 66–67.

16. William Pride and O.C. Ferrell, *Marketing*, 5th ed. (Boston: Houghton Mifflin, 1987).

17. John B. Clark, *Marketing Today: Successes, Failures, and Turnarounds* (Englewood Cliffs, NJ: Prentice-Hall, 1987), p. 32.

18. Michael Allen, "Devoloping new line of low-priced PCs shakes up Compaq," *Wall Street Journal*, June 15, 1992, pp. A1, A4.

19. Marina Strauss, "Towel War Turns to Name-Naming," *The Globe and Mail*, December 5, 1995, pp. B1, B10.

20. "Regulators wary of ads rapping rivals," *The Globe and Mail*, May 23, 1991, p. B4.

21. "Pepsi got the right one for promoting itself," *The Globe and Mail*, January 30, 1992, p. B4.

22. Stuart Elliot, "Topsy-turvey becomes darling of print ads," *The Globe and Mail*, February 25, 1992, pp. B1, B6.

23. Marina Strauss, "This billboard wants to pass you by," *The Globe and Mail*, February 27, 1992, p. B4.

24. Laurie Ward, "Big rock brews strong U.S. growth," *The Financial Post*, September 25, 1993, p. 7.

25. Lawrence Surtees, "Ads, Scores and More Coming to a Phone Near You," *The Globe and Mail*, November 6, 1996, pp. B1, B5.

26. Marina Strauss, "Small shops quake over IBM's earth-shaking move," *The Globe and Mail*, May 26, 1994, p. B4.

27. Ann Gibbon, "Ad group tries to demystify Quebec," *Globe and Mail*, November 25, 1993, p. B6.

28. "Regulators wary of ads rapping rivals," *The Globe and Mail*, May 23, 1991, p. B4.

29. Raju Narisetti, "Move to Drop Coupons Puts Procter & Gamble in a Sticky PR Situation," *The Wall Street Journal*, April 17, 1997, pp. A1, A10.

30. "Point-of-purchase rush is on," *Advertising Age*, February 8, 1988, p. 47.

31. Lois Therrien, "Want shelf space at the supermarket? Ante up," *Business Week*, August 7, 1989, pp. 60–61.

32. Jennifer Lawrence, "Free samples get emotional reaction," *Advertising Age*, September 30, 1991, p. 10.

34. "Pageant Runner-Up Looks for Compensation," *Winnipeg Free Press*, February 3, 1998, p. A4.

35. Joseph Periera, "Toy Story: How Shrewd Marketing Made Elmo a Hit," *The Wall Street Journal*, December 16, 1996, pp. B1, B8.

36. Pam Weisz, "Border Crossings: Brands Unify Image to Counter Cult of Culture," *Brandweek*, October 31, 1994, p. 26.

37. "Does the 'Special Relationship' Include Ketchup and Cola?" *Adweek*, December 13, 1993, p. 17.

38. Shelley Garcia, "Philips Seeks Shop," *Adweek*, December 5, 1994, pp. 1, 46; Rosalyn Retkwa, "T1 Buys $10 Million Facelift," *Business Marketing*, 78, 4 (April 1993), 6.

Chapter 17

1. Rahul Jacob, "Beyond quality and value," *Fortune*, Autumn/Winter 1993, pp. 8–11.

2. Calmetta Y. Coleman, "How Burger King Finally Became a Contender," *The Wall Street Journal*, February 27, 1997, pp. B1, B4.

3. Stephen Kindel, "Tortoise gains on hare," *Financial World*, February 23, 1988, pp. 18–20.

4. Bruce Nussbaum, *Good Intentions* (New York: Atlantic Monthly Press, 1990), pp. 176+; Brian O'Reilly, "The inside story of the AIDS drug," *Fortune*, November 5, 1990, pp. 112+; Julia Flynn with John Carey, "Wellcome's AZT faces attacks on two fronts," *Business Week*, July 26, 1993, p. 36.

5. Stewart A. Washburn, "Establishing Strategy and Determining Cost in the Pricing Decision," *Business Marketing*, July 1985, pp. 64–78.

6. John Saunders, "Retailer's Pricing Strategies Seen As Confusing," *The Globe and Mail*, February 28, 1997, p. B6.

7. Scott McCartney, "Gap Grows Between Business, Leisure Fares," *The Globe and Mail*, November 12, 1997, pp. A16, A18.

8. "Odd prices hurt image of prices," *Business Month*, July 1987, p. 23.

9. Randall Litchfield, "The pressure on prices," *Canadian Business*, February 1992, pp. 30–35.

10. Stephanie Anderson Forest, "The education of Michael Dell," *Business Week*, March 22, 1993, pp. 82–86; Lois Therrien, "Why gateway is racing to answer on the first ring," *Business Week*, September 13, 1993, pp. 92–93; Peter Burrows, "The computer is in the mail (really)," *Business Week*, January 23, 1995, pp. 76–77; Scott McCartney, "Michael Dell—and his company—grow up," *Wall Street Journal*, January 31, 1994, pp. B1, B2.

11. Dale M. Lewison, *Retailing*, 5th ed. (New York: Macmillan, 1994), p. 454; Louis Stern and Adel I. El-Ansary, *Marketing Channels*, 4th ed. (Englewood Cliffs, NJ: Prentice Hall, 1992), pp. 129–30.

12. Zachary Schiller and Wendy Zellner, "Making the middleman an endangered species," *Business Week*, June 6, 1994, pp. 114–15.

13. Ronald Henkoff, "Delivering the goods," *Fortune*, November 28, 1994, pp. 64–66+; Gene Bylinsky, "The digital factory," *Fortune*, November 14, 1994, pp. 92–95+.

14. Kenneth Kidd, "Canadian Tire opts for austerity," *The Globe and Mail*, July 17, 1991, pp. B1–B2; also John Heinzl, "Canadian Tire treads new ground in warehouse stores," *The Globe and Mail*, October 7, 1991, pp. B1–B2.

15. Barnaby Feder, "McDonald's makes a comeback," *The Globe and Mail*, January 22, 1994, p. B8.

16. Julie Iovine, "Cher's gothic look, by mail," *New York Times*, September 8, 1994, p. C8.

17. Murray McNeill, "Vending Machine Franchiser Expanding to 3 Big Cities," *Winnipeg Free Press*, July 11, 1997, p. B7.

18. Philip Kotler and Gary Armstrong, *Marketing: An Introduction*, 3rd ed. (Englewood Cliffs, NJ: Prentice Hall, 1993), p. 362; Scott Donaton and Joe Mandese, "GM, Hachette to test TV show," *Advertising Age*, September 13, 1993, p. 1.

19. Andrew Tausz, "Getting there fast—by truck," *The Globe and Mail*, March 1, 1994, p. B23.

20. Andrew Allentuck, "Arctic delivery tough sailing," *The Globe and Mail*, March 1, 1994, p. B23.

21. Rick Tetzeli, "Cargo that phones home," *Fortune*, November 15, 1993, p. 143.

22. Bill Redekop, "The crow subsidy is history," *Winnipeg Free Press*, February 28, 1995, p. 1.

23. Dan Lett, "What's to Crow About?" *The Winnipeg Free Press*, February 28, 1997, p. B4.

Chapter 18

1. Terence P. Paré, "How to Find Out What They Want," *Fortune*, Autumn-Winter 1993, pp. 39–41.

2. John Rockart, "Chief executives define their own data needs," *Harvard Business Review*, March-April 1979, pp. 81–93.

3. Andrew McIntosh, "Computerized bus system set for Hull region," *The Globe and Mail*, July 5, 1985, p. B10.

4. Patrick Conlon, "Use of computer dispatching means fewer squawks for taxis," *The Globe and Mail*, December 5, 1988, p. B7.

5. Bruce Gates, "Hard-to-police software pirates cost industry millions," *The Financial Post*, March 11, 1991, p. 13.

6. Geoffrey Rowan, "Speed is object of new technology," *The Globe and Mail*, June 15, 1994, pp. B1, B19.

7. This section is based on Larry Long, *Computers and Information Systems*, 4th ed. (Englewood Cliffs, NJ: Prentice Hall, 1994), pp. 450–51.

8. "Pirates Peddle Half the Software," *The Globe and Mail*, May 28, 1997, p. B10.

9. Frank Lenk, "Piracy Costs Software Firms Billions," *The Globe and Mail*, May 18, 1994, p. B5.

10. Jonathan Chevreau, "SoftCop Tackles the Software Pirates," *The Financial Post*, March 12, 1994, p. 16.

11. Catherine Arnst et al., "The Information Appliance," *Business Week*, November 22, 1993, pp. 98–102+.

12. Jack B. Rochester, *Computers: Tools for Knowledge Workers* (Homewood, IL: Irwin, 1993), pp. 164, 167; Robert D. Hof with Neil Gross, "The Gee-Whiz Company," *Business Week*, July 18, 1994, pp. 56–59+.

13. Otis Port et al., "Wonder Chips," *Business Week*, July 4, 1994, pp. 86–92.

14. Richard Brandt, "Bill Gates's vision," *Business Week*, June 27, 1994, pp. 56–62.

15. Bruce Nussbaum et al., "Winners: The best product designs of the year," *Business Week*, June 7, 1993, p. 68; Long and Long, *Computers*, pp. 27–29, 473–74.
16. Gary McWilliams, "Computers are finally learning to listen," *Business Week*, November 1, 1993, pp. 100–101; Gene Bylinski, "At last! Computers you can talk to," *Fortune*, May 3, 1993, pp. 88–91; Brandt, "Bill Gates's vision," p. 60.
17. Geoffrey Rowan, "Unique Software Thinks Like a Human," *The Globe and Mail*, December 31, 1996, pp. B1, B4.
18. Andrzej J. Taramina, "Expert systems in manufacturing," *P&IM Review with APICS News*, December 1990, pp. 42, 45.
19. Deidre A. Depke and Richard Brandt, "PCs: What the future holds," *Business Week*, August 12, 1991, pp. 58–64.
20. Long and Long, *Computers*, p. 470.
21. John Wilke, "Togetherness, the PC way," *The Globe and Mail*, December 11, 1993, pp. B1, B5.
22. David Caruso, "Making sense of new information technologies," *APICS—The Performance Advantage*, October 1991, pp. 32–35; John J. Kanet, "Real decision support for production scheduling and support," *Production and Inventory Management*, September 1991, pp. 24–25; Gene Bylinsky, "The payoff from 3-D computing," *Fortune*, Autumn 1993, pp. 32–34+.
23. Rochester, *Computers*, pp. 449–50.
24. Brandt, "Bill Gates's vision," p. 62; Arnst et al., "The information appliance," p. 100.
25. Brandt, "Bill Gates's vision," p. 58.
26. "Small business computing," *Nation's Business*, December 1989, pp. 34-35; also Deidre A. Depke, "Software's big guns take aim at small business," *Business Week*, September 25, 1989, pp. 216–18.
27. Kirkpatrick, "How PCs will take over your home," p. 101; Barbara Kantrowitz, "In Quicken they trust," *Newsweek*, May 2, 1994, pp. 65–66.

Chapter 19

1. Ronald Hilton, *Managerial Accounting*, 2nd ed. (New York: McGraw-Hill, 1994), p. 7.
2. M. Rothkopf, "No more easy questions on the uniform CPA examination," *Accounting Horizons*, Vol. 1, No. 4, December 1987, pp. 79–85.
3. Elizabeth MacDonald, "Accounting Sleuths Ferret Hidden Assets," *The Wall Street Journal*, December 18, 1996, pp. B1–B2.
4. Elizabeth MacDonald, "More Accounting Firms Bar Risky Clients," *The Wall Street Journal*, April 25, 1997, p. A2.
5. Philip Mathias, "Non-profits fight move to GAAP accounting," *The Financial Post*, March 5, 1994, p. 15.
6. L.A. Nikolai, J.D. Bazley, and J.C. Stallman, *Principles of Accounting*, 3rd ed. (Boston: PWS-Kent, 1990).
7. C.T. Horngren and G.I. Sundem, *Introduction to Financial Accounting* (Englewood Cliffs, NJ: Prentice-Hall, 1987).
8. Ronald Hilton, *Managerial Accounting*, 2nd ed. (New York: McGraw-Hill, 1994), pp. 402–403.
9. Douglas Lavin, "GM would have to cut 20,000 workers to match Ford efficiency, report says," *Wall Street Journal*, June 24, 1994, p. C22.

Chapter 20

1. P.S. Rose and D.R. Fraser, *Financial Institutions*, 3rd ed. (Plano, TX: Business Publications, Inc., 1988).
2. Robert E. Calem, "Taking the worry out of paying with plastic," *New York Times*, November 14, 1993, Sec. 3, p. 9.
3. William Cantrell, "Why are all of those Canadian issuers selling?" *Credit Card Management*, December 1991, pp. 26-31; Thomas Holden, "The Japanese discover the perils of plastic," *Business Week*, February 10, 1992, p. 42; Richard L. Holman, "Korea curbs credit cards," *Wall Street Journal*, December 22, 1994, p. A10.
4. Russell Mitchell, "The Smart Money Is on Smart Cards," *Business Week*, August 14, 1995, pp. 68–69; Nikhil Deogun, "The Smart Money

Is on 'Smart Cards,' but Electronic Cash Seems Dumb to Some," *Wall Street Journal*, August 5, 1996, pp. B1, B8.
5. Kelly Holland and Greg Burns, "Plastic Talks," *Business Week*, February 14, 1994, pp. 105–107; Saul Hansell, "An End to the 'Nightmare' of Cash," *New York Times*, September 6, 1994, pp. D1, D5; Thomas McCarroll, "No Checks. No Cash. No Fuss?" *Time*, May 9, 1994, pp. 60–62; Marla Matzer, "Plastic Mania," *Forbes*, October 24, 1994, pp. 281–82.
6. Kelly Holland and Amy Cortese, "The Future of Money," *Business Week*, June 12, 1995, pp. 66–72+.
7. Grep Ip, "Ottawa Set to Lose Millions When Reserve Rules Dropped," *The Financial Post*, July 17, 1991, p. 3.
8. Karen Horcher, "Reconstruction Zone," *CGA Magazine*, June 1997, p. 19.
9. "Big MacCurrencies," *The Economist*, April 9, 1994, p. 88.
10. Robert J. Carbaugh, *International Economics*, 5th ed. (Cincinnati: South-Western, 1995), Chapter 11.

Chapter 21

1. *The Value Line Investment Survey*, January 28, 1994, p. 1095.
2. Karen Howlett, "An Era Ends as the TSE Closes Trading Floor After 145 Years," *The Globe and Mail*, April 24, 1997, pp. B1.
3. George G. Kaufman, *The U.S. Financial System: Money, Markets, and Institutions*, 6th ed. (Englewood Cliffs, NJ: Prentice Hall, 1995), p. 432.
4. *NYSE Fact Book: 1995 Data* (New York: New York Stock Exchange, 1996), pp. 7, 43.
5. Nicholas D. Kristof, "Don't jolt about this stock market," *New York Times*, May 9, 1993, Sec. 3, pp. 1, 6; Jane Perlez, "Warsaw's exuberant exchange," *New York Times*, December 25, 1993, pp. 47–48.
6. *Moody's Bond Survey*, August 2, 1993, p. 4138.
7. Karen Horcher, "Reconstruction Zone," *CGA Magazine*, June 1997, p. 21.
8. Amey Stone, "Futures: Dare you defy the odds?" *Business Week*, February 28, 1994, pp. 12–13.
9. Steven Greenhouse, "Exchanges thrive as Russians pursue market economy," *Winnipeg Free Press*, November 3, 1991, p. B13.

Chapter 22

1. John Heinzl, "Good strategy gone awry, top retailer's tale of woe," *The Globe and Mail*, March 7, 1992, pp. B1, B4.
2. *Financial World*, April 4, 1989, p. 106; also *Mutual Fund Profiles* (New York: Standard and Poor's Corp., May 1989), p. ix; also *Stock Reports Index* (New York: Standard and Poor's Corp., November 1989), p. 38.
3. *The State of Small Business*, 1989 Annual Report on Small Business in Ontario (Toronto: Ministry of Industry, Trade and Technology, 1990).
4. J.W. Duncan, *D&B Reports*, September-October 1991, p. 8.
5. E.F. Brigham, *Fundamentals of Financial Management*, 5th ed. (Chicago: Dryden, 1989).
6. Barry Critchley, "Risk management now Bhalla's full-time business," *The Financial Post*, September 17, 1990, p. 29.
7. Thomas P. Fitch, *Dictionary of Banking Terms*, 2nd ed. (Hauppauge, NY: Barron's, 1993), p. 531.
8. This section is based on Phillip L. Zweig et al., "Managing risk," *Fortune*, October 31, 1994, pp. 86–90+.
9. Figure estimated from *1988-89 Property/Casualty Fact Book*, p. 19.
10. Gayle MacDonald, "How an Eaton's Supplier Cut Risk," *The Globe and Mail*, March 17, 1997, p. B7.
11. *The Financial Post*, July 1995, p. 172.

Source Notes

Chapter 1

Opening Case Summarized from Gary Lamphier, "Diamond Fields' Dream," *The Globe and Mail*, April 22, 1995, pp. B1, B4; also Tim Falconer, "Boomtown Jitters," *Report on Business*, November 1995, pp. 122–34; also "The Big Nickel," *The Financial Post*, June 8, 1996, p. 33; also Jacquie McNish, "Inco Digs Deep with Gamble on Voisey's Bay," *The Globe and Mail*, December 22, 1997, pp. B1, B8. **International Report** Summarized from Ken Wells, "African Game Ranchers See a New Way to Save Endangered Species," *The Wall Street Journal*, January 7, 1997, pp. A1, A11. **Figure 1.6** *Bank of Canada Review*, Summer 1997, Table A1, p. S7. **International Report** Summarized from Peter Cook, "Brazil campaigns against inflation," *The Globe and Mail*, May 16, 1994, p. B1; also Katherine Ellison, "Heart attacks price of Brazil's chaotic economy," *The Financial Post*, January 17, 1994, p. C8; also Peter Cook, "Brazil's inflation fight gets real," *The Globe and Mail*, July 4, 1994, p. B1; also Isabel Vincent, "Argentina's miracle more of a paradox," *The Globe and Mail*, March 17, 1994, p. B1; also Bruce Little, "Deflation returns after 40 years," *The Globe and Mail*, June 18, 1994, pp. B1, B3; also Barrie McKenna, "Is it the last gasp for inflation?" *The Globe and Mail*, February 17, 1994, pp. B1, B8. **Figure 1.7** *Bank of Canada Review*, Summer 1997, Table H5, p. S89. **Concluding Case 1-1** Summarized from Brent Jang, "An Oil Boom Dawns on Newfoundland," *The Globe and Mail*, March 7, 1997, pp. B1, B6; also Allanna Sullivan, "Four Decades Later, Oil Field Off Canada Is Ready to Produce," *The Wall Street Journal*, April 1, 1997, pp. A1, A6; also Brent Jang, "The Economics of Hibernia," *The Globe and Mail*, May 17, 1997, pp. B1, B3. **Concluding Case 1-2** Lisa Bannon, "Disney Decides World Isn't So Small, Creating Education Resort for Boomers," *The Wall Street Journal*, March 1, 1996, p. B1; "Celebrated Pro Gary Player to Design Golf Program at New Disney Institute," *Business Wire*, February 2, 1996; Greg Dawson, "Spirituality, Serenity? Spend a Day at Disney," *Orlando Sentinel*, March 5, 1996, p. B1; Leslie Doolittle, "Disney Executives Thinking Big—and Small—for Upcoming Asian Smalltrip," *Orlando Sentinel*, March 5, 1996, p. B1; Monika Guttman, "Facing the Facts of Life," *U.S. News & World Report*, April 22, 1996, pp. 57–58; Kerry Hannon, "The Joys of a Working Vacation," *U.S. News & World Report*, June 10, 1996, pp. 89–94; Dick Marlowe, "Will Institute Start Revolution?" *Orlando Sentinel*, July 24, 1995, p. 3; Christine Shenot, "Disney Breaks New Ground with Institute," *Orlando Sentinel*, February 7, 1996, p. A1; Shenot, "Disney Offers Alternative Vacation," *Orlando Sentinel*, December 18, 1995, p. 5.

Chapter 2

Opening Case Summarized from Gail Lem, "Algoma Chief Shares Pain, Gives Up $400 000 Bonus," *The Globe and Mail*, May 4, 1994, pp. B1–B2; also Patricia Commins, "United Airlines Unions Bet on Success," *The Globe and Mail*, December 24, 1993, p. B5; also Robin Sidel, "Employee Ownership Seen as Industry Trend," *The Globe and Mail*, December 24, 1993, p. B5; also David Roberts, "The Brew Crew Takes Over," *The Globe and Mail*, December 21, 1993, p. B20; also Hugh McBride, "How to Lose Freedom and Gain the World," *The Globe and Mail*, January 25, 1994; also Kimberley Noble, "Can the Workers Make a Go of It?" *The Globe and Mail*, August 17, 1991, p. B18; also Nattalia Lea, "Study of a Spinoff: Workers to Owners," *The Globe and Mail*, April 3, 1995, p. B6; also Martin Cash, "Salvage Could Turn Golden," *Winnipeg Free Press*, September 5, 1997, p. B4; also Janet McFarland, "Employees at the Controls," *The Globe and Mail*, March 5, 1996, p. B8. **International Report** Adapted from Madelaine Drohan, "Lloyd's ends tradition of un-limited liability," *The Globe and Mail*, April 30, 1993, pp. B1, B8; also "Investors revel in Lloyd's suit win," *Winnipeg Free Press*, October 5, 1994, p. C12; "Lloyd's Offers $6 Billion Solution," *The Globe and Mail*, May 24, 1995, p. B8; also "Lloyd's Rings Bell to Celebrate Rescue," *The Globe and Mail*, September 5, 1996, p. B9. **Table 2.3** *The Financial Post*, 1997 Annual Edition, p. 120; *Fortune*, April 28, 1997, p. F-1. **The Canadian Business Scene** Summarized from Patrick Brethour, "The Price of Going Public," *The Globe and Mail*, April 30, 1997, p. B12. **The Canadian Business Scene** Summarized from Gayle MacDonald, "Board seat a hotter place to sit," *The Financial Post*, November 19, 1990, p. 36; see also Arthur Johnson, "Directors: New breed in a hot seat," *Canadian Business*, June 1991, pp. 74-83; see also Patricia Lush, "Being a director means being a worker," *The Globe and Mail*, March 16, 1987, pp. B1, B8; see also Drew Fagan, "Despite recent gains, women still a rare breed on company boards," *The Globe and Mail*, May 2, 1990, p. B7. **Table 2.5** *The Financial Post*, 1997 Annual Edition, pp. 120–35. **International Report** Summarized from Scott Kilman, "Hard-Pressed Ranchers Dream of Marketing Own Beef," *The Wall Street Journal*, March 26, 1997, pp. A1, A9. **Concluding Case 2-1** Summarized from John Saunders, "Could We Stop Meeting Like This?" *The Globe and Mail*, March 15, 1997, pp. B1, B5; also "How to Get the Most out of an Annual Meeting," *The Globe and Mail*, March 15, 1997, p. B5. **Concluding Case 2-2** Summarized from Robert Tomsho, "Costly Funerals Spur a Co-op Movement to Hold Down Bills," *The Wall Street Journal*, November 12, 1996, pp. A1, A5.

Chapter 3

Opening Case Summarized from Greg Ip, "Jobs Cut Despite Hefty Profits," *The Globe and Mail*, February 6, 1996, pp. A1, A4; also Greg Ip, "Shareholders vs. Jobholders," *The Globe and Mail*, March 23, 1996, pp. B1, B4. **Figure 3.1** *Historical Statistics of Canada*, F.H. Leacy (ed) Series D266-317 (1950–1970); see also *The Labour Force*, 71-001 (1980 and 1985). Used by permission of the Minister of Supply and Services Canada; also *The Bank of Canada Review*, "General Economic Statistics Section, Catalogue Number FB12-1; also *The Labour Force*, 71-001, 1996, p. B25. **The Canadian Business Scene** Summarized from Allan Robinson and Kimberley Noble, "Lac makes a deal," *The Globe and Mail*, August 25, 1994, pp. B1, B4; also Allan Robinson, "Lac rivals await poison pill ruling," *The Globe and Mail*, August 20, 1994, p. B1; also Allan Robinson, "Royal Oak asked to extend offer," *The Globe and Mail*, August 19, 1994, pp. B1, B6; also Allan Robinson, "Lac slams bid from Royal Oak," *The Globe and Mail*, July 19, 1994, p. B1; also Jacquie McNish, "Time pops poison pill; Seagram gets headache," *The Globe and Mail*, January 21, 1994, pp. B1, B5; also Casey Mahood, "MDC challenges Regal poison pill," *The Globe and Mail*, August 27, 1994, p. B18; also Kimberley Noble, "Cangene resisting takeover bid," *The Globe and Mail*, July 9, 1994, p. B18; also John Partridge, "Poison pill a sore point between Nova, Fairvest," *The Globe and Mail*, June 27, 1994; also Harvey Enchin, "Emerson trargets old client," *The Globe and Mail*, February 14, 1994, pp. B1, B4; also Marina Strauss, "Labatt shareholders reject poison pill," *The Globe and Mail*, September 14, 1994, pp. B1, B5; also Andrew Willis, "OSC Cuts Down Tarxien Poison Pill," *The Globe and Mail*, November 16, 1996, p. B7. **The Canadian Business Scene** Summarized from Brian Hutchinson, "Cheers!" *Canadian Business*, November 1994, pp. 23-28. **Table 3.1** Reproduced by permission of the Minister of Supply and Services Canada. **Figure 3.4** Summarized from Brian Owen, "Business Managers' Influence (or Lack of Influence) on Government," *Business Quarterly*, Autumn 1976. **Table 3.3** *The Financial Post*, 1997 Annual Edition, p. 178. **International Report** Summarized from Madelaine Drohan, "Corrupt officials line road to capitalism," *The Globe and Mail*, May 2, 1994, p. B8; also "Entrepreneurship still viewed as a criminal activity by some," *The Globe and Mail*, May 26, 1994, p. B8. **The Canadian Business Scene** Summarized from Paul King, "Trading Places," *Canadian Business*, May 1991, pp. 78–81; see also Douglas Forster, "Trading Places," *Report on Business Magazine*, March 1992, pp. 17–27. **Figure 3.6** (a) *Historical Statistics of Canada*, F.H. Leacy (ed.), Series D8-55 (1921–1971); see also *The Labour Force*, 71-001 (1981); see also Cansim database; see also *The Labour Force*, 71-001, December 1996, p. B25 (1996). Used by permission of the Minister of Supply and Services Canada. (b) Cansim database (label #C892583). (c) *Historical Statistics of Canada*, F.H. Leacy (ed.), Series C85-97 (1931–1971); see also *The Labour Force*, 71-001 (1981, 1986, and 1993); see also *The Labour Force*, 71-001, December 1996, p. B3 (1996). Used by permission of the Minister of Supply and Services Canada. **Figure 3.8** *Bank of Canada Review*, Autumn 1994, p. S74; also *Bank of Canada Review*, Summer 1997, Table G1, p. 573. **Figure 3.9** Statistics Canada, *Industrial R & D Statistics*, catalogue number 88-202, p. 21; see also chart 1.1, 1989, p. 15; see also Statistics Canada, 88-202, *Industrial Research & Development Statistics*, p. 15. **Concluding Case 3-1** Summarized from John Heinzl, "The Plane Truth," *The Globe and Mail*, January 4, 1997, pp. B1, B3. **Concluding Case 3-2** Summarized from Ann Gibbon, "PQ Behind Firing, Suit Says," *The Globe and Mail*, September 14, 1995, pp. B1–B2.

Chapter 4

Opening Case Summarized from Gayle MacDonald, "Purdy's Test Asia's Sweet Tooth," *The Globe and Mail*, June 9, 1997, p. B7. **Table 4.1** *Market Research Handbook*, 63-224, 1995, p. 37. **Figure 4.1** *Bank of Canada Review*, Summer 1997, p. S96. **International Report** Summarized from David Rocks, "Czech Currency Falls on Hard Times," *The Globe and Mail*, June 10, 1997, p. B7; also Craig Torres and Paul Carroll, "Mexico Reverses Currency Policy," *The Wall Street Journal*, December 21, 1994, pp. A3, A6; also Paul Carroll and Craig Torres, "Mexico Unveils Program of Harsh Fiscal Medicine," *The Wall Street Journal*, March 10, 1995, pp. A3, A11; also Craig Torres, "Mexican Markets Are Hit by Fresh Blows," *The Wall Street Journal*, February 16, 1995, p. A11; also Michael Urlocker and Frances Misutka, "Russians Learn to Love the Greenback," *The Financial Post*, September 11, 1993, p. 9; also "Russia Tumbles, Russia Reels," *The Globe and Mail*, October 12, 1994, pp. B1, B20. Laura Eggertson, "Peso Crisis Lingers for Many Mexicans," *The Globe and Mail*, October 7, 1997, pp. B1, B12. **Figure 4.3** Griffin/Ebert, *Business*, Fourth Edition (Englewood Cliffs, NJ: Prentice Hall, 1996). **International Report** Summarized from Jonathan Kaufman, "Tethered to Pittsburgh For Years, an Engineer Thrives on Trips to Asia," *The Wall Street Journal*, November 19, 1996, pp. A1, A8. **Table 4.2** *International Trade Statistics*, Volume II, 1995, pp. S2–S16. **International Report** Summarized from Phillip Day, "A-OK? Not for this Moscow Crowd, after Clinton Gives 'em the Finger," *Winnipeg Free Press*, June 18, 1994, p. C6; also Tamsen Tillson, "The art of the deal in China," *The Globe and Mail*, September 5,

1994, pp. B1-B2. **International Report** Norihiko Shirouzu, "Snapple in Japan: How a Splash Dried Up," *Wall Street Journal*, April 15, 1996, p. B1; Edith Hill Updike, "Is Cavalier Japanese for Edsel?" *Business Week*, June 24, 1996, p. 39. **International Report** Summarized from Casey Mahood, "Mags on the Move," *The Globe and Mail*, May 23, 1993, p. B13. **Table 4.4** *The Financial Post*, Annual Edition, 1997, p. 150. **Concluding Case 4-1** Summarized from Bob Ortega, "Wal-Mart's invasion of Mexico far from a revolution," *The Globe and Mail*, August 4, 1994, p. B1. **Concluding Case 4-2** Marcus W. Brauchli, "The Outlook: China's Big Advantage Is a Young Population," *Wall Street Journal*, April 14, 1996, p. A1; Kathy Chen, "Young Chinese Loosen the Purse Strings," *Wall Street Journal*, July 15, 1996, p. A9; Pete Engardio, "Microsoft's Long March," *Business Week*, June 24, 1996, pp. 52–54; Seth Faison, "U.S. and China Agree on Pact to Fight Piracy," *New York Times*, June 18, 1996, p. A6; David E. Sanger, "Software Pirates Growing in Number in China, U.S. Says," *New York Times*, May 8, 1996, pp. A1, A9; Jarie H. Lili, "Boom-at-a-Glance," *New York Times Magazine*, February 16, 1996, pp. 26–27.

Chapter 5

Opening Case Margot Franssen, "Beyond Profits," *Business Quarterly*, Autumn 1993, pp. 15–20; also Raymond Cote et al. (eds.), *Business Meets the Environmental Challenge: Essays with Profiles of N.S. Companies*. Hantsport, Nova Scotia: Lancelot Press, 1993, p. 177; also Jon Entine, "Rain-Forest Chic," *Report on Business Magazine*, October 1995, pp. 41–52; Web sites http://www.think-act-change.com and http://www.the-body-shop.ca. A book is available on The Body Shop: Anita Roddick, *Body and Soul*. London: Ebury Press, 1992. **International Report** Summarized from Madelaine Drohan, "To bribe or not to bribe," *The Globe and Mail*, February 14, 1994, p. B7; see also Margaret Shapiro, "A Country on the Take," *Winnipeg Free Press*, November 21, 1994, p. A7. **Figure 5.2** Guiding Principles of Great West Life Assurance Company, Winnipeg, Manitoba. Reproduced with permission. **The Canadian Business Scene** Summarized from Catherine Collins, "The Greening of Dow," *Report on Business Magazine*, November 1991, pp. 21-35; see also Jeb Blount, "Battle of the Clamshell," *Report on Business Magazine*, April 1991, pp. 40-47. **International Report** Lawrence K. Altman, "U.S. Officials Confident That Mad Cow Disease of Britain Has Not Occurred Here," *New York Times*, March 27, 1996, p. A12; Gina Kolata, "Study Questions Top Theory on Cause of Mad Cow Disease," *New York Times*, January 17, 1997, p. A19; Patrick Barrett, "Beef Industry Takes Stock," *Marketing*, March 28, 1996, p. 14; John Darnton, "British Beef Banned in France and Belgium," *New York Times*, March 22, 1996, p. A8; Darnton, "For the British Beef War: A Truce but No Victory," *New York Times*, June 24, 1996, p. A9; Mary Kay Melvin, "Food Managers in England Report on Impact of Mad Cow Disease," *Amusement Business*, April 15, 1996, p. 16; Richard L. Papiernik, "U.S. Chains Switch Beef Sources in U.K.," *Nation's Restaurant News*, April 8, 1996, p. 1. **Table 5.1** The Conference Board of Canada's *Canadian Centre for Business in the Community*. **International Report** Andrea Gerlin, "A Matter of Degree: How a Jury Decided That a Coffee Spill Is Worth $2.9 Million," *The Wall Street Journal*, September 1, 1994, pp. A1, A5; Aric Press with Ginny Carroll and Steven Waldman, "Are Lawyers Burning America?" *Newsweek*, March 20, 1995, pp. 32–35; Neil A. Lewis, "Senate Backs Plan to Limit Damages in All Civil Suits," *The New York Times*, May 4, 1995, pp. A1, A20; Lewis, "Senate Agrees on Bill to Cut Civil-Court Damage Awards," *The New York Times*, May 10, 1995, pp. A1, D20. **Concluding Case 5-1** Summarized from Kimberley Noble and Dan Westell, "Better Business Bungle," *The Globe and Mail*, September 23, 1995, pp. B1, B4; Tamsen Tillson, "Thumbs Down for the Critic," *Canadian Business*, August 1995, pp. 66–67; John Heinzl, "Tuz Charged with Defrauding BBB," *The Globe and Mail*, December 12, 1996, p. B5. **Concluding Case 5-2** Kevin Kelly and Kathleen Kerwin, "There's another side to the López saga," *Business Week*, August 23, 1993, p. 26; John Templeman and Peggy Salz-Trautman, "VW figures its best defense may be a good offense," *Business Week*, August 9, 1993, p. 29; Templeman and David Woodruff, "The aftershock from the López affair," *Business Week*, August 19, 1993, p. 31; Doron Levin, "Executive who left G.M. denies taking documents and sues," *The New York Times*, May 25, 1993, pp. A1, D21; Ferdinand Protzman, "VW hums tightfisted López tune," *The New York Times*, April 30, 1994, pp. 39, 47; Gabriella Mitchener, "VW Agrees To Big Settlement with GM," *The Wall Street Journal*, January 10, 1997, p. A3.

Chapter 6

Opening Case Summarized from Brian Milner, "The Dying Game," *The Globe and Mail*, December 16, 1995, pp. B1, B4; also Brian Milner, "Loewen Settles Mississippi Suit," *The Globe and Mail*, January 30, 1996, pp. B1, B4; also Brian Milner, "Loewen Licks Its Wounds," *The Globe and Mail*, January 31, 1996, pp. B1, B4. **The Canadian Business Scene** Summarized from Henry Mintzberg, *The Nature of Managerial Work* (New York: Harper and Row, 1973), Chapter 3. **The Canadian Business Scene** Interviews with Sterling McLeod and Wayne Walker, senior vice-presidents of sales for Investors. **The Canadian Business Scene** Summarized from Gabriella Stern, "How a Young Manager Shook Up the Culture at Old Chrysler Plant," *The Wall Street Journal*, April 21, 1997, pp. A1, A6. **Concluding Case 6-1** Summarized from "A Message

from Mudville," *Canadian Business*, March 1996, pp. 36–37; also Scott Taylor, "Baseball Develops Class Systems," *Winnipeg Free Press*, December 15, 1996, p. A8; also David Napier, "Beeston Plays Hardball," *The Financial Post Magazine*, September 1992, pp. 28–32. **Concluding Case 6-2** Summarized from Thomas E. Ricks, "Army Devises System to Decide What Does, and Does Not, Work," *The Wall Street Journal*, May 23, 1997, pp. A1, A10.

Chapter 7

Opening Case Summarized from Ann Gibbon, "CP Rail Moving to Calgary," *The Globe and Mail*, November 21, 1995, pp. B1, B19; also Ann Gibbon, "Reorganization of CP Draws Applause," *The Globe and Mail*, November 22, 1995, p. B2. **The Canadian Business Scene** Interview with Tom Ward, Operations Manager for Genstar Shipyards Ltd. **The Canadian Business Scene** Summarized from Owen Edwards, "Leak soup," *GQ*, April 1989, pp. 224+; see also Beatryce Nivens, "When to Listen to the office grapevine," *Essence*, March 1989, p. 102; John S. Tompkins, "Gossip: Silicon Valley's secret weapon," *Science Digest*, August 1986, pp. 58+; see also "Why you need the grapevine," *Glamour*, August 1986, pp. 126+. **Concluding Case 7-1** Susan Chandler, "United We Own," *Business Week*, March 18, 1996, pp. 96–100; Perry Flint, "The Buck Stops Lower," *Air Transport World*, September 1995, pp. 28–32. **Concluding Case 7-2** Summarized from Robert Collison, "How Bata rules the world," *Canadian Business*, September 1990, pp. 28–34.

Chapter 8

Opening Case Awards for Business Excellence, *1989 Winners' Profiles*, Industry, Science and Technology Canada; also Rod McQueen, "Jobless in recovery," *The Financial Post*, October 14, 1995, p. 14. **Figure 8.1** Quality of Work in the Service Sector, Statistics Canada, 11-612E, No. 6, 1992. **The Canadian Business Scene** Diane Francis, "What makes Jim Pattison run—and whistle," *The Financial Post*, March 5, 1994, p. S3. **Figure 8.2** Allan J. Magrath, "The thorny management issues in family-owned business," *Business Quarterly*, Spring 1988, p. 73. Reprinted with permission of *Business Quarterly*, published by the Western Business School, The University of Western Ontario, London, Ontario. **The Canadian Business Scene** Summarized from Al Emid, "Trend to micro-enterprises helps neophytes," *The Globe and Mail*, March 13, 1990, p. C5; see also Laura Fowlie, "How to feel at home in your home office," *The Financial Post*, June 25, 1990, p. 34; see also Douglas and Diana Lynn Gray, *Home Inc.: The Canadian Home-Based Business Guide* (Toronto: McGraw-Hill Ryerson, 1990). **International Report** Summarized from Richard T. Ashman, "Born in the U.S.A.," *Nation's Business*, November 1986, pp. 41+; see also "Canadian franchisees start to fight abuses," *Wall Street Journal*, October 6, 1988, p. B1; see also Ted Holden et al., "Who says you can't break into japan?" *Business Week*, October 16, 1989, p. 49; see also Joann S. Lublin, "For U.S. franchisers, a common tongue isn't a guarantee of success in the U.K.," *Wall Street Journal*, August 16, 1988, p. 25; see also Matt Moffitt, "For U.S. firms, franchising in Mexico gets more appetizing, thanks to Michael Selz," *Wall Street Journal*, January 3, 1991, p. A6; see also Michael Selz "Europe offers expanding opportunities to franchisers," *Wall Street Journal*, July 20, 1991, p. B2; see also Jeffrey A. Tannenbaum, "Franchisers see a future in East Bloc," *Wall Street Journal*, June 5, 1990, pp.B1+; see also Jeffrey A. Tannenbaum, "Small businesses join franchise push in Japan," *Wall Street Journal*, May 17, 1989, p. B1; see also Andrew Tanzer, "A form of flattery," *Forbes*, June 2, 1986, pp. 110+; see also Russell G. Todd, "U.S. fast-food franchises go East in American international venture," *Wall Street Journal*, November 15, 1988, p. B2; see also Meg Whittemore, "International franchising," *Inc.*, April 1988, pp.116+. **International Report** Ebert/Griffin, *Business Essentials* (Englewood Cliffs, NJ: Prentice Hall, 1995), p. 166 and Wilton Woods, "Products to watch: Heavy artillery," *Fortune*, May 30, 1994, p. 163; David Whitford, "Opposite attractions," *Inc.*, December 1994, pp. 60-64+. **Table 8.3** Mel Scott and Richard Bruce, "Five stages of growth in small business," *Long Range Planning*, 20, 1987, p. 48. **Table 8.5** Starke/Sexty, *Contemporary Management in Canada*, Scarborough: Prentice Hall Canada (1995). **Concluding Case 8-1** Summarized from John Southerst, "Ontario Proposals Hit Sore Point with Franchisors," *The Globe and Mail*, November 25, 1996, p. B6; also Ellen Roseman, "Flowering Firm Faces Branch Battles," *The Globe and Mail*, November 28, 1995, p. B13; also John Lorinc, "War and Pizza," *Canadian Business*, November 1995, pp. 87–97; also John Lorinc, *Opportunity Knocks*. Scarborough: Prentice-Hall Canada Inc., 1995. **Concluding Case 8-2** Glenn Collins, "Growing Pains for a Doll Maker," *New York Times*, September 17, 1996, pp. D1, D19; Sally Lodge, "Magic Attic Club Casts a Spell," *Publishers Weekly*, June 19, 1995, p. 23.

Chapter 9

Opening Case Summarized from John Heinzl, "Women Take Charge at Canadian Units," *The Globe and Mail*, November 29, 1996, p. B10; also Greg Keenan, "Ford Canada Gets New CEO," *The Globe and Mail*, April 9, 1997, p. B1; also Joseph White and Carol Hymowitz, "Watershed Generation of Women Executives is Rising to the Top," *The Globe and Mail*, February 10, 1997, pp. A1, A6; also Greg Keenan, "Woman at the Wheel," *The Globe and Mail*, July 8, 1995, pp. B1, B6. Greg Keenan and

Janet McFarland, "The Boys' Club," *The Globe and Mail*, September 27, 1997, pp. B1, B5. **The Canadian Business Scene** Bruce Little, "Employment sweepstakes requires flexible ticket," *The Globe and Mail*, January 13, 1993, pp. B1, B6. **Table 9.1** *The Financial Post*, 1997 Annual Edition, p. 152. **The Canadian Business Scene** Summarized from Rose Fisher, "Screen Test," *Canadian Business*, May 1992, pp. 62–64. **The Canadian Business Scene** Summarized from Timothy Schellhardt, "It's Time to Evaluate Your Work, and All Involved Are Groaning," *The Wall Street Journal*, November 19, 1996, pp. A1, A5. **The Canadian Business Scene** Summarized from Diane Forrest, "Guess who you can't fire," *Canadian Business*, November 1991, pp. 97-100; see also Margot Gibb-Clark, "Campeau faces hurdles in lawsuit," *The Globe and Mail*, July 13, 1991, p. B1. **The Canadian Business Scene** Summarized from John Saunders, "What Executives Earn," *The Globe and Mail*, April 3, 1993, pp. B1, B4; also Lawrence Surtees, "Stern Farewell to Cost NorTel $3 Million," *The Globe and Mail*, April 3, 1993, pp. B1, B4; also Alexander Ross, "Sixty-Five and Ouch," *Canadian Business*, July 1992, p. 44; also Susan Noakes, "CEO pay-packets come under greater scrutiny," *The Financial Post*, May 8, 1993, p. 24; also J. Castro, "How's Your Pay?" *Time*, April 15, 1991, pp. 40–41; also A. Byrne, "The Flap Over Executive Pay," *Business Week*, May 6, 1991, pp. 90–96; also T. McCarroll, "Motown's Fat Cats," *Time*, January 20, 1992, pp. 34–35; also Frances Misutka, "The Biggest Headache Money Can Buy," *Canadian Business*, July 1992, pp. 50–54; also Kimberley Noble Stone, "Executive Pay Highest in Canada," *The Globe and Mail*, May 5, 1990, p. B1; also John Partridge, "How Top Pay Matches Performance," *The Globe and Mail*, May 12, 1987, pp. B1–B2; also Frances Russell, "Tycoons Set Own Salaries and Keep Them Secret," *Winnipeg Free Press*, November 21, 1990; also Janet McFarland, "Mintzberg Takes Aim at Business-Style Government," *The Globe and Mail*, April 19, 1996, p. B9; also John Saunders, "A League of Their Own," *The Globe and Mail*, April 13, 1996, pp. B1, B4; John Saunders, "Dollars and Sense," *The Globe and Mail*, April 12, 1997, pp. B1, B6. **Concluding Case 9-1** Starke/Sexty, *Contemporary Management in Canada* (Scarborough, ON: Prentice Hall Canada, 1992), p. 351. **Concluding Case 9-2** Summarized from Mark Brender, "Free isn't easy," *The Globe and Mail*, August 9, 1994, p.B18; also Margot Gibb-Clark, "Temps take on new tasks," *The Globe and Mail*, December 22, 1993, p. B1; also Merle MacIsaac, "New broom sweeps schools," *The Globe and Mail*, March 22, 1994, p. B22; also Robert Williamson, "Tradition gives way to world of freelancers," *The Globe and Mail*, January 15, 1993, pp. B1, B4; also Sally Ritchie, "Rent-a-manager," *The Globe and Mail*, August 17, 1993, p. B22.

Chapter 10

Opening Case Mark Stevenson, "Be nice for a change," *Canadian Business*, November 1993, pp. 81-85; also Michael Smyth, "Union leaders claim violence was a setup," *Winnipeg Free Press*, November 26, 1994, p. C6. **The Canadian Business Scene** Alan Farnham, "The trust gap," *Fortune*, December 4, 1989, pp. 56+; Anne B. Fisher, "Morale crisis," *Fortune*, November 18, 1991, pp. 70+; Anne B. Fisher, "CEOs think that morale is dandy," *Fortune*, November 18, 1991, pp. 83+; Walter Kiechell III, "How important is morale, really?" *Fortune*, February 13, 1989, pp. 121+. **The Canadian Business Scene** Summarized from Arthur Bragg, "Should you make a lateral move?" *Sales & Marketing Management*, June 1989, pp. 70+; Carey W. English, "Money Isn't Everything," *U.S. News & World Report*, June 23, 1986, pp. 64+; see also "Family Ties," *Inc.*, August, 1989, p. 112; see also Curtis Hartman and Steven Pearlstein, "The joy of working," *Inc.*, November 1987, pp. 61+; see also John Naisbitt and Patricia Aburdene, "When companies are great places to work," *Reader's Digest*," January 1987, pp. 141+. **Figure 10.2** Griffin/Ebert, *Business*, Second Edition (Englewood Cliffs, NJ: Prentice Hall, 1996). **Figure 10.3** Griffin/Ebert, *Business*, Second Edition (Englewood Cliffs, NJ: Prentice Hall, 1996). **The Canadian Business Scene** Summarized from Bruce McDougall, "Perks with pizzazz," *Canadian Business*, June 1990, pp. 78-79; see also Don Champion, "Quality—a way of life at B.C. Tel," *Canadian Business Review*, Spring 1990, p. 33; see also Margot Gibb-Clark, "Companies find merit in using pay as a carrot," *The Globe and Mail*, May 9, 1990, p. B1; also Margot Gibb-Clark, "The right reward," *The Globe and Mail*, August 10, 1990, p. B5; see also Peter Matthews, "Just rewards—the lure of pay for performance," *Canadian Business*, February 1990, pp. 78-79; also Ian Allaby, "Just Rewards," *Canadian Business*, May 1990, p. 39; see also David Evans, "The myth of customer service," *Canadian Business*, March 1991, pp. 34-39; also Bud Jorgensen, "Do bonuses un-scrupulous brokers make?" *The Globe and Mail*, May 28, 1990, p. B5; also Wayne Gooding, "Ownership is the best motivator," *Customer Business*, March 1990, p. 6. **International Report** Summarized from Brenton Schlender, "Japan's white collar blues," *Fortune*, March 21, 1994, pp. 97-100; also Brenton Schlender, "Japan: Is it changing for good?" *Fortune*, June 13, 1994, pp. 124-134; also Edith Terry, "Japan lives with tradition," *The Globe and Mail*, May 14, 1994, pp. B1, B4; also William Ouchi, *Theory Z* (Reading, Mass.: Addison-Wesley, 1981); also Suzanne McGee, "How Japanese managers are trained," *The Financial Post*, June 1, 1985, p. 25; also Chalmers Johnson, "Japanese-style management in America," *California Management Review*, Summer 1988, pp. 34-45; N. Coates, "Determinants of Japan's business success: Some Japanese executives'

views," *Academy of Management Executive*, February 1988, 2, pp. 69-72. **Concluding Case 10-1** Summarized from Alan Farnham, "Mary Kay's lesson in Leadership," *Fortune*, September 20, 1993, pp. 68-77. **Concluding Case 10-2** Summarized from Aaron Bernstein and Wendy Zellner, "Detroit vs. the UAW: At odds over teamwork," *Business Week*, August 24, 1987, pp. 54+; see also Peter Downs, "Drudgery at Wentzville: The team concept strikes out," *Commonweal*, September 9, 1988, pp. 453+; see also John Hoerr, "Is teamwork," *Business Week*, July 10, 1989, pp. 56+; see also John Holusha, "A new spirit at U.S. auto plants," *New York Times*, December 29, 1987, p. D1+.

Chapter 11

Opening Case Summarized from John Heinzl and Marina Strauss, "Wal-Mart's Cheer Fades," *The Globe and Mail*, February 15, 1997, pp. B1, B4; also Margot Gibb-Clark, "Why Wal-Mart Lost the Case," *The Globe and Mail*, February 14, 1997, p. B10. Susan Bourette, "Organized Labour Lures Growing Number of Youth," *The Globe and Mail*, July 4, 1997, pp. B1, B4; also Susan Bourette, "Women Make Strides in Union Movement," *The Globe and Mail*, August 29, 1997, pp. B1–B2. **The Canadian Business Scene** Summarized from "Progress on Child Labor Hailed," *The Winnipeg Free Press*, February 28, 1997, p. B1. **Table 11.1** Labour Canada, *Labour Organizations in Canada*, 1989, pp. xiii and xiv. Used by permission of the Minister of Supply and Services Canada. **Figure 11.1** *Labour Organizations in Canada*, 1996, p. xiv. **International Report** Joyce Barnathan and Matt Forney, "Damping labor's fires," *Business Week*, August 1, 1994, p. 41; Jane Perlez, "Solidarity forever? Well, it's not the 80's anymore," *The New York Times*, July 20, 1994, p. A4; Allen R. Myerson, "Big labor's strategic raid in Mexico," *The New York Times*, September 12, 1994, pp. D1, D4; Bill Keller, "The revolution won, workers are still unhappy," *The New York Times*, July 23, 1994, p. A2. **Table 11.2** *Labour Organizations in Canada*, 1996, p. xv. **Table 11.3** *Labour Organizations in Canada*, 1996, p. xvii. **Figure 11.2** Griffin/Ebert, *Business*, Second Edition (Englewood Cliffs, NJ: Prentice Hall, 1996). **The Canadian Business Scene** Summarized from Marina Strauss and Harvey Enchin, "Strike is no ball for business," *The Globe and Mail*, August 22, 1994, pp. B1, B5; also Marina Strauss, "Broadcasters body-checked," *The Globe and Mail*, October 1, 1994, pp. B1, B2; also Scott Feschuk, "Hockey shutout costs provinces millions," *The Globe and Mail*, December 8, 1994, pp. B1, B10; also Marina Stauss, "Broadcasters worry: When the games return, will advertisers follow?" *The Globe and Mail*, December 3, 1994, pp. B1, B7; also Harvey Enchin, "Hockey loss cross-checks Maple Leaf Gardens," *The Globe and Mail*, November 11, 1994, pp. B1, B4. **Figure 11.3** Labour Canada, *Labour Organizations in Canada*, 1991, p. xxv. Used by permission of the Minister of Supply and Services Canada. **Concluding Case 11-1** Summarized from "Posties Return to Work; Vow to Sabotage Service," *Winnipeg Free Press*, December 5, 1997, p. B4; also Paul Samyn, "Back-to-Work Legislation in the Mail," *Winnipeg Free Press*, December 2, 1997, p. B1; also Nahiah Ayed, "Postal Workers Picket Manning's Residence," *Winnipeg Free Press*, December 1, 1997, p. B1; also Jennifer Ditchburn, "Commons Passes Back-to-Work Law," *Winnipeg Free Press*, December 3, 1997, p. B3. **Concluding Case 11-2** Kennith Labich, "Will United fly?" *Fortune*, August 22, 1994, pp. 70+; Adam Bryant, "After seven years, employees win United Airlines," *The New York Times*, July 13, 1994, p. A1, D13; Bryant, "Buyout of UAL by its unions looks like winning alternative," *The New York Times*, May 13, 1994, p. D6; Aaron Bernstein and Kevin Kelly, "This give-and take may actually fly," *Business Week*, December 27, 1993, p. 37; Susan Chandler, "United: So many cuts, so little relief," *Business Week*, December 5, 1994, p. 42; "United Airlines' parent posts first yearly profit since 1990," *The New York Times*, January 25, 1995, p. D8.

Chapter 12

Opening Case Summarized from Alexander Ross and Randall Litchfield, "The new industrial revolution," *Canadian Business*, December 1993, pp. 23-33; also Jacquie McNish, "Throng of firms moves to the U.S. to slash costs," *The Globe and Mail*, July 2, 1991, pp. B1, B4; also Ian Allaby, "Why everybody's flying south," *Canadian Business*, December 1990, pp. 2-47. **International Report** Summarized from Gene Bylinsky, "The digital factory," *Fortune*, November 14, 1994, pp. 92-110. **The Canadian Business Scene** Summarized from Gordon Bock, "Limping along in robot land," *Time*, July 13, 1987, pp. 46+; see also Gene Bylinsky, "Invasion of the service robots," *Fortune*, September 14, 1987, pp. 81+; "*Ecce Robo*," *The Economist*, October 15, 1988, pp. 19+; see also Bill Lawren, "Humans make a comeback," *Omni*, August 1987, pp. 32+; see also "Living with smart machines," *The Economist*, May 21, 1988, pp. 79+; see also Wally Dennison, "Robotics paint system makes splash at CN," *Winnipeg Free Press*, October 6, 1988, p. 30; see also "Robots aren't for burning," *Canadian Business*, September 1984, p. 45; see also Renate Lerch, "More firms finding place for robots on factory floor," *The Financial Post*, June 29, 1985, p. C6; see also Carolyn Leitch, "When boxes have brains," *The Globe and Mail*, April 12, 1994, p. B26. **Concluding Case 12-1** Doron P. Levin, "Compaq Storms the PC Heights from Its Factory Floor," *The New York Times*, November 13, 1994, Sec. 3, p. 5; Jim Carlton, "Study Says

Compaq Has Surpassed IBM in Personal Computer Unit Shipments," *The Wall Street Journal*, December 23, 1994, pp. A3, A12; Peter Burrows, "Compaq Stretches for the Crown," *Business Week*, July 11, 1994, pp. 140–42; Stephanie Losee, "How Compaq Keeps the Magic Going," *Fortune*, February 21, 1994, pp. 90–92; Gary McWilliams, "At Compaq, a Desktop Crystal Ball," *Business Week*, March 20, 1995, pp. 96–97; Kyle Pope, "Out for Blood: For Compaq and Dell, Accent Is on Personal in the Computer Wars," *The Wall Street Journal*, July 2, 1993, pp. A2, A4. **Concluding Case 12-2** Summarized from Fred Bleakley, "Who's that on the factory floor?" *The Globe and Mail*, January 31, 1995, p. B26.

Chapter 13

Opening Case Summarized from Bruce Little, "Stock Answers," *The Globe and Mail*, June 6, 1995, p. B12. **The Canadian Business Scene** Summarized from David Evans, "The myth of customer service," *Canadian Business*, March 1991, pp. 34–39. **Table 13.2** Adapted from Richard Chase, "Where does the customer fit in a service operation?" *Harvard Business Review*, November/December 1978, pp. 137–42. **The Canadian Business Scene** Summarized from Scott McCartney, "The Inexact Science of Keeping an Airline on Schedule," *The Wall Street Journal*, September 11, 1996, pp. B1, B4; also Gayle MacDonald, "The Eye of a Storm," *The Globe and Mail*, January 11, 1996, p. B13. **International Report** Summarized from Geoffrey York, "Beeg Maks on a Roll," *The Globe and Mail*, September 12, 1996, pp. B1, B17; also Peter Foster, "McDonald's Excellent Soviet Venture?" *Canadian Business*, May, 1991, pp. 51–64 **Concluding Case 13-1** Summarized from Geoffrey Rowan, "How software star solved service slips," *The Globe and Mail*, December 13, 1994, p. B24. **Concluding Case 13-2** Starke/Sexty, *Contemporary Management in Canada*, Second Edition (Scarborough, ON: Prentice Hall Canada, 1995), pp. 31–32.

Chapter 14

Opening Case Alex Taylor III, "Shaking up Jaguar," *Fortune*, September 6, 1993, pp. 65-68; John Templeman, "These repair jobs are taking a little longer than expected," *Business Week*, April 27, 1992, pp. 117, 121; "Will your next Jaguar be built at Von Braun's lane?" *Road & Track*, May 1993, pp. 39-40; Julia Flynn and James B. Treece, "Is the jinx finally off Jaguar?" *Business Week*, October 10, 1994, p. 62; Valerie Reitman and Oscar Suris, "Can the very British Jaguar be made in Japan?" *The Wall Street Journal*, December 9, 1994, p. B1; Michael Clements, "Jaguar has a lot riding on XJ series," *USA Today*, December 19, 1994, pp. B1, B2. **International Report** Summarized from Harvey Enchin, "Canada urged to stop living off fat of the land," *The Globe and Mail*, October 25, 1991, pp. B1, B6. **The Canadian Business Scene** Starke/Sexty, *Contemporary Management in Canada*, Second Edition (Scarborough, ON: Prentice Hall Canada, 1995), p. 564. **International Report** Ebert/Griffin, *Business Essentials* (Englewood Cliffs, NJ: Prentice Hall, 1995), pp. 272-3. **International Report** "Air reservation merger is off," *The New York Times*, October 16, 1991, p. D3; "Best practice companies;" *Financial World*, September 17, 1991, pp. 36+; "The computer network that keeps American flying," *Fortune*, September 24, 1990, p. 46; Max D. Hopper, "Rattling SABRE— New ways to compete on information," *Harvard Business Review*, May-June 1990, pp. 188+; "Hotels find better lodging in airline reservation systems," *Business Week*, July 10, 1989, p. 84E; Kenneth Lambich, "American takes on the world," *Fortune*, September 24, 1990, pp. 40+. **Concluding Case 14-1** Summarized from Scott Rankine, "The Last Picture Show," *The Globe and Mail*, July 26, 1994, p. B22; "Mitsubishi Closing Ontario Plant," *Winnipeg Free Press*, March 23, 1996, p. B24. **Concluding Case 14-2** Brian S. Moskal, "Born to Be Real," *Industry Week*, August 2, 1993, pp. 14–18; Robert L. Rose, "Vrooming Back: After Nearly Stalling, Harley-Davidson Finds New Crowd of Riders," *The Wall Street Journal*, August 31, 1990, pp. A1, A6; Peter C. Reid, *Well Made in America* (New York: McGraw-Hill, 1990); John Holusha, "How Harley Outfoxed Japan with Exports," *The New York Times*, August 12, 1990, Sec. 3, p. 5.

Chapter 15

Opening Case Summarized from Elizabeth Jensen, "Networks Blast Nielsen, Blame Faulty Ratings For Drop in Viewership," *The Wall Street Journal*, November 22, 1996, pp. A1, A8; also R. Turner and J.R. Emshwiller, "FlimFlam? Movie Research Czar Is Said by Some to Sell Manipulated Findings," *The Wall Street Journal*, December 17, 1993, pp. A1, A7. **International Report** Summarized from Shawn Tully, "Teens: The most global market of all," *Fortune*, May 16, 1994, pp. 90–97. **The Canadian Business Scene** Summarized from Suanne Kelman, "Consumers on the couch," *Report on Business Magazine*, February 1991, pp. 50–53. **The Canadian Business Scene** Summarized from Gina Mallet, "Greatest romance on earth," *Canadian Business*, August 1993, pp. 19–23. **International Report** Griffin/Ebert, *Business*, Third Edition. **Concluding Case 15-2** Summarized from William M. Bulkeley, "Wring in the New: Washers That Load from Front Are Hot," *The Wall Street Journal*, April 29, 1997, pp. A1, A5.

Chapter 16

Opening Case Summarized from Daniel Stoffman, "Bombardier's billion-dollar space race," *Canadian Business*, June 1994, pp. 91–101. **The Canadian Business Scene** Summarized from Jared Mitchell, "Wonders and Blunders," *Report on Business*, September 1995, pp. 152–62. **Table 16.1** Philip Kotler and Gary Armstrong, *Marketing: An Introduction*, 3rd ed. (Englewood Cliffs, NJ: Prentice Hall), p. 274; William J. Stanton, Michael J. Etzel, and Bruce J. Walker, *Fundamentals of Marketing*, 10th ed. (New York: McGraw-Hill, 1994), p. 247; William P. Pride and O.C. Ferrell, *Marketing: Concepts and Strategies*, 9th ed. (Boston: Houghton Mifflin, 1995), pp. 307–13. **International Report** Summarized from Carla Rapaport, "Nestle's brand building machine," *Fortune*, September 19, 1994, pp. 147–56. **International Report** Summarized from Robert Berner, "The Rolls-Royce of Leather Jackets Is Hard to Come By," *The Wall Street Journal*, November 22, 1996, pp. A1, A10. **Figure 16.8** *Marketing Magazine*, April 15, 1996, p. 1. **Figure 16.9** *Media Digest*, 1996, p. 11. **The Canadian Business Scene** Marina Strauss, "Battery companies battle over ads," *The Globe and Mail*, November 29, 1994, pp. B1, B10; also Marina Strauss, "Frozen pie crust ruling puts chill on comparative ads," *The Globe and Mail*, October 6, 1994, p. B4. **Table 16.2** "Total measured U.S. ad spending by category and media," *Advertising Age*, September 28, 1994, p. 8. **Table 16.3** *The Financial Post*, Annual Edition, 1997, p. 188. **The Canadian Business Scene** Summarized from Shona McKay, "Make room, Madison Avenue," *Canadian Business*, January 1993, pp. 33-36. **Concluding Case 16-1** Ian Fisher, "A New Jordan Sneaker Inspires a Frenetic Run," *New York Times*, July 4, 1996, pp. B1, B4; Leigh Gallagher, "Industry Retailers See Swoosh as Double-Edged Sword," *Sporting Goods Business*, April 1996, p. 8; Robert McAllister, "Jordan Fever Is Heating Up Retailers," *Footwear News*, March 20, 1995, pp. 2–3; Catherine Salfino, "Pro Name Game Gives Nike, Reebok Foothold in Apparel Arena," *Daily News Record*, February 28, 1996, p. 3. **Concluding Case 16-2** Summarized from Gail Lem, "Cott profit soars as revenues double," *The Globe and Mail*, April 9, 1994, p. B18; also Patricia Sellers, "Brands: It's thrive or die," *Fortune*, August 23, 1993, pp. 52–56; also Madelaine Drohan, "British await Coke's reply to grocer's look-alike cola," *The Globe and Mail*, August 29, 1994; Marina Strauss and John Saunders, "Cott to Write Off $40 million, Cut Operations," *The Globe and Mail*, November 23, 1995, pp. B1, B16; "Cott Executives Sold Stock," *The Globe and Mail*, November 28, 1995, p. B6; "How the Cola Giants Stopped Cott," *The Globe and Mail*, November 30, 1995, p. B11; Paul Waldie, "Cott's Profit Jumps 48 percent in Quarter," *The Globe and Mail*, June 14, 1997, p. B1.

Chapter 17

Opening Case Summarized from Ian McGugan, "Eaton's on the Brink," *Canadian Business*, March 1996, pp. 38–48, 65–73; also "Eaton's Stuns Nation," *Winnipeg Free Press*, February 28, 1997, pp. A1, A3; John Heinzl and Paul Waldie, "Eaton's Drowning in Red Ink," *The Globe and Mail*, February 28, 1997, pp. B1; John Heinzl, Carolyn Leitch, John Saunders, Marina Strauss, and Paul Waldie, "Inside the Debacle at Eaton's," *The Globe and Mail*, March 1, 1997, pp. B1, B4; Rob Ferguson, "Eaton's Gets on With It," *Winnipeg Free Press*, September 9, 1997, p. B3. **Table 17.2** *The Financial Post*, 1997 Annual Edition, pp. 121–22. **International Report** Summarized from John Heinzl, "Canadian Tire pulls out of U.S.," *The Globe and Mail*, December 2, 1994, pp. B1, B6; also William C. Symonds, "Invasion of the retail snatchers," *Business Week*, May 9, 1994, pp. 72–73; also Carla Rapaport, "The new U.S. push into Europe," *Fortune*, January 10, 1994, pp. 73–74; also Marina Strauss, "Imasco sells stores," *The Globe and Mail*, June 26, 1990, pp. B1–B2; also Karen Howlett, "Once bitten in the U.S. market, Canadian Tire not shy about re-entering," *The Globe and Mail*, May 6, 1988, p. B3; also Kenneth Kidd, "Success breeds prudence as Canadian Tire peers over 49th parallel," *The Globe and Mail*, January 31, 1990, p. 36; also Frances Phillips, "Canadian Tire finds Texas trails a bit bumpy," *The Financial Post*, March 26, 1983, p. 18; also Jean Matthews and Greg Boyd, "Can Lionel Robbins rescue Dylex?" *Canadian Business*, November 1990, pp. 106–14; also Beppi Crosariol, "What makes the U.S. so tough," *Financial Times of Canada*, October 8, 1990, p. 14; also *The Financial Post* Information Service, History Sections on Canadian Tire Corporation and Dylex Ltd. **The Canadian Business Scene** Summarized from Mark Stevenson, "The store to end all stores," *Canadian Business*, May 1994, pp. 20–29. **Table 17.3** *The Financial Post*, 1997 Annual Edition, p. 164. **Concluding Case 17-1** Robert Berner, "Retired General Speeds Deliveries, Cuts Costs, Helps Sears Rebound," *Wall Street Journal*, July 16, 1996, pp. A1, A7; June Carolyn Erlick, "Pagonis Takes Battle Plan to Sears," *HFD—The Weekly Home Furnishings Newspaper*, April 24, 1994, p. 12; "From Moving Tanks to Moving Merchandise," *Management Review*, June 1994, pp. 30–32. **Concluding Case 17-2** Keith Bradsher, "Sticker Shock: Car Buyers Miss Haggling Ritual," *New York Times*, June 13, 1996, pp. D1, D23; Bradley J. Fikes, "Haggling Over Price Is No Longer Automatic," *San Diego Business Journal*, October 3, 1994, pp. 17–18; Greg Keenan, "Revolution on the Car Lot," *The Globe and Mail*, March 22, 1997, pp. B1, B4.

Chapter 18

Opening Case Robert Williamson, "Cyber Seadogs," *The Globe and Mail*, July 18, 1995, p. B18. **The Canadian Business Scene** Summarized from Carolyn Leitch, "Paper chase goes high tech," *The Globe and Mail*, October 11, 1994, p. B26. **The Canadian Business Scene** Summarized from Geoffrey Rowan, "Date Digit Glitch Bedevils Computers," *The Globe and Mail*, April 9, 1996, p. B8; Lee Gomes, "Why Prepping Mainframes for 2000 Is So Tough," *The Wall Street Journal*, December 9, 1996, pp. B1, B8; Patrick Brethour, "Report Warns of '2000 crisis'," *The Globe and Mail*, October 8, 1997, pp. B1, B14; Murray McNeill, "Firm Cashing in on Millenium," *Winnipeg Free Press*, June 11, 1997; Thomas Petzinger, "Programmer Attacks the Millennium Bug," *The Globe and Mail*, June 20, 1997, p. B6. **Figure 18.6** Based on a study by W. Lambert Gardiner, GAMMA, Montreal, Quebec. Reproduced by permission. **The Canadian Business Scene** James Kaminsky, "Computers that fly," *Vis a Vis*, October 1991, pp. 39+; Peter H. Lewis, "One day, laptops could rule the world," *The New York Times*, March 31, 1991, p. F4; Thayer C. Taylor, ed., "Small is beautiful: Making laptops easier to love," *Sales & Marketing Management*, May 1990, p. 103; Thayer C. Taylor, ed., "The PC evolution: desktop...laptop...palmtop...? Top," *Sales & Marketing Management*, February 1991, pp. 50+. **Table 18.1** *The Financial Post*, 1997 Annual Edition, p. 162. **The Canadian Business Scene** Summarized from G. Pascal Zachary, "Executives jam e-mail signals," *The Globe and Mail*, June 23, 1994, p. B7; also John Wilke, "Togetherness, the PC way," *The Globe and Mail*, December 11, 1993, pp. B1, B5; also Alex Markels, "Memo 4/8/97, FYI: Messages Inundate Office," *The Wall Street Journal*, April 8, 1997, pp. B1, B10. **The Canadian Business Scene** Peter H. Lewis, "Getting down to business on the Net," *The New York Times*, June 19, 1994, Sec. 3, p. 1; John W. Verity and Robert D. Hof, "The Internet: How it will change the way you do business," *Business Week*, November 14, 1994, pp. 80–86+; Steven Dickman, "Catching customers on the Web," *Inc. Technology*, Summer 1995, pp. 56–60; Stephen D. Solomon, "Staking a claim on the Internet," *Inc. Technology*, March 1995, pp. 87–90+; Alan R. Earls, "Incubators of agility," *Computerworld*, January 23, 1995, pp. 81–82; Hof, "From the man who brought you silicon graphics...," *Business Week*, October 24, 1994, pp. 90–91; Lewis, "Netscape knows fame and aspires to fortune," *The New York Times*, March 1, 1995, pp. D1, D6. **Concluding Case 18-1** Summarized from Victoria Burrus, "The virtual stockyard," *The Globe and Mail*, September 27, 1994, p. B28. **Concluding Case 18-2** Summarized from Gary Lamphier, "Flower power," *The Globe and Mail*, March 29, 1994, p. B30.

Chapter 19

Opening Case Summarized from John Southerst, "Suddenly, it all makes sense," *Canadian Business*, March 1994, pp. 39–42; also Bruce Little, "A foundry finds its way," *The Globe and Mail*, October 5, 1993, p. B28; also Terence Pare, "A new tool for managing costs," *Fortune*, June 14, 1993, pp. 124–29. **Table 19.1** *The Financial Post*, Annual Edition 1997, p. 188. **The Canadian Business Scene** Summarized from Edward Clifford, "Big accounting firms face insurance crunch," *The Globe and Mail*, November 13, 1993, p. B3; also "Cooperants' Auditors Sued," *The Financial Post*, October 30, 1993, p. 8; also Patricia Lush, "Gap widens between views on auditor's role in Canada," *The Globe and Mail*, February 14, 1986, p. B3; also Chris Robinson, "Auditors' Role Raises Tough Questions," *The Financial Post*, June 22, 1985. **International Report** Lee Berton, "College Courses on Accounting Get Poor Grades," *The Wall Street Journal*, August 12, 1994, pp. B1, B7; "Focus on Accounting Education," *Journal of Accountancy*, June 1994, pp. 44–45; Gary Siegel and James Sorensen, *What Corporate America Wants in Entry-Level Accountants* (New York: The Institute of Management Accountants, August 1994). **Concluding Case 19-1** Reed Abelson, "The Shell Game of Hollywood 'Net Profits'," *New York Times*, March 4, 1996, pp. D1, D6; Elizabeth Lesly, "Fatal Subtraction?" *Business Week*, March 11, 1996, pp. 66–68; Tim Carvell, "Accounting, Hollywood-Style," *Fortune*, November 11, 1996, p. 48. **Concluding Case 19-2** Summarized from Karen Howlett and Murray Wood, "Standard directors sue Peat Marwick," *The Globe and Mail*, June 5, 1992, pp. B1, B10; see also Allan Robinson, "OSC says Standard ignored warning signals," *The Globe and Mail*, June 2, 1992, p. B10.

Chapter 20

Opening Case Summarized from Anne Reifenberg, "Dialing for Dinars: Iraqis Turn on Radio To Set Exchange Rate," *The Wall Street Journal*, September 20, 1996, pp. A1, A4. **The Canadian Business Scene**, Ebert/Griffin, *Business Essentials*, p. 252. **Table 20.1** *The Financial Post*, Annual Edition 1997, p. 180. **The Canadian Business Scene** Summarized from Sandy Fife, "Have a nice day," *Report on Business Magazine*, October 1991, pp. 49–57. **International Report** Summarized from Sean Silcoff, "No Frills. Unbeatable Prices. It Worked for Wal-Mart," *Canadian Business*, August 1997, pp. 34–42. **The Canadian Business Scene** Summarized from Janet McFarland, "A royal loss of trust: 1993's sorriest debacle," *The Financial Post*, December 25, 1993, p.

9; also Gordon Pitts, "The Man on Royal Trustco's Hot Seat," *The Financial Post*, November 25, 1991, p. 7. **Table 20.2** *The Financial Post*, Annual Edition 1997, p. 184. **Table 20.3** *The Financial Post*, Annual Edition 1997, p. 188. **Concluding Case 20-1** Ken Wells, "Its New ATMs in Place, a Bank Reaches Out to South Africa's Poor," *Wall Street Journal*, June 13, 1996, pp. A1, A10; "Taking Microchips to Townships: South Africa's Banks Are Going Boldly Where Few Banks Have Gone Before," *The Economist*, July 8, 1995, pp. 71–73. **Concluding Case 20-2** Summarized from David West, "Why we need a cheaper buck," *Canadian Business*, July 1990. p. 21; see also Randall Litchfield, "Our Strong Dollar: The right medicine," *Canadian Business*, January 1992, p. B10.

Chapter 21

Opening Case Summarized from Brian Hutchinson, "The Prize," *Canadian Business*, March 1997, pp. 26–48 and 65–72; also Andrew Willis, "Bre-X's Winners and Losers," *The Globe and Mail*, May 7, 1997, pp. B1, B6; also Karen Howlett, "David Walsh: Naive or Scandal-Plagued?," *The Globe and Mail*, May 31, 1997, pp. B1, B6; also Philip Mathias, "The Sad, Twisted Tale," *The Financial Post*, October 19, 1996, pp. 6–7; also Paul Waldie, Michael Den Tandt, "How Bre-X Samples Were Salted," *The Globe and Mail*, May 8, 1997; also Stephen Northfield, "Delgratia Says Gold Results Fake," *The Globe and Mail*, May 20, 1997, pp. B1, B9. **The Canadian Business Scene** Summarized from Patricia Lush, "Matkin lowers the boom on VSE," *The Globe and Mail*, January 26, 1994, pp. B1, B7; also Douglas Gould, "Who needs brokers?" *Report on Business Magazine*, June 1990, pp. 35–37; also John Lorinc, "Making your firm a stock market star," *Canadian Business*, January 1992, pp. 51–54. **International Report** Vanessa O'Connell, "Stock Answer," *Wall Street Journal*, June 17, 1996, p. R8; "With the World Wide Web, Who Needs Wall Street?" *Business Week*, April 29, 1996, pp. 120–21. **The Canadian Business Scene** Summarized from Karen Howlett, "Funds told to inform public," *The Globe and Mail*, February 1, 1995, pp. B1, B12; also Karen Howlett, "Mutual fund industry put under spotlight," *The Globe and Mail*, January 30, 1995, pp. B1–B2; *The Globe and Mail*, December 12, 1995, pp. B1, B23; Andrew Bell, "OSC To Ban Fund Freebies," *The Globe and Mail*, July 9, 1996, pp. B1, B17; Karen Howlett, "Fund Crusader Reported on the Outs at OSC," *The Globe and Mail*, February 13, 1997, pp. B1, B10. **The Canadian Business Scene** Summarized from Karen Howlett and Susan Bourette, "Pension, Mutual Funds Dominate TSE Trading," *The Globe and Mail*, July 21, 1995, pp. B1, B6; also Jacquie McNish, "Pension Fund Power," *The Globe and Mail*, June 17, 1995, pp. B1, B3; also Karen Howlett, "How the Altamira Case Reveals OSC's Failings," *The Globe and Mail*, September 22, 1997, pp. B1, B13. **Concluding Case 21-1** David J. Jefferson, "Bam! Aargh! Little comics get trounced," *The Wall Street Journal*, January 22, 1990, pp. B1+; Douglas A. Kass, "Pow! Smash! Kerplash!" *Barron's*, February 17, 1992, pp. 14+; Floyd Norris, "Boom in comic books lifts new marvel stock offering," *The New York Times*, July 15, 1991, pp. D1, D8; Mark Landler with Laura Zinn, "The new Ron Perelman has an old problem," *Business Week*, June 14, 1993, pp. 94–95; Gene G. Marcial, "Ron Perelman: Vegas or bust?" *Business Week*, January 16, 1995, p. 72; Marvin Shankin, "Interview: Ron Perelman," *Cigar Aficionado*, Spring 1995, p. 65; Jeff Jensen, "Comics' high-tech weapons," *Advertising Age*, September 12, 1994, pp. 20, 24; "Is This The End of Marvel? Or ...", *Winnipeg Free Press*, December 28, 1996, p. B11. **Concluding Case 21-2** Summarized from Daniel Stoffman, "Look who's calling the shots," *Canadian Business*, July 1990, pp. 45–47.

Chapter 22

Opening Case Summarized from Kimberly Noble, "How Bramalea Gambled—and Lost," *The Globe and Mail*, April 1, 1995, pp. B1, B4. **The Canadian Business Scene** Summarized from Jacquie McNish and Margaret Philp, "O & Y backs away from commercial paper," *The Globe and Mail*, March 6, 1992, pp. B1, B7; see also Brian Milner, Margaret Philp, Alan Freeman, Drew Fagan, and John Saunders, "Reichmanns call in cavalry; U.S. banker to head O & Y," *The Globe and Mail*, March 25, 1992, pp. B1, B4; see also Brian Milner and Margaret Philp, "Reichmann shuffle gives Camdev stake to Albert," *The Globe and Mail*, March 28, 1992, pp. B1, B8; see also Jacquie McNish, Margaret Philp, and Brian Milner, "O & Y's hard times stem from shift to short-term debt," *The Globe and Mail*, April 4, 1992, pp. B1, B8; see also Madelaine Drohan, "O & Y has no plans for bankruptcy filing," *The Globe and Mail*, April 23, 1992, pp. B1, B6; see also Madelaine Drohan and Jacquie McNish, "O & Y reported on verge of bankruptcy protection," *The Globe and Mail*, May 15, 1992, pp. B1, B5; see also Brian Milner and Margaret Philp, "O & Y puts on brave face to mask predicament," *The Globe and Mail*, May 16, 1992, pp. B1, B4. **Table 22.2** *The Financial Post*, Annual Edition 1997, p. 186. **International Report** Summarized from Leslie Scism, "If Disaster Strikes This 'Titanic', Chubb Could Lose Millions," *The Wall Street Journal*, April 9, 1997, pp. A1, A4; also Leslie Scism, "Maybe Julie Andrews Could Offer Insurers a Spoonful of Sugar," *The Wall Street Journal*, April 4, 1997, pp. A1, A4. **The Canadian Business Scene** Summarized from Denyse O'Leary, "The Scams That Drive Up Premiums," *The Globe and Mail*, May 2, 1995, p. B1; also Denyse

O'Leary, "Insurers United Against Fraud Face Serious Obstacles," *The Globe and Mail*, May 2, 1995, p. B1. **International Report** Summarized from Patrick Reilly, "Insurers Are Downbeat on Rap Concert Tours," *The Wall Street Journal*, March 26, 1997, pp. B1, B12. **Concluding Case 22-1** Sara Webb et al., "A royal mess: Britain's Barings PLC bets on derivatives—and the cost is dear," *The Wall Street Journal*, February 27, 1995, pp. A1, A6; Marcus W. Brauchli, Nicholas Bray, and Michael R. Sesit, "Broken bank: Barings PLC officials may have been aware of trader's po-

sition," *The Wall Street Journal*, March 6, 1995, pp. A1, A7; Richard W. Stevenson, "Markets shaken as a British bank takes a big loss," *The New York Times*, February 27, 1995, pp. A1, D5; Paula Dwyer et al., "The lesson from Barings' straits," *Business Week*, March 13, 1995, pp. 30–32; Glenn Whitney, "Dutch concern agrees to buy Barings assets," *The Wall Street Journal*, March 5, 1995, pp. A3, A5; "Leeson's Six-and-a-half Year Sentence Greeted with Mixed Reviews," *The Globe and Mail*, December 4, 1995, pp. B1, B10.

Photo Credits

Chapter 1: Al Harvey/The Slide Farm, page 2; Voisey Bay Mills/Advantage productions, page 4; Susan McCartney; Al Harvey;/The Slide Farm; Bettmann Archives; Junebug Clark, page 9; Angela Baur; Al Harvey/The Slide Farm, page 15; Kathleen Bellesiles/Little Apple Studio, page 18

Chapter 2: Spruce Falls Mill, page 28; The Granger Collection, page 32; First Light/D. Pollack, page 35; Imperial Oil Limited, page 42; Al Harvey/The Slide Farm, page 45

Chapter 3: Toronto Sun Syndicate, page 54; Allelix Biopharmaceuticals Inc., Mississauga, Ontario, page 56; Courtesy IBM; Courtesy BASF, page 58; Canapress/Fred Chartrand, page 63; Ontario Ministry of Natural Resources, page 65; VIA Rail Canada Inc., page 68; Dave Repp/Black Star, page 71; Ports Canada, page 74; Ontario Hydro, page 80

Chapter 4: Purdy's Chocolate Stores, page 91; Nortel/M.A. Malfavon Y Associates, page 103; Canapress/Jacques Boissinot, page 108; Palliser Furniture, page 112; Motorola, page 116

Chapter 5: The Body Shop Canada, page 124; Al Harvey/The Slide Farm, page 127; David R. Frazier/Photo Researchers, page 131; Courtesy of Construction Association of Ontario, page 138; McDonald's Restaurant, page 139; Canapress/Frank Gunn, page 147

Chapter 6: Canapress/Frank Gunn, page 164; AP/Wide World Photos/Ed Andrieski, page 171; Prentice Hall Archives, page 172; Gabe Palmer/The Stock Market, page 175; Will McIntyre, page 177; Tom Hollyman/Photo Researchers, page 178; Henley & Savage/The Stock Market; Han Feingersh/The Stock Market; Courtesy Control Data Corporation; Al Harvey/The Slide Farm; Federal Express Customer Service, page 179; Tom Hollyman/Photo Researchers, page 184; Takeshi Takahara, page 186

Chapter 7: Canadian Pacific Railway, page 193; Nelvana Studios, page 196; Eaton's, page 199; First Light/Jose L. Pelrez, page 201; Tony Stone Images/Frank Siteman, page 204; Telus Corporation, page 205; Renee Lynn/Photo Researchers, page 208

Chapter 8: Lawrence Zepf, page 216; S. Houston, page 219; Dick Hemmingway, page 221; The Pattison Group, page 222; Canapress, page 224; Midas Canada Inc., page 229

Chapter 9: Norco Bicycles, page 248; Canapress/Frank Gunn, page 250; Hunt Personnel, page 256; Canapress/Jacques Brinon, page 260; Canapress/Frank Gunn, page 262; Prentice Hall Archives, page 263; David Starrett/The Cover Studios, page 270; MacMilliam Bloedel, page 277

Chapter 10: Corbis, page 282; Courtesy Western Electric, page 283; Ed Bock/The Stock Market, page 286; Al Harvey/The Slide Farm, page 291; Dick Hemmingway, page 295

Chapter 11: Walmart Canada, page 302; Prentice Hall Archives, page 306; VIA Rail Canada Inc., page 313; Canapress/Dan Janisse, page 316; Canapress/Adrian Wyld, page 317; AP/Wide World Photos/J. Pat Carter, page 322

Chapter 12: Al Harvey/The Slide Farm, page 340; Canapress Photo Service, page 345; Toyota Motor Manufactuing Canada Inc., page 350; Larry Mulvehill/Photo Researchers, page 356; Courtesty Calma Company, page 362

Chapter 13: Livingston Healthcare Services/Ken Davies, page 367; Al Harvey/The Slide Farm, page 372; Dick Hemmingway, page 375; Dick Hemmingway, page 379; Courtesy of Four Seasons Hotels and Resorts, page 382

Chapter 14: Jaguar Canada Inc., page 391; Hank Morgan/Photo Researchers, page 396; UPI/Corbis-Bettmann, page 397; Chris Jones/The Stock Market, page 401; Dofasco Canada, page 407

Chapter 15: Dick Hemmingway, page 424; Loblaws Brands Limited; Toronto Zoo/Chiat Day/Ill. Doug Martin, page 429; Will McIntyre/Photo Researchers, page 432; Al Harvey/The Slide Farm, page 441; Prentice Hall Archives, page 444; The Body Shop Canada, page 445; Feathercraft Products Ltd., page 448

Chapter 16: Bombardier Canadair, page456; Dick Hemmingway, page 469; Boy Scouts of Canada; Joseph Rodriguez/Black Star; Duncan Roban/Alpha; Prime Minister's Office, page 475; Used with permission of Kellogg Canada Inc., copyright 1995, page 482; Paul Barton/The Stock Market, page 486

Chapter 17: Canapress/Jeff Goode, page 498; Richard Hutchings/Photo Researchers, page 506; IBM Canada, page 512; Larry Mulvehill/Photo Researchers, page 516; Canadian National, page 523

Chapter 18: Trudy Woodcock's Image Network/Al Harvey, page 542; Wayne Farrar Photography, page 544; Northern Telecom, page 547; Dick Hemmingway, page 560; IBM Canada, page 563; IBM Canada, page 567

Chapter 19: Walt Hodges/Tony Stone Images, page 577; Al Harvey/The Slide Farm, page 579; Deloitte & Touche, page 584; Courtesy The Coca-Cola Company, page 591

Chapter 20: Canapress, page 612; Canapress/Jassim Mohammed, page 614; The Granger Collection, page 616; Dick Hemmingway, page 619; Kathleen Bellesiles, page 624; Bob Carroll/Leucar, page 625; Prentice Hall Archives

Chapter 21: Canapress/Jim Wells, page 642; Toronto Star/D. Loek, page 651; Dick Hemmingway, page 653; Canapress Photo Service, page 658

Chapter 22: The Financial Post, page 669; David Pollack/The Stock Market, page 674; Reuters/Corbis-Bettman, page 682; Lawrence Migdale, Ulrich Welch, Eunice Harris/Photo Researchers, page 687; Kent and Donna Dannen/Photo Researchers, page 694

INDEX

Name and Organization Index

Subject Index